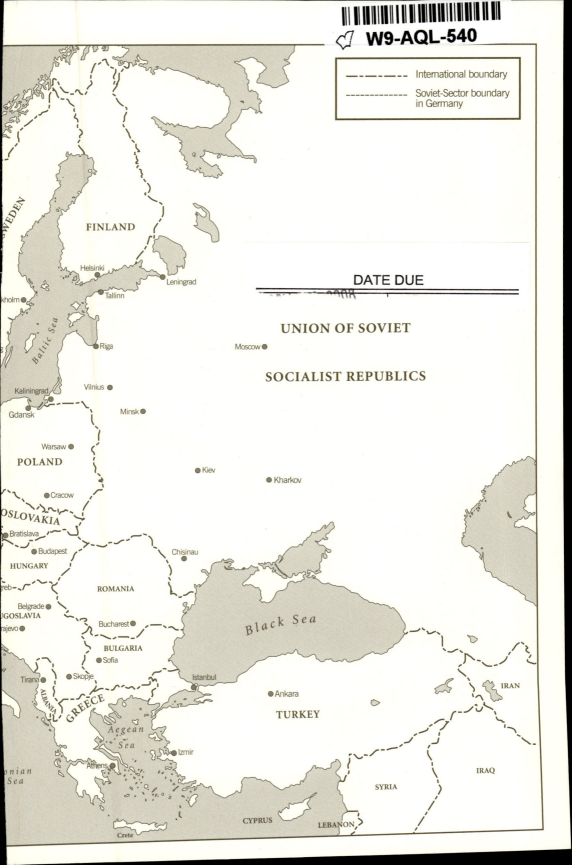

W9-AQL-540

| International boundary |
| Soviet-Sector boundary in Germany |

DATE DUE

FINLAND

Helsinki
Leningrad
Tallinn

UNION OF SOVIET

SOCIALIST REPUBLICS

Moscow

Riga

Kaliningrad
Gdansk
Vilnius
Minsk
Warsaw
POLAND
Kiev
Kharkov
Cracow
OSLOVAKIA
Bratislava
Budapest
Chisinau
HUNGARY
greb
ROMANIA
Belgrade
UGOSLAVIA
Bucharest
ajevo
BULGARIA
Sofia
Tirana
Skopje
Istanbul
IRAN
GREECE
Ankara
TURKEY
Aegean Sea
Izmir
IRAQ
Athens
onian Sea
SYRIA
CYPRUS
LEBANON
Crete

Baltic Sea
kholm
Black Sea
ALBANIA

Postwar

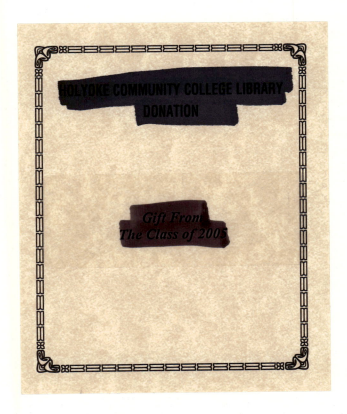

ALSO BY TONY JUDT

The Politics of Retribution in Europe
(with Jan Gross and István Deák)

The Burden of Responsibility: Blum, Camus, Aron,
and the French Twentieth Century

Language, Nation and State: Identity Politics in a Multilingual Age
(edited with Denis Lacorne)

With Us or Against Us: Studies in Global Anti-Americanism
(edited with Denis Lacorne)

A Grand Illusion? An Essay on Europe

Past Imperfect: French Intellectuals, 1944–1956

Marxism and the French Left: Studies on Labour
and Politics in France 1830–1982

Resistance and Revolution in Mediterranean Europe 1939–1948
(edited by Tony Judt)

Socialism in Provence 1871–1914:
A Study in the Origins of the Modern French Left

La reconstruction du Parti Socialiste 1921–1926

Postwar

A HISTORY OF EUROPE SINCE 1945

Tony Judt

THE PENGUIN PRESS

New York

2005

THE PENGUIN PRESS
Published by the Penguin Group
Penguin Group (USA) Inc., 375 Hudson Street, New York, New York 10014, U.S.A. ·
Penguin Group (Canada), 90 Eglinton Avenue East, Suite 700, Toronto, Ontario,
Canada M4P 2Y3 (a division of Pearson Penguin Canada Inc.) · Penguin Books Ltd,
80 Strand, London WC2R 0RL, England · Penguin Ireland, 25 St. Stephen's Green,
Dublin 2, Ireland (a division of Penguin Books Ltd) · Penguin Books Australia Ltd,
250 Camberwell Road, Camberwell, Victoria 3124, Australia (a division of Pearson
Australia Group Pty Ltd) · Penguin Books India Pvt Ltd, 11 Community Centre,
Panchsheel Park, New Delhi – 110 017, India · Penguin Group (NZ), Cnr Airborne
and Rosedale Roads, Albany, Auckland 1310, New Zealand (a division of Pearson
New Zealand Ltd) · Penguin Books (South Africa) (Pty) Ltd, 24 Sturdee Avenue,
Rosebank, Johannesburg 2196, South Africa

Penguin Books Ltd, Registered Offices:
80 Strand, London WC2R 0RL, England

First published in 2005 by The Penguin Press,
a member of Penguin Group (USA) Inc.

1 2 3 4 5 6 7 8 9 10

LIBRARY OF CONGRESS CATALOGING IN PUBLICATION DATA

ISBN 1-59420-065-3

Printed in the United States of America

For Jennifer

Is not the pastness of the past the more profound, the more legendary,
the more immediately it falls before the present?
THOMAS MANN, *The Magic Mountain*

Contents

Preface & Acknowledgements

Europe is the smallest continent. It is not really even a continent—just a sub-continental annexe to Asia. The whole of Europe (excluding Russia and Turkey) comprises just five and a half million square kilometers: less than two thirds the area of Brazil, not much more than half the size of China or the US. It is dwarfed by Russia, which covers seventeen million square kilometers. But in the intensity of its internal differences and contrasts, Europe is unique. At the last count it comprised forty-six countries. Most of these consist of states and nations with their own languages; quite a few of them incorporate additional nations and languages without states; all have their distinct and overlapping histories, politics, cultures and memories; and every one of them has been copiously studied. Even for the brief, sixty-year period of Europe's history since the end of the Second World War—indeed, for this period above all—the secondary literature in English alone is inexhaustible.

No one, then, can aspire to write a fully comprehensive or definitive history of contemporary Europe. My own inadequacy to the task is aggravated by proximity: born not long after the war ended, I am a contemporary to most of the events described in this book and can remember learning about or watching—or even participating in—much of this history as it unfolded. Does this make it easier for me to understand the story of post-war Europe, or harder? I don't know. But I do know that it can sometimes render the dispassionate disengagement of the historian quite difficult to find.

This book attempts no such Olympian detachment. Without, I hope, abandoning objectivity and fairness, *Postwar* offers an avowedly personal interpretation of the recent European past. In a word that has acquired undeservedly pejorative connotations, it is *opinionated*. Some of its judgments will perhaps be controversial, some will surely prove mistaken. All are fallible. For good and ill they are my own—as are any mistakes which are bound to have crept into a work of this length and scope. But if the errors are contained, and at least some of the assessments and conclusions in this book prove durable, then I owe this in large measure to the many scholars and friends on whom I have relied in the course of researching and writing it.

A book of this kind rests, in the first instance, on the shoulders of other books.[1]

[1] In the chapters that follow the footnotes are, for the most part, of the traditional sort: that is, they comment on the text rather than identify a source. To avoid adding to what is already a very long book addressed to a general readership, a full apparatus of references is not provided here. Instead, the sources for *Postwar*, together with a full bibliography, will in due course be available for consultation on the Remarque Institute website [*http://www.nyu.edu/pages/remarque/*].

The classics of modern history writing to which I have looked for inspiration and example include Eric Hobsbawm's *The Age of Extremes*, George Lichtheim's *Europe in the Twentieth Century*, A J P Taylor's *English History 1914–1945* and the late François Furet's *The Passing of an Illusion*. Utterly different in every other respect, these books and their authors share an assurance born of wide learning and the sort of intellectual self-confidence rarely found among their successors—as well as a clarity of style that should be a model for every historian.

Among those scholars from whose own writings on recent European history I have learned the most I should especially mention and thank Harold James, Mark Mazower and Andrew Moravcsik. The imprint of their work will be clear in the pages that follow. To Alan S. Milward I—along with everyone who studies modern Europe—owe a special debt for his learned, iconoclastic studies of the post-war economy.

To the extent that I can claim familiarity with the history of central and eastern Europe—a subject often slighted by general European histories, written as they are by specialists in the continent's western half—I owe this to the work of a gifted cohort of younger scholars, including Brad Abrams, Catherine Merridale, Marci Shore and Timothy Snyder, as well as to my friends Jacques Rupnik and István Deák. From Timothy Garton Ash I have learned not only about central Europe (a subject that for many years he made his own) but also and especially about the two Germanies in the era of *Ostpolitik*. In the course of many years of conversation with Jan Gross—and thanks to his path-breaking writings—I have learned not only some Polish history but also how to understand the social consequences of war, a subject on which Jan has written with matchless insight and humanity.

The sections on Italy in this book owe a transparent debt to the work of Paul Ginsborg, just as the chapters dealing with Spain reflect what I have learned from reading and listening to the remarkable Victor Perez-Diaz. To both of these, and to Annette Wieviorka—whose magisterial analysis of post-war France's ambivalent response to the Holocaust, *Déportation et Génocide*, has deeply marked my account of that troubled story—I owe particular thanks. My closing reflections on 'Europe as a Way of Life' were much influenced by the writings of a brilliant international lawyer, Anne-Marie Slaughter, whose work on 'disaggregated states' argues forcefully for the EU form of international governance not because it is inherently better or because it represents an ideal model but because—in the world in which we find ourselves—nothing else will work.

All across Europe, friends, colleagues and audiences have taught me far more about the continent's recent past and its present than I could ever have gleaned from books and archives. I am especially grateful to Krzysztof Czyzewski, Peter Kellner, Ivan Krastev, Denis Lacorne, Krzysztof Michalski, Mircea Mihaes, Berti Musliu, Susan Neiman and David Travis for their hospitality and their help. I am indebted to Istvan Rév for his invaluable insistence that—however distasteful the experience—I must visit Budapest's House of Terror. In New York my friends and

colleagues Richard Mitten, Katherine Fleming and Jerrold Seigel have been generous with their time and ideas. Dino Buturovic kindly scrutinized my account of the
Yugoslav linguistic imbroglio.

I am grateful to successive deans of the Faculty of Arts & Sciences at New York
University—Philip Furmansky, Jess Benhabib and Richard Foley—for supporting
both my own research and the Remarque Institute which I founded to encourage
others to study and discuss Europe. I could not have developed the Remarque Institute—which hosted many of the workshops and lectures from which I have
learned so much—without the generous support and patronage of Yves-André
Istel; and I could not have written this book while running Remarque without the
uncomplaining and ultra-efficient collaboration of its Administrative Director
Jair Kessler.

Like so many, I am deeply beholden for friendship and advice to my agents Andrew Wylie and Sarah Chalfant; they have been unfailingly supportive of a project
that took longer—and grew larger—than they can ever have anticipated. In thank-
ing my editors Ravi Mirchandani and Scott Moyers, I should especially single out
Scott and his colleague Jane Fleming at The Penguin Press in New York—they
know how much I owe them for bringing this book successfully to publication.
Thanks to the hospitality of Leon Wieseltier, some of the evaluations and opinions
that surface in Chapters 12 and 14 were first published in essay form in the remarkable arts pages that he cultivates at the back of *The New Republic*. By far my
greatest professional debt is to Robert Silvers, peerless editor of *The New York Review of Books*, who over the years has encouraged me to roam an ever larger political and historical compass, with all the risks and benefits such adventurism entails.

This book has benefitted greatly from the contribution of students at New York
University. Some of them—in particular Drs Paulina Bren, Daniel Cohen (now at
Rice University) and Nicole Rudolph—have contributed to my understanding of
the period through their own historical research, which they will find acknowledged
in these pages. Others—Jessica Cooperman and Avi Patt—did invaluable work as
research assistants. Michelle Pinto, along with Simon Jackson, transformed herself
uncomplainingly into a skilled picture researcher; she was responsible for locating
many of the most engaging illustrations, notably the wrapped Lenin that graces the
end of Part III. Alex Molot diligently identified and accumulated the published and
unpublished statistical reports and data series on which a book of this sort inevitably and very properly depends. I truly could not have written it without them.

My family has lived with postwar Europe for a very long time—in the case of
my children for the whole of their young lives. Not only have they been tolerant of
the absences, travels and obsessions to which it has given rise, but they have made
distinctive contributions to its content. To Daniel, the book owes its title; to
Nicholas, the reminder that not all good stories get a happy ending. To my wife Jennifer the book also owes a lot—not least two very careful and constructive readings. But its author owes much, much more. *Postwar* is dedicated to her.

Postwar

Introduction

'Every epoch is a sphinx that plunges into the abyss
as soon as its riddle has been solved'.
Heinrich Heine

'Circumstances (which with some gentlemen pass for nothing!) give in
reality to every political principle its distinguishing colour and
discriminating effect'.
Edmund Burke

'Events, dear boy, events'.
Harold Macmillan

World history is not the soil in which happiness grows.
Periods of happiness are empty pages in it'.
Georg Wilhelm Friedrich Hegel

I first decided to write this book while changing trains at the Westbahnhof, Vienna's main railway terminus. It was December 1989, a propitious moment. I had just returned from Prague, where the playwrights and historians of Václav Havel's *Civic Forum* were dislodging a Communist police state and tumbling forty years of 'real existing Socialism' into the dustbin of history. A few weeks earlier the Berlin Wall had been unexpectedly breached. In Hungary as in Poland, everyone was taken up with the challenges of post-Communist politics: the old regime—all-powerful just a few months before—was receding into irrelevance. The Communist Party of Lithuania had just declared itself for immediate independence from the Soviet Union. And in the taxi on the way to the railway station Austrian radio carried the first reports of an uprising against the nepotistic dictatorship of Nicolae Ceauşescu in Romania. A political earthquake was shattering the frozen topography of post-World War II Europe.

An era was over and a new Europe was being born. This much was obvious. But with the passing of the old order many longstanding assumptions would be called into question. What had once seemed permanent and somehow inevitable would take on a more transient air. The Cold-War confrontation; the schism separating East from West; the contest between 'Communism' and 'capitalism'; the separate and non-communicating stories of prosperous western Europe and the Soviet bloc

1

satellites to its east: all these could no longer be understood as the products of ideological necessity or the iron logic of politics. They were the accidental outcomes of history—and history was thrusting them aside.

Europe's future would look very different—and so, too, would its past. In retrospect the years 1945–89 would now come to be seen not as the threshold of a new epoch but rather as an interim age: a post-war parenthesis, the unfinished business of a conflict that ended in 1945 but whose epilogue had lasted for another half century. Whatever shape Europe was to take in the years to come, the familiar, tidy story of what had gone before had changed for ever. It seemed obvious to me, in that icy central-European December, that the history of post-war Europe would need to be rewritten.

The time was propitious; so, too, was the place. Vienna in 1989 was a palimpsest of Europe's complicated, overlapping pasts. In the early years of the twentieth century Vienna *was* Europe: the fertile, edgy, self-deluding hub of a culture and a civilization on the threshold of apocalypse. Between the wars, reduced from a glorious imperial metropole to the impoverished, shrunken capital of a tiny rump-state, Vienna slid steadily from grace: finishing up as the provincial outpost of a Nazi empire to which most of its citizens swore enthusiastic fealty.

After Germany was defeated Austria fell into the Western camp and was assigned the status of Hitler's 'first victim'. This stroke of doubly unmerited good fortune authorized Vienna to exorcise its past. Its Nazi allegiance conveniently forgotten, the Austrian capital—a 'Western' city surrounded by Soviet 'eastern' Europe—acquired a new identity as outrider and exemplar of the free world. To its former subjects now trapped in Czechoslovakia, Poland, Hungary, Romania and Yugoslavia, Vienna stood for 'central Europe': an imagined community of cosmopolitan civility that Europeans had somehow mislaid in the course of the century. In Communism's dying years the city was to become a sort of listening post of liberty, a rejuvenated site of encounters and departures for eastern Europeans escaping West and Westerners building bridges to the East.

Vienna in 1989 was thus a good place from which to 'think' Europe. Austria embodied all the slightly self-satisfied attributes of post-war western Europe: capitalist prosperity underpinned by a richly-endowed welfare state; social peace guaranteed thanks to jobs and perks liberally distributed through all the main social groups and political parties; external security assured by the implicit protection of the Western nuclear umbrella—while Austria itself remained smugly 'neutral'. Meanwhile, across the Leitha and Danube rivers just a few kilometres to the east, there lay the 'other' Europe of bleak poverty and secret policemen. The distance separating the two was nicely encapsulated in the contrast between Vienna's thrusting, energetic Westbahnhof, whence businessmen and vacationers boarded sleek modern expresses for Munich or Zurich or Paris; and the city's grim, uninviting Südbahnhof: a shabby, dingy, faintly menacing hangout of penurious foreigners descending filthy old trains from Budapest or Belgrade.

Just as the city's two principal railway stations involuntarily acknowledged the geographical schism of Europe—one facing optimistically, profitably west, the other negligently conceding Vienna's eastern vocation—so the very streets of the Austrian capital bore witness to the chasm of silence separating Europe's tranquil present from its discomforting past. The imposing, confident buildings lining the great Ringstrasse were a reminder of Vienna's one-time imperial vocation—though the Ring itself seemed somehow too big and too grand to serve as a mere quotidian artery for commuters in a medium-sized European capital—and the city was justifiably proud of its public edifices and civic spaces. Indeed, Vienna was much given to invoking older glories. But concerning the more recent past it was decidedly reticent.

And of the Jews who had once occupied many of the inner city's buildings and who contributed decisively to the art, music, theatre, literature, journalism and ideas that *were* Vienna in its heyday, the city was most reticent of all. The very violence with which the Jews of Vienna had been expelled from their homes, shipped east from the city and stamped out of its memory helped account for the guilty calm of Vienna's present. Post-war Vienna—like post-war western Europe—was an imposing edifice resting atop an unspeakable past. Much of the worst of that past had taken place in the lands that fell under Soviet control, which was why it was so easily forgotten (in the West) or suppressed (in the East). With the return of eastern Europe the past would be no less unspeakable: but now it would, unavoidably, have to be spoken. After 1989 nothing—not the future, not the present and above all not the past—would ever be the same.

Although it was in December 1989 that I decided to undertake a history of post-war Europe, the book did not get written for many years to come. Circumstances intervened. In retrospect this was fortunate: many things which have become a little clearer today were still obscure back then. Archives have opened. The inevitable confusions attendant upon a revolutionary transformation have sorted themselves out and at least some of the longer-term consequences of the upheaval of 1989 are now intelligible. And the aftershocks of 1989 did not soon abate. The next time I was in Vienna the city was struggling to house tens of thousands of refugees from neighbouring Croatia and Bosnia.

Three years after that Austria abandoned its carefully-cultivated post-war autonomy and joined the European Union, whose own emergence as a force in European affairs was a direct consequence of the east-European revolutions. Visiting Vienna in October 1999 I found the Westbahnhof covered in posters for the Freedom Party of Jörg Haider who, despite his open admiration for the 'honourable men' of the Nazi armies who 'did their duty' on the eastern front, won 27 percent of the vote that year by mobilizing his fellow Austrians' anxiety and incomprehension at the changes that had taken place in their world over the past decade. After nearly half a century of quiescence Vienna—like the rest of Europe—had re-entered history.

. . .

This book tells the story of Europe since the Second World War and so it begins in 1945: *Stunde nul,* as the Germans called it—Zero hour. But like everything else in the twentieth-century its story is back-shadowed by the thirty-year war that began in 1914, when the European continent embarked upon its descent into catastrophe. The First World War itself was a traumatic killing field for all the participants— half of Serbia's male population between 18 and 55 died in the fighting—but it re- solved nothing. Germany (contrary to widespread belief at the time) was not crushed in the war or the post-war settlement: in that case its rise to near-total dom- ination of Europe a mere twenty-five years later would be hard to explain. Indeed, because Germany didn't pay its First World War debts the cost of victory to the Al- lies exceeded the cost of defeat to Germany, which thus emerged relatively *stronger* than in 1913. The 'German problem' that had surfaced in Europe with the rise of Prussia a generation before remained unsolved.

The little countries that emerged from the collapse of the old land empires in 1918 were poor, unstable, insecure—and resentful of their neighbours. Between the wars Europe was full of 'revisionist' states: Russia, Germany, Austria, Hungary and Bul- garia had all been defeated in the Great War and awaited an occasion for territorial redress. After 1918 there was no restoration of international stability, no recovered equilibrium between the powers: merely an interlude born of exhaustion. The vi- olence of war did not abate. It metamorphosed instead into domestic affairs—into nationalist polemics, racial prejudice, class confrontation and civil war. Europe in the Twenties and especially the Thirties entered a twilight zone between the after- life of one war and the looming anticipation of another.

The internal conflicts and inter-state antagonisms of the years between the world wars were exacerbated—and in some measure provoked—by the accompa- nying collapse of the European economy. Indeed economic life in Europe was struck a triple blow in those years. The First World War distorted domestic em- ployment, destroyed trade and devastated whole regions—as well as bankrupting states. Many countries—in central Europe above all—never recovered from its ef- fects. Those that did were then brought low again in the Slump of the Thirties, when deflation, business failures and desperate efforts to erect protective tariffs against foreign competition resulted not only in unprecedented levels of unemployment and wasted industrial capacity but also the collapse of international trade (be- tween 1929 and 1936 Franco-German commerce fell by 83 percent), accompanied by bitter inter-state competition and resentment. And then came the Second World War, whose unprecedented impact upon the *civilian* populations and domestic economies of the affected nations is discussed in Part One of this book.

The cumulative impact of these blows was to destroy a civilization. The scale of the disaster that Europe had brought upon itself was perfectly clear to contempo- raries even as it was happening. Some, on the far Left and far Right alike, saw the self-immolation of bourgeois Europe as an opportunity to fight for something better. The Thirties were Auden's 'low, dishonest decade'; but they were also an age of commitment and political faith, culminating in the illusions and lives lost to the civil war in Spain. This was the Indian summer of nineteenth-century radical visions, now invested in the violent ideological engagements of a grimmer age: 'What an enormous longing for a new human order there was in the era between the world wars, and what a miserable failure to live up to it.'(Arthur Koestler)

Despairing of Europe, some fled: first to the remaining liberal democracies of far-western Europe, thence—if they could get out in time—to the Americas. And some, like Stefan Zweig or Walter Benjamin, took their own lives. On the eve of the continent's final descent into the abyss the prospect for Europe appeared hopeless. Whatever it was that had been lost in the course of the implosion of European civilization—a loss whose implications had long since been intuited by Karl Kraus and Franz Kafka in Zweig's own Vienna—would never be recaptured. In Jean Renoir's eponymous film classic of 1937, the *Grand Illusion* of the age was the resort to war and its accompanying myths of honour, caste and class. But by 1940, to observant Europeans, the grandest of all Europe's illusions—now discredited beyond recovery—was 'European civilisation' itself.

In the light of what had gone before it is thus understandably tempting to narrate the story of Europe's unexpected recovery after 1945 in a self-congratulatory, even lyrical key. And this, indeed, has been the dominant underlying theme of histories of post-war Europe, above all those written before 1989—just as it was the tone adopted by European statesmen when reflecting upon their own achievements in these decades. The mere survival and re-emergence of the separate states of continental Europe after the cataclysm of total war; the absence of inter-state disputes and the steady extension of institutionalized forms of intra-European cooperation; the sustained recovery from thirty years of economic meltdown and the 'normalization' of prosperity, optimism and peace: all these invited a hyperbolic response. Europe's recovery was a 'miracle'. 'Post-national' Europe had learned the bitter lessons of recent history. An irenic, pacific continent had risen, 'Phoenix-like', from the ashes of its murderous—suicidal—past.

Like many myths, this rather agreeable account of Europe in the second half of the twentieth century contains a kernel of truth. But it leaves out a lot. Eastern Europe—from the Austrian border to the Ural Mountains, from Tallinn to Tirana—doesn't fit. *Its* post-war decades were certainly peaceful when contrasted with what went before, but only thanks to the uninvited presence of the Red Army: it was the peace of the prison-yard, enforced by the tank. And if the satellite countries of the Soviet bloc engaged in international cooperation superficially comparable to developments further west, this was only because Moscow imposed 'fraternal' institutions and exchanges upon them by force.

The history of the two halves of post-war Europe cannot be told in isolation from one another. The legacy of the Second World War—and the pre-war decades and the war before that—forced upon the governments and peoples of east and west Europe alike some hard choices about how best to order their affairs so as to avoid any return to the past. One option—to pursue the radical agenda of the popular front movements of the 1930s—was initially very popular in *both* parts of Europe (a reminder that 1945 was never quite the fresh start that it sometimes appears). In eastern Europe some sort of radical transformation was unavoidable. There could be no possibility of returning to the discredited past. What, then, would replace it? Communism may have been the wrong solution, but the dilemma to which it was responding was real enough.

In the West the prospect of radical change was smoothed away, not least thanks to American aid (and pressure). The appeal of the popular-front agenda—and of Communism—faded: both were prescriptions for hard times and in the West, at least after 1952, the times were no longer so hard. And so, in the decades that followed, the uncertainties of the immediate post-war years were forgotten. But the possibility that things might take a different turn—indeed, the likelihood that they *would* take a different turn—had seemed very real in 1945; it was to head off a return of the old demons (unemployment, Fascism, German militarism, war, revolution) that western Europe took the new path with which we are now familiar. Post-national, welfare-state, cooperative, pacific Europe was not born of the optimistic, ambitious, forward-looking project imagined in fond retrospect by today's Euro-idealists. It was the insecure child of anxiety. Shadowed by history, its leaders implemented social reforms and built new institutions as a prophylactic, to keep the past at bay.

This becomes easier to grasp when we recall that authorities in the Soviet bloc were in essence engaged in the same project. They, too, were above all concerned to install a barrier against political backsliding—though in countries under Communist rule this was to be secured not so much by social progress as through the application of physical force. Recent history was re-written—and citizens were encouraged to forget it—in accordance with the assertion that a Communist-led social revolution had definitively erased not just the shortcomings of the past but also the conditions that had made them possible. As we shall see, this claim was also a myth; at best a half-truth.

But the Communist myth bears unintended witness to the importance (and the difficulty) in *both* halves of Europe of managing a burdensome inheritance. World War One destroyed old Europe; World War Two created the conditions for a new Europe. But the whole of Europe lived for many decades after 1945 in the long shadow cast by the dictators and wars in its immediate past. That is one of the experiences that Europeans of the post-war generation have in common with one another and which separates them from Americans, for whom the twentieth century taught rather different and altogether more optimistic lessons. And it is the necessary point of departure for anyone seeking to understand European history before 1989—and to appreciate how much it changed afterwards.

. . .

In his account of Tolstoy's view of history, Isaiah Berlin drew an influential distinction between two styles of intellectual reasoning, citing a famous line from the Greek poet Archilochus: 'The fox knows many things but the hedgehog knows one big thing.' In Berlin's terms this book is decidedly not a 'hedgehog'. I have no big theory of contemporary European history to propose in these pages; no one overarching theme to expound; no single, all-embracing story to tell. It does not follow from this, however, that I think the post-World War Two history of Europe has no thematic shape. On the contrary: it has more than one. Fox-like, Europe knows many things.

In the first place, this is a history of Europe's reduction. The constituent states of Europe could no longer aspire, after 1945, to international or imperial status. The two exceptions to this rule—the Soviet Union and, in part, Great Britain—were both only half-European in their own eyes and in any case, by the end of the period recounted here, they too were much reduced. Most of the rest of continental Europe had been humiliated by defeat and occupation. It had not been able to liberate itself from Fascism by its own efforts; nor was it able, unassisted, to keep Communism at bay. Post-war Europe was liberated—or immured—by outsiders. Only with considerable effort and across long decades did Europeans recover control of their own destiny. Shorn of their overseas territories Europe's erstwhile seaborne empires (Britain, France, the Netherlands, Belgium, Portugal) were all shrunk back in the course of these years to their European nuclei, their attention re-directed to Europe itself.

Secondly, the later decades of the twentieth century saw the withering away of the 'master narratives' of European history: the great nineteenth-century theories of history, with their models of progress and change, of revolution and transformation, that had fuelled the political projects and social movements that tore Europe apart in the first half of the century. This too is a story that only makes sense on a pan-European canvas: the decline of political fervor in the West (except among a marginalized intellectual minority) was accompanied—for quite different reasons—by the loss of political faith and the discrediting of official Marxism in the East. For a brief moment in the 1980s, to be sure, it seemed as though the intellectual *Right* might stage a revival around the equally nineteenth-century project of dismantling 'society' and abandoning public affairs to the untrammelled market and the minimalist state; but the spasm passed. After 1989 there was no overarching ideological project of Left *or* Right on offer in Europe—except the prospect of liberty, which for most Europeans was a promise now fulfilled.

Thirdly, and as a modest substitute for the defunct ambitions of Europe's ideological past, there emerged belatedly—and largely by accident—the 'European model'. Born of an eclectic mix of Social Democratic and Christian Democratic legislation and the crab-like institutional extension of the European Community and its successor Union, this was a distinctively 'European' way of regulating social intercourse and inter-state relations. Embracing everything from child-care to inter-state legal norms, this European approach stood for more than just the bureaucratic practices of the European Union and its member states; by the beginning of the twenty-first century it had become a beacon and example for aspirant EU members and a global challenge to the United States and the competing appeal of the 'American way of life'.

This decidedly unanticipated transformation of Europe from a geographical expression (and a rather troubled one at that) into a rôle-model and magnet for individuals and countries alike was a slow, cumulative process. Europe was not, in Alexander Wat's ironic paraphrase of the delusions of inter-war Polish statesmen, 'doomed to greatness'. Its emergence in this capacity could certainly not have been predicted from the circumstances of 1945, or even 1975. This new Europe was not a preconceived common project: no-one set out to bring it about. But once it became clear, after 1992, that Europe *did* occupy this novel place in the international scheme of things, its relations with the US in particular took on a different aspect—for Europeans and Americans alike.

This is the fourth theme interwoven into this account of post-war Europe: its complicated and frequently misunderstood relationship to the United States of America. Western Europeans wanted the US to involve itself in European affairs after 1945—but they also resented that involvement and what it implied about Europe's decline. Moreover, despite the US presence in Europe, especially in the years after 1949, the two sides of the 'West' remained very different places. The Cold War was perceived quite differently in western Europe from the rather alarmist response it aroused in the US, and the subsequent 'Americanisation' of Europe in the Fifties and Sixties is often exaggerated, as we shall see.

Eastern Europe, of course, saw America and its attributes rather differently. But there, too, it would be misleading to overstate the exemplary influence of the US upon eastern Europeans both before and after 1989. Dissident critics in both halves of Europe—Raymond Aron in France, for example, or Václav Havel in Czecho-slovakia—were careful to emphasize that they did not regard America as any sort of model or example for their own societies. And although a younger generation of post-'89 eastern Europeans did aspire for a while to liberalize their countries on the American model, with limited public services, low taxes and a free market, the fashion has not caught on. Europe's 'American moment' lay in the past. The future of eastern Europe's 'little Americas' lay squarely in Europe.

Finally, Europe's post-war history is a story shadowed by silences; by absence. The continent of Europe was once an intricate, interwoven tapestry of overlapping languages, religions, communities and nations. Many of its cities—particularly the smaller ones at the intersection of old and new imperial boundaries, such as Trieste, Sarajevo, Salonika, Cernovitz, Odessa or Vilna—were truly multicultural societies *avant le mot*, where Catholics, Orthodox, Muslims, Jews and others lived in familiar juxtaposition. We should not idealise this old Europe. What the Polish writer Tadeusz Borowski called 'the incredible, almost comical melting-pot of peoples and nationalities sizzling dangerously in the very heart of Europe' was periodically rent with riots, massacres and *pogroms*—but it was real, and it survived into living memory.

Between 1914 and 1945, however, *that* Europe was smashed into the dust. The tidier Europe that emerged, blinking, into the second half of the twentieth century had fewer loose ends. Thanks to war, occupation, boundary adjustments, expulsions and genocide, almost everybody now lived in their own country, among their own people. For forty years after World War Two Europeans in both halves of Europe lived in hermetic national enclaves where surviving religious or ethnic minorities—the Jews in France, for example—represented a tiny percentage of the population at large and were thoroughly integrated into its cultural and political mainstream. Only Yugoslavia and the Soviet Union—an empire, not a country and anyway only part-European, as already noted—stood aside from this new, serially homogenous Europe.

But since the 1980s, and above all since the fall of the Soviet Union and the enlargement of the EU, Europe is facing a multicultural future. Between them refugees; guest-workers; the denizens of Europe's former colonies drawn back to the imperial metropole by the prospect of jobs and freedom; and the voluntary and involuntary migrants from failed or repressive states at Europe's expanded margins have turned London, Paris, Antwerp, Amsterdam, Berlin, Milan and a dozen other places into cosmopolitan world cities whether they like it or not.

This new presence of Europe's living 'others'—perhaps fifteen million Muslims in the EU as currently constituted, for example, with a further eighty million awaiting admission in Bulgaria and Turkey—has thrown into relief not just Europe's current discomfort at the prospect of ever greater variety, but also the ease with which the dead 'others' of Europe's past were cast far out of mind. Since 1989 it has become clearer than it was before just how much the stability of post-war Europe rested upon the accomplishments of Josef Stalin and Adolf Hitler. Between them, and assisted by wartime collaborators, the dictators blasted flat the demographic heath upon which the foundations of a new and less complicated continent were then laid.

This disconcerting kink in the smooth narrative of Europe's progress towards Winston Churchill's 'broad sunlit uplands' was left largely unmentioned in both halves of postwar Europe—at least until the Sixties, after which it was usually invoked uniquely in reference to the extermination of Jews by Germans. With only the occasional controversial exception, the record of other perpetrators—and other victims—was kept closed. The history and memory of the Second World War were typically confined to a familiar set of moral conventions: Good versus Evil, Anti-Fascists against Fascists, Resisters against Collaborators and so forth.

Since 1989—with the overcoming of long-established inhibitions—it has proven possible to acknowledge (sometimes in the teeth of virulent opposition and denial) the moral price that was paid for Europe's rebirth. Poles, French, Swiss, Italians, Romanians and others are now better placed to know—if they wish to know—what really happened in their country just a few short decades ago. Even Germans, too, are revisiting the received history of their country—with paradoxical consequences. Now—for the first time in many decades—it is *German* suffering and *German* victimhood, whether at the hands of British bombers, Russian soldiers or Czech expellers—that are receiving attention. The Jews, it is once again being tentatively suggested in certain respectable quarters, were not the only victims . . .

Whether these discussions are a good or a bad thing is a matter for debate. Is all this public remembering a sign of political health? Or is it sometimes more prudent, as De Gaulle among others understood all too well, to forget? This question will be taken up in the Epilogue. Here I would simply note that these latest hiccups of disruptive recall need not be understood—as they sometimes are understood (notably in the United States), when juxtaposed to contemporary outbreaks of ethnic or racial prejudice—as baleful evidence of Europe's Original Sin: its inability to learn from past crimes, its amnesiac nostalgia, its ever-imminent propensity to return to 1938. This is not, in the words of Yogi Berra, 'déjà vu all over again'.

Europe is not re-entering its troubled wartime past—on the contrary, it is leaving it. Germany today, like the rest of Europe, is more conscious of its twentieth-century history than at any time in the past fifty years. But this does not mean that it is being drawn *back* into it. For that history never went away. As this book tries to show, the long shadow of World War Two lay heavy across postwar Europe. It could not, however, be acknowledged in full. Silence over Europe's recent past was the necessary condition for the construction of a European future. Today—in the wake of painful public debates in almost every other European country—it seems somehow fitting (and in any case unavoidable) that Germans, too, should at last feel able openly to question the canons of well-intentioned official memory. We may not be very comfortable with this; it may not even be a good portent. But it *is* a kind of closure. Sixty years after Hitler's death, his war and its consequences are entering history. Postwar in Europe lasted a very long time, but it is finally coming to a close.

PART ONE

Post-War: 1945–1953

the Soviet Union, a further 20 million in Germany—500,000 of them in Hamburg alone), the rubble-strewn urban landscape was the most immediate reminder of the war that had just ended. But it was not the only one. In Western Europe transport and communications were seriously disrupted: of 12,000 railway locomotives in pre-war France, only 2,800 were in service by the time of the German surrender. Many roads, rail tracks and bridges had been blown up—by the retreating Germans, the advancing Allies or the French Resistance. Two-thirds of the French merchant fleet had been sunk. In 1944–45 alone, France lost 500,000 dwellings.

But the French—like the British, the Belgians, the Dutch (who lost 219,000 hectares of land flooded by the Germans and were reduced by 1945 to 40 percent of their pre-war rail, road and canal transport), the Danes, the Norwegians (who had lost 14 percent of the country's pre-war capital in the course of the German occupation), and even the Italians—were comparatively fortunate, though they did not know it. The true horrors of war had been experienced further east. The Nazis treated western Europeans with some respect, if only the better to exploit them, and western Europeans returned the compliment by doing relatively little to disrupt or oppose the German war effort. In eastern and south-eastern Europe the occupying Germans were merciless, and not only because local partisans—in Greece, Yugoslavia and Ukraine especially—fought a relentless if hopeless battle against them.

The material consequences in the East of the German occupation, the Soviet advance and the partisan struggles were thus of an altogether different order from the experience of war in the West. In the Soviet Union, 70,000 villages and 1,700 towns were destroyed in the course of the war, along with 32,000 factories and 40,000 miles of rail track. In Greece, two-thirds of the country's vital merchant marine fleet was lost, one-third of its forests were ruined and a thousand villages were obliterated. Meanwhile the German policy of setting occupation-cost payments according to German military needs rather than the Greek capacity to pay generated hyper-inflation.

Yugoslavia lost 25 percent of its vineyards, 50 percent of all livestock, 60 percent of the country's roads, 75 percent of all its ploughs and railway bridges, one in five of its pre-war dwellings and a third of its limited industrial wealth—along with 10 percent of its pre-war population. In Poland three-quarters of standard gauge rail tracks were unusable and one farm in six was out of operation. Most of the country's towns and cities could barely function (though only Warsaw was totally destroyed).

But even these figures, dramatic as they are, convey just a part of the picture: the grim physical background. Yet the material damage suffered by Europeans in the course of the war, terrible though it had been, was insignificant when set against the human losses. It is estimated that about thirty-six and a half million Europeans died between 1939 and 1945 from war-related causes (equivalent to the *total* population of France at the outbreak of war)—a number that does not include deaths from natural causes in those years, nor any estimate of the numbers of children not conceived or born then or later because of the war.

The overall death toll is staggering (the figures given here do not include Japanese, US or other non-European dead). It dwarfs the mortality figures for the Great War of 1914–18, obscene as those were. No other conflict in recorded history killed so many people in so short a time. But what is most striking of all is the number of non-combatant civilians among the dead: at least 19 million, or more than half. The numbers of civilian dead exceeded military losses in the USSR, Hungary, Poland, Yugoslavia, Greece, France, the Netherlands, Belgium and Norway. Only in the UK and Germany did military losses significantly outnumber civilian ones.

Estimates of civilian losses on the territory of the Soviet Union vary greatly, though the likeliest figure is in excess of 16 million people (roughly double the number of Soviet military losses, of whom 78,000 fell in the battle for Berlin alone). Civilian deaths on the territory of pre-war Poland approached 5 million; in Yugoslavia 1.4 million; in Greece 430,000; in France 350,000; in Hungary 270,000; in the Netherlands 204,000; in Romania 200,000. Among these, and especially prominent in the Polish, Dutch and Hungarian figures, were some 5.7 million Jews, to whom should be added 221,000 gypsies (Roma).

The causes of death among civilians included mass extermination, in death camps and killing fields from Odessa to the Baltic; disease, malnutrition and starvation (induced and otherwise); the shooting and burning of hostages—by the Wehrmacht, the Red Army and partisans of all kinds; reprisals against civilians; the effects of bombing, shelling and infantry battles in fields and cities, on the eastern Front throughout the war and in the West from the Normandy landings of June 1944 until the death of Hitler the following May; the deliberate strafing of refugee columns and the working to death of slave labourers in war industries and prison camps.

The greatest *military* losses were incurred by the Soviet Union, which is thought to have lost 8.6 million men and women under arms; Germany, with 4 million casualties; Italy, which lost 400,000 soldiers, sailors and airmen; and Romania, some 300,000 of whose military were killed, mostly fighting with the Axis armies on the Russian front. In proportion to their populations, however, the Austrians, Hungarians, Albanians and Yugoslavs suffered the greatest military losses. Taking all deaths—civilian and military alike—into account, Poland, Yugoslavia, the USSR and Greece were the worst affected. Poland lost about one in five of her pre-war population, including a far higher percentage of the educated population, deliberately targeted for destruction by the Nazis.[1] Yugoslavia lost one person in eight of the country's pre-war population, the USSR one in 11, Greece one in 14. To point up the contrast, Germany suffered a rate of loss of 1/15; France 1/77; Britain 1/125.

---

[1] Or by Stalin, who ordered the shooting of 23,000 Polish officers in Katyn forest in 1940 and then blamed it on the Germans.

The Soviet losses in particular include prisoners of war. The Germans captured some 5.5 million Soviet soldiers in the course of the war, three quarters of them in the first seven months following the attack on the USSR in June 1941. Of these, 3.3 million died from starvation, exposure and mistreatment in German camps—more Russians died in German prisoner-of-war camps in the years 1941–45 than in all of World War One. Of the 750,000 Soviet soldiers captured when the Germans took Kiev in September 1941, just 22,000 lived to see Germany defeated. The Soviets in their turn took 3.5 million prisoners of war (German, Austrian, Romanian and Hungarian for the most part); most of them returned home after the war.

In view of these figures, it is hardly surprising that post-war Europe, especially central and eastern Europe, suffered an acute shortage of men. In the Soviet Union the number of women exceeded men by 20 million, an imbalance that would take more than a generation to correct. The Soviet rural economy now depended heavily on women for labour of every kind: not only were there no men, there were almost no horses. In Yugoslavia—thanks to German reprisal actions in which all males over 15 were shot—there were many villages with no adult men left at all. In Germany itself, two out of every three men born in 1918 did not survive Hitler's war: in one community for which we have detailed figures—the Berlin suburb of Treptow—in February 1946, among adults aged 19–21 there were just 181 men for 1,105 women.

Much has been made of this over-representation of women in post-war Germany especially. The humiliated, diminished status of German males—reduced from the supermen of Hitler's burnished armies to a ragged troupe of belatedly returning prisoners, bemusedly encountering a generation of hardened women who had perforce learned to survive and manage without them—is not a fiction (the German Chancellor Gerhard Schroeder is just one of many thousands of German children who grew up after the war without fathers). Rainer Fassbinder put this image of post-war German womanhood to effective cinematic use in the *Marriage of Maria Braun* (1979), where the eponymous heroine turns her good looks and her cynical energies to advantage, despite her mother's entreaties to do nothing 'that might harm your soul'. But whereas Fassbinder's Maria carried the burden of a later generation's resentful disillusion, the real women of 1945 Germany faced more immediate difficulties.

In the final months of the war, as the Soviet armies pushed west into central Europe and eastern Prussia, millions of civilians—most of them German—fled before them. George Kennan, the American diplomat, described the scene in his memoirs: 'The disaster that befell this area with the entry of the Soviet forces has no parallel in modern European experience. There were considerable sections of it where, to judge by all existing evidence, scarcely a man, woman or child of the indigenous population was left alive after the initial passage of Soviet forces ... The Russians ... swept the native population clean in a manner that had no parallel since the days of the Asiatic hordes.'

Chief among the victims were adult males (if any remained) and women of any age. 87,000 women in Vienna were reported by clinics and doctors to have been raped by Soviet soldiers in the three weeks following the Red Army's arrival in the city. A slightly larger number of women in Berlin were raped in the Soviet march on the city, most of them in the week of May 2nd–7th, immediately preceding the German surrender. Both of these figures are surely an underestimate, and they do not include the uncounted number of assaults on women in the villages and towns that lay in the path of the Soviet forces in their advance into Austria and across western Poland into Germany.

The behaviour of the Red Army was hardly a secret. Milovan Djilas, Tito's close collaborator in the Yugoslav partisan army and at the time a fervent Communist, even raised the matter with Stalin himself. The dictator's response, as recorded by Djilas, is revealing: 'Does Djilas, who is himself a writer, know what human suffering and the human heart are? Can't he understand the soldier who has gone through blood and fire and death, if he has fun with a woman or takes a trifle?'

In his grotesque way, Stalin was half right. There was no leave policy in the Soviet army. Many of its infantry and tank crews had fought their way back for three terrible years in an unbroken series of battles and marches across the western USSR, through Russia and Ukraine. In the course of their advance they saw and heard copious evidence of German atrocities. The Wehrmacht's treatment of war prisoners, of civilians, of partisans and indeed of anyone or anything that got in its way, first in its proud advance to the Volga and the gates of Moscow and Leningrad, then in its bitter, bloody retreat, had left its mark on the face of the land and in the soul of the people.

When the Red Army finally reached central Europe, its exhausted soldiers encountered another world. The contrast between Russia and the West was always great—Czar Alexander I had long ago regretted allowing Russians to see how Westerners lived—and it had grown even sharper during the war. While German soldiers wreaked devastation and mass murder in the East, Germany itself remained prosperous—so much so that its civilian population had very little sense of the material cost of war until quite late in the conflict. Wartime Germany was a world of towns, of electricity, of food and clothing and shops and consumer goods, of reasonably well-fed women and children. The contrast with his own devastated homeland must have seemed unfathomable to the common Soviet soldier. The Germans had done terrible things to Russia; now it was their turn to suffer. Their possessions and their women were there for the taking. With the tacit consent of its commanders, the Red Army was turned loose on the civilian population of the newly-conquered German lands.

On its route west the Red Army raped and pillaged (the phrase, for once, is brutally apt) in Hungary, Romania, Slovakia and Yugoslavia; but German women suffered by far the worst. Between 150,000 and 200,000 'Russian babies' were born in the Soviet-occupied zone of Germany in 1945–46, and these figures make no allowance for untold numbers of abortions, as a result of which many women died along with their unwanted foetuses. Many of the surviving infants joined the growing number of children now orphaned and homeless: the human flotsam of war.

In Berlin alone, there were some 53,000 lost children by the end of 1945. The Quirinale gardens in Rome became briefly notorious as a gathering place for thousands of Italy's mutilated, disfigured and unclaimed children. In liberated Czechoslovakia there were 49,000 orphaned children; in the Netherlands, 60,000; in Poland it was estimated that there were about 200,000 orphans, in Yugoslavia perhaps 300,000. Few of the younger children were Jewish—such Jewish children as survived the pogroms and exterminations of the war years were mostly adolescent boys. In Buchenwald, 800 children were found alive at the liberation of the camp; in Belsen just 500, some of whom had even survived the death march from Auschwitz.

Surviving the war was one thing, surviving the peace another. Thanks to early and effective intervention by the newly formed United Nations Relief and Rehabilitation Administration (UNRRA) and the occupying allied armies, large-scale epidemics and the uncontrolled spread of contagious diseases were avoided—the memory of the Asian 'flu that swept through Europe in the wake of the First World War was still fresh. But the situation was grim enough. For much of 1945 the population of Vienna subsisted on a ration of 800 calories per day; in Budapest in December 1945 the officially provided ration was just 556 calories per day (children in nurseries received 800). During the Dutch 'hunger winter' of 1944–45 (when parts of the country had already been liberated) the *weekly* calorie ration in some regions fell below the *daily* allocation recommended by the Allied Expeditionary Force for its soldiers; 16,000 Dutch citizens died, mostly old people and children.

In Germany, where the average adult intake had been 2,445 calories per day in 1940–41 and was 2,078 calories per day in 1943, it had fallen to 1,412 calories for the year 1945–46. But this was just an average. In June 1945, in the American Zone of occupation, the official daily ration for 'normal' German consumers (excluding favoured categories of worker) stood at just 860 calories. These figures gave rueful significance to the wartime German joke: 'Better enjoy the war—the peace will be terrible.' But the situation was not much better in most of Italy and somewhat worse in some districts of Yugoslavia and Greece. [2]

The problem lay partly in destroyed farms, partly in disrupted communications and mostly in the sheer numbers of helpless, unproductive mouths needing to be fed. Where Europe's farmers *could* grow food they were reluctant to supply it to the towns. Most European currencies were worthless; and even if there had been the wherewithal to pay peasants for their food in some hard currency, the latter held little attraction for them—there was nothing to buy. So food did appear on

---

[2] By way of comparison—the average daily calorie consumption in France in 1990 was 3,618.

the black market, but at prices that only criminals, the rich and the occupiers could pay.

In the meantime, people starved and they fell sick. One third of the population of Piraeus, in Greece, suffered from trachoma in 1945 due to acute vitamin deficiency. During an outbreak of dysentery in Berlin during July 1945—the result of damaged sewage systems and polluted water supplies—there were 66 infant deaths for every 100 live births. Robert Murphy, the US political adviser for Germany, reported in October 1945 that an average of ten people daily were dying at the Lehrter railway station in Berlin from exhaustion, malnutrition and illness. In the British Zone of Berlin, in December 1945, the death rate of children under one year was one in four, while during that same month there were 1,023 new cases of typhoid and 2,193 cases of diphtheria.

For many weeks after the end of the war, in the summer of 1945, there was a serious risk, in Berlin especially, of disease from rotting corpses. In Warsaw, one person in five suffered from tuberculosis. The Czechoslovak authorities in January 1946 reported that half of the 700,000 needy children in the country were infected with the disease. Children all over Europe were suffering from sicknesses of deprivation: tuberculosis and rickets especially, but also pellagra, dysentery and impetigo. Sick children had little recourse: for the 90,000 children of liberated Warsaw there was just one hospital, with fifty beds. Otherwise healthy children died from a shortage of milk (millions of head of European cattle were slaughtered in the battles across southern and eastern Europe in 1944–45) and most were chronically undernourished. Infant mortality in Vienna during the summer of 1945 was nearly four times the rate in 1938. Even in the relatively prosperous streets of western cities children went hungry and food was strictly rationed.

The problem of feeding, housing, clothing and caring for Europe's battered civilians (and the millions of imprisoned soldiers of the former Axis powers) was complicated and magnified by the unique scale of the refugee crisis. This was something new in the European experience. All wars dislocate the lives of non-combatants: by destroying their land and their homes, by disrupting communications, by enlisting and killing husbands, fathers, sons. But in World War Two it was state policies rather than armed conflict that did the worst damage.

Stalin had continued his pre-war practice of transferring whole peoples across the Soviet empire. Well over a million people were deported east from Soviet-occupied Poland and the western Ukraine and Baltic lands between 1939–41. In the same years the Nazis too expelled 750,000 Polish peasants eastwards from western Poland, offering the vacated land to *Volksdeutsche*, ethnic Germans from occupied eastern Europe who were invited to 'come home' to the newly-expanded Reich. This offer attracted some 120,000 Baltic Germans, a further 136,000 from Soviet-occupied Poland, 200,000 from Romania and others besides—all of whom would in their turn be expelled a few years later. Hitler's policy of racial transfers and genocide in Germany's conquered eastern lands must thus be understood in direct relation to the Nazis' project of returning to the Reich (and settling in the newly-cleared property of their victims) all the far-flung settlements of Germans dating back to medieval times. The Germans removed Slavs, exterminated Jews and imported slave workers from west and east alike.

Between them Stalin and Hitler uprooted, transplanted, expelled, deported and dispersed some 30 million people in the years 1939–43. With the retreat of the Axis armies, the process was reversed. Newly-resettled Germans joined millions of es-tablished German communities throughout eastern Europe in headlong flight from the Red Army. Those who made it safely into Germany were joined there by a pul-lulating throng of other displaced persons. William Byford-Jones, an officer with the British army, described the situation in 1945 thus:

'Flotsam and jetsam! Women who had lost husbands and children, men who had lost their wives; men and women who had lost their homes and children; families who had lost vast farms and estates, shops, distilleries, factories, flour-mills, mansions. There were also little children who were alone, carry-ing some small bundle, with a pathetic label attached to them. They had somehow got detached from their mothers, or their mothers had died and been buried by other displaced persons somewhere along the wayside.'

From the east came Balts, Poles, Ukrainians, Cossacks, Hungarians, Romanians and others: some were just fleeing the horrors of war, others escaping West to avoid being caught under Communist rule. A *New York Times* reporter described a col-umn of 24,000 Cossack soldiers and families moving through southern Austria, 'no different in any major detail from what an artist might have painted in the Napoleonic wars'.

From the Balkans came not just ethnic Germans but more than 100,000 Croats from the fallen wartime fascist regime of Ante Pavelic, fleeing the wrath of Tito's partisans.[3] In Germany and Austria, in addition to the millions of Wehr-macht soldiers held by the Allies and newly released Allied soldiers from German p-o-w camps, there were many non-Germans who had fought against the Allies alongside the Germans or under German command: the Russian, Ukrainian and other soldiers of General Andrei Vlasov's anti-Soviet army; volunteers for the *Waf-fen SS* from Norway, the Netherlands, Belgium and France; and auxiliary German fighters, concentration camp staff and others liberally recruited in Latvia, Ukraine, Croatia and elsewhere. All had good reason to seek refuge from Soviet retribution.

Then there were the newly-released men and women who had been recruited by the Nazis to work in Germany. Brought into German farms and factories from all across the continent, they numbered many millions, spread across Germany

---

[3]They had good grounds for fear. The British army in Austria would later hand them over to the Yu-goslav authorities (under an Allied agreement to return such prisoners to the government against whom they had fought) and at least 40,000 of them were killed.

proper and its annexed territories, constituting the largest single group of Nazi-displaced persons in 1945. Involuntary *economic* migration was thus the primary social experience of World War Two for many European civilians, including 280,000 Italians forcibly removed to Germany by their former ally after Italy's capitulation to the Allies in September 1943.

Most of Germany's foreign workers had been brought there against their will—but not all. Some foreign workers caught in the slipstream of German defeat in May 1945 had come of their own free will—like those unemployed Dutchmen who accepted offers of work in Nazi Germany before 1939 and stayed on.[4] Even at the derisory wages paid by wartime German employers, men and women from eastern Europe, the Balkans, France and the Benelux countries were often better off there than staying at home. And Soviet labourers (of whom there were upwards of two million in Germany by September 1944), even if they had been brought to Germany by force, were not necessarily sorry to be there—as one of them, Elena Skrjabena, recalled after the war: 'None of them complain about how the Germans had sent them to work in German industry. For all of them that was the only possibility of getting out of the Soviet Union.'

Another group of displaced persons, the survivors of the concentration camps, felt rather differently. Their 'crimes' had been various—political or religious opposition to Nazism or Fascism, armed resistance, collective punishment for attacks on Wehrmacht soldiers or installations, minor transgressions of Occupation regulations, real or invented criminal activities, falling foul of Nazi racial laws. They survived camps which by the end were piled high with dead bodies and where diseases of every kind were endemic: dysentery, TB, diphtheria, typhoid, typhus, broncho-pneumonia, gastro-enteritis, gangrene and much else. But even these survivors were better off than the Jews, since they had not been systematically and collectively scheduled for extermination.

Few Jews remained. Of those who were liberated 4 out of 10 died within a few weeks of the arrival of Allied armies—their condition was beyond the experience of Western medicine. But the surviving Jews, like most of Europe's other homeless millions, found their way into Germany. Germany was where the Allied agencies and camps were to be situated—and anyway, eastern Europe was still not safe for Jews. After a series of post-war pogroms in Poland many of the surviving Jews left for good: 63,387 Jews arrived in Germany from Poland just between July and September 1946.

What was taking place in 1945, and had been underway for at least a year, was thus an unprecedented exercise in ethnic cleansing and population transfer. In part this was the outcome of 'voluntary' ethnic separation: Jewish survivors leaving a Poland where they were unsafe and unwanted, for example, or Italians departing

---

[4]Yet they, too, had little real choice—during the Depression years anyone who refused a proffered work contract from Germany risked losing his Dutch unemployment benefits.

the Istrian peninsula rather than live under Yugoslav rule. Many ethnic minorities who had collaborated with occupying forces (Italians in Yugoslavia, Hungarians in Hungarian-occupied northern Transylvania now returned to Romanian rule, Ukrainians in the western Soviet Union, etc) fled with the retreating Wehrmacht to avoid retribution from the local majority or the advancing Red Army, and never returned. Their departure may not have been legally mandated or enforced by local authorities, but they had little option.

Elsewhere, however, official policy was at work well before the war ended. The Germans of course began this, with the removal and genocide of the Jews, and the mass expulsions of Poles and other Slav nations. Under German aegis between 1939 and 1943 Romanians and Hungarians shunted back and forth across new frontier lines in disputed Transylvania. The Soviet authorities in their turn engineered a series of forced population exchanges between Ukraine and Poland; one million Poles fled or were expelled from their homes in what was now western Ukraine, while half a million Ukrainians left Poland for the Soviet Union between October 1944 and June 1946. In the course of a few months what had once been an intermixed region of different faiths, languages and communities became two distinct, mono-ethnic territories.

Bulgaria transferred 160,000 Turks to Turkey; Czechoslovakia, under a February 1946 agreement with Hungary, exchanged the 120,000 Slovaks living in Hungary for an equivalent number of Hungarians from communities north of the Danube, in Slovakia. Other transfers of this kind took place between Poland and Lithuania and between Czechoslovakia and the Soviet Union; 400,000 people from southern Yugoslavia were moved to land in the north to take the place of 600,000 departed Germans and Italians. Here as elsewhere, the populations concerned were not consulted. But the largest affected group was the Germans.

The Germans of eastern Europe would probably have fled west in any case: by 1945 they were not wanted in the countries where their families had been settled for many hundreds of years. Between a genuine popular desire to punish local Germans for the ravages of war and occupation, and the exploitation of this mood by post-war governments, the German-speaking communities of Yugoslavia, Hungary, Czechoslovakia, Poland, the Baltic region and the western Soviet Union were doomed and they knew it.

In the event, they were given no choice. As early as 1942 the British had privately acceded to Czech requests for a post-war removal of the Sudeten German population, and the Russians and Americans fell into line the following year. On May 19th 1945, President Edouard Benes of Czechoslovakia decreed that ' we have decided to eliminate the German problem in our republic once and for all'.[5] Germans

---

[5]In a speech in Bratislava on May 9th 1945, Benes declared that Czechs and Slovaks no longer wished to live in the same state as Hungarians and Germans. This sentiment, and the actions that followed, has haunted Czech-German and Slovak-Hungarian relations ever since.

(as well as Hungarians and other 'traitors') were to have their property placed under state control. In June 1945 their land was expropriated and on August 2nd of that year they lost their Czechoslovak citizenship. Nearly three million Germans, most of them from the Czech Sudetenland, were then expelled into Germany in the course of the following eighteen months. Approximately 267,000 died in the course of the expulsions. Whereas Germans had comprised 29 percent of the population of Bohemia and Moravia in 1930, by the census of 1950 they were just 1.8 percent.

From Hungary a further 623,000 Germans were expelled, from Romania 786,000, from Yugoslavia about half a million and from Poland 1.3 million. But by far the greatest number of German refugees came from the former eastern lands of Germany itself: Silesia, East Prussia, eastern Pomerania and eastern Brandenburg. At the Potsdam meeting of the US, Britain and the USSR (July 17th–August 2nd 1945) it was agreed, in the words of Article XIII of the subsequent agreement, that the three governments 'recognize that the transfer to Germany of German populations, or elements thereof, remaining in Poland, Czechoslovakia and Hungary, will have to be undertaken.' In part this merely recognized what had already taken place, but it also represented a formal acknowledgement of the implications of shifting Poland's frontiers westwards. Some seven million Germans would now find themselves in Poland, and the Polish authorities (and the occupying Soviet forces) wanted them removed—in part so that Poles and others who lost land in the eastern regions now absorbed into the USSR could in their turn be resettled in the new lands to the west.

The upshot was *de jure* recognition of a new reality. Eastern Europe had been forcibly cleared of its German populations: as Stalin had promised in September 1941, he had returned 'East Prussia back to Slavdom, where it belongs.' In the Potsdam Declaration it was agreed 'that any transfers that take place should be effected in an orderly and humane manner', but under the circumstances this was hardly likely. Some Western observers were shocked at the treatment of the German communities. Anne O'Hare McCormick, a *New York Times* correspondent, recorded her impressions on October 23rd 1946: 'The scale of this resettlement, and the conditions in which it takes place, are without precedent in history. No one seeing its horrors first hand can doubt that it is a crime against humanity for which history will exact a terrible retribution.'

History has exacted no such retribution. Indeed, the 13 million expellees were settled and integrated into West German society with remarkable success, though memories remain and in Bavaria (where many of them went) the subject can still provoke intense feeling. To contemporary ears it is perhaps a little jarring to hear the German expulsions described as a 'crime against humanity' a few months after the revelation of crimes on an altogether different scale committed in the name of those same Germans. But then the Germans were alive and present, whereas their victims—Jews above all—were mostly dead and gone. In the words of Telford Taylor, the US prosecutor at the Nuremberg trials of the Nazi leadership, writing many decades later: there was a crucial difference between the post-war expulsions and the wartime population clearances, 'when the expellers accompany the expelled to ensure that they are kept in ghettos and then either kill them or use them as forced labor.'

At the conclusion of the First World War it was borders that were invented and adjusted, while people were on the whole left in place.[6] After 1945 what happened was rather the opposite: with one major exception boundaries stayed broadly intact and people were moved instead. There was a feeling among Western policymakers that the League of Nations, and the minority clauses in the Versailles Treaties, had failed and that it would be a mistake even to try and resurrect them. For this reason they acquiesced readily enough in the population transfers. If the surviving minorities of central and eastern Europe could not be afforded effective international protection, then it was as well that they be dispatched to more accommodating locations. The term 'ethnic cleansing' did not yet exist, but the reality surely did—and it was far from arousing wholesale disapproval or embarrassment.

The exception, as so often, was Poland. The geographical re-arrangement of Poland—losing 69,000 square miles of its eastern borderlands to the Soviet Union and being compensated with 40,000 square miles of rather better land from German territories east of the Oder-Neisse rivers—was dramatic and consequential for Poles, Ukrainians and Germans in the affected lands. But in the circumstances of 1945 it was unusual, and should rather be understood as part of the general territorial adjustment that Stalin imposed all along the western rim of his empire: recovering Bessarabia from Romania, seizing the Bukovina and Sub-Carpathian Ruthenia from Romania and Czechoslovakia respectively, absorbing the Baltic states into the Soviet Union and retaining the Karelian peninsula, seized from Finland during the war.

West of the new Soviet frontiers there was little change. Bulgaria recovered a sliver of land from Romania in the Dobrudja region; the Czechoslovaks obtained from Hungary (a defeated Axis power and thus unable to object) three villages on the right bank of the Danube opposite Bratislava; Tito was able to hold on to part of the formerly Italian territory around Trieste and in Venezia Giulia that his forces occupied at the end of the war. Otherwise land seized by force between 1938 and 1945 was returned and the *status quo ante* restored.

With certain exceptions, the outcome was a Europe of nation states more ethnically homogenous than ever before. The Soviet Union of course remained a multi-national empire. Yugoslavia lost none of its ethnic complexity, despite bloody

[6]With the significant exception of Greeks and Turks, following the Lausanne Treaty of 1923.

inter-communal fighting during the war. Romania still had a sizeable Hungarian minority in Transylvania and uncounted numbers—millions—of gypsies. But Poland, whose population was just 68 percent Polish in 1938, was overwhelmingly populated by Poles in 1946. Germany was nearly all German (not counting temporary refugees and displaced persons); Czechoslovakia, whose population before Munich was 22 percent German, 5 percent Hungarian, 3 percent Carpathian Ukrainians and 1.5 percent Jewish, was now almost exclusively Czech and Slovak: of the 55,000 Czechoslovak Jews who survived the war, all but 16,000 would leave by 1950. The ancient diasporas of Europe—Greeks and Turks in the south Balkans and around the Black Sea, Italians in Dalmatia, Hungarians in Transylvania and the north Balkans, Poles in Volhynia (Ukraine), Lithuania and the Bukovina, Germans from the Baltic to the Black Sea, from the Rhine to the Volga, and Jews everywhere—shriveled and disappeared. A new, 'tidier' Europe was being born.

Most of the initial management of the displaced persons and refugees—gathering them up, establishing camps for them and providing food, clothing and medical help was undertaken by the Allied armies occupying Germany, the US Army especially. There was no other authority in Germany but also in Austria and in northern Italy, the other areas in which refugees congregated. Only the army had the resources and the organizational capacity to administer the demographic equivalent of a medium-sized country. This was an unprecedented charge for a huge military machine that, just a few weeks before, had been devoted almost exclusively to the business of fighting the Wehrmacht. As General Dwight D. Eisenhower (the Supreme Allied Commander) expressed it, reporting to President Harry Truman on October 8th 1945 in response to criticisms directed at the military's handling of refugees and concentration camp survivors: 'In certain instances we have fallen below standard, but I should like to point out that a whole army has been faced with the intricate problem of adjusting from combat to mass repatriation and then to the present static phase with its unique welfare problems.'

Once the system of camps had been set in place, however, responsibility for the care and eventual repatriation or resettlement of the displaced millions fell increasingly on the United Nations Relief and Rehabilitation Administration. UNRRA was founded in November 9th 1943 at a Washington meeting of representatives from 44 future UN members, held in anticipation of likely post-war needs, and went on to play a vital role in the post-war emergency. The agency spent $10 billion between July 1945 and June 1947, almost all of it furnished by the governments of the USA, Canada and the United Kingdom. A lot of that aid went directly to former allies in eastern Europe—Poland, Yugoslavia and Czechoslovakia—and to the Soviet Union, as well as to the administration of displaced persons in Germany and elsewhere. Of the former Axis countries only Hungary received UNRRA assistance, and not very much at that.

In late 1945 UNRRA was operating 227 camps and relief centers for displaced persons and refugees in Germany, with a further 25 in neighbouring Austria and a handful in France and the Benelux countries. By June 1947 it had 762 such units in Western Europe, the overwhelming majority in the Western Zones of Germany. At its peak, in September 1945, the number of liberated United Nations civilians (i.e. not including citizens of former Axis countries) being cared for or repatriated by UNRRA and other Allied agencies was 6,795,000—to whom should be added a further 7 million under Soviet authority and many millions of displaced Germans. In nationality the largest groups were from the Soviet Union: released prisoners and former forced labourers. Then came 2 million French (prisoners of war, labourers and deportees), 1.6 million Poles, 700,000 Italians, 350,000 Czechs, more than 300,000 Dutch, 300,000 Belgians and countless others.

UNRRA food supplies played a vital part in feeding Yugoslavia especially: without the agency's contributions, many more people would have died in the years 1945–47. In Poland UNRRA helped maintain food consumption at 60 percent of pre-war levels, in Czechoslovakia at 80 percent. In Germany and Austria it shared responsibility for handling displaced persons and refugees with the International Refugee Organisation (IRO), whose statutes were approved by the General Assembly of the UN in December 1946.

The IRO, too, was largely funded from the Western allied powers. In its first (1947) budget the United States' share was 46 percent, rising to 60 percent by 1949; the United Kingdom contributed 15 percent, France 4 percent. Because of disagreement between the Western allies and the Soviet Union over the issue of forced repatriations, the IRO was always regarded by the USSR (and later by the Soviet bloc) as a purely Western instrument and its services were thus confined to refugees in areas controlled by Western armies of occupation. Moreover, since it was devoted to servicing the needs of refugees, German displaced persons were also debarred from its benefits.

This distinction between displaced persons (assumed to have, somewhere, a home to go to) and refugees (who were classified as homeless) was just one of many nuances that were introduced in these years. People were treated differently depending on whether they were nationals of a wartime ally (Czechoslovakia, Poland, Belgium, etc) or a former enemy state (Germany, Romania, Hungary, Bulgaria, etc). This distinction was also invoked when establishing priorities for the repatriation of refugees. The first to be processed and sent home were UN nationals liberated from concentration camps; then came UN nationals who had been prisoners of war, followed by UN nationals who were displaced persons (former forced labourers in many cases), then displaced persons from Italy and finally the nationals of former enemy states. Germans were to be left in place and absorbed locally.

Returning French, Belgian, Dutch, British or Italian citizens to their country of origin was relatively straightforward and the only impediments were logistic: determining who had a right to go where and finding enough trains to take them there. By June 18th 1945, all but 40,550 of the 1.2 million French nationals found in

Germany at the surrender a month earlier were back in France. Italians had to wait longer, as former enemy nationals and because the Italian government had no co-ordinated plan to repatriate its citizens. But even they were all home by 1947. In the east, however, there were two significant complications. Some displaced persons from eastern Europe were technically stateless and had no country to which to return. And many of them had no wish to go home. This puzzled Western administrators at first. Under an agreement signed at Halle, in Germany, in May 1945 all former prisoners of war and other citizens of the Soviet Union were to return home, and it was assumed that they would wish to do so. There was one exception: the western Allies did not recognize Stalin's wartime absorption of the Baltic states into the USSR and Estonians, Latvians and Lithuanians in displaced persons camps in the western zones of Germany and Austria were therefore to be given the option of returning east or finding new homes in the West.

But it was not just the Balts who did not wish to go back. A large number of former Soviet, Polish, Romanian and Yugoslav citizens also preferred to remain in temporary camps in Germany rather than return to their countries. In the case of Soviet citizens this reluctance often arose from a well-founded fear of reprisals against anyone who had spent time in the West, even if that time had been passed in a prison camp. In the case of Balts, Ukrainians, Croats and others there was a reluctance to return to countries now under Communist control in fact if not yet in name: in many cases this reluctance was prompted by fear of retribution for real or imputed war crimes, but it was also driven by a simple desire to escape west into a better life.

Throughout 1945 and 1946 Western authorities preferred to ignore such feelings on the whole and oblige Soviet and other east European citizens to return home, sometimes by force. With Soviet officials actively rounding up their own people from German camps, refugees from the East sought desperately to convince bemused French, American or British officials that they did not want to return 'home' and would rather stay in Germany—of all places. They were not always successful: between 1945 and 1947, 2,272,000 Soviet citizens were returned by the Western Allies.

There were terrible scenes of desperate struggle, particularly in the early postwar months, as Russian émigrés who had never been Soviet citizens, Ukrainian partisans and many others were rounded up by British or American troops and pushed—sometimes literally—across the border into the arms of the waiting NKVD.[7] Once in Soviet hands they joined hundreds of thousands of other repatriated Soviet nationals, as well as Hungarians, Germans and other former enemies deported east by the Red Army. By 1953 a total of five and a half million So-

---

[7]At the end of May 1945 the British Army turned over to Yugoslav authorities 10,000 Slovenian soldiers and civilians who had fled to Austria. Most of them were trucked south to the Kocevje forests and summarily shot.

viet nationals had been repatriated. One in five of them ended up shot or dispatched to the Gulag. Many more were sent directly into Siberian exile or else assigned to labour battalions.

Only in 1947 did forced repatriation cease, with the onset of the Cold War and a new willingness to treat displaced persons from the Soviet bloc as *political* refugees (the 50,000 Czech nationals still in Germany and Austria at the time of the February 1948 Communist coup in Prague were immediately accorded this status). A total of one and a half million Poles, Hungarians, Bulgarians, Romanians, Yugoslavs, Soviet nationals and Jews thus successfully resisted repatriation. Together with Balts these formed the overwhelming majority of displaced persons left in the western zones of Germany and Austria, and in Italy. In 1951 the European Convention on Human Rights would codify the protection to which such displaced aliens were entitled, and finally guarantee them against forcible return to persecution.

The question remained, however: what was to become of them? The refugees and DPs themselves were in no doubt. In the words of Genêt (Janet Flanner), writing in *The New Yorker* in October 1948, '[The displaced persons] are willing to go anywhere on earth except home.' But who would take them? West European states, short of labour and in the midst of economic and material reconstruction, were initially quite open to importing certain categories of stateless person. Belgium, France and Britain especially needed coalminers, construction workers and agricultural labourers. In 1946–47 Belgium took in 22,000 displaced persons (along with their families) to work in the mines of Wallonia. France took in 38,000 people for manual employment of various kinds. Britain took 86,000 persons in this way, including many veterans of the Polish army and Ukrainians who had fought in the *Waffen SS* 'Halychnya' Division.[8]

The criteria for admission were simple—western European states were interested in strong (male) manual workers, and were not embarrassed to favour Balts, Poles and Ukrainians on those grounds, whatever their wartime record. Single women were welcome as manual workers or domestics—but the Canadian Labor Department in 1948 rejected girls and women applying to emigrate to Canada for jobs in domestic service if there was any sign that they had education beyond secondary school. And no-one wanted older people, orphans or single women with children. Refugees in general, then, were not met with open arms—post-war polls in the US and western Europe revealed very little sympathy for their plight. Most people expressed a desire to see immigration reduced rather than increased.

The problem of the Jews was distinctive. At first the Western authorities treated Jewish DPs like any other, corralling them in camps in Germany alongside many

---

[8]The Halychnya or Galician Division of the Waffen SS was made up of Ukrainians who had been citizens of inter-war Poland and whose region of origin was incorporated into the USSR after the war. They were thus not repatriated to the Soviet Union, despite having fought against it alongside the Wehrmacht, and were treated by Western authorities as stateless persons.

of their former persecutors. But in August 1945 President Truman announced that separate facilities should be provided for all Jewish DPs in the American Zone of Germany: in the words of a report the President had commissioned to look into the problem, the previously integrated camps and centers were 'a distinctly unrealistic approach to the problem. Refusal to recognize the Jews as such has the effect . . . of closing one's eyes to their former and more barbaric persecution.' By the end of September 1945, all Jews in the US Zone were being cared for separately.

There had never been any question of returning Jews to the east—no-one in the Soviet Union, Poland or anywhere else evinced the slightest interest in having them back. Nor were Jews particularly welcome in the west, especially if educated or qualified in non-manual professions. And so they remained, ironically enough, in Germany. The difficulty of 'placing' the Jews of Europe was only solved by the creation of the state of Israel: between 1948 and 1951 332,000 European Jews left for Israel, either from IRO centers in Germany or else directly from Romania, Poland and elsewhere, in the case of those still left in these countries. A further 165,000 eventually left for France, Britain, Australia and North or South America.

There they would be joined by the remaining displaced persons and refugees from World War Two, to whom should be added a new generation of political refugees from east-central European countries in the years 1947–49. Overall the US admitted 400,000 people in these years, with another 185,000 arriving in the course of the years 1953–57. Canada allowed in a total of 157,000 refugees and DPs, Australia took 182,000 (among them 60,000 Poles and 36,000 Balts).

The scale of this achievement needs to be emphasized. Some people, notably certain categories of ethnic Germans from Yugoslavia and Romania, were left in limbo because the Potsdam agreements did not cover their case. But in the course of half a dozen years, operating in a scarred, embittered and impoverished continent emerging from six years of terrible war and already anticipating the divisions of the Cold War, the Allied Military Governments and the UN civilian agencies succeeded in repatriating, integrating or resettling unprecedented numbers—many millions— of desperate people from all across the continent and dozens of different nations and communities. By the end of 1951, when UNRRA and the IRO were replaced by the newly-established United Nations High Commission for Refugees, there were just 177,000 people left in displaced persons camps in Europe—mostly the aged and the infirm, because no-one wanted them. The last DP camp in Germany, at Foehrenwald in Bavaria, closed in 1957.

The displaced persons and refugees of Europe had survived not just a general war but a whole series of local, civil wars. Indeed, from 1934 through 1949, Europe saw an unprecedented sequence of murderous civil conflicts within the boundaries of existing states. In many cases subsequent foreign occupation—whether by Germans, Italians or Russians—served above all to facilitate and legitimize the pursuit of pre-war political agendas and antagonisms by new and violent means. The oc-cupiers were not neutral, of course. Typically they joined forces with factions within the occupied nation to fight a common foe. In this way, a political tendency or eth-nic minority that had been at a disadvantage in peacetime politics was able to ex-ploit the altered circumstances to settle local scores. The Germans, especially, were pleased to mobilize and exploit such sentiments not merely to divide and thus more easily conquer, but also to reduce the trouble and cost of administering and policing their conquered territories: they could rely on local collaborators to do it for them.

Since 1945 the term 'collaborators' has acquired a distinctive and pejorative moral connotation. But wartime divisions and affiliations often carried local im-plications altogether more complicated and ambiguous than the simple post-war attributions—of 'collaboration' and 'resistance'—would imply. Thus in occupied Belgium some Flemish-speakers, repeating a mistake they had already made in the First World War, were tempted by the promise of autonomy and a chance to break the French-speaking elite's hold on the Belgian state, and welcomed German rule. Here as elsewhere the Nazis willingly played the communal card so long as it suited their purposes—Flemish-speaking Belgian prisoners of war were released in 1940 when hostilities ceased, whereas French-speaking Walloons remained in p-o-w camps throughout the war.

In France and Belgium, as also in Norway, resistance against the Germans was real, especially in the last two years of the occupation when Nazi efforts to press-gang young men into forced labour in Germany drove many of them to opt for the *maquis* (forests) as a lesser risk. But not until the very end of the occupation did the number of active resisters exceed the numbers of those who collaborated with the Nazis out of belief, venality or self-interest—in France it has been estimated that the likely numbers of fully engaged men and women was about the same on both sides, between 160,000–170,000 at most. And their main enemy, more often than not, was each other: the Germans were largely absent.

In Italy, circumstances were more complicated. The Fascists had been in power for twenty years when Mussolini was overthrown in a palace coup in July 1943. Per-haps for this reason, there was little local resistance to the regime; most active anti-Fascists were in exile. After September 1943, when the country officially became a 'co-belligerent' on the Allied side, the German-occupied north of the country was torn between a puppet regime—Mussolini's 'Republic of Salò'—and a small but courageous partisan resistance co-operating with and sometimes supported by the advancing Allied armies.

But here, too, what was presented by both camps as a majority of right-thinking Italians locked in conflict with a marginal band of murderous terrorists in league with a foreign power was actually, for the years 1943–45, a genuine civil war, with significant numbers of Italians engaged on either side. The Fascists of Salò were in-deed the unrepresentative collaborators of a brutal occupier; but the domestic support they could count on at the time was not negligible, and certainly not obviously less than that of their most aggressive opponents, the Communist-led partisans. The anti-Fascist resistance was in reality one side in a struggle among Italians whose memory came to be conveniently occluded in the post-war decades.

In eastern Europe matters were more complicated still. Slovaks and Croats took advantage of the German presence to establish notionally independent states in accordance with the cherished projects of pre-war separatist parties. In Poland the Germans were not looking for collaborators; but further north—in the Baltic States and even Finland—the Wehrmacht was initially welcomed as an alternative to occupation and absorption by the Soviet Union. Ukrainians especially did their best to capitalize on German occupation after 1941 to secure their long-sought independence, and the lands of eastern Galicia and western Ukraine saw a murderous civil conflict between Ukrainian and Polish partisans under the aegis of both anti-Nazi and anti-Soviet partisan warfare. In these circumstances, fine distinctions between ideological warfare, inter-communal conflict and the battle for political independence lost their meaning: not least for the local populations, the primary victims in every case.

Poles and Ukrainians fought with or against the Wehrmacht, the Red Army and each other according to the moment and the place. In Poland this conflict, which after 1944 transmuted into guerilla warfare against the Communist state, took the lives of some 30,000 Poles in the years 1945–48. In the Soviet-occupied Ukraine, the last partisan commander, Roman Shukhevych, was killed near Lviv in 1950, though sporadic anti-Soviet activity persisted for a few years more in Ukraine and Estonia in particular.

It was in the Balkans, however, that the Second World War was experienced above all as a civil war, and a uniquely murderous one at that. In Yugoslavia the meaning of conventional labels—collaborator, resister—was particularly opaque. What was Draza Mihajlović, the Serb leader of the Chetnik[9] partisans? A patriot? A resister? A collaborator? What was it that moved men to fight? Resistance against the (German, Italian) occupier? Revenge against domestic political enemies from the inter-war Yugoslav state? Inter-community conflicts among Serbs, Croats and Muslims? Pro- or anti-Communist goals? For many people more than one motive was in play.

Thus Ante Pavelic's *Ustase* regime in the Croatian puppet state murdered Serbs (well over 200,000) and Muslims. But Mihajlović's (mostly Serb) royalist partisans also killed Muslims. For this reason if no other the Muslims of Bosnia sometimes cooperated with the German armies in their own defence. Tito's Communist partisans, despite their strategic goal of ridding Yugoslavia of German and Italian forces, devoted time and resources to destroying the Chetniks first—not least just

---

[9]The wartime 'Chetnik' partisans were named after upland guerilla bands who had fought against Serbia's Ottoman rulers in the eighteenth century.

because this was an objective within their reach. Writing a decade later and already disillusioned with the outcome of the battles between partisans and Chetniks in which he himself played a heroic role, Milovan Djilas bore witness to the real experience of war and resistance in occupied Yugoslavia: 'For hours both armies clambered up rocky ravines to escape annihilation or to destroy a little group of their countrymen, often neighbours, on some jutting peak six thousand feet high, in a starving, bleeding, captive land. It came to mind that this was what had become of all our theories and visions of the workers' and peasants' struggle against the bourgeoisie.'

Further south, Greece—like Yugoslavia—experienced World War Two as a cycle of invasion, occupation, resistance, reprisals and civil war, culminating in five weeks of clashes in Athens between Communists and the royalist-backing British forces in December 1944, after which an armistice was agreed upon in February 1945. Fighting broke out again in 1946, however, and lasted three more years, ending with the rout of the Communists from their strongholds in the mountainous north. While there is no doubt that the Greek resistance to the Italians and the Germans was more effective than the better known resistance movements in France or Italy— in 1943–44 alone it killed or wounded over 6,000 German soldiers—the harm it brought to Greeks themselves was greater still by far. The KKE (Communist) guerillas and the Athens-based and western-backed government of the king terrorized villages, destroyed communications and divided the country for decades to come. By the time the fighting was over, in September 1949, 10 percent of the population was homeless. The Greek civil war lacked many of the ethnic complexities of the fighting in Yugoslavia and Ukraine,[10] but in human terms it was costlier still

The post-war impact of these European civil wars was immense. In a simple sense they meant that the war in Europe did not finish in 1945, with the departure of the Germans: it is one of the traumatic features of civil war that even after the enemy is defeated he remains in place; and with him the memory of the conflict. But the internecine struggles of these years did something else. Together with the unprecedented brutality of the Nazi and, later, Soviet occupations they corroded the very fabric of the European state. After them, nothing would ever be the same. In the truest sense of a much-abused term, they transformed World War Two— Hitler's war—into a social revolution.

To begin with, the serial occupation of territory by foreign powers inevitably eroded the authority and legitimacy of local rulers. Purportedly autonomous in name, the Vichy regime in France—like Father Józef Tiso's Slovak state or Pavelic's Ustase regime in Zagreb—was a dependent agent of Hitler and most people knew it. At municipal level the collaborating local authorities in Holland or Bohemia retained a degree of initiative, but only by avoiding any conflict with the wishes of

---

[10]But not all—the Greek Communists' opportunistic post-war support for the annexation to Communist Bulgaria of ethnically Slav regions of northern Greece did little to advance their cause.

their German masters. Further east the Nazis and later the Soviets replaced pre-existing institutions with men and machinery of their own, except where it suited them to exploit for a while local divisions and ambitions for their own advantage. Ironically, it was only in those countries allied with the Nazis—Finland, Bulgaria, Romania and Hungary—and thus left to rule themselves that a degree of real local independence was preserved, at least until 1944.

With the exception of Germany and the heartland of the Soviet Union, every continental European state involved in World War Two was occupied at least twice: first by its enemies, then by the armies of liberation. Some countries—Poland, the Baltic states, Greece, Yugoslavia—were occupied three times in five years. With each succeeding invasion the previous regime was destroyed, its authority dismantled, its elites reduced. The result in some places was a clean slate, with all the old hierarchies discredited and their representatives compromised. In Greece, for example, the pre-war dictator Metaxas had swept aside the old parliamentary class. The Germans removed Metaxas. Then the Germans too were pushed out in their turn, and those who had collaborated with them stood vulnerable and disgraced.

The liquidation of old social and economic elites was perhaps the most dramatic change. The Nazis' extermination of Europe's Jews was not only devastating in its own right. It had significant social consequences for those many towns and cities of central Europe where Jews had constituted the local professional class: doctors, lawyers, businessmen, professors. Later, often in the very same towns, another important part of the local bourgeoisie—the Germans—was also removed, as we have seen. The outcome was a radical transformation of the social landscape—and an opportunity for Poles, Balts, Ukrainians, Slovaks, Hungarians and others to move up into the jobs (and homes) of the departed.

This leveling process, whereby the native populations of central and eastern Europe took the place of the banished minorities, was Hitler's most enduring contribution to European social history. The German plan had been to destroy the Jews and the educated local intelligentsia in Poland and the western Soviet Union, reduce the rest of the Slav peoples to neo-serfdom and place the land and the government in the hands of resettled Germans. But with the arrival of the Red Army and the expulsion of the Germans the new situation proved uniquely well adapted to the more truly radicalizing projects of the Soviets.

One reason for this was that the occupation years had seen not just rapid and bloodily-enforced upward social mobility but also the utter collapse of law and the habits of life in a legal state. It is misleading to think of the German occupation of continental Europe as a time of pacification and order under the eye of an omniscient and ubiquitous power. Even in Poland, the most comprehensively policed and repressed of all the occupied territories, society continued to function in defiance of the new rulers: the Poles constituted for themselves a parallel underground world of newspapers, schools, cultural activities, welfare services, economic exchange and even an army—all of them forbidden by the Germans and carried on outside the law and at great personal risk.

But that was precisely the point. To live normally in occupied Europe meant breaking the law: in the first place the laws of the occupiers (curfews, travel regulations, race laws, etc) but also conventional laws and norms as well. Most common people who did not have access to farm produce were obliged, for example, to resort to the black market or illegal barter just to feed their families. Theft—whether from the state, from a fellow citizen or from a looted Jewish store—was so widespread that in the eyes of many people it ceased to be a crime. Indeed, with gendarmes, policemen and local mayors representing and serving the occupier, and with the occupying forces themselves practicing organized criminality at the expense of selected civilian populations, common felonies were transmuted into acts of resistance (albeit often in post-liberation retrospect).

Above all, violence became part of daily life. The ultimate authority of the modern state has always rested *in extremis* on its monopoly of violence and its willingness to deploy force if necessary. But in occupied Europe authority was a function of force alone, deployed without inhibition. Curiously enough, it was precisely in these circumstances that the state *lost* its monopoly of violence. Partisan groups and armies competed for a legitimacy determined by their capacity to enforce their writ in a given territory. This was most obviously true in the more remote regions of Greece, Montenegro and the eastern marches of Poland where the authority of modern states had never been very firm. But by the end of World War Two it also applied in parts of France and Italy.

Violence bred cynicism. As occupying forces, both Nazis and Soviets precipitated a war of all against all. They discouraged not just allegiance to the defunct authority of the previous regime or state, but any sense of civility or bond between individuals, and on the whole they were successful. If the ruling power behaved brutally and lawlessly to your neighbour—because he was a Jew, or a member of an educated elite or ethnic minority, or had found disfavour in the eyes of the regime or for no obvious reason at all—then why should you show any more respect for him yourself? Indeed, it was often prudent to go further and curry pre-emptive favour with the authorities by getting your neighbour in trouble.

Throughout German-occupied (and even unoccupied) Europe until the very end, the incidence of anonymous reports, personal accusations and plain rumours was strikingly high. Between 1940 and 1944 there were huge numbers of denunciations to the SS, the Gestapo and local police in Hungary, Norway, the Netherlands and France. Many were not even for reward or material gain. Under Soviet rule, too—notably in Soviet-occupied eastern Poland from 1939–41—the Jacobin-style encouragement of informers and the (French) revolutionary habit of casting doubt on the loyalty of others flourished unrestrained.

Everyone, in short, had good reason to be afraid of everyone else. Suspicious of other people's motives, individuals were quick to denounce them for some presumed deviation or illicit advantage. There was no protection to be had from above: indeed, those in power were often the most lawless of all. For most Europeans in the years 1939–45 *rights*—civil, legal, political—no longer existed. The state ceased to be the repository of law and justice; on the contrary, under Hitler's New Order government was itself the leading predator. The Nazis' attitude to life and limb is justifiably notorious; but their treatment of *property* may actually have been their most important practical legacy to the shape of the post-war world.

Under German occupation, the right to property was at best contingent. Europe's Jews were simply stripped of money, goods, homes, shops and businesses. Their property was divided up among Nazis, collaborators and their friends, with the residue made available for looting and theft by the local community. But sequestration and confiscation went far beyond the Jews. The 'right' of possession was shown to be fragile, often meaningless, resting exclusively on the goodwill, interests or whim of those in power.

There were winners as well as losers in this radical series of involuntary property transactions. With Jews and other ethnic victims gone, their shops and apartments could be occupied by local people; their tools, furniture and clothes were confiscated or stolen by new owners. This process went furthest in the 'killing zone' from Odessa to the Baltic, but it happened everywhere—returning concentration camp survivors in Paris or Prague in 1945 often found their home occupied by wartime 'squatters' who angrily asserted their own claim and refused to leave. In this way hundreds of thousands of ordinary Hungarians, Poles, Czechs, Dutch, French and others became complicit in the Nazi genocide, if only as its beneficiaries.

In every occupied country factories, vehicles, land, machinery and finished goods were expropriated without compensation for the benefit of the new rulers in what amounted to wholesale *de facto* nationalization. In central and eastern Europe especially, substantial private holdings and a number of financial institutions were taken over by the Nazis for their war economy. This was not always a radical break with precedent. The disastrous turn to autarky in the region after 1931 had entailed a high level of state intervention and manipulation and in Poland, Hungary and Romania the state-owned business sector had expanded considerably in the immediate pre-war and early war years, as a pre-emptive defense against German economic penetration. State-direction of the economy in eastern Europe did not begin in 1945.

The post-war dispossession of the German populations from Poland to Yugoslavia completed the radical transformation that had begun with the Germans' own removal of the Jews. Many ethnic Germans in the Sudetenland, Silesia, Transylvania and northern Yugoslavia owned significant holdings in land. When these were taken into state hands for redistribution the impact was immediate. In Czechoslovakia, goods and property seized from the Germans and their collaborators amounted to one-quarter of the national wealth, while the redistribution of farmland alone directly benefited over 300,000 peasants, agricultural labourers and their families. Changes on this scale can only be described as revolutionary. Like the war itself, they represented both a radical caesura, a clear break with the past, and a preparation for even bigger changes still to come.

In liberated *western* Europe there was little German-owned property to redistribute and the war had not been experienced as quite the cataclysm that it was further east. But there, too, the legitimacy of constituted authorities was cast into question. The local administrations in France, Norway and the Benelux countries had not covered themselves in glory. On the contrary, they had on the whole performed with alacrity the occupiers' bidding. In 1941 the Germans were able to run occupied Norway with just 806 administrative personnel. The Nazis administered France with just 1,500 of their own people. So confident were they of the reliability of the French police and militias that they assigned (in addition to their administrative staff) a mere 6,000 German civil and military police to ensure the compliance of a nation of 35 million. The same was true in the Netherlands. In post-war testimony the head of German security in Amsterdam averred that 'the main support of the German forces in the police sector and beyond was the Dutch police. Without it, not 10 percent of the German occupation tasks would have been fulfilled.' Contrast Yugoslavia, which required the unflagging attention of entire German military divisions just to contain the armed partisans.[11]

This was one difference between western and eastern Europe. Another was the Nazis' own treatment of occupied nations. The Norwegians, Danes, Dutch, Belgians, French and, after September 1943, the Italians were humiliated and exploited. But unless they were Jews, or Communists or resisters of one kind or another they were, on the whole, left alone. In consequence, the liberated peoples of western Europe could imagine a return to something resembling the past. Indeed, even the parliamentary democracies of the inter-war years now looked a bit less shabby thanks to the Nazi interlude—Hitler had successfully discredited at least one radical alternative to political pluralism and the rule of law. The exhausted populations of continental western Europe aspired above all to recover the trappings of normal life in a properly regulated state.

The situation in the newly liberated states of western Europe, then, was bad enough. But in central Europe, in the words of John J McCloy of the US Control Commission in Germany, there was 'complete economic, social and political collapse . . . the extent of which is unparalleled in history unless one goes back to the collapse of the Roman Empire.' McCloy was speaking of Germany, where the Al-

---

[11]Note though that the Protectorate of Bohemia was run in 1942 by just 1,900 German bureaucrats. In these as other respects, Czechoslovakia was at least partly western.

lied Military Governments had to build everything from scratch: law, order, services, communications, administration. But at least they had the resources to do it. Further east, matters were worse still.

Thus it was Hitler, at least as much as Stalin, who drove a wedge into the continent and divided it. The history of central Europe—of the lands of the German and Habsburg Empires, the northern parts of the old Ottoman Empire and even the westernmost territories of the Russian Czars—had always been different in degree from that of the nation states of the West. But it had not necessarily differed in kind. Before 1939 Hungarians, Romanians, Czechs, Poles, Croats and Balts might look enviously upon the more fortunate inhabitants of France or the Low Countries. But they saw no reason not to aspire to similar prosperity and stability in their own right. Romanians dreamed of Paris. The Czech economy in 1937 outperformed its Austrian neighbour and was competitive with Belgium.

The war changed everything. East of the Elbe, the Soviets and their local representatives inherited a sub-continent where a radical break with the past had already taken place. What was not utterly discredited was irretrievably damaged. Exiled governments from Oslo, Brussels or the Hague could return from London and hope to take up the legitimate authority they had been forced to relinquish in 1940. But the old rulers of Bucharest and Sofia, Warsaw, Budapest and even Prague had no future: their world had been swept aside by the Nazis' transformative violence. It remained only to decide the political shape of the new order that must now replace the unrecoverable past.

II

Retribution

'Belgians and French and Dutch had been brought up in the war to believe
that their patriotic duty was to cheat, to lie, to run a black market, to
discredit and to defraud: these habits became ingrained after five years'.
Paul-Henri Spaak (Foreign Minister of Belgium)

'Vengeance is pointless, but certain men did not have a place in the world
we sought to construct'.
Simone de Beauvoir

'Let a hard and just sentence be given and carried out,
as the honour of the nation demands and its greatest traitor deserves'.
*Resolution of Czechoslovak resistance organizations,
demanding severe punishment for Father Józef Tiso, November 1946*

In order for the governments of liberated Europe to be legitimate, to claim for
themselves the authority of properly-constituted states, they had first to deal with
the legacy of the discredited wartime regimes. The Nazis and their friends had
been defeated, but in view of the scale of their crimes this was obviously not
enough. If post-war governments' legitimacy rested merely on their military victory over Fascism, how were they better than the wartime Fascist regimes themselves? It was important to define the latter's activities as crimes and punish them
accordingly. There was good legal and political reasoning behind this. But the desire for retribution also addressed a deeper need. For most Europeans World War
Two was experienced not as a war of movement and battle but as a daily degradation, in the course of which men and women were betrayed and humiliated, forced
into daily acts of petty crime and self-abasement, in which everyone lost something
and many lost everything.

Moreover, and in marked contrast to the still living memory of the Great War
in many places, there was in 1945 little of which to be proud and much about which
to feel embarrassed and more than a little guilty. As we have seen, most Europeans
experienced the war passively—defeated and occupied by one set of foreigners and
then liberated by another. The only source of collective national pride were the
armed partisan resistance movements that had fought the invader—which is why
it was in western Europe, where real resistance had actually been least in evidence,
that the myth of Resistance mattered most. In Greece, Yugoslavia, Poland or

Ukraine, where large numbers of real partisans had engaged the occupation forces and each other in open battle, things were, as usual, more complicated.

In liberated Poland, for example, the Soviet authorities did not welcome public praise for armed partisans whose sentiments were at least as much anti-Communist as anti-Nazi. In post-war Yugoslavia, as we have seen, some resisters were more equal than others—at least in the eyes of Marshall Tito and his victorious Communist fighters. In Greece, as in Ukraine, the local authorities in 1945 were rounding up, imprisoning or shooting every armed partisan they could find.

'Resistance', in short, was a protean and unclear category, in some places an invented one. But 'collaboration' was another matter. Collaborators could be universally identified and execrated. They were men and women who worked or slept with the occupier, who threw in their lot with Nazis or Fascists, who opportunistically pursued political or economic advantage under cover of war. Sometimes they were a religious or national or linguistic minority and thus already despised or feared for other reasons; and although 'collaboration' was not a pre-existing crime with legal definitions and stated penalties, collaborators could plausibly be charged with treason, a real crime carrying satisfactorily severe punishment.

The punishment of collaborators (real and imagined) began before the fighting ended. Indeed it had been going on throughout the war, on an individual basis or under instructions from underground resistance organizations. But in the interval between the retreat of the German armies and the establishment of effective control by Allied governments, popular frustrations and personal vendettas, often coloured by political opportunism and economic advantage, led to a brief but bloody cycle of score-settling. In France some 10,000 people were killed in 'extra-judicial' proceedings, many of them by independent bands of armed resistance groups, notably the *Milices Patriotiques*, who rounded up suspected collaborators, seized their property and in many cases shot them out of hand.

About a third of those summarily executed in this way were dispatched before the Normandy landings of June 6th 1944, and most of the others fell victim during the next four months of fighting on French soil. If anything, the numbers are rather low considering the level of mutual hatred and suspicion abroad in France after four years of occupation and Marshall Pétain's regime at Vichy; no-one was surprised at the reprisals—in the words of one elderly former French prime minister, Edouard Herriot, 'France will need first to pass through a blood bath before republicans can again take up the reins of power'.

The same sentiment was felt in Italy, where reprisals and unofficial retribution, especially in the Emilia-Romagna and Lombardy regions, resulted in death tolls approaching 15,000 in the course of the last months of the war—and continued, sporadically, for at least three more years. Elsewhere in western Europe the degree of bloodshed was much lower—in Belgium about 265 men and women were lynched or executed in this way, in the Netherlands less than 100. Other forms of revenge were widespread, however. Accusations against women, for what French-speaking cynics were already calling 'collaboration horizontale', were very common: 'moffenmeiden' in the Netherlands were tarred and feathered, and all over France there were scenes of women stripped and shaved in public squares, often on the day of local liberation from the occupiers or very shortly thereafter.

The frequency with which women were charged—often by other women—with consorting with Germans is revealing. There was some truth to many of the accusations: offering sexual services in exchange for food or clothing or personal help of one kind or another was one avenue, often the only one, open to women and families in desperate straits. But the popularity of the charge and the vindictive pleasure taken in the punishment is a reminder that for men and women alike the occupation was experienced above all as a *humiliation*. Jean-Paul Sartre would later describe collaboration in distinctly sexual terms, as 'submission' to the power of the occupier, and in more than one French novel of the 1940s collaborators are depicted as either women or weak ('effeminate') men, seduced by the masculine charms of their Teutonic rulers. Wreaking revenge on fallen women was one way to overcome the discomforting memory of personal and collective powerlessness.

Anarchic acts of retributive violence in liberated eastern Europe were also widespread but took different forms. In the West the Germans had actively sought collaborators; in occupied Slav lands they ruled directly and by force. The only collaboration they encouraged on a sustained basis was that of local separatists, and even then only so long as it served German ends. As a result, once the Germans retreated the first victims of spontaneous retribution in the East were ethnic minorities. The Soviet forces and their local allies did nothing to discourage this. On the contrary, spontaneous score-settling (some of it not altogether unprompted) contributed towards a further removal of local elites and politicians who might prove an impediment to post-war Communist ambitions. In Bulgaria, for example, the newly-constituted Fatherland Front encouraged unofficial retribution against wartime collaborators of all colours, invoking the charge of 'Fascist sympathiser' on a wholesale basis and inviting denunciations of anyone suspected of pro-Western sentiments.

In Poland, the main target of popular vengeance was frequently Jews—150 Jews were killed in liberated Poland in the first four months of 1945. By April 1946 the figure was nearly 1,200. Attacks on a smaller scale took place in Slovakia (at Velké Topolčany in September 1945) and in Kunmadaras (Hungary) in May 1946, but the worst pogrom occurred in Kielce (Poland), on July 4th 1946, where 42 Jews were murdered and many more injured following a rumour of the abduction and ritual murder of a local child. In a sense these, too, were reprisals against collaborators, for in the eyes of many Poles (including former anti-Nazi partisans) Jews were suspected of sympathy for the Soviet occupiers.

The exact number of people killed in Soviet-occupied eastern Europe, or in Yugoslavia, during the first months of 'unauthorised' purging and killing is not known. But nowhere did the unregulated settling of accounts last very long. It was not in the interest of fragile new governments, far from universally accepted and often distinctly makeshift, to allow armed bands to roam the countryside arresting, torturing and killing at will. The first task of the new authorities was to assert a monopoly of force, legitimacy and the institutions of justice. If anyone was to be arrested and charged with crimes committed during the occupation, this was the responsibility of the appropriate authorities. If there were to be trials, they should take place under the rule of law. If there was to be bloodletting, then this was the exclusive affair of the state. This transition took place as soon as the new powers felt strong enough to disarm the erstwhile partisans, impose the authority of their own police and damp down popular demands for harsh penalties and collective punishment.

The disarming of the resisters proved surprisingly uncontentious in western and central Europe at least. A blind eye was turned to murders and other crimes already committed in the frenzied liberation months: the provisional government of Belgium issued an amnesty for all offences committed by and in the name of the Resistance for a period of 41 days following the official date of the country's liberation. But it was tacitly understood by all that newly re-constituted institutions of government must take upon themselves the task of punishing the guilty.

Here the problems began. What was a 'collaborator'? With whom had they collaborated and to what end? Beyond straightforward cases of murder or theft, of what were 'collaborators' guilty? Someone had to pay for the suffering of the nation, but how was that suffering to be defined and who could be assigned responsibility for it? The shape of these conundrums varied from country to country but the general dilemma was a common one: there was no precedent for the European experience of the preceding six years.

In the first place, any law addressing the actions of collaborators with the Germans would necessarily be retroactive—before 1939 the crime of 'collaboration with the occupier' was unknown. There had been previous wars in which occupying armies sought and obtained cooperation and assistance from the people whose land they had overrun, but except in very particular instances—like that of the Flemish nationalists in German-occupied Belgium during 1914–18—this was regarded not as an invitation to crime but simply as part of the collateral damage of war.

As noted, the only sense in which the crime of collaboration could be said to fall under existing law was when it amounted to treason. To take a representative instance, many collaborators in France—whatever the details of their behaviour—were brought to trial and convicted under Article 75 of the 1939 Penal Code, for 'intelligence with the enemy'. But men and women brought before French courts had often worked not for the Nazis but rather with the regime of Vichy, led and administered by Frenchmen and ostensibly the legitimate heir to the pre-war French state. Here, as in Slovakia, Croatia, the Protectorate of Bohemia, Mussolini's Social

Republic at Salò, Marshal Ion Antonescu's Romania and in wartime Hungary, collaborators could and did claim in their defence that they had only ever worked for or with the authorities of their own state.

In the case of senior police or government officials who were palpably guilty of serving Nazi interests via the puppet regimes that employed them, this defence was at best disingenuous. But lesser figures, not to speak of the many thousands charged with accepting employment in these regimes or in agencies or businesses that worked with them, could point to a genuine confusion. Was it right, for example, to charge someone with membership after May 1940 of a political party that had been legally represented in a pre-war parliament but had gone on to collaborate with the Germans during the occupation?

The French, Belgian and Norwegian governments-in-exile had tried to anticipate these dilemmas by issuing wartime decrees warning of harsh post-war retribution. But these were intended to deter people from cooperating with the Nazis; they did not address the broader questions of jurisprudence and fairness. Above all, they could not resolve in anticipation the problem of weighing individual against collective responsibility. The balance of political advantage in 1944–45 lay in assigning blanket responsibility for war crimes and crimes of collaboration to predetermined categories of people: members of certain political parties, military organizations and government agencies. But such a procedure would still pass over many individuals whose punishment was widely demanded; it would include people whose chief offence was inertia or cowardice; and above all it would entail a form of collective indictment, something anathema to most European jurists.

Instead, it was individuals who were brought to trial, with results that varied greatly with time and place. Many men and women were unfairly singled out and punished. Many more escaped retribution altogether. There were multiple procedural irregularities and ironies, and the motives of governments, prosecutors and juries were far from unsullied—by self-interest, political calculation or emotion. This was an imperfect outcome. But as we assess the criminal proceedings and associated public catharsis that marked the transition in Europe from war to peace, we need to keep constantly in mind the drama of what had just taken place. In the circumstances of 1945 it is remarkable that the rule of law was re-established at all—never before, after all, had an entire continent sought to define a new set of crimes on such a scale and bring the criminals to something resembling justice.

The numbers of people punished, and the scale of their punishments, varied enormously from country to country. In Norway, a country with a population of just 3 million, the entire membership of the Nasjonal Sammlung, the main organisation of pro-Nazi collaborators, was tried, all 55,000 of them, along with nearly 40,000 others; 17,000 men and women received prison terms and thirty death sentences were handed down, of which twenty-five were carried out.

Nowhere else were the proportions so high. In the Netherlands 200,000 people were investigated, of whom nearly half were imprisoned, some of them for the crime of giving the Nazi salute; 17,500 civil servants lost their jobs (but hardly anyone in business, education or the professions); 154 people were condemned to death, forty of them executed. In neighbouring Belgium many more death sentences were passed (2,940), but a smaller percentage (just 242) carried out. Roughly the same numbers of collaborators were sent to prison but whereas the Dutch soon amnestied most of those convicted, the Belgian state kept them in prison longer and former collaborators convicted of serious crimes never recovered their full civil rights. Contrary to longstanding post-war myth the Flemish population was not disproportionately targeted for punishment, but by effectively repressing the (mostly Flemish) supporters of the wartime New Order the pre-war Belgian elites—Catholic, Socialist, Liberal—re-established their control of Flanders and Wallonia alike.

The contrast between Norway, Belgium, the Netherlands (and Denmark), where the legitimate governments had fled into exile, and France, where for many people the Vichy regime *was* the legitimate government, is suggestive. In Denmark the crime of collaboration was virtually unknown. Yet 374 out of every 100,000 Danes were sentenced to prison in post-war trials. In France, where wartime collaboration was widespread, it was for just that reason punished rather lightly. Since the state itself was the chief collaborator, it seemed harsh and more than a little divisive to charge lowly citizens with the same crime—the more so since three out of four of the judges at the trials of collaborators in France had themselves been employed by the collaborationist state. In the event, 94 people in every 100,000—less than 0.1 percent of the population—went to prison for wartime offences. Of the 38,000 imprisoned, most were released under the partial amnesty of 1947 and all but 1,500 of the remainder under an amnesty in 1951.

In the course of the years 1944–51, official courts in France sentenced 6,763 people to death (3,910 in absentia) for treason and related offences. Of these sentences only 791 were carried out. The main punishment to which French collaborators were sentenced was that of 'national degradation', introduced on August 26th 1944, immediately after the Liberation of Paris and sardonically described by Janet Flanner: 'National degradation will consist of being deprived of nearly everything the French consider nice—such as the right to wear war decorations; the right to be a lawyer, notary, public-school teacher, judge or even a witness; the right to run a publishing, radio or motion-picture company; and above all the right to be a director in an insurance company or a bank.'

49,723 Frenchmen and women received this punishment. Eleven thousand civil servants (1.3 percent of state employees, but a far smaller number than the 35,000 who had lost their jobs under Vichy) were removed or otherwise sanctioned, but most of them were re-instated within six years. All in all the *épuration* (purge), as it was known, touched some 350,000 persons, most of whose lives and careers were not dramatically affected. No-one was punished for what we should now describe as crimes against humanity. Responsibility for these, like other war crimes, was imputed to the Germans alone.

The Italian experience was distinctive, for a number of reasons. Although a former Axis power, Italy was authorized by the Allied governments to carry out its own trials and purges—it had, after all, switched sides in September 1943. But there was considerable ambiguity as to what and who should be prosecuted. Whereas elsewhere in Europe most collaborators were by definition tarred with 'Fascism', in Italy the term embraced too broad and ambiguous a constituency. Having been governed by its own Fascists from 1922–43, the country was initially liberated from Mussolini's rule by one of his own marshals, Pietro Badoglio, whose first anti-Fascist government itself consisted largely of former Fascists.

The only obviously prosecutable Fascist crime was collaboration with the enemy after (the German invasion of) September 8th 1943. As a result, most of those charged were in the occupied north and were connected to the puppet government installed at Salò on Lake Garda. The much-mocked 'Were you a Fascist?' questionnaire (the 'Scheda Personale') circulated in 1944 focused precisely on the difference between Salò and non-Salò Fascists. Sanctions against the former rested on Decree #159, passed in July 1944 by the interim legislative Assembly, which described 'acts of special gravity which, while not in the bounds of crime, [were] considered contrary to the norms of sobriety and political decency'.

This obscure piece of legislation was designed to get around the difficulty of prosecuting men and women for acts committed while in the employ of recognised national authorities. But the High Court established in September 1944 to try the more important prisoners was staffed by judges and lawyers who were themselves mostly ex-Fascists, as were the personnel of the Extraordinary Assize Courts set up to punish minor employees of the collaborationist regime. In these circumstances the proceedings were hardly calculated to garner much respect among the population at large.

Unsurprisingly, the outcome satisfied no-one. By February 1946, 394,000 government employees had been investigated, of whom just 1,580 were dismissed. Most of those questioned claimed gattopardismo ('leopardism' or 'spot-changing'), arguing that they had played a subtle double game in the face of Fascist pressure— after all, membership of the Fascist Party had been obligatory for civil servants. Since many of those doing the questioning could just as easily have found themselves on the other side of the table, they were decidedly sympathetic to this line of defense. Following the highly-publicized trials of a few senior Fascists and generals the promised purge of government and administration petered out.

The High Commission assigned the task of administering the purge was shut down in March 1946 and three months later the first amnesties were announced, including the cancellation of all prison sentences under five years. Virtually every prefect, mayor and mid-level bureaucrat purged in the years 1944–45 would get his job back or avoid payment of the fines imposed, and most of the nearly 50,000 Italians imprisoned for Fascist activities spent little time in jail.[1] At most 50 people were judicially executed for their crimes, but that does not include 55 Fascists massacred by partisans in Schio Prison on July 17th 1945.

During the Cold War, Italy's suspiciously painless transition from Axis power to democratic ally was often blamed upon foreign (American) pressure as well as the political influence of the Vatican. In reality matters were more complex. To be sure, the Catholic Church got off very lightly indeed, in view of Pius XII's warm relations with Fascism and the pro-actively blind eye he turned to Nazi crimes in Italy and elsewhere. Church pressure *was* brought to bear. And the Anglo-American military authorities certainly *were* reluctant to remove compromised administrators while they were trying to re-establish normal life throughout the peninsula. And on the whole the purge of Fascists *was* more efficiently carried out in regions where the left-wing Resistance and its political representatives held sway.

But it was Palmiro Togliatti, the 51–year old leader of the Italian Communist Party who, as Minister of Justice in the post-war coalition government, drafted the June 1946 Amnesty. After two decades in exile and many years as a high-ranking official in the Communist International, Togliatti had few illusions about what was and what was not possible in the aftermath of the European war. Upon his return from Moscow, in March 1944, he announced in Salerno his Party's commitment to national unity and parliamentary democracy—to the confusion and surprise of many of his followers.

In a country where many millions of people, by no means all of them on the political Right, were compromised by their association with Fascism, Togliatti saw little advantage in pushing the nation to the brink of civil war—or, rather, in prolonging a civil war already under way. Far better to work for the re-establishment of order and normal life, leave the Fascist era behind, and seek power through the ballot box. Moreover Togliatti, from his privileged standpoint as a senior figure in the international Communist movement whose strategic perspective reached beyond the shores of Italy, had the Greek situation in mind as a caution and a warning.

In Greece, despite a significant level of wartime collaboration among the bureaucratic and business elites, post-war purges were directed not at the Right but the Left. This was a unique case but a revealing one. The civil war of 1944–45 had convinced the British that only the firm re-establishment of a conservative regime in Athens would stabilize this small but strategically vital country. To purge or otherwise threaten businessmen or politicians who had worked with Italians or Germans could have radical implications in a country where the revolutionary Left seemed poised to seize power.

---

[1]As late as 1960, 62 out of the 64 prefects responsible for Italy's provincial administration had held office under Fascism, as had all 135 police chiefs.

In short order, then, the threat to stability in the Aegean and south Balkans switched from the retreating German army to the well-dug-in Greek Communists and their partisan allies in the mountains. Very few people were severely punished for wartime collaboration with the Axis powers, but the death penalty was liberally assigned in the war against the Left. Because no consistent distinction was drawn in Athens between left-wing partisans who had fought against Hitler and Communist guerillas trying to bring down the post-war Greek state (and indeed, more often than not, they were the same men), it was wartime resisters rather than their collaborationist enemies who were likely to find themselves tried and imprisoned in the coming years—and excluded from civil life for decades afterwards: even their children and grandchildren would pay the price, often being refused employment in the bloated state sector until well into the 1970s.

The purges and trials in Greece were thus blatantly political. But so, in a sense, were the more conventional proceedings in western Europe. Any judicial process brought about as the direct consequence of a war or a political struggle is political. The mood at the trials of Pierre Laval or Philippe Pétain in France, or the police chief Pietro Caruso in Italy, was hardly that of a conventional judicial proceeding. Score-settling, blood-letting, revenge and political calculation played a crucial role in these and many other post-war trials and purges. This consideration needs to be borne in mind as we turn to official post-war retribution in central and eastern Europe.

There is no doubt that from the point of view of Stalin and the Soviet occupation authorities throughout the territories under Red Army control, the trials and other punishments of collaborators, Fascists and Germans were always and above all a way of clearing the local political and social landscape of impediments to Communist rule. The same applied to Tito's Yugoslavia. Many men and women were accused of Fascist felonies when their major crime was membership of the wrong national or social group, association with an inconvenient religious community or political party, or simply an awkward visibility or popularity in the local community. Purges, land expropriation, expulsions, prison sentences and executions aimed at extirpating incriminated political opponents were important staging points in a process of social and political transformation, as we shall see. But they also targeted and punished genuine Fascists and war criminals

Thus in the course of his attack on the Catholic church in Croatia Tito also prosecuted the notorious Cardinal Alois Stepinac of Zagreb, apologist for some of the worst crimes of the Croat *Ustase* regime, who might well have considered himself fortunate to spend the next fourteen years under house arrest before dying in his bed in 1960. Draza Mihajlović, the Chetnik leader, was tried and executed in July 1946. In his wake many tens of thousands of other non-Communists were killed in the two years following Yugoslavia's liberation. They were all victims of a politically-motivated policy of revenge; but considering their wartime actions in the Chetniks, the Ustasa, the Slovenian White Guard or as armed Domobranci many of them would have received heavy sentences under any system of law.[2] The Yugoslavs executed and deported many ethnic Hungarians for their role in Hungarian military massacres in the Vojvodina during January 1942, and their land was made over to non-Hungarian supporters of the new regime. This was a calculated political move, but in many cases the victims were surely guilty as charged.

Yugoslavia was a particularly tangled case. Further north, in Hungary, post-war Peoples' Courts really did begin by trying actual war criminals, notably activists in the pro-German regimes of Döme Sztójay and Ferenc Szálasi during 1944. The ratio of fascists and collaborators condemned in Hungary did not exceed the numbers found guilty in post-war Belgium or the Netherlands—and there is no doubt that they committed serious crimes, including anticipating and enthusiastically executing German plans to round up and transport to their death hundreds of thousands of Hungarian Jews. Only later did the Hungarian authorities add categories like 'sabotage' and 'conspiracy', whose overt purpose was to net a broader range of opponents and others likely to resist a Communist takeover.

In Czechoslovakia the Extraordinary Peoples' Courts, established by Presidential Decree on May 19th 1945, handed out 713 death sentences, 741 life sentences and 19,888 shorter prison terms to 'traitors, collaborators and fascist elements from the ranks of the Czech and Slovak nation'. The language is redolent of Soviet legalspeak and certainly anticipates Czechoslovakia's grim future. But there really had been traitors, collaborators and Fascists in occupied Czechoslovakia; one of them, Father Tiso, was hanged on April 18th 1947. Whether Tiso and others received a fair trial—whether they *could* have received a fair trial in the atmosphere of the time— is a legitimate question. But the treatment they got was no worse than that accorded to, say, Pierre Laval. Post-war Czech justice was much preoccupied with the troubling and vague category of 'crimes against the nation', a device for visiting collective punishment on Sudeten Germans especially. But the same was true of French justice in those years, with perhaps less cause.

It is hard to judge the success of the post-war trials and anti-Fascist purges in formerly-occupied Europe. The pattern of sentencing was much criticized at the time—those who were tried while the war was still going on, or immediately following a country's liberation, were apt to receive tougher punishments than those prosecuted later. As a result, minor offenders dealt with in the spring of 1945 received far longer prison terms than major collaborators whose cases did not come to court for another year or more. In Bohemia and Moravia a very high percentage (95 percent) of death sentences was carried out because of a rule requiring that prisoners be executed within two hours of the passing of judgment; elsewhere,

---

[2]The Domobran was the wartime Croatian Home Guard. Of course Tito's Communist partisans had frequently behaved no better: but they won.

anyone who avoided immediate execution could anticipate a commutation of his sentence.

Death sentences were frequent at the time and provoked scant opposition: the wartime devaluation of life made them seem less extreme—and better warranted—than under normal circumstances. What caused greater offence, and may ultimately have undercut the value of the whole proceedings in some places, was the manifest inconsistency of the punishments, not to mention that many of them were being passed by judges and juries whose own wartime record was spotty or worse. Writers and journalists, having left a written record of their wartime allegiance, came off worst. Highly publicized trials of prominent intellectuals—like that of Robert Brasillach in Paris in January 1945—provoked protests from bona fide resisters like Albert Camus, who thought it both unjust and imprudent to condemn and execute men for their opinions, however ghastly these might be.

In contrast, businessmen and high officials who had profited from the occupation suffered little, at least in western Europe. In Italy the Allies insisted that men like Vittorio Valletta of FIAT be left in place, despite his notorious engagement with the Fascist authorities. Other Italian business executives survived by demonstrating their erstwhile opposition to Mussolini's Social Republic at Salò—and indeed they *had* often opposed it, precisely for being too 'social'. In France, prosecutions for economic collaboration were pre-empted by selective nationalization—of the Renault factories, for example, in retribution for Louis Renault's considerable contribution to the German war effort. And everywhere small businessmen, bankers and officials who had helped administer occupation regimes, build the 'Atlantic Wall' against an invasion of France, supply German forces and so forth were left in place to perform similar services for the successor democracies and provide continuity and stability.

Such compromises were probably inevitable. The very scale of destruction and moral collapse in 1945 meant that whatever was left in place was likely to be needed as a building block for the future. The provisional governments of the liberation months were almost helpless. The unconditional (and grateful) cooperation of the economic, financial and industrial elites seemed vital if food, clothing and fuel were to be supplied to a helpless and starving population. Economic purges could be counter-productive, even crippling.

But a price for this was paid in political cynicism and a sharp falling away from the illusions and hopes of the liberation. As early as December 27th 1944, the Neapolitan writer Guglielmo Giannini wrote as follows in *L'Uomo Qualunque*, the newspaper of a new Italian party of the same name that appealed precisely to this sentiment of derisive disenchantment: 'I am the guy who, meeting an ex-*gerarca*, asks 'how did you get to be a purger?'... I am the guy who looks around and says, 'These are Fascists methods and systems'... I am the guy who no longer believes in anything or anyone.'

Italy, as we have seen, was a hard case. But sentiments like those of Giannini were widespread in Europe by late 1945 and prepared the way for a rapid shift in mood. Having assigned blame for the recent past, and punished those whose cases were the most egregious or psychologically satisfying, the majority of people in the lands recently occupied by the Germans were more interested in putting uncomfortable or unpleasant memories behind them and getting on with their fractured lives. In any case, very few men and women at the time were disposed to blame their countrymen for the worst crimes. For these, it was universally agreed, the Germans must take full responsibility.

Indeed, so widespread was the view that ultimate blame for the horrors of World War Two must fall on German shoulders alone that even Austria was held exempt. Under an Allied agreement of 1943, Austria had been officially declared Hitler's 'first victim' and was thus assured different treatment from Germany at the war's end. This appealed to Winston Churchill's insistence on the Prussian origins of Nazism, a view driven by his generation's obsession with the emergence of the Prussian threat to European stability in the course of the last third of the nineteenth century. But it also suited the other Allies—Austria's pivotal geographical position and the uncertainty over central Europe's political future made it seem prudent to detach her fate from that of Germany.

Nevertheless, Austria could hardly be treated as just another Nazi-occupied country whose local Fascists and Nazi-collaborators would need to be punished, after which normal life could be resumed. In a country of under 7 million inhabitants there had been 700,000 NSDAP members: at the war's end there were still 536,000 registered Nazis in Austria; 1.2 million Austrians had served in German units during the war. Austrians had been disproportionately represented in the SS and in concentration camp administrations. Austrian public life and high culture were saturated with Nazi sympathizers—45 out of 117 members of the Viennese Philharmonic Orchestra were Nazis (whereas the Berlin Philharmonic had just 8 Nazi Party members out of 110 musicians).

In the circumstances, Austria got off lightly, astonishingly so. 130,000 Austrians were investigated for war crimes, of whom 23,000 were tried, 13,600 condemned, 43 sentenced to death and just 30 executed. Some 70,000 civil servants were dismissed. The four occupying Allied powers agreed in the autumn of 1946 to let Austria thenceforth handle its own criminals and 'denazification'. The education system, particularly infested, was duly denazified: 2,943 primary school teachers were dismissed and 477 secondary school teachers, but just 27 university professors—despite the notoriously pro-Nazi sympathies of many senior academics.

In 1947 the Austrian authorities passed a law distinguishing between 'more' and 'less' incriminated Nazis. 500,000 of the latter were amnestied the following year and their voting rights restored. The former—about 42,000 in all—would all be amnestied by 1956. After that Austrians simply forgot about their involvement with

Hitler altogether. One reason for the ease with which Austria emerged from its dalliance with Nazism is that it suited all local interests to adjust the recent past to their advantage: the conservative People's Party, heir to the pre-war Christian Social Party, had every reason to burnish its own and Austria's 'un-German' credentials so as to divert attention from the corporatist regime they had imposed by force in 1934. The Austrian Social Democrats, indisputably anti-Nazi, had nonetheless to overcome the record of their pre-1933 calls for *Anschluss* with Germany. Another reason is that all parties were interested in massaging and flattering the votes of ex-Nazis, a significant electoral constituency that would shape the country's political future. And then, as we shall see, there were the new configurations shaped by the onset of the Cold War.

Calculations like these were far from absent in Germany. But there the local population was not offered a say in its own fate. In the same Moscow Declaration of October 30th 1943 that relieved Austria of responsibility for its Nazi allegiance, the Allies warned the Germans that they would be held responsible for their war crimes. And so they were. In a series of trials between 1945 and 1947 the Allied occupying powers in Germany prosecuted Nazis and their collaborators for crimes of war, crimes against humanity, murder and other common felonies committed in pursuit of Nazi goals.

Of these procedures the International Military Tribunal at Nuremberg that tried the major Nazi leadership between October 1945 and October 1946 is the best known, but there were many others: US, British and French military courts tried lower-level Nazis in their respective zones of occupied Germany and together with the Soviet Union they delivered Nazis to other countries—notably Poland and France—for trial in the places where their crimes had been committed. The programme of War Crimes Trials continued throughout the Allied occupation of Germany: in the Western zones more than 5,000 people were convicted of war crimes or crimes against humanity, of whom just under 800 were condemned to death and 486 eventually executed—the last of these in Landsberg prison in June 1951 over vociferous German appeals for clemency.

There could hardly be a question of punishing Germans merely for *being* Nazis, despite the Nuremberg finding that the Nazi Party was a criminal organization. The numbers were too great and the arguments against collective guilt too compelling. In any case, it was not clear what could follow from finding many millions of people guilty in this way. The responsibilities of the Nazi leaders were clear, however, and there was never any doubt about their likely fate. In the words of Telford Taylor, one of the US prosecutors at Nuremberg and Chief Prosecutor at subsequent trials: 'Too many people believed they had been *wrongfully* hurt by the leaders of the Third Reich and wanted a *judgment* to that effect.'

From the outset the German War Crimes trials were as much about pedagogy as justice. The main Nuremberg Trial was broadcast twice daily on German radio, and the evidence it amassed would be deployed in schools, cinemas and re-education centers throughout the country. However, the exemplary benefits of trials were not always self-evident. In an early series of trials of concentration camp commanders and guards, many escaped punishment altogether. Their lawyers exploited the Anglo-American system of adversarial justice to their advantage, cross-examining and humiliating witnesses and camp survivors. At the Lüneberg trial of the staff of Bergen-Belsen (September 17th–November 17th 1945), it was *British* defence lawyers who argued with some success that their clients had only been obeying (Nazi) laws: 15 of the 45 defendants were acquitted.

It is thus hard to know how far the trials of Nazis contributed to the political and moral re-education of Germany and the Germans. They were certainly resented by many as 'victors' justice', and that is just what they were. But they were also real trials of real criminals for demonstrably criminal behaviour and they set a vital precedent for international jurisprudence in decades to come. The trials and investigations of the years 1945–48 (when the UN War Crimes Commission was disbanded) put an extraordinary amount of documentation and testimony on record (notably concerning the German project to exterminate Europe's Jews), at the very moment when Germans and others were most disposed to forget as fast as they could. They made clear that crimes committed by individuals for ideological or state purposes were nonetheless the responsibility of individuals and punishable under law. Following orders was not a defense.

There were, however, two unavoidable shortcomings to the Allied punishment of German war criminals. The presence of Soviet prosecutors and Soviet judges was interpreted by many commentators from Germany and Eastern Europe as evidence of hypocrisy. The behaviour of the Red Army, and Soviet practice in the lands it had 'liberated', were no secret—indeed, they were perhaps better known and publicized then than in later years. And the purges and massacres of the 1930s were still fresh in many people's memory. To have the Soviets sitting in judgment on the Nazis—sometimes for crimes they had themselves committed—devalued the Nuremberg and other trials and made them seem exclusively an exercise in anti-German vengeance. In the words of George Kennan: 'The only implication this procedure could convey was, after all, that such crimes were justifiable and forgivable when committed by the leaders of one government, under one set of circumstances, but unjustifiable and unforgivable, and to be punished by death, when committed by another government under another set of circumstances.'

The Soviet presence at Nuremberg was the price paid for the wartime alliance and for the Red Army's pre-eminent role in Hitler's defeat. But the second shortcoming of the trials was inherent in the very nature of judicial process. Precisely because the personal guilt of the Nazi leadership, beginning with Hitler himself, was so fully and carefully established, many Germans felt licensed to believe that the rest of the nation was innocent, that Germans in the collective were as much passive victims of Nazism as anyone else. The crimes of the Nazis might have been 'committed in the name of Germany' (to quote the former German Chancellor Helmut

Germany and Austria: Allied Occupation Sectors

DENMARK

Flensburg
Kiel
Rostock
Lübeck
Wilhelmshaven
Bremerhaven
Hamburg
Szczecin
Groningen
Oldenburg
Bremen

POLAND

NETHERLANDS

Osnabrück
Hannover
Brandenburg
Berlin
Frankfurt an der Oder
Braunschweig
Münster

G E R M A N Y

Magdeburg
Dortmund
Kassel
Leipzig
Düsseldorf
Köln
Görlitz
Aachen
BONN
Erfurt
Dresden
Vrodaw
KarlMarxStadt
Koblenz
Frankfurt am Main
LUXEMBOURG
PRAGUE
SAARLAND
Würzburg
Bamberg
CZECHOSLOVAKIA
Ludwigshafen
Mannheim
Kaiserslautern
Heidelberg
Nürnberg
Karlsruhe
Regensburg
Strasbourg
Stuttgart

FRANCE

Mulhouse
Freiburg
Munich
Linz
VIENNA
St Pölten
Salzburg
Wr Neustadt
Basel
AUSTRIA
Zurich
Luzerne
LIECHTENSTEIN
Innsbruck
BERN
SWITZERLAND
Graz

Klagenfurt

0 20 40 60 80 100 miles
0 40 80 120 160 200 kilometres

ITALY
Udine
Ljubljana
YUGOSLAVIA
Zagreb

DIVIDED BERLIN 1945-89

FRENCH SECTOR
SOVIET SECTOR
BRITISH SECTOR
Brandenburg Gate
West Berlin
East Berlin
AMERICAN SECTOR

Boundaries of Allied military sectors, 1945-8
Berlin Wall, 1961-89
American sectors
British sectors
French sectors
Soviet sectors
International borders
Zone boundaries

DIVIDED VIENNA 1945-55

X Inter-Allied sector

AMERICAN SECTOR
SOVIET SECTOR
FRENCH SECTOR
X
Danube
BRITISH SECTOR
SOVIET SECTOR
BRITISH SECTOR

Kohl, speaking half a century later), but there was little genuine appreciation that they had been perpetrated *by* Germans.

The Americans in particular were well aware of this and immediately initiated a programme of re-education and denazification in their zone, whose objective was to abolish the Nazi Party, tear up its roots and plant the seeds of democracy and liberty in German public life. The US Army in Germany was accompanied by a host of psychologists and other specialists, whose assigned task was to discover just why the Germans had strayed so far. The British undertook similar projects, though with greater skepticism and fewer resources. The French showed very little interest in the matter. The Soviets, on the other hand, were initially in full agreement and aggressive denazification measures were one of the few issues on which the Allied Occupation authorities could agree, at least for a while.

The real problem with any consistent programme aimed at rooting out Nazism from German life was that it was simply not practicable in the circumstances of 1945. In the words of General Lucius Clay, the American Military Commander, 'our major administrative problem was to find reasonably competent Germans who had not been affiliated or associated in some way with the Nazi regime . . . All too often, it seems that the only men with the qualifications . . . are the career civil servants . . . a great proportion of whom were more than nominal participants (by our definition) in the activities of the Nazi Party.'

Clay did not exaggerate. On May 8th 1945, when the war in Europe ended, there were 8 million Nazis in Germany. In Bonn, 102 out of 112 doctors were or had been Party members. In the shattered city of Cologne, of the 21 specialists in the city waterworks office—whose skills were vital for the reconstruction of water and sewage systems and in the prevention of disease—18 had been Nazis. Civil administration, public health, urban reconstruction and private enterprise in post-war Germany would inevitably be undertaken by men like this, albeit under Allied supervision. There could be no question of simply expunging them from German affairs.

Nevertheless, efforts were made. Sixteen million *Fragebogen* (questionnaires) were completed in the three western zones of occupied Germany, most of them in the area under American control. There, the US authorities listed 3.5 million Germans (about one quarter of the total population of the zone) as 'chargeable cases', though many of them were never brought before the local denazification tribunals, set up in March 1946 under German responsibility but with Allied oversight. German civilians were taken on obligatory visits to concentration camps and made to watch films documenting Nazi atrocities. Nazi teachers were removed, libraries restocked, newsprint and paper supplies taken under direct Allied control and reassigned to new owners and editors with genuine anti-Nazi credentials.

There was considerable opposition even to these measures. On May 5th 1946, the future West German Chancellor Konrad Adenauer spoke out against the denazification measures in a public speech in Wuppertal, demanding that the 'Nazi fellow travellers' be left in peace. Two months later, in a speech to his newly-formed Christian Democratic Union, he made the same point: Denazification was lasting much too long and doing no good. Adenauer's concern was genuine. In his view, confronting Germans with the crimes of the Nazis—whether in trials, tribunals or re-education projects—was more likely to provoke a nationalist backlash than induce contrition. Just because Nazism *did* have such deep roots in his country, the future Chancellor thought it more prudent to allow and even encourage silence on the subject.

He was not altogether mistaken. Germans in the 1940s had little sense of the way the rest of the world saw them. They had no grasp of what they and their leaders had done and were more preoccupied with their own post-war difficulties—food shortages, housing shortages and the like—than the sufferings of their victims across occupied Europe. Indeed they were more likely to see themselves in the role of victim and thus regarded trials and other confrontations with Nazi crimes as the victorious Allies' revenge on a defunct regime.[3] With certain honorable exceptions, Germany's post-war political and religious authorities offered scant contradiction to this view, and the country's natural leaders—in the liberal professions, the judiciary, the civil service—were the most compromised of all.

Thus the questionnaires were treated with derision. If anything they served mostly to whitewash otherwise suspect individuals, helping them get certificates of good character (the so-called 'Persil' certificates, from the laundry soap of the same name). Re-education had a decidedly limited impact. It was one thing to oblige Germans to attend documentary films, quite another to make them watch, much less think about what they were seeing. Many years later the writer Stephan Hermlin described the scene in a Frankfurt cinema, where Germans were required to watch documentary films on Dachau and Buchenwald before receiving their ration cards: 'In the half-light of the projector, I could see that most people turned their faces away after the beginning of the film and stayed that way until the film was over. Today I think that that turned-away face was indeed the attitude of many millions ... The unfortunate people to which I belonged was both sentimental and callous. It was not interested in being shaken by events, in any "know thyself." '[4]

By the time the western Allies abandoned their denazification efforts with the coming of the Cold War, it was clear that these had had a decidedly limited impact. In Bavaria about half the secondary schoolteachers had been fired by 1946, only to be back in their jobs two years later. In 1949 the newly-established Federal Republic ended all investigations of the past behaviour of civil servants and army officers. In Bavaria in 1951, 94 percent of judges and prosecutors, 77 percent of finance min-

---

[3]In 1946 the West German Länderrat (Council of regions) recommended to the Allied authorities that in view of current shortages in Germany, food rations for displaced persons be reduced. General Lucius Clay confined his reply to a reminder that the food in question was provided by other European nations, victims of Germany's own war of aggression.

[4]Stephan Hermlin, *Bestimmungsorte* (Berlin, 1985), p. 46, quoted in Frank Stern, *The Whitewashing of the Yellow Badge* (1992), p. xvi

istry employees and 60 percent of civil servants in the regional Agriculture Ministry were ex-Nazis. By 1952 one in three of Foreign Ministry officials in Bonn was a former member of the Nazi Party. Of the newly-constituted West German Diplomatic Corps, 43 percent were former SS men and another 17 percent had served in the SD or Gestapo. Hans Globke, Chancellor Adenauer's chief aide throughout the 1950s, was the man who had been responsible for the official commentary on Hitler's 1935 Nuremberg Laws. The chief of police in the Rhineland-Palatinate, Wilhelm Hauser, was the *Obersturmführer* responsible for wartime massacres in Byelorussia.

The same pattern held true outside the civil service. Universities and the legal profession were the *least* affected by denazification, despite their notorious sympathy for Hitler's regime. Businessmen also got off lightly. Friedrich Flick, convicted as a war criminal in 1947, was released three years later by the Bonn authorities and restored to his former eminence as the leading shareholder in Daimler-Benz. Senior figures in the incriminated industrial combines of I.G. Farben and Krupp were all released early and re-entered public life little the worse for wear. By 1952 Fordwerke, the German branch of Ford Motor Company, had reassembled *all* its senior management from the Nazi years. Even the Nazi judges and concentration camp doctors convicted under American jurisdiction saw their sentences reduced or commuted (by the American administrator, John J McCloy).

Opinion poll data from the immediate post-war years confirm the limited impact of Allied efforts. In October 1946, when the Nuremberg Trial ended, only 6 percent of Germans were willing to admit that they thought it had been 'unfair', but four years later one in three took this view. That they felt this way should come as no surprise, since throughout the years 1945–49 a consistent majority of Germans believed that 'Nazism was a good idea, badly applied'. In November 1946, 37 per cent of Germans questioned in a survey of the American zone took the view that 'the extermination of the Jews and Poles and other non-Aryans was necessary for the security of Germans'.

In the same poll of November 1946, one German in three agreed with the proposition that 'Jews should not have the same rights as those belonging to the Aryan race'. This is not especially surprising, given that respondents had just emerged from twelve years under an authoritarian government committed to this view. What *does* surprise is a poll taken six years later in which a slightly higher percentage of West Germans—37 percent—affirmed that it was better for Germany to have no Jews on its territory. But then in that same year (1952) 25 percent of West Germans admitted to having a 'good opinion' of Hitler.

In the Soviet-occupied zone the Nazi legacy was treated a little differently. Although Soviet judges and lawyers took part in the Nuremberg trials, the main emphasis in denazification in the East was on the collective punishment of Nazis and the extirpation of Nazism from all areas of life. The local Communist leadership was under no illusions about what had taken place. As Walter Ulbricht, the future leader of the German Democratic Republic, put it in a speech to German Communist Party representatives in Berlin just six weeks after the defeat of his country, 'The tragedy of the German people consists in the fact that they obeyed a band of criminals . . . The German working class and the productive parts of the population failed before history.'

This was more than Adenauer or most West German politicians were willing to concede, at least in public. But Ulbricht, like the Soviet authorities to whom he answered, was less interested in extracting retribution for Nazi crimes than in securing Communist power in Germany and eliminating capitalism. As a consequence, although denazification in the Soviet zone actually went further in some instances than it did in the West, it was based upon two misrepresentations of Nazism: one integral to Communist theory, the other calculatedly opportunistic.

It was a Marxist commonplace and Soviet official doctrine that Nazism was merely Fascism and that Fascism, in turn, was a product of capitalist self-interest in a moment of crisis. Accordingly, the Soviet authorities paid little attention to the distinctively racist side of Nazism, and its genocidal outcome, and instead focused their arrests and expropriations on businessmen, tainted officials, teachers and others responsible for advancing the interests of the social class purportedly standing behind Hitler. In this way the Soviet dismantling of the heritage of Nazism in Germany was not fundamentally different from the social transformation that Stalin was bringing about in other parts of central and eastern Europe.

The opportunistic dimension of Soviet policy towards ex-Nazis was a function of weakness. The Communists in occupied Germany were not a strong movement—and their arrival in the baggage train of the Red Army was hardly calculated to endear them to voters. Their only political prospect, beyond brute force and electoral fraud, lay in appealing to calculated self-interest. To the east and south Communists did this by encouraging the expulsion of ethnic Germans and offering themselves as guarantor and protector for the new Polish/Slovak/Serb occupants of the Germans' vacated farms, businesses and apartments. This was obviously not an option in Germany itself. In Austria the local Communist Party made the mistake, in elections held in late 1945, of rejecting the potentially crucial support of minor Nazis and former Party members. In doing so it doomed the prospects for Communism in post-war Austria. The lesson was not lost on Berlin. The German Communist Party (KPD) decided instead to offer its services and its protection to millions of former Nazis.

The two perspectives—doctrine and calculation—were not necessarily in conflict. Ulbricht and his colleagues certainly believed that the way to expunge Nazism from Germany was by effecting a socio-economic transformation: they were not particularly interested in individual responsibility or moral re-education. But they also understood that Nazism was not just a trick perpetrated on an innocent German proletariat. The German working class, like the German bourgeoisie, had failed in its responsibilities. But for precisely that reason it would be more, not less likely to adapt itself to Communist goals, given the right combination of stick and carrot. And in any event the authorities in eastern Germany, like those in the West, had little choice—with whom else should they run the country if not ex-Nazis?

Thus on the one hand Soviet occupation forces fired from their jobs huge numbers of ex-Nazis—520,000 by April 1948—and appointed 'anti-Fascists' to administrative posts in their zone of occupation. On the other hand, German Communist leaders actively encouraged former Nazis whose records were not too publicly compromised to join them. Not surprisingly, they were very successful. Ex-Nazis were only too happy to expunge their past by throwing in their lot with the victors. As party members, local administrators, informers and policemen they proved uniquely well-adapted to the needs of the Communist state.

The new system, after all, was remarkably like the one they had known before: the Communists simply took over Nazi institutions like Labor Fronts or residential block-wardens and gave them new names and new bosses. But the adaptability of ex-Nazis was also a product of their vulnerability to blackmail. The Soviet authorities were quite prepared to conspire with their former enemies in lying about the nature and extent of Nazism in eastern Germany—asserting that Germany's capitalist and Nazi heritage was confined to the western zones and that the future German Democratic Republic was a land of workers, peasants and anti-Fascist heroes—but they also knew better and had the Nazi files to prove it, should the need arise. Black-marketeers, war profiteers and ex-Nazis of all sorts thus made excellent Communists, for they had every incentive to please.

By the early 1950s, more than half the rectors of East German institutes of higher education were former Nazi Party members, as were over 10 percent of the parliament a decade later. The newly-formed Stasi (state security agency) took over not just the role and the practices of the Nazi Gestapo but many thousands of its employees and informers. Political victims of the incoming Communist regime, often charged in a blanket manner as 'Nazi criminals', were arrested by ex-Nazi policemen, tried by ex-Nazi judges and guarded by ex-Nazi camp guards in Nazi-era prisons and concentration camps taken over en bloc by the new authorities.

The ease with which individuals and institutions switched from Nazism or Fascism over to Communism was not unique to East Germany, except perhaps in scale. The wartime resistance in Italy harboured quite a few ex-Fascists of various kinds, and the post-war moderation of the Italian Communist Party probably owed something to the fact that many of its potential supporters were compromised with Fascism. In post-war Hungary the Communists openly courted former members of the Fascist Arrow Cross, even going so far as to offer them support against Jews seeking the return of their property. In wartime London the Slovak Communists Vlado Clementis and Eugen Löbl were stalked by Soviet agents recruited from pre-war Czech Fascist parties, whose testimony would be used against them in their show trial a decade later.

Communists were not alone in turning a blind eye to people's Nazi or Fascist pasts in return for post-war political services. In Austria, former Fascists were often favoured by Western authorities and allowed to work in journalism and other sensitive occupations: their association with the corporatist, authoritarian regime of pre-war Austria was neutralized by the Nazi invasion and by their altogether credible and increasingly serviceable antipathy for the Left. The Allied Military Government in the frontier zone of north-east Italy protected former Fascists and collaborators, many of them wanted by the Yugoslavs, while Western intelligence services everywhere recruited experienced and well-informed ex-Nazis—including the 'Butcher of Lyon', the Gestapo officer Klaus Barbie—for future use: not least against the ex-Nazis in Soviet service, whom they were well-placed to identify.

In his first official address to the parliament of the Federal Republic of Germany, on September 20th 1949, Konrad Adenauer had this to say about denazification and the Nazi legacy: 'The government of the Federal Republic, in the belief that many have subjectively atoned for a guilt that was not heavy, is determined where it appears acceptable to do so to put the past behind us.' There is no doubt that many Germans heartily endorsed this assertion. If denazification aborted, it was because for political purposes Germans had spontaneously 'denazified' themselves on May 8th 1945.

And the German people were not alone. In Italy the daily newspaper of the new Christian Democrat Party put out a similar call to oblivion on the day of Hitler's death: 'We have the strength to forget!', it proclaimed. 'Forget as soon as possible!' In the East the Communists' strongest suit was their promise to make a revolutionary new beginning in countries where everyone had something to forget— things done to them or things they had done themselves. All over Europe there was a strong disposition to put the past away and start afresh, to follow Isocrates' recommendation to the Athenians at the close of the Peloponnesian Wars: 'Let us govern collectively as though nothing bad had taken place.'

This distrust of short-term memory, the search for serviceable myths of anti-Fascism—for a Germany of anti-Nazis, a France of Resisters or a Poland of victims—was the most important invisible legacy of World War Two in Europe. In its positive form it facilitated national recovery by allowing men like Marshall Tito, Charles De Gaulle or Konrad Adenauer to offer their fellow countrymen a plausible and even prideful account of themselves. Even East Germany claimed a noble point of origin, an invented tradition: the fabled and largely fabricated Communist 'uprising' in Buchenwald in April 1945. Such accounts allowed countries that had suffered war passively, like the Netherlands, to set aside the record of their compromises, and those whose activism had proven misguided, like Croatia, to bury it in a blurred story of competing heroisms.

Without such collective amnesia, Europe's astonishing post-war recovery would not have been possible. To be sure, much was put out of mind that would subsequently return in discomforting ways. But only much later would it become clear just how much post-war Europe rested on foundation myths that would fracture and shift with the passage of years. In the circumstances of 1945, in a continent covered with rubble, there was much to be gained by behaving as though the past was indeed dead and buried and a new age about to begin. The price paid was a certain amount of selective, collective forgetting, notably in Germany. But then, in Germany above all, there was much to forget.

III

The Rehabilitation of Europe

'All of us know by now that from this war there is no way back to a laissez-
faire order of society, that war as such is the maker of a silent revolution by
preparing the road to a new type of planned order'.
Karl Mannheim

'The all but general opinion seems to be that capitalist methods will be
unequal to the task of reconstruction'.
Joseph Schumpeter

'A lot of us were disappointed in the Britain that we came back to . . .
nobody could make it change overnight into the Britain we wanted'.
*Mrs Winnie Whitehouse (in Paul Addison, **Now The War Is Over**)*

'The remedy lies in breaking the vicious circle and restoring the confidence
of the European people in the economic future of their own countries and
of Europe as a whole'.
George C. Marshall

The sheer scale of the European calamity opened new opportunities. The war
changed everything. A return to the way things had been before 1939 was out of the
question almost everywhere. This was naturally the view of the young and the radical, but it was just as evident to perspicacious observers of an older generation.
Charles De Gaulle, 54 years old when France was liberated and born into the conservative Catholic bourgeoisie of northern France, put the matter with characteristic precision: 'During the catastrophe, beneath the burden of defeat, a great change
had occurred in men's minds. To many, the disaster of 1940 seemed like the failure
of the ruling class and system in every realm.'

But the problems had not begun in 1940, either in France or elsewhere. Anti-
Fascist resisters everywhere saw themselves in battle not just with the wartime occupiers and their local surrogates but with an entire political and social system
which they held directly responsible for the disasters their countries had undergone.
It was the politicians and bankers and businessmen and soldiers of the inter-war
years who had brought their countries to catastrophe, who had betrayed the sacrifices of the First World War and laid the ground for the Second. These, in the
words of a British pamphlet excoriating Conservative advocates of appeasement be-

fore 1940, were the 'Guilty Men'. They, and their system, were the target of wartime plans for post-war change.

Resistance was thus everywhere implicitly revolutionary. This was inherent in its logic. To reject a society that had produced Fascism led one naturally 'to a dream of revolution which would take off from a *tabula rasa*' (Italo Calvino). In much of eastern Europe the slate was indeed wiped clean, as we have seen. But even in western Europe there was widespread expectation of dramatic and rapid social transformation: who, after all, would stand in its way?

Seen from the point of view of the wartime Resistance movements, post-war politics would be the continuation of their wartime struggle, a natural projection and extension of their clandestine existence. Many young men and women who came to the fore in the wartime underground had known no other form of public life: in Italy since 1924, in Germany, Austria and most of Eastern Europe since the early thirties, and throughout occupied continental Europe since 1940, normal politics were unknown. Political parties had been banned, elections rigged or abolished. To oppose the authorities, to advocate social change or even political reform, was to place your self beyond the law.

For this new generation, politics was therefore *about* resistance—resistance to authority, resistance to conventional social or economic arrangements, resistance to the past. Claude Bourdet, an activist in the French resistance and a prominent left-wing magazine editor and writer in the post-war years, captured the mood in his memoirs, *L'aventure incertaine*: 'The Resistance', he wrote, 'turned us all into *contestataires* in every sense of the word, towards men as much as towards the social system.' From resisting Fascism to resisting a post-war retreat to the errors of the thirties seemed a natural step. Out of this came the oddly optimistic mood upon which many observers remarked in the immediate aftermath of Liberation. In spite of the destitution all around—indeed, because of it—something new and better was bound to emerge. 'None of us' wrote the editors of the Italian review *Società* in November 1945, 'recognizes his own past. It seems incomprehensible to us . . . Our life today is dominated by a sense of stupor and by an instinctive search for a direction. We are simply disarmed by the facts.'

The chief impediment to radical change in the aftermath of Hitler's defeat was not the reactionaries or Fascists, who had thrown in their lot with the dictators and been swept away with them, but the legitimate governments-in-exile, most of which had sat out the war in London planning their return. They saw the local resistance organizations in their countries as a problem rather than as allies: careless youngsters who would need to be disarmed and returned to civilian life, leaving public affairs in the hands of a political class duly cleansed of collaborators and traitors. Anything less would mean anarchy—or else an indefinite occupation by Allied armies.

The wartime resistance groups, organized by 1944–45 into various political movements, were just as suspicious in return. For them, the politicians, functionaries and courtiers who had escaped the Occupation were doubly discredited: by their pre-war errors and by their subsequent absence. In France and Norway the legislators elected in 1936 were disqualified by their actions in 1940. In Belgium and the Netherlands their absence in the intervening five years had cut off the returning governments from any appreciation of local suffering and the change in public mood brought about under Nazi occupation. In central and eastern Europe, with the important exception of Czechoslovakia, the former governments were rendered irrelevant by the arrival of the Red Army (though they were sometimes slow to grasp this).

The returning authorities were quite willing to compromise in matters of policy—in particular on social and economic reforms, as we shall see. What they insisted upon, however, was what De Gaulle and others perceived as an 'orderly transition'. Since this was also the preference of the Allied occupying forces, West and East, the illusions of the Resistance were soon shattered. In eastern Europe (with the exception of Yugoslavia) it was the Soviets who determined the shape of post-war governments and who directed their actions. In western Europe, provisional authorities took office pending new elections. And in every case the resistance movements were encouraged and eventually forced to hand in their weapons and disband their organizations.

It is striking, in retrospect, how little resistance there was to this restoration of the institutional *status quo*. In Poland and parts of the western Soviet Union armed partisan groups survived for a few more years, but theirs was a specifically national and anti-Communist struggle. In Norway, Belgium, France and Italy the organized resistance merged peacefully into post-war political parties and unions with only muted protests. In Belgium in November 1944 armed members of the wartime resistance were given two weeks to hand over their weapons. This led to a large protest rally in Brussels on November 25th at which the police opened fire, injuring 45 people. But such incidents were uncommon.[1] More typically, 200,000 French resistance fighters were successfully integrated into the regular army when their organization, the *Forces Françaises de l'Intérieur*, was disbanded without protest.

The demobilization of the resistance was greatly facilitated by Soviet strategy, which favoured the restoration of parliamentary regimes in western Europe (as, nominally, in eastern Europe too). Communist leaders like Maurice Thorez in France and Palmiro Togliatti in Italy played a major role in ensuring the peaceful cooperation of their (sometimes bemused) followers. But many were willing to believe that the energies and ambitions of the resistance would now be channeled into political projects for national renewal.

Contacts made in the Resistance *did* sometimes survive—the post-war 'depillarization' of Dutch society, for example, the breaking down of the centuries-long

---

[1]The last armed Italian partisans were rounded up in a series of military operations around Bologna in the autumn of 1948.

denominational divide between communities of Catholics and Protestants, began with personal links forged in wartime. But plans for a post-war 'Resistance Party' failed everywhere. They came closest to fruition in Italy, where Ferrucio Parri became Prime Minister in June 1945 and promised that his Action Party would pursue the spirit and goals of the Resistance. But Parri was no politician and when he fell, six months later, political power shifted definitively into the hands of the traditional parties. De Gaulle, in France, was a far better political strategist but he, too, abandoned office (one month after Parri) rather than accommodate his wartime ambitions to parliamentary routine—thus paying unintended tribute to his own success in re-establishing the continuity of the Republic.

Rather than being governed by a new, fraternal community of resisters, then, most Europeans in the immediate post-war years instead found themselves ruled by coalitions of left and left-centre politicians rather similar to the Popular Fronts of the 1930s. This made sense. The only pre-war political parties able to operate normally in these years were those with anti-Fascist credentials—or, in Soviet-occupied eastern Europe, those to whom it suited the new authorities to ascribe such credentials at least for the time being. In practice this meant Communists, Socialists and a handful of liberal or radical groups. These, together with the newly-prominent Christian Democratic parties, thus constituted the parties of government in the first post-war years and they brought with them many of the policies and men of the Popular Front era.

The existing parties of the Left had gained immensely by their engagement in the wartime resistance: especially in France, where the Communists' succeeded in converting their (sometimes exaggerated) wartime exploits into political capital and convinced even dispassionate observers of their unique moral standing—'the great heroes of the Resistance' as Janet Flanner described them in December 1944. It is thus not especially odd that the reform programs of post-war European governments echoed and recapitulated the unfinished business of the 1930s.

If experienced party politicians had so little difficulty displacing wartime activists after 1945 this was because, although they shared a common anti-Fascist ethos and a widespread desire for change, the Resistance and its heirs were rather vague on specifics. The Action Party in Italy sought to abolish the monarchy, nationalize large capital and industry and reform agriculture. The Action Programme of the French National Resistance Council had no king to depose, but its ambitions were otherwise similarly imprecise. Resistance units had been too preoccupied fighting, or just surviving, to busy themselves with detailed plans for post-war legislation.

But above all the resisters were handicapped by a lack of experience. Among clandestine organizations only the Communists had practical knowledge of politics, and except in the French case not much of that. But Communists in particular were reluctant to tie their hands with detailed programmatic statements that might alienate future tactical allies. The Resistance thus bequeathed little in the way of post-war projects beyond high-minded statements of intent and broad generalities—and even these, as the otherwise sympathetic François Mauriac noted in August 1944, were 'hastily typed fantasy programs'.

On one thing, however, all were agreed—resisters and politicians alike: 'planning'. The disasters of the inter-war decades—the missed opportunities after 1918, the great depression that followed the stock-market crash of 1929, the waste of unemployment, the inequalities, injustices and inefficiencies of laissez-faire capitalism that had led so many into authoritarian temptation, the brazen indifference of an arrogant ruling elite and the incompetence of an inadequate political class—all seemed to be connected by the utter failure to organize society better. If democracy was to work, if it was to recover its appeal, it would have to be *planned*.

It is sometimes suggested that this faith in planning, the political religion of post-war Europe, derived from the example of the Soviet Union: a planned economy that had ostensibly escaped the traumas of capitalist Europe, withstood the Nazi assault and won the Second World War thanks to a series of detailed Five Year Plans. This is entirely mistaken. In post-war western and central Europe only Communists put their faith in Soviet-style Plans (about which they knew very little), and even they had no notion of how such Plans might be applied to their local circumstances. The Soviet obsession with numerical targets, production quotas and centralized direction was alien to all but a few of the contemporary western advocates of planning. The latter—and they came in many varieties—were drawing on a very different set of sources.

The vogue for plans and planning began long before 1945. Throughout the inter-war depression, from Hungary to Great Britain, voices were raised in support of a planned economy of one kind or another. Some of the ideas propounded, notably in Austria and among the British Fabians, derived from an older Socialist tradition, but many more had their origins in pre-1914 liberal reformism. The nineteenth-century 'caretaker' state, its attention confined to security and policing, was outmoded, so the argument ran. If only on prudential grounds—to forestall political upheaval—it would now be necessary to intervene in economic affairs to regulate imbalances, eliminate inefficiencies and compensate for the inequities and injustice of the market.

Before 1914 the main emphasis in such reformist projects was confined to calls for progressive taxation, protection of labour and, occasionally, state ownership of a restricted number of natural monopolies. But with the collapse of the international economy and the ensuing war, planning took on a greater urgency and ambition. Competing proposals for a national Plan, in which the state would intervene actively to support, discourage, facilitate and if necessary direct key economic sectors, circulated widely among young engineers, economists and civil servants in France and Germany.

For most of the inter-war years, would-be planners and their supporters languished in frustration at the political margins. The older generation of politicians was deaf to their appeals: to many on the conservative Right and Center state intervention in the economy was still abhorrent, while on the socialist Left it was generally believed that only a post-revolutionary society could plan its economic affairs rationally. Until then, capitalism was condemned to suffer and eventually collapse of its own contradictions. The idea that one might 'plan' a capitalist economy seemed to both sides a non-sense. The frustrated advocates of economic planning thus frequently found themselves attracted to authoritarian parties of the radical Right, distinctly more hospitable to their approach.

It was not by chance, therefore, that Oswald Mosley and some other British Labourites turned to Fascism out of frustration at their Party's inadequate response to the Great Depression. In Belgium Hendrik de Man likewise failed to convince his fellow Socialists of the viability of his 'Plan' and began propounding more authoritarian solutions. In France a number of the brightest young leaders of the Socialist Party broke away to form new movements, frustrated at their party's failure to respond imaginatively to the economic crisis. Many of these and others like them ended up as Fascists.

Mussolini's cheerleaders in France and Britain, before 1940, envied what they saw as his success in overcoming Italy's economic disadvantages through state-led planning and the establishment of umbrella agencies for whole economic sectors. Albert Speer, the administrator of Hitler's New Order, was much admired abroad for his programme of economic direction and regulation. In September 1943, Speer and Jean Bichelonne, Vichy's Minister of Industrial Production, worked out a system of tariff reductions based on inter-war 'plan-ist' ideas that closely anticipated European trading relations and Franco-German economic coordination in later years. In 'Jeune Europe', a club founded in 1933 for young thinkers and politicians keen to set a new direction in policy making, the future Belgian statesman and Europhile Paul-Henri Spaak exchanged ideas about an enhanced role for the state with similarly-minded contemporaries from across the continent, including Otto Abetz, the future Nazi administrator of wartime Paris.

'Planning', in short, had a complicated history. Many of its advocates got their first experience, as civil servants and business administrators, in wartime occupation regimes—in France, Italy, Belgium and Czechoslovakia, not to speak of Germany and Italy. Britain was not occupied but there, too, it was the war that introduced and domesticated the hitherto rather abstract notion of governmental 'planning'. Indeed in Britain it was the war above all that placed the government at the heart of economic life. The Emergency Powers Bill of May 1940 authorised the government to direct anyone to do anything in the national interest, to control any property and assign any industrial plant to any national end it chose. In the words of Kenneth Harris, the biographer of Clement Attlee, Britain's post-war Labour leader: 'National planning and national ownership, which in the period 1945–51 seemed the result of a Labour government putting socialist principles into effect, were to a great degree the legacy of a state which had been organized to fight a total war.'

Fascism and war were thus the bridge linking heterodox, marginal and often controversial notions of economic planning with mainstream post-war economic policy. Yet this compromised heritage had little impact on planning's appeal—whatever its associations with far Right, far Left, occupation or war, planning was quite distinctly *not* associated with the discredited politics of the inter-war years, a point widely held in its favour. What planning was really about was faith in the state. In many countries this reflected a well-founded awareness, enhanced by the experience of war, that in the absence of any other agency of regulation or distribution, only the state now stood between the individual and destitution. But contemporary enthusiasm for an interventionist state went beyond desperation or self-interest. The vision of Clement Attlee, the British Labour leader whose party defeated Churchill's Conservatives in the dramatic election upset of 1945, nicely captured the contemporary mood: what was needed now were 'well-planned, well-built cities and parks and playing fields, homes and schools, factories and shops.'

There was a great faith in the ability (and not just the duty) of government to solve large-scale problems by mobilizing and directing people and resources to collectively useful ends. Obviously this way of seeing things was particularly attractive to socialists; but the idea that a well-planned economy meant a richer, fairer and better-regulated society was taken up by a very broad constituency, including the Christian Democratic parties then rising to prominence all over Western Europe. The English historian A. J. P. Taylor told BBC listeners in November 1945 that '[n]obody in Europe believes in the American way of life—that is, private enterprise; or, rather, those who believe in it are a defeated party which seems to have no more future than the Jacobites in England after 1688'. Taylor exaggerated as always, he was wrong in the long run (but who isn't?) and he might have been surprised to learn about the planist enthusiasms of many New Dealers prominent in the contemporary US administration of Germany. But at the time he was broadly correct.

What *was* 'Planning'? The term is misleading. What all planners had in common was belief in an enhanced role for the state in social and economic affairs. Beyond this there was great variation, usually a consequence of distinctive national political traditions. In Britain, where very little actual *planning* ever took place, the real issue was *control*—of industries and social and economic services—through state ownership as an end in itself. Thus nationalization—notably of mines, railways, goods transportation and utilities—and the provision of medical services lay at the heart of the Labour Party programme after 1945. The 'commanding heights' of the economy, in short, were taken over. But that was all.

In Italy the Fascist institutional legacy—which had brought large tracts of the economy under state oversight—was left largely intact after the war. What changed was the political colour of the parties now benefiting from the industrial and financial power base afforded them by holding companies and state-owned agencies. In West Germany, after 1948, the economy would remain mostly in private hands but with detailed, publicly-approved arrangements for factory management, employer-employee relations and conditions of employment and distribution. In the Netherlands central planning entailed a variable mix of predictive and prescriptive edicts for the use of private enterprise.

Most countries of western Europe had rapidly growing public sectors, when measured by government expenditure or the number of public-sector employees. But only in France did rhetorical enthusiasm for state planning translate into the real thing. Like the British, post-war French governments nationalized: air transportation, banks, thirty two insurance companies, utilities, mines, munitions industries, aircraft manufacturing and the giant Renault concern (as punishment for its owner's contribution to the German war effort). One fifth of France's total industrial capacity was in state ownership by May 1946.

Meanwhile, on December 4th 1945, Jean Monnet presented President De Gaulle with his *Plan de Modernisation et d'Équipement*. A month later the *Commissariat Général du Plan* was established, with Monnet at its head. In the course of the following months Monnet set up Modernization Commissions for various industries (mining, electricity, transportation, building materials, steel and agricultural machinery; oil, chemicals, fertilizers, shipping and synthetic fibres would later be added) and these in turn delivered proposals and sectoral plans. Exactly one year after its creation, in January 1947, the *Commissariat* saw its first national Plan approved by the French Cabinet—without discussion.

The Monnet Plan was unique. It was the work of an unusual man.[2] But above all it was the product of a political culture already favourably disposed to authoritarian decision-making and consensus building by governmental *fiat*. Under its auspices France became the first western country to commit itself wholeheartedly to economic growth and modernization as public policy. The Plan depended heavily on assumptions about French access to German raw materials and markets, and thus the story of its success is part of the narrative of France's relations with Germany and the rest of Europe in the post-war decade: a story of many false starts, constraints and frustrations.

The first Monnet Plan was largely an emergency measure to address France's post-war crisis. Only later was it extended and adapted to the terms of Marshall Aid.

---

[2]Jean Monnet was born in Cognac in 1888, the son of a brandy merchant. Upon leaving school he spent many years living and working abroad, notably in London; after the First World War he was named Secretary General of the new League of Nations. He passed much of the Second World War in the US, negotiating arms supplies on behalf of the British government and the Free French. His devotion to economic planning and his later contribution to the Schuman Plan for European economic cooperation thus drew upon a familiarity with large-scale organization and inter-state collaboration that was strikingly unusual for a Frenchman of his class and time.

But the basic outline of post-war French economic strategy was present from the start. French planning was never more than 'indicative': it only ever set targets, not production quotas. In this respect it was quite unlike Soviet planning, whose characteristic feature (and prime defect) was its insistence upon arbitrary and rigid output figures by sector and by commodity. The Monnet Plan confined itself to providing government with a strategy and levers for actively fostering certain favoured objectives. At the time this was a strikingly original undertaking.

In Czechoslovakia a Central Planning Commission with some Monnet-like features and aspirations was established in June 1946 to guide and coordinate the sizeable public sector nationalized by President Benes in 1945. In the year *before* the Prague Communist coup of February 1948, 93 percent of all those employed in transport and 78 percent of those in industry already worked for the state. Banks, mines, insurance companies, major utilities, steel and chemical works, food processing industries and all large enterprises had been taken over: 2,119 firms comprising some 75 percent of all manufacturing output.

In the Czechoslovak case nationalization and state planning of the economy thus began well in advance of the Communist take-over and represented the policy preferences of a genuine majority of the electorate—only in February 1949, a year after the Communist coup, was the Planning Commission purged and renamed as the 'State Planning Office', with a very different remit. Elsewhere in the region large-scale nationalizations, like those mandated under Poland's January 1946 Nationalization Law, were the work of coalition governments in which Communists dominated. But here, too, there were pre-Communist roots: back in 1936 the authoritarian government of the pre-war Polish Republic had inaugurated a 'Four-Year Investment Plan' with a rudimentary system of centralized directive planning.

The chief purpose of planning in post-war continental Europe was public investment. At a time of acute capital shortage and with huge demand for investment in every sector, government planning consisted of hard choices: where to place the limited resources of the state and at whose expense. In eastern Europe the emphasis was inevitably upon basic expenditure—on roads, railways, factories, utilities. But that left very little over for food and housing, much less medical, educational and other social services; and nothing at all for non-essential consumer goods. This was not a pattern of expenditure likely to endear itself to any electorate, especially in countries that had already suffered years of material deprivation, and it is not surprising that this sort of planning under conditions of dire shortage was almost always accompanied, sooner or later, by authoritarian rule and the police state.

But the situation in the West was not so very different. The British, as we shall see, were constrained to accept years of 'austerity' as the price for economic recovery. In France or Italy, where there was almost no long-term private capital market, all major investments had to be publicly funded—which was why the first Monnet Plan was skewed towards capital investment in major industries at the expense of domestic consumption, housing and services. The political consequences of this were predictable: by 1947 France, like Italy, was threatened with strikes, violent demonstrations and a steady increase in support for the Communist Party and its trade unions. Deliberate neglect of the consumer goods sector and the diversion of scarce national resources to a handful of key industrial sectors made long-term economic sense: but it was a high-risk strategy.

The economics of Planning drew directly upon the lessons of the 1930s—a successful strategy for post-war recovery must preclude any return to economic stagnation, depression, protectionism and above all unemployment. The same considerations lay behind the creation of the modern European welfare state. In the conventional wisdom of the 1940s, the political polarizations of the last inter-war decade were born directly of economic depression and its social costs. Both Fascism and Communism thrived on social despair, on the huge gulf separating rich and poor. If the democracies were to recover, the 'condition of the people' question must be addressed. In the words of Thomas Carlyle a hundred years earlier, 'if something be not done, something will *do* itself one day, and in a fashion that will please nobody.'

But the 'welfare state'—*social* planning—was more than just a prophylactic against political upheaval. Our present discomfort with notions of race, eugenics, 'degeneration' and the like obscures the important part these played in European public thinking during the first half of the twentieth century: it wasn't only the Nazis who took such matters seriously. By 1945 two generations of European doctors, anthropologists, public health officials and political commentators had contributed to widespread debates and polemics about 'race health', population growth, environmental and occupational well-being and the public policies through which these might be improved and secured. There was a broad consensus that the physical and moral condition of the citizenry was a matter of common interest and therefore part of the responsibility of the state.

As a consequence, rudimentary welfare provisions of one kind or another were already widespread before 1945, although their quality and reach varied widely. Germany was typically the most advanced country, having already instituted pension, accident and medical insurance schemes under Bismarck, between 1883 and 1889. But other countries began to catch up in the years immediately before and after World War One. Embryonic national insurance and pension schemes were introduced in Britain by Asquith's Liberal governments in the first decade of the century; and both Britain and France established ministries of health immediately following the end of the Great War, in 1919 and 1920 respectively.

Compulsory unemployment insurance, first introduced in Britain in 1911, was instituted in Italy (1919), Austria (1920), Ireland (1923), Poland (1924), Bulgaria (1925), Germany and Yugoslavia (1927) and Norway (1938). Romania and Hungary already had accident and sickness insurance schemes in place before World War

One, and all the countries of eastern Europe introduced national pension systems between the wars. Family allowances were a key element in plans to increase the birth rate—a particular obsession after 1918 in countries badly hit by wartime losses—and were introduced first in Belgium (1930), next in France (1932) and in Hungary and the Netherlands just before the outbreak of war.

But none of these arrangements, not even those of the Nazis, represented comprehensive welfare systems. They were cumulative *ad hoc* reforms, each addressing a particular social problem or improving upon the demonstrated shortcomings of previous schemes. The various pensions and medical insurance systems introduced in Britain, for example, had very restricted benefits and applied only to working men: wives and other dependents were excluded. Eligibility for unemployment benefits in inter-war Britain rested on a 'Means Test'. This drew on the nineteenth-century Poor Law principle of 'least eligibility' and required an applicant for public assistance to demonstrate his virtual destitution in order to qualify. Nowhere was there yet any recognition of an obligation upon the state to guarantee a given set of services to all citizens, whether male or female, employed or workless, old or young.

It was the war that changed all this. Just as World War One had precipitated legislation and social provisions in its wake—if only to deal with the widows, orphans, invalids and unemployed of the immediate post-war years—so the Second World War transformed both the role of the modern state and the expectations placed upon it. The change was most marked in Britain, where Maynard Keynes correctly anticipated a post-war 'craving for social and personal *security*'. But everywhere (in the words of the historian Michael Howard) 'war and welfare went hand in hand'. In some countries nutrition and medical provision actually improved during the war: mobilizing men and women for total war meant finding out more about their condition and doing whatever was necessary to keep them productive.

The post-1945 European welfare states varied considerably in the resources they provided and the way they financed them. But certain general points can be made. The provision of social *services* chiefly concerned education, housing and medical care, as well as urban recreation areas, subsidized public transport, publicly-funded art and culture and other indirect benefits of the interventionary state. Social *security* consisted chiefly of the state provision of insurance—against illness, unemployment, accident and the perils of old age. Every European state in the post-war years provided or financed most of these resources, some more than others.

The important differences lay in the schemes set in place to pay for the new public provisions. Some countries collected revenue through taxation and provided free or heavily-subsidized care and services—this was the system chosen in Britain, where it reflected the contemporary preference for state monopolies. In other countries cash benefits were paid to citizens according to socially-determined criteria of eligibility, with the beneficiaries left to purchase services of their own choice. In France and some smaller countries citizens would be expected to pay up front for certain categories of medical provision, for example, but could then claim back much of their expenses from the state.

These differences reflected varying systems of national finance and accounting, but they also signified a fundamental strategic choice. In isolation, social insurance, however generous, was not in principle politically radical—we have seen how relatively early it was introduced in even the most conservative of regimes. *Comprehensive* welfare systems, however, are inherently re-distributive. Their universal character and the sheer scale on which they operate require the transfer of resources—usually through taxation—from the privileged to the less well off. The welfare state was thus in itself a radical undertaking, and the variations among the European welfare states after 1945 reflected not just institutional procedures but also political calculation.

In eastern Europe, for example, the Communist regimes after 1948 on the whole did *not* usually favour universal welfare systems—they did not need to, since they were at liberty to redistribute resources by force without spending scarce state funds on public services. Peasants, for instance, were frequently excluded from the social insurance and pension arrangements on political grounds. In western Europe only six countries—Belgium, Italy, Norway, Austria, the Federal Republic of Germany and the UK—introduced compulsory and universal unemployment insurance after 1945. Subsidized voluntary schemes remained in the Netherlands until 1949, in France through 1967, in Switzerland until the mid-1970s. In Catholic Europe long-established local and communal coverage against unemployment probably impeded the development of universal systems of insurance by reducing the need for them. In countries where inter-war unemployment had been especially traumatic—the UK, or Belgium—welfare spending was driven in part by the desire to maintain full or close to full employment. Where it had not been so significant—in France or Italy, for example—this was reflected in a rather different balance of priorities.

Although Sweden and Norway (but not Denmark) were in the vanguard of benefit provision across a broad range of social services, and West Germany kept in place the welfare provisions inherited from past regimes (including Nazi-era programmes aimed at encouraging a high-birth rate), it was in Britain that the most ambitious efforts were made to build, from scratch, a genuine 'Welfare State'. In part this reflected the unique position of Britain's Labour Party, which won an outright victory at the elections of July 1945 and—unlike the governments of most other European countries—was free to legislate its entire electoral programme unconstrained by coalition partners. But it also derived from the rather distinctive sources of British reformism.

The social legislation of post-war Britain was based on the justly famous wartime report by Sir William Beveridge, published in November 1942 and an immediate best-seller. Beveridge was born in 1879, the son of a British judge in imperial India, and his sensibilities and ambitions were those of the great reforming

Liberals of Edwardian Britain. His Report was at once an indictment of the social injustices of pre-1939 British society and a policy template for root and branch reform once the war was over. Even the Conservative Party did not dare to oppose its core recommendations and it became the moral basis for the most popular and enduring elements in Labour's post-war programme.

Beveridge made four assumptions about post-war welfare provision, all of which were to be incorporated in British policy for the next generation: that there should be a national health service, an adequate state pension, family allowances and near-full employment. The last of these was not a welfare provision in itself, but it underpinned everything else since it took for granted that the normal situation of a healthy post-war adult was to be in full-time paid work. On this assumption generous provision could be made for unemployment insurance, pensions, family allowances, medical and other services, since these would be paid for by levies on wage packets, as well as by progressive taxation of the working population at large.

The implications were significant. Non-working women with no private health insurance of their own got coverage for the first time. The humiliation and social dependency of the old Poor Law/Means Test system was done away with—on the (presumptively) rare occasion when the citizen of the Welfare State needed public assistance he or she was now entitled to it by right. Medical and dental services were provided free of charge at the point of service, pension provision was made universal, family allowances (at 5/- [25 p] per week for second and subsequent children) were introduced. The main parliamentary Bill legislating these provisions received the Royal Assent in November 1946 and the National Health Service (NHS) Act—the core of the welfare system—was introduced into law on July 5th 1948.

The British Welfare State was both the completion of an earlier cycle of reforms, with its roots in the mid-nineteenth century Factory Acts, and a genuinely radical departure. The contrast between the Britain of George Orwell's *Road to Wigan Pier* (published in 1937) and that of Conservative Prime Minister Harold Macmillan's famous put-down to a heckler twenty years later ('You've never had it so good') is a tribute to the National Health Service and the provisions for security, income maintenance and employment that accompanied it. It is all too easy, looking back today upon the miscalculations of the first post-war reformers, to minimize and even dismiss their achievement. Within a few years many of the universal provisions of the NHS proved unsustainably expensive; the quality of the services provided has not been maintained across the years; and over time it has become clear that certain of the fundamental actuarial assumptions—including the optimistic prediction of permanent full employment—were short-sighted or worse. But anyone who grew up (like the present writer) in post-war Britain has good reason to be grateful for the Welfare State.

The same is true for the post-war generation all across the European continent, although nowhere outside Britain was comprehensive social coverage attempted on so generous a scale and all at once. Thanks to the coming of welfare states Europeans ate more and (mostly) better, lived longer and healthier lives, were better housed and clothed than ever before. Above all, they were more secure. It is not by chance that most Europeans, when asked what they think of their public services, nearly always speak first of the safety net of insurance and pension provisions which the post-war state has provided for them. Even in Switzerland, a country distinctly under-provisioned by European welfare standards, the December 1948 Federal Old Age and Survivors' Insurance Act is regarded by many citizens as one of their country's finest achievements.

The Welfare State did not come cheap. Its cost, to countries not yet recovered from the slump of the thirties and the destruction of the war, was very considerable. France, which devoted just 5 percent of its Gross Domestic Product (GDP) to social services in 1938, was committing 8.2 percent in 1949—a 64 percent increase. In Britain by 1949 nearly 17 percent of all public expenditure was on social security alone (that is, not including the public provision of services and facilities not included under this heading), a 50 percent increase over the 1938 level at a moment of severe strain on the country's finances. Even in Italy, a much poorer country whose governments tried to avoid carrying high social security costs by diverting services and provisions into the private sector or the workplace, government spending on social services as a share of GDP rose from 3.3 percent in 1938 to 5.2 percent in 1949.

Why were Europeans willing to pay so much for insurance and other long-term welfare provisions, at a time when life was still truly hard and material shortages endemic? The first reason is that, precisely because times *were* difficult, the post-war welfare systems were a guarantee of a certain minimum of justice, or fairness. This was not the spiritual and social revolution for which many in the wartime Resistance had dreamed, but it was a first step away from the hopelessness and cynicism of the pre-war years.

Secondly, the welfare states of western Europe were not politically divisive. They *were* socially re-distributive in general intent (some more than others) but not at all revolutionary—they did not 'soak the rich'. On the contrary: although the greatest immediate advantage was felt by the poor, the real long-term beneficiaries were the professional and commercial middle class. In many cases they had not previously been eligible for work-related health, unemployment or retirement benefits and had been obliged, before the war, to purchase such services and benefits from the private sector. Now they had full access to them, either free or at low cost. Taken with the state provision of free or subsidized secondary and higher education for their children, this left the salaried professional and white-collar classes with both a better quality of life and more disposable income. Far from dividing the social classes against each other, the European welfare state bound them closer together than ever before, with a common interest in its preservation and defense.

But the chief basis of support for state-funded welfare and social service provisions lay in the popular sense that these corresponded to the proper tasks of government. The post-war state all across Europe was a 'social' state, with implicit (and often constitutionally explicit) responsibility for the well-being of its citizens. It had an obligation to provide not only the institutions and services necessary for a well-regulated, safe and prosperous land, but also to *improve* the condition of the population, as measured by a broad and expanding range of indices. Whether it could actually meet all these demands was another matter.

Obviously it would prove easier to achieve the ideals of the social state, 'from cradle to grave', in the small population of a wealthy, homogenous country like Sweden than in one like Italy. But faith in the state was at least as marked in poor lands as in rich ones—perhaps more so, since in such places only the state could offer hope or salvation to the mass of the population. And in the aftermath of depression, occupation and civil war, the state—as an agent of welfare, security and fairness—was a vital source of community and social cohesion. Many commentators today are disposed to see state-ownership and state-dependency as the European problem, and salvation-from-above as the illusion of the age. But for the generation of 1945 some workable balance between political freedoms and the rational, equitable distributive function of the administrative state seemed the only sensible route out of the abyss.

The post-1945 urge for change went well beyond the provision of welfare. The years following World War Two were a sort of foreshortened Age of Reform, during which many long-pressing problems were belatedly addressed. One of the most important of these was the matter of agrarian reform, which many well-informed contemporaries saw as Europe's most pressing dilemma. The weight of the past still hung heavily upon the continent's peasantry. Only in England, the Low Countries, Denmark, the Alpine lands and parts of France was it possible to speak of a prosperous, independent class of farmers. The overwhelming majority of Europe's predominantly rural population lived in conditions of indebted penury.

One reason for this was that large tracts of the best arable and, especially, pasture land were still in the hands of a relatively few wealthy landowners, often absent and in many cases adamantly opposed to any improvement in the conditions of their land, their tenants or their workers. Another factor was the long decline in agricultural prices relative to industrial ones, a process exacerbated since the eighteen-seventies by the importation of cheap grain and later meat from the Americas and the British Dominions. By the 1930s European peasants had lived for nearly three generations with this relentless deterioration in their circumstances. Many—from Greece, Southern Italy, the Balkans, central and eastern Europe—had emigrated: to the US, Argentina and elsewhere. Those who stayed behind had often proved easy prey for nationalist and Fascist demagogues. After the war it was thus widely believed, particularly on the Left, that Fascism appealed especially to desperate peasants and that any revival of Fascism in Europe would begin in the countryside. The agrarian problem was thus twofold: how to improve the economic prospects of the peasant and thereby wean him from authoritarian temptation.

The first objective had already been attempted after World War One through a series of land reforms—notably in Romania and Italy but in some measure virtually everywhere—whose goal was to redistribute large holdings, reduce the number of 'microfundia' (inefficient plotlets) and give farmers a better chance of producing efficiently for the market. But these reforms failed in their goal—partly because in the disastrous economic circumstances of inter-war Europe, with prices falling even faster than before 1914, the newly 'independent' landholding peasants were actually more vulnerable than ever.

After World War Two agrarian reform was once again attempted. In a Romanian land reform of March 1945, one million hectares of land were taken out of the hands of 'kulaks' and 'war criminals' and distributed to upwards of 600,000 hitherto poor or landless peasants. In Hungary, where the inter-war regime of Admiral Horthy had blocked any significant land redistribution, one-third of the country's surface area was expropriated from the previous owners, in accordance with the December 1944 Szeged Programme of the provisional post-war coalition government. The wartime Czechoslovak National Front government drew up a similar programme the same year and duly redistributed significant tracts of land—notably farms seized from Sudeten Germans and Hungarians—in the immediate post-war months. Between 1944 and 1947 every east European country saw the creation of a large class of smallholders beholden to the new authorities for their land. A few years later those same smallholders would in their turn be dispossessed by the Communist regimes in their drive for collectivization. But in the meantime whole classes of landed gentry and large farmers, in Poland, East Prussia, Hungary, Romania and Yugoslavia simply disappeared.

In western Europe only Southern Italy saw anything comparable to the dramatic changes further East. Sweeping reform laws in 1950 announced the redistribution of estate land across Sicily and the *Mezzogiorno*, following land seizures and occupations in Basilicata, the Abruzzi and Sicily. But for all the fuss, little changed—much of the land redistributed from the old *latifundia* lacked water, roads or housing. Of 74,000 hectares redistributed in Sicily after World War Two, 95 percent was 'marginal' or inferior land, unsuited to cultivation. The impoverished peasants to whom it was offered had no money and no access to credit; they could do little with their new holdings. The land reforms in Italy failed. Their stated goal—the solution of the 'Southern Question'—would only be met a decade later, and then only in part, when the surplus peasantry of the South abandoned the soil and went in search of work to the booming northern cities of the Italian 'miracle'.

But southern Italy was a hard case. New legal rights for tenant farmers in France and elsewhere gave them an incentive to invest in their smallholdings, while innovative credit systems and rural banks made it possible for them to do so. State-subsidized farm price support systems helped reverse the decades-long decline in agricultural prices by encouraging farmers to produce as much as possible while guaranteeing to purchase their output at a fixed, minimum rate. Meanwhile the unprecedented post-war demand for labour in the cities drained off surplus workers from poorer rural districts, leaving a more efficient farming population with fewer mouths to feed.

The political dimensions of the agrarian problem were indirectly addressed in the broader package of political reforms introduced in the first post-war years. Many of these were constitutional in nature, once again completing the unfinished business of 1918. In Italy, France and Belgium women finally secured the vote. In June 1946 the Italians voted to become a Republic, but the margin was narrow (12.7 million votes in favour of abolishing the monarchy, 10.7 million for retaining it) and the country's historical divisions were if anything further exacerbated by the outcome: the South, except for the region of Basilicata, voted overwhelmingly for the king (by a ratio of 4:1 in Naples).

The Greeks, in contrast, voted in September 1946 to retain their monarchy. Belgians kept theirs, too, but removed the incumbent, King Leopold III, as punishment for his cooperation with the Nazis. This decision, taken under public pressure in 1950 against the wishes of a slight majority of the population, sharply divided the country along communal and linguistic lines: francophone Walloons voted to remove Leopold from the throne, whereas 72 percent of Dutch-speaking Flamands expressed a preference for letting him stay. The French had no monarch on whom to vent their memory of wartime humiliation, and merely voted in 1946 to replace the disgraced Third Republic with a numerical successor. Like the German Basic Law of 1949, the constitution of the Fourth Republic was designed to eliminate so far as possible the risk of any surrender to authoritarian or caesarist sirens—an aspiration which was to prove singularly unsuccessful.

The Provisional or Constituent Assemblies which promulgated these post-war constitutions, proposed popular referenda on controversial topics and voted major institutional reforms were mostly canted to the Left. In Italy, France and Czechoslovakia Communist Parties did well after the war. In the Italian elections of 1946 the Partito Communista Italiano (PCI) obtained 19 percent of the vote; the Parti Communiste Français (PCF) won 28.6 percent of the vote in the second French elections of that year, its best result ever. In Czechoslovakia, in the free elections of May 1946, the Communists secured 38 percent of the national vote (40 percent in the Czech lands). Elsewhere Communists did not fare so well in free elections, though better than they would ever manage again, ranging from 13 percent in Belgium to just 0.4 percent in the United Kingdom.

The Communists' initial political leverage in western Europe came from their association with Socialist parties, most of which before 1947 were reluctant to break with the Popular Front-style alliance that had re-formed itself in the resistance movements. Socialist parties in France and Italy did almost as well as the Communists in initial post-war elections and considerably better in Belgium. In Scandinavia the Social Democrats vastly outscored any other party, obtaining between 38 and 41 percent of the votes in Denmark, Norway and Sweden in elections held between 1945 and 1948.

Nevertheless, outside Britain and the Nordic countries the 'old Left' of Communists and Socialists was never able to govern alone. In western Europe the balance was always held, and in many cases dominated by, a new political animal, the Christian Democratic parties. Catholic parties were familiar in continental Europe—they had long thrived in the Netherlands and Belgium. Wilhelminian and Weimar Germany had a Catholic Center Party and the conservative wing of Austrian politics has long been closely bound up with the (Catholic) People's Party. Even 'Christian Democracy' itself was not an altogether new idea—its origins lay in early-twentieth-century Catholic reformism and Catholic movements of the political center that tried without success to make their way in the turbulent years following World War One. But after 1945 the situation was quite different and wholly to their advantage.

In the first place, these parties—especially the Christian Democratic Union (CDU) in West Germany, the Christian Democrats (DC) in Italy and the Popular Republican Movement (MRP) in France—now had a near-monopoly of the Catholic vote. In 1945 Europe, that still mattered a lot: the Catholic vote was still heavily conservative, especially on social questions and in regions of high Catholic practice. Traditional Catholic voters in Italy, France, Belgium, the Netherlands and southern and western Germany would rarely vote Socialist and almost never Communist. But, and this was the peculiarity of the post-war era, even conservative Catholics in many countries often had no choice but to vote Christian Democrat, despite the reformist bent of Christian Democrat politicians and policies, because conventional right-wing parties were either under a shadow or else banned outright. Even non-Catholic conservatives turned increasingly to the Christian Democrats, as a bar to the 'Marxist' Left.

Secondly, and for related reasons, Christian Democrat parties were the major beneficiaries of women's votes—in 1952 some two-thirds of practicing Catholic women in France voted for the MRP. No doubt the influence of the pulpit played a role. But a large part of the Christian Democratic parties' appeal to women lay in their programme. In contrast to the lingering insurrectionary undertone to even the most domesticated Socialist and Communist rhetoric, prominent Christian Democrats—Maurice Schumann and Georges Bidault in France, Alcide de Gasperi in Italy and Konrad Adenauer in the Federal Republic—always emphasised reconciliation and stability,.

Christian Democracy avoided class-based appeals and emphasized instead social and moral reforms. In particular, it insisted upon the importance of the *family*, a properly Christian theme with significant policy implications at a time when the needs of single-parent, homeless and destitute families had never been greater. Thus Christian Democratic parties were ideally placed to capitalize on virtually every aspect of the post-war condition: the desire for stability and security, the expectation of renewal, the absence of traditional right-wing alternatives and the expectations vested in the state—for in contrast to conventional Catholic politicians of an earlier generation, the leaders of Christian Democratic parties and their more radical younger followers had no inhibitions about enrolling the power of the state in pursuit of their goals. If anything, Christian Democrats of the first post-war years saw free-market liberals rather than the collectivist Left as their main opponents and were keen to demonstrate that the modern state could be adapted to non-socialist forms of benevolent intervention.

As a consequence, in Italy and West Germany Christian Democrat parties secured (with some American assistance) a near monopoly of political power for many years to come. In France—thanks to the corrosive effects of two colonial wars, followed in 1958 by De Gaulle's return to power—the MRP did rather less well. But even there it remained the arbiter of power until the mid-fifties, with an uncontested claim to certain key ministries (notably Foreign Affairs). Catholic parties of a Christian Democrat bent exercised unbroken power in the Benelux countries for more than a generation, in Austria through 1970.

The leaders of Christian Democratic parties, like Britain's Winston Churchill, were men of an earlier time: Konrad Adenauer was born in 1876, Alcide de Gasperi five years later, Churchill himself in 1874. This was no mere coincidence or biographical curiosity. By 1945 many continental European countries had lost two generations of potential leaders: the first to death and injury in the Great War, the second to the temptation of Fascism or else to murder at the hands of Nazis and their friends. This shortfall manifested itself in the generally rather mediocre quality of younger politicians in these years—Palmiro Togliatti (who had spent much of the previous twenty years as a political operative in Moscow) was an exception. The special appeal of Léon Blum, who returned to public life in France after imprisonment by Vichy and incarceration in Dachau and Buchenwald, was not just his heroism but also his age (he was born in 1872).

At first sight it may seem rather odd that so much of the rehabilitation of post-war Europe was the work of men who reached maturity and entered politics many decades before. Churchill, who first entered Parliament in 1901, always described himself as a 'child of the Victorian Age'. Clement Attlee, too, was a Victorian, born in 1883. But it is perhaps not so very surprising after all. In the first place such older men were rather unusual in surviving politically and ethically unscathed from thirty years of turmoil—their political credibility enhanced, as it were, by their scarcity value. Secondly, they all came from the remarkable generation of European social reformers who reached maturity during the years 1880–1910—whether as socialists (Blum, Attlee), liberals (Beveridge, or the future Italian President Luigi Einaudi, born in 1874) or progressive Catholics (De Gasperi, Adenauer). Their instincts and interests were very well suited to the post-war mood.

But thirdly, and perhaps most important, the old men who rebuilt Western Europe represented continuity. The vogue between the wars had been for the new and the modern. Parliaments and democracies were seen by many—and not just Fascists and Communists—as decadent, stagnant, corrupt and in any case inadequate to the tasks of the modern state. War and occupation dispelled these illusions, for voters if not for intellectuals. In the cold light of peace, the dull compromises of constitutional democracy took on a new appeal. What most people longed for in 1945 was social progress and renewal, to be sure, but combined with the reassurance of stable and familiar political forms. Where the First World War had a politicizing, radicalizing effect, its successor produced the opposite outcome: a deep longing for normality.

Statesmen whose experience reached back beyond the troubled inter-war decades to the more settled and self-confident era before 1914 thus had a particular attraction. In the continuity of their person they could facilitate a difficult transition from the over-heated politics of the recent past to a coming era of rapid social transformation. Whatever their party 'label', the elder statesmen of Europe were all, by 1945, skeptical, pragmatic practitioners of the art of the possible. This personal distance from the over-confident dogmas of inter-war politics faithfully reflected the mood of their constituents. A post-'ideological' age was beginning.

The prospects for political stability and social reform in post-World War Two Europe all depended, in the first place, on the recovery of the continent's economy. No amount of state planning or political leadership could conjure away the Himalayan task facing Europeans in 1945. The most obvious economic impact of the war was on housing stock. The damage to London, where three and a half million homes in the metropolitan area were destroyed, was greater than that wrought by the Great Fire of 1666. Ninety percent of all homes in Warsaw were destroyed. Only 27 percent of the residential buildings in Budapest in 1945 were habitable. Forty percent of German housing stock was gone, 30 percent of British, 20 percent of French. In Italy 1.2 million homes were destroyed, mostly in cities of 50,000 or more people. The problem of homelessness, as we have seen, was perhaps the most obvious consequence of war in the immediate post-war era—in West Germany and Britain the housing shortage would last well into the mid-1950s. As one middle-class woman expressed it, upon emerging from a Post-War Homes Exhibition in London: 'I'm so desperate for a house I'd like anything. Four walls and a roof is the height of my ambition.'[3]

The second area of evident damage was in transport—merchant fleets, railway lines, rolling stock, bridges, roads, canals and tramways. There were no bridges across the Seine between Paris and the sea, just one left intact across the Rhine. As

---

[3]Quoted in Maureen Waller, *London 1945* (2004), page 150.

a consequence, even if mines and factories could produce necessary goods they could not move them—many European coal mines were working again by December 1945 but the city of Vienna was still without coal.

The visual impact was the worst: many countries *looked* as though they had been battered and broken beyond any hope of recovery. And it was true that in almost every European country involved in the Second World War the national economy stagnated or shrunk when compared even with the mediocre performance of the inter-war years. But war is not always an economic disaster—on the contrary, it can be a powerful stimulus to rapid growth in certain sectors. Thanks to World War Two the US surged into an unassailable commercial and technological lead, much as Britain had done during the Napoleonic wars.

And indeed, as Allied surveyors soon realized, the destructive *economic* impact of the war against Hitler was by no means as total as they had first thought, even in Germany itself. The bombing campaign, for all its human costs, had wrought less economic damage than its advocates expected. Little more than 20 percent of German industrial plant had been destroyed by May 1945; even in the Ruhr, where much Allied bombing had been concentrated, two thirds of all plant and machinery had survived intact. Elsewhere, in the Czech lands for example, industry and agriculture thrived under the German occupation and emerged virtually unscathed—Slovakia, like parts of Hungary, saw accelerated industrialization during the war years and actually emerged better off than before.

The dramatically skewed nature of much of the damage, such that it was people and places that suffered terribly while factories and goods were relatively spared, contributed to an unexpectedly speedy recovery after 1945 of core economic sectors. Engineering industries flourished during the war. The UK, the USSR, France, Italy and Germany (as well as Japan and the USA) *all* emerged with a larger stock of machine tools than they started with. In Italy only the aeronautic and shipbuilding industries suffered serious damage. Engineering firms situated in the North, and thus out of reach of the heaviest fighting during the Italian campaign, did rather well (as they had in World War One), their wartime output and investment more than compensating for any harm they suffered. As for the machine tool industry in what became West Germany, it lost just 6.5 percent of its equipment through war damage.

In some countries, of course, there *was* no war damage. Ireland, Spain, Portugal, Switzerland and Sweden all remained neutral throughout the conflict. This does not mean that they were not affected by it. On the contrary, most of the European neutrals were intimately engaged, albeit indirectly, in the Nazi war effort. Germany depended heavily on Franco's Spain for its wartime supply of manganese. Tungsten reached Germany from Portugal's colonies, via Lisbon. Forty percent of Germany's wartime requirements in iron ore were met from Sweden (delivered to German ports in Swedish ships). And all this was paid for in gold, much of it stolen from Germany's victims and channeled through Switzerland.

The Swiss did more than act as money-launderer and conduit for German payments, in itself a substantial contribution to Hitler's war. In 1941–42 60 percent of Switzerland's munitions industry, 50 percent of its optical industry and 40 percent of its engineering output was producing for Germany, remunerated in gold. The Bührle-Oerlikon small arms firm was still selling rapid-fire guns to the Wehrmacht in April 1945. All told, the German Reichsbank deposited the gold equivalent of 1,638,000,000 Swiss francs in Switzerland during the Second World War. And it was Swiss authorities before the outbreak of the conflict who asked that German passports indicate whether their holders were Jewish, the better to restrict unwanted arrivals.

The Swiss authorities, in their defence, had good reason to keep the Nazis friendly. Although the Wehrmacht high command postponed its June 1940 plans for an invasion of Switzerland, it never abandoned them; the experience of Belgium and the Netherlands was a grim reminder of the fate awaiting vulnerable neutral states that got in Hitler's way. For similar reasons the Swedes also extended their cooperation to Berlin, on whom they were historically dependent for coal. Selling iron ore to Germany was something Sweden had been doing for many years— even before the war half of German iron-ore imports came across the Baltic, and three-quarters of all Swedish iron-ore exports went to Germany. In any case, Swedish neutrality had long been slanted toward Germany out of fear of Russian ambitions. Co-operation with the Nazis—allowing the transit of 14,700 Wehrmacht troops at the start of Operation Barbarossa, as well as German soldiers on leave from Norway passing through on their way home, deferring the draft for Swedish iron mine workers so as to ensure regular deliveries to Germany—was thus not a departure from habit.

After the war the Swiss (though not the Swedes) were initially the object of resentful international suspicion as accomplices to Germany's war effort; in the Washington Accords of May 1946 they were constrained to offer a 'voluntary' contribution of 250 million Swiss francs to European reconstruction, as a final settlement of all claims relating to Reichsbank transactions through Swiss banks. But by that time Switzerland was already rehabilitated as a prosperous island of fiscal rectitude: its banks highly profitable, its farms and engineering industries set to supply food and machinery to needy European markets.

Before the war neither Switzerland nor Sweden had been especially prosperous—indeed they contained significant regions of rural poverty. But the lead they secured in the course of the war has proved lasting: both are now at the top of the European league and have been there steadily for four decades. Elsewhere the path to recovery was a little steeper. But even in Eastern Europe the economic infrastructure at least was repaired with remarkable speed. Despite the worst efforts of the retreating Wehrmacht and the advancing Red Army, the bridges, roads, railways and cities of Hungary, Poland and Yugoslavia were rebuilt. By 1947, transportation networks and rolling stock in central Europe had been brought up to or surpassed their pre-war levels. In Czechoslovakia, Bulgaria, Albania and Romania, where there was less war-related destruction, this process took less time than in Yugoslavia or Poland. But even the Polish economy recovered quite rapidly—in part because the western territories newly seized from Germany were actually more fertile and better supplied with industrial towns and factories.

In western Europe, too, material damage was repaired with remarkable speed—quickest, on the whole in Belgium, somewhat slower in France, Italy and Norway, slowest in the Netherlands, where the worst harm (to farms, dykes, roads, canals and people) had all come in the last months of the war. The Belgians benefited from Antwerp's privileged status as the only major European port more or less intact at the end of the war, and from the high concentration of Allied troops in their country, pumping a steady flow of hard cash into an economy that had long specialized in coal, cement and semi-finished metals, all vital for reconstruction work.

Norway, by contrast, was considerably worse off. Half the nation's vital fishing and merchant fleet was lost in the war. Thanks to deliberate German destruction in the course of the Wehrmacht's retreat, Norway's industrial output in 1945 was just 57 per cent that of its 1938 level, with nearly a fifth of the country's capital stock gone. In later years the contrast with Sweden was not lost on embittered Norwegians. But even Norway was able to restore most of its rail and road network by the end of 1946; and in the course of the following year, as in the rest of western and most of eastern Europe, fuel shortages and inadequate communications were no longer an impediment to economic recovery.

To contemporary observers, however, it was *Germany's* capacity to recover which seemed the most remarkable of all. This was a tribute to the efforts of the local population who worked with a striking singularity of purpose to rebuild their shattered country. The day Hitler died, 10 percent of German railways were operational and the country was at a literal standstill. A year later, in June 1946, 93 percent of all German rail tracks had been re-opened and 800 bridges had been rebuilt. In May 1945 German coal production was barely one-tenth that of 1939; a year later it had quintupled in output. In April 1945 it seemed to Saul K. Padover, a psychologist with the advancing US Army in western Germany, that it would surely take the flattened city of Aachen 20 years to rebuild. But within a few weeks he was already recording the re-opening of the city's tyre and textile factories and the beginnings of economic life.

One reason for the speed of Germany's initial recovery was that once the workers' houses had been rebuilt, and the transport networks put back in place, industry was more than ready to deliver the goods. At the Volkswagen works 91 percent of the machinery had survived wartime bombing and post-war looting, and by 1948 the factory was equipped to produce one in every two cars made in western Germany. Ford of Germany was largely undamaged. Thanks to wartime investment, one-third of German industrial equipment was less than five years old in 1945, compared to just 9 percent in 1939. And the industries in which wartime Germany had invested most heavily—optics, chemicals, light engineering, vehicles, non-ferrous metals—were precisely those which would lay the foundations for the boom of the Fifties. By early 1947 the chief impediment to a German recovery was no longer war damage, but rather raw material and other shortages—and, above all, uncertainty over the country's political future.

The year 1947 was to prove crucial, the hinge on which was suspended the fate of the continent. Until then Europeans had been consumed with repairs and reconstruction, or else were busy putting in place the institutional infrastructure for long-term recovery. In the course of the first eighteen months following the Allied victory the mood of the continent swung from relief at the mere prospect of peace and a fresh start, to stony resignation and growing disillusion in the face of the magnitude of the tasks still ahead. By the beginning of 1947 it was clear that the hardest decisions had not yet been taken and that they could not be postponed much longer.

To begin with, the fundamental problem of food supply was not yet overcome. Food shortages were endemic everywhere except Sweden and Switzerland. Only UNRRA supplies built up in the spring of 1946 kept Austrians from starving in the twelve months that followed. Caloric provision in the British Zone of Germany fell from 1,500 per day per adult in mid-1946 to 1,050 in early 1947. Italians, who suffered two consecutive years of hunger in 1945 and 1946, had the lowest average food levels of all the west European populations in the spring of 1947. In French opinion polls taken in the course of 1946 'food', 'bread', 'meat' consistently outpaced everything else as the public's number one preoccupation.

Part of the problem was that western Europe could no longer turn to the granaries of eastern Europe on which it had traditionally depended. For there, too, no-one had enough to eat. In Romania the 1945 harvest failed, through mismanaged land reforms and bad weather. From western Wallachia through Moldavia, into the western Ukraine and the middle Volga region of the USSR, poor harvests and drought led to near-famine conditions in the autumn of 1946, with aid agencies describing one-year old children weighing just three kilograms and sending back reports of cannibalism. Relief workers in Albania described the situation there as one of 'terrifying distress'.

Then came the brutal winter of 1947, the worst since 1880. Canals froze, roads were impassable for weeks at a time, frozen points paralyzed whole rail networks. The incipient post-war recovery came to a grinding halt. Coal, still in short supply, could not keep up with domestic demand and anyway could not be moved. Industrial production slumped—steel output, having just begun to recover, promptly fell back by 40 percent over the previous year. When the snows melted, many parts of Europe were flooded. A few months later, in June 1947, the continent entered one of the hottest, driest summers since records began. It was clear that the harvest would be inadequate, in some places for the third year running: agricultural yields fell by about a third even over the previous year's meager crop. The shortfall in coal could be made up in part from American imports (34 million tonnes in 1947). Food, too, could be purchased from America and the British Dominions. But all these imports had to be paid for in hard currency, usually dollars.

Two structural dilemmas underlay the European crisis of 1947. One was the effective disappearance of Germany from the European economy. Before the war Germany had been a major market for most of central and eastern Europe, as well as the Netherlands, Belgium and the Mediterranean region (until 1939, for example, Germany bought 38 percent of Greece's exports and supplied about one-third of the country's imports). German coal was a vital resource for French steel manufacturers. But until its political future was resolved Germany's economy—for all its restored potential—remained frozen, effectively blocking the economic recovery of the rest of the continent.

The second problem concerned not Germany but the USA, though the two were connected. In 1938, 44 percent of Britain's machinery imports by value came from the USA, 25 percent from Germany. In 1947 the figures were 65 percent and 3 percent respectively. The situation was similar in other European countries. This sharply increased demand for American goods was, ironically, an indication of an upswing in European economic activity—but to buy American products or materials required American dollars. Europeans had nothing to sell to the rest of the world; but without hard currency they could not buy food to stop millions from starving, nor could they import the raw materials and machinery needed to move forward their own production.

The dollar crisis was serious. In 1947 the UK, whose national debt had increased fourfold since 1939, was buying nearly half its total imports from the USA and fast running out of cash. France, the world's largest importer of coal, was running an annual payments deficit with the US of $2,049 million. Most other European countries did not even have currencies in which to trade. Romanian inflation was at its worst in August 1947. The inflation in neighbouring Hungary, the worst in recorded history and far exceeding that of 1923 Germany, peaked at 5 quintillion (5^{30}) paper *pengos* to the dollar—meaning that by the time the *pengo* was replaced by the *forint* in August 1946 the dollar value of all Hungarian banknotes in circulation was just one-thousandth of one cent.

In Germany there was no functioning currency. The black market flourished and cigarettes were the accepted medium of exchange: teachers in DP camps were paid 5 packs a week. The value of a carton of American cigarettes in Berlin ranged from $60–$165, an opportunity for soldiers in the American occupation forces to make serious money converting and re-converting their cigarette allocation: in the first four months of the Allied occupation US troops in Berlin alone sent home $11 million more than they received in wages. In Braunschweig, 600 cigarettes would buy you a bicycle—a necessity in Germany no less than in Italy, as depicted unforgettably in Vittorio de Sica's 1948 film *Bicycle Thieves*.

The seriousness of the European crisis was not lost on the Americans. As we shall see, it was one of their main reasons for pressing forward with a solution to the problem of Germany with or without Soviet cooperation. In the opinion of well-informed Presidential counselors like George Kennan, Europe in the spring of 1947 was teetering on the edge. The frustrations of western Europeans, who had initially been led to expect quicker recovery and a return to normal economic conditions, and the hopelessness of Germans and other central Europeans, compounded by the unanticipated subsistence crisis of 1947, could only strengthen the appeal of Communism or else the risk of a descent into anarchy.

The attraction of Communism was real. Although the Communist parties of Italy, France and Belgium (as well as those of Finland and Iceland) remained in governing coalitions until May 1947, through their trade union affiliates and popular demonstrations they were able to mobilize popular anger and capitalize on the failures of their own governments. The electoral successes of local Communists, combined with the aura of the invincible Red Army, made an Italian (or French, or Czech) 'road to Socialism' seem plausible and seductive. By 1947 907,000 men and women had joined the French Communist Party. In Italy the figure was two and a quarter million, far more than in Poland or even Yugoslavia. Even in Denmark and Norway, one voter in eight was initially attracted to the promise of a Communist alternative. In the western zones of Germany the Allied authorities feared that nostalgia for the better days of Nazism, together with a reaction against denazification programmes, food shortages and endemic minor crime, could yet turn to neo-Nazi or even Soviet advantage.

The west European states were perhaps fortunate that their Communist parties in the spring of 1947 were still pursuing the moderate, democratic path adopted in 1944. In France, Maurice Thorez was still urging coalminers to 'produce'. In Italy the British ambassador described Togliatti as a moderating influence on his more 'hotheaded' Socialist allies. For his own reasons Stalin was not yet encouraging his many supporters in central and western Europe to exploit popular anger and frustration. But even so, the spectre of civil war and revolution was never far away. In Belgium, Allied observers described communal and political tensions as serious and ranked the country with Greece and Italy as 'unstable'.

In France the economic hardships of the winter of 1947 were already leading to popular disillusion with the new post-war Republic. In a French opinion poll of July 1st 1947, 92 percent of those questioned thought that things in France were going 'badly or rather badly'. In Britain the Labour Chancellor Hugh Dalton, reflecting on the punctured enthusiasms of the first post-war years, confided to his diary: 'Never bright confident morning again'. His French counterpart, André Philip, the Socialist Minister of National Economy, made the same point more dramatically in a speech in April 1947: 'We are threatened,' he declared, 'with total economic and financial catastrophe'.

This sense of hopelessness and impending disaster was everywhere. 'For the past two months', reported Janet Flanner from Paris in March 1947, 'there has been a climate of indubitable and growing malaise in Paris, and perhaps all over Europe, as if the French people, or all European people, expected something to happen, or, worse, expected nothing to happen.' The European continent, as she had noted a few months before, was slowly entering a new ice age. George Kennan would have agreed. In a Policy Planning Staff paper six weeks later he suggested that the real problem was not Communism, or if so then only indirectly. The true source of the European malaise was the effects of war and what Kennan diagnosed as 'profound exhaustion of physical plant and spiritual vigour'. The hurdles the continent faced seemed too great, now that the initial burst of post-war hope and rebuilding had drained away. Hamilton Fish, editor of *Foreign Affairs*, the influential house journal of the American foreign policy establishment, described his impressions of Europe in July 1947:

'There is too little of everything—too few trains, trams, buses and automobiles to transport people to work on time, let alone to take them on holidays; too little flour to make bread without adulterants, and even so not enough bread to provide energies for hard labor; too little paper for newspapers to report more than a fraction of the world's news; too little seed for planting and too little fertilizer to nourish it; too few houses to live in and not enough glass to supply them with window panes; too little leather for shoes, wool for sweaters, gas for cooking, cotton for diapers, sugar for jam, fats for frying, milk for babies, soap for washing.'

It is widely believed by scholars today that for all the contemporary gloom the initial post-war recovery and the reforms and plans of the years 1945–47 laid the groundwork for Europe's future well being. And to be sure, for western Europe at least 1947 would indeed prove the turning point in the continent's recovery. But at the time none of this was obvious. Quite the contrary. World War Two and its uncertain aftermath might well have precipitated Europe's terminal decline. To Konrad Adenauer like many others, the scale of European chaos seemed worse even than in 1918. With the precedent of the post-World War One mistakes uppermost in their thoughts, many European and American observers indeed feared the worst. At best, they calculated, the continent was in for decades of poverty and struggle. German residents of the American Zone expected it to be at least twenty years before their country recovered. In October 1945 Charles de Gaulle had imperiously informed the French people that it would take twenty-five years of 'furious work' before France would be resuscitated.

But long before that, in the pessimists' view, continental Europe would collapse back into civil war, Fascism and Communism. When US Secretary of State George C. Marshall returned on April 28th 1947 from a Moscow meeting of Allied Foreign Ministers, disappointed at Soviet unwillingness to collaborate in a solution for Germany and shaken by what he had seen of the economic and psychological state of western Europe, he was clear in his own mind that something rather dramatic would have to be done, and very soon. And judging from the resigned, doom-laden mood in Paris, Rome, Berlin and elsewhere, the initiative would have to come from Washington.

Marshall's plan for a European Recovery Program, discussed with his advisers over the next few weeks and made public in a famous Commencement Address at Harvard University on June 5th 1947, was dramatic and unique. But it did not come out of nowhere. Between the end of the war and the announcement of the Marshall Plan, the United States had already spent many billions of dollars in grants and loans to Europe. The chief beneficiaries by far had been the UK and France, which had received $4.4 billion and $1.9 billion in loans respectively, but no country had been excluded—loans to Italy exceeded $513 million by mid-1947 and Poland ($251 million), Denmark ($272 million), Greece ($161 million) and many other countries were indebted to the US as well.

But these loans had served to plug holes and meet emergencies. American aid hitherto was not used for reconstruction or long-term investment but for essential supplies, services and repairs. Furthermore, the loans—especially those to the major western European states—came with strings attached. Immediately following the Japanese surrender President Truman had imprudently cancelled the wartime Lend-Lease agreements, causing Maynard Keynes to advise the British Cabinet, in a memorandum on August 14th 1945, that the country faced an 'economic Dunkirk'. Over the course of the following months Keynes successfully negotiated a substantial American loan agreement to supply the dollars that Britain would need to buy goods no longer available under Lend-Lease, but the American terms were unrealistically restrictive—notably in their requirement that Britain give up imperial preferences for its overseas dominions, abandon exchange controls and make sterling fully convertible. The result, as Keynes and others predicted, was the first of many post-war runs on the British pound, the rapid disappearance of Britain's dollar reserves and an even more serious crisis the following year.

The terms of the loan negotiated in Washington in May 1946 between the US and France were only slightly less restrictive. In addition to a write-off of $2.25 billion of wartime loans, the French got hundreds of millions of dollars in credits and the promise of low-interest loans to come. In return, Paris pledged to abandon protectionist import quotas, allowing freer entry to American and other foreign products. Like the British loan, this agreement was designed in part to advance the US agenda of freer international trade, open and stable currency exchanges and closer international cooperation. In practice, however, the money was gone within a year and the only medium-term legacy was increased popular resentment (much played upon by the Left) at America's exploitation of its economic muscle.

By the spring of 1947, then, Washington's bilateral approaches to Europe's economic troubles had manifestly failed. The trading deficit between Europe and the US in 1947 would reach $4,742 million, more than double the figure for 1946. If this was a 'hiccup of growth', as later commentators have suggested, then Europe was close to choking. That is why Ernest Bevin, the British Foreign Minister, responded to Marshall's Commencement Address by describing it as 'one of the greatest speeches in world history', and he was not wrong.

Marshall's proposals were a clean break with past practice. To begin with, beyond certain framing conditions it was to be left to the Europeans to decide whether to take American aid and how to use it, though American advisers and specialists would play a prominent role in the administration of the funds. Secondly, the assistance was to be spread across a period of years and was thus from the start a strategic programme of recovery and growth rather than a disaster fund.

Thirdly, the sums in question were very substantial indeed. By the time Marshall Aid came to an end, in 1952, the United States had spent some $13 billion, more than all previous US overseas aid combined. Of this the UK and France got by far the largest sums in absolute amounts, but the relative impact on Italy and the smaller recipients was probably greater still: in Austria, 14 percent of the country's income in the first full year of the European Recovery Program (ERP), from July 1948 to June 1949, came from Marshall Aid. These figures were enormous for the time: in cash terms the ERP was worth about $100 billion in today's (2004) dollars, but as an equivalent share of America's Gross Domestic Product (it consumed about 0.5 percent of the latter in the years 1948–1951) a Marshall Plan at the beginning of the twenty-first century would cost about $201 billion.

Immediately following Marshall's speech the foreign ministers of Britain, France and the USSR met in Paris, at Bevin's suggestion, to consider their response. On July 2nd the Soviet foreign minister Vyacheslav Molotov walked out and two days later Britain and France formally invited representatives of 22 European countries (excluding only Spain and the Soviet Union) to discuss the proposals. On July 12th sixteen European states took part in these discussions. All of these—Britain, France, Italy, Belgium, Luxemburg, Netherlands, Denmark, Norway, Sweden, Switzerland, Greece, Turkey, Ireland, Iceland, Austria and Portugal—would be among the eventual beneficiaries. But despite the initial interest shown by Poland, Czechoslovakia, Hungary, Bulgaria and Albania, no future Communist state took part in the European Recovery Programme or received a dollar in Marshall aid

It is worth pausing to consider the implications of this. The fact that the money was to be confined to the West (with Greece and Turkey as honorary west Europeans) undoubtedly made it easier for Truman to secure passage of the ERP through Congress the following year. But by then much had changed and Congress was willing to be convinced that Marshall Aid was an economic barrier to Soviet expansion. In June 1947, however, the offer of aid through Marshall's new programme was made to all European countries without distinction. Stalin and Molotov were of course suspicious of American motives—the terms Marshall was proposing were quite incompatible with the closed Soviet economy—but their sentiments were not widely shared elsewhere in eastern Europe, in what was not yet a *bloc*.

Thus Jan Masaryk, Czechoslovakia's non-Communist Foreign Minister, enthusiastically accepted the joint Franco-British invitation of July 4th. The very next day the Czech Communist Party leader and Prime Minister, Klement Gottwald, was summoned to Moscow and initially instructed to attend the Paris conference. But his orders were clear: he was to use his presence in Paris to demonstrate 'the unacceptability of the Anglo-French plan, prevent the adoption of unanimous decisions, and then leave the conference, taking as many delegates of other countries as possible.'

Four days later Stalin reconsidered. Gottwald was told to withdraw his country's acceptance of the invitation to Paris. Meeting with a delegation from the Czech government, including Masaryk, Stalin advised the Czechs that '[w]e consider this matter to be a fundamental question on which [Czech] friendship with the USSR depends. If you go to Paris, you will show that you want to cooperate in an action aimed at isolating the Soviet Union.' The next day the Czech coalition government duly announced that it would not be sending a delegation to Paris. 'Czechoslovak participation would be construed as an act directed against friendship with the Soviet Union and the rest of our allies. That is why the government unanimously decided it will not take part in this conference.'

Why did the Czechs give way? Their Polish and Hungarian neighbours, with the Communists already in charge and the Red Army in close attendance, had no option but to follow Soviet 'guidance'. But the Red Army had long since left Czechoslovakia and the Communists did not yet have a monopoly of power. Yet Masaryk and his colleagues buckled at the first display of Stalin's displeasure. Had the non-Communist Czech parties insisted on accepting Marshall Aid they would have carried the overwhelming majority of their fellow citizens (and quite a few Czech Communists) with them, making it that much harder for Stalin to justify enforcing his will. In the broader context of post-Munich politics the Czech decision to favour the Soviet embrace was understandable; but it almost certainly paved the way for the Communists' successful coup in Prague seven months later.

Czechoslovakia's exclusion from the Marshall Aid programme was an economic and political catastrophe for the country. The same is true of the 'choice' imposed on every other country in the region, and above all, perhaps, for the Soviet Union itself. His decision to stand aside from the European Recovery Program was one of Stalin's greatest strategic mistakes. Whatever their private calculations, the Americans would have had no choice but to include eastern Europe in the ERP, having made the offer available to all, and the consequences for the future would have been immeasurable. Instead, the aid was confined to the West and marked a parting of the ways between the two halves of the continent.

Marshall Aid was from the start intended to be self-limiting. Its goal, as Marshall himself set it out in his Harvard speech, was to 'break the vicious circle and restore the confidence of the European people in the economic future of their own countries and of Europe as a whole.' Rather than merely offering aid in cash it proposed the provision of goods, free of charge, delivered to European countries on the basis of annual requests formulated as part of a four-year plan by each recipient state. These goods, when sold in each country, would generate so-called 'counterpart funds' in the local currency which could be used according to bilateral agreements reached between Washington and each national government. Some countries used these funds to purchase more imports; others, like Italy, transferred them into their national reserves in anticipation of future foreign exchange needs.

This unusual way of furnishing assistance carried innovative implications. The programme obliged European governments to plan ahead and calculate future investment needs. It laid upon them a requirement to negotiate and confer not just with the United States but with each other, since the trading and exchanges implied in the programme were intended to move from the bilateral to the multilateral as soon as possible. It constrained governments, businesses and labour unions to collaborate in planning increased rates of output and the conditions likely to facilitate them. And above all, it blocked any return to the temptations that had so stymied the inter-war economy: under-production, mutually destructive protectionism, and a collapse of trade.

Although the US administrators of the Plan made no secret of their expectations, they left it to Europeans to take responsibility for determining the level of aid and the manner of its distribution. European politicians—accustomed to the blunt self-interest of the US in earlier bilateral loan negotiations—were rather taken by surprise. Their confusion was understandable. Americans themselves were divided as to the goals of the Plan. Idealists in the New Deal mould—and there were many in post-war American administrations—saw an opportunity to reconstruct Europe in the American image, emphasizing modernization, infrastructural investment, industrial productivity, economic growth and labour-capital cooperation.

Thus 'productivity missions', funded by the Marshall Plan, brought to the US many thousands of managers, technicians and trade unionists to study the American way of business—five thousand from France alone (one in four of the overall total) between 1948 and 1952. One hundred and forty-five 'European productivity teams' arrived in the US just between March and July 1951—in most cases consisting of men (rarely women) who had never before set foot outside Europe. Meanwhile enthusiastic New Dealers in the Organization for European Economic

Cooperation (OEEC), set up in 1948 as a conduit for ERP funds, urged upon their European colleagues the virtues of freer trade, international collaboration and inter-state integration.

These American urgings met, it must be said, with limited immediate success. Most European politicians and planners were not yet ready to contemplate grand projects of international economic integration. The Marshall Planners' greatest achievement in this respect was perhaps the European Payments Union, proposed in December 1949 and inaugurated a year later. Its limited objective was to 'multi-lateralize' European trade by establishing a sort of clearing-house for debits and credits in European currencies. This was designed to overcome the risk that each European country might try to save badly needed dollars by restricting imports from other European countries, to everyone's eventual disadvantage.

Using the Bank of International Settlements as their agent, European states were encouraged to secure credit lines proportional to their trading requirements. Then, instead of using up scarce dollars they could settle their obligations through an intra-European transfer of credits. All that mattered was not whom you traded with but the overall balance of credits and debits in European currencies. By the time it was wound up in 1958, the Payments Union had quietly contributed not merely to the steady expansion of intra-European trade but to an unprecedented degree of mutually advantageous collaboration—financed, it should be noted, by a substantial injection of US dollars to furnish the initial credit pool.

From a more conventional American perspective, however, free trade and its attendant benefits were themselves a sufficient objective and justification for the ERP programme. The United States had been particularly hard hit by the trading and export slump of the thirties and spared no effort to convince others of the importance to post-war recovery of liberalized tariff regimes and convertible currencies. Like English Liberals' enthusiasm for free trade in the era before 1914, such American pleas for the unrestricted movement of goods were not altogether un-self-interested.

Nevertheless, this self-interest was distinctly enlightened. After all, as CIA Director Allen Dulles observed: 'The Plan presupposes that we desire to help restore a Europe which can and will compete with us in the world markets and for that very reason will be able to buy substantial amounts of our products.' In a few cases there were more immediate benefits: back in the US, organized labour's backing for the Marshall Plan was secured through the promise that all in-kind transfers from America would be despatched in US-owned ships loaded by American dockworkers unionized in the AFL-CIO. But this was a rare case of direct and immediate advantage. For the most part Dulles was right: the Marshall Plan would benefit the USA by restoring her major trading partner, rather than by reducing Europe to an imperial dependency.

Yet there was more to it than that. Even if not everyone saw it at the time, Europe in 1947 faced a choice. One part of that choice was recovery or collapse, but the deeper question was whether Europe and Europeans had lost control of their destiny, whether thirty years of murderous intra-European conflict had not passed the fate of the continent over to the two great peripheral powers, the US and the Soviet Union. The Soviet Union was quite content to await such a prospect—as Kennan noted in his memoirs, the pall of fear hanging over Europe in 1947 was preparing the continent to fall, like a ripe fruit, into Stalin's hands. But for American policymakers, Europe's vulnerability was a problem, not an opportunity. As a CIA report argued in April 1947, '(t)he greatest danger to the security of the United States is the possibility of economic collapse in western Europe and the consequent accession to power of Communist elements'.

A Special Ad Hoc group of the State, War and Navy Departments' coordinating committee spelled the point out more fully in a report dated April 21st 1947: 'It is important to maintain in friendly hands areas which contain or protect sources of metals, oil and other natural resources, which contain strategic objectives or areas strategically located, which contain substantial industrial potential, which possess manpower and organized military forces in substantial quantities, or which for political or psychological reasons enable the US to exert a greater influence for world stability, security and peace.' This is the broader context of the Marshall Plan, a lowering political and security landscape in which American interests were inextricably interwoven with those of a fragile and sickly European sub-continent.

The better-informed European recipients of Marshall Aid, notably Bevin and Georges Bidault, his counterpart at the French Foreign Ministry on the Quai d'Orsay, understood this perfectly well. But European domestic interest in the European Recovery Program itself, of course, and the uses to which it was put, varied considerably from country to country. In Belgium, where American assistance was probably least urgently needed, the Marshall Plan may even have had a long-term prejudicial impact, allowing the government to spend heavily on investment in traditional industrial plants and politically-sensitive industries like coal mining without counting the long-term cost.

In most cases, though, Marshall Aid was applied as intended. In the Plan's first year, aid to Italy was largely devoted to urgently needed imports of coal and grain, together with help for struggling industries like textiles. But thereafter 90 percent of Italian counterpart funds went directly to investment: in engineering, energy, agriculture and transportation networks. In fact, under Alcide De Gasperi and the Christian Democrats, Italian economic planning at the end of the forties rather resembled its east European counterpart, with consumer goods deliberately disfavoured, food consumption held down to pre-war levels and resources diverted to infrastructural investment. This was almost too much of a good thing: American observers became nervous and tried unsuccessfully to encourage the government to introduce more progressive taxes, relax its austere approach, allow reserves to fall and avoid bringing about a recession. Here, as also in western Germany, American Marshal Planners would have liked to see social and economic policies slanted more to the Centre and away from traditional deflationist policies.

In France, Marshall Aid very much served the goals of the 'planners'. As Pierre Uri, one of Monnet's associates, later acknowledged: 'we used the Americans to impose on the French government what we deemed necessary', ignoring the American desire for liberalization but responding enthusiastically to US exhortations to invest and modernize. ERP dollars—$1.3 million in 1948–49 and a further $1.6 million in the next three years—financed almost fifty percent of French public investment under the Monnet Plan during the Marshall years, and the country could never have managed without it. It is thus more than a little ironic that it was in France that the Marshall Plan faced the greatest popular criticism. In mid-1950 only one French adult in three acknowledged having even heard of the Marshall Plan and of these 64 percent declared it to be 'bad' for their country!

The Plan's relatively poor image in France represented a partial public relations success for the French Communists, perhaps their greatest.[4] In Austria the local Communists—backed by Soviet forces still occupying the eastern region of the country—never made any dent in the popularity of Americans and their aid; the latter put food in people's mouths and this was what mattered most. In Greece the situation was clearer still. In the circumstances of a brutal civil war Marshall Aid, extended to Greece in April 1948, made the difference between survival and destitution. The $649 million of American aid to Greece under the ERP supported refugees and staved off hunger and disease: the mere delivery of mules to indigent farmers made the difference between life and death for thousands of peasant families. In 1950 Marshall Aid was credited with furnishing half of the country's GNP.

How successful was the European Recovery Program? Western Europe indubitably recovered, and precisely over the period (1948–1951) of the Marshall Plan. By 1949 French industrial and agricultural production both exceeded 1938 levels for the first time. By the same criterion sustained recovery was achieved in 1948 by the Netherlands, in 1949 by Austria and Italy, in 1950 by Greece and West Germany. Of those countries occupied during the war, only Belgium, Denmark and Norway recovered sooner (in 1947). Between 1947 and 1951 the combined GNP of western Europe rose by 30 percent.

In the short-term the chief contribution of the Program to this recovery was surely the provision of dollar credits. These underwrote trade deficits, facilitated the large-scale importation of urgently needed raw materials and thus carried Western Europe through the crisis of mid-'47. Four-fifths of all the wheat consumed

---

[4]Note, though, that 4 out of 10 Communist voters in France were in favour of accepting Marshall Aid, despite the Party's opposition. French suspicion of the Marshall Plan was not so much political as cultural; many people seem to have been especially offended by what were described as 'des questionnaires insipides et nombreux' emanating from American bureaucracies—a particularly irritating reminder of their subordination to an inferior civilisation.

by Europeans in the years 1949–51 came from dollar-zone countries. Without Marshall Aid it is not clear how the fuel shortages, food shortages, cotton shortages and other commodity scarcities could have been overcome at a politically acceptable price. For while the economies of western Europe surely *could* have continued to grow without American assistance, this could only have been achieved by repressing home demand, cutting back on newly-introduced social services and further reducing the local standard of living.

This was a risk most elected governments were understandably reluctant to run. In 1947 the coalition governments of western Europe were trapped and they knew it. It is all very well for us to recognize in hindsight that Marshall Aid 'merely' broke a logjam born of renewed demand, that Washington's new approach overcame a 'temporary' dollar shortfall. But no-one in 1947 could know that the $4.6 billion gap was 'temporary'. And who at the time could be sure that the logjam was not sweeping the fragile European democracies over a roaring cataract? Even if the ERP did no more than buy time, that was a crucial contribution, for time was precisely what Europe appeared to lack. The Marshall Plan was an economic program but the crisis it averted was political.

The longer run benefits of the Marshall Plan are harder to assess. Some observers were disappointed at the Americans' apparent failure to persuade Europeans to co-operate in integrating their planning as much as they had initially hoped. And it is true that whatever collaborative habits and institutions the Europeans did eventually acquire were only indirectly indebted to American efforts, if at all. But in the light of Europe's recent past, *any* moves in this direction represented progress; and Marshall's invitation did at least oblige the mutually-suspicious European states to sit down together and co-ordinate their responses and, ultimately, much else. *The Times* was not so very wide of the mark when it stated, in a leader on January 3rd 1949, that '(w)hen the cooperative efforts of the last year are contrasted with the intense economic nationalism of the inter-war years, it is surely permissible to suggest that the Marshall Plan is initiating a new and hopeful era in European history.'

The real benefits were psychological. Indeed, one might almost say that the Marshall Plan helped Europeans feel better about themselves. It helped them break decisively with a legacy of chauvinism, depression and authoritarian solutions. It made co-ordinated economic policy-making seem normal rather than unusual. It made the beggar-your-neighbour trade and monetary practices of the thirties seem first imprudent, then unnecessary and finally absurd.

None of this would have been possible had the Marshall Plan been presented as a blueprint for the 'Americanization' of Europe. On the contrary, post-war Europeans were so aware of their humiliating dependence upon American aid and protection that any insensitive pressure from that quarter would certainly have been politically counter-productive. By allowing European governments to pursue policies that had emerged from domestic compromises and experiences, and by avoiding a one-size-fits-all approach to recovery programmes, Washington actually had to forego some of its hopes for western European integration, at least in the short term.

For the ERP was not parachuted into a vacuum. Western Europe was able to benefit from American help because it was a long-established region of private property, market economics and, except in recent years, stable polities. But for just this reason, western Europe had to make its own decisions and would ultimately insist on doing so. As the British diplomat Oliver Franks put it: 'The Marshall Plan was about putting American dollars in the hands of Europeans to buy the tools of recovery.' The rest—convertible currencies, good labour relations, balanced budgets and liberalized trade—would depend on Europeans themselves.

The obvious comparison, however, was not between American visions and European practices but between 1945 and 1918. In more respects than we now recall, the two post-war eras were uncannily alike. In the 1920s Americans were already encouraging Europeans to adopt US production techniques and labour relations. In the 1920s many American observers saw Europe's salvation in economic integration and capital investment. And in the 1920s Europeans, too, looked across the Atlantic for guidance about their own future and for practical aid in the present.

But the big difference was that after World War One the US gave only loans, not grants; and these were nearly always supplied through the private capital market. As a result they carried a price tag and were usually short-term. When they were called in at the onset of the Depression, the effect was disastrous. The contrast in this respect is striking—after initial stumbles in 1945–47, American policymakers went to some lengths to correct the mistakes of the previous post-war era. The Marshall Plan is significant not just for what it did but for what it was careful to avoid.

There was one European problem, however, that the European Recovery Plan could neither solve nor avoid, yet everything else depended upon its resolution. This was the German Question. Without German recovery French planning would come to nought: France was to use Marshall counterpart funds to build huge new steel mills in Lorraine, for example, but without German coal these would be useless. Marshall credits with which to buy German coal were all very well; but what if there *was* no coal? In the spring of 1948 German industrial output was still only half that of 1936. The British economy would never recover while the country was spending unprecedented sums ($317 million in 1947 alone) just to sustain the helpless population of its zone of occupation in northwest Germany. Without Germany to buy their produce the trading economies of the Low Countries and Denmark were moribund.

The logic of the Marshall Plan required the lifting of all restrictions upon (West) German production and output, so that the country might once again make its crucial contribution to the European economy. Indeed, Secretary of State Marshall made clear from the outset that his Plan meant an end to French hopes of war reparations from Germany—the point, after all, was to develop and integrate Germany, not make of it a dependent pariah. But in order to avoid a tragic re-run of the events of the 1920s—in which frustrated efforts to extract war reparations from a prostrate Germany had led, as it seemed in retrospect, directly to French insecurity, German resentment and the rise of Hitler—it was clear to the Americans and their friends that the Marshall Plan would only work as part of a broader political settlement in which French and Germans alike could see real and lasting advantage. There was no mystery to this—a post-war settlement in Germany was the key to Europe's future, and this was as obvious in Moscow as it was in Paris, London or Washington. But the shape such a settlement should take was an altogether more contentious matter.

IV

The Impossible Settlement

'Those who were not alive at the time may find it difficult to appreciate the
extent to which European politics in the post-war years were governed by
the fear of a German revival and directed to making sure that this never
happened again'.
Sir Michael Howard

'Make no mistake, all the Balkans, except Greece, are going to be
Bolshevised, and there is nothing I can do to prevent it. There is nothing I
can do for Poland, either'.
Winston Churchill, January 1945

'Reminded me of the Renaissance despots—no principles, any methods,
but no flowery language—always Yes or No, though you could only count
on him if it was No'.
Clement Attlee on Stalin

'In the space of five years we have acquired a formidable
inferiority complex'.
Jean-Paul Sartre (1945)

'Nobody in the world can understand what Europeans feel about the Germans
until one talks to Belgians, Frenchmen or Russians. To them the only good Germans
are dead Germans.' The author of these words, written to his diary in 1945, was Saul
K. Padover, the psychologist with the American armies whom we met in Chapter
Three. His observation should be borne in mind in any account of the post-war
division of Europe. The point of the Second World War in Europe was to defeat
Germany, and almost all other considerations were set aside so long as the fighting continued.

The Allies' chief wartime concern had been to keep one another in the war. The
Americans and British worried incessantly that Stalin might make a separate peace
with Hitler, especially once the Soviet Union had recovered territory lost after June
1941. Stalin, for his part, saw the delay in establishing a Second (Western) Front as
a ploy by the Western Allies to bleed Russia dry before coming forward to benefit
from her sacrifices. Both parties could look to pre-war appeasement and pacts as

evidence of the other's unreliability; they were bound together only by a common enemy.

This mutual unease illuminates the wartime accords and understandings reached by the three major Allied governments. At Casablanca, in January 1943, it was agreed that the war in Europe could only end with an unconditional German surrender. At Teheran, eleven months later, the 'Big Three' (Stalin, Roosevelt and Churchill) agreed in principle upon a post-war dismantling of Germany, a return to the so-called 'Curzon Line'[1] between Poland and the USSR, recognition of Tito's authority in Yugoslavia and Soviet access to the Baltic at the former East Prussian port of Königsberg.

The obvious beneficiary of these agreements was Stalin, but then since the Red Army played by far the most important role in the struggle with Hitler, this made sense. For the same reason, when Churchill sat down with Stalin in Moscow in October 1944 and initialed the notorious 'percentages agreement', he was merely conceding to the Soviet dictator ground that the latter was already sure to seize. In this agreement, scribbled in haste by Churchill and passed across a table to Stalin who 'took his blue pencil and made a large tick upon it', Britain and the USSR agreed to exercise control over post-war Yugoslavia and Hungary on a 50:50 basis; Romania would be 90 percent under Russian control and Bulgaria 75 percent, while Greece would be 90 percent 'British'.

Three points are worth making about this secret 'deal'. The first is that the percentages for Hungary and Romania were purely formulaic: the real issue was the Balkans. Secondly, the deal was largely upheld on both sides, as we shall see. But thirdly, and however heartless this must seem from the point of view of the countries concerned, it really wasn't significant. The same applies to the discussions at Yalta in February 1945. 'Yalta' has entered the lexicon of central European politics as a synonym for Western betrayal, the moment when the Western Allies sold out Poland and the other small states between Russia and Germany.

But Yalta actually mattered little. To be sure, the Allies all signed the Declaration on Liberated Europe—'To foster the conditions in which the liberated peoples may exercise those [democratic] rights, all three governments will jointly assist the people in any European liberated state or former Axis satellite state in Europe . . . ' to form representative governments, facilitate free elections, etc. And it was the post-war cynicism of the Soviet Union with regard to this commitment that would be thrown in the face of the West by understandably aggrieved spokesmen for the imprisoned nations. But nothing was decided at Yalta that had not already been agreed at Teheran or elsewhere.

The most that can be said of the Yalta Conference was that it offers a striking

---

[1] The frontier between Poland and Soviet Russia as proposed by the British Foreign Secretary after the First World War.

study in misunderstanding, with Roosevelt in particular a victim of his own illusions. For by then Stalin hardly needed Western permission to do whatever he wished in eastern Europe, as the British at least understood perfectly well. The eastern territories ceded to Stalin under the secret protocols of the Nazi-Soviet pacts of 1939 and 1940 were firmly in Soviet hands once again: at the time of the Yalta meeting (February 4th–11th 1945) the 'Lublin Committee' of Polish Communists brought west in the Soviet baggage train to run post-war Poland was already installed in Warsaw.[2]

In fact, Yalta left the truly important issue—arrangements for post-war Germany—off the table precisely because it *was* so important and intractable. And it is unlikely that the Western leaders could have got a better deal out of Stalin during these last months of the war, even if it had occurred to them to try. The only hope for the Poles and others was that Stalin would be generous to them in return for Western goodwill. But he had the latter in any case, and long after the defeat of Hitler it was the Western Allies who sought Stalin's cooperation, not the other way around. The Soviet Union had to be kept in the war against Germany (and later, as it was then supposed, Japan); the problem of central Europe could wait upon the peace. Had it been otherwise Roosevelt and Churchill might have protested more strongly in August 1944, when 200,000 Poles were killed by the Germans in a hopeless uprising in Warsaw while the Red Army looked on from the other side of the Vistula.

Western leaders may not have shared Stalin's view of the Poles' underground Home Army as 'a handful of power-hungry adventurers and criminals', but they were certainly not about to antagonize their major military ally just six weeks after the D-Day landings in Normandy. For Poles then and since this was a betrayal of the very purpose of the war—after all, Britain and France had declared war on Hitler in September 1939 over his violation of Poland. But for the Western Allies the case for leaving Stalin a free hand in the east was self evident. The point of the war was to defeat Germany.

This remained the primary impulse to the very end. In April 1945, with Germany already beaten in all but name, Roosevelt could still declare that, even with regard to post-war arrangements for Germany itself, 'our attitude should be one of study and postponement of final decision.' There were good reasons for taking this stance—the search for a settlement of the German Question was going to prove horribly difficult, as perceptive observers could already see, and it made sense to sustain for as long as possible the anti-German alliance that bound the wartime partners together. But as a result, the shape of post-war Europe was dictated in the

---

[2]Stalin had broken off relations with the Polish government-in-exile in London in 1943 following the latter's demand for an international examination of the Katyn massacre. The Germans, who uncovered the site, correctly claimed that it was the location of a mass execution by the Soviets of captured Polish officers. The Soviet authorities and their Western supporters, then and for the next half century, angrily denied it.

first instance not by wartime deals and accords but rather by the whereabouts of occupying armies when the Germans surrendered. As Stalin explained to Molotov, when the latter expressed doubts over the wording of the well-meaning 'Declaration on Liberated Europe': 'We can fulfill it in our own way. What matters is the correlation of forces.'

In south-east Europe the war was over by the end of 1944, with Soviet forces in full control of the northern Balkans. By May 1945, in central and eastern Europe, the Red Army had liberated and re-occupied Hungary, Poland and most of Czecho-slovakia. Soviet troops were through Prussia and into Saxony. In the West, where the British and Americans were fighting virtually separate wars in north-western and south-western Germany respectively, Eisenhower certainly *could* have reached Berlin before the Russians but was discouraged by Washington from doing so. Churchill would have liked to see a Western advance on Berlin but Roosevelt was conscious both of his generals' concern for loss of life (one fifth of all US troop losses in World War Two were sustained at the Battle of the Bulge in the Belgian Ardennes in the previous winter) and of Stalin's interest in the German capital.

As a result, in Germany and in Czechoslovakia (where the US army initially advanced 18 miles short of Prague and liberated the Pilsen region of western Bohemia, only to hand it over to the Red Army shortly afterwards), the line dividing what were not yet 'eastern' and 'western' Europe fell a little further west than the outcome of the fighting might have suggested. But only a little: however hard Generals Patton or Montgomery might have pressed forward, the final outcome would not have been significantly altered. Meanwhile, further south, on May 2nd 1945 the Yugoslav Army of National Liberation and the British Eighth Army came face to face in Trieste drawing through that most cosmopolitan of central European cities a line that would become the first true frontier of the Cold War.

Of course the 'official' Cold War still lay in the future. But in certain respects it had begun long before May 1945. So long as Germany remained the enemy it was easy to forget the deeper disputes and antagonisms separating the Soviet Union from its wartime allies. But they were there. Four years of wary cooperation in a life or death struggle with a common foe had done little to obliterate nearly thirty years of mutual suspicion. For the fact is that in Europe the Cold War began not after the Second World War but following the end of the First.

This point was perfectly clear in Poland, which fought a desperate war with the new Soviet Union in 1920; in Britain, where Churchill built his inter-war reputation in part upon the Red Scare of the early 20s and the theme of anti-Bolshevism; in France, where anti-Communism was the Right's strongest suit in domestic affairs from 1921 until the German invasion of May 1940; in Spain where it suited Stalin and Franco alike to play up the importance of Communism in the Spanish civil war; and above all, of course, in the Soviet Union itself, where Stalin's monopoly of power and his bloody purges of Party critics relied heavily on the charge that the West and its local associates were plotting to undermine the Soviet Union and destroy the Communist experiment. The years 1941–45 were just an interlude in an international struggle between Western democracies and Soviet totalitarianism, a struggle whose shape was obscured but not fundamentally altered by the threat posed to both sides by the rise of Fascism and Nazism at the heart of the continent.

It was Germany that brought Russia and the West together in 1941, much as it had succeeded in doing before 1914. But the alliance was foredoomed. From 1918–34 the Soviet strategy in central and western Europe—splitting the Left and encouraging subversion and violent protest—helped shape an image of 'Bolshevism' as fundamentally alien and hostile. Four years of troubled and controversial 'Popular Front' alliances did something to dispel this impression, despite the contemporary trials and mass murders in the Soviet Union itself. But the Molotov-Ribbentrop Pact of August 1939, and Stalin's collaboration with Hitler in his dismemberment of their common neighbours the following year, considerably undermined the propaganda gains of the Popular Front years. Only the heroism of the Red Army and Soviet citizens in the years 1941–45, and the unprecedented crimes of the Nazis, helped dispel these earlier memories.

As for the Soviets, they never lost their distrust of the West—a distrust whose roots go back far beyond 1917, of course, but which were well irrigated by Western military intervention during the civil war of 1917–21, by the Soviet Union's absence from international agencies and affairs for the next fifteen years, by the well-founded suspicion that most Western leaders preferred Fascists to Communists if forced to choose, and by the intuition that Britain and France especially would not be sorry to see the Soviet Union and Nazi Germany engage in mutually destructive conflict to others' advantage. Even after the wartime alliance was forged and the common interest in defeating Germany was clear, the degree of mutual mistrust is striking: there was, revealingly, very little wartime exchange of sensitive intelligence between West and East.

The unraveling of the wartime alliance and the subsequent division of Europe were thus not due to a mistake, to naked self-interest or malevolence; they were rooted in history. Before the Second World War relations between the US and the UK on the one hand, and the USSR on the other, had always been tense. The difference was that none of them had had responsibility for large tracts of the European continent. Moreover they had been separated by, among other considerations, the presence of France and Germany. But with French humiliation in 1940 and German defeat five years later, everything was different. The renewed Cold War in Europe was always likely, but it was not inevitable. It was brought about by the ultimately incompatible goals and needs of the various interested parties.

Thanks to German aggression the United States was now, for the first time, a power in Europe. That the US had overwhelming strength was self-evident, even to those mesmerized by the achievements of the Red Army. US GNP had doubled in the course of the war, and by the spring of 1945 America accounted for half the world's manufacturing capacity, most of its food surpluses and virtually all international financial reserves. The United States had put 12 million men under arms to fight Germany and its allies, and by the time Japan surrendered the American fleet was larger than all other fleets in the world combined. What would the US do with its power? In the aftermath of the First World War Washington had chosen not to exercise it; how different would things be after the Second World War? What did America want?

So far as Germany was concerned—and 85 percent of the American war effort had gone on the war against Germany—the initial American intent was quite severe. A directive from the Joint Chiefs of Staff, JCS 1067, was presented to President Truman on April 26th 1945, two weeks after Roosevelt's death. Reflecting the views of, among others, Henry Morgenthau, the US Secretary of the Treasury, it recommended that:

'It should be brought home to the Germans that Germany's ruthless warfare and the fanatical Nazi resistance has destroyed the German economy and made chaos and suffering inevitable and that the Germans cannot escape responsibility for what they have brought upon themselves. Germany will not be occupied for the purpose of liberation but as a defeated enemy nation'. Or, as Morgenthau himself put it, 'It is of the utmost importance that every person in Germany should realize that this time Germany is a defeated nation.'

The point, in short, was to avoid one of the major mistakes of the Versailles Treaty, as it seemed in retrospect to the policy makers of 1945: the failure to bring home to Germans the extent of their sins and the nemesis visited upon them. The logic of this initial American approach to the German question was thus demilitarization, denazification, deindustrialization—to strip Germany of her military and economic resources and re-educate the population. This policy was duly applied, at least in part: the Wehrmacht was formally dissolved (on August 20th 1946); denazification programs were set in place in the US-occupied zone especially, as we saw in Chapter Two; and strict limits were placed upon German industrial capacity and output, with steel-making particularly severely restricted under the March 1946 'Plan for the Level of the Post-War (German) Economy'.

But from the outset the 'Morgenthau strategy' was vigorously criticized within the US Administration itself. What good would be served by reducing (American-controlled) Germany to a virtually pre-industrial condition? Most of pre-war Germany's best agricultural land was now under Soviet control or else had been transferred to Poland. Meanwhile western Germany was awash in refugees who had access neither to land nor food. Restrictions on urban or industrial output might keep Germany prostrate but they wouldn't feed it or rebuild it. That burden, a very considerable one, would fall on the victorious occupiers. Sooner or later they would need to offload this responsibility onto Germans themselves, at which point the latter would *have* to be allowed to rebuild their economy.

To these concerns, American critics of the initial US 'hard' line added a further consideration. It was all very well forcibly bringing Germans to a consciousness of their own defeat, but unless they were given some prospect of a better future the outcome might be the same as before: a resentful, humiliated nation vulnerable to demagogy from Right or Left. As former President Herbert Hoover expressed it to Truman himself, in 1946, 'You can have vengeance, or peace, but you can't have both.' If, in American treatment of Germany, the balance of advantage swung increasingly to 'peace' this was largely due to the darkening prospect for US-Soviet relations.

Among a restricted circle of Washington insiders, it was obvious from the outset that the incompatibility of Soviet and Western interests would lead to conflict and that clearly delimited zones of power might be a prudent solution to post-war problems. This was the view of George Kennan. Why, he wrote on January 26th 1945, 'could we not make a decent and definite compromise with [the USSR]?—divide Europe frankly into spheres of influence—keep ourselves out of the Russian sphere and the Russians out of ours? . . . And within whatever sphere of action was left to us we could at least . . . (try) to restore life, in the wake of the war, on a dignified and stable foundation.'

Six weeks later a more pessimistic and implicitly confrontational response to Soviet actions in eastern Europe was proposed to President Roosevelt in a memo from Averell Harriman, the US ambassador in Moscow: 'Unless we wish to accept the 20th century barbarian invasion of Europe, with repressions extending further and further in the East as well, we must find ways to arrest the Soviet domineering policy . . . If we don't face the issues squarely now, history will record the period of the next generation as the Soviet age.'

Harriman and Kennan differed implicitly on how to respond to Soviet actions, but they did not disagree in their account of what Stalin was doing. Other American leaders were much more sanguine, however, and not just in the spring of 1945. Charles Bohlen, another US diplomat and the recipient of the Kennan letter quoted above, believed in the possibility of a post-war settlement based on broad principles of self-determination and Great Power cooperation. Recognising the need to maintain Soviet cooperation in working out a solution in Germany itself, Bohlen and others—like the post-war Secretary of State James Byrnes—placed their faith in Allied military occupation of the former Axis states and their satellites, together with free elections along the lines adumbrated at Yalta. Only later—after observing the workings of Soviet power under the auspices of Allied Control Councils in Romania and Bulgaria especially—did they accept the incompatibility of these goals and come to share Kennan's preference for the *realpolitik* of separate spheres.

One ground for initial optimism was the widely held view that Stalin had no interest in provoking confrontation and war. As General Eisenhower himself put it to President Truman and his Joint Chiefs of Staff in June 1946, 'I don't believe the

Reds want a war. What can they gain now by armed conflict? They've gained just about all they can assimilate.' In a limited sense Eisenhower was correct: Stalin was not about to go to war with the USA (although the reasonable conclusion to be drawn, that the Soviet Union thus had an interest in cooperating fully with its erstwhile ally, did not in fact follow). And in that case the US, which had a monopoly of atomic weapons, risked little by keeping communications open with the Soviet Union and seeking mutually compatible solutions to common problems.

Another element in US policy in the initial post-war period were the new international institutions that the Americans had helped bring about and whose success they sincerely desired. Of these the United Nations, whose Charter was ratified on October 24th 1945 and whose General Assembly first met in January 1946, is obviously the best known; but it was the financial and economic agencies and agreements associated with 'Bretton Woods' which perhaps mattered more to policymakers at the time.

The economic meltdown of the inter-war years seemed to Americans especially to be the root source of the European (and world) crisis. Unless currencies were convertible and nations stood to benefit mutually from increased trade, there was nothing to prevent a return to the bad days of September 1931, when the post-World War One monetary system fell apart. Led by Maynard Keynes—the moving spirit behind the July 1944 meeting at the Bretton Woods conference center in New Hampshire—economists and statesmen sought an alternative to the international financial system of pre-war days: something less rigid and deflationary than the gold standard, but more reliable and mutually sustaining than a floating-rate currency regime. Whatever this new regime was to be, it would need, Keynes argued, something resembling an international bank, functioning rather like the central bank of a domestic economy, to administer it: to maintain the fixed exchange rate while at the same time encouraging and facilitating foreign exchange transactions.

That, in essence, is what was agreed at Bretton Woods. An International Monetary Fund was set up (with US cash) 'to facilitate the expansion and balanced growth of international trade' (Article I). The initial Executive Board, modeled on the UN Security Council, had representatives from the US, UK, France, China and the USSR. An International Trading Organisation was proposed, which would eventually take shape in 1947 as the General Agreement on Trade and Tariffs (later the World Trade Organisation). Members agreed to tariff and other concessions for contracting partners, as well as codes for trade practices and procedures for handling breaches and disputes. All of this was in itself a dramatic break from earlier 'mercantilist' approaches to trade and was intended, in due course, to inaugurate a new age of open commerce.

Implicit in the Bretton Woods goals and institutions, which also included a new 'World Bank', was an unprecedented degree of external interference in national practices. Moreover currencies were to become convertible, a necessary condition for sustained and predictable international commerce, on the basis of their relationship to the US dollar. In practice this proved problematic: both Britain and France resisted convertibility, the British because of their protected 'sterling area'[3] and the weakness of their post-war economy, the French through a longstanding obsession with a 'strong franc' and their wish to preserve multiple exchange rates for different sectors and products, the neo-Colbertian heritage of a bygone era. Full convertibility took over a decade to achieve, with the franc and the pound finally joining the Bretton Woods system in 1958 and 1959 respectively (they would be followed by the *Deutschmark* in May 1959 and the Italian *lira* in January 1960).

Thus the post-war Bretton Woods system did not come about all at once. The participants at Bretton Woods had anticipated universal international convertibility by the end of the 1940s, but their calculations did not allow for the political and economic consequences of the coming of the Cold War (or, indeed, of the Marshall Plan). Put differently, the high ideals of those setting out plans and institutions for a better international system presumed a stable era of international cooperation from which all would gain. The Soviet Union was originally integral to the financial system proposed at Bretton Woods—it was to be the third-largest contributor to the International Monetary Fund quota. It was perhaps naïve for the Americans (and some British) to imagine that these proposals would be acceptable to Russian—or indeed French—policy-makers; in any case, they got around this impediment by the simple expedient of drawing up their plans without consulting the Russians or the French or anyone else.

Nevertheless, they sincerely expected that the mutual benefits to be had from an increase in international commerce and financial stability would eventually overcome national traditions and political mistrust. So when the Soviet Union abruptly announced, at the beginning of 1946, that it would not be joining the Bretton Woods institutions, the United States Treasury Department was genuinely bewildered; and it was to explain the thinking that lay behind Stalin's move that George Kennan sent from Moscow, on the night of February 22nd 1946, his famous Long Telegram, the first significant move in America's acknowledgement of the coming confrontation.

Putting the matter thus has the effect of depicting the makers of US foreign policy, Kennan aside, as remarkably innocent. And so, perhaps, they were, and not only those like Senator Estes Kefauver or Walter Lippmann, who simply refused to believe what they were told about Soviet actions in eastern Europe and elsewhere. At least through mid-1946, many US leaders spoke and acted as though they truly be-

---

[3] India and some of the British overseas Dominions had substantial holdings in sterling, built up as credit during the war years especially. Had the pound been freely convertible into dollars in the immediate post-war era many of these holdings might have been run down, thus further weakening Britain's already fragile stock of foreign exchange. That is why, after an initial, disastrous experiment with convertibility imposed from Washington as a condition for the US loan, Britain re-imposed sterling controls in 1947.

lieved in the continuation of their wartime partnership with Stalin. Even Lucretius Patrascanu, a senior figure in the Romanian Communist leadership (and later victim of a show trial in his own country), was moved to comment, at the time of the Paris Peace Treaty negotiations in the summer of 1946, that '[t]he Americans are crazy. They are giving even more to the Russians than [they] are asking and expecting.'[4]

But there was more to American policy than innocence. The United States in 1945 and for some time to come seriously expected to extricate itself from Europe as soon as possible, and was thus understandably keen to put in place a workable settlement that would not require American presence or supervision. This aspect of American post-war thinking is not well remembered or understood today, but it was uppermost in American calculations at the time—as Roosevelt had explained at Yalta, the US did not expect to remain in occupation of Germany (and thus in Europe) more than two years at most.

There was strong pressure on Truman to fulfill this undertaking. The abrupt ending of Lend-Lease was part of a general cutting back of economic and military commitments to Europe. The American defense budget was reduced by five-sixths between 1945 and 1947. At the end of the war in Europe the US had 97 combat-ready ground divisions in place; by mid-1947 there were just twelve divisions, most of them under strength and engaged in administrative tasks. The rest had gone home and been demobilized. This met the expectations of American voters, only 7 percent of whom in October 1945 placed foreign problems ahead of domestic concerns; but it played havoc with America's European allies, who began seriously to fear a reprise of inter-war isolationism. They were only half-mistaken; as the British knew, in the event of a Soviet invasion of western Europe after 1945 American strategy consisted of an immediate retreat to peripheral bases in Britain, Spain and the Middle East.

But even as they were reducing their military commitment to Europe, American diplomats were being taken through a steep learning curve. The same Secretary Byrnes who had initially placed his faith in wartime accords and Soviet goodwill gave a speech at Stuttgart, on September 6th 1946, in which he sought to reassure his German audience: 'As long as an occupation force is required in Germany, the Army of the United States will be a part of that occupation force.' It was hardly a ringing commitment to European defense but, prompted perhaps by a letter from Truman in June ('I'm tired of babying the Russians'), it reflected growing US frustration at the difficulty of working with the Soviet Union.

The Germans were not the only people who needed reassuring—the British especially were anxious at the Americans' apparent desire to escape their European

---

[4]According to Kennan, '[O]ur national leaders in Washington had no idea at all, and would probably have been incapable of imagining, what a Soviet occupation, supported by the Russian secret police of Beria's time, meant for the people who were subjected to it.'

encumbrance. Britain was not universally loved in Washington. In a speech on April 12th 1946, Vice-President Henry Wallace reminded his audience that 'aside from our common language and common literary tradition, we have no more in common with Imperialistic England than with Communist Russia'. Wallace, of course, was notoriously 'soft' on Communism, but his distaste for American involvement with Britain and Europe was widely shared across the political spectrum. When Winston Churchill gave his famous 'iron curtain' speech in Fulton, Missouri, in March 1946, the *Wall Street Journal* acidly commented: 'The country's reaction to Mr Churchill's Fulton speech must be convincing proof that the US wants no alliance, or anything that resembles an alliance, with any other nation.'

Churchill above all would not have been surprised, either by Wallace or the editorialist of the *Wall Street Journal*. As early as 1943 he had taken the full measure of Roosevelt's desire to see the liquidation of the British Empire—indeed, there were times when Roosevelt seemed at least as concerned with reducing post-war Britain as with containing Soviet Russia. If it is possible to speak of a coherent US strategy spanning the years 1944–47 it would be this: reach a continental European settlement with Stalin; pressure Britain to abandon its overseas empire and embrace open trade and sterling convertibility; and withdraw from Europe with all due speed. Of these, only the second objective was achieved—the third falling victim to the impossibility of the first.

The British perspective was quite different. A Cabinet sub-committee in 1944 listed four areas of primary concern to be borne in mind when dealing with the Soviet Union: i) Middle-Eastern oil; ii) the Mediterranean basin; iii) 'vital sea communications'; iv) the maintenance and protection of British industrial strength. None of these, it might be noted, directly concerned Europe proper—except the second point, which explains British engagement in Greece. There was no mention of eastern Europe. If British leaders were wary in their dealings with Stalin it was not from any anxiety over his plans in central Europe but rather in anticipation of future Soviet moves in Central Asia and the Near East.

This made sense in the light of Britain's continuing priorities—in East Asia, India, Africa and the Caribbean. But those selfsame Imperial illusions (as some, and not only in Washington, were already calling them) made British strategists much more realistic than their American allies when it came to Europe. From London's point of view, the war had been fought to defeat Germany, and if the price for this was a Soviet imperium in eastern Europe, then that was how things would be. The British continued to see European affairs in terms of a balance of power: in the words of Sir William Strang, of the Foreign Office, '[i]t is better that Russia should dominate eastern Europe than that Germany should dominate western Europe'.

Strang was writing in 1943. By 1945, when the extent of Russian domination was becoming clear, British leaders were less optimistic than their American counterparts. Following the Russian-engineered coup in Bucharest in February 1945, and subsequent heavy-handed Soviet pressure in both Romania and Bulgaria, it was obvious that the local price of Soviet hegemony was going to be high. But the British harboured no fond hopes for improvement in the region—as Foreign Secretary Ernest Bevin put it to his US counterpart Byrnes: 'In these countries we must be prepared to exchange one set of crooks for another.'

The real British fear in Europe was not that the USSR might control eastern Europe—by late 1944 that was a *fait accompli*—but that it might draw a prostrate, resentful Germany into its orbit as well and thus establish mastery over the whole continent. To prevent this, as the British Chiefs of Staff concluded in the autumn of 1944, it would probably be necessary to divide Germany and then occupy the western part. In that case, as a confidential British Treasury Paper of March 1945 concluded, one answer to the German problem might be to forget about an all-German resolution and instead incorporate such a western German Zone fully into the western European economy. As General Alan Brooke, Chief of the Imperial General Staff, had confided to his diary on July 27th 1944, 'Germany is no longer the dominating power in Europe. Russia is . . . She . . . cannot fail to become the main threat in fifteen years from now. Therefore, foster Germany, gradually bring her up and bring her into a Federation of Western Europe. Unfortunately, all this must be done under the cloak of a holy alliance of Russia, England and America.'

This, of course, is more or less what happened four years later. Of all the Allied powers it was Britain which came closest to anticipating and even seeking the settlement that finally emerged. But the British were in no position to impose such an outcome, nor indeed to impose very much at all, on their own. By the end of the war it was obvious that London was no match for Washington and Moscow. Britain had exhausted itself in the epic struggle with Germany and could not much longer sustain even the outer trappings of a great power. Between Victory-in-Europe Day in 1945 and the spring of 1947 British forces were reduced from a peak of 5.5 million men and women under arms to just 1.1 million. In the autumn of 1947 the country was even forced to cancel naval manoeuvres in order to save fuel oil. In the words of the American Ambassador William Clayton, a far from unsympathetic observer, 'the British are hanging in by their eyelashes to the hope that somehow or other with our help they will be able to preserve the British Empire and their leadership of it.'

In these circumstances the British were understandably concerned not that the Russians would attack—British policy was predicated on the assumption that Soviet aggression might take any form *except* war—but that the Americans would retreat. A minority within the governing British Labour Party would have been happy to see them go, placing their post-war faith instead in a neutrally-inclined European defense alliance. But Prime Minister Clement Attlee had no such delusions and explained why, in a letter to his Labour Party colleague Fenner Brockway:

'Some [in the Labour Party] thought we ought to concentrate all our efforts on building up a Third Force in Europe. Very nice, no doubt. But there wasn't either a spiritual or a material basis for it at that time. What remained of Europe wasn't strong enough to stand up to Russia by itself. You had to have a world force because you were up against a world force . . . Without the stopping power of the Americans, the Russians might easily have tried sweeping right forward. I don't know whether they would, but it wasn't a possibility you could just ignore.'

But could the Americans be counted on? British diplomats had not forgotten the 1937 Neutrality Act. And of course they understood very well the American ambivalence about overseas engagement, for it was not so different from their own stance in earlier days. From the mid-eighteenth century through to the dispatch of the British Expeditionary Force to France in 1914, the English had preferred to fight by proxy, maintaining no standing army, avoiding protracted continental engagements and keeping no permanent force on European soil. In the past, a maritime power seeking to fight a European war with someone else's soldiers could look to the Spanish, the Dutch, the Swiss, the Swedes, the Prussians and of course the Russians for allies. But times had changed.

Hence the British decision, in January 1947, to go ahead with their own atomic weapons programme. The significance of that choice lay in the future, however. In the circumstances of the initial post-war years Britain's best hope lay in encouraging continued American engagement in Europe (which meant publicly espousing the American faith in a negotiated settlement) while collaborating with the Soviets in so far as this was still realistic. So long as the fear of German revanchism took precedence over anything else, this policy could just about be sustained.

By early 1947, however, it was clearly crumbling. Whether or not the Soviet Union constituted a real and present danger was unclear (as late as December 1947 even Bevin though Russia less of a threat than a future, resurgent Germany). But what *was* painfully clear was that the limbo in Germany, where the country's economy was held hostage to unresolved political discussions and the British were footing enormous bills in their zone of occupation, could not long continue. The German economy needed to be revived, with or without Soviet agreement. It was the British—who had fought two long wars against Germany from beginning to end and had been brought low by their hard-won victories—who were thus most keen to close that chapter, establish some *modus vivendi* in continental affairs and move on.

In better times the British would have retreated to their Isles, much as they suspected the Americans of wanting to retreat to their continent, and left the security of western Europe to its traditional guardians, the French. As recently as 1938 this had been the basis of British strategic calculation: that France, the strongest military power on the continent, could be relied on as a counterweight not just to German ambitions in central Europe but even against future Soviet threats further east. This image of France as a—*the*—European Great Power was shaken at Munich, but outside the chancelleries of Eastern Europe it was not yet broken. The seismic shock that ran through Europe in May and June 1940, when the great French army collapsed and fell apart before the Panzer onslaught across the Meuse and through Picardy, was thus all the greater for being so unexpected.

In six traumatic weeks, the cardinal reference points of European inter-state relations changed forever. France ceased to be not just a Great Power but even a power, and despite De Gaulle's best efforts in later decades it has never been one since. For the shattering defeat of June 1940 was followed by four years of humiliating, demeaning, subservient occupation, with Marshall Pétain's Vichy regime playing Uriah Heep to Germany's Bill Sikes. Whatever they said in public, French leaders and policymakers could not but know what had happened to their country. As one internal French policy paper put it, a week after the Liberation of Paris in 1944: 'If France should have to submit to a third assault during the next generation, it is to be feared that . . . it will succumb forever.'

That was in private. In public, post-war French statesmen and politicians insisted upon their country's claim to recognition as a member of the victorious Allied coalition, a world power to be accorded equal standing with her peers. This illusion could be sustained, in some degree, because it suited the other powers to pretend it was so. The Soviet Union wanted a tactical ally in the West who shared its suspicion of the 'Anglo-Americans'; the British wanted a revived France to take its place in the counsels of Europe and relieve Great Britain of continental obligations; even the Americans saw some advantage, though not much, in granting Paris a seat at the top table. So the French were given a permanent seat on the new United Nations Security Council, they were offered a role in the joint military administrations of Vienna and Berlin, and (at British insistence) an occupation district was carved for them out of the American zone in south-west Germany, in an area contiguous to the French frontier and well west of the Soviet front line.

But the net effect of these encouragements was to pour further humiliation upon an already humbled nation. And the French responded at first with predictable prickliness. On the Allied Control Council in Germany they consistently blocked or vetoed the implementation of decisions taken at the Potsdam Conference of the Big Three on the grounds that France had not been party to them. The French provisional authorities initially refused to cooperate with UNRRA and Allied military governments in the handling of displaced persons on the grounds that *French* refugees and DPs should be located and administered as part of an independent and exclusively *French* operation.

Above all, French post-war governments felt very strongly their sense of exclusion from the highest councils of Allied decision-making. The British and the Americans were not to be trusted separately, they thought (remembering the American retreat from Europe after 1920 and the July 1940 British destruction of the French fleet at Mers-el-Kebir); but above all they were not to be trusted together— a sentiment felt especially acutely by De Gaulle, haunted by recollections of his demeaning wartime status as a guest in London and his low standing in the eyes of FDR. Decisions were being taken in Washington and London, the French came to believe, that directly concerned them but over which they had no influence

Like Britain, France was an Empire, at least on paper. But Paris had become estranged from its colonial holdings in the course of the occupation. In any case, and despite the country's significant possessions in Africa and South-East Asia, France was first and always a continental power. Soviet moves in Asia, or the coming crisis in the Middle East, were matters with which the French, unlike the British, were by now only indirectly concerned. Precisely because France was now shrunk, Europe loomed larger in its field of vision. And in Europe, Paris had grounds for concern. French influence in eastern Europe, an arena where French diplomacy had been most active between the wars, was finished: in October 1938 a shell-shocked Edouard Benes famously confided that his 'great mistake before History . . .will have been my fidelity to France', and his disillusion was widespread in the region.

France's attention was now fixed, indeed fixated, upon Germany. This was not unreasonable: between 1814 and 1940 French soil had been invaded and occupied by Germans on five distinct occasions, three of them within living memory. The country had paid an incalculable price in territorial and material loss and in human lives and suffering. The failure after 1918 to put in place a system of controls and alliances capable of restraining a renascent, vengeful Germany haunted the Quai d'Orsay, home of the French Foreign Ministry. The country's first priority after the defeat of Hitler was to ensure that this mistake was not repeated.

Thus France's initial position on the German problem was very clear, and drew directly upon the lessons of 1918–24: so much so, indeed, that to outsiders it appeared an attempt to re-run the script of the post-World War One years, only this time with someone else's army. What French policy makers sought was the complete disarmament and economic dismantling of Germany: arms and arms-related production were to be prohibited, reparations were to be made (including obligatory labour service in France for German workers), agricultural produce, timber, coal and machinery were to be requisitioned and removed. The mining districts of the Ruhr, the Saarland and parts of the Rhineland should be separated from the German state, their resources and output placed at French disposal.

Such a schedule, had it been imposed, would surely have destroyed Germany for many years to come: that was its half-acknowledged object (and an attractive political programme in France). But it would also have served the purpose of placing Germany's huge primary resources at the service of France's own plans for recovery—indeed, the Monnet Plan presumed the availability of German coal deliveries in particular, without which the French steel industry was helpless. Even in 1938 France had been the world's biggest importer of coal, buying from abroad some 40 percent of its requirements in coal and coke. By 1944 French domestic coal output had fallen to less than half that of 1938. The country was even more dependent upon foreign coal. But in 1946, when domestic coal production regained

1938 levels, French coal imports—at 10 million tons—were still desperately short of the required amounts. Without German coal and coke, the post-war French recovery would be stillborn.

There were, however, a number of shortcomings to French calculations. In the first place they fell foul of the same objections raised by Keynes to French policy a quarter century earlier. It made little sense to destroy German resources if they were vital to France's own recovery; and there was simply no way to oblige Germans to work for France while being held down to a low standard of living at home with little prospect for improvement. The risk of provoking a nationalist backlash in Germany against post-war foreign oppression appeared at least as great in the 1940s as it had twenty years earlier.

But the most serious objection to French plans for post-war Germany was that they took little account of the interests or plans of France's Western allies, an imprudent oversight at a time when France was utterly dependent on those same allies not just for her security but for her very livelihood. On secondary issues—such as a customs and monetary union with the Saarland, on which the French got their way in 1947—the Western Allies could accommodate French demands. But on the central issue of Germany's future, Paris had no leverage with which to oblige the 'Anglo-Americans' to do its bidding.

France's relationship with the Soviet Union was a little different. France and Russia had been in and out of alliances together for the past half century and Russia still held a special place in French public affection: opinion polls in post-war France consistently revealed a substantial reserve of sympathy for the Soviet Union.[5] French diplomats in the aftermath of German defeat could thus hope that a natural concordance of interests—shared fear of Germany and suspicion of the 'Anglo-Americans'—might translate into sustained Soviet support for French diplomatic goals. Like Churchill, De Gaulle thought and spoke of the USSR as 'Russia' and reasoned in grand historical analogies: on his way to Moscow in December 1944, to negotiate a rather meaningless Franco-Russian Treaty against any revival of German aggression, the French leader observed to his entourage that he was dealing with Stalin as François I[e] had with Suleiman the Magnificent four centuries earlier: with the difference 'that in sixteenth-century France there wasn't a Muslim party'.

Stalin, however, did not share French illusions. He had no interest in serving as a counterweight to assist the French in offsetting the foreign policy heft of London and Washington, though this was only finally made clear to the French in April 1947, at the Moscow gathering of Allied foreign ministers, when Molotov refused to back Georges Bidault's proposals for a separate Rhineland and foreign control of the Ruhr industrial belt. Yet the French continued to dream up alternative ways to secure an impossible independence of policy. There were aborted negotiations with

---

[5]In February 1945, when asked who would do most to help France recover, 25 percent of those polled said the USSR, 24 percent the USA.

Czechoslovakia and Poland aimed at securing coal and markets for French steel and farm produce. And the French Ministry of War could—confidentially—propose, as late as 1947, that France should adopt a stance of international neutrality, making preventive ententes or alliances with the USA *and* the USSR and lining up against whichever of the two initiated aggression against her.

If France finally abandoned these fantasies and came round to the position of her Western partners in 1947, it was for three reasons. In the first place, French strategies for Germany had failed: there was to be no dismantling of Germany and there would be no reparations. France was in no position to impose a German solution of her own, and no-one else wanted the one she was proposing. The second reason for France's retreat from her initial positions was the desperate economic situation of mid-1947: like the rest of Europe, France (as we have seen) urgently needed not just American aid but German recovery. The former was indirectly but unambiguously dependent upon French agreement on a strategy for the latter.

But thirdly, and decisively, French politicians and the French national mood shifted definitively in the second half of 1947. Soviet rejection of Marshall Aid and the advent of the Cominform (to be discussed in the next chapter) transformed the powerful French Communist Party from an awkward coalition partner in government to the unrestrained critic of all French policies at home and abroad: so much so that through the latter part of 1947 and most of 1948 France seemed to many to be heading into civil war. At the same time there was something of a war scare in Paris, coupling the country's continued worries about German revanchism with new talk of an impending Soviet invasion.

In these circumstances, and following their rebuff by Molotov, the French turned reluctantly towards the West. Asked by US Secretary of State George Marshall in April 1947 whether America 'could rely on France', Foreign Minister Bidault replied 'yes'—given time and if France could avoid a civil war. Marshall was understandably not much impressed, any more than he was eleven months later when he described Bidault as having 'a case of the jitters'. Marshall found France's preoccupation with the German threat 'outmoded and unrealistic'.[6]

What Marshall said of France's fears about Germany was doubtless true, but it suggests a lack of empathy for France's recent past. It was thus a matter of no small significance when the French parliament approved Anglo-American plans for western Germany in 1948, albeit by a significantly close vote of 297–289. The French had no choice and they knew it. If they wanted economic recovery *and* some level of American and British security guarantees against German revival or Soviet expansion, then they had to go along—especially now that France was embroiled in a costly colonial war in Indo-China for which she urgently needed American help.

The Americans and British could guarantee France against a renascent military

---

[6]Marshall was probably not much reassured to learn from Bidault that this public emphasis upon the *German* threat was strictly for domestic consumption.

threat from Germany; and American policy could hold out the promise of economic recovery in Germany. But none of this resolved France's long-standing dilemma—how to secure privileged French access to the materials and resources located there. If these objectives were not to be obtained by force or by annexation, then an alternative means had to be found. The solution, as it emerged in French thinking in the course of the ensuing months, lay in 'Europeanising' the German Problem: as Bidault, once again, expressed it in January 1948: 'On the economic plane, but also on the political plane one must . . . propose as an objective to the Allies and to the Germans themselves, the integration of Germany into Europe . . . it is . . . the only means to give life and consistency to a politically decentralized, but economically prosperous Germany.'

In short, if you could not destroy Germany, then join her up to a European framework in which she could do no harm militarily but much good economically. If the idea had not occurred to French leaders before 1948 this was not through a shortage of imagination, but because it was clearly perceived as a *pis aller*, a second-best outcome. A 'European' solution to France's German problem could only be adopted once a properly 'French' solution had been abandoned, and it took French leaders three years to accept this. In those three years France had, in effect, to come to terms with the abrupt negation of three hundred years of history. In the circumstances this was no small achievement.

The situation of the Soviet Union in 1945 was precisely the opposite of that of France. After two decades of effective exclusion from the affairs of Europe, Russia had re-surfaced. The resilience of the Soviet population, the successes of the Red Army and, it must be said, the Nazis' capacity to turn even the most sympathetic anti-Soviet nations against them, had brought Stalin credibility and influence, in the counsels of governments and on the streets.

This newfound Bolshevik appeal was founded on the seduction of power. For the USSR was very powerful indeed: despite their huge losses in the first six months of the German invasion—when the Red Army lost 4 million men, 8,000 aircraft and 17,000 tanks—the Soviet armies had recovered to the point where, in 1945, they constituted the greatest military force Europe had ever seen: in Hungary and Romania alone they maintained, through 1946, a military presence of some 1,600,000 men. Stalin had direct or (in the case of Yugoslavia) indirect control of a huge swathe of eastern and central Europe. His armies had only narrowly been blocked, by the rapid advance of the British under Montgomery, from moving forward through north Germany as far as the Danish border.

As Western generals well knew, there was absolutely nothing to stop the Red Army advancing to the Atlantic if Stalin ordered it. To be sure, the Americans and the British had a clear advantage in strategic bombing capacity, and America had the atomic bomb, as Stalin knew even before Truman told him so at Potsdam in

July 1945. There is no doubt that Stalin wanted a Soviet atomic bomb—it is one of the reasons why he insisted on Soviet control of those parts of eastern Germany and, especially, Czechoslovakia where there were uranium deposits; within a few years 200,000 east Europeans would be working in these mines as part of the Soviet atomic programme.[7]

But the atomic bomb, though it worried the Soviet leaders and made Stalin even more suspicious of American motives and plans than he already was, did little to alter Soviet military calculations. These derived directly from Stalin's political goals, which in turn drew on longstanding Soviet and Russian objectives. The first of these was territorial: Stalin wanted back the land the Bolsheviks had lost, at the 1918 Treaty of Brest-Litovsk and in the course of the war with Poland two years later. This goal had been partly achieved in the secret clauses of his 1939 and 1940 pacts with Hitler. The rest he owed to Hitler's decision to invade the Soviet Union in June 1941, allowing the Red Army in turn to reoccupy the disputed territories in the course of its advance on Berlin. That way, the Soviet occupation and annexation of Bessarabia (from Romania), the Bukovina (from Romania), sub-Carpathian Ruthenia (from Czechoslovakia), western Ukraine (from Poland), eastern Finland, the three independent Baltic republics and Königsberg/Kaliningrad in East Prussia could all be presented as the spoils of victory, rather than deriving from unsavoury deals with the Fascist enemy.

For the Soviet Union the point of this territorial aggrandizement was twofold. It ended its pariah status. This was a matter of some importance to Stalin, who now became the leader of a huge Eurasian bloc in world affairs, its newfound power symbolized by the Soviet Union's insistence on a system of vetoes in the new UN Security Council. However, land represented not just prestige but also and above all security. From the Soviet viewpoint a *glacis* to its west, a broad swathe of land across which Germans especially would have to pass if they wished to attack Russia, was a vital security concern. At Yalta and again at Potsdam Stalin made explicit his insistence that these territories between Russia and Germany, if they were not to be wholly absorbed into the USSR itself, must be run by friendly regimes 'free of fascist and reactionary elements'.

The interpretation of that last phrase would prove, to say the least, contentious. But in 1945 the Americans and British were not disposed to give Stalin an argument on the matter. The Soviets had earned, it was felt, the privilege of defining their security as they saw fit; just as it was initially agreed that Moscow was within its rights to extract reparations, booty, labour and *materiel* from former Axis countries (Germany, Austria, Hungary, Romania, Bulgaria and Finland). Looking back, we may be tempted to see in these territorial seizures and economic spoliation the first stages of the bolshevization of Europe's eastern half, and so of course they

---

[7]Under the terms of a secret Czech-Soviet agreement of March 1945, the USSR had the right to mine and extract uranium from the Jachymov deposits in Western Bohemia.

proved. But at the time this was not obvious to everyone—to Western observers there was even something familiar and reassuringly traditional about Moscow's initial post-war stance.[8] And there was a precedent.

Overall, it is not possible to understand the Communist regime in Russia unless we take seriously its ideological claims and ambitions. But there were moments, and the years 1945–47 are one of them, when even if one knew little of Bolshevik doctrine it would be possible to make reasonably good sense of Soviet *foreign* policy simply by looking to the policies of the czars. It was Peter the Great, after all, who introduced the strategy by which Russia would dominate through 'protection' of its neighbours. It was Catherine the Great who drove the Empire forward to the south and south-west. And it was Czar Alexander I, above all, who established the template for Russian imperial engagement in Europe.

At the Vienna Congress of 1815, where—as in 1945—the victorious and mutually suspicious allied powers met to re-establish continental equilibrium following the defeat of a tyrant, Alexander's purposes had been quite explicit. The concerns of small nations were to be subordinated to those of the Great Powers. Since British interests lay overseas and no other continental power matched that of Russia, the Czar would serve as arbiter of a post-war continental arrangement. Local protests would be treated as threats to the arrangement at large and put down with appropriate energy. Russian security would be defined by the territory under Czarist control—never again must a Western army be able to reach Moscow unimpeded—and by the success with which its occupants were forcibly reconciled to the new system.

There is nothing in that account which does not apply to Soviet calculations in 1945. Indeed, Alexander and his ministers would have seen nothing with which to cavil in a policy memorandum written by Ivan Maisky, the Deputy People's Commissar for Foreign Affairs, in November 1944: 'The most advantageous situation for us would be the existence in Europe after the war of only one mighty continental power—the USSR, and one mighty maritime power—Britain.' Of course, at a distance of 130 years nothing is ever quite the same: in 1945 Stalin was more concerned with Central Asia and the Near East than Alexander had been (though Alexander's immediate successors were very active there); conversely, Soviet strategists did not fully share the Czarist obsession with Constantinople, the Straits and the south Balkans. But the continuities of policy far outweigh the differences. They are linked, as it were, by the calculations of Sazunov (Russia's foreign minister on the outbreak of war in 1914), who was already envisaging the future of eastern Europe as a cluster of small, vulnerable, states; nominally independent but effectively clients of Great Russia.

To these enduring themes of Czarist foreign policy in Europe, Stalin added distinctive calculations of his own. He truly expected the coming economic collapse

---

[8]In Poland, of course, it was anything but reassuring—just because it was so familiar.

of the West—extrapolating from inter-war precedent as well as Marxist dogma—and he exaggerated the 'inevitable' conflict between Britain and the US as imperial competitors for a shrinking world market. From this he deduced not just a coming time of increased turbulence—and thus the need for the Soviet Union to nail down its gains—but the real possibility of 'splitting' the Western allies: over the Middle East especially but perhaps over Germany as well. That was one reason why he evinced no haste in reaching a settlement there—time, Stalin believed, was on his side.

But this did not make him any more secure. On the contrary, defensiveness and a wary suspicion characterized all aspects of Soviet foreign policy—'the Kremlin's neurotic view of world affairs' as George Kennan described it in 1946. Hence the famous February 9th 1946 speech at the Bolshoi Theatre, where Stalin announced that the Soviet Union was returning to its pre-war emphasis on industrialization, war-preparedness, and the inevitability of conflict between capitalism and Communism, and made explicit what was already obvious, that henceforth the Soviet Union would cooperate with the West only when it suited her.

There was nothing new here: Stalin was retreating to the 'hard' line taken by the Bolsheviks before 1921 and again between 1927 and the onset of the Popular Fronts. The Bolshevik regime had always been insecure—it was born, after all, of a minority coup in unpropitious circumstances and a highly unsympathetic environment—and Stalin, like all tyrants, needed to invoke threats and enemies, whether domestic or foreign. Moreover Stalin knew better than most that World War Two had been a close run thing: if the Germans had invaded a month earlier in 1941 (as Hitler's original schedule required) the Soviet Union might very well have folded. Like the USA after Pearl Harbor, but with rather better cause, the Soviet leadership was obsessed to the point of paranoia with 'surprise attacks' and challenges to its new-won standing. And the Russians (even more than the French) continued for many decades to see Germany as the main threat.[9]

What, then, did Stalin want? That he anticipated a coming cooling of relations with the West and was out to make the best of his assets and take advantage of Western weakness is doubtless true. But it is far from obvious that Stalin had any clear strategy beyond that. As Norman Naimark, the historian of the Soviet occupation of post-war East Germany, concludes, 'The Soviets were driven by concrete events in the zone, rather than by preconceived plans or ideological imperatives'. This fits with what we know of Stalin's general approach, and it applies beyond the East German case as well.

The Soviets were certainly not planning for World War Three in the near term. Between June 1945 and the end of 1947 the Red Army was reduced from 11,365,000

---

[9]In 1990 Edvard Shevardnadze, the Soviet Foreign Secretary, reportedly observed that despite a forty-year-long Cold War with the United States, when his grandchildren played war games, Germany was still the enemy.

personnel to 2,874,000—a rate of cutback comparable to that in US and British forces (though leaving a far larger contingent still in the field, comprising many well-armed, motorized divisions). Of course, Soviet calculations were by no means self-evident to western contemporaries, and even those who read Stalin as a cautious pragmatist could not be absolutely certain. However, Molotov is surely telling the truth when he suggests in his memoirs that the Soviet Union preferred to take advantage of propitious situations but was not going to take risks in order to bring them about: 'Our ideology stands for offensive operations when possible, and if not, we wait.'

Stalin himself was famously risk-averse, which is why some commentators then and since regretted the West's failure to exercise 'containment' sooner and further forward. But no-one wanted another war in these years, and whereas Stalin could readily be dissuaded from trying to destabilize Paris or Rome (since he had no armies there), the Soviet presence further east was a non-negotiable affair, as everyone recognized. In the Allied Control Councils in Bulgaria or Romania the Soviets did not even pretend to take note of British or American wishes, much less those of the locals. Only in Czechoslovakia was there a degree of ambiguity, the Red Army having long since withdrawn.

From his standpoint, Stalin operated in what passed in Moscow for good faith. He and his colleagues assumed that the Western Allies understood that the Soviets planned to occupy and control 'their' half of Europe; and they were willing to treat Western protests at Soviet behaviour in their zone as *pro forma*, the small change of democratic cant. When it seemed to them that the West was taking its own rhetoric too seriously, demanding freedom and autonomy in Eastern Europe, the Soviet leadership responded with genuine indignation. A note from Molotov in February 1945, commenting upon Western interference over Poland's future, captures the tone: 'How governments are being organized in Belgium, France, Greece, etc, we do not know. We have not been asked, although we do not say that we like one or another of these governments. We have not interfered, because it is the Anglo-American zone of military action.'

Everyone expected World War Two to end, like its predecessor, with an all-embracing Peace Treaty, and five separate treaties were indeed signed in Paris in 1946. These settled territorial and other business in Romania, Bulgaria, Hungary, Finland and Italy, though not in Norway, which remained technically in a state of war with Germany until 1951.[10] But however much these developments mattered for the peoples concerned (and in the case of Romania, Bulgaria and Hungary they sig-

---

[10] Italy lost all of its colonies, paid $360 million in reparations to the USSR, Yugoslavia, Greece, Albania and Ethiopia, and ceded the Istrian peninsula to Yugoslavia. The disposition of the border city of Trieste remained in dispute for eight more years.

naled their definitive consignment to Soviet domination), such agreements could be reached because in the end none of the Great Powers were willing to risk confrontation over them.

The business of Germany, however, was starkly different. To the Russians especially, Germany mattered very much indeed. Just as the war had been about Germany, so was the peace, and the spectre of German revanchism haunted Soviet calculations every bit as much as it did those of the French. When Stalin, Truman and Churchill met at Potsdam (from July 17th to August 2nd 1945, with Attlee replacing Churchill following Labour's victory in the British General Election), it proved possible to reach agreement on the expulsion of Germans from Eastern Europe, the administrative sub-division of Germany for occupation purposes and the goals of 'democratization', 'denazification' and 'decartelization'. Beyond this level of general common intention, however, the difficulties began.

Thus it was agreed to treat the German economy as a single unit, but the Soviets were also granted the right to extract and remove goods, services and financial assets from their own zone. They were further accorded 10 percent of reparations from the Western zones in exchange for food and raw materials to be supplied from eastern Germany. But these accords introduced a contradiction, by treating the economic resources of East and West as separate and distinct. Reparations were thus to be a divisive issue from the start (as they had been after the First World War): the Russians (and the French) wanted them, and the Soviet authorities did not hesitate to dismantle and remove German plant and equipment from the outset, with or without the consent of their fellow occupiers.

There was no final agreement on Germany's new frontiers with Poland and even the common ground of democratization posed practical difficulties in implementation. Accordingly, the Allied leaders agreed to differ and to defer, instructing their Foreign Ministers to meet and continue the talks at a later date. There thus began two years of meetings of the Allied Foreign Ministers—representing the Soviet, American, British and, latterly, French governments: the first gathering took place in London two months after Potsdam, the last in December 1947, again in London. Their goal, in principle, was to draw up definitive arrangements for post-war Germany and prepare Peace Treaties between the Allied Powers and German and Austria. It was in the course of these encounters—notably in Moscow during March and April 1947—that the gap separating Soviet and Western approaches to the German problem became clear.

The Anglo-American strategy was driven in part by calculations of political prudence. If the Germans in the Western zone of occupation remained beaten down and impoverished, and were offered no prospect of improvement, then they would sooner or later turn back to Nazism—or else to Communism. In the regions of Germany occupied by American and British military governments, therefore, the emphasis switched quite early to reconstructing civic and political institutions and giving Germans responsibility for their domestic affairs. This offered emerging German politicians considerably more leverage than they could have hoped for when the war ended and they didn't hesitate to exploit it—intimating that unless matters improved and the occupiers followed their advice, they could not answer for the future political allegiance of the German nation.

Fortunately for the Western allies, Communist occupation policies in Berlin and the Soviet-occupied territory of eastern Germany were not such as to attract disaffected German sentiments and votes. However unpopular the Americans or British or French might be in the eyes of resentful Germans, the alternative was far worse: if Stalin sincerely wanted Germany to remain united, as he instructed German Communists to demand in the initial post-war years, then Soviet tactics were grievously ill-chosen. From the outset, the Soviets established in their zone of occupation a *de facto* Communist-led government without Allied consent and set about rendering superfluous the Potsdam accords by ruthlessly extracting and dismantling whatever fell within their grasp.

Not that Stalin had much choice. There was never any prospect of the Communists gaining control of the country or even the Soviet zone except by force. In the Berlin city elections on October 20th 1946, Communist candidates came far behind both the Social Democrats and Christian Democrats. With that, Soviet policy perceptibly hardened. But by this time the Western occupiers were running into difficulties of their own. By July 1946 Britain had been forced to import 112,000 tons of wheat and 50,000 tons of potatoes to feed the local population of its zone (the urban and industrial north-west of Germany), paid for out of an American loan.

The British were extracting at most $29 million in reparations from Germany; but the occupation was costing London $80 million a year, leaving the British taxpayer to foot the bill for the difference even as the British government was forced to impose bread rationing at home (an expedient that had been avoided throughout the war). In the opinion of the British Chancellor of the Exchequer, Hugh Dalton, the British were 'paying reparations to the Germans.' The Americans were not under the same economic constraints and their zone had not suffered as much war damage, but the situation appeared no less absurd to them—the US Army in particular was not well pleased, since the cost of feeding millions of hungry Germans fell on its own budget. As George Kennan observed: 'the unconditional surrender of Germany . . . left us with the sole responsibility for a section of Germany which had never been economically self-supporting in modern times and the capacity of which for self-support had been catastrophically reduced by the circumstances of the war and the German defeat. At the moment we accepted that responsibility we had no program for the rehabilitation of the economy of our zone, preferring to leave all that to later settlement by international agreement.'

Faced with this dilemma, and growing German resentment at the dismantling of plant and installations for shipment east, the US military governor, General Clay, unilaterally suspended deliveries of reparations from the American zone to the Soviet Union (or anywhere else) in May 1946, observing that Soviet authorities had failed to keep their part of the Potsdam arrangements. The British followed suit two months later. This signaled a first parting of the ways, but no more than that. The French, like the USSR, still wanted reparations, and all four Allies were still formally committed to the 1946 'Levels-of-Industry' agreement under which Germany was to be held down to a standard of living no higher than the European average (excluding Britain and the Soviet Union). Moreover the British Cabinet, meeting in May 1946, was still reluctant to accept a formal division of occupied Germany into eastern and western halves, with all the implications that would have for European security.

But it was becoming obvious that the four Occupying Powers were not about to reach an agreement. Once the main Nuremberg Trial ended in October 1946 and the terms of the Paris Peace Treaties were finalized the following month, the wartime Allies were bound by little more than their co-responsibility for Germany, the contradictions of which thus came increasingly to the fore. The Americans and British agreed at the end of 1946 to fuse the economies of their two occupation zones into a so-called 'Bizone'; but even this did not yet signify a firm division of Germany, much less a commitment to integrating the Bizone into the West. On the contrary: three months later, in February 1947, the French and British ostentatiously signed the Dunkirk Treaty in which they committed themselves to mutual support against any future *German* aggression. And US Secretary of State Marshall was still optimistic, in early 1947, that whatever arrangements were made to resolve the German economic conundrum need not result in a divided Germany. On this, at least, East and West were still in formal accord.

The real break came in the spring of 1947, at the (March 10th–April 24th) Moscow meeting of the Foreign Ministers of the US, Britain, France and the Soviet Union, convened once again to seek agreement on a Peace Treaty for Germany and Austria. By now the fault lines were clear. The British and Americans were determined to build up the Western German economy, in order that the Germans might support themselves but also to contribute to the revival of the European economy in general. The Soviet representatives wanted a restoration of reparations from the Western zones of Germany and, to this end, a united German administration and economy as initially envisaged (albeit vaguely) at Potsdam. But by now the Western Allies were no longer seeking a single German administration. For this would entail not just the abandonment of the population of the western zones of Germany—by now a political consideration in its own right—but the effective handing over of the country to the Soviet sphere of control, given the military asymmetry of the time.

As Robert K. Murphy, the political adviser to the US Military Government in Germany, recognized, 'it was the Moscow Conference of 1947 . . . which really rang down the Iron Curtain.' Ernest Bevin had abandoned any serious hope of agreement over Germany before he even arrived in Moscow, but for Marshall (and Bidault) it was the defining moment. For Molotov and Stalin as well, no doubt. By the time the four Foreign Ministers next met, in Paris from June 27th–July 2nd to discuss Marshall's dramatic new Plan, the Americans and British had already agreed (on May 23rd) to permit German representation on a new Bizone 'Economic Council', the embryonic prelude to a West German government.

From this point on, things moved rapidly forward. Neither side made or sought any further concessions: the Americans and British, who had long feared a separate Russo-German Peace and had countenanced delays and compromises in order to forestall it, ceased to take into account an eventuality they could now discount. In August they unilaterally increased output in the Bizone (to a chorus of Soviet *and* French criticism). The Joint Chiefs of Staff directive JCS 1067 (the 'Morgenthau plan') was replaced by JCS 1779 which formally acknowledged the new American goals: economic unification of the western zone of Germany and the encouragement of German self-government. For the Americans especially, Germans were rapidly ceasing to be the enemy.[11]

The Foreign Ministers—Molotov, Bevin, Marshall and Bidault—met one last time, in London, from November 25th through December 16th 1947. It was a curious gathering, since their relations had already in practice broken down. The Western Allies were moving forward with independent plans for West European recovery, while two months earlier Stalin had established the Cominform, instructed the Communist parties of France and Italy to take an intransigent line in their countries' affairs and clamped down sharply on the Communist-controlled countries in what was now a Soviet bloc. The Ministers discussed, as in the past, the prospects for an all-German government under Allied control and other terms for an eventual Peace Treaty. But there was no further agreement on the common administration of Germany or plans for its future and the meeting broke up without scheduling any future gatherings.

Instead Britain, France and the US began tripartite discussions on Germany's future at an extended conference, once again held in London, beginning on February 23rd, 1948. In that same week the Communist Party in Czechoslovakia staged its successful coup, signaling Stalin's definitive abandonment of his earlier strategy and his acceptance of the inevitability of confrontation rather than agreement with the West. In the shadow of the Prague coup, France and Britain extended their Dunkirk Treaty into the Brussels Pact of March 17th, binding Britain, France and the Benelux countries in a mutual defense alliance.

There was now nothing to inhibit the Western leaders and the London Conference rapidly agreed to extend the Marshall Plan to western Germany and lay down schemes for an eventual government for a West German state (an arrangement ap-

---

[11]This proved an easy accommodation. In the words of one American GI, pleasantly surprised at his reception in Germany following the rather frosty French response to their liberators, 'Hell, these people are cleaner and a damned sight friendlier than the French. They're our kind of people.' Quoted in Earl Ziemke, *The U.S.Army in the Occupation of Germany, 1944–46* (Washington DC, 1985), p. 142.

proved by the French delegation in exchange for the—temporary—separation of the Saar from Germany and a proposal for an independent authority to oversee the industry of the Ruhr). These plans constituted an explicit departure from the spirit of the Potsdam accords and General Vassily Sokolovsky, the Soviet representative on the Allied Control Council (ACC) in Berlin, duly protested (neglecting to acknowledge the Soviet Union's own frequent breaches of those same accords).

On March 10th, Sokolovsky condemned plans for western Germany as the enforced imposition of capitalist interests upon a German population denied the chance to demonstrate its desire for Socialism, and repeated Soviet assertions that Western powers were abusing their presence in Berlin—which he claimed was part of the Soviet Zone—to interfere in eastern German affairs. Ten days later, at an ACC meeting in Berlin on March 20th, Sokolovsky denounced the 'unilateral actions' of the Western Allies, 'taken in Western Germany and which are against the interests of the peaceful countries and peace-loving Germans who seek the peaceful unity and democratization of their country'. He then swept out of the room, followed by the rest of the Soviet delegation. No date was set for a further meeting. The joint Allied occupation of Germany was over: less than two weeks later, on April 1st, the Soviet military authorities in Berlin began to interfere with surface traffic between western Germany and the Western Allies' zones of occupation in Berlin. The real Cold War in Europe had begun.

It should be clear from this narrative that there is little to be gained from asking 'who started the Cold War?' To the extent that the Cold War was about Germany, the final outcome—a divided country—was probably preferred by all parties to a Germany united against them. No one planned this outcome in May 1945, but few were deeply discontented with it. Some German politicians, notably Konrad Adenauer himself, even owed their career to the division of their country: had Germany remained a quadri-zonal or united country, an obscure local politician from the far-western Catholic Rhineland would almost certainly not have made it to the top.

But Adenauer could hardly have espoused the division of Germany as a goal, however much he welcomed it in private. His chief opponent in the first years of the Federal Republic, the Social Democrat Kurt Schumacher, was a Protestant from West Prussia and a tireless advocate of German unity. In contrast to Adenauer *he* would readily have accepted a neutralized Germany as the price for a single German state, which was what Stalin appeared to be offering. And Schumacher's position was probably the more popular one in Germany at the time, which was why Adenauer had to tread carefully and ensure that the responsibility for a divided Germany fell squarely on the occupying forces.

By 1948 the United States, like Great Britain, was not unhappy to see the emergence of a divided Germany, with American influence dominant in the larger, western segment. But although there were some, like George Kennan, who had perceptively anticipated this outcome (as early as 1945 he had concluded that the USA had 'no choice but to lead her section of Germany . . . to a form of independence so prosperous, so secure, so superior, that the east cannot threaten it'), they were in the minority. The Americans, like Stalin, were improvising in these years. It is sometimes suggested that certain key American decisions and declarations, notably the Truman Doctrine of March 1947, precipitated Stalin's retreat from compromise to rigidity and that in this sense the responsibility for European divisions lay with Washington's insensitivity or, worse, its calculated intransigence. But this is not so.

For the Truman Doctrine, to take this example, had remarkably little impact on Soviet calculations. President Truman's March 12th 1947 announcement to Congress that 'It must be the policy of the United States to support free peoples who are re-sisting attempted subjugation by armed minorities or outside pressure' was a direct response to London's inability to continue with aid to Greece and Turkey following the British economic crisis of February 1947. America would have to take over Britain's role. Truman thus sought Congressional approval for a $400 million increase in his budget for overseas aid: to secure the funding he presented the request in the context of a crisis of Communist insurgency.

Congress took him seriously, but Moscow did not. Stalin was not much interested in Turkey and Greece—the chief beneficiaries of the aid package—and he understood perfectly well that his own sphere of interest was unlikely to be affected by Truman's grandstanding. On the contrary, he continued to suppose that there were very good prospects for a split within the Western camp of which the American assumption of erstwhile British responsibilities in the Eastern Mediterranean was a sign and precursor. Whatever led Stalin to adjust his calculations in Eastern Europe, it was decidedly not the rhetoric of American domestic politics.[12]

The immediate cause of the division of Germany and Europe lies rather in Stalin's own errors in these years. In central Europe, where he would have preferred a united Germany, weak and neutral, he squandered his advantage in 1945 and subsequent years by uncompromising rigidity and confrontational tactics. If Stalin's hope had been to let Germany rot until the fruit of German resentment and hopelessness fell into his lap, then he miscalculated seriously—though there were moments when the Allied authorities in western Germany wondered whether he might yet succeed. In that sense the Cold War in Europe was an unavoidable outcome of the Soviet dictator's personality and the system over which he ruled.

But the fact remains that Germany was at his feet, as his opponents well knew—'The trouble is that we are playing with fire which we have nothing with which to

---

[12]In September 1947 Andrej Zdanov, speaking as always for his master, would inform delegates at the founding Congress of the Cominform that the Truman Doctrine was directed at least as much against Britain as against the USSR, 'because it signifies Britain's expulsion from its sphere of influence in the Mediterranean and the Near East'.

put out', as Marshall put it to the National Security Council on February 13th 1948. All the Soviet Union needed to do was accept the Marshall Plan and convince a majority of the Germans of Moscow's good faith in seeking a neutral, independent Germany. In 1947 this would radically have shifted the European balance of advantage. Whatever Marshall, Bevin or their advisers might have thought of such maneuvers, they would have been helpless to prevent them. That such tactical calculations were beyond Stalin cannot be credited to the West. As Dean Acheson put it on another occasion, 'We were fortunate in our opponents.'

Looking back, it is somewhat ironic that after fighting a murderous war to reduce the power of an over-mighty Germany at the heart of the European continent, the victors should have proven so unable to agree on post-war arrangements to keep the German colossus down that they ended up dividing it between them in order to benefit separately from its restored strength. It had become clear—first to the British, then to the Americans, belatedly to the French and finally to the Soviets— that the only way to keep Germany from being the problem was to change the terms of the debate and declare it the solution. This was uncomfortable, but it worked. In the words of Noel Annan, a British intelligence officer in occupied Germany, 'It was odious to find oneself in alliance with people who had been willing to go along with Hitler to keep Communism at bay. But the best hope for the West was to encourage the Germans themselves to create a Western democratic state.'

V

The Coming of the Cold War

'Imagine the Austrian Empire fragmented into a multitude of greater and
lesser republics. What a nice basis for universal Russian monarchy'.
František Palacký (April, 1848)

'The Yugoslavs want to take Greek Macedonia. They want Albania, too,
and even parts of Austria and Hungary. This is unreasonable. I do not like
the way they are acting'.
Josef Stalin, 1945

'All that the Red Army needed in order to reach the North Sea was boots'.
Dennis Healey

'The idea of a European order is not an artificial creation of Germany
but a necessity'.
Paul-Henri Spaak (April, 1942)

'This is something which we know, in our bones, we cannot do'.
Anthony Eden (January, 1952)

'This war is not as in the past; whoever occupies a territory also imposes upon it
his own social system. Everyone imposes his own system as far as his army can
reach. It cannot be otherwise.' Josef Stalin's famous aphorism—reported by Milovan Djilas in his *Conversations with Stalin*—was not quite as original as it appeared.
World War Two was by no means the first European war in which military outcomes determined social systems: the religious wars of the sixteenth century ended
in 1555 at the Peace of Augsburg, where the principle of *cuius regio eius religio* authorised rulers to establish in their own territory the religion of their choice; and
in the initial stages of the Napoleonic conquests in early nineteenth-century Europe, military success translated very quickly into social and institutional revolution on the French model.

Nevertheless, Stalin's point was clear—and put to Djilas well in advance of the
Communist take-over of eastern Europe. From the Soviet side the war had been
fought to defeat Germany and restore Russian power and security on its western
frontiers. Whatever was to become of Germany itself, the region separating Ger-

many and Russia could not be left in uncertainty. The territories running in a north-south arc from Finland to Yugoslavia comprised small, vulnerable states whose inter-war governments (with the partial exception of Czechoslovakia) had been uniformly hostile to the Soviet Union. Poland, Hungary and Romania in particular had been consistently unfriendly to Moscow and suspicious of Soviet intentions towards them. The only acceptable outcome for Stalin was the establishment—in those parts of the region not preemptively absorbed into the USSR itself—of governments that could be relied upon never to pose a threat to Soviet security.

But the only way to guarantee such an outcome was to align the political system of the states of eastern Europe with that of the Soviet Union and this, from the start, was what Stalin wanted and intended. On the one hand it might seem that this goal was straightforward enough: the old elites in countries like Romania or Hungary had been discredited and it would not be difficult to remove them and begin afresh. In many places the Soviet occupiers were at first welcomed as liberators and harbingers of change and reform.

On the other hand, however, the Soviet Union had almost no leverage in the domestic affairs of its western neighbours beyond the authority of its overwhelming military presence. Communists in much of the region had been banned from public life and legal political activity for most of the previous quarter century. Even where Communist parties were legal, their identification with Russia and the rigid, sectarian tactics imposed from Moscow for most of the period after 1927 had reduced them to a marginal irrelevance in East European politics. The Soviet Union had further contributed to their weakness by imprisoning and purging many of the Polish, Hungarian, Yugoslav and other Communists who had taken refuge in Moscow: in the Polish case the leadership of the inter-war Polish Communist Party was almost completely wiped out.

Thus when Mátyás Rákosi, the leader of the Hungarian Communist Party, was returned from Moscow to Budapest in February 1945, he could count on the support of perhaps 4,000 Communists in Hungary. In Romania, according to the Romanian Communist leader Ana Pauker herself, the Party had less than 1,000 members in a population of nearly 20 million. The situation in Bulgaria was not much better: in September 1944 the Communists numbered about 8,000. Only in the industrial regions of Bohemia and in Yugoslavia, where the Party was identified with the victorious partisan resistance, did Communism have anything resembling a mass base.

Characteristically cautious, and in any case still maintaining working relations with the Western powers, Stalin thus initially pursued a tactic already familiar from the Popular Front years of the thirties and from Communist practice during the Spanish Civil War: favouring the formation of 'Front' governments, coalitions of Communists, Socialists and other 'anti-Fascist' parties, which would exclude and punish the old regime and its supporters but would be cautious and 'democratic', reformist rather than revolutionary. By the end of the war, or very shortly thereafter, every country in eastern Europe had such a coalition government.

In view of continuing scholarly disagreement over responsibility for the division of Europe, it is perhaps worth emphasizing that neither Stalin nor his local representatives were in any doubt as to their long-term goal. Coalitions were the route to power for Communist parties in a region where they were historically weak; they were only ever a means to this end. As Walter Ulbricht, leader of the East German Communists, explained privately to his followers when they expressed bemusement at Party policy in 1945: 'It's quite clear—it's got to look democratic, but we must have everything in our control.'

Control, in fact, mattered much more than policies. It was not by chance that in every coalition government—'Fatherland Front', 'Unity Government' or 'bloc of anti-Fascist parties'—in eastern Europe, Communists sought control of certain key ministries: the Ministry of the Interior, which gave the Party authority over the police and security forces as well as the power to grant or withhold licenses to print newspapers; the Ministry of Justice, with control over purges, tribunals and judges; the Ministry of Agriculture, which administered land reforms and redistribution and was thus in a position to confer favours and buy the loyalty of millions of peasants. Communists also put themselves in key positions on 'denazification' committees, district commissions and in the trade unions.

Conversely, Communists in eastern Europe were in no hurry to claim the offices of President, Prime Minister or Foreign Minister, often preferring to leave these to their coalition allies in Socialist, Agrarian or Liberal Parties. This reflected the initial post-war disposition of government places—with the Communists in a minority—and reassured Western observers. The local population was not fooled and took its own precautions—Romanian Communist Party membership rose to 800,000 by the end of 1945—but in many respects Communist strategy really was reassuringly moderate. Far from collectivizing land, the Party was urging its distribution among the landless. Beyond the confiscation of 'Fascist' property, the Party was not pressing for nationalization or state ownership—certainly no more and usually rather less than some of its coalition partners. And there was very little talk of 'Socialism' as a goal.

The Communists' stated objective in 1945 and 1946 was to 'complete' the unfinished bourgeois revolutions of 1848, to re-distribute property, guarantee equality and affirm democratic rights in a part of Europe where all three had always been in short supply. These were plausible goals, at least on the surface, and they appealed to many in the region and in western Europe who wanted to think well of Stalin and his purposes. Their appeal to Communists themselves, however, was sharply diminished in a series of local and national elections in eastern Germany, Austria and Hungary. There it became clear very early (in the Hungarian case at the Budapest municipal elections of November 1945) that however successfully they had inserted themselves into positions of local influence, Communists were never going to achieve public power through the ballot box. Despite every advantage of military occupation and economic patronage, Communist candidates were consistently defeated by representatives of the old Liberal, Social Democratic and Agrarian/Smallholder parties.

The result was that Communist parties adopted instead a strategy of covert pressure, followed by open terror and repression. In the course of 1946 and into 1947 electoral opponents were maligned, threatened, beaten up, arrested, tried as 'Fascists' or 'collaborators' and imprisoned or even shot. 'Popular' militias helped create a climate of fear and insecurity which Communist spokesmen then blamed on their political critics. Vulnerable or unpopular politicians from non-Communist parties were targeted for public opprobrium, while their colleagues consented to this mistreatment in the hope it would not be applied to them. Thus in Bulgaria, as early as the summer of 1946, seven out of twenty-two members of the 'Praesidium' of the Agrarian Union and thirty-five out of the eighty members of its governing Council were in prison. Typical of the charges was one against the Agrarian journalist Kunev, accusing him of having, in an article, 'in a truly criminal manner called the Bulgarian government political and economic dreamers'.

Agrarians, Liberals and other mainstream parties proved an easy target, tarred with the brush of Fascism or anti-national sentiment and picked off in stages. The more complicated impediment to Communist ambitions were the local Socialist and Social-Democratic parties who shared the Communists' own reforming ambitions. It was not easy to charge Social Democrats in central or eastern Europe with 'Fascism' or collaboration—they had usually been as much the victim of repression as Communists. And in so far as there was an industrial working-class constituency in overwhelmingly rural eastern Europe, its allegiance was traditionally Socialist, not Communist. Thus since the Socialists could not easily be beaten, the Communists chose instead to join them.

Or, rather, to make the Socialists join *them*. This was a venerable Communist device. Lenin's initial tactic from 1918 to 1921 had been to split Europe's Socialist Parties, hive off the radical left element into new-formed Communist movements, and condemn the rump as reactionary and overtaken by history. But when Communist parties found themselves in the minority during the course of the next two decades, Moscow's approach altered and the Communists instead held out to the (mostly larger) Socialist Parties the prospect of Left 'unity'—but under Communist auspices. In the circumstances of post-liberation eastern Europe this seemed to many socialists a sensible proposition.

Even in western Europe some left-leaning members of the French and Italian Socialist Parties were seduced by Communist invitations to merge into a single political force. In eastern Europe the pressure proved, literally, irresistible. The process began in the Soviet Zone of Germany where (at a secret meeting in Moscow in February 1946) the Communists determined upon a merger with their much larger Socialist 'allies'. This merger was consummated two months later with the birth of the

Socialist Unity Party (it was characteristic of these mergers that the term 'Communist' was deliberately eschewed by the freshly united party). Quite a few former leaders of the Social Democrats in eastern Germany proved amenable to the merger and were given honorific posts in the new Party and subsequent East German government. Socialists who protested or opposed the new Party were denounced, expelled and at the very least forced out of public life or into exile.

In the rest of the Soviet bloc these Communist-Socialist 'unions', similarly structured, came a little later, in the course of 1948: in Romania in February 1948; in Hungary and Czechoslovakia in June; in Bulgaria in August; and in Poland in December. By then the Socialist parties had been split and split again over the issue of fusion, so that long before they disappeared they had ceased to be an effective political force in their country. And, as in Germany, former Social-Democrats who threw in their lot with the Communists were duly rewarded with empty titles: the first Head of State in Communist Hungary—appointed on July 30th 1948—was Árpád Szakasits, a former Socialist.

The Social Democrats in eastern Europe were in an impossible position. Western Socialists often encouraged them to merge with the Communists, either in the innocent belief that everyone would benefit, or else in the hope of moderating Communist behaviour. As late as 1947 independent Socialist Parties in eastern Europe (i.e. Socialists who refused to cooperate with their Communist comrades) were barred from joining international Socialist organizations on the grounds that they were an impediment to the alliance of 'progressive' forces. Meanwhile, at home, they were subject to humiliation and violence. Even when they accepted the Communist embrace their situation hardly improved—at the February 1948 'fusion' Congress of the two parties in Romania, the Communist leader Ana Pauker accused her erstwhile Socialist colleagues of systematic sabotage, servility to reactionary governments and anti-Soviet 'calumnies'.

Following the decimation, imprisonment or absorption of their main opponents, Communists did indeed do rather better at elections in 1947 and thereafter, with some help from violent assaults on their remaining opponents, intimidation at polling stations and blatantly abusive vote counts. There then, typically, followed the formation of governments in which the Communist, or newly-united 'Worker' or 'Unity' Party was now blatantly dominant: coalition partners, if any, were reduced to nominal and empty roles. In keeping with this transition from united front coalitions to a Communist monopoly of power, Soviet strategy in the course of 1948 and 1949 reverted to a radical policy of state control, collectivization, destruction of the middle-class and purges and punishment of real and imagined opponents.

This account of the initial Soviet take-over in eastern Europe describes a process common to all the countries of the region. Stalin's calculations were typically indifferent to national variety. Where Communists could reasonably hope to secure power by legal or ostensibly legal means this appears to have been Stalin's preference, at least through the autumn of 1947. But the point was power, not legality, which is why Communists' tactics became more confrontational and less embarrassed by judicial or political constraints, even at the cost of alienating foreign sympathy, once it was clear that electoral success would elude them.

Nonetheless, there were significant local variations. In Bulgaria and Romania the Soviet hand was heaviest—in part because both countries had been at war with the USSR, in part because of local Communist weakness, but mostly just because they were so obviously consigned by geography to the Soviet sphere from the outset. In Bulgaria the Communist leader (and former Comintern Secretary) Georgy Dimitrov declared bluntly as early as October 1946 that anyone who voted for the anti-Communist opposition would be regarded as a traitor. Even so, the Communists' opponents won 101 out of 465 parliamentary seats in the ensuing general election. But the opposition was fore-doomed—the only thing preventing the occupying Red Army and its local allies from openly destroying all dissent right away was the need to work with the Western Allies on a Peace Treaty for Bulgaria and to secure Anglo-American recognition of a Communist-led government as Bulgaria's legitimate authority.

Once the peace treaties were signed, the Communists had nothing to gain by waiting and the chronology of events is thus revealing. On June 5th 1947 the US Senate ratified the Paris Peace Treaties with Bulgaria, Romania, Hungary, Finland and Italy, despite the misgivings of American diplomats in Sofia and Bucharest. The very next day the leading anti-Communist politician in Bulgaria, the Agrarian leader Nikola Petkov (who had refused to follow more accommodating Agrarians into the Communists' Fatherland Front), was arrested. His trial lasted from August 5th to 15th. On September 15th the Bulgarian Peace Treaty officially came into force and four days later the USA offered to extend diplomatic recognition to the government in Sofia. Within 96 hours Petkov was executed, his sentence having been delayed until the official American announcement. With Petkov judicially murdered, the Bulgarian Communists need fear no further impediments. As the Soviet general Biryuzov observed in retrospect, discussing Red Army support for the Bulgarian Communists against the 'bourgeois' parties: 'We did not have the right to withhold assistance to the efforts of the Bulgarian people to crush this reptile.'

In Romania, the Communists' position was even weaker than Bulgaria, where at least there was a history of philo-Russian sentiment on which the Party could try to draw.[1] Although the Soviets guaranteed the return to Romania of northern Translyvania (assigned to Hungary under duress in 1940), Stalin had no intention

---

[1] The Bulgarians had actually oscillated quite markedly over the years from enthusiastic pro-Germanism to ultra-Slavophilism. Neither served them well. As a local commentator remarked at the time, Bulgaria always chooses the wrong card . . . and *slams* it on the table!

of returning Bessarabia or the Bukovina, both incorporated into the USSR, nor the Southern Dobrudja region of south-east Romania now attached to Bulgaria: as a consequence, the Romanian Communists were forced to justify a significant territorial loss, much as, during the inter-war years, they had been hobbled by the Soviet claim on Bessarabia, then Romanian territory.

Worse, the Romanian Communist leaders were frequently not even Romanian, at least by traditional Romanian criteria. Ana Pauker was Jewish, Emil Bodnaras was Ukrainian, Vasile Luca was of Transylvanian German background. Others were Hungarian or Bulgarian. Perceived as an alien presence, the Romanian Communists were utterly dependent on the Soviet forces. Their domestic survival rested not upon winning the popular vote—never remotely considered as a practical objective—but upon the speed and efficiency with which they could occupy the state and divide and destroy their opponents in the 'historic' parties of the Liberal center, a task at which they proved decidedly adept—as early as March 1948 the government list won 405 out of 414 seats in national elections. In Romania as in Bulgaria (or Albania, where Enver Hodxa mobilized the southern Tosk communities against tribal resistance from the northern Ghegs), subversion and violence were not one option among others—they were the only road to power.

The Poles, too, were fore-doomed to the Soviet sphere after World War Two. This was because of their location, on the route from Berlin to Moscow; their history, as longstanding impediments to Russian imperial ambitions in the west; and because in Poland, too, the prospects of a Soviet-friendly government emerging spontaneously by popular choice were minimal. The difference between Poland and the Balkan states, however, was that Poland had been a victim of Hitler, not his ally; hundreds of thousands of Polish soldiers had fought with the Allied armies on Eastern and Western fronts; and the Poles nursed expectations about their post-war prospects.

As it transpired, those prospects were not so very bad. The Polish Communists in the so-called 'Lublin Committee'—set up in July 1944 by the Soviet authorities so that they would have a ready-made government to put in office when they reached Warsaw—could hardly claim a mass base, but they had a degree of local support, especially among the young, and they could point to some real benefits of Soviet 'friendship': an effective guarantee against German territorial revanchism (a genuine consideration at the time) and a policy of national exchanges whereby Poland was 'cleansed' of its remaining Ukrainian minority and ethnic Poles from the east were resettled within the new national frontiers. These considerations allowed Polish Communists, for all their marginality (many of them, too, were of Jewish origin), to claim a place in Polish national and even nationalist political traditions.

Nevertheless, Poland's Communists too would always have been an insignificant minority in electoral terms. The Polish Peasant Party of Stanislaw Mikołajczyk counted some 600,000 members in December 1945, ten times the number of activists in the Communists' Polish Workers' Party (the Polish *United* Workers' Party after its absorption of the Socialists in December 1948). But Mikołajczyk, prime minister of the wartime government-in-exile, was fatally handicapped by his party's characteristically Polish insistence on being *both* anti-Nazi *and* anti-Soviet.

Stalin was more or less indifferent to the success of 'Socialism' in Poland, as later events would reveal. But he was far from indifferent to the general tenor of Polish policy, especially Polish foreign policy. Indeed, together with the outcome of the German standoff, it was more important to him than anything else, at least in Europe. Accordingly the Peasant Party was steadily edged aside, its supporters threatened, its leaders attacked, its credibility impugned. In the blatantly rigged Polish parliamentary elections of January 1947, the Communist-led 'Democratic bloc' obtained 80 percent of the votes, the Peasant Party just 10 percent.[2] Nine months later, in fear of his life, Mikołajczyk fled the country. Remnants of the wartime Home Army continued to fight a guerilla war with the Communist authorities for a few more years, but theirs, too, was a hopeless cause.

In Poland, the Soviet Union had so obvious an interest in the political complexion of the country that the Poles' wartime illusions—before and after Yalta—can seem quixotic. In Hungary, however, notions of a 'Hungarian road to Socialism' were not altogether fanciful. Hungary's chief post-war interest for Moscow was as a safe conduit for Red Army troops, should these need to move west into Austria (or—later—south into Yugoslavia). Had there been widespread public support for the local Communists their Soviet advisers might have been willing to play out the 'democratic' tactic longer than they did.

But in Hungary, too, the Communists proved consistently unpopular, even in Budapest. Despite being targeted as reactionary and even Fascist, the Smallholders Party (Hungary's equivalent of Agrarian parties elsewhere) secured an absolute majority in the national elections of November 1945. With the backing of the Socialists (whose leader Anna Kéthly refused to believe that the Communists would stoop to election-rigging), the Communists succeeded in expelling some of the Smallholder deputies from parliament and charged them in February 1947 with conspiracy and, in the case of their leader Béla Kovács, espionage against the Red Army (Kovács was sent to Siberia, whence he returned in 1956). In new elections in August 1947, shamelessly falsified by the Communist Interior Minister László Rajk, the Communists still managed to secure only 22 percent of the vote, although the Smallholders were duly reduced to a 15 percent share. In these circumstances Hungary's road to Socialism converged rapidly with that of its eastern neighbours.

[2]This was not the first time armed Russians had personally supervised crucial Polish elections: during the local parliamentary elections of 1772 at which Poles were asked to chose representatives who would confirm the partition of their country, foreign troops stood menacingly by to ensure the desired outcome.

By the next elections, in May 1949, the 'People's Front' was credited with 95.6 percent of the vote.

It is easy, in retrospect, to see that hopes for a democratic Eastern Europe after 1945 were always forlorn. Central and Eastern Europe had few indigenous democratic or liberal traditions. The inter-war regimes in this part of Europe had been corrupt, authoritarian and in some cases murderous. The old ruling castes were frequently venal. The real governing class in inter-war Eastern Europe was the bureaucracy, recruited from the same social groups who would furnish the administrative cadre of the Communist states. For all the rhetoric of 'Socialism', the transition from authoritarian backwardness to Communist 'popular democracy' was a short move and an easy one. It is not so very surprising that history took the turn it did.

Moreover the alternative of a return to the politicians and policies of pre-1939 Romania or Poland or Hungary significantly weakened the anti-Communist case, at least until the full force of Soviet terror was felt after 1949. After all, as the French Communist leader Jacques Duclos slyly asked in the Communist daily *l'Humanité* on July 1st 1948, was not the Soviet Union these countries' best guarantee not just against a return to the bad old days but of their very national independence? That was indeed the way it seemed to many at the time. As Churchill observed: 'One day the Germans would want their territory back and the Poles would not be able to stop them.' The Soviet Union was now the self-appointed protector of the new borders of Romania and Poland, not to speak of the redistributed land of expelled Germans and others all across the region.

This was a reminder, as though it were needed, of the omnipresence of the Red Army. The 37th Army of the 3rd Ukrainian Front was detached from the forces occupying Romania in September 1944 and stationed in Bulgaria, where it remained until the Peace Treaties were signed in 1947. Soviet forces remained in Hungary until the mid-Fifties (and again after 1956), in Romania until 1958. The German Democratic Republic was under Soviet military occupation throughout its forty-year life and Soviet troops transited regularly across Poland. The Soviet Union was not about to leave this part of Europe, whose future was thus intimately bound up with the fate of its giant neighbour, as events were to show.

The apparent exception was of course Czechoslovakia. Many Czechs welcomed the Russians as liberators. Thanks to Munich they had few illusions about the Western powers and Edvard Beneš's London-based government-in-exile was the only one that made unambivalent overtures to Moscow well before 1945. As Beneš himself expressed his position to Molotov in December 1943, 'in regard to issues of major importance, [we] . . . would always speak and act in a fashion agreeable to the representatives of the Soviet government.' Beneš may not have been as alert as his mentor, the late President Tomáš Masaryk, to the risks of a Russian or Soviet embrace, but he was not a fool either. Prague was going to be friendly with Moscow for the same reason it had sought close links to Paris before 1938: because Czechoslovakia was a small, vulnerable country in central Europe and needed a protector.

Thus despite being in many ways the most western of 'eastern' European countries—with a historically pluralist political culture, a significant urban and industrial sector, a flourishing capitalist economy before the war and a Western-oriented social-democratic policy after it—Czechoslovakia was also the Soviet Union's closest ally in the region after 1945, in spite of losing its easternmost district of sub-Carpathian Ruthenia to Soviet territorial 'adjustments'. That is why Beneš, alone of the east- and south-east European wartime prime-ministers-in-exile, was able to bring his government home—where, in April 1945, he reconfigured it with seven Communists and eleven ministers from the other four parties.

The Czech Communists under their leader Klement Gottwald genuinely believed that their chances of coming to power through the ballot box were good. They had made a respectable showing at the last pre-war Czechoslovak elections, obtaining 849,000 votes (10 percent of the total) in 1935. They were not dependent on the Red Army, which withdrew from Czechoslovakia in November 1945 (though in Prague as elsewhere the Soviet Union maintained a significant intelligence and secret police presence through its diplomatic establishment). In the genuinely free, albeit psychologically fraught Czechoslovak elections of May 1946, the Communist Party won 40.2 percent of the vote in the Czech districts of Bohemia and Moravia, 31 percent in largely rural and Catholic Slovakia. Only the Slovak Democrat Party did better, and its appeal was by definition confined to the Slovak third of the population.[3]

The Czech Communists anticipated continuing success, which is why they initially welcomed the prospect of Marshall Aid and undertook recruitment drives to bolster their prospects at future polls—party membership of some 50,000 in May 1945 rose to 1,220,000 in April 1946 and reached 1,310,000 in January 1948 (in a national population of just 12 million). The Communists were certainly not beyond using patronage and pressure to secure support. And, as elsewhere, they had taken the precaution of obtaining the vital ministries and placing their men in crucial positions within the police and elsewhere. But in anticipation of the elections of 1948 the homegrown Communists of Czechoslovakia were preparing to come to full power by a 'Czech road' that still looked quite different from those to the east.

Whether the Soviet leadership believed Gottwald's assurances that the Czechoslovak Communist Party would triumph unaided is unclear. But at least until the autumn of 1947 Stalin left Czechoslovakia alone. The Czechs had expelled the Sudeten Germans (which exposed them to German hostility and thus made their country even more dependent on Soviet protection) and the emphasis in

---

[3]The Agrarian Party in the Czech lands and its partner, the People's Party in Slovakia, were banned after the war for connivance with Nazi policies.

Beneš's post-war governments on economic planning, state ownership and hard work reminded at least one French journalist in May 1947 of the rhetoric and mood of early Soviet stakhanovism. Prague billboards carried portraits of Stalin alongside those of President Benes himself, long before the Communists had even established a government of their own, much less secured a monopoly of power. We have seen that Foreign Minister Jan Masaryk and his colleagues did not hesitate, in the summer of 1947, to decline Marshall Aid at Moscow's behest. Stalin, in short, had nothing to complain of in Czechoslovak behaviour.

Nevertheless, in February 1948 the Communists engineered a political coup in Prague, taking advantage of the imprudent resignation of non-Communist ministers (over an important but obscure issue of Communist infiltration of the police) to seize control of the country. The Prague coup was of enormous significance, precisely because it came in a more or less democratic country that had seemed so friendly to Moscow. It galvanized the Western allies, who inferred from it that Communism was on the march westwards.[4] It probably saved the Finns: thanks to the problems that the Czech coup caused him in Germany and elsewhere, Stalin was forced in April 1948 to compromise with Helsinki and sign a Friendship Treaty (having initially tried to impose on Finland an eastern-European solution by splitting the Social Democrats, forcing them to merge with the Communists in a 'Finnish People's Defense League'—and thus bringing the latter to power).

In the West, Prague awoke Socialists to the realities of political life in eastern Europe. On February 29th 1948 the ageing Léon Blum published in the French Socialist paper *Le Populaire* a hugely influential article, criticizing western Socialists' failure to speak out about the fate of their comrades in eastern Europe. Thanks to Prague, a significant part of the non-Communist Left in France, Italy and elsewhere would now firmly situate itself in the Western camp, a development that consigned Communist parties in countries beyond Soviet reach to isolation and growing impotence.

If Stalin engineered the Prague coup without fully anticipating these consequences, it was not just because he had always planned to enforce his writ in a certain way throughout the *bloc*. Nor was it because Czechoslovakia mattered much in the grand scheme of things. What happened in Prague—and what was happening at the same time in Germany, where Soviet policy was moving swiftly from stonewalling and disagreement to open confrontation with her former allies—was a return by Stalin to the style and strategy of an earlier era. This shift was driven in general terms by Stalin's anxiety at his inability to shape European and German affairs as he wished; but also and above all by his growing irritation with Yugoslavia.

---

[4]Western public opinion was also influenced by Masaryk's death on March 10th 1948—he was reported to have 'fallen' from his window into the courtyard of the Foreign Ministry. The exact circumstances of his death have never been elucidated.

. . .

In 1947, the Communist government in Yugoslavia under Josip Broz Tito had a unique status. Alone of the Communist parties in Europe, the Yugoslavs had come to power by their own efforts, depending neither on local allies nor foreign help. To be sure, the British in December 1943 had stopped sending aid to the rival Chetnik partisans and had swung their support behind Tito, and in the immediate postwar years the United Nations Relief and Rehabilitation Administration (UNRRA) spent more money (US$415 million) in aid to Yugoslavia than anywhere else in Europe, 72 percent of that money coming from the United States. But for contemporaries what mattered was that the Yugoslav Communist partisans had fought the only successful resistance war against the German and Italian occupiers.

Buoyed by their victory, Tito's Communists had no truck with coalitions of the kind being set up elsewhere in liberated eastern Europe and set about immediately destroying *all* their opponents. In the first post-war elections, in November 1945, voters were presented with an unambiguous choice: Tito's 'People's Front' . . . or an urn publicly labeled 'opposition'. In January 1946 the Communist Party of Yugoslavia introduced a constitution directly modeled on that of the USSR. Tito pressed forward with mass arrests, imprisonment and execution of his opponents, together with forced collectivization of the land, at a time when Communists in neighbouring Hungary and Romania were still carefully calibrating a more accommodating image. Yugoslavia, it seemed, was on the hard, cutting edge of European Communism.

On the surface, Yugoslav radicalism and the success of the Communist Party of Yugoslavia in taking firm control of a strategically crucial region appeared to Soviet advantage and relations between Moscow and Belgrade were warm. Moscow lavished unstinting praise on Tito and his party, evinced great enthusiasm for their revolutionary achievements and held Yugoslavia up as a model for others to emulate. The Yugoslav leaders in return took every occasion to insist on their respect for the Soviet Union; they saw themselves as introducing the Bolshevik model of revolution and government into the Balkans. As Milovan Djilas recalled, 'all of us were pre-disposed towards [the USSR] in spirit. And all of us would have remained devoted to it, but for its own Great Power standards of loyalty'.

But Yugoslav devotion to Bolshevism was, from Stalin's point of view, always a little *too* enthusiastic. Stalin, as we have already seen, was interested less in revolution than in power. It was for Moscow to determine the strategy of Communist parties, for Moscow to decide when a moderate approach was called for and when a radical line should be adopted. As the origin and fountainhead of world revolution, the Soviet Union was not *a* model for revolution but *the* model. Under the appropriate circumstances lesser Communist parties might follow suit, but they were ill advised to trump the Soviet hand. And this was Tito's besetting weakness in Stalin's eyes. In his ambition to plant the Communist standard in south-east Europe, the

Stalin's monopoly of power and a conflict was inevitable: Stalin needed to break Tito in order to make very clear to Tito's fellow Communists that Moscow would brook no dissent.

Tito, of course, was not broken. But both he and his country were more vulnerable than they seemed at the time, and without growing Western backing Tito would have been hard put to survive the Soviet economic boycott—in 1948 46 percent of Yugoslav trade was with the Soviet bloc, a figure that was reduced to 14 percent one year later—and credible threats of Soviet intervention. The Yugoslavs certainly paid a high rhetorical price for their opinionated actions. In the course of the next two years Cominform attacks were steadily ratcheted up. In the well-oiled lexicon of Leninist abuse, Tito became 'Judas Tito and his abettors', 'the new Czar of the Pan-Serbs and of the entire Yugoslav bourgeoisie'. His followers were 'despicable traitors and imperialist hirelings', 'sinister heralds of the camp of war and death, treacherous warmongers and worthy heirs of Hitler'. The Yugoslav Communist Party was condemned as a 'gang of spies, provocateurs and murderers', 'dogs tied to American leashes, gnawing imperialist bones and barking for American capital'.

It is significant that the attacks on Tito and his followers coincided with the full flowering of the Stalinist personality cult and the purges and show trials of the coming years. For there is little doubt that Stalin truly did see in Tito a threat and a challenge, and feared his corrosive effect on the fealty and obedience of other Communist regimes and parties. The Cominform's insistence, in its journals and publications, on the 'aggravation of the class struggle in the transition from capitalism to socialism' and on the 'leading role' of the Party risked reminding people that these had been precisely the policies of the Yugoslav Party since 1945. Hence the accompanying emphasis on loyalty to the Soviet Union and Stalin, the rejection of all 'national' or 'particular' roads to Socialism and the demand for a 're-doubling of vigilance'. The second Stalinist ice age was beginning.

If Stalin went to such trouble to assert and re-assert his authority in eastern Europe, it was in large measure because he was losing the initiative in Germany.[7] On June 1st 1948 the Western Allies, meeting in London, announced plans to establish a separate West German state. On June 18th a new currency, the *Deutsche Mark*, was announced; three days later it was placed in circulation (the banknotes had been printed in great secrecy in the US and transported to Frankfurt under US Army escort). The old *Reichsmark* was withdrawn, with every German resident entitled to exchange just forty of them for the new marks at a 1:1 ratio, thereafter at a ratio of 10:1. Initially unpopular (because it destroyed savings, pushed up real prices and

---

[7]It was no coincidence that Soviet advisers were withdrawn from Yugoslavia on March 18th 1948, just forty-eight hours before General Sokolovski walked out of the Allied Control Council meeting in Germany.

put goods beyond most people's reach) the currency was quickly accepted, as stores filled up with goods that farmers and traders were now willing to sell at fixed prices for a reliable medium of exchange.

On June 23rd, the Soviet authorities responded by issuing a new, East German *Mark* and cutting the rail lines linking Berlin to western Germany (three weeks later they would close the canals as well). The following day the Western military government in Berlin blocked Soviet efforts to extend the new Eastern zone currency to West Berlin—an important point of principle, since the city of Berlin was under four-power rule and the Western zone had not hitherto been treated as part of Soviet-occupied eastern Germany. As the Soviet troops tightened their control over surface connections into the city, the American and British governments decided upon an airlift to provision their own zones and on June 26th the first transport plane landed at Tempelhof airfield in (West) Berlin.

The Berlin airlift lasted until May 12th 1949. Over those eleven months the Western allies shipped some 2.3 million tons of food on 277,500 flights, at the cost of the lives of 73 Allied airmen. Stalin's purpose in blockading Berlin was to force the West to choose between quitting the city (taking advantage of the absence in the Potsdam protocols of any written guarantee of Allied surface access to it), or else abandoning their plans for a separate West German state. This was what Stalin really wanted—Berlin for him was always a negotiating chip—but in the end he secured neither objective.

Not only did the Western allies hang on to their share of Berlin (somewhat to their own surprise, and to the amazed gratitude of the—West—Berliners themselves), but the Soviet blockade, following hard on the Prague coup, only made them more determined to move ahead with plans for West Germany, just as it made a division of the country more acceptable to Germans themselves. France joined the Bizone in April 1949, creating a single West German economic unit of 49 million inhabitants (against just 17 million in the Soviet Zone)

Like most of Stalin's diplomatic adventures the Berlin blockade was an improvisation, not part of any calculated aggressive design (though the West could hardly be blamed for not knowing this at the time). Stalin was not about to go to war for Berlin.[8] Accordingly, when the blockade failed, the Soviet leader changed tack. On January 31st 1949 he publicly proposed lifting the blockade in exchange for a postponement of plans for a West German state. The Western allies had no intention of making any such concession, but it was agreed to convene a meeting to discuss the matter and on May 12th the Soviet Union ended the blockade in exchange for nothing more than a conference of Foreign Ministers scheduled for May 23rd.

The conference duly took place and lasted for a month, but predictably found

---

[8] Had he wished to do so, there was little practical impediment. In the spring of 1948 the Soviet Union had three hundred divisions within reach of Berlin. The US had only 60,000 soldiers in all of Europe, fewer than 7,000 of them in Berlin.

no common ground. Indeed it had only just begun when the West German parliamentary council in Bonn formally passed into effect the 'Basic Law' establishing
a West German government; a week later Stalin responded by announcing plans
for a complementary East German state, formally created on October 7th.[9] By the
time the conference broke up, on June 20th, the military government in West Germany had been replaced by High Commissioners from the US, Britain and France.
The Federal Republic of Germany had come into being, though the Allies reserved
certain powers of intervention and even the right to resume direct rule if they
judged it necessary. On September 15th 1949, following his Christian Democratic
Party's success at the elections a month earlier, Konrad Adenauer became the Republic's first Chancellor.

The Berlin crisis had three significant outcomes. In the first place, it led directly
to the creation of two German states, an outcome none of the Allies had sought four
years earlier. For the Western powers this had become an attractive and attainable
objective; indeed, for all the lip service thenceforth paid to the desirability of German unification, no-one would be in any hurry to see it happen. As the British
Prime Minister Harold Macmillan replied to President Charles De Gaulle nine
years later, when De Gaulle asked how he felt about a united Germany: 'In theory.
In theory we must always support reunification. There is no danger in that.' For
Stalin, once he appreciated that he could neither compete with the Allies for the
allegiance of the Germans nor force them to abandon their plans, a separate East
German Communist state was the least bad outcome.

Secondly, the Berlin crisis committed the United States for the first time to a significant military presence in Europe for the indefinite future. This was the achievement of Ernest Bevin, the British Foreign Minister—it was Bevin who successfully
urged the Americans to lead the airlift to Berlin, once Truman had been assured
by Marshall and General Clay (the US commander in Berlin) that the risk was
worth taking. The French were all the less involved in the Berlin crisis because
from July 18th to September 10th 1948 the country was in the midst of a political
crisis with no clear governing majority in the Assemblée Nationale.

But thirdly, and this followed from the first two, the Berlin crisis led directly to
a reappraisal of Western military calculations. If the West was going to protect its
German clients from Soviet aggression then it would need to give itself the means
to do so. The Americans had stationed strategic bombers in Britain at the start of
the Berlin crisis and these were equipped to carry atomic bombs, of which the US
had 56 at the time. But Washington had no established policy on the use of atomic
bombs (Truman himself was especially reluctant to consider using them) and in
the event of a Soviet advance US strategy in Europe still presumed a retreat from
the continent.

---

[9]The Basic Law was deliberately *provisional*—'to give a new order to political life for a transitional period': i.e. until the country was reunited.

Central and Eastern Europe after World War Two

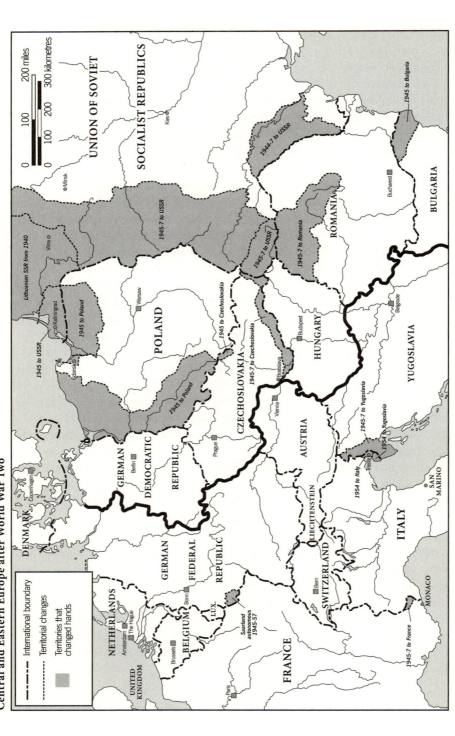

Legend:
- — · — · International boundary
- ·········· Territorial changes
- ▨ Territories that changed hands

Scale:
- 0 100 200 miles
- 0 100 200 300 kilometres

UNION OF SOVIET SOCIALIST REPUBLICS

DENMARK
Copenhagen

NETHERLANDS
Amsterdam
The Hague

UNITED KINGDOM

BELGIUM
Brussels

LUX.

GERMAN FEDERAL REPUBLIC
Bonn

Saarland autonomous 1945–57

FRANCE
Paris

1945–7 to France

GERMAN DEMOCRATIC REPUBLIC
Berlin

Prague

POLAND
Warsaw
Gdansk
Kaliningrad

1945 to USSR
1945 to Poland
1945 to Poland

Lithuanian SSR from 1940
Vilna

Mirsk

Kiev

1945–7 to USSR

1944–7 to USSR

CZECHOSLOVAKIA
1945 to Czechoslovakia
1945–7 to Czechoslovakia
Bratislava

1945–7 to USSR

HUNGARY
Budapest

ROMANIA
Bucharest

1945–7 to Romania

BULGARIA
1945 to Bulgaria

AUSTRIA
Vienna

LIECHTENSTEIN

SWITZERLAND
Bern

ITALY

SAN MARINO

MONACO

YUGOSLAVIA
Belgrade

1945–7 to Yugoslavia
1954 Italy
Trieste
1954 to Yugoslavia
1954 Italy

The military rethinking began with the Czech coup. In its aftermath Europe entered a period of heightened insecurity, with much talk of war. Even General Clay, not typically given to hyperbole, shared the prevailing fear: 'For many months, based on logical analysis, I have felt and held that war was unlikely for at least ten years. Within the last few weeks I have felt a subtle change in Soviet attitude which I cannot define, but which now gives me a feeling it may come with dramatic suddenness.' It was in this atmosphere that the US Congress passed the Marshall Plan legislation and the European allies signed the Brussels Pact, on March 17th 1948. The Brussels Pact, however, was a conventional 50-Year Treaty binding Britain, France and the Benelux countries to 'collaborate in measures of mutual assistance in the event of a renewal of German aggression', whereas European politicians were becoming markedly more aware of their helpless exposure to *Soviet* pressure. In this respect they were as vulnerable as ever: as Dirk Stikker, the Dutch Foreign Minister, would note in retrospect, 'We in Europe had only a verbal pledge from President Truman of American support.'

It was the British who initiated a new approach to Washington. In a speech to Parliament on January 22nd 1948, Bevin had committed Britain to engagement with her continental neighbours in a common defense strategy, a 'Western European Union', on the grounds that British security needs were no longer separable from those of the continent—a significant break with past British thinking. This western European Union was officially inaugurated with the Brussels Pact, but as Bevin explained to Marshall in a message of March 11th, such an arrangement would be incomplete unless extended to the concept of North Atlantic security as a whole—a point to which Marshall was all the more sympathetic because Stalin was just then applying considerable pressure on Norway to get it to sign a 'non-aggression' pact with the Soviet Union.

At Bevin's urging, then, secret discussions took place in Washington between British, US and Canadian representatives to draft a treaty for Atlantic defense. On July 6th 1948, ten days after the start of the Berlin airlift and immediately following Yugoslavia's expulsion from the Cominform, these talks were opened to other members of the Brussels Pact, among whom the French were not well pleased to discover that once again the 'Anglo-Americans' had been arranging the world behind their back. By April of the following year the North Atlantic Treaty Organisation (NATO) had been agreed and signed by the US, Canada, and ten European states.

NATO was a remarkable development. As late as 1947 few would have predicted that the United States would commit itself to a European military alliance. Indeed, there were many in the US Congress who were notably reluctant to approve Article V of the Treaty (which bound NATO members to come to one another's aid if attacked), and the Treaty only secured Congressional approval, after three months of discussion, because it was represented as an *Atlantic* defense pact, rather than a Euro-American alliance. Indeed, when Dean Acheson presented the Administration's case before the Senate, he took care to insist that America would *not* be deploying substantial ground forces in Europe.

And this was indeed the American intention. If the United States was committing itself to an entangling European alliance for the first time, it was because many people in Washington saw NATO much as they saw the Marshall Plan: as a device to help Europeans feel better about themselves and manage their own affairs—in this case, their own defense. In itself, NATO changed nothing in the European military balance: of the fourteen divisions stationed in Western Europe, only two were American. The Western allies were still outnumbered on the ground 12:1. The US Chiefs of Staff in 1949 calculated that it would be 1957 at the earliest before an effective defense on the Rhine could be mounted. It was by no means inappropriate that at the NATO Treaty-signing ceremony in Constitutional Hall, Washington, on April 9th 1949, the band played 'I've Got Plenty of Nothing . . .'.

Nevertheless, things looked rather different from the European side. The Americans did not ascribe much significance to military alliances; but Europeans, as Walter Bedell Smith advised his colleagues on the State Department Policy Planning Staff, 'do attach far more importance to the scrap of paper pledging support than we ever have.' This was not perhaps altogether surprising—they had nothing else. The British, at least, were still an island. But the French, like everyone else, were as vulnerable as ever: to the Germans *and* now to the Russians as well.

NATO thus had a double attraction for Paris especially: it would place the line of defense against Soviet forces further east than hitherto—as Charles Bohlen had observed, some months before the Treaty was signed, 'the one faint element of confidence which [the French] cling to is the fact that American troops, however strong in number, stand between them and the Red Army.' And perhaps more important, it would serve as a reinsurance policy against German revanchism. Indeed it was only because of the promise of NATO protection that the French government, with the outcome of World War One still firmly in mind, conceded its approval for a West German state.

The French thus welcomed NATO as the guarantee against a revived Germany that they had been unable to obtain by diplomatic means in the previous three years. The Dutch and Belgians also saw in NATO an impediment to future German revanchism. The Italians were included to help shore up Alcide De Gasperi's domestic support against Communist critics. The British regarded the NATO Treaty as a signal achievement in their struggle to keep the US engaged in Europe's defense. And the Truman Administration sold the agreement to Congress and the American people as a barrier to Soviet aggression in the North Atlantic. Hence the famous *bon mot* of Lord Ismay, who took up his post as NATO's first Secretary General in 1952: the purpose of the North Atlantic Treaty Organization was 'to keep the Russians out, the Americans in and the Germans down.'

NATO was a bluff. As Denis Healey, a future British defense minister, observed in his memoirs, 'for most of the Europeans, NATO was worthless unless it could prevent another war; they were not interested in fighting one'. The originality of the Treaty lay not so much in what it could achieve but in what it represented: like the Marshall Plan—and the Brussels Treaty from which it sprang—NATO illustrated the most significant change that had come over Europe (and the US) as a result of the war—a willingness to share information and cooperate in defense, security, trade, currency regulations and much else. An integrated Allied command in peacetime, after all, was an unheard of departure from practice.

But NATO did not leap fully formed from the agreements of 1949. In the spring of 1950 Washington was still worrying about how to explain to the French and other Europeans that the only realistic hope for West European defense was to rearm Germany, a subject that made everyone uneasy and was thought likely to provoke an unpredictable response from Stalin. In any case, no-one wanted to spend precious resources on rearmament. The appeal of neutrality—as an alternative to defenseless confrontation—was growing, in Germany and France alike. If the Korean War had not broken out just at this moment (a reasonable counter-factual, since it nearly didn't) the contours of recent European history might look very different indeed.

Stalin's support for Kim Il Sung's invasion of South Korea on June 25th 1950 was his most serious miscalculation of all. The Americans and West Europeans immediately drew the (erroneous) conclusion that Korea was a diversion or prelude, and that Germany would be next—an inference encouraged by Walter Ulbricht's imprudent boast that the Federal Republic would be next to fall. The Soviet Union had successfully tested an atomic bomb just eight months earlier, leading American military experts to exaggerate Soviet preparedness for war; but even so, the budget increases requested in National Security Council paper #68 (presented on April 7th 1950) would almost certainly not have been approved but for the Korean attack.

The risk of a European war was greatly exaggerated, but not completely absent. Stalin *was* contemplating a possible assault—on Yugoslavia, not West Germany—but abandoned the idea in the face of Western rearmament. And just as the West misread the Soviet purpose in Korea, so Stalin—accurately advised by his intelligence services of the rapid US military build-up that followed—mistakenly assumed that the Americans had aggressive designs of their own on his sphere of control in eastern Europe. But none of these assumptions and miscalculations was clear at the time, and politicians and generals proceeded as best they could on the basis of limited information and past precedent.

The scale of Western rearmament was dramatic indeed. The US defense budget rose from $15.5 billion in August 1950 to $70 billion by December of the following year, following President Truman's declaration of a National Emergency. By 1952–53 defense expenditure consumed 17.8 percent of the US GNP, compared with just 4.7 percent in 1949. In response to Washington's request, America's allies in NATO also increased their defense spending: after falling steadily since 1946, British defense costs rose to nearly 10 percent of GNP in 1951–52, growing even faster than in the hectic rearmament of the immediate pre-war years. France, too, increased defense spending to comparable levels. In every NATO member state, defense spending increased to a post-war peak in the years 1951–53.

The economic impact of this sudden leap in military investment was equally unprecedented. Germany especially was flooded with orders for machinery, tools, vehicles and other products that the Federal Republic was uniquely well-placed to supply, all the more so because the West Germans were forbidden to manufacture arms and could thus concentrate on everything else. West German steel output alone, 2.5 million tonnes in 1946 and 9 million tonnes in 1949, grew to nearly 15 million tonnes by 1953. The dollar deficit with Europe and the rest of the world fell by 65 percent in the course of a single year, as the United States spent huge sums overseas on arms, equipment stockpiles, military emplacements and troops. FIAT in Turin got its first American contracts, for ground-support jet aircraft (a contract urged upon Washington for political reasons by its Rome embassy).

But the economic news was not all good. The British government was forced to divert public expenditure away from welfare services to meet its defense commitments, a choice that split the governing Labour Party and helped bring about its defeat at the elections of 1951. The cost of living in West Europe went up as government spending fuelled inflation—in France consumer prices rose 40 percent in the two years following the outbreak of war in Korea. The West Europeans, who had only just begun to reap the benefits of Marshall Aid, were clearly in no condition to sustain for very long what amounted to a war economy and the 1951 US Mutual Security Act recognized this, effectively closing out the Marshall Plan and transforming it into a programme of military assistance. By the end of 1951 the US was transferring nearly $5 billion of military support to Western Europe.

From a psychological boost to European confidence, NATO thus became a major military commitment, drawing on the seemingly limitless resources of the US economy and committing the Americans and their allies to an unprecedented peacetime build up of men and matériel. General Eisenhower returned to Europe as Supreme Allied Commander and Allied military headquarters and administrative facilities were established in Belgium and France. The North Atlantic Treaty Organisation was now, unambiguously, an *alliance*. Its primary task was what military planners called the 'forward defense' of Europe: i.e. confrontation with the Red Army in the middle of Germany. To perform this role, it was agreed at the NATO Council meeting in Lisbon in February 1952 that the alliance would need to raise at least ninety-six new divisions within two years.

But even with a significant and ever-growing American military presence there was only one way in which NATO could meet its targets: by rearming the West Germans. Thanks to Korea the Americans had felt obliged to bring up this sensitive matter (Dean Acheson first raised it formally at a Foreign Ministers' meeting in September 1950), even though President Truman himself was initially reluctant. On the one hand no-one wanted to put weapons in the hands of Germans just five years after the liberation of Europe; on the other hand, and on the analogy of the economic difficulties of the Bizone just three years previous, there was something perverse about spending billions of dollars to defend the West Germans from Russian attack without asking them to make a contribution of their own. And if Germany was to become, as some anticipated, a sort of buffer zone and future battlefield, then the risk of alienating German sympathies and encouraging neutralist sentiments could not be ignored.

Moscow, of course, would not take kindly to West German rearmament. But after June 1950 Soviet sensibilities were no longer a prime consideration. The British, however reluctantly, saw no option but to find some device for arming Germany while keeping it firmly under Allied control. It was the *French* who had always been most firmly opposed to putting weapons in German hands, and France had certainly not joined NATO just to see it become an umbrella for German re-militarisation. France managed to block and postpone the rearmament of Germany until 1954. But long before then French policy had been undergoing a signal transformation, allowing Paris to accept with some equanimity a limited restoration of Germany. Unhappy and frustrated at being reduced to the least of the great powers, France had embarked upon a novel vocation as the initiator of a new Europe.

The idea of European union, in one form or another, was not new. The nineteenth century had seen a variety of more or less unsuccessful customs unions in central and western Europe and even before World War One there had been occasional idealistic talk, drawing on the idea that Europe's future lay in a coming together of its disparate parts. World War One itself, far from dissipating such optimistic visions, seems to have given them greater force: as Aristide Briand—the French statesman and himself an enthusiastic author of European pacts and proposals—insisted, the time had come to overcome past rivalries and think European, speak European, feel European. In 1924 the French economist Charles Gide joined other signatories across Europe in launching an International Committee for a European Customs Union. Three years later a junior minister in the British Foreign Office would profess himself 'astonished' at the extent of continental interest in the 'pan-European' idea.

More prosaically, the Great War had brought French and Germans, in a curious way, to a better appreciation of their mutual dependence. Once the post-war disruption had subsided and Paris had abandoned its fruitless efforts to extract German reparations by force, an international Steel Pact was signed, in September 1926, by France, Germany, Luxembourg, Belgium and the (then autonomous) region of the Saar, to regulate steel production and prevent excess capacity. Although the Pact was joined the following year by Czechoslovakia, Austria and Hungary, it was only ever a cartel of the traditional kind; but the German Prime Minister Gustav Stresemann certainly saw in it the embryonic shape of future trans-national accords. He was not alone.

Like other ambitious projects of the 1920s, the Steel Pact barely survived the 1929 crisis and ensuing depression. But it recognized what was already clear to French ironmasters in 1919: that France's steel industry, once it had doubled in size as a result of the return of Alsace-Lorraine, would be utterly dependent on coke and coal from Germany and would therefore need to find a basis for long-term collaboration. The situation was equally obvious to Germans, and when the Nazis occupied France in 1940 and reached agreement with Pétain on a system of payments and deliveries amounting to the forced application of French resources to the German war effort, there were nevertheless many on both sides who saw in this latest Franco-German 'collaboration' the germ of a new 'European' economic order.

Thus Pierre Pucheu, a senior Vichy administrator later to be executed by the Free French, envisaged a post-war European order where customs barriers would be eliminated and a single European economy would encompass the whole continent, with a single currency. Pucheu's vision—which was shared by Albert Speer and many others—represented a sort of updating of Napoleon's Continental System under Hitlerian auspices, and it appealed to a younger generation of continental bureaucrats and technicians who had experienced the frustrations of economic policy making in the 1930s.

What made such projects especially seductive was that they were typically presented in terms of a shared, pan-European interest, rather than as self-interested projections of separate national agendas. They were 'European' rather than German or French, and they were much admired during the war by those who wanted desperately to believe that some good might come out of the Nazi occupation. The fact that the Nazis themselves had apparently unified much of Europe in a technical sense—removing frontiers, expropriating property, integrating transportation networks and so forth—made the idea even more plausible. And the attraction of a Europe liberated from its past and its mutual antagonisms was not lost abroad, either. Four years after Nazism's defeat, in October 1949, George Kennan would confess to Dean Acheson that while he could understand apprehension at Germany's growing importance in Western European affairs, 'it often seemed to me, during the war living over there, that what was wrong with Hitler's new order was that it was Hitler's.'

Kennan's remark was made in private. In public, after 1945, few were willing to say a good word about the wartime New Order—whose inefficiency and bad faith Kennan rather underestimated. The case for intra-European economic cooperation was of course undiminished—Jean Monnet, for example, continued to believe after the war as he had in 1943 that to enjoy 'prosperity and social progress . . . the states of Europe must form . . . a 'European entity', which will make them a single unit'. And there were enthusiasts for the 'Movement for European Unity' formed in January 1947 at Churchill's instigation.

Winston Churchill had been an early and influential advocate of a European assembly of some kind. On October 21st 1942 he wrote to Anthony Eden: 'I must admit that my thoughts rest primarily in Europe, in the revival of the glory of Europe . . . it would be a measureless disaster if Russian bolshevism overlaid the culture and independence of the ancient states of Europe. Hard as it is to say now, I trust that the European family may act unitedly as one, under a Council of Europe.' But the post-war political circumstances seemed unpropitious for such ideals. The best that might be expected was the creation of a sort of forum for European conversation, which is what a May 1948 Congress of the European Unity Movement in The Hague proposed. The 'Council of Europe' which grew out of this suggestion was inaugurated in Strasbourg in May 1949 and held its first meeting there in August of that year; delegates from Britain, Ireland, France, the Benelux countries, Italy, Sweden, Denmark and Norway took part.

The Council had no power and no authority; no legal, legislative or executive status. Its 'delegates' represented no-one. Its most important asset was the mere fact of its existence, though in November 1950 it issued a 'European Convention on Human Rights' that would assume greater significance in decades to come. As Churchill himself had recognized, in a speech given in Zurich on September 19th 1946, 'The first step in the re-creation of the European family must be a partnership between France and Germany.' But in those first post-war years the French, as we have seen, were in no mood to envisage such a partnership.

Their small neighbours to the north were moving rather faster, however. Even before the war ended the exiled governments of Belgium, Luxembourg and the Netherlands signed the 'Benelux Agreement', eliminating tariff barriers and looking forward to the eventual free movement of labour, capital and services between their countries. The Benelux Customs Union came into effect on January 1st 1948, and there followed desultory conversations between the Benelux countries, France and Italy over projects to extend such cooperation across a larger space. But these half-formed projects for a 'Little Europe' all came to grief on the shoals of the German problem.

Everyone agreed, as the Marshall Plan negotiators in Paris in July 1947 concluded, that the 'German economy should be integrated into the economy of Europe in such a way as to contribute to a raising of the general standard of life.' The question was how? Western Germany, even after it became a state in 1949, had no organic links to the rest of the continent except via the mechanisms of the Marshall Plan and the Allied occupation—both of them temporary. Most Western Europeans still thought of Germany as a threat, not a partner. The Dutch had always been economically dependent on Germany—48 percent of Dutch 'invisible' earnings before 1939 came from German trade passing through the harbours and waterways of the Netherlands—and Germany's economic revival was vital for them. But in 1947 only 29 percent of the Dutch population had a 'friendly' view of Germans and for the Netherlands it was important that an economically revived Germany be politically and militarily weak. This view was heartily endorsed in Belgium. Neither country could envisage an accommodation with Germany unless it was balanced by the reassuring involvement of Great Britain.

The deadlock was broken by the international events of 1948–49. With the Prague coup, the agreement on a West German state, the Berlin blockade and the plans for NATO it became clear to French statesmen like Georges Bidault and Robert Schuman that France must re-think its approach to Germany. There was now to be a West German political entity including the Ruhr and the Rhineland—only the tiny Saarland had been temporarily separated from the main body of Germany, and the coal of the Saar region was not suitable for coking. How were the resources of this new Federal Republic to be both contained and yet mobilized to French advantage?

On October 30th 1949, Dean Acheson appealed to Schuman for France to take the initiative in incorporating the new West German state into European affairs. The French were well aware of the need to do *something*—as Jean Monnet would later remind Georges Bidault, the US would surely encourage a newly-independent West Germany to increase its steel production, at which point it might well flood the market, force France to protect its own steel industry and thus trigger a retreat to trade wars. As we saw in Chapter Three, Monnet's own plan—and with it the revival of France—depended upon a successful resolution of this dilemma.

It was in these circumstances that Jean Monnet proposed to France's Foreign Minister what became known to history as the 'Schuman Plan'. This constituted a genuine diplomatic revolution, albeit one that had been five years in the making. In essence it was very simple. In Schuman's words, 'The French government proposes that the entire French-German coal and steel production be placed under a joint High Authority within the framework of an organization which would also be open to the participation of the other countries of Europe.' More than a coal and steel cartel, but far, far less than a blueprint for European integration, Schuman's proposal represented a practical solution to the problem that had vexed France since 1945. In Schuman's scheme the High Authority would have the power to encourage competition, set pricing policy, direct investment and buy and sell on behalf of participating countries. But above all it would take control of the Ruhr and other vital German resources out of purely German hands. It represented a European solution to a—*the*—French problem.

Robert Schuman announced his Plan on May 9th 1950, informing Dean Acheson the day before. The British received no advance notice. The Quai d'Orsay took a certain sweet pleasure in this: the first of many small retaliations for Anglo-American decisions taken without consulting Paris. The most recent of these had been Britain's unilateral devaluation of the pound sterling by 30 percent just eight months before, when only the Americans had been pre-advised and the rest of Europe had been obliged to follow suit.[10] Ironically, it was this reminder of the risks of renewed economic self-interest and non-communication among European states that had prompted Monnet and others to think their way forward to the solution they were now proposing

The German government immediately welcomed Schuman's proposal, as well they might: in Konrad Adenauer's delighted reply to Schuman he declared that 'this plan of the French government has given the relations between our two countries, which threatened to be paralysed by mistrust and reserve, a fresh impetus towards constructive cooperation.' Or, as he put it more bluntly to his aides: '*Das ist unser Durchbruch*'—this is our breakthrough. For the first time the Federal Republic of Germany was entering an international organization on equal terms with other independent states—and would now be bound to the Western alliance, as Adenauer wished.

The Germans were the first to ratify the Schuman Plan. Italy and the Benelux countries followed suit, though the Dutch were at first reluctant to commit themselves without the British. But the British declined Schuman's invitation and without Britain there was no question of the Scandinavians signing on. So it was just six West European states that signed the April 1951 Paris Treaty founding the European Coal and Steel Community (ECSC).

It is perhaps worth pausing to remark on a feature of the Community which did not escape notice at the time. All six foreign ministers who signed the Treaty in 1951 were members of their respective Christian Democratic parties. The three dominant statesmen in the main member states—Alcide De Gasperi, Konrad Adenauer and Robert Schuman—were all from the margins of their countries: De Gasperi from the Trentino, in north-east Italy; Adenauer from the Rhineland; Schuman from Lorraine. When De Gasperi was born—and well into his adult life—the Trentino was part of the Austro-Hungarian Empire and he studied in Vienna. Schuman grew up in a Lorraine that had been incorporated into the German Empire. As a young man, like Adenauer, he joined Catholic associations—indeed the same ones that the Rhinelander had belonged to ten years earlier. When they met, the three men conversed in German, their common language.

For all three, as for their Christian Democrat colleagues from bi-lingual Luxembourg, bi-lingual and bi-cultural Belgium, and the Netherlands, a project for European cooperation made cultural as well as economic sense: they could reasonably see it as a contribution to overcoming the crisis of civilization that had shattered the cosmopolitan Europe of their youth. Hailing from the fringes of their own countries, where identities had long been multiple and boundaries fungible, Schu-

---

[10]The French Finance Minister Henri Queuille complained to the US Ambassador to France of Britain's 'complete lack of loyalty.'

man and his colleagues were not especially troubled at the prospect of some merging of national sovereignty. All six member countries of the new ECSC had only recently seen their sovereignty ignored and trampled on, in war and occupation: they had little enough sovereignty left to lose. And their common Christian Democratic concern for social cohesion and collective responsibility disposed all of them to feel comfortable with the notion of a trans-national 'High Authority' exercising executive power for the common good.

But further north, the prospect was rather different. In the Protestant lands of Scandinavia and Britain (or to the Protestant perspective of a North German like Schumacher), the European Coal and Steel Community carried a certain whiff of authoritarian incense. Tage Erlander, the Swedish Social Democratic Prime Minister from 1948–68, actually ascribed his own ambivalence about joining to the overwhelming Catholic majority in the new Community. Kenneth Younger, a senior adviser to Bevin, noted in his diary entry for May 14th 1950—five days after learning of the Schuman Plan—that while he generally favoured European economic integration the new proposals might 'on the other hand, . . . be just a step in the consolidation of the Catholic 'black international' which I have always thought to be a big driving force behind the Council of Europe.' At the time this was not an extreme point of view, nor was it uncommon.

The ECSC was not a 'black international'. It was not really even a particularly effective economic lever, since the High Authority never did exercise the kind of power Monnet intended. Instead, like so many of the other international institutional innovations of these years, it provided the psychological space for Europe to move forward with a renewed self-confidence. As Adenauer explained to Macmillan ten years later, the ECSC was not really even an economic organization at all (and Britain, in his view, had thus been right to stand aside from it). It was not a project for European integration, Monnet's flights of fantasy notwithstanding, but rather the lowest common denominator of West European mutual interest at the time of its signing. It was a political vehicle in economic disguise, a device for overcoming Franco-German hostility.

Meanwhile, the problems that the European Coal and Steel Community was designed to address began to resolve themselves. In the last quarter of 1949 the Federal Republic of Germany regained the industrial output levels of 1936; by the end of 1950 it had surpassed them by one-third. In 1949 West Germany's trade balance with Europe was based on the export of raw materials (essentially coal). A year later, in 1950, that trade balance was negative, as Germany was consuming its own raw materials to fuel local industry. By 1951 the balance was once again positive and would stay so for many years to come, thanks to the German export of *manufactured* goods. By the end of 1951 German exports had grown to over six times the level of 1948 and German coal, finished goods and trade were fuelling a European economic renaissance—indeed by the late Fifties western Europe was suffering the effects of a glut of coal. How much of this can be attributed to the ECSC is a matter of some doubt—it was Korea, not Schuman, that sent the West German industrial machine into high gear. But in the end it did not much matter.

If the European Coal and Steel Community was so much less than was claimed for it—if the French commitment to supranational organisms was simply a device to control a Germany that they continued to distrust, and if the European economic boom owed little to the actions of a High Authority whose impact on competition, employment and prices was minimal—why, then, did the British refuse to join it? And why did it seem to matter so much that they stood apart?

The British had nothing against a European customs union—they were quite in favour of one, at least for other Europeans. What made them uncomfortable was the idea of a supranational executive implied in the institution of a High Authority, even if it only directed the production and pricing of two commodities. London had been clear about this for some time—in 1948, when Bevin discussed with the Labour Cabinet American proposals for a future Organisation for European Economic Cooperation, his main concern was that 'effective control should be in the hands of the national delegations . . . to prevent the secretariat (or an 'independent' chairman) from taking action on its own . . . There should be no question of instructions being given by the organization to individual members.'

This British reluctance to relinquish any national control was obviously incompatible with Monnet's purpose in the ECSC. But the British saw the ECSC as the thin edge of a continental wedge in British affairs, whose implications were the more dangerous for being unclear. As Bevin explained to Acheson when justifying Britain's refusal to join, 'Where matters of such vital importance are at stake we cannot buy a pig in a poke, and [I am] pretty sure that if the Americans had been placed in a similar position they would have thought the same.' Or, as he put it more colourfully to his aides when expressing his misgivings over the Council of Europe: 'If you open that Pandora's Box, you never know what Trojan 'orses will jump out'.

Some of the British reasoning was economic. The British economy—particularly that part of it which relied on trade—appeared in far healthier condition than that of its continental neighbours. In 1947 British exports represented, by value, the sum of the exports of France, Italy, western Germany, the Benelux countries, Norway and Denmark combined. Whereas western European states at that time traded chiefly with one another, Britain had extensive commerce with the whole world—indeed, Britain's trade with Europe in 1950 was much *less* than it had been in 1913.

In the eyes of British officials, therefore, the country had more to lose than to gain by committing itself to participation in binding economic arrangements with countries whose prospects looked very uncertain. A year before Schuman's proposal, the UK position, expressed in private by senior civil servants, was that 'there is no attraction for us in long-term economic cooperation with Europe. At best it will be a drain on our resources. At worst it can seriously damage our economy.'

To which should be added the Labour Party's particular anxiety at joining continental arrangements of a kind that might limit its freedom to pursue 'socialist' policies at home, policies closely tied to the corporate interests of the old industrial unions who had founded the Labour Party fifty years earlier: as acting Prime Minister Herbert Morrison explained to the Cabinet in 1950, when Schuman's invitation was (briefly) considered: 'It's no good, we can't do it, the Durham Miners won't wear it.'

And then there was the Commonwealth. In 1950 the British Commonwealth covered large tracts of Africa, South Asia, Australasia and the Americas, much of it still in British hands. Colonial territories from Malaya to the Gold Coast (Ghana) were net dollar earners and kept significant sums in London—the notorious 'sterling balances'. The Commonwealth was a major source of raw materials and food, and the Commonwealth (or Empire as most people still referred to it) was integral to British national identity, or so it seemed at the time. To most policymakers it was obviously imprudent—as well as practically impossible—to make Britain part of any continental European system that would cut the country off from this other dimension of its very existence.

Britain, then, was part of Europe but also part of a world-wide Anglophone imperial community. And it had a very particular relationship with the United States. The British people tended to be ambivalent about America—perceiving it from afar as a 'paradise of consumer splendours' (Malcolm Bradbury) in contrast to their own constricted lives, but resenting it for just that reason. Their governments, however, continued to profess faith in what would later be called the 'special relationship' between the two countries. In some degree this derived from Britain's presence at the wartime 'top table', as one of the three Great Powers at Yalta and Potsdam, and as the third nuclear Power following the successful test of a British bomb in 1952. It drew, too, on the close collaboration between the two countries during the war itself. And it rested, a little, on the peculiarly English sense of superiority towards the country that had displaced them at the imperial apex.[11]

The Americans were frustrated by the UK's reluctance to merge its fate with Europe and irritated by Britain's insistence upon preserving its imperial standing. However, there was more to London's stance in 1950 than imperial self-delusion or bloody-mindedness. Britain, as Jean Monnet would later acknowledge in his memoirs, had not been invaded or occupied: 'she felt no need to exorcise history.' The British experienced World War Two as a moment of national reconciliation and rallying together, rather than as a corrosive rent in the fabric of the state and nation,

---

[11] A point of view nicely captured in lines anonymously penned during the negotiations on Britain's postwar loan:

> 'In Washington Lord Halifax
> Once whispered to Lord Keynes:
> "It's true they have the moneybags
> But *we* have all the brains."'

which was how it was remembered across the Channel. In France the war had revealed everything that was wrong with the nation's political culture; in Britain, it had seemed to confirm everything that was right and good about national institutions and habits. World War Two, for most Britons, had been fought between Germany and Great Britain and the British had emerged triumphant and vindicated.[12]

This sense of quiet pride at the country's capacity to suffer, endure and win through had marked Britain off from the continent. It also shaped the political culture of the post-war years. In the elections of 1945 Labour won a clear parliamentary majority for the first time in its history and, as we have seen, pressed through a broad range of nationalizations and social reforms culminating in the constitution of the world's first universal welfare state. The government's reforms were mostly popular—in spite of prompting remarkably little change in the deepest habits and affinities of the nation. In the words of J.B. Priestley, writing in the *New Statesman* in July 1949, 'We are a Socialist Monarchy that is really the last monument of Liberalism.'

Domestic politics in post-war Britain were taken up with matters of social justice and the institutional reforms it required. This was to a considerable degree the result of a cumulative failure on the part of previous governments to address social inequalities; the belated re-centering of debate around urgently needed public expenditure—on health, education, transport, housing, pensions and the like—seemed to many to constitute a well-earned reward for the country's recent sacrifices. But it also meant that most British voters (and many British Members of Parliament) had absolutely no idea of how poor their country was and what it had cost them to win their epic struggle with Germany.

In 1945 Britain was insolvent. The British mobilized more completely, and for longer than any other country: in 1945 10 million men and women were under arms or making them, in an employed population of 21.5 million adults. Rather than tailor the British war effort to the country's limited means, Winston Churchill had gone for broke: borrowing from the Americans and selling British overseas assets to keep money and matériel flowing. As one wartime Chancellor of the Exchequer put it, these years saw 'England's transition from a position of the world's largest creditor nation to the world's largest debtor nation.' The cost of World War Two to Britain was twice that of World War One; the country lost one quarter of its national wealth.

This accounts for Britain's recurrent post-war currency crises, as the country struggled to pay off huge dollar-denominated debts from a drastically reduced income. That is one reason why the Marshall Plan in Britain had almost no impact upon investment or modernization in industry: 97 percent of the counterpart

---

[12]Germans understandably did *not* remember the war in this light and would be mystified in decades to come when subjected to English football supporters' chants and British tabloid newspaper headlines referring to 'Huns', 'Krauts' and the like.

funds (more than anywhere else) were used to pay off the country's massive debt. These problems would have been bad enough for any medium-sized European country in Britain's straitened post-war circumstances; they were hugely exacerbated in this case by the global scale of British imperial responsibilities.

The cost to Britain of remaining a Great Power had greatly increased since 1939. The country's expenditure on all military and diplomatic activity in the years 1934–38 was £6 million per annum. In 1947, on military expenditure alone, the government budgeted £209 million. In July 1950, on the eve of the Korean War— i.e. *before* the increase in defense spending that followed the outbreak of war— Britain had a full naval fleet in the Atlantic, another in the Mediterranean and a third in the Indian Ocean, as well as a permanent 'China station'. The country maintained 120 Royal Air Force squadrons worldwide and had armies or parts of armies permanently based in: Hong Kong, Malaya, the Persian Gulf and North Africa, Trieste and Austria, West Germany and the United Kingdom itself. In addition there was a large and expensive diplomatic, consular and intelligence establishment spread worldwide, together with the colonial civil service, a significant bureaucratic and administrative burden in its own right even though it had recently been reduced by Britain's departure from India.

The only way for the country to pay its way in these overstretched circumstances was for the British to impose on themselves unprecedented conditions of restraint and voluntary penury—which accounts for the much remarked upon feature of these years: that proud, victorious Great Britain seemed somehow tighter, poorer, grayer and grimmer than any of the erstwhile defeated, occupied and ravished lands across the water. Everything was rationed, restricted, controlled. The editor and essayist Cyril Connolly, admittedly a pessimistic soul at the best of times, nonetheless captured the mood of the times all too well in a comparison between America and Britain in April 1947:

'Here the ego is at half-pressure; most of us are not men and women but members of a vast, seedy, overworked, over-legislated neuter class, with our drab clothes, our ration books and murder stories, our envious, strict, old-world apathies—a care-worn people. And the symbol of this mood is London, now the largest, saddest and dirtiest of great cities, with its miles of unpainted, half-inhabited houses, its chopless chop-houses, its beerless pubs, its once vivid quarters losing all personality, its squares bereft of elegance . . . its crowds mooning around the stained green wicker of the cafeterias in their shabby raincoats, under a sky permanently dull and lowering like a metal dish-cover.'

This was the age of austerity. In order to increase the country's exports (and thus earn vital foreign currency) almost anything was either rationed or simply unavailable: meat, sugar, clothes, cars, gasoline, foreign travel, even sweets. Bread rationing, never imposed during the war, was introduced in 1946 and not abandoned until July 1948. The government ostentatiously celebrated a 'bonfire of controls' on November 5th 1949; but many of those same controls had to be re-imposed with the belt-tightening of the Korean War, and basic food rationing in Britain only ended in 1954—long after the rest of western Europe. Street scenes in post-war Britain would have been familiar to citizens in the Soviet bloc—in the words of one English housewife, recalling these years, 'It was queues for everything, you know, even if you didn't know what you were queuing for . . . you joined it because you knew there was something at the end of it.'

The British proved remarkably tolerant of their deprivations—in part because of a belief that these were, at least, shared fairly across the community—although the accumulated frustration with rations and regulations, and a certain air of puritanical paternalism that clung to some Labour ministers (notably the Chancellor of the Exchequer, Sir Stafford Cripps), contributed to Conservative electoral recovery in the 1950s. The sense that there was no choice and that the government knew best made the first generation of post-war England, in novelist David Lodge's recollections of his youth, 'cautious, unassertive, grateful for small mercies and modest in our ambition,' in marked contrast to the generation that would succeed them. And the mercies did not seem so very small. As Sam Watson, the veteran leader of the Durham miners union, reminded the Labour Party's annual conference in 1950: 'Poverty has been abolished. Hunger is unknown. The sick are tended. The old folks are cherished, our children are growing up in a land of opportunity.'

Britain remained a deferential, class-divided society—and the welfare state, as we have seen, benefited the 'middling sort' above all. But income and wealth really *were* redistributed as a result of post-war legislation—the share of the national wealth held by the richest 1 percent of the population fell from 56 percent in 1938 to 43 percent in 1954; and the effective disappearance of unemployment pointed an optimistic contrast with the grim pre-war decade. Between 1946 and 1948 150,000 Britons migrated to Canada, Australia and New Zealand and many more contemplated following in their footsteps; but beginning in 1951 it seemed as though the worst of the austerity years were over and the country offered itself the optimistic spectacle of a 'Festival of Britain', marking the centennial of Prince Albert's great Exhibition of 1851.

The feelings of the moment are nicely captured in Humphrey Jennings' contemporary film documentary of England in 1951, 'Family Portrait'. The title itself points to something distinctive about the country—no documentary film-maker in France or Italy or Germany or Belgium would have thought to use it. The film is a celebration of Englishness, strongly coloured by shared recollections of suffering and glory in the recent war, and it is suffused with an only partly self-conscious pride in the peculiarities of the place. There is much emphasis upon science and progress, design and work. And there is no reference whatsoever to England's (*sic*) neighbours or allies. The country is presented in 1951 as it truly stood in 1940: alone.

In 1828, the German poet Heinrich Heine made the already familiar observation that 'it is rarely possible for the English, in their parliamentary debates, to give utterance to a principle. They discuss only the utility or disutility of a thing, and produce facts, for and against.' The British rejected Robert Schuman's invitation in 1950 because of what they took to be the disutility of joining a European economic project, and because of their longstanding discomfort with continental entanglements. But the British decision to stand aside from the ECSC was above all an instinctive, psychological and even emotional one, a product of the utter peculiarity of recent British experience. In Anthony Eden's summary of the British decision, to a New York audience in January 1952, 'This is something which we know, in our bones, we cannot do.'

The decision was not final; but, taken when it was, it proved fateful. In the absence of Britain (and, in Britain's wake, the Scandinavians) power within the 'little Europe' of the West fell by default to France. The French duly did what the British might have done in other circumstances and made 'Europe' in their own image, eventually casting its institutions and policies in a mould familiar from French precedent. At the time it was the continental Europeans, not the British, who expressed regret at the course of events. Many prominent European leaders deeply wanted Britain to join them. As Paul-Henri Spaak, the Belgian and European statesman, noted in regretful retrospect: 'This moral leadership—it was yours for the asking.' Monnet, too, would later look back and wonder how different things might have been had Britain chosen to take the initiative at a moment when her authority was still unrivalled. Ten years later, it is true, the British would think again. But in post-war Europe ten years was a very long time and by then the die was cast.

VI
Into the Whirlwind

'Say what you will—the Communists were more intelligent. They had a grandiose program, a plan for a brand-new world in which everyone would find his place . . . From the start there were people who realized they lacked the proper temperament for the idyll and wished to leave the country. But since by definition an idyll is one world for all, the people who wished to emigrate were implicitly denying its validity. Instead of going abroad, they went behind bars'.
Milan Kundera

'And so it was necessary to teach people not to think and make judgments, to compel them to see the non-existent, and to argue the opposite of what was obvious to everyone'.
Boris Pasternak, **Doctor Zhivago**

'I met many people in the camp who managed to combine a shrewd sense of what was going on in the country at large with a religious cult of Stalin'.
Evgenia Ginsburg, **Journey into the Whirlwind**

'Stalinism means the killing of the inner man. And no matter what the sophists say, no matter what lies the communist intellectuals tell, that's what it all comes down to. The inner man must be killed for the communist Decalogue to be lodged in the soul'.
Alexander Wat

'Here they hang a man first and then they try him'.
Molière, **Monsieur de Pourceaugnac**

To Western observers in the years after 1945, the Soviet Union presented a daunting prospect. The Red Army marched on foot and hauled its weapons and supplies on carts powered by draught animals; its soldiers were granted no leave and, if they hesitated, no quarter: 157,593 of them had been executed for 'cowardice' in 1941 and 1942 alone. But after a halting start, the USSR had out-produced and out-fought the Nazi colossus, ripping the heart from the magnificent German military machine. For its friends and foes alike, the Soviet victory in World War Two bore witness to the Bolsheviks' achievement. Stalin's policies were vindicated, his pre-war crimes largely forgotten. Success, as Stalin well understood, is a winning formula.

But Soviet victory was bought at a uniquely high price. Of all the victors in World War Two—indeed of all the participant countries, victors and vanquished alike—the USSR was the only one to suffer permanent economic damage. The measurable losses in people and resources were immense, and would be felt for decades to come. Zdeněk Mlynář, a Czech Communist studying in Moscow in 1950, recalled the capital as mired in 'poverty and backwardness . . . a huge village of wooden cottages.' Away from the cities the situation was far worse. Roads, bridges, railways had been deliberately destroyed across much of Byelorussia, Ukraine and western Russia. The grain harvest in the early fifties was smaller than that of 1929, which in turn had been far less than the last peacetime harvest under the czars. The war had been fought across some of the Soviet Union's best arable land, and hundreds of thousands of horses, cows, pigs and other animals had been killed. Ukraine, which had never recovered from the deliberate, punitive famine of the thirties, faced another—this time unplanned—in the winter and spring of 1946–47.

But the war years had also seen what would prove an enduring semi-militarization of Soviet life. Centralised direction and a relentless focus upon the production of tanks, guns and planes had turned the wartime USSR into a surprisingly effective war machine, careless of human life and welfare but otherwise well-adapted to fighting a total war. The cohort of Party bureaucrats formed in the war—the Brezhnev generation—equated power and success with large-scale output in the defense industries, and they were to run the country for the next forty years with that model always in mind. Longstanding Leninist metaphors of class struggle and confrontation could now be linked with proud memories of a real war. The Soviet Party-State acquired a new foundation myth: the Great Patriotic War.

Thanks to the Nazis' treatment of the lands and people they overran, the war of 1941–45 in Russia *was* a great patriotic war. Stalin had encouraged autonomous expressions of Russian national and religious sentiment, allowing the Party and its goals to be temporarily displaced by an aura of common purpose in the titanic battle against the German invaders. And that same emphasis upon the Soviet Union's roots in Russia's imperial past served Stalin's purposes in his post-war foray into central Europe.

What Stalin wanted in Europe above all, as we have seen, was security. But he was also interested in the economic benefits to be had from his victories in the West. The little states of central Europe, from Poland to Bulgaria, had lived under the shadow of German dominion long before World War Two: in the 1930s especially, Nazi Germany was their main trading partner and source of foreign capital. During the war this relationship had been simplified into one of master and slave, with Germany extracting for its war effort the maximum possible output from land

and people. What happened after 1945 was that the Soviet Union took over, quite literally, where the Germans had left off, attaching eastern Europe to its own economy as a resource to be exploited at will.

The Soviet Union extracted reparations from Hungary and Romania, as former allies of Hitler. These reparations, like those taken in kind from the Soviet Zone in Germany, did relatively little to compensate for Russia's losses but they represented substantial sacrifices for the donor countries: by 1948, Romanian reparations to the USSR represented 15 percent of that country's national income; in Hungary the figure was 17 percent. From countries that had not fought against him Stalin was no less demanding, but on 'fraternal' rather than punitive terms.

It is estimated that until the late 1950s the Soviet Union exacted from the GDR, Romania and Hungary considerably more than it spent to control them. In Czechoslovakia it broke even. Bulgaria and especially Poland probably cost Moscow rather more in aid, between 1945 and 1960, than they furnished in trade and other deliveries. Such a pattern of mixed economic benefit in economic relations between metropole and colony is familiar to historians of colonialism and in this respect the relationship between the USSR and the lands to its west was conventionally 'imperial' (except that in the Soviet case the imperial center was actually poorer and more backward than its subjugated periphery).

Where Stalin differed from other empire-builders, even the czars, was in his insistence upon reproducing in the territories under his control forms of government and society *identical* to those of the Soviet Union. Just as he had done in eastern Poland between 1939 and 1941, and in the Baltic states in 1940 and again (following their re-conquest from the Nazis) in 1945, Stalin set out to re-mould eastern Europe in the Soviet image; to reproduce Soviet history, institutions and practices in each of the little states now controlled by Communist parties.

Albania, Bulgaria, Romania, Hungary, Czechoslovakia, Poland and the German Democratic Republic were to become, in the felicitous words of one scholar, 'geographically contiguous replica states'.[1] Each was to have a constitution modeled on the Soviet one (the first of these was adopted in Bulgaria in December 1947, the last in Poland in July 1952). Each was to undergo economic 'reforms' and adopt Five Year Plans to bring its institutions and practices into line with those of the Soviet Union. Each was to become a police state on the Soviet template. And each was to be governed by the apparatus of a Communist Party subservient (in fact if not name) to the ruling Communist Party in Moscow.[2]

Stalin's motives for reproducing Soviet society in the satellite states were once again very simple. The widespread desire in post-war Eastern Europe for peace,

---

[1]Professor Kenneth Jowett of UC Berkeley.
[2]The institutions of the German Democratic Republic were somewhat distinct, reflecting its interim standing in Soviet eyes. But the spirit of its laws and practices was impeccably orthodox.

land, food and a new beginning might have eased the Communists' path to power, but it was no guarantee of local support for Soviet policies. The preference for Communists over Fascists, or for some form of democratic Socialism, could not be counted upon to survive practical experience of Communist rule. Even the appeal of Soviet guarantees against German revanchism might wane in time.

Stalin needed to secure his satellite neighbours' unswerving allegiance, and he knew only one way to do this. First, the Party had to secure a monopoly of power. In the words of the Hungarian Constitution of August 1949, it was to take and keep a 'leading role', extinguishing or absorbing all other political parties. The Party became the only medium of social mobility, the sole source of patronage and the dispenser—through its control of the courts—of justice. Inseparable from the state whose institutions it monopolized, and taking its instructions directly from Moscow, the local Party and its state security apparatus were the most direct lever of Soviet command.

Secondly, the Party-State was to exercise a monopoly over economic decisions. This was not a simple matter. The economies of the east European states varied considerably. Some were modern, urban and industrial, with a sizeable working-class; others (the majority) were rural and impoverished. Some, like Poland and Hungary, had quite sizeable state sectors, dating from pre-war strategies of protection against German economic penetration. In others, like Czechoslovakia, property and business had been mostly in private hands before the war. Some countries and regions had a thriving commercial sector; others resembled parts of the Soviet Union itself. Most of the region had suffered seriously from the effects of the Depression and the autarkic protectionist policies adopted to combat it; but, as we have seen, during the war certain industrial sectors—in Hungary and Slovakia especially—had actually benefited from German investment in war production.

Notwithstanding this variety, the Communist seizures of power were followed in short order by the imposition of economic uniformity across the region. First, in keeping with the Leninist redefinition of 'socialism' as a matter of ownership rather than social relations, the state expropriated large-scale firms in service, commerce and industry, where these were not already in public hands. Next, the state took over, taxed or squeezed out of business all firms employing more than fifty people. In Czechoslovakia, by December 1948, there were hardly any private businesses left with more than 20 employees. By that same date 83 percent of Hungarian industry was in state hands, 84 percent of Polish industry, 85 percent of Romanian industry and fully 98 percent of Bulgarian industry.

One of the means at hand for eliminating the property-owning middle class in eastern Europe was currency reform. This was an effective device for destroying the cash savings of peasants and businessmen alike, an updating of older exactions like the forced capital levy. In Romania it was undertaken twice, in August 1947 (when it had the legitimate objective of ending hyperinflation) and in January 1952, when peasants who had built up savings over the previous four years (there was little for them to spend their money on) saw them wiped out.

As in the Soviet Union, so in Soviet-run eastern Europe, the peasantry were doomed. The initial post-war reforms in the countryside had distributed small parcels of land to large numbers of farmers. But however politically popular, these reforms simply exacerbated the longstanding agrarian crisis of the region: too little investment in machinery and fertilizer, too many underemployed laborers and five decades of steadily falling prices for farm produce. Until they were firmly ensconced in power, the Communist parties of eastern Europe actively encouraged inefficient land redistribution. But from 1949 they moved, with increasing urgency and aggression, to destroy the 'nepmen' and 'kulaks'.

In the early stages of rural collectivization, small peasant landowners—few large landholders remained by this time—were penalized by punitive taxation (often exceeding their money income), differential prices and quotas that favored the new collective and state farms, the withholding of ration books, and discrimination against their children, who were denied access to post-primary education. Even under such conditions a surprising number of independent peasants held on, though mostly on economically insignificant 'microfundia' of two hectares or less.

In Romania, where tens of thousands of peasants were forcibly registered on collective farms in the autumn of 1950 and where the regime was uninhibited in its resort to force, it was not until 1962 that future President Nicolae Ceauşescu could proudly announce the completion of rural collectivization 'three years ahead of schedule'. In Bulgaria, in the course of the first two Five-Year Plans beginning in 1949, viable agricultural land had been completely removed from private hands. In the Czech lands, where collectivization began quite late (in 1956 most arable land was still privately farmed), 95 percent of agricultural land would be taken over in the next ten years, rather less (85 percent) in backward and inaccessible regions of Slovakia. But here, as in Hungary and throughout the region, independent farmers survived only in name. The measures taken against them and the destruction of markets and distribution networks ensured their impoverishment and ruin.

The irrational, occasionally surreal quality of Soviet economic practice was faithfully reproduced throughout the bloc. On September 30th 1948, Gheorghe Gheorghiu-Dej of the Romanian Communist Party announced that 'We want to achieve a socialist accumulation at the expense of the capitalist elements in the countryside'—in a country where 'capitalist elements' in the rural economy were conspicuously absent. In Slovakia, in the course of 1951, there were even efforts to send urban clerks and government functionaries out into the fields. 'Operation 70,000 Must Be Productive', as it was called, proved disastrous and was quickly abandoned; but this exercise in Maoism *avant l'heure*, just fifty miles east of Vienna, says much about the mood of the times. Meanwhile, as in the newly Sovietized

Baltic lands, the consequence of Communist land reform was long-term institutionalized scarcity, in countries where food had hitherto been abundant and cheap.[3]

To address this palpable policy failure, the authorities introduced Soviet-style laws criminalizing 'parasitism', 'speculation' and 'sabotage'. In the words of Dr Zdenka Patschová, judge and member of the Czechoslovak National Assembly, addressing her fellow legislators on March 27th 1952: 'The unmasking of the true face of the village rich is the foremost task of criminal proceedings . . . Non-deliveries and non-fulfillment of the [agricultural] production plan must be severely punished as sabotage.' As this faithful echo of Soviet rhetoric from the 1930s suggests, antipathy towards the peasant, and successful implementation of rural collectivization, were one of the chief tests of Stalinist orthodoxy.

In the short run, implementation of Soviet-inspired plans for *industry* was not so obviously a disaster: there are some things that command economies can manage quite well. Collectivisation of land and the destruction of small businesses released an abundant supply of men and women for work in mines and factories; the single-minded Communist emphasis upon investment in heavy goods production at the expense of consumer products and services ensured unprecedented increases in output. Five Year Plans were everywhere adopted, with wildly ambitious targets. In terms of gross production figures the growth rates in this first generation of industrialization were impressive, notably in countries like Bulgaria or Romania which started from virtually nothing.

The number of people employed in agriculture even in Czechoslovakia, the most urbanized state in the region, dropped by 18 percent between 1948 and 1952. In the Soviet Zone of Germany raw steel output rose from 120,000 tons in 1946 to over 2 million tons by 1953. Parts of Eastern Europe (south-west Poland, the industrial belt north-west of Bucharest) were transformed almost overnight: whole new cities were built, like Nowa Huta near Crakow, to house the thousands of workers turning out iron, steel and machine tools. On an appropriately smaller scale the semi-militarized, monolithic, first-generation industrialization of the interwar Soviet Union was being re-run throughout the Soviet bloc. Much as they had set out to do in Russia, the Communists in eastern Europe were reproducing a foreshortened and accelerated version of western Europe's nineteenth-century industrial revolution.

Seen in this light, the economic history of eastern Europe after 1945 bears a passing resemblance to the pattern of West European recovery in the same years. In western Europe, too, investment in productivity and growth was given priority over the provision of consumer goods and services, though the Marshall Plan soft-

---

[3]The Baltic states, fully incorporated into the Soviet Union itself, were even worse off than the rest of eastern Europe. In 1949 kolkhozes in northern Estonia were required to begin grain deliveries even before the harvest had begun, in order to keep in line with Latvia, four hundred kilometers to the south. By 1953 rural conditions in hitherto prosperous Estonia had deteriorated to the point where cows blown over by the wind were too weak to get back on their feet unaided.

ened the pain of this strategy. In Western Europe, too, certain industrial sectors and regions took off from low starting points, and a dramatic transition from countryside to town took place in the course of the 1950s in Italy and France in particular. But there the similarity ends. The distinctive feature of the economic history of Communist eastern Europe is that, in addition to coal, steel, factories and apartment blocks, first-generation Soviet industrialization produced grotesque distortions and contradictions, more so even than in the USSR itself.

Following the establishment in January 1949 of Comecon (the Council for Mutual Economic Assistance[4]), the rules for inter-state Communist trade were laid down. Each country was to trade bilaterally with the Soviet Union (another echo of Nazi-era requirements, with Moscow once again substituting for Berlin) and was assigned a non-negotiable role in the international Communist economy. Thus East Germany, Czechoslovakia and Hungary would supply finished industrial products to the USSR (at prices set by Moscow), while Poland and Romania were to specialize in producing and exporting food and primary industrial products. In return the Soviet Union would trade raw materials and fuel.

Except for the curious inversion we have already noted—with the imperial power furnishing raw materials and the colonies exporting finished goods—this structure is reminiscent of European overseas colonization. And as in the case of non-European colonies, so in eastern Europe: the indigenous economies suffered deformation and under-development. Some countries were prevented from manufacturing finished goods, others were instructed to make certain products in abundance (shoes in Czechoslovakia, trucks in Hungary) and sell them to the USSR. No attention was paid to the economics of comparative advantage.

The Soviet model of the thirties, improvised to address uniquely Soviet circumstances of vast distance, abundant raw materials and endless, cheap, unskilled labor, made no sense at all for tiny countries like Hungary or Czechoslovakia, lacking raw materials but with a skilled industrial labor force and long-established international markets for high-value-added products. The Czech case is a particularly striking one. Before World War Two, the Czech regions of Bohemia and Moravia (already the industrial heartland of the Austro-Hungarian Empire before 1914) had a higher per capita output than France, specializing in leather goods, motor vehicles, high-tech arms manufacture and a broad range of luxury goods. Measured by industrial skill levels, productivity, standard of living and share of foreign markets, pre-1938 Czechoslovakia was comparable to Belgium and well ahead of Austria and Italy.

By 1956, Communist Czechoslovakia had not only fallen behind Austria, Bel-

---

[4]The initial Comecon participants were Bulgaria, Czechoslovakia, Hungary, Poland, Romania and the USSR, joined shortly thereafter by Albania and the GDR. In later years Yugoslavia, Mongolia, China, North Korea and North Vietnam also became members. In 1963 Comecon countries' share of international trade was 12 percent; by 1979 it was 9 percent and falling.

gium and the rest of Western Europe, but was far less efficient and much poorer than it had been twenty years earlier. In 1938, per capita car ownership in Czechoslovakia and Austria was at similar levels; by 1960 the ratio was 1:3. Even the products in which the country still had a competitive edge—notably small arms manufacture—no longer afforded Czechs any benefit, since they were constrained to direct their exports exclusively to their Soviet masters. As for the establishment of manufacturing mammoths like the Gottwald Steelworks in Ostrava, identical to steelworks in Poland, the German Democratic Republic, Hungary, Romania, Bulgaria and the USSR, these represented for the Czechs not rapid industrialization but enforced backwardness (crash programs of industrialization based on the manufacture of steel were pursued in spite of Czechoslovakia's very limited resources in iron ore). Following the one-time start-up benefits from unprecedented growth in primary industries, the same was true for every other satellite state. By the midfifties, Soviet Eastern Europe was already beginning its steady decline into 'planned' obsolescence.

There are two partial exceptions to this brief account of the economies of the Soviet bloc. While primitive industrialization was undertaken just as enthusiastically in Poland as elsewhere, land collectivization was not. Stalin seems to have grasped the impracticality of forcing Polish peasants onto collective farms, but this consideration alone would hardly have caused him to hesitate. Soviet caution when dealing with Poland (we shall have occasion to meet it again) was strictly instrumental. In marked contrast to the other subject peoples of eastern Europe, there were a lot of Poles, their capacity and propensity to rebel against Russian servitude was familiar to generations of Russian officers and bureaucrats, and Soviet rule was more obviously resented in Poland than anywhere else.

From the Soviet point of view, Polish opposition was an annoyance—remnants of the Polish wartime underground carried on a guerilla war against the Communist regime until at least the end of the 1940s—and seemingly undeserved. Had not the Poles gained 40,000 square miles of rather good agricultural land in exchange for the 69,000 square miles of eastern marches transferred to the USSR after the war? And was not Moscow the Poles' (only) guarantee against a Germany whose revival everyone anticipated? Moreover Poland was now free of its pre-war minorities: the Jews had been murdered by the Germans, and the Germans and Ukrainians had been expelled by the Soviets. If Poland was now more 'Polish' than at any time in its complicated history, it had Moscow to thank.

But inter-state relations, above all in the Soviet bloc, did not hinge on gratitude or its absence. Poland's use value to Moscow was above all as a buffer against German or Western aggression. It was desirable that Poland become socialist, but it was imperative that it remain stable and reliable. In return for Polish domestic calm Stalin was willing to tolerate a class of independent farmers, however inefficient and ideologically untidy, and a publicly active Catholic Church, in ways that would have been unimaginable further south or east. Polish universities were also left virtually intact, in contrast to the purges that stripped out the teaching staff of higher educational institutions in neighbouring Czechoslovakia and elsewhere.

The other exception, of course, was Yugoslavia. Until the Stalin-Tito split, Yugoslavia was, as we have seen, the most 'advanced' of all the east European states along the path to socialism. Tito's first Five Year Plan outdid Stalin by aiming at a higher rate of industrial investment than anywhere else in the Soviet bloc. Seven thousand collective farms had been set up before collectivization had even begun in the other satellite states; and post-war Yugoslavia was well on the way to outdoing Moscow itself in the efficiency and ubiquity of its apparatus of repression. The partisans' wartime security services were expanded into a full-scale police network whose task, in Tito's words, was 'to strike terror into the hearts of those who do not like this sort of Yugoslavia.'

Yugoslavia's per capita income at the time of the break with Stalin was the lowest in Europe save for neighboring Albania; an already impoverished land had been beaten into penury in the course of four years of occupation and civil war. The bitter heritage of Yugoslavia's war experience was further complicated by its ethnic composition, the last genuinely multi-national state in Europe: according to the 1946 census Yugoslavia's 15.7 million people comprised 6.5 million Serbs, 3.8 million Croats, 1.4 million Slovenes, 800,000 Muslims (mostly in Bosnia), 800,000 Macedonians, 750,000 Albanians, 496,000 Hungarians, 400,000 Montenegrins, 100,000 Vlachs and an uncertain number of Bulgars, Czechs, Germans, Italians, Romanians, Russians, Greeks, Turks, Jews and Gypsies.

Of these only Serbs, Croats, Slovenes, Montenegrins and Macedonians were accorded separate recognition under the 1946 Constitution, though encouraged to see themselves, like all the others, as 'Yugoslavs'.[5] As Yugoslavs, their prospects seemed grim indeed. Writing from Belgrade to a Greek friend at the end of the 1940s, Lawrence Durrell had this to say of the country: 'Conditions are rather gloomy here—almost mid-war conditions, overcrowding, poverty. As for Communism— my dear Theodore a short visit here is enough to make one decide that Capitalism is worth fighting for. Black as it may be, with all its bloodstains, it is less gloomy and arid and hopeless than this inert and ghastly police state.'

In the initial months following the split with Stalin, Tito actually became *more* radical, more 'Bolshevik', as if to prove the legitimacy of his claim and the mendacity of his Soviet critics. But the posture could never have been sustained very long. Without external help, and faced with the very real prospect of Soviet invasion, he turned to the West for aid. In September 1949 the US Export-Import Bank loaned Belgrade $20 million. The following month Yugoslavia borrowed $3 million from

---

[5]Under the 1946 Constitution the constituent republics—Serbia, Croatia, Slovenia, Bosnia, Macedonia and Montenegro—were free to secede from the Federation, a right of which they were deprived seven years later.

the International Monetary Fund, and in December of that same year signed a trade agreement with Great Britain and received $8 million in credits.

The Soviet threat forced Tito to increase his defense spending (as a share of Yugoslavia's meager national income) from 9.4 percent in 1948 to 16.7 percent in 1950; the country's munitions industries were moved for safety into the mountains of Bosnia (a matter of some consequence in the wars of the 1990s). In 1950 the US Congress, now convinced of Yugoslavia's possible significance in the global Cold War, offered a further $50 million in aid under the Yugoslav Emergency Relief Act of 1950, and followed this in November 1951 with an accord that allowed Yugoslavia to receive military aid under the terms of the Mutual Security Act. By 1953 the Yugoslav national deficit on current account was fully covered by American aid; over the course of the years 1949–55 Tito's aid from all Western sources amounted to $1.2 billion, of which just $55 million was repaid. The stand-off over Trieste, which had bedeviled Yugoslavia's relations with Italy and the West since May 1945, was finally resolved in a Memorandum of Understanding signed by Yugoslavia, Italy, Britain and the US on October 5th 1954.

Western aid allowed the Yugoslav regime to continue favoring heavy industry and defense, as it had been doing before the 1948 split. But while the League of Yugoslav Communists retained all the reins of authoritarian power, the ultra-Bolshevism of the post-war years was abandoned. By the spring of 1951 only the postal service, together with rail, air and river transport, was left under federal (i.e. central government) control. Other services, and all economic enterprises, were in the hands of the separate republics. By 1954, 80 percent of agricultural land was back in private hands, following a March 30th 1953 decree permitting peasants to withdraw themselves and their land from the collective. Of the 7,000 collective farms, just 1,000 remained.

Stalin had emerged from his victory over Hitler far stronger even than before, basking in the reflected glory of 'his' Red Army, at home and abroad. The personality cult around the Soviet dictator, already well advanced before the war, now rose to its apogee. Popular Soviet documentaries on World War Two showed Stalin winning the war virtually single-handed, planning strategy and directing battles with not a general in sight. In almost every sphere of life, from dialectics to botany, Stalin was declared the supreme and unchallenged authority. Soviet biologists were instructed to adopt the theories of the charlatan Lysenko, who promised Stalin undreamed-of agricultural improvements if his theories about the inheritability of acquired characteristics were officially adopted and applied to Soviet farming—as they were, to disastrous effect.[6] On his 70th birthday in December 1949 Stalin's

---

[6]It is significant that Stalin left his nuclear physicists alone and never presumed to second guess *their* calculations. Stalin may well have been mad, but he was not stupid.

image, picked out by searchlights hung from balloons, lit the night sky over the Kremlin. Poets outdid one another in singing the Leader's praises—a 1951 couplet by the Latvian poet V. Lukss is representative:

> Like beautiful red yarn into our hearts we wove,
> Stalin, our brother and father, your name.

This obsequious neo-Byzantine anointing of the despot, the attribution to him of near-magical powers, unfolded against a steadily darkening backdrop of tyranny and terror. In the last years of the war, under the cloak of Russian nationalism, Stalin expelled east to Siberia and Central Asia a variety of small nations from western and south-western border regions, the Caucasus in particular: Chechens, Ingush, Karachays, Nalkars, Kalmyks, Crimean Tatars and others, in the wake of the Volga Germans deported in 1941. This brutal treatment of small nations was hardly new—Poles and Balts had been exiled east by the hundreds of thousands between 1939 and 1941, Ukrainians in the 1930s and others before them, back to 1921.

The initial post-war trials of collaborators and traitors across the region echoed nationalist sentiment as well. Peasant party leaders in Poland, Hungary and Bulgaria were arrested, tried and shot between 1945 and 1947 for a mixed bag of real and imaginary crimes, ranging from Fascist sympathies through wartime collaboration to spying for the West; but in every case prosecutors took particular care to impugn their patriotism and credibility as representatives of the Bulgarian/Hungarian/Polish 'people'. Socialists who refused the embrace of the Communist Party, like the Bulgarian Krastyn Partakhov (tried in 1946 and sentenced to prison where he died three years later), were also singled out for punishment as enemies of the people.

What is striking about the non-Communist victims of these early public trials is that—with the exception of those who really had thrown in their lot with the Germans and whose activities were thus common knowledge—they conspicuously refused to plead guilty or confess to their alleged 'anti-national' crimes. In the palpably rigged Sofia show trial of Agrarian Party leader Nikola Petkov and his 'co-conspirators', in August 1947, four out of the five accused proclaimed their innocence in spite of torture and false testimony.[7]

With the Yugoslav crisis of 1948, Stalin's attitude shifted. As an alternative to Moscow, Belgrade had a certain appeal to many. Unlike Stalin, Tito posed no imperial threat (except within the local Balkan context); and by liberating his country and leading it to Communism with no help from Moscow, the Yugoslav leader

---

[7]They were executed nonetheless. Three weeks after his death, the regime published Petkov's posthumous 'confession'. But this was so obviously faked that it rapidly became an embarrassment, even in Communist Bulgaria. The authorities ceased to speak of it and the Bulgarian secret police chief who had injudiciously arranged for its publication was duly shot.

had set an attractive precedent for any Communist in eastern Europe still tempted to ground a local revolution in national sentiment. Stalin was notoriously paranoid about threats to his monopoly of power; but that does not mean that he was altogether mistaken to see in Tito and 'Tito-ism' a genuine danger. Henceforward, therefore, nationalism ('small-state nationalism', 'bourgeois nationalism') ceased to be a local asset and became instead the main enemy. The term 'nationalist' was first deployed pejoratively in Communist rhetoric at the June 1948 meeting of the Cominform to condemn the Yugoslav 'deviation'.

But with all domestic non-Communist opponents now dead, imprisoned or in exile, to what genuine risks was the Soviet monopoly of power exposed? Intellectuals could be bought off or intimidated. The military were firmly under the thumb of the occupying Soviet forces. Mass popular protest posed the only significant threat to Communist regimes, as it would seriously erode the credentials of the 'worker and peasant' state. But in their early years the Peoples' Democracies were by no means always unpopular with the proletarians they claimed to represent. On the contrary: the destruction of the middle classes and the expulsion of ethnic minorities opened prospects of upward mobility for rural peasants, industrial workers and their children.

Opportunities abounded, particularly at the lower rungs of the ladder and in government employ: there were jobs to be had, apartments to be occupied at subsidized rents, places in schools reserved for the children of workers and closed to the children of the 'bourgeoisie'. Competence mattered less than political reliability, employment was guaranteed, and the burgeoning Communist bureaucracy sought out reliable men and women for everything from block organizer to police interrogator.[8] Most of the population of Soviet eastern Europe, especially in the more backward regions, accepted their fate without protest, at least in these years.

The two best-known exceptions to this generalization both occurred in the most urban and advanced corners of the bloc: in industrial Bohemia and in the streets of Soviet-occupied Berlin. The 'currency reform' of May 31st 1953 in Czechoslovakia, ostensibly 'a crushing blow against the former capitalists', had the effect of cutting industrial wages by 12 percent (because of the price rises that followed). Together with the steadily worsening working conditions in what had once been an advanced industrial economy based on well-remunerated skilled labor, this triggered mass demonstrations by 20,000 workers at the Škoda plant in Plzeň, a major industrial center in western Bohemia, followed by a march on the city hall, on June 1st 1953, by thousands of workers carrying portraits of Beneš and pre-war president Tomáš Masaryk.

The Plzeň demonstrations, confined to one provincial city, fizzled out. But a few days later a far larger protest was sparked off a few dozen miles to the north by sub-

---

[8]As late as 1966, four-fifths of Polish state employees had only a primary school education. The country was run by a strikingly under-educated administrative caste.

stantial (unpaid) increases in the German Democratic Republic's official work norms. These were imposed by an unpopular regime, already (and not for the last time) far more rigid than its Soviet masters in Moscow, whose advice to the East German Communist leadership to accept reforms and compromises to stem the hemorrhage of skilled workers to the West had been ignored. On June 16th some 400,000 workers went on strike across East Germany, with the biggest demonstrations in Berlin itself.

As with the Plzeň protesters, the German workers were easily put down by the *Volkspolizei*, but not without cost. Nearly three hundred were killed when Red Army tanks were called in; many thousands more were arrested, of whom 1,400 were given long prison sentences. Two hundred 'ringleaders' were shot. The Berlin Uprising was the occasion for Berthold Brecht's only overt literary dissent from the Communist regime to which he had—somewhat ambivalently—committed himself:

> Following the June Seventeenth uprising
> the secretary of the Writers' League
> had leaflets distributed on Stalin Allee
> where one could read that the people
> had forfeited the confidence of the government
> and could regain it only through redoubled efforts.
> Wouldn't it be simpler under these circumstances
> for the government to dissolve the people
> and elect another one?

Angry, disaffected workers on the industrialized western edge of the Soviet empire were a poor advertisement for Communism, but they hardly represented a threat to Soviet power—and it is not coincidental that both the Plzeň and Berlin uprisings took place *after* Stalin's death. In Stalin's time the truly threatening challenge came, as it seemed, from within the Communist apparatus itself. This was the real implication of the Yugoslav schism, and it was in direct response to 'Titoism' that Stalin thus reverted to earlier methods, updated and adapted to circumstances. From 1948 through 1954, the Communist world underwent a second generation of arrests, purges and, above all, political 'show trials'.

The chief precedent for the purges and trials of these years was of course the Soviet Terror of the 1930s. Then, too, the main victims had been Communists themselves, the goal being to purge the Party of 'traitors' and other challenges to the policy and person of the General Secretary. In the 1930s the presumptive ringleader was Leon Trotsky—like Tito, a genuine Communist hero un-beholden to Stalin and with views of his own about Communist strategy and practice. The Terror of the thirties had secured and illustrated Stalin's untrammeled power and authority, and the purges of the post-war years would serve a similar objective in Eastern Europe.

But whereas the Moscow Trials of the 1930s, particularly the 1938 trial of Niko-lai Bukharin, had been *sui generis*, theatrical innovations whose shock value lay in the grisly spectacle of the Revolution consuming not just its children but its very architects, the trials and purges of later decades were shameless copies, deliberately modeled on past Soviet practice, as though the satellite regimes hardly merited even an effort at verisimilitude. And they came, after all, at the end of a long string of judicial purges.

In addition to the post-war trials for treason and the political trials of anti-Communist politicians, the Communist regimes of Eastern Europe had used the courts to punish and close down the churches everywhere except Poland, where open confrontation with the Catholic Church was deemed too risky. In 1949 the leaders of the United Protestant Church in Bulgaria were tried for conspiracy to 're-store capitalism'. The previous year the Uniate Church in Romania was forcibly merged with the more pliable Romanian Orthodox church by the new Commu-nist regime, in keeping with a long tradition of persecution reaching back to the Russian czars of the eighteenth-century. Selected Catholic priests were tried on two separate occasions in Prague on charges of spying for the Vatican (and the USA), receiving sentences ranging from ten years to life imprisonment; by the early 1950s there were eight thousand monks and nuns in Czechoslovak prisons. Mon-signor Grosz, who succeeded the imprisoned Cardinal Mindszenty as head of the Catholic Church in Hungary in January 1949, was found guilty of working to re-store the Habsburgs *and* of plotting with Titoists to arm Hungarian Fascists.

The trials of Communists themselves fell into two distinct groups. The first, be-ginning in 1948 and lasting through 1950, were immediate responses to the Tito-Stalin rift. In Albania, Communist Interior Minister Koçi Xoxe was tried in May-June 1949, found guilty and hanged the following month. Charged with Tito-ism, Xoxe had the distinction of really having *been* a supporter of Tito and his plans for the Balkans, at a time when these had Moscow's backing. In this respect his case was a little unusual, as was the fact that it was handled in secret.

The Albanian trial was followed by the arrest, trial and execution in Bulgaria of Traicho Kostov, one of the founders of the Bulgarian Communist Party. Kostov, crippled by his sufferings at the hands of Bulgaria's inter-war rulers[9], was if any-thing a known opponent of Tito and critic of the latter's plans to absorb Bulgaria into a Balkan Federation (Tito disliked Kostov and the sentiment was mutual). But Stalin distrusted him anyway—Kostov had imprudently criticized a Soviet-Bulgarian economic agreement as unfavorable to his country—and he was an ideal candidate for a trial intended to illustrate the crimes of nationalism.

He and his 'group' ('The Treacherous Espionage and Wrecking Group of Trai-

---

[9]In 1924 the 27-year-old Kostov was arrested and tortured by the Bulgarian police. Afraid that he might betray the (underground) Communists he leaped from a fourth-floor window at police headquarters in Sofia and broke both his legs.

cho Kostov') were charged in December 1949 with collaboration with pre-war Bulgarian Fascists, espionage on behalf of British intelligence and conspiring with Tito. After finally giving in under sustained torture and signing his 'confession' of guilt, Kostov refused to speak the pre-agreed text in his courtroom appearance, publicly retracted his statement to his interrogators and was carried out of the courtroom protesting his innocence. Two days later, on December 16th 1949, Kostov was hanged, and his 'co-conspirators' sentenced to long imprisonment in accordance with decisions taken by Stalin and his police chief Lavrenti Beria before the trial had begun. Kostov's case was unusual in that he was the only East European Communist who retracted his confession and protested his innocence at a public trial. This caused some minor international embarrassment for the regime (Kostov's trial was broadcast on radio and widely reported in the West) and instructions were given that this must never happen again. It did not.

Shortly before Kostov's execution the Hungarian Communists had staged a show trial of *their* would-be 'Tito', Communist Interior Minister László Rajk. The text was the same as in Bulgaria—literally so, with only the names changed. Accusations, details, confessions were all identical, which is not surprising since both trials were scripted in Moscow. Rajk himself was no innocent; as Communist Interior Minister he had sent many others to prison and worse. But in his case the indictment took particular care to emphasize his 'traitorous work' as 'a paid agent of a foreign power'; the Soviet occupation was especially unpopular in Hungary and Moscow did not want to run the risk of turning Rajk into a hero of 'national Communism'.

In the event there was no such danger. Rajk duly spoke his lines, acknowledging his service as an Anglo-American agent working to bring down Communism in Hungary, informing the Court that his real name was Reich (and thus of German, not Hungarian origin), and that he had been recruited in 1946 by Yugoslav intelligence who threatened to expose his wartime collaboration with the Hungarian Nazis 'if I did not carry out all of their wishes.' The proceedings of the Tribunal trying Rajk and his fellow 'conspirators', including Rajk's own confession of September 16th 1949, were broadcast live by Radio Budapest. The pre-determined verdict was announced on September 24th; Rajk and two others were condemned to death. The executions, by hanging, were carried out on October 15th.

The public trials of Rajk and Kostov were only the tip of an iceberg of secret trials and tribunals set off by the hunt for Titoists in the Communist parties and governments of the region. The worst affected were the 'southern tier' of Communist states closest to Yugoslavia: Bulgaria, Romania, Albania and Hungary. In Hungary alone—where Stalin's fear of creeping Titoism was marginally more credible given the proximity of Yugoslavia, the large Hungarian minority in the Vojvodina region of Serbia, and the close alignment of Hungarian and Yugoslav foreign policy during 1947—some 2,000 Communist cadres were summarily executed, a further 150,000 sentenced to terms of imprisonment and about 350,000 expelled from the

Party (which frequently meant loss of jobs, apartments, privileges and the right to higher education).

The persecutions in Poland and East Germany, while they put thousands of men and women in prison, did not result in any major show trials. There *was* a candidate in Poland for the role of Tito-Kostov-Rajk: Władisław Gomułka, Secretary General of the Polish United Workers Party and Vice-President of the Polish Council of Ministers. Gomułka had openly criticized plans for land collectivization in Poland and was publicly associated with talk of a Polish 'national path' to socialism. Indeed, he had been criticized for this by loyal Stalinists in the Polish party, and in August 1948 he was replaced as General Secretary by Bolesław Bierut. Five months later he resigned from his ministerial post, in November 1949 he was expelled from the Party and that December Bierut publicly accused Gomułka and his 'group' of nationalism and Titoism.

Reduced to the post of administrator for Social Assurance in Warsaw, Gomułka was finally arrested in July 1951 and only released in September 1954. Yet he was not harmed and there was no Titoism trial in Warsaw. There *were* trials in Poland—one of them, in which a group of officers was charged with anti-state plotting, began on the day of Gomułka's arrest in 1951. And in a scheme devised by the secret services in Moscow, Gomułka was to have been linked to Rajk, Tito *et al.* via a complex network of real or invented contacts centering on an American, Noel Field, director of the Unitarian Church's relief efforts in post-war Europe. Based in Budapest, Field's imaginary network of master spies and Titoists had already been invoked in the charges against Rajk and others and was to have been the main evidence against Gomułka.

But the Poles were able to resist Soviet pressure to conduct full-scale public witch-hunts on the Hungarian model. The decimation of the exiled Polish Communist Party, at Stalin's hands in Moscow ten years earlier, had given Bierut a foretaste of his own probable fate if Poland too entered the vortex of arrests, purges and trials. The Poles were fortunate in their timing too: delays in preparing the dossier on Gomułka—he had refused to break under interrogation or sign a fabricated confession—meant that Stalin died and his henchman Beria was killed before a Polish trial could be mounted. Finally, some Soviet leaders undoubtedly judged it imprudent in these early years to tear the Polish Communist leadership apart in full public view.

No such inhibitions applied in Czechoslovakia, however, where the biggest show trial of them all was to be staged in Prague in November 1952. A major Czech show trial had been planned from 1950, in the immediate wake of the Rajk and Kostov purges. But by the time it was finally mounted, the emphasis had shifted. Tito was still the enemy and accusations of espionage for the West still figured prominently in the indictments. But of the fourteen defendants at the 'Trial of the Leadership of the Anti-State Conspiracy Centre', eleven were Jews. On the very first page of the charge sheet it was made abundantly clear that this was no accident. The 'Trotskyite-

Titoite bourgeois-nationalist traitors and enemies of the Czechoslovak people' were also, and above all, 'Zionists'.

Stalin was an anti-Semite and always had been. But until the Second World War his dislike for Jews was so comfortably embedded in his destruction of other categories of person—Old Bolsheviks, Trotskyites, Left- and Right-deviationists, intellectuals, bourgeois and so on—that their Jewish origin seemed almost incidental to their fate. In any case, it was a matter of dogma that Communism had no truck with racial or religious prejudice; and once the Soviet cause was attached to the banner of 'anti-Fascism', as it was from 1935 until August 1939 and again from June 1941, the Jews of Europe had no greater friend than Josef Stalin himself.

That last claim is only partly ironic. The European Communist parties, especially those of central and eastern Europe, counted significant numbers of Jews among their members. The Jews of inter-war Poland, Czechoslovakia, Hungary and Romania were an oppressed and disliked minority. Young, secular Jews had few political options: Zionism, Bundism[10], Social Democracy (where it was legal) or Communism. As the most uncompromisingly anti-national and ambitious of these, Communism had a distinctive appeal. Whatever its passing defects, the Soviet Union offered a revolutionary alternative at a time when central and eastern Europe appeared to be facing a choice between an authoritarian past and a Fascist future.

The appeal of the USSR was further accentuated by the experience of war. Jews who found themselves in Soviet-occupied Poland after the Germans attacked in 1939 were frequently deported eastwards and many died of disease and hardship. But they were not systematically exterminated. The advance of the Red Army through Ukraine and Byelorussia into the Baltic States, Romania, Hungary, Czechoslovakia, Poland and Germany saved the remaining Jews in these lands. It was the Red Army that liberated Auschwitz. Stalin most certainly did *not* fight the Second World War for the Jews; but had Hitler won—had the Germans and their collaborators remained in control of the territories they had captured up to the Battle of Stalingrad—millions more Jews would have been exterminated.

When the Communist parties took over in eastern Europe, many of their leading cadres were of Jewish origin. This was particularly marked at the level just below the top: the Communist police chiefs in Poland and Hungary were Jewish, as were economic policy makers, administrative secretaries, prominent journalists and Party theorists. In Hungary the Party leader (Mátyás Rákosi) was Jewish; in Romania, Czechoslovakia and Poland the Party leader was not Jewish but most of the core leadership group were. Jewish Communists throughout the Soviet bloc owed

[10]The *Bund* was a Jewish labor movement whose roots lay in pre-war czarist Russia and whose interwar activities were confined to Poland.

everything to Stalin. They were not much welcome in the countries to which they had returned, often after long exile: neither as Communists nor as Jews. Experience of war and occupation had made the local populations even more resentful of the Jews than before ('Why have you come back?' one neighbor asked Heda Margolius when she escaped from the Auschwitz death march and made her way back to Prague at the very end of the war[11]); the eastern European Jewish Communists could be counted on, more perhaps than anyone else, to do Stalin's bidding.

In the first post-war years Stalin displayed no hostility to his Jewish subordinates. At the United Nations the Soviet Union was an enthusiastic supporter of the Zionist project, favoring the creation of a Jewish state in the Middle East as an impediment to British imperial ambitions. At home Stalin had looked favorably on the work of the Jewish Anti-Fascist Committee, formed during the war to mobilize Jewish opinion in the USSR and (especially) abroad behind the Soviet struggle against the Nazis. Soviet Jews, like many others under Moscow's rule, fondly supposed that the more ecumenical mood of the war years, when Stalin sought and accepted help from any likely quarter, would translate into easier times after victory.

In fact, the opposite happened. Before the war had even ended Stalin, as we have seen, was exiling whole nations to the east and doubtless harbored similar plans for the Jews. As in central Europe, so in the lands of the Soviet Union: even though Jews had lost more than anyone else, it was easy and familiar to blame those same Jews for everyone else's sufferings. The wartime invocation of the banner of Russian nationalism brought Soviet rhetoric a lot closer to the Slav-exclusivist language of old-time Russian anti-Semites; this was certainly not to the regime's disadvantage. For Stalin himself it represented a return to familiar territory, his own anti-Jewish instincts underscored by his observation of Hitler's successful exploitation of popular anti-Semitism.

For various reasons it had always suited the Soviet purpose to downplay the distinctively *racist* character of Nazi brutality: the massacre of Ukrainian Jews at Babi Yar was officially commemorated as the 'murder of peaceful Soviet citizens', just as the post-war memorial at Auschwitz confined itself to general references to 'victims of Fascism'. Racism had no place in the Marxist lexicon; dead Jews were posthumously assimilated into the same local communities that had so disliked them when they were alive. But now the presumptively cosmopolitan qualities of Jews—the international links from which Stalin had hoped to benefit in the dark months following the German attack—began once more to be held against them as the battle lines of the Cold War settled into place and international wartime contacts and communications became in Stalin's eyes a retroactive liability.

The first victims were the Jewish leaders of the wartime Anti-Fascist Commit-

---

[11]See Heda Margolius Kovaly, *Under a Cruel Star* (1986). In the eighteen months following the end of World War Two more Jews were killed in Poland, Hungary and Czechoslovakia than in the ten years preceding the war.

tee itself. Solomon Mikhoels, its prime mover and a major figure in Russia's Yiddish Theatre, was murdered on January 12th 1948. The arrival in Moscow of Israeli Ambassador Golda Meir on September 11th 1948 was the occasion for spontaneous outbursts of Jewish enthusiasm, with street demonstrations on Rosh Hashana and Yom Kippur and chants of 'Next Year in Jerusalem' outside the Israeli legation. This would have been provocative and unacceptable to Stalin at any time. But he was rapidly losing his enthusiasm for the new State of Israel: whatever its vaguely socialist proclivities it clearly had no intention of becoming a Soviet ally in the region; worse, the Jewish state was demonstrating alarmingly pro-American sensibilities at a sensitive moment. The Berlin blockade had just begun and the Soviet split with Tito was entering its acute phase.

On September 21st 1948 *Pravda* published an article by Ilya Ehrenburg indicating clearly the change of line on Zionism. From January 1949 articles began to appear in *Pravda* attacking 'cosmopolitans without a fatherland', 'unpatriotic groups of theater critics', 'rootless cosmopolitans', 'persons without identity' and 'passportless wanderers'. Yiddish schools and theatres were shut down, Yiddish newspapers banned and libraries closed. The Jewish Anti-Fascist Committee itself had been suppressed on November 20th 1948. Its remaining leaders, artists, writers and government functionaries were arrested the following month and kept in prison for three years. Pressured under torture to confess to an 'anti-Soviet' conspiracy, they were clearly being prepared for a show trial.

The security forces colonel who conducted the investigation, Vladimir Komarov, sought to broaden the charges out to encompass a large-scale Jewish conspiracy against the USSR directed from Washington and Tel Aviv. As he put it to Solomon Lozovsky, one of the prisoners: 'Jews are low, dirty people, all Jews are lousy bastards, all opposition to the Party consists of Jews, Jews all over the Soviet Union are conducting an anti-Soviet whispering campaign. Jews want to annihilate all Russians.'[12] Such overt anti-Semitism might have been embarrassing even to Stalin, however; in the end the fifteen defendants (all Jewish) were secretly tried in the summer of 1952 by a Military Tribunal. All but one were executed; the sole survivor, Lina Shtern, received ten years in prison.

Meanwhile the anti-Semitic tide was gathering strength in the satellite states. In Romania, where a substantial part of the Jewish population had survived the war, an anti-Zionist campaign was launched in the autumn of 1948 and sustained with varying degrees of energy for the next six years. But the size of the Romanian Jewish community and its links to the United States inhibited direct attacks on it; in-

---

[12] *Stalin's Secret Pogrom: The Postwar Inquisition of the Jewish Anti-Fascist Committee* (Yale University Press, 2002), edited by Joshua Rubenstein and Vladimir Naumov, page 52. Following a familiar pattern, Komarov himself would later be imprisoned and executed—pleading to the last his anti-Semitic credentials.

deed the Romanians for some time toyed with the idea of letting their Jews leave—applications for visas were allowed from the spring of 1950 and not halted until April 1952, by which time 90,000 Romanian Jews had left for Israel alone.

Plans for a show trial in Romania centred on the (non-Jewish) Romanian Communist leader Lucretius Pǎtrǎşcanu. Pǎtrǎşcanu's publicly voiced doubts over rural collectivization made him a natural candidate for a Romanian 'Rajk trial' based on charges of pro-Titoism, and he was arrested in April 1948. But by the time his interrogators were ready to bring him to trial the goalposts had moved and Pǎtrǎşcanu's case was bundled with that of Ana Pauker. Pauker *was* Jewish; the daughter of a Jewish *shochet* (a ritual slaughterer) from Moldavia she was the first Jewish government minister in Romania's history (and the first female foreign minister anywhere in the world). She was also a notorious hard-liner in doctrinal and policy matters, which made her an exemplary target for a Romanian leadership trying to curry favor with the local population.

Stalin's death aborted the plans of Romanian Communist leader Gheorghe Gheorghiu-Dej to stage a show trial of Pauker and others. Instead, during 1953 and early '54, the Romanian Party conducted a series of secret trials of lesser fry accused of being Zionist spies in the pay of 'imperial agents'. Victims ranging from genuine members of the (right-wing) Revisionist Zionists to Jewish Communists tarred with the Zionist brush were accused of illegal relations with Israel and of collaborating with Nazis during the war. They were sentenced to prison for periods varying from ten years to life. Finally Pǎtrǎşcanu himself was tried in April 1954, after languishing in prison for six years; charged with spying for the British, he was found guilty and executed.

Pauker was more fortunate: protected by Moscow (first by Stalin, later by Molotov) she was never directly targeted as a 'Zionist', and survived her September 1952 expulsion from the Party, disappearing into obscurity until her death in 1960. The Romanian Communist Party, smaller and more isolated than any of the other east European parties, had always been rent by infighting, and the defeat of the 'rightist' Pǎtrǎşcanu and the 'leftist' Pauker was above all a factional victory for the viciously effective dictator Gheorghiu-Dej, whose governing style (like that of his successor Nicolae Ceauşescu) was morbidly reminiscent of old-style authoritarian rule in the Balkans.

Jews were purged from Romanian party and government posts in these years, as they were in East Germany and Poland, two other countries where one faction of the Party could mobilize popular anti-Jewish sentiment against the Party's own 'cosmopolitans'. East Germany was especially fertile territory. In January 1953, as the 'Doctors' Plot' was unfolding in Moscow, prominent East German Jews and Jewish Communists fled west. One member of the East German Central Committee, Hans Jendretsky, demanded that Jews—'enemies of the state'—be excluded from public life. But by luck, by timing or out of prudence, all three states avoided a full-scale anti-Semitic show trial of the kind planned in Moscow and carried through in Prague.

The Slánský Trial, as it became known, is the classic Communist show trial. It was meticulously prepared over three years. First to be 'investigated' were a group of Slovak Communist leaders, notably the Czechoslovak Foreign Minister Vladimír Clementis, arrested in 1950 and accused of 'bourgeois nationalism'. To them were added various mid-level Czech Communists, accused with the Slovaks of having taken part in a Titoist-Trotskyist conspiracy along lines familiar from the Rajk case. But none of those implicated and held in prison during 1950 and 1951 was senior enough to serve as figurehead and ringleader for the major public trial that Stalin was demanding.

In the spring of 1951 Soviet Police Chief Beria instructed the Czechs to shift the emphasis of their investigations from a Titoist to a Zionist plot. From now on the whole enterprise was in the hands of the Soviet secret services—Colonel Komarov and another officer were sent to Prague to take the investigations in hand, and the Czech security police and Communist leadership received their orders from them. The need for a prominent victim had focused Soviet attention on the second figure in the Czech hierarchy after President Klement Gottwald: Party General Secretary Rudolf Slánský. Unlike Gottwald, who was a serviceable figurehead and pliable Party loyalist, Slánský, though eminently Stalinist (like Rajk before him), was a Jew.

At first Gottwald was reluctant to have Slánský arrested—the two of them had worked closely together in purging their colleagues over the past three years and if the General Secretary was implicated, Gottwald himself might be next. But the Soviets insisted, presenting forged evidence linking Slánský to the CIA, and Gottwald gave way. On November 23rd 1951 Slánský was arrested; in the days that followed prominent Jewish Communists still at liberty followed him into prison. The security services now set themselves the task of extracting confessions and 'evidence' from their many prisoners in order to construct a major case against Slánský and his collaborators. Thanks to a certain amount of resistance by their victims (notably the former General Secretary himself) even in the face of barbaric torture, this task took them the best part of a year.

Finally, by September 1952, the indictment was completed. The text of the confessions, the indictment, the predetermined sentences and the script of the trial were then sent to Moscow for Stalin's personal approval. Back in Prague a 'dress rehearsal' of the full trial was conducted—and tape-recorded. This was to provide an alternative text for 'live transmission' in the unlikely event that one of the defendants retracted his confession in open court, like Kostov. It was not needed.

The trial lasted from November 20th to November 27th 1952. It followed well-established precedent: the accused were charged with having done and said things they had not (on the basis of confessions extracted by force from other witnesses, including their fellow defendants); they were blamed for things that they *had* done but to which new meanings were attached (thus three of the accused men were charged with having favored Israel in trade deals, at a time when this was still Soviet policy); and prosecutors charged Clementis with having met with Tito ('the executioner-of-the-Yugoslav-people and lackey-of-imperialism Tito')—at a time when Clementis was Czechoslovakia's Vice-Minister of Foreign Affairs and Tito was still in Soviet good graces.

Two characteristics marked this trial out from all those preceding it. Prosecutors and witnesses repeatedly emphasized the Jewishness of most of the accused—'the cosmopolitan Rudolf Margolius', 'Slánský . . . the great hope of all the Jews in the Communist Party', 'representatives of international Zionism', etc. 'Jewish origin' (sometimes 'Zionist origin') served as a presumption of guilt, of anti-Communist, anti-Czech intentions. And the language of the prosecutors, broadcast over Czechoslovak radio, harked back to and even improved upon the crude vituperation of Prosecutor Vyshinsky in the Moscow Trials: 'repulsive traitors', 'dogs', 'wolves', 'wolfish successors of Hitler' and more in the same vein. It was also recapitulated in the Czech press.

On the fourth day of the trial the Prague Communist daily *Rudé Právo* editorialized thus: 'One trembles with disgust and repulsion at the sight of these cold, unfeeling beings. The Judas Slánský', the paper continued, was betting on 'these alien elements, this rabble with its shady past.' No Czech, the writer explained, could have committed such crimes: 'only cynical Zionists, without a fatherland . . . clever cosmopolitans who have sold out to the dollar. They were guided in this criminal activity by Zionism, bourgeois Jewish nationalism, racial chauvinism.'

Eleven of the fourteen accused were sentenced to death and executed, three were condemned to life imprisonment. Addressing the National Conference of the Czechoslovak Communist Party a month later, Gottwald had this to say about his former comrades: 'Normally bankers, industrialists, former kulaks don't get into our Party. But if they were of Jewish origin and Zionist orientation, little attention among us was paid to their class origins. This state of affairs arose from our repulsion at anti-Semitism and our respect for the suffering of the Jews.'

The Slánský trial was a criminal masquerade, judicial murder as public theatre.[13] Like the trial of the Anti-Fascist Committee in Moscow which preceded them, the Prague proceedings were also intended as an overture to the arrest of the Soviet Jewish doctors whose 'plot' was announced by *Pravda* on January 13th 1953. These Jewish physicians—'a Zionist terrorist gang' accused of murdering Andrei Zdanov, conspiring with the 'Anglo-American bourgeoisie', and advancing the cause of 'Jewish nationalism' in connivance with the American Jewish Joint Distribution

---

[13] The survivors were all released in later years, though they and their fellow victims would not be fully rehabilitated and exonerated until 1968.

Committee (as well as the late 'bourgeois Jewish nationalist' Solomon Mikhoels)—were to go on trial within three months of the Slánský verdicts.

Indications are that this trial in its turn was envisaged by the Kremlin as a preamble and excuse for mass round-ups of Soviet Jews and their subsequent expulsion to Birobidzhan (the 'homeland' in the east assigned to Jews) and Soviet Central Asia, where many Polish Jews had previously been sent between 1939 and 1941: the MVD publishing house had printed and prepared for distribution one million copies of a pamphlet explaining 'Why Jews Must Be Resettled from the Industrial Regions of the Country.' But even Stalin appears to have hesitated (Ilya Ehrenburg warned him of the devastating impact a show trial of the Jewish doctors would have upon Western opinion); in any case, before he could make a decision he died, on March 5th 1953.

Stalin's prejudices do not require an explanation: in Russia and Eastern Europe anti-Semitism was its own reward. Of greater interest are Stalin's purposes in mounting the whole charade of purges, indictments, confessions and trials. Why, after all, did the Soviet dictator need trials at all? Moscow was in a position to eliminate anyone it wished, anywhere in the Soviet bloc, through 'administrative procedures'. Trials might seem counter-productive; the obviously false testimonies and confessions, the unembarrassed targeting of selected individuals and social categories, were hardly calculated to convince foreign observers of the *bona fides* of Soviet judicial procedures.

But the show trials in the Communist bloc were not about justice. They were, rather, a form of public pedagogy-by-example; a venerable Communist institution (the first such trials in the USSR dated to 1928) whose purpose was to illustrate and exemplify the structures of authority in the Soviet system. They told the public who was right, who wrong; they placed blame for policy failures; they assigned credit for loyalty and subservience; they even wrote a script, an approved vocabulary for use in discussion of public affairs. Following his arrest Rudolf Slánský was only ever referred to as 'the spy Slánský', this ritual naming serving as a form of political exorcism. [14]

Show trials—or tribunals, in the language of Vyshinsky's 1936 *Soviet Manual of Criminal Investigation*—were explicitly undertaken for the 'mobilisation of proletarian public opinion'. As the Czechoslovak 'Court Organisation Act' of January 1953 baldly summed it up, the function of the courts was 'to educate the citizens in de-

---

[14]The script was *very* precise. When André Marty was unofficially 'tried' by the Central Committee of the French Communist Party in December 1952, his 'prosecutor', Léon Mauvais, accused him of speaking of 'the Trotskyist International' rather than 'Trotskyist scum' or 'group of Trotskyist police spies', which were the Communists' 'natural and habitual' terms for use when referring to Trotskyists. This linguistic slippage alone placed Marty under grave suspicion.

votion and loyalty toward the Czechoslovak Republic, etc.' Robert Vogeler, a defendant at a Budapest trial in 1948, noted at the time: 'To judge from the way our scripts were written, it was more important to establish our allegorical identities than it was to establish our "guilt". Each of us, in his testimony, was obliged to "unmask" himself for the benefit of the Cominform Press and the radio.'

The accused were reduced from presumptive political critics or opponents to a gaggle of unprincipled conspirators, their purposes venal and traitorous. The clumsiness of Soviet imperial style sometimes masks this objective—what is one to make of a rhetoric designed to mobilize public opinion in metropolitan Budapest by reiterating the errors of those who opposed 'the struggle against the kulaks'? But the 'public' were not being asked to believe what they heard; they were merely being trained to repeat it.

One use of the public trials was to identify scapegoats. If Communist economic policy was not producing its pre-announced successes, if Soviet foreign policy was blocked or forced to compromise, someone must take the blame. How else were the mis-steps of the infallible Leader to be explained? There were many candidates: Slánský was widely disliked inside and outside the Czechoslovak Communist Party. Rajk had been a harsh Stalinist interior minister. And precisely because they had carried out unpopular policies now seen to have failed, any and all Communist leaders and ministers were potential victims in waiting. Just as defeated generals in the French Revolutionary wars were frequently charged with treason, so Communist ministers confessed to sabotage when the policies they had implemented failed—often literally—to deliver the goods.

The advantage of the confession, in addition to its symbolic use as an exercise in guilt-transferal, was that it confirmed Communist doctrine. There were no disagreements in Stalin's universe, only heresies; no critics, only enemies; no errors, only crimes. The trials served both to illustrate Stalin's virtues and identify his enemies' crimes. They also illuminate the extent of Stalin's paranoia and the culture of suspicion that surrounded him. One part of this was a deep-rooted anxiety about Russian, and more generally 'Eastern' inferiority, a fear of Western influence and the seduction of Western affluence. In a 1950 trial in Sofia of 'The American Spies in Bulgaria', the accused were charged with propagating the view 'that the chosen races live only in the West, in spite of the fact that geographically they have all started from the East'. The indictment went on to describe the accused as exhibiting 'a feeling for servile under-valuation' that Western spies had successfully exploited.

The West, then, was a threat that had to be exorcised, repeatedly. There *were* Western spies, of course: real ones. In the early 1950s, following the outbreak of war in Korea, Washington did consider the possibility of destabilizing eastern Europe and US intelligence made a number of unsuccessful attempts to penetrate the Soviet bloc, lending superficial verisimilitude to the confessions of Communists who had purportedly worked with the CIA or spied for the British Secret Service. And

Stalin in his last years seems genuinely to have expected a war; as he explained in an 'interview' in *Pravda* in February 1951, a confrontation between capitalism and communism was inevitable, and now increasingly likely. From 1947 through 1952 the Soviet bloc was on a permanent war footing: arms production in Czechoslovakia increased seven-fold between 1948 and 1953, while more Soviet troops were moved to the GDR and plans for a strategic bomber force drawn up.

Thus the arrests and purges and trials were a public reminder of the coming confrontation; a justification for Soviet war fears; and a strategy (familiar from earlier decades) for slimming down the Leninist party and preparing it for combat. The 1949 charge that Rajk had conspired with the US and Britain to overthrow the Communists seemed believable to many Communists and their sympathizers in the West. Even the otherwise *outré* accusations against Slánský et al. drew on the widely recognized truth that Czechoslovakia had many more links with the West than other states in the bloc. But why Rajk? Why Slánský? How were the scapegoats chosen?

In Stalin's eyes any Communist who had spent time in the West, out of Soviet reach, was to be regarded with suspicion—whatever he or she was doing there. Communists who had been active in Spain during the Civil War of the thirties—and there had been many from Eastern Europe and Germany—were the first to fall under suspicion. Thus László Rajk had served in Spain (as a political commissar of the 'Rákosi battalion'); so had Otto Sling, one of Slánský's co-defendants. Following Franco's victory, many of the Spanish veterans had escaped into France, where they ended up in French internment camps. From there a significant number of them had joined the French Resistance, where they teamed up with German and other foreign Communists who had taken refuge in France. There were enough such men and women for the French Communist Party to have organized them into a sub-section of the Communist underground, the *Main d'Oeuvre Immigré* (MOI). Prominent post-war Communists like Artur London (another Slánský trial defendant) made many Western contacts through their wartime work in the MOI and this, too, aroused Stalin's suspicions and was later held against them.

The wartime Jewish Anti-Fascist Committee in the USSR had been instructed to make Western contacts and document Nazi atrocities—the very activities that later formed the basis of the criminal charges against them. German Communists like Paul Merker who spent the war years in Mexico; Slovak Communists like the future Foreign Minister Clementis who worked in London; anyone who remained in Nazi-occupied Europe: all were vulnerable to accusations that they had contacted Western agents or worked too closely with non-Communist resisters. Josef Frank, a Czech Communist who survived imprisonment at Buchenwald, was charged at the Slánský trial with using his time in the camp to make suspect acquaintances, 'class enemies'.

The only Communists who were not *prima facie* objects of Stalin's misgivings were those who had spent long periods of time in Moscow, under Kremlin scrutiny.

These could be counted on twice over: having spent many years in full view of the Soviet authorities they had few if any foreign contacts; and if they had survived the purges of the thirties (in which most of the exiled leadership of the Polish, Yugoslav and other Communist parties had been eliminated) they could be counted on to obey the Soviet dictator without question. 'National' Communists on the other hand, men and women who had remained on home soil, were deemed unreliable. They usually had a more heroic track record in domestic resistance than their Moscow confrères, who had returned after the war courtesy of the Red Army, and thus a more popular local image. And they were prone to form their own views on a local or national 'road to Socialism'.

For these reasons the 'national' Communists were almost always the main victims of the post-war show trials. Thus Rajk was a 'national' Communist, whereas Rákosi and Gerö—the Hungarian Party leaders who stage-managed his trial— were 'Muscovites' (though Gerö had also been active in Spain). There was little else to distinguish them. In Czechoslovakia, the men who had organized the Slovak national uprising against the Nazis (including Slánský) were ready-made victims of Soviet suspicion; Stalin did not enjoy sharing the credit for Czechoslovakia's liberation. The Kremlin preferred reliable, unheroic, unimaginative 'Muscovites' whom it knew: men like Klement Gottwald.

Traicho Kostov had led the Bulgarian Communist partisans during the war, until his arrest; after the war he took second place to Georgii Dimitrov, newly returned from Moscow, until his wartime record was turned against him in 1949. In Poland Gomułka had organized armed resistance under the Nazis, together with Marian Spychalski; after the war Stalin favored Bierut and other Moscow-based Poles. Spychalski and Gomułka were both later arrested and, as we have seen, narrowly avoided starring in their own show trial.

There were exceptions. In Romania it was one 'national' Communist, Dej, who engineered the downfall of another 'national' Communist, Pătrăşcanu, as well as the eclipse of the impeccably Muscovite and Stalinist Ana Pauker. And even Kostov had spent the early thirties in Moscow, at the Comintern's Balkan desk. He was also a well-attested critic of Tito (although for his own reasons: Kostov saw in Tito the heir to Serbian territorial ambitions at Bulgarian expense). Far from saving him, however, this just exacerbated his crime—Stalin was not interested in agreement or even consent, only unswerving obedience.

Lastly, there was a considerable element of personal score-settling and cynical instrumentalism in the selection of trial victims and the charges against them. As Karol Bacílek explained to the National Conference of the Czech Communist Party on December 17th 1952, 'The question as to who is guilty and who is innocent will in the end be decided upon by the Party with the help of the National Security Organs.' In some instances the latter fabricated cases against people out of coincidence or fantasy; in others they deliberately claimed the opposite of what they knew to be the case. Thus two of the defendants in the Slánský trial were accused of over-billing Moscow for Czech products. Typically, goods made in the satellite states were deliberately under-priced to Soviet advantage; only Moscow could authorize exceptions. The 'over-billing' in the Czech case, however, was established Soviet practice, as the prosecutors well knew: a way of funneling cash through Prague and on to the West, for use in intelligence operations.

Similarly cynical—and part of a campaign of personal vilification—was the charge against Ana Pauker, who was accused of Rightist and Leftist 'deviationism' simultaneously: first she had been 'critical' of rural collectivization, then she forced peasants to collectivize against their will. Rajk was accused of dissolving the Communist Party's network within the Hungarian police in 1947; in fact he had done this (on the eve of the 1947 elections and with official approval) as a cover for the dissolution of the far stronger Social Democratic police organization. Later he had secretly re-established the Communist network while maintaining the ban on other parties. But his actions, impeccably orthodox at the time, were grist to the Soviet mill when the time came to remove him.

The defendants at the major show trials were all Communists. Other Communists were purged without public trials or without any judicial process at all. But the overwhelming majority of Stalin's victims, in the Soviet Union and the satellite states, were of course not Communists at all. In Czechoslovakia, in the years 1948–54, Communists represented just one-tenth of 1 percent of those condemned to prison terms or work camps, one in twenty of those condemned to death. In the GDR the Stasi was created on February 8th 1950, with the task of overseeing and controlling not just Communists but the whole of society. Stalin was routinely suspicious not only of Communists with contacts or experience in the West, but of *anyone* who had lived outside the Soviet bloc.

It thus went without saying that virtually the entire population of eastern Europe fell under Kremlin suspicion in those years. Not that the post-war repression *within* the Soviet Union was any less all-embracing: just as Russians' exposure to Western influence in the years 1813–15 was believed to have paved the way for the Decembrist Revolt of 1825, so Stalin feared contamination and protest as a result of wartime contacts in his own day. Any Soviet citizen or soldier who survived Nazi occupation or imprisonment was thus an object of suspicion. When the Presidium of the Supreme Soviet passed a law in 1949, punishing soldiers who committed rape with 10 to 15 years in a labour camp, disapproval of the Red Army's rampage across eastern Germany and Austria was the least of its concerns. The real motive was to fashion a device with which to punish returning Soviet soldiers at will.

The scale of the punishment meted out to the citizens of the USSR and Eastern Europe in the decade following World War Two was monumental—and, outside the Soviet Union itself, utterly unprecedented. Trials were but the visible tip of an archipelago of repression: prison, exile, forced labor battalions. In 1952, at the height of the second Stalinist terror, 1.7 million prisoners were held in Soviet labor camps, a further 800,000 in labor colonies, and 2,753,000 in 'special settlements'. The 'normal' Gulag sentence was 25 years, typically followed (in the case of survivors) by exile to Siberia or Soviet Central Asia. In Bulgaria, from an industrial workforce of just under half a million, two persons out of nine were slave laborers.

In Czechoslovakia it is estimated that there were 100,000 political prisoners in a population of 13 million in the early 1950s, a figure that does not include the many tens of thousands working as forced laborers in everything but name in the country's mines. 'Administrative liquidations', in which men and women who disappeared into prison were quietly shot without publicity or trial, were another form of punishment. A victim's family might wait a year or more before learning that he or she had 'disappeared'. Three months later the person was then legally presumed dead, though with no further official acknowledgement or confirmation. At the height of the terror in Czechoslovakia some thirty to forty such announcements would appear in the local press every day. Tens of thousands disappeared this way; many hundreds of thousands more were deprived of their privileges, apartments, jobs.

In Hungary, during the years 1948–53, about one million people (of a total population of less than ten million) are estimated to have suffered arrest, prosecution, imprisonment or deportation. One Hungarian family in three was directly affected. Relatives suffered commensurately. Fritzi Loebl, the wife of one of Slánský's 'co-conspirators', was kept for a year in the prison at Ruzyn, outside Prague, and interrogated by Russians who called her a 'stinking yid prostitute'. Upon her release she was exiled to a factory in north Bohemia. The wives of prisoners and deportees lost their employment, their apartments and their personal effects. At best, if they were lucky, they were then forgotten, like Josephine Langer, whose husband Oskar Langer, a witness at the Slánský trial, was later sentenced in a secret trial to 22 years in prison. She and her daughters lived for six years in a cellar.

Romania saw perhaps the worst persecution, certainly the most enduring. In addition to well over a million detainees in prisons, labor camps and slave labor on the Danube-Black Sea Canal, of whom tens of thousands died and whose numbers don't include those deported to the Soviet Union, Romania was remarkable for the severity of its prison conditions and various 'experimental' prisons; notably the one at Pitești where, for three years from December 1949 through late 1952, prisoners were encouraged to 're-educate' one another through physical and psychological torture. Most of the victims were students, 'Zionists' and non-Communist political detainees.

The Communist state was in a permanent condition of undeclared war against its own citizens. Like Lenin, Stalin understood the need for enemies, and it was in the logic of the Stalinist state that it was constantly mobilizing against its foes—external, but above all domestic. In the words of Stephan Rais, Czechoslovak Justice Minister, addressing the June 11th 1952 Conference of Czechoslovak Attorneys:

[the attorney] must . . . rely on the most mature, solely correct and truthful science in the world, on Soviet legal science, and thoroughly avail himself of the experiences of Soviet legal practice . . . An inevitable necessity of our period is the ever increasing class struggle.

The martial vocabulary so beloved of Communist rhetoric echoed this conflict-bound condition. Military metaphors abounded: class conflict required alliances, liaison with the masses, turning movements, frontal attacks. Stalin's assertion that class warfare *accentuated* as socialism approached was adduced to account for the curious fact that even as elections everywhere showed 99 percent support for the Party, its enemies were nevertheless multiplying, the battle had to be fought with ever firmer resolve, and the domestic history of the USSR had to be painstakingly reproduced across the Soviet bloc.

The main enemies were ostensibly the peasant and the bourgeois. But in practice intellectuals were often the easiest target, just as they had been for the Nazis. Andrei Zdanov's venomous attack on Anna Akhmatova—'a nun or a whore, or rather a nun *and* a whore, who combines harlotry with prayer. Akhmatova's poetry is utterly remote from the people'[15]—echoes most of the conventional Stalinist anti-intellectual themes: religion, prostitution, alienation from the masses. Had Akhmatova been Jewish, like much of the central European intelligentsia, the caricature would have been complete.

Political repression, censorship, even dictatorship were by no means unknown in Europe's eastern half before the coming of Stalinism, although there was universal agreement among those in a position to compare that the interrogators and prisons of inter-war Hungary, Poland or Romania were much to be preferred to those of the 'popular democracies'. The instruments of control and terror through which the Communist state operated after 1947 were perfected by Stalin's men, but for the most part they did not need to be imported from the East; they were already in place. It was not by chance that Piteşti prison was set up and run for the Communist Securitate by one Eugen Turcanu, who in an earlier incarnation had been a student activist at Iaşi University for the Iron Guard, Romania's inter-war Fascist movement.

What distinguished the Party-State of the Communists from its authoritarian predecessors, however, was not so much the sheer efficiency of its repressive apparatus; but rather that power and resources were now monopolized and abused for the near-exclusive benefit of a *foreign* power. Soviet occupation succeeded Nazi occupation with minimal transitional disruption and drew Europe's eastern half steadily deeper into the Soviet orbit (for the citizens of East Germany, emerging

---

[15]Catherine Merridale, *Night of Stone: Death and Memory in 20th-Century Russia* (2000), page 249.

POSTWAR: A HISTORY OF EUROPE SINCE 1945

from twelve years of Nazi dictatorship, the transition was smoother still). This process and its consequences—the 'Sovietization' and 'Russification' of everything in Eastern Europe from manufacturing processes to academic titles—would sooner or later alienate the allegiance of all but the most inveterate Stalinists.

And it had the ancillary effect of blurring many people's recollection of their initial ambivalence in the face of the Communist transformation. In later years it was easy to forget that the anti-Semitic and frequently xenophobic tone of Stalinist public language had found a sympathetic audience in much of eastern Europe, just as it did in the Soviet Union itself. Economic nationalism had popular local roots too, so that expropriation, nationalization, controls and state regulation of work were by no means unfamiliar. In Czechoslovakia, for example, under the Two-Year Plan introduced in 1946, recalcitrant workers could be exiled to labor camps (though it is also true that most Czech judges in the years 1946–48 refused to apply these penalties).

In its initial phases, then, the Soviet take-over of eastern Europe was not quite as one-sided and brutal a transition as it would appear in retrospect, even if we discount the high hopes vested in the Communist future by a minority of young people in Warsaw or Prague. But just as the Nazis' brutality had alienated potentially friendly local sentiment in the territories they 'liberated' from the USSR in 1941–42, so Stalin soon dispersed illusions and expectations in the satellite states.

The result of imposing an accelerated version of the Soviet Union's own dismal economic history upon the more developed lands to its west has already been noted. The only resource upon which Communist managers could consistently rely was labor-intensive production pressed to the breaking point. That is why the Stalinist terror of 1948–53 in Eastern Europe so closely resembled its Soviet counterpart of twenty years before: both were tied to a policy of coercive industrialization. The centrally planned economies were actually quite effective at extracting surplus-value from miners and factory workers by force; but this was all they could do. Soviet-bloc agriculture slipped further and further backwards, its occasionally surreal inefficiencies exemplified in the USSR by the bureaucrats in Frunze (now Bizkek, in Kirghizstan) who in 1960 encouraged local peasants to meet their (arbitrary and unattainable) butter delivery quotas by buying up stocks from local shops . . .

The trials and purges, and the accompanying chorus of mendacious commentary, helped degrade whatever remained in eastern Europe of the public sphere. Politics and government became synonymous with corruption and arbitrary repression, practiced by and for the benefit of a venal clique, itself rent by suspicion and fear. This was hardly a new experience in the region, of course. But there was a distinctively cynical quality to *Communist* misrule: old-fashioned abuses were now laboriously embedded in a rhetorical cant of equality and social progress, a hypocrisy for which neither the inter-war oligarchs nor the Nazi occupiers had felt the need. And, once again, it was a form of misrule adapted for the near-exclusive benefit of a foreign power, which was what made Soviet rule so resented outside the Soviet Union's own borders.

The effect of the Sovietization of eastern Europe was to draw it steadily away from the western half of the continent. Just as Western Europe was about to enter an era of dramatic transformation and unprecedented prosperity, eastern Europe was slipping into a coma: a winter of inertia and resignation, punctured by cycles of protest and subjugation, that would last for nearly four decades. It is symptomatic and somehow appropriate that during the very years when the Marshall Plan injected some $14 billion *into* Western Europe's recovering economy, Stalin— through reparations, forced deliveries and the imposition of grossly disadvantageous trading distortions—extracted approximately the same amount *from* eastern Europe.

Eastern Europe had always been different from western Europe. But the distinction between eastern and western Europe had not been the only one by which the continent understood itself, nor even the most important. Mediterranean Europe was markedly different from North-West Europe; religion had far greater salience than politics in the historic boundaries within and between states. In Europe before World War Two, the differences between North and South, rich and poor, urban and rural, counted for more than those between East and West.

The impact of Soviet rule upon the lands east of Vienna was thus in certain respects even more marked than it had been upon Russia itself. The Russian Empire, after all, had only ever been part-European; and the European identity of post-Petrine Russia was itself much contested in the course of the century preceding Lenin's coup. In brutally cutting the Soviet Union adrift from its ties to European history and culture the Bolsheviks did great and lasting violence to Russia. But their suspicion of the West and their fear of Western influence was not unprecedented; it had deep roots in self-consciously Slavophil writings and practices long before 1917.

There were no such precedents in central and eastern Europe. It was, indeed, part of the insecure small-state nationalism of Poles, Romanians, Croats and others that they saw themselves not as some far-flung outriders at the edge of European civilization; but rather as the under-appreciated defenders of Europe's core heritage—just as Czechs and Hungarians understood themselves, reasonably enough, as dwelling at the very heart of the continent. Romanian and Polish intellectuals looked to Paris for fashions in thought and art, much as the German-speaking intelligentsia of the late Habsburg Empire, from Sub-Carpathian Ruthenia to Trieste, had always looked to Vienna.

That integrated, cosmopolitan Europe had of course only ever existed for a minority—and it died in 1918. But the new states hatched at Versailles were fragile and somehow impermanent from the very start. The inter-war decades had thus been a sort of interregnum, neither peace nor war, in which the fate of post-imperial central and eastern Europe remained somehow undecided. The likeliest outcome—that a renascent Germany would be the *de facto* heir to the old empires in the territories stretching from Stettin to Istanbul—was narrowly averted only by Hitler's own errors.

Instead, the imposition of a Russian rather than a German solution cut Europe's vulnerable eastern half away from the body of the continent. At the time this was not a matter of great concern to western Europeans themselves. With the exception of the Germans, the nation most directly affected by the division of Europe but also ill-placed to voice displeasure at it, western Europeans were largely indifferent to the disappearance of eastern Europe. Indeed, they soon became so accustomed to it, and were anyway so preoccupied with the remarkable changes taking place in their own countries, that it seemed quite natural that there should be an impermeable armed barrier running from the Baltic to the Adriatic. But for the peoples to the *east* of that barrier, thrust back as it seemed into a grimy, forgotten corner of their own continent, at the mercy of a semi-alien Great Power no better off than they and parasitic upon their shrinking resources, history itself ground slowly to a halt.

VII

Culture Wars

'We all rejected the preceding era. I knew it chiefly through literature, and it seemed to me to have been an era of stupidity and barbarity'.
Milan Šimečka

'Every action, in the middle of the twentieth century, presupposes and involves the adoption of an attitude with regard to the Soviet enterprise'.
Raymond Aron

'I was right to be wrong, while you and your kind were wrong to be right'.
Pierre Courtade (to Edgar Morin)

'Like it or not, the construction of socialism is privileged in that to understand it one must espouse its movement and adopt its goals'.
Jean-Paul Sartre

'You can't help people being right for the wrong reasons ... This fear of finding oneself in bad company is not an expression of political purity; it is an expression of a lack of self-confidence'.
Arthur Koestler

With an alacrity that would perplex future generations, the struggle in Europe between Fascism and Democracy was hardly over before it was displaced by a new breach: that separating Communists from anti-Communists. The staking out of political and intellectual positions for and against the Soviet Union did not begin with the post-World War Two division of Europe. But it was in these post-war years, between 1947 and 1953, that the line dividing East from West, Left from Right, was carved deep into European cultural and intellectual life.

The circumstances were unusually propitious. Between the wars the far Right had been better supported than it suited most people to recall. From Brussels to Bucharest the polemical journalism and literature of the 1930s abounded in racism, anti-Semitism, ultra-nationalism, clericalism and political reaction. Intellectuals, journalists and teachers who before and during the war had espoused Fascist or ultra-reactionary sentiments had good reason after 1945 vociferously to affirm their new-found credentials as progressives or radicals (or else retreat into temporary or lasting obscurity). Since most parties and journals of a Fascist or even ultra-conservative persuasion were in any case now banned (except in the Iberian Peninsula, where the opposite was true), public expressions of political allegiance were confined to the center and left of the spectrum. Right-wing thought and opinion in Europe had been eclipsed.

But although the *content* of public writing and performance was spectacularly metamorphosed by the fall of Hitler, Mussolini and their followers, the *tone* stayed much the same. The apocalyptic urgency of the Fascists; their call for violent, 'definitive' solutions, as though genuine change *necessarily* led through root-and-branch destruction; the distaste for the compromise and 'hypocrisy' of liberal democracy and the enthusiasm for Manichean choices (all or nothing, revolution or decadence): these impulses could serve the far Left equally well and after 1945 they did so.

In their preoccupation with nation, degeneration, sacrifice and death, inter-war Fascist writers had looked to the First World War. The intellectual Left after 1945 was also shaped by the experience of war, but this time as a clash of incompatible moral alternatives, excluding all possibility of compromise: Good versus Evil, Freedom against Enslavement, Resistance against Collaboration. Liberation from Nazi or Fascist occupation was widely welcomed as an occasion for radical political and social change; an opportunity to turn wartime devastation to revolutionary effect and make a new beginning. And when, as we have seen, that opportunity was seemingly thwarted and 'normal' life was summarily restored, frustrated expectations turned readily enough to cynicism—or else to the far Left, in a world once more polarized into irreconcilable political camps.

Post-war European intellectuals were in a hurry and impatient with compromise. They were young. In World War One a generation of young men was killed. But after the Second World War it was largely an older, discredited cohort that disappeared from the scene. In its place emerged writers, artists, journalists and political activists who were too young to have known the war of 1914–18, but who were impatient to make up the years lost in its successor. *Their* political education had come in the era of the Popular Fronts and anti-Fascist movements; and when they achieved public acclaim and influence, often as a result of their wartime activities, it was at an unusually early age by traditional European standards.

In France, Jean-Paul Sartre was 40 when the war ended; Simone de Beauvoir was 37; Albert Camus, the most influential of them all, just 32. Of the older generation only Francois Mauriac (born in 1885) could match them in influence, precisely because he was not tainted by any Vichyite past. In Italy only the Neapolitan philosopher Benedetto Croce (born in 1866) remained from an earlier generation of Italian public figures. In post-Fascist Italy Ignazio Silone, born in 1900, was among the more senior of the influential intellectual figures; the novelist and political commentator Alberto Moravia was 38, the Communist editor and writer Elio Vittorini a year younger. In Germany, where Nazi sympathies and the war had taken the heaviest toll on public intellectuals and writers, Heinrich Böll—the most talented of a self-consciously new generation of writers who came together two years after Hitler's defeat to form the 'Group 47'—was only 28 when the war ended.

In eastern Europe, where the intellectual elites of the pre-war years were tainted with ultra-conservatism, mystical nationalism or worse, the social promotion of youth was even more marked. Czesław Miłosz, whose influential essay *The Captive Mind* was published in 1951 when he was just 40 and already in political exile, was not at all atypical. Jerzy Andrzejewski (who appears in Miłosz's book in a less than flattering light) published *Ashes and Diamonds,* his acclaimed novel of post-war Poland, while in his thirties. Tadeusz Borowski, born in 1922, was still in his mid-twenties when he published his memoir of Auschwitz: *This Way to the Gas, Ladies and Gentlemen.*

The leaders of the East European Communist parties were, typically, slightly older men who had survived the inter-war years as political prisoners or else in Moscow exile, or both. But just below them was a cohort of very young men and women whose idealistic commitment to the Soviet-backed takeovers played an important part in their success. In Hungary, Géza Losonczy, who would fall victim to the Soviet repression after the 1956 Hungarian revolt, was still in his twenties when he and hundreds like him schemed to bring the Hungarian Communist Party to power. Heda Kovaly's husband, Rudolf Margolius, one of the defendants at the Slánský trial in December 1952, was 35 when he was appointed minister in the Communist government of Czechoslovakia; Artur London, another of the accused at that trial, was younger still, 33 years old when the Communists seized power. London had received his political education in the French resistance; like many in the Communist underground, he learned how to exercise political and military responsibilities at a very young age.

Youthful enthusiasm for a Communist future was widespread among middle-class intellectuals, in East and West alike. And it was accompanied by a distinctive complex of inferiority towards the proletariat, the blue-collar working class. In the immediate post-war years, skilled manual workers were at a premium—a marked contrast with the Depression years still fresh in collective memory. There was coal to be mined; roads, railways, buildings, power lines to be rebuilt or replaced; tools to be manufactured and then applied to the manufacture of other goods. For all these jobs there was a shortage of trained labor; as we have seen, young, able-bodied men in the Displaced Persons camps had little difficulty finding work and asylum, in contrast to women with families—or 'intellectuals' of any sort.

One consequence of this was the universal exaltation of industrial work and workers—a distinct political asset for parties claiming to represent them. Left-leaning, educated, middle-class men and women embarrassed by their social origin could assuage their discomfort by abandoning themselves to Communism. But even if they didn't go so far as to join the Party, many artists and writers in France and Italy especially 'prostrated themselves before the proletariat' (Arthur Koestler) and elevated the 'revolutionary working class' (typically imagined in a rather Socialist-Realist/Fascist light as stern, male and muscular) to near iconic status.

Although the phenomenon was pan-European in scope and transcended Communist politics (the best-known intellectual exponent of 'workerism' in Europe was Jean-Paul Sartre, who never joined the French Communist Party), it was in eastern Europe that such sentiments had real consequences. Students, teachers, writers and artists from Britain, France, Germany and elsewhere flocked to (pre-schismatic) Yugoslavia to help rebuild railways with their bare hands. In August 1947 Italo Calvino wrote enthusiastically about young volunteers from Italy similarly engaged in Czechoslovakia. Devotion to a new beginning, the worship of a real or imagined community of workers, and admiration for the Soviets (and their all-conquering Red Army) separated a young post-war generation from its social roots and the national past.

The decision to become a Communist (or a 'Marxist', which in the circumstances of the time usually meant Communist) was typically made at a young age. Thus Ludek Pachman, a Czech: 'I became a Marxist in the year 1943. I was 19 years old and the idea that suddenly I understood everything and could explain everything enchanted me, as well as the idea that I would march with proletarians of the whole world, first against Hitler and then against the international bourgeoisie.' Even those, like Czesław Miłosz, who were not swept off their feet by the charms of its dogma, unambiguously welcomed Communism's social reforms: 'I was delighted to see the semi-feudal structure of Poland finally smashed, the universities opened to young workers and peasants, agrarian reform undertaken and the country finally set on the road to industrialization.' As Milovan Djilas observed, recalling his own experience as Tito's close adjunct: 'Totalitarianism at the outset is enthusiasm and conviction; only later does it become organizations, authority, careerism.'

Communist parties initially flattered intellectuals, for whom Communism's ambitions stood in appealing contrast to the small-state parochialism of their homelands as well as the violent anti-intellectualism of the Nazis. For many young intellectuals, Communism was less a matter of conviction than an affair of faith—as Alexander Wat (another subsequently ex-Communist Pole) would observe, the secular intelligentsia of Poland hungered after a 'refined catechism'. Although it was only ever a minority of East European students, poets, playwrights, novelists, journalist or professors who became active Communists, these were often the most talented men and women of their generation.

Thus Pavel Kohout, who in later decades would achieve international renown as a dissident and post-Communist essayist and playwright, first came to the public eye in his native Czechoslovakia as an ultra-enthusiast for his country's new regime. Looking back in 1969 he described his 'sensation of certainty' upon watching Party Leader Klement Gottwald in Prague's crowded Old Town Square on the day of the February 1948 Czech coup. Here, 'in that human mass which set out to search for justice and in this man [Gottwald] who is leading them into the decisive battle', the 20-year-old Kohout found 'the *Centrum Securitatis* that Comenius tried to find in vain.' Four years later, embraced in the faith, Kohout wrote 'A Cantata to our very own Communist Party':

Let us sing greetings to the party!
Her youth is marked by young shock workers
She has the reason of a million heads
And the strength of millions of human hands
And her battalion is the
words of Stalin and Gottwald.

In the midst of blooming May
Into far-away confines
Above the old Castle the flag swaying
With the words 'The truth prevails!'
The words gloriously fulfilled themselves:
Workers truth has prevailed!
Towards a glorious future our country rises.
Glory to Gottwald's party!
Glory!
Glory! [1]

This sort of faith was widespread in Kohout's generation. As Milosz would observe, Communism operated on the principle that writers need not *think*, they need only *understand*. And even understanding required little more than commitment, which was precisely what young intellectuals in the region were looking for. 'We were children of the war,' wrote Zdeněk Mlynář (who joined the Czechoslovak Communist Party in 1946, at the age of fifteen), 'who, having not actually fought against anyone, brought our wartime mentality with us into these first postwar years, when the opportunity to fight for something presented itself at last.' Mlynář's generation knew only the years of war and Nazi occupation, during which 'it was either one side or the other—there was no middle ground. Thus our unique experience drummed into us the notion that the victory of the correct conception meant quite simply the liquidation, the destruction, of the other.'[2]

The innocent enthusiasm with which some young East Europeans plunged into Communism ('I'm in that revolutionary mood . . .', as the writer Ludvík Vaculík would exclaim to his girlfriend upon joining the Czech Party) does not diminish

---

[1] Translation by Professor Marci Shore of the University of Indiana, slightly amended by TJ. I am also indebted to Professor Shore for the quotation from Ludek Pachman.
[2] Zdeněk Mlynář, *Night Frost in Prague* (London, 1980), page 2.

the responsibility of Moscow for what was, in the end, a Soviet take-over of their countries. But it helps account for the scale of disenchantment and disillusion that followed. Slightly older Communists, like Djilas (born in 1911), probably always understood, in his words, that 'the manipulation of fervor is the germ of bondage.' But younger converts, particularly intellectuals, were stunned to discover the rigors of Communist discipline and the reality of Stalinist power.

Thus the imposition of Zdanov's 'two cultures' dogma after 1948, with its insistence upon the adoption of 'correct' positions on everything from botany to poetry, came as a particular shock in the popular democracies of eastern Europe. Slavish intellectual adherence to a party line, long-established in the Soviet Union where there was in any case a pre-Soviet heritage of repression and orthodoxy, came harder to countries that had only recently emerged from the rather benign regimen of the Habsburgs. In nineteenth-century central Europe, intellectuals and poets had acquired the habit and responsibility of speaking on behalf of the nation. Under Communism their role was different. Where once they had represented an abstract 'people' they were now little more than cultural mouthpieces for (real) tyrants. Worse, they would soon be the victim of choice—as cosmopolitans, 'parasites' or Jews—for those same tyrants in search of scapegoats for their errors.

Thus most of the Eastern European intellectuals' enthusiasm for Communism—even in Czechoslovakia, where it was strongest—had evaporated by Stalin's death, though it would linger on for some years in the form of projects for 'revision', or for 'reform Communism'. The division within Communist states was no longer between Communism and its opponents. The important distinction was once again between those in authority—the Party-State, with its police, its bureaucracy and its house intelligentsia—and everyone else.

In this sense the Cold War fault-line fell not so much between East and West as *within* Eastern and Western Europe alike. In Eastern Europe, as we have seen, the Communist Party and its apparatus were in a state of undeclared war with the rest of society, and closer acquaintance with Communism had drawn up new battle-lines: between those for whom Communism brought practical social advantage in one form or another, and those for whom it meant discrimination, disappointment and repression. In *Western* Europe the same fault-line found many intellectuals on both sides; but enthusiasm for Communism in theory was characteristically present in inverse proportion to direct experience of it in practice.

This widespread ignorance of the fate of contemporary Eastern Europe, coupled with growing Western indifference, was a source of bewilderment and frustration to many in the East. The problem for East European intellectuals and others was not their peripheral situation—this was a fate to which they had long been resigned. What pained them after 1948 was their *double* exclusion: from their own history, thanks to the Soviet presence, and from the consciousness of the West, whose best-known intellectuals took no account of their experience or example. In East

European writings about West Europe in the early fifties there is a reiterated tone of injury and bewildered surprise: of 'disappointed love' as Miłosz described it in *The Captive Mind*. Does Europe not realize, wrote the exiled Romanian Mircea Eliade in April 1952, that she has been amputated of a part of her very flesh? 'For . . . all these countries *are in* Europe, all these peoples belong to the European community.'

But they did not belong to it anymore, and that was the point. Stalin's success in gouging his defensive perimeter deep into the center of Europe had removed Eastern Europe from the equation. European intellectual and cultural life after the Second World War took place on a drastically reduced stage, from which the Poles, Czechs and others had been summarily removed. And despite the fact that the challenge of Communism lay at the heart of Western European debates and disputes, the practical experience of 'real existing Communism' a few score miles to the east was paid very little attention: and by Communism's most ardent admirers, none at all.

The intellectual condition of post-war Western Europe would have been unrecognizable to a visitor from even the quite recent past. German-speaking central Europe—the engine room of European culture for the first third of the twentieth century—had ceased to exist. Vienna, already a shadow of its former self after the overthrow of the Habsburgs in 1918, was divided like Berlin among the four allied powers. It could hardly feed or clothe its citizens, much less contribute to the intellectual life of the continent. Austrian philosophers, economists, mathematicians and scientists, like their contemporaries in Hungary and the rest of the former Dual Monarchy, had either escaped into exile (to France, Britain, the British Dominions or the US), collaborated with the authorities or else been killed.

Germany itself lay in ruins. The German intellectual emigration after 1933 had left behind almost no-one of standing not compromised by his dealings with the regime. Martin Heidegger's notorious flirtation with the Nazis was atypical only in its controversial implications for his influential philosophical writings; tens of thousands of lesser Heideggers in schools, universities, local and national bureaucracies, newspapers and cultural institutions were similarly compromised by the enthusiasm with which they had adapted their writings and actions to Nazi demands.

The post-war German scene was further complicated by the existence of *two* Germanies, one of them claiming a monopolistic inheritance of the 'good' German past: anti-Fascist, progressive, enlightened. Many intellectuals and artists were tempted to throw in their lot with the Soviet Zone and its successor, the German Democratic Republic. Unlike the Federal Republic of Bonn, incompletely de-Nazified and reluctant to stare the recent German past in the face, East Germany proudly insisted upon its anti-Nazi credentials. Communist authorities welcomed historians or playwrights or film-makers who wanted to remind their audiences of the crimes of the 'other' Germany—so long as they respected certain taboos. Some of the best talent that had survived from Weimar Republic days migrated east.

One reason for this was that because Soviet-occupied East Germany was the only state in the eastern bloc with a Western *doppelganger*, its intellectuals had access to a Western audience in a way not open to Romanian or Polish writers. And if censorship and pressure became intolerable, there remained the option of returning west, through the Berlin crossing points, at least until 1961 and the building of the Wall. Thus Berthold Brecht opted to live in the GDR; young writers like Christa Wolf chose to remain there; and younger writers still, like the future dissident Wolf Biermann, actually migrated east to study and write (in Biermann's case at the age of 17, in 1953).[3]

What appealed to radical intellectuals from the 'materialist' West was the GDR's self-presentation as progressive, egalitarian and anti-Nazi, a lean and sober alternative to the Federal Republic. The latter seemed at once heavy with a history it preferred not to discuss, and yet at the same time curiously weightless, lacking political roots and culturally dependent on the Western Allies, the US above all, who had invented it. Intellectual life in the early Federal Republic lacked political direction. Radical options at either political extreme were expressly excluded from public life, and young writers like Böll were reluctant to engage in party politics (in sharp contrast to the generation that would follow).

There was certainly no lack of cultural outlets: by 1948, once shortages of paper and newsprint had been overcome and distribution networks rebuilt, over two hundred literary and political journals were circulating in the Western Zone of Germany (though many of these disappeared following the currency reform), and the new Federal Republic could boast an unusual range of quality newspapers, notably the new weekly *Die Zeit*, published in Hamburg. And yet West Germany was, and would for many years remain, peripheral to the mainstream of European intellectual life. Melvin Lasky, a Western journalist and editor based in Berlin, wrote of the German intellectual condition in 1950 that 'Never in modern history, I think, has a nation and a people revealed itself to be so exhausted, so bereft of inspiration or even talent.'

The contrast with Germany's earlier cultural pre-eminence accounts in part for the disappointment many domestic and foreign observers felt when contemplating the new Republic: Raymond Aron was not the only person to recall that in earlier years this had looked to be Germany's century. With so much of Germany's cultural heritage polluted and disqualified by its appropriation for Nazi purposes, it was no longer clear just what Germans could now contribute to Europe. German writers and thinkers were obsessed, understandably enough, with peculiarly *Ger-*

---

[3]Brecht, characteristically, hedged his bets by retaining an Austrian passport.

man dilemmas. It is significant that Karl Jaspers, the only major figure from the pre-Nazi intellectual world who took an active part in post-1945 debates, is best known for a singular contribution to an *internal* German debate: his 1946 essay on *The Question of German Guilt.* But it was West German intellectuals' studious avoidance of ideological politics that did most to marginalize them in the first post-war decade, at a time when public conversation in western Europe was intensely and divisively politicized.

The British, too, were mostly peripheral to European intellectual life in these years, though for very different reasons. The political arguments that were splitting Europe were not unknown in Britain—inter-war confrontations over pacifism, the Depression and the Spanish Civil War had divided the Labor Party and the intellectual Left, and these divisions were not forgotten in later years. But in inter-war Britain neither Fascists nor Communists had succeeded in translating social dissent into political revolution. The Fascists were largely confined to the poorer quarters of London, where they traded for a while in the 1930s on popular anti-Semitism; the Communist Party of Great Britain (CPGB) never gathered much support outside its early strongholds in the Scottish shipbuilding industry, some mining communities and a handful of factories in the West Midlands of England. Even at its brief electoral peak, in 1945, the Party won just 102,000 votes (0.4 percent of the national vote) and elected two members to Parliament—both of whom lost their seats at the 1950 elections. By the election of 1951 the CPGB attracted just 21,000 voters in a population of some 49 million.

Communism in the UK, then, was a political abstraction. This in no way inhibited intellectual sympathy for Marxism, among the London intelligentsia and in the universities. Bolshevism had from the outset held a certain appeal to British Fabian Socialists like H. G. Wells, who recognized in the policies of Lenin and even Stalin something familiar and sympathetic: social engineering from above by those who know best. And the British mandarin Left, like their contemporaries in the Foreign Office, had little time for the travails of the small countries between Germany and Russia, whom they had always regarded as something of a nuisance.

But whereas these matters would stir heated debate across the English Channel, Communism did not mobilize or divide intellectuals in Britain to anything like the same extent. As George Orwell observed in 1947, 'the English are not sufficiently interested in intellectual matters to be intolerant about them.' Intellectual and cultural debate in England (and to a lesser extent in the rest of Britain) was focused instead upon a domestic concern: the first intimations of a decades-long anxiety about national 'decline'. It is symptomatic of the ambivalent mood of post-war England that the country had just fought and won a six-year war against its mortal enemy and was embarked upon an unprecedented experiment in welfare capitalism—yet cultural commentators were absorbed by intimations of failure and deterioration.

Thus T. S. Eliot, in his *Notes Towards the Definition of Culture* (1948), asserted 'with some confidence that our own period is one of decline; that the standards of culture are lower than they were fifty years ago; and that the evidences of this decline are visible in every department of human activity.' Motivated by comparable concerns, the British Broadcasting Corporation began its Third Programme on the radio in 1946: a high-minded, high-cultural product explicitly intended for the encouragement and dissemination of 'quality', and directed at what in continental Europe would be thought of as the 'intelligentsia'; but whose mix of classical music, topical lectures and serious discussion was unmistakably English in its studious avoidance of divisive or politically sensitive topics.

The British were not uninterested in European affairs. European politics and letters were regularly covered in weekly and periodical magazines, and British readers could be well-informed if they wished. Nor were the British unaware of the scale of the trauma that Europe had just passed through. Cyril Connolly, writing in his own journal, *Horizon*, in September 1945, had this to say about the contemporary European condition: 'Morally and economically Europe has lost the war. The great marquee of European civilization in whose yellow light we all grew up, and read, or wrote, or loved, or traveled has fallen down; the side-ropes are frayed, the centre pole is broken, the chairs and tables are all in pieces, the tent is empty, the roses are withered on their stands . . . '

But notwithstanding this concern for the state of the Continent, British (and especially English) commentators stood a little aside; as though the problems of Europe and of Britain, while recognizably related, were nevertheless different in crucial respects. With certain notable exceptions,[4] British intellectuals did not play an influential part in the great debates of continental Europe, but observed them from the sidelines. Broadly speaking, affairs that were urgently *political* in Europe aroused only intellectual interest in Britain; while topics of *intellectual* concern on the Continent were usually confined to academic circles in the UK, if indeed they were noticed at all.

The situation in Italy was almost exactly the opposite. Of all the countries of western Europe, it was Italy that had most directly *experienced* the plagues of the age. The country had been governed for twenty years by the world's first Fascist regime. It had been occupied by the Germans, then liberated by the Western Allies, in a snail-paced war of attrition and destruction that had lasted nearly two years, covered three quarters of the country, and reduced much of the land and its people to near-destitution. Moreover, from September 1943 to April 1945 the north of Italy was convulsed in what amounted in all but name to a full-scale civil war.

As a former Axis state Italy was an object of suspicion to West and East alike. Until Tito's split with Stalin, Italy's unresolved border with Yugoslavia was the most

---

[4]The best-known of course was Arthur Koestler—but then he might as readily be described as Hungarian, or Austrian, or French or Jewish.

unstable and potentially explosive frontier of the Cold War, and the country's un-easy relationship to its Communist neighbor was complicated by the presence in Italy of the largest Communist Party outside the Soviet bloc: 4,350,000 votes (19 percent of the total) in 1946, rising to 6,122,000 (23 percent of the total) in 1953. In that same year the *Partito Communista Italiano* (PCI) boasted a paid-up member-ship of 2,145,000. The Party's local influence was further strengthened by its near-monopoly of power in certain regions (notably the Emilia-Romagna, around the city of Bologna); the support it could rely on from Pietro Nenni's *Partito Socialista Italiano (PSI)*;[5] and the widespread popularity of its subtle and thoughtful leader, Palmiro Togliatti.

For all these reasons, intellectual life in post-war Italy was highly politicized and intimately tied to the problem of Communism. The overwhelming majority of young Italian intellectuals, including even some of those tempted by Fascism, had been formed in the shadow of Benedetto Croce. Croce's distinctive blend of Hegelian idealism in philosophy and nineteenth-century liberalism in politics had provided an ethical reference for a generation of intellectual anti-Fascists; but in the post-war circumstances it seemed manifestly insufficient. The real choice fac-ing Italians appeared as a stark alternative: politicized clericalism—the alliance of a conservative Vatican (under Pius XII) and the US-backed Christian Democrats—or else political Marxism.

The PCI had a special quality that distinguished it from other Communist par-ties, East and West. From the outset, it had been led by intellectuals. Togliatti, like Antonio Gramsci and the Party's other youthful founders of twenty years earlier, was markedly more intelligent—and respectful of intelligence—than the leaders of most of the other Communist parties of Europe. In the decade following World War Two, moreover, the Party openly welcomed intellectuals—as members and as allies—and took care to tone down those elements in Party rhetoric likely to put them off. Indeed, Togliatti consciously tailored Communism's appeal to Italian in-tellectuals with a formula of his own devising: 'half Croce and half Stalin.'

The formula was uniquely successful. The path from Croce's liberal anti-Fascism to political Marxism was taken by some of the Italian Communist Party's most tal-ented younger leaders: men like Giorgio Amendola, Lucio Lombardo Radice, Pietro Ingrao, Carlo Cassola and Emilio Sereni, all of whom came to Communist politics from the world of philosophy and literature. They were joined after 1946 by men and women disillusioned by the Action Party's failure to put into practice the as-pirations of the wartime Resistance, signaling the end of hopes for a secular, radi-cal and non-Marxist alternative in Italian public life. 'Shamefaced Crocians', one writer called them at the time.

Presented as the voice of progress and modernity in a stagnant land, and as the

---

[5]The PSI in these years was unique among West European Socialist parties in its proximity and subor-dination to the Communists—a pattern much more familiar in *Eastern* Europe.

best hope for practical social and political reform, the PCI gathered around itself a court of like-minded scholars and writers, who gave to the Party and its politics an aura of respectability, intelligence and even ecumenicalism. But with the division of Europe, Togliatti's strategy came under growing pressure. The criticism addressed by the Soviets to the PCI at the first Cominform meeting in September 1947 revealed Stalin's determination to bring the Italian Communists (like the French) under tighter control; their political tactics were to be more closely coordinated with Moscow and their latitudinarian approach to cultural affairs was to be replaced by Zdanov's uncompromising thesis of the 'two cultures'. Meanwhile, with America's brazen but successful intervention on behalf of the Christian Democrats in the elections of 1948, Togliatti's post-war policy of working within the institutions of liberal democracy began to seem naïve.

Whatever his doubts, then, Togliatti had no option but to exercise tighter control and impose Stalinist norms. This provoked public dissent among some Party intellectuals, who had hitherto felt at liberty to distinguish between the Party's political authority, which they did not question, and the terrain of 'culture' where they prized their autonomy. As Vittorini, the editor of the Communist cultural journal *Il Politechnico*, had reminded Togliatti in an Open Letter back in January 1947, 'culture' cannot be subordinated to politics, except at its own expense and at the price of truth.

Togliatti, who had spent the 1930s in Moscow and had played a leading role in the Comintern's Spanish operations in 1937–38, knew otherwise. In a Communist Party everyone took their instructions from above, everything was subordinate to politics. 'Culture' was not a protected zone in which the Soviet writ need not run. Vittorini and his companions would have to accept the Party line in literature, art and ideas, or else leave. Over the course of the next few years the Italian Party cleaved more closely to Soviet authority and Vittorini and many other intellectuals duly drifted away. But despite Togliatti's unswerving loyalty to Moscow, the PCI never altogether lost a certain un-dogmatic 'aura', as the only major Communist Party that tolerated and even embraced intelligent dissent and autonomy of thought; this reputation would serve it well in later decades.

Indeed, Togliatti's critics on the non-Communist Left were consistently wrong-footed by the widespread perception at home and (especially) abroad that the PCI was not like other Communist parties. As Ignazio Silone would later acknowledge, Italian Socialists and others had only themselves to blame. The close relations between Communists and Socialists in Italy, at least until 1948, and the consequent reluctance of non-Communist Marxists to criticize the Soviet Union, inhibited the emergence in Italian politics of a clear left-leaning alternative to Communism.

But if Italy was unusual in Western Europe for the relatively *simpatico* quality of its Communists, it was also of course atypical for another reason. The overthrow of Mussolini in 1943 could not obscure the complicity of many Italian intellectuals in his twenty-year rule. Mussolini's ultra-nationalism had been directed, among other things, against foreign culture and influence; and Fascism had blatantly favored 'national' intellectuals by applying to literature and the arts autarkic policies of protection and substitution similar to those imposed against more commonplace foreign products.

Inevitably, many Italian intellectuals (especially younger ones) had accepted support and subsidies from the Fascist state: the alternative was exile or silence. Elio Vittorini himself had won prizes in Fascist literary competitions. Vittorio de Sica was a well-known actor in Fascist-era films before becoming the leading exponent of post-war Neo-Realism. His fellow Neo-Realist director Roberto Rossellini, whose post-war films were distinctly Communist in their political sympathies, had just a few years before made documentaries and feature films in Mussolini's Italy with help from the authorities, and his was not an isolated case. By 1943 Mussolini's rule was the normal order of things for the many millions of Italians who had no adult memory of any other peacetime government.[6]

The moral standing of the vast majority of Italian intellectuals in the post-war years thus mirrored the rather ambivalent international position of the country as a whole, too uncomfortably implicated in its authoritarian past to take center stage in post-war European affairs. In any case, Italy had long been oddly peripheral to modern European culture, perhaps because of its own centrifugal history and arrangements: Naples, Florence, Bologna, Milan and Turin each formed little worlds of their own, with their own universities, newspapers, academies and intelligentsias. Rome was the source of authority, the fount of patronage and locus of power. But it never monopolized the nation's cultural life.

In the end, then, there could be only one place for a properly *European* intellectual life in the years after World War Two: only one city, one national capital whose obsessions and divisions could both reflect and define the cultural condition of the continent as a whole. Its competitors were imprisoned, had destroyed themselves or else were parochially absorbed. Ever since the 1920s, as one European state after another fell to the dictators, political refugees and intellectual exiles had headed for France. Some had remained during the war and joined the Resistance, where many had fallen victim to Vichy and the Nazis. Some had escaped to London, or New York, or Latin America, but would return after the Liberation. Others, like Czesław Miłosz or the Hungarian historian and political journalist François Fejtö, did not emigrate until the Soviet coups in Eastern Europe forced them to flee—at which point it seemed only natural that they would go straight to Paris.

The result was that, for the first time since the 1840s, when Karl Marx, Heinrich

---

[6]In De Sica's *Sciuscià* (made in 1946 and set in that same year) the director of a boys' prison not only gives the Fascist salute—a habit he cannot break—but alludes with undisguised nostalgia to the low crime figures back in Mussolini's time.

Heine, Adam Mickiewicz, Giuseppe Mazzini and Alexander Herzen all lived in Parisian exile, France was once again the natural European home of the disinherited intellectual, a clearing house for modern European thought and politics. Post-war Parisian intellectual life was thus doubly cosmopolitan: men and women from all over Europe partook of it—and it was the only European stage on which local opinions and disputes were magnified and transmitted to a wide, international audience.

And so, despite France's shattering defeat in 1940, its humiliating subjugation under four years of German occupation, the moral ambiguity (and worse) of Marshall Pétain's Vichy regime, and the country's embarrassing subordination to the US and Britain in the international diplomacy of the post-war years, French culture became once again the center of international attention: French intellectuals acquired a special international significance as spokesmen for the age, and the tenor of French political arguments epitomized the ideological rent in the world at large. Once more—and for the last time—Paris was the capital of Europe.

The irony of this outcome was not lost on contemporaries. It was historical chance that thrust French intellectuals into the limelight in these years, for their own concerns were no less parochial than anyone else's. Post-war France was as much taken up with its own problems of score-settling, scarcity and political instability as any other country. French intellectuals re-interpreted the politics of the rest of the world in the light of their own obsessions, and the narcissistic self-importance of Paris within France was projected un-self-critically onto the world at large. As Arthur Koestler memorably described them, post-war French intellectuals ('the Little Flirts of Saint Germain des Prés') were 'peeping Toms who watch History's debauches through a hole in the wall.' But History had afforded them a privileged perch.

The divisions that would characterize the French intellectual community in later years were not immediately in evidence. When Jean-Paul Sartre founded *Les Temps Modernes* in 1945 the editorial board included not only Simone de Beauvoir and Maurice Merleau-Ponty but also Raymond Aron, reflecting a broad consensus around left-wing politics and 'existentialist' philosophy. The latter label also encompassed (rather to his discomfort) Albert Camus, at the time close friends with Sartre and De Beauvoir and, from his column on the editorial pages of the daily newspaper *Combat*, the most influential writer in post-war France.

All of them shared a certain 'résistantialiste' attitude (though only Camus had taken an active part in the Resistance itself—Aron was with the Free French in London and the others made their way more or less untroubled through the Occupation years). In Merleau-Ponty's words, the wartime struggle had overcome for French intellectuals the dilemma of 'being versus doing'. Henceforth they were 'in' History and must *engage* with it to the full. Their situation no longer afforded intellectuals the luxury of refusing to commit themselves to political choices; true freedom consisted of accepting this truth. In Sartre's words, 'To be free is not to do what one wants, but to want to do what one can'.

Another lesson that Sartre and his generation claimed to have learnt from the war was the inevitability—and thus in certain measure the desirability—of political violence. This was far from being a distinctively French interpretation of recent experience: by 1945 many Europeans had lived through three decades of military and political violence. Young people all across the continent were inured to a level of public brutality, in words and actions, that would have shocked their nineteenth-century forebears. And modern political rhetoric offered a 'dialectic' with which to domesticate calls for violence and conflict: Emmanuel Mounier, editor of the magazine *Esprit* and an influential presence on the Christian Left, undoubtedly spoke for many in 1949 when he asserted that it was hypocrisy to oppose violence or class-struggle when 'white violence' was practiced on the victims of capitalism every day.

But in France the appeal of violent solutions represented more than just a projection forward of recent experience. It was also the echo of an older heritage. Accusations of collaboration, betrayal and treason, demands for punishment and a fresh start did not begin with the Liberation. They recapitulated a venerable French tradition. Ever since 1792 the Revolutionary and counter-Revolutionary poles of French public life exemplified and reinforced the two-fold division of the country: for and against the Monarchy, for and against the Revolution, for and against Robespierre, for and against the Constitutions of 1830 and 1848, for and against the Commune. No other country had such a long and unbroken experience of bipolar politics, underscored by the conventional historiography of the national Revolutionary myth as inculcated to French schoolchildren for many decades.

Moreover France, more than any other Western nation-state, was a country whose intelligentsia approved and even worshipped violence as a tool of public policy. George Sand records a walk along the Seine in 1835 with a friend who was urgently pressing the case for bloody proletarian revolution: only when the Seine runs red, he explained, when Paris burns and the poor take their rightful place, can justice and peace prevail. Almost exactly one century later the English essayist Peter Quennell described in the *New Statesman* 'the almost pathological worship of violence which seems to dominate so many French writers.'

Thus when the elderly Radical Party politician Edouard Herriot, president of the French National Assembly until his death in 1957 at the age of 85, announced at the Liberation that normal political life could not be restored until 'France has first passed through a bloodbath', his language did not sound out of the ordinary to French ears, even coming as it did from a pot-bellied provincial parliamentarian of the political center. French readers and writers had long since been familiarized with the idea that historical change and purgative bloodshed go hand in hand. When Sartre and his contemporaries insisted that Communist violence was a form of 'proletarian humanism', the 'midwife of History', they were more conventional than they realized.

This familiarity of revolutionary violence in the French *imaginaire*, together with sepia-tinted memories of the old Franco-Russian alliance, pre-disposed intellectuals in France to greet Communist apologetics for Soviet brutality with a distinctly sympathetic ear. Dialectics helped, too. Commenting on the Slánský trial for Sartre's *Temps Modernes*, Marcel Péju reminded his readers that there is nothing wrong with killing one's political enemies. What was amiss in Prague was that 'the ceremony with which they are killed [i.e. the show trial] seems a caricature of what it could be if this violence were justified in a Communist perspective. The charges, after all, are not *prima facie* implausible.'

French intellectuals visiting the Soviet bloc waxed more lyrically enthusiastic than most at the sight of Communism under construction. Thus the poet and surrealist Paul Eluard, addressing a (doubtless bemused) audience in Bucharest in October 1948: 'I come from a country where no-one laughs any more, where no-one sings. France is in shadow. But you have discovered the sunshine of Happiness.' Or the same Eluard in Soviet-occupied Hungary, the following year: 'A people has only to be master in its own land and in a few years Happiness will be the supreme law and Joy the daily horizon.'

Eluard was a Communist, but his sentiments were widespread even among the many intellectuals and artists who never joined the Party. In 1948, following the Czech coup, Simone de Beauvoir was sure the Communists were on the path to victory everywhere: as her contemporary Paul Nizan had written many years before, a revolutionary philosopher can only be effective if he chooses the class that bears the Revolution, and the Communists were the self-anointed representatives of that class. Engaged intellectuals were obliged to take a stand on the side of progress and History, whatever the occasional moral vicissitudes.[7]

The importance of the Communist question for intellectuals in France was also a consequence of the ubiquitous presence of the French Communist Party (PCF). Though never as large as the Italian party (with 800,000 members at its peak), the PCF in the immediate post-war years was even more electorally successful, with 28 percent of the vote in 1946. And unlike the Italians the French Communists did not have to face a unified center-right Catholic Party. Conversely, the French Socialist Party, thanks to its long inter-war experience of Communist tactics, did not align itself unquestioningly with the Communists in the early stages of the Cold War (though a minority of its members would have liked to see it do so). And so the PCF was both stronger and more isolated than any other Communist party.

---

[7]Despite his own misgivings about Soviet cultural policy, Paul Eluard refused to criticize Zdanovism in front of the working-class comrades of his local Party cell. As he explained to Claude Roy, 'Poor things, it would just discourage them. One must not upset those taking part in the struggle; they wouldn't understand.'

It was also peculiarly unsympathetic to intellectuals. In marked contrast to the Italians, the PCF had always been led by hard-nosed, blunt-minded Party bureaucrats, exemplified by the ex-miner Maurice Thorez who ran the Party from 1932 until his death in 1964. For Stalin, Thorez's most important quality was that—like Gottwald in Czechoslovakia—he could be relied on to do what he was told and ask no questions. It was no coincidence that, having deserted from the French army during the phony war of 1939–40, Thorez spent the next five years in Moscow. The French Communist Party was thus a reliable if somewhat rigid satellite party, a serviceable vehicle for declaiming and practicing the Stalinist line.

To the post-war student generation, looking for leadership, direction, discipline and the promise of action in harness with 'the workers', the PCF's very rigidity had a certain appeal, at least for a few years: much as its Czech or Polish counterparts initially inspired enthusiasm among their peers further east. But to more established French intellectuals, the fervor that the PCF's cultural commissars brought to the imposition of orthodoxy in the turgid pages of the Party daily L'Humanité and elsewhere posed a daily challenge to their progressive beliefs. Writers or scholars who threw in their lot with the PCF could not expect, like Vittorini in Italy or the Communist Party Historians' Group in London, to be allowed any leeway.[8]

For this reason the affinities of the Parisian intelligentsia are our soundest guide to the fault-lines of faith and opinion in Cold War Europe. In Paris, as nowhere else, intellectual schisms traced the contours of political ones, at home and abroad. The East European show trials were debated in Paris with special intensity because so many of their Communist victims had lived and worked in France: László Rajk had been interned in France after the Spanish Civil War; Artur London had worked in the French Resistance, was married to one prominent French Communist and was the future father-in-law of another; 'André Simone' (Otto Katz, another Slánský trial victim) was widely known in Parisian journalistic circles for his work there during the thirties; Traicho Kostov was well-remembered from his days in Bulgarian foreign service in Paris—his arrest in Sofia actually made the front page of Camus's Combat.

Paris was even the site for two influential political trials of its own. In 1946 Victor Kravchenko, a mid-level Soviet bureaucrat who defected to the US in April 1944, published his memoirs, I Chose Freedom. When these appeared in France in May of the following year, under the title J'ai choisi la Liberté, they caused a sensation for their account of the Soviet purges, massacres, and in particular the Soviet concentration camp system, the Gulag. In November 1947, two months after the Cominform meeting in Poland where PCF leaders had been raked over the coals for their failure to toe the new Soviet hard line, the Party's intellectual periodical

---

[8]François Fejtö, living in Paris, noted some years later that whereas the Italian Communists gave a warm, if guarded, welcome to his history of Eastern Europe, the PCF condemned it as the work of just another renegade.

Les Lettres françaises ran a series of articles asserting that Kravchenko's book was a tissue of lies, fabricated by the American secret services. When the paper repeated and amplified these charges in April 1948, Kravchenko sued for libel.

At the trial, which lasted from January 24th to April 4th 1949, Kravchenko brought forward a stream of rather obscure witnesses in his support; but the defendants could flourish a sheaf of depositions from major French non-Communist intellectuals: the Resistance novelist Vercors, the physicist and Nobel Prize winner Frédéric Joliot-Curie, the art critic, Jean Cassou, Resistance hero and director of the Museum of Modern Art in Paris, and many others. These all attested to the impeccable Resistance record of the French Communist Party, the indisputable revolutionary credentials of the Soviet Union, and the unacceptable implications of Kravchenko's assertions—even if true. In the judgment Kravchenko was awarded a single franc of insultingly symbolic damages.

This 'moral' victory for the Progressive Left coincided with the first round of major show trials in Eastern Europe, and the adoption of intellectual positions for and against the Soviet Union—as Sartre had begun to insist a few months earlier, 'One must choose between the USSR and the Anglo-Saxon bloc.' But for many critics of the Soviet Union, Kravchenko had been a less than ideal spokesman. A longtime Soviet apparatchik who had chosen exile in the USA, he held no appeal for those anti-Communist European intellectuals, perhaps the majority, who were as concerned to keep their distance from Washington as they were to deny Moscow a monopoly of progressive credentials. With such a person, wrote Sartre and Merleau-Ponty in January 1950, we can have no feelings of fraternity: he was the living proof of the decline 'of Marxist values in Russia itself'.

But another trial proved harder to ignore. On November 12th 1949, four weeks after the execution in Budapest of László Rajk, David Rousset published in *Le Figaro littéraire* an appeal to former inmates of Nazi camps to assist him in establishing an enquiry into *Soviet* concentration camps. Basing himself on the Soviet Union's own Code of Corrective Labor, he argued that these were not re-education centers as officials asserted, but rather a system of concentration camps integral to the Soviet economy and penal system. A week later, again in *Les Lettres françaises*, the Communist writers Pierre Daix and Claude Morgan accused him of inventing his sources and caricaturing the USSR in a base calumny. Rousset sued for defamation.

The *dramatis personae* in this confrontation were unusually interesting. Rousset was no Kremlin defector. He was French; a longtime socialist; a sometime Trotskyist; a Resistance hero and survivor of Buchenwald and Neuengamme; a friend of Sartre and co-founder with him in 1948 of a short-lived political movement, the *Rassemblement démocratique révolutionnaire*. For such a man to accuse the Soviet Union of operating concentration or labor camps broke sharply with the conventional political alignments of the time. Daix, too, had been arrested for Resistance activities and deported, in his case to Mauthausen. For two left-wing former

Resisters and camp survivors to clash in this way illustrated the degree to which past political alliances and allegiances were now subordinated to the single question of Communism.

Rousset's witness list included a variety of highly credible first-hand experts on the Soviet prison system, culminating in dramatic testimony from Margarete Buber-Neumann, who testified to experience not only in Soviet camps but also in Ravensbrück, to which she had been sent after Stalin handed her back to the Nazis in 1940, part of the small change of the Molotov-Ribbentrop Pact. Rousset won his case. He even had some impact upon the conscience and consciousness of his contemporaries. Following the announcement of the verdict in January 1950, Maurice Merleau-Ponty confessed that 'the facts put altogether into question the meaning of the Russian system'. Simone de Beauvoir felt sufficiently constrained to insert in her new roman-à-clef, *Les Mandarins*, a series of anguished debates between her protagonists over the news of the Soviet camps (though she flatteringly re-adjusted the chronology to make it seem that Sartre and his friends had been aware of such matters as early as 1946).

To counter Rousset and his like—and keep 'progressive' intellectuals in line—Communist parties exercised the moral lever of 'anti-Fascism'. This had the appeal of familiarity. For many Europeans their first experience of political mobilization was in the anti-Fascist, Popular-Front leagues of the 1930s. For most people the Second World War was remembered as a victory over Fascism, and celebrated as such in France and Belgium especially in the post-war years. 'Anti-Fascism' was a reassuring, ecumenical link to a simpler time.

At the core of anti-Fascist rhetoric as deployed by the official Left was a simple binary view of political allegiance: we are what they are not. They (the Fascists, Nazis, Franco-ists, Nationalists) are Right, we are Left. They are reactionary, we are Progressive. They stand for War, we stand for Peace. They are the forces of Evil, we are on the side of Good. In the words of Klaus Mann, in Paris in 1935: whatever Fascism is, we are not and we are against it. Since most of the anti-Fascists' opponents made a point of defining their own politics as above all anti-Communist (this was part of Nazism's wartime appeal to conservative elites in countries as far apart as Denmark and Romania), this tidy symmetry worked to the Communists' polemical advantage. Philo-Communism, or at least anti-anti-Communism, was the logical essence of anti-Fascism.[9]

The Soviet Union, of course, had every interest in directing attention to its anti-Fascist credentials in the post-war years, especially once the US replaced Germany as its enemy. Anti-Fascist rhetoric was now directed against America, accused first of defending revanchist Fascists and then, by extension, described as a proto-Fascist threat in its own right. What made this Communist tactic particularly effective, of

---

[9]Thus Emmanuel Mounier, in *Esprit*, February 1946: 'Anti-Communism . . . is the necessary and sufficient crystallizing force for a return of Fascism.'

course, was the widespread and genuine fear in Europe of a revival of Fascism itself, or at least a surge of neo-Fascist sympathy out of the ruins.

'Anti-Fascism', with its sub-text of resistance and alliance, was also related to the lingering favorable image of the wartime Soviet Union, the genuine sympathy that many Western Europeans felt for the heroic victors of Kursk and Stalingrad. As Simone de Beauvoir put it in her memoirs, in a characteristically sweeping claim: 'There were no reservations in our friendship for the USSR: the sacrifices of the Russian people had proved that its leaders embodied its wishes.' Stalingrad, according to Edgar Morin, swept away all doubts, all criticisms. It helped, too, that Paris had been liberated by the *Western* Allies, whose sins thus loomed larger in local memory.

But there was more to intellectual Russophilia than this. It is important to recall what was happening just a few miles to the east. Western intellectual enthusiasm for Communism tended to peak not in times of 'goulash Communism' or 'Socialism with a human face', but rather at the moments of the regime's worst cruelties: 1935–39 and 1944–56. Writers, professors, artists, teachers and journalists frequently admired Stalin not in spite of his faults, but *because* of them. It was when he was murdering people on an industrial scale, when the show trials were displaying Soviet Communism at its most theatrically macabre, that men and women beyond Stalin's grasp were most seduced by the man and his cult. It was the absurdly large gap separating rhetoric from reality that made it so irresistible to men and women of goodwill in search of a Cause.[10]

Communism excited intellectuals in a way that neither Hitler nor (especially) liberal democracy could hope to match. Communism was exotic in locale and heroic in scale. Raymond Aron in 1950 remarked upon 'the ludicrous surprise . . . that the European Left has taken a pyramid-builder for its God.' But was it really so surprising? Jean-Paul Sartre, for one, was most attracted to the Communists at precisely the moment when the 'pyramid-builder' was embarking upon his final, crazed projects. The idea that the Soviet Union was engaged upon a momentous quest whose very ambition justified and excused its shortcomings was uniquely attractive to rationalist intellectuals. The besetting sin of Fascism had been its parochial objectives. But Communism was directed towards impeccably universal and transcendent goals. *Its* crimes were excused by many non-Communist observers as the cost, so to speak, of doing business with History.

But even so, in the early years of the Cold War there were many in Western Europe who might have been more openly critical of Stalin, of the Soviet Union and of their local Communists had they not been inhibited by the fear of giving aid and comfort to their political opponents. This, too, was a legacy of 'anti-Fascism', the insistence that there were 'no enemies on the Left' (a rule to which Stalin himself,

---

[10] Likewise, the cult of Mao in the West reached its zenith at the height of the Cultural Revolution, just when and *just because* Mao was persecuting writers, artists and teachers.

it must be said, paid little attention). As the progressive Abbé Boulier explained to François Fejtö, when trying to prevent him from writing about the Rajk trial: drawing attention to Communist sins is 'to play the imperialists' game'.[11]

This fear of serving anti-Soviet interests was not new. But by the early fifties it was a major calculation in European intellectual debates, above all in France. Even after the East European show trials finally led Emmanuel Mounier and many in his *Esprit* group to distance themselves from the French Communist Party, they took special care to deny any suggestion that they had become 'anti-Communist'—or worse, that they had ceased to be 'anti-American'. Anti-anti-Communism was becoming a political and cultural end in itself.

On one side of the European cultural divide, then, were the Communists and their friends and apologists: progressives and 'anti-Fascists'. On the other side, far more numerous (outside of the Soviet bloc) but also distinctly heterogeneous, were the anti-Communists. Since anti-Communists ran the gamut from Trotskyists to neo-Fascists, critics of the USSR frequently found themselves sharing a platform or a petition with someone whose politics in other respects they abhorred. Such unholy alliances were a prime target for Soviet polemic and it was sometimes difficult to persuade liberal critics of Communism to voice their opinions in public for fear of being tarred with the brush of reaction. As Arthur Koestler explained to a large audience at Carnegie Hall, New York, in 1948: 'You can't help people being right for the wrong reasons . . . This fear of finding oneself in bad company is not an expression of political purity; it is an expression of a lack of self-confidence.'

Genuinely reactionary intellectuals were thin on the ground in the first decade after the war. Even those, like Jacques Laurent or Roger Nimier in France, who styled themselves as unashamedly of the Right, took a certain pleasure in acknowledging the hopelessness of their cause, fashioning a sort of neo-Bohemian nostalgia for the discredited past and parading their political irrelevance as a badge of honor. If the Left had the wind in its sails and History on its side, then a new generation of Right-wing literati would take pride in being defiant losers, turning the genuine decadence and death-seeking solipsism of inter-war writers like Drieu la Rochelle and Ernst Jünger into a social and sartorial style—thereby anticipating the 'young fogeys' of Mrs Thatcher's Britain.

More representative, in France and Britain at least, were intellectual conservatives whose dislike of Communism had changed little in thirty years. In both countries, as in Italy, actively Catholic intellectuals played a prominent part in anti-Communist polemics. Evelyn Waugh and Graham Greene succeeded Hilaire Belloc and G. K. Chesterton in the space reserved in English cultural life for gifted,

---

[11]In these years 'progressivism', as Raymond Aron mordantly observed, consisted in 'presenting Communist arguments as though they emanated spontaneously from independent speculation.'

dyspeptic Catholic traditionalists. But where English conservatives might rage at the vacuity of modern life or else retreat from it altogether, a *French* Catholic like François Mauriac was drawn quite naturally into polemical exchanges with the political Left.

Throughout Mauriac's long post-war engagement with public affairs (he wrote regularly for *Le Figaro* into his eighties—he died in 1970 aged 85) his arguments were almost always cast in an ethical vein—first with Albert Camus over the propriety of the post-war purges, later with his fellow conservatives over the war in Algeria—of which he disapproved—and always with the Communists, whom he abominated. As he explained to the readers of *Le Figaro* on October 24th 1949, the French Communists' justification for the Budapest show trial—then under way— was *'une obscénité de l'esprit'*. But Mauriac's moral clarity about the crimes of Communism was accompanied in these years by an equally moralized distaste for the 'alien values' of American society: like many European conservatives, he was always a little uncomfortable about the alignment with America that the Cold War required of them.

This was not a problem for liberal realists like Raymond Aron. Like many other 'Cold Warriors' of the European political center, Aron had only limited sympathy for the United States—'the U.S. economy seems to me', he wrote, 'a model neither for humanity nor for the West'. But Aron understood the central truth about European politics after the war: domestic and foreign conflicts were henceforth intertwined. 'In our times', he wrote in July 1947, 'for individuals as for nations the choice that determines all else is a global one, in effect a geographical choice. One is in the universe of free countries or else in that of lands placed under harsh Soviet rule. From now on everyone in France will have to state his choice.' Or, as he put it on another occasion, 'It is never a struggle between good and evil, but between the preferable and the detestable.'

Liberal intellectuals, then, whether of the continental persuasion like Aron or Luigi Einaudi, or in the British sense like Isaiah Berlin, were always distinctly more comfortable than most conservatives with the American connection that history had imposed upon them. The same was true, curious as it may seem, of Social Democrats. This was in part because the memory of FDR was still fresh, and many of the American diplomats and policy-makers with whom Europeans dealt in these years were New Dealers, who encouraged an active role for the state in economic and social policy and whose political sympathies fell to the left of center.

But it was also a direct consequence of American policy. The AFL-CIO, the US intelligence services and the State Department saw moderate, trade union-based social democratic and labor parties as the best barrier to Communist advance in France and Belgium especially (in Italy, where the political configuration was different, they vested their hopes and the bulk of their funds in Christian Democracy). Until mid-1947 this would have been an uncertain bet. But following the expulsion of Communist parties from government in France, Belgium and Italy that spring, and especially after the Prague coup in February 1948, west European Socialists and Communists drew apart. Violent clashes between Communist and Socialist workers' unions, and between Communist-led strikers and troops ordered in by Socialist ministers, together with the news from eastern Europe of Socialists arrested and imprisoned, turned many Western Social Democrats into confirmed foes of the Soviet bloc and ready recipients of covert American cash.

For Socialists like Léon Blum in France or Kurt Schumacher in Germany, the Cold War imposed political choices which were in one respect at least familiar: they knew the Communists of old and had been around long enough to remember bitter fratricidal battles in the grim years before the Popular Front alliances. Younger men lacked this comfort. Albert Camus—who had briefly joined and then quit the Communist Party in Algeria during the 1930s—emerged from the war a firm believer, like so many of his contemporaries, in the Resistance coalition of Communists, Socialists and radical reformers of every shade. 'Anticommunism', he wrote in Algiers in March 1944, 'is the beginning of dictatorship.'

Camus first began to have doubts during France's post-war trials and purges, when the Communists took a hard line as *the* Party of the Resistance and demanded exclusions, imprisonments and the death penalty for thousands of real or imagined collaborators. Then, as the arteries of political and intellectual allegiance began to harden from 1947, Camus found himself increasingly prone to doubt the good faith of his political allies—doubts he at first stifled out of habit and for the sake of unity. He handed over control of the newspaper *Combat* in June 1947, no longer so politically confident or optimistic as he had been three years before. In his major novel *La Peste* (*The Plague*), published the same year, it was clear that Camus was not comfortable with the hard-edged political realism of his political bedmates. As he put it, through the mouth of one of his characters, Tarrou: 'I have decided to reject everything that, directly or indirectly, makes people die or justifies others in making them die.'

Nevertheless, Camus was still reluctant to come out in public and break with his former friends. In public he still tried to balance honest criticism of Stalinism with balanced, 'objective' references to American racism and other crimes committed in the capitalist camp. But the Rousset trial and the East European show trials ended any illusions he might have retained. To his private notebooks he confided: 'One of my regrets is to have conceded too much to objectivity. Objectivity, at times is an accommodation. Today things are clear and we must call something "*concentrationnaire*" if that is what it is, even if it is socialism. In one sense, I shall never again be polite.'

There is here a perhaps unconscious echo of a speech at the International Conference of the Pen Club two years earlier, in June 1947, where Ignazio Silone—speaking on '*La Dignité de l'Intelligence et l'Indignité des Intellectuels*' ('The Dignity of Intelligence and the Unworthiness of Intellectuals')—publicly regretted his own silence and that of his fellow Left intellectuals: 'We placed on the shelves, like tanks stored in a depôt, the principles of liberty for all, human dignity, and the rest.' Like Silone, who would go on to contribute one of the better essays in Richard Crossman's 1950 collection, *The God That Failed*, Camus became thenceforth an ever more acerbic critic of 'progressivist' illusions, culminating in the condemnation of revolutionary violence in his 1951 essay *L'Homme révolté* that provoked the final break with his erstwhile friends on the Parisian intellectual Left. For Sartre, the first duty of a radical intellectual was not to betray the workers. For Camus, like Silone, the most important thing was not to betray oneself. The battle lines of the Cultural Cold War were drawn up.

It is difficult, looking back across the decades, to recapture in full the stark contrasts and rhetoric of the Cold War in these early years. Stalin was not yet an embarrassment—on the contrary. As Maurice Thorez expressed it in July 1948, 'people think they can insult us Communists by throwing the word "Stalinists" at us. Well, for us that label is an honor that we try hard to merit to the full.' And many gifted non-Communists, as we have seen, were likewise reluctant to condemn the Soviet leader, seeking out ways to minimize his crimes or excuse them altogether. Hopeful illusions about the Soviet realm were accompanied by widespread misgivings—and worse—about America.[12]

The United States, together with the new Federal Republic of Germany, bore the brunt of Communist rhetorical violence. It was an astute tactic. The US was not wildly popular in western Europe, despite and in some places because of its generous help in Europe's economic reconstruction. In July 1947 only 38 percent of French adults believed that Marshall Aid did not pose a serious threat to French independence, a suspicion of American motives that was further fuelled by the war scares of 1948 and the fighting in Korea two years later. Fabricated Communist charges that the US Army was using biological weapons in Korea found a receptive audience.

In cultural matters, the Communists did not even need to take the initiative. Fear of American domination, of the loss of national autonomy and initiative, brought into the 'progressive' camp men and women of all political stripes and none. Compared with its impoverished West European dependencies, America seemed economically carnivorous and culturally obscurantist: a deadly combination. In October 1949—in the second year of the Marshall Plan and just as plans for NATO were being finalized—the French cultural critic Pierre Emmanuel informed readers of *Le Monde* that America's chief gift to post-war Europe had been . . . the phallus; even in the land of Stendhal 'the phallus is on its way to becoming a God'. Three years later the Christian editors of *Esprit* reminded their readers that 'we have,

---

[12]These sentiments are unintentionally caricatured in this report from a child's first class with a Communist primary teacher, in Prague, April 1948: 'Children, you all know that in America people live in holes dug in the ground and are slaves for a few capitalists, who take all the profit. But in Russia everyone is happy, and we in Prague are very happy too, owing to the government of Klement Gottwald. Now children, repeat loudly with me: "We are very contented and approve the Gottwald government". '

from the outset, warned of the dangers posed to our national well-being by an American culture which attacks the very roots of the mental and moral cohesion of the peoples of Europe.'

Meanwhile, an insidious American artifact was spreading across the continent. Between 1947 and 1949 the Coca-Cola Company opened bottling plants in the Netherlands, Belgium, Luxembourg, Switzerland and Italy. Within five years of its creation West Germany would have 96 such plants and became the largest market outside the US itself. But while some voices had been raised in protest in Belgium and Italy, it was in France that Coca-Cola's plans unleashed a public storm. When *Le Monde* revealed that the company had set a target of 240 million bottles to be sold in France in 1950, there were loud objections—encouraged but not orchestrated by the Communists, who confined themselves to the warning that Coke's distribution services would do double duty as a US espionage network. As *Le Monde* editorialized on March 29th 1950, 'Coca-Cola is the Danzig of European Culture.'

The furor over 'Coca-Colonisation' had its light side (there were rumours that the company planned to attach its logo, in neon, to the Eiffel Tower . . .), but the sentiments underlying it were serious. The crassness of American culture, from films to beverages, and the self-interest and imperialist ambitions behind the US presence in Europe were commonplaces for many Europeans of Left and Right. The Soviet Union might pose an immediate threat to Europe but it was America that presented the more insidious long-term challenge. This view gained credence after the outbreak of war in Korea, when the US began to press for the rearmament of the West Germans. Communists could now blend their attacks on the 'ex-Nazis' in Bonn with the charge that America was backing 'Fascist revanchism'. Nationalist hostility to 'Anglo-Americans', encouraged under the wartime occupation but silent since the liberation, was dusted off and drafted into service in Italy, France and Belgium—and also in Germany itself, by Brecht and other East German writers.

Seeking to capitalize on this inchoate but widespread fear of war, and suspicion of things American among European elites, Stalin launched an international Movement for Peace. From 1949 to Stalin's death 'Peace' was the centerpiece of Soviet cultural strategy. The Peace Movement was launched in Wrocław, Poland, in August 1948 at a 'World Congress of Intellectuals'. The Wrocław meeting was followed by the first 'Peace Congresses', in April 1949, conducted more or less simultaneously in Paris, Prague and New York. As a prototypical 'front' organization, the Peace Movement itself was ostensibly led by prominent scientists and intellectuals like Frédéric Joliot-Curie; but Communists controlled its various committees and its activities were closely coordinated with the Cominform, whose own journal, published in Bucharest, was now re-named 'For a Lasting Peace, for a Popular Democracy'.

On its own terms the Peace Movement was quite a success. An appeal, launched in Stockholm in March 1950 by the 'Permanent Committee of the World Congress of Partisans of Peace', obtained many millions of signatures in Western Europe (in addition to the tens of millions of signatories rounded up in the Soviet bloc). Indeed, gathering these signatures was the Movement's main activity, especially in France, where it had its strongest support. But under the umbrella of the Peace Movement other front organizations also pressed home the message: the Soviet Union was on the side of peace, while the Americans (and their friends in Korea, Yugoslavia and Western European governments) were the party of war. Writing from Paris for *The New Yorker*, in May 1950, Janet Flanner was impressed: 'At the moment, Communist propaganda is enjoying the most extraordinary success, especially among non-Communists, that it has ever had in France.'

The Communists' attitude towards their mass movements was strictly instrumental—the Peace Movement was only ever a vehicle for Soviet policy, which is why it suddenly adopted the theme of 'peaceful co-existence' in 1951, taking its cue from a shift in Stalin's international strategy. Privately, Communists—especially in the eastern bloc—had little but scorn for the illusions of their fellow-travellers. During organized visits to the popular democracies, Peace Movement supporters (overwhelmingly from France, Italy and India) were fêted and honored for their support; behind their backs they were derided as 'pigeons', a new generation of Lenin's 'useful idiots'.

The Communists' success in securing at least the conditional sympathy of many in Western Europe, and the great play that Communist parties in France and Italy especially made with their support among a cultural elite suspicious of America, prompted a belated but determined response from a group of Western intellectuals. Worried that in the cultural battle Stalin would win by default, they set about establishing a cultural 'front' of their own. The founding meeting of the Congress for Cultural Freedom (CCF) was held in Berlin in June 1950. The Congress was planned as a response to Moscow's Peace Movement initiative of the previous year, but it coincided with the outbreak of war in Korea, which gave it added significance. The decision to hold the meeting in Berlin rather than Paris was deliberate: from the outset the Congress was going to take the cultural battle to the Soviets.

The Congress for Cultural Freedom was formed under the official patronage of Bertrand Russell, Benedetto Croce, John Dewey, Karl Jaspers and Jacques Maritain, the French Catholic philosopher. These old men conferred respectability and authority upon the new venture, but the political drive and intellectual energy behind it came from a glittering middle generation of liberal or ex-Communist intellectuals—Arthur Koestler, Raymond Aron, A. J. Ayer, Margarete Buber-Neumann, Ignazio Silone, Nicola Chiaromonte and Sidney Hook. They, in turn, were assisted by a group of younger men, mostly American, who took responsibility for the day to day planning and administration of the CCF's activities.

The CCF would eventually open up offices in thirty-five countries worldwide, but the focus of its attention was on Europe, and within Europe on France, Italy and Germany. The goal was to rally, energize and mobilize intellectuals and scholars for the struggle with Communism, primarily through the publication and dissemination of cultural periodicals: *Encounter* in Britain, *Preuves* in France, *Tempo Presente* in Italy and *Der Monat* in Germany. None of these journals ever reached a large audience—*Encounter*, the most successful, boasted a circulation of 16,000 copies by 1958; in the same year *Preuves* had just 3,000 subscribers. But their contents were of an almost unvaryingly high quality, their contributors were among the best writers of the post-war decades, and they filled a crucial niche—in France especially, where *Preuves* provided the only liberal, anti-Communist forum in a cultural landscape dominated by neutralist, pacifist, fellow-traveling or straightforwardly Communist periodicals.

The Congress and its many activities were publicly supported by the Ford Foundation and privately underwritten by the CIA—something of which nearly all its activists and contributors were quite unaware until it became public many years later. The implications—that the US government was covertly subsidizing anti-Communist cultural outlets in Europe—were perhaps not as serious as they appear in retrospect. At a time when Communist and 'front' journals and all sorts of cultural products were covertly subsidized from Moscow, American backing would certainly not have embarrassed some of the CCF writers. Arthur Koestler, Raymond Aron or Ignazio Silone did not need official American encouragement to take a hard line against Communism, and there is no evidence that their own critical views about the US itself were ever toned down or censored to suit the paymasters in Washington.

The US was a newcomer to culture wars of this kind. The Soviet Union established its 'Society for Cultural Relations with Foreign Nations' in 1925; French, Germans and Italians had been actively underwriting overseas 'cultural diplomacy' since before 1914. The Americans did not begin to budget for such activities until just before World War Two, and it was only in 1946, with the establishment of the Fulbright Program, that they entered the field seriously. Until the autumn of 1947 American cultural and educational projects in Europe were directed towards 'democratic reorientation'; only then did anti-Communism become the primary strategic goal.

By 1950 the US Information Agency had taken overall charge of American cultural exchange and information programs in Europe. Together with the Information Services Branch of the US Occupation authorities in western Germany and Austria (which had full control of all media and cultural outlets in the US Zone in these countries), the USIA was now in a position to exert huge influence in Western European cultural life. By 1953, at the height of the Cold War, US foreign cultural programs (excluding covert subsidies and private foundations) employed 13,000 people and cost $129 million, much of it spent on the battle for the hearts and minds of the intellectual elite of Western Europe.

The 'fight for peace', as the Communist press dubbed it, was conducted on the cultural 'front' by the 'Battle of the Book' (note the characteristically militarized Leninist language). The first engagements were undertaken in France, Belgium and Italy in the early spring of 1950. Prominent Communist authors—Elsa Triolet, Louis Aragon—would travel to a variety of provincial cities to give talks, sign books and put on display the literary credentials of the Communist world. In practice this did little to promote the Communist case—two of the best-selling books in post-war France were Arthur Koestler's *Darkness at Noon* (which sold 420,000 copies in the decade 1945–55) and Viktor Kravchenko's *I Chose Freedom* (503,000 copies in the same period). But the point was not so much to sell books as to remind readers and others that Communists stood for culture—French culture.

The American response was to set up 'America Houses', with libraries and newspaper-reading rooms, and host lectures, meetings and English-language classes. By 1955 there were sixty-nine such America Houses in Europe. In some places their impact was quite considerable: in Austria, where the Marshall Plan years saw 134 million copies of English-language books distributed nationwide, a significant percentage of the population of Vienna and Salzburg (the former under Four Power administration, the latter in the US Zone of Occupation) visited their local America House to borrow books and read the papers. The study of English replaced French and the classical languages as the first choice of Austrian high-school students.

Like American-supported radio networks (Radio Free Europe was inaugurated in Munich one month after the outbreak of the Korean War), the America House programs were sometimes undermined by the crude propaganda imperatives emanating from Washington. At the peak of the McCarthy years the directors of America Houses spent much of their time *removing* books from their shelves. Among dozens of authors whose works were deemed inappropriate were not only the obvious suspects—John Dos Passos, Arthur Miller, Dashiell Hammett and Upton Sinclair—but also Albert Einstein, Thomas Mann, Alberto Moravia, Tom Paine and Henry Thoreau. In Austria, at least, it seemed to many observers that in the 'Battle of Books' the US was sometimes its own most effective foe.

Fortunately for the West, American popular culture had an appeal that American political ineptitude could do little to tarnish. Communists were at a severe disadvantage in that their official disapproval of decadent American jazz and American cinema closely echoed the views of Josef Goebbels. While east European Communist states were banning jazz as decadent and alien, Radio Free Europe was broadcasting into eastern Europe three hours of popular music every weekday afternoon, interspersed with news on the hour for ten minutes. Cinema, the other universal medium of the time, could be regulated in states under Communist control; but throughout *western* Europe the appeal of American films was universal. Here, Soviet propaganda had nothing with which to compete and even Western progressives, often drawn to American music and cinema, were out of sympathy with the Party line.

The cultural competition of the early Cold War years was asymmetrical. Among European cultural elites there was still a widespread sentiment that they shared, across ideological divides and even bridging the Iron Curtain, a common culture to which America posed a threat. The French in particular took this line, echoing the early post-war efforts of their diplomats to trace an international policy independent of American control. Symptomatically, the head of the French Cultural Mission in occupied Berlin, Félix Lusset, got on much better with his Soviet counterpart (Alexander Dymschitz) than he did with the British or American representatives in the city and dreamed, like his masters in Paris, of a restored cultural axis reaching from Paris to Berlin and on to Leningrad.

The US spent hundreds of millions of dollars trying to win over European sympathies, but many of the resulting publications and products were heavy-handed and counter-productive, merely confirming the European intelligentsia's innate suspicions. In Germany, America's excessive attention to Communist crimes was seen by many as a deliberate ploy to forget or relativise the crimes of the Nazis. In Italy the lurid anti-Communist campaigns of the Vatican undercut the anti-Stalinist arguments of Silone, Vittorini and others. Only in art and literature, where the absurdities of Stalinist cultural policy impinged directly upon the territory of painters and poets, did Western intellectuals consistently distance themselves from Moscow—and even here their opposition was muted for fear of offering hostages to American 'propaganda'.[13]

On the other hand, in the struggle for the sympathies of the large mass of the Western European population, the Soviets were rapidly losing ground. Everywhere except Italy the Communist vote fell steadily from the late 1940s, and—if opinion polls are to be believed—even those who did vote Communist often saw their vote either as a symbolic protest or else as an expression of class or communal solidarity. Well before the cataclysms of 1956, when the sympathies of most European intellectuals would swing sharply away from the Soviet bloc, the Atlantic orientation of most other Western Europeans had been decided.

---

[13]'We were intolerant of idiocy in the domains we knew well ', wrote the French poet Claude Roy, who joined the PCF during the war after an earlier romance with the far Right Action Française, 'but forgiving of crimes in matters of which we knew little.'

CODA

The End of Old Europe

'Life changed surprisingly little after the war'.
David Lodge

'I spent my early years in factory towns and their adjacent suburbs, amid bricks and soot and smokestacks and cobbled streets. We took streetcars for short trips and trains for long ones. We bought food fresh for every meal, not because we were gourmets but because we lacked a refrigerator (less perishable substances were kept in the root cellar). My mother got up every morning in the chill and made a fire in the parlor stove. Running water came in only one temperature: frigid. We communicated by mail and got our news chiefly from newspapers (we were sufficiently modern, though, in that we owned a radio roughly the size of a filing cabinet). My early classrooms featured pot-bellied stoves and double desks with inkwells, into which we dipped our nibs. We boys wore short pants until the ceremony of *communion solennelle*, at age twelve. And so on. But this wasn't any undiscovered pocket of the Carpathians, it was postwar western Europe, where "postwar" was a season that stretched for nearly twenty years.'[1]

This description of industrial Wallonia in the 1950s, by the Belgian author Luc Sante, could as well be applied to most of western Europe in these years. The present author, who grew up after the war in the inner-London district of Putney, recalls frequent visits to a murky sweetshop run by a wizened old woman who advised him reproachfully that she had 'been selling gobstoppers to little boys like you since the Queen's Golden Jubilee'—i.e. since 1887: she meant Victoria of course—*the* Queen.[2] In the same street the local grocery store—Sainsbury's—had sawdust on the floor and was staffed by beefy men in striped shirts and sprightly young women in starched aprons and caps. It looked exactly like the sepia photos on the wall taken when the store was first opened in the 1870s.

In many of its essential features, daily life in the first decade after World War Two would have been thoroughly familiar to men and women of fifty years earlier. In these years coal still met nine-tenths of Britain's fuel requirements, 82 percent of the needs of Belgium and the other countries of the new European Coal and Steel

---

[1] Luc Sante, *The Factory of Facts* (1998), p.27.
[2] She was not alone in her Victorian allusions. The British Prime Minister at the time, Winston Churchill, used to remind audiences that he had ridden in the last cavalry charge of the British Army—at Omdurman in the Sudan—in September 1898.

Community. Thanks in part to the omnipresence of coal-fires London—a city of trams and docks—was still periodically shrouded in the damp fog so familiar from images of the industrial city of late-Victorian times. British films from those years have a distinctly Edwardian feel—either in their social setting (e.g. *The Winslow Boy* of 1948) or else in their period tone. In *The Man in a White Suit* (1951) contemporary Manchester is depicted as nineteenth-century in all its essentials (hand carts, housing, social relations); bosses and union leaders concur in treating entrepreneurial amateurism as a moral virtue, whatever the price in productive efficiency. Three million British men and women went to licensed dance halls every week, and there were seventy working-men's clubs just in the Yorkshire town of Huddersfield in the early fifties (though both sorts of social activity were losing their appeal to the young).

The same sense of suspended time hung over much of continental Europe too. Rural life in Belgium could have been depicted by Millet: the hay gathered with wooden rakes, the straw beaten with flails, fruits and vegetables handpicked and transported on horse-drawn carts. Like French provincial towns, where men in berets really did collect a baguette on their way home from the corner Café de la Paix (typically named in 1919), or Spain, sealed in aspic by Franco's authoritarian rule, Belgium and Britain hung in a sort of delayed Edwardian limbo. Post-war Europe was still warmed by the fading embers of the nineteenth-century economic revolution that had almost run its course, leaving behind sedimentary evidence of cultural habits and social relations increasingly at odds with the new age of airplanes and atomic weapons. If anything, the war had set things in reverse. The modernizing fervor of the 1920s and even the 1930s had drained away, leaving behind an older order of life. In Italy, as in much of rural Europe, children still entered the job market upon completing (or more likely not completing) their primary education; in 1951 only one Italian child in nine attended school past the age of thirteen.

Religion, especially the Catholic religion, basked in a brief Indian summer of restored authority. In Spain the Catholic hierarchy had both the means and the political backing to re-launch the Counter-Reformation: in a 1953 concordat, Franco granted the Church not merely exemption from taxation and all state interference, but also a right to request censorship of any writing or speech to which it objected. In return the ecclesiastical hierarchy maintained and enforced the conservative conflation of religion with national identity. Indeed, the Church was now so thoroughly integrated into narratives of national identity and duty that the leading primary school history textbook, *Yo soy español* ['I Am Spanish'] (first published in 1943) taught Spanish history as a single, seamless story: beginning in the Garden of Eden and ending with the Generalissimo.[3]

---

[3] In high-school history textbooks the message of Franco's ascent to power was unambiguous: 'The future of Spain united, after three centuries, to the destiny of the past! ... The ancient procession has not

To this was added a new cult of the dead—the 'martyrs' of the victorious side in the recent Civil War. At the thousands of memorial sites dedicated to victims of anti-clerical Republicanism, the Spanish Church organized countless ceremonies and memorials. A judicious mix of religion, civic authority and victory commemoration reinforced the spiritual and mnemonic monopoly of the clerical hierarchy. Because Franco needed Catholicism even more than the Church needed him—how else maintain Spain's tenuous post-war links to the international community and the 'West'?—he gave it, in effect, unrestricted scope to re-create in modern Spain the 'Crusading' spirit of the *ancien régime*.

Elsewhere in Western Europe the Catholic Church had to reckon with competing and hostile claims on popular allegiance; but even in Holland the Catholic hierarchy felt confident enough to excommunicate electors who voted for its Labour opponents in the first post-war elections. As late as 1956, two years before the death of Pius XII marked the end of the old order, seven out of ten Italians regularly attended Sunday Mass. As in Flanders, the Church in Italy did especially well among Monarchists, women and the elderly—a clear majority of the population as a whole. Article 7 of the Italian Constitution approved in March 1947 judiciously confirmed the terms of Mussolini's 1929 Concordat with the Church: the Catholic hierarchy retained its influence in education and its oversight power in everything pertaining to marriage and morals. At Togliatti's insistence even the Communist Party voted reluctantly for the law, though this did not stop the Vatican excommunicating Italians who voted for the PCI the following year.

In France, the Catholic hierarchy and its political supporters felt sufficiently confident to press for special educational privileges in a '*guerre scolaire*' that briefly echoed the church-state struggles of the 1880s. The main battleground was the old issue of state funding for Catholic schools; a traditional demand but well chosen. While the energy that had fuelled nineteenth-century anti-clericalism, in France as in Italy or Germany, had mostly dissolved, or else was channeled into updated ideological conflicts, the cost and quality of their children's education was one of the few issues that could be counted on to mobilize even the most intermittent churchgoers.

Of Europe's traditional religions, only the Catholics were increasing the number of their active constituents in the forties and fifties. This was partly because only the Catholic Church had political parties directly associated with it (and in some cases beholden to it for support)—in Germany, the Netherlands, Belgium, Italy, France and Austria; and partly because Catholicism was traditionally implanted in

---

ceased . . . Along its path advance the dead and the living, bursting with Christianity, in which a world disoriented and in catastrophic convulsions centers and anchors itself . . . This is the grand task that God has saved for the Spain of today . . . An exceptional destiny . . . Through the Empire, to God!' Feliciano Cereceda, *Historia del imperio espanol y de la hispanidad* (Madrid, 1943), pp. 273–74, quoted in Carolyn Boyd, *Historia Patria: Politics, History and National Identity in Spain, 1875–1975* (Princeton, 1997), p. 252.

just those regions of Europe which were the slowest to change in these years. But above all the Catholic Church could offer its members something that was very much missing at the time: a sense of continuity, of security and reassurance in a world that had altered violently in the past decade and was about to be transformed even more dramatically in the years to come. It was the Catholic Church's association with the old order, indeed its firm stand against modernity and change, which gave it a special appeal in these transitional years.

The various Protestant churches of north-west Europe had no such allure. In Germany a significant segment of the non-Catholic population was now under Communist rule; the standing of the German Evangelical churches was in any case somewhat diminished by their compromise with Hitler, as the Stuttgart Confession of Guilt by the Protestant leaders in 1945 half-conceded. But the main problem, in West Germany as elsewhere, was that Protestant churches did not offer an alternative to the modern world but rather a way to live in harmony with it.

The spiritual authority of the Protestant pastor or the Anglican vicar was by convention offered not as a competitor to the state, but rather as its junior partner—which is one reason why the Protestant churches of central Europe were unable to withstand the pressure of the Communist state in these years. But at a time when the West European state was embarking on a much enhanced role as the spiritual and material guardian of its citizens, the distinction between church and state as arbiters of public manners and morals became rather blurred. The late forties and early fifties thus appear as a transitional age, in which conventions of social deference and claims of rank and authority still held sway, but where the modern state was beginning to displace church and even class as the arbiter of collective behavior.

The character of the age is nicely encapsulated in an instruction booklet (*BBC Variety Programmes. Policy Guide for Writers and Producers*, 1948) prepared by the BBC for internal use in 1948. The sense of *moral* responsibility that the public broadcasting corporation chose to place upon itself is quite explicit: 'The influence that [the BBC] can exert upon its listeners is immense and the responsibility for a high standard of taste correspondingly high.' Jokes about religion were forbidden, as was the description of old-fashioned musical taste as 'B.C.'—'Before Crosby'.[4] There were to be no references to 'lavatories' and no jokes about 'effeminacy in men'. Writers were forbidden to use jokes that had become popular in the relaxed ambiance of the war, or make suggestive *double-entendre* allusions to ladies' underwear as in 'winter draws on'. Sexual allusions of any kind were banned—there was to be no talk of 'rabbits', or suchlike 'animal habits'.[5]

---

[4] Bing.
[5] Wartime humour in Britain had typically concentrated on material shortcomings, mild sexual innuendo and an undercurrent of resentment at over-privileged American GIs. Sometimes on all three at once: 'Have you heard about the new Utility underpants? One Yank and they're off!'

Furthermore: Members of Parliament were not to appear on radio programs that might be 'undignified or unsuitable' for public figures, nor were there to be any jokes or references that might encourage 'Strikes or industrial disputes. The Black Market, Spivs and drones.' These terms—'spivs' and 'drones' for louche types and minor criminals, the 'black market' as an all-purpose term for traders and customers circumventing rationing and other restrictions—show how much Britain at least lived for some years in the shadow of the war. Well into the 1950s the BBC could reprimand one producer, Peter Eton of the popular radio comedy *The Goon Show*, for allowing 'Major Dennis Bloodnok' (played by Peter Sellers) to be awarded an OBE (Order of the British Empire) for 'emptying dustbins in the heat of battle' (and for permitting an actor to 'imitate the Queen's voice trying to shoo away pigeons at Trafalgar Square').

Such strictures, and their accompanying note of high-collared, Edwardian-era reformism, were perhaps distinctive to Britain. But their tone would have been familiar all across the continent. In school, in church, on state-run radio, in the confident, patronizing style of the broadsheet and even the tabloid press, and in the speech and dress of public figures, Europeans were still very much subject to the habits and regulations of an earlier time. We have already noted how many of the political leaders of the age were men of another time—Britain's Clement Attlee would not have been out of place in a Victorian mission to the industrial slums, and it was altogether fitting that the prime minister who oversaw Britain's transition to a modern welfare state should have begun his public career performing good works in the East End of pre-World War One London.

Against this image of an older Europe—moving at the pace of earlier days, at once changed by the war and restrained by pre-war routines and habits—we must set the unmistakably *modern* form of its primary source of entertainment. This was the golden age of the cinema. In Britain, cinema attendance peaked quite soon after the end of the war, with 1,700 million seats sold in the country's five thousand cinemas in 1946. In that year one person in three went every week to the local cinema. Even in 1950, when attendance had already started to decline, the average English man or woman went to the cinema twenty-eight times a year, a figure that was nearly 40 percent higher than in the last year before the war.

Whereas the British cinema audience was to slip steadily through the fifties, in continental Europe it continued to grow. One thousand new picture houses opened in France during the first half of the 1950s, about the same number in West Germany; in Italy three thousand new cinemas appeared, bringing the national total to some 10,000 by 1956. The previous year cinema attendance in Italy peaked at around 800 million seats sold (half the UK figure for about the same size population). French audiences, which were at their largest at the end of the 1940s, were nowhere near as large as those of Britain or even Italy[6]. Nor were those of West

---

[6]But note that France had more publications devoted to cinema than the other two combined.

Germany, although in the Federal Republic cinema attendance did not peak until 1959. But by any other measure audiences were large indeed; as they were even in Spain, where cinema attendance per head of the adult population in 1947 was among the highest in Europe.

Part of the reason for this post-war enthusiasm for films was the pent-up wartime demand, especially for American films—stoked by the ban on most US films imposed by the Nazis, by Mussolini (after 1938) and by the Pétain regime in France, and more generally by wartime shortages. In 1946, 87 percent of box-office receipts in Italy were for foreign (mostly American) films; of about 5,000 films shown in Madrid between 1939 and the end of the 1950s, 4,200 were foreign (again, mostly American). In 1947 the French film industry produced 40 films, in contrast with 340 that were imported from the United States. And American films were not just available in overwhelming numbers, they were also popular: the most commercially successful films in post-war Berlin were Chaplin's *Gold Rush* and *The Maltese Falcon* (made in 1941 but not available in Europe until the end of the war).

American domination of post-war European cinema did not come about through the vagaries of popular taste alone, however. There was a political context: 'positive' American films flooded into Italy in time for the pivotal 1948 elections; Paramount was encouraged by the State Department to re-issue *Ninotchka* (1939) that year to help get out the anti-Communist vote. Conversely, Washington requested that John Ford's *Grapes of Wrath* (made in 1940) be held back from distribution in France: its unfavorable portrayal of Depression-era America might be exploited by the French Communist Party. In general, American films were part of America's appeal, and as such significant assets in the cultural Cold War. Only intellectuals were likely to be sufficiently moved by Sergei Eisenstein's depiction of Odessa in the *Battleship Potemkin* to translate their aesthetic appreciation into political affinity; but everyone—intellectuals included—could appreciate Humphrey Bogart.

However, American cinema's drive into Europe was above all prompted by economic considerations. US films had always been exported to Europe and made money there. But after World War Two American producers, squeezed between falling domestic cinema attendance and the rising cost of film-making, pressed especially hard for access to European markets. European governments, by contrast, were more than ever reluctant to open up their home market to American products: the local film industry, still a significant factor in Britain and Italy especially, needed protection against American 'dumping'; and dollars were too scarce and valuable to be spent on importing American films.

As early as 1927 the UK Parliament had passed a law instituting a quota system, under which 20 percent of all films released in Britain by 1936 had to be British made. After World War Two the British Government's goal was to set this quota at 30 percent for 1948. The French, Italians and Spanish all pursued similar or even more ambitious objectives (the German film industry, of course, was in no position to demand such protection). But heavy lobbying by Hollywood kept State Department pressure on European negotiators, and agreement to allow entry for US films was part of every major bipartite trade deal or loan agreement reached by the US and its European allies in the first post-war decade.

Thus, under the terms of the Blum-Byrnes accords of May 1946, the French government very reluctantly reduced its protectionist quota from 55 percent French-made films per annum to 30 percent—with the result that within a year domestic film production was halved. The British Labour Government similarly failed to keep out US imports. Only Franco succeeded in restricting US film imports into Spain (despite an attempted 'boycott' of the Spanish market by US producers from 1955 to 1958), in large measure because he had no need to respond to public opinion or anticipate the political fall-out of his decisions. But even in Spain, as we have seen, American movies vastly outnumbered home-grown products.

The Americans knew what they were doing: when European governments after 1949 took to taxing cinema receipts in order to subsidize domestic film producers, American producers began investing directly in foreign productions, their choice of European venue for the making of a film or group of films often depending on the level of local 'domestic' subsidy then available. In time, then, European governments found themselves indirectly subsidizing Hollywood itself, via local intermediaries. By 1952, 40 percent of the US film industry's revenue was generated overseas, most of it in Europe. Six years later that figure would stand at 50 percent.

As a result of American domination of the European market, the *European* films of this period are not always the most reliable guide to European filmgoers' experience or sensibilities. The British viewer especially was quite likely to form a sense of contemporary Englishness as much from Hollywood's presentation of England as from his or her own direct experience. It is a matter of some note that among the films of the forties, *Mrs Miniver* (1942)—a very *English* tale of domestic fortitude and endurance, of middle-class reticence and perseverance, set symptomatically around the disaster at Dunkirk where all these qualities were taken to be most on display—was a pure product of Hollywood. Yet for the English generation that first saw it the film would long remain the truest representation of national memory and self-image.

What made American films so appealing, beyond the glamour and lustre that they brought to the gray surroundings in which they were viewed, was their 'quality'. They were well-made, usually on a canvas far beyond the resources of any European producer. They were not, however, 'escapist' in the manner of 1930s 'screwball' comedies or romantic fantasies. Indeed, some of the most popular American films of the late forties were (as later continental admirers would dub them) 'film noir'. Their setting might be a detective story or social drama, but the mood—and cinematographic texture—were darker and more sombre than American films of earlier decades.

It was *Europeans* who were often more likely to make escapist films at this time—

like the frothy German romances of the early fifties, set in fairy-tale landscapes of the Black Forest or Bavarian Alps, or British-made lightweight genre comedies like *Piccadilly Incident* (1946), *Spring in Park Lane* (1948) or *Maytime in Mayfair* (1949), all made by Herbert Wilcox, set in London's fashionable (and comparatively undamaged) West End, and starring Anna Neagle, Michael Wilding or Rex Harrison as witty debutantes and capricious aristocrats. Their no-less-forgettable Italian and French equivalents were usually updated costume dramas, with peasants and aristocrats occasionally replaced by mechanics or businessmen.

The best European films of the post-war decade—those that later viewers can most readily appreciate—inevitably dealt in one way or another with the war. The Liberation saw a brief spate of 'Resistance' films—*Peleton d'execution* (1945), *Le Jugement dernier* (1945), and *La Bataille du Rail* (1946) in France; *Roma: città aperta* (1945), *Paisan* (1946), and *Un Giorno della vita* (1946) in Italy—in all of which a moral chasm separates heroic resisters from craven collaborators and brutal Germans. These were closely followed by a group of films set in the rubble (literal and spiritual) of Berlin: Roberto Rosselini's *Germania anno zero* (1947); *A Foreign Affair* (1948)—American but by the Austrian émigré director Billy Wilder; and *Murderers Are Among Us* (1946) by Wolfgang Staudte, notable in its time as the only German film to even begin to engage the moral implications of Nazi atrocities (but in which the word 'Jew' is never spoken).

Three of these films, *Open City, Paisan* and *Germania anno zero* were by Roberto Rossellini. Together with Vittorio De Sica, who directed *Sciuscià* (1946), *Bicycle Thieves* (1948) and *Umberto D* (1952), Rossellini was responsible for the cycle of neo-realist films made in the years 1945–52 that propelled Italian filmmakers to the front rank of international cinema. Like one or two of the contemporary English comedies made at the Ealing Studios, notably *Passport to Pimlico* (1949), the neo-realist films took the damage and destruction of war, especially in the cities, as the setting and in some measure the subject for post-war cinema. But even the best of the English films never approached the sombre humanism of the Italian masterpieces.

The simple 'verities' of these films reflect not so much the European world as it then was as that same world passed through the grid of wartime memories and myths. Workers, the undamaged countryside, above all young children (boys especially) stand for something good and uncorrupted and real—even in the midst of urban destruction and destitution—when set against false values of class, wealth, greed, collaboration, *luxe et volupté*. For the most part Americans are absent (except for the GIs having their shoes shined in the eponymous *Sciuscià*, or the posters of Rita Hayworth that appear in *Bicycle Thieves*, juxtaposed to the impoverished bill poster himself); this is a Europe of Europeans, living on the half-built, half-destroyed margins of their cities, filmed almost as documentary (and owing something, therefore, to documentary film-making experience gained with armies during the war). Like the world of post-war Europe itself they disappear after

1952—though neo-realism had a kind of curious half-after life in Spain, where Luis Garcia Berlanga directed *Bienvenido Mister Marshall* in 1953 and Juan Antonio Bardem made *Death of a Cyclist* three years later.

Like other amusements of its era, cinema-going was a collective pleasure. In small Italian towns the weekly film would be watched and commented on by most of the population, a public entertainment publicly discussed. In England, at Saturday morning shows for children, songs were flashed on the screen, with the audience encouraged to sing along in harmony with a little white ball that bounced from word to word. One such song from around 1946 is recalled in a memoir of childhood in post-war South London:

> We come along on Saturday morning
> Greeting everybody with a smile.
> We come along on Saturday morning
> Knowing it's well worthwhile.
> As members of the Odeon we all intend to be
> Good citizens when we grow up
> And champions of the Free.[7]

The didactic tone was not representative—at least not in so overt a form—and would disappear within a few years. But the ingenuous, old-fashioned note nicely captures the moment. Popular workingmen's recreations like pigeon-raising, speedway and greyhound racing reached their peak in these years before entering upon a steady decline that accelerated from the later 1950s. Their roots in late-Victorian times could be seen in the sort of headgear worn by spectators: the beret (France) and flat workingmen's cap (England) both became popular around the 1890s and were still the norm in 1950. Boys still dressed like their grandfathers, except for the ubiquitous short trousers.

Dancing, too, was popular, in large part thanks to the American GIs, who introduced swing and be-bop which were widely performed at dance halls and nightclubs and popularized by radio (few could afford record-players before the mid-1950s and the juke-box had not yet killed off live dance bands). The generation gap of the next decade was hardly yet in evidence. Christian Dior's 'New Look' of February 1947—an aggressively indulgent style meant to contrast with wartime shortages of cloth, with ankle-length skirts, stuffed 'leg of mutton' shoulders and a plethora of bows and pleats—was favored, where they could afford it, by women of all ages; external appearance was still a function of class (and income) rather than age.

There were, of course, inter-generational tensions. During the war, American-

---

[7]Trevor Grundy, *Memoir of a Fascist Childhood* (1998), page 19.

influenced 'zoot suits' were worn by London spivs and Parisian 'zazous' alike, much to the appalled disapproval of their elders; and in the later forties the enthusiasm among bohemians and intellectuals for the duffle-coat, an adaptation of what had until then been the traditional outerwear of Belgian fishermen, hinted at the coming fashion among the young for dressing *down* rather than up. In the ultra-fashionable Parisian nightclub *Le Tabou*, which opened in April 1947, sartorial permissiveness was treated with great seriousness, while a French film of 1949, *Rendezvous de Juillet*, makes much of the spoilt younger generation's lack of *gravitas*: at lunch, the conventional father of a traditional bourgeois household is appalled at the behavior of his youngest son, above all by his insistence on eating without a tie.

But all this was the small change of adolescent revolt, hardly new. Most people of all ages in post-war Europe were chiefly concerned with making do. At the beginning of the 1950s, one Italian family in four lived in poverty and most of the rest were little better off. Less than one house in two had an indoor toilet, only one in eight boasted a bathroom. In the worst-off regions of the far south-east of Italy poverty was endemic: in the village of Cuto, in the Marchesato di Crotone, the fresh water supply to the town's 9,000 inhabitants consisted of a single public fountain.

The Mezzogiorno was an extreme case. But in West Germany in 1950 17 million of the country's 47 million residents were still classed as 'needy', chiefly because they had nowhere to live. Even in London a family whose name was on the waiting list for a house or flat could expect on average to wait seven years before being housed; in the meantime they were placed in post-war 'prefabs'—metal boxes installed on empty lots around the city to shelter the homeless until the construction of new dwellings could catch up with need. In post-war polls, 'housing' always topped the list of popular concerns; in De Sica's *Miracle in Milan* (1951) the homeless crowd chants, 'We want a home to live in, so we and our children can believe in tomorrow'.

The consumption patterns of post-war Europe reflected the continuing penury of the continent and the enduring impact of the Depression and the war. Rationing continued longest in Britain, where bread rationing was introduced between July 1946 and July 1948, clothes coupons remained in force until 1949, the wartime utility clothing and furniture regime was not abandoned until 1952, and food rationing on meat and many other foods was not finally ended until the summer of 1954—though it was temporarily suspended for the Coronation of Queen Elizabeth II in June 1953, when everyone was allocated an extra pound of sugar and four ounces of margarine.[8] But even in France, where rationing (and therefore the black market) disappeared rather sooner, the wartime obsession with food supply did not abate until 1949 at the earliest.

---

[8]Rationing in Eastern Europe was not abolished until 1953 in Czechoslovakia, Hungary, Poland and Bulgaria; 1954 in Romania, 1957 in Albania and 1958 in East Germany. But since the Communist economy induced shortage systemically, comparisons with Western Europe are inappropriate.

Almost everything was either in short supply or else small (the recommended size of the much-coveted new family dwellings being built by the Labour Government in Britain was just 900 square feet for a 3-bedroom house). Very few Europeans possessed a car or a fridge—working-class women in the UK, where the standard of living was higher than most countries on the continent, shopped twice a day for food, either on foot or by public transport, much as their mothers and grandmothers had done before them. Goods from distant lands were exotic and expensive. The widespread sense of restriction and limits and containment was further reinforced by controls on international travel (to save valuable foreign currency) and legislation keeping out foreign workers and other migrants (the post-war Republic in France maintained in force all the legislation from the 1930s and the Occupation designed to bar foreign labor and other undesirable aliens, allowing exceptions, mostly for skilled manual laborers, only according to need).

In many ways, Europe in the late 1940s and early 1950s was less open, less mobile and more insular than it had been in 1913. It was certainly more dilapidated, and not just in Berlin, where only one quarter of the rubble of battle had been cleared by 1950. The English social historian Robert Hewison describes the British in these years as 'a worn-out people working with worn-out machinery.' Whereas in the US by the end of the 1940s most industrial equipment was under five years old, in post-war France the average age of machinery was twenty years. A typical French farmer produced food for five fellow Frenchmen; the American farmer was already producing at three times this rate. Forty years of war and economic depression had taken a heavy toll.

'Post-war', then, lasted a long time; longer, certainly, than historians have sometimes supposed, recounting the difficult post-war years in the flattering light of the prosperous decades to come. Few Europeans in that time, well-informed or otherwise, anticipated the scale of change that was about to break upon them. The experience of the past half-century had induced in many a skeptical pessimism. In the years preceding World War One Europe was an optimistic continent whose statesmen and commentators looked to a confident future. Thirty years on, after World War Two, people had their eyes firmly and nervously fixed upon the terrible past. Many observers anticipated more of the same: another post-war depression, a re-run of the politics of extremism, a third world war.

But the very scale of the collective misery that Europeans had brought upon themselves in the first half of the century had a profoundly de-politicizing effect: far from turning to extreme solutions, in the manner of the years following World War One, the European publics of the gloomy post-World War Two years turned *away* from politics. The implications of this could be discerned only vaguely at the time—in the failure of Fascist or Communist parties to cash in upon the difficulties of daily existence; in the way in which economics displaced politics as the goal and language of collective action; in the emergence of domestic recreations and domestic consumption in place of participation in public affairs.

And something else was happening. As *The New Yorker*'s Janet Flanner had noticed back in May 1946, the second highest priority (after underclothes) in France's post-war agenda for 'utility' products was baby-carriages. For the first time in many years, Europeans were starting to have babies again. In the UK the birthrate in 1949 was up by 11 percent on 1937; in France it had risen by an unprecedented 33 percent. The implications of this remarkable burst of fertility, in a continent whose leading demographic marker since 1913 had been premature death, were momentous. In more ways than most contemporaries could possibly have foreseen, a new Europe was being born.

Shortly after Germany's defeat in 1945, a child walks past the corpses of hundreds of former inmates of Bergen-Belsen concentration camp, laid out along a country road. Like most adult Germans in the post-war years, he averts his gaze.

German soldiers publicly hanged in Kiev in 1946 following their conviction for war crimes. However mixed the Soviet motivation in staging post-war trials and executions, the appalling crimes committed by the German army, the SS and their local collaborators were real enough.

Draza Mihailović, wartime leader of Yugoslavia's Chetnik (nationalist) resistance, before a military court in June 1946. For Communist partisans the Chetniks posed almost as great a threat as the foreign occupiers; after the war Tito suppressed them ruthlessly. Mihailović himself was shot on July 18, 1946.

Accused of 'horizontal collaboration' with the German occupiers, a Frenchwoman is shaved and paraded around the town of Laval a few hours after its liberation by American troops in August 1944. Thousands of women in France, Belgium and the Netherlands suffered similar retribution.

Women queuing for coal in London at the height of the bitter winter of February 1947. The fuel shortage was so acute that most of these women had to wait all day to collect their weekly ration. The prams are for transporting coal, not babies.

A mother and her children drawing their family allowance in Stratford, east London, on August 6th 1946—the day the allowances were first introduced. Europe's post-war welfare states wrought an authentic social revolution, dramatically improving the life-chances of middle and working classes alike.

Marshall Aid i). The first delivery of Marshall Plan sugar from the Caribbean arrives at London's docks on February 3rd 1949 (greeted by the Labour Minister John Strachey, left, and Elmer Holmgreen, the Marshall Plan representative, center).

Marshall Aid ii). Athens, Christmas 1949: Bread made from 'Marshall Plan flour' being distributed to Greek orphans. Even in impoverished Greece the Plan's morale-boosting functions were at least as important as its material contribution to economic recovery.

Marshall Aid iii): 'The people of the world do not want a repetition of the sorrows of war'— J. Stalin (the rifle accompanying the eggs is wrapped in a document marked 'North Atlantic Pact'). Note that the USSR's Western supporters are marching under a French banner.

Czechs assemble in Prague's Wenceslas Square on February 25th 1948 to hear Klement Gottwald announce the formation of a new government. Note the range of contrasting emotions among the spectators—the Communist coup was by no means greeted with universal dismay.

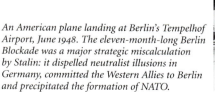

Josip Broz Tito's image adorns a Belgrade building, July 1948. Stalin broke with Communist Yugoslavia in the spring of 1948 not because of its policies but in irritation at Tito's insubordination, his personality cult and his growing challenge to Moscow's monopoly of Communist authority.

An American plane landing at Berlin's Tempelhof Airport, June 1948. The eleven-month-long Berlin Blockade was a major strategic miscalculation by Stalin: it dispelled neutralist illusions in Germany, committed the Western Allies to Berlin and precipitated the formation of NATO.

Present at the Creation. From left to right: Dean Acheson, US Secretary of State and moving spirit behind the policy of 'containment'; Ernest Bevin, the post-war UK Foreign Minister who first conceived of an Atlantic Alliance; Robert Schuman, the French statesman who proposed a European Coal & Steel Community.

Socialism with a human face: 'Uncle Joe' on a receiving stand in Moscow, 1949. 'Reminded me of the Renaissance despots—no principles, any methods, but no flowery language— always Yes or No, though you could only count on him if it was No.' (Clement Attlee, British Prime Minister)

The uprising in East Berlin, on June 17th 1953, was the first sign in the Soviet bloc that the people might 'forfeit the confidence of the government'. The option (proposed derisively by Brecht) of 'dissolving the people and electing another one' proved unattainable, though not for want of trying.

László Rajk (center) on the final day of his trial, September 23rd 1949. As Communist Interior Minister, Rajk had himself been responsible for the death of many innocents; but his trial and subsequent execution turned him into a martyr for future generations.

Workers in the Soviet gulag, circa 1952. In that year, at the height of the second Stalinist terror, 1.7 million prisoners were held in Soviet labor camps, a further 800,000 in labor colonies and 2,753,000 in 'special settlements'. The 'normal' gulag sentence was 25 years.

Jean-Paul Sartre admiring rare books in the Leningrad National Library, June 23rd 1954. Sartre's indulgence for Communism in these years derived from romantic illusions (and anti-Americanism) rather than ideology; but in subsequent decades it was to sully his international reputation and dim his post-war lustre.

Raymond Aron (left) visiting Radio Free Europe in Munich, 1952. Aron was a liberal in an illiberal age; his political choices were often incomprehensible to many of his fellow intellectuals: 'In politics the choice is never between good and evil but between the preferable and the detestable'.

PART TWO

Prosperity and Its Discontents: 1953–1971

VIII

The Politics of Stability

'To most people it must have been apparent, even before the Second World War made it obvious, that the time when European nations could quarrel among themselves for world dominion is dead and gone. Europe has nothing more to look for in this direction, and any European who still hankers after world power must fall victim either to despair or to ridicule, like the many Napoleons in lunatic asylums'.
Max Frisch (July, 1948)

'Because we have had our troops there, the Europeans had not done their share. They won't make the sacrifices to provide the soldiers for their own defense'.
Dwight Eisenhower

'The chief argument against the French having nuclear information has been the effect it would have on the Germans, encouraging them to do the same'.
John F. Kennedy

'Treaties, you see, are like girls and roses: they last while they last'.
Charles de Gaulle

'Political institutions alone are capable of forming the character of a nation'.
Madame de Stael

In his classic study of the growth of political stability in early-eighteenth-century England, the English historian J. H. Plumb wrote: 'There is a general folk belief, derived largely from Burke and the nineteenth-century historians, that political stability is of slow, coral-like growth; the result of time, circumstances, prudence, experience, wisdom, slowly building up over the centuries. Nothing is, I think, farther from the truth (. . .) Political stability, when it comes, often happens to a society quite quickly, as suddenly as water becomes ice.'[1]

---

[1] J. H. Plumb, *The Growth of Political Stability in Early Eighteenth-Century England 1675–1725* (London, 1967), p. xvii.

Something of the sort occurred in Europe, quite unexpectedly, in the first half of the 1950s.

From 1945 until early 1953, Europeans lived, as we have seen, in the shadow of the Second World War and in anxious anticipation of a third. The failed settlement of 1919 was still fresh in the minds of statesmen and public alike. The imposition of Communism in Eastern Europe was a pointed reminder of the revolutionary instability that had followed World War One. The Prague coup, the tensions in Berlin and the Korean War in the Far East seemed uncomfortably reminiscent of the serial international crises of the thirties. In July 1951 the Western Allies had declared their 'state of war' with Germany to be over, but in the circumstances of a rapidly intensifying Cold War there was still no Peace Treaty, and little prospect of one to come. Nor could anyone be confident that Fascism would not once again find fertile soil in the unresolved problem of Germany, or indeed anywhere else.

The expanding web of international alliances, agencies and accords offered little guarantee of international harmony. With the benefit of hindsight we can now see that between them the Council of Europe, the European Coal and Steel Community, the European Payments Union and above all the North Atlantic Treaty Organization were the germ of a new and stable system of inter-state relations. Documents like the Council of Europe's 1950 Convention for the Protection of Human Rights would acquire lasting significance in the decades to come. But at the time such documents, like the agencies that published them, rather closely resembled the well-meaning but doomed pacts and leagues of the 1920s. Skeptical contemporaries could be forgiven for paying them little attention.

Nevertheless, with the death of Stalin and the end of the Korean War, Western Europe stumbled half unawares into a remarkable era of political stability. For the first time in four decades the states of the continent's western half were neither at war nor under the threat of imminent war, at least among themselves. Domestic political strife subsided. Communist parties everywhere except Italy began their slow retreat to the political margins. And the threat of a Fascist revival no longer carried conviction, except perhaps at Communist political rallies.

Western Europeans owed their newfound well-being to the uncertainties of the Cold War. The internationalization of political confrontations, and the consequent engagement of the United States, helped draw the sting from domestic political conflicts. Political issues that in an earlier age would almost certainly have led to violence and war—the unresolved problem of Germany, territorial conflicts between Yugoslavia and Italy, the future of occupied Austria—were all contained, and would in due course be addressed, within the context of Great Power confrontations and negotiations over which Europeans had very little say.

The German Question remained unanswered. Even after the panic of 1950 had subsided, and Western leaders recognized that Stalin had no immediate plans to 'do a Korea' in central Europe, the two sides were no closer to agreement. The official Western position was that the two Germanies that had emerged in 1949 should be reunited in a single democratic state. But until all Germans were free to choose for themselves the political regime under which they would live, such reunification was not possible. In the meantime the Federal Republic of (West) Germany would be treated as the representative of all German citizens. *Unofficially*, the Americans, like the West Europeans, were not at all unhappy to see Germany divided indefinitely. As John Foster Dulles would put it to President Eisenhower in February 1959, there was 'a great deal to be said for the status quo', but this wasn't 'a position we could take publicly'.

The Soviet position was ironically quite similar. In his last years Stalin continued to maintain the official Soviet stance, that Moscow sought a united Germany and would even be willing to accept that such a Germany be neutral, so long as it was unarmed. In a series of Notes in the spring of 1952 Stalin proposed that the four occupying powers draw up a Peace Treaty aimed at establishing such a united Germany, neutral and demilitarized, with all occupying forces removed and its government chosen by free, all-German elections. Historians have criticized Washington for its failure to take Stalin up on these proposals—a 'missed opportunity' to end the Cold War or at least to draw the sting from its most dangerous point of confrontation.

It is certainly true that Western leaders did not take Stalin's Notes very seriously and refused to take the Soviet Union up on its offer. As it turns out, though, they were right. The Soviet leaders themselves attached little importance to their own proposals and didn't seriously expect the Americans, British and French to withdraw their occupying troops and allow a neutral, unarmed Germany to float loose in the middle of a divided continent. If anything, Stalin and his successors were not unhappy to see a continuing American military presence on German soil; from the point of view of the Soviet leaders of this generation, the presence of US troops in West Germany was one of the more reliable guarantees against German revanchism. It was worth risking that guarantee in exchange for a demilitarized Germany in the Soviet shadow (an objective for which Moscow would happily have abandoned its East German clients and their Democratic Republic), but not for anything short of that.

What the Russians decidedly did *not* want at any price was a re-militarized West Germany. The point of the Soviet *démarches* was not to reach an agreement with the West on German reunification, but to head off the impending prospect of German rearmament. The Americans had raised the matter, a mere five years after Hitler's defeat, as a direct consequence of the Korean War. If Congress were to accede to the Truman Administration's requests for increased military aid overseas, then America's allies—Germans included—had to be seen to make their own contribution to their continent's defense.

When the US Secretary of State Dean Acheson first initiated discussions about German rearmament with Britain and France, in September 1950, the French vehemently opposed the idea. It confirmed all their earlier suspicions that NATO, far from representing a firm American commitment to protect France on her eastern flank, was simply a stalking horse for the remilitarization of Germany. Even the Germans were reluctant, though for their own reasons. Konrad Adenauer understood perfectly well the opportunity afforded him by these altered circumstances: far from leaping at the opportunity to rearm, the Federal Republic would hold back. In return for a German contribution to Western defense Bonn would insist upon full international recognition of the FRG and an amnesty for German war criminals held in Allied custody.

Anticipating some such deal being cut behind their back, the French pre-empted further discussion of a German military contribution to NATO by making a counter-proposal of their own. In October 1950, René Pleven, the French Prime Minister, suggested that a European Defense Community be established, analogous to the Schuman Plan. In addition to an Assembly, a Council of Ministers and a Court of Justice, this Community would have its own European Defense Force (EDF). The Americans, like the British, were not happy with the idea but agreed to go along with it as a second-best solution to the problem of defending Europe.

The European Defense Community (EDC) Treaty was accordingly signed on May 27th 1952, along with contingent documents affirming that once all the signatory countries had ratified the Treaty, the US and Great Britain would cooperate fully with an EDF and that the military occupation of Germany would come to an end. It was *this* accord that the Soviet Union had tried unsuccessfully to derail with its offers of a Peace Treaty demilitarizing Germany. The West German Bundestag ratified the EDC Treaty in March 1953, and the Benelux countries followed suit.[2] It only remained for the French National Assembly to ratify the Treaty and Western Europe would have acquired something resembling a European army, with integrated and intermingled national contingents, including a German one.

The French, however, were still unhappy. As Janet Flanner shrewdly observed in November 1953, 'for the French as a whole the EDC problem is Germany—not Russia, as it is for the Americans.' France's hesitations frustrated the Americans— at a NATO Council meeting in December 1953 John Foster Dulles, Eisenhower's new Secretary of State, threatened an 'agonising reappraisal' of American policy if the EDC were to fail. But even though the Pleven Plan was the brainchild of a French prime minister, public debate had revealed the extent of French reluctance to countenance German rearmament under any conditions. Moreover, the proposals for German rearmament and a European army could not have come at a worse time: the French army was facing defeat and humiliation in Vietnam, and the new French Prime Minister, Pierre Mendès-France, rightly calculated that it would be impru-

---

[2]In March 1951, under US pressure, the Dutch, overcoming considerable domestic neutralist sentiment, had reluctantly agreed to double their defense budget and ready five divisions for deployment by 1954.

dent to stake the future of his fragile coalition government on an unpopular proposal to re-arm the national enemy.

Accordingly, when the EDC Treaty finally came to the National Assembly for ratification, Mendès-France forbore to make of it an issue of confidence, and the Treaty was rejected, on August 30th 1954, by a vote of 319–264. The plan for a European Defense Community, and with it a re-armed Germany in a European army, was finished. In private conversation with Belgian Foreign Minister Paul-Henri Spaak and Luxembourg Prime Minister Joseph Bech, a frustrated Adenauer attributed Mendès's behavior to his 'Jewishness'—for which he was, according to the German Chancellor, overcompensating by aligning himself with French nationalist sentiment. More plausibly, Mendès himself explained the failure of the EDC thus: 'In the EDC there was too much integration and too little England.'

The Europeans and their American ally were back where they had begun. But the circumstances were now very different. The Korean War was over, Stalin was dead, NATO was a fixture on the international scene. The French had successfully postponed the problem of European defense for a while but they could not put it off much longer. Within a few weeks of the National Assembly vote on the EDC the Western Allied powers—the US, Britain and France—met twice, at hastily convened conferences in London and Paris. At the initiative of the British foreign secretary Anthony Eden a set of proposals[3]—the so-called London Agreements—was rapidly approved which, when finalized in the subsequent Paris Treaties, were to form the basis of European defense policy for the next half century.

To overcome the problem of 'too little England', Eden offered to commit British forces (four divisions) to a permanent presence in continental Europe (for the first time since the Middle Ages). The Brussels Treaty of 1948 would be extended into a Western European Union (WEU), and Germany and Italy would join it (even though the 1948 Treaty, as we saw, was drawn up for the explicit purpose of mutual protection *against* Germany). In return, the French would agree to allow the Federal Republic an army of no more than half a million men; and Germany would join NATO as a sovereign state.[4]

When these treaties were ratified and went into effect, the German occupation statute would lapse and in all but name the Western Allies would have made formal peace with their erstwhile enemy. Allied troops would remain in the Federal Republic to guard against German recidivism, but as part of a European presence and by mutual agreement. The French were by no means unanimous in welcoming these new plans, but having shot down their own alternative proposals they were ill-placed to protest, even though West Germany achieved more generous terms

---

[3]Based, according to Eden, on an idea dreamed up in his morning bath.
[4]The only explicit restriction placed on German rearmament was an absolute prohibition of any German nuclear arms program, then or ever.

under the 1954 Treaties than it would have got from the Pleven Plan. Not for the first time in international disputes over Germany, France was its own worst enemy. Understandably, French support for the Paris Treaties was more than a little ambivalent. When the National Assembly voted to ratify them, on December 30th 1954, they passed by 287–260, a majority of just 27 votes.

If the French were hesitant, the Russians were distinctly displeased. On May 15th 1955, ten days after the formal incorporation of West Germany into NATO and the abolition of the Allied High Commission in the Federal Republic, the Soviet Union announced the formation of its Warsaw Pact. Poland, Czechoslovakia, Hungary, Romania, Bulgaria, Albania and the Soviet Union formed an alliance of 'friendship, cooperation and mutual assistance' under a unified command. Moscow abrogated its wartime treaties of alliance with Britain and France and, accepting the inevitable, asserted the full sovereignty of the East German Democratic Republic and incorporated it into the Warsaw Pact. The German Question had not exactly been answered; but with both parts fully integrated into their respective international alliances it would now be set aside for a while, its place to be taken in due course by the still unresolved dilemma of the divided former capital, Berlin.

Now that the immediate future of Germany had been resolved, both sides hastened to address secondary conflicts and tensions. The new men in the Kremlin, Nikita Khrushchev in particular, took seriously their own agenda for 'peaceful coexistence' in Europe and shared the American desire to minimize the risk of future confrontations. The day after the Warsaw Pact was announced, the four occupying powers signed the Austrian State Treaty. Austria was to be independent and neutral, attached neither to NATO nor the Warsaw Pact and free to choose its own path.[5] All four armies of occupation were to withdraw—though the Soviet Union, which had already extracted about $100 million from its Zone of Occupation in eastern Austria, secured a final pound of flesh in the form of an obligation on Austria to 'buy out' Soviet economic interests in the country's eastern sector for a further $150 million.

Meanwhile, just to the south, Yugoslavia and Italy had agreed to end their standoff over Trieste. In an agreement brokered by the Americans and the British in October 1954, the city of Trieste would remain with Italy while its surrounding hinterland, overwhelmingly populated by Slovenes, would revert to Yugoslavia. The Trieste accords, like so much else in these years, were facilitated by the understanding that they would be regarded as 'provisional': in the words of the Italian ambassador to the US, Alberto Tarchiani, the agreement on Trieste 'had merely a resemblance of being provisional while in reality it was final'.

The accords over Austria, Yugoslavia and Italy were made possible by a new mood of 'détente' in European affairs, symbolized by the July 1955 Summit Meet-

---

[5]Austrian neutrality was not in the original text; it was inserted by the Austrian parliament during the debate over the State Treaty.

ing at Geneva (the first since Potsdam) and the admission of sixteen new member states to the United Nations, breaking a ten-year East-West deadlock. Beyond the atmospherics of friendly exchanges between Eisenhower, Khrushchev and Eden, the most important issue resolved at Geneva was the fate of some 10,000 German prisoners of war still in Soviet hands. In return for Adenauer's visit to Moscow in September 1955 and the establishment of diplomatic relations, the Soviet leaders consented to the return of these men: 9,626 of them were released that same year, and the remainder by the end of January 1956. Meanwhile Germany's small western neighbors also achieved some degree of closure with Bonn. The Danes reached agreement on minor border issues and compensation for German war crimes in 1955, the Belgians a year later (the Grand Duchy of Luxembourg, however, did not come to an agreement with the Germans until 1959, and the Dutch only in 1960). Without anyone actually saying so, the book was closing on the crimes and punishments of the European war and its aftermath.

These reassuring developments were unfolding against the backdrop of a major international arms race. This paradox—that a peaceful European settlement was taking shape even as the two Great Powers of the day were arming themselves to the hilt and preparing for the eventuality of a thermonuclear war—was not so bizarre as it might appear. The growing emphasis in US and Soviet strategic thinking on nuclear weapons, and the intercontinental missiles with which to deliver them, released European states from the need to compete in an arena where they could not hope to match the resources of the superpowers, even though central Europe remained the most likely terrain over which any future war might be fought. For this reason, the Cold War in Western Europe was experienced quite differently in these years from the way it was felt in the United States, or indeed in the USSR.

The United States' nuclear arsenal had grown rapidly through the 1950s. From 9 in 1946, 50 in 1948 and 170 at the beginning of the decade, the stockpile of nuclear weapons at the disposal of the US armed forces had reached 841 by 1952 before expanding to around 2,000 by the time of Germany's entry into NATO (it would reach 28,000 on the eve of the Cuban crisis seven years later). To deliver these bombs the US Air Force had a fleet of forward-based B-29 bombers that grew from around 50 at the onset of the 1948 Berlin blockade to well over 1,000 five years later; the first intercontinental B-52 bombers entered service in June 1955. Given the Soviet Union's overwhelming advantage in manpower and conventional weapons in Europe, these airborne nuclear weapons were inevitably to become central to Washington's strategy, especially following President Truman's secret order of March 10th 1950 to accelerate development of a hydrogen bomb.

Truman's decision was prompted by the Soviet Union's successful test in August 1949 of a Soviet atomic bomb. The gap between American and Soviet nuclear capability was shrinking: the first successful US thermonuclear test was carried out on the Pacific atoll of Elugelab on November 1st 1952; the first such Soviet test, at Semipalatinsk, was announced just ten months later, on August 12th 1953. American battlefield nuclear weapons first began arriving in West Germany the following month; the next January Dulles announced Eisenhower's 'New Look' policy. NATO was to be 'nuclearised': the threat to use tactical nuclear weapons on the European battlefield was to become part of the Alliance's defense strategy. In order for the Soviet Union to believe that the West might really fire them, the distinction between nuclear and conventional arms was to be abolished. As Dulles explained to a NATO Council meeting in April 1954: 'The US considers that the ability to use atomic weapons is essential for the defense of the NATO area in the face of the present threat. In short, such weapons must now be treated as in fact having become conventional.'

The coincidence of NATO's nuclearization with the stabilization of the Continent was no accident. From the Soviet point of view as well, conventional warfare in central and Western Europe was of diminishing strategic interest. Moscow too was stockpiling nuclear weapons—starting with just 5 in 1950 it had built some 1,700 by the end of the decade. But the chief Soviet emphasis was on developing the means to deliver them not on the European battlefield but across oceans, to compensate for American plans to base nuclear weapons in Germany, just a few hundred miles from Russia itself.

The notorious 'missile gap' of which John F. Kennedy spoke when campaigning for the US presidency in 1960 was a myth, a successful exercise in Soviet propaganda; the same was true of widespread contemporary accounts of Soviet educational and technical superiority. Two decades before German Chancellor Helmut Schmidt made the observation, Khrushchev and some of his senior colleagues already understood intuitively that the empire they ruled over was basically 'Upper Volta with missiles'. But the USSR certainly *was* expending great efforts on the development of its ballistic capabilities. The first successful Soviet test of an intercontinental ballistic missile came in August 1957, five months ahead of the Americans. The subsequent launching of Sputnik on October 4th 1957 showed what it could do (to American horror[6]).

Ballistic weapons—intercontinental missiles capable of delivering nuclear warheads from the Soviet hinterland to American targets—had considerable appeal for Nikita Khrushchev in particular. They were cheaper than conventional weapons. They allowed Khrushchev to maintain good relations with heavy industry and the military while diverting resources to consumer goods production. And they had the curious consequence, as both sides would come to appreciate, of making a major

---

[6]The Americans were not the only ones panicked by displays of Soviet hardware. In 1960 the British Conservative Prime Minister Harold Macmillan privately concluded that 'They [the USSR] are no longer frightened of aggression. They have at least as powerful nuclear forces as the West. They have interior lines [of communication]. They have a buoyant economy and will soon outmatch capitalist society in the race for material wealth.'

war much less likely than hitherto. Nuclear weapons made both Moscow and Washington more belligerent in form—it was important to seem ready and willing to use them—but far more restrained in practice.

For the Americans they had an added appeal. The US was still trying to find a way to extricate itself from the European entanglement into which it had slipped despite its leaders' best intentions. The nuclearization of Europe would be a way of managing this. It would no longer be necessary to envisage a huge American military presence indefinitely stationed in the heart of Europe—statesmen and military strategists alike looked forward to the day when Europe would be able to defend itself virtually alone, backed only by the firm promise of massive American nuclear retaliation in the event of a Soviet attack. As Eisenhower had reiterated in 1953, the US presence in Europe was only ever supposed to be a 'stopgap operation to bring confidence and security to our friends overseas.'

There are various reasons why the Americans were never able to realize their plans for quitting Europe. Towards the end of the 1950s the US was pressing the case for a European nuclear deterrent, under collective European command. But neither the British nor the French were happy with the idea. This was not because their governments were opposed in principle to nuclear weapons. The British exploded their first plutonium bomb in the Australian desert in August 1952; fourteen months later the first British atomic bomb was delivered to the Royal Air Force. For military and economic reasons the British governments of the time were quite keen to switch from a strategy of continental defense to one of nuclear deterrence: indeed, British urgings had played a role in persuading Eisenhower to come up with his 'New Look' strategy, and the British offered no objection to the stationing of nuclear-capable US bombers on British soil.[7]

The French also had an atomic weapons program, approved by Mendès-France in December 1954, although the first independent French bomb was not successfully exploded until February 1960. However, neither the British nor the French were willing to relinquish control of nuclear weapons to a European defense entity; the French especially were suspicious of any hint that the Americans might allow Germans access to a nuclear trigger. The Americans reluctantly conceded that their presence in Europe was indispensable—which was just what their European allies wanted to hear.[8]

A second issue binding the Americans to Europe was the problem of Berlin. Thanks to the defeat of the blockade in 1948–49, the former capital of Germany re-

---

[7] It was left unclear what say, if any, the British would have in their use. At the time (1952) a joint Churchill-Truman communiqué rather obscurely declared that 'the use of these bases in an emergency would be a matter for joint decision . . . in the light of circumstances prevailing at the time.'

[8] American pressure on the British and French to withdraw from Suez in November 1956 (see Chapter Nine) had led to fears among the NATO countries that when it came to a war the US might retreat to its hemisphere, abandoning the exposed Europeans. Hence the perceived need in Washington to 'stand firm', first on Berlin and later on Cuba, in order to reassure America's vulnerable allies.

mained something of an open city; East and West Berlin were linked by phone lines and transport networks criss-crossing the various zones of occupation. It was also the only transit route from East Europe into the West. Germans fleeing west could come to East Berlin from anywhere in the German Democratic Republic, make their way from the Russian Zone of occupation into the Western Zones and thence along the road and rail corridor linking West Berlin to the rest of the Federal Republic. Once there, they were automatically entitled to citizenship in West Germany.

The journey was not entirely risk free, and refugees could bring only what they could carry; but neither consideration inhibited younger East Germans from undertaking it. Between the spring of 1949 and August 1961 somewhere between 2.8 and 3 million East Germans went through Berlin to the West, around 16 percent of the country's population. Many of them were educated, professional men and women—East Germany's future; but the numbers also included thousands of farmers who fled rural collectivization in 1952, and workers who abandoned the regime after the violent repression of June 1953.

Berlin's curious status was thus a standing embarrassment and public-relations disaster for East Germany's Communist regime. As the Soviet Ambassador to the GDR tactfully advised Moscow in December 1959: 'The presence in Berlin of an open and, to speak to the point, uncontrolled border between the socialist and the capitalist worlds unwittingly prompts the population to make a comparison between both parts of the city, which, unfortunately, does not always turn out in favour of Democratic Berlin.' The situation in Berlin had its uses for Moscow, of course, as for others—the city had become the primary listening post and spy center of the Cold War; some 70 different agencies were operating there by 1961, and it was in Berlin that Soviet espionage agencies scored some of their greatest successes.

However, now that the Soviet leaders had accepted the division of Germany and elevated the eastern zone into a fully fledged sovereign state, they could not continue indefinitely to ignore the steady haemorrhage of its human resources. Nevertheless, when Moscow did once again direct international attention to Berlin and generate a three-year international crisis over the city's status, it was not out of consideration for the wounded sensibilities of the East German rulers. By 1958 the Soviet Union was once again worried that the Americans might be planning to arm their West German clients, this time with nuclear weapons. This, as we have seen, was not an entirely unreasonable fear—it was, after all, shared by some West Europeans. And so Khrushchev set out to use Berlin—a city to whose fate the Russians were otherwise indifferent—as a lever to block the nuclearization of Bonn, about which they felt very strongly indeed.

The first move in the 'Berlin crisis' came on November 10th 1958, when Khrushchev made a public speech in Moscow, addressed to the Western powers:

The imperialists have turned the German question into an abiding source of international tension. The ruling circles of Western Germany are doing everything to whip up military passions against the German Democratic Republic . . . Speeches by Chancellor Adenauer and Defense Minister Strauss, the atomic arming of the Bundeswehr and various military exercises all speak of a definite trend in the policy of the ruling circles of West Germany . . . The time has obviously arrived for the signatories of the Potsdam Agreement to give up the remnants of the occupation regime in Berlin and thereby make it possible to create a normal situation in the capital of the German Democratic Republic. The Soviet Union, for its part, would hand over to the sovereign German Democratic Republic the functions in Berlin that are still exercised by Soviet agencies.

The ostensible objective of Khrushchev's offensive, which took on a greater urgency when the Soviet leader demanded two weeks later that the West make up its mind to withdraw from Berlin within six months, was to get the Americans to abandon Berlin and allow it to become a 'free city'. If they did so, the credibility of their general commitment to the defense of Western Europe would be seriously dented, and neutralist, anti-nuclear sentiment in West Germany and elsewhere would probably grow. But even if the Western powers insisted on staying put in Berlin, the USSR might be able to exchange its consent to this for a firm Western commitment to deny Bonn any nuclear weapons.

When Western leaders refused any concessions over Berlin, claiming that the Soviet Union itself had broken its Potsdam undertakings by integrating East Berlin fully into the government and institutions of the East German state before any final Treaty had been agreed, Khrushchev tried again. Following an unsuccessful series of foreign ministers' discussions in Geneva in the summer of 1959, he repeated his demands, first in 1960 and then again in June 1961. The Western military presence in Berlin must end. Otherwise the Soviet Union would unilaterally withdraw from Berlin, conclude a separate Peace Treaty with the GDR and leave the West to negotiate the fate of its zones of occupation with an independent East German state. From November 1958 through the summer of 1961 the crisis over Berlin simmered, diplomatic nerves frayed and the exodus of East Germans grew to a flood.

Khrushchev's June 1961 ultimatum was delivered at a summit meeting with John F. Kennedy, the new American President, held in Vienna. The last such summit meeting, between Khrushchev and Eisenhower in May 1960, had been abandoned when the Soviets shot down US Air Force pilot Gary Powers in his U2 plane and the Americans reluctantly conceded that they had indeed been conducting high-altitude espionage (having first denied all knowledge of the matter). In his talks with Kennedy, Khrushchev threatened to 'liquidate' Western rights in Berlin if there was no settlement there by the end of the year.

In public Kennedy, like Eisenhower before him, took a hard line, insisting that the West would never abandon its commitments. Washington was standing by its rights under the Potsdam accords and increasing the national defense budget specifically to buttress the US military presence in Germany. But off the record the US was much more accommodating. The Americans—unlike their West German clients—accepted the reality of an East German state, and understood Soviet anxiety over the aggressive tone of recent speeches by Adenauer and, especially, his Defense Minister Franz Josef Strauss. Something had to be done to move the German situation forward—as Eisenhower said to Macmillan on March 28th 1960, the West couldn't 'really afford to stand on a dime for the next fifty years.' In a similar spirit, Kennedy assured Khrushchev at Vienna that the United States did not 'wish to act in a way that would deprive the Soviet Union of its ties in Eastern Europe': a veiled acknowledgement that what the Russians had, they could hold, including the eastern zone of Germany and the former German territories now in Poland, Czechoslovakia and the Soviet Union.[9]

Shortly after Kennedy returned to Washington, the East German authorities began imposing travel restrictions on would-be emigrants. In direct response, the US President publicly re-asserted the Western commitment to *West* Berlin—thereby implicitly conceding that the city's eastern half was in the Soviet sphere of influence. The rate of exodus through Berlin grew faster than ever: 30,415 people left for the West in July; by the first week of August 1961 a further 21,828 had followed, half of them under twenty-five years of age. At this rate the German Democratic Republic would soon be empty.

Khrushchev's response was to cut the Gordian knot of Berlin. After the Allied foreign ministers, meeting in Paris on August 6th, rejected yet another Soviet note threatening a separate Peace Treaty with the GDR if a settlement was not reached, Moscow authorized the East Germans to draw a line, literally, separating the two sides once and for all. On August 19th 1961 the East Berlin authorities set soldiers and workmen to the task of building a partition across the city. Within three days a rough wall had been erected, sufficient to foreclose casual movement between the two halves of Berlin. Over the ensuing weeks it was raised and strengthened. Searchlights, barbed wire and guard posts were added; the doors and windows of buildings abutting the wall were first blocked off, and then bricked up. Streets and squares were cut in half and all communications across the divided city were subjected to close policing or else broken off altogether. Berlin had its Wall.

Officially the West was horrified. For three days in October 1961 Soviet and American tanks confronted one another across the checkpoint separating their respective zones—one of the last remaining links between them—as the East German authorities tested the Western powers' willingness to affirm and assert their continuing right of access to the eastern zone in keeping with the original Four-Power Agreement. Faced with the intransigence of the local American military commander—who refused to recognize any *East German* right to impede Allied

---

[9]Kennedy's remark was not only confidential at the time, it was even kept out of the documents from the summit meeting when they were first published thirty years later.

252

movements—the Soviets reluctantly granted the point; for the next thirty years all four occupying powers remained in place, although both sides conceded *de facto* administration of their respective zones of control to the local German authorities.

Behind the scenes many Western leaders were secretly relieved at the appearance of the Wall. For three years Berlin had threatened to be the flashpoint for an international confrontation, just as it had been in 1948. Kennedy and other Western leaders privately agreed that a wall across Berlin was a far better outcome than a war—whatever was said in public, few Western politicians could seriously imagine asking their soldiers to 'die for Berlin'. As Dean Rusk (Kennedy's Secretary of State) quietly observed, the Wall had its uses: 'the probability is that in realistic terms it would make a Berlin settlement easier.'

The outcome of the Berlin crisis showed that the two Great Powers had more in common than they sometimes appreciated. If Moscow undertook not to raise again the question of Allied status in Berlin, Washington would accept the reality of East German government there and would resist West German pressure for nuclear weapons. Both sides had an interest in stability in central Europe; but more to the point, the US and the USSR were both tired of responding to the demands and complaints of their respective German clients. The first decade of the Cold War had given German politicians on either side of the divide unparalleled leverage over their patrons in Washington and Moscow. Afraid of losing credibility with 'their' Germans, the Great Powers had allowed Adenauer and Ulbricht to blackmail them into 'hanging tough'.

Moscow, which as we have seen had never set out to establish a client state in the eastern zone of occupied Germany, but had settled for it as a second best, devoted inordinate effort to shoring up a weak and unloved Communist regime in Berlin. The East German Communists in their turn were always half-afraid that their Soviet patrons would sell them out.[10] The Wall thus offered them some reassurance, although they were disappointed by Khrushchev's refusal to keep pressing for a Peace Treaty once the barrier had gone up. As for Bonn, the longstanding fear there was that the 'Amis' (Americans) would just get up and walk away. Washington had always bent over backwards to reassure Bonn that it had America's unswerving support, but after the Wall went up and the Americans conspicuously acquiesced, West German anxiety only increased. Hence the reiterated post-Wall promises from Washington that the US would never quit their zone—the background to Kennedy's famous 'Ich bin ein Berliner' (*sic*) declaration in June 1963. With 250,000 troops in Europe by 1963, the Americans like the Russians were clearly there for the duration.

The Wall ended Berlin's career as the crisis zone of world and European affairs. Although it took ten years to reach formal agreement on issues of access, after No-

---

[10]As they were to discover in 1990, their fears were not unfounded.

vember 1961 Berlin ceased to matter and West Berlin began its steady descent into political irrelevance. Even the Russians lost interest in it. Curiously, this was not immediately clear to the West. When the Cuba crisis broke out the following year, Kennedy and his advisers were convinced that Khrushchev was engaged in a complex, Machiavellian ploy to achieve his longstanding German objectives. The lessons of 1948–50 had been learned too well.

Just as Truman and Acheson had seen the Korean incursion as a possible prelude to a Soviet probe across the divided frontier of Germany, so Kennedy and his colleagues saw in the missile emplacements in Cuba a Soviet device to blackmail a vulnerable America into giving way in Berlin. Hardly an hour passed during the first ten days of the Cuba crisis without American leaders reverting to the subject of West Berlin, and the need to 'neutralize' Khrushchev's anticipated countermove in the divided city. As Kennedy explained on October 22nd 1962 to British Prime Minister Harold Macmillan: 'I need not point out to you the possible relation of this secret and dangerous move on the part of Khrushchev to Berlin.'

The problem was that Kennedy had taken recent Soviet bluster and propaganda all too seriously and built his understanding of US-Soviet relations around the Berlin question. This dramatically ratcheted up the apparent significance of the Cuban crisis, leading Kennedy to inform his closest advisers, on October 19th: 'I don't think we've got any satisfactory alternatives ... Our problem is not merely Cuba but it is also Berlin. And when we recognize the importance of Berlin to Europe, and recognize the importance of our allies to us, that's what has made this thing be a dilemma for these days. Otherwise, our answer would be quite easy.' Three days earlier, as the Cuba crisis began, Secretary of State Dean Rusk had summarized his own interpretation of the Soviet actions: 'I think also that Berlin is very much involved in this. For the first time, I'm beginning really to wonder whether maybe Mr. Khrushchev is entirely rational about Berlin.'

But Khrushchev, as it transpired, was *entirely* rational about Berlin. The Soviet Union had indeed maintained a vast superiority of conventional forces in Europe and could have occupied West Berlin (and most of Western Europe) any time it wished. But now that the US had sworn to defend the freedom of West Berlin by all means (which in practice meant nuclear weapons), Khrushchev had no intention of risking nuclear war for Germany. As the Soviet ambassador to Washington later observed in his memoirs, 'Kennedy overestimated the readiness of Khrushchev and his allies to take decisive actions on Berlin, the most aggressive of which really was the erection of the Berlin Wall.'[11]

With Berlin and Cuba behind them, the superpowers moved with surprising

---

[11] Anatoly Dobrynin, *In Confidence* (Times Books, 1995), p. 46. Khrushchev's aversion to war was genuine. As he wrote to Kennedy on October 26th, at the height of the Cuba crisis: 'If indeed war should break out, then it would not be in our power to stop it, for such is the logic of war. I have participated in two wars and I know that war ends when it has rolled through cities and villages, everywhere sowing death and destruction.'

alacrity to resolve the uncertainties of the first Cold War. On June 20th 1963 a 'hot-line' was established between Washington and Moscow; a month later talks in Moscow between the US, the Soviet Union and the UK culminated in a Limited Nuclear Test-Ban Treaty. This Treaty, which came into force on October 10th, had considerable significance for Europe—less because of its overt objectives than on account of the 'sub-text' underlying it.

Both great powers wanted to keep nuclear weapons out of the hands of China and West Germany and this was the real purpose of the Treaty. The promise of a non-nuclear Germany was the *quid pro quo* Moscow sought for the Berlin compromise; that is why the Americans were willing to court unpopularity in Bonn in order to achieve it. The West Germans somewhat resentfully accepted the veto on German nuclear arms, just as they had accepted the division of Berlin, as the price of a continued American presence. Meanwhile the Treaty confirmed a distinct shift in Soviet strategic concerns, away from Europe and towards other continents.

The stabilization of the Cold War in Europe, the reduced likelihood of it ever becoming 'hot', and the fact that these matters lay largely out of their hands, induced among West Europeans the rather comfortable conviction that conventional armed conflict was obsolete. War, it seemed to many observers in the years 1953–63, was unthinkable, at least on the European continent (it never ceased to be the preferred approach to conflict resolution elsewhere). If war were to come, the huge nuclear arsenals of the Great Powers meant that it must surely entail unimaginably terrible consequences, and could only therefore be the result of a miscalculation on someone's part. In that case, there would be very little that Europeans could do to mitigate the consequences.

Not everyone saw things thus. Among a minority, the same evidence inspired movements calling urgently for nuclear disarmament. The British Campaign for Nuclear Disarmament (CND) was launched in London on February 17th 1958. From the outset it was squarely in the great dissenting tradition of British radical politics: most of its supporters were educated, left-leaning and non-violent, and their demands were addressed in the first instance to their own government, not to the Russians or Americans (both major parties in Britain were convinced of the need for an independent British nuclear deterrent, even though it was clear by the end of the 1950s that without American-provided missiles and submarines a British bomb would never reach its target).

At its peak, in 1962, the CND was able to turn out 150,000 supporters on the annual protest march to the Atomic Weapons Establishment at Aldermaston. But, together with like-minded disarmament movements in West Germany and the Benelux countries, the British campaign shriveled in the course of the sixties. The anti-nuclear campaigners lost their relevance after the Test Ban Treaty; it was increasingly difficult to claim with any credibility that Europe faced imminent annihilation and new topics had displaced disarmament from the radical agenda. Even in the Soviet Union the dissenting atomic physicist Andrei Sakharov became less concerned with the risk of imminent nuclear holocaust—turning, as he put it, 'from world wide problems to the defense of individual people'.

There is no doubt that most West Europeans, when they thought about it at all, were in favor of nuclear disarmament: polls taken in 1963 showed that Italians in particular would welcome the abolition of all nuclear weapons. The French were somewhat less overwhelmingly abolitionist, while Germans and British were divided, though with a clear anti-nuclear majority in each case. But in contrast with the fraught debates over disarmament of the 1920s and early '30s, the nuclear question in Europe did not move people much. It was too abstract. Only the British and (nominally) the French had nuclear arms, and of the others only a minority of the West German political establishment sought them.

Italians, Danes and the Dutch worried on occasion about having US bases on their soil, which exposed them to danger should a war break out. But the weapons that caused concern belonged to the superpowers; and most Europeans, reasonably enough, concluded that they could do nothing to influence decisions made in Moscow and Washington. Indeed, the hard *ideological* edge of American Cold War rhetoric allowed many in Western Europe, once the immediate threat of nuclear war had passed, to tell themselves that they were in effect doing the United States a favor by allowing it to defend them. And so, rather than engage one way or the other in debates over disarmament, they cultivated their gardens instead.

The most remarkable aspect of the European political scene in the 1950s was not the changes it saw but the changes it *didn't* see. The re-emergence in post-war Europe of self-governing democratic states—with neither the means nor the desire to make war, and led by elderly men whose common if unstated political creed was 'No experiments'—came as something of a surprise. Notwithstanding widespread expectations to the contrary, the political temperature of Western Europe retreated from the fevered heights of the past forty years. With the calamities of the recent past still fresh in public memory, most Europeans turned away with relief from the politics of mass mobilization. The provision of administration and services replaced revolutionary hopes and economic despair as the chief concern of voters (who in many places now included women for the first time): governments and political parties responded accordingly.

In Italy the change was especially striking. Unlike Europe's other Mediterranean states—Portugal, Spain and Greece—Italy became a democracy, however imperfect, and remained a democracy throughout the post-war decades. This was no small achievement. Italy was a profoundly divided country. Indeed, its very existence *as* a country had long been a controversial issue—and would become so again in later years. Studies from the early 1950s suggest that fewer than one adult Italian in five communicated exclusively in Italian: many Italians continued to identify above all with their locality or region, and used its dialect or language for most of their daily exchanges. This was especially true of those—the overwhelming majority of the population in those years—who did not have a secondary-school education.

The backwardness of southern Italy, the *Mezzogiorno*, was notorious—Norman Lewis, a British army officer stationed for a while in wartime Naples, was particularly struck by the ubiquitous Neapolitan water-carriers, 'hardly changed from representations of them in the frescoes of Pompeii.' Carlo Levi, a doctor from Piedmont exiled by Mussolini as punishment for his activities in the Resistance, recorded similar observations in *Christ Stopped in Eboli* (first published in 1945), his classic account of life in a remote village in the barren uplands of southern Italy. But the South was not only unchanging, it was poor. A parliamentary enquiry of 1954 revealed that 85 percent of Italy's poorest families lived south of Rome. A rural laborer in Apulia, in south-eastern Italy, could expect to earn at best half the wages of his counterpart in the province of Lombardy. Taking the average Italian per capita income in that year to be 100, the figure for Piedmont, in Italy's wealthy North-West, was 174; that of Calabria, in the far South, just 52.

The war had further exacerbated the historical division of Italy: whereas the North, beginning in September 1943, had experienced nearly two years of German rule and political resistance, followed by Allied military occupation of its radicalized cities, the South of Italy had been effectively taken out of the war by the arrival of the Western Allied troops. In the *Mezzogiorno* the social and administrative structures inherited from the Fascists thus survived unscathed the bloodless coup that replaced Mussolini by one of his generals. To the longstanding political and economic contrasts between northern and southern Italy were now added markedly different memories from the war.

The failure of post-war agrarian reforms led Italian governments to adopt a new approach to the country's vexed 'Southern Question'. In August 1950 the Italian Parliament established a *Cassa per il Mezzogiorno*, a Southern Fund, to channel national wealth to the impoverished South. In itself this was not a new idea—efforts by Rome to address the poverty and hopelessness of the South date back at least to the reform-minded early-twentieth-century governments of Giovanni Giolitti. But previous efforts had achieved little and the only effective solution to the woes of Italy's southerners was still, as it had been ever since the birth of modern Italy, emigration. However, the *Cassa* represented a far greater commitment of resources than any previous plan and had a better prospect of success because it fitted rather well into the core political mechanisms of the new Italian republic.

The function of the Republican state was not very different from its Fascist predecessor—from whom it had inherited most of its bureaucrats[12]: the role of

---

[12] As late as 1971, 95 percent of Italy's senior civil servants had begun their careers before the overthrow of Fascism.

Rome was to provide employment, services and welfare to the many Italian citizens for whom it was the only refuge. Through a variety of intermediaries and holding agencies—some of them, like the *IRI* (Institute for Industrial Reconstruction) or the *INPS* (the National Institute for Social Security) founded by Mussolini, others like the *ENI* (the National Agency for Hydrocarbons) established in the 1950s—the Italian state either owned or controlled large sections of the Italian economy: energy, transport, engineering, chemicals and food-production in particular.

Whatever the economic arguments against such a strategy (its roots lay partly in the inter-war Fascist drive for economic autarky), its social and political advantages were clear. At the beginning of the 1950s the *IRI* employed 216,000 people; other agencies, including the many branches of the national bureaucracy, employed hundreds of thousands more. Contract work financed by the *Cassa*—for road-building, urban housing, rural irrigation projects—and state subsidies for new factories and commercial services were another, and a substantial source of centralized funding, as was state employment itself: by the mid-fifties nearly three civil servants in five were from the South, even though that region represented little more than a third of the country's population.

The opportunities that these arrangements afforded for corruption and crime were considerable; here too the Republic sat squarely in a tradition dating from the early years of the unified state. Whoever controlled the Italian state was peculiarly well placed to dispense favors, directly and indirectly. Politics in post-war Italy, then, whatever their patina of religious or ideological fervor, were primarily a struggle to occupy the state, to gain access to its levers of privilege and patronage. And when it came to securing and operating these levers, the Christian Democrats under Alcide De Gasperi and his successors demonstrated unmatched skill and enterprise.

In 1953, and again in 1958, the CDs secured more than 40 percent of the vote (their share did not slip below 38 percent until the later 1970s). In coalition with small parties of the Center they ran the country without interruption until 1963, when they switched to a partnership with the minority parties of the non-Communist Left. Their strongest support, outside the traditionally Catholic voters of Venice and the Veneto, came in the South: in Basilicata, Molise, Calabria and the islands of Sardinia and Sicily. Here it was not faith but services that drew small-town voters to the Christian Democrats and kept them loyal for generations. A Christian Democrat mayor in a southern town hall or a representative in the national parliament was elected and re-elected on the promise of electricity, indoor plumbing, rural mortgages, roads, schools, factories and jobs—and thanks to the Party's monopoly of power, he could deliver.

Christian Democracy in Italy resembled in many respects similar parties in West Germany, the Netherlands and Belgium. It lacked ideological baggage. To be sure, De Gasperi and his successors took care to meet regularly with the Vatican authorities and never to propose or support any legislation of which the Vatican disapproved; post-war Italy was in some respects the Church's moment of revenge for the aggressively anti-clerical secularism of the new Italian state after 1861. But the active role of the Catholic Church in Italian politics was smaller than both its defenders and its critics liked to assert. The main vehicle for social control was the powerful central ministries—it is significant that De Gasperi, like the Communist parties of eastern Europe in the immediate post-war years, took care to keep the Interior Ministry securely under CD direction.

In time, the clientelistic system of patronage and favors put in place by the Christian Democrats came to characterize national Italian politics as a whole. Other parties were constrained to follow suit: in cities and districts controlled by the PCI, most notably 'Red' Bologna and the surrounding Emilia region, the Communists supported *their* friends and favored *their* clients, the urban workers and rural small-holders of the lower Po valley. If there was a difference, it lay in the Communists' emphasis upon the propriety and honesty of their municipal administration, in contrast with the widely acknowledged corruption and rumored Mafia links of the CD municipalities of the South. In the 1950s, large-scale corruption was a near-monopoly of Christian Democrats; in later decades the Socialists who governed the great cities of the North emulated them with considerable success. In politics, corruption is largely a by-product of opportunity.

Government Italian-style was not especially edifying, but it worked. Over time whole areas of public and civic activity were carved up *de facto* into political families. Entire industries were 'colonised' by the Christian Democrats. Control and employment at newspapers and radio—later television—were divided among Christian Democrats, Socialists and Communists; occasional allowance was made for the somewhat shrunken constituency of old-school anti-clerical liberals. Jobs and favors were created and delivered proportional to local, regional and national political clout. Every social organism from trade unions to sporting clubs was split among Christian Democrat, Socialist, Communist, Republican and Liberal variants. From the point of view of Economic Man the system was grossly wasteful, and in-imical to private initiative and fiscal efficiency. The Italian 'economic miracle' (as we shall see) happened in spite of it rather than because of it.

And yet: Italy's post-war stability was the crucial permissive condition for the country's economic performance and subsequent social transformation. And that stability rested, paradoxical as it may appear, upon the rather peculiar institutional arrangements just described. The country lacked a stable majority in favor of any one party or program, and the complicated electoral system of proportional representation generated parliaments too divided to agree on substantial or controversial legislation: the post-war Republican constitution did not acquire a Constitutional Court to adjudicate its laws until 1956, and the much-discussed need for regional autonomy was not voted upon in Parliament until fourteen years later.

Accordingly, as in Fourth Republic France and for some of the same reasons,

Italy was in practice run by un-elected administrators working in central government or one of the many para-state agencies. This distinctly un-democratic outcome has led historians to treat the Italian political system with some disdain. The opportunities for graft, bribery, corruption, political favoritism and plain robbery *were* extensive and they worked above all to the advantage of the virtual one-party monopoly of the Christian Democrats.[13] Yet under the umbrella of these arrangements, state and society in Italy proved remarkably resilient in the face of inherited challenges and new ones ahead. When measured by the standards of Canada or Denmark, Italy in the 1950s might appear wanting in public probity and institutional transparency. But by the standards of Italy's strife-ridden national past, or by those prevailing in the other states of Mediterranean Europe with which the country was traditionally compared, Italy had taken a remarkable leap forward.

In important respects Italy's condition after the war stood comparison with that of Austria. Both countries had fought alongside Germany and had suffered accordingly after the war (Italy paid a total of $360 million in reparations to the Soviet Union, Greece, Yugoslavia, Albania and Ethiopia). Like Italy, Austria was a poor and unstable country whose post-war renaissance could hardly have been predicted from her recent past. The country's two dominant political groupings had spent the inter-war years in bitter conflict. Most Austrian Social Democrats had regarded the emergence in 1918 of a truncated Austrian state out of the ruins of the Habsburg Empire as an economic and political nonsense. In their view the German-speaking remnant of the old Dual Monarchy ought logically to have joined its fellow Germans in an *Anschluss* (union), and would have done so had the self-determination clauses of the Versailles agreements been applied consistently.

The Austrian Left had always received its strongest backing from working-class Vienna and the urban centers of eastern Austria. During the inter-war years of the First Austrian Republic, most of the rest of the country—rural, Alpine and deeply Catholic—voted for the Christian Socials, a provincial and conservative party suspicious of change and outsiders. Unlike the Social Democrats, the Christian Socials had no pan-German urge to be absorbed into an urban and mostly Protestant Germany. But nor did they have any sympathy for the Social Democratic policies of the Viennese workers' movement; in 1934 a coup engineered by the Right destroyed the Social Democrats' bastion in 'Red Vienna' and with it Austrian democracy. From 1934 until the Nazi invasion Austria was ruled by an authoritarian clericalist regime in which the Catholic party exercised a monopoly of power.

The legacy of Austria's first, unhappy experience with democracy lay heavily on

---

[13]Though in the light of Italy's earlier history it is not entirely fair to lay the blame for the country's institutional corruption on American foreign policy. See Eric J. Hobsbawm, *The Age of Extremes. A History of the World, 1914–1991* (New York, 1994), pp. 238–39.

the post-war Republic. The Christian Socials, reborn as the Austrian People's Party, boasted proudly of their opposition in 1938 to the German takeover; but they were conspicuously silent on their singular contribution to the destruction of Austrian democracy just four years earlier. The Socialists, as the Social Democrats were now known, could reasonably claim to have been the victims twice over: first of the civil war in 1934 and then at the hands of the Nazis. What this obscured, however, was their erstwhile enthusiasm for the *Anschluss*. Dr Karl Renner, the Socialist leader and first president of the independent Republic established by the Austrian State Treaty of 1955, had maintained his principled enthusiasm for a union of Austria and Germany as late as 1938.

Both parties thus had an interest in putting the past behind them—we have seen what became of initial attempts at de-Nazification in post-war Austria. The Socialists were the majority party in Vienna (which comprised one-quarter of the country's population), while the People's Party had a lock on the allegiance of voters in the countryside and small towns of the Alpine valleys. In political terms the country was divided almost exactly in half: in the elections of 1949 the People's Party outpolled the Socialists by just 123,000 votes; in 1953 the Socialists led by 37,000; in 1956 the People's Party again won, by 126,000 votes; in 1959 the result favored the Socialists, by 25,000 votes; and in 1962 it was reversed yet again, with the Peoples Party winning by a mere 64,000 votes in a total of over four and a quarter million.

These uniquely narrow margins recalled the similarly close elections of the inter-war Republic. Catholic Austria and Socialist Austria thus faced the renewed prospect of parliamentary politics degenerating into a cultural civil war. Even with the help of a third party—the Liberals, who depended to an embarrassing extent on the vote of ex-Nazis, and whose vote in any case fell steadily at each election—neither Austrian party could hope to form a stable government, and any controversial legislation would risk resurrecting bitter memories. The prognosis for Austrian democracy was not promising.

Yet Austria not only succeeded in avoiding a re-run of its history, but managed in a short space of time to repackage itself as a model Alpine democracy: neutral, prosperous and stable. In part this was due to the uncomfortable proximity of the Red Army, occupying Lower Austria until 1955 and thence withdrawn just a few kilometers to the east—a reminder that Austria's neighbors now included three Communist states (Yugoslavia, Hungary and Czechoslovakia) and that the country's vulnerable location made it prudent to pursue conciliatory and uncontentious policies at home and abroad. In addition, the Cold War assigned Austria an identity by association—as Western, free, democratic—that it might have been hard put to generate from within.

But the main source of Austria's successful post-war political settlement lay in the widely acknowledged need to avoid ideological confrontations of the sort that had torn the country apart before the war. Since Austria had to be—there could be no question after 1945 of annexing it to its German neighbor—its political communities would have to find a way to co-exist. The solution on which the country's leaders settled was to eliminate the very possibility of confrontation by running the country in permanent tandem. In politics, the two major parties agreed to collaborate in office: from 1947 to 1966 Austria was governed by a 'Grand Coalition' of Socialists and People's Party. Ministries were carefully divided up, with the People's Party typically providing the Prime Minister, the Socialists the Foreign Minister and so on.

In public administration—which in post-war Austria comprised all public services, most of the media and much of the economy, from banking to logging—a similar division of responsibilities was reached, known as *Proporz*. At almost every level jobs were filled, by agreement, with candidates proposed by one of the two dominant parties. Over time this system of 'jobs for the boys' reached deep into Austrian life, forming a chain of interlocking patrons and clients who settled virtually every argument either by negotiation or else through the exchange of favors and appointments. Labor disputes were handled by arbitration rather than confrontation, as the bi-cephalous state sought to head off dissent by incorporating contending parties into its shared system of benefits and rewards. The unprecedented prosperity of these years allowed the Grand Coalition to paper over disagreements or conflicts of interest and, in effect, purchase the consensus on which the country's equilibrium rested.

Some groups in Austrian society were inevitably left out—small shopkeepers, independent artisans, isolated farmers, anyone whose work or awkward opinions placed them outside the grid of allocated benefits and positions. And in districts where one or other side had an overwhelming advantage, proportionality would sometimes be ignored in favor of a monopoly of posts and favors for members of that party. But the pressure to avoid confrontation usually triumphed over local self-interest. Just as Austria's newfound neutrality was enthusiastically adopted as the country's identity tag, displacing awkward memories of more contentious identities from the past—'Habsburg', 'German', 'Socialist', 'Christian'—so the post-ideological (indeed post-political) implications of government-by-coalition and administration-by-*Proporz* came to define Austrian public life.

At first sight this would seem to distinguish the Austrian solution to political instability from the Italian variant; after all, the major political cleavage in Italy separated Communists from Catholics, a juxtaposition that hardly suggests the description 'post-ideological'.[14] But in fact the two cases were quite similar. The singular quality of Togliatti and his party was the importance they attached, throughout the post-war decades, to political stability: to the preservation and strengthening of the institutions of democratic public life, even at a cost to the

---

[14]In the elections of 1945 the Austrian Communists received just 174,000 votes—5 percent—and elected four deputies to the parliament. Thereafter they played no role in Austrian politics.

Communists' own credibility as the revolutionary vanguard. And Italy, too, was administered through a system of favors and jobs that bore a certain resemblance to *Proporz*, albeit skewed heavily to the advantage of one side.

If Italy paid a price for political stability in an ultimately intolerable level of public corruption, the cost to Austrians was less tangible but just as pernicious. A Western diplomat once described post-war Austria as 'an opera sung by the understudies', and the point is well taken. As a result of the First World War Vienna lost its raison d'être as an imperial capital; in the course of Nazi occupation and the Second World War the city lost its Jews, a significant proportion of its most educated and cosmopolitan citizens.[15] Once the Russians left in 1955, Vienna lacked even the *louche* appeal of divided Berlin. Indeed, the measure of Austria's remarkable success in overcoming its troubled past was that to many visitors its most distinctive feature was its reassuringly humdrum quality.

Behind the tranquil appeal of an increasingly prosperous 'Alpine Republic', however, Austria too was corrupt in its own way. Like Italy, it won its newfound security at the price of a measure of national forgetting. But whereas most other European countries—Italy especially—could boast at least a myth of national resistance to the occupying Germans, Austrians could not plausibly put their wartime experience to any such service. And unlike the West Germans, they had not been constrained to acknowledge, at least in public, the crimes they had committed or allowed. In a curious way Austria resembled *East* Germany, and not only in the rather monotonously bureaucratic quality of its civic facilities. Both countries were arbitrary geographical expressions whose post-war public life rested on a tacit agreement to fabricate for common consumption a flattering new identity—except that the exercise proved considerably more successful in the Austrian case.

A reform-minded Christian Democrat party, a parliamentary Left, a broad consensus not to press inherited ideological or cultural divisions to the point of political polarization and destabilization, and a de-politicized citizenry; these were the distinctive traits of the post-World War Two settlement in Western Europe. In various configurations the Italian or Austrian pattern can be traced almost everywhere. Even in Scandinavia there was a steady descent from the high point of political mobilization reached in the mid-1930s: the annual sales of May Day badges in Sweden fell consistently from 1939 to 1962 (with a brief blip at the end of the war) before rising again with the enthusiasms of a new generation.

In the Benelux countries the various constitutive communities (Catholics and Protestants in Holland, Walloons and Flemings in Belgium) had long been organized into separate community-based structures—*zuilen* or *pillars*—that encompassed most human activities. Catholics in predominantly Protestant Holland not only prayed differently and attended a different church from their Protestant fel-

---

[15]On the eve of the 1938 *Anschluss* there were 189,000 Jews in Vienna. When the city was liberated in 1945 there were fewer than 1,000 remaining.

low citizens. They also voted differently, read a different newspaper and listened to their own radio programmes (and in later years watched different television channels). Of Dutch Catholic children in 1959, 90 percent attended Catholic elementary schools; 95 percent of Dutch Catholic farmers in that same year belonged to Catholic farmers' unions. Catholics traveled, swam, cycled and played football in Catholic organizations; they were insured by Catholic societies, and when the time came they were of course buried separately as well.

Similar lifelong distinctions shaped the routines of Dutch-speakers in northern Belgium and marked them off absolutely from the French-speakers of Wallonia, even though in this case both communities were overwhelmingly Catholic. In Belgium, though, the *pillars* defined not just linguistic communities but also political ones: there were Catholic unions and Socialist unions, Catholic newspapers and Socialist newspapers, Catholic radio channels and Socialist radio channels—each in turn divided into those serving the Dutch-speaking community and those serving French-speakers. Appropriately enough, the smaller Liberal tendency in both countries was less emphatically communitarian.

The experience of war and occupation, and the memory of contentious civic divisions in earlier decades, encouraged a greater tendency towards cooperation across these communitarian divides. The more extreme movements, notably the Flemish nationalists, were discredited by their opportunistic collaboration with the Nazis; and in general the war served to diminish people's identification with the established *political* parties, though not with the community services associated with them. In both Belgium and the Netherlands a Catholic Party—the Christian Social Party in Belgium, the Catholic People's Party in the Netherlands—established itself as a fixture in government from the late 1940s until the late sixties and beyond.[16]

The Catholic parties of the Benelux countries were moderately reformist in rhetoric and functioned very much like Christian Democrat parties elsewhere—to protect the interests of the Catholic community, colonize government at every level from state to municipality, and make provision through the state for the needs of their broad social constituency. Except for the reference to religion this description also fits the main opposition parties—the Labour Party in the Netherlands and the Belgian Workers' (later Socialist) Party. Both of these approximated more closely to the northern European model of a trade union-based labor movement than to the Mediterranean socialist parties with their more radicalised heritage and frequently anti-clerical rhetoric, and they evinced only limited discomfort in competing for power (and sharing its spoils) with the Catholics.

It was this distinctive post-war mix of self-sustaining cultural communities and

---

[16]In Belgium the long-established *Catholic* Party changed its name to *Christian* to emphasize its cross-denominational appeal and its more modern, reforming aspirations. In the Netherlands, where intra-Christian distinctions actually mattered, the Catholic Party kept its old title.

reformist parties of the left- and right-center that established political equilibrium in the Low Countries. It had not always been thus. Belgium especially had seen serious political violence in the 1930s when the Flemish separatists and Léon Degrelle's Fascist *Rexistes* had between them threatened the parliamentary regime, and the country would experience a new and even more disruptive bout of inter-community strife beginning in the 1960s. But the old political and administrative elites (and local Catholic hierarchy), whose rule had been briefly threatened in 1945, regained their power while allowing considerable latitude for welfare and other reforms. The *pillars* thus survived into the 1960s—anachronistic echoes of a pre-political age that lasted just long enough to serve as cultural and institutional stabilizers during a period of hectic economic transformation.

The most dramatic instance of political stabilization in post-war Europe, and certainly the most important, is also in retrospect the least surprising. By the time it joined NATO in 1955, the Federal Republic of [West] Germany was already well on the way to the *Wirtschaftswunder* (economic miracle) for which it liked to be known. But the Bonn Republic was even more noteworthy for its success in wrong-footing the many observers in both camps who had anticipated the worst. Under Konrad Adenauer's direction West Germany had navigated safely between the Scylla of neo-Nazism and the Charybdis of philo-Soviet neutralism, and was anchored securely within the Western alliance, despite the misgivings of critics at home and abroad.

The institutions of post-war Germany were deliberately shaped so as to minimize the risk of a re-run of Weimar. Government was decentralized: primary responsibility for administration and the provision of services was devolved upon the *Länder*, the regional units into which the country was divided. Some of these, like Bavaria or Schleswig-Holstein, corresponded to once-independent German states that had been absorbed into Imperial Germany in the course of the nineteenth century. Others, like Rhineland-Westphalia in the north-west, were administrative conveniences that combined or bisected older territorial units.

West Berlin became a *Land* in 1955 and was duly represented in the *Bundesrat*, the Upper House where the regions' delegates sat (although its deputies in the directly elected Lower House, the *Bundestag*, could not vote in plenary sessions). The powers of the central government were on the one hand considerably restricted when compared to those of its predecessors—the Western Allies blamed the rise of Hitler upon the Prussian tradition of authoritarian government and set out to prevent any recurrence. On the other hand, the Bundestag could not casually unseat a Chancellor and his government once elected; to do so they were obliged to have ready in advance a candidate for the succession with sufficient parliamentary votes to assure his success. The purpose of this constraint was to prevent the kind of serial political instability and weak government that had characterized the

Weimar Republic's last years; but it also contributed to the longevity and author-ity of strong Chancellors like Konrad Adenauer, and after him Helmut Schmidt and Helmut Kohl.

This concern to deflect or contain conflict shaped the whole public culture of the Bonn Republic. 'Social market' legislation was aimed at reducing the risk of labor conflicts or the politicization of economic disputes. Under a Co-Determination Law of 1951, large firms in the heavy industries of coal, steel and iron were obliged to include employee representatives on their supervisory boards, a practice that was later extended to other sectors and smaller businesses. The Fed-eral Government and the *Länder* were active in many economic sectors; and, de-spite objecting in principle to nationalized monopolies, the Christian Democratic-run state of the fifties owned or controlled 40 percent of all coal and iron production, two-thirds of electricity-generating plants, three quarters of alu-minium manufacturing and, crucially, a majority of German banks.

The decentralization of power, in other words, did not mean hands-off gov-ernment. By maintaining an active economic presence either directly or indirectly (through holding companies), West German regional and national governments were in a position to encourage policies and practices conducive to social peace as well as private profit. Banks, acting as intermediaries between government and the businesses on whose boards bankers typically sat, played a crucial role. Older Ger-man economic practices returned, notably price-setting and consensual market-sharing. At the local level especially there had been very little stripping out of Nazi-era bureaucrats, businessmen or bankers, and by the later 1950s much of the West German economy was run in a manner that would have been familiar to the giant trusts and cartels of earlier decades.

This *de facto* corporatism was not perhaps what its American overseers had in mind for the new German republic—trusts and their powers were widely believed to have contributed to the rise of Hitler and were anyway inimical to the free mar-ket. Had the economist Ludwig Erhard—leader of the Free Democrats, Germany's third political party—got his way, the West German economy and with it West German social relations might have looked quite different. But regulated markets and close government-business relations sat comfortably in the Christian Democratic schema, both on general social principles and from pragmatic calcu-lation. Trade unions and business groups cooperated for the most part—the eco-nomic cake grew fast enough in these years for most demands to be accommodated without conflict.

The Christian Democrat Union ruled without interruption from the first FRG elections in 1949 until 1966; until Konrad Adenauer resigned in 1963 at the age of 87, he had unbroken charge of the affairs of the Bonn Republic. There were vari-ous reasons why the CDU, with Adenauer as Chancellor, enjoyed such a long pe-riod of continuous power. One was the strong position of the Catholic Church in post-war West Germany: with the predominantly Protestant regions of Brandenburg, Prussia and Saxony now in Communist hands, Catholics represented just over half the West German population. In Bavaria, where conservative Catholics constituted the overwhelming majority of the voters, the local Christian Social Union had an impregnable power base and used it to secure for itself a permanent place as junior coalition partner in the Adenauer governments.

Adenauer himself was old enough to remember the early years of the Wilhelminian Empire when the Catholic Church had been the target of Bismarck's *Kulturkampf*; he was wary of profiting excessively from the new balance of forces and thereby risking renewed conflict around the relations of church and state, especially in the aftermath of the German churches' distinctly un-heroic record under the Nazis. From the outset, therefore, he sought to make of his party a nationwide *Christian* electoral vehicle rather than an exclusively Catholic one, emphasizing the socially ecumenical appeal of Christian Democracy. In this he was distinctly successful: the CDU/CSU only narrowly beat the Social Democrats in the first elections of 1949, but by 1957 their vote had almost doubled and the winners' share of the turnout topped 50 percent.

A related reason for the success of the CDU/CSU alliance (between them the two parties would always henceforth secure 44 percent or more of the national vote) was that, like the Christian Democrats in Italy, it appealed to a broad electorate. The Bavarian Christian Socials, like their homologues in the Low Countries, had a restricted appeal, attracting votes from a conservative, church-going community in a single region. But Adenauer's CDU, though traditionally conservative in cultural matters—in many smaller towns and rural communities local CDU activists allied with the Catholic Church and other Christian groups to control and censor cinema programs, for example—was otherwise quite ecumenical: particularly in social policy.

In this way, Germany's Christian Democrats established a trans-regional, cross-denominational base in German politics. They could count on votes from the countryside and the towns, from employers and from workers. Whereas the Italian Christian Democrats colonized the state, in Germany the CDU colonized the issues. On economic policy, on social services and welfare, and especially on the still sensitive topics of the East-West divide and the fate of Germany's many expellees, the CDU under Adenauer was firmly entrenched as an umbrella party of the majority center—a new departure in German political culture.

The chief victim of the CDU's success was the Social Democratic Party, the SPD. On the face of things, the SPD ought to have been better placed, even allowing for the loss of traditionally Socialist voters in northern and eastern Germany. Adenauer's anti-Nazi record was spotty: as late as 1932 he had believed that Hitler could be brought to behave responsibly, and he was perhaps rather fortunate to have been an object of Nazi suspicion both in 1933 (when he was ousted from his post as mayor of Cologne) and again in the last months of the war when he was briefly imprisoned as an opponent of the regime. Without these points to his credit it is doubtful whether the Western Allies would have sponsored his rise to prominence.

The Socialist leader Kurt Schumacher, on the other hand, had been a resolute anti-Nazi from the outset. In the Reichstag on February 23rd 1932 he had famously denounced National Socialism as 'a continuous appeal to the inner swine in human beings', unique in German history in its success in 'ceaselessly mobilizing human stupidity.' Arrested in July 1933 he spent most of the next twelve years in concentration camps, which permanently damaged his health and shortened his life. Gaunt and stooped, Schumacher, with his personal heroism and his unswerving insistence after the war on Germany's obligation to acknowledge its crimes, was not just the natural leader of the Socialists but the only national politician in postwar Germany who might have provided his fellow Germans with a clear moral compass.

But Schumacher, for all his many qualities, was curiously slow to grasp the new international regime in Europe. Born in Kreisstadt, in Prussia, he was reluctant to abandon the prospect of a united, neutral Germany. He disliked and distrusted Communists and had no illusions about them; but he seems seriously to have believed that a demilitarized Germany would be left in peace to determine its fate, and that such circumstances would be propitious for the Socialists. He was thus virulently opposed to Adenauer's Western orientation and his apparent willingness to countenance an indefinite division of Germany. For the Socialists, the restoration of a sovereign, unified and politically neutral Germany must take precedence over all international entanglements.

Schumacher was particularly aroused by Adenauer's enthusiasm for the project of West European integration. In Schumacher's view, the 1950 Schuman Plan was intended to produce a Europe that would be 'conservative, capitalist, clerical and dominated by cartels.' Whether or not he was altogether mistaken is besides the point here. The trouble was that Schumacher's Social Democrats had nothing practical to offer instead. By combining their traditional socialist program of nationalizations and social guarantees with the demand for unification and neutrality they did respectably in the first FRG elections of 1949, receiving 29.2 percent of the vote and the support of 6,935,000 voters (424,000 less than the CDU/CSU). But by the mid-fifties, with West Germany firmly tied into the Western Alliance and the incipient project of European union, and with the Socialists' doom-laden economic prophecies demonstrably falsified, the SPD was stymied. In the elections of 1953 and 1957 the Socialist vote increased only slightly and their share of the electorate stagnated.

Only in 1959, seven years after Schumacher's premature death, did a new generation of German Socialists formally abandon the party's seventy-year-old commitment to Marxism and make a virtue of the necessity of compromise with West German reality. The function of Marxism in post-war German socialism had only ever been rhetorical—the SPD had ceased to harbor genuinely revolutionary ambitions by 1914 at the latest, if indeed it ever really had any. But the decision to relinquish the ageing formulas of Socialist maximalism also released Germany's Socialists to adapt the substance of their thinking. Although many remained unhappy with Germany's role in the new European Economic Community, they did reconcile themselves both to Germany's participation in the Western Alliance and to the need to become a cross-class *Volkspartei*—rather than rely on their working-class core—if they were ever seriously to challenge Adenauer's monopoly of power.

In due course the SPD reformers were successful: the improvement in the Party's performance at the elections of 1961 and 1965 led to a 'grand' coalition government in 1966 with the Social Democrats, now led by Willy Brandt, in office for the first time since Weimar days. But they would pay an ironic price for this improvement in their prospects. So long as Germany's Social Democrats maintained their principled opposition to most of Adenauer's policies, they contributed inadvertently to the political stability of the West German Republic. The Communist Party had never done well in the FRG (in 1947 it received just 5.7 percent of the vote, in 1953 2.2 percent, and in 1956 it was banned by the West German Constitutional Court). The SPD thus had a monopoly on the political Left and absorbed within itself whatever youthful and radical dissent there was at the time. But once it joined the Christian Democrats in office and adopted a moderate and reformist agenda, the SPD lost the allegiance of the far Left. A space would now open up *outside* parliament for a new and destabilizing generation of political radicals.

West Germany's political leaders did not need to worry about the rise of a direct successor to the Nazis, since any such party was explicitly banned under the Basic Law of the Republic. There were, however, many millions of former Nazi voters, most of them divided among the various parties of the mainstream. And there was now an additional constituency: the *Vertriebene*—ethnic Germans expelled from East Prussia, Poland, Czechoslovakia and elsewhere. Of the approximately thirteen million German expellees, nearly nine million had initially settled in the western zones; by the mid-1960s, with the steady flow of refugees west through Berlin, a further 1.5 million Germans expelled from the eastern lands had arrived in West Germany.

Predominantly small farmers, shopkeepers and businessmen, the *Vertriebene* were too numerous to ignore—as 'ethnic Germans' (*Volksdeutsche*) their rights as citizens and refugees were enshrined in the 1949 Basic Law. In the early years of the Republic they were more likely than other Germans to be without proper housing or employment, and they were strongly motivated to turn out at elections, their politics shaped by one issue above all others: the right of return to their land and property in the countries of the Soviet bloc, or, failing that, the claim to compensation for their losses.

In addition to the *Vertriebene* there were the many millions of war veterans—even more after Khrushchev agreed to return the remaining POWs in 1955. Like the expellees, the war veterans and their spokesmen saw themselves above all as the unjustly abused victims of the war and the post-war settlement. Any suggestion that Germany, and especially the German armed forces, had behaved in ways that precipitated or justified their suffering was angrily dismissed. The preferred self-image of Adenauer's Germany was that of a victim thrice over: first at Hitler's hands—the huge success of films like *Die Letzte Brücke* (*The Last Bridge*, 1954), about a female doctor resisting the Nazis, or *Canaris* (1955) helped popularize the notion that most good Germans had spent the war resisting Hitler; then at the hands of their enemies—the bombed-out cityscapes of post-war Germany encouraged the idea that on the home front as in the field, Germans had suffered terribly at the hands of their enemies; and finally thanks to the malicious 'distortions' of post-war propaganda, which—it was widely believed—deliberately exaggerated Germany's 'crimes' while downplaying her losses.

In the early years of the Federal Republic there were some indications that these sentiments might translate into a significant political backlash. Already at the 1949 elections 48 parliamentary seats—three times as many as the Communists and almost as many as the Free Democrats—went to various populist parties of the nationalist Right. Once refugees were permitted to organize politically there emerged the 'Bloc of Expellees and Disenfranchised': in local elections in Schleswig-Holstein (formerly a rural stronghold of the Nazi Party) the 'Bloc' won 23 percent of the vote in 1950. The following year, in nearby Lower Saxony, a *Sozialistische Reichspartei*—appealing to a similar constituency—scored 11 percent. It was with this by no means insignificant constituency in mind that Konrad Adenauer took great care to avoid direct criticisms of the recent German past, and explicitly blamed the Soviet Union and the Western Allies for Germany's continuing problems, especially those resulting from the Potsdam accords.

To assuage the demands of refugees and their supporters, Adenauer and the CDU kept a hard line towards the East. In international relations Bonn insisted that Germany's 1937 frontiers remain legally in force until a final Peace Conference. Under the Hallstein Doctrine propounded in 1955, the Federal Republic refused diplomatic relations with any country that recognized the GDR (and thereby implicitly denied Bonn's claim under the 1949 Basic Law to represent *all* Germans). The only exception was the Soviet Union. Bonn's rigidity was demonstrated in 1957 when Adenauer broke off diplomatic relations with Yugoslavia after Tito recognized East Germany. For the next ten years Germany's relations with eastern Europe were effectively frozen.

In domestic affairs, in addition to devoting considerable resources to helping the refugees, returning prisoners and their families integrate into West German society, the governments of the nineteen-fifties encouraged a distinctly uncritical approach to Germany's recent past. In 1955 the Foreign Ministry formally protested against the showing at that year's Cannes Film Festival of Alain Resnais's documentary *Night and Fog*. With the Federal Republic about to enter NATO as a full partner the film could harm West Germany's relations with other states: in the words of the official protest it 'would disturb the international harmony of the festival by its emphatic reminder of the painful past.' The French government duly complied and the film was withdrawn.[17]

This was no momentary aberration. Until 1957 the West German Ministry of the Interior banned any screenings of Wolfgang Staudte's (East German) film of Heinrich Mann's *Der Untertan* ('Man of Straw', 1951)—objecting to its suggestion that authoritarianism in Germany had deep historical roots. This might seem to confirm the view that post-war Germany was suffering from a massive dose of collective amnesia; but the reality was more complex. Germans did not so much forget as selectively remember. Throughout the fifties West German officialdom encouraged a comfortable view of the German past in which the Wehrmacht was heroic, while Nazis were in a minority and had been properly punished.

In the course of a series of amnesties, hitherto-imprisoned war criminals were steadily released back into civilian life. Meanwhile, most of the worst German war crimes—those committed in the East and in the camps—were never investigated. Although a Central Office of *Land* Justice Departments was set up in Stuttgart in 1956, local prosecutors studiously failed to pursue any investigations until 1963, when Bonn began to pressure them to do so—and to greater effect after 1965, when the Federal Government extended the twenty-year statute of limitations on murder.

Adenauer's own attitude to these matters was complicated. On the one hand he clearly felt that a prudent silence was better than a provocative public recital of the truth—Germans of that generation were too morally compromised for democracy to work, except at this price. Anything else risked a right-wing revival. Unlike Schumacher, who spoke publicly and movingly of the sufferings of the Jews at German hands, or the German President Theodor Heuss, who declared at Bergen-Belsen in November 1952 that *'Diese Scham nimmt uns niemand ab,'*[18] Adenauer said very little on the subject. Indeed, he only ever spoke of Jewish victims, never of German perpetrators.

On the other hand, he acknowledged the irresistible pressure to make restitution. In September 1952 Adenauer reached agreement with Israeli Prime Minister Moshe Sharett to pay to Jewish survivors what would amount, through the years, to over DM100 billion. In making this agreement Adenauer ran some domestic political risk: in December 1951, just 5 percent of West Germans surveyed admitted feeling 'guilty' towards Jews. A further 29 percent acknowledged that Germany owed some restitution to the Jewish people. The rest were divided between those (some two-fifths of respondents) who thought that only people 'who really committed something' were responsible and should pay, and those (21 percent) who

---

[17]To which Resnais responded, 'Naturally I hadn't realized that the National Socialist regime would be represented at Cannes. But now, of course, I do.'
[18]'No-one can take this shame from us.'

thought 'that the Jews themselves were partly responsible for what happened to them during the Third Reich.' When the restitution agreement was debated in the Reichstag on March 18th 1953, the Communists voted against, the Free Democrats abstained and both the Christian Social Union and Adenauer's own CDU were divided, with many voting against any *Wiedergutmachen* (reparations). In order to get the agreement approved Adenauer depended on the votes of his Social Democratic opponents.

On more than one occasion Adenauer exploited widespread international nervousness over a possible Nazi revival in Germany to nudge West Germany's allies in the direction he wanted them to move. If the Western Allies wanted German cooperation in European defense, he suggested, then they had better abstain from criticizing German behaviour or evoking troubled pasts. If they wanted to head off domestic backlash, then they should stand firm with Adenauer in rejecting Soviet plans for East Germany. And so forth. The Western Allies understood perfectly well what Adenauer was up to. But they too read the German opinion polls. And so they allowed him considerable leeway, accepting his insistence that only he stood between them and a far less amenable alternative, and his claim to need foreign concessions if he was to head off trouble at home. In January 1951 even Eisenhower was brought to declare that he had been wrong to conflate the Wehrmacht with the Nazis—'the German soldier fought bravely and honorably for his homeland.' In a similar vein General Ridgeway, Eisenhower's successor as Supreme Allied Commander in Europe, asked Allied High Commissioners in 1953 to pardon all German officers previously convicted of war crimes on the Eastern Front.

Adenauer's behaviour did not endear him to his interlocutors—Dean Acheson in particular rather resented Bonn's insistence on setting conditions before agreeing to join the community of civilized nations, as though West Germany were doing the victorious Western Allies a favor. But on those rare occasions when Washington or London displayed their frustration in public, or whenever there was any suggestion that they might be talking to Moscow behind Bonn's back, Adenauer was quick to turn the situation to political advantage—reminding German voters of the fickleness of Germany's allies and of how he alone could be counted upon to look after the national interest.

Domestic support for German rearmament was not especially strong in the 1950s, and the creation of a new West German army, the *Bundeswehr*, in 1956—a mere eleven years after the defeat—did not arouse widespread enthusiasm. Even Adenauer himself had been ambivalent, insisting—with what was by his lights a modicum of sincerity—that he was responding to international pressure. One of the achievements of the Soviet-backed 'Peace Movement' of the early 1950s was its success in convincing many West Germans that their country could be both reunified and secure if it declared itself 'neutral'. Over a third of adults polled in the early fifties favored a neutral, united Germany under any circumstances, and almost 50 percent wanted the Federal Republic to declare neutrality in the event of a war.

Given that the most likely trigger for a Third World War in Europe was the German situation itself, these aspirations may seem curious. But it was one of the oddities of post-war West Germany that their country's privileged position as a *de facto* American protectorate was for some of its citizens as much a source of resentment as of security. And such sentiments were only strengthened when it became clear from the later fifties that a war in Germany might see the use of battlefield nuclear weapons—under the exclusive control of others.

Back in 1956 Adenauer had warned that the Federal Republic could not remain a 'nuclear protectorate' forever. When it became clear in the early 1960s that the Western Allies had come to terms with Moscow on this sensitive subject, and that between them they would never allow Germany access to *nuclear* weapons, he was furious.[19] For a brief period it seemed as though the Bonn Republic's allegiance to Washington might be transferred to De Gaulle's Paris, with whom it was bound by a common resentment at high-handed Anglo-American treatment and a shared suspicion that the US was wriggling free of obligations to its European clients.

Certainly, the French desire for an independent nuclear deterrent offered a tempting precedent to West Germany, one that De Gaulle skillfully exploited in his efforts to wean Bonn away from its American friends. As De Gaulle phrased it, at the same January 14th 1963 press conference where he responded 'Non!' to British membership in the EEC, he 'sympathized' with West Germany's aspirations to nuclear status. And the following week he translated that 'sympathy' into a Treaty of Franco-German friendship. But the Treaty, for all its accompanying fanfare, was hollow. Adenauer's apparent switch of loyalties was disavowed by many in his own party; later that same year his colleagues conspired to bring about his removal from power and reaffirm their loyalty to NATO. As for De Gaulle, he of all people harbored no illusions about the Germans. Six months earlier, in Hamburg, the French President had told a wildly enthusiastic crowd *'Es lebe die Deutsch-französiche Freundschaft! Sie Sind ein grosses Volk!'* ('Long live Franco-German friendship! You are a great people!'); but to an aide he commented, 'If they really were still a great people, they wouldn't be cheering me so.'

In any event, however cool their relations, no West German leader dared break with Washington for the sake of an illusory French alternative. Nonetheless, Adenauer's foreign policy intrigues played to an underlying mood of resentment at Germany's unavoidable subservience to the US. In retrospect we too readily assume that the post-war Federal Republic enthusiastically welcomed everything American; that the GIs spread across central and southern Germany in these years, with

---

[19]With unintentionally revealing hyperbole he described the Nuclear Non-Proliferation Treaty as a 'Morgenthau Plan squared'.

their military installations, bases, convoys, movies, music, food, clothes, chewing gum and cash were universally loved and adopted by the people whose freedom they were there to secure.

The reality was more complicated. Individual American (and British) soldiers were certainly liked, for the most part. But after the initial relief at having been 'liberated' (*sic*) by the West (and not the Red Army) had worn off, other feelings surfaced. The hard post-war years of the Allied occupation contrasted unfavorably with life under the Nazis. During the Cold War some blamed America for putting Germany at the center of 'its' conflict with the Soviet Union and exposing the country to risk. Many conservatives, particularly in the Catholic South, attributed the rise of Hitler to the 'secularizing' influence of the West and argued that Germany should steer a 'middle way' between the triple evils of modernity: Nazism, Communism and 'Americanism'. And West Germany's growing prominence on the eastern edge of the Western alliance subliminally recalled Nazi Germany's self-assigned role as Europe's cultural bulwark facing down the Asiatic Soviet hordes.

Moreover the Americanising of West Germany—and the omnipresence of foreign occupiers—contrasted revealingly with the sanitized Germany of popular desires, nourished in the early fifties especially on a diet of nostalgic domestic films. These, the so-called '*Heimat*' ('homeland') cinema, were typically set in the mountain landscapes of southern Germany and featured tales of love, loyalty and community, in period or regional costume. Shamelessly kitschy, these hugely popular entertainments were often close copies of Nazi-era films, sometimes with identical titles (e.g. *Black Forest Maiden*, of 1950, a re-make of a film with the same title from 1933): the work of directors like Hans Deppe, who had flourished under the Nazis, or else younger men like Rudolf Schündler who were trained by them.

The titles—*Green Is the Heath* (1951), *Land of Smiles* (1952), *When the White Lilacs Bloom Again* (1953), *Victoria and Her Hussar* (1954), *The Faithful Hussar* (1954), *The Gay Village* (1955), *When the Alpine Roses Bloom* (1955), *Rosie from the Black Forest* (1956) and dozens more in this vein—evoke a land and a people untroubled by bombs or refugees, 'deep Germany': wholesome, rural, uncontaminated, happy and blond. And their very timelessness carried comforting intimations of a country and people free not just of occupiers from East and West but clean, too, of guilt and undefiled by Germany's recent past.

The *Heimat* films reflected the provinciality and conservatism of the early Federal Republic, a heartfelt desire to be left alone. This demobilization of Germans was perhaps facilitated by the disproportionate presence of women among the adult population. In the first post-war census of 1950, one-third of all West German households were headed by a divorced woman or a widow. Even after the surviving prisoners of war returned from the USSR in 1955 and 1956, the disproportions remained: in 1960 females in the Federal Republic outnumbered males in a proportion of 126:100. As in Britain or France, only more so, family and domestic concerns were uppermost in the public mind. In this world of women, many of them in full-time work and raising children alone[20]—with terrible private memories of the last months of war and the immediate post-war era—the rhetoric of nation, nationalism, rearmament, military glory or ideological confrontation held little appeal.

The adoption of substitute public goals to replace the discredited ambitions of the past was quite deliberate. As Konrad Adenauer explained to his cabinet on February 4th 1952, when outlining the Schuman Plan's importance for his countrymen: 'The people must be given a new ideology. It can only be a European one.' West Germany was distinctive in that it alone stood to *recover* its sovereignty by joining international organizations; and the idea of Europe could itself substitute for the void opened up in German public life by the evisceration of German nationalism—as Schuman explicitly hoped that it would.

For the intellectual and political elites, this diversion of energies proved effective. But for the woman in the street, the real substitute for the old politics was not the new 'Europe' but the business of surviving—and prospering. At the end of the war, according to the British Labour politician Hugh Dalton, Winston Churchill had expressed the wish that Germany might grow 'fat but impotent'. And so it did, faster and to greater effect than Churchill could have dared to hope. The attention of West Germans in the two decades after Hitler's defeat did not need to be *diverted* away from politics and towards producing and consuming: it moved wholeheartedly and single-mindedly in that direction.

Making, saving, getting and spending became not just the primary activity of most West Germans, but also the publicly affirmed and approved purpose of national life. Reflecting many years later on this curious collective transformation, and on the concentrated zeal with which the citizens of the Federal Republic went about their work, the writer Hans Magnus Enzensberger observed that 'one cannot understand the puzzling energy of the Germans if one resists the idea that they have turned their defects into virtues. They had, in a quite literal sense, lost their minds and that was the condition of their future success.'

Internationally condemned after Hitler's fall for blindly obeying immoral orders, Germans thus turned the defect of their industrious obedience into a national virtue. The shattering impact of their country's total defeat and subsequent occupation made West Germans amenable to the imposition of democracy in a way that few could have imagined a decade earlier. In place of the 'devotion for its rulers' that Heine had first observed in the German people a century before, Germans in the nineteen-fifties attracted international respect for their similarly wholehearted devotion to efficiency, detail, and quality in the manufacture of finished products.

By older Germans especially, this newfound devotion to building prosperity was

---

[20]Many of modern Germany's senior public figures (including the Federal Chancellor and Foreign Minister at the time of writing—2005) were children of this time, raised in single-parent families by a working mother.

unambiguously welcome. Well into the nineteen-sixties, many Germans over sixty years old—which included almost everyone in a position of authority—still thought that life had been better under the Kaiser. But in view of what had followed, the security and tranquility afforded them by the passive routines of daily life in the Federal Republic were more than acceptable as a substitute. *Younger* citizens, however, were more suspicious. The 'skeptical generation'—men and women born in the last days of the Weimar Republic, and thus old enough to have experienced Nazism but young enough to bear no responsibility for its crimes—were particularly mistrustful of the newfound German order.

For men like the writer Günther Grass, or the social theorist Jürgen Habermas, both born in 1927, West Germany was a democracy without democrats. Its citizens had vaulted with shocking ease from Hitler to consumerism; they had salved their guilty memories by growing prosperous. In the German turn away from politics towards private accumulation, Grass and others saw a denial of civic responsibilities past and present. They ardently seconded the dissent from Bertold Brecht's aphorism *'Erst kommt das Fressen, dann kommt die Moral'* ('Eating comes first, then morality') expressed by Ernst Reuter, the mayor of West Berlin, in March 1947: 'No sentence is more dangerous than "Eating comes first, then morality". We are hungry and freezing because we permitted the erroneous doctrine which this sentence expresses.'

Habermas would later be closely identified with the search for *Verfassungspatriotism* ('constitutional patriotism'), the only sort of national sentiment that he felt it appropriate—and prudent—to encourage in his countrymen. But as early as 1953 he came to public attention for an article in the *Frankfurter Allgemeine Zeitung* attacking Martin Heidegger for allowing his Heidelberg lectures to be republished with the original allusions to the 'inner greatness' of Nazism. At the time the incident was isolated—it aroused little international attention. But it put down a marker all the same, foreshadowing the bitter interrogations of a later decade.

In his 1978 film *The Marriage of Maria Braun*, Rainer Werner Fassbinder (born in 1945) acidly dissects the serial defects of the Federal Republic as they appeared to its youthful critics. The eponymous heroine picks up her life in the rubble of defeat, in a Germany where 'all the men look shrunken', and coolly puts the past behind her, announcing that 'it's a bad time for emotions'. Maria then devotes herself with unflinching single-mindedness to the national preoccupation with making money, at which she proves strikingly adept. Along the way the heroine, her initial vulnerability now encrusted with cynicism, exploits the resources, affections and credulity of men—including a (black) American soldier—while remaining 'loyal' to Hermann, her German soldier-husband incarcerated in the Soviet Union and whose wartime exploits are left studiously vague.

All Maria's relations, achievements and comforts are measured in cash, culminating in a new, gadget-filled house into which she plans to welcome her restored husband. They are about to be reconciled in connubial bliss when they and their worldly goods are blown to pieces by an oversight: an open gas tap (*sic*) in their ultra-modern kitchen. Meanwhile the radio acclaims hysterically West Germany's victory in the 1954 football World Cup. For Fassbinder and a coming generation of angrily dissenting West Germans, the newfound qualities of the new Germany in its new Europe—prosperity, compromise, political demobilization and a tacit agreement not to arouse the sleeping dogs of national memory—did not deflect attention from the old defects. They *were* the old defects, in a new guise.

IX
Lost Illusions

'Indië verloren, rampspoed geboren.' [If the Indies are lost, we're done for'.]
Dutch saying, widely cited in 1940s

'The wind of change is blowing through this continent and, whether we
like it or not, this growth of [African] consciousness is a political fact'.
Harold Macmillan, speech at Cape Town, February 3rd 1960

'Great Britain has lost an Empire and has not yet found a role'.
Dean Acheson, speech at West Point, December 5th 1962

'This is Imre Nagy, chairman of the Council of Ministers of the Hungarian
People's Republic, speaking. In the early hours of this morning, the Soviet
troops launched an attack against our capital city with the obvious
intention of overthrowing the lawful, democratic, Hungarian Government.
Our troops are fighting. The Government is in its place. I inform the
people of the country and world public opinion of this'.
Imre Nagy on Hungarian radio, 5.20 a.m. on November 4th 1956

'It is a grave error to call upon foreign troops to teach one's people
a lesson'.
Josip Broz Tito, November 11th 1956

At the close of the Second World War, the peoples of Western Europe—who were
hard put to govern or even feed themselves—continued to rule much of the non-
European world. This unseemly paradox, whose implications were not lost on indigenous elites in the European colonies, had perverse consequences. To many in
Britain, France or the Netherlands, their countries' colonies and imperial holdings
in Africa, Asia, the Middle East and the Americas were balm for the suffering and
humiliations of the war in Europe; they had demonstrated their material value in
that war as vital national resources. Without access to the far-flung territory, supplies and men that came with colonies, the British and French especially would have
been at an even greater disadvantage in their struggle with Germany and Japan than
they already were.

This appeared particularly obvious to the British. To anyone raised (like the
present author) in post-war Britain, 'England', 'Britain' and 'British Empire' were

near-synonymous terms. Elementary school maps showed a world heavily daubed in imperial red; history textbooks paid close attention to the history of British conquests in India and Africa especially; cinema newsreels, radio news bulletins, newspapers, illustrated magazines, children's stories, comics, sporting contests, biscuit tins, canned fruit labels, butcher shop windows: everything was a reminder of England's pivotal presence at the historical and geographical heart of an international sea-borne empire. The names of colonial and dominion cities, rivers and political figures were as familiar as those of Great Britain itself.

The British had lost their 'first' empire in North America; its successor, if not exactly acquired in 'a fit of absent-mindedness', was anything but the product of design. It cost a lot to police, service and administer; and—like the French imperium in North Africa—it was most fervently appreciated and defended by a small settler class of farmers and ranchers, in places like Kenya or Rhodesia. The 'white' dominions—Canada, Australia, New Zealand—and South Africa were independent; but their formal allegiance to the Crown, their affective ties to Britain, the food and raw materials they could supply and their armed forces were regarded as national assets in all but name. The material value of the rest of Britain's Empire was less immediately obvious than its strategic uses: British holdings in East Africa—like the various British-controlled territories and ports in the Middle East and around the Arabian peninsula and the Indian Ocean—were esteemed above all as adjuncts to Britain's main imperial asset: India, which at the time included what would later become Pakistan and Bangladesh, as well as Sri Lanka and Burma.

All the European empires had been acquired sporadically, episodically and (with the exception of the land and sea routes servicing British India) with little sustained attention to logistic consistency or economic gain. The Spanish had already lost most of their empire, first to the British, later to demands for independence from their own settlers, most recently to the rising power of the United States—a source of lingering anti-American sentiment in Spain, then and now. What remained were mere enclaves in Morocco and Equatorial Guinea, to be abandoned by Franco (ever the realist) between 1956 and 1968.

But much of Africa and Asia was still in European hands: governed either directly from the imperial capitals, through a locally recruited governing caste of European-educated intellectuals, or else via indigenous rulers in subservient alliance with European masters. Politicians in post-war Europe who knew only such people were thus largely unaware of the rapid growth of nationalist sentiment among a coming generation of activists throughout the empires (except perhaps in India, but even there they long underestimated its scale and determination).

Thus neither the British, nor any of the other remaining European colonial powers, anticipated the imminent collapse of their holdings or influence overseas. As the British historian Eric Hobsbawm has attested, the end of the European colonial empires seemed very far off in 1939 even to students at a seminar for young Communists from Britain and her colonies. Six years later, the world was still divided between rulers and ruled, powerful and powerless, wealthy and poor, to an extent that seemed unlikely to be bridged in the near future. Even in 1960, well after the worldwide movement towards independence had gathered steam, 70 percent of the world's gross output and 80 percent of the economic value added in manufacturing industry came from Western Europe and North America.

Tiny Portugal—smallest and poorest of the European colonial powers—extracted raw materials at highly favorable prices from its colonies in Angola and Mozambique; these also offered a captive market for Portuguese exports, otherwise internationally uncompetitive. Thus Mozambique grew cotton for the Portuguese commodity market rather than food for its people, a distortion that issued in sizeable profits and regular local famines. In these circumstances and despite unsuccessful revolts in the colonies and military coups at home, Portugese decolonization was postponed as long as possible.[1]

Even if the European states could manage without their empires, few at the time could conceive of the colonies themselves surviving alone, unsupported by foreign rule. Even liberals and socialists who favored autonomy and eventual independence for Europe's overseas subjects expected it to be many years before such goals would be realized. It is salutary to be reminded that as recently as 1951 the British foreign secretary, Labour's Herbert Morrison, regarded independence for African colonies as comparable to 'giving a child of ten a latch-key, a bank account and a shotgun.'

The world war, however, had wrought greater changes in the colonies than most Europeans yet understood. Britain had lost its East Asian territories to Japanese occupation during the war, and although these territories were recovered after the defeat of Japan the standing of the old colonial power had been radically undermined. The British surrender in Singapore in February 1942 was a humiliation from which the British Empire in Asia never recovered. Even though British forces were able to prevent Burma and thence India falling to the Japanese, the myth of European invincibility was shattered for good. After 1945 the colonial powers in Asia would face growing pressure to relinquish their traditional claims.

For the Netherlands, the oldest colonial power in the region, the consequences were particularly traumatic. The Dutch East Indies, and the trading company that had developed them, were part of the national myth, a direct link to the Golden Age and a symbol of Dutch commercial and seafaring glory. It was also widely assumed, especially in the gloomy, impoverished post-war years, that the raw mate-

---

[1]The Portuguese dictator Dr Antonio de Oliveira Salazar was asked in 1968 (seven years into the Angolan revolt that began in February 1961) when he envisaged independence for Portugal's African colonies, Angola and Mozambique: 'It is a problem for centuries', he replied. 'Within five hundred years. And in the meantime they will have to go on participating in the process of development.' (See Tom Gallagher, *Portugal. A Twentieth-Century Interpretation*, 1983, page 200.) But then Salazar's principled denial of the modern world was legendary: for most of the 1950s he succeeded in keeping Coca-Cola out of his country, something even the French could not manage.

rials of the Indies—rubber especially—would be the Netherlands' economic salvation. Yet within two years of the Japanese defeat, the Dutch were once again at war: the Dutch-held territories of South-East Asia (today's Indonesia) were tying down 140,000 Dutch soldiers (professionals, conscripts and volunteers) and the revolution for Indonesian independence was generating admiration and imitation throughout the remaining Dutch imperium in the Pacific, the Caribbean and South America.

The ensuing guerilla war lasted for four years and cost the Netherlands more than 3,000 military and civilian casualties. Indonesian independence, unilaterally asserted by the nationalist leader Sukarno on November 17th 1945, was finally conceded by the Dutch authorities (and a tearful Queen Juliana) at a conference in The Hague, in December 1949. A steady stream of Europeans (actually many of them were born in the Indies and had never seen the Netherlands) made their way 'home'. By the end of 1957, when President Sukarno closed Indonesia to Dutch businessmen, Dutch 'repatriates' numbered many tens of thousands.

The experience of decolonization had an embittering effect on Dutch public life, already hard hit by the war and its sufferings. Many ex-colonials and their friends pressed what became known as 'the Myth of Good Rule', blaming the Left for the Dutch failure to reassert colonial authority following the interregnum of Japanese occupation. On the other hand conscripted soldiers (the overwhelming majority) were just glad to be home in one piece, after a colonial war of which no-one was proud, in which many felt that military success had been impeded by UN insistence on a negotiated transfer of power, and that was very quickly consigned to a national memory hole.

In the longer run the enforced Dutch retreat from the colonies facilitated a growing national sentiment for 'Europe'. World War Two had demonstrated that the Netherlands could not stand aside from international affairs, particularly those of its large neighbors, and the loss of Indonesia was a timely reminder of the country's real standing as a small and vulnerable European state. Making a virtue of necessity, the Dutch retooled as ultra-enthusiastic proponents of European economic and later political integration. But the process did not just happen painlessly, nor was it an overnight switch in the collective sensibilities of the nation. Until the spring of 1951, the military calculations and expenditures of post-war Dutch governments were targeted not for European defense (despite Dutch participation in the Brussels Pact and NATO) but to hold on to the colonies. Only slowly, and with some suppressed regret, did Dutch politicians pay undivided attention to European affairs and abandon their ancient priorities.

The same was true, in varying degrees, of all the colonial and ex-colonial powers of Western Europe. American scholars, projecting the experience and preoccupations of Washington onto the rest of the West, sometimes miss this distinctive feature of post-World War Two Europe. In the United States, the Cold War was what mattered and foreign and domestic priorities and rhetoric reflected this. But in The

Hague, in London or in Paris, these same years were much taken up with costly guerrilla wars in far-flung and increasingly ungovernable colonies. National independence movements were the strategic headache for much of the 1950s, not Moscow and its ambitions—though in some cases the two overlapped.

The French Empire, like the British, had benefited from the re-distribution after 1919 of Asian and African holdings seized from the defeated Central Powers. Thus in 1945 liberated France ruled once again over Syria and Lebanon, as well as substantial swaths of sub-Saharan Africa and some island holdings in the Caribbean and the Pacific. But the 'jewels' in France's imperial crown were her territories in Indo-China and, especially, the old-established French settlements along the Mediterranean coast of North Africa: Tunisia, Morocco and most of all Algeria. In French history texts, however, the place of colonies was perhaps more ambiguous than across the English Channel—in part because France was a Republic in which imperial dominion had no natural place, in part because so many of France's early conquests had long since been taken over by English-speaking rulers. In 1950 there were still millions of French men and women who remembered the 'Fashoda Incident' of 1898, when France backed down from a confrontation with Britain over control of Egypt, Sudan and the Upper Nile. To speak of Empire in France was to be reminded of defeat as well as victory.

On the other hand French schoolchildren were insistently presented with the image of 'France' itself as a trans-oceanic continuum, a place in which the civic and cultural attributes of Frenchness were open to all; where elementary schools from Saigon to Dakar taught about *'nos ancêtres les Gallois'* ('our ancestors the Gauls') and proclaimed—if only in principle—the virtues of a seamless cultural assimilation that would have been quite unthinkable to the administrators of British, Dutch, Belgian, Spanish or Portugese colonies.[2] Only in France could the metropolitan authorities seriously treat their most valued colonial possessions not as foreign soil but as administrative extensions of France itself. Thus 'Algeria' was but a geographical expression; the area it denoted was administered as three departments of France (in which, however, only its *European* residents enjoyed full civil rights).

During the war, the French, like the British and Dutch, had lost their prized South-East Asian colonies to the Japanese. But in the French case the Japanese occupation came late—until March 1945 French Indo-China remained under the tutelage of the Vichy authorities—and was anyway incomparably less traumatic than France's own defeat at home in 1940. France's humiliation in Europe accentuated the symbolic significance of its overseas empire: if the French were not, in their own eyes, quite reduced to a 'helpless, hopeless mass of protoplasm' (Eisenhower's description of them in 1954) this was in large measure due to their con-

---

[2]There was occasional substance to the French claim: Félix Eboué, the governor-general of French Equatorial Africa in 1945, was a high French colonial functionary—and he was black.

tinued credibility as a leading colonial power, which was thus a matter of some importance.

In Africa, De Gaulle had re-established France's presence at the Brazzaville Conference of early February 1944. There, in the capital of French Equatorial Africa across the river from the Belgian Congo, the leader of the Free French had given characteristic expression to his vision of France's colonial future:

'In French Africa, as in every land where men live under our flag, there can be no true progress unless men are able to benefit from it morally and materially on their native soil, unless they can raise themselves little by little to a level where they can partake in the management of their own affairs. It is the duty of France to bring this about.'

What exactly De Gaulle meant is—as so often—unclear, perhaps deliberately so. But he was certainly *understood* to be referring to colonial emancipation and eventual autonomy. The circumstances were propitious. French public opinion was not inhospitable to colonial reforms—André Gide's excoriation of forced labor practices in his *Voyage au Congo* (1927) had raised pre-war public awareness of European crimes in central Africa—while the Americans were making ominously anti-colonial noises. US Secretary of State Cordell Hull had recently spoken approvingly of the prospect of international control for the less advanced European colonies and early self-government for the rest.[3]

Reformist talk in impoverished, isolated francophone Africa was cheap, especially before metropolitan France itself was even liberated. South-East Asia was another matter. On September 2nd 1945 Ho Chi Minh, the Vietnamese nationalist leader (and a founder member of the French Communist Party, thanks to his youthful presence at its December 1920 Congress in Tours), proclaimed the independence of his nation. Within two weeks British forces began to arrive in the southern city of Saigon, followed a month later by the French. Meanwhile the northern districts of Vietnam, hitherto under Chinese control, were restored to the French in February 1946.

At this point there was a serious prospect of negotiated autonomy or independence, as the authorities in Paris opened talks with nationalist representatives. But on June 1st 1946 the French admiral and local plenipotentiary Thierry d'Argenlieu unilaterally proclaimed the separation of Cochin China (the southern part of the country) from the nationalist-dominated north, sabotaging his own government's tentative efforts to reach a compromise and breaking off government conversations with Ho. By the autumn of that same year the French had bombed Haiphong harbor, the nationalist Vietminh had attacked the French in Hanoi and the first Vietnam War had begun.

France's post-war struggle to re-establish its authority in Indo-China was a po-

---

[3]According to some sources, De Gaulle discouraged open talk of colonial self-government lest European settlers, notably in Algeria, seize the occasion to secede from France and establish a segregationist state, on the South African model. This was not an unreasonable anxiety, as subsequent events would show.

litical and military catastrophe. Ho Chi Minh received double credit among the French domestic Left, as a fighter for national independence and as a Communist revolutionary—two identities as inextricably intertwined in his own thinking as they were in his burnished international image.[4] Sending young men to fight and die in a 'dirty war' in Indo-China made little sense to most French voters; and letting Hanoi take over was not obviously more ill-advised than supporting the palpably inadequate Bao Dai, whom the French established as the country's new 'emperor' in March 1949.

The French officer corps, on the other hand, was certainly keen to pursue the struggle in Vietnam; there, as later in Algeria, France's martial heritage (or what remained of it) seemed at stake and the French High Command had a point to prove. But the French economy could never have sustained a long drawn out war in a far-flung colony without significant external aid. France's war in Indo-China was funded by the Americans. At first, Washington's contribution was indirect: thanks to US loans and aid, the French were able to divert considerable resources to an increasingly expensive and unsuccessful struggle to defeat the Vietminh. In effect, the USA underwrote post-war French economic modernization while France dedicated its own scarce resources to the war.

From 1950, American aid took a more direct form. Starting in July of that year (one month after the outbreak of war in nearby Korea) the US sharply increased its military assistance to French forces in South-East Asia. The French bargained hard before consenting to support the doomed European defense project and conceding West German membership in NATO: what they got in return (for allowing the US to protect them, as it seemed to aggrieved Washington insiders) was very substantial American military aid. Of all the European states France, by 1953, was by far the most dependent on US support, in cash and kind alike.

Only in 1954 did Washington call a halt, rejecting increasingly desperate French pleas for airborne help to save the doomed French garrison at Dien Bien Phu. After nearly eight years of fruitless and bloody struggle, it was clear to Washington not merely that the French could not re-establish their former authority in Indo-China, but that they were no match for Ho Chi Minh's regular and guerilla forces. In America's view the French had frittered their money away and were an increasingly risky investment. When Dien Bien Phu surrendered on May 7th 1954 and the French requested a cease-fire, no-one was surprised.

The fall of French Indo-China precipitated the collapse of the last of the French coalition governments that had tried to hold it, and the succession to the premiership of Pierre Mendès-France. Led by 'PMF' the French negotiated an agreement, signed at Geneva on July 21st 1954, under whose terms France withdrew

---

[4]For friend and foe alike, Ho Chi Minh's incarnation as an international Communist icon was confirmed on January 14th 1950, when Mao and Stalin were the first to recognize his newly declared Democratic Republic of Vietnam.

from the region, leaving two separate entities—'North' and 'South' Vietnam—whose political relationship and institutions were to be determined by future elections. Those elections were never held, and the burden of sustaining the southern half of France's former colony now fell to the Americans alone.

Few in France were sorry to see Indo-China go. Unlike the Dutch, the French had not been in the region very long; and even though America paid for the first Vietnam War (something of which very few Frenchmen were aware at the time), it was French soldiers who fought and died there. French politicians of the Right in particular castigated Mendès-France and his predecessors for their failure to prosecute the war more effectively, but no-one had anything better to propose and almost all were secretly pleased to put Vietnam behind them. Only the French Army—or more precisely the professional officer corps—harbored continuing grievances. Some younger officers, notably those who had first served in the Resistance or with the Free French and acquired there the habit of independent political judgment, began to nourish inchoate but dangerous resentments. Once again, they murmured, French troops in the field had been ill served by their political masters in Paris.

With the loss of Indo-China, French attention turned to North Africa. In one respect this was almost literally true—the Algerian insurrection began on November 1st 1954, just fourteen weeks after the signing of the Geneva accords. But North Africa had been at the center of Parisian concerns long since. Ever since the French first arrived in present-day Algeria in 1830, the colony there had been part of a larger French ambition, dating back further still, to dominate Saharan Africa from the Atlantic to Suez. Thwarted in the east by the British, the French had settled instead for primacy in the western Mediterranean and across the Sahara into west-central Africa.

Outside of the far older settlement in Quebec, and some islands of the Caribbean, Northern Africa (Algeria in particular) was the only French colony in which Europeans had established themselves permanently in large numbers. But many of the Europeans were not French in origin but rather Spanish, Italian, Greek or something else. Even an emblematically French Algerian like Albert Camus was part-Spanish, part-French; and his French forebears were very recent arrivals. It was a long time since France had had an excess of people; and unlike Russia, Poland, Greece, Italy, Spain, Portugal, Scandinavia, Germany, Ireland, Scotland (and even England), France had not been a land of emigrants for many generations. The French were not natural colonizers.

Nevertheless, if there was a France-outside-France it was in Algeria—confirmed, as we have seen, by Algeria's technical presence *inside* France as part of the metropolitan administrative structure. The closest analogy elsewhere was Ulster, another overseas enclave in a former colony, institutionally incorporated into the 'mainland' and with a long-established settler community for whom the attachment to the imperial heartland mattered far more than it did to the metropolitan majority. The idea that Algeria might one day become independent (and thus Arab-ruled, given the overwhelming numerical predominance of Arabs and Berbers in its population) was unthinkable to its European minority.

Accordingly, French politicians had long avoided thinking about it. No French government except Léon Blum's short-lived Popular Front of 1936 paid serious attention to the grievous mis-rule practiced by colonial administrators in French North Africa. Moderate Algerian nationalists like Ferhat Abbas were well known to French politicians and intellectuals before and after World War Two, but no-one really expected Paris to concede their modest goals of self-government or 'home rule' any time soon. Nevertheless, the Arab leadership was initially optimistic that the defeat of Hitler would usher in long-awaited reforms, and when they issued a manifesto on February 10th 1943, in the wake of the Allied landings in North Africa, they took great care to emphasize their loyalty to the ideals of 1789 and their affection for the 'culture of France and the West that they had received and cherished'.

Their appeals went unheard. The government of liberated France showed little concern for Arab sentiment, and when this indifference resulted in an uprising in the Kabylia region east of Algiers in May 1945, the insurgents were uncompromisingly crushed. For the following decade Parisian attention was turned elsewhere. By the time these years of pent-up anger and thwarted expectations culminated in the outbreak of organized insurrection, on November 1st 1954, compromise was no longer on the agenda. The Algerian FLN—*Front de Libération Nationale*—was led by a younger generation of Arab nationalists who scorned the moderate, Francophile strategies of their elders. Their objective was not 'home rule' or reform but independence, a goal that successive French governments could not contemplate. The result was eight murderous years of civil war.

Belatedly, the French authorities proposed reforms. The new Socialist government of Guy Mollet granted independence in March 1956 to the neighboring French colonies of Tunisia and Morocco—the first surrender of colonial power on the African continent. But when Mollet visited Algiers, a crowd of European settlers pelted him with rotten fruit. Paris was caught between the implacable demands of the clandestine FLN and the refusal of Algeria's European residents, now led by a Committee for the Defense of French Algeria (*l'Algérie française*), to accept any compromise with their Arab neighbors. The French strategy, if it merits the name, was now to defeat the FLN by force before putting pressure on the settlers to accept political reforms and some power-sharing measures.

The French army duly undertook a bitter war of attrition against the guerrillas of the FLN. Both sides regularly resorted to intimidation, torture, murder and outright terrorism. After a particularly gruesome series of Arab assassinations and European reprisals in December 1956, Mollet's political representative Robert Lacoste gave French paratroop colonel Jacques Massu a free hand to destroy the nationalist insurgents in Algiers by whatever means necessary. By September 1957 Massu was victorious, having broken a general strike and crushed the insurgents in the Battle of Algiers. The Arab population paid a terrible price, but the reputation of France was irrevocably sullied. And the European settlers remained as suspicious as ever of Paris's long-term intentions.[5]

In February 1958 the newly installed government of Felix Gaillard was embarrassed by the French air force's bombing of Sakhiet, a town across the border in Tunisia suspected of serving as a base for Algerian nationalists. The resulting international outcry, and offers of Anglo-American 'good offices' to help solve the Algerian imbroglio, led to growing fears among the Europeans of Algeria that Paris was planning to abandon them. Policemen and soldiers in Paris and Algiers began openly to demonstrate their sympathy for the settlers' cause. The Gaillard government, France's third in eleven months, resigned on April 15th. Ten days later there was a huge demonstration in Algiers demanding the preservation in perpetuity of French Algeria and the return to power of De Gaulle; the organizers of the gathering formed themselves into a Committee of Public Safety, provocatively echoing the French Revolutionary institution of the same name.

On May 15th, forty-eight hours after yet another French government, led by Pierre Pfimlin, had been inaugurated in Paris, General Raoul Salan—the French military commander in Algeria—shouted out De Gaulle's name to a cheering crowd in the Forum in Algiers. De Gaulle himself, who had been conspicuously silent since retreating from public life to his home village of Colombey in eastern France, reappeared in public to address a press conference on May 19th. Armed rebels seized control of the island of Corsica and Paris was gripped by rumours of imminent paratroop landings. On May 28th Pfimlin resigned and President René Coty called upon De Gaulle to form a government. Without even pretending to demur, De Gaulle took office on June 1st and was voted full powers by the National Assembly the following day. His first act was to fly to Algiers, where on June 4th he announced delphically to an enthusiastic crowd of cheering soldiers and grateful Europeans: *'Je vous ai compris'* ('I have understood you').

The new French Prime Minister had indeed understood his Algerian supporters, better than they knew. He was immensely popular among the Europeans of Algeria, who saw him as their saviour: in the referendum of September 1958 De Gaulle secured 80 percent of the vote in France, but 96 percent of the vote in Algeria.[6] But among De Gaulle's many distinctive traits was an unwavering appreciation for order and legitimacy. The hero of the Free French, the implacable critic of Vichy, the man who had restored the credibility of the French state after August 1944 was no friend of the Algerian rebels (many of them former Pétainists), much less the free-thinking insurrectionary young officers who had taken their part. His first

---

[5]These events are memorably depicted in Gilles Pontecorvo's 1965 film *La Battaglia di Algeri* (*The Battle of Algiers*).

[6]The referendum established a new, Fifth Republic. De Gaulle was elected its first President three months later.

task, as he understood it, was to restore the authority of government in France. His second and related objective was to resolve the Algerian conflict that had so dramatically undermined it.

Within a year it was clear that Paris and Algiers were on a collision course. International opinion was increasingly favorable to the FLN and its demand for independence. The British were granting independence to their African colonies. Even the Belgians finally released the Congo in June 1960 (albeit in an irresponsible manner and with disastrous results).[7] Colonial Algeria was fast becoming an anachronism, as De Gaulle fully understood. He had already established a 'Communauté Française' as the first step towards a 'commonwealth' of France's former colonies. South of the Sahara, formal independence would be granted rapidly to French-educated elites of countries that were far too weak to stand alone and would thus be utterly dependent on France for decades to come. In September 1959, just one year after coming to power, the French President proposed 'self-determination' for Algeria.

Infuriated by what they regarded as evidence of a coming sell-out, officers and settlers in Algeria began planning a full-scale revolt. There were plots, coups and talk of revolution. In January 1960 barricades went up in Algiers and 'ultra-patriots' shot at French gendarmes. But the revolt collapsed in the face of De Gaulle's intransigence and unreliable senior officers (including Massu and his superior, General Maurice Challe) were carefully re-assigned away from Algeria. The disturbances continued, however, culminating in an unsuccessful military *putsch* in April 1961, inspired by the newly formed *OAS* (Organisation de l'Armée Secrète). But the conspirators failed to shift De Gaulle, who went on French national radio to denounce the 'military *pronunciamento* by a handful of retired generals'. The chief victim of the coup was the morale and the international image (what remained of it) of the French Army. An overwhelming majority of Frenchmen and women, many of them with sons serving in Algeria, drew the conclusion that Algerian independence was not just inevitable but desirable—and for the sake of France, the sooner the better.[8]

De Gaulle, ever the realist, began negotiations with the FLN at the spa town of Evian on Lake Geneva. Initial talks, conducted in June 1960 and again during June and July 1961, had failed to find common ground. A renewed attempt, in March 1962, was more successful, after just ten days of discussion the two sides reached agreement and on March 19th, after nearly eight years of unbroken fighting, the FLN declared a cease-fire. On the basis of the terms agreed at Evian De Gaulle called a referendum on Sunday July 1st and the French people voted overwhelmingly to free themselves of the Algerian shackle. Two days later Algeria became an independent state.

---

[7]When the Belgians abandoned the Congo in 1960 they left behind just thirty Congolese university graduates to fill four thousand senior administrative positions.
[8]Between 1954 and 1962, 2 million French soldiers served in Algeria; 1.2 million of them were conscripts.

The Algerian tragedy did not end there. The OAS grew into a fully fledged underground organization, committed first to preserving French Algeria and then, after that failed, to punishing those who had 'betrayed' their cause. In February 1962 alone, OAS operatives and bombs killed 553 people. Spectacular assassination attempts on French Culture Minister André Malraux and on De Gaulle himself were unsuccessful, though at least one plan to ambush the President's car as he drove through the Parisian suburb of Petit Clamart came perilously close to succeeding. For a few years in the early sixties France was in the grip of a determined and increasingly desperate terrorist threat. The French intelligence services ultimately broke the OAS, but the memory lingered.

Meanwhile, millions of Algerians were forced into French exile against their will. The European *pieds-noirs* settled for the most part in southern France; the first generation harbored longstanding grievances against the French authorities for betraying their cause and forcing them off their property and out of their jobs. Algeria's Jews also abandoned the country, some for Israel, many—like the Moroccan Jews before them—for France, where they would come in time to constitute the largest (and predominantly Sephardic) Jewish community in Western Europe. Many Arabs, too, quit independent Algeria. Some left in anticipation of the repressive, dogmatic rule of the FLN. Others, notably those who had worked with the French or served as auxiliaries with French police and military authorities—the so-called *harkis*—fled the predictable wrath of the victorious nationalists. Many were caught and suffered horrible retribution; but even those who made it safely to France got no thanks from the French and scant acknowledgement or recompense for their sacrifices.

France was in a hurry to forget its Algerian trauma. The Evian Agreements of 1962 put an end to nearly five decades of war or fear of war in French life. The population was weary—weary of crises, weary of fighting, weary of threats and rumours and plots. The Fourth Republic had lasted just twelve years. Unloved and unlamented, it was cruelly weakened from the outset by the absence of an effective executive—a legacy of the Vichy experience, which had made post-war legislators reluctant to establish a strong presidency. It was handicapped by its parliamentary and electoral systems, which favored multiple parties and produced unstable coalition governments. It oversaw unprecedented social changes but these generated a divisive political backlash. Pierre Poujade, a bookseller from St Céré in the deep south-west of France, formed Europe's first single-issue protest party to defend '*des petits, des matraqués, des spoliés, des laminés, des humiliés*': the ripped-off, lied-to, humiliated little men and women left behind by history. Fifty-two anti-system, 'poujadist' deputies won parliamentary seats in the national elections of 1956.

But above all, the first post-war French republic was brought low by its colonial struggles. Like the Ancien Régime, the Fourth Republic was crippled by the costs of war. Between December 1955 and December 1957 France lost two-thirds of its currency reserves, despite the steady growth of the economy. Exchange controls, multiple exchange rates (comparable to those operated by the Soviet bloc in later decades), foreign debt, budget deficits and chronic inflation were all attributable to the uncontrolled expenses of unsuccessful colonial wars, from 1947 to 1954 and again from 1955 onwards. Governments of every hue divided and fell when faced with these hurdles. Even without a disaffected army, the Fourth Republic would have been hard pressed to face down such challenges just a decade after the worst military defeat in the nation's history and a humiliating four-year occupation. The wonder is that it lasted as long as it did.

The institutions of Charles de Gaulle's Fifth French Republic were designed to avoid precisely the defects of its predecessor. The Assembly and the political parties were reduced in significance, the executive was dramatically strengthened: the constitution gave the President considerable control and initiative in the making of policy, and absolute sway over prime ministers whom he could appoint and dismiss virtually at will. In the aftermath of his success in ending the Algerian conflict, De Gaulle proposed that the President of the Republic be henceforth elected by direct universal suffrage (rather than indirectly, by the Assembly, as hitherto); this amendment to the constitution was duly approved in a referendum of October 28th 1962. Sustained by his institutions, his record and his personality—and French memories of the alternative—the French President now had more power than any other freely elected head of state or government in the world.

In domestic affairs, De Gaulle was for the most part content to leave daily business to his prime ministers. The radical economic reform program that began with the issuing of a new franc on December 27th 1958 was in line with earlier recommendations from the International Monetary Fund, and it contributed directly to the stabilization of France's troubled finances. For all his mandarin allure De Gaulle was a natural radical, unafraid of change: as he had written in *Vers l'armée de métier* ('The Army of the Future'), a youthful treatise on military reform: 'Nothing lasts unless it is incessantly renewed.' It is thus not surprising that many of the most significant transformations in French transportation infrastructure, town planning and state-directed industrial investment were conceived and begun under his authority.

But like much else in De Gaulle's pursuit of domestic modernization, notably Malraux's ambitious plans to restore and clean all of France's stock of historic public buildings, these changes were always part of a larger, political objective: the restoration of French *grandeur*. Like Spain's General Franco (with whom he otherwise had nothing in common), De Gaulle understood economic stabilization and modernization largely as weapons in the struggle to restore national glory. France had been in steady decline at least since 1871, a grim trajectory marked by military defeat, diplomatic humiliation, colonial retreat, economic deterioration and domestic instability. De Gaulle's goal was to close out the era of French decay. 'All my life', he wrote in his war memoirs, 'I have had a certain idea of France'. Now he was to put it into effect.

The French President's chosen arena was foreign policy, an emphasis dictated by personal taste and *raison d'état* alike. De Gaulle had long been sensitive to France's serial *humiliation*—less by its German foe in 1940 than at the hands of its Anglo-American allies ever since. De Gaulle never forgot his own embarrassing isolation as France's impoverished and largely ignored spokesman in wartime London. His grasp of military reality kept him from expressing the pain that he shared with other Frenchmen at the British sinking of France's proud Mediterranean fleet at Mers-el-Kebir in July 1940; but the symbolism of the act rankled nonetheless.

De Gaulle had particular cause to feel ambivalent towards Washington, where Franklin Roosevelt never took him seriously. The United States maintained good relations with the wartime Vichy regime far longer than was decent or prudent. France was absent from the wartime Allied negotiations; and even though this allowed De Gaulle in later years cynically to disclaim responsibility for a Yalta agreement of which he privately approved, the memory rankled. But the worst humiliations came after the war was won. France was effectively shut out of all major decisions over Germany. Intelligence-sharing between Britain and the US was never extended to France (which was rightly assumed to be dangerously leaky). The nuclear 'club' did not include France, reduced thereby to unprecedented irrelevance in international military calculations.

Worse still, France had been utterly dependent on the USA in its colonial war in Asia. In October 1956, when Britain, France and Israel conspired to attack Nasser's Egypt, it was President Eisenhower who pressured the British into withdrawing, to France's impotent fury. A year later, in November 1957, French diplomats fumed helplessly when British and American arms were delivered to Tunisia, despite French fears that these would end up in Algerian rebel hands. Shortly after taking office in 1958, De Gaulle himself was bluntly informed by General Norstad, the American commander of NATO, that he was not entitled to learn details of the American deployment of nuclear weapons on French soil.

This is the background to De Gaulle's foreign policy once he assumed full presidential powers. Of the Americans he expected little. From nuclear weapons to the dollar's privileged international status as a reserve currency, the US was in a position to impose its interests on the rest of the Western alliance and could be expected to do so. The US could not be trusted, but it was at least predictable; the important thing was not to be dependent on Washington, as French policy had been in Indo-China and again at Suez. France must stand its ground as best it could—for example, by acquiring its own nuclear weapon. De Gaulle's attitude to Britain, however, was more complicated.

Like most observers, the French President reasonably and correctly assumed that Great Britain would strive to maintain its position halfway between Europe and America—and that, if forced to chose, London would opt for its Atlantic ally over its European neighbors. This was brought home very forcibly in December 1962, when the British Prime Minister Harold Macmillan met President Kennedy at Nassau, in the Bahamas, and accepted an arrangement whereby the US would furnish Britain with Polaris submarine-based nuclear missiles (as part of a multilateral force that effectively subsumed Britain's nuclear arms under US control).

De Gaulle was furious. Before traveling to Nassau, Macmillan had held talks with De Gaulle at Rambouillet; but he had given the French President no indication of what was to come. Nassau, then, was yet another 'Anglo-American' arrangement cooked up behind France's back. To this injury was added further insult when Paris was itself offered the same Polaris missiles, on similar conditions, without even having been party to the discussions. It was against this background that President De Gaulle announced, at his press conference on January 14th 1963 that France was vetoing Britain's application to join the European Economic Community. If Britain wished to be a US satellite, so be it. But it could not be 'European' as well. Meanwhile—as we have seen—De Gaulle turned towards Bonn and signed the highly symbolic if utterly insubstantial Treaty with the Federal Republic.

The idea that France could compensate for its vulnerability to Anglo-American pressure by aligning with its old enemy across the Rhine was hardly new. Back in June 1926 the French diplomat Jacques Seydoux had minuted in a confidential note to his political bosses that 'it is better to work with the Germans to dominate Europe than to find ourselves against them ... a Franco-German rapprochement will allow us to get out all the quicker from the Anglo-American grip'.[9] Similar thinking had lain behind the calculations of conservative diplomats who backed Pétain in 1940. But in the circumstances of 1963 the Treaty with Germany made little practical difference. The French had no plans to leave the Western alliance, and De Gaulle had not the least intention of being dragged into any German schemes to revise the post-war settlement in the East.

What the Treaty of 1963 and the new Franco-German condominium really confirmed was France's decisive turn towards Europe. For Charles de Gaulle, the lesson of the twentieth century was that France could only hope to recover its lost glories by investing in the European project and shaping it into the service of French goals. Algeria was gone. The colonies were going. The Anglo-Americans were as unsympathetic as ever. The serial defeats and losses of the past decades left France with no other option, if it hoped to recover some of its past influence: as Adenauer had reassured French Prime Minister Guy Mollet on the day that the French were forced by US pressure and British compliance to halt their operations at Suez, 'Europe will be your revenge.'

With one important exception, the British retreat from empire was very different from that of the French. Britain's colonial inheritance was larger and more com-

---

[9]Quoted in Fernand L'Huillier, *Dialogues Franco-Allemandes 1925–1933* (Strasbourg, 1971), pp. 35–36.

plicated. The British Empire, like the Soviet one, survived the war intact, if battered. Great Britain depended heavily on imperial growers for basic foodstuffs (unlike France, which was self-sufficient in foodstuffs and whose overwhelmingly tropical imperial territories produced very different commodities); and in certain theatres of the war—North Africa in particular—Commonwealth troops had outnumbered British soldiers. The residents of Britain itself were, as we have seen, far more conscious of Empire than their French counterparts—one reason why London was so much bigger than Paris was that it had thrived on its imperial role as port, commercial entrepôt, manufacturing center and financial capital. The BBC guidelines in 1948 advised broadcasters to be mindful of their predominantly non-Christian overseas audience: 'Disrespectful, let alone derogatory, references to Buddhists, Hindus, Moslems and so on . . . may cause deep offense and are to be avoided altogether.'

But the British after 1945 had no realistic hope of holding on to their imperial heritage. The country's resources were hopelessly overstretched, and the costs of maintaining even the Indian empire were no longer balanced by economic or strategic advantage: whereas exports to the Indian sub-continent in 1913 were nearly one-eighth of the British total, after World War Two they were just 8.3 percent and falling. In any case it was obvious to almost everyone that the pressure for independence was now irresistible. The Commonwealth, created by the 1931 Statute of Westminster, had been intended by its framers to obviate the need for rapid moves to colonial independence, offering instead a framework for autonomous and semi-autonomous territories to remain bound by allegiance and obedience to the British Crown, while relieving them of the objectionable trappings of Imperial domination. But it was now to become instead a holding club for former colonies, independent states whose membership in the British Commonwealth constrained them only to the extent of their own interests and sentiments.

India, Pakistan and Burma were granted independence in 1947, Ceylon the following year. The process was hardly bloodless—millions of Hindus and Muslims were massacred in ethnic cleansing and population exchanges that followed—but the colonial power itself withdrew relatively unscathed. A Communist insurgency in neighboring Malaya, however, led the British government in June 1948 to declare a State of Emergency that would only be lifted twelve years later with the rebels' decisive defeat. But on the whole, and in spite of the accompanying retreat from India and its neighbors of thousands of colonial residents and administrators, Britain's departure from South Asia was both more orderly and less traumatic than might have been expected.

In the Middle East, matters were more complicated. In the British Mandate territory of Palestine, Great Britain abandoned its responsibilities in 1948 under humiliating but (again, from the British point of view) relatively bloodless circumstances—it was only after the British had quit the scene that Arabs and Jews set upon one another in force. In Iraq, where Britain and America had common oil interests, the US progressively displaced the UK as the dominant imperial influence. But it was in Egypt, paradoxically a country that had never been a British colony in the conventional sense, that Britain experienced the ironies and drama of de-colonization and suffered a defeat of historic proportions. In the Suez Crisis of 1956 Britain underwent for the first time the sort of international humiliation—illustrating and accelerating the country's decline—that had become so familiar to the French.

The British interest in Egypt stemmed directly from the importance of India, to which was added in later years the need for oil. British troops first seized Cairo in 1882, thirteen years after the opening of the Suez Canal, administered from Paris by the Suez Canal Company. Until World War One Egypt was ruled in fact if not in name by a British Resident (for much of this period the redoubtable Lord Cromer). From 1914 to 1922 Egypt was a British Protectorate, after which it became independent. Relations between the two countries remained stable for a while, formalized in a 1936 Treaty. But in October 1952 the new government in Cairo, led by army officers who had overthrown the Egyptian King Farouk, abrogated the Treaty. In response the British, fearful for the loss of their privileged access to a strategically crucial waterway, re-occupied the Canal Zone.

Within two years one of the revolutionary officers, Gamal Abdul Nasser, had become head of the government and was pressing for the departure of British soldiers from Egyptian soil. The British were disposed to compromise—they needed Egyptian cooperation. The UK was increasingly reliant on cheap oil, imported via the Suez Canal and paid for in sterling. If this supply was disrupted, or the Arabs rejected payment in sterling, Britain would have to use her precious currency reserves to buy dollars and get the oil elsewhere. Moreover, as Anthony Eden, then Foreign Secretary, had advised the British Cabinet in February 1953: 'Military occupation could be maintained by force, but in the case of Egypt the base upon which it depends is of little use if there is no local labour to man it.'

Accordingly, London signed an agreement in October 1954 to evacuate the Suez base by 1956—but on the understanding that the British military presence in Egypt could be 're-activated' if British interests were threatened by attacks on or by states in the region. The agreement held and the last British soldiers were duly evacuated from Suez on June 13th 1956. But by then Colonel Nasser—who had declared himself President of Egypt in November 1954—was becoming a problem in his own right. He was a prominent player in the newly formed movement of independent states from Asia and Africa, which met at a conference in Bandung (Indonesia) in April 1955 and condemned 'colonialism in all of its manifestations.' He was a charismatic beacon for Arab radicals across the region. And he was beginning to attract Soviet interest: in September 1955 Egypt announced a major arms deal with Czechoslovakia.

By 1956, then, the British were coming increasingly to regard Nasser as a threat—both in his own right as a radical despot sitting athwart a vital waterway, and by the example he was setting to others. Eden and his advisers regularly compared him to Hitler; a threat to be addressed, not appeased. Paris shared this view, though French dislike of Nasser had to do less with his threat to Suez or even his growing friendship with the Soviet bloc, than with his disruptive influence on France's North African subjects. The United States, too, was not well pleased with Egypt's President. At a meeting with Tito in Yugoslavia on July 18th 1956, Nasser—together with India's Prime Minister Jawaharlal Nehru—issued a joint statement of 'Non-Alignment', explicitly disassociating Egypt from any dependence on the West. The Americans took offense: despite having initiated talks in November 1955 on American financing for Egypt's Aswan High Dam on the Nile, US Secretary of State Dulles now broke these off, on July 19th. A week later, on July 26th, Nasser nationalized the Suez Canal Company.[10]

The initial reaction of the Western powers was a united front: Britain, the US and France convened a conference in London to decide on their response. The conference duly met, and on August 23rd drew up a 'plan' that the Australian Prime Minister Robert Menzies was to present to Nasser. But Nasser rejected it. The London conferees then met again, from September 19th to the 21st, this time agreeing to form a Suez Canal Users Association. Meanwhile the British and French announced that they would refer the dispute over Suez to the United Nations.

Up to this point the British especially had taken care to align their own response to Nasser's acts with that of Washington. Britain was still heavily indebted to the US, paying interest on outstanding loans; pressure on sterling in 1955 had even led London to consider seeking a temporary waiver of these payments. London was always more than a little skeptical of American motives in the region: Washington, it was believed, harbored plans to supplant Britain in the Middle East, which was why American spokesmen indulged in occasional anti-colonialist rhetoric, the better to seduce local elites. But relations between the two countries were generally good. Korea—and the dynamic of the Cold War—had papered over the mutual resentments of the 1940s, and the British felt they could rely on American sympathy for Britain's international interests and commitments. And so, even though they had been told by Eisenhower himself that they were worrying altogether too much about Nasser and the threat he posed, British leaders took it for granted that the US would always support them if matters came to a head.

It was in this context that the British Prime Minister Anthony Eden (who had succeeded the ageing Churchill the previous year) set out to deal once and for all with the troublesome Egyptian. Whatever their public posture, the British and French were impatient with the UN and its cumbersome procedures. They didn't *want* a diplomatic solution. Even as the various conferences and international plans provoked by Nasser's actions were being convened and discussed, the British gov-

---

[10]The Canal itself had always been within Egyptian territory and indisputably a part of Egypt. But most of its revenues went to the foreign-owned company.

ernment began secret negotiations with France, planning a joint military invasion of Egypt. On October 21st these plans were extended to include the Israelis, who joined the French and British in top-secret negotiations at Sèvres. The Israeli interest was quite straightforward: the border separating Egypt and Israel had been secured by armistice in February 1949, but both sides regarded it as impermanent and there were frequent raids, notably across the frontier at Gaza. The Egyptians had blockaded the Gulf of Aqaba as early as July 1951, a restriction on Israeli trade and freedom of movement that Jerusalem was determined to remove. Israel was out to reduce Nasser and secure its territorial and security interests in and around Sinai.

At Sèvres the plotters reached agreement. Israel would attack the Egyptian army in Sinai, pressing forward to occupy the whole peninsula, including the Suez Canal on its western edge. The French and British would issue an ultimatum requiring that both sides withdraw and then, ostensibly as disinterested third parties acting on behalf of the international community, France and Britain would attack Egypt: first by air and then by sea. They would seize control of the Canal, assert that Egypt was incompetent to run so important a resource fairly and efficiently, restore the *status quo ante* and fatally undermine Nasser. The plan was kept very secret indeed—in Britain only Eden and four senior cabinet ministers were aware of the protocol signed at Sèvres after three days of discussion, October 21st–24th.

At first everything proceeded according to schedule. On October 29th, two weeks after the UN Security Council failed to agree on a solution for Suez (thanks to a Soviet veto), and just one week after the Sèvres meeting, Israeli forces crossed into Sinai. Simultaneously, British vessels sailed east from their base in Malta. The following day, October 30th, Britain and France vetoed a UN motion calling for Israel to withdraw, and issued an ultimatum to Israel and Egypt, disingenuously calling on *both* sides to cease fighting and accept an Anglo-French military occupation of the Canal Zone. The next day British and French planes attacked Egyptian airfields. Within forty-eight hours the Israelis completed their occupation of Sinai and Gaza, ignoring a UN General Assembly call for a cease-fire; the Egyptians for their part sank boats in the Suez Canal, effectively closing it to shipping. Two days later, on November 5th, the first Anglo-French ground troops landed in Egypt.

And then the plot began to unravel. On November 6th Dwight Eisenhower was re-elected President of the United States. The Administration in Washington was furious at the Anglo-French deception and deeply resentful at the lies it had been told about its allies' real intentions: London and Paris had patently ignored both the letter and the spirit of the 1950 Tripartite Declaration, which committed Britain, France and the US to acting against the aggressor in the event of any Israel-Arab conflict. The US began to place considerable public and private pressure on Britain in particular to put a stop to its invasion of Egypt, even threatening to 'pull the plug' on the British pound. Shocked at such direct American opposition, but unable to withstand the accelerating run on sterling, Eden hesitated briefly but then capitulated. On November 7th, just two days after the first British paratroopers landed at

Port Said, the British and French forces ceased fire. That same day the UN authorized the dispatch to Egypt of a Peacekeeping Force, which Nasser accepted on November 12th, provided that Egyptian sovereignty was not infringed. Three days later the UN Peacekeeping Force arrived in Egypt and on December 4th it moved into Sinai.

Meanwhile the British and French announced their own withdrawal from Suez, a retreat that was completed on December 22nd. Britain, whose sterling and dollar reserves had fallen by $279 million in the course of the crisis, was promised American financial aid (and received it in the form of a $500 million line of credit from the US Export-Import Bank); on December 10th the IMF announced that it had approved a $561.47 million loan for Britain, and a stand-by commitment for a further $738 million. Israel, having secured a public US commitment to its right of passage through the Gulf of Aqaba and the Straits of Tiran, withdrew its own troops from Gaza in the first week of March 1957. Clearance of the Suez Canal began a week after the completion of the Anglo-French withdrawal and the Canal was reopened on April 10th 1957. It remained in Egyptian hands.

Each country took its own lesson away from the Suez débâcle. The Israelis, despite their dependence on French military hardware, saw very clearly that their future lay in aligning their interests as closely as possible with those of Washington—the more so following the US President's announcement of the 'Eisenhower Doctrine' in January 1957, stating that the US would use armed force in the event of 'International Communist' aggression in the Middle East. Nasser's standing in the non-aligned world was greatly enhanced by his apparent success in facing down the old colonial powers—as the French had feared, his moral influence and example upon Arab nationalists and their supporters now reached new heights. The failure in Egypt presaged more trouble for the French in Algeria.

For the United States, the Suez adventure was a reminder of its own responsibilities, as well as an opportunity to flex its muscles. Eisenhower and Dulles resented the way Mollet and Eden had taken American support for granted. They were annoyed with the French and British: not just for secretly undertaking so ill-conceived and poorly executed an expedition, but also for their timing. The Suez crisis coincided almost to the hour with the Soviet occupation of Hungary. By indulging in so patently imperialist a plot against a single Arab state, ostensibly in retribution for the exercise of its territorial sovereignty, London and Paris had drawn the world's attention away from the Soviet Union's invasion of an independent state and destruction of its government. They had placed their own—as it seemed to Washington, anachronistic—interests above those of the Western alliance as a whole.

Worse, they had given Moscow an unprecedented propaganda gift. The USSR exercised almost no role in the Suez crisis itself—a Soviet note of November 5th, threatening military action against France, Britain and Israel unless they accepted a cease-fire, played little part in the proceedings, and Khrushchev and his colleagues had no plans to follow through on the threat. But by allowing Moscow to perform, even if only symbolically, the role of protector to the injured party, France and Britain had initiated the Soviet Union into a role that it would improvise with gusto in the coming decades. Thanks to the Suez crisis, the divisions and rhetoric of the Cold War were to be imported deep into the Middle East and Africa.

It was on Britain that the impact of the Suez miscalculation was felt most acutely. It would be many years before the full extent of the conspiracy against Nasser was made public, though many suspected it. But within weeks, Anthony Eden was forced to resign, humiliated by the incompetence of the military strategy he had approved and by the very public American refusal to back it. Although the ruling Conservative Party itself did not especially suffer at the polls—under the leadership of Harold Macmillan, who had somewhat reluctantly taken part in the planning of the Suez expedition, the Conservatives won the general elections of 1959 quite comfortably—the British government was forced into a radical re-appraisal of its foreign policy.

The first lesson of Suez was that Britain could no longer maintain a global colonial presence. The country lacked the military and economic resources, as Suez had only too plainly shown, and in the wake of so palpable a demonstration of British limitations the country was likely now to be facing increased demands for independence. After a pause of nearly a decade, during which only the Sudan (in 1956) and Malaya (in 1957) had severed their ties with Britain, the country thus entered upon an accelerated phase of de-colonization, in Africa above all. The Gold Coast was granted its freedom in 1957 as the independent state of Ghana, the first of many. Between 1960 and 1964, seventeen more British colonies held ceremonies of independence as British dignitaries traveled the world, hauling down the Union Jack and setting up new governments. The Commonwealth, which had just eight members in 1950, would have twenty-one by 1965, with more to come.

When compared to the trauma of Algeria or the catastrophic consequences of Belgium's abandonment of the Congo in 1960, the dismantling of the British Empire was relatively peaceful. But there were exceptions. In eastern and, especially, southern Africa, the unraveling of empire proved more controversial than it had in West Africa. When Harold Macmillan informed South Africans, in a famous speech at Cape Town in 1960, that 'the wind of change is blowing through this continent, and, whether we like it or not, this growth of [African] consciousness is a political fact,' he did not expect a friendly reception and he did not get one. To preserve the system of apartheid rule in force since 1948, the white settlers of South Africa declared themselves a republic in 1961 and left the Commonwealth. Four years later, in neighboring Southern Rhodesia, the white colonists unilaterally pronounced themselves independent and self-governing. In both countries the ruling minority succeeded for a few years longer in ruthlessly suppressing opposition to their rule.

But southern Africa was unusual. Elsewhere—in East Africa for example—

comparably privileged white settler communities accepted their fate. Once it became clear that London had neither the resources nor the appetite for enforcing colonial rule against majority opposition—something that had not been self-evident as recently as the early fifties, when British forces conducted a brutal and secretive dirty war of their own against the Mau-Mau revolts in Kenya—the European colonists accepted the inevitable and went quietly.

In 1968 the Labour government of Harold Wilson drew the final, ineluctable conclusion from the events of November 1956 and announced that British forces would henceforth be withdrawn permanently from the various bases, harbors, entrepôts, fuelling ports and other imperial-era establishments that the country had maintained 'East of Suez'—notably at the fabulous natural harbor of Aden on the Arabian peninsula. The country could no longer afford to pretend to power and influence across the oceans. By and large this outcome was met with relief in Britain itself: as Adam Smith had foreseen, in the twilight of Britain's first empire in 1776, forsaking the 'splendid and showy equipage of empire' was the best way to contain debt and allow the country to 'accommodate her future views and designs to the real mediocrity of her circumstances.'

The second lesson of Suez, as it seemed to the overwhelming majority of the British establishment, was that the UK must never again find itself on the wrong side of an argument with Washington. This didn't mean that the two countries would always agree—over Berlin and Germany, for example, London was far more disposed to make concessions to Moscow, and this produced some coolness in Anglo-American relations between 1957 and 1961. But the demonstration that Washington could not be counted on to back its friends in all circumstances led Harold Macmillan to precisely the opposite conclusion to that drawn by his French contemporary De Gaulle. Whatever their hesitations, however ambivalent they might feel about particular US actions, British governments would henceforth cleave loyally to US positions. Only that way could they hope to influence American choices and guarantee American support for British concerns when it mattered. This strategic re-alignment was to have momentous implications, for Britain and for Europe.

The lasting consequences of the Suez crisis were felt in British society. Great Britain, and England especially, was distinctly optimistic in the early 1950s. The election of a Conservative government in 1951, and the first intimations of an economic boom, had dispersed the egalitarian gloom of the early post-war years. In the first years of the reign of the new Queen, the English basked in a cozy Indian summer of self-satisfied well-being. Englishmen were the first to conquer Everest (1953)—with the help of an appropriately colonial guide—and to run the mile in under four minutes (in 1954). Moreover it was Britons, the country was frequently reminded, who had split the atom, invented radar, discovered penicillin, designed the turbo-jet engine and more besides.

The tone of those years—somewhat over-enthusiastically dubbed a 'new Elizabethan age'—is well caught in the cinema of the time. The most popular British films of the first half of the Fifties—comedies like *Genevieve* (1953) or *Doctor in the House* (1954)—depict a rather perky, youthful, affluent and self-confident southern England. The settings and characters are no longer grey or downtrodden, but in other respects all remains firmly traditional: everyone is bright, young, educated, middle-class, well-spoken, respectful and deferential. This was an England in which debutantes were still received at Court (an anachronistic and increasingly absurd ritual that the Queen finally abandoned in 1958); where one in five Conservative parliamentarians had gone to Eton; and where the percentage of students of working-class origin attending university in 1955 was no higher than it had been in 1925.

In addition to benign social comedy, English cinema in these years flourished on a steady diet of war films: *The Wooden Horse* (1952), *The Cruel Sea* (1953), *The Dam Busters* (1954), *Cockleshell Heroes* (1955), *The Battle of the River Plate* (1956). All based more or less faithfully on episodes of British heroism from World War Two (with a particular emphasis upon naval warfare), these films were a comforting reminder of the reasons the British had for feeling proud of themselves—and self-sufficient. Without glorifying combat, they cultivated the myth of Britain's war, paying special attention to the importance of comradeship across class and occupation. When social tensions or class distinctions were hinted at, the tone was usually one of street-wise wit and skepticism rather than conflict or anger. Only in Charles Crichton's *Lavender Hill Mob* (1951), the sharpest of the Ealing Comedies, does more than a hint of social commentary come across—and here it is an English variant of poujadism: the resentment and dreams of the meek little men in the middle.

From 1956, however, the tone began to darken discernibly. War films like *The Bridge on the River Kwai* (1957) or *Dunkirk* (1958) carried undertones of questioning and doubt, as though the confident heritage of 1940 was starting to crack. By 1960, *Sink the Bismarck*, a war film firmly set in the older mould, appeared curiously anachronistic and quite at odds with the prevailing temper. The new mood was set by John Osborne's path-breaking play *Look Back in Anger*, first produced in London in 1956 and made into an impressively faithful film two years later. In this drama of frustration and disillusion the protagonist, Jimmy Porter, stifles in a society and marriage that he can neither abandon nor change. He abuses his wife Alison for her bourgeois background. She, in turn, is trapped between her angry working-class husband and her aging ex-colonial father, confused and wounded by a world he no longer understands. As Alison admonishes him, 'You're hurt because everything's changed. Jimmy's hurt because everything's the same. And neither of you can face it.'

This diagnosis of Britain's unstable mood at the moment of Suez was not perhaps terribly nuanced, but it rang true. By the time *Look Back in Anger* arrived in the cinemas it was accompanied by a shoal of similarly minded films, most of them drawn from novels or plays written in the second half of the 1950s: *Room at the Top* (1959), *Saturday Night and Sunday Morning* (1960), *The Loneliness of the Long-Distance Runner* (1962), *A Kind of Loving* (1962), *This Sporting Life* (1963). The films of the early fifties had all starred either well-groomed middle-class actors with BBC accents—Kenneth More, Dirk Bogarde, John Gregson, Rex Harrison, Geoffrey Keene—or else lovable London 'types' usually portrayed by Jewish character actors (Sidney James, Alfie Bass, Sidney Tafler or Peter Sellers). The later films, dubbed 'kitchen-sink dramas' for their gritty depiction of everyday life, starred a new cohort of younger actors—Tom Courtenay, Albert Finney, Richard Harris and Alan Bates. They were typically set in northern working-class communities, with accents and language to match. And they represented England as a divided, embittered, cynical, jaundiced and hard-faced world, its illusions shattered. About the only thing that the cinema of the early fifties and early sixties had in common was that women almost always played a secondary role, and everyone was white.

If the illusions of Empire died at Suez, the insular confidence of middle England had been under siege for some time. The disaster of 1956 merely accelerated its collapse. The symbolism of the English national cricket team's first defeat by a team from the West Indies (in 1950 and on the 'hallowed soil' of the home of the game at the Lord's cricket ground in London) was driven home three years later when England's soccer team was thrashed in 1953 at its national stadium—by a team from lowly Hungary and by the unprecedented margin of six goals to three. In the two international games that Englishmen had spread across the world, England itself was no longer supreme.

These non-political measures of national decline had all the more impact because Britain in these years was a largely apolitical society. The British Labour Party, in opposition at the time of Suez, was unable to turn Eden's failure to its advantage because the electorate no longer filtered experience through a primarily party-political grid. Like the rest of Western Europe, the British were increasingly interested in consuming and being entertained. Their interest in religion was waning, and with it their taste for collective mobilization of any kind. Harold Macmillan, a conservative politician with liberal instincts—a middle-class political trimmer masquerading as an Edwardian country gentleman—was very much the appropriate leader for this transitional moment, selling colonial retreat abroad and prosperous tranquility at home. Older voters were well enough pleased with this outcome; only the young were increasingly disenchanted.

The retreat from Empire contributed directly to a growing British anxiety about the loss of national direction. Absent imperial glory, the Commonwealth served Britain largely as a source of food. Thanks to Commonwealth preferences (i.e. tariffs favoring imports from Commonwealth member states), food from the Commonwealth was cheap, and constituted nearly one-third by value of all imports to the UK at the start of the 1960s. But Britain's own exports to Commonwealth countries represented a steadily *falling* share of national exports, more of which were now heading to Europe (in 1965, for the first time, British trade with Europe would overtake its trade with the Commonwealth). After the Suez débâcle Canada, Australia, South Africa and India had all taken the measure of British decline and were re-orienting their trade and their policies accordingly: towards the US, towards Asia, to what would soon be dubbed the 'third' world.

As for Britain itself: America might be the indispensable ally, but it could hardly furnish the British with a renewed sense of purpose, much less an updated national identity. On the contrary, Britain's very dependence on America illustrated the nation's fundamental weakness and isolation. And so, even though little in their instincts, their culture or their education pointed them toward continental Europe, it was becoming obvious to many British politicians and others—not least Macmillan himself—that one way or another, the country's future lay across the Channel. Where else but to Europe could Great Britain now look to recover its international standing?

The 'European project', in so far as it ever existed outside the heads of a few idealists, had stalled by the mid-nineteen-fifties. The French National Assembly had vetoed the proposed European army, and with it any talk of enhanced European coordination. Various regional accords on the Benelux model had been reached— notably the Scandinavian 'Common Nordic Labor Market' in 1954—but nothing more ambitious was on the agenda. Advocates of European cooperation could point only to the new European Atomic Energy Community, announced in the spring of 1955; but this—like the Coal and Steel Community—was a French initiative and its success lay, symptomatically, in its narrow and largely technical mandate. If the British were still as skeptical as ever about the prospects for European unity, theirs was not an altogether unreasonable view.

The push for a fresh start came, appropriately enough, from the Benelux countries, who had the most experience of cross-border union and the least to lose from diluted national identities. It was now clear to leading European statesmen— notably Paul-Henri Spaak, foreign minister of Belgium—that political or military integration was not feasible, at least for the present. In any event, by the mid-fifties European concerns had shifted markedly away from the military preoccupations of the previous decade. The emphasis, it seemed clear, should be placed on European *economic* integration, an arena in which national self-interest and cooperation could be pursued in concert without offending traditional sensibilities. Spaak, together with his Dutch counterpart, convened a meeting at Messina, in June 1955, to consider this strategy.

The participants at the Messina conference were the ECSC six, together with a (low-ranking) British 'observer'. Spaak and his collaborators put forward a range of suggestions for customs union, trading agreements and other quite conventional projects of trans-national coordination, all of them carefully packaged to avoid offending the sensibilities of Britain or France. The French were cautiously enthusiastic; the British decidedly doubtful. After Messina the negotiations continued in an international planning committee chaired by Spaak himself, with the task of making firm recommendations for a more integrated European economy, a 'common market'. But by November 1955 the British had dropped out, alarmed at the prospect of just the sort of pre-federal Europe they had always suspected.

The French, however, decided to take the plunge. When the Spaak Committee reported back in March 1956 with a formal recommendation in favor of a Common Market, Paris concurred. British observers remained doubtful. They were certainly aware of the risks of being left out—as a British government committee confidentially observed just a few weeks before Spaak's recommendations were made public, 'should the Messina powers achieve economic integration without the United Kingdom, this would mean German hegemony in Europe'.[11] But in spite of this, the urgings of the Anglophile Spaak, and the fragility of the international sterling area as revealed a few months later at Suez, London could not bring itself to throw in its lot with the 'Europeans'. When the Treaty establishing a European Economic Community (and Euratom, the atomic energy authority) was signed at Rome on March 25th 1957, and became effective on January 1st 1958, the new EEC— its headquarters in Brussels—comprised the same six countries that had joined the Coal and Steel Community seven years before.

It is important not to overstate the importance of the Rome Treaty. It represented for the most part a declaration of future good intentions. Its signatories laid out a schedule for tariff reductions and harmonization, offered up the prospect of eventual currency alignments, and agreed to work towards the free movement of goods, currencies and labor. Most of the text constituted a framework for instituting procedures designed to establish and enforce future regulations. The only truly significant innovation—the setting up under Article 177 of a European Court of Justice to which national courts would submit cases for final adjudication—would prove immensely important in later decades but passed largely unnoticed at the time.

The EEC was grounded in weakness, not strength. As Spaak's 1956 report emphasized, 'Europe, which once had the monopoly of manufacturing industries and obtained important resources from its overseas possessions, today sees its external position weakened, its influence declining and its capacity to progress lost in its divisions.' It was precisely because the British did not—*yet*—understand their situation in this light that they declined to join the EEC. The idea that the European Common Market was part of some calculated strategy to challenge the growing power of the United States—a notion that would acquire a certain currency in Washington policy circles in later decades—is thus quite absurd: the new-formed

---

[11]Quoted in Alan Milward, *The European Rescue of the Nation-State* (Berkeley and Los Angeles, U of California Press, 1992), page 429.

EEC depended utterly upon the American security guarantee, without which its members would never have been able to afford to indulge in economic integration to the exclusion of all concern with common defense.

Not everyone even in the member states was entirely pleased with the new proposals. In France many conservative (including Gaullist) deputies voted against ratification of the Rome Treaty on 'national' grounds', while some socialists and left radicals (including Pierre Mendès-France) opposed the formation of a 'little Europe' without the reassuring presence of Great Britain. In Germany, Adenauer's own Economics Minister, the enthusiastic free-trader Ludwig Erhard, remained critical of a neo-mercantilist 'customs union' that might damage Germany's links with Britain, restrict trade flows and distort prices. In Erhard's view, the EEC was a 'macro-economic nonsense'. As one scholar has perceptively observed, things could well have turned out differently: 'If Erhard had ruled Germany, the likely result would have been an Anglo-German Free Trade Association with no agricultural component, and the effects of economic exclusion would eventually have forced France to join'.[12]

But it didn't happen that way. And the final shape of the EEC did have a certain logic to it. In the course of the 1950s the countries of continental Western Europe traded increasingly with one another. And they each traded above all with West Germany, on whose markets and products the European economic recovery had thus come increasingly to depend. Moreover, every post-war European state was now deeply involved in economic affairs: through planning, regulation, growth targeting and subsidies of all sorts. But the promotion of exports; the redirection of resources from old industries to new ones; the encouragement of favored sectors like agriculture or transport: all these required cross-border cooperation. None of the West European economies was self-sufficient.

This trend towards mutually advantageous coordination was thus driven by national self-interest, not the objectives of Schuman's Coal and Steel Authority, which was irrelevant to economic policy making in these years. The same concern to protect and nourish local interests that had turned Europe's states inwards before 1939 now brought them closer together. The removal of impediments and the lessons of the recent past were perhaps the most important factors in facilitating this change. The Dutch, for example, were not altogether happy at the prospect of high EEC external tariffs that would inflate local prices, and like their Belgian neighbors they worried about the absence of the British. But they could not risk being cut off from their major trading partners.

German interests were mixed. As Europe's main exporting nation Germany had a growing interest in free trade within Western Europe—the more so because German manufacturers had lost their important markets in eastern Europe and had

[12]Andrew Moravcsik, *The Choice for Europe. Social Purpose and State Power from Messina to Maastricht* (Ithaca, Cornell University Press, 1998), page 137.

no former colonial territories to exploit. But a tariff-protected European customs union confined to six countries was not necessarily a rational German policy objective, as Erhard understood. Like the British, he and many other Germans might have preferred a broader, looser European free trade area. But as a principle of foreign policy, Adenauer would never break with France, however divergent their interests. And then there was the question of agriculture.

In the first half of the twentieth century, too many inefficient European peasants produced only just sufficient food for a market that could not pay them enough to live on. The result had been poverty, emigration and rural fascism. In the hungry years immediately after World War Two all sorts of programs were put in place to encourage and assist arable farmers in particular to produce more. To reduce dependence on dollar-denominated food imports from Canada and the US, the emphasis was placed upon encouraging output rather than efficiency. Farmers did not need to fear a return of the pre-war price deflation: until 1951 agricultural output in Europe did not recover to pre-war levels, and between protection and government price-supports farmers' income was anyway effectively guaranteed. In a manner of speaking, the Forties were thus a golden age for Europe's farmers. In the course of the 1950s, output continued to increase even as surplus rural labor was drained off into new jobs in the cities: Europe's peasants were becoming increasingly efficient farmers. But they continued to benefit from what amounted to permanent public welfare.

The paradox was particularly acute in France. In 1950 the country was still a net food importer. But in the years that followed the country's agricultural output soared. French production of butter increased by 76 percent in the years 1949–56; cheese output by 116 percent between 1949 and 1957. Beet sugar production in France rose 201 percent from 1950 to 1957. The barley and maize crops grew by an astonishing 348 percent and 815 percent respectively in the same period. France now was not merely self-sufficient; it had food surpluses. The third Modernization Plan, covering the years 1957–61, favored still more investment in meat, milk, cheese, sugar and wheat (the staple products of northern France and the Paris basin, where the influence of France's powerful farming syndicates was greatest). Meanwhile the French government, always conscious of the symbolic significance of the land in French public life—and the very real importance of the rural vote—sought to maintain price supports and find export markets for all this food.

This issue played a vital role in the French decision to join the EEC. France's chief economic interest in a European common market was the preferential access it would afford to foreign—especially German (or British)—markets for meat, dairy and grain products. This, together with the promise of continued price supports and a commitment by its European partners to buy up superfluous French farm output, was what convinced the National Assembly to vote for the Rome Treaty. In exchange for an undertaking to open their home market to German non-agricultural exports, the French effectively shifted their domestic system of rural guarantees onto the backs of fellow EEC members, thereby relieving Paris of an intolerably expensive (and politically explosive) long-term burden.

This is the background to the EEC's notorious Common Agricultural Policy (CAP), inaugurated in 1962 and formalized in 1970 after a decade of negotiations. As fixed European prices rose, *all* of Europe's food production became too expensive to compete on the world market. Efficient Dutch dairy combines were no better off than small and unproductive German farms, since all were now subject to a common pricing structure. In the course of the 1960s the EEC devoted its energies to forging a set of practices and regulations designed to address this problem. Target prices would be established for all food items. EEC external tariffs would then bring the cost of imported agricultural products up to these levels—which were typically keyed to the highest priced and least efficient producers in the Community.

Each year, the EEC would henceforth buy up all its members' surplus agricultural output, at figures 5–7 percent below the 'target' prices. It would then clear the surplus by subsidizing its re-sale outside the Common Market at below-EU prices. This manifestly inefficient proceeding was the result of some very old-fashioned horse-trading. Germany's small farms needed heavy subsidies to remain in business. French and Italian farmers were not especially high-priced, but no-one dared instruct them to restrict production, much less require that they take a market price for their goods. Instead each country gave its farmers what they wanted, passing the cost along in part to urban consumers but above all to taxpayers.

The CAP was not wholly unprecedented. The grain tariffs of late-nineteenth-century Europe, directed against cheap imports from North America, were partly analogous. There were various attempts at the depths of the Slump of the early 1930s to shore up farm prices by buying surpluses or paying farmers to produce less. In a never-implemented 1938 agreement between Germany and France, Germany would have promised to take French agricultural exports in return for France opening its domestic market to German chemical and engineering products (a wartime exhibition in occupied Paris devoted to 'La France européenne' emphasized France's agrarian wealth, and the benefits that would accrue to it from participation in Hitler's New Europe).

Modern agriculture has never been free of politically motivated protections of one kind or another. Even the US, whose external tariffs fell by 90 percent between 1947 and 1967, took care (and still does) to exclude agriculture from this liberalization of trade. And farm products were from an early stage excluded from the deliberations of GATT. The EEC, then, was hardly unique. But the perverse consequences of the Common Agricultural Policy were perhaps distinctive all the same. As European producers became ever more efficient (their guaranteed high incomes allowing them to invest in the best equipment and fertilizer), output vastly exceeded demand, especially in those commodities favored by the policy: the latter was markedly skewed in favor of the cereal and livestock in which big French agri-businesses tended to specialize, while doing little for the fruit, olive and vegetable farmers of southern Italy.

As world food prices fell in the late 1960s, EEC prices were thus stranded at absurdly high levels. Within a few years of the inauguration of the Common Agricultural Policy, European maize and beef would be selling at 200 percent of world prices, European butter at 400 percent. By 1970 the CAP employed four out of five of the Common Market's administrators, and agriculture was costing 70 percent of the budget, a bizarre situation for some of the world's most industrialized states. No single country could have sustained so absurd a set of policies, but by transferring the burden to the Community at large, and tying it to the broader objectives of the Common Market, each national government stood to gain, at least in the short run. Only the urban poor (and non-EEC farmers) lost out from the CAP, and the former at least were typically compensated in other ways.

At this stage most West European countries were of course *not* members of the EEC. A year after the Common Market was inaugurated, the British—still trying to head off the emergence of a super-national European bloc—suggested that the EEC be expanded into an industrial free-trade zone including the EEC member-states, other European countries and the British Commonwealth. De Gaulle, predictably, rejected the idea. In response, and at the initiative of the UK, a number of countries then met in Stockholm in November 1959 and formed themselves into the European Free Trade Association (EFTA). The member states—Austria, Switzerland, Denmark, Norway, Sweden, Portugal and the UK, later joined by Ireland, Iceland and Finland—were mostly prosperous, peripheral, and enthusiastic proponents of free trade. Their agriculture, with the exception of Portugal, was small-scale but highly efficient and oriented to the world market.

For these reasons, and because of their close links to London (especially in the case of the Scandinavian countries), they had little use for the EEC. But EFTA was (and remains) a minimalist organization, a reaction to the defects of Brussels rather than a genuine alternative. It was only ever a free-trade zone for *manufactured* goods; farm products were left to find their own price level. Some of the smaller member-states, like Austria, Switzerland or Sweden, could thrive in a niche market for their high-value-added industrial goods and their attraction for tourists. Others, like Denmark, depended heavily on Britain as a market for their meat and dairy products.

But Britain itself needed a vastly larger industrial export market than its tiny Scandinavian and Alpine allies could provide. Recognizing the inevitable—though still hoping to influence the shape of EEC policy—Harold Macmillan's government formally applied to join the European Economic Community in July 1961, six years after London's disdainful disengagement from the Messina talks. Ireland and Denmark, their economies umbilically linked to that of the UK, applied alongside it. Whether the British application would have been successful is uncertain—most of the EEC member states still wanted Britain in, but they were also justifiably skeptical of London's commitment to the core goals of the Rome Treaty. But the issue was moot—De Gaulle, as we have seen, publicly vetoed Britain's entry in January 1963. It is an indication of the speed with which events had unfolded since the Suez crisis that Britain's rejection from the hitherto disparaged European community prompted the following despairing entry in Macmillan's private diary: 'It is the end . . . to everything for which I have worked for many years. All our policies at home and abroad are in ruins.'

The British had little recourse but to try again, which they did in May 1967—only to be vetoed once more, six months later, by a calmly vengeful French President. Finally, in 1970, following De Gaulle's resignation and subsequent death, negotiations between Britain and Europe were opened for a third time, culminating this time in a successful application (in part because British trade with the Commonwealth had fallen so far that London was no longer pressing a reluctant Brussels to guarantee third-party trading preferences to non-EEC nations). But by the time Britain, Denmark and Ireland finally joined, in 1973, the European Economic Community had taken shape and they were in no position to influence it as British leaders had once fondly hoped.

The EEC was a Franco-German condominium, in which Bonn underwrote the Community's finances and Paris dictated its policies. The West German desire to be part of the European Community was thus bought at a high price, but for many decades Adenauer and his successors would pay that price without complaining, cleaving closely to the French alliance—rather to British surprise. The French, meanwhile, 'Europeanized' their farm subsidies and transfers, without paying the price of a loss of sovereignty. The latter concern had always been uppermost in French diplomatic strategy—back at Messina in 1955 the French foreign minister Antoine Pinay had made France's objectives perfectly clear: supra-national administrative institutions were fine, but only if subordinated to decisions taken unanimously at the inter-government level.

It was with this goal in mind that De Gaulle browbeat the other member-states of the European Economic Community in the course of its first decade. Under the original Rome Treaty all major decisions (except for the admission of new members) were to be taken by majority vote in the inter-governmental Council of Ministers. But by withdrawing from inter-governmental talks in June 1965 until his fellow leaders agreed to adapt its agricultural funding to French demands, the French President hobbled the workings of the Community. After holding out for six months the other countries gave in; in January 1966 they reluctantly conceded that in future the Council of Ministers would no longer be able to pass measures by a majority vote. It was the first breach of the original Treaty and a remarkable demonstration of raw French power.

The early achievements of the EEC were nonetheless impressive. Intra-Community tariffs were removed by 1968, well ahead of schedule. Trade between the six member-states quadrupled in the same period. The farming workforce fell steadily, by some 4 percent each year, while agricultural production per worker rose in the Sixties at an annual rate of 8.1 percent. By the end of its first decade, and notwithstanding the shadow of De Gaulle, the European Economic Community had acquired an aura of inevitability, which is why other European states began lining up to join it.

But there were problems, too. A high-priced, self-serving customs union, directed from Brussels by a centralized administration and an unelected executive, was not an unalloyed gain for Europe or the rest of the world. Indeed, the network of protective agreements and indirect subsidies put into place at France's bidding was altogether out of keeping with the spirit and institutions of the international trading system that had emerged in the decades following Bretton Woods. To the (considerable) extent that the EEC's system of governance was modeled on that of France, its Napoleonic heritage was not a good omen.

Lastly, France's influence in the European Community's early years helped forge a new 'Europe' that was vulnerable to the charge that it had reproduced all the worst features of the nation-state on a sub-continental scale: there was always more than a little risk that the price to be paid for the recovery of Western Europe would be a certain Euro-centric provincialism. For all its growing wealth the world of the EEC was quite petty. In certain respects it was actually a lot smaller than the world that the French, or Dutch, had known when their nation-states opened on to people and places flung far across the seas. In the circumstances of the time this hardly mattered to most West Europeans, who in any case had little option. But it would lead in time to a distinctly parochial vision of 'Europe', with troubling implications for the future.

Josef Stalin's death in March 1953 had precipitated a power struggle among his nervous heirs. At first the head of the secret police, Lavrenti Beria, appeared likely to emerge as the dictator's sole heir. But for just that reason, his colleagues conspired to assassinate him in July of that same year and after a brief detour via Georgy Malenkov it was Nikita Khrushchev—by no means the best-known of Stalin's inner circle—who was confirmed two months later as the First Secretary of the Communist Party of the Soviet Union. This was somewhat ironic: for all his psychotic disposition, Beria was an advocate of reforms and even of what was not yet called 'de-Stalinization'. In the brief period of time separating Stalin's death from his own arrest, he repudiated the Doctors' Plot, released some prisoners from the Gulag and even proposed reforms in the satellite states, to the confusion of the local Party leaders there.

The new leadership, collective in name but with Khrushchev increasingly *primus inter pares*, had little choice but to follow the path that Beria had advocated. Stalin's death, following many years of repression and impoverishment, had precipitated widespread protests and demand for change. In the course of 1953 and 1954 there were revolts in Siberian labor camps at Norilsk, Vorkuta and Kengir; it took tanks, planes and a considerable deployment of troops for the Kremlin to bring these under control. But once 'order' had been restored, Khrushchev reverted to Beria's strategy. In the course of the years 1953–56 some five million prisoners were released from the Gulag.

In the people's democracies the post-Stalin era was marked not just by the 1953 Berlin revolt (see Chapter Six) but by opposition even in such obscure and typically cowed imperial outposts as provincial Bulgaria, where workers in tobacco factories rioted in May and June of that same year. Nowhere was Soviet rule seriously threatened, but the authorities in Moscow took very seriously the scale of public discontent. The task now facing Khrushchev and his colleagues was to bury Stalin and his excesses without putting at risk the system that Stalinist terror had built and the advantages that accrued to the Party from its monopoly of power.

Khrushchev's strategy, as it emerged in the following years, was fourfold. First, as we have seen, he needed to stabilize relations with the West, following the re-armament of West Germany, its incorporation into NATO and the establishment of the Warsaw Pact. At the same time Moscow began building bridges to the 'non-Aligned' world—starting with Yugoslavia, which Khrushchev and Marshal Bulganin visited in May 1955 (just one month after the signing of the Austrian State Treaty) in order to rekindle Soviet-Yugoslav relations after seven years of very cold storage. Thirdly, Moscow started to encourage Party reformers in the satellite states, allowing circumspect criticism of the 'mistakes' of the Stalinist old guard and rehabilitation of some of their victims, and bringing to an end the cycle of show trials and mass arrests and Party purges.

It was in this context that Khrushchev gingerly advanced to the fourth (and in his understanding, final) stage of controlled reform: the break with Stalin himself. The setting for this was the 20th Party Congress of the CPSU, in February 1956, at which Khrushchev delivered his now-famous 'secret speech', denouncing the crimes, errors and 'cult' of the General Secretary. In retrospect this speech has taken on a mythical aura, but its epochal significance should not be overstated. Nikita Khrushchev was a Communist, a Leninist and at least as much a true believer as his contemporaries in the Party leadership. He had set himself the tricky objective of acknowledging and detailing Stalin's deeds, while confining responsibility for them to the man himself. His task, as he saw it, was to confirm the legitimacy of the Communist project by heaping obloquy and responsibility upon the corpse of Uncle Joe.

The speech, delivered on February 25th, was entirely conventional in length and language. It was addressed to the Party élite and confined itself to describing the 'perversions' of Communist doctrine of which Stalin was guilty. The dictator was accused of 'ignoring the norms of Party life and trampling upon the Leninist principles of collective Party leadership': which is to say that he made his own decisions.

His junior colleagues (of whom Khrushchev had been one since the early 1930s) were thus absolved of responsibility both for his criminal excesses and, more importantly, for the failure of his policies. Khrushchev took the calculated risk of detailing the scale of Stalin's personal failings (and thus shocking and offending the sensibilities of the obedient cadres in his audience), in order to preserve and even enhance the unsullied standing of Lenin, the Leninist system of government and Stalin's own successors.

The secret speech achieved its purpose, at least within the CPSU. It drew a firm line under the Stalinist era, acknowledging its monstrosities and disasters while preserving the fiction that the present Communist leadership bore no responsibility. Khrushchev was thus secure in power and had won a relatively free hand to reform the Soviet economy and liberalize the apparatus of terror. Old Stalinists were now marginalized—Molotov was removed from the post of foreign minister on the eve of Tito's return visit to Moscow in June. As for Khrushchev's contemporaries, and younger apparatchiks like Leonid Brezhnev, these men were just as guilty as Khrushchev of collaborating in Stalin's crimes and they were thus in no position either to deny his assertions or attack his credibility. Controlled de-Stalinization suited nearly everyone.

But Khrushchev's attack on Stalin could not be kept a secret, and therein lay the seeds of its failure. The speech would not be officially published in the Soviet Union until 1988, but Western intelligence agencies had wind of it within days. So did Western Communist parties, even though they had not been made privy to Khrushchev's intentions. As a consequence, within a few weeks rumours of Khrushchev's denunciations of Stalin were everywhere. The effect was intoxicating. For Communists, the denunciation of Stalin and his works was confusing and troubling; but it was also a relief. Henceforth, as it seemed to many, Communists would no longer have to excuse or deny the more outrageous charges of their critics. Some Western Party members and sympathizers dropped away, but others remained, their faith renewed.

In Eastern Europe, the impact of Khrushchev's reported abjuration of Stalin was even more dramatic. Read in the context of the Soviet leader's recent reconciliation with Tito, and his dissolution of the moribund Cominform on April 18th, Khrushchev's repudiation of Stalin seemed to suggest that Moscow would now look favorably upon different 'roads to socialism', and had rejected terror and repression as a tool of Communist control. Now, or so it was believed, it would be possible to speak openly for the first time. As the Czech author Jaroslav Seifert explained to a Writers' Congress in Prague in April 1956, 'Again and again, we hear it said at this Congress that it is necessary for writers to tell the truth. This means that in recent years they did not write the truth . . . All that is now over. The nightmare has been exorcised.'

In Czechoslovakia—whose Communist leaders maintained a tight-lipped silence about their own Stalinist past—the memory of terror was still too fresh for rumours from Moscow to translate into political action.[13] The impact of the shock wave of de-Stalinization in neighboring Poland was very different. In June the Polish army was called out to put down demonstrations in the western city of Poznan, sparked (like those of East Berlin three years before) by disputes over wages and work-rates. But this only fanned widespread discontent throughout the autumn, in a country where Sovietization had never been carried through as thoroughly as elsewhere and whose Party leaders had survived the post-war purges largely unscathed.

In October 1956, worried at the prospect of losing control over the popular mood, the Polish United Workers Party decided to remove Soviet Marshal Konstanty Rokossowski from his post as Poland's defense minister and expel him from the Politburo. At the same time the Party elected Wladisław Gomułka to the position of First Secretary, replacing the Stalinist Boleslaw Bierut. This was a dramatic symbolic move: Gomułka had been in prison just a few years before and narrowly escaped trial. He represented, for the Polish public, the 'national' face of Polish Communism and his promotion was widely understood as an act of implicit defiance by a Party forced to choose between its national constituency and the higher authority in Moscow.

That, certainly, is how Soviet leaders saw the matter. Khrushchev, Mikoyan, Molotov and three other senior figures flew to Warsaw on October 19th, intending to block Gomułka's appointment, forbid the ouster of Rokossowski and restore order in Poland. To ensure that their intentions were clear, Khrushchev simultaneously instructed a brigade of Soviet tanks to move towards Warsaw. But in heated discussions with Gomułka himself, conducted in part on the airport tarmac, Khrushchev concluded that Soviet interests in Poland might be best served by accepting the new situation in the Polish Party, rather than forcing matters to a head and almost certainly provoking violent confrontations. Gomułka, in return, assured the Russians that he could restore control and had no intention of abandoning power, taking Poland out of the Warsaw Pact, or demanding that Soviet troops leave his country.

Considering the disproportion in power between Khrushchev and Gomułka, the new Polish leader's success in averting a catastrophe for his country was remarkable. But Khrushchev had read his interlocutor well—as he explained to the Soviet Politburo upon his return to Moscow the following day, the Soviet Ambassador in Warsaw, Ponomarenko, had been 'grossly mistaken in his assessment of Gomułka'. The price of Communist control in Poland might be some personnel changes and liberalization of public life, but Gomułka was a sound Party man and had no intention of abandoning power to the streets or to the Party's opponents. He was also

---

[13]The Stalinist leadership remained firmly in place, trials continued *in camera* for two more years and on May 1st 1955 a grotesque, over-sized statue of Stalin was erected on a hill overlooking Prague. De-Stalinization would not reach Czechoslovakia until a decade later, with dramatic consequences.

a realist: if *he* could not calm Poland's turbulence, the alternative was the Red Army. De-Stalinization, as Gomułka appreciated, did not mean that Khrushchev planned to relinquish any of the Soviet Union's territorial influence or political monopoly.

The 'Polish October', then, had a fortuitously benign outcome—few at the time knew just how close Warsaw had come to a second Soviet occupation. In Hungary, however, things were to take a different turn. This was not immediately obvious. As early as July 1953 the Hungarian Stalinist leadership had been replaced (at Moscow's initiative) with a reform-minded Communist, Imre Nagy. Nagy, like Gomułka, had been purged and imprisoned in earlier days and thus carried little responsibility for the season of terror and misgovernment through which his country had just passed; indeed, his first act as Party leader was to present, with Beria's backing, a programme of liberalizations. Internment and labor camps were to be closed, peasants were to be permitted to leave kolkhozes if they wished. In general agriculture was to get more encouragement, and unrealistic industrial targets were abandoned: in the characteristically veiled language of a confidential Hungarian Party resolution of June 28th 1953, '[t]he false economic policy revealed a certain boastfulness as well as risk-taking, in so far as the forced development of heavy industry presupposed resources and raw materials that were in part just not available.'

Nagy was certainly not a conventional option, from Moscow's point of view. In September 1949 he had been critical of the ultra-Stalinist line of Mátyás Rákosi and was one of only two Hungarian Politburo members who had opposed the execution of László Rajk. This, together with his criticisms of rural collectivization, had led to his expulsion from the Party leadership and a public 'self-criticism', in which Nagy conceded his 'opportunist attitude' and his failure to stay close to the Party line. But he was nonetheless a logical choice, once the time came to make changes in a country whose political elite, like its economy, had been ravaged by Stalinist excesses. Under Rákosi some 480 public figures had been executed between 1948 and 1953—not including Rajk and other Communist victims; and over 150,000 people (in a population of less than 9 million) had been imprisoned in those same years.

Nagy remained in office until the spring of 1955. At that time Rákosi and other Hungarian Party stalwarts, who had been working to undermine their troublesome colleague ever since his return to office, succeeded in convincing Moscow that he could not be counted on to maintain firm control, at a moment when the Soviet Union was facing the threat of an expanded NATO and neighboring Austria was about to become an independent, neutral state. The Soviet Central Committee duly condemned Nagy's 'rightist deviations', he was removed from office (and later expelled from the Party), and Rákosi and his friends returned to power in Budapest. This retreat from reform, just eight months before Khrushchev's speech, illustrates in anticipation how little the Soviet leader planned, when dismantling Stalin's reputation, to disrupt the smooth exercise of Communist power.

313

For a year or so the unofficial 'Nagy group' in the Hungarian Party functioned as a sort of informal 'reform' opposition, the first such in post-war Communism. Meanwhile, it was Rákosi's turn to attract the unfavorable attention of Moscow. Khrushchev, as we have seen, was keen to rebuild Soviet links to Yugoslavia. But in the course of the anti-Tito hysteria of earlier days Rákosi had played a particularly prominent role. It was not by chance that the accusation of 'Tito-ism' had figured so prominently in the Hungarian show trials, above all in the trial of Rajk himself—the Hungarian Party had been assigned the role of prosecutor in these developments and the Party's leadership had carried out their task with enthusiasm.

Rákosi, then, was becoming an embarrassment, an anachronistic impediment to Soviet projects. With high-level Soviet-Yugoslav negotiations taking place in Moscow in June 1956, it seemed unnecessarily provocative to maintain in power in Budapest an unreconstructed Stalinist so closely associated with the bad old days—the more so as his past record and present intransigence were beginning to provoke public protests in Hungary. Despite Rákosi's best efforts—in March 1956 he contributed to the Hungarian newspaper *Szabad Nép* an enthusiastic denunciation of Beria and his Hungarian police lieutenant Gábor Péter, closely echoing Khrushchev's denunciation of the 'personality cult' and celebrating the 'unmasking' of such men for their criminal persecution of the innocent—his time was past. On July 17th 1956 Anastas Mikoyan flew into Budapest and unceremoniously removed Rákosi from office, for the last time.

In Rákosi's place the Soviets promoted Ernö Gerö, another Hungarian of impeccably Stalinist pedigree. This proved a mistake; Gerö could neither lead change nor suppress it. On October 6th, as a gesture to Belgrade especially, the authorities in Budapest permitted the public reburial of László Rajk and his fellow show-trial victims. Béla Szász, one of the survivors of the Rajk trial, spoke at the graveside:

> Executed as a result of trumped up charges, László Rajk's remains rested for seven years in an unmarked grave. Yet his death has become a warning signal for the Hungarian people and for the whole world. For the hundreds of thouands who pass by this coffin desire to honor not only the dead man; it is their passionate hope and their firm resolve to bury an entire epoch. The lawlessness, arbitrariness and moral decay of those shameless years must be buried forever; and the danger posed by Hungarian practitioners of rule by force and of the personality cult must be banned forever.

There was a certain irony in the sympathy now aroused by the fate of Rajk, a man who had himself sent so many innocent (non-Communist) victims to the gallows. But ironic or not, the reburial of Rajk provided the spark that was to ignite the Hungarian revolution.

On October 16th 1956, university students in the provincial city of Szeged organized themselves into a 'League of Hungarian Students', independent of the official Communist student organizations. Within a week, student organizations had sprung up all across the country, culminating on October 22nd with a 'Sixteen Point' manifesto formulated by the students of the Technical University in Budapest itself. The student demands encompassed industrial and agrarian reforms, greater democracy and the right to free speech, and an end to the manifold petty restrictions and regulations of life under Communist rule. But they also included, more ominously, the desire to see Imre Nagy installed as prime minister, Rákosi and his colleagues tried for their crimes, and Soviet troops withdrawn from their country.

The following day, October 23rd, students began to assemble in Budapest's Parliament Square to demonstrate in support of their demands. The regime was at a loss how to respond: Gerö first prohibited and then permitted the demonstration. After it went ahead that same afternoon, Gerö proceeded to denounce the meeting and its organizers in a speech broadcast by Hungarian radio that evening. An hour later enraged demonstrators tore down the statue of Stalin in the center of the city, Soviet troops entered Budapest to attack the crowds, and the Hungarian Central Committee met through the night. The following morning, at 8.13 a.m., it was announced that Imre Nagy had been installed as Prime Minister of Hungary.

If the Party leaders hoped that the return of Nagy would put an end to the revolution, they miscalculated badly. Nagy himself was certainly keen enough to restore order: he declared martial law within an hour of assuming power. In talks with Suslov and Mikoyan (who arrived by plane from Moscow that same day), he and the other members of the new Hungarian leadership insisted on the need to negotiate with the demonstrators. As the Russians reported back to a special meeting of the Soviet Party Presidium on October 26th, János Kádár[14] had explained to them that it was possible and important to distinguish between the loyal masses, who had been alienated from the Party by its past mistakes, and the armed counter-revolutionaries whom the Nagy government hoped to isolate.

Kádár's distinction may have convinced some of the Soviet leaders, but it did not reflect Hungarian reality. Student organizations, workers' councils and revolutionary 'national committees' were spontaneously forming all over the country. Clashes between police and demonstrators provoked counter-attacks and lynchings. Against the advice of some of its members, the Hungarian Party leadership initially refused to recognize the uprising as a democratic revolution, insisting instead on regarding it as a 'counterrevolution', and thereby missing the occasion to co-opt it. Only on October 28th, nearly a week after the initial demonstrations, did Nagy go on the radio to propose a truce in the armed clashes, acknowledge the legitimacy and revolutionary character of recent protests, promise to abolish the de-

---

[14]Kádár, whom Nagy had released from prison three years before, was appointed First Secretary of the Hungarian Party on October 25th. He replaced Gerö, whose security forces had fired on unarmed demonstrators in Parliament Square that same morning.

spised Secret Police, and announce the impending departure of Soviet troops from Budapest.

The Soviet leadership, whatever their doubts, had decided to endorse the new approach of the Hungarian leader. Suslov, reporting back on the day of Nagy's radio address, presented the new concessions as the price to be paid for bringing the mass movement under Party control. But events in Hungary were outpacing Moscow's calculations. Two days later, on October 30th, following attacks on the Communist Party's Budapest headquarters and the death of twenty-four of the building's defenders, Imre Nagy again went on Hungarian radio. This time he announced that his government would henceforth be based 'on democratic cooperation between the coalition parties, reborn in 1945.' In other words, Nagy was forming a multi-party government. Far from confronting the opposition, Nagy was now basing his authority increasingly on the popular movement itself. In his final sentence, celebrating a 'free, democratic and independent' Hungary, he even omitted, for the first time, the discredited adjective 'socialist'. And he appealed publicly to Moscow 'to begin the withdrawal of Soviet troops', from Budapest and the rest of Hungary as well.

Nagy's gamble—his sincere belief that he could restore order in Hungary, and thus stave off the unspoken threat of Soviet intervention—was supported by the other Communists in his Cabinet. But he had relinquished the initiative. Popular insurrectionary committees, political parties and newspapers had sprung up all over the country. Anti-Russian sentiment was everywhere, with frequent references to the Imperial Russian suppression of the Hungarian revolt of 1848–49. And, most important of all, the Soviet leaders were losing confidence in him. By the time Nagy announced, on the afternoon of October 31st, that he was beginning negotiations to secure Hungary's withdrawal from the Warsaw Pact, his fate was probably sealed.

Khrushchev and his colleagues had always taken the view that, in Hungary—as earlier in Poland—they would have to intervene if the 'counterrevolution' got out of control. But they appear to have been initially reluctant to pursue this option. As late as October 31st the Presidium of the Central Committee put out a statement declaring its willingness 'to enter into the appropriate negotiations' with the Hungarian leadership regarding the withdrawal of Soviet troops from Hungarian territory. But even as they made this concession they were getting reports of student demonstrations in Timişoara (Romania) and of 'hostile sentiments' among Bulgarian intellectuals sympathetic to the Hungarian revolutionaries. This was beginning to sound like the start of the contamination effect that the Soviet leaders had long feared, and it prompted them to adopt a new approach.

Accordingly, the day after it had promised to negotiate troop withdrawals, the Soviet Presidium was advised by Khrushchev that this was now out of the question. 'The imperialists' would interpret such a withdrawal as evidence of Soviet weakness. On the contrary, the USSR would now have 'to take the initiative in restoring order in Hungary'. Soviet army divisions in Romania and Ukraine were duly ordered to move towards the Hungarian border. On learning of this, the Hungarian Prime Minister summoned the Soviet Ambassador (Yuri Andropov) and informed him that in protest against the renewed Soviet troop movements, Hungary was unilaterally renouncing its membership in the Warsaw Pact. That evening, at 7.50 p.m. on November 1st, Nagy announced on the radio that Hungary was henceforth a neutral country and asked that the UN recognize its new status. This declaration was widely approved in the country; the Workers' Councils of Budapest, who had been on strike since the revolt began, responded by calling for a return to work. Nagy had finally won over most of those in Hungary who had been suspicious of his intentions.

The same evening that Nagy made his historic announcement, János Kádár was secretly spirited away to Moscow, where Khrushchev convinced him of the need to form a new government in Budapest, with Soviet backing. The Red Army would come in and restore order in any case; the only question was which Hungarians would have the honour of collaborating with them. Any reluctance that Kádár may have felt about betraying Nagy and his fellow Hungarians was overcome by Khrushchev's insistence that the Soviets now knew they had made a mistake when they installed Gerö in July. That error would not be repeated once order was restored in Budapest. Khrushchev then set off for Bucharest to meet Romanian, Bulgarian and Czech leaders and coordinate plans for intervention in Hungary (a lower-level delegation had met Polish leaders the previous day). Meanwhile Nagy continued to protest against the increased Soviet military activity; and on November 2nd he asked UN Secretary-General Dag Hammerskjöld to mediate between Hungary and the USSR, and seek Western recognition of Hungary's neutrality.

The following day, November 3rd, the Nagy government opened (or thought it was opening) negotiations with the Soviet military authorities about the withdrawal of troops. But when the Hungarian negotiating team returned that evening to Soviet army headquarters at Tököl, in Hungary, they were immediately arrested. Shortly afterwards, at 4 a.m. on the morning of November 4th, Soviet tanks attacked Budapest, followed an hour later by a broadcast from Soviet-occupied eastern Hungary announcing the replacement of Imre Nagy by a new government. In response, Nagy himself made a final radio address to the Hungarian people, calling for resistance against the invader. Then he and his closest colleagues took refuge in the Yugoslav embassy in Budapest, where they were granted asylum.

The military outcome was never in question: despite intense resistance, Soviet forces took Budapest within seventy-two hours, and the government of János Kádár was sworn in on November 7th. Some Workers' Councils survived for another month—Kádár preferring not to attack them directly—and sporadic strikes lasted into 1957: according to a confidential report submitted to the Soviet Central Committee on November 22nd 1956, Hungary's coalmines had been reduced to working at 10 percent of capacity. But within a month the new authorities felt confident enough to take the initiative. On January 5th, the death penalty was established for 'provocation to strike' and repression began in earnest. In addition to around 2,700 Hungarians who died in the course of the fighting a further 341 were tried and executed in the years that followed (the last death sentence was carried out in 1961). Altogether, some 22,000 Hungarians were sentenced to prison (many for five years or more) for their role in the 'counter revolution'. A further 13,000 were sent to internment camps and many more were dismissed from their jobs or placed under close surveillance until a general amnesty was declared in March 1963.

An estimated 200,000 people—over 2 percent of the population—fled Hungary in the aftermath of the Soviet occupation, most of them young and many from the educated professional élite of Budapest and the urbanized west of the country. They settled in the US (which took in some 80,000 Hungarian refugees), Austria, Britain, West Germany, Switzerland, France and many other places. For a while the fate of Nagy and his colleagues remained uncertain. After spending nearly three weeks in the Yugoslav Embassy in Budapest they were tricked into leaving on November 22nd, immediately arrested by the Soviet authorities, and abducted to prison in Romania.

It took Kádár many months to decide what to do with his erstwhile friends and comrades. Most of the reprisals against young workers and soldiers who had taken part in street fighting were kept as quiet as possible, to avoid arousing international protest; even so there were international demands for clemency in the case of a number of prominent figures, such as the writers József Gáli and Gyula Obersovszky. The fate of Nagy himself was an especially sensitive issue. In April 1957 Kádár and his colleagues decided to return Nagy and his 'accomplices' to Hungary to face trial, but the proceedings themselves were delayed until June 1958, and even then they were held in strict secrecy. On June 15th 1958, the accused were all found guilty of fomenting counter-revolution, and variously sentenced to death or long prison terms. The writers István Bibó and Árpád Göncz (future president of post-Communist Hungary) received life sentences. Two others—József Szilágyi and Géza Lozonczy—were killed in prison before their trial began. Imre Nagy, Pál Maléter and Miklós Gimes were executed at dawn on June 16th 1958.

The Hungarian uprising, a brief and hopeless revolt in a small outpost of the Soviet empire, had a shattering impact on the shape of world affairs. In the first place, it was an object lesson for Western diplomats. Until then the United States, while officially acknowledging the impossibility of detaching Eastern European satellites from Soviet control, continued to encourage the 'spirit of resistance' there. Covert actions and diplomatic support were directed, in the words of National Security Council Policy paper No. 174 (December 1953) to 'fostering conditions which would make possible the liberation of the satellites at a favorable moment in the future.'

But, as a later confidential policy document, drawn up in July 1956 to take account of that year's upheavals, was to emphasize, 'the United States is not prepared to resort to war to eliminate Soviet domination of the satellites' (NSC5608/1 'U.S. Policy toward the Soviet satellites in Eastern Europe').

Indeed, ever since the repression of the Berlin revolt in 1953, the State Department had concluded that the Soviet Union was, for the foreseeable future, in unshakeable control of its 'zone'. 'Non-intervention' was the West's *only* strategy for Eastern Europe. But the Hungarian rebels could not know this. Many of them sincerely hoped for Western assistance, encouraged by the uncompromising tone of American public rhetoric and by emissions from Radio Free Europe, whose émigré broadcasters encouraged Hungarians to take up arms and promised imminent foreign support. When no such backing was forthcoming, the defeated rebels were understandably embittered and disillusioned.

Even if Western governments had wished to do more, the circumstances of the moment were highly unpropitious. On the very day that the Hungarian revolt broke out, representatives of France and Britain were at Sèvres, in secret talks with the Israelis. France in particular was pre-occupied with its North African problems: as Christian Pineau, the Foreign Minister, explained on October 27th in a highly confidential memo to France's representative on the UN Security Council, 'It is essential that the draft resolution which will be put to the Security Council on the Hungarian question should not contain any disposition which may disturb our action in Algeria . . . We are particularly against the formation of a committee of inquiry.' The British Foreign Minister Selwyn Lloyd wrote to Prime Minister Anthony Eden in a similar vein four days later, in response to a suggestion from the British Ambassador to Moscow that London appeal directly to the Soviet leadership to desist from intervention in Hungary: 'I do not myself think that this is a moment for such a message.'

As Khrushchev had explained to his Central Committee Presidium colleagues on October 28th, 'the English and French are in a real mess in Egypt'.[15] As for Eisenhower, he was in the final week of an election campaign—the day of his re-election saw some of the heaviest fighting in Budapest. His National Security Council did not even discuss Hungary until three days after the Soviet invasion; they had been slow to take the full measure of Nagy's actions, notably his abandonment of one-party rule, in a country of little significance for US grand strategy (the recent crisis in Poland had received far more attention in Washington). And when Hungary did appear on the NSC agenda, at a meeting on November 8th, the general consensus—from Eisenhower down—was that it was all the fault of the French and British. If they hadn't invaded Egypt, the Soviet Union would not have had the

---

[15]That the Soviet leader could know this as early as October 28th, three days before the Anglo-French invasion began, suggests that Soviet intelligence was even better than the Western Allies feared at the time.

cover to move against Hungary. The Eisenhower Administration had a clean conscience.

Soviet leaders, then, saw their advantage and seized it. In Communist eyes the real threat posed by Nagy was neither his liberalization of the economy nor the relaxation of censorship. Even the Hungarian declaration of neutrality, though it was regarded in Moscow as 'provocative', was not the occasion for Nagy's downfall. What the Kremlin could not condone was the Hungarian Party's abandonment of a monopoly of power, the 'leading role of the Party' (something Gomułka, in Poland, had taken care never to allow). Such a departure from Soviet practice was the thin edge of a democratic wedge that would spell doom for Communist parties everywhere. That is why the Communist leaders in every other satellite state went along so readily with Khrushchev's decision to depose Nagy. When the Czechoslovak Politburo met on November 2nd and expressed its willingness to make an active contribution to 'maintaining with every necessary measure the people's democracy in Hungary', the sentiment was unquestionably genuine and heartfelt.[16]

Even Tito eventually conceded that the breakdown of Party control in Hungary, and the collapse of the state security apparatus, set a dangerous example. The Yugoslav leader had initially welcomed the changes in Hungary as further evidence of de-Stalinization. But by the end of October the course of events in Budapest was changing his mind—Hungary's proximity to Yugoslavia, the presence of a large Hungarian minority in the Vojvodina region of his country, and the consequent risks of contagion were very much on his mind. When Khrushchev and Malenkov took the trouble, on November 2nd, to fly to Tito's Adriatic island retreat and brief him on the coming invasion, Tito proved anxious but understanding. His main concern was that the puppet government to be installed in Hungary not include Rákosi and other unreconstructed Stalinists. On this score Khrushchev was happy to reassure him.

Khrushchev was distinctly less pleased when, just two days later, Tito granted asylum to Nagy, fifteen members of his government, and their families. The Yugoslav decision appears to have been made in the heat of the Hungarian crisis, and on the assumption that the Russians had no interest in making martyrs. But when the Soviet leaders expressed their displeasure, and especially following the abduction of Nagy and the others upon their departure from the Yugoslav Embassy with a promise of safe conduct from Kádár himself, Tito was placed in an uncomfortable position. In public the Yugoslav leader continued to express approval of Kádár's new government; but unofficially he made no effort to hide his displeasure at the course of events.

---

[16]Even Gomułka, in Poland, acceded readily enough to Soviet arguments. In Poland, Nagy's departure from the Warsaw Pact *was* a source of anxiety—the Poles' fear of German territorial revisionism gave them a special interest in the security arrangements guaranteed by Soviet arms. It should be noted, though, that in a meeting with Khrushchev in May 1957 Gomułka tried hard, albeit without success, to dissuade the Soviet leader from putting Nagy on trial.

The precedent of unconstrained Soviet interference in the affairs of a fraternal Communist state was not calculated to endear the Soviet leadership to the Yugoslavs. Relations between Moscow and Belgrade deteriorated once more, and the Yugoslav regime initiated overtures to the West and the non-aligned countries of Asia. Tito's response to the Soviet invasion of Hungary was thus mixed. Like the Soviet leaders he was relieved at the restoration of Communist order; but the way in which it had been accomplished set a dangerous precedent and left a bad taste.

Elsewhere the response was altogether less ambivalent. Khrushchev's secret speech, once it leaked out in the West, had marked the end of a certain Communist faith. But it also allowed for the possibility of post-Stalinist reform and renewal, and by sacrificing Stalin himself in order to preserve the illusion of Leninist revolutionary purity, Khrushchev had offered Party members and fellow-traveling progressives a myth to which they could cling. But the desperate street fighting in Budapest dispelled any illusions about this new, 'reformed' Soviet model. Once again, Communist authority had been unambiguously revealed to rest on nothing more than the barrel of a tank. The rest was dialectics. Western Communist parties started to hemorrhage. By the Italian Communist Party's own count, some 400,000 members left between 1955 and 1957. As Togliatti had explained to the Soviet leaders at the height of the Hungarian crisis, 'Hungarian events have developed in a way that renders our clarifying action in the party very difficult, it also makes it difficult to obtain consensus in favor of the leadership.'

In Italy, as in France, Britain and elsewhere, it was younger, educated Party members who left in droves.[17] Like non-Communist intellectuals of the Left, they had been attracted both to the promise of post-Stalin reforms in the USSR *and* to the Hungarian revolution itself, with its workers' councils, student initiatives and the suggestion that even a ruling Soviet-bloc Party could adapt and welcome new directions. Hannah Arendt, for one, thought it was the rise of the councils (rather than Nagy's restoration of political parties) that signified a genuine upsurge of democracy against dictatorship, of freedom against tyranny. Finally, as it seemed, it might be possible to speak of Communism and freedom in the same breath. As Jorge Semprun, then a young Spanish Communist working clandestinely in Paris, would later express it, 'The secret speech released us; it gave us at least the chance to be freed from . . . the sleep of reason.' After the invasion of Hungary, that moment of hope was gone.

A few Western observers tried to justify Soviet intervention, or at least explain it, by accepting the official Communist claim that Imre Nagy had led—or been swept up in—a *counter*-revolution: Sartre characteristically insisted that the Hun-

---

[17]In particularly backward organizations, like the French Communist Party (which for a long time denied all knowledge of Khrushchev's denunciations of Stalin), many members abandoned the Party not so much because of what was happening in the Soviet bloc, but because the local leadership forbade any discussion of it.

garian uprising had been marked by a 'rightist spirit'. But whatever the motives of the insurgents in Budapest and elsewhere—and these were far more varied than was clear at the time—it was not the Hungarians' revolt but rather the Soviet repression which made the greater impression on foreign observers. Communism was now forever to be associated with oppression, not revolution. For forty years the Western Left had looked to Russia, forgiving and even admiring Bolshevik violence as the price of revolutionary self-confidence and the march of History. Moscow was the flattering mirror of their political illusions. In November 1956, the mirror shattered.

In a memorandum dated September 8th 1957, the Hungarian writer István Bibo observed that 'in crushing the Hungarian revolution, the USSR has struck a severe, maybe mortal blow at "fellow-traveler" movements (Peace, Women, Youth, Students, Intellectuals, etc) that contributed to Communism's strength.' His insight proved perceptive. Shorn of the curious magnetism of Stalinist terror, and revealed in Budapest in all its armored mediocrity, Soviet Communism lost its charm for most Western sympathizers and admirers. Seeking to escape the 'stink of Stalinism', ex-Communists like the French poet Claude Roy turned 'our nostrils towards other horizons'. After 1956, the secrets of History were no longer to be found in the grim factories and dysfunctional kolkhozes of the People's Democracies but in other, more exotic realms. A shrinking minority of unreconstructed apologists for Leninism clung to the past; but from Berlin to Paris a new generation of Western progressives sought solace and example outside of Europe altogether, in the aspirations and upheavals of what was not yet called the 'Third World'.

Illusions were shattered in Eastern Europe too. As a British diplomat in Budapest reported on October 31st, at the height of the first round of fighting: 'It is nothing short of a miracle that the Hungarian people should have withstood and turned back this diabolical onslaught. They will never forget nor forgive.' But it was not only the Hungarians who would take to heart the message of the Soviet tanks. Romanian students demonstrated in support of their Hungarian neighbors; East German intellectuals were arrested and put on trial for criticizing Soviet actions; in the USSR it was the events of 1956 that tore the veil from the eyes of hitherto committed Communists like the young Leonid Pliushch. A new generation of intellectual dissidents, men like Paul Goma in Romania or Wolfgang Harich in the GDR, was born in the rubble of Budapest.

The difference in Eastern Europe, of course, was that the disillusioned subjects of a discredited regime could hardly turn their faces to distant lands, or rekindle their revolutionary faith in the glow of far-off peasant revolts. They were perforce obliged to live in and with the Communist regimes whose promises they no longer believed. East Europeans experienced the events of 1956 as a distillation of cumulative disappointments. Their expectations of Communism, briefly renewed with the promise of de-Stalinization, were extinguished; but so were their hopes of Western succor. Whereas Khrushchev's revelations about Stalin, or the hesitant moves to rehabilitate show-trial victims, had suggested up until then that Communism might yet contain within itself the seeds of renewal and liberation, after Hungary the dominant sentiment was one of cynical resignation.

This was not without its benefits. Precisely because the populations of Communist Eastern Europe were now quiescent, and the order of things restored, the Khrushchev-era Soviet leadership came in time to allow a limited degree of local liberalization—ironically enough, in Hungary above all. There, in the wake of his punitive retaliation against the insurgents of 1956 and their sympathizers, Kádár established the model 'post-political' Communist state. In return for their unquestioning acceptance of the Party's monopoly of power and authority, Hungarians were allowed a strictly limited but genuine degree of freedom to produce and consume. It was not asked of anyone that they believe in the Communist Party, much less its leaders; merely that they abstain from the least manifestation of opposition. Their silence would be read as tacit consent.

The resulting 'goulash Communism' secured the stability of Hungary; and the memory of Hungary ensured the stability of the rest of the Bloc, at least for the next decade. But this came at a cost. For most people living under Communism, the 'Socialist' system had lost whatever radical, forward-looking, utopian promise once attached to it, and which had been part of its appeal—especially to the young—as recently as the early fifties. It was now just a way of life to be endured. That did not mean it could not last a very long time—few after 1956 anticipated an early end to the Soviet system of rule. Indeed, there had been rather more optimism on that score *before* the events of that year. But after November 1956 the Communist states of Eastern Europe, like the Soviet Union itself, began their descent into a decades-long twilight of stagnation, corruption and cynicism.

The Soviets too would pay a price for this—in many ways, 1956 represented the defeat and collapse of the revolutionary myth so successfully cultivated by Lenin and his heirs. As Boris Yeltsin was to acknowledge many years later, in a speech to the Hungarian Parliament on November 11th 1992, 'The tragedy of 1956 . . . will forever remain an indelible spot on the Soviet regime.' But that was nothing when compared with the cost the Soviets had imposed on their victims. Thirty-three years later, on June 16th 1989, in a Budapest celebrating its transition to freedom, hundreds of thousands of Hungarians took part in another ceremonial reburial: this time of Imre Nagy and his colleagues. One of the speakers over Nagy's grave was the young Viktor Orbán, future Prime Minister of his country. 'It is a direct consequence of the bloody repression of the Revolution,' he told the assembled crowds, 'that we have had to assume the burden of insolvency and reach for a way out of the Asiatic dead end into which we were pushed. Truly, the Hungarian Socialist Workers' Party robbed today's youth of its future in 1956.'

X

The Age of Affluence

'Let us be frank about it: most of our people have never had it so good'.
Harold Macmillan, July 20th 1957

'Admass is my name for the whole system of an increasing productivity,
plus inflation, plus a rising standard of living, plus high-pressure
advertising and salesmanship, plus mass communications, plus cultural
democracy and the creation of the mass mind, the mass man'.
J. B. Priestley

'Look at these people! Primitives!'
'Where do they come from?'
'Lucania.'
'Where's that?'
'Down at the bottom!'
Rocco and His Brothers, *dir. Luchino Visconti (1960)*

'We're going where the sun shines brightly,
We're going where the sea is blue.
We've seen it in the movies—
Now let's see if it's true.'
*Cliff Richard, from **Summer Holiday** (1959)*

'It's pretty dreary living in the American age—
unless of course you're American'.
*Jimmy Porter, in **Look Back in Anger** (1956)*

In 1979, the French writer Jean Fourastié published a study of the social and economic transformation of France in the thirty years following World War Two. Its title—*Les trente glorieuses: ou, La Révolution invisible de 1946 à 1975*—was well chosen. In Western Europe the three decades following Hitler's defeat were indeed 'glorious'. The remarkable acceleration of economic growth was accompanied by the onset of an era of unprecedented prosperity. In the space of a single generation, the economies of continental Western Europe made good the ground lost in forty years of war and Depression, and European economic performance and patterns of consumption began to resemble those of the US. Less than a decade after staggering uncertainly out of the rubble, Europeans entered, to their amazement and with some consternation, upon the age of affluence.

The economic history of post-war western Europe is best understood as an inversion of the story of the immediately preceding decades. The 1930s Malthusian emphasis on protection and retrenchment was abandoned in favor of liberalized trade. Instead of cutting their expenditure and budgets, governments increased them. Almost everywhere there was a sustained commitment to long-term public and private investment in infrastructure and machinery; older factories and equipment were updated or replaced, with attendant gains in efficiency and productivity; there was a marked increase in international trade; and an employed and youthful population demanded and could afford an expanding range of goods.

The post-war economic 'boom' differed slightly in its timing from place to place, coming first to Germany and Britain and only a little later to France and Italy; and it was experienced differently according to national variations in taxation, public expenditure or investment emphasis. The initial outlays of most post-war governments went above all on infrastructure modernization—the building or upgrading of roads, railways, houses and factories. Consumer spending in some countries was deliberately held back, with the result—as we have seen—that many people experienced the first post-war years as a time of continuing, if modified, penury. The degree of relative change also depended, of course, on the point of departure: the wealthier the country, the less immediate and dramatic it seemed.

Nevertheless, every European country saw steadily growing rates of *per capita* GDP and GNP—Gross Domestic Product and Gross National Product—the newly sanctified measures of national strength and well-being. In the course of the 1950s, the average *annual* rate at which *per capita* national output grew in West Germany was 6.5 percent; in Italy 5.3 percent; in France 3.5 percent. The significance of such high and sustained growth rates is best appreciated when they are compared with the same countries' performance in earlier decades: in the years 1913–1950 the German growth rate *per annum* was just 0.4 percent, the Italian 0.6 percent, the French 0.7 percent. Even in the prosperous decades of the Wilhelminian Empire after 1870, the German economy had only managed an annual average of 1.8 percent.

By the 1960s the rate of increase began to slow down, but the western European economies still grew at historically unusual levels. Overall, between 1950 and 1973, German GDP per head of the population more than tripled in real terms. GDP per head in France grew by 150 percent. The Italian economy, starting from a lower base, did even better. Historically poor countries saw their economic performance improve spectacularly: between 1950 and 1973 *per capita* GDP in Austria rose from $3,731 to $11,308 (in 1990 dollars); in Spain from $2,397 to $8,739. The Dutch economy grew by 3.5 percent each year from 1950–1970—*seven* times the average annual growth rate for the preceding forty years.

A major contributory factor in this story was the sustained increase in overseas trade, which grew much faster than overall national output in most European countries. Merely by removing impediments to international commerce, the governments of the post-war West went a long way towards overcoming the stagnation of previous decades.[1] The chief beneficiary was West Germany, whose share of the world's export of manufactured goods rose from 7.3 percent in 1950 to 19.3 percent just ten years later, bringing the German economy back to the place it had occupied in international exchange before the Crash of 1929.

In the forty-five years after 1950 worldwide exports by volume increased sixteen-fold. Even a country like France, whose share of world trade remained steady at around 10 percent throughout these years, benefited greatly from this huge over-all increase in international commerce. Indeed, *all* industrialized countries gained in these years—the terms of trade moved markedly in their favor after World War Two, as the cost of raw materials and food imported from the non-Western world fell steadily, while the price of manufactured goods kept rising. In three decades of privileged, unequal exchange with the 'Third World', the West had something of a license to print money.[2]

What distinguished the western European economic boom, however, was the de-gree of *de facto* European integration in which it resulted. Even before the Treaty of Rome, the future member states of the European Economic Community were trading primarily with one another: in 1958, 29 percent of Germany's exports (by value) were going to France, Italy and the Benelux countries, and a further 30 per-cent to other European states. On the eve of the signing of the Rome Treaty, 44 per-cent of Belgian exports were already going to its future EEC partners. Even countries like Austria, or Denmark, or Spain, which would not officially join the European Community until many years later, were already integrated into its trad-ing networks: in 1971, twenty years before it joined the future European Union, Aus-tria was taking more than 50 percent of its imports from the original six EEC member states. The European Community (later Union) did not lay the basis for an economically integrated Europe; rather, it represented an institutional expres-sion of a process already under way.[3]

Another crucial element in the post-war economic revolution was the increased productivity of the European worker. Between 1950 and 1980 labor productivity in western Europe rose by three times the rate of the previous eighty years: GDP per hour worked grew even faster than GDP per head of the population. Consid-ering how many more people were in work, this points to a marked increase in ef-ficiency and, almost everywhere, much improved labour relations. This, too, was in some measure a consequence of catching-up: the political upheavals, mass un-

---

[1] One should not, however, overstate the speed with which old regulations were swept aside. Well into the 1960s the Italian government, for example, found it politically prudent to maintain Fascist-era tar-iffs and quotas on foreign cars, the better to protect domestic producers (essentially FIAT). British gov-ernments pursued similar strategies.

[2] Much of which would be recycled as loans to that same Third World, now saddled with crippling debts.

[3] Great Britain, as so often, was different. In 1956, 74 percent of the UK's exports went outside of Europe, mostly to its colonies and to the Commonwealth. Even in 1973, when the UK finally entered the EEC, only one-third of its export trade was directed at the twelve countries that would form the European Union in 1992.

employment, under-investment and physical destruction of the previous thirty years left most of Europe at a historically low starting point after 1945. Even without the contemporary interest in modernization and improved techniques, economic performance would probably have seen some improvement.

Behind the steady increase in productivity, however, lay a deeper, permanent shift in the nature of work. In 1945, most of Europe was still pre-industrial. The Mediterranean countries, Scandinavia, Ireland and Eastern Europe were still primarily rural and, by any measure, backward. In 1950, three out of four working adults in Yugoslavia and Romania were peasants. One working person in two was employed in agriculture in Spain, Portugal, Greece, Hungary and Poland; in Italy, two people in every five. One out of every three employed Austrians worked on farms; in France, nearly three out of every ten employed persons was a farmer of one kind or another. Even in West Germany, 23 percent of the working population was in agriculture. Only in the UK, where the figure was just 5 percent, and to a lesser extent in Belgium (13 percent), had the industrial revolution of the nineteenth century truly ushered in a post-agrarian society.[4]

In the course of the next thirty years vast numbers of Europeans abandoned the land and took up work in towns and cities, with the greatest changes taking place during the 1960s. By 1977, just 16 percent of employed Italians worked on the land; in the Emilia-Romagna region of the northeast, the share of the active population engaged in agriculture dropped precipitately, from 52 percent in 1951 to just 20 percent in 1971. In Austria the national figure had fallen to 12 percent, in France to 9.7 percent, in West Germany to 6.8 percent. Even in Spain only 20 percent were employed in agriculture by 1971. In Belgium (at 3.3 percent) and the UK (at 2.7 percent) farmers were becoming statistically (if not politically) insignificant. Farming and dairy production became more efficient and less labor-intensive—especially in countries like Denmark or the Netherlands, where butter, cheese and pork products were now profitable exports and mainstays of the domestic economy.

As a percentage of GDP, agriculture fell steadily: in Italy, its share of national production slipped from 27.5 percent to 13 percent between 1949 and 1960. The chief beneficiary was the tertiary sector (including government employment), where many of the former peasants—or their children—ended up. Some places—Italy, Ireland, parts of Scandinavia and France—moved directly from an agricultural to a service-based economy in a single generation, virtually bypassing the industrial stage in which Britain or Belgium had been caught for nearly a century.[5] By the end of the 1970s, a clear majority of the employed population of Britain, Germany,

---

[4]By way of comparison it might be noted that the figure for the USA in 1950 was 12 percent employed in agriculture.

[5]Sweden constitutes a partial exception—the key to Swedish post-war prosperity was the creation of a manufacturing specialty in high-value products. But the Swedes had access to a pool of cheap and readily available (Finnish) immigrant workers, as well as a hydroelectric power industry that cushioned the country from oil-price shocks. Like Switzerland, and for similar reasons, they constitute a special case.

France, the Benelux countries, Scandinavia and the Alpine countries worked in the service sector—communications, transport, banking, public administration and the like. Italy, Spain and Ireland were very close behind.

In Communist Eastern Europe, by contrast, the overwhelming majority of former peasants were directed into labour-intensive and technologically retarded mining and industrial manufacture; in Czechoslovakia, employment in the tertiary, service sector actually *declined* during the course of the 1950s. Just as the output of coal and iron-ore was tailing off in mid-1950s Belgium, France, West Germany and the UK, so it continued to increase in Poland, Czechoslovakia and the GDR. The Communists' dogmatic emphasis on raw material extraction and primary goods production did generate rapid initial growth in gross output and *per capita* GDP. In the short run the industrial emphasis of the Communist command economies thus appeared impressive (not least to many Western observers). But it boded ill for the region's future.

The decline of agriculture alone would have accounted for much of Europe's growth, just as the shift from country to town, and farming to industry, had accompanied Britain's rise to pre-eminence a century before. Indeed, the fact that there was no remaining surplus agricultural population in Britain to transfer into low-wage manufacturing or service employment, and therefore no gain in efficiency to be had from a rapid transition out of backwardness, helps explain the relatively poor performance of the UK in these years, with growth rates consistently lagging behind those of France or Italy (or Romania, come to that). For the same reason, the Netherlands outperformed its industrialized Belgian neighbor in these decades, benefiting from the 'one-time' transfer of a surplus rural workforce into hitherto undeveloped industrial and service sectors.

The role of government and planning in the European economic miracle is harder to gauge. In some places it appeared all but superfluous. The 'new' economy of northern Italy, for example, drew much of its energy from thousands of small firms—composed of family employees who often doubled as seasonal agricultural workers—with low overheads and investment costs, and paying little or no tax. By 1971, 80 percent of the country's workforce was employed in establishments with fewer—often far fewer—than 100 employees. Beyond turning a blind eye to fiscal, zoning, construction and other infractions, the part played by the Italian central authorities in sustaining the economic efforts of these firms is unclear.

At the same time the role of the state was crucial in financing large-scale changes that would have been beyond the reach of individual initiative or private investment: non-governmental European capital funding remained scarce for a long time, and private investment from America did not begin to substitute for Marshall Aid or military assistance until the later fifties. In Italy, the *Cassa per il Mezzogiorno*, backed by a large loan from the World Bank, invested initially in infrastructure and agrarian improvements: land reclamation, road building, drainage, viaducts, etc. Later it turned to supporting new industrial plants. It offered incentives—loans, grants, tax concessions—for private firms willing to invest in the South; it served as the vehicle through which state holdings were directed to locate up to 60 percent of their new investment in the South; and in the decades after 1957 it established twelve 'growth areas' and thirty 'growth nuclei' spread throughout the southern third of the peninsula.

Like large-scale state projects elsewhere, the *Cassa* was inefficient, and more than a little corrupt. Most of its benefits went to the favored coastal regions; much of the new industry that it brought in was capital-intensive and thus created few jobs. Many of the smaller, 'independent' farms formed in the wake of agrarian reform in the region remained dependent on the state, making of Italy's *Mezzogiorno* a sort of semi-permanent welfare region. Nevertheless, by the mid-1970s *per capita* consumption in the South had doubled, local incomes had risen by an average of 4 percent per annum, infant mortality had halved and electrification was well on the way to completion—in what had been, within the memory of a generation, one of the most forlorn and backward regions of Europe. Given the speed at which the industrial North was taking off—in some measure, as we shall see, thanks to Southern workers—what is striking is not the failure of the *Cassa* to work an economic miracle south of Rome, but the fact that the region was able to keep up at all. For this, the authorities in Rome deserve some credit.

Elsewhere, the role of government varied; but it was never negligible. In France, the state confined itself to what became known as 'indicative planning'—using the levers of power to direct resources into selected regions, industries and even products, and consciously compensating for the crippling Malthusian under-investment of the pre-war decades. Government officials were able to exercise fairly effective control over domestic investment especially because, throughout these initial post-war decades, currency laws and the limited mobility of international capital held back foreign competition. Restricted in their freedom to seek out more profitable short-term returns abroad, bankers and private lenders in France and elsewhere invested at home.[6]

In West Germany, where the abiding inter-war memory was of conflict and instability (political and monetary alike), the authorities in Bonn were much less active than their French or Italian counterparts in designing or directing economic behavior, but paid far closer attention to arrangements aimed at preventing or mitigating social conflict, notably between employers and workers. In particular, they encouraged and underwrote negotiations and 'social contracts' designed to reduce the risk of strikes or wage inflation. As a consequence, private industries (and the banks with whom they worked or who owned them) were more disposed to

---

[6]The contrast with past practice is revealing. In earlier stages of French industrialization even the great Parisian investment banks had lacked the resources to support the modernization of the country's industrial infrastructure, and had received no help or encouragement from the government. The dilapidated condition of French factories, roads, rail networks and utilities in 1945 bore eloquent testament to these shortcomings.

invest for their future because they could count on long-term wage restraint from their workers. Shop-floor workers in West Germany, as in Scandinavia, were compensated for this comparative docility by the assurance of employment, low inflation and, above all, comprehensive public welfare services and benefits financed out of sharply progressive rates of taxation.

In Britain, the government intervened more directly in the economy. Most of the nationalizations undertaken by the Labour government of 1945–51 were left in place by the Conservative governments that succeeded it. But both parties foreswore long-term economic planning or aggressive intervention in labour-management relations. Such active involvement as there was took the form of demand-management—manipulating interest rates and marginal tax bands to encourage saving or spending. These were short-term tactics. The main *strategic* objective of British governments of all colors in these years was to prevent a return to the traumatic levels of unemployment of the 1930s.

Throughout Western Europe, then, governments, employers and workers conspired to forge a virtuous circle: high government spending, progressive taxation and limited wage increases. As we have seen, these goals were already inscribed in the widespread consensus, forged during and after the war, on the need for planned economies and some form of 'welfare state'. They were thus the product of government policies and collective intention. But the facilitating condition for their unprecedented success lay beyond the direct reach of government action. The trigger for the European economic miracle, and the social and cultural upheaval that followed in its wake, was the rapid and sustained increase in Europe's population.

Europe had seen demographic growth spurts in the past—most recently in the mid-nineteenth century. But these had not typically ushered in sustained population increases: either because traditional agriculture could not support too many mouths, or because of wars and disease, or else because the newly excess population, especially the young adults, emigrated overseas in search of a better life. And in the twentieth century, war and emigration had kept population growth in Europe well below what might have been expected from the increased birth rate of earlier decades.

By the eve of World War Two, the knock-on effects of the loss of a generation of young men in World War One, together with the economic Depression and the civil wars and political uncertainty of the 1930s, had reduced the birth rate in parts of Western Europe to historic lows. In the UK there were just 15.3 live births per thousand people; in Belgium 15.4; in Austria 12.8. In France, where the birth rate in 1939 stood at 14.6 per thousand, deaths exceeded births not only during World War One and in 1919 and again in 1929, but also for every year from 1935 to 1944. There, as in civil war-era Spain, the national population was steadily falling. In the rest of Mediterranean Europe and east of Vienna the birth rate was higher, sometimes double the rate of the West. But elevated levels of infant mortality and higher death rates in all age groups meant that even there population growth was unremarkable.

It is against this background, and that of the additional demographic calamity of the Second World War itself, that the post-war baby boom has to be understood. Between 1950 and 1970 the population of the UK rose by 13 percent; that of Italy by 17 percent. In West Germany the population grew in these years by 28 percent; in Sweden by 29 percent; in the Netherlands by 35 percent. In some of these cases the indigenous increase was boosted by immigration (of returning colonials to the Netherlands, of East German and other refugees to the Federal Republic). But exogenous factors played only a small role in France: between the first post-war census of 1946 and the end of the sixties, the French population grew by almost 30 percent—the fastest rate of increase ever recorded there.

The striking feature of Europe in the nineteen fifties and sixties—it can immediately be gleaned from any contemporary street scene—was thus the number of children and youths. After a forty-year hiatus, Europe was becoming young again. The peak years for post-war births in most countries were 1947–1949—in 1949 869,000 babies were born in France, compared to just 612,000 in 1939. By 1960, in the Netherlands, Ireland and Finland, 30 percent of the population was under fifteen years old. By 1967, in France, one person in three was under twenty. It was not just that millions of children had been born after the war: an unprecedented number of them had survived.

Thanks to improved nutrition, housing and medical care, the infant mortality rate—the number of children per thousand live births who died before reaching their first birthday—fell sharply in Western Europe in these decades. In Belgium it dropped from 53.4 in 1950 to 21.1 in 1970, with most of the change coming in the first decade. In Italy it fell from 63.8 to 29.6, in France from 52.0 to 18.2. Old people lived longer too—at least in Western Europe, where the death rate fell steadily over the same period. The survival rate of infants in Eastern Europe also improved, admittedly from a far worse starting figure: in Yugoslavia, child mortality rates fell from 118.6 per thousand in 1950 to 55.2 twenty years later.[7] In the Soviet Union itself, rates fell from 81 per thousand in 1950 to 25 in 1970, though with wide variations among the different republics. But fertility rates in Communist states tailed off rather sooner than in the West, and from the mid-sixties they were more than matched by steadily worsening death rates (especially among men).

There are many explanations for the recovery of European fertility after World War Two, but most of them reduce to a combination of optimism plus free milk. During the long demographic trough of 1913–1945, governments had sought in

---

[7]By 1950, Yugoslavia, Poland, Romania and Albania were the only European countries where more than one child in ten died before the age of one. In west Europe the last-placed country was Portugal, where the infant mortality rate in 1950 was 94.1 per thousand.

vain to foster procreation: compensating through patriotic urging, family 'codes' and other legislation for the chronic shortage of men, housing, jobs and security. Now—even before post-war growth had translated into secure employment and a consumer economy—the coincidence of peace, security and a measure of state encouragement sufficed to achieve what no amount of pro-natal propaganda before 1940 had been able to bring about.

Demobilized soldiers, returning prisoners of war and political deportees, encouraged by rationing and allocation schemes that favored married couples with children, as well as cash allowances for each child, took the first opportunity to marry and start a family. And there was something else. By the early nineteen-fifties, the countries of western Europe could offer their citizens more than just hope and a social safety net: they also provided an abundance of jobs. Through the course of the 1930s the average unemployment rate in western Europe had been 7.5 percent (11.5 percent in the UK). By the 1950s it had fallen below 3 percent everywhere except Italy. By the mid-1960s the European average was just 1.5 percent. For the first time since records were kept, western Europe was experiencing full employment. In many sectors there were now endemic labor shortages.

In spite of the leverage this afforded to organized labor, trade unions (with the distinctive exception of Britain) were either weak or else reluctant to exercise their power. This was a legacy of the inter-war decades: militant or political unions never fully recovered from the impact of the Depression and Fascist repression. In return for their newfound respectability as national negotiating partners, union representatives through the fifties and early sixties often preferred to collaborate with employers rather than exploit labour shortages to their immediate advantage. In 1955, when the first ever productivity agreement in France was struck between the car workers' representatives and the nationalized car manufacturer Renault, it was symptomatic of the shift in perspective that the workers' major gain came not in wages but in the innovatory concession of a third week of paid holiday.[8]

Another reason why the old blue-collar unions were no longer so significant in Western Europe is that their constituency—skilled male manual workers—was in decline. Employment in coal, steel, textiles and other nineteenth-century industries was shrinking, though this did not become obvious until the sixties. More and more jobs were opening up in the tertiary sector, and many of those taking them were women. Some occupations—textile manufacture, domestic labor—had been heavily feminized for many decades. But after the war employment opportunities in both of these diminished sharply. The female labor force no longer consisted of single women working as servants or mill girls. Instead it was increasingly composed of older women (often married) working in shops, offices, and certain low-

---

[8]The following year, in March 1956, this right was extended to all French workers. Renault workers obtained a fourth week of paid vacation in 1962, but on this occasion it took seven years before the rest of the country followed suit.

paid professions: nursing and teaching in particular. By 1961, one-third of the employed labour force in the UK was female; and two out of every three employed women worked in clerical or secretarial jobs. Even in Italy, where older women had traditionally not joined the ranks of the (officially) employed, 27 percent of the labour force was female by the end of the 1960s.

The insatiable demand for labour in Europe's prosperous northwest quadrant accounts for the remarkable mass migrations in the 1950s and early 1960s. These took three forms. In the first place, men (and to a lesser extent women and children) abandoned the countryside for the city and moved to more developed regions of their own country. In Spain over one million residents of Andalucia moved north to Catalonia in the two decades after 1950: by 1970, 1.6 million Andalucian-born Spaniards lived outside their native region, 712,000 of them in Barcelona alone. In Portugal a substantial percentage of the residents of the impoverished Alentejo region departed for Lisbon. In Italy, between 1955 and 1971, an estimated nine million people moved from one region of their country to another.

This pattern of population movement was not confined to the Mediterranean. The millions of young people who abandoned the German Democratic Republic for West Germany between 1950 and 1961 may have been opting for political freedom, but in heading west they were also seeking well-paid jobs and a better life. In this respect they differed little from their Spanish or Italian contemporaries—or the quarter of a million Swedes from the rural centre and north of their country who moved to the cities in the decade after 1945. Much of this movement was driven by income disparities; but the desire to escape hardship, isolation, the bleakness of village life and the hold of traditional rural hierarchies also played a part, especially for young people. One incidental benefit was that the wages of those who remained behind, and the amount of land available to them, increased as a consequence.

A second route taken by migrants involved moving from one European country to another. European emigration, of course, was nothing new. But the fifteen million Italians who left their country between 1870 and 1926 had typically departed across the ocean: for the United States or Argentina. The same was true of the millions of Greeks, Poles, Jews and others who emigrated in the same years, or the Scandinavians, Germans and Irish of an earlier generation. After World War One, to be sure, there had been a steady trickle of miners and farm workers from Italy and Poland into France, for example; and the 1930s saw political refugees fleeing west from Nazism and Fascism. But intra-European migration, especially in search of work, remained the exception.

By the end of the 1950s, all this changed. Cross-border labor movement had begun shortly after the end of the war—following an agreement of June 1946, tens of thousands of young Italian workers traveled in organized convoys to work in the mines of Wallonia, in return for a Belgian undertaking to supply coal to Italy. But in the course of the 1950s the economic expansion of northwest Europe was outrunning local population growth: the 'baby-boom' generation had yet to enter the workforce but demand for labor was peaking. As the German economy in particular began to accelerate, the Bonn government was forced to seek out cheap labour from abroad.

By 1956 Chancellor Adenauer was in Rome, offering free transport to any Italian laborer who would make the journey to Germany and seeking official Italian cooperation to funnel unemployed southerners across the Alps. In the course of the next decade the Bonn authorities would sign a series of accords not just with Italy but also encompassing Greece and Spain (1960), Turkey (1961), Morocco (1963), Portugal (1964), Tunisia (1964) and Yugoslavia (1968). Foreign ('guest') workers were encouraged to take up employment in Germany—on the understanding that their stay was strictly temporary: they would eventually return to their country of origin. Like Finnish migrant workers in Sweden, or Irish laborers in Britain, these men—most of them under 25—came in almost every case from poor, rural or mountainous regions. The majority were unskilled (although some accepted 'de-skilling' in order to get work). Their earnings in Germany and other northern countries played an important part in sustaining the economies of the regions they had left behind, even as their departure alleviated local competition for jobs and housing. In 1973, the remittances of workers abroad represented 90 percent of Turkish export earnings, 50 percent of export earnings in Greece, Portugal and Yugoslavia.

The demographic impact of these population transfers was significant. Although the migrants were officially 'temporary' they had in practice left their homes for good. If they returned, it would only be many years later, to retire. Seven million Italians left their country between 1945 and 1970. In the years 1950–1970 a quarter of the entire Greek labor force left to find work abroad: at the height of the emigration, in the mid-Sixties, 117,000 Greeks left their country every year.[9] It is estimated that between 1961 and 1974, one and a half million Portugese workers found jobs abroad—the greatest population movement in Portugal's history, leaving behind in Portugal itself a workforce of just 3.1 million. These were dramatic figures for a country whose total population in 1950 had been only eight and one third million. The emigration of young women in search of domestic employment in Paris and elsewhere had a particularly marked effect on the countryside, where the shortfall of young adults was only partly made good by the arrival of immigrants from Portugal's colonies in the Cape Verde Islands and Africa. In one Portuguese municipality, Sabugal in the rural north, emigration reduced the local population from 43,513 in 1950 to just 19,174 thirty years later.

The economic benefit to the 'importing' country was considerable. By 1964, foreign (mostly Italian) workers were one quarter of the work force of Switzerland,

---

[9]With the result that as tourism began to develop towards the end of the Sixties there was actually a shortage of workers in Greece itself, for the most menial jobs.

whose tourist trade depended heavily upon cheap, seasonal labor: easily hired, readily fired. In West Germany, in the peak year of 1973, there were 2.8 million foreign workers, mostly in the building trades and in metalworking and car manufacture. They constituted one worker in eight of the national labour force. In France the 2.3 million foreign workers recorded that year were 11 percent of the total working population. Many of them were women in domestic work, employed as cooks, cleaners, concierges and babysitters—overwhelmingly of Portuguese origin.

Most of these men and women had no permanent rights of residence, and they were not included in the agreements signed by unions and employers providing for the security, welfare and retirement of local employees. They thus represented very little commitment or long-term cost to the employer and country to which they had come. Well into the 1980s, 'guest-workers' in Germany were held back at entry-level positions and wages. They lived as best they could, sending most of their earnings home: however little they were paid in marks or francs, it was worth many times their earning potential in their villages of origin. Their condition resembled that of the forlorn Italian waiter in Luzerne lightly caricatured in Franco Brusati's 1973 film *Pane e Cioccolata* (*Bread and Chocolate*).

By 1973 in West Germany alone there were nearly half a million Italians, 535,000 Yugoslavs and 605,000 Turks.[10] The Germans—like the Swiss, French, Belgians or British—did not especially welcome the sudden eruption of so many foreigners on their soil. The experience of living among so many people from unknown foreign lands was unfamiliar to most Europeans. If it was tolerated reasonably well, with only occasional outbreaks of prejudice and violence against communities of foreign workers, this was in some measure because the latter lived apart from the local population, in the drearier outer suburbs of the larger cities; because they posed no economic threat in an era of full employment; because at least in the case of Christians from Portugal, Italy and Yugoslavia they were physically and culturally 'assimilable'—i.e. not dark or Muslim; and because it was widely understood that they would one day be gone.

Such considerations did not apply, however, to a third source of imported labour: immigrants from past and present European colonies. The number of people in this category was not initially significant. Many of the people who had returned to the Netherlands, Belgium and France from former imperial holdings in Asia, Africa, South America and the Pacific were white professionals, or else retired farmers. Even the Algerian nationals living in France by 1969 numbered just 600,000, less than the local population of Italians or Spaniards.

Even in Britain, where the governments of the 1950s had actively encouraged immigration from the Caribbean to staff the country's trains, buses and municipal services, the figures were not especially striking. In the 1951 census there were

---

[10] Just fifteen years earlier, in 1958, there had been 25,000 Italians, 4,000 Yugoslavs and not enough Turks to be recorded in official censuses.

15,000 people from the West Indies (mostly Barbados) resident in the UK: 4,000 of them in London. By 1959 West Indian immigration to the UK was running at around 16,000 people per year. Immigration from other parts of the Commonwealth was even smaller—in 1959 there were just 3,000 immigrant arrivals from India and Pakistan. The numbers would increase in later years—notably when the British government reluctantly agreed to admit the East African Asians expelled by the Ugandan dictator Idi Amin—but as late as 1976 there were still only 1.85 million 'non-whites' in the UK population, 3 percent of the total. And 40 percent of these had been born there.

What made the difference, of course, was that these people were brown or black—and, being Commonwealth citizens, had a presumptive right of permanent residence and eventually citizenship in the imperial metropole. Already in 1958, race riots in west London alerted the government to the perceived risk of permitting 'too many' immigrants to enter a historically white society. And so, even though the economic case for unskilled immigrants remained strong and the overall totals insignificant, the UK brought in the first of many controls on non-European immigration. The Commonwealth Immigration Act of 1962 introduced 'employment vouchers' for the first time, and placed rigorous controls on non-white immigration to the UK. A successor Act of 1968 tightened these still further, restricting UK citizenship to persons with at least one British parent; and in 1971 a further Act, overtly directed at non-whites, severely restricted the admission of the dependents of immigrants already in Britain.[11]

The net effect of these laws was to end non-European immigration into Britain less than twenty years after it had begun. Henceforth, the growing share of non-whites in the UK population would be a function of high African, Caribbean and South Asian birth rates within the UK. On the other hand, these drastic restrictions on the right of blacks and Asians to enter the UK were accompanied, in due course, by a considerable improvement in their life chances once there. A Race Relations Act of 1965 banned discrimination in public places, introduced remedies for job discrimination, and set out penalties for incitement to race hatred. A successor Act eleven years later finally outlawed *all* discrimination based on race and established a Commission for Racial Equality. In certain respects, the new, non-European populations of the UK (and, later, France) were more fortunate than the second-class Europeans who found work north of the Alps. English landladies could no longer display signs announcing 'No Blacks, Irish or Dogs'; but notices forbidding entry to 'dogs and Italians' were not unknown in Swiss parks for some years to come.

---

[11]These draconian restrictions on colonial immigration reflected mainstream opinion in both major parties. However, less than a generation before and in rather different circumstances, the Labour Prime Minister Clement Attlee had written thus, in July 1948: 'It is traditional that British subjects, whether of Dominion or Colonial origin (and of whatever race or colour), should be freely admissible to the United Kingdom. That tradition is not, in my view, to be lightly discarded, particularly at a time when we are importing foreign labour in large numbers.'

In northern Europe the situation of foreign labourers and other residents was kept deliberately precarious. The Dutch government encouraged workers from Spain, Yugoslavia, Italy (and later Turkey, Morocco and Surinam), to come and take up jobs in textiles, mines and shipbuilding. But when the old industries shut down, it was these workers who lost their jobs, often without any insurance or social safety net to cushion the impact on them and their families. In West Germany a Foreigners' Law of 1965 incorporated within its text 'Police Regulations for Foreigners' first promulgated by the Nazis in 1938. Foreign workers were described and treated as a temporary presence, at the mercy of the authorities. By 1974, however, when the European economy had slowed to a crawl and many of the immigrant workers were no longer required, they had become permanent residents. In that year, 17.3 percent of all children born in West Germany were the children of 'foreigners'.

The net impact of these movements of people is hard to overestimate. Taken all in all, they amounted to some forty million people in transit, moving within countries, between countries and into Europe from overseas. Without cheap and abundant labour in this vulnerable and mostly unorganized form, the European boom would not have been possible. The post-war European states—and private employers—benefited greatly from a steady flow of docile, low-paid workers for whom they frequently avoided paying the full social cost. When the boom ended and it came time to lay off excess labour, the immigrant and migrant workforce was the first to suffer.

Like everyone else, the new workers not only made things; they bought them. This was something quite new. Throughout recorded history, most people in Europe—as elsewhere in the world—had possessed just four kinds of things: those they inherited from their parents; those they made themselves; those they bartered or exchanged with others; and those few items they had been obliged to purchase for cash, almost always made by someone they knew. Industrialization in the course of the nineteenth century had transformed the world of town- and city-dwellers; but in many parts of rural Europe the traditional economy operated largely unchanged up to and even beyond the Second World War.

By far the largest expense in a traditional household budget was food and clothing, which together with housing took up much of a family's earnings. Most people did not shop or 'consume' in the modern sense; they subsisted. For the overwhelming majority of the European population up to the middle of the twentieth century, 'disposable income' was a contradiction in terms. As recently as 1950, the average *western* European household spent more than half its cash outlay on necessities: food, drink and tobacco (*sic*). In Mediterranean Europe the figure was distinctly higher. Once clothing and rent were added, there was not much left over for non-essential items.

In the next generation, all this was to change. In the two decades after 1953, real wages almost tripled in West Germany and the Benelux countries. In Italy the rate of income growth was higher still. Even in Britain the purchasing power of the average citizen nearly doubled in these years. By 1965, food and clothing absorbed just 31 percent of consumer spending in Britain; by 1980 the average for northern and western Europe as a whole was less than one quarter.

People had money to spare and they were spending it. In 1950, West German retailers sold just 900,000 pairs of ladies' nylon stockings (the emblematic 'luxury' item of the immediate post-war years). Four years later, in 1953, they moved 58 million pairs. In more traditional commodities the major impact of this revolution in spending came in the way goods were packaged and the scale on which they were sold. Supermarkets began to appear, notably in the 1960s, the decade when the impact of the increase in purchasing power was felt most dramatically. In the Netherlands, which boasted just seven supermarkets in 1961, there were 520 ten years later. In the same decade, the number of supermarkets in neighboring Belgium rose from 19 to 456; in France from 49 to 1,833.[12]

The rationale for supermarkets was that shoppers (housewives for the most part) would spend more in any one shopping trip if most of what they wanted— or could be tempted into wanting—was conveniently available in one place. But this in turn presumed that women had somewhere to put their food when they got it home; and that implied, increasingly, the presence of a fridge. In 1957 most west European households still did not possess a fridge (the figure ranging from 12 percent in West Germany to less than 2 percent in Italy). The reason was not so much technical (by the mid-1950s virtually all of western Europe had full electricity service, with the exception of parts of rural Norway and southern and upland regions of Italy) as logistic: until housewives could afford to buy a lot of perishable food at one outing, and could transport it home, there was not much point in spending large sums of money on a fridge.[13]

It is thus symptomatic of many other related changes that, by 1974, the absence of a fridge in most places would have been remarked upon: in Belgium and the UK, 82 percent of households had one; in France, 88 percent; in the Netherlands and West Germany, 93 percent. Most remarkable of all, 94 percent of Italian households now owned a fridge, the highest ratio in Europe. Indeed, Italy had become Europe's largest manufacturer of refrigerators and other 'white goods'. In 1951 Italian facto-

---

[12]The exception was Italy, where in 1971 less than 5 percent of all purchases were made in the country's 538 supermarkets and almost everyone continued to use local, specialized shops. This was still true twenty years later: in 1991, by which time the number of food outlets in West Germany had fallen to 37,000 and in France to a mere 21,500, there were fully 182,432 food stores in Italy. Per head of the population, only Poland had more.

[13]There were 'cultural' objections as well. In 1952 the French Communist author Roger Vailland asserted that, '[i]n a country like France, where—except for two months a year, and not every year—it is always so cold that a food-box on the window ledge will keep the roast for a weekend, and more, a fridge is a "symbol", an (American) "mystification".'

ries made just 18,500 fridges; two decades later Italy was producing 5,247,000 a year—almost as many as the USA, and more than the rest of Europe put together.

Like the domestic fridge, the washing machine made its appearance in these years. It too was aimed at easing the work of the newly affluent housewife and encouraging her to extend her range of purchases. The washing machine, however, took longer to catch on than the fridge—partly because in the mid-1950s running water had still not arrived in more than half of all households in Belgium, Italy, Austria, Spain and many parts of France and Scandinavia, partly because the electricity grid in many places could not support two large appliances in a single residence.[14] Even in 1972, by which time most west Europeans lived in homes equipped with indoor toilets and full plumbing, only two households in three owned a washing machine, a ratio that increased steadily but slowly with each decade. Washing machines remained for many years beyond the reach of the poor, especially large families that had greatest need of them. Partly for this reason, the washing machine—like dishwashers after the mid-1970s—remained associated in commercial imagery with the domestic accoutrements of the affluent middle class.

Washing machines and fridges were becoming cheaper. Like toys and clothes, they were being made on a far larger scale than ever before, as investment at one end and sustained high demand at the other brought prices down: even in France, where mass production always lagged a little behind, turnover in the toy industry increased 350 percent in the early baby-boom years 1948–1955. But the virtuous circle of millions of newly employed commodity-consumers had its most significant impact not in the home but outside. The greatest single measure of European prosperity was the revolution wrought by the family car.

Until the 1950s, the motor car was a luxury for most Europeans and in many parts was scarcely to be seen. Even in major cities its arrival had been very recent. Most people did not travel great distances for pleasure, and when travelling to work or school they used public transport: trains, trams and buses. At the beginning of the 1950s there were just 89,000 private cars (not counting taxis) in Spain: one for every 314,000 persons. In 1951, just one French household in twelve possessed a car. Only in Great Britain was car ownership a mass phenomenon: there were 2,258,000 private cars there in 1950. But the geographical distribution was uneven: nearly a quarter of all cars were registered in London—much of rural Britain was as empty of cars as France or Italy. And even so, many Londoners didn't own a car and there were thousands of market traders, costermongers and others who still depended in their work upon a horse and cart.

Car ownership was to increase spectacularly in the next two decades. In Britain, where an initial take-off in the 1930s had been stalled by war and post-war shortages, it doubled in each decade from 1950 to 1980. From two and a quarter million

---

[14]Only in 1963 did *Electricité de France* begin upgrading their urban power lines to permit the running of multiple appliances—the countryside followed some years later.

vehicles in 1950, British car ownership had risen to 8 million by 1964, and reached 11.5 million by the end of the Sixties. Italians, who owned just 270,000 private cars at the outbreak of the war and 342,000 in 1950 (less than the number of cars in Greater London alone), had two million vehicles by 1960, five and a half million by 1965, over ten million in 1970 and an estimated 15 million five years later—two cars for every seven residents of the country.[15] In France, car ownership rose from less than two million to nearly six million vehicles in the course of the 1950s, then doubled again in the next ten years. Symptomatically, parking meters were introduced at the end of the 1950s—beginning in Britain, then spreading through France and elsewhere in the course of the Sixties.[16]

If Europeans could buy cars for their personal use in such unprecedented numbers it was not merely because they had more money to spend. There were many more cars available to meet the pent-up demand of decades of Depression and war. Well before 1939, a number of European car manufacturers (Porsche in Germany, Renault and Citroën in France, Morris in Britain), anticipating a post-Depression lift in demand for private automobiles, had begun to think about a new kind of family car—analogous in function to Henry Ford's Model T of twenty years before: reliable, mass-produced and affordable. The war delayed the appearance of these models, but by the early 1950s they were rolling off newly installed production lines in ever-increasing number.

In each Western European country there was a dominant local make and model of car, but in essence they were all remarkably alike. The Volkswagen Beetle, the Renault 4cv, the FIAT 500 and 600, the Austin A30 and the Morris Minor were tiny, two-door units of family transport: cheap to buy, cheap to run and easy to fix. They had thin, tinny frames; small, under-powered engines (designed to consume as little fuel as possible); and were equipped with the minimum of accessories and fixtures. The Volkswagens, Renaults and Fiats were rear-engined and had rear-wheel drive, leaving the compartment in front of the driver to accommodate a small amount of luggage, as well as the battery, spare wheel, crank handle and tools.

The front-engined Morris, like its contemporary and competitor the Ford Popular (American-owned but made at Ford's UK plant in Dagenham, near London, for the domestic market), aspired to a slightly higher level of comfort—and would later spawn a four-door model, as befitted the rather greater prosperity of Britain in the years of its first appearance. Citroën of France introduced its utterly distinctive 2CV (initially marketed to farmers seeking to upgrade or replace their ox wagon), complete with four doors, removable roof and seats, and the engine of a

---

[15]An exponential increase nicely captured in the opening scene of Fellini's *8 1/2* (1963). Even by Fellini's own standards, this urban traffic jam would have been bizarrely implausible just a few years earlier.

[16]Local response to this innovation followed historical precedent: English motorists, regarding meter charges as a form of unauthorized taxation, withheld payment. The French registered their disapproval by decapitating Parisian meters.

medium-sized motorbike. Despite these cultural variations the little cars of the fifties had a common purpose: to render automobile ownership accessible and affordable for almost every west European family.

For some years after the start of Europe's post-war transport revolution, the supply of cars could not keep up with demand (a situation that remained the case in Eastern Europe right up to 1989). Thus bikes, motorcycles and motorcycle-sidecar combinations flourished for a while—the latter as a makeshift family vehicle for those who could not afford a car or could not yet get hold of one. Motor scooters appeared on the scene—in France and especially Italy, where the first national motor-scooter rally, held in Rome on November 13th 1949, was followed by an explosive growth in the market for these convenient and reasonably priced symbols of urban freedom and mobility, popular with young people and duly celebrated—the Vespa model in particular—in every contemporary film from or about Italy.

But by the beginning of the sixties the car was firmly in command in Western Europe, displacing traffic from rails to roads and from public to private means of transport. Railway networks had peaked in length and user-volume in the years following World War One; now, unprofitable services were cut back and thousands of miles of track pulled up. In the UK the railways carried 901 million passengers in 1946, close to their historic peak. But thereafter the numbers declined each year. Elsewhere in Western Europe, train traffic held up rather better; in small, crowded countries with efficient networks—like Belgium, the Netherlands and Denmark—it actually grew; but far slower than road traffic.

The number of people using buses also began to decline for the first time ever, as more and more people went to work by car. Between 1948 and 1962, in Britain's congested capital, the overall passenger traffic on London Transport's buses, trams, trolleys and underground network fell from 3,955 million people a year to 2,485, as commuters took to their cars instead. Despite the distinctly inadequate condition of Europe's roads—outside of Germany there had been no significant upgrading of any national road network since the late 1920s—individuals and especially families used cars increasingly for discretionary travel: for shopping trips to hypermarkets newly situated at the edge of cities, and above all for weekend excursions and on annual holidays.[17]

Recreational travel in Europe was not new, though it had hitherto been confined first to the aristocracy and latterly to the better-heeled and more culturally ambitious middle classes. But like every other economic sector, 'tourism' had suffered through war and economic recession. The Swiss tourist industry in 1913 boasted 21.9 million nights of lodging; it would not recover such numbers until the mid-

---

[17]The first European hypermarkets, defined as stores with at least 25,000 square feet of space on a single level and typically located at least two miles from a town center, began to appear at the end of the 1960s. By 1973 there were about 750 of these giant stores in Western Europe, 620 of them in France and West Germany alone. In Italy in that same year there were just three. Twenty years later there were fully 8,000 hypermarkets and superstores in France . . . but still just 118 in Italy.

1950s. And when it came, the tourist boom of the 1950s was different. It was facilitated and encouraged by the availability of private transport and above all by the growing number of people enjoying paid vacations: by 1960 most employees in continental Europe were legally entitled to two weeks of paid holiday (three in Norway, Sweden, Denmark and France) and increasingly they took that holiday away from home.

Leisure travel was becoming mass tourism. Coach companies blossomed, extending the tradition of factory and farm workers' annual char-à-banc seaside trips into commercial services within and between countries. Fledgling airline entrepreneurs like Britain's Freddie Laker, who had bought up war-surplus Dakota turbo-prop planes, developed charter services to newly opened summer vacation resorts in Italy, France and Spain. Camping—already popular before the war among less affluent vacationers and outdoor enthusiasts—became a major industry in the later Fifties, spawning coastal and pastoral camp-sites, camping equipment emporia, printed guides and specialized clothing outlets. Older holiday resorts—along the coasts and in the countryside of northern and western Europe—thrived. Freshly discovered (or re-discovered) locations emerged, gaining prominence in glossy brochures and popular mythology. The French Riviera, once a sedate wintering escape for Edwardian gentry, was given a seductive and youthful makeover in a new genre of 'fun-in-the-sun' movie: in 1956 Roger Vadim 'invented' St Tropez as a showcase for his new starlet Brigitte Bardot in *Et Dieu . . . créa la femme*.

Not everyone could afford St Tropez or Switzerland—though the French and Italian coasts and mountains were still inexpensive for travelers from Britain or Germany, exchanging sterling and Deutschmarks for the undervalued francs and lire of the day. But *domestic* seaside holidays, still much sought-after by British, Dutch and Germans in particular, were now truly cheap. Billy Butlin, a Canadian fairground worker who opened his first operation at Skegness in 1936, went on in the Fifties to make a fortune selling 'cheap and cheerful', all-in family vacations in holiday camps strategically set along the seashore of industrial England: 'Walmart with overnight accommodations' as one critic dismissed them in cynical retrospect. But Butlin's was immensely popular in its day—and was the unacknowledged institutional ancestor of France's Club Med, the collective recreational preference of a later, more cosmopolitan generation: even down to the *'gentils moniteurs'* (or 'Redcoats', as Butlin called them).

For the slightly more adventurous there were also the newly opened resorts of Spain's Mediterranean coast, where visitors could choose between bed-and-breakfast establishments, *pensións* or modest seaside hotels block-booked by a new breed of package-tour operators. And all of these could now be reached by car. Dressed in summer leisure clothing (itself a new product—and evidence of the new affluence), millions of families would squeeze into their Fiats, Renaults, Volkswagens and Morrises—often on the same day, since official vacation dates tended to cluster around a block of weeks in August—and make their way to distant coasts, along narrow, inadequately serviced roads designed for an earlier age of travel.

The result was unprecedented and quite awful traffic jams that grew worse every year from the late 1950s. They followed predictable arteries: the A303 road south-west from London to Cornwall; the *Routes Nationales* 6 and 7 from Paris to the Mediterranean coast; the *Route Nationale* 9 from Paris to the Spanish border (from a few thousand tourists in 1955, French visitors to Spain numbered three million by 1962, seven million two years later—in Franco's Spain even the French franc went a long way, especially after the Gaullist revaluation).[18] German tourists followed the medieval trade route south, pouring through the Austrian Tyrol and over the Bren-ner Pass into Italy in ever increasing numbers. Many continued on into Yugoslavia which, like Spain, opened itself to foreign tourism in these years: already at 1.7 million in 1963, foreign travelers to the only accessible Communist country in Europe (blessed with a long and very cheap Adriatic coastline) numbered nearly 6.3 million per annum a decade later.

Mass tourism, it has been well observed, may be environmentally insensitive but it has distinct re-distributive benefits. As prosperous northerners flocked to hith-erto impoverished Mediterranean lands, jobs opened up for building workers, cooks, waiters, chambermaids, taxi-drivers, prostitutes, porters, airport mainte-nance crews and others. For the first time, unskilled young men and women in Greece, Yugoslavia, Italy and Spain could find low-paying, seasonal work at home instead of seeking it abroad. Rather than migrate to the expanding economies of the north, they now serviced those same economies in their own lands.

Foreign travel may not have broadened the mind: the more popular a foreign des-tination, the quicker it came to resemble—in all essential features save climate—the tourist's point of origin. Indeed, the success of large-scale tourism in the 1960s and after depended upon making Brits, Germans, Dutch, French and other neophyte travelers feel as comfortable as possible, surrounded by fellow-countrymen and in-sulated from the exotic, the unfamiliar and the unexpected. But the mere fact of going somewhere distant on a regular (annual) basis, and the novel means of transport used to get there—private car, charter flight—offered millions of hitherto insular men and women (and especially their children) a window onto a far bigger world.

Until the 1960s, the chief source of information, opinion and entertainment available to the overwhelming majority of Europeans was the radio. It was from the radio that people got the news, and if there was a common national culture it was shaped far more by what people heard than from what they saw or read. In every European country at this time radio was regulated by the state (in France the na-

---

[18]Between 1959 and 1973, the number of visitors to Spain rose from 3 million to 34 million. Already in 1966 the number of annual tourists in Spain—17.3 million—far surpassed the totals for France or Italy. In parts of the north-east and Spain's Mediterranean littoral, the transition from a pre-industrial econ-omy to the age of the credit card was accomplished in half a generation. The aesthetic and psycholog-ical impact was not always positive.

tional broadcasting network closed down at midnight). Broadcasting stations, transmitters and wavelengths were licensed and typically owned by national governments: symptomatically, the few radio stations transmitting from outside national frontiers were usually situated on ships or islands and colloquially referred to as 'pirates'.

Ownership of radios, already widespread before the war, was near universal by 1960: in that year there was one radio for every five people in the USSR, one for every four people in France, Austria and Switzerland, one for every three people in Scandinavia and East Germany. In effect, almost every family owned a radio.[19] Most domestic radio sets had evolved little from the large, unwieldy, valve-driven wireless units of the inter-war decades. There was usually one per family. It occupied a prime site in the parlor or kitchen and the family had perforce to listen to it while gathered in one place. Even car radios altered little in this respect—the family that traveled together, listened together, and parents chose the programs. Wireless radio was thus a naturally conservative medium, both in its content and in the social patterns that it encouraged and sustained.

Transistors would change all this. The transistor radio was still rare in 1958—in all of France, for example, there were just 260,000. But three years later, in 1961, the French owned two and a quarter million transistor radios. By 1968, when nine out of every ten people in France owned a radio, two thirds of those radios were portable models. Teenagers no longer needed to sit around with their families, listening to news and drama directed at the taste of adults and scheduled for 'family listening hours', usually following the evening meal. They now had their own programmes—'Salut les Copains' on French national radio, 'Pick of the Pops' on the BBC, etc. Individualized radios bred targeted programming; and when the state radio systems proved slow to adapt, 'peripheral' radio stations—Radio Luxemburg, Radio Monte Carlo, Radio Andorra, transmitting legally but from across state frontiers and financed by commercial advertising—seized the opportunity.

Battery-driven transistor radios were light and portable, and thus well adapted to an age of increasing mobility—their natural habitat was the tourist beach or public park. But radio was still an aural medium, and thus restricted in its capacity to adapt to what was an increasingly visual age. For older people radio remained a primary source of information, enlightenment and entertainment. In Communist states the radio set was also the only means of access, however inadequate, to uncensored news and opinion, from Radio Free Europe, the Voice of America and, above all, the BBC World Service. But young people everywhere now listened to radio above all for popular music. For everything else they turned increasingly to television.

---

[19]With the exception of the Iberian peninsula and the southern Balkans, where radio ownership in 1960 was roughly comparable to that of Western Europe thirty-five years earlier, and where people still clustered in cafés to listen to news and music.

Television service came slowly to Europe and in some places quite late. In Britain, regular transmitting began in the 1940s and many people watched Queen Elizabeth's June 1953 coronation live on television. By 1958 more television licenses were issued than radio licenses: the country had ten million sets in domestic use even before the Sixties began. France, by contrast, boasted just 60,000 television sets in June 1953 (at a time when there were already 200,000 in West Germany and fifteen million in the USA); even in 1960 only one French family in eight owned a television, one-fifth the UK figure for a comparable population. In Italy the figures were smaller still.

In the course of the Sixties, however, television caught on almost everywhere— small black-and-white television sets had become an affordable and increasingly essential item of domestic furniture in even the most modest household. By 1970 there was on average one television set for every four people in western Europe— more in the UK, rather less in Ireland. In some countries at this time—France, the Netherlands, Ireland, Italy (Europe's biggest manufacturer of television sets as well as fridges)—a family was more likely to own a television than a telephone, though by later standards they did not watch it very much: three quarters of Italian adults watched less than thirteen hours per week. Two East German households in three possessed a television (whereas less than half owned a fridge); Czechs, Hungarians and Estonians (who could watch Finnish television broadcasting from as early as 1954) were close behind.

The impact of television was complicated. Its subject matter was not, at first, especially innovative—state-owned television channels ensured that the political and moral content of programs for children and adults alike was strictly regulated. Commercial television began in Britain in 1955, but it did not come elsewhere until much later and in most European countries there was no question of allowing private television channels until well into the 1970s. Most television programming in the early decades of the medium was conventional, stuffy and more than a little patronizing—confirming rather than undermining traditional norms and values. In Italy Filiberto Guala, head of RAI (*Radio Audizioni Italiane*—the Italian national broadcasting network) from 1954–56, instructed his employees that their programs were 'not to undermine the institution of the family' or portray 'attitudes, poses or particulars which might arouse base instincts'.[20]

There was very little choice—one or at best two channels in most places—and the service operated only for a few hours of the afternoon and evening. Nevertheless, television *was* a medium of social subversion. It contributed hugely to ending the isolation and ignorance of far-flung communities, by providing everyone with the same experience and a common visual culture. Being 'French', or 'German' or 'Dutch' was now something shaped less by primary education or public festivities

---

[20]Paul Ginsborg, *A History of Contemporary Italy. Society and Politics 1943–1988* (1990), p. 240.

than by one's understanding of the country as gleaned from the images thrust into each home. 'Italians', for good or ill, were forged more by the shared experience of watching sport or variety shows on RAI than by a century of unified national government.

Above all, television put national politics onto the domestic hearth. Until television, politics in Paris or Bonn, Rome or London were an élite affair, conducted by distant leaders known only from their disembodied voices on radio, lifeless newspaper photographs or brief, stylized appearances on formulaic cinema newsreels. Now, within the span of less than two decades, political leaders had to become television-friendly: capable of conveying authority and confidence while feigning egalitarian ease and warm familiarity to a mass audience—a performance for which most European politicians were much less well-prepared than their US counterparts. Many older politicians failed miserably when faced with television cameras. Younger, more adaptable aspirants stood to profit immensely. As the British Conservative politician Edward Heath was to remark in his memoirs, à propos the media success of his nemesis, the Labour Party leader Harold Wilson: television was 'open to abuse by any charlatan who was capable of manipulating it properly. So it proved in the following decade.'

As a visual medium, television was a direct challenge to cinema. Not only did it offer alternative screen entertainment, but it could also bring feature films into people's homes, obviating the need to go out to see anything but the latest releases. In the UK, cinemas lost 56 percent of their customers between 1946 and 1958. Numbers fell more slowly elsewhere in Europe, but sooner or later they fell everywhere. Cinema attendance held up longest in Mediterranean Europe—especially in Italy, where audience levels remained fairly constant until the mid-1970s. But then Italians not only went to see films on a regular (usually weekly) basis, they also made them: in mid-1950s Rome the film industry was the second largest employer after the construction trades, making not only classical films by famous *auteurs*, but also (and more profitably) a steady stream of forgettable movies starring beauty queens and evanescent starlets—'*le maggiorate fisiche*' (the 'physically advantaged').

Eventually, even the Italian film industry, and Italian cinema attendance, languished. European film producers, lacking the resources of Hollywood, could not hope to compete with American films in scale or 'production values' and confined themselves increasingly to 'ordinary life' cinema, whether 'new wave', kitchen sink or domestic comedy. Cinema in Europe declined from a social activity to an art form. Whereas audiences in the 1940s and 1950s had automatically gone to see whatever happened to be showing at the local cinema, they now went only if they were attracted by a particular film. For random entertainment, to see whatever was 'on', they turned instead to television.

Despite being a 'young' medium, television had a particular attraction for older audiences, especially in its early, state-regulated, culturally cautious years. Where once they would have listened to the radio, or else gone out to the cinema, mature men and women stayed at home and watched television instead. Commercial sport, especially traditional spectator sports like soccer or dog racing, suffered: firstly because their audience now had an alternative source of entertainment, more convenient and comfortable; and secondly because sport soon began to be televised, usually at the weekends. Only young people went out in large numbers. And their tastes in entertainment were starting to change.

By the end of the 1950s, the European economy was beginning to feel the full commercial impact of the baby boom. First there had been the explosion in products for babies, toddlers and children: baby carriages, cribs, diapers, baby food, children's clothing, sporting equipment, books, games and toys. Then came a vast expansion in schools and education services, bringing in its wake a new market for school uniforms, desks, schoolbooks, school equipment and an ever-widening range of educational products (including teachers). But the buyers for all these goods and services had been adults: parents, relatives, school administrators and central governments. Around 1957, for the first time in European history, young people started buying things themselves.

Until this time, young people had not even existed as a distinct group of consumers. Indeed, 'young people' had not existed at all. In traditional families and communities, children remained children until they left school and went to work, at which point they were young adults. The new, intermediate category of 'teenager', in which a generation was defined not by its status but by its age—neither child nor adult—had no precedent. And the notion that such persons—teenagers—might represent a distinct group of consumers would have been quite unthinkable a few years before. For most people the family had always been a unit of production, not consumption. To the extent that any young person within the family had independent cash earnings, these were part of the family income and used to help defray collective expenses.

But with real wages rising rapidly, most families could subsist—and better—on the income of the primary wage-earner; all the more so if both parents were employed. A son or daughter who had left school at fourteen (the typical school-leaving age for most young west Europeans in these years), who was living at home, and who had a steady or just a part-time job, was no longer automatically expected to hand over all his or her earnings every Friday. In France, by 1965, 62 percent of all 16- to 24-year-olds still living with their parents were retaining all their own earnings to spend as they wished.

The most immediately obvious symptom of this new adolescent spending power was sartorial. Well before the baby-boom generation itself discovered miniskirts and long hair, its immediate predecessor—the generation born during the war rather than just after it—asserted its presence and its appearance in the gang cults of the late Fifties. Dressed in dark, skin-hugging outfits—sometimes leather, sometimes suede, always sharply cut and vaguely threatening—the *blouson noirs* (France), *Halbstarker* (Germany and Austria) or *skinknuttar* (Sweden), like the teddy boys of

London, affected a cynical, indifferent demeanour, something between Marlon Brando (in *The Wild One*) and James Dean (*Rebel Without a Cause*). But despite occasional bursts of violence—most seriously in Britain, where gangs of leather-clad youths attacked Caribbean immigrants—the chief threat that these young people and their clothes posed was to their elders' sense of propriety. They *looked* different.

Age-specific clothing was important, as a statement of independence and even revolt. It was also new—in the past, young adults had had little option but to wear the same clothes as their fathers and mothers. But it was not, economically speaking, the most important change wrought by teenage spending habits: young people were spending a lot of money on clothes, but even more—far more—on music. The association of 'teenager' and 'pop music' that became so automatic by the early Sixties had a commercial as well as a cultural basis. In Europe as in America, when the family budget could dispense with a teenager's contribution, the first thing the liberated adolescent did was to go out and buy a gramophone record.

The long-playing record was invented in 1948. The first 45rpm 'single', with one song on each side, was marketed by RCA the following year. Sales in Europe did not take off as fast as in America—where turnover from record sales rose from $277 million in 1955 to $600 million four years later. But they rose nonetheless. In Britain, where young people were initially more exposed to American popular music than their continental contemporaries, observers dated the pop music explosion from the showing of the 1956 film *Rock Around the Clock*, starring Bill Haley and the Comets and the Platters. The film itself was mediocre even by the undemanding standards of rock music movie vehicles; but its eponymous title song (performed by Haley) galvanized a generation of British teenagers.

Working-class teenagers for whom jazz had never held much appeal were immediately attracted to the American (and in its wake, British) revolution in popular music: driving, tuneful, accessible, sexy and, above all, their own.[21] But there was nothing very angry about it, much less violent, and even the sex was kept firmly under wraps by record company producers, marketing managers and radio broadcasting executives. This is because the initial pop music revolution was a Fifties phenomenon: it did not accompany the cultural transformation of the Sixties but preceded it. As a consequence it was frequently the object of official criticism. Disapproving local council watch committees banned *Rock Around the Clock*—as they did Elvis Presley's decidedly superior rock musical, *Jailhouse Rock*.

The city fathers of Swansea in Wales thought the British skiffle player Lonnie

---

[21]It is perhaps worth emphasizing the marginality of jazz. Like American folk music in the sixties, jazz was only ever appreciated and bought by a small number of people in western Europe: usually educated, bourgeois or bohemian (or, typically, both) and rather older than the average rock-and-roll enthusiast. The situation in eastern Europe was a little different. There jazz was American (and black), therefore both exotic and subversive, Western yet radical—and carried a charge quite lacking further West.

Donegan 'unsuitable'. Tommy Steele, a moderately energetic British rock singer of the late Fifties, was not allowed to perform in Portsmouth on the Sabbath. Johnny Hallyday, a half-successful French attempt to clone US rockers of the Gene Vincent or Eddie Cochran mould, inspired outrage among a generation of French conservative intellectuals when his first record appeared in 1960. In retrospect, the horrified response of parents, teachers, clerics, pundits and politicians across Western Europe appears quaintly disproportionate. Within less than a decade Haley, Donegan, Steele, Hallyday and their like would seem hopelessly outdated, relics of an innocent prehistory.

European teenagers of the late fifties and early sixties did not aspire to change the world. They had grown up in security and a modest affluence. Most of them just wanted to look different, travel more, play pop music and buy stuff. In this they reflected the behavior and tastes of their favorite singers, and the disc-jockeys whose radio programs they listened to on their transistors. But all the same they were the thin end of a revolutionary wedge. More even than their parents, they were the target of the advertising industry that followed, accompanied and prophesied the consumer boom. More and more goods were being made and purchased, and they came in unprecedented variety. Cars, clothes, baby carriages, packaged foods and washing powder all now came to market in a bewildering variety of shapes and sizes and colors.

Advertising had a long history in Europe. Newspapers, especially the popular newspapers that flourished from the 1890s, had always carried advertisements. Roadside hoardings and placards were a longstanding blight in Italy well before the nineteen fifties, and any traveler in mid-century France would have been familiar with the exhortations painted high up on the side of rural farmhouses and urban terraces to drink *St Raphael* or *Dubonnet*. Commercial jingles as well as still photographs had long accompanied newsreels and the second feature in cinemas across Europe. But such traditional advertising took little account of targeted product placement, or markets segmented by age or taste. From the mid-1950s, by contrast, consumer choice became a major marketing consideration; and advertising, still a relatively small business expense in pre-war Europe, took on a prominent role.

Moreover, whereas the cleaning products and breakfast cereals advertised on early commercial television in Britain were directed towards housewives and children, commercial breaks on Radio Monte Carlo and elsewhere were aimed above all at the 'young adult' market. Teenage discretionary spending—on tobacco, alcohol, mopeds and motor bikes, modestly-priced fashion clothing, footwear, makeup, hair care, jewelry, magazines, records, record-players, radios—was a huge, and hitherto untapped, pool of cash: advertising agencies flocked to take advantage of it. Expenditure on retail advertising in Great Britain rose from £102 million a year in 1951 to £2.5 billion in 1978.

In France, spending on magazine adverts aimed at adolescents rose by 400 percent in the crucial years 1959–1962. For many people, the world as depicted in advertisements was still beyond their reach: in 1957 a majority of young people polled in France complained that they lacked access to entertainment of their choice, the vacation of their imaginings, a means of transport of their own. But it is symptomatic that those polled already regarded these goods and services as rights of which they were deprived, rather than fantasies to which they could never aspire. Across the English Channel, in that same year, a group of middle-class activists, perturbed at the unmediated impact of commercial advertising and the efflorescence of commodities it was selling, published the first-ever consumer guide in Europe. Significantly, they named it not 'What' but *Which?*

This was the brave new world that the British novelist J. B. Priestley described in 1955 as 'admass'. For many other contemporary observers it was, very simply, 'Americanization': the adoption in Europe of all the practices and aspirations of modern America. A radical departure though it seemed to many, this was not in fact a new experience. Europeans had been 'Americanizing'—and dreading the thought—for at least thirty years.[22] The vogue for US-style production lines and 'Taylorized' work rates, like the fascination with American films and fashions, was an old story even before World War Two. European intellectuals between the wars had bemoaned the 'soulless' world of American modernity that lay ahead for everyone; and Nazis and Communists both made great play with their role as the preservers of culture and values in the face of unrestricted American capitalism and a 'mongrelized' rootless cosmopolitanism symbolized by New York and its spreading example.

And yet, for all its presence in the European imagination—and the very physical reality of American soldiers based all over western Europe—the United States was still a great unknown for most Europeans. Americans spoke English—not a language with which most continental Europeans had any acquaintance in these years. The history and geography of the USA were not studied in European schools; its writers were unknown even to an educated minority; its political system was a mystery to all but a privileged few. Hardly anyone had made the long and expensive journey to the US: only the wealthy (and not many of them); hand-picked trade unionists and others paid from Marshall funds; a few thousand exchange students—and a number of Greek and Italian men who had emigrated to America after 1900 and returned to Sicily or the Greek islands in old age. East Europeans often had more links to the US than westerners, since many Poles or Hungarians knew a friend or relative who had gone to America, and many more would have gone if they could.

To be sure, the US government and various private agencies—notably the Ford Foundation—were doing their best to overcome the gulf separating Europe from America: the 1950s and early 1960s were the great age of overseas cultural invest-

---

[22]The American writer William Stead published *The Americanization of the World* in 1902: anticipating his subject, perhaps, but not by much.

ment, from America Houses to Fulbright Scholars. In some places—notably the Federal Republic of Germany—the consequences were profound: between 1948 and 1955, 12,000 Germans were brought to America for extended stays of one month or more. A whole generation of West Germans grew up in the military, economic and cultural shadow of the United States; Ludwig Erhard once described himself as 'an American invention.'

But it is important to emphasize that this sort of American influence and example depended curiously little on direct American economic involvement. America in 1950 had three fifths of the capital stock of the West and about the same share of output, but very little of the proceeds flowed across the Atlantic. Post-1945 investment came above all from the US government. In 1956, US private investment in Europe amounted to just $4.15 billion. It then began to rise sharply, taking off in the 1960s (notably in Britain) and reaching $24.52 billion in 1970—by which time it had provoked a flurry of anxious publications warning of the rise of American economic power, notably J-J Servan-Schreiber's 1967 essay, *Le Défi Américain* (The American Challenge).

The American economic presence in Europe was felt less in direct economic investment or leverage than in the consumer revolution that was affecting America and Europe alike. Europeans were now gaining access to the unprecedented range of products with which American consumers were familiar: phones, white goods, televisions, cameras, cleaning products, packaged foods, cheap colorful clothing, cars and their accessories, etc. This was prosperity and consumption as a way of life—the 'American way of life'. For young people the appeal of 'America' was its aggressive contemporaneity. As an abstraction, it stood for the opposite of the past; it was large, open, prosperous—and youthful.

One aspect of 'Americanization', already noted, was popular music—though even this was not in itself a new pattern: 'ragtime' was first performed in Vienna in 1903 and American dance bands and jazz groups were widely circulating before and after World War Two. Nor was it a uniquely one-way process: most modern popular music was a hybridization of imported and local genres. 'American' music in Britain was subtly different from 'American' music in France or Germany. French taste in particular was influenced by black performing artists who made their way to Paris to escape prejudice at home—one reason why the idea of 'America' in French culture was markedly infused with the image of racism.

By the 1950s, the impact of American example on a European audience came overwhelmingly through the medium of film. European audiences had near-unrestricted access to anything Hollywood could export: by the later 1950s, the US was marketing about 500 films a year, to Europe's collective output of about 450. American films suffered the disadvantage of language, of course (though in many places, notably Italy, they were simply dubbed en masse into the local tongue). And partly for this reason audiences above a certain age continued to prefer the domestic product. But their children felt otherwise. Younger audiences increasingly appreciated American feature films—often made by European directors who had fled Hitler or Stalin.

Contemporary critics worried that the smug conformism of American popular culture, combined with the manifest or subliminal political messages conveyed in films aimed at mass audiences, would corrupt or tranquilize the sensibilities of European youth. If anything, the effect seems rather to have been the opposite. Young European audiences filtered out the propaganda content of mainstream American movies—envying the 'good life' as depicted on screen, much as their parents had done twenty years before, but laughing out loud at the bathos and naiveté of American romance and domestic routine. Meanwhile, however, they paid very close attention to the often-subversive *style* of the performers.

The music that was played in American films would re-surface on radio, in cafés, bars and dance halls. The body language of rebellious American youth—as seen on film—became a fashion statement for their European contemporaries. Young Europeans began to dress 'American'—when 'genuine Levi' jeans first appeared on sale in Paris, at the *Marché aux Puces* in May 1963, demand far outran supply. The American youth uniform of jeans and tee-shirts carried very little connotation of class (at least until both were appropriated by expensive high-end fashion designers, and even then the distinction that emerged was not of social rank but material resources); indeed, worn by middle class and working class alike, jeans were a revealing inversion of the traditional 'trickle down' development of dress style, having trickled *up* from a genuine item of work clothing. They were also distinctively *young*: like many other form-fitting fashions imitated from the films of the late 1950s, they did not flatter the older figure.

Within a very short time, jeans—like motorbikes, Coca-Cola, big hair (male and female) and pop stars—had spawned locally adapted variations across western Europe (both the films and the products they flaunted were unavailable further east). This was part of a broader pattern. Stock American film themes—science-fiction, detective stories, Westerns—were domesticated in stylized European versions. Millions of West Germans learned about cowboys from paperback novels written by local authors who had never been to America; by 1960 German-language 'Western' novels were selling at the rate of ninety-one million a year in the Federal Republic alone. The second most popular European cartoon character after the Belgian boy-detective *Tintin* was another Belgian product: *Lucky Luke*, a hapless and appealing cowpoke featured weekly in French- and Dutch-language comics. America, real or imagined, was becoming the natural setting for light entertainment of all genres.

The American impact on young Europeans contributed directly to what was already being widely bemoaned as the 'generation gap'. Their elders observed and regretted the propensity of young Europeans everywhere to pepper their conversations with real or imagined Americanisms. One study estimated that such 'Americanisms' increased fourteen-fold in the Austrian and German press over the course of the sixties; in 1964 the French critic René Etiemble published *Parlez-vous Franglais?*, an entertaining (and, as some might now say, prophetic) account of the damage being done to the French language by anglophone pollution.

Anti-Americanism—the principled distrust and dislike of American civilization and all its manifestations—was typically confined to cultural elites whose influence made it appear more widespread than it was. Cultural conservatives like André Siegfried in France—whose 1954 *Tableau des États-Unis* reprised all the resentments and some of the anti-semitism of inter-war polemics—agreed with cultural radicals like Jean-Paul Sartre (or Britain's Harold Pinter in later decades): America was a land of hysterical puritans, given over to technology, standardization and conformism, bereft of originality of thought. Such cultural insecurities had more to do with the pace of change in Europe itself than with the challenge or threat posed by America. Just as European teenagers identified the future with an America they hardly knew, so their parents blamed America for the loss of a Europe that had never really been, a continent secure in its identity, its authority and its values, and impervious to the sirens of modernity and mass society.

These sentiments were not yet widely encountered in Germany or Austria, or even Italy, where many older people still regarded Americans as liberators. Conversely, anti-Americanism was more frequently espoused in England and France, the two former colonial powers directly displaced by the rise of the United States. As Maurice Duverger informed the readers of the French weekly *L'Express* in March 1964, Communism was no longer a threat: 'There is only one immediate danger for Europe, and that is the American civilization'—'a civilization of bathtubs and frigidaires', as the poet Louis Aragon had dismissed it thirteen years before. But notwithstanding the haughty disdain of Parisian intellectuals, a civilization of bathtubs and frigidaires—and indoor plumbing and central heating and television and cars—was what most Europeans now wanted. And they wanted these commodities not because they were American but because they represented comfort and a degree of ease. For the first time in history, ease and comfort were now within the reach of most people in Europe.

POSTSCRIPT:

A Tale of Two Economies

'Germany is a land teeming with children. It is a terrifying thought that, in long range terms, the Germans may have won the war after all'.
Saul Padover, 1945

'Of course, if we succeeded in losing two world wars, wrote off all our debts—instead of having nearly £30 million in debts—got rid of all our foreign obligations, and kept no force overseas, then we might be as rich as the Germans'.
Harold Macmillan

'The prosperity and strength of the British economy which [UK Chancellor of the Exchequer R.A.] Butler celebrated in several speeches in 1953 and 1954 was but the last wash of prosperity breaking on British shores from the wake of the German economy as it surged ahead, pulling its attendant European flotilla with it. In retrospect, 1954 looks like the last grand summer of illusion for the United Kingdom'.
Alan Milward

A striking feature of the history of post-war western Europe was the contrast between the economic performance of West Germany and Great Britain. For the second time in one generation, Germany was the defeated power—its cities shattered, its currency destroyed, its male workforce dead or in prison camps, its transportation and service infrastructure pulverized. Britain was the only European state to emerge unambiguously victorious from World War Two. Bomb damage and human losses aside, the fabric of the country—roads, railways, shipyards, factories and mines—had survived the war intact. Yet by the early 1960s, the Federal Republic was the booming, prosperous powerhouse of Europe, while Great Britain was an underperforming laggard, its growth rate far behind that of the rest of Western Europe.[1] Already by 1958 the West German economy was larger than that of Britain. In the eyes of many observers the UK was well on its way to becoming the sick man of Europe.

---

[1] In 1960 the German economy grew at a rate of 9.0 percent per annum, the British economy by 2.6 percent: the slowest rate in the developed world, except for Ireland—which at this time was still far from 'developed'.

The sources of this ironic reversal of fate are instructive. The background to the German economic 'miracle' of the fifties was the recovery of the *thirties*. The investments of the Nazis—in communications, armaments and vehicle manufacture, optics, chemical and light engineering industries and non-ferrous metals—were undertaken for an economy geared to war; but their pay-off came twenty years later. The social market economy of Ludwig Erhard had its roots in the policies of Albert Speer—indeed, many of the young managers and planners who went on to high position in post-war West German business and government got their start under Hitler; they brought to the committees, planning authorities and firms of the Federal Republic policies and practices favored by Nazi bureaucrats.

The essential infrastructure of German business survived the war undamaged. Manufacturing firms, banks, insurance companies, distributors were all back in business by the early '50s, supplying a voracious foreign market with their products and services. Even the increasingly high-valued Deutschmark did not impede German progress. It made imported raw materials cheap, without restricting foreign demand for German products—these were typically high-value and technically advanced, and they sold on quality, not price. In any case, during the first post-war decades there was little competition: if Swedish or French or Dutch firms wanted a certain sort of engineering product or tool, they had little option but to buy it from Germany, and at the asking price.

German business costs were kept down by sustained investment in new and efficient production methods—and by a compliant workforce. The Federal Republic benefited from a virtually inexhaustible supply of cheap labor—skilled young engineers fleeing East Germany, semi-skilled machine minders and assembly workers from the Balkans, unskilled laborers from Turkey, Italy and elsewhere. All of these were grateful for stable hard-currency wages in return for steady employment, and—like an un-protesting older generation of German workers inherited from the Thirties—they were not disposed to make trouble.

The results can be illustrated with reference to a single industry. By the 1960s German car manufacturers had successfully established a reputation for engineering quality and manufacturing reliability, such that companies like Mercedes-Benz in Stuttgart and BMW in Munich could sell increasingly expensive cars to a near-captive market, first at home and increasingly overseas. The Bonn government unashamedly supported such 'national champions', just as the Nazis had done before it, nurturing them in early years with favorable loans and encouraging the banking-business nexus that provided German companies with ready cash for investment.

In the case of Volkswagen, the groundwork had already been laid by 1945. Like so much of post-war West German industry, Volkswagen benefited from all the advantages of a free-market economy—notably growing demand for its products—without suffering any of the drawbacks of competition or the costs of research, development and tooling. The company had been given inexhaustible resources before 1939. Nazism, war and military occupation had all done well by it—the Allied Military Government looked kindly on Volkswagen precisely because its productive capacity had been built up before the war and could be put to work without further ado. There was no serious domestic competition for the VW Beetle when demand for mass-produced small family cars took off, and even at a fixed and low price the cars turned a profit—thanks to the Nazis, the company had no old debt to pay off.

In Britain, too, there was a 'national champion'—the British Motor Corporation (BMC), a conglomerate of various formerly independent car manufacturers like Morris or Austin, and itself later merged with Leyland Motors to produce British Leyland (BL). As late as 1980, BL was selling its products as emblematically British: 'Drive the flag—buy an Austin Morris'. And like the German manufacturers, British carmakers laid increasing emphasis on the overseas market. But there the similarities ended.

After the war, successive British governments urged BMC especially (they had less influence over US-owned Ford, or General Motors' subsidiaries in the UK) to sell every car they could overseas—as part of the desperate search for foreign currency earnings to offset the country's huge war debts (the official government export target at the end of the 1940s was 75 percent of all UK car production). The company duly and deliberately neglected quality control in favor of rapid output. The resulting shoddy quality of British cars mattered little at first. British firms had a captive market: demand both at home and in Europe exceeded available supply. And continental European manufacturers could not compete on volume: in 1949 the UK produced more passenger cars than the rest of Europe combined. But once the reputation for low quality and poor service was established, it proved impossible to shake. European buyers abandoned British cars in droves as soon as better home-produced alternatives became available

When they did decide to update their fleets and modernize their production lines, British car firms had no affiliated banks to turn to for investment cash and loans, in the German manner. Nor (unlike FIAT in Italy or Renault in France) could they count on the state to make up the shortfall. Yet under heavy political pressure from London, they built plants and distribution centers in uneconomic parts of the country—to conform to official regional policies and to appease local politicians and unions. Even after this economically irrational strategy was abandoned and some consolidization undertaken, British automobile firms remained hopelessly atomized: in 1968 British Leyland consisted of sixty different plants.

Governments actively encouraged the inefficiency of British producers. After the war, the authorities distributed scarce supplies of steel to manufacturers on the basis of their *pre-war* market share, thus freezing a major sector of the economy in the mould of the past and decisively penalizing new, and potentially more efficient producers. The guarantee of supplies, the artificially high demand for anything they could make, and political pressure to behave in economically inefficient ways all combined to lead British firms down into bankruptcy. By 1970 European and Japanese producers were taking over their markets and beating them on quality *and* price. The oil crisis of the early 1970s, entry into the EEC and the end of the UK's last protected markets in the dominions and colonies finally destroyed the independent British car industry. In 1975 British Leyland, the country's only independent mass automobile maker, collapsed and had to be bailed out via nationalization. A few years later its profitable parts would be bought up for a song . . . by BMW.

The decline and eventual disappearance of an autonomous British automobile sector can stand for British economic experience at large. The British economy did not initially do so very badly: in 1951 Britain was still the major manufacturing center of Europe, producing twice as much as France and Germany combined. It provided full employment and it did grow, albeit more slowly than everywhere else. It suffered, however, from two crippling disadvantages, one a product of historical misfortune, the other self-imposed.

The UK's endemic balance of payments crisis was in large measure a result of the debts racked up to pay for the six-year war against Germany and Japan, to which should be added the enormous costs of supporting an effective post-war defense establishment (8.2 percent of the national income in 1955, against a German outlay of less than half that figure). The pound—still a major unit of international transactions in the 1950s—was overvalued, which made it hard for Britain to sell enough abroad to compensate for sterling's chronic deficit against the dollar. An island country, utterly dependent on imports of food and vital raw materials, Britain had historically compensated for this structural vulnerability by its privileged access to protected markets in the Empire and Commonwealth.

But this dependence on far-flung markets and resources, an advantage in the initial post-war years as the rest of Europe struggled to recover, became a serious liability once Europe—and especially the EEC zone—took off. The British could not compete with the US, and later Germany, in any unprotected overseas market, while British exports to Europe itself lagged ever further behind those of other European producers. British manufactured exports represented 25 percent by value of the world's total in 1950; twenty years later they constituted just 10.8 percent. The British had lost their share of the world market, and their traditional suppliers—in Australia, New Zealand, Canada and the African colonies—were now turning to other markets as well.

In some measure the relative economic decline of Britain was thus inevitable. But Britain's own contribution should not be underestimated. Even before World War Two, Britain's manufacturing industry had gained a well-deserved reputation for inefficiency, for coasting on past success. It was not that the British were overpriced. Quite the contrary. As Maynard Keynes pointed out in a sardonic commentary on Britain's post-war economic prospects: 'The hourly wage in this country is (broadly) 2/- per hour; in the US it is 5/- per hour . . . Even the celebrated inefficiency of British manufacturers can scarcely (one hopes) be capable of offsetting over wide ranges of industry the whole of this initial cost-difference in their favour, though admittedly they have managed it in some important cases ... The available statistics suggest that, provided we have never made the product before, we have the whole world licked on cost'.[2]

One problem was the workforce. Britain's factories were staffed by men (and some women) who were traditionally organized into—literally—hundreds of long-established craft unions: British Leyland's car factories in 1968 counted 246 different trade unions with whom management had separately to negotiate every detail of work rates and wages. This was an era of full employment. Indeed, the maintenance of full employment was the cardinal social objective of every British government in these years. The determination to avoid a return to the horrors of the thirties, when men and machines decayed in idleness, thus trumped any consideration of growth, productivity or efficiency. Trade unions—and especially their local representatives, the factory shop stewards—were more powerful than ever before or since. Strikes—a symptom of labour militancy and incompetent management alike—were endemic to post-war British industrial life.

Even if Britain's trade union leadership had followed the German example and offered amicable shop-floor relations and wage restraint in return for investment, security and growth, it is unlikely that most of their employers would have taken the bait. Back in the 1930s the future Labour Prime Minister Clement Attlee had accurately identified the British economic malaise as a problem of under-investment, lack of innovation, labour immobility and managerial mediocrity. But, once in office, there seemed little that he or his successors could do to stop the rot. Whereas German industry inherited all the advantages of the changes wrought by Nazism and war, Britain's old-established, uncompetitive industries inherited stagnation and a deep fear of change.

Textiles, mines, shipbuilding, steel and light engineering plants would all need restructuring and retooling in the post-war decades; but just as they chose to accommodate trade unions rather than attack inefficient labour practices, so British factory managers preferred to operate in a cycle of under-investment, limited research and development, low wages and a shrinking pool of clients, rather than risk a fresh start with new products in new markets. The solution was not obvious. Keynes, once again: 'If by some sad geographical slip the American Air Force (it is too late now to hope for much from the enemy) were to destroy every factory on the North East coast and in Lancashire (at an hour when the Directors were sitting there and no-one else) we should have nothing to fear. How else are we to regain the exuberant inexperience which is necessary, it seems, for success, I cannot surmise.'

In France, a similar heritage of managerial incompetence and inertia was over-

---

[2]Quoted in Peter Hennessy, *Never Again. Britain 1945–1951* (1993), p.117.

come by public investment and aggressive indicative planning. British governments, however, confined themselves to collective bargaining, demand management and exhortation. For a state that had nationalized such sweeping tracts of the economy after 1945, and that was by 1970 responsible for spending 47 percent of the country's GNP, this caution seems a curious paradox. But the British state, although it owned or operated most of the transport, medical, educational and communications sectors, never boasted any overall national strategic ambition; and the economy was for practical purposes left to its own devices. It fell to a later generation of free-market reformers—and a radically state-averse Conservative prime minister—to apply the full force of central government to the problem of Britain's economic stagnation. But by then some of the strictures levelled at Britain's maladapted 'old' economy were being levelled, for different reasons, at the faltering German economy too.

XI

The Social Democratic Moment

'The important thing for Government is not to do things which
individuals are doing already, and to do them a little better or a little
worse; but to do those things which at present are not done at all'.
John Maynard Keynes (1926)

'The challenge is not going to come from the U.S, . . . from Western
Germany or from France; the challenge is going to come from those
nations who, however wrong they may be—and I think they are wrong in
many fundamental respects—nevertheless are at long last being able to
reap the material fruits of economic planning and of public ownership'.
Aneurin Bevan (1959)

'Our nation stands for democracy and proper drains'.
John Betjeman

'I want to throw open the windows of the Church so that we can see out
and the people can see in'.
Pope John XXIII

'Photography is truth. The cinema is truth twenty-four times per second'.
Jean-Luc Godard

The 1960s saw the apogee of the European state. The relation of the citizen to the
state in Western Europe in the course of the previous century had been a shifting
compromise between military needs and political claims: the modern rights of
newly enfranchised citizens offset by older obligations to defend the realm. But
since 1945 that relationship had come increasingly to be characterised by a dense
tissue of social benefits and economic strategies in which it was the state that served
its subjects, rather than the other way around.

In later years the all-encompassing ambitions of the Western European welfare
states would lose some of their appeal—not least because they could no longer fulfill their promise: unemployment, inflation, ageing populations and economic
slowdown placed insuperable constraints upon the efforts of states to deliver their
half of the bargain. Transformations in international capital markets and modern
electronic communications hamstrung governments' capacity to plan and enforce

domestic economic policy. And, most important of all, the very legitimacy of the interventionist state itself was undermined: at home by the rigidities and inefficiencies of public-sector agencies and producers, abroad by the incontrovertible evidence of chronic economic dysfunction and political repression in the Socialist states of the Soviet bloc.

But all of this lay in the future. In the peak years of the modern European welfare state, when the administrative apparatus still exercised broad-ranging authority and its credibility remained unassailed, a remarkable consensus was achieved. The state, it was widely believed, would always do a better job than the unrestricted market: not just in dispensing justice and securing the realm, or distributing goods and services, but in designing and applying strategies for social cohesion, moral sustenance and cultural vitality. The notion that such matters might better be left to enlightened self-interest and the workings of a free market in commodities and ideas was regarded in mainstream European political and academic circles as a quaint relic of pre-Keynesian times: at best a failure to learn the lessons of the Depression, at worst an invitation to conflict and a veiled appeal to the basest human instincts.

The state, then, was a good thing; and there was a lot of it. Between 1950 and 1973, government spending rose from 27.6 percent to 38.8 percent of the gross domestic product in France, from 30.4 percent to 42 percent in West Germany, from 34.2 percent to 41.5 percent in the UK and from 26.8 percent to 45.5 percent in the Netherlands—at a time when that domestic product was itself growing faster than ever before or since. The overwhelming bulk of the increase in spending went on insurance, pensions, health, education and housing. In Scandinavia the share of national income devoted to social security alone rose 250 percent in Denmark and Sweden between 1950 and 1973. In Norway it tripled. Only in Switzerland was the share of post-war GNP spent by the state kept comparatively low (it did not reach 30 percent until 1980), but even there it stood in dramatic contrast to the 1938 figure of just 6.8 percent.

The success story of post-war European capitalism was everywhere accompanied by an enhanced role for the public sector. But the nature of state engagement varied considerably. In most of continental Europe the state eschewed direct ownership of industry (though not of public transport or communications), preferring to exercise indirect control; often through notionally autonomous agencies, of which Italy's tentacular IRI was the biggest and best known (see Chapter 8).

Conglomerates such as IRI serviced not just their employees and consumers, but also a variety of political parties, trade unions, social service agencies and even churches whose patronage they dispensed and whose influence they enhanced. Italy's Christian Democrat Party 'colonised' at every level from village to national capital a protean range of public services and state-controlled or state-subsidized products: transport, electronic media, banks, energy, engineering and chemical industries, the building trades, food production. The primary beneficiaries, after the

Party itself, were the millions of children and grandchildren of landless peasants who found secure employment in the bureaucracies that resulted. The Italian National Institute for War Orphans employed 12 people for every 70 orphans and spent 80 percent of its annual budgetary allocation on salaries and administration.

In a similar way, control of public-sector companies in Belgium allowed the national government in Brussels to buffer local resentments and bribe contending regional and linguistic interests with services, jobs and costly infrastructure investment. In France the post-war nationalizations established long-lasting networks of influence and patronage. *Electricité de France* (EDF) was the country's primary energy provider. But it was also one of the country's largest employers. By an agreement dating from the initial post-war legislation, one percent of EDF's French turnover was handed annually to a social fund managed by the then-dominant trade union movement, the Confédération Générale du Travail (CGT). The vacation and other benefits paid from this fund (not to mention the employment opportunities for its staff) represented for decades to come a lucrative and politically significant lever of patronage for the CGT's own patron, the French Communist Party.

The state thus lubricated the wheels of commerce, politics and society in numerous ways. And it was responsible, directly or indirectly, for the employment and remuneration of millions of men and women who thus had a vested interest in it, whether as professionals or bureaucrats. Graduates from Britain's leading universities, like their contemporaries in French *grandes écoles*, typically sought employment not in private-sector professions, much less industry and commerce, but in education, medicine, the social services, public law, state monopolies or government service. By the end of the 1970s, 60 percent of all university graduates in Belgium took up employment in the public services or publicly subsidized social sector. The European state had forged a unique market for the goods and services it could provide. It formed a virtuous circle of employment and influence that attracted near-universal appreciation.

Doctrinal differences over the ostensible goals of the state might noisily oppose Left and Right, Christian Democrats and Communists, Socialists and Conservatives, but almost everyone had something to gain from the opportunities the state afforded them for income and influence. Faith in the state—as planner, coordinator, facilitator, arbiter, provider, caretaker and guardian—was widespread and crossed almost all political divides.[1] The welfare state was avowedly social, but it was far from socialist. In that sense welfare capitalism, as it unfolded in Western Europe, was truly post-ideological.

---

[1] Liberal parties and thinkers in Germany and Italy, like the small free-market wing of Britain's Conservative Party, did not join in this consensus. But at the time—and in part for this reason—they wielded little influence.

Nevertheless, within the general post-war European consensus there *was* a distinctive vision, that of the Social Democrats. Social Democracy had always been a hybrid; indeed, this was just what was held against it by enemies to the Right and Left alike. A practice in lifelong search of its theory, Social Democracy was the outcome of an insight vouchsafed to a generation of European socialists early in the twentieth century: that radical social revolution in the heartlands of modern Europe—as prophesied and planned by the socialist visionaries of the nineteenth century—lay in the past, not the future. As a solution to the injustice and inefficiency of industrial capitalism, the nineteenth-century paradigm of violent urban upheaval was not only undesirable and unlikely to meet its goals; it was also redundant. Genuine improvements in the condition of all classes could be obtained in incremental and peaceful ways.

It did not follow from this that the fundamental nineteenth-century socialist tenets were discarded. The overwhelming majority of mid-twentieth-century European Social Democrats, even if they kept their distance from Marx and his avowed heirs, maintained as an article of faith that capitalism was inherently dysfunctional and that socialism was both morally *and economically* superior. Where they differed from Communists was in their unwillingness to commit to the inevitability of capitalism's imminent demise or to the wisdom of hastening that demise by their own political actions. Their task, as they had come to understand it in the course of decades of Depression, division and dictatorship, was to use the resources of the state to eliminate the social pathologies attendant on capitalist forms of production and the unrestricted workings of a market economy: to build not economic utopias but good societies.

The politics of social democracy were not always seductive to impatient young people, as later events were to show. But they were intuitively appealing to men and women who had lived through the terrible decades since 1914, and in certain parts of Western Europe social democracy by the mid-Sixties was no longer so much a politics as a way of life. Nowhere was this more evident than in Scandinavia. Between 1945 and 1964 the Danish Social Democratic Party's share of the vote in national elections rose from 33 percent to 42 percent; in the same years the Norwegian Labour Party won between 43 and 48 percent; as for the Swedish Social Democrats, their share of the post-war vote never fell below 45 percent. In the elections of 1968 it even exceeded 50 percent.

What was remarkable about these voting figures was not the numbers themselves—the Austrian Socialist Party did almost as well on occasion and in the British general elections of 1951 Clement Attlee's Labour Party had won 48.8 percent of the vote (though the Conservatives, with a smaller overall vote, got more parliamentary seats). It was their consistency. Year in, year out, Scandinavian Social Democratic parties secured over two-fifths of their countries' votes, and the result was decades of unbroken control of government, occasionally at the head of a coalition of small and compliant junior partners but usually alone. Between 1945 and 1968, eight out of ten Danish governments were led by Social Democrats; in the same years there were five Norwegian governments, three of them Social Democratic, and four Swedish governments, all Social Democratic. There was consistency in personnel, too: Norway's Einar Gerhardsen led two Social Democratic governments for a total of fourteen years; in Sweden, Tage Erlander ruled both his party and his country for twenty-three years, from 1946–1969.[2]

Scandinavian societies inherited certain advantages. Small and socially homogenous, with no overseas colonies or imperial ambitions, they had been constitutional states for many years. The Danish constitution of 1849 had introduced limited parliamentary government but extensive press and religious freedom. The Swedish (and at the time Norwegian) constitution of 1809 established modern political institutions, including proportional representation and the exemplary system of the *ombudsman*—the latter adopted throughout Scandinavia in later years—and provided the stable framework within which the party political system could develop. It would remain in force until 1975.

But Scandinavia was historically poor—a region of forests, farms, fisheries and a handful of primary industries, most of them in Sweden. Labour relations in Sweden and Norway especially were chronically troubled by conflict—the strike rate in both countries was among the highest in the world during the first decades of the twentieth century. During the Depression of the 1930s unemployment in the region was chronic. In 1932–33 one third of the Swedish labour force was out of work; in Norway and Denmark 40 percent of the adult workforce had no jobs—figures comparable to the worst years of joblessness in Britain, Weimar Germany or the industrial states of the US. In Sweden the crisis led to violent confrontations, notably at Ådalen in 1931 where a strike at a paper-mill was suppressed by the army (memorably recalled by Swedish director Bo Widerberg in a 1969 film, *Ådalen 31*).

If Scandinavia—and Sweden in particular—did not follow the path of other economically depressed societies on the European margin between the wars, much of the credit belongs to the Social Democrats. After World War One the Scandinavian socialist parties largely abandoned the radical dogma and revolutionary ambitions they had shared with the German and other Socialist movements of the Second International; and in the course of the 1930s they moved towards a historic compromise between capital and labour. At Saltsjöbaden in 1938, representatives of Swedish employers and labour signed a Pact that was to form the basis of the country's future social relations—a foretaste of the neo-corporatist social partnerships

---

[2]Contrast Italy, which had 13 different governments and 11 different prime ministers in the same period—or France, which had 23 governments and 17 prime ministers between 1945 and 1968. Long-serving party leaders were a Swedish speciality: Erlander's predecessor as Chairman of the Swedish Social Democratic Party, Per Albin Hansson, had held the post from 1926–1946.

formed in Germany and Austria after 1945, but which were virtually unknown before the war, except under Fascist auspices.[3]

Scandinavian Social Democrats were open to such compromises because they had no illusions about the putative 'proletarian' constituency on whom other socialist parties relied for their core support. Had they depended upon urban working-class votes alone, or even working-class votes allied to middle-class reformers, the Socialist parties of Scandinavia would forever have remained in the minority. Their political prospects rested upon extending their appeal to the overwhelmingly rural populations of the region. And thus, unlike almost every other socialist or social-democratic party of Europe, Scandinavian social democrats were not scarred by the instinctive antipathy to the countryside that characterized much of the European Left, from Marx's remarks about the 'idiocy of rural life' to Lenin's distaste for 'kulaks'.

The embittered and destitute peasants of inter-war central and southern Europe formed a ready constituency for Nazis, Fascists or single-issue Agrarian populists. But the equally troubled farmers, loggers, crofters and fisherman of Europe's far north turned in growing numbers to the Social Democrats, who actively supported agrarian cooperatives—especially important in Denmark, where commercial farming was widespread and efficient, but very small-scale—and thereby blurred the longstanding socialist distinctions between private production and collectivist goals, 'backward' country and 'modern' town that were so electorally disastrous in other countries.

This alliance of labour and farming—facilitated by the unusual independence of Scandinavian peasants, conjoined in fervently Protestant communities unconstrained by traditional rural subservience to priest or landlord—was to form the long-term platform on which Europe's most successful social democracies were built. 'Red-green' coalitions (at first between Agrarian and Social Democratic parties, later within the latter alone) were unthinkable everywhere else; in Scandinavia they became the norm. The Social Democratic parties were the vehicle through which traditional rural society and industrial labour together entered the urban age: in that sense Social Democracy in Scandinavia was not just one politics among many, it was the very form of modernity itself.

The Scandinavian welfare states that evolved after 1945 had their origins, then, in the two social pacts of the 1930s: between employees and employers, and between labour and farming. The social services and other public provisions that came to

---

[3]The Saltsjöbaden Pact resembled in certain respects the *Arbeitsfrieden* (Labour Peace) reached in Switzerland the previous year, in which employers and workers agreed to establish a system of non-confrontational collective bargaining that was to prove an enduring cornerstone of the country's future stability and prosperity. However, whereas the Swiss *Arbeitsfrieden* was intended to keep government *out* of economic bargaining, the Saltsjöbaden Pact committed the government to working in harmony with owners and employees for the common interest.

characterize the Scandinavian 'model' reflected these origins, emphasizing universality and equality—universal social rights, equalized incomes, flat-rate benefits paid from steeply progressive taxation. They thus stood in marked contrast to the typical continental European version in which the state transferred or returned income to families and individuals, enabling them to pay in cash for what were, in essence, subsidized private services (insurance and medicine in particular). But except for education, which was already universal and comprehensive before 1914, the Scandinavian system of welfare was not conceived and implemented all at once. It came about incrementally. Health care in particular lagged behind: in Denmark, universal health coverage was achieved only in 1971, twenty-three years after Aneurin Bevan's National Health Service was inaugurated across the North Sea in the United Kingdom.

Moreover, what looked from the outside like a single Nordic system was in reality quite varied by country. Denmark was the least 'Scandinavian'. Not only was it critically dependent upon an overseas market for farm produce (dairy and pork products especially) and thus more sensitive to policies and political developments elsewhere in Europe; but its skilled work force was much more divided by traditional craft-based loyalties and organisations. In this respect it resembled Britain more than, say, Norway; indeed, Denmark's Social Democrats were constrained on more than one occasion in the Sixties to emulate British governments and seek to impose price and wage controls on an unstable labour market. By British standards the policy was a success; but by more demanding Scandinavian measures, Danish social relations and Denmark's economic performance were always somewhat troubled.

Norway was the smallest and most homogenous of all the Nordic societies (save Iceland). It had also suffered most from the war. Moreover, even before oil was discovered off the coast, Norway's situation was distinctive. A front-line state in the Cold War and therefore committed to much greater defense outlays than tiny Denmark or neutral Sweden, it was also the most elongated of the northern countries, its tiny population of less than four million people strung along a 1,752 kilometre coastline, the longest in Europe. Many of the farther-flung towns and villages were and are utterly dependent on fishing for their livelihood. Social Democratic or not, the government of Oslo was bound to apply the resources of the state to social and communal objectives: subsidies flowing from centre to periphery (for transport, communications, education and the supply of professionals and services, notably to the third of the country lying north of the Arctic Circle) were the lifeblood of the Norwegian nation state.

Sweden, too, was distinctive—though *its* peculiarities came over time to be thought of as the Scandinavian norm. With a population almost the size of Norway and Denmark combined (greater Stockholm alone was home to the equivalent of 45 percent of Norway's inhabitants), Sweden was by far the richest and most industrialized of the Scandinavian societies. By 1973 its output of iron ore was comparable to that of France, Britain and West Germany put together and was almost half that of the USA. In paper production, wood pulp and shipping it was a world leader. Where Norwegian social democracy consisted for many years in marshalling, rationing and distributing scarce resources in a poor society, Sweden was by the 1960s already one of the world's wealthiest countries. Social democracy there was about allocating and equalizing wealth and services for the common good.

Throughout Scandinavia, but in Sweden especially, the private ownership and exploitation of the means of production were never put into question. Unlike the British Labour movement, whose core doctrine and program ever since 1918 rested on an ineradicable faith in the virtues of state ownership, Swedish Social Democrats were content to leave capital and initiative in private hands. The example of the UK's British Motor Corporation, a helpless guinea pig for government experiments in centralized resource allocation, was never followed in Sweden. Volvo, Saab and other private businesses were left free to flourish or fail.

Indeed, industrial capital in 'socialist' Sweden was concentrated into fewer private hands than anywhere else in western Europe. The government never interfered either with private wealth accumulation or with the marketplace for goods and capital. Even in Norway, after fifteen years of Social Democratic government, the directly state-owned or state-run sector of the economy was actually smaller than that of Christian Democratic West Germany. But in both countries, as in Denmark and Finland, what the state *did* do was ruthlessly and progressively tax and redistribute private profits for public ends.

To many foreign observers and most Scandinavians the results appeared to speak for themselves. By 1970 Sweden (along with Finland) was one of the world's four leading economies, measured by purchasing power per head of the population (the other two were the USA and Switzerland). Scandinavians lived longer, healthier lives than most other people in the world (something that would have amazed the isolated, impoverished Nordic peasantry of three generations before). The provision of educational, welfare, medical, insurance, retirement and leisure services and facilities was unequalled (not least in the US and indeed Switzerland), as were the economic and physical security in which the citizens of Nordic Europe pursued their contented lives. By the mid-1960s, Europe's 'frozen north' had acquired near-mythic status: the Scandinavian Social Democratic model might not be replicated readily elsewhere, but it was universally admired and widely envied.

Anyone familiar with Nordic culture, from Ibsen and Munch through Ingmar Bergman, will recognise another side of Scandinavian life: its self-interrogating, incipiently melancholic quality—popularly understood in these years as a propensity to depression, alcoholism and high suicide rates. In the 1960s and at times since, it pleased conservative critics of Scandinavian politics to blame these shortcomings on the moral paralysis induced by too much economic security and centralised direction. And then there was the concurrent propensity of Scandinavians to take off their clothes in public (and on film) and—so it was widely rumoured—

make love with perfect strangers: further evidence, to some observers, of the psychic damage wrought by an over-mighty state that provides everything and forbids nothing.[4]

If this was the worst that could be said against the Scandinavian 'model' then the Social Democrats of Sweden and elsewhere could be forgiven for laughing (or, as it were, complaining) all the way to the bank. But the critics had a point: there was indeed a darker side to the all-embracing state. Early-twentieth-century confidence in the capacity of the state to make a better society had taken many forms: Scandinavian Social Democracy—like the Fabian reformism of Britain's welfare state—was born of a widespread fascination with social engineering of all kinds. And just a little beyond the use of the state to adjust incomes, expenditures, employment and information there lurked the temptation to tinker with individuals themselves.

Eugenics—the 'science' of racial improvement—was more than an Edwardian-era fad, like vegetarianism or rambling (though it often appealed to the same constituencies). Taken up by thinkers of all political shades, it dovetailed especially well with the ambitions of well-meaning social reformers. If one's social goal was to improve the human condition wholesale, why pass up the opportunities afforded by modern science to add retail amelioration along the way? Why should the prevention or abolition of imperfections in the human condition not extend to the prevention (or abolition) of imperfect human beings? In the early decades of the twentieth century the appeal of scientifically manipulated social or genetic planning was widespread and thoroughly respectable; it was only thanks to the Nazis, whose 'hygienic' ambitions began with ersatz anthropometrics and ended in the gas chamber, that it was comprehensively discredited in post-war Europe. Or so it was widely supposed.

But, as it emerged many years later, Scandinavian authorities at least had not abandoned an interest in the theory—and practice—of 'racial hygiene'. Between 1934 and 1976 sterilization programmes were pursued in Norway, Sweden and Denmark, in each case under the auspices and with the knowledge of Social Democratic governments. In these years some 6,000 Danes, 40,000 Norwegians and 60,000 Swedes (90 percent of them women) were sterilized for 'hygienic' purposes: 'to improve the population'. The intellectual driving force behind these programmes—the Institute of Racial Biology at the University of Uppsala in Sweden—had been set up in 1921, at the peak of the fashion for the subject. It was not dismantled until fifty-five years later.

What, if anything, this sad story tells us about Social Democracy is unclear—

---

[4]The suicide rate in western Europe by 1973 was indeed highest in the most developed and prosperous countries: Denmark, Austria, Finland and West Germany. It was lowest at the poorer fringes: per head of population, the Danish suicide rate was six times that of Italy, fourteen times that of Ireland. What this suggests about the depressant effect of prosperity, climate, latitude, diet, religion, family structures or the welfare state was obscure to contemporaries and remains unclear today.

distinctly *un*socialist and *un*democratic societies and governments have done more and worse. The legitimacy of the state in post-war Scandinavia, the authority and initiative accorded it by a mostly unquestioning citizenry, left government free to act in what it took to be the common interest with remarkably little oversight. It does not seem ever to have occurred to an *ombudsman* to investigate abuse of those who stood outside the rights-bearing community of tax-paying citizens. The line separating progressive taxation and paternity-leave from forcible interference in the reproductive capacities of 'defective' citizens seems not to have been altogether clear to some post-war governments in Social Democratic Scandinavia. If nothing else this suggests that the moral lessons of World War Two were not as clear as was once supposed—precisely (and not perhaps coincidentally) in countries like Sweden whose collective conscience was widely presumed clear.

Outside of Scandinavia, the closest approximation to the Social Democratic ideal was achieved in another small, neutral country on the edge of Western Europe: Austria. Indeed, the superficial similarities were such that observers took to referring to the 'Austro-Scandinavian model'. In Austria as in Sweden or Norway, an overwhelmingly rural, historically poor country had been transformed, as we have seen, into a prosperous, stable, politically tranquil oasis of state-furnished well-being. In Austria, too, a *de facto* pact had been agreed, in this case between the Socialists and the conservative People's Party, to avoid any return to the open conflicts of the inter-war decades. But there the similarities ended.

Austria was indeed 'social' (and had, after Finland, the largest nationalized sector of any Western European democracy), but it was not particularly Social Democratic. It was only in 1970 that the country got its first post-war Socialist head of government, when Bruno Kreisky became Chancellor. Although Austria over time instituted many of the social services and public policies associated with Scandinavian Social Democratic society—child care, generous unemployment insurance and public pensions, family support, universal medical and educational provision, exemplary state-subsidized transportation—what distinguished Austria from Sweden, for example, was the near-universal allocation of employment, influence, favours and funds according to *political* affiliation. This appropriation of the Austrian state and its resources to stabilize the market in political preferences had less to do with social ideals than with the memory of past traumas. In the wake of their inter-war experience, Austria's socialists were more interested in stabilizing their country's fragile democracy than in revolutionizing its social policies.[5]

Like the rest of Austrian society, the country's Social Democrats proved remarkably adept at putting their past behind them. Social Democratic parties else-

---

[5]Ironically, it was the Swedish Social Democrats who for a long time showed more interest in Vienna's early-twentieth-century 'Austro-Marxist' theorists Otto Bauer and Rudolf Hilferding. Their Austrian successors, by contrast, were typically happy to put all that behind them—save for the occasional echo, as in the Austrian Socialist Party's 1958 program, where it was opaquely asserted that 'democratic socialism occupies a position between capitalism and dictatorship'...

where took somewhat longer to abandon a certain nostalgia for radical transformation. In West Germany the SPD waited until 1959 and its Congress at Bad Godesberg to recast its goals and purposes. The new Party Program adopted there baldly stated that 'Democratic socialism, which in Europe is rooted in Christian ethics, in humanism, and in classical philosophy, has no intention of proclaiming absolute truths.' The state, it was asserted, should 'restrict itself mainly to indirect methods of influencing the economy'. The free market in goods and employment was vital: 'The totalitarian directed economy destroys freedom'.[6]

This belated acknowledgement of the obvious contrasts with the decision of Belgium's Labour Party (the *Parti Ouvrier Belge*) the following year to re-confirm the Party's founding charter of 1894, with its demand for the collectivisation of the means of production; and the refusal of Britain's Labour Party, also in 1960, to follow the recommendation of its reformist leader Hugh Gaitskell and delete the identical commitment as enshrined in Clause IV of the Party's 1918 programme. Part of the explanation for this contrast in behaviour lay in recent experience: the memory of destructive struggles and the close proximity of the totalitarian threat, whether in the immediate past or just across a border, helped focus the attention of German and Austrian Social Democrats—like Italian Communists—on the virtues of compromise.

Britain's Labour Party had no such nightmares to exorcise. It was also, like its Belgian (and Dutch) counterparts in this respect, from its origins a *labour* movement rather than a *socialist* party, motivated above all by the concerns (and cash) of its trade union affiliates. It was thus less ideological—but more blinkered. If asked, Labour Party spokesmen would readily accede to the general objectives of continental European Social Democrats; but their own interests were much more practical and parochial. Precisely *because* of the built-in stability of British (or at least English) political culture, and thanks to its long-established—albeit shrinking—working-class base, the Labour Party showed little interest in the innovative settlements that had shaped the Scandinavian and German-speaking welfare states.

Instead, the British compromise was characterized by demand-manipulating fiscal policy and costly universal social provisions, supported by sharply progressive taxation and a large nationalized sector, and set against a background of unstable and historically adversarial industrial relations. Except for the Labourite emphasis on the intrinsic virtues of nationalization, these ad hoc arrangements were largely supported by the mainstream of the Conservative and Liberal Parties. If there was any sense in which British politics, too, were shaped by past shocks it came in the widespread, cross-party acknowledgement that a return to mass unemployment must be avoided at almost any cost.

---

[6]For this translation, see Bark & Gress, *From Shadow to Substance. A History of West Germany*, Volume 1 (1992), Chapter 16.

Even after the new Labour leader Harold Wilson took his party back into power in 1964 after thirteen years of opposition, and spoke enthusiastically of the 'white hot technological revolution' of the age, very little changed. Wilson's narrow margin of victory in the election of 1964 (a parliamentary majority of four) hardly disposed him to take political risks, and even though Labour did better in elections called two years later there was to be no radical departure in economic or social policy. Wilson himself was heir to the Attlee-Beveridge tradition of Fabian theory and Keynesian practice and showed little interest in economic (or political) innovation. Like most British politicians of every stripe he was deeply conventional and pragmatic, with a proudly myopic view of public affairs: as he once put it, 'a week is a long time in politics.'

Nevertheless, there *was* a certain distinctiveness about the British Social Democratic state, beyond the insular refusal of all parties concerned to describe it thus. What the British Left (and, at the time, much of the Centre and Centre-Right of the political spectrum) were taken up with above all was the goal of *fairness*. It was the manifest injustice, the unfairness of life before the war that drove both the Beveridge reforms and the overwhelming vote for Labour in 1945. It was their promise that they could liberalize the economy while maintaining a *fair* distribution of rewards and services that brought the Conservatives to power in 1951 and kept them there for so long. The British accepted progressive taxation and welcomed universal health provision not because these were presented as 'socialist', but because they were more intuitively just.

In the same way, the curiously regressive workings of the British flat-rate systems of benefits and services—which disproportionately favoured the better-heeled professional middle class—were broadly acceptable because they were egalitarian, if only in appearance. And the most important innovation of the Labour governments of the nineteen sixties—the introduction of un-streamed comprehensive secondary education and the abolition of entrance examinations to selective grammar schools, a longstanding Labour commitment judiciously ignored by Attlee after 1945—was welcomed less on its intrinsic merits than because it was deemed 'anti-elitist' and thus 'fair'. That is why the educational reform was even pursued by Conservative governments after Wilson's departure in 1970, despite warnings from all sides of the perverse consequences such changes might have.[7]

The Labour Party's dependence on trade union backing led it to postpone the sorts of industrial reforms that many (including some of its own leaders) knew to

---

[7]The destruction of the selective state schools of England merely drove more of the middle class to the private sector, thus improving the prospects and profits of the fee-charging 'public schools' that Labour's radicals so despised. Meanwhile selection continued, but by income rather than merit: parents who could afford it bought a home in a 'good' school district, leaving the children of the poor at the mercy of the weakest schools and the worst teachers, and with much reduced prospect of upward educational mobility. The 'comprehensivisation' of British secondary education was the most socially retrograde piece of legislation in post-war Britain.

be long overdue. British industrial relations remained mired in adversarial shop-floor confrontations and craft-based piece-rate and wage disputes of a kind virtually unknown in Scandinavia, Germany, Austria or the Netherlands. Labour ministers made half-hearted attempts to break clear of this encumbering inheritance, but without much success; and partly for this reason the achievements of continental social democracy were never quite emulated in Britain.

Moreover, the universal features of Britain's system of welfare, introduced two or even three decades before those of France, or Italy, for example, hid from view the very limited practical achievements of the British state even in the field of material equality: as late as 1967, 10 percent of the UK population still possessed 80 percent of all personal wealth. The net effect of the re-distributive policies of the first three post-war decades was to shift income and assets from the top 10 percent to the next 40 percent; the bottom 50 percent gained very little, for all the general improvement in security and welfare.

Any overall audit of the era of the welfare state in Western Europe will inevitably be side-shadowed by our knowledge of the problems it would face in later decades. Thus today it is easy to see that initiatives like the West German Social Security Reform Act of 1957, which guaranteed workers a pension keyed to their wage at the point of retirement and linked to a cost-of-living index, would prove an intolerable budgetary burden in changed demographic and economic circumstances. And with hindsight it is clear that radical income-levelling in Social Democratic Sweden reduced private savings and thus inhibited future investment. Even at the time it was obvious that government transfers and flat-rate social payments benefited those who knew how to take full advantage of them: notably the educated middle class, who would fight to hold on to what amounted to a new set of privileges.

But the achievements of Europe's 'nanny states' were real all the same, whether introduced by Social Democrats, paternalist Catholics, or prudentially disposed conservatives and liberals. Beginning with core programmes of social and economic protection, the welfare states moved on to systems of entitlement, benefits, social justice and income redistribution—and managed this substantial transformation at almost no political cost. Even the creation of a self-interested class of welfare bureaucrats and white-collar beneficiaries was not without its virtues: like the farmers, the much-maligned 'lower middle class' now had a vested interest in the institutions and values of the democratic state. This was good for Social Democrats and Christian Democrats alike, as such parties duly noted. But it was also bad for Fascists and Communists, which mattered rather more.

These changes reflected the demographic transformations already noted, but also unprecedented levels of personal security and a new intensity of educational and social mobility. As west Europeans were now less likely to remain in the place, the occupation, the income bracket and the social class into which they had been born, so they were less disposed to identify automatically with the political movements and social affiliations of their parents' world. The generation of the 1930s was content to find economic security and turn its back on political mobilization and its attendant risks; their children, the much larger generation of the 1960s, had only ever known peace, political stability and the welfare state. They took these things for granted.

The rise in the influence of the state upon the employment and welfare of its citizens was accompanied by a steady reduction in its authority over their morals and opinions. At the time this was not seen as a paradox. Liberal and Social Democratic advocates for the European welfare state saw no reason in principle why government should not pay close attention to the economic or medical welfare of the population, guaranteeing citizens' well-being from cradle to grave, while keeping its nose firmly out of their views and practices on strictly personal matters like religion and sex, or artistic taste and judgement. The Christian Democrats of Germany or Italy, for whom the state still had a legitimate interest in the manners and *mores* of its subjects, could not so readily make this distinction. But they too faced growing pressure to adapt.

Until the early 1960s, public authorities throughout Western Europe (with the partial exception of Scandinavia) had exercised firm and mostly repressive control over the private affairs and opinions of the citizenry. Homosexual intercourse was illegal almost everywhere, and punishable by long prison terms. In many countries it could not even be depicted in art. Abortion was illegal in most countries. Even contraception was technically against the law in some Catholic states, albeit often condoned in practice. Divorce was everywhere difficult, in some places impossible. In many parts of Western Europe (Scandinavia once again being a partial exception) government agencies still enforced censorship of theatre, cinema and literature, and radio and television were public monopolies almost everywhere, operating as we have seen under strict rules as to content and with very little tolerance for dissent or 'disrespect'. Even in the UK, where commercial television was introduced in 1955, it too was strictly regulated and carried a publicly mandated obligation to provide 'enlightenment and information' as well as entertainment and advertisements.

Censorship, like taxation, was driven forward by war. In Britain and France some of the most stringent constraints on behaviour and the expression of opinion had been introduced during the First or Second World Wars and never repealed. Elsewhere—in Italy, West Germany and some of the countries they had occupied—post-war regulations were a legacy of Fascist laws that democratic legislators had preferred to maintain in place. Relatively few of the most repressive 'moral' powers still in force by 1960 dated back beyond the nineteenth century (the most obviously anachronistic being perhaps the Office of the Lord Chamberlain in Britain, responsible for pre-censorship of the theatre, where the posts of Examiner and Deputy Examiner of Plays were created early in 1738). The outstanding exception to this rule, of course, was the Catholic Church.

Ever since the First Vatican Council of 1870, held under the influence and auspices of the avowedly reactionary Pope Pius IX, the Catholic Church had taken an all-embracing and decidedly dogmatic view of its responsibilities as moral guardian of its flock. Precisely because it was being steadily squeezed out of the realm of political power by the modern state, the Vatican made uncompromising demands upon its followers in other ways. Indeed, the long and—in retrospect— controversial papacy of Eugenio Pacelli, Pope Pius XII (1939–1958) not only maintained its spiritual claims, but actually brought the official Church back into politics.

Avowedly on the side of political reaction, from the Vatican's close ties to Mussolini and ambivalent response to Nazism to its enthusiasm for Catholic dictators in Spain and Portugal, Pacelli's papacy also took an uncompromising line in the domestic politics of the democracies. Catholics in Italy especially were left in no doubt as to the spiritual impropriety, and worse, of voting against the Christian Democrats; but even in relatively liberal Belgium or Holland the local Catholic hierarchy was under strict instructions to turn out the Catholic vote for the Catholic parties and only them. Not until 1967, nine years after the death of Pius XII, did a Dutch bishop dare suggest in public that Dutch Catholics might vote for a non-Catholic party without risking excommunication.

In such circumstances, it is hardly surprising that the post-war Catholic hierarchy also took an uncompromising line in questions having to do with the family, or moral behavior or inappropriate books and films. But younger Catholic laymen, and a new generation of priests, were uncomfortably aware that by the end of the 1950s the Vatican's authoritarian rigidity in public and private matters alike was both anachronistic and imprudent. Back in 1900, most marriages in Italy had lasted around twenty years, before being dissolved by the death of a spouse. By the end of the third quarter of the century marriages lasted in excess of thirty-five years, and demand for the right to divorce was steadily growing.

Meanwhile, the post-war baby boom had undercut the demographic case against contraception, isolating the ecclesiastical authorities in their uncompromising opposition. Attendance at mass was down everywhere in western Europe. Whatever the reasons—the geographical and social mobility of hitherto acquiescent villagers, the political emancipation of women, the declining importance of Catholic charities and parochial schools in the age of the welfare state—the problem was real and, as it seemed to the more perceptive Catholic leaders, could not be addressed by appeals to tradition and authority, or suppressed by invoking anti-Communism in the style of the late 1940s.

Upon Pacelli's death, his successor Pope John XXIII called a new Vatican Council, to attend to these difficulties and bring up to date the attitudes and practices of the Church. Vatican II, as it became known, convened on October 11th 1962. In the course of its work over the next few years it transformed not only the liturgy and language of Catholic Christianity (quite literally—Latin was no longer to be used in daily Church practice, to the uncomprehending fury of a traditionalist minority) but also, and more significantly, the response of the Church to the dilemmas of modern life. The pronouncements of the Second Vatican Council made it clear that the Church was no longer frightened by change and challenge, was not an opponent of liberal democracy, mixed economies, modern science, rational thought and even secular politics. The first—very tentative—steps were taken towards reconciliation with other Christian denominations and there was some (not much) acknowledgement of the Church's responsibility to discourage anti-Semitism by re-casting its longstanding account of Jewish responsibility for the death of Jesus. Above all, the Catholic Church could no longer be counted upon to support authoritarian regimes—quite the contrary: in Asia, Africa and especially Latin America, it was at least as likely to be on the side of their opponents.

These changes were not universally welcomed even among the Catholic Church's own reformers—one delegate to Vatican II, a young priest from Crakow, would later rise to the papacy and see it as his task to restore the full weight of moral authority and influence of an uncompromising Catholic hierarchy. Nor did Vatican II achieve a reversal of the steady fall in religious practice among European Catholics: even in Italy, attendance at mass fell from 69 percent of all Catholics in 1956 to 48 percent twelve years later. But since the decline of religion in Europe has by no means been confined to the Catholic faith, this was probably beyond their powers. What Vatican II did achieve—or at least facilitate and authorize—was the final divorce between politics and religion in continental Europe.

After the death of Pius XII, no pope and almost no bishop again presumed to threaten Catholics with serious consequences should they fail to vote the correct way; and the once-close link between Church hierarchy and Catholic or Christian Democratic parties in the Netherlands, Belgium, West Germany, Austria and Italy was prised open.[8] Even in Franco's Spain, where the local Catholic hierarchy had enjoyed unusual privileges and powers, Vatican II wrought dramatic changes. Until the mid-sixties the Spanish leader forbade all outward manifestations of non-Catholic religious belief or practice. But in 1966 he felt constrained to pass a law allowing other Christian churches to subsist, though still privileging Catholicism, and within four years full freedom of (Christian) worship was authorized. By lobbying successfully for this belated 'disestablishment' of the Catholic Church in Spain and thus putting daylight between the Church and the regime during Franco's lifetime, the Vatican was to spare the Spanish Church at least some of the consequences of its long and troubling association with the 'ancien régime'.

This *rupture culturelle*, as it became known in Belgium and elsewhere, between religion and politics and between the Catholic Church and its recent past, played a crucial role in the making of 'the sixties'. There were, of course, limits to the Vat-

---

[8] With the demise of clerical politics, political anti-clericalism lost its raison d'être—ending a cycle of quarrels and obsessions that had endured for nearly two centuries.

ican's reforming mood—for many of its participants the strategic impulse behind Vatican II was not to embrace radical change, but to head it off. When the rights to abortion and the liberalization of divorce were put to the vote a few years later, in predominantly Catholic countries like Italy, France or West Germany, the ecclesiastical authorities vigorously if unsuccessfully opposed them. But even on these sensitive issues the Church did not go to the wall, and its opposition no longer risked fragmenting the community. In a society well on the way to being 'post-religious', the Church accepted its reduced place and made the best of it.[9]

In non-Catholic societies—which meant Scandinavia, the UK, parts of the Netherlands and a minority of German-speaking western Europe—the liberation of the citizen from traditional moral authority was necessarily more diffuse, but even more dramatic when it came. The transition was most striking in Britain. Until the end of the 1950s, British citizens were still forbidden to gamble; to read or to see anything that their betters judged 'obscene' or politically sensitive; to advocate (much less engage in) homosexual acts; to practice abortions on themselves or others; or to get divorced without great difficulty and public humiliation. And if they committed murder or certain other major offences, they could be hanged.

Then, beginning in 1959, the skein of convention began to unravel. Following the Obscene Publications Act of that year, an uncensored work of adult literature could be shielded from charges of 'obscenity' if it was deemed to be 'in the interests of science, literature, art or learning'. Henceforward, publishers and authors could defend themselves in court by invoking the worth of the work as a whole, and could invoke 'expert' opinion in their defense. In October 1960 came the notorious test case of *Lady Chatterley's Lover*, in which Penguin Books were prosecuted for publishing in Britain the first unexpurgated edition of D. H. Lawrence's otherwise unremarkable novel. The *Chatterley* case was of particular interest to the British not just because of the hitherto illicit passages to which they were now exposed, but also thanks to the inter-class eroticism on which its notoriety rested. Upon being asked by the prosecuting counsel whether this was a novel he would let his 'wife or maidservant' (*sic*) read, one witness replied that this would not trouble him in the least: but he would never let it into the hands of his gamekeeper.

Penguin Books were acquitted of obscenity, having called thirty-five expert witnesses in their defense, and the decline of the moral authority of the British Establishment can be dated from that acquittal. In the same year gambling was legalized in the United Kingdom. Four years later the death penalty was abolished by the incoming Labour Government, and under the leadership of Roy Jenkins, a remarkable reforming Home Secretary, Labour oversaw the introduction of state-financed family planning clinics, reform of the law on homosexuality and the legalization of abortion in 1967, and the abolition of theatre censorship in the following year. In 1969

---

[9]In Ireland, however, the authority of the Church and its involvement in daily politics was sustained rather longer—well into the nineties.

there followed the Divorce Act, which did not so much precipitate a dramatic transformation in the institution of marriage as reveal its extent: whereas in the last year before World War Two there had been just one divorce for every fifty-eight marriages in England and Wales, forty years later the ratio would approach one in three.

The liberal and liberalizing reforms of 1960s Britain were emulated across northwest Europe, albeit with varying delays. The Social Democratic-led coalition governments of West Germany, under Willy Brandt, introduced similar changes there in the course of the later Sixties and Seventies, constrained in their case less by law or precedent than by the reluctance of their coalition partners—notably the economically liberal but socially conservative Free Democrats. In France, abolition of the death penalty had to await the arrival in power of François Mitterrand's Socialists in 1981, but there—as in Italy—the laws on abortion and divorce were rewritten in the course of the early Seventies. In general, with the exception of Britain and Scandinavia, the liberated 'Sixties' did not actually arrive in Europe until the Seventies. Once the legal changes were in place, however, the social consequences flowed rapidly enough: the crude divorce rate in Belgium, France and the Netherlands tripled between 1970 and 1985.

The diminishing standing of public authorities in matters of morality and personal relationships in no way supposed a decline in the role of the state in the cultural affairs of the nation. Quite the contrary. The broad Western European consensus of the age held that only the state had the resources to service the cultural needs of its citizens: left to themselves, individuals and communities would lack both means and initiative. It was the responsibility of a well-run public authority to deliver cultural nourishment no less than food, lodging and employment. In such matters Social and Christian Democrats thought alike, and both were heir to the great Victorian-era improvers, though with far greater resources to hand. The aesthetic revolt of the Sixties changed little in this respect: the new ('counter-') culture demanded and obtained the same funding as the old.

The 1950s and 1960s were the great age of the cultural subsidy. Back in 1947 the British Labour government added sixpence to local taxes to pay for local artistic initiatives—theatres, philharmonic societies, regional opera and the like: a prelude to the Arts Council of the 1960s, which spread public largesse across an unprecedented range of local and national festivals and institutions, as well as arts education. The financially strapped French Fourth Republic was less forthcoming, except to traditional, prestige venues for high culture—museums, the Paris Opéra, the Comédie Française—and the state-monopolized radio and television stations. But after De Gaulle returned to power and installed André Malraux as his Minister for Culture, the situation there was transformed.

The French state had long played the part of *mécène*. But Malraux conceived of his role in a wholly new way. Traditionally, the power and purse of the royal Court and its republican successors had been deployed to bring artists and art to Paris (or Versailles), sucking the rest of the country dry. Now the government would spend money to place performers and performances in the provinces. Museums, galleries, festivals and theatres began to sprout across provincial France. The best known of these, the Avignon summer festival under the direction of Jean Vilar, began in 1947; but it took flight in the course of the fifties and sixties when Vilar's productions played a major part in the transformation and renewal of French theatre. Many of France's best known actors—Jeanne Moreau, Maria Casarès, Gérard Philipe—worked in Avignon. It was there, as well as in such unlikely venues as Saint-Étienne, Toulouse, Rennes or Colmar, that the French artistic renaissance began.

Malraux's encouragement of provincial cultural life depended of course on centralized initiative. Even Vilar's own project was typically Parisian in its iconoclastic objectives: the point was not to bring culture to the regions but to break with the conventions of mainstream theatre—'to bring life back into theatre, into collective art . . . to help it breath free again, released from cellars and drawing rooms: to reconcile architecture and dramatic poetry'—something that could be more easily accomplished away from Paris, but with central government funds and ministerial backing. In a genuinely decentralized country like the Federal Republic of Germany, on the other hand, culture and the arts were a direct outgrowth of local policy and regional self-interest.

In Germany, as elsewhere in Western Europe, public spending on the arts expanded quite dramatically in the post-war decades. But because cultural and educational matters in West Germany fell under the authority of the *Länder*, there was considerable duplication of effort. Every *Land* and most significant towns and cities had an opera company, orchestra and concert halls, a dance company, subsidized theatre and arts groups. By one estimate there were 225 local theatres in West Germany by the time of reunification, their budget subsidized by an amount varying from 50–70 percent, either by *Land* or by city. As in France, this system had its roots in the past—in Germany's case the pre-modern micro-principalities, duchies and ecclesiastical fiefs, many of which had maintained full-time court musicians and artists, and regularly commissioned new works.

The benefits were considerable. Despite the cultural self-doubt of post-Nazi West Germany, the country's generously financed cultural institutions became a Mecca for artists of all kinds. The Stuttgart Ballet, the Berlin Symphony Orchestra, the Cologne Opera and dozens of smaller institutions—the Mannheim National Theatre, the Staatstheater of Wiesbaden and so on—offered steady work (as well as unemployment benefits, medical coverage and pensions) to thousands of dancers, musicians, actors, choreographers, theatre technicians and office staff. Many of the dancers and musicians especially came from abroad, the US included. They, no less than the local audiences who paid subsidized rates to watch and hear them perform, benefited hugely from the flourishing European cultural scene.

Just as the 1960s never really happened in many places until the early seventies, so the stereotyped 1950s—staid, stuffy, sterile, stagnant—were largely mythical. In *Look Back in Anger,* John Osborne has Jimmy Porter revile the phoniness of post-war prosperity and self-satisfaction; and there is no doubt that the veneer of polite conformity that was not swept away until the end of the decade was intensely frustrating to many observers and especially the young.[10] But in fact the 1950s saw much original work—a lot of it, in theatre, literature and cinema especially, of more enduring interest than what was to follow. What Western Europe had lost in power and political prestige it was now making up for in the arts. Indeed, the late fifties were something of an Indian summer for the 'high' arts in Europe. The circumstances were unusually propitious: 'European quality' (the scare quotes had yet to acquire the ironic deprecation of later decades) was being underwritten for the first time by large-scale public funding, but was not yet exposed to populist demands for 'accessibility', 'accountability' or 'relevance'.

With the premiere in Paris's Théâtre de Babylone of Samuel Beckett's *En Attendant Godot,* in March 1953, European theatre entered a golden age of modernism. Across the Channel, the English Stage Company at London's Royal Court Theatre adopted Beckett and East Germany's Berthold Brecht, as well as performing works by John Osborne, Harold Pinter and Arnold Wesker, all of whose plays married stylistic minimalism to aesthetic disdain in a technique that was often hard to place on the conventional political spectrum. Even mainstream British theatre became more adventurous. In the late fifties an unparalleled generation of English theatrical knights—Olivier, Gielgud, Richardson, Redgrave, Guinness—was joined by younger performers fresh from the universities (Cambridge for the most part) and a remarkable pool of innovative directors and producers including Peter Brook, Peter Hall and Jonathan Miller.

First proposed in 1946, Britain's National Theatre was formally established in 1962 with Lawrence Olivier as its founding director and the theatre critic Kenneth Tynan as his adviser and assistant, though its permanent home on London's South Bank was not opened until 1976. Together with the Royal Shakespeare Company, the National Theatre—which was to become the leading sponsor and venue for new British drama—was a prime beneficiary of Arts Council munificence. That did not mean, it should be noted, that theatre became a more *popular* form of entertainment. On the contrary: ever since the decline of the music halls, theatre had been the purview of the middling sort—even when the subject matter was ostensibly proletarian. Playwrights might write about working-class life, but it was the middle class that came to watch.

Just as Beckett and his work migrated readily to Britain, so British theatre and its leading figures worked very comfortably abroad; after making his reputation in

---

[10]In a representative outburst, Osborne writes of British royalty as 'the gold filling in a mouthful of decay'.

London productions of Shakespeare (most famously *A Midsummer Night's Dream*), Peter Brook would establish himself permanently in Paris, straddling aesthetic and linguistic frontiers with ease. By the early 1960s it was becoming possible to speak of a 'European' theatre, or at least a theatre that took as its material controversial, contemporary European themes. Rolf Hochhuth's *The Deputy*, first performed in Germany in 1963 and shortly afterwards in Britain, attacked Pope Pius XII for his wartime failure to help the Jews; but in his next work, *Soldiers* (1967), Hochhuth turned on Winston Churchill for the wartime fire-bombing of German cities, and the play was initially banned in the UK.

It was in the 1950s, too, that the European arts were swept by a 'new wave' of writers and film directors whose break with narrative convention and attention to sex, youth, politics and alienation anticipated much of what the generation of the Sixties came to think of as its own achievement. The most influential west European novels of the Fifties—Alberto Moravia's *Il Conformista* (1951), Albert Camus's *La Chute* (The Fall), published in 1956, or Günter Grass's *Die Blechtrommel* (The Tin Drum, 1959)—were all in various ways more original and certainly more courageous than anything that came later. Even Françoise Sagan's *Bonjour Tristesse* (1953) or Colin Wilson's *The Outsider* (1956), narcissistic accounts of post-adolescent self-absorption (coloured in Wilson's case with more than a hint of authoritarian misanthropy), were original in their day. Written when their authors were respectively eighteen and twenty-four years of age, their subject matter—and their success—anticipated the 'youth revolution' of the sixties by a full decade.

Notwithstanding the decline in cinema attendance already noted, it was in the course of the second half of the 1950s and early 1960s that European films acquired a lasting reputation for artistry and originality. Indeed, there was probably a connection, as cinema in Western Europe graduated (or declined) from popular entertainment into high culture. Certainly the renaissance of European cinema was not driven by audience demand—had it been left to viewers, French cinema would have remained confined to the 'quality' costume dramas of the early fifties, German cinemas would have continued to show romantic 'Heimat' films set in the Black Forest, and British audiences would have thrived on a diet of war films and increasingly suggestive light comedy. In any case, European mass audiences continued to show a marked preference for American popular films.

Ironically, it was their own admiration for American films, particularly the sombre, unadorned *film noir* style of the late 1940s, which stimulated a revolution among a new cohort of French *cinéastes*. Despairing of the thematic clichés and rococo décor of their elders, a group of young Frenchmen—dubbed 'The New Wave' in 1958 by the French critic Pierre Billard—set out to re-invent film-making in France: first in theory, then in practice. The theoretical aspect, adumbrated in the new journal *Cahiers du Cinéma*, centred around the notion of the director as 'auteur': what these critics admired in Alfred Hitchcock or Howard Hawks, for example, or in the work of the Italian neo-realists, was their 'autonomy'—the way they had managed to 'sign' their own films even when working within studios. For the same reason they championed—then neglected—the films of an earlier generation of French directors, notably Jean Vigo and Jean Renoir.

While all this suggested intuitive good taste, the theoretical penumbra in which it was packaged was of little interest—indeed often incomprehensible—beyond a very restricted circle. But the practice, at the hands of Louis Malle, Jean-Luc Godard, Claude Chabrol, Jacques Rivette, Eric Rohmer, Agnès Varda and above all François Truffaut, changed the face of film. Between 1958 and 1965, French studios turned out an astonishing body of work. Malle directed *Ascenseur pour l'échafaud* and *Les Amants*, both in 1958; *Zazie dans le métro* (1960); *La Vie privée* (1961) and *Le Feu follet* (1963). Godard directed *À bout de souffle* (1960), *Une femme est une femme* (1961), *Vivre sa vie* (1962), *Bande à part* (1964) and *Alphaville* (1965). Chabrol's oeuvre from the same years includes *Le Beau Serge* (1958), *À double tour* (1959), *Les bonnes femmes* (1960) and *L'Oeil du malin* (1962).

Rivette's more interesting work came a little later. Like Varda, best known in these years for *Cléo de 5 à 7* (1961) and *Le Bonheur* (1965), he often lapsed into self-indulgence; but this was never true of Eric Rohmer, the oldest of the group, later to become internationally famous for his elegiac 'moral tales', of which the first two, *La Boulangère de Monceau* and *La Carrière de Suzanne*, were both made in 1963. But it was the incomparable François Truffaut who would come to incarnate the style and impact of the New Wave. Renowned above all for a series of films starring Jean-Pierre Léaud as Antoine Doinel (Truffaut's autobiographical 'hero')—notably *Les Quatre cents coups* (1959), *L'Amour à vingt ans* (1962), and *Baisers volés* (1968)—Truffaut was not only the main theorist behind the revolution in French cinema, he was also by far its most consistently successful practitioner. Many of his individual films—*Jules et Jim* (1962), *La Peau douce* (1964), *Fahrenheit 451* (1966) or *Le dernier Métro* (1980)—are classics of the art.

It was one of the strengths of the best New Wave directors that, while they always looked upon their work as intellectual statements rather than diversionary entertainment (contributors to *Cahiers du Cinéma* frequently invoked their debts to what was still referred to as 'existentialism'), their films entertained all the same (no-one ever said of Truffaut or Malle—as it was whispered of later work by Godard and Rivette—that viewing their films was like watching paint dry). And it was this combination of intellectual seriousness and visual accessibility that was so important for foreign emulators. As the response to Alain Resnais's *Hiroshima mon amour* (1959) suggests, French film had become the preferred vehicle for international moral debate.

Thus, when a group of 26 young German film directors gathered at Oberhausen in 1962 to proclaim 'the collapse of the conventional German film' and declared their intention to 'create the new German feature film . . . free from the conventions of the established industry, from the control of special interest groups', they openly acknowledged the influence of the French. Just as Jean-Luc Godard had eulogized Ingmar Bergman in a famous 1957 *Cahiers du cinéma* essay entitled "Bergmanorama", in which he claimed that the Swedish 'auteur' was 'the most original film-maker of the European cinema', so Edgar Reitz and his colleagues in Germany, like young film directors all across western Europe and Latin America, took their cue from Godard and his friends.[11]

What Truffaut, Godard and their colleagues had admired in the black-and-white American films of their youth was a lack of 'artifice'. What American and other observers envied in the French directors' *own* riffs on American realism were their subtlety and intellectual sophistication: the uniquely French ability to invest small human exchanges with awe-inspiring cultural significance. In Eric Rohmer's *Ma Nuit Chez Maud* (1969) Jean-Louis—a provincial philosophy professor played by Jean-Louis Trintignant—spends a snow-bound night on the sofa at the home of Maud (Françoise Fabian), the seductively intelligent girlfriend of an acquaintance. A Catholic, Jean-Louis agonises over the ethical implications of the situation and whether or not he should/should not have slept with his host, occasionally pausing to swap moral reflections with a Communist colleague. Nothing happens and he goes home.

It is hard to imagine an American or even a British film director making such a film, much less getting it distributed. But to a new generation of Euro-American intellectuals, Rohmer's film captured everything that was sophisticated, world-weary, witty, allusive, mature and European about French cinema. Contemporary Italian films, though quite widely distributed abroad, did not have the same impact. The more successful products played too self-consciously off the new image of Italy and Italians as rich and 'sexy'—often built around the corporeal attributes of Sophia Loren or the comic roles assigned to Marcello Mastroianni as a disabused roué: e.g. in *Divorzio all'Italiana* (Divorce Italian Style, 1961) or *Matrimonio all'italiana* (Marriage Italian Style, 1964).

Mastroianni had first played this role, but in an altogether more sombre key, in Federico Fellini's *Dolce Vita* (1960). Fellini himself had a loyal following in many of the same circles as Truffaut and Godard, notably following the appearance of *8½* (1963) and *Giulietta degli spiriti* (1965). An older generation of gifted Italian directors had not yet left the scene—Vittorio De Sica directed *I Sequestrati di Altona* (1962), from Sartre's play, co-directed *Boccaccio '70* (1962) with Fellini and would go on to direct *Il Giardino dei Finzi-Contini* at the end of the decade—but their work never recaptured the political and aesthetic impact of the great neo-realist films of the 1940s with which De Sica above all was forever linked. More influential were men like Michelangelo Antonioni. In *L'Avventura* (1960), *L'Eclisse* (1962) and *Il Deserto rosso* (1964), all starring Monica Vitti, Antonioni's hard-edged cinematography and unappealing, cynical, disabused characters anticipated the disaf-

[11]Godard in particular had decidedly eclectic tastes. He is reported to have been 'mesmerized' by Nicholas Ray's *Johnny Guitar* (1954) starring Joan Crawford.

fected and detached world of later sixties art, self-consciously captured by Antonioni himself in *Blow Up* (1966).

Italian cinema lacked the seductive intellectuality of French (or Swedish) films, but what they shared in abundance was *style*. It was this European style—a variable balance of artistic self-confidence, intellectual pretension and cultivated wit—that distinguished the continental European scene for foreign (especially American) observers. By the end of the 1950s western Europe had not merely recovered from depression and war; it was once again a magnet for aspiring sophisticates. New York had the money and perhaps, too, the modern art. But America was still, as it seemed even to many Americans, a little raw. Part of the attraction of John F. Kennedy, as candidate and as President, was the cultivated cosmopolitanism of his Washington entourage: 'Camelot'. And Camelot, in turn, owed much to the European background and continental self-presentation of the President's wife.

If Jacqueline Kennedy imported European style to the White House, this was hardly surprising. European 'design' in the later Fifties and Sixties flourished as never before, the *imprimatur* of status and quality. A European label—attached to a commodity, an idea or a person—ensured distinction, and thus a price premium. This development was actually quite recent. To be sure, *'articles de Paris'* had a longstanding place in the luxury goods trade, dating at least to the late eighteenth century; and Swiss watches had been well regarded for many decades. But the notion that cars made in Germany would *ipso facto* be better crafted than others, or that Italian-designed clothing, Belgian chocolates, French kitchenware or Danish furniture were unquestionably the best to be had: this would have seemed curious indeed just a generation before.

If anything, it was English manufacture that had until quite recently carried this reputation, a legacy of Britain's nineteenth-century industrial supremacy. British-made domestic goods, vehicles, tools or weapons had for long been highly prized on foreign markets. But in the course of the 1930s and 1940s British producers had so successfully undermined their own standing in almost every commodity save men's clothing that the only niche left to Britain's retail merchants by the 1960s was high profile, low quality 'trendy' fads—a market they were to exploit ruthlessly in the following decade.

What was remarkable about European commercial style was its segmentation by product as well as country. Italian cars—FIAT, Alfa Romeo, Lancia—were notoriously shoddy and unreliable; yet their embarrassing reputation did no discernible harm to Italy's elevated standing in other markets, such as leather goods, *haute couture* and even, in a less exalted sector, domestic white goods.[12] International demand for Ger-

---

[12]Italians could certainly *design* cars, as any motor racing enthusiast would confirm. It was Italian coach-builders who first removed mudguards, running boards and other redundant excrescences from small family cars—much as Milanese tailors in the same years were eliminating trouser turn-ups and inventing the sharp, clean lines and cut of the modern Italian suit. What Italian car manufacturers appeared unable to do with any consistency was *build* the cars that their draughtsmen had imagined.

man clothing or food products was all but non-existent, and deservedly so. But by 1965, anything turned on a German lathe or conceived by German-speaking engineers could walk out of a British or American showroom at a price of its own asking. Only Scandinavia had acquired a general reputation for quality across an eclectic range of products, but even there the market had distinctive variations. Well-heeled foreigners filled their homes with high-styled Swedish or Danish furniture, even if it was a little fragile, because it was so 'modern'. But the same consumer would be attracted to Sweden's Volvo cars, despite their resolute *lack* of style, precisely because they appeared indestructible. Both qualities, however—'style' and 'value'—were now inextricably identified with 'Europe': often in contrast with America.

Paris remained the capital of high fashion in women's clothing. But Italy, with lower labour costs and unconstrained by textile rationing (unlike France or Britain), was already a serious competitor as early as 1952, when the first international Men's Fashion Festival was staged in San Remo. However innovative its styling, French *haute couture*—from Christian Dior to Yves St Laurent—was quite socially conventional: as late as 1960, magazine editors and columnists in France and elsewhere not only wore hats and gloves when attending annual fashion shows, they wore them at their desks too. So long as middle-class women took their clothing cues from a handful of Parisian designers and fashion houses, the latter's status (and profits) remained secure. But by the early sixties European women—like men—were no longer wearing formal hats, styled outer garments or evening wear as a matter of routine. The mass market in clothing was taking its cues as much from below as from above. Europe's reputation as the capital of style and chic was secure, but the future lay with more eclectic vogues, many of them European adaptations of American and even Asian prototypes, something at which Italians proved especially adept. In clothing as in ideas, Paris dominated the European scene and would do so for a little while to come. But the future lay elsewhere.

At a March 1955 gathering in Milan of the Congress for Cultural Freedom, Raymond Aron proposed as a topic for discussion 'the End of the Ideological Age'. At the time some of his audience found the suggestion a touch premature—after all, across the Iron Curtain, and not only there, ideology appeared all too alive and well. But Aron had a point. The western European state, as it emerged in those years, was increasingly detached from any doctrinal project; and, as we have seen, the rise of the welfare state had defused the old political animosities. More people than ever before had a direct interest in the policies and expenditures of the state, but they no longer came to blows over who should control it. Western Europeans seemed to have arrived rather sooner than anticipated at the 'broad, sunlit uplands' (Churchill) of prosperity and peace: where politics was giving way to government, and government was increasingly confined to administration.

However: the predictable consequence of the nanny state, even the post-ideological nanny state, was that for anyone who had grown up knowing nothing different it was the duty of the state to make good on its promise of an ever better society—and thus the fault of the state when things did not turn out well. The apparent routinization of public affairs in the hands of a benevolent caste of overseers was no guarantee of public apathy. In this respect, at least, Aron's prognosis was off target. Thus it was that the very generation which came of age in the Social Democratic paradise of its parents' longings was most irritated and resentful at its shortcomings. A pregnant symptom of this paradox can be seen—quite literally—in an area of public planning and works in which the progressive state on both sides of the Cold War divide was unusually active.

The post-World War Two combination of demographic growth and rapid urbanization placed unprecedented demands upon urban planners. In Eastern Europe, where many urban centers had been destroyed or half abandoned by the end of the war, twenty million people moved from the countryside into towns and cities in the first two post-war decades. In Lithuania by 1970 half the population lived in towns; twenty years before the figure had been just 28 percent. In Yugoslavia, where the agricultural population declined by 50 percent between the liberation and 1970, there was a great surge of migration from the countryside to the cities: between 1948 and 1970 the Croatian capital, Zagreb, doubled in size, from 280,000 inhabitants to 566,000; likewise the national capital, Belgrade, which grew from 368,000 to 746,000.

Bucharest grew from 886,000 to 1,475,000 between 1950 and 1970. In Sofia the number of inhabitants rose from 435,000 to 877,000. In the USSR, where the urban population overtook the rural one in 1961, Minsk—the capital of the Belorussian Republic—went from 509,000 in 1959 to 907,000 just twelve years later. The result in all these cities, from Berlin to Stalingrad, was the classic Soviet-era housing solution: mile upon mile of identical gray or brown cement blocks; cheap, poorly-constructed, with no distinguishing architectural features and lacking any aesthetic indulgence (or public facilities).

Where the inner city had survived undamaged (as in Prague), or had been carefully rebuilt from old plans (Warsaw, Leningrad), most of the new building took place on the edge of the city, forming a long string of suburban dormitories reaching into the countryside. Elsewhere—in the Slovak capital Bratislava, for example—the new slums were erected in the very heart of the town. As for smaller towns and rural villages, constrained to absorb the tens of thousands of former peasants now recycled as miners or steelworkers, they had nothing to preserve and were transformed, virtually overnight, into industrial dormitories, lacking even the grace of a remnant of an old town. Collective farm workers were forced into agro-towns, pioneered in the 1950s by Nikita Khrushchev and later perfected by Nicolae Ceaușescu. Such new public architecture as there was—Technical School, Culture House, Party offices—was carefully modeled on the Soviet precedent: sometimes consciously Socialist Realist, always oversize, rarely attractive.

Forced industrialization, rural collectivization and an aggressive disdain for private needs help explain the calamity of Communist town planning. But Western European city fathers did not do much better. In Mediterranean Europe especially, the mass migration from countryside to cities placed comparable strains on urban resources. Greater Athens grew from 1,389,000 people in 1951 to 2,540,000 in 1971. Milan's population rose from 1,260,000 to 1,724,000 in the same period; Barcelona's from 1,280,000 to 1,785,000. In all these places, as in smaller towns across northern Italy and in the rapidly expanding outer suburbs of London, Paris, Madrid and elsewhere, planners could not keep up with demand. Like their contemporaries in Communist city offices, their instinct was to construct large blocks of homogenous housing—either on space cleared by war and urban renewal, or else on green-field sites at the edges of cities. In Milan and Barcelona in particular, where the first generation of migrants from the south began moving from shanty towns into high-rise apartments in the course of the 1960s, the result was depressingly reminiscent of the Soviet bloc—but with the additional handicap that many would-be tenants could not afford to rent anywhere near their place of work. They were thus forced into long daily journeys on inadequate public transport—or else in their newly-acquired cars, further straining the urban infrastructure.

But the distinctive ugliness of urban architecture in Western Europe in these years cannot be attributed to demographic pressures alone. The 'New Brutalism' (as it was dubbed by the architectural critic Rayner Banham) was not an accident or oversight. In West Germany, where many of the country's major cities were re-built with a breathtaking lack of imagination and vision; or in London—where the Architect's Department of the London County Council authorized mass housing projects like the aggressively linear, windswept, Le Corbusier-inspired Alton estate in Roehampton—ugliness appeared almost deliberate, the product of careful design. Milan's awful Torre Velasco, a reinforced concrete skyscraper built between 1957 and 1960 by a private Anglo-Italian consortium, was typical of the aggressive hyper-modernism of the age, in which the point was to break all attachments to the past. When, in March 1959, the Council of Buildings of France approved the design for the future Tour Montparnasse, their report concluded: 'Paris cannot afford to lose herself in her past. In the years to come, Paris must undergo imposing metamorphoses.'

The result was not just the Tour Montparnasse (or its natural child, the hideous complex of buildings at La Défense) but a rash of new towns: ultra-high density, multiple housing block-units (*'grands ensembles'*, as they were symptomatically designated), bereft of employment opportunities or local services, parked at the edge of greater Paris. The earliest and therefore best known of these, at Sarcelles, north of Paris, grew from a population of just 8,000 in 1954 to 35,000 seven years later. Sociologically and aesthetically it was rootless, resembling contemporary worker-dormitory suburbs in other countries (like the remarkably similar settlement of Lazdynai at the edge of Vilnius, in Lithuania) far more than anything in indigenous French housing design or urban tradition.

This break with the past was deliberate. The European 'style' so much admired in other spheres of life was here nowhere in evidence. Indeed, it was consciously and carefully eschewed. The architecture of the 1950s and, especially, the 1960s was self-consciously ahistorical; it broke with the past in design, in scale and in materials (steel, glass and reinforced concrete being much the most favoured).[13] The result was not necessarily any more imaginative than what had gone before: on the contrary, the 'urban redevelopment' schemes that transformed the face of so many European towns in these decades were a colossal missed opportunity.

In Britain as elsewhere, urban 'planning' was at best tactical, a patch-up: no long-term strategies were worked out to integrate housing, services, jobs or leisure (hardly any of the new towns and housing complexes had cinemas, much less sports facilities or adequate public transport).[14] The goal was to clear urban slums and accommodate growing populations, quickly and cheaply: between 1964 and 1974, 384 tower blocks were thrown up in London alone. Many of these would be abandoned within twenty years. One of the most egregious, 'Ronan Point' in London's East End, actually had the good taste to fall down of its own accord in 1968.

Public architecture fared little better. The Pompidou Center (a 1960s design, though not opened until January 1977)—like the Halles complex to its west—may have brought an assortment of popular cultural resources to central Paris but it failed miserably in the longer run to integrate with the surrounding district or complement the older architecture around it. The same was true of London University's new Institute of Education, ostentatiously installed on Woburn Square, at the heart of old Bloomsbury—'uniquely hideous', in the words of Roy Porter, the historian of London. In a similar vein, London's South Bank complex brought together an invaluable assortment of performing arts and artistic services; but its grim, low elevations, its windswept alleys and cracking concrete facades, remain a depressing testimony to what the urban critic Jane Jacobs called 'the Blight of Dullness'.

Just why post-war European politicians and planners should have made so very many mistakes remains unclear, even if we allow that in the wake of two world wars and an extended economic depression there was a craving for anything fresh, new and unlinked to the past. It is not as though contemporaries were unaware of the ugliness of their new environment: the occupants of the giant housing complexes,

---

[13]In the admiring commentary of one Parisian critic the thousands of identical apartments squeezed into the new *grands ensembles* were 'veritable tiny houses incorporated into a vertical structure, like so many different bottles in the same wine rack.' See Pierre Agard, 'L'Unité de résidence' in *Esprit*, October–November 1953. I am grateful to Dr Nicole Rudolph for the reference.
[14]But contrast Rotterdam: gutted by German bombs and rebuilt in stages through the following decades, the Dutch port was a consciously and genuinely 'designed' city.

tower blocks and new towns never liked them, and they said so clearly enough to anyone who cared to enquire. Architects and sociologists may not have understood that their projects would, within one generation, breed social outcasts and violent gangs, but that prospect was clear enough to the residents. Even European cinema—which only a few years before had paid loving, nostalgic attention to old cities and city life—now focused instead on the cold, hard impersonality of the modern metropolis. Directors like Godard or Antonioni took an almost sensuous pleasure in filming the tawdry new urban and industrial environment in films like *Alphaville* (1965) or *The Red Desert* (1964).

A particular victim of post-war architectural iconoclasm was the railway station, the lapidary incarnation of Victorian achievement and often a significant architectural monument in its own right. Railway stations suffered in the United States, too (the destruction of New York's Pennsylvania Station in 1966 is still remembered by many as the defining moment of official hooliganism); but American city planners at least had the excuse that, squeezed between the car and the airplane, the prospects for rail travel appeared grim. But in the overcrowded circumstances of a small continent, the future of train travel was never seriously in question. The stations that were torn down in Europe were replaced by insipid, unappealing buildings performing the identical function. The destruction of Euston Station in London, or Paris's Gare Montparnasse, or the elegant Anhalter Bahnhof in Berlin had no practical purpose and was aesthetically indefensible.

The sheer scale of urban destruction, the pan-European urge to have done with the past and leap in one generation from ruins to ultra-modernity, was to prove its own nemesis (thankfully aided by the recession of the 1970s, which trimmed public and private budgets alike and brought the orgy of renewal to a halt). As early as 1958, even before the paroxysm of city renovation had peaked, a group of preservationists in Britain founded the Victorian Society. This was a typically British volunteer organization, devoted to identifying and saving the country's threatened architectural heritage; but similarly inspired networks emerged all across Western Europe in the following decade, pressing residents, academics and politicians to act in concert to avert further loss. Where they were too late to save a particular district or building, they at least managed to preserve whatever was left—as in the case of the façade and inner cloister of the Palazzo delle Stelline on Milan's Corso Magenta: all that remains of a seventeenth-century city orphanage, the rest of which was torn down in the early 1970s.

In the physical history of the European city, the 1950s and 1960s were truly terrible decades. The damage that was done to the material fabric of urban life in those years is the dark, still half-unacknowledged underside of the 'thirty glorious years' of economic development—analogous in its way to the price paid for the industrial urbanization of the previous century. Although certain amends would be made in later decades—notably in France, where planned modernization and heavy investment in roads and transport networks brought a distinct improvement in the quality of life to some of the grimmer outer suburbs—the damage could never be wholly undone. Major cities—Frankfurt, Brussels, London above all—discovered too late that they had sold their urban birthright for a mess of brutalist pottage.

It is one of the ironies of the 1960s that the ruthlessly 'renewed' and rebuilt cityscapes of the age were deeply resented above all by the *young* people who lived there. Their houses, streets, cafés, factories, offices, schools and universities might be modern and relentlessly 'new'. But except for the most privileged among them, the result was an environment experienced as ugly, soulless, stifling, inhuman, and—in a term that was acquiring currency—'alienating'. It is altogether appropriate that when the well-fed, well-housed, well-educated children of Europe's benevolent service states grew up and revolted against 'the system', the first intimations of the coming explosion would be felt in the pre-fabricated cement dormitories of a soulless university 'extension campus', heedlessly parked among the tower blocks and traffic jams of an overspill Parisian suburb.

XII

The Spectre of Revolution

'Sexual intercourse began in 1963,
Between the end of the Chatterley
ban and the Beatles' first LP'.
Philip Larkin

'The Revolution—we loved it so much'.
Daniel Cohn-Bendit

'The rebellion of the repentant bourgeoisie against the complacent and
oppressive proletariat is one of the queerer phenomena of our time'.
Sir Isaiah Berlin

'Now all the journalists of the world are licking your arses . . . but not me,
my dears. You have the faces of spoilt brats, and I hate you, like I hate your
fathers . . . When yesterday at Valle Giulia you beat up the police, I
sympathized with the police because they are the sons of the poor'.
Pier Paolo Pasolini (June 1968)

'We are not with Dubček. We are with Mao'.
(Italian student slogan, 1968)

Moments of great cultural significance are often appreciated only in retrospect. The Sixties were different: the transcendent importance contemporaries attached to their own times—and their own selves—was one of the special features of the age. A significant part of the Sixties was spent, in the words of The Who, 'talking about My Generation'. As we shall see, this was not a wholly unreasonable preoccupation; but it led, predictably, to some distortions of perspective. The 1960s were indeed a decade of extraordinary consequence for modern Europe, but not everything that seemed important at the time has left its mark upon History. The self-congratulatory, iconoclastic impulse—in clothing or ideas—dated very fast; conversely, it would be some years before the truly revolutionary shift in politics and public affairs that began in the late 1960s could take full effect. And the political geography of the Sixties can be misleading—the most important developments were not always in the best-known places.

By the middle of the 1960s, the social impact of the post-war demographic explosion was being felt everywhere. Europe, as it seemed, was full of young people—in France, by 1968, the student-age cohort, of persons aged 16 to 24, was eight million strong, constituting 16.1 percent of the national total. In earlier times such a population explosion would have placed huge strains upon a country's food supply; and even if people could be fed, their job prospects would have been grim. But in a time of economic growth and prosperity, the chief problem facing European states was not how to feed, clothe, house and eventually employ the growing number of young people, but how to educate them.

Until the 1950s, most children in Europe left school after completing their primary education, usually between the ages of 12 and 14. In many places compulsory primary education itself, introduced at the end of the nineteenth century, was only weakly enforced—the children of peasants in Spain, Italy, Ireland and pre-Communist eastern Europe typically dropped out of school during the spring, summer and early fall. Secondary education was still a privilege confined to the middle and upper classes. In post-war Italy, less than 5 percent of the population had completed secondary school.

In anticipation of future numbers, and as part of the broader cycle of social reforms, governments in post-war Europe introduced a series of major educational changes. In the UK the school-leaving age was raised to 15 in 1947 (and later to 16 in 1972). In Italy, where in practice most children in the early-post war years still left school at 11, it was raised to 14 in 1962. The number of children in full-time schooling in Italy doubled in the course of the decade 1959–1969. In France, which boasted a mere 32,000 *bacheliers* (high-school graduates) in 1950, the numbers would increase more than five-fold over the next twenty years: by 1970, *bacheliers* represented 20 percent of their age cohort.

These educational changes carried disruptive implications. Hitherto, the cultural fault-line in most European societies had fallen between those—the overwhelming majority—who had left school after learning to read, write, do basic arithmetic and recite the outlines of national history; and a privileged minority who had remained in school until 17 or 18, been awarded the highly-valued secondary-school leaving certificate, and gone on to professional training or employment. The grammar schools, *lycées* and *Gymnasiums* of Europe had been the preserve of a ruling élite. Heirs to a classical curriculum once closed to the children of the rural and urban poor, they were now opened to an ever-expanding pool of young people from every social milieu. As more and more children entered and passed through the secondary school systems, a breach opened up between their world and the one their parents had known.

This new and wholly unprecedented generation gap constituted a *de facto* social revolution in its own right—albeit one whose implications were still confined to the realm of the family. But as tens of thousands of children poured into hastily constructed secondary schools, placing great strain upon the physical and financial fabric of an education system designed for a very different age, planners were already becoming concerned at the implications of these changes for what had until then been the preserve of an even tinier élite: the universities.

If most Europeans before 1960 never saw the inside of a secondary school, fewer still could even have dreamed of attending university. There had been some expansion of traditional universities in the course of the nineteenth century, and an increase in the number of other establishments of tertiary education, mostly for technical training. But higher education in Europe in the 1950s was still closed to all but a privileged few, whose families could forgo the earnings of their children to keep them in school until 18, and who could afford the fees charged by secondary schools and universities alike. There were, of course, scholarships, open to children of the poor and middling sort. But except in the admirably meritocratic and egalitarian institutions of the French Third and Fourth Republics, these scholarships rarely covered the formal costs of additional schooling; nowhere did they compensate for lost income.

Despite the best intentions of an earlier generation of reformers, Oxford, Cambridge, the *École Normale Supérieure*, the Universities of Bologna or Heidelberg and the rest of Europe's ancient establishments of learning remained off-limits to almost everyone. In 1949 there were 15,000 university students in Sweden, in Belgium 20,000. There were just 50,000 university students in all of Spain, less than double that number in the United Kingdom (in a population of 49 million). The French student population that year barely exceeded 130,000. But with Europe now on the cusp of mass secondary education there would soon be irresistible pressure to expand higher education too. A lot would have to change.

In the first place, Europe was going to need many more universities. In many places there was no 'system' of tertiary education as such. Most countries had inherited a randomly configured network of individual institutions: an infrastructure of small, ancient, nominally independent establishments designed to admit at most a few hundred entrants each year and frequently situated in provincial towns with little or no public infrastructure. They had no space for expansion and their lecture halls, laboratories, libraries and residential buildings (if any) were quite incapable of accommodating thousands more young people.

The typical European university town—Padua, Montpellier, Bonn, Leuven, Fribourg, Cambridge, Uppsala—was small and often some distance from major urban centers (and deliberately chosen many centuries before for just this reason): the University of Paris was an exception, albeit an important one. Most European universities lacked campuses in the American sense (here it was the British universities, Oxford and Cambridge above all, that were the obvious exception) and were physically integrated into their urban surroundings: their students lived in the town and depended upon its residents for lodging and services. Above all, and despite being hundreds of years old in many cases, the universities of Europe had almost no material resources of their own. They were utterly dependent on city or state for funding.

If higher education in Europe was to respond in time to the ominous demographic bulge pushing up through the primary and secondary schools, the initiative would thus have to come from the center. In Britain and to a lesser extent in Scandinavia, the problem was addressed by building new universities on 'greenfield' sites outside provincial cities and county towns: Colchester or Lancaster in England, Aarhus in Denmark. By the time the first post-secondary cohort began to arrive, these new universities, however architecturally soulless, were at least in place to meet the increased demand for places—and create job openings for an expanding pool of post-graduate students seeking teaching posts.

Rather than open these new universities to a mass constituency, British educational planners chose to integrate them into the older, elite system. British universities thus preserved their right to select or refuse students at the point of admission: only candidates who performed above a certain level in national high school-leaving exams could hope to gain entry to university and each university was free to offer places to whomsoever it wished—and to admit only as many students as it could handle. Students in the UK remained something of a privileged minority (no more than 6 percent of their age group in 1968) and the long-term implications were unquestionably socially regressive. But for the fortunate few, the system worked very smoothly—and insulated them from almost all the problems faced by their peers elsewhere in Europe.

For on the Continent, higher education moved in a very different direction. In the majority of Western European states there had never been any impediment to movement from secondary to higher education: if you took and passed the national school-leaving exams you were automatically entitled to attend university. Until the end of the 1950s this had posed no difficulties: the numbers involved were small and universities had no cause to fear being overwhelmed with students. In any case, academic study in most continental universities was by ancient convention more than a little detached and unstructured. Haughty and unapproachable professors offered formal lectures to halls full of anonymous students who felt little pressure to complete their degrees by a deadline, and for whom being a student was as much a social rite of passage as a means to an education.[1]

Rather than construct new universities, most central planners in Europe simply decreed the expansion of existing ones. At the same time they imposed no additional impediments or system of pre-selection. On the contrary, and for the best of reasons, they frequently set about removing those that remained—in 1965 the

[1]Obviously this did not apply to small, élite academies like France's *École Polytechnique*, or *École Normale Supérieure*, which admitted their few students by a rigorous selective exam and then taught them very well indeed. But these were unusual and highly atypical.

Italian Ministry of Education abolished all university entrance examinations and fixed subject quotas. Higher education, once a privilege, would now be a right. The result was catastrophic. By 1968 the University of Bari, for example, which traditionally enrolled about 5,000 people, was trying to cope with a student body in excess of 30,000. The University of Naples in the same year had 50,000 students, the University of Rome 60,000. Those three universities alone were enrolling between them more than the total student population of Italy a mere eighteen years earlier; many of their students would never graduate.[2]

By the end of the 1960s, one young person in seven in Italy was attending university (compared to one in twenty ten years before). In Belgium the figure was one in six. In West Germany, where there had been 108,000 students in 1950, and where the traditional universities were already beginning to suffer from overcrowding, there were nearly 400,000 by the end of the Sixties. In France, by 1967, there were as many university students as there had been *lycéens* in 1956. All over Europe there were vastly more students than ever before—and the quality of their academic experience was deteriorating fast. Everything was *crowded*—the libraries, the dormitories, the lecture halls, the refectories—and in distinctly poor condition (even, indeed especially, if it was new). Post-war government spending on education, which had everywhere risen very steeply, had concentrated upon the provision of primary and secondary schools, equipment and teachers. This was surely the right choice, and in any case one dictated by electoral politics. But it carried a price.

At this juncture it is worth recalling that even by 1968 most young people in every European country were *not* students (a detail that tends to be overlooked in accounts of this period), especially if their parents were peasants, workers, unskilled or immigrants, whether from peripheral provinces or abroad. Of necessity, this non-student majority experienced the Sixties rather differently: particularly the later Sixties, when so much seemed to turn on events in and around universities. Their opinions, and especially their politics, should not be inferred from those of their student contemporaries. In other respects, however, young people shared what was already a distinctive—and common—culture.

Every generation sees the world as new. The Sixties generation saw the world as new and *young*. Most young people in history have entered a world full of older people, where it is their seniors who occupy positions of influence and example. For the generation of the mid-1960s, however, things were different. The cultural eco-system was evolving much faster than in the past. The gap separating a large, prosperous, pampered, self-confident and culturally autonomous generation from the unusually small, insecure, Depression-scarred and war-ravaged generation of its parents was greater than the conventional distance between age groups. At the very least, it seemed to many young people as though they had been born into a

---

[2]In the mid-1960s only 44 percent of Italian university students graduated; these figures were to deteriorate still further in the course of the 1970s.

society reluctantly transforming itself—its values, its style, its rules—before their very eyes and at their behest. Popular music, cinema and television were full of young people and increasingly appealed to them as its audience and market. By 1965 there were radio and television programs, magazines, shops, products and whole industries that existed exclusively for the young and depended upon their patronage.

Although each national youth culture had its distinctive icons and institutions, its exclusively local reference points (the June 22nd 1963 *Fête des Copains* in Paris's Place de la Nation was the founding event of Sixties youth culture in France, yet it passed virtually unnoticed elsewhere), many of the popular cultural forms of the age flowed with unprecedented ease across national boundaries. Mass culture was becoming international as a matter of definition. A trend (in music, or clothing) would begin in the English-speaking world, often in England itself, and would then move south and east: facilitated by an increasingly visual (and therefore cross-border) culture and only occasionally impeded by locally generated alternatives or, more often, by political intervention. [3]

The new fashions were perforce addressed to the more prosperous young: the children of Europe's white middle-class, who could afford records, concerts, shoes, clothes, make-up and modish hair-styling. But the presentation of these wares cut ostentatiously athwart conventional lines. The most successful musicians of the time—the Beatles and their imitators—took the rhythms of American blues guitarists (most of them black) and paired them with material drawn directly from the language and experience of the British working class. [4] This highly original combination then became the indigenous, trans-national culture of European youth.

The content of popular music mattered quite a lot, but its form counted for more. In the 1960s people paid particular attention to *style*. This, it might be thought, was hardly new. But it was perhaps a peculiarity of the age that style could substitute so directly for substance. The popular music of the 1960s was insubordinate in *tone*, in the *manner* of its performance—whereas its lyrics were frequently anodyne and anyway at best half-understood by foreign audiences. In Austria, to perform or listen to British or American pop music was to cock a snoot at one's shocked parents, the generation of Hitler; the same applied, *mutatis mutandis*, just

---

[3] In the Communist bloc 'the Sixties' as pop culture were of necessity experienced at second-hand. But this difference should not be exaggerated. To apply the Ur-reference of the age: everyone in Eastern Europe knew who the Beatles were and many people had heard their music. And not just the Beatles: when the French rock star Johnny Hallyday performed in the small town of Košice in Slovakia, in 1966, 24,000 people turned out to hear him.

[4] The Beatles came from the Liverpool working class—or, in the case of Paul McCartney, from a notch or two above. The other iconic rock band of the Sixties, the Rolling Stones, was more conventionally bohemian in its subject matter, as befitted its members' middle-class London background. This handicap was overcome by a calculated roughness of style and by the Stones' well-publicized and ostentatiously raunchy private lives.

across the border in Hungary or Czechoslovakia. The music, so to speak, protested on your behalf.

If much of the mainstream musical culture of the Sixties seemed to be about sex—at least until it shifted, briefly, into drugs and politics—this, too, was largely a matter of style. More young people lived away from their parents, and at a younger age than hitherto. And contraceptives were becoming safer, easier and legal.[5] Public displays of flesh and representations of unconstrained sexual abandon on film and in literature became more common, at least in north-west Europe. For all these reasons, the older generation was convinced that sexual restraints had completely collapsed—and it pleased their children to nourish the nightmare.

In fact, the 'sexual revolution' of the Sixties was almost certainly a mirage for the overwhelming majority of people, young and old alike. So far as we can know, the sexual interests and practices of most young Europeans did not change nearly as rapidly or as radically as contemporaries liked to claim. On the evidence of contemporary surveys, even the sex lives of students were not very different from those of earlier generations. The liberated sexual style of the Sixties was typically contrasted with the Fifties, depicted (somewhat unfairly) as an age of moral rectitude and constipated emotional restraint. But when compared with the 1920s, or the European fin-de-siècle, or the demi-monde of 1860s Paris, the 'Swinging Sixties' were quite tame.

In keeping with the emphasis upon style, the generation of the Sixties placed unusual insistence upon *looking* different. Clothing, hair, make-up and what were still called 'fashion accessories' became vital generational and political identification tags. London was the source of such trends: European taste in clothing, music, photography, modeling, advertising and even mass-market magazines all took their cues from there. In view of the already-established British reputation for drab design and shoddy construction this was an unlikely development, a youthful inversion of the traditional order of such things, and it proved short-lived. But the false dawn of 'Swinging London'—as *Time* magazine dubbed it in April 1966—cast a distinctive light upon the age.

By 1967 there were over 2,000 shops in the British capital describing themselves as 'boutiques'. Most of them were shameless imitations of the clothing stores that had sprung up along Carnaby Street, a long-time haunt of male homosexuals now recycled as the epicentre of 'mod' fashion for homosexuals and heterosexuals alike. In Paris the clothing boutique 'New Man', the first French intimation of the sartorial revolution, opened in the rue de l'Ancienne Comédie on April 13th 1965. Within

---

[5]Note, though, that for most of the Sixties it was still forbidden in many parts of Western and Eastern Europe alike to dispense information about contraception. Britain was exceptional in approving the contraceptive pill for use in 1961—across the Channel the singer Antoine sold a million records in 1966 plaintively imagining a France where the Pill would one day 'be sold in Monoprix stores'.

a year it was followed by a trail of imitators, all of them dubbed with fashionably British-sounding names—'Dean', 'Twenty', 'Cardiff', etc.

The Carnaby Street style—cloned all across Western Europe (though less markedly in Italy than elsewhere)—emphasized colorful, contoured outfits tending to the androgynous and deliberately mal-adapted to anyone over thirty. Tight red corduroy pants and fitted black shirts from 'New Man' became the staple uniform of Parisian street demonstrators for the next three years and were widely copied everywhere. Like everything else about the Sixties they were made by men, for men; but young women could wear them too and increasingly did so. Even the mainstream fashion houses of Paris were affected: from 1965, the city's couturiers turned out more slacks than skirts.

They also cut back on their output of hats. It was symptomatic of the primacy of the juvenile market that hair replaced headgear as the ultimate self-expression, with traditional hats confined to formal occasions for the 'elderly'.[6] Hats did not by any means disappear, though. In a second stage of the sartorial transition, the cheerful, primary colors of 'mod gear' (inherited from the late-Fifties) were displaced by more 'serious' outer garments, reflecting a similar shift in music. Young people's clothing was now cut and marketed with more than half an eye to the 'proletarian' and 'radical' sources of its inspiration: not only blue jeans and 'work shirts', but also boots, dark jackets and leather 'Lenin' caps (or felt-covered variants, echoing the 'Kossuth caps' of 19th-century Hungarian insurgents). This more self-consciously political fashion never really caught on in Britain, but by the end of the decade it was quasi-official uniform for German and Italian radicals and their student followers.[7]

Overlapping with both sets of fashions were the gypsy-like drapes of the hippies. In contrast to the 'Carnaby Street' and 'Street-fighting Man' looks, which were indigenously European in origin, the hippie look—obscurely 'utopian' in its non-western, 'counter-cultural', asexual ethic of conspicuous under-consumption—was an American import. Its commercial utility was obvious, and many of the outlets that had sprung up to service the demand for skin-tight, sharply cut fashions in the mid-sixties were soon working hard to adapt their stock accordingly. They even tried, briefly, to market the 'Mao look'. A shapeless jacket with a sharply tailored collar, paired with the ubiquitous 'proletarian' cap, the Mao look neatly combined aspects of all three styles, particularly when 'accessorized' by the Chinese dictator's *Little Red Book* of revolutionary insights. But despite Godard's 1967 film *La Chinoise*, in which a group of French students dutifully study Mao and try to follow his example, the 'Mao look' remained a minority taste—even among 'Maoists'.

---

[6]There was a time lag in the farther-flung provinces, however, where black berets, cloth caps and even women's bonnets were still in daily use. For a little while longer, headgear remained a reliable traditional indicator of regional origin and social class.

[7]It was also to evolve with little difficulty into the skinhead attire of the following decade.

Counter-cultural politics and their symbols took on a harder edge after 1967, by association with romanticized accounts of 'Third World' guerrilla insurgents. But even so, they never fully caught on in Europe. We should not be misled by Che Guevara's remarkable after-life as the martyred, Christ-like poster-boy for disaffected Western adolescents: the European Sixties were always Eurocentric. Even the 'hippy revolution' never quite crossed the Atlantic. At most it washed up on the shores of Great Britain and Holland, leaving behind some sedimentary evidence in the form of a more developed drug culture than elsewhere—and one spectacularly original long-playing record.

The frivolous side of the Sixties—fashion, pop culture, sex—should not be dismissed as mere froth and show. It was a new generation's way of breaking with the age of the grandpas—the gerontocracy (Adenauer, De Gaulle, Macmillan—and Khrushchev) still running the continent's affairs. To be sure, the attention-catching, *poseur* aspects of the Sixties—the narcissistic self-indulgence that will forever be associated with the era—ring false when taken all at once. But in their day, and to their constituency, they seemed new and fresh. Even the cold, harsh sheen of contemporary art, or the cynical films of the later Sixties, appeared refreshing and authentic after the cozy bourgeois artifice of the recent past. The solipsistic conceit of the age—that the young would change the world by 'doing their own thing', 'letting it all hang out' and 'making love, not war'—was always an illusion, and it has not worn well. But it was not the only illusion of the time, and by no means the most foolish.

The 1960s were the great age of Theory. It is important to be clear what this means: it certainly does not refer to the truly path-breaking work then being undertaken in biochemistry, astrophysics or genetics, since this was largely ignored by non-specialists. Nor does it describe a renaissance in European social thought: the mid-twentieth century produced no social theorists comparable to Hegel, Comte, Marx, Mill, Weber or Durkheim. 'Theory' did not mean philosophy, either: the best-known western European philosophers of the time—Bertrand Russell, Karl Jaspers, Martin Heidegger, Benedetto Croce, Maurice Merleau-Ponty, Jean-Paul Sartre—were either dead, old or otherwise engaged, and the leading thinkers of *eastern* Europe—Jan Patočka or Leszek Kołakowski—were still mostly unknown outside their own countries. As for the sparkling cohort of economists, philosophers and social theorists who had flourished in Central Europe before 1934: most of the survivors had gone into permanent exile in the US, Great Britain or the Antipodes, where they formed the intellectual core of modern 'Anglo-Saxon' scholarship in their fields.

In its newly fashionable usage, 'Theory' meant something quite different. It was largely taken up with 'interrogating' (a contemporary term of art) the method and objectives of academic disciplines: above all the social sciences—history, sociology, anthropology—but also the humanities and even, in later years, the laboratory sciences themselves. In an age of vastly expanded universities, with periodicals, journals and lecturers urgently seeking 'copy', there emerged a market for 'theories' of every kind—fuelled not by improved intellectual supply but rather by insatiable consumer demand.

At the forefront of the theory revolution were the academic disciplines of History and the softer social sciences. The renewal of historical study in Europe had begun a generation before: the *Economic History Review* and *Annales: Économies, Sociétés, Civilizations* were both founded in 1929, their revisionist projects implicit in their titles. In the 1950s had come the Historians' Group of the Communist Party of Great Britain and the influential social history journal *Past & Present*; the Cultural Studies unit at England's Birmingham University, inspired by the work of Richard Hoggart and Raymond Williams; and, a little later, the Social History school centered around Hans-Ulrich Wehler at Bielefeld University in West Germany.

The scholarship produced by the men and women associated with these groups and institutions was not necessarily iconoclastic; indeed, though usually of very high quality, it was often quite methodologically conventional. But it was self-consciously *interpretive*, typically from a non-dogmatic but unmistakably left-leaning position. Here was history informed by social theory, and by an insistence upon the importance of class, particularly the lower classes. The point was not just to narrate or even explain a given historical moment; the point was to reveal its deeper meaning. Historical writing in this vein seemed to bridge the gap between past and present, between scholarly speculation and contemporary engagement, and a new generation of students read (and, not infrequently, mis-read) it in this light.

But for all its political applications, History is a discipline peculiarly impervious to high theoretical speculation: the more Theory intrudes, the farther History recedes. Although one or two of the leading historians of the Sixties went on to achieve iconic status in old age none of them—however subversive his scholarship—quite emerged as a cultural guru. Other disciplines fared better—or worse, depending on one's point of view. Borrowing from an earlier vein of speculation in the field of linguistics, cultural anthropologists—led by Claude Lévi-Strauss—proposed a comprehensive new explanation for variations and differences across societies. What counted was not surface social practices or cultural symptoms but the inner essences, the deep structures of human affairs.

'Structuralism', as it came to be called, was intensely seductive. As a way of sorting human experience it bore a family resemblance to the *Annales* school of history—whose best-known contemporary exponent, Fernand Braudel, had built his reputation on the study of the *longue durée*, a bird's-eye view of history describing slowly shifting geographical and social structures across long periods—and thus fitted comfortably into the academic style of the time. But of greater relevance was structuralism's immediate accessibility to intellectuals and non-specialists. As explicated by Lévi-Strauss's admirers in cognate disciplines, structuralism was not even a representational theory: the social codes, or 'signs', that it described related not to any particular people or places or events but merely to other signs, in a closed system. It was thus not subject to empirical testing or disproof—there was no sense in which structuralism could ever be demonstrated to be *wrong*—and the iconoclastic ambition of its assertions, allied to this impermeability to contradiction, guaranteed it a wide audience. Anything and everything could be explained as a combination of 'structures': as Pierre Boulez noted when labeling one of his compositions *Structures*, 'it is the key word of our time.'

In the course of the 1960s there emerged a plethora of applied structuralisms: in anthropology, history, sociology, psychology, political science and of course literature. The best-known practitioners—usually those who combined in the right doses scholarly audacity with a natural talent for self-promotion—became international celebrities, having had the good fortune to enter the intellectual limelight just as television was becoming a mass medium. In an earlier age Michel Foucault might have been a drawing-room favourite, a star of the Parisian lecture circuit, like Henri Bergson fifty years earlier. But when *Les Mots et les Choses* sold 20,000 copies in just four months after it appeared in 1966 he acquired celebrity status almost overnight.

Foucault himself foreswore the label 'structuralist', much as Albert Camus always insisted he had never been an 'existentialist' and didn't really know what that was.[8] But as Foucault at least would have been constrained to concede, it didn't really matter what he thought. 'Structuralism' was now shorthand for any ostensibly subversive account of past or present, in which conventional linear explanations and categories were shaken up and their assumptions questioned. More importantly, 'structuralists' were people who minimized or even denied the role of individuals and individual initiative in human affairs.[9]

But for all its protean applications, the idea that everything is 'structured' left something vital unexplained. For Fernand Braudel, or Claude Lévi-Strauss, or even Michel Foucault, the goal was to uncover the deep workings of a cultural system. This might or might not be a subversive scholarly impulse—it certainly was not in Braudel's case—but it does gloss over or minimize change and transition. Decisive political events in particular proved resistant to this approach: you could explain why things *had* to change at a given stage, but it wasn't clear just *how* they did so, or why individual social actors opted to facilitate the process. As an interpretation of human experience, any theory dependent on an arrangement of structures from

---

[8] By 1960 'existentialism' (like 'structuralism' a few years later) had become a general-purpose catchword, roughly approximating to 'bohemian' in earlier decades: the unemployed art students who came to hear the Beatles on the Reeperbahn in Hamburg all called themselves 'Exis'.

[9] In which case it might seem odd that the fashionable psychoanalytical theorist Jacques Lacan should have been popularly assimilated to the category. But Lacan was a special case. Even by the lax standards of Sixties-era Paris he remained quite remarkably ignorant of contemporary developments in medicine, biology and neurology, with no discernible harm to his practice or reputation.

which human choice had been eliminated was thus hobbled by its own assumptions. Intellectually subversive, structuralism was politically passive.

The youthful impulse of the Sixties was not about understanding the world; in the words of Karl Marx's *Eleventh Thesis on Feuerbach*, written when Marx himself was just 26 years old and much cited in these years: 'The philosophers have only interpreted the world, in various ways; the point, however, is to change it.' When it came to changing the world there was still only one grand theory purporting to relate an interpretation of the world to an all-embracing project of change; only one Master Narrative offering to make sense of everything while leaving open a place for human initiative: the political project of Marxism itself.

The intellectual affinities and political obsessions of the Sixties in Europe only make sense in the light of this continuing fascination with Marx and Marxism. As Jean-Paul Sartre put it in 1960, in his *Critique of Dialectical Reason*: 'I consider Marxism to be the unsurpassable philosophy of our time.' Sartre's unshaken faith was not universally shared, but there was general agreement across the political spectrum that anyone wishing to understand the world must take Marxism and its political legacy very seriously. Raymond Aron—Sartre's contemporary, erstwhile friend and intellectual nemesis—was a lifelong anti-Communist. But he, too, freely acknowledged (with a mixture of regret and fascination) that Marxism was the dominant idea of the age: the secular religion of its epoch.

Between 1956 and 1968 Marxism in Europe lived—and, as it were, thrived—in a state of suspended animation. Stalinist Communism was in disgrace, thanks to the revelations and events of 1956. The Communist parties of the West were either politically irrelevant (in Scandinavia, Britain, West Germany and the Low Countries); in slow but unmistakable decline (France); or else, as in the Italian case, striving to distance themselves from their Muscovite inheritance. Official Marxism, as incarnated in the history and teachings of Leninist parties, was largely discredited—especially in the territories over which it continued to rule. Even those in the West who chose to vote Communist evinced little interest in the subject.

At the same time there was widespread intellectual and academic interest in those parts of the Marxist inheritance that could be distinguished from the Soviet version and salvaged from its moral shipwreck. Ever since the Founder's death, there had always been Marxist and *marxisant* sects and splinter groups—well before 1914 there were already tiny political parties claiming the True Inheritance. A handful of these, like the Socialist Party of Great Britain (SPGB), were still in existence: vaunting their political virginity and asserting their uniquely correct interpretation of the original Marxist texts.[10] But most late-nineteenth-century Socialist move-

---

[10]The SPGB continues to the time of writing. Impervious to change, and too small to be adversely affected by its own irrelevance, it will presumably survive indefinitely.

ments, circles, clubs and societies had been absorbed into the general-purpose Socialist and Labour parties that coalesced in the years 1900–1910. Modern Marxist disputes have their roots in the Leninist schism that was to follow.

It was the factional struggles of the early Soviet years that gave rise to the most enduring Marxist 'heresy', that of Trotsky and his followers. A quarter century after Trotsky's death in Mexico at the hands of a Stalinist assassin (and in no small measure because of it), Trotskyist parties could be found in every European state that did not explicitly ban them. They were typically small and led, in the image of their eponymous founder, by a charismatic, authoritarian chief who dictated doctrine and tactics. Their characteristic strategy was 'entryism': working inside larger left-wing organizations (parties, trade unions, academic societies) to colonize them or nudge their policies and political alliances in directions dictated by Trotskyist theory.

To the outsider, Trotskyist parties—and the evanescent Fourth (Workers') International to which they were affiliated—appeared curiously indistinguishable from Communists, sharing a similar allegiance to Lenin and separated only by the bloody history of the power struggle between Trotsky and Stalin. There *was* a crucial distinguishing point of dogma—Trotskyists continued to speak of 'permanent revolution' and to accuse official Communists of having aborted the workers' revolution by confining it to a single country—but in other respects the only obvious difference was that Stalinism had been a political success, whereas the Trotskyist record was one of unblemished failure.

It was that very failure, of course, which Trotsky's latter-day followers found so appealing. The past might look grim, but their analysis of what had gone wrong—the Soviet revolution had been hi-jacked by a bureaucratic reaction analogous to the Thermidorian coup that put paid to the Jacobins in 1794—would, they felt, assure them success in the years ahead. Yet even Trotsky carried the whiff of power—he had, after all, played a crucial role in the first years of the Soviet regime and bore some responsibility for its deviations. To a new and politically innocent generation, the *truly* appealing failures were European Communism's lost leaders, the men and women who never had a chance to exercise any political responsibilities at all.

Thus the 1960s saw the rediscovery of Rosa Luxemburg, the Polish-Jewish Socialist assassinated by German *Frei Korps* soldiers in the doomed Berlin revolution of January 1919; György Lukacs, the Hungarian Communist thinker whose political writings of the 1920s briefly suggested an alternative to official Communist interpretations of history and literature before he was forced publicly to abjure them; and above all Antonio Gramsci, co-founder of the Italian Communist Party and author of a cycle of brilliant, unpublished papers on revolutionary politics and Italian history, most of them written in the Fascist prisons where he languished from 1926 until his death, at the age of 46, in April 1937.

In the course of the 1960s all three were copiously re-published, or published for the first time, in many languages. They had little in common, and most of what they did share was negative: none had exercised power (except in Lukacs's case as the Commissar for Culture in Béla Kun's brief Communist dictatorship in Budapest, from March to August 1919); all of them had at one time disagreed with Leninist practices (in Luxemburg's case even before the Bolsheviks took power); and all three, like so many others, had fallen into long neglect under the shadow of official Communist theory and practice.

The exhumation of the writings of Luxemburg, Lukacs, Gramsci and other forgotten early-twentieth century Marxists[11] was accompanied by the rediscovery of Marx himself. Indeed, the unearthing of a new and ostensibly very different Marx was crucial to the attraction of Marxism in these years. The 'old' Marx was the Marx of Lenin and Stalin: the Victorian social scientist whose neo-positivist writings anticipated and authorized democratic centralism and proletarian dictatorship. Even if this Marx could not be held directly responsible for the uses to which his mature writings had been put, he was irrevocably associated with them. Whether in the service of Communism or Social Democracy, they were of the *old* Left.

The *new* Left, as it was starting to call itself by 1965, sought out new texts—and found them in the writings of the young Karl Marx, in the metaphysical essays and notes written in the early 1840s when Marx was barely out of his teens, a young German philosopher steeped in Hegelian historicism and the Romantic dream of ultimate Freedom. Marx himself had chosen not to publish some of these writings; indeed, in the aftermath of the failed revolutions of 1848 he had turned decisively away from them and towards the study of political economy and contemporary politics with which he was henceforth to be associated.

Accordingly, many of the writings of the early Marx were not widely known even to scholars. When they were first published in full, under the auspices of the Marx-Engels Institute in Moscow in 1932, they attracted little attention. The revival of interest in them—notably the *Economic and Philosophical Manuscripts* and *The German Ideology*—came thirty years later. Suddenly it was possible to be a Marxist while jettisoning the heavy, soiled baggage of the traditional Western Left. The Young Marx was seemingly preoccupied with strikingly modern problems: how to transform 'alienated' consciousness and liberate human beings from ignorance of their true condition and capacities; how to reverse the order of priorities in capitalist society and place human beings at the center of their own existence; in short, how to change the world.

To an older generation of Marx scholars, and to the established Marxist parties, this perverse insistence upon the very writings that Marx himself had chosen not to publish seemed deeply unserious. But it was also implicitly subversive: if anyone could just go to the texts themselves and interpret Marx at will, then the authority of the Communist (and in this case also the Trotskyist) leadership must

---

[11]Like Gramsci's near-contemporary the German Marxist Karl Korsch, or the Austro-Marxist writers Otto Bauer and Rudolf Hilferding.

crumble, and with it much of the justification for mainstream revolutionary politics as then understood. Not surprisingly, the Marxist Establishment fought back. Louis Althusser—the French Communist Party's leading theoretician, an internationally known expert on Marxism and a teacher at France's *École Normale Supérieure*—built his professional reputation and passing fame upon the claim to have constructed a firewall between a 'young', Hegelian Marx and the 'mature', materialist Marx. Only the later writings, he insisted, were scientific and thus properly Marxist.[12]

What Communists and other conservative Marxists rightly foresaw was how easily this new, humanist Marx could be adapted to contemporary tastes and fashions. The complaints of an early-nineteenth-century Romantic like Marx against capitalist modernity and the dehumanizing impact of industrial society were well adapted to contemporary protests against the 'repressive tolerance' of post-industrial Western Europe. The prosperous, liberal West's apparently infinite flexibility, its sponge-like capacity to absorb passions and differences, infuriated its critics. Repression, they insisted, was endemic in bourgeois society. It could not just evaporate. The repression that was missing on the streets must perforce have gone *somewhere*: it had moved into people's very souls—and, above all, their bodies.

Herbert Marcuse, a Weimar-era intellectual who had ended up in Southern California—where he handily adapted his old epistemology to his new environment—offered a helpful conflation of all these strands of thought. Western consumer society, he explained, no longer rested upon the straightforwardly economic exploitation of a class of property-less proletarians. Instead it diverted human energy away from the search for fulfillment (notably sexual fulfillment) and into the consumption of goods and illusions. Real needs—sexual, social, civic—are displaced by false ones, whose fulfillment is the purpose of a consumer-centered culture. This was pushing even the very young Marx further than he might have wished to go, but it attracted a broad audience: not just for the few who read Marcuse's essays, but for many more who picked up the language and the general drift of the argument as it acquired broad cultural currency.

The emphasis upon *sexual* fulfillment as a radical goal was quite offensive to an older generation of Left-wingers. Free love in a free society was not a new idea—some early nineteenth-century Socialist sects had espoused it, and the first years of the Soviet Union had been distinctly morally relaxed—but the mainstream tradition of European radicalism was one of moral and domestic rectitude. The Old Left had never been *culturally* dissident or sexually adventurous even when it was

---

[12]Althusser's claim rested on a bizarre structuralist account of Marx, whose contemporary appeal to youthful seekers after Theory was directly proportional to its Jesuitical opacity (older scholars were unimpressed). But the assertion of authority was clear enough: there is only one proper way to think about Marx, he insisted, and it is mine. In France, Althusser's star waned with the fall of the Party whose cause he espoused; today his obscurantist appeal is confined to the outer fringes of Anglo-Saxon academia.

young: that had been the affair of bohemians, aesthetes and artists, often of an individualistic or even politically reactionary bent.

But however discomfiting, the conflation of sex and politics presented no real threat—indeed, as more than one Communist intellectual took pains to point out, the new emphasis on private desires over collective struggles was *objectively* reactionary.[13] The truly subversive implications of the New Left's adaptation of Marx lay elsewhere. Communists and others could dismiss talk of sexual liberation. They were not even bothered by the anti-authoritarian aesthetic of a younger generation, with its demands for self-government in the bedroom, the lecture hall and the shop floor; all *that* they perhaps imprudently dismissed as a passing disturbance in the natural order of things. What caused far deeper offence was the emerging tendency of young radicals to identify Marxist theory with revolutionary practices in exotic lands, where none of the established categories and authorities seemed to apply.

The core claim of the historical Left in Europe was that it represented, indeed in Communism's case *incarnated*, the proletariat: the blue-collar industrial working class. This close identification of Socialism with urban labor was more than just an elective affinity. It was the distinguishing mark of the ideological Left, separating it from well-intentioned liberal or Catholic social reformers. The working-class vote, especially the *male* working-class vote, was the foundation of the power and influence of the British Labour Party, the Dutch and Belgian workers' parties, the Communist parties of France and Italy and the Social Democratic parties of German-speaking central Europe.

Except in Scandinavia, the majority of the working population had never been Socialist or Communist—its allegiances were spread right across the political spectrum. Traditional Left-wing parties were nonetheless heavily dependent on the votes of the working class and thus identified closely with it. But by the mid-1960s this class was disappearing. In the developed countries of Western Europe miners, steelworkers, shipbuilders, metalworkers, textile hands, railway men and manual workers of every sort were retiring in large numbers. In the coming age of the service industry their place was being taken by a very different sort of working population.

This ought to have been a source of some anxiety to the conventional Left: trade union and party memberships and funds depended heavily on this mass base. But even though the incipient disappearance of the classical European proletariat was widely announced in contemporary social surveys, the older Left continued to insist upon its working-class 'base'. Communists especially remained intransigent.

---

[13]They had a point. Thus Raoul Vaneigem, a Belgian Situationist, writing in 1967: 'With a world of ecstatic pleasures to gain, we have nothing to lose but our boredom.' It is hard to be sure, in retrospect, whether such slogans were witty, innocent or merely cynical. In any event, they did little to imperil the status quo.

There was only one revolutionary class: the proletariat; only one party that could represent and advance the interests of that class: the Communists; and only one correct outcome to the workers' struggle under Communist direction: the Revolution, as patented in Russia fifty years before.

But for anyone not wedded to this version of European history, the proletariat was no longer the only available vehicle of radical social transformation. In what was now increasingly referred to as the 'Third' world, there were alternative candidates: anti-colonial nationalists in North Africa and the Middle East; black radicals in the US (hardly the third world but closely identified with it); and peasant guerillas everywhere, from Central America to the South China Sea. Together with 'students' and even simply the young, these constituted a far larger and more readily mobilized constituency for revolutionary hopes than the staid and satisfied working masses of the prosperous West. In the wake of 1956, young west European radicals turned away from the dispiriting Communist record in Europe's east and looked further afield for inspiration.

This new taste for the exotic was fuelled in part by contemporary decolonization and the aspirations of national liberation movements, in part by the projection on to others of Europe's own lost illusions. It rested on remarkably little local knowledge, despite an emerging academic cottage industry in 'peasant studies'. The revolutions in Cuba and China especially were invested with all the qualities and achievements so disappointingly lacking in Europe. The Italian Marxist writer Maria-Antonietta Macciocchi waxed lyrical over the contrast between the miserable condition of contemporary Europe and the post-revolutionary utopia of Mao's China, then at the height of the Cultural Revolution: 'In China there are no signs of alienation, nervous disorders or of the fragmentation within the individual that you find in a consumer society. The world of the Chinese is compact, integrated and absolutely whole.'

The peasant revolutions in the non-European world had a further attribute that appealed to West European intellectuals and students at the time: they were violent. There was, of course, no shortage of violence just a few hours to the east, in the Soviet Union and its satellites. But that was the violence of the state, of official Communism. The violence of third-world revolts was a liberating violence. As Jean-Paul Sartre famously explained, in his 1961 preface to the French edition of Frantz Fanon's *The Wretched of the Earth*, the violence of anti-colonial revolutions was 'man recreating himself . . . to shoot down a European is to kill two birds with one stone, to destroy an oppressor and the man he oppresses at the same time: there remain a dead man and a free man; the survivor, for the first time, feels a *national* soil under his foot.'

This self-abnegating admiration for alien models was not new in Europe—Tocqueville had long ago remarked upon its attractions for the pre-revolutionary intelligentsia of eighteenth-century France, and it had once played a part in the appeal of the Soviet Revolution itself. But in the 1960s the example of the Far East, or the far south, was now being held up for European emulation. Student radicals in Milan and Berlin were urged to imitate successful oriental stratagems: in a revealing combination of Maoist rhetoric and Trotskyist tactics, the German student leader Rudi Dutschke urged his followers in 1968 to undertake 'a long march through the institutions.'

For their conservative elders, this casual invocation of extraneous models illustrated the undisciplined ease with which the venerable revolutionary syntax of old Europe was unraveling into an ideological Babel. When Italian students proposed that, in the new service economy, universities constituted the epicenters of knowledge production and students were thus the new working class, they were stretching the terms of Marxist exchange to the limit. But at least they had dialectical precedent on their side and were playing within the accepted rules. A few years later, when *Re Nudo*, a Milanese student paper, proclaimed 'Proletarian Youth of Europe, Jimi Hendrix unites us!', dialectics had descended into parody. As their critics had insisted from the outset, the boys and girls of the Sixties just weren't serious.

And yet—the Sixties were also an intensely significant decade. The third world was in turmoil, from Bolivia to South-East Asia. The 'Second' world of Soviet Communism was stable only in appearance, and even then not for long, as we shall see. And the leading power of the West, shaken by assassinations and race riots, was embarking on a full-scale war in Vietnam. American defense expenditure rose steadily through the mid-sixties, peaking in 1968. The Vietnam War was not a divisive issue in Europe—it found disfavor all across the political spectrum—but it served as a catalyst for mobilization across the continent: even in Britain, where the largest demonstrations of the decade were organized explicitly to oppose US policy. In 1968 the Vietnam Solidarity Campaign marched many tens of thousands of students through the streets of London to the US Embassy in Grosvenor Square, angrily demanding an end to the war in Vietnam (and the British Labour government's halfhearted support of it).

It says something about the peculiar circumstances of the Sixties, and the social background of the most prominent public activists, that so many of the disputes and demands of the time were constructed around a political agenda and not an economic one. Like 1848, the Sixties was a Revolution of the Intellectuals. But there *was* an economic dimension to the discontents of the hour, even if many of the participants were still oblivious to it. Though the prosperity of the post-war decades had not yet run its course and unemployment in Western Europe was at a historic low, a cycle of labor disputes throughout Western Europe in the early sixties hinted at troubles ahead.

Behind these strikes, and those that were to come in 1968–69, was some discontent at declining real wages, as the post-war growth wave passed its peak; but the real source of complaint was working conditions; and in particular relations between employees and their bosses. Except in the distinctive cases of Austria, Germany and Scandinavia, management-worker relations in European factories and offices were not good: on a typical shop floor in Milan—or Birmingham, or the Paris industrial belt—resentful, militant workers were overseen by intransigently autocratic employers, with very little communication between them. 'Industrial relations' in parts of Western Europe was an oxymoron.

Much the same was true in parts of the service and professional world too: France's national Radio and Television organization, the *ORTF*, and the *Commissariat à l'Energie Atomique*, to take just two prominent cases, seethed with resentful technical staff, from journalists to engineers. Traditional styles of authority, discipline and address (or, indeed, dress) had failed to keep pace with the rapid social and cultural transformations of the past decade. Factories and offices were run from the top down with no input from below. Managers could discipline, humiliate or fire their staff at will. Employees were often accorded little respect, their opinions unheeded. There were widespread calls for greater worker initiative, more professional autonomy, even 'self-management' (*autogestion* in French).

These were issues that had not featured prominently in European industrial conflicts since the Popular Front occupations of 1936. They had largely escaped the attention of unions and political parties, focused as they were on more traditional and easily manipulated demands: higher wages, shorter hours. But they overlapped readily enough with the rhetoric of the student radicals (with whom shop-floor militants had little else in common) who voiced similar complaints about their overcrowded, poorly managed universities.

The sense of exclusion, from decision-making and thus from power, reflected another dimension of the Sixties whose implications were not fully appreciated at the time. Thanks to the system of two-round legislative elections and presidential election by universal suffrage, political life in France had coalesced by the mid-Sixties into a stable system of electoral and parliamentary coalitions built around two political families: Communist and Socialists on the Left, centrists and Gaullists on the Right. By tacit agreement across the spectrum, smaller parties and fringe groups were forced either to merge with one of the four big units or else be squeezed out of mainstream politics.

For different reasons, the same thing was happening in Italy and Germany. From 1963, a broad Center-Left coalition in Italy occupied most of the national political space, with only Communist and ex-Fascist parties excluded. The Federal Republic of Germany was governed from 1966 by a 'Grand Coalition' of Christian Democrats and Social Democrats who, together with the Free Democrats, monopolized the Bundestag. These arrangements ensured political stability and continuity; but as a consequence, in the three major democracies of western Europe, radical opposition was pushed not just to the fringes but out of parliament altogether. 'The system' seemed indeed to be run exclusively by 'them', as the New Left had for some time been insisting. Making a virtue of necessity, radical students declared themselves the 'extra-parliamentary' opposition, and politics moved into the streets instead.

The best-known instance of this, in France during the spring of 1968, was also the shortest-lived. It owes its prominence more to shock value, and to the special symbolism of insurgency in the streets of *Paris*, than to any enduring effects. The May 'Events' began in the autumn of 1967 in Nanterre, a dreary inner suburb of western Paris and the site of one of the hastily constructed extensions to the ancient University of Paris. The student dormitories at Nanterre had for some time been home to a floating population of legitimate students, 'clandestine' radicals and a small number of drug-sellers and users. Rent passed unpaid. There was also considerable nocturnal movement to and fro between the male and female dormitories, in spite of strict official prohibitions.[14]

The academic administration at Nanterre had been reluctant to provoke trouble by enforcing the rules, but in January 1968 they expelled one 'squatter' and threatened disciplinary measures against a legitimate student, Daniel Cohn-Bendit, for insulting a visiting government minister.[15] Further demonstrations followed, and on March 22nd, following the arrest of student radicals who attacked the American Express building in central Paris, a Movement was formed, with Cohn-Bendit among its leaders. Two weeks later the Nanterre campus was closed down following further student clashes with police, and the Movement—and the action—shifted to the venerable university buildings in and around the Sorbonne, in central Paris.

It is worth insisting upon the parochial and distinctly self-regarding issues that sparked the May Events, lest the ideologically charged language and ambitious programs of the following weeks mislead us. The student occupation of the Sorbonne and subsequent street barricades and clashes with the police, notably on the nights of May 10th–11th and May 24th–25th, were led by representatives of the (Trotskyist) *Jeunesse Communiste Révolutionnaire*, as well as officials from established student and junior lecturer unions. But the accompanying Marxist rhetoric, while familiar enough, masked an essentially anarchist spirit whose immediate objective was the removal and humiliation of authority.

In this sense, as the disdainful French Communist Party leadership rightly insisted, this was a party, not a revolution. It had all the symbolism of a traditional

---

[14]This was a longstanding source of friction. In January 1966, after months of dispute at a student dormitory complex in Antony, in southern Paris, a newly appointed director had introduced what was then a radical regime. Girls and boys over twenty one could henceforth entertain members of the opposite sex in their dormitory rooms. Those under twenty one could do so with *written permission* from their parents. No such liberalizations were introduced anywhere else.

[15]The Minister for Youth, one François Missoffe, had come to Nanterre to open a new sports facility. Cohn-Bendit, a local student *enragé*, asked why the Education Ministry was doing nothing to address the dormitory disputes (or 'sexual problems', as he put it). The Minister, rising to the provocation, suggested that if Cohn-Bendit had sexual problems he should jump in the splendid new swimming pool. 'That', replied the part-German Cohn-Bendit, 'is what the Hitler Youth used to say.'

French revolt—armed demonstrators, street barricades, the occupation of strategic buildings and intersections, political demands and counter-demands—but none of the substance. The young men and women in the student crowds were overwhelmingly middle-class—indeed, many of them were from the Parisian bourgeoisie itself: '*fils à papa*' ('daddy's boys'), as the PCF leader Georges Marchais derisively called them. It was their own parents, aunts and grandmothers who looked down upon them from the windows of comfortable bourgeois apartment buildings as they lined up in the streets to challenge the armed power of the French state.

Georges Pompidou, the Gaullist Prime Minister, rapidly took the measure of the troubles. After the initial confrontations he withdrew the police, despite criticism from within his own party and government, leaving the students of Paris in *de facto* control of their university and the surrounding *quartier*. Pompidou—and his President, De Gaulle—were embarrassed by the well-publicized activities of the students. But, except very briefly at the outset when they were taken by surprise, they did not feel threatened by them. When the time came the police, especially the riot police—recruited from the sons of poor provincial peasants and never reluctant to crack the heads of privileged Parisian youth—could be counted on to restore order. What troubled Pompidou was something far more serious.

The student riots and occupations had set the spark to a nationwide series of strikes and workplace occupations that brought France to a near-standstill by the end of May. Some of the first protests—by reporters at French Television and Radio, for example—were directed at their political chiefs for censoring coverage of the student movement and, in particular, the excessive brutality of some riot policemen. But as the general strike spread, through the aircraft manufacturing plants of Toulouse and the electricity and petro-chemical industries and, most ominously, to the huge Renault factories on the edge of Paris itself, it became clear that something more than a few thousand agitated students was at stake.

The strikes, sit-ins, office occupations and accompanying demonstrations and marches were the greatest movement of social protest in modern France, far more extensive than those of June 1936. Even in retrospect it is difficult to say with confidence exactly what they were about. The Communist-led trade union organization, the *Confédération Générale du Travail* (CGT) was at first at a loss: when union organizers tried to take over the Renault strike they were shouted down, and an agreement reached between government, unions and employers was decisively rejected by the Renault workers, despite its promise of improved wages, shorter hours and more consultation.

The millions of men and women who had stopped work had one thing at least in common with the students. Whatever their particular local grievances, they were above all frustrated with their conditions of existence. They did not so much want to get a better deal at work as to change something about their way of life; pamphlets and manifestos and speeches explicitly said as much. This was good news for the public authorities in that it diluted the mood of the strikers and directed their attention away from political targets; but it suggested a general malaise that would be hard to address.

France was prosperous and secure and some conservative commentators concluded that the wave of protest was thus driven not by discontent but by simple boredom. But there *was* genuine frustration, not only in factories like those of Renault where working conditions had long been unsatisfactory, but everywhere. The Fifth Republic had accentuated the longstanding French habit of concentrating power in one place and a handful of institutions. France was run, and was seen to be run, by a tiny Parisian élite: socially exclusive, culturally privileged, haughty, hierarchical and unapproachable. Even some of its own members (and especially their children) found it stifling.

The ageing De Gaulle himself failed, for the first time since 1958, to understand the drift of events. His initial response had been to make an ineffective televised speech and then to disappear from sight.[16] When he did try to turn what he took to be the anti-authoritarian national mood to his advantage in a referendum the following year, and proposed a series of measures designed to decentralize government and decision-making in France, he was decisively and humiliatingly defeated; whereupon he resigned, retired and retreated to his country home, to die there a few months later.

Pompidou, meanwhile, had proven right to wait out the student demonstrations. At the height of the student sit-ins and the accelerating strike movement some student leaders and a handful of senior politicians who should have known better (including former premier Pierre Mendès-France and future president François Mitterrand) declared that the authorities were helpless: power was now there for the taking. This was dangerous talk, and foolish: as Raymond Aron noted at the time, 'to expel a President elected by universal suffrage is not the same thing as expelling a king.' De Gaulle and Pompidou were quick to take advantage of the Left's mistakes. The country, they warned, was threatened with a Communist coup.[17] At the end of May De Gaulle announced a snap election, calling upon the French to choose between legitimate government and revolutionary anarchy.

To kick off its election campaign the Right staged a huge counter-demonstration. Far larger even than the student *manifestations* of two weeks before, the massed crowds marching down the Champs Elysées on May 30th gave the lie to the Left's assertion that the authorities had lost control. The police were given instructions to re-occupy university buildings, factories and offices. In the ensuing parliamentary elections, the ruling Gaullist parties won a crushing victory,

---

[16]To visit the French Army in Germany, as it transpired, and assure himself of its loyalty and availability were it to be called upon. But this was not known at the time.
[17]This was palpably untrue. The French Communist Party had no coherent strategy in 1968, beyond pouring scorn on the student radicals and trying to preserve its influence in the labor movement. Seizing political power was quite beyond its ability or imagination.

increasing their vote by more than a fifth and securing an overwhelming majority in the National Assembly. The workers returned to work. The students went on vacation.

The May Events in France had a psychological impact out of all proportion to their true significance. Here was a revolution apparently unfolding in real time and before an international television audience. Its leaders were marvelously telegenic; attractive and articulate young men leading the youth of France through the historical boulevards of Left Bank Paris.[18] Their demands—whether for a more democratic academic environment, an end to moral censorship, or simply a nicer world—were accessible and, despite the clenched fists and revolutionary rhetoric, quite unthreatening. The national strike movement, while mysterious and unsettling, merely added to the aura of the students' own actions: having quite by accident detonated the explosion of social resentment, they were retrospectively credited with anticipating and even articulating it.

Above all, the May Events in France were curiously peaceful by the standards of revolutionary turbulence elsewhere, or in France's own past. There was quite a lot of violence to property, and a number of students and policemen had to be hospitalized following the 'Night of the Barricades' on May 24th. But both sides held back. No students were killed in May 1968; the political representatives of the Republic were not assaulted; and its institutions were never seriously questioned (except the French university system, where it all began, which suffered sustained internal disruption and discredit without undergoing any significant reforms).

The radicals of 1968 mimicked to the point of caricature the style and the props of past revolutions—they were, after all, performing on the same stage. But they foreswore to repeat their violence. As a consequence, the French 'psychodrama' (Aron) of 1968 entered popular mythology almost immediately as an object of nostalgia, a stylized struggle in which the forces of Life and Energy and Freedom were ranged against the numbing, gray dullness of the men of the past. Some of the prominent crowd pleasers of May went on to conventional political careers: Alain Krivine, the charismatic graduate leader of the Trotskyist students is today, forty years on, the sexagenarian leader of France's oldest Trotskyist party. Dany Cohn-Bendit, expelled from France in May, went on to become a respected municipal councilor in Frankfurt and thence a Green Party representative in the European Parliament.

But it is symptomatic of the fundamentally apolitical mood of May 1968 that the best-selling French books on the subject a generation later are not serious works of historical analysis, much less the earnest doctrinal tracts of the time, but collections of contemporary graffiti and slogans. Culled from the walls, notice-

---

[18]There were no women among the student leaders. In contemporary photographs and newsreels girls can be seen prominently perched on the shoulders of their boyfriends, but they were at best the auxiliary foot soldiers of the student army. The youth revolt of 1968 talked a lot about sex, but was quite unconcerned with inequalities of gender.

boards and streets of the city, these witty one-liners encourage young people to make love, have fun, mock those in authority, generally do what feels good—and change the world almost as a by-product. *Sous le pavé*, as the slogan went, *la plage*. ('Under the paving stones—the beach'). What the slogan writers of May 1968 never do is invite their readers to do anyone serious harm. Even the attacks on De Gaulle treat him as a superannuated impediment rather than as a political foe. They bespeak irritation and frustration, but remarkably little *anger*. This was to be a victimless revolution, which in the end meant that it was no sort of revolution at all.

The situation was very different in Italy, despite superficial similarities in the rhetoric of the student movements. In the first place, the social background to Italy's conflicts was quite distinctive. The extensive migration from south to north in the course of the first half of the decade had generated, in Milan, Turin and other industrial towns of the north, a demand for transport, services, education and above all housing that the governments of the country had never managed to address. The Italian 'economic miracle' arrived later than elsewhere, and the transition out of an agrarian society had been more abrupt.

As a consequence, the disruptions of first-generation industrialization overlapped and collided with the discontents of modernity. Unskilled and semi-skilled workers—typically from the south, many of them women—were never absorbed into the established unions of skilled male workers in the industrialized north. Traditional worker/employer tensions were now multiplied by disputes between skilled and unskilled, unionized and unorganized workers. The better-paid, better-protected, skilled employees in the factories of FIAT, or the Pirelli Rubber Company, demanded a greater say in management decisions—over shift hours, wage differentials and disciplinary measures. Unskilled workers sought some of these goals and opposed others. *Their* main objection was to exhausting piece rates, the unrelenting pace of mechanized mass production lines, and unsafe working conditions.

Italy's post-war economy was transformed by hundreds of small engineering, textile and chemical firms, most of whose employees had no legal or institutional recourse against their bosses' demands. The Italian welfare state in the 1960s was still a rather rough-and-ready edifice that would not reach maturity until the following decade (in large part thanks to the social upheavals of the Sixties), and many unskilled workers and their families were still without workplace rights or access to family benefits (in March 1968 there was a nationwide strike to demand a comprehensive national pension scheme). These were not issues that the traditional parties and unions of the Left were equipped to address. On the contrary, their main concern at the time was the dilution of the old labor institutions by this new and undisciplined workforce. When semi-skilled women workers sought backing from the Communist trade union in their complaints about accelerated work-rates they were encouraged instead to demand higher compensation.

In these circumstances, the chief beneficiaries of Italy's social tensions were not the established organizations of the Left, but a handful of informal networks of the 'extra-parliamentary' Left. Their leaders—dissident Communists, academic theoreticians of worker autonomy, and spokesmen for student organizations—were quicker to identify the new sources of discontent at the industrial workplace and absorb them into their projects. Moreover, the universities themselves offered an irresistible analogy. There, too, a new and unorganized workforce (the massive influx of first-generation students) faced conditions of life and work that were deeply unsatisfactory. There, too, an old élite exercised untrammeled decision-making power over the student masses, imposing workload, tests, grades and penalties at will.

From this perspective, administrators and established unions and other professional organizations in schools and universities—no less than in factories and workshops—shared a vested, 'objective' interest in the *status quo*. The fact that Italy's student population was drawn overwhelmingly from the urban middle class was no impediment to such reasoning—as producers and consumers of knowledge, they represented (in their own eyes) an even greater threat to power and authority than the traditional forces of the proletariat. In the thinking of the New Left it was not the social origin of a group that counted, but rather its capacity to disrupt the institutions and structures of authority. A lecture hall was as good a place to begin as a machine shop.

The protean adaptability of Italian radical politics in these years is well captured in the following set of demands circulated in a *liceo* (secondary school) in Milan: the goals of the student movement, it declared, were 'the control and eventual elimination of marks and failures, and therefore the abolition of selection in school; the right of everyone to an education and to a guaranteed student grant; freedom to hold meetings; a general meeting in the morning; accountability of teachers to students; removal of all reactionary and authoritarian teachers; setting of the curriculum from below'.[19]

The late-Sixties cycle of protests and disruptions in Italy began in Turin in 1968 with student objections to plans to move part of the university (the science faculty) to the suburbs—an echo of the protests taking place in suburban Nanterre at exactly the same time. There was a parallel, too, in the subsequent closure, in March 1968, of the University of Rome following student riots there in protest of a parliamentary bill to reform the universities. But unlike the French student movements, the Italian student organizers' interest in the reform of academic institutions was always secondary to their identification with the workers' movement, as the names of their organizations—*Avanguardia Operaia* or *Potere Operaio* ('Workers' Vanguard', 'Workers' Power')—suggest.

---

[19]Quoted in Robert Lumley, *States of Emergency. Cultures of Revolt in Italy from 1968 to 1978* (London, 1990), p.96

The labor disputes that began in the Pirelli company's Milan factories in September 1968 and lasted through November 1969 (when the government pressured Pirelli into conceding the strikers' main demands) furnished an industrial counterpoint and encouragement to the student protesters. The strike movement of 1969 was the largest in Italian history, and had a mobilizing and politicizing impact upon young Italian radicals out of all proportion to France's brief, month-long protests of the previous year. The 'hot autumn' of that year, with its wildcat strikes and spontaneous occupations by small groups of workers demanding a say in the way factories were run, led a generation of Italian student theorists and their followers to conclude that their root and branch rejection of the 'bourgeois state' was the right tactic. Workers' autonomy—as tactic and as objective—was the path of the future. Not only were reforms—in schools and factories alike—unattainable, they were undesirable. Compromise was defeat.

Just why 'unofficial' Italian Marxists should have taken this turn remains a matter of debate. The traditionally subtle and accommodating strategy of the Italian Communist Party left it exposed to the charge of working inside 'the system', of having a vested interest in stability and thus being, as its left-wing critics charged, 'objectively reactionary'. And the Italian political system itself was both corrupt and seemingly impermeable to change: in the parliamentary elections of 1968 the Christian Democrats and Communists *both* increased their vote, and every other party came nowhere. But while this might account for the disaffection of the extra-parliamentary Left, it cannot fully explain their turn to violence.

'Maoism'—or at any rate, an uncritical fascination with the Chinese Cultural Revolution then in full swing—was more extensive in Italy than anywhere else in Europe. Parties, groups and journals of a Maoist persuasion, recognizable by their insistence upon the adjective 'Marxist-Leninist' (to distinguish them from the despised official Communists), sprung up in quick succession in these years, inspired by China's Red Guards and emphasizing the identity of interests binding workers and intellectuals. Student theorists in Rome and Bologna even mimicked the rhetoric of the Beijing doctrinaires, dividing academic subjects into 'pre-bourgeois remnants' (Greek and Latin), the 'purely ideological' (e.g. history) and the 'indirectly ideological' (physics, chemistry, mathematics).

The putatively Maoist combination of revolutionary romanticism and workerist dogma was incarnated in the journal (and movement) *Lotta Continua* ('Continuous Struggle')—whose name, as was often the case, encapsulates its project. *Lotta Continua* first appeared in the autumn of 1969, by which time the turn to violence was well under way. Among the slogans of the Turin student demonstrations of June 1968 were 'No to social peace in the factories!' and 'Only violence helps where violence reigns.' In the months that followed, university and factory demonstrations saw an accentuation of the taste for violence, both rhetorical ('Smash the state, don't change it!') and real. The most popular song of the Italian student movement in these months was, appropriately enough, *La Violenza*.

The ironies of all this were not lost on contemporaries. As the film-maker Pier Paolo Pasolini remarked in the wake of student confrontations with the police in Rome's Villa Borghese gardens, the class roles were now reversed: the privileged children of the bourgeoisie were screaming revolutionary slogans and beating up the underpaid sons of southern sharecroppers charged with preserving civic order. For anyone with an adult memory of the recent Italian past, this turn to violence could only end badly. Whereas French students had played with the idea that public authority might prove vulnerable to disruption from below, a caprice that Gaullism's firmly-grounded institutions allowed them to indulge with impunity, Italy's radicals had good reason to believe that they might actually succeed in rending the fabric of the post-Fascist Republic—and they were keen to try. On April 24th 1969, bombs were planted at the Milan Trade Fair and the central railway station. Eight months later, *after* the Pirelli conflicts had been settled and the strike movement ended, the Agricultural Bank on the Piazza Fontana in Milan was blown up. The 'strategy of tension' that underlay the lead years of the Seventies had begun.

Italian radicals in the Sixties could be accused of having forgotten their country's recent past. In West Germany, the opposite was true. Until 1961, a post-war generation had been raised to see Nazism as responsible for war and defeat; but its truly awful aspects were consistently downplayed. The trial that year in Jerusalem of Adolf Eichmann, followed from 1963 to 1965 by the so-called 'Auschwitz trials' in Frankfurt, belatedly brought to German public attention the evils of the Nazi regime. In Frankfurt, 273 witnesses attested to the scale and depth of German crimes against humanity, reaching far beyond the 23 men (22 SS and 1 camp *kapo*) on charge. In 1967, Alexander and Margarete Mitscherlich published their hugely influential study of *Die Unfähigkeit zu trauen* ('The Inability to Mourn'), arguing that the official West German recognition of Nazi evil had never been accompanied by genuine individual recognition of responsibility.

West German intellectuals vigorously took up this idea. Established writers, playwrights and film-makers—Günter Grass, Martin Walser, Hans-Magnus Enzensberger, Jürgen Habermas, Rolf Hochhuth, Edgar Reitz, all born between 1927 and 1932—now focused their work increasingly upon Nazism and the failure to come to terms with it. But a younger cohort of intellectuals, born during or just after World War Two, took a harsher stance. Lacking direct knowledge of what had gone before, they saw all Germany's faults through the prism of the failings not so much of Nazism as of the Bonn Republic. Thus for Rudi Dutschke (born in 1940), Peter Schneider (1940), Gudrun Ensslin (1940) or the slightly younger Andreas Baader (born in 1943) and Rainer Werner Fassbinder (1945), West Germany's postwar democracy was not the solution; it was the problem. The apolitical, consumerist, American-protected cocoon of the *Bundesrepublik* was not just imperfect and amnesiac; it had actively conspired with its Western masters to deny the German past, to bury it in material goods and anti-Communist propaganda. Even its constitutional attributes were inauthentic: as Fassbinder put it, 'Our democracy was decreed for the Western occupation zone, we didn't fight for it ourselves.'

The youthful radical intelligentsia of the German Sixties accused the Bonn Republic of covering up the crimes of its founding generation. Many of the men and women born in Germany during the war and immediate post-war years never knew their fathers: who they were, what they had done. In school they were taught nothing about German history post-1933 (and not much more about the Weimar era either). As Peter Schneider and others would later explain, they lived in a vacuum constructed over a void: even at home—indeed, especially at home—no-one would talk about 'it'.

Their parents, the cohort of Germans born between 1910 and 1930, did not just refuse to discuss the past. Skeptical of political promises and grand ideas, their attention was relentlessly and a trifle uneasily focused on material well-being, stability and respectability. As Adenauer had understood, their identification with America and 'the West' derived in no small measure from a wish to avoid association with all the baggage of 'Germanness'. As a result, in the eyes of their sons and daughters they stood for *nothing*. Their material achievements were tainted by their moral inheritance. If ever there was a generation whose rebellion really was grounded in the rejection of everything their parents represented—*everything*: national pride, Nazism, money, the West, peace, stability, law and democracy—it was 'Hitler's children', the West German radicals of the Sixties.

In their eyes the Federal Republic exuded self-satisfaction and hypocrisy. First there was the *Spiegel* Affair. In 1962 Germany's leading weekly news magazine had published a series of articles investigating West German defense policy that hinted at shady dealings by Adenauer's Bavarian defense minister, Franz-Josef Strauss. With Adenauer's authorization and at Strauss's behest, the government harassed the paper, arrested its publisher and ransacked its offices. This shameless abuse of police powers to suppress unwelcome reporting attracted universal condemnation—even the impeccably conservative *Frankfurter Allgemeine Zeitung* observed that 'this is an embarrassment to our democracy, which cannot live without a free press, without indivisible freedom of the press.'

Then, four years later in December 1966, the ruling Christian Democrats selected as Chancellor in succession to Ludwig Erhard the former Nazi Kurt-Georg Kiesinger. The new Chancellor had been a paid-up Party member for twelve years, and his appointment was taken by many as conclusive evidence of the Bonn Republic's unrepentant cynicism. If the head of the government was not embarrassed to have supported Hitler for twelve years, who could take seriously West German professions of repentance or commitment to liberal values at a time when neo-Nazi organizations were once again surfacing at the political fringe? As Grass expressed it in an open letter to Kiesinger at a moment of neo-Nazi resurgence:

'How are young people in our country to find arguments against the Party that died two decades ago but is being resurrected as the NPD if you burden the Chancellorship with the still very considerable weight of your own past?'

Kiesinger headed the government for three years, from 1966–1969. In those years the German Extra-Parliamentary Left (as it had taken to describing itself) moved into the universities with dramatic success. Some of the causes taken up by the SDS, the Socialist Students Union, were by now commonplace across continental Western Europe: overcrowded dormitories and classes; remote and inaccessible professors; dull and unimaginative teaching. But the burning issues of these years were peculiar to West Germany. The liveliest campus was at the Free University of Berlin (founded in 1948 to compensate for the imprisonment of the established Humboldt University campus in the Communist Zone), where many students had gone to avoid conscription.[20]

Anti-militarism had a special place in German student protest as a tidy way to condemn both the Federal Republic and its Nazi predecessor. With the growth of opposition to the Vietnam War this conflation between past and present extended to West Germany's military mentor. America, always 'fascist' in the rhetoric of a minority of radicals, now became the enemy for a far broader constituency. Indeed, attacking 'Amerika' (*sic*) for its criminal war in Vietnam served almost as a surrogate for discussion of Germany's own war crimes. In Peter Weiss's 1968 play *Vietnam-Discourse* the parallel between the United States and the Nazis is explicitly drawn.

If America was no better than the Hitler regime—if, in a slogan of the time, US=SS—then it was but a short step to treating Germany itself as Vietnam: both countries were divided by foreign occupiers, both were helplessly caught up in other people's conflicts. This way of talking allowed West German radicals to despise the Bonn Republic both for its present imperialist-capitalist associations *and* for its past fascist ones. More ominously, it authorized the radical Left to recycle the claim that it was Germans themselves who were the true victims—an assertion hitherto identified with the far Right.[21]

We should not, then, be surprised to learn that for all their anger at the 'Auschwitz generation', young Germans of the Sixties were not really much concerned with the Jewish Holocaust. Indeed, like their parents, they were uncomfortable with the 'Jewish Question'. They preferred to subsume it in academic demands for classes on '*Faschismustheorie*', obscuring the racist dimension of Nazism and emphasizing instead its links to capitalist production and imperial

---

[20]West Berlin itself had taken on something of a counter-cultural tone in these years. Fossilized by its peculiar isolation at the heart of international political tensions, dependant on handouts from Bonn and Washington, its future lastingly impermanent, the city was suspended in time and space. This made it rather appealing to dissidents, radicals and others who sought out the political and cultural fringe. The irony of West Berlin's situation—that its survival as a bohemian outpost of the West depended entirely on the presence of American soldiers—was lost on many of its youthful residents.

[21]Echoes of this inversion were to be heard again at the time of the first Gulf War in 1991, when its German opponents did not hesitate to cast America as the twentieth century's leading war criminal . . . and Germany as its first victim.

power—and thence forward to Washington and Bonn. The truly 'repressive state apparatus' was the imperial lackeys in Bonn; their victims were those who opposed America's war in Vietnam. In this peculiar logic the populist, down-market tabloid *Bild Zeitung*, with its withering criticisms of student politics, was a revived *Der Stürmer*; students were the new 'Jews'; and Nazi concentration camps were just a serviceable metaphor for the crimes of imperialism. In the words of a slogan graffitoed across the walls of Dachau in 1966 by a group of radicals: 'Vietnam is the Auschwitz of America'.

The German extra-parliamentary Left thus lost touch with its roots in the anti-Nazi mainstream. Furious with Willy Brandt's Social Democratic Party for entering a governing coalition with Kiesinger, the erstwhile Social Democratic student organizations moved rapidly to the fringes. More ostentatiously anti-Western than Sixties movements elsewhere in Europe, their constituent sects adopted deliberately third world names: Maoists, of course, but also 'Indians', 'Mescaleros' and the like. This anti-Western emphasis in turn nourished a counter-culture that was self-consciously exotic and more than a little bizarre, even by the standards of the time.

One distinctively German variant of Sixties cultural confusion saw sex and politics more closely entangled than elsewhere. Following Marcuse, Erich Fromm, Wilhelm Reich and other twentieth-century German theorists of sexual and political repression, radical circles in Germany (and Austria, or at least Vienna) sung the praises of nudity, free love and anti-authoritarian childrearing. Hitler's much advertised sexual neuroses were freely adduced to account for Nazism. And once again, a bizarre, chilling analogy was drawn in certain quarters between Hitler's Jewish victims and the youth of the 1960s, martyrs to the sexually repressive regime of their parents.

'Kommune 1', a Maoist micro-sect that aggressively promoted sexual promiscuity-as-liberation, circulated a self-portrait in 1966: seven nude young men and women splayed against a wall—'Naked Maoists Before a Naked Wall' as the caption read when the photo ran in *Der Spiegel* in June 1967. The emphasis on nudity was explicitly designed to recall pictures of helpless, naked concentration camp bodies. Look, it said: first came Hitler's victims, now the rebelliously unclothed bodies of Maoist revolutionaries. If Germans can look at the truth about *our* bodies, they will be able to face other truths as well.

The 'message'—that adolescent promiscuity would force the older generation to be open about sex, and thence about Hitler and everything else—provoked SDS leader Rudi Dutschke (in such matters a conventional Left moralist of the older sort) to condemn the 'Kommunards' as 'neurotics'. As no doubt they were. But their aggressively anachronistic narcissism, casually conflating mass murder and sexual exhibitionism in order to titillate and shock the bourgeoisie, was not without consequences: one member of 'Kommune 1', who proudly declared his orgasm to be of greater revolutionary consequence than Vietnam, would resurface in the 1970s in a guerrilla training camp in the Middle East. The path from self-indulgence to violence was even shorter in Germany than elsewhere.

In June 1967, at a Berlin demonstration against the Shah of Iran, police shot and killed Benno Ohnesorg, a student. Dutschke declared Ohnesorg's death a 'political murder' and called for a mass response; within days, 100,000 students demonstrated across West Germany. Jürgen Habermas, hitherto a prominent critic of the Bonn authorities, warned Dutschke and his friends a few days later of the risk of playing with fire. 'Left Fascism', he reminded the SDS leader, is as lethal as the right-wing kind. Those who talked loosely of the 'hidden violence' and 'repressive tolerance' of the peaceful Bonn regime—and who set out deliberately to provoke the authorities into repression by voluntaristic acts of real violence—did not know what they were doing.

In March of the following year, as radical student leaders called repeatedly for confrontation with the Bonn 'regime' and the government threatened to retaliate against violent provocation in West Berlin and elsewhere, Habermas—joined by Grass, Walser, Enzensberger and Hochhuth—again appealed for democratic reason to prevail, calling upon students and government alike to respect republican legality. The following month Dutschke himself would pay the price of the violent polarization he had encouraged, when he was shot in Berlin by a neo-Nazi sympathizer, on April 11th 1968. In the angry weeks that followed, two people were killed and four hundred wounded in Berlin alone. The Kiesinger government passed Emergency Laws (by 384 votes to 100, with backing from many Social Democrats) authorizing Bonn to rule by decree if necessary—and arousing widespread fear that the Bonn Republic was on the verge of collapse, like Weimar just thirty-five years earlier.

The increasingly violent fringe sects of German student politics—*K-Gruppen*, the *Autonome*, the sharp end of the SDS—were all ostensibly 'Marxist', usually Marxist-Leninist (i.e., Maoist). Many of them were quietly financed from East Germany or Moscow, though this was not common knowledge at the time. Indeed, in Germany as elsewhere, the New Left kept its distance from official Communism—which in West Germany was in any case a political irrelevance. But like much of the West German Left (and not only the Left), the radicals had an ambiguous relationship with the German Democratic Republic to their East.

Quite a few of them had been born in what was now East Germany, or else in other lands to the east from which their ethnic German families had been expelled: East Prussia, Poland, Czechoslovakia. Perhaps not surprisingly, their parents' nostalgia for a lost German past was unconsciously echoed in their own dreams of an alternative, better Germany to the East. East Germany, despite (because of?) its repressive, censorious authoritarianism, had a special attraction for hard-core young radicals: it was everything Bonn was not and it did not pretend otherwise.

Thus the radicals' hatred for the 'hypocrisies' of the Federal Republic made them uniquely susceptible to the claims of East Germany's Communists to have faced up to German history and purged *their* Germany of its fascist past. Moreover, the anti-Communism that bound West Germany into the Atlantic Alliance and that constituted its core political doctrine was itself a target for the New Left, particularly in the years of the Vietnam War, and helps account for their anti-anti-Communism. Emphasis upon the crimes of Communism was just a diversion from the crimes of capitalism. Communists, as Daniel Cohn-Bendit had expressed it in Paris, might be 'Stalinist scoundrels'; but liberal democrats were no better.

Thus the German Left turned a deaf ear to rumblings of discontent in Warsaw or Prague. The face of the Sixties in West Germany, as in Western Europe at large, was turned resolutely inwards. The cultural revolution of the era was remarkably parochial: if Western youth looked beyond their borders at all, it was to exotic lands whose image floated free of the irritating constraints of familiarity or information. Of alien cultures *closer* to home, the Western Sixties knew little. When Rudi Dutschke paid a fraternal visit to Prague, at the height of the Czech reform movement in the spring of 1968, local students were taken aback at his insistence that pluralist democracy was the real enemy. For them, it was the goal.

XIII

The End of the Affair

'Revolution is the act of an enormous majority of society directed against the rule of a minority. It is accompanied by a crisis of political power and by a weakening of the apparatus of coercion. That is why it does not have to be carried out by force of arms'.
Jacek Kuroń and Karel Modzelewski, **Open Letter to the Party (March 1965)**

'Each Communist party is free to apply the principles of Marxism-Leninism and socialism in its own country, but it is not free to deviate from these principles if it is to remain a Communist party'.
Leonid Brezhnev (August 3rd 1968)

'It was only after the Prague Spring of 1968 that one began to see who was who'.
Zdeněk Mlynář

'Yesterday came suddenly'.
Paul McCartney

The Sixties in the Soviet bloc were of necessity experienced very differently from the West. De-Stalinization after 1956 stimulated demands for change much as de-colonization and the Suez débâcle did in the West, but the destruction of the Hungarian revolt made it clear from the outset that reforms would come only under the auspices of the Party. This in turn served as a reminder that the mainspring of Communism was the authority of Moscow; it was the mood and policies of the Soviet leadership that counted. Until his overthrow in 1964, it was Nikita Khrushchev who determined the history of Europe's eastern half.

Khrushchev's generation of Soviet leaders still believed in the international class struggle. Indeed, it was Khrushchev's romanticized projection of Soviet revolutionary memories onto Latin American uprisings that led him to make the missteps that produced the Cuba crisis of 1962 and his own downfall. The struggle with China that emerged into the open in 1960, and afforded Moscow's leftist critics a 'Maoist' alternative to the Soviet model, was not merely a struggle for geopolitical primacy; it was also in part a genuine conflict for the soul of 'world revolution'. In this guise, the competition with Beijing placed Moscow's post-Stalinist rulers in a contradictory position. As the homeland of anti-capitalist revolution they continued to advertise their seditious ambitions and insist upon the undiminished authority of the Party, in the USSR and in its satellites. On the other hand the Kremlin continued to favour co-existence with the Western powers—and with its own citizens.

The Khrushchev years did see real improvements. From 1959, Stalin's 'Short Course' was no longer the authoritative source of Soviet history and Marxist theory.[1] The reign of terror abated, though not the institutions and practices to which it had given rise: the Gulag was still in place, and tens of thousands of political prisoners still languished in camps and in exile—half of them Ukrainians. Under Khrushchev, Stalin-era laws restricting job mobility were abandoned, the official workday was shortened, minimum wages were established and a system of maternity leave introduced, along with a national pension scheme (extended to collective farmers after 1965). In short, the Soviet Union—and its more advanced satellite states—became embryonic welfare states, at least in form.

However, Khrushchev's more ambitious reforms failed to produce the promised food surpluses (another reason why his colleagues were to dump him in October 1964). The cultivation of hitherto 'virgin' lands in Kazakhstan and southern Siberia was especially disastrous: half a million tons of topsoil washed away each year from land that was wholly unsuited to forced grain planting, and what harvest there was frequently arrived infested with weeds. In a tragic-comic blend of centralized planning and local corruption, Communist bosses in Kyrgyzstan urged collective farmers to meet official farm delivery quotas by buying up supplies in local shops. There were food riots in provincial cities (notably in Novocherkassk in June 1962). By January 1964, following the disastrous 1963 harvest, the USSR was reduced to importing grain from the West.

At the same time, the private micro-farms that Khrushchev had sporadically encouraged were almost embarrassingly successful: by the early sixties, the 3 percent of cultivated soil in private hands was yielding over a third of the Soviet Union's agricultural output. By 1965, two thirds of the potatoes consumed in the USSR and three quarters of the eggs came from private farmers. In the Soviet Union as in Poland or Hungary, 'Socialism' depended for its survival upon the illicit 'capitalist' economy within, to whose existence it turned a blind eye.[2]

The economic reforms of the fifties and sixties were from the start a fitful attempt to patch up a structurally dysfunctional system. To the extent that they implied a half-hearted willingness to decentralize economic decisions or authorize *de*

---

[1]Though it was replaced by a newly mythologized version in which Stalin himself—and his crimes—passed half unacknowledged.

[2]The credibility of the Soviet system rested to a quite extraordinary extent upon its capacity to get results from the land. For most of its eighty-year life, agriculture was on an emergency footing in one way or another. This would not have struck an eighteenth-century European or even a twentieth-century African observer as especially unusual; but the Soviet Union was held to rather higher standards of performance.

facto private production, they were offensive to hardliners among the old guard. But otherwise the liberalizations undertaken by Khrushchev, and after him Brezhnev, presented no immediate threat to the network of power and patronage on which the Soviet system depended. Indeed, it was just because economic improvements in the Soviet bloc were always subordinate to political priorities that they achieved so very little.

Cultural reform was another matter. Lenin had always worried more about his critics than his principles; his heirs were no different. Intellectual opposition, whether or not it was likely to find a wider echo in the party or outside, was something to which Communist leaders, Khrushchev included, were intensely sensitive. Following his first denunciations of Stalin in 1956 there was widespread optimism, in the Soviet Union as elsewhere, that censorship would relax and a space would open up for cautious dissent and criticism (that same year Boris Pasternak unsuccessfully submitted the manuscript of his novel *Dr Zhivago* to the literary periodical *Novy Mir*). But the Kremlin was soon worried by what it saw as the rise of cultural permissiveness; within three years of the Twentieth Party Congress Khrushchev was making aggressive public speeches defending official Socialist Realism in the arts and threatening its critics with serious consequences if they continued to disparage it, even in retrospect. At the same time, in 1959, the authorities clamped down on Orthodox priests and Baptists, a form of cultural dissidence that had been allowed a certain freedom since Stalin's fall.

However, Khrushchev himself, if not his colleagues, was reliably unpredictable. The 22nd Congress of the CPSU, in October 1961, revealed the extent of the schism between China and the USSR (the following month the Soviets closed their embassy in Albania, Beijing's European *locum*), and in the competition for global influence Moscow set out to present a new face to its confused and vacillating foreign constituency. In 1962 an obscure provincial schoolteacher, Aleksandr Solzhenitsyn, was allowed to publish his pessimistic and implicitly subversive novel *One Day in the Life of Ivan Denisovitch* in *Novy Mir*—the same journal that had rejected Pasternak not six years before.

The relative tolerance of Khrushchev's last years did not extend to direct criticism of the Soviet leadership: Solzhenitsyn's later work would certainly never have been allowed into print even at the height of the 'thaw'. But in comparison with what had gone before, the early Sixties were a time of literary freedom and cautious cultural experimentation. With the Kremlin coup of October 1964, however, everything changed. The plotters against Khrushchev were irritated at his policy failures and his autocratic style; but above all it was his inconsistencies that made them uneasy. The First Secretary himself might know exactly what was permissible and what was not, but others could be tempted to misunderstand his apparent tolerance. Mistakes might be made.

Within months of taking control, the new Kremlin leadership began to press down upon the intelligentsia. In September 1965 two young writers, Andrei

Sinyavsky and Yuli Daniel, were arrested. Under the pseudonyms Abram Tertz and Nikolay Arzhak they had smuggled out for publication in the West various works of fiction. Tertz-Sinyavsky had also published—abroad—a short, critical essay on modern Soviet literature, *On Socialist Realism*. In February 1966 the two men were put on trial. Since no law in the Soviet Union prohibited the publication of works abroad, the authorities claimed that the content of their works was itself evidence of the crime of anti-Soviet activity. The two men were found guilty and sentenced to labor camps: Sinyavsky for seven years (though he was released after six) and Daniel for five.

The Sinyavsky-Daniel trial was held *in camera*, although a press campaign vilifying the two writers had drawn public attention to their fate. But the trial proceedings were secretly recorded and transcribed by several people admitted to the courtroom and they were published both in Russian and English a year later, generating international petitions and demands for the men's release.[3] The unusual aspect of the affair was that for all the brutality of the Stalin decades, no-one had hitherto been arrested and imprisoned *solely* on the basis of the content of their (fictional) writings. Even if material evidence had been freely invented for the purpose, intellectuals in the past had always been accused of *deeds*, not merely *words*.

Contrasting as it did with the comparative laxity of the Khrushchev years, the treatment of Sinyavsky and Daniel aroused unprecedented protests within the Soviet Union itself. The dissident movement of the last decades of the Soviet Union dates from this moment: underground 'samizdat' ('self-publication') began in the year of the arrests and because of them, and many of the most consequential figures in Soviet dissident circles of the seventies and eighties made their first appearance as protesters against the treatment of Sinyavsky and Daniel. Vladimir Bukovsky, then a 25-year-old student, was arrested in 1967 for organizing a demonstration in Pushkin Square in defense of civil rights and freedom of expression. Already in 1963 he had been arrested by the KGB, charged with possession of anti-Soviet literature and committed to a psychiatric hospital for compulsory treatment. Now he was sentenced to three years in labor camp for 'anti-Soviet activities'.

The Sinyavsky-Daniel affair and the response it aroused seemed to mark out very clearly the situation in the Soviet Union: what had changed and what had not. By any standards save those of its own history, the regime was immovable, repressive and inflexible. The mirage of 1956 had faded. The prospects for truth telling about the past, and reform in the future, seemed to have receded. The illusions of the Khrushchev era were shattered. Whatever face it presented to the Western powers, the Soviet regime at home was settling in for an indefinite twilight of economic stagnation and moral decay.

In the satellite states of the Soviet bloc in Eastern Europe, however, the prospects

---

[3] A year after his release, Sinyavsky emigrated to France and took up a post teaching Russian literature at the Sorbonne. Daniel stayed in Russia, where he died in 1988.

for change seemed distinctly more propitious. On the face of it, this is a paradox. After all, if the citizens of the Soviet Union were powerless in the face of the post-Stalinist dictatorship, then the inhabitants of Hungary or Czechoslovakia and their neighbors were doubly helpless: not only did they live under a repressive regime, but their own rulers were themselves in thrall to the real authority in the imperial capital. The principles of the Soviet imperium had been handily illustrated in Budapest in November 1956. Moreover, in Czechoslovakia and Romania some of the surviving victims of the show trials of earlier years were still languishing in prison a decade later.

And yet, Eastern Europe *was* different—in part, of course, just because it was a recent colonial extension of Communist rule. By the 1960s, Communism was the only form of rule most inhabitants of the Soviet Union had ever known; in the shadow of the Great Patriotic War it had even acquired a certain legitimacy. But further West the memory of Soviet occupation and the enforced Soviet take-over was still fresh. The mere fact that they *were* Moscow's puppets and thus lacked local credibility made the Party leaders of the satellite states more sensitive to the benefits of accommodating local sentiment.

This seemed the more possible because domestic critics of the Party regimes in Eastern Europe between 1956 and 1968 were by no means anti-Communist. Responding to Sartre's assertion in 1956 that Hungary's revolution had been marked by a 'rightist spirit', the Hungarian refugee scholar François Fejtö had replied that it was the Stalinists who stood on the Right. *They* were the 'Versaillais'. '*We* remain men of the Left, faithful to our ideas, our ideals and our traditions.' Fejtö's insistence on the credibility of an anti-Stalinist *Left* catches the tone of east European intellectual opposition for the following twelve years. The point was not to condemn Communism, much less overthrow it; the goal, rather, was to think through what had gone so horribly wrong and propose an alternative within the terms of Communism itself.

This was 'revisionism': a term first used in this context by Poland's leader Władislaw Gomułka at a May 1957 meeting of the Central Committee of the Polish United Workers' Party, to describe his intellectual critics. These 'revisionists'—in Poland the best known was the young Marxist philosopher Leszek Kołakowski—had in many cases been orthodox Marxists until 1956. They did not overnight foreswear this allegiance. Instead they spent the next twelve years, in the words of the Slovak writer Milan Šimečka, 'trying to find the fault in the blueprint.' Like most contemporary Western Marxists they were wedded to the notion that it was possible to distinguish clearly between the credibility of Marxism and the crimes of Stalin.

For many Eastern European Marxists, Stalinism was a tragic parody of Marxist doctrine and the Soviet Union a permanent challenge to the credibility of the project of Socialist transformation. But unlike the New Left in the West, the intellectual revisionists of the East continued to work with, and often within, the Communist Party. This was partly from necessity, of course; but partly too from sincere conviction. In the longer run this affiliation would isolate and even discredit the reform Communists of these years, notably in the eyes of a rising generation increasingly attuned to the mood of their Western peers and whose point of reference was not the Stalinist past but the capitalist present. But from 1956 to 1968, the revisionist moment in Eastern Europe afforded writers, filmmakers, economists, journalists and others a brief window of optimism about an alternative Socialist future.

In Poland the most important critical space was that afforded by the Catholic Church and the protection it could offer those working under its auspices—notably at the Catholic University of Lublin and on the journals *Znak* and *Tygodnik Powszechny*. It was a peculiarity of Poland in the Gomułka years that Marxist philosophers and Catholic theologians could find some common ground in their defense of free speech and civil liberties—an embryonic anticipation of the alliances that would be forged in the Seventies. Elsewhere, however, the Communist Party itself was the only forum in which such criticisms could safely be voiced. The most propitious terrain for 'helpful' criticism was the Communist management of the economy.

One reason for this was that conventional Marxism was purportedly grounded in political economy, so that economic policy (once liberated from the dead hand of Stalin) was a permissible arena of intellectual dissent. Another reason was that many east European intellectuals of the time still took Marxism very seriously and treated the problem of Communist economics as a vital theoretical starting point for serious reforms. But the main explanation was simply that, by the early Sixties, the economies of Europe's Communist states were showing the first intimations of serious disrepair.

The failings of Communist economies were hardly a secret. They were only just able to furnish their citizens with sufficient food (in the Soviet Union they often failed to manage even this). They were committed to the mass production of redundant primary industrial goods. The commodities—consumer goods above all—for which there *was* a growing demand were not produced, or else not in sufficient quantity, or of the necessary quality. And the system of distribution and sale of such goods as were available was so badly managed that genuine shortages were exacerbated by artificially induced scarcity: bottlenecks, skimming, corruption, and—in the case of food and other perishables—high levels of wastage.

The peculiar inefficiencies of Communism had been partly camouflaged in the first post-war decade by the demands of post-war reconstruction. But by the early Sixties, following Khrushchev's boast that Communism would 'overtake' the West and official proclamations about the now completed transition to Socialism, the gap between Party rhetoric and daily penury could no longer be bridged by exhortations to repair war damage or produce more. And the charge that it was saboteurs—kulaks, capitalists, Jews, spies or Western 'interests'—who were responsible for impeding Communism's forward march, though still heard in certain quarters, was now associated with the time of terror: a time that most Communist leaders, following Khrushchev, were anxious to put behind them. The problems, it was increasingly conceded, must lie in the Communist economic system itself.

Self-styled 'reform economists' ('revisionist' carried pejorative connotations) were thickest on the ground in Hungary. In 1961 János Kádár had let it be known that the Party-State would assume henceforth that anyone not actively opposing it was for it; and it was thus under the auspices of the Kádárist regime that critics of Communist economic practice first felt safe to speak.[4] Reform economists acknowledged that the land collectivization of the forties and fifties had been a mistake. They also recognized, though more cautiously, that the Soviet obsession with the large-scale extraction and production of primary industrial goods was an impediment to growth. In short, they conceded—though not in so many words—that the blanket application to eastern Europe of the Soviet Union's own forced industrialization and destruction of private property had been a disaster. And even more radically, they began to seek ways in which Communist economies might incorporate price signals and other market incentives into a collectivist system of property and production.

The Sixties debates on economic reform in eastern Europe had to walk a fine line. Some Party leaders were sufficiently pragmatic (or worried) to acknowledge the technical mistakes of the past—even the neo-Stalinist Czech leadership abandoned the emphasis on heavy industry in 1961, halfway through its disastrous Third Five-Year Plan. But admitting the failure of central planning or collective property was another matter. Reform economists like Ota Sik or the Hungarian János Kornai sought instead to define a 'third way': a mixed economy in which the non-negotiable fact of common ownership and central planning would be mitigated by increased local autonomy, some price signals and the relaxation of controls. The economic arguments, after all, were incontrovertible: without such reforms, the Communist system would degenerate into stagnation and poverty—'reproducing shortage', as Kornai put it in a famous paper.

In Hungary alone, Kádár did respond to his critics by allowing a measure of genuine reform: the New Economic Mechanism inaugurated in 1968. Collective farms were granted substantial autonomy and not just permitted but actively encouraged to support private plots on the side. Some monopolies were broken up. Certain commodity prices were tied to the world market and allowed to fluctuate via multiple exchange rates. Private retail outlets were authorized. The point of the

---

[4]Although the best-known reform economist of the Sixties was a Czech, Ota Sik, it was the Hungarian school that had the broadest influence and the most practical impact.

exercise was not so much to construct a working middle way between two in-compatible economic systems, but rather to introduce the maximum of market ac-tivity (and thus, it was hoped, contentment-inducing consumer prosperity) compatible with undiluted political control of the commanding heights of the economy.

In retrospect it is clear that the reformers were deluding themselves if they sup-posed that a 'third way' between Communism and capitalism was ever realistic. But this was not because of any formal shortcoming in their economic analysis. Their true error lay in a curiously naïve misreading of the system under which they lived. What mattered to the Communist leadership was not economics but politics. The ineluctable implication of the economic reformers' theories was that the central au-thority of the Party-State would need to be weakened if normal economic life was to be resumed. But faced with *that* choice the Communist Party-States would al-ways opt for economic abnormality.

In the meantime, however, the regimes were interested above all in stability. For this there were three emerging models. The first, 'Kádárism', was not readily exportable—and it was very much part of the Hungarian leader's own strategy to assure the Kremlin authorities that there *was* no Hungarian 'model', merely a lim-ited practical solution to local difficulties. Hungary's situation was indeed unique, with Kádár cynically dangling access to the prosperous West before his travel-starved fellow Hungarians as a sort of reward for good behaviour—a tacit confes-sion of Communism's own failure. The country was now run by and for the 'New Class', as the Yugoslav dissident Milovan Djilas had called it in an influential 1957 book: an educated technocracy of bureaucrats and professionals, pragmatically concerned above all with feathering its nest and ensuring its own survival. Genuine liberation was unthinkable, but a reversion to repression highly unlikely.

Kádár's Hungary—'the best barracks in the *laager*'—was much envied, though only fitfully emulated. The second model, Tito's Yugoslavia, was even more obvi-ously *sui generis*. This was not because Yugoslavia had managed to avoid the prob-lems of its neighbors. Many of the economic dysfunctions of the Soviet satellites were just as familiar to Yugoslavs, a reminder that their country's suspended ani-mation between East and West was a product of historical chance rather than ide-ological choice. But in the course of the Fifties and Sixties Tito had introduced some decentralization in decision-making and allowed experiments with factory and worker 'autonomy'.

These innovations were born of ethnic and geographical divisions as well as eco-nomic necessity. In a federal state whose constituent republics and peoples shared little beyond unhappy and mutually antagonistic memories, the imposition of uni-form instructions from Belgrade looked a lot like a return to pre-war practices. The difficult topography of the region favored local initiative; and thanks to the break with Stalin, Tito's own version of proletarian dictatorship was no longer under pressure to replicate in detail every error of the Soviet Union's own path to industrial modernity. It was these considerations—rather than the creative, alternative Socialist blueprint with which his Western admirers wishfully credited Tito in these years—that shaped the Yugoslav model.

But Yugoslavia was different all the same: not necessarily kinder to its critics, as Djilas and others found to their cost when dissenting from Titoist orthodoxy,[5] but more flexible in handling the needs and wants of the population at large (not least thanks to Western aid). When the Yugoslav essayist Dubravka Ugrešić writes of her nostalgia for the lost Yugoslavia of her youth, what comes to mind are 'real "winkle-pickers", plastic macs, the first nylon underwear . . . the first trip to Trieste.' Such a checklist of cheap consumer goods would have been much less to the fore in Bulgarian or Romanian memory, for example—and the 'first trip to Trieste' would have been quite out of the question. Yugoslavs were not prosperous and they were not free; but nor were they imprisoned in a hermetic system. 'Titoism' was oppressive rather than repressive. At the time this distinction mattered.

A third route to stability was 'national Stalinism'. This was the Albanian option—a closed, impoverished society under the absolute rule of a local Party autocrat, paranoid and all-powerful. But it was also, increasingly, the Romanian model too. Nikita Khrushchev, who actively disliked Romania (a sentiment widespread in his generation of Russians), had sought to assign it a uniquely agricultural role in the international Communist distribution of labor. But the Bucharest Party leaders had no intention of being reduced to supplying raw materials and food to more prosperous and advanced Communist economies.

Having played an accommodating role in the imprisonment and suppression of the Hungarian revolt, the Romanians secured the withdrawal of Soviet forces from Romanian territory in 1958 and took an increasingly independent path. Under Dej and (from 1965) Ceauşescu, Romania declined to get involved in Moscow's quarrels with China and even refused to allow Warsaw Pact maneuvers on its territory. The Romanian leaders made overtures to Tito (whose own relations with the Warsaw Pact were formal rather than friendly), Dej even addressing the Yugoslav National Assembly in 1963; and they underwrote Romania's neo-Stalinist industrialization with money and machinery obtained from Western Europe. Romania's dealings with the West steadily increased; while trade with Comecon countries fell—from 70 percent of Romania's overall foreign trade at the start of the 1960s to 45 percent ten years later.

This much trumpeted 'Romania-first' strategy was not unpopular at home—indeed, one of the ways Romania's Communist Party had compensated in office for its distinctly un-Romanian origins was to wrap itself in the mantle of nationalism. Dej began this, and Ceauşescu merely went further still. But the strategy was even

---

[5]Djilas was imprisoned for four years when *The New Class* appeared in the West, and re-incarcerated for a further four years shortly after his release.

more successful abroad. Whereas Albania, China's European surrogate, held no attraction for anyone save nostalgic Stalinists and ultra-besotted Maoists, the international image of Communist Romania was curiously positive. Simply by distancing themselves from Moscow, the men in Bucharest gleaned a host of unlikely Western admirers. *The Economist*, in August 1966, called Ceauşescu 'the De Gaulle of Eastern Europe.'

As for De Gaulle himself, on a visit to Bucharest in May 1968 he observed that while Ceauşescu's Communism would not be appropriate for the West, it was probably well suited to Romania: "*Chez vous un tel régime est utile, car il fait marcher les gens et fait avancer les choses.*" ("For you such a regime is useful, it gets people moving and gets things done."). De Gaulle was doubtless right that Romanian Communism would not have been appropriate for the West. Communism in Romania was peculiarly vicious and repressive: by distancing themselves from the Soviet Union after 1958 Dej and Ceauşescu were also freeing themselves of any need to echo the de-Stalinization and reforms associated with the Khrushchev era. In contrast to other satellite states Romania allowed no space for any internal opposition—Bucharest intellectuals in the Sixties, cut off from their own society, played no part in domestic debates (there were none) and had to be satisfied with reading the latest *nouveaux romans* from Paris and participating vicariously in a cosmopolitan French culture for which educated Romanians had always claimed a special affinity.

But far from condemning the Romanian dictators, Western governments gave them every encouragement, After Romania breached the Soviet veto and formally recognized West Germany in January 1967, relations grew warmer still: Richard Nixon became the first US President to visit a Communist state when he went to Bucharest in August 1969. National Communism—'He may be a Commie but he's our Commie'—paid off for Ceauşescu: in due course Romania was the first Warsaw Pact state to enter GATT (in 1971), the World Bank and the IMF (1972), to receive European Community trading preferences (1973) and US Most-Favored-Nation status (1975).[6]

What Western diplomats thought they saw in Bucharest's anti-Russian autocrats were the germs of a new Tito: stable, biddable and more interested in local power than international disruption. In one sense, at least, they were correct. Tito and Ceauşescu, like Kádár and the neo-Stalinist leadership in the GDR, successfully negotiated the shoals of the Sixties. Each in his own way, they assured their authority and control at home while maintaining at least a *modus vivendi* with Moscow. The Communist leaders in Warsaw and Prague had no such success.

---

[6]Richard Nixon was by no means the last American to be seduced by the Romanian dictator. Impressed by Nicolae Ceauşescu during a visit to Romania in 1978, Senator George McGovern praised him as "among the world's leading proponents of arms control"; and as late as September 1983, when the awful truth about Ceauşescu's regime was already widely known, Vice President George Bush memorably described him as "one of Europe's good Communists."

. . .

The peaceful outcome to the Polish uprisings of 1956 had been achieved at a price. While Catholic institutions and writers were permitted in Gomułka's Poland, opposition within the Party itself was severely constrained. The Polish United Workers' Party remained deeply conservative, even though it had successfully avoided violent purges in the Stalin years. Nervous at the prospect of a re-run of the disturbances of 1956, the Party leadership treated any criticism of its policies as a direct threat to its political monopoly. The result was deep frustration among 'revisionist' intellectuals, not just at the regime in general but at the lost opportunity for a new direction, the unfinished business of the Polish October.

In the summer of 1964, two graduate students at Warsaw University, Jacek Kuroń and Karel Modzelewski, drafted an academic critique of the political and economic system of People's Poland. Their dissertation was unimpeachably Marxist in tone and content, but that did not stop them being expelled from the Party and the Union of Socialist Youth and being denounced in official circles for spreading anti-Party propaganda. Their response was to publish an Open Letter to the Party, submitted to the Warsaw University Party branch in March 1965. In the Letter the authors depicted a bureaucratic, autocratic regime, deaf to the interests of all but the ruling elite that it served, ruling incompetently over an impoverished working population and censoring all commentary and criticism. Poland's only hope, Kuroń and Modzelewski concluded, was a genuine revolution, based on workers' councils, freedom of the press and the abolition of the political police.

The day after presenting their Letter the two men were arrested and charged with advocating the overthrow of the state. On July 19th 1965 they were sentenced to prison terms of three and three and a half years respectively. The authorities were particularly sensitive to the impeccably Marxist terms of their critique, its effective use of social data to point up the regime's shabby economic performance, and its call for a workers' revolution to replace the current bureaucratic dictatorship (a neo-Trotskyist touch that did not help the authors' case[7]). Above all, perhaps, the Party was determined to head off precisely the combination of intellectual diagnosis and proletarian action for which the Kuroń-Modzelewski letter called.

The Kuroń-Modzelewski Affair sparked a heartfelt response in the university. The secret trial of the two students came as a shock, and there were demands not merely for their release but for their Letter and earlier research paper to be made public. Senior scholars took up their case. Leszek Kołakowski, professor of philosophy at Warsaw University, addressed students of the History Institute the following year, on the 10th anniversary of the Polish Party's plenary session of October

---

[7]The French translation of the *Open Letter* that circulated in Paris the following year was distributed by *Jeunesse Communiste Révolutionnaire*, a Trotskyist organization.

1956. The Polish October was a missed opportunity, he explained. Ten years later Poland was a land of privilege, inefficiency and censorship. The Communists had lost touch with the nation, and the repression of Kuroń, Modzelewski and the criticisms they espoused was a sign of the Party's—and the country's—decline.

Kołakowski was duly expelled from the Party as a 'bourgeois-liberal', though his colleagues at Warsaw University valiantly asserted his internationally recognized Marxist credentials. Twenty-two prominent Polish Communist writers and intellectuals then wrote to the Central Committee defending 'Comrade Kołakowski' as the spokesman of a 'free and authentic socialist culture and democracy.' They in turn were expelled from the Party. By the spring of 1967 the clumsy Polish leadership, enraged by criticism from its Left, had succeeded in forging a genuine intellectual opposition; and Warsaw University had become a center of student revolt—in the name of free speech and in defense, among other things, of their persecuted professors.

The issue of free speech at Warsaw University took an additional twist in January 1968. Since late November 1967 the University theatre had been running a production of *Forefathers' Eve*, a play by Adam Mickiewicz, Poland's national poet. Written in 1832 but dangerously contemporary in its portrayal of nineteenth-century rebels struggling against oppression, the play had attracted lively and distinctly engaged audiences. In late January the Communist authorities announced that the play would have to be cancelled. Following the last performance, hundreds of students marched to the Mickiewicz monument in the Polish capital denouncing censorship and demanding 'free theater'. Two of the students, Henryk Szlajfer and Adam Michnik, described the situation to *Le Monde*'s Warsaw correspondent, whose report was then carried on Radio Free Europe: Michnik and his colleague were duly expelled from the University.

The response was a wave of student-organized petitions to the Polish Parliament, sympathetic resolutions at the Warsaw branch of the Polish Writers' Association and speeches by Kołakowski and other prominent professors and writers in defense of the students. One writer publicly denounced the Communists' treatment of culture as 'the dictatorship of the dumb'. On March 8th a meeting of students in Warsaw University to protest the expulsion of Michnik and Szlajfer was violently broken up by police. There followed nationwide student demonstrations three days later and a strike at Warsaw University itself. Neo-Stalinist circles within the Party began to speak ominously of the Party's loss of control, some of them even alerting Moscow to the dangers of Czechoslovak-style 'revisionism'.

The Gomułka regime struck back decisively. The strike and ensuing protests were crushed with considerable violence—enough to provoke one Politburo member and two senior cabinet ministers to resign in protest. Thirty-four more students and six professors (including Kołakowski) were dismissed from Warsaw University. Then, following the crushing of the Prague Spring in neighboring Czechoslovakia (see below), the authorities arrested the organizers of protests and petitions against the Soviet invasion and brought them to trial. In a long series of trials held between September 1968 and May 1969, students and other intellectuals from Warsaw, Wrocław, Cracow and Łodz were sentenced to terms ranging from six months to three years for 'participation in secret organizations', 'distribution of anti-State publications' and other crimes. The harshest sentences were handed out to those like Adam Michnik, Jan Litynski and Barbara Toruńczyk who had also been active in the initial student protests.

A disproportionate number of the students and professors arrested, expelled and imprisoned in Poland in the years 1967–69 were of Jewish origin, and this was not a coincidence. Ever since Gomułka's return to power in 1956, the conservative (neo-Stalinist) wing of the Polish Party had been seeking an occasion to undo even the limited liberalizations he had introduced. Under the direction of Mieczysław Moczar, the Interior Minister, this inner-party opposition had coalesced around the cause of anti-Semitism.

From Stalin's death until 1967, anti-Semitism—though endemic in eastern Europe and the Soviet Union itself—was kept out of official Communist rhetoric. After the war most of Eastern Europe's surviving Jews had gone west, or to Israel. Of those who remained, many fled, if they could, in the course of the persecutions of Stalin's last years. There were still substantial communities of Jews remaining, in Poland and (especially) Hungary; but most of these were not practicing Jews and typically did not think of themselves as Jewish at all. In the case of those born after the war, they often did not even know that they were—their parents had thought it prudent to keep quiet.[8]

In Poland especially, the still considerable numbers of Jewish Communists—some of them holding political office, others in universities and the professions—were mostly indifferent to their Jewish background, some of them naïve enough to suppose that their indifference was shared by Poles at large. But they offered an irresistible target for anyone seeking a route to power within the Party and demagogic popularity in the country at large.[9] All that was lacking was the opportunity, and the Six Day War between Israel and its Arab neighbors duly afforded this in June 1967. Soviet support for the Arab cause legitimized vocal criticism of Israel, Zionism—and Jews.

Thus in a speech on June 19th 1967, condemning those who had backed Israel in the recent conflict, Gomułka brazenly conflated his Jewish critics and the Zionist state: 'I wish to announce that we shall not prevent Polish citizens of Jewish na-

---

[8]Of the approximately 30,000 Jews in mid-Sixties Poland, less than 7,500 belonged to the official Jewish organizations.
[9]In 1966 a Polish-language edition of the anti-Semitic forgery *The Protocols of the Elders of Zion* was unofficially circulated in Party groups, universities and the army.

tionality from returning [*sic*] to Israel if they wish to do so. Our position is that every Polish citizen should have one country: the People's Poland . . . Let those who feel that these words are addressed to them, irrespective of their nationality, draw the proper conclusion. We do not want a Fifth Column in our country.' The reference to Jews as Poland's Fifth Column was carried on radio and television and heard by millions of Poles. Its message was unambiguous.

Whether Gomulka was expressing his own views; was seeking scapegoats for the policy failures of the past decade; or was merely anticipating Moczar's efforts to unseat him and had decided to outflank his Stalinist opponents, was never clear. But the consequences of his decision were dramatic. The Polish authorities unleashed a flood of prejudice against Jews: throughout Poland, but especially in the Party and in academic institutions. Party apparatchiks spread suggestions that the economic shortages and other problems were the work of Jewish Communists. Distinctions were openly drawn between 'good' Communists, with national Polish interests at heart, and others (Jews) whose true affiliation lay elsewhere.

In 1968, the parents and other relatives of Jewish students arrested or expelled were themselves sacked from official positions and academic posts. Prosecutors paid special attention to the names and origins of students and professors who appeared in court—familiar from the Slánský and other trials of the Fifties but a first for Communist Poland. At the height of the anti-Semitic frenzy, newspapers were defining Jews by criteria derived directly from the Nuremberg Laws—unsurprising, perhaps, in view of the presence of recycled Polish fascists among the Stalinist wing of the ruling Party.

Jews were now invited to leave the country. Many did so, under humiliating conditions and at great personal cost. Of Poland's remaining 30,000 Jews some 20,000 departed in the course of 1968–69, leaving only a few thousand behind, mostly the elderly and the young—including Michnik and his fellow students, now serving terms in prison. Among the beneficiaries of this upheaval were Moczar and his supporters who took over the Party and government posts vacated by their Jewish occupants. The losers, beyond Poland's Jews, were the country's educational institutions (which lost many of their finest scholars and teachers, including Kolakowski—not himself a Jew but married to one); Gomulka, who realized too late what he had unleashed and was himself removed two years later; and Poland itself, its international reputation once again—and for many years to come—inextricably associated with the victimization of its Jewish minority.

The relative ease with which Poland's rulers were able to isolate and destroy the student protesters derived from their success in separating the intellectuals and their discontents from the rest of the nation—a strategy in which anti-Semitism naturally played a useful role. The students themselves had some responsibility for this, perhaps: at Warsaw University especially it was the privileged sons and daughters of Poland's Communist *nomenklatura* who took the most prominent roles in the protests and demonstrations, and their concerns were focused on issues of free speech and political rights above all. As their neo-Stalinist enemies were quick to point out, Warsaw's dissident intelligentsia paid little attention to the bread and butter concerns of the working population. In return, the mass of the Polish people was studiously indifferent to the persecution of Jews and students alike, and Jewish students especially.

Two years later, in 1970, when the government raised food prices by 30 percent and the shipyard workers of Gdansk struck in protest, the compliment was tragically if unintentionally returned: there was no one to take up the cause. But the lesson of these years—that if Poland's workers and intellectuals wanted to challenge the Party they would need to bridge their mutual indifference and forge a political alliance—would in due course be well-learned and applied with historic effect, above all by Adam Michnik and Jacek Kuroń themselves. In this respect, at least, 1968 in Poland had one positive outcome, albeit deferred. The same could not be said of neighbouring Czechoslovakia.

Czechoslovakia in the early Sixties was a hybrid, caught in an uncomfortable transition from national Stalinism to reform Communism. The show trials and purges of the 1950s had come late to Prague and their impact had been both greater and more enduring than elsewhere. There was no rotation of the old Stalinist elite, no Czech Gomułka or Kádár. The old guard of the regime remained in place. Two investigating Commissions were established to inquire into the Slánský and other trials: the first sat from 1955–57, the second from 1962–63. The purpose behind both commissions was somehow to acknowledge the regime's recent criminal past without loosening any control of the present.

In the short run this goal was achieved. Victims of the Stalinist trials were released and rehabilitated—in many instances at the behest of the same politicians, judges, prosecutors and interrogators who had condemned them in the first place. The ex-prisoners received back their Party membership card, some money, coupons (e.g. for a car) and in certain cases even their apartments. Their wives and children could once again find work and attend school. But despite this *de facto* acknowledgement of past injustices, the Party and its Stalin-era leadership remained intact and in office.

Like the French Communist leader Maurice Thorez, First Secretary Antonin Novotný waited many years to be sure which way the wind was blowing before following Khrushchev's example and denouncing the Soviet dictator. The Czech experience of high Stalinist terror was so recent and so extreme that the Party leaders were reluctant to risk any admission of 'error'—lest the consequences of doing so dwarf the '56 upheavals in Poland or even Hungary. De-Stalinization in Czechoslovakia was thus deliberately delayed as long as possible—even the monumental statue of Stalin on the heights overlooking Prague, like the rather smaller copy in the Slovak capital Bratislava, was left untouched until October 1962.[10]

The consequences of the Communist social revolution had been felt more dramatically in Czechoslovakia than elsewhere, in large part precisely because, as we have seen, it really was a developed, bourgeois society—in contrast with every other country subjected to Soviet rule. The leading victims of Stalinist terror in Czechoslovakia had all been intellectuals, usually of middle-class origin, many of them Jews. Other classes of Czechoslovak society had not suffered as much. Upward social mobility for workers—or, more precisely, downward social mobility for everyone else—was a distinguishing feature of the 1950s in the Czech and Slovak lands. The percentage of working-class children in non-vocational higher education in Czechoslovakia rose from under 10 percent in 1938 to 31 percent by 1956, nearly 40 percent in 1963. Income distribution in Czechoslovakia by the early Sixties was the most egalitarian in Soviet Europe.

The Communist leadership had thus indeed advanced Czechoslovakia to 'full Socialism', as the new Constitution of 1960 proclaimed. However, this achievement had been accomplished at the price of a level of stagnation that was unacceptable even by Soviet standards. Hence the decision of the Party authorities, at the 12th Party Congress in December 1962, to 'adapt the national economy' to the country's advanced stage of socialist development—i.e. to accept the inevitable and allow a minimum of non-socialist reforms in order to invigorate the stagnant economy. However, the changes proposed by Ota Sik and other Party reform economists—such as linking worker incentives to a share of factory profits rather than the fulfillment of official Plans or norms—were not popular with Party hardliners and were only finally endorsed at the 13th Congress four years later.

By then, as the leadership had feared all along, the combination of public rehabilitations, cautious acknowledgement of Stalin's faults, and the prospect of even mild economic reforms had opened the way to much more serious questioning of the Party's stranglehold on public life. The economic reforms begun in 1963 might not be universally welcomed by shop-floor employees; but among writers, teachers, filmmakers and philosophers the prospect of a loosening of the Stalinist shackles released an avalanche of criticisms, hopes and expectations.

Thus a writers' conference in Liblice in 1963 was devoted to Franz Kafka. Hitherto this was a taboo subject: in part because Kafka had been a Prague Jew writing in German, and thus a reminder of Bohemia's lost history; but mostly because of the embarrassingly penetrating anticipation in many of Kafka's writings of the

---

[10]Novotný was not the only one afraid of a backlash. On April 5th 1963, the Italian Communist leader Palmiro Togliatti secretly wrote to ask Novotný and his colleagues to delay news of the rehabilitation of Slánský and other trial victims until after the forthcoming Italian elections. As the PCI's chief well understood, it was not only Czechs who had good cause to be disgusted at their leaders' collaboration in covering up large-scale judicial murder just ten years before.

logic of totalitarian rule. And thus the authorization to discuss Kafka appeared to presage a much broader liberalization of public debate: from the discussion of forbidden writers to the mention of murdered leaders was a small step. In April 1963, Ladislav Novomeský, a rehabilitated Slovak writer, made open and admiring mention at the Slovak Writers' Congress of his 'comrade and friend' Clementis, a Slánský trial victim. The desire to speak—to talk about the past—was now taking center stage, albeit still couched in carefully 'revisionist' language: when the young novelist Milan Kundera contributed an article to the Prague cultural periodical *Literární Noviny* in June 1963, his criticisms were cautiously confined to the Stalinist 'deviation' in Czech literature and the need to tell the truth about it.

The relatively liberal mood of these years was a belated Czech echo of the Khrushchev thaw. Despite the changed tone in Moscow following Brezhnev's coup, the artistic renaissance in Czechoslovakia continued to unfold, impeded only by sporadic censorship and pressure. To foreigners, the best-known symptom was a rash of new films, cautiously addressing subjects that would have been forbidden a few years before—Jiří Menzel's *Closely Observed Trains* (1966), gently debunking the core Communist myth of wartime anti-Nazi resistance, was co-written by Josef Škvorecký (author of *The Cowards*, a novel whose similar theme, gingerly adumbrated, had established his reputation a few years before). But playwrights, poets and novelists—many of whom, Kundera included, doubled as screenwriters in these years—played an even more important role.

In 1966 Ludvík Vaculík published *The Axe*, a fictional account drawing on his own father's Communist ideals—and the son's subsequent disillusionment. In 1967 another writer, Ladislas Mňačko, published a biting critique of Novotný and the Party *nomenklatura*, loosely disguised in novel form, under the transparent title *The Taste of Power*. In the same year Kundera himself published *The Joke*, a neo-existentialist and avowedly autobiographical novel of the Stalinist generation in Czechoslovakia. Those years, 'the era of building socialism' as they were officially known, were now fair game for intellectual condemnation, and at the Fourth Czechoslovak Writers' Congress in the summer of 1967 Kundera, Vaculík, the poet and playwright Pavel Kohout and the young playwright Václav Havel attacked the Communist leadership of the time for the material and moral devastation it had wrought. They called for a return to the literary and cultural heritage of Czechoslovakia and for the country to take up once again its 'normal' place in the center of a free Europe.

The implied attack on Czechoslovakia's *current* leadership was obvious to all—certainly, as we now know, the Kremlin leadership was already watching the situation in Prague with some misgivings: Brezhnev had long regarded Czechoslovakia as the least ideologically reliable element in the Warsaw Pact. It was because they knew this that the aging Stalinists in Prague Castle had tried for so long to hold the line. If they did not clamp down firmly on the intellectual opposition emerging in 1967 it was not for want of trying. But they were held back by two constraints: the need to pursue the recently implemented economic reforms, which implied a degree of openness and tolerance of dissenting opinion along Hungarian lines; and the emerging difficulties in Slovakia.

Czecho-Slovakia (as it was initially known) had always been an uneasy and unbalanced state. The Slovak minority in the south and east of the country was poorer and more rural than the Czechs to the northwest. Released from Hungarian rule in 1918, Slovaks were the poor relations in multi-ethnic inter-war Czechoslovakia and were not always treated well by Prague. Many Slovak political leaders had thus welcomed the breakup of the country in 1939 and the Nazi-sponsored appearance of an 'independent' puppet state with its capital in Bratislava. Conversely it was the urban and heavily Social Democratic Czechs of Bohemia and Moravia who had backed Communist candidates in the post-war elections, while the Catholic Slovaks remained indifferent or opposed.

All the same, Slovakia had not done badly under Communism. Slovak intellectuals fell victim to Communist purges, accused of bourgeois nationalism or anti-Communist plotting (or both). And the small number of surviving Slovak Jews suffered along with their Czech confrères. But 'bourgeois nationalists', Communists, Jews and intellectuals were fewer in number in Slovakia and much more isolated from the rest of society. Most Slovaks were poor and worked in the countryside. For them the rapid urbanization and industrialization of the first post-war decade carried real benefits. In contrast to Czechs, they were by no means displeased with their lot.

The mood in the Slovak region of the country changed sharply after 1960, however. The new 'Socialist' Constitution made even fewer concessions to local initiative or opinion than its predecessor and such autonomy as had been accorded Slovakia in the post-war reconstruction of the country was now taken back. Of more immediate consequence for most Slovaks, however, was the stagnation of the economy (by 1964 Czechoslovakia's rate of growth was the slowest in the bloc), which hit the heavy industry of central Slovakia harder than anywhere else.

In January 1967 Novotný had been due to begin implementing the overdue economic reforms recommended by his own Party experts. The reform economists' proposals for decentralization of decision-making and increased local autonomy had been welcomed in Bratislava—though some of the reforms, such as profit-related wage incentives, were hardly calculated to appeal to the unskilled workers in Slovakia's inefficient industrial plants. But all Novotný's instincts told him to resist such loosening of Party control, and instead he encouraged amendments to the proposed changes, with the goal of shoring up the institutions of central planning. This not only sabotaged the proposals of Sik and other Party economists; it further alienated Slovak opinion. Slovak Communists themselves now began to talk of the need for federalization and of the difficulties of collaborating with the aging Communist *apparatchiks* in Prague. Echoing a longstanding complaint of Slovak cleaners, building workers, teachers and shop assistants, they felt slighted and ignored by the Czech majority. There was talk of long-forgotten pre-war indignities, as well as the Stalinist purges of Slovak Communists.

Meanwhile, and for the first time in years, there was a hint of troubles of yet another order. On October 31st 1967, a group of students from Prague's Technical University organized a street demonstration in the district of Strahov to protest electricity cuts at their dormitories: however, their calls for 'More light!' were rightly interpreted as extending beyond local housekeeping difficulties. The 'Strahov Events', as they were later dubbed, were efficiently and violently suppressed by the police; but they added to the charged atmosphere of the moment, all the more so because they seemed to suggest that a Communist state might not be immune to the student mood in the West.

Novotný, like Gomulka in Poland, was uncertain how to respond to such challenges. Lacking the anti-Semitic option, he turned to Brezhnev for help in dealing with his local critics. But when the Soviet leader arrived in Prague in December 1967 he offered only the rather obscure recommendation that the Czechoslovak President do as he saw fit: 'It's your business.' Novotný's colleagues seized the opportunity: on January 5th 1968 the Central Committee of the Czechoslovak Communist Party elected a new First Secretary, Alexander Dubček.

The new man was young (at 47 he was sixteen years Novotný's junior), from the reform wing of the Party and, above all, a Slovak. As leader of the Slovak Communist Party for the past three years he appeared to many to be a credible compromise candidate: a longstanding Communist *apparatchik* who would nevertheless support reforms and appease Slovak resentments. Dubček's early moves seemed to confirm this reading: a month after his appointment the Party leadership gave its unstinting approval to the stalled economic reform program. Dubček's rather artless manner appealed to the young in particular, while his indisputable loyalty to the Party and to 'Socialism' reassured for the time being the Kremlin and other foreign Communist leaders looking anxiously on.

If Dubček's intentions were obscure to observers, this is probably because he himself was far from sure just where to go. At first this ambiguity worked in his favor, as different factions competed for his support and offered to strengthen his hand. Public rallies in Prague in the weeks following his election demanded an end to censorship, greater press freedom and a genuine inquiry into the purges of the fifties and the responsibilities of the old guard around Novotný (who remained President of the country even after being ousted from the Party leadership). Carried on this wave of popular enthusiasm, Dubček endorsed the call for a relaxation of censorship and initiated a purge of Novotnýites from the Party and from the Czech army.

On March 22nd Novotný reluctantly resigned the presidency and was replaced a week later by General Ludvík Svoboda. Five days after that, the Central Committee adopted an 'Action Program' calling for equal status and autonomy for Slovakia, the rehabilitation of past victims and 'democratization' of the political and economic system. The Party was now officially endorsing what the Program called 'a unique experiment in democratic Communism': 'Socialism with a human face' as it became colloquially known. Over a period of time (the document spoke of a ten-year transition) the Czechoslovak Communist Party would allow the emergence of other parties with whom it would compete in genuine elections. These were hardly original ideas, but publicly pronounced from the official organs of a ruling Communist Party they triggered a political earthquake. The Prague Spring had begun.

The events of the spring and summer of 1968 in Czechoslovakia hinged on three contemporary illusions. The first, widespread in the country after Dubček's rise and especially following publication of the Action Program, was that the freedoms and reforms now being discussed could be folded into the 'Socialist' (i.e. Communist) project. It would be wrong to suppose, in retrospect, that what the students and writers and Party reformers of 1968 were 'really' seeking was to replace Communism with liberal capitalism or that their enthusiasm for 'Socialism with a human face' was mere rhetorical compromise or habit. On the contrary: the idea that there existed a 'third way', a Democratic Socialism compatible with free institutions, respecting individual freedoms *and* collective goals, had captured the imagination of Czech students no less than Hungarian economists.

The distinction that was now drawn between the discredited Stalinism of Novotný's generation and the renewed idealism of the Dubček era, was widely accepted—even, indeed especially, by Party members.[11] As Jiří Pelikán asserted, in his preface to yet a third report on the Czech political trials (commissioned in 1968 by Dubček but suppressed after his fall) 'the Communist Party had won tremendous popularity and prestige, the people had spontaneously declared themselves for socialism'.[12] That is perhaps a little hyperbolic, but it was not wildly out of line with contemporary opinion. And this, in turn, nourished a second illusion.

If the people believed the Party could save Socialism from its history, so the Party leadership came to suppose that they could manage this without losing control of the country. A new government headed by Oldřich Černík was installed on April 18th and, encouraged by huge public demonstrations of affection and support (notably in the traditional May Day celebrations), it relaxed virtually all formal controls on public expressions of opinion. On June 26th censorship of press and media was formally abolished. The same day it was announced that Czechoslovakia was to become a genuinely federal state, comprising a Czech Socialist republic and a Slovak Socialist republic (this was the *only* one of Dubček's reforms to survive the subsequent repression, becoming law on October 28th 1968).

But having relaxed all controls on opinion, the Communist leadership was now

---

[11]In December 1967 Party members constituted 16.9 percent of the Czechoslovak population—the highest share of any Communist state.
[12]Jiří Pelikán, ed., *The Czechoslovak Political Trials. The Suppressed Report of the Dubček Government's Commisson of Inquiry, 1968* (Stanford, 1971), p. 17.

pressed from every side to pursue the logic of its actions. Why wait ten years for free and open elections? Now that censorship had been abolished, why retain formal control and ownership of the media? On June 27th *Literárny Listy* and other Czech publications carried a manifesto by Ludvík Vaculík, 'Two Thousand Words', addressed to 'workers, farmers, officials, artists, scholars, scientists and technicians.' It called for the re-establishment of political parties, the formation of citizens' committees to defend and advance the cause of reform, and other proposals to take the initiative for further change out of the control of the Party. The battle was not yet won, Vaculík warned: the reactionaries in the Party would fight to preserve their privileges and there was even talk of 'foreign forces intervening in our development'. The people needed to strengthen the arm of the Communists' own reformers by pressing them to move forward even faster.

Dubček rejected Vaculík's manifesto and its implication that the Communists should abandon their monopoly of power. As a lifelong Communist he would not countenance this crucial qualitative shift ('bourgeois pluralism') and anyway saw no need to do so. For Dubček the Party itself was the only appropriate vehicle for radical change if the vital attributes of a Socialist system were to be preserved. The more popular the Party, the more changes it could safely institute. But as Vaculík's manifesto made cruelly clear, the Party's popularity and its credibility would increasingly rest upon its willingness to pursue changes that might ultimately drive it from power. The fault line between a Communist state and an open society was now fully exposed.

And this, in turn, directed national attention in the summer of 1968 to the third illusion, the most dangerous of all: Dubček's conviction that he could keep Moscow at bay, that he would succeed in assuring his Soviet comrades that they had nothing to fear from events in Czechoslovakia—indeed, that they had everything to gain from the newfound popularity of the Czechoslovak Communist Party and the renewed faith in a rejuvenated socialist project. If Dubček made this mortal miscalculation it was above all because the Czech reformers had crucially misinterpreted the lesson of 1956. Imre Nagy's mistake, they thought, had been his departure from the Warsaw Pact and declaration of Hungarian neutrality. So long as Czechoslovakia stayed firmly in the Pact and unambiguously allied to Moscow, Leonid Brezhnev and his colleagues would surely leave them alone.

But by 1968, the Soviet Union was worried less about military security than the Party's loss of monopoly control. As early as March 21st, at a meeting of the Soviet Politburo, Ukrainian Party leader Petro Shelest was complaining of contamination from the Czechoslovak example: rumors from Prague were having an adverse impact on the mood among young Ukrainians, he reported. Polish and East German leaders made similar remonstrations to their Soviet colleagues at a meeting in Dresden the same month (Gomuƚka, with his own troubles at home, was especially angered by public criticism in Prague at Poland's turn to anti-Semitism). Unbeknownst to Prague, the KGB chief Yuri Andropov was already speaking of a possible need for 'concrete military measures'; and in April Soviet Defense Minister Andrei Grechko was quietly authorized to draw up a contingent plan for military operations in Czechoslovakia—a first draft of what would become 'Operation Danube'.

With every liberalizing step in Prague, Moscow grew ever more uneasy. Dubček must have been aware of this: on May 4th–5th he and other Czech Communists visited Moscow and were presented by Eastern bloc leaders with a menu of complaints about developments in their country. But while Dubček continued to insist that the Party had everything under control, and that however free Czech speech became there was no question of the country breaking with its fraternal obligations, the reliability of the Czech army was now coming into question, and the uncensored Czech press was publishing Soviet dissidents. Russian students visiting Prague could now read and hear people and opinions long since banned at home. Prague was becoming a window into the West.

By July 1968, Moscow had come to the conclusion that events in Prague were spinning out of the Party's control—and so, indeed, they may have been. At a meeting in Moscow on July 14th of Party leaders from the USSR, Poland, East Germany, Bulgaria and Hungary—but not the Czechs themselves—it was agreed to send a fraternal Letter to the Czechoslovak Party warning it of the risk of counter-revolution and listing measures that needed to be taken: 'The situation in Czechoslovakia jeopardizes the common vital interests of other socialist countries.' Two weeks later the Soviet and Czech leaders met on the Czechoslovak-Soviet frontier, at Čierna nad Tisou, and Dubček tried once again to convince Brezhnev that the Communist Party was not jeopardizing its position by enacting reforms, but was actually strengthening its public support.

The Soviet leader was not merely unconvinced; he came away increasingly skeptical of Dubček's prospects. The Warsaw Pact announced forthcoming maneuvers near the Czech border. At a Warsaw Pact meeting in Bratislava on August 3rd (which Romania's Ceauşescu declined to attend), Brezhnev propounded the Doctrine that would henceforth be associated with his name: 'Each Communist party is free to apply the principles of Marxism-Leninism and socialism in its own country, but it is not free to deviate from these principles if it is to remain a Communist party . . . The weakening of any of the links in the world system of socialism directly affects all the socialist countries, and they cannot look indifferently upon this.'

This pronouncement, a lightly veiled assertion of the Kremlin's right to act *preventively* to head off a threat to socialism in any socialist country, may well have given Dubček pause. But there was little he could do, and so he continued to insist that his domestic reforms posed no threat to the socialist system. On August 13th, in a telephone conversation with a mistrustful Brezhnev, Dubček painstakingly explained that he was trying to suppress popular criticisms of the Soviet Union but that 'this issue cannot just be solved by a directive from above.' Had he known that five of his colleagues on the Czechoslovak Praesidium had secretly handed the

Russians a letter on August 3rd, describing an imminent threat to Communist order in Czechoslovakia and requesting military intervention, he might have felt differently.[13]

The Soviet decision to invade Czechoslovakia was not formally taken until August 18th. Brezhnev seems to have been reluctant—intuitively sensing that however easy the victory, its aftershocks might prove troublesome—but it had become all but inevitable well before then. The Soviet leaders anticipated that the forthcoming 14th Czechoslovak Communist Party Congress might see a definitive take-over by the Party's reformist wing, and they were by now truly frightened of the infectious impact of the Czech example upon its neighbors. As Grechko put it when informing the assembled Soviet military leaders of the decision to invade: 'The invasion will take place even if it leads to a third world war.' But the Soviet leaders knew perfectly well that there was no such risk, and not just because Washington had its hands full in Vietnam. Just five weeks earlier, Washington and Moscow had co-signed a Treaty of Nuclear Non-proliferation; the US was not about to jeopardize such gains for the sake of a few million misguided Czechs. And so, on August 21st 1968, 500,000 Warsaw Pact troops from Poland, Hungary, Bulgaria, the DDR and the Soviet Union marched into Czechoslovakia.[14]

The invasion met some passive resistance and quite a lot of street protests, especially in Prague; but at the urgent behest of the Czech government it was otherwise unopposed. The unfriendly reception was a source of some surprise to the Soviet leadership, who had been led to expect that their tanks would encounter widespread support. Having at first arrested Dubček and his leading colleagues, flown them to Moscow and obliged them to sign a paper renouncing parts of their program and agreeing to the Soviet occupation of their country, the Kremlin was now perforce obliged to accept that the reformers had the support of the Czech and Slovak people and allow them to retain formal charge of their country, at least for the moment. It was clearly imprudent to do otherwise.

Nevertheless, the repression of the Prague reforms—'normalization', as it became known—began almost immediately. The forthcoming Party Congress was cancelled, censorship was re-introduced and all talk of implementing the Action Program ended. Among the Soviet leaders there was considerable support for the imposition on Prague of a military dictatorship. This was the preference not only

[13] The request was hardly spontaneous. Two weeks earlier—at a secret meeting near Lake Balaton in Hungary hosted by János Kádár—Vasil Bil'ak (one of Dubček's opponents within the Czechoslovak Party leadership) was advised by Shelest that Moscow would like a 'letter of invitation'. The ensuing letter refers explicitly to the Party's 'loss of control', the likelihood of a 'counter-revolutionary coup' and the 'risks to socialism' before inviting Moscow's 'intervention and all round assistance'. It ends: 'we request that you treat our statement with the utmost secrecy, and for that reason we are writing to you, personally, in Russian.'
[14] Because Ceaușescu refused to take part in the invasion or allow Warsaw Pact troops to cross Romanian territory, the Bulgarian contingent had to be airlifted to Ukraine instead. Their presence hardly justified the trouble; but the importance of spreading responsibility for the attack across the largest possible number of fraternal states overrode other considerations.

of Andropov and Shelest but also—revealingly—of the GDR's Walter Ulbricht, Bulgaria's Todor Zhivkov and Poland's Gomułka. But Brezhnev chose instead to let Dubček stay in office a few months longer, pursue the federalization of the country (with the aim of splitting Slovaks, their chief demand now conceded, from the more radical Czechs) and see how events unfolded—while retaining a Warsaw Pact presence just in case.

There were occasional student demonstrations in defense of the reforms, and in the industrial towns of Bohemia and Moravia there emerged, briefly, a network of workers' councils on the model of 1956 in Hungary (at their peak, in January 1969, these councils claimed to represent one in six of the national workforce, though they were very weak in Slovakia). And there was the suicide of Jan Palach, a 20-year-old student at Charles University who set fire to himself on the steps of the National Museum in Prague's Wenceslas Square in protest against the Soviet invasion and its aftermath. Palach lived for three days before dying of his burns on January 19th 1969. His funeral, on January 25th, was an occasion for national mourning: for Palach and for Czechoslovakia's lost democracy.

The next time pro-democracy demonstrators took to the streets (following Czechoslovakia's victory over the USSR in a game of ice hockey), the Kremlin exploited the occasion to remove Dubček and replace him, on April 17th 1969, with one of his erstwhile colleagues, Gustav Husák. As a Slovak and former trial victim (he had been imprisoned in the Stalin years for 'nationalism'), Husák was the ideal candidate to purge the land of the reformist heresy without prompting accusations of a return to Stalinism. The repression that followed was less obtrusive than in the past, but highly effective. Public trials were eschewed, but in the course of the next two years the Czechoslovak Communist Party was purged of all its 'unreliable' elements (nine out of ten of those expelled were Czechs). Men and women who had been active or prominent in the Prague Spring were 'interviewed' and asked to sign statements renouncing their actions and rejecting the Dubcek reforms. Most signed. Those who refused lost their jobs and, along with their relatives and children, became social pariahs. By far the largest group of victims was those, whether in or out of the Party, who had played a visible role in recent years: journalists, television announcers, essayists, novelists, playwrights, film directors or student leaders.[15]

The 'screening' and purging of these intellectuals was carried out by lower ranking bureaucrats, policemen and party officials—more often than not the victims' own colleagues. Their goal was to extract petty confessions—not so much in order to incriminate their victims but rather to humiliate them and thus secure their col-

---

[15]After 1989 it emerged that the Czech Secret Police in the normalization years had established a special unit to monitor and target the country's Jews: an echo of Czechoslovakia's own past as well as contemporary Poland. It had not escaped the authorities' notice that only one of Dubček's leading colleagues had refused to sign the Moscow document renouncing his actions. He was František Kriegel—the only Jew in the group.

laboration in the self-subjugation of a troublesome society. The message went out that the country had passed through a mass psychosis in 1968, that false prophets had exploited the ensuing 'hysteria', and that the nation needed to be directed firmly back to the correct path: induced by the carrot of consumer goods and the stick of omnipresent surveillance.

The threat of violence was of course always implicit, but the fact that it was rarely invoked merely added to the collective humiliation. Once again, as in 1938 and again in 1948, Czechoslovakia was being made complicit in its own defeat. By 1972—with poets and playwrights forced to clean boilers and wash windows; university lecturers stacking bricks, and their more troublesome students expelled; the police files full of useful 'confessions'; and reform Communists cowed or else in exile—'order', in the words of a brilliant, bitter essay by one of normalization's victims, had been 'restored'.[16]

There were ripples of protest throughout the Communist bloc. On August 25th 1968 demonstrators in Red Square protesting the occupation of Czechoslovakia included Pavel Litvinov (grandson of Stalin's foreign minister) and Larissa Daniel (wife of the imprisoned Soviet novelist). East European army units engaged in the invasion of Czechoslovakia had been led to believe that they were defending the country against West German or American invaders, and some of them had later to be quietly withdrawn, their reliability—notably that of Hungarian units occupying Slovakia—seriously in question. In Poland, as we have seen, the repression in Prague both stimulated student protests and strengthened the hand of the authorities in stamping them down. In April 1969 in the Latvian capital Riga, a Jewish student, Ilia Rips, set herself on fire to draw attention to the Soviet treatment of Dubček. The attitude of Czechs and Slovaks themselves, hitherto among the most pro-Russian nations in the Soviet bloc, now shifted irrevocably to a stance of sullen acquiescence.

But all this was easily contained. The Kremlin had made its point—that fraternal socialist states had only limited sovereignty and that any lapse in the Party's monopoly of power might trigger military intervention. Unpopularity at home or abroad was a small price to pay for the stability that this would henceforth ensure. After 1968, the security of the Soviet zone was firmly underwritten by a renewed appreciation of Moscow's willingness to resort to force if necessary. But never again—and this was the true lesson of 1968, first for the Czechs but in due course for everyone else—never again would it be possible to maintain that Communism rested on popular consent, or the legitimacy of a reformed Party, or even the lessons of History.

In Prague, the evisceration of the reform movement left an especially bitter taste. Many of the most enthusiastic purgers had been among the loudest enthu-

---

[16]Milan Šimečka, *Obnovení Pořádku* (*The Restoration of Order*), (Bratislava, 1984—in *samizdat*). Eighty thousand Czechs and Slovaks fled into exile following the Soviet invasion.

Nikita Khrushchev visiting a collective farm. 'Mr K' fancied himself an agrarian expert, though his experiments were usually disastrous failures. But his contributions to de-Stalinization (notably the 'Secret Speech' of February 1956) were invaluable—albeit the consequences exceeded his wishes.

Imre Nagy (center) following his appeal to the UN, November 1st 1956. Nagy paid dearly for his role in the doomed Hungarian revolt but in the long run Moscow paid the higher price, extinguishing the illusions of its own followers.

Building the Berlin Wall, August 19th 1961. Despite their protests to the contrary Western governments were not sorry to see the perennial crisis over Berlin resolved by the Soviet Union's decision to erect a physical barrier between the two halves of the occupied city.

The Marriage of Maria Braun *(1978), film director Rainer Fassbinder's acid dissection of the shortcomings of the post-war Federal Republic. To its youthful critics, West Germany's obsession with prosperity, political demobilization and collective forgetting were just the old German defects in a new guise.*

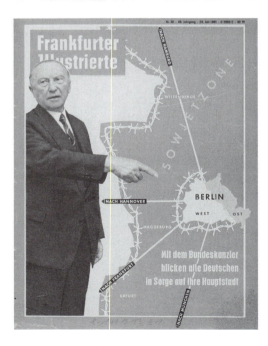

'Together with the Chancellor all Germans are anxiously watching their capital city'. In reality Konrad Adenauer (who hailed from the Catholic Rhineland) heartily disliked Prussian Berlin. But he was not above wielding the divided city as a lever to extract concessions from his Western Allies.

Portraits of Dutch governors being moved out of the palace in Jakarta on December 26th 1949—the day before the inauguration of the Indonesian Republic. The loss of their 'Indies' was traumatic for the Dutch, who had now to settle for a reduced role back in Europe.

Vietminh troops escorting French soldiers into captivity after the battle of Dien Bien Phu, May 1954. France's humiliating expulsion from Vietnam contributed to a disastrous reluctance, particularly on the part of the army, to relinquish the country's remaining holdings in North Africa.

Egyptians demanding the withdrawal of Anglo-French forces, December 1956. The Suez débâcle was a watershed in post-war Europe: it accelerated the European retreat from empire and re-cast (in very different ways) the political trajectory of France and Britain alike.

'All my life I have had a certain idea of France'. Charles de Gaulle seized power in May 1958 in a virtual coup; but he re-established France as a presence in world affairs and his Fifth Republic has proven more stable than its predecessors.

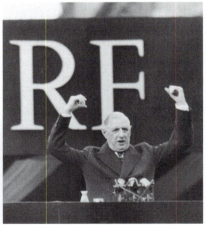

The OAS (Secret Army Organization) waged a bloody war of vengeful terror against those it held responsible for the loss of Algeria. Its rancour was directed above all at De Gaulle for betraying the cause (note the broken Cross of Lorraine, the Gaullist emblem).

Europeans from the Congo escaping to Tanzania, July 1960. Belgium's retreat from empire was an irresponsible fiasco: when the Belgians abandoned the Congo in 1960, following decades of exploitation, they left behind just thirty Congolese university graduates to fill four thousand senior administrative positions.

Dean Acheson's famous 1962 quip about Britain's post-imperial discomfiture prompted the cartoonist Vicky to depict British Prime Minister Harold Macmillan's humiliating and obsequious 'special relationship' with Washington in terms that remain, over four decades later, as depressingly timely as ever.

Icons of modernity i). A Czech-made Tatra-603 on display at the Brno Trade Fair, September 1959. Soviet-bloc automobiles encapsulated much that was wrong with the economies of the Communist bloc: they were poorly designed and available only to a privileged few. They were, however, remarkably durable.

Icons of modernity ii). Three ladies peering into a limousine, London 1960. Although modern consumer durables—cars, fridges, washing machines—were now within reach of many west European households, vast distinctions of wealth, class and privilege remained. The limousine was probably still driven by a personal chauffeur.

And God Created Woman. Fun in the sun was now a realistic aspiration for a growing number of European holidaymakers. Bardot remained for a while on the Côte d'Azur she had made famous but many of her friends moved away, fleeing the onslaught of mass tourism.

All across post-war
Europe, 'slum clearance'
and town planning
ushered in a generation
of high-rise apartment
buildings: unpopular
with their residents and
typically subject to early
decay and premature
demolition. 'Moss
Heights' in Glasgow,
shown here under
construction,
was representative.

Teddy boys at the Elephant & Castle, London,
July 1955. The 1950s' 'lost generation'—
teenagers caught between their Depression-
era parents and the baby-boomers to follow—
lacked entertainment or recreation facilities.
Many—the blouson noirs (France),
Halbstarker (Germany) or skinknuttar
(Sweden)—turned to gang violence.

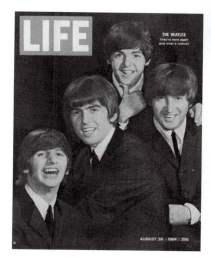

The Beatles really did matter. Four decades later
they remain the outstanding—perhaps the only—
common reference point for Sixties-generation
memories worldwide. And they made very good
music indeed—even if Sergeant Pepper was not
(quite) a 'decisive moment in the history of Western
Civilization' (Kenneth Tynan).

Students occupying the Sorbonne, Paris 1968. Notwithstanding the Marxian iconography—Mao, Stalin, Engels and Marx atop a flag with hammer and sickle—the rebels of 1968 were not notably doctrinaire. Most of them weren't especially serious, either. As one of them recalled, we just 'loved the Revolution' (Dany Cohn-Bendit).

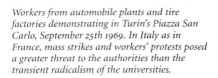

Workers from automobile plants and tire factories demonstrating in Turin's Piazza San Carlo, September 25th 1969. In Italy as in France, mass strikes and workers' protests posed a greater threat to the authorities than the transient radicalism of the universities.

Prague, August 1968. 'Each Communist party is free to apply the principles of Marxism-Leninism . . . but it is not free to deviate from these principles if it is to remain a Communist party' (Leonid Brezhnev, August 3rd 1968). The Soviet invasion extinguished the Prague Spring—and any remaining illusions about Communism itself.

siasts for Dubček just a few months before—'it was only after the Prague Spring of 1968', wrote Zdeněk Mlynář, one of the Communist Party's leading reformers, 'that one began to see who was who.' The apparent ease with which first Dubček, then the Party, and finally the whole society seemed to cave before the Soviet over-lords and their local hirelings was not merely humiliating (unflattering compar-isons were made with Hungary twelve years before); it cast a retroactively skeptical light upon the ideals and hopes of the reform era itself.

Reflecting in later years upon his memories of August 21st 1968, when Red Army troops burst into a meeting of Czech party leaders and a soldier lined up behind each Politburo member, Mlynář recalled that 'at such a moment one's concept of socialism moves to last place. But at the same time you know that it has a direct connection of some sort with the automatic weapon pointing at your back.' It is that connection which marked the definitive turning point in the history of Com-munism, more even than the Hungarian tragedy of 1956.

The illusion that Communism was reformable, that Stalinism had been a wrong turning, a mistake that could still be corrected, that the core ideals of democratic pluralism might somehow still be compatible with the structures of Marxist col-lectivism: that illusion was crushed under the tanks on August 21st 1968 and it never recovered. Alexander Dubček and his Action Program were not a beginning but an end. Never again would radicals or reformers look to the ruling Party to carry their aspirations or adopt their projects. Communism in Eastern Europe staggered on, sustained by an unlikely alliance of foreign loans and Russian bayo-nets: the rotting carcass was finally carried away only in 1989. But the soul of Com-munism had died twenty years before: in Prague, in August 1968.

The Sixties ended badly everywhere. The closing of the long post-war cycle of growth and prosperity dispelled the rhetoric and the projects of the New Left; the optimistic emphasis on post-industrial alienation and the soulless quality of mod-ern life would soon be displaced by a renewed attention to jobs and wages.[17] In the East the message of the Sixties was that you could no longer work within 'the sys-tem'; in the West there appeared no better choice. On both sides of the Iron Cur-tain illusions were swept aside. Only the truly radical stuck with their determination to remain outside the political consensus—a commitment which in Germany and Italy, as in the US and Latin America, led them into clandestinity, violence and crime.

In the short run, the practical achievements of the Sixties seemed rather thin. Eighteen-year-olds got the vote: first in Britain, then elsewhere. Universities tried,

---

[17]The baby-boom generation itself never wanted for employment. It was its immediate successor, the cohort born after 1953, which entered the employment market just as jobs were getting harder to find. Not surprisingly, the politics of the successor generation were markedly different.

with mixed success, to upgrade their facilities and courses and render themselves more open to student demands. In the course of the next decade access to divorce, abortion and contraception was facilitated almost everywhere, and restrictions upon sexual behavior—whether as depicted or practiced—largely disappeared. In the *Statuto dei Lavoratori* of May 1970, Italian workers won the right to protection against unfair dismissal. Taken all in all, such changes constitute an underlying cultural transformation of European society; but they were hardly the 'revolution' envisaged in the slogans and actions of the generation of 1968.[18]

Indeed, that revolution had from the start been self-defeating. The same movements that purported to despise and abhor 'consumer culture' were from the outset an object of cultural consumption, reflecting a widespread disjunction between rhetoric and practice. Those in Paris or Berlin who aggressively declared their intention to 'change the world' were often the people most devoted to parochial and even bodily obsessions—anticipating the solipsistic 'me' politics of the decade to follow—and absorbed in the contemplation of their own impact. 'The Sixties' were a cult object even before the decade had passed.

But if the Sixties seemed at last to pass un-mourned and with few enduring monuments, this was perhaps because the changes that they did bring about were *so* all-embracing as to seem natural and, by the early Seventies, wholly normal. At the start of the decade Europe was run by and—as it seemed—for old men. Authority, whether in the bedroom, the home, the streets, educational establishments, workplaces, the media or politics, passed unquestioned. Yet within ten years the old men (Churchill, Adenauer, De Gaulle) were dead. Authority had either been withdrawn from most spheres of social life, or else was acknowledged only in the breach. In some places—France, Italy—the transition had been quite dramatic. Elsewhere—Britain, perhaps—the transition was spread over a period of years and its dimensions could only be fully appreciated in retrospect.[19]

It was one of the self-delusions of the age that the Sixties were an era of heightened political consciousness. 'Everyone' (or at least everyone under twenty-five attending an educational establishment and drawn to radical ideas) was in the streets and mobilized for a cause. The deflation of the causes—and the demobilization of the coming decades—thus confers in retrospect an air of failure upon a decade of frenetic political activity. But in certain important respects the Sixties were actually a vital decade for the opposite reason: they were the moment when Europeans in both halves of the continent began their definitive turn *away* from ideological politics.

---

[18]Only in Spain, where the cycle of social protest lasted into the mid-Seventies before blending into the movement for a return to parliamentary democracy, did the upheavals of the Sixties herald a genuine political transformation—a story to be taken up in Chapter 16.

[19]Britain's Profumo Affair of 1963—a deliciously multifaceted scandal of sex, class, drugs, race, politics and spies that absorbed the country for months—would have been unthinkable a few years later. The peccadilloes of a fallen élite might continue to arouse a certain prurient interest, but after the Sixties they could no longer *shock*.

Thus the slogans and projects of the Sixties' generation, far from re-awakening a revolutionary tradition whose language and symbols they so energetically sought to reinvigorate, can be seen in hindsight to have served as its swansong. In Eastern Europe, the 'revisionist' interlude and its tragic dénouement saw off the last illusions of Marxism as a practice. In the West, Marxist and para-Marxist theories soared clear of any relationship to local reality, disqualifying themselves from any future role in serious public debate. In 1945 the radical Right had discredited itself as a legitimate vehicle for political expression. By 1970, the radical Left was set fair to emulate it. A 180-year cycle of ideological politics in Europe was drawing to a close.

PART THREE

Recessional: 1971–1989

XIV

Diminished Expectations

'The dollar is our currency but your problem'.
John Connally, US Treasury Secretary, 1971

'It might or might not be right to kill, but sometimes it is necessary'.
Gerry Adams

'The death of a worker weighs heavily like a mountain, while that of a
bourgeois weighs as lightly as a feather'.
Mao Zedong

'This is the Hour of Lead-
Remembered, if outlived'.
Emily Dickinson

'Punk might have been invented for the cultural theorists—and the partial
truth is that it was'.
Robert Hewison

Even before the effervescence of the Sixties had subsided, the unique circumstances that made it possible had passed forever. Within three years of the end of the most prosperous decade in recorded history, the post-war economic boom was over. Western Europe's 'thirty glorious years' gave way to an age of monetary inflation and declining growth rates, accompanied by widespread unemployment and social discontent. Most of the radicals of the Sixties, like their followers, abandoned 'the Revolution' and worried instead about their job prospects. A few opted for violent confrontation; the damage they wrought—and the response their actions elicited from the authorities—led to much nervous talk of the 'ungovernable' condition of Western societies. Such anxieties proved overwrought: under stress, the institutions of Western Europe showed more resilience than many observers had feared. But there was to be no return to the optimism—or the illusions—of the first post-war decades.

The impact of economic slowdown was only just beginning to be felt when two external shocks brought the Western European economy to a shuddering halt. On August 15th 1971, US President Richard Nixon unilaterally announced that his country was abandoning the system of fixed exchange rates. The US dollar, the anchor of the international monetary system since Bretton Woods, would henceforth float against other currencies. The background to this decision was the huge military burden of the Vietnam War and a growing US Federal budget deficit. The dollar was tied to a gold standard, and there was a growing fear in Washington that foreign holders of US currency (including Europe's central banks) would seek to exchange their dollars for gold, draining American reserves.[1]

The decision to float the dollar was not economically irrational. Having opted to fight an expensive war of attrition on the other side of the world—and pay for it with borrowed money—the US could not expect to maintain the dollar indefinitely at its fixed and increasingly over-valued rate. But the American move nonetheless came as a shock. If the dollar was to float, then so must the European currencies, and in that case all of the carefully constructed certainties of the postwar monetary and trading systems were called into question. The fixed rate system, established before the end of the Second World War in anticipation of a controlled network of national economies, was over. But what would replace it?

Following some months of confusion, two successive devaluations of the dollar, and the 'floating' of the British pound in 1972 (belatedly bringing to an inglorious end sterling's ancient and burdensome role as an international 'reserve' currency), a conference in Paris, in March 1973, formally buried the financial arrangements so laboriously erected at Bretton Woods and agreed to establish in its place a new floating-rate system. The cost of this liberalization, predictably enough, was inflation. In the aftermath of the American move of August 1971 (and the subsequent fall in the value of the dollar) European governments, hoping to head off the anticipated economic downturn, adopted deliberately reflationary policies: allowing credit to ease, domestic prices to rise, and their own currencies to fall.

Under normal circumstances this controlled 'Keynesian' inflation might have succeeded: only in West Germany was there a deep-seated historical aversion to the very idea of price inflation. But the uncertainty produced by America's retreat from a dollar-denominated system encouraged growing currency speculation, which international accords on floating-rate regimes were powerless to restrain. This in turn undermined the efforts of individual governments to manipulate local interest rates and maintain the value of their national currency. Currencies fell. And as they fell, so the cost of imports rose: between 1971 and 1973, the world price of non-fuel commodities increased by 70 percent, of food by 100 percent. And it was in this already unstable situation that the international economy was hit by the first of the two oil shocks of the 1970s.

On October 6th 1973, Yom Kippur (The Day of Atonement) in the Jewish cal-

---

[1]The US federal budget deficit grew from $1.6 billion in 1965 to $25.2 billion in 1968.

endar, Egypt and Syria attacked Israel. Within twenty-four hours major Arab oil-exporting states had announced plans to reduce oil production; ten days later they announced an oil embargo against the US in retaliation for its support for Israel and increased the price of petroleum by 70 percent. The Yom Kippur War itself ended with an Egyptian-Israeli cease-fire on October 25th, but Arab frustration at Western support for Israel did not abate. On December 23rd the oil-producing nations agreed to a further increase in the price of oil. Its cost had now more than doubled since the start of 1973.

To appreciate the significance of these developments for Western Europe especially, it is important to recall that the price of oil, unlike almost every other primary commodity on which the modern industrial economy rests, had remained virtually unchanged over the decades of economic growth. One barrel of Saudi light crude—a benchmark measure—cost $1.93 in 1955; in January 1971 it went for just $2.18. Given the modest price inflation of those years, this meant that in real terms oil had actually got cheaper. OPEC, formed in 1960, had been largely inert and showed no inclination to constrain its major producers to use their oil reserves as a political weapon. The West had grown accustomed to readily available and remarkably cheap fuel—a vital component in the long years of prosperity.

Just how vital can be seen from the steadily growing place of oil in the European economy. In 1950, solid fuel (overwhelmingly coal and coke) had accounted for 83 percent of Western Europe's energy consumption; oil for just 8.5 percent. By 1970 the figures were 29 percent and 60 percent respectively. Seventy-five percent of Italy's energy requirements in 1973 were met by importing oil; for Portugal the figure was 80 percent.[2] The UK, which would for a while become self-sufficient thanks to newly discovered reserves of oil in the North Sea, had only begun production in 1971. The consumer boom of the late fifties and sixties had greatly increased European dependence on cheap oil: the tens of millions of new cars on the roads of Western Europe could not run on coal, nor on the electricity now being generated—in France especially—by nuclear power.

Hitherto, imported fuel had been priced in fixed dollars. Floating exchange rates and oil price increases thus introduced an unprecedented element of uncertainty. Whereas prices and wages had risen steadily, if moderately, over the course of the previous two decades—an acceptable price for social harmony in an age of rapid growth—monetary inflation now took off. According to the OECD, the inflation rate in non-Communist Europe for the years 1961–1969 was steady at 3.1 percent; from 1969–1973 it was 6.4 percent; from 1973–1979 it averaged 11.9 percent. Within this overall figure there was considerable national variation: whereas West Germany's rate of inflation from 1973–1979 was held to a manageable 4.7 percent, Swe-

---

[2]As a point of comparison American oil imports, at the height of the 1973 crisis, represented no more than 36 percent of US domestic consumption.

den experienced a level twice as high. French prices inflated at an average of 10.7 percent per annum in those years. In Italy the inflation rate averaged 16.1 percent; in Spain over 18 percent. The UK average was 15.6 percent, but in its worst year (1975) the British inflation rate exceeded 24 percent per annum.

Price and wage inflation at these levels was not historically unprecedented. But after the stable rates of the fifties and sixties it was a new experience for most people—and for their governments. Worse still, the European inflation of the seventies—compounded by a second oil price rise in 1979, when the overthrow of the Shah of Iran produced panic in the oil markets and a 150 percent price increase between December 1979 and May 1980—did not conform to previous experience. In the past, inflation was associated with growth, often over-rapid growth. The great economic depressions of the late nineteenth century and the 1930s had been accompanied by *de*flation: precipitate falls in prices and wages caused, as it seemed to observers, by over-rigid currencies and chronic under-spending by governments and citizens alike. But in 1970s Europe the conventional pattern seemed no longer to apply.

Instead, western Europe began to experience what was inelegantly dubbed 'stagflation': wage/price inflation and economic slowdown at the same time. In retrospect this outcome is less surprising than it seemed to contemporaries. By 1970 the great European migration of surplus agricultural labor into productive urban industry was over; there was no more 'slack' to be taken up and rates of productivity increase began inexorably to decline. Full employment in Europe's major industrial and service economies was still the norm—as late as 1971 unemployment in the UK was 3.6 percent, in France just 2.6 percent: but this meant that organized workers who had grown accustomed to bargaining from a position of strength were now facing employers whose generous profit margins were starting to shrink.

Pointing in justification to the increased rate of inflation from 1971, workers' representatives were pressing their case for higher wages and other compensation upon economies that were already showing signs of exhaustion even before the crisis of 1973. Real wages had begun to outstrip productivity growth; profits were declining; new investment fell away. The excess capacity born of enthusiastic post-war investment strategies could only be absorbed by inflation or unemployment. Thanks to the Middle East crisis, Europeans got both.

The depression of the 1970s seemed worse than it was because of the contrast with what had gone before. By historical standards the average rates of Gross Domestic Product (GDP) growth in western Europe through the 1970s were not especially low. They ranged from 1.5 percent in the UK to 4.9 percent in Norway and were thus actually a distinct improvement over the 1.3 percent average growth rates achieved by France, Germany and the UK over the years 1913–1950. But they contrasted sharply with the figures of the immediate past: from 1950–1973 French growth per annum had averaged 5 percent, West Germany had grown at nearly 6 percent and even Britain had maintained an average rate above 3 percent. It was not the 1970s that were unusual so much as the '50s and '60s.[3]

Nevertheless, the pain was real, made worse by growing export competition from new industrial countries in Asia and ever more costly import bills as commodities (and not just oil) increased in price. Unemployment rates started to rise, steadily but inexorably. By the end of the decade the numbers out of work in France exceeded 7 percent of the workforce; in Italy 8 percent; in the UK 9 percent. In some countries—Belgium, Denmark—unemployment levels in the seventies and early eighties were comparable to those experienced in the 1930s; in France and Italy they were actually worse.

One immediate result of the economic down-turn was a hardening of attitudes towards 'foreign' workers of all sorts. If published unemployment rates in West Germany (close to zero in 1970) did not climb above 8 percent of the labor force despite a slump in demand for manufactured goods, it was because most of the unemployed workers in Germany were not German—and thus not officially recorded. When Audi and BMW, for example, laid off large numbers of their workforce in 1974 and 1975, it was the 'guest workers' who went first; four out of five BMW employees who lost their jobs were not German citizens. In 1975 the Federal Republic permanently closed its recruiting offices in North Africa, Portugal, Spain and Yugoslavia. As the 1977 Report of a Federal Commission expressed the point in its 'Basic Principle #1': 'Germany is not an immigrant country. Germany is a place of residence for foreigners who will eventually return home voluntarily.' Six years later the Federal Parliament would pass an Act to 'Promote the Preparedness of Foreign Workers to Return'.

Voluntarily or otherwise, many of them did indeed return 'home'. In 1975, 290,000 immigrant workers and their families left West Germany for Turkey, Yugoslavia, Greece and Italy. In that same year, 200,000 Spaniards returned to Spain in search of work; returnees to Italy now outnumbered emigrants for the first time in modern memory, as they were shortly to do in Greece and Portugal. By the mid-seventies, nearly a third of a million Yugoslav emigrants had been obliged to return to the Balkans, where their expectation of employment was no better than in Germany or France. The northern European jobs crisis was being re-exported to the Mediterranean. Meanwhile France imposed strict restrictions on immigration from Algeria and its former African colonies, and the United Kingdom placed ever tighter limits on would-be immigrants from the South Asian sub-continent.

The combination of structural unemployment, rising oil import bills, inflation

---

[3]An average, of course, is just an average. In the particularly bleak year of 1976, when British unemployment passed one million for the first time since the war and annual inflation approached 25 percent, rates of growth everywhere hit a low point—in Italy the national economy actually shrank, for the first time since the war.

and declining exports led to budget deficits and payments crises all across Western Europe. Even West Germany, the continent's manufacturing capital and leading exporter, was not spared. The country's balance-of-payments surplus of $9,481 million in 1973 fell within a year to a deficit of $692 million. The British national accounts were by now chronically in deficit—so much so that by December 1976 there appeared a serious risk of a national debt default and the International Monetary Fund was called in to bail Britain out. But others were little better off. French payments balances fell into the red in 1974 and remained there for most of the ensuing decade. Italy, like Britain, was forced in April 1977 to turn to the IMF for help. As in the British case its leaders could then blame 'international forces' for the unpopular domestic policy measures that ensued.

In Keynesian thinking, budget shortfalls and payments deficits—like inflation itself—were not inherently evil. In the Thirties they had represented a plausible prescription for 'spending your way' out of recession. But in the Seventies all Western European governments *already* spent heavily on welfare, social services, public utilities and infrastructure investment. As the British Labour Prime Minister James Callaghan glumly explained to his colleagues, 'We used to think that you could just spend your way out of a recession . . . I tell you, in all candour, that that option no longer exists.' Nor could they look to the liberalization of trade to save them, as it had done after World War Two: the recent Kennedy round of trade negotiations in the mid-Sixties had already taken industrial tariffs to a historic low. If anything, the risk now was of growing domestic pressure to re-impose protection against competition.

There was a further complicating element in the choices facing policymakers in the 1970s. The economic crisis, however circumstantial and conjunctural its triggers, coincided with a far-reaching transformation which governments could do little to arrest. In the course of a generation, Western Europe had undergone a third 'industrial revolution'; the smokestack industries that had been so much a part of daily life just a few years before were on their way out. If steelworkers, miners, car workers and mill hands were losing jobs, it wasn't just because of a cyclical downturn in the local economy, or even a by-product of the oil crisis. The venerable manufacturing economy of Western Europe was disappearing.

The evidence was incontrovertible, though policymakers had for some years been trying hard to ignore its implications. The number of miners had been slipping steadily ever since West European coal output peaked in the 1950s: the great Sambre-Meuse mining basin of southern Belgium, which generated 20.5 million tonnes of coal in 1955, produced just six million tonnes by 1968 and negligible amounts ten years later. Between 1955 and 1985 100,000 mining jobs disappeared in Belgium; ancillary trades of various kinds suffered accordingly. Even greater losses were experienced in British mining, though spread across a longer period. In 1947 the UK boasted 958 coal mines in 1947; forty-five years later just fifty of them remained. The mining workforce was to fall from 718,000 to 43,000: most of those jobs were lost in the course of the decade 1975–85.

Steel, the other staple industry of industrial Europe, suffered a similar fate. It was not that demand for steel had fallen so very dramatically—unlike coal, it could not so readily be replaced. But as more non-European countries entered the industrial ranks, competition increased, the price fell and the market for expensively produced European steel collapsed. Between 1974 and 1986 British steelworkers lost 166,000 jobs (though in the latter year the UK's major manufacturer, the British Steel Corporation, made a profit for the first time in over a decade). Shipbuilding declined for similar reasons; motor car manufacturing and textiles likewise. Courtaulds, the UK's leading textile and chemical combine, reduced its workforce by 50 percent in the years 1977–83.

The recession of the Seventies saw an acceleration of job losses in virtually every traditional industry. Before 1973 the transformation was already under way in coal, iron, steel, engineering; thereafter it spread to chemicals, textiles, paper and consumer goods. Whole regions were traumatized: between 1973 and 1981 the British West Midlands, home of small engineering firms and car plants, lost one in four of its workforce. The industrial zone of Lorraine, in north-west France, lost 28 percent of its manufacturing jobs. The industrial workforce in Lüneburg, West Germany, fell by 42 percent in the same years. When FIAT of Turin began its switch to robotization at the end of the 1970s, 65,000 jobs (out of a total of 165,000) were lost in just three years. In the city of Amsterdam, 40 percent of the workforce was employed in industry in the 1950s; a quarter of a century later the figure was just one employee in seven.

In the past, the social cost of economic change on this scale, and at this pace, would have been traumatic, with unpredictable political consequences. Thanks to the institutions of the welfare state—and perhaps the diminished political enthusiasms of the time—protest was contained. But it was far from absent. In the years 1969–1975 there were angry marches, sit-ins, strikes and petitions all across industrial Western Europe, from Spain (where 1.5 million days were lost to industrial strikes in the years 1973–75) to Britain, where two major strikes by coalminers—in 1972 and 1974—persuaded a nervous Conservative government that it might be the better part of valor to postpone major mine closures for a few more years, even at the cost of further subsidies charged to the population at large.

The miners and steelworkers were the best-known and perhaps the most desperate of the organized protesters of the time, but they were not the most militant. The decline in the number of workers in old industries had shifted the balance of strength in trade union movements to the service-sector unions, whose constituency was rapidly growing. In Italy, even as the older, Communist-led industrial organizations lost members, teachers and civil service unions grew in size and militancy. The old unions evinced scant sympathy for the unemployed: most were anxious above all to preserve jobs (and their own influence) and shied away from open confrontations. It was the combative service-sector unions—*Force Ouvrière* in France, NALGO, NUPE and ASTMS in Britain[4]—which enthusiastically took up the cause of the young and the jobless.

Faced with an unprecedented raft of demands for job security and wage protection, European leaders initially resorted to proven past practice. Inflationary wage settlements were negotiated with powerful unions in Britain and France; in Italy a flat-rate indexing system linking wages to prices, the *Scala Mobile*, was inaugurated in 1975. Ailing industries—steel especially—were taken under the wing of the state, much as in the initial round of post-war nationalizations: in the UK the 'Steel Plan' of 1977 saved the industry from collapse by cartelizing its price structure and effectively abolishing local price competition; in France the bankrupt steel combines of Lorraine and the industrial center of the country were regrouped into state-regulated conglomerates underwritten from Paris. In West Germany the Federal government, following form, encouraged private consolidation rather than state control, but with similar cartelizing outcomes. By the mid-seventies one holding company, *Ruhrkohle AG*, was responsible for 95 percent of the mining output of the Ruhr district.

What remained of the domestic textile industries of France and Britain was preserved, for the sake of the jobs it offered in depressed regions, by substantial direct job subsidies (paying employers to keep on workers they didn't need) and protective measures against third-world imports. In the Federal Republic the Bonn government undertook to cover 80 percent of the wage costs of industrial employees put on part-time work. The Swedish government poured cash into its unprofitable but politically sensitive shipyards.

There were national variations in these responses to economic downturn. The French authorities pursued a practice of micro-economic intervention, identifying 'national champions' by sector and favoring them with contracts, cash and guarantees; whereas the UK Treasury continued its venerable tradition of macro-economic manipulation through taxes, interest rates and blanket subsidies. But what is striking is how little variation there was along *political* lines. German and Swedish Social Democrats, Italian Christian Democrats, French Gaullists and British politicians of every stripe instinctively clung at first to the post-war consensus: seeking full employment if possible, compensating in its absence with wage increases for those in work, social transfers for those out of work and cash subsidies for ailing employers in private and public sector alike.

But over the course of the seventies a growing number of politicians came to the conviction that inflation now posed greater risks than high levels of unemployment—especially since the human and political costs of joblessness were

---

[4]National Association of Local Government Officers; National Union of Public Employees; Association of Scientific, Technical and Managerial Staffs.

institutionally alleviated. Inflation could not be addressed without some sort of international arrangements for the regulation of currencies and exchange rates, to replace the Bretton Woods system precipitately overthrown by Washington. The six original member states of the European Economic Community had responded by agreeing in 1972 to establish the 'snake in a tunnel': an accord to maintain semi-fixed ratios between their currencies, allowing a margin of 2.25 percent movement either side of the approved rates. Initially joined by Britain, Ireland and the Scandinavian countries, this compromise lasted just two years: the British, Irish and Italian governments—unable or unwilling to withstand domestic pressures to devalue beyond the established bands—were all forced to withdraw from the arrangement and let their currencies fall. Even the French were twice forced out of the 'snake', in 1974 and again in 1976. Clearly, something more was needed.

In 1978 the West German Chancellor Helmut Schmidt proposed recasting the snake into something altogether more rigorous: a European Monetary System (EMS). A grid of fixed bilateral exchange rates would be set up, linked by a purely notional unit of measure, the European Currency Unit (the *écu*[5]), and underwritten by the stability and anti-inflationary priorities of the German economy and the Bundesbank. Participant countries would commit themselves to domestic economic rigour in order to sustain their place in the EMS. This was the first German initiative of its kind and it amounted in fact if not in name to the recommendation that, for Europe at least, the Deutschmark replace the dollar as the currency of reference.

Some countries stayed out—notably the UK, where Labour Prime Minister James Callaghan correctly understood that the EMS would prevent Britain adopting reflationary policies to address the country's unemployment problem. Others joined precisely for that reason. As a '*solution de rigueur*', the EMS would function rather like the International Monetary Fund (or the European Commission and the euro in later years): it would oblige governments to take unpopular decisions which they could hope to blame on rules and treaties framed from abroad. Indeed, this was the true long-term significance of the new arrangements. It was not so much that they succeeded in time in driving out the demon of inflation (though they did), but that they did so by steadily depriving national governments of their initiative in domestic policy.

This was a momentous shift, of greater consequence than was sometimes appreciated at the time. In the past, if a government opted for a 'hard money' strategy by adhering to the gold standard or declining to lower interest rates, it had to answer to its local electorate. But in the circumstances of the later 1970s, a government in London—or Stockholm, or Rome—facing intractable unemployment, or

---

[5]This acronym had a distinct political use: by reviving the name of an eighteenth-century French silver coin it helped assuage Parisian discomfort at having to acknowledge West Germany's emerging primacy in the affairs of Europe.

failing industries, or inflationary wage demands, could point helplessly at the terms of an IMF loan, or the rigours of pre-negotiated intra-European exchange rates, and disclaim liability. The tactical benefits of such a move were obvious: but they would come at a price.

If the European state could no longer square the circle of full employment, high real wages and economic growth, then it was bound to face the wrath of those constituents who felt betrayed. As we have noted, the instinctive reaction of politicians everywhere was to assuage the anxieties of the blue-collar male proletariat: partly because they were the worst affected, but mostly because precedent suggested that this was the social constituency most likely to mount effective protests. But as it transpired, the real opposition lay elsewhere. It was the heavily-taxed middle classes—white-collar public and private employees, small tradesmen and the self-employed—whose troubles translated most effectively into political opposition.

The greatest beneficiaries of the modern welfare state, after all, were the middle classes. When the post-war system started to unravel in the 1970s it was those same middle classes who felt not so much threatened as cheated: by inflation, by tax-financed subsidies to failing industries and by the reduction or elimination of public services to meet budgetary and monetary constraints. As in the past, the redistributive impact of inflation, made worse by the endemic high taxation of the modern service state, was felt most severely by citizens of the middling sort.

It was the middle classes, too, who were most disturbed by the issue of 'ungovernability'. The fear, widely expressed in the course of the 1970s, that Europe's democracies had lost control of their fate derived from a number of sources. In the first place there was a backlog of nervousness provoked by the iconoclastic rebellions of the 1960s; what had seemed curious and even exciting in the confident atmosphere of those days now looked more and more like a harbinger of uncertainty and anarchy. Then there was the more immediate anxiety born of job losses and inflation, about which governments seemed helpless to act.

Indeed, the very fact that European leaders appeared to have lost control was itself a source of public angst—all the more so in that politicians, as we have seen, found some advantage in insisting upon their own inadequacy. Denis Healey, Chancellor of the Exchequer in the hapless Labour government of the mid-Seventies, bemoaned the billions of Eurodollars washing around the continent, the work of 'the faceless men who managed the growing atomic clouds of footloose funds, which had accumulated in the Euro-markets to evade control by national governments'.[6] Ironically, Healey's own party had been elected in 1974 because of the Conservatives' apparent inability to allay public discontent—only to find itself accused of comparable impotence, and worse, in the coming years.

In Britain there was even passing talk of the inadequacy of democratic institu-

---

[6]Quoted in Harold James, *International Monetary Cooperation since Bretton Woods* (NY, Oxford, 1996), p. 180.

tions in the face of modern crises, and some speculation in the press about the benefits of government by disinterested outsiders, or 'corporatist' coalitions of 'nonpolitical' experts. Like De Gaulle (in May 1968), some senior British political figures in these years thought it prudent to meet with police and military leaders to reassure themselves of their support in the event of public disorder. Even in Scandinavia and the Low Countries, where the core legitimacy of representative institutions was never seriously called into question, the disarray of the world financial system, the apparent unraveling of the post-war economy and the disaffection of traditional electorates called into question the easy confidence of the post-war generation.

Behind these nebulous stirrings of doubt and disillusion there was a very real and, as it seemed at the time, present threat. Since the end of the Second World War, Western Europe had been largely preserved from civil conflict, much less open violence. Armed force had been deployed to bloody effect all across Eastern Europe, in the European colonies, and throughout Asia, Africa and South America. The Cold War notwithstanding, heated and murderous struggles were a feature of the post-war decades, with millions of soldiers and civilians killed from Korea to the Congo. The United States itself had been the site of three political assassinations and more than one bloody riot. But Western Europe had been an island of civil peace.

When European policemen did beat or shoot civilians, the latter were usually foreigners, often dark-skinned.[7] Aside from occasional violent encounters with Communist demonstrators, the forces of order in Western Europe were rarely called upon by their governments to handle violent opposition and, when they were, the violence was often of their own perpetrating. By the standards of the inter-war decades, Europe's city streets were quite remarkably safe—a point that was frequently underscored by commentators contrasting Europe's well-regulated society with the rampant and uncaring individualism of urban America. As for the student 'riots' of the Sixties, they served, if anything, to confirm this diagnosis: Europe's youth might play at revolution but it was mostly show. The 'street-fighting men' ran little risk of actually getting hurt.

In the 1970s, the prospect suddenly darkened. Just as eastern Europe, in the wake of the invasion of Prague, was stifled in the fraternal embrace of the Party patriarchs, western Europe appeared to be losing its grip on public order. The challenge did not come from the conventional Left. To be sure, Moscow was well pleased with the balance of international advantage in these years: Watergate and the fall of Saigon had decidedly reduced America's standing while the USSR, as the world's

---

[7]Most notoriously on October 17th 1961, when the French police murdered an estimated two hundred Algerians, many of them drowned in the Seine, following a protest march through Paris. The Chief of Police at the time was Maurice Papon, later indicted and found guilty of crimes against humanity for his collaboration in the wartime rounding up and despatch of French Jews to Auschwitz. See Epilogue.

largest petroleum producer, did very well out of the Middle East crises. But the publication in English of Aleksandr Solzhenitsyn's *Gulag Archipelago* and his subsequent expulsion from the Soviet Union in February 1974, followed within a few years by the massacres in Cambodia and the plight of the Vietnamese 'boat people', ensured that there would be no revival of illusions about Communism.

Nor, except in a very few marginal instances, was there a credible revival of the far Right. Italy's neo-Fascist *Movimento Sociale Italiano* (MSI) never received more than 6.8 percent of the vote in national elections and in any case took care to present itself as a legitimate political party. The nationalists in West Germany were less concerned with such niceties of appearance, but like comparable parties of the nationalist fringe in Belgium, France or Britain, they had negligible electoral significance. In short, Communism and Fascism, in their classic incarnations, had no future in Western Europe. The real threat to civic peace came from another direction altogether.

In the course of the 1970s, Western European society faced two violent challenges. The first of these was pathological, in the sense that it was born of a longstanding malaise, albeit cast in a very modern form. In the Basque region of northern Spain, in the Catholic minority of Northern Ireland, in Corsica and elsewhere, old grievances flared into violent revolt. This was hardly a new experience for Europeans: Flemish nationalists in Belgian Flanders and German-speaking 'Austrians' in Italy's Alto Adige (the former South Tyrol) had long resented their 'subjection', resorting variously to graffiti, demonstrations, assault, bombs and even the ballot box.

But by 1970 the problem of the South Tyrol had been resolved by the creation of an autonomous bi-lingual region which appeased all but the most extreme critics; and although the Flemish nationalists of the *Volksunie* and *Vlaams Blok* parties never abandoned their ultimate goal of separation from French-speaking Wallonia, the new prosperity of Flanders, together with far-reaching legislation to federalize Belgium, had temporarily removed the sting from their demands: from a resentful pariah movement Flemish nationalism had been transformed into a revolt of Dutch-speaking taxpayers reluctant to subsidize unemployed Walloon steelworkers (see Chapter 22). The Basques and the Ulster Catholics, however, were another matter altogether.

The Basque country of northern Spain had always been a particular target of Franco's ire: partly because of its identification with the Republican cause in the Spanish Civil War, partly because the Basques' longstanding demand to be recognized as *different* ran counter to the deepest centralizing instincts and self-ascribed, state-preserving role of the Spanish officer corps. Anything and everything distinctively *Basque* was aggressively repressed throughout the Franco years: language, customs, politics. Contradicting his own centripetal instincts, the Spanish dictator even favored Navarre (a region whose sense of self and separateness never remotely approached that of the Basques or Catalans) with rights, privileges and its own leg-islature, for no other reason than to rub in the fact that the neighboring Basques could expect no such favors.

The emergence of modern Basque terrorism was a direct response to Franco's policies, though its spokesmen and defenders always claimed deeper roots in their region's frustrated dreams of independence. ETA—*Euskadi Ta Askatasuna* (Basquia and Freedom)—was formed in December 1958 to lead the armed struggle for Basque independence. From its earliest days as an underground organization it es-tablished working links—later given somewhat specious ideological justification—with similar groups abroad, who helped it secure money, weapons, training, safe havens and publicity: the Baader-Meinhof Group in Germany, the Irish Republi-can Army, the Palestine Liberation Organisation, as well as the OAS in France.

The strategy of ETA—and its political supporters in *Herri Batasuna*, the Basque separatist party formed in 1978—was a straightforward one of instrumental vio-lence: to raise the price of keeping Basques in Spain to a politically intolerable level. But like the IRA and other comparable organizations, ETA also had ambitions to function as a society within the state. Catholic, stern and moralistic—in a man-ner ironically redolent of Franco himself—ETA activists targeted not just Spanish policemen (their first victim was killed in June 1968) and moderate Basque politi-cians and notables, but also symbols of 'Spanish' decadence in the region: cinemas, bars, discothèques, drug pushers and the like.

In the waning years of the Franco era, ETA's activities were restricted by the very repression that had led to its emergence: by the end of the dictatorship, in the early 1970s, one quarter of Spain's armed police were stationed in the Basque country alone. This did not prevent ETA from assassinating Franco's Prime Minister (Ad-miral Luis Carrero Blanco) in Madrid on December 20th 1973, or killing twelve civilians in a bomb attack in the capital nine months later. Nor did the execution of five ETA gunmen in September 1975, shortly before Franco's death, have any moderating impact upon the group's activities. The coming of democracy, on the other hand, offered new opportunities.

ETA and its supporters wanted full independence. What the Basque region got, under Spain's post-Franco constitution (see Chapter 16), was a Statute of Auton-omy, approved by referendum in 1979. Infuriated—not least at the prospect of los-ing the support of moderate sympathizers satisfied by self-government and the right to linguistic and cultural self-expression—ETA stepped up its campaigns of bombing and assassination. In 1979–80 the organization killed 181 people; in the course of the next decade its murder rate averaged 34 a year. But in spite of this, and the fragility of Spain's infant democracy, ETA and its political allies failed to turn their terrorist campaign to political advantage: their one success, in provok-ing a small group of right-wing army officers to hold up the Cortes in February 1981 in the name of law, order and the integrity of the state, turned to fiasco.

One reason for ETA's limited impact, despite the horrific scale and wide public impact of its killing sprees, was that most Basques identified neither with its means nor with its ends. Indeed, many Basques were not really even Basques. The economic transformations of Spain in the 1960s, and the large-scale migrations within the country and abroad, had wrought changes that the old nationalists and their fanatical young followers simply did not grasp. By the mid-eighties, less than half the population of the Basque region had Basque parents, much less Basque grandparents. Such people rightly saw ETA and *Herri Batasuna* as a threat to their well-being (and implicitly to their very presence in the region).

As its political project lost touch with social reality ETA became ever more extreme—having forgotten its aim it redoubled its efforts, to cite George Santayana's definition of fanaticism. Financed by crime and extortion, its operatives increasingly constrained to function from across the border in the Basque *départements* of south-west France, ETA survived and it survives still, murdering the occasional politician or village policeman. But it has failed either to mobilize Basque sentiment in support of political independence, or to bludgeon the Spanish state into conceding its case. ETA's greatest 'success' came early in the 1980s, when its actions prompted the Socialist Prime Minister Felipe González to allow counter-terrorist hit men (the *Grupos Antiterroristas de Liberación*) to base themselves illegally on French soil and pick off ETA operatives, twenty-six of whom were killed between 1983 and 1987. González's decision, only revealed many years later (see Chapter 22), has cast a retrospective shadow across the early post-Franco years of constitutional democracy in Spain; but in the circumstances it was arguably a remarkably moderate response.

The Provisional IRA was much like ETA in its methods, and in some of its proclaimed objectives. Just as ETA sought to make the Basque provinces ungovernable and thereby secure their exit from Spain, so the Irish Republican Army aimed at making Northern Ireland ungovernable, expelling the British, and uniting the six northern provinces with the rest of Ireland. But there were significant differences. Since an independent Ireland already existed, there was—at least in principle—a practicable national goal for the rebels to hold out to their supporters. On the other hand, there was more than one Northern Irish community, and the distinctions between them went back a very long way.

Like French Algeria, Northern Ireland—Ulster—was both a colonial remnant and an integral part of the metropolitan nation itself. When London finally relinquished Ireland to the Irish, in 1922, the UK retained the six northern counties of the island on the reasonable enough grounds that the overwhelmingly Protestant majority there was intensely loyal to Britain and had no desire to be governed from Dublin—and incorporated into a semi-theocratic republic dominated by the Catholic episcopate. Whatever they said in public, the political leaders of the new Republic were themselves not altogether unhappy to forgo the presence of a compact and sizeable community of angrily recalcitrant Protestants. But for a minority of Irish nationalists this abandonment constituted a betrayal, and under the banner of the IRA they continued to demand the unification—by force if need be— of the entire island.

This situation remained largely unchanged for four decades. By the 1960s the official stance in Dublin somewhat resembled that of Bonn: acknowledging the desirability of national re-unification but quietly content to see the matter postponed *sine die*. Successive British governments, meanwhile, had long chosen to ignore so far as possible the uneasy situation they had inherited in Ulster, where the Protestant majority dominated local Catholics through gerrymandered constituencies, political clientelism, sectarian pressure on employers, and a monopoly of jobs in crucial occupations: civil service, judiciary and above all the police.

If politicians on the British mainland preferred not to know about these matters, it was because the Conservative Party depended on its 'Unionist' wing (dating from the nineteenth-century campaign to maintain Ireland united with Britain) for a crucial block of parliamentary seats; it was thus committed to the *status quo*, with Ulster maintained as an integral part of the United Kingdom. The Labour Party was no less closely identified with the powerful labour unions in Belfast's shipbuilding and allied industries, where Protestant workers had long received preferential treatment.

As this last observation suggests, the divisions in Northern Ireland were unusually complicated. The religious divide between Protestants and Catholics was real and corresponded to a communal divide replicated at every stage of life: from birth to death, through education, housing, marriage, employment and recreation. And it was ancient—references to seventeenth- and eighteenth-century quarrels and victories might appear to outsiders absurdly ritualistic, but the history behind them was real. But the Catholic/Protestant divide was never a class distinction in the conventional sense, despite the IRA's efforts to import Marxist categories into its rhetoric. There were workers and priests—and to a lesser extent landowners, businessmen and professionals—on both sides.

Moreover, many Ulster Catholics felt no urgent desire to be ruled from Dublin. In the 1960s Ireland was still a poor and backward country and the standard of living in the North, while below that of most of the rest of the UK, was still considerably above the Irish average. Even for Catholics, Ulster was a better economic bet. Protestants, meanwhile, identified very strongly with the UK. This sentiment was by no means reciprocated by the rest of Britain, which thought little of Northern Ireland (when it thought of it at all). The old industries of Ulster, like those of the rest of the UK, were in decline by the end of the 1960s, and it was already clear to planners in London that the overwhelmingly Protestant blue-collar workforce there had an uncertain future. But beyond this, it is fair to say that the British authorities had not given Ulster serious thought for many decades.

The IRA had declined to a marginal political sect, denouncing the Irish Republic as illegitimate because incomplete while reiterating its 'revolutionary' aspiration to forge a different Ireland, radical and united. The IRA's wooly, anachronistic rhetoric had little appeal to a younger generation of recruits (including the seventeen-year-old, Belfast-born Gerry Adams, who joined in 1965) more interested in action than doctrine and who formed their own organization, the clandestine, 'Provisional' IRA.[8] The 'Provos', recruited mainly from Derry and Belfast, emerged just in time to benefit from a wave of civil rights demonstrations across the North, demanding long overdue political and civil rights for Catholics from the Ulster government in Stormont Castle and encountering little but political intransigence and police batons for their efforts.

The 'Troubles' that were to take over Northern Irish—and to some extent British—public life for the next three decades were sparked by street battles in Derry following the traditional Apprentice Boys' March in July 1969, aggressively commemorating the defeat of the Jacobite and Catholic cause 281 years before. Faced with growing public violence and demands from Catholic leaders for London to intervene, the UK government sent in the British Army and took over control of policing functions in the six counties. The army, recruited largely in mainland Britain, was decidedly less partisan and on the whole less brutal than the local police. It is thus ironic that its presence provided the newly formed Provisional IRA with its core demand: that the British authorities and their troops should leave Ulster, as a first stage towards re-uniting the island under Irish rule.

The British did not leave. It is not clear how they could have left. Various efforts through the 1970s to build inter-community confidence and allow the province to run its own affairs fell foul of suspicion and intransigence on both sides. Catholics, even if they had no liking for their own armed extremists, had good precedent for mistrusting promises of power-sharing and civic equality emanating from the Ulster Protestant leadership. The latter, always reluctant to make real concessions to the Catholic minority, were now seriously fearful of the intransigent gunmen of the Provisionals. Without the British military presence the province would have descended still further into open civil war.

The British government was thus trapped. At first London was sympathetic to Catholic pressure for reforms; but following the killing of a British soldier in February 1971 the government introduced internment without trial and the situation deteriorated rapidly. In January 1972, on 'Bloody Sunday', British paratroopers killed thirteen civilians in the streets of Derry. In that same year 146 members of the security forces and 321 civilians were killed in Ulster, and nearly five thousand people injured. Buoyed up by a new generation of martyrs and the obstinacy of its opponents, the Provisional IRA mounted what was to become a thirty-year campaign, in the course of which it bombed, shot and maimed soldiers and civilians in Ulster and across mainland Britain. It made at least one attempt to assassinate the British Prime Minister. Even if the British authorities had wanted to walk away

---

[8]The Provisionals took their name from the April 24th 1916 declaration in Dublin, when the insurrectionists proclaimed a provisional government.

from Ulster (as many mainland voters might have wished), they could not. As a referendum of March 1973 showed and later polls confirmed, an overwhelming majority of the people of Ulster wished to maintain their ties to Britain.[9]

The IRA campaign did not unite Ireland. It did not remove the British from Ulster. Nor did it destabilize British politics, though the assassination of politicians and public figures (notably Lord Mountbatten, former Viceroy of India and godfather of the Prince of Wales) genuinely shocked public opinion on both sides of the Irish Sea. But the Irish 'Troubles' further darkened an already gloomy decade in British public life and contributed to the 'ungovernability' thesis being touted at the time, as well as to the end of the carefree optimism of the 1960s. By the time the Provisional IRA—and the Protestant paramilitary groups that had emerged in its wake—finally came to the negotiating table, to secure constitutional arrangements that the British government might have been pleased to concede almost from the outset, 1,800 people had been killed and one Ulster resident in five had a family member killed or wounded in the fighting.

Against this background, the other 'pathologies' of 1970s Europe were small indeed, though they contributed to the widespread atmosphere of unease. A self-styled 'Angry Brigade', purportedly acting on behalf of the unrepresented unemployed, planted bombs around London in 1971. Francophone separatists in the Swiss Jura, modeling their tactics on those of the Irish, rioted in 1974 at their enforced incorporation into the (German-speaking) canton of Bern. Crowds of rioters in Liverpool, Bristol and the Brixton district of London battled with police over control of 'no-go' inner-city slums.

In one key or another, all such protests and actions were, as I have suggested, pathologies of politics: however extreme their form, their goals were familiar and their tactics instrumental. They were trying to achieve something and would—by their own account—have desisted if their demands were met. ETA, the IRA and their imitators were terrorist organizations; but they were not irrational. In due course most of them ended up negotiating with their enemies, in the hope of securing their objectives if only in part. But such considerations were never of interest to protagonists of the second violent challenge of the times.

In most of Western Europe, the airy radical theorems of the 1960s dissipated harmlessly enough. But in two countries in particular they metamorphosed into a psychosis of self-justifying aggression. A small minority of erstwhile student radicals, intoxicated by their own adaptation of Marxist dialectics, set about 'revealing' the 'true face' of repressive tolerance in Western democracies. If the parliamentary regime of capitalist interests were pushed hard enough, they reasoned, it would shed the cloak of legality and show its true face. Confronted with the truth about its oppressors, the proletariat—hitherto 'alienated' from its own in-

---

[9]It was estimated at the time that the cost of maintaining a British presence in Northern Ireland was £3 billion per annum, at a time when London was hard pushed to balance its budget.

terest and victim of 'false consciousness' about its situation—would take up its proper place on the barricades of class warfare.

Such a summary gives too much credit to the terrorist underground of the 1970s—and too little. Most of the young men and women swept up in it, however familiar they were with the justificatory vocabulary of violence, played little part in its formulation. They were the foot soldiers of terrorism. On the other hand, especially in West Germany, the emotional energy invested in their hatred of the Federal Republic drew on sources deeper and darker than the mal-adapted rhetorical gymnastics of nineteenth-century radicalism. The urge to bring the architecture of security and stability crashing down on the heads of their parents' generation was the extreme expression of a more widespread skepticism, in the light of the recent past, about the local credibility of pluralist democracy. It was not by chance, therefore, that 'revolutionary terror' took its most menacing form in Germany and Italy.

The link between extra-parliamentary politics and outright violence first emerged in Germany as early as April 1968, when four young radicals—among them Andreas Baader and Gudrun Ensslin—were arrested on suspicion of burning two department stores in Frankfurt. Two years later Baader escaped from prison in the course of an armed raid planned and led by Ulrike Meinhof. She and Baader then issued their 'Concept City Guerrilla Manifesto', announcing the formation of a '*Rote Armee Fraktion*' (Red Army Fraction—RAF) whose goal was to dismantle the Federal Republic by force. The acronym RAF was chosen deliberately: just as Britain's Royal Air Force had attacked Nazi Germany from the air, so the Baader-Meinhof Group, as they were colloquially known, would bomb and shoot its successor into submission from below.

Between 1970 and 1978, the RAF and its ancillary offshoots pursued a strategy of deliberately random terror, assassinating soldiers, policemen and businessmen, holding up banks and kidnapping mainstream politicians. In addition to killing 28 people and wounding a further 93 in the course of bombings and shootings in these years, they took 162 hostages and carried out over 30 bank robberies—partly to finance their organization, partly to advertise their presence. In the early years they also targeted American Army bases in West Germany, killing and injuring a number of soldiers, notably in the late spring of 1972.

In their peak year of 1977, the RAF kidnapped and subsequently executed Hans Martin Schleyer, the chairman of Daimler Benz and President of the West German Federation of Industries, and assassinated both Siegfried Buback, the West German Attorney General, and Jürgen Ponto, the head of Dresdner Bank. But this was to be their swansong. Already, in May 1976, Meinhof (captured in 1972) had been found dead in her Stuttgart prison cell. She had apparently hung herself, though rumors persisted that she had been executed by the state. Baader, seized in a shoot-out in Frankfurt in 1972, was in prison serving a life sentence for murder when he, too, was found dead in his cell on October 18th 1977, on the same day as Gudrun Ensslin and another imprisoned terrorist. Their underground organization persisted into the eighties, albeit much reduced: in August 1981 it bombed the US Air Force HQ at Ramstein in West Germany, and the following month the 'Gudrun Ensslin Kommando' tried unsuccessfully to assassinate the US Supreme Commander in Europe.

Since the German terrorist underground had no defined goals, its achievements can only be measured by the extent of its success in disrupting German public life and undermining the institutions of the Republic. In this it clearly failed. The most distinctively repressive governmental action of the time was the passing of the *Berufsverbot* in 1972 by the Social Democratic government of Willy Brandt. This decree excluded from state employment any person who engaged in political acts considered detrimental to the Constitution, and was ostensibly aimed at keeping supporters of Left and Right political extremes out of sensitive posts. In a culture already preternaturally disposed to public conformity this certainly aroused fears of censorship and worse; but it was hardly the prelude to dictatorship that its critics feared and—at the outer extreme—hoped.

Neither the terrorist Left nor the apparently renascent neo-Nazi Right—notably responsible for killing 13 people and wounding 220 others in a bomb attack on Munich's *Oktoberfest* in 1980—succeeded in destabilizing the Republic, although they did provoke careless talk in conservative political circles of the need to curb civil liberties and enforce 'Order'. Much more worrying was the extent to which the Baader-Meinhof Group in particular was able to tap into a fund of generalized sympathy for its ideas among otherwise law-abiding intellectuals and academics.[10]

One source of local sympathy was a growing nostalgia in literary and artistic circles for Germany's lost past. Germany, it was felt, had been doubly 'disinherited': by the Nazis, who had deprived Germans of a respectable, 'usable' past; and by the Federal Republic, whose American overseers had imposed upon Germany a false image of itself. In the words of Hans-Jürgen Syberberg, the film director, the nation had been 'spiritually disinherited and dispossessed . . . we live in a country without homeland, without *Heimat*.' The distinctly nationalist tinge to German extreme-Left terrorism—its targeting of American occupiers, multinational corporations and the 'international' capitalist order—rang a chord, as did the terrorists' claim that it was *Germans* who were now the victims of the manipulations and interests of others.

These same years saw an outpouring of films, speeches, books, television programs and public commentary on the country's problematic history and identity.

---

[10]The unimpeachably law-abiding French Socialist Party even formed a 'Committee for the Defense of Human Rights' in the Federal Republic, offering to provide expertise and practical help to defendants accused of terrorist acts there.

Just as the Red Army Fraktion claimed to be fighting 'Fascism'—by proxy, so to speak—so West Germany's intellectuals, Left and Right, battled for control of Germany's true heritage. Syberberg's fellow film director Edgar Reitz directed a hugely popular, sixteen-hour television mini-series: 'Heimat: A German Chronicle'. The story of a family from the Hunsrück countryside of the Rhineland Palatinate, it traced contemporary German history through a domestic narrative reaching from the end of World War One to the present.

In Reitz's film the inter-war years especially are bathed in a sepia-like afterglow of fond memory; even the Nazi era is hardly permitted to intrude upon fond recollections of better times. The Americanized world of the post-war Federal Republic, on the other hand, is presented with angry, icy disdain: its materialist neglect of national values and its destruction of memory and continuity are depicted as violently corrosive of human values and community. As in Fassbinder's *Marriage of Maria Braun* the main character—also 'Maria'—does duty for a victimized Germany; but *Heimat* is quite explicitly nostalgic and even xenophobic in its contempt for foreign values and longing for the lost soul of 'deep Germany'.

Reitz, like Syberberg and others, was publicly scornful of the American television series 'Holocaust', first shown on German television in 1979. If there were to be depictions of Germany's past, however painful, then it was the business of Germans to produce them. 'The most radical process of expropriation there is,' wrote Reitz, 'is the expropriation of one's own history. The Americans have stolen our history through *Holocaust*.' The application of a 'commercial aesthetic' to Germany's past was America's way of controlling it. The struggle of German directors and artists against American 'kitsch' was part of the struggle against American capitalism.

Reitz and Fassbinder were among the directors of *Deutschland im Herbst* ('Germany in Autumn') a 1978 collage of documentary, movie clips and interviews covering the events of the autumn of 1977, notably the kidnapping and killing of Hans Martin Schleyer and the subsequent suicide of Ensslin and Baader. The film is notable not so much for its expressions of empathy for the terrorists as for the distinctive terms in which these are conveyed. By careful inter-cutting, the Third Reich and the Federal Republic are made to share a family resemblance. 'Capitalism', 'the profit system' and National Socialism are presented as equally reprehensible and indefensible, with the terrorists emerging as latter-day resisters: modern Antigones struggling with their consciences and against political repression.

Considerable cinematic talent was deployed in *Deutschland im Herbst*—as in other contemporary German films—to depict West Germany as a police state, akin to Nazism if only in its (as yet unrevealed) capacity for repression and violence. Horst Mahler, a semi-repentant terrorist then still in prison, explains to the camera that the emergence of an extra-parliamentary opposition in 1967 was the 'anti-fascist revolution' that did not happen in 1945. The true struggle against Germany's Nazi demons was thus being carried through by the country's young radical underground—albeit by the use of remarkably Nazi-like methods, a paradox Mahler does not address.

The implicit relativizing of Nazism in *Deutschland im Herbst* was already becoming quite explicit in intellectual apologias for anti-capitalist terror. As the philosopher Detlef Hartmann explained in 1985, 'We can learn from the obvious linkage of money, technology and extermination in New Order Nazi imperialism . . . (how) to lift the veil covering the civilized extermination technology of the New Order of Bretton Woods.' It was this easy slippage—the thought that what binds Nazism and capitalist democracy is more important than their differences, and that it was Germans who had fallen victim to both—that helped account for the German radical Left's distinctive insensitivity on the subject of Jews.

On September 5th 1972, the Palestinian organization Black September attacked the Israeli team at the Munich Olympics and killed eleven athletes, as well as one German policeman. Almost certainly, the killers had local assistance from the radical Left (though it is a curiosity of German extremist politics of the time that the far Right would have been no less pleased to offer its services). The link between Palestinian organizations and European terrorist groups was already well-established—Ensslin, Baader and Meinhof all 'trained' at one time with Palestinian guerillas, along with Basques, Italians, Irish Republicans and others. But only Germans went the extra mile: when four gunmen (two Germans, two Arabs) hijacked an Air France plane in June 1976 and flew it to Entebbe, in Uganda, it was the Germans who undertook to identify and separate the Jewish passengers from the rest.

If this action, so unmistakably reminiscent of selections of Jews by Germans in another time and place, did not definitively discredit the Baader-Meinhof gang in the eyes of its sympathizers it was because its arguments, if not its methods, attracted quite broad consent: Germans, not Jews, were now the victims; and American capitalism, not German National Socialism, was the perpetrator. 'War crimes' were now things that Americans did to—e.g.—Vietnamese. There was a 'new patriotism' abroad in West Germany, and it is more than a little ironic that Baader, Meinhof and their friends, whose violent revolt was initially directed against the Germany-first self-satisfaction of their parents' generation, should find themselves co-opted by the reverberations of that same nationalist heritage. It was altogether appropriate that Horst Mahler, one of the few surviving founders of Left terrorism in West Germany, should end up three decades later on the far Right of the political spectrum.

In external respects, contemporary Italian terrorism was not markedly different from the German kind. It too drew on para-Marxist rhetoric from the Sixties, and most of its leaders received their political education in the university protests of that time. The main underground organization of Left terror, the self-styled *Brigate Rosse* ('Red Brigades', BR) first came to public attention in October 1970, when it distributed leaflets describing goals that closely resembled those of the Red

Army Fraktion. Like Baader, Meinhof and others, the leaders of the BR were young (the best known of them, Renato Curcio, was just 29 in 1970), mostly former students, and devoted to armed underground struggle for its own sake.

But there were also some important differences. From the outset, Italian Left terrorists placed far greater emphasis upon their purported relationship to the 'workers'; and indeed in certain industrial towns of the north, Milan in particular, the more respectable fringes of the ultra-Left *did* have a small popular following. Unlike the German terrorists, grouped around a tiny hard core of criminals, the Italian far Left ranged from legitimate political parties through urban guerrilla networks to micro-sects of armed political bandits, with a fair degree of overlap in membership and objectives.

These groups and sects replicated in miniature the fissiparous history of the mainstream European Left. In the course of the 1970s each violent act would be followed by assertions of responsibility by hitherto unknown organizations, frequently by sub-sections and breakaways from the original unit. Beyond the terrorists themselves orbited a loose constellation of semi-clandestine movements and journals whose sententious 'theoretical' pronouncements offered ideological cover for terrorist tactics. The names of these various groups, cells, networks, journals and movements are beyond parody: in addition to the Red Brigades there were *Lotta Continua* ('Ongoing Struggle'), *Potere Operaio* ('Workers' Power'), *Prima Linea* ('Front Line') and *Autonomia Operaia* ('Workers' Autonomy'); *Avanguardia Operaia* ('Workers' Avant-garde'), *Nuclei Armati Proletari* ('Armed Proletarian Nuclei') and *Nuclei Armati Rivoluzionari* ('Revolutionary Armed Nuclei); *Formazione Comuniste Combattenti* ('Fighting Communist Formations'), *Unione Comunisti Combattenti* ('Fighting Communist Unions'), *Potere Proletario Armato* ('Armed Proletarian Power'), and others besides.

If this list suggests in retrospect a desperate desire to inflate the social and revolutionary significance of a few thousand ex-students and their followers at the disaffected edges of the labour movement, the impact of their efforts to bring themselves to public attention should not be underestimated. Curcio, his companion Mara Cagol and their friends may have been living out in fantasy a romanticized fairy tale of revolutionary bandits (derived in large measure from the popularized image of revolutionary guerrillas in Latin America), but the damage they wrought was real enough. Between 1970 and 1981 not a year passed in Italy without murders, mutilations, kidnapping, assaults and sundry acts of public violence. In the course of the decade three politicians, nine magistrates, sixty-five policemen and some three hundred others fell victim to assassination.

In their first years, the Red Brigades and others confined their actions largely to the kidnapping and occasional shooting of factory managers and lesser businessmen: 'capitalist lackeys', '*servi del padrone*' ('the bosses' hacks'), reflecting their initial interest in direct democracy on the shop floor. But by the mid-seventies they had progressed to political assassination—at first of right-wing politicians, then policemen, journalists and public prosecutors—in a strategy designed to 'strip away the mask' of bourgeois legality, force the state into violent repression and thus polarize public opinion.

Until 1978 the Red Brigades had failed to provoke the desired backlash, despite a rising crescendo of attacks in the course of the previous year. Then, on March 16th 1978, they kidnapped their most prominent victim: Aldo Moro, a leader of the Christian Democrat Party and former Prime Minister and Foreign Minister. Moro was held hostage for two months; backed by the Communists and most of his own party, the Christian Democrat Prime Minister Giulio Andreotti refused even to consider the kidnappers' demand for the release of 'political prisoners' in exchange for Moro's life. In spite of unanimous condemnation across the Italian political spectrum and appeals from the Pope and the Secretary General of the UN, the terrorists refused to relent. On May 10th Aldo Moro's body was found in a car brazenly parked on a street in the centre of Rome.

The Moro Affair certainly illustrated the incompetence of the Italian state—the Interior Minister resigned the day after the body was found. After eight years of frantic anti-terrorist legislation and nationwide manhunts, the police had manifestly failed to break the terrorist underground.[11] And the reverberations of the Red Brigades' success in committing political murder at the very heart of the state and its capital city were significant. It was now clear to everyone that Italy faced a real challenge to its political order: less than two weeks after Moro's corpse was found, the BR killed the head of the anti-terrorist squad in Genoa; in October 1978 they assassinated the Director General of Penal Affairs in Rome's Justice Ministry. Two weeks later the *Formazione Comuniste Combattenti* assassinated a senior public prosecutor.

But the very scale of the terrorists' challenge to the state now began to extract a price. The Italian Communist Party threw its weight firmly and unambiguously behind the institutions of the Republic, making explicit what was by now clear to almost everyone: namely, that whatever their roots in popular movements of the Sixties, the terrorists of the Seventies had now placed themselves beyond the spectrum of radical politics. They were simple criminals and should be hunted down as such. And so should those who provided them with ideological cover, and perhaps more: in April 1979 the University of Padua lecturer Toni Negri, together with other leaders of *Autonomia Operaia*, was arrested and charged with plotting armed insurrection against the state.

Negri and his supporters insisted (and continue to insist) that the radical 'autonomists', neither clandestine nor armed, should not be confused with illegal secret societies, and that the political decision to go after them represented precisely the retreat from 'bourgeois order' that the Red Brigades had prophesied and sought

---

[11] As in Germany, the police had actually found the leaders at one point, only to lose them again. Arrested in 1974, Renato Curcio escaped from prison in February 1975, only to be recaptured eleven months later.

to bring about. But Negri himself had condoned at the University of Padua violent attacks on teachers and administrators falling only just short of terrorist tactics. The slogans of 'mass illegality', 'permanent civil war' and the need to organize 'militarily' against the bourgeois state were widely declaimed in respectable academic circles—including Negri's own paper *Rosso*. A year after the kidnapping and murder of Moro, Negri himself wrote in celebration of 'the annihilation of the adversary': 'The pain of my adversary does not affect me: proletarian justice has the productive force of self-affirmation and the faculty of logical conviction'.[12]

The idea that political violence might have the 'productive force of self-affirmation' was not unfamiliar in modern Italian history, of course. What Negri was affirming, and what the Red Brigades and their friends were practicing, was no different from the 'cleansing power of force' as exalted by Fascists. As in Germany, so in Italy: the far Left's hatred of the 'bourgeois state' had led it back to the 'proletarian' violence of the anti-democratic Right. By 1980 both the targets and the methods of terrorist Left and terrorist Right in Italy had become indistinguishable. Indeed, the Red Brigades and their offspring were by no means responsible for all the violence of Italy's *anni di piombo* ('Lead Years'). The conspiratorial, anti-republican Right resurfaced in these years (and perpetrated the single worst crime of the age, the bombing of Bologna's railway station in August 1980, killing 85 and wounding 200 more); and in the *Mezzogiorno* the Mafia, too, adopted a more aggressive strategy of terror in its war with magistrates, police and local politicians.

But to the extent that the re-emergence of neo-Fascist terror and the resurgence of Mafia violence illustrated and exacerbated the vulnerability of democratic institutions, their undertakings were—perhaps correctly—interpreted by Left terrorists as a sign of their own success. Both extremes sought to destabilize the state by rendering normal public life intolerably dangerous—with the difference that the far Right could count on some protection and collaboration from the very forces of order they sought to subvert. Shadowy right-wing conspiratorial networks, reaching up into the higher ranks of the police, the banking community and the ruling Christian Democrat Party, authorized the murder of judges, prosecutors and journalists.[13]

That democracy and the rule of law in Italy survived these years is a matter of no small note. From 1977 to 1982 especially, the country was under siege from random acts of extreme violence by far Left, far Right and professional criminals alike—it was in these same years that the Mafia and other criminal networks as-

---

[12]Initially released, Negri was re-arrested in 1983. In June 1984 he was tried and condemned to thirty years in prison.
[13]One such network, the infamous 'P2 Lodge', was a mysterious Masonic web of right-wing politicians, bankers, soldiers and policemen, organized by Licio Gelli, a former militant in Mussolini's 'Social Republic' from 1943 to 1945. Its 962 members included thirty generals, eight admirals, forty-three parliamentary deputies, three active Cabinet Ministers and a fair cross-representation of the highest ranks of the Catholic Church, industry and the private banking sector.

sassinated police chiefs, politicians, prosecutors, judges and journalists, sometimes with apparent near-impunity. While the more serious threat came from the extreme Right—better organized and much closer to the heart of the state—the 'Red' terrorists made the greater impact upon the public imagination. This was in part because, like the Red Army Fraktion in Germany, they traded upon widespread local sympathy for radical ideas. Official Communists correctly saw this appropriation of the revolutionary heritage as the terrorists' chief asset, as well as a symptom of the risk that they posed for the credibility of the mainstream Left.

Ironically, and unbeknown to local Communists themselves, the Red Brigades and the Red Army Fraktion—like the similarly motivated but ineffectual *Cellules communistes combattantes* in Belgium, *Action Directe* in France and other, even smaller operations elsewhere—were financed in part with money supplied by the Soviet secret services. This cash was not part of any coherent strategy: it was paid out, rather, on general principles—the enemies of our enemies, however absurd and insignificant, are still our friends. But in this case the undertaking backfired: the one incontrovertible achievement of left-wing terrorism in Western Europe in these years was the thoroughness with which it expunged any remaining revolutionary illusions from the local body politic.

All the mainstream political organizations of the Left, Communists especially, were constrained to take and maintain their distance from violence of any kind. Partly this was a spontaneous response to the threat terror posed to them as well as others—trade unionists and other representatives of the traditional labor movement were among the most vilified targets of the underground networks. But partly it was because the 'lead years' of the 1970s served to remind everyone of just how fragile liberal democracies might actually be—a lesson occasionally neglected in the heady atmosphere of the sixties. The net effect of years of would-be revolutionary subversion at the heart of Western Europe was not to polarize society, as the terrorists had planned and expected, but rather to drive politicians of all sides to cluster together in the safety of the middle ground.

In the life of the mind, the nineteen seventies were the most dispiriting decade of the twentieth century. In some measure this can be attributed to the circumstances described in this chapter: the sharp and sustained economic downturn, together with widespread political violence, encouraged the sentiment that Europe's 'good times' had gone, perhaps for many years to come. Most young people were now less concerned with changing the world than with finding a job: the fascination with collective ambitions gave way to an obsession with personal needs. In a more threatening world, securing one's self-interest took precedence over advancing common causes.

There is no doubt that this change in mood was also a response to the heady indulgence of the previous decade. Europeans who only recently had enjoyed an unprecedented explosion of energy and originality in music, fashion, cinema and the arts could now contemplate at leisure the cost of their recent revelries. It was not so much the idealism of the Sixties that seemed to have dated so very fast as the *innocence* of those days: the feeling that whatever could be imagined could be done; that whatever could be made could be possessed; and that transgression—moral, political, legal, aesthetic—was inherently attractive and productive. Whereas the Sixties were marked by the naive, self-congratulatory impulse to believe that everything happening was new—and everything new was significant—the Seventies were an age of cynicism, of lost illusions and reduced expectations.

Mediocre times, wrote Albert Camus in *The Fall*, beget empty prophets. The 1970s offered a rich harvest of them. It was an age depressingly aware of having come *after* the big hopes and ambitious ideas of the recent past, and having nothing to offer but breathless and implausible re-runs and extensions of old thoughts. It was, quite self-consciously, a 'post-everything' era, whose future prospects appeared cloudy. As the American sociologist Daniel Bell observed at the time, 'The use of the hyphenated prefix post- indicates [a] sense of living in interstitial time.' As a description of the real world—'post-war', 'post-imperial', and most recently 'post-industrial'—the term had its uses, even if it left uncertain what might follow. But when applied to categories of thought—as in 'post-Marxist', 'post-structuralist' and, most elusively of all, 'post-modern'—it merely added to the obscurities of an already confused time.

The culture of the Sixties had been rationalistic. Mild drugs and utopian revelries notwithstanding, the social thought of the age, like its music, operated in a familiar and coherent register, merely 'expanded'. It was also strikingly communitarian: students, like 'workers', 'peasants', 'negroes' and other collectives, were presumed to share interests and affinities that bound them in a special relationship with one another and—albeit antagonistically—to the rest of society. The projects of the Sixties, however fantastic, presumed a relationship between individual and class, class and society, society and state, that would have been familiar in its form if not its content to theorists and activists at any point in the previous century.

The culture of the Seventies turned not on the collective but the individual. Just as anthropology had displaced philosophy as the Ur-discipline of the Sixties, so psychology now took its place. In the course of the Sixties the notion of 'false consciousness' had been widely taken up by young Marxists to explain the failure of workers and others to liberate themselves from identification with the capitalist interest. In a perverted variant this idea formed, as we have seen, the core premise of Left terrorism. But it also took on a curious afterlife in less politicized circles: adapting Marxist background language to Freudian subjects, self-styled 'post-Freudians' now emphasized the need to liberate not social classes but aggregated individual subjects.

Theorists of liberation now surfaced, in Western Europe as in North America, whose goal was to release the human subject not from socially enforced bondage but from self-imposed illusions. The sexual variant on this theme—the idea that social and sexual repression were integrally linked—was already a truism in certain milieux of the late Sixties. But Marcuse, or Wilhelm Reich, stood in clear line of descent from both Freud *and* Marx—seeking collective transformation through individual liberation. The followers of Jacques Lacan on the other hand, or contemporary theorists of feminism like Kate Millett and Annie Leclerc, were both less ambitious and more. They were not much concerned with traditional projects of social revolution (which the feminists correctly identified with political movements led by and primarily for men). Instead they sought to undermine the very concept of the human subject that had once underlain them.

Two widespread assumptions lay behind such thinking, shared very broadly across the intellectual community of the time. The first was that power rested not—as most social thinkers since the Enlightenment had supposed—upon control of natural and human resources, but upon the monopoly of *knowledge*: knowledge about the natural world; knowledge about the public sphere; knowledge about oneself; and above all, knowledge about the way in which knowledge itself is produced and legitimized. The maintenance of power in this account rested upon the capacity of those in control of knowledge to maintain that control at the expense of others, by repressing subversive 'knowledges'.

At the time, this account of the human condition was widely and correctly associated with the writings of Michel Foucault. But for all his occasional obscurantism Foucault was a rationalist at heart. His early writings tracked quite closely the venerable Marxist claim that in order to liberate workers from the shackles of capitalism one had first to substitute a different account of history and economics for the self-serving narrative of bourgeois society. In short, one had to substitute revolutionary knowledge, so to speak, for that of the masters: or, in the language of Antonio Gramsci so fashionable a few years earlier, one had to combat the 'hegemony' of the ruling class.

A second assumption, one that was to acquire an even stronger grip on intellectual fashions, went considerably further. This was the seductive insistence upon subverting not just old certainties but the very possibility of certainty itself. All behavior, all opinion, all knowledge, precisely because it was socially derived and therefore politically instrumental, should be regarded with suspicion. The very idea that judgments or evaluations might stand independent of the person making them came to be treated in certain quarters as itself the expression and representation of a partisan (and implicitly conservative) social position.

All iterations of judgment or belief could in principle be reduced in this way. Even critical intellectuals could themselves be thus 'positioned'. In the words of the French sociology professor Pierre Bourdieu, the most influential European exponent of the new sociology of knowledge, 'professorial discourse' is but the expression of 'the dominated fraction of the dominating class.' What this beguilingly subversive way of positioning all knowledge and opinion did not disclose was how to determine whether one 'discourse' was truer than another: a dilemma resolved by treating 'truth' as itself a socially positioned category—a stance that would soon become fashionable in many places. The natural outcome of such developments was a growing skepticism towards *all* rational social argument. The French philosopher Jean-François Lyotard, whose 1979 essay on the subject, *The Post-modern Condition*, nicely summarized the *air du temps*, put the point clearly enough: 'I define *postmodern* as incredulity towards meta-narratives.'

The underlying and usually unacknowledged source of these predominantly French intellectual influences was, as so often in past decades, German. The Italian writer Elio Vittorini once observed that ever since Napoleon, France had proved impermeable to any foreign influence except that of German romantic philosophy: and what was true when he wrote that in 1957 was no less true two decades later. Whereas the humanist sensibilities of an earlier generation had been drawn to Marx and Hegel, the self-doubting Seventies were seduced by an altogether darker strain in German thought. Michel Foucault's radical skepticism was in large measure an adaptation of Nietzsche. Other influential French authors, notably the literary critic Jacques Derrida, looked instead to Martin Heidegger for their critique of human agency and their 'de-construction', as it was becoming known, of the cognitive human subject and his textual subject matter.

To scholarly specialists on Heidegger or his German contemporary Carl Schmitt (whose historicist realism was attracting attention among students of international affairs), this interest was more than a little odd. Both Heidegger and Schmitt, after all, were identified with Nazism—Heidegger quite explicitly thanks to his acceptance of academic office under Nazi auspices. But the renewed interest in criticizing optimistic assumptions about progress, in questioning the underpinnings of enlightened rationalism and its political and cognitive by-products, established a certain affinity between early-twentieth-century critics of modernity and technical progress like Heidegger and the disabused skeptics of the 'post-modern' age— and allowed Heidegger and others to launder their earlier associations.

By the time German philosophy had passed through Parisian social thought into English cultural criticism—the forms in which it was familiar to most readers of the time—its inherently difficult vocabulary had attained a level of expressive opacity that proved irresistibly appealing to a new generation of students and their teachers. The junior faculty recruited to staff the expanded universities of the time were themselves in most cases graduates of the Sixties, raised in the fashions and debates of those years. But whereas European universities of the previous decade were preoccupied with grand theories of various sorts—society, the state, language, history, revolution—what trickled down to the next generation was above all a preoccupation with Theory as such. Seminars in 'Cultural Theory', or 'General Theory' displaced the conventional disciplinary boundaries that had still dominated even radical academic debate a few years before. 'Difficulty' became the measure of intellectual seriousness. In their disabused commentary on the heritage of ''68

Thought', the French writers Luc Ferry and Alain Renault tartly concluded that 'the greatest achievement of the thinkers of the Sixties was to convince their audience that incomprehensibility was the sign of greatness.'

With a ready-made audience in the universities, newly lionised theorists like Lacan and Derrida elevated the vagaries and paradoxes of language into full-fledged philosophies, infinitely flexible templates for textual and political explication. In institutions such as Birmingham University's Centre for Contemporary Cultural Studies, the new theoreticism blended smoothly into the old. Marxism was relieved of its embarrassingly atavistic attachment to economic categories and political institutions and recycled as cultural criticism. The inconvenient reluctance of the revolutionary proletariat to vanquish the capitalist bourgeoisie was no longer an impediment. As Stuart Hall, the leading British spokesman for Cultural Studies in those years, expressed it in 1976: 'The idea of the "disappearance of the class as a whole" is replaced by the far more complex and differentiated picture of how the different sectors and strata of a class are driven into different courses and options by their determining socio-economic circumstances.'

Hall himself would in later years concede that his Centre was 'for a time, over-preoccupied with these difficult theoretical issues.' But in fact this narcissistic obscurantism was very much of its time, its detachment from daily reality bearing unconscious witness to the exhaustion of an intellectual tradition. Moreover, it was by no means the only symptom of cultural depletion in these years. Even the sparkling originality of 1960s French cinema declined into self-conscious artistry. In 1974 Jacques Rivette, the witty and original director of *Paris Nous Appartient* (1960) and *La Religieuse* (1966), directed *Céline et Julie vont en bateau* ('Céline and Julie Go Boating'). At 193 minutes in length, a plot-less, stylized parody (albeit unintended) of the French New Wave, *Céline et Julie* marked the end of an age. Artistic theorizing was displacing art.

If one strand in the heritage of the Sixties was high-cultural pretension, the other, its intimate inversion, was a hardening crust of knowing cynicism. The relative innocence of rock and roll was increasingly displaced by media-wise pop bands whose stock in trade was a derisive appropriation and degradation of the style forged by their immediate precursors. Much as popular romances and tabloid journalism had once fastened on to mass literacy for commercial advantage, so 'punk' rock appeared in the Seventies in order to exploit the market for popular music. Presented as 'counter-cultural' it was in fact parasitic upon mainstream culture, invoking violent images and radical language for frequently mercenary ends.

The avowedly politicized language of punk rock bands, exemplified in the Sex Pistols' 1976 hit 'Anarchy in the UK', caught the sour mood of the time. But the punk bands' politics were as one-dimensional as their musical range, the latter all too often restricted to three chords and a single beat and dependent upon volume for its effect. Like the Red Army Fraction, the Sex Pistols and other punk rock groups wanted above all to *shock*. Even their subversive appearance and manner came packaged in irony and a certain amount of camp: 'Remember the Sixties?' they seemed to say; 'Well, like it or not, we are what's left.' Musical subversion now consisted of angry songs decrying 'hegemony', their counterfeit political content masking the steady evisceration of musical form.[14]

However bogus their politics and their music, the punk generation's *cynicism* at least was real, and honestly come by. They were the sour and mostly untalented end of a growing spectrum of disrespect: for the past, for authority, for public figures and public affairs. In its wittier incarnations, this scorn for pomposity and tradition took its cue from the disabused young British political satirists who had first surfaced nearly two decades earlier: the theatre review *Beyond the Fringe*; the BBC late-night show *That Was the Week That Was*; and the weekly magazine *Private Eye*. Exploiting the rapidly growing television audience and the steady retreat of state censorship, *Monty Python* and its successors and imitators blended broad slapstick, ribald social commentary and sardonic political mockery—a mixture last seen in the trenchant political cartoons of Gillray and Cruikshank. The close interplay between rock music and the new burlesque is nicely illustrated in the financial backing for two of the Python films, *Monty Python and the Holy Grail* (1974) and *Life of Brian* (1979): underwritten respectively by Pink Floyd and Led Zeppelin, and by George Harrison of the Beatles.

The low standing of public figures offered rich pickings to weekly television shows like *Spitting Image* or France's *Bebête Show*, where leading politicians were routinely held up to a degree of ridicule and scorn that would have been unthinkable a few years before (and still is in the United States). Satirists and political comedians replaced writers and artists as the intellectual heroes of the hour: when French students were asked in the early Eighties which public figures they most admired, older commentators were shocked to learn that the late Jean-Paul Sartre had been replaced by Coluche, a ribald and occasionally licentious television comedian who sardonically acknowledged his newfound standing by running for President of his country.

Yet the same public television channels that broadcast pointed and irreverent parodies of popular and middlebrow culture also provided humorists with copious raw material. Perhaps the most widely celebrated object of ridicule was the 'Eurovision Song Contest', an annual television competition first broadcast in 1970. A commercial exercise glossed as a celebration of the new technology of simultaneous television transmission to multiple countries, the show claimed hundreds of millions of spectators by the mid-Seventies. The Eurovision Song Contest—in

---

[14]West European punk left a particularly ugly aftertaste in the waning years of Communist Eastern Europe, where it was taken up by nihilistic underground bands cynically fastening on to a heritage of political and musical dissidence for their own ends. In a repellent blend of pornography and political incorrectness, the *Spions*, a Hungarian punk group of the Eighties, recorded 'Anna Frank': 'A little forced intercourse before they come and take you away, Anna Frank! Make love to me! Anna Frank! Cry you bitch! Anna Frank! Otherwise I'll give you up! Anna Frank—the boys are waiting for you.'

which B-league crooners and unknowns from across the continent performed generic and forgettable material before returning in almost every case to the obscurity whence they had briefly emerged—was so stunningly banal in conception and execution as to defy parody. It would have been out of date fifteen years earlier. But for just that reason it heralded something new.

The enthusiasm with which the Eurovision Song Contest promoted and celebrated a hopelessly dated format and a stream of inept performers reflected a growing culture of nostalgia, at once wistful and disabused. If punk, post-modern and parody were one response to the confusions of a disillusioned decade, 'retro' was another. The French pop group *Il Était Une Fois* ('Once Upon a Time') sported 1930s clothing, one of many short-lived sartorial revivals from 'granny skirts' to the neo-Edwardian hairstyles of the 'New Romantics'—the latter reprised for the second time in three decades. In clothing and music (and buildings) the temptation to recycle old styles—mixing and matching with little self-confidence—substituted for innovation. The Seventies, a self-questioning time of troubles, looked backward, not forward. The Age of Aquarius had left in its wake a season of pastiche.

XV

Politics in a New Key

'Je déclare avoir avorté' ("I have had an abortion').
Simone de Beauvoir (and 342 other women), April 5th 1971

'Within a generation at most, the French and Italian Communist parties
will either break their ties with Moscow or shrivel into insignificance'.
Denis Healey (1957)

'With this Treaty, nothing is lost that had not long since been
gambled away'.
Chancellor Willy Brandt, August 1970

'When two states wish to establish better relations they often reach for the
highest common platitude'.
Timothy Garton Ash

In the 1970s the political landscape of western Europe started to fracture and fragment. Since the end of the First World War, mainstream politics had been divided between two political 'families', Left and Right, themselves internally split between 'moderates' and 'radicals'. Since 1945 the two sides had drawn ever closer, but the pattern had not radically altered. The spectrum of political options available to European voters in 1970 would not have been unfamiliar to their grandparents.

The longevity of Europe's political parties derived from a remarkable continuity in the ecology of the electorate. The choice between Labour and Conservatives in Britain, or Social Democrats and Christian Democrats in West Germany, no longer reflected deep divisions over particular policies, much less profound 'lifestyle' preferences as they would come to be known. In most places it was an echo of longstanding, trans-generational voting habits, determined by the class, religion or locality of the voter rather than by the party's program. Men and women voted as their parents had voted, depending on where they lived, where they worked and what they earned.

But beneath the surface continuity a tectonic shift was taking place in the political sociology of European voters. The block vote of the white, male, employed working class—the universal bedrock of Communist and Socialist party support— was contracting and splitting. In much the same way, the 'ideal-typical' conservative voter—older, female, churchgoing—could no longer be counted upon to furnish the core electorate of Christian Democrat or Conservative parties. To the extent that they persisted, such traditional voters were no longer the majority. Why?

In the first place, social and geographical mobility over the course of the post-war decades had diluted fixed social categories almost beyond recognition. The Christian voting bloc in rural western France or the small towns of the Veneto, the proletarian industrial strongholds of southern Belgium or northern England, were now fissured and fragmented. Men and women no longer lived in the same places as their parents and often did very different jobs. Unsurprisingly, they saw the world rather differently as well; their political preferences began to reflect these changes, though slowly at first.

Secondly, the prosperity and social reforms of the Sixties and early Seventies had effectively exhausted the programs and vision of the traditional parties. Their very success had deprived politicians of moderate Left and Right alike of a credible agenda, especially after the spate of liberal reforms of the Sixties. The institutions of the state itself were not in dispute, nor were the general objectives of economic policy. What remained was the fine-tuning of labour relations, legislation against discrimination in housing and employment, the expansion of educational facilities and the like: serious public business, but hardly the stuff of great political debate.

Thirdly, there were now alternative denominators of political allegiance. Ethnic minorities, often unwelcome in the white working-class communities of Europe where they had arrived, were not always invited into local political or labour organizations and their politics reflected this exclusion. And lastly, the generational politics of the Sixties had introduced into public discussion concerns utterly unfamiliar to an older political culture. The 'New Left' might have lacked a program, but it was not short of themes. Above all, it introduced new constituencies. The fascination with sex and sexuality led naturally to sexual politics; women and homosexuals, respectively subordinate and invisible in traditional radical parties, now surfaced as legitimate historical subjects, with rights and claims. Youth, and the enthusiasms of youth, moved to center stage, especially as the voting age fell to eighteen in many places.

The prosperity of the time had encouraged a shift in people's attention from production to consumption, from the necessities of existence to the quality of life. In the heat of the Sixties few troubled themselves much over the moral dilemmas of prosperity—its beneficiaries were too busy enjoying the fruits of their good fortune. But within a few years, many—notably among the educated young adults of north-west Europe—came to look upon the commercialism and material well-being of the Fifties and Sixties as a burdensome inheritance, bringing tawdry commodities and false values. The price of modernity, at least to its main beneficiaries, was starting to look rather high; the 'lost world' of their parents and grandparents rather appealing.

The politicization of these cultural discontents was typically the work of activists familiar with the tactics of more traditional parties in which they or their families had once been active. The logic of politics thus changed relatively little: the point was still to mobilize like-minded persons around a program of legislation to be enacted by the state. What was new was the organizing premise. Hitherto—in Europe—political constituencies had emerged from the elective affinities of large groups of voters defined by class or occupation, bound by a common, inherited, and often rather abstract set of principles and objectives. Policies had mattered less than allegiances.

But in the Seventies *policies* moved to the forefront. 'Single-issue' parties and movements emerged, their constituencies shaped by a variable geometry of common concerns: often narrowly focused, occasionally whimsical. Britain's remarkably successful Campaign For Real Ale (CAMRA) is a representative instance: founded in 1971 to reverse the trend to gaseous, homogenized 'lager' beer (and the similarly homogenized, 'modernized' pubs where it was sold), this middle-class pressure group rested its case upon a neo-Marxist account of the take-over of artisanal beer manufacture by mass-producing monopolists who manipulated beer-drinkers for corporate profit—alienating consumers from their own taste buds by meretricious substitution.

In its rather effective mix of economic analysis, environmental concern, aesthetic discrimination and plain nostalgia, CAMRA foreshadowed many of the single-issue activist networks of years to come, as well as the coming fashion among well-heeled bourgeois-bohemians for the expensively 'authentic'.[1] But its slightly archaic charm, not to mention the disproportion between the intensity of its activists' engagement and the tepid object of their passion, made this particular single-issue movement necessarily somewhat quaint.

But there was nothing whimsical or quaint about other single-issue political networks, most of them—like CAMRA—organized by and for the middle class. In Scandinavia a variety of protest parties emerged in the early seventies, notably the Rural Party (later the Real Finn Party) in Finland; Morgens Glistrup's Danish Progress Party and Anders Lange's Norwegian Progress Party. All of them were energetically and at first uniquely devoted to the cause of tax reduction—the founding title for the Norwegian party in 1973 had been 'Anders Lange's Party for a Drastic Reduction in Taxes, Rates and State Intervention', its program a single sheet of paper reiterating the demands of its name.

The Scandinavian experience was perhaps distinctive—nowhere else were tax

---

[1]In Britain this trend could be traced to longstanding enthusiasms for vegetarianism, 'authentic' building and clothing materials and the like—often overlapping with networks of socialist societies and rambling clubs: the Left's response to the hunting, shooting and fishing of the conservative set. In continental Europe the cultures of both Left and Right reflected a very different history. Whereas Britain's *Good Food Guide* was founded and edited by Fabian socialists and presented from the outset as a contribution to class warfare on the gastronomic front, France's *Guide Michelin* was always and only a commercial enterprise, albeit directed to much the same audience.

rates so high nor public services so extensive—and certainly no single-issue parties outside the region ever did as well as Glistrup's party, which won 15.9 percent of the Danish national vote in 1973. But anti-tax parties were not new. Their model was Pierre Poujade's *Union de Défense des Commerçants et Artisans* (UDCA), founded in 1953 to protect small shopkeepers against taxes and supermarkets and which won brief fame by securing 12 percent of the vote in the French elections of 1956. But Poujade's movement was singular. Most of the protest parties that emerged after 1970 proved enduring—the Norwegian Progress Party achieved its strongest vote to date (15.3 percent) a quarter of a century later, in 1997.

The anti-tax parties, like the agrarian protest parties of inter-war Europe, were primarily reactive and negative—they were against unwelcome change and asked of the state above all that it remove what they saw as unreasonable fiscal burdens. Other single-issue movements had more positive demands to make of the state, or the law, or institutions. Their concerns ranged from prison reform and psychiatric hospitals through access to education and medical services and into the provision of safe food, community services, the amelioration of urban environments and access to cultural resources. All were 'anti-consensus' in their reluctance to confine their support to any one traditional political constituency and their willingness—of necessity—to consider alternative ways of publicizing their concerns.

Three of the new political groupings—the women's movement, environmentalism, and peace activism—are of particular significance, for their scale and their lasting impact. For obvious reasons, the women's movement was the most diverse and far-reaching. In addition to the interests they shared with men, women had distinctive concerns that were only just then beginning to enter the European legislative arena: childcare, wage equality, divorce, abortion, contraception, domestic violence.

To these should be added the attention paid by the more radical women's groups to homosexual (lesbian) rights, and the growing feminist concern with pornography. The latter illustrates rather well the new moral geography of politics: sexually explicit literature and film had only recently and partially been liberated from the control of the censors, thanks to the concerted efforts of old liberals and new Left. Yet within a decade it was again under fire, this time from networks of women's groups, often led by coalitions of radical feminists and traditional conservatives who united around this one issue.

The women's movement in Europe was from the outset a variable mix of intersecting objectives. In 1950, one quarter of West German married women were in paid employment outside the home, by 1970 the number had risen to one married woman in two; of one and a half million new entrants to the labour force in Italy between 1972 and 1980, one and a quarter million were women. By the mid-1990s women constituted over 40 percent of the total (official) labour force in every European country except Portugal and Italy. Many of the new women workers were employed part-time, or in entry-level clerical jobs where they were not entitled to full benefits. The flexibility of part-time jobs suited many working mothers, but in the straitened economic circumstances of the Seventies this did not compensate for poor wages and job insecurity. Equal pay and the workplace provision of childcare facilities thus emerged early as the main demands of most working women in the West and have remained at the forefront ever since.

Working (and non-working) women increasingly sought assistance in caring for their children; but they did not necessarily wish for more children of their own. Indeed, with increased prosperity and more time spent working outside the home, they wanted fewer—or at least more say in the matter. The demand for access to contraceptive information, and contraceptives, dates to the early years of the twentieth century, but it gathered speed within a decade of the peak of the baby boom. The French *Association Maternité* was formed in 1956 to press for contraceptive rights; four years later it was succeeded by the *Mouvement Français pour le Planning Familial*, the change in name a clear indication of a shift in mood.

As pressure grew through the liberalizing Sixties for sexual freedoms of all kinds, laws regulating contraception were everywhere relaxed (except in certain countries of Eastern Europe like Romania, where national 'reproduction strategies' continued to forbid it). By the early seventies contraception was widely available throughout Western Europe, though not in remote rural districts or regions where Catholic authorities held moral sway over the local population. Even in towns and cities, however, it was middle class women who benefited most from the new freedom; for many working-class married women, and the overwhelming majority of unmarried ones, the leading form of birth control remained what it had long been: abortion.

It is thus not surprising that the demand for reform of abortion laws became a *leitmotif* of the new women's politics—a rare point of intersection where the politics of radical feminism encountered the needs of apolitical everywoman. In Britain abortion had been decriminalized in 1967, as we have seen. But in many other places it was still a crime: in Italy it carried a five-year prison sentence. But legal or otherwise, abortions were part of the life experience of millions of women—in tiny Latvia, in 1973, there were 60,000 abortions for 34,000 live births. And where abortion was illegal the risks it entailed, both legal and medical, united women across class, age and political affiliation.

On April 5th 1971, the French weekly magazine *Le Nouvel Observateur* published a petition signed by 343 women declaring that they had all had abortions, and thus broken the law, and demanding revision of the penal code. The signatories were all well known, some of them—the writers Simone de Beauvoir and Françoise Sagan, the actresses Catherine Deneuve, Jeanne Moreau and Marie-France Pisier, the lawyers and political activists Yvette Roudy and Gisèle Halimi—very well known indeed. And they were joined by obscure but militant activists from the feminist movements that had sprung up in the wake of 1968. Although over three hundred women had been found guilty of the crime of abortion in the previous year, the government prudently forbore to prosecute the signatories of the open letter.

The petition had been organized by the *Mouvement de Libération des Femmes* (MLF), founded the previous year; the political stir aroused by their action prompted Halimi and de Beauvoir to form *Choisir*, a political organization dedicated to ending the ban on abortion. In January 1973, at a press conference, French President Georges Pompidou conceded that French law had fallen behind the evolution of public opinion. He could hardly do otherwise: in the course of 1972–73, over 35,000 French women made their way to Britain to undergo legal abortions. Pompidou's successor, Valéry Giscard D'Estaing, instructed his health minister, Simone Weil, to present parliament with a revision of the law and on January 17th 1975, the *Assemblée Nationale* legalized abortion (during the first ten weeks of pregnancy) in France.

The French example was studied closely by women throughout Western Europe. In Italy the newly-formed *Movimento della Liberazione delle Donne Italiane* (Italian Women's Liberation Movement) joined forces with the small Radical Party to raise 800,000 signatures on a petition to change the law on abortion, supported by a march on Rome of 50,000 women in April 1976. Three years after the belated introduction in 1975 of a new 'family code' to replace that of the Fascists, the Italian parliament voted—on May 29th 1978, three weeks after the discovery of Aldo Moro's corpse—to legalise abortion.

The decision was indirectly confirmed at a national referendum in May 1981, when Italian voters rejected *both* a proposal to loosen further the existing restrictions on legal abortion *and* a move to re-criminalize it, proposed by a newly formed Pro-Life Movement. If the pace of reform in Italy lagged somewhat behind Britain or France, it was less through the opposition of the Catholic Church than because so many Italian feminists had cut their teeth in the movements of the extra-parliamentary 'autonomous' Left (revealingly, the first *Lotta Femminista* manifesto of 1971 had focused upon the demand for salaries for housework—a ritual extension to the domestic realm of an older, 'workerist' vision of modern society as one huge factory). They were thus slow to exploit established political institutions in pursuit of their goals.

In Spain, the French strategy was followed more closely still, accelerated by the energies released by the collapse of the old regime. The first feminist demonstration in Spain was organized in January 1976, within two months of Franco's death. Two years later adultery was de-criminalized and contraception legalized. In 1979 one thousand women, including prominent public figures, signed a public statement declaring themselves to have broken the law by undergoing an abortion—a reminder that Spain under Franco's rule had one of Europe's highest rates of illegal abortion, comparable to those of Eastern Europe and driven by the same authoritarian, pro-natalist disapproval of all forms of birth control. But even in post-Franco Spain the cultural pressures working against abortion-law reform remained strong; when the Cortes finally approved a law permitting abortion in May 1985, it restricted permission to cases of rape, a deformed foetus, or where the mother's life was at risk.

Together with the right to divorce, the successful battle over abortion rights was the main achievement of women's political groups in these years. As a consequence, the personal circumstances of millions of women were inestimably improved. The availability of abortion, in conjunction with effective and available contraception, not only improved the life chances of many, especially the poor, but also offered working women the option of postponing their first child to a historically late point in their childbearing years.

The result was a steady fall in the number of children born. The Spanish birth rate per woman fell by nearly 60 percent between 1960 and 1996; Italy, West Germany and the Netherlands were close behind. Within a few years of the reforms of the Seventies, *no* west European country except Ireland had a birthrate sufficient to replace the previous generation. In Britain the annual birthrate fell in the three decades after 1960 from 2.71 children per woman to 1.84; in France from 2.73 to 1.73. Married women were increasingly choosing to have one child or none at all—were it not for extra-marital births the rates would have been lower still: by the end of the 1980s, extra-marital births as a percentage of the annual total were at 24 percent in Austria, 28 percent in the UK, 29 percent in France and 52 percent in Sweden.

As the economy slowed and the emancipation of women gathered pace, the demography of Europe was changing—with ominous implications for the welfare state in years to come. The social changes wrought by the women's movement were not, however, mirrored in politics itself. No 'women's party' emerged, capable of siphoning off votes and getting its representatives elected. Women remained a minority in national legislatures and governments.

The Left proved generally more open to electing women than the Right (but not everywhere—in both Belgium and France, Christian parties of the Center-Right were for many years more likely than their Socialist opponents to nominate women to safe constituencies), but the best predictor of women's prospects in public life was not ideology but geography. Between 1975 and 1990 the number of women in Finland's parliament rose from 23 percent to 39 percent; in Sweden from 21 percent to 38 percent; in Norway from 16 percent to 36 percent; and in Denmark from 16 percent to 33 percent. Farther south, in the parliaments of Italy and Portugal, women constituted just one in twelve of parliamentary deputies in 1990. In the UK House of Commons they were just 7 percent of the total; in France's *Assemblée Nationale*, a mere 6 percent.

Environmentalists, men and women alike, had considerably more success in translating their sentiments into electoral politics. At one level 'environmentalism' (a neologism dating from the Thirties) was indeed a new departure: the collective expression of middle-class fears about nuclear power stations and galloping urbanization, motorways and pollution. But the Green Movement in Europe would never have been so effective had it been just a footnote to the Sixties: well-heeled weekend Luddites in stone-washed natural fibres triangulating between their instincts and their interests. The longing for a more 'natural' world and the search for a personal politics of 'authenticity' had deep roots on both sides of the ideological divide, traceable to the Romantics and their horror at the depredations of early industrialism. By the early twentieth century both Left and Right had their cycling clubs, vegetarian restaurants, *Wandervogel* movements and ramblers, affiliated variously to socialist or nationalist dreams of emancipation and return.

The German nostalgia for uniquely *German* landscapes, for the mountains and rivers of the Harz and the Pfalz, for *Heimat*; the French nationalist dream of peasant harmony in *la France profonde*, unsullied by cities and cosmopolitanism; the English reverie of a once and future country harmony, Blake's lost Jerusalem: these had more in common than any of their followers might have felt comfortable admitting. And whereas the Left had for many decades watched in admiration as Communist 'output' strove to outstrip that of the West, by the Seventies voices on Right and Left alike were starting to express some unease at the collateral costs of progress, productivity and 'modernity'.[2]

The modern environmentalist revolution thus benefited twice over: it was a break from the callous nostrums of the recent past—and it had roots in a more distant history, unremembered but atavistically reassuring. Environmentalism (like pacifism) often aroused in its wake a revival of nationalism—or regionalism—but with a human face. The '*Alternativen*' of West Berlin, or the anti-nuclear protesters of Austria who won a 1978 referendum forbidding their government from activating the nuclear power station at Zwentendorf, would never have identified themselves as nationalists or even patriots. But their anger against the pollution of the *local* environment above all (and their relative indifference to similar havoc being wreaked elsewhere) suggests otherwise. The 'not in my backyard' quality of the incipient Green Movement harked back to an earlier model.

There was thus nothing contradictory in the enthusiasm with which Portugal's ageing dictator António Salazar enforced the same environmental controls being urged upon their democratic governments by post-'68 radicals in Vienna or Amsterdam. Distrustful of 'materialism' and determined to keep the twentieth century at bay, Salazar was, in his way, a genuine enthusiast for ecological objectives—attained in his case by the simple expedient of maintaining his fellow countrymen in a condition of unparalleled economic torpor. He would certainly have approved

---

[2]By 1980 the Soviet Union was releasing almost as much carbon dioxide into the atmosphere as the United States—a statistic that would until very recently have been a source of pride rather than embarrassment for its admirers.

of the achievement of the French protesters who in 1971 blocked a planned military base at Larzac, on the high plains of south-central France.

The symbolism of Larzac—where uninhabited grasslands were defended against the massed power of the French state by an insurgent regiment of environmentalists—was immense, and not just in France: an emotional victory had been secured less for the indigenous sheep of the Massif uplands than for their distinctly un-local shepherds, many of them young radicals who had only recently left Paris or Lyon to recycle themselves as farmers on the wilder shores of 'deep France'. The battlefront had decidedly shifted—at least in Western Europe.

In Eastern Europe, of course, the doctrine of unrestricted primary production—and the absence of any official countervailing voices—left the environment at the mercy of official polluters of every sort. Whereas Austria might be constrained by internal opposition to abandon nuclear power, her Communist neighbors had no such compunction about building nuclear reactors in Czechoslovakia, planning massive dams just downstream along the Danube, in Czechoslovakia and Hungary, or steadily increasing output and air pollution a few dozen miles north in Nowa Huta, Poland's 'purpose-built' steel town. But for all that, the moral and human costs of rampant industrial pollution and environmental degradation had not passed unnoticed in the Eastern bloc.

Thus the cynical indifference of the post-'68 Husák regime in Prague—its willingness to wreak havoc along the common Danube frontier in pursuit of domestically generated kilowatts—triggered a rising backlash among otherwise politically quiescent Hungarians. Implausible as it would have seemed in earlier days, the proposed Gabčikovo-Nagymaros dam was to become a significant source of domestic opposition to the Budapest regime itself—as well as a major embarrassment to relations between the two 'fraternal' neighbors.[3]

In Czechoslovakia, an older distaste for technological modernity had passed to a new generation of intellectuals via the writings of the philosophers Jan Patočka and Václav Bělohradský especially; the latter working from exile in Italy after 1970, his neo-Heideggerian musings read in *samizdat* back in his country of origin. The idea that the effort to subdue and dominate nature to human ends—the project of the Enlightenment—might come at too high a price was already familiar to readers on both sides of the Cold War divide through the writings of the Frankfurt School, notably Theodor Adorno and Max Horkheimer in their *Dialectic of Enlightenment*, published in 1944. With a Heideggerian twist—the suggestion that Communism itself was an illicit Western import, touched with the hubristic illusion of endless material progress—these ruminations formed the basis of an in-

---

[3]Within certain limits environmental protest—because of its ostensibly apolitical character—offered a safe space for political action and national self-expression in otherwise restrictive regimes. By 1983 the problem of water pollution had brought fully 10 percent of the population of Soviet Lithuania into a 'Lithuanian Nature Protection Association'.

tellectual opposition that would surface in the Seventies, combining ethical dissent with ecological critiques, and led by Patočka and one of Bělohradský's most enthusiastic readers, the playwright Václav Havel.[4]

In time, a common environmentalist critique would serve as a bridge between new forms of protest in East and West. But in the circumstances of the early Seventies neither side yet knew—nor in the Western case cared—much about the views or problems of their counterparts across the Iron Curtain. The west European environmentalists especially were far too busy building their local political constituency to pay attention to international politics, except in so far as these affected the unique object of their attentions. In this, however, they were singularly successful.

It was in 1973 that the first 'ecology' candidates stood in local elections in France and Britain—the same year that saw the founding Bauern (farmers') Congress in West Germany, forerunner to the Greens. Fuelled by the first oil crisis, the West German environmental movement moved rapidly into the political mainstream. From sit-ins, protest marches and citizens' initiatives at the start of the decade, the Greens—variously backed by farmers, environmentalists, pacifists and urban squatters—had progressed by 1979 to the point of securing their own representation in the parliaments of two of the German *Länder*. Four years later, in the wake of the second oil shock, their support at the Federal elections of 1983 increased from 568,000 to 2,165,000 (5.6 percent of the vote) and won them parliamentary representation (twenty-seven seats) for the first time. By 1985 the Greens were in a major regional government, ruling Hesse in coalition with the SPD (and with the young Green politician Joschka Fischer as Hesse's Minister for environment and energy).

The German Greens' success was not immediately repeated elsewhere, although in time the Austrian and especially the French parties would do quite respectably. West Germans were perhaps unusual. In these years they were growing averse to the very sources of their own post-war revival: between 1966 and 1981 the share of the population that looked favorably upon 'technology' and its achievements fell precipitately, from 72 percent to 30 percent. The West German Greens also benefited from the German system of proportional representation, whereby even quite small parties could make their way into the regional and Federal parliaments—although a roughly comparable system in Italy did little for environmentalists there: by 1987 the Italian 'Greens' had secured less than a million votes and just 13 seats out of 630. In Belgium the two ecological parties (one French-speaking, one Flemish) also improved steadily: from 4.8 percent of the vote at their first appearance in 1981 they rose steadily, passing 7.1 percent in 1987. In Britain, however, the

---

[4]Heideggerian existentialism in this key opened another link to the West: the French philosopher Emmanuel Mounier had many years before claimed to see in the existentialism of his contemporaries (like Sartre) a 'subjective barrier' against what he excoriated as 'objective materialism' and 'technology'. In later decades, Mounier's intellectual heirs in the circle of writers on the journal *Esprit* would be among the first in Western Europe to publish and celebrate Havel and his fellow dissidents.

voting system was designed to disadvantage small or fringe parties and did just that.

In Scandinavia, the prospects for single-issue parties like environmentalists (or pacifists, or feminists) were restricted by the ecumenical range of the existing political groupings—why 'waste' a vote on the Greens when Social Democrats, or Agrarian Parties, purported to share similar concerns? Environmentalism in Norway, for example, was at least as widely embraced as in Germany—as early as 1970 the Labour government's plans to exploit Northern Europe's largest waterfall, at Mardola in the Arctic Circle, for hydro-electric power provoked widespread national outrage and prompted the emergence of environmental politics in Norway. But neither the Mardola affair nor subsequent protests at the prospect of nuclear power stations ever translated into a separate political movement: protests—and compromises—were negotiated within the governing majority.

Greens did a little better in Sweden, where they finally entered Parliament in 1988; and in Finland, where individual environmentalists first won election in 1987 and only then formed the Green Association, an environmental party, the following year (not surprisingly, perhaps, the Finnish Greens did far better in the prosperous, urban, 'yuppie' south of the country than in the poorer, rural center and north). But Finland and Sweden were unusual: pacifists, feminists, environmentalists, the handicapped and other single-issue activists were so sure of a generally sympathetic cultural environment for their concerns that they could afford to split from the mainstream and risk dividing their own supporters without jeopardizing either the governing majority or the prospects for their own agenda.

Single-issue parties, as we have seen, often emerged in the wake of a crisis, a scandal or an unpopular proposal: thus Austria's environmentalists, to the extent that they became a national force, owed their rise to bitter confrontation with the authorities over a 1984 proposal to build a hydro-electric plant in a wetland forest at Hainburg in eastern Austria. The Green cause received a strong boost from the ensuing confrontation between the Socialist-led coalition government and environmental activists: and even though the government subsequently backed down, the incident led to a sharp increase in support for the Greens from disillusioned Socialist voters, notably among intellectuals and liberal professionals.

The proliferation of single-issue parties and programs, and their steady absorption into mainstream public life, took its toll upon the traditional organizations of the Left in particular. Communist parties in Western Europe, undermined by the steady erosion of their proletarian constituency and discredited by the invasion of Czechoslovakia, were most vulnerable. The French Communist Party was led by semi-unreconstructed Stalinists who had never really taken their distance from the events of 1956, much less those of 1968. Inherently conservative and suspicious of any issue or person it could not subordinate and control, the Party saw its share of the vote fall steadily at every election: from a post-war peak of 28 percent in 1946 to 18.6 percent in 1977 and thence, in a vertiginous collapse, to under 10 percent in the elections of the 1980s.

The Italian Communists did rather better. Where the French Communist hierarchy was almost universally mediocre and unattractive—reflecting in this, as almost everything else, the PCF's slavish imitation of the Soviet example—the PCI, from Palmiro Togliatti to Enrico Berlinguer (Party Secretary from 1972 until his early death, at the age of 62, in 1984), was blessed with intelligent and even appealing leaders. Both parties, like every other Communist organization, were deeply dependent on Soviet funding: between 1971 and 1990 Soviet agencies channeled $50 million to the French Communists, $47 million to the Italians.[5] But the Italians did at least express public disapproval for egregious Soviet actions—notably the invasion of Czechoslovakia.

The (relative) autonomy of the Italian Communists was complemented by Berlinguer's 1973 decision to commit his party to the defense of Italian democracy, even if it meant abandoning its outright opposition to the Christian Democrats: this was the so-called 'historic compromise'. This shift was driven in part by the shock of the 1973 coup d'état in Chile, which convinced Berlinguer and other Communist intellectuals that even if the Communists won a parliamentary majority they would never be allowed—by the Americans, or their allies in Italian military, business and Church circles—to form a government of their own. But it was also a reaction, as we saw in the previous chapter, to the very real threat to Italian democracy itself from Right and Left terrorists for whom the Communist Party was as much the enemy as the Italian state.

These changes brought temporary electoral dividends. The Communist electorate in Italy grew steadily—from 6.7 million votes at the elections of 1958 to 9 million in 1972 and reaching a peak four years later, in the elections of June 1976, when the PCI culled 12.6 million votes and 228 parliamentary seats. With 34.4 percent of the votes cast, it was just four percentage points and 34 seats short of the ruling Christian Democrats, an unprecedented score for a Western Communist party. The PCI was making a credible attempt to present itself as a 'system' party, perhaps even (as Henry Kissinger and many foreign observers feared) an alternative government-in-waiting.[6]

The new approach of the Italian Party, and rather less convincing efforts by the French Party to emulate its success if not its ideas, became known as 'Eurocommunism'—a term first coined at a November 1975 meeting of Italian, French and Spanish Communists and given official currency by the secretary-general of the

---

[5]In the same years Moscow even funded the minuscule American Communist Party to the tune of $42 million, a revealing exercise in undiscriminating generosity.

[6]On April 13th 1976, just nine weeks before the Italian elections, Kissinger publicly declared that the US would 'not welcome' a Communist role in the government of Italy—thereby confirming Berlinguer's intuitions.

Spanish Communists, Santiago Carrillo, in his 1977 essay *Eurocommunism and the State*. The Spanish Party was only just emerging from decades of clandestinity and its leaders were keen to establish their democratic credentials. Like their Italian comrades, they understood that the best way to achieve this was by taking their distance, both from the contemporary Soviet Union but also, and more significantly, from their common Leninist past.

'Eurocommunism' proved briefly seductive, though less to electors than to intellectuals and academics who mistook for a political revival of Marxism what was in fact an expression of doctrinal exhaustion. If Western Communists were to overcome the burden of their history and reprogram themselves as a—*the*—democratic movement of the Left, they needed to jettison more than just 'the dictatorship of the proletariat' and other rhetorical dogmas abandoned in a bonfire of the ideological vanities during the course of the 1970s. They also needed very publicly to abandon their association with Soviet Communism itself, and this even Berlinguer and Carrillo were unable to do.

Eurocommunism was thus a contradiction in terms, despite the best efforts of its spokesmen. Subordination to Moscow was, as Lenin had always intended, the primary identification tag of any Communist party. Until the disappearance of the Soviet Union itself the Communist parties of Western Europe were shackled to it—if not in their own eyes then most assuredly in the opinion of voters. In Italy, where the PCI had uniquely succeeded in establishing itself in certain regions as the natural party of (local) governance, the Communists held on to a sizeable vote, though never again scaling the heights of their 1976 successes. But elsewhere Eurocommunism's steady decline continued almost uninterrupted. The Spanish Communists, who invented it, saw their share of the vote fall to just 4 percent by 1982.

Ironically, Leonid Brezhnev in Moscow actually gave his blessing to the Eurocommunists' efforts to secure their local base by distancing themselves from him. The Soviet move, a by-product of the strategy of international détente then being pursued, did little for the would-be Communist reformers. But then, for all the support they continued to furnish in cash and kind, the Soviet leaders were losing interest in Western Communist parties, who had limited political impact and seemed unlikely to take power in the foreseeable future. Social Democrats, however, especially those in positions of influence, were another matter. And Social Democrats in Germany, still the crucible of a divided continent, were of very particular interest indeed.

In 1969, the West German Social Democratic Party (SPD), led by Willy Brandt, won a majority at the Federal elections and took office in a coalition with the Free Democratic Party, pushing the conservative Christian Democrats into opposition for the first time since the founding of the Federal Republic. Brandt had already served three years as foreign minister in Kiesinger's Grand Coalition, and there, in close collaboration with the head of his policy-planning staff, Egon Bahr, he had begun to formulate a new departure for German foreign policy, a new approach to Germany's relations with the Soviet bloc: *Ostpolitik*.

Hitherto, West German foreign policy had been dominated by Adenauer's view that the new Republic, firmly tied to the West through the West European Union, the European Economic Community and NATO, must be unwavering in its refusal to recognize the German Democratic Republic (GDR) to its east. Claiming that the FRG alone represented Germany, Adenauer had also refused to recognize states that had diplomatic relations with the GDR, with the exception of the Soviet Union. His successor, Ludwig Erhard, had opened trade missions in Bucharest, Sofia, Warsaw and Budapest; but the first real breach of the principle had come only in 1967, when at Brandt's encouraging Bonn established diplomatic relations with Romania, followed a year later by Yugoslavia.

Adenauer had always insisted that the division of Germany, and unresolved frontier disputes to its east, had to be addressed before there could be any détente or military disengagement in central Europe. But by refusing to contest the construction of the Berlin Wall in 1961, the United States had demonstrated its unwillingness to risk war to keep the Berlin frontier open: and America, as President Lyndon Johnson confirmed in October 1966, would no longer allow its foreign policy to be held hostage to the principle of future German reunification. The message was clear: instead of insisting on the resolution of the 'German problem' as a precondition for détente, a new generation of German diplomats would have to reverse their priorities if they wished to achieve their objectives.

If Willy Brandt was willing to risk a breach with the conventions of West German politics it was in large measure because of his experience as Mayor of West Berlin. Indeed it is no coincidence that some of the most enthusiastic proponents of *Ostpolitik* in all its forms were former mayors of Berlin—Brandt himself, future Federal President Richard von Weizsäcker, and Hans-Jochen Vogel, Brandt's successor at the head of the SPD. To these men it was obvious that the Western Allies would take no untoward risks to overcome the division of Europe—an interpretation reconfirmed by the West's passive acceptance of the Warsaw Pact invasion of Czechoslovakia. If West Germans wanted to break the central European stalemate, they would have to do it themselves, by dealing directly with the authorities in the East.

With these considerations always in mind, Brandt and Bahr devised their approach to the east in order to achieve what Bahr called '*Wandel durch Annäherung*'—change through rapprochement. The aim was to 'overcome Yalta' through a multitude of contacts—diplomatic, institutional, human; and thereby to 'normalize' relations between the two Germanies and within Europe, without provoking disquiet at home or abroad. In a characteristic rhetorical innovation, Brandt quietly abandoned West German insistence upon the illegitimacy of the GDR and the non-negotiable demand for reunification. Henceforth, Bonn would continue to affirm the fundamental unity of the German people, but the undeniable *facticity* of East Germany would be acknowledged: 'one German nation, two German states'.[7]

Between 1970 and 1974 Brandt and his foreign minister, Walter Scheel of the Free Democratic Party, negotiated and signed a series of major diplomatic accords: treaties with Moscow and Warsaw in 1970, recognizing the *de facto* existence and inviolability of the post-war intra-German and German-Polish frontiers ('the existing boundary line . . . shall constitute the western state frontier of the People's Republic of Poland') and offering a new relationship between Germany and its eastern neighbors 'on the basis of the political situation as it exists in Europe'; a quadripartite agreement over Berlin in 1971, in which Moscow agreed not to make any unilateral changes there and to facilitate cross-border movement, followed by a Basic Treaty with the GDR, ratified by the Bundestag in 1973, in which Bonn, while continuing to grant automatic citizenship to any inhabitant of the GDR who succeeded in coming west, relinquished its longstanding claim to be the *sole* legitimate representative of all Germans; a treaty with Prague (1973); and the exchange of 'Permanent Representatives' with the GDR in May 1974.

For these achievements, and in the aftermath of a moving pilgrimage to Warsaw, where he knelt in homage to the memory of the Warsaw Ghetto, Willy Brandt was awarded the Nobel Peace Prize. He triumphed at home, too—in the elections of 1972 his SPD emerged for the first time as the leading party in the Federal Parliament. Despite side-stepping Bonn's longstanding insistence that no final settlement of frontiers and peoples had been reached, that the Yalta divisions had no *de jure* status, and that the legal fiction of the continuity of the December 1937 frontiers of Germany must be maintained, Brandt was very popular at home in Germany.[8] And not just in the West: on his journey in 1970 to the city of Erfurt, the first visit to East Germany by a West German leader, Brandt was greeted by rapturous crowds.

After Brandt was forced out of office by a spy scandal in 1974 his successors in the Chancellery—the Socialist Helmut Schmidt and the Christian Democrat Helmut Kohl—never deviated from the general line of *Ostpolitik*, pursuing it not only in public diplomacy but also through multiple links with the GDR, official and unofficial, all designed to facilitate human contacts, smooth relations, alleviate fears of West German revanchism and generally 'normalize' Bonn's relations with her eastern neighbors—accepting, in Brandt's words after signing the Moscow Treaty

---

[7]One of Brandt's first decisions upon taking office in 1969 was to rename the 'Ministry for All-German Questions' as the 'Ministry for Inter-German Relations': to allay East German fears that the Federal Republic would continue to assert its legal claim to speak for all Germans, and to indicate his readiness to treat with the GDR as a distinctive and enduring entity.

[8]This legal fiction, and the emotional issues surrounding it, account for the Christian Democratic Party's initial reluctance to sign the 1973 Basic Treaty which established relations with East Germany—and for the CD's continuing insistence upon keeping open the issue of the eastern frontiers right up to 1990.

that acknowledged Germany's post-war frontiers, that 'with this Treaty, nothing is lost that had not long since been gambled away'.

There were three distinct constituencies whom the framers of *Ostpolitik* had to consider if they were to succeed in their ambitions. Western Europeans needed reassurance that Germany was not turning East. French President Georges Pompidou's first response to the Moscow Treaty had been to make encouraging overtures to Great Britain—British membership of the European Community now held out the attraction of providing a counterweight to a less pliable Germany. The French were eventually appeased by German promises to anchor the Federal Republic ever more firmly in West European institutions (much as Pompidou's successors would be reassured by Germany's commitment to a common European currency following German unification two decades later); but in Paris as in Washington, remarks such as those of Finance Minister Helmut Schmidt in 1973, depicting a 'changing world' in which 'the traditional categories of East and West' were losing significance, were not soon forgotten.

The second constituency was Germans on both sides of the divide. For many of them Brandt's *Ostpolitik* brought real dividends. Contact and communication between the two Germanies burgeoned. In 1969 a mere half-million phone calls had been placed from West to East Germany. Twenty years later there were some forty million. Telephone contact between the two halves of Berlin, virtually unknown in 1970, had reached the level of ten million calls per year by 1988. By the mid-Eighties most East Germans had virtually unrestricted access to West German television; indeed, the East German authorities even went so far as to lay cable into the 'valley of the clueless' around Dresden (so-called because of local topographical impediments to West German television signals), in the wishful belief that if East Germans could watch West German television at home they would not feel the need to emigrate. These and other arrangements, including the reuniting of families and the release to the West of political prisoners, redounded to the credit of *Ostpolitik* and reflected the Communists' growing confidence in the West German policy of 'stability' and 'no surprises.'

The rulers of East Germany had particularly good reason to be pleased with these developments. In September 1973 the United Nations recognized and admitted East and West Germany as sovereign states; within a year the German Democratic Republic was diplomatically recognized by eighty countries, including the USA. In an ironic echo of changes in Bonn, the GDR's own leaders stopped referring to 'Germany' and instead began speaking with growing confidence of the GDR as a distinctive and legitimate *German* state in its own right, with a future of its own—rooted, they now insisted, not just in 'good', anti-Fascist Germans but in the soil and heritage of Prussia. Whereas the 1968 constitution of the GDR spoke of a commitment to unification on the basis of democracy and socialism, the phrase is absent in the amended constitution of 1974, replaced by a vow to remain 'forever and irrevocably allied with the USSR.'

There were also more immediate and mercenary grounds for official GDR interest in *Ostpolitik*. Since 1963 the GDR had been 'selling' political prisoners to Bonn for cash, the sum depending upon the 'value' and qualifications of the candidate. By 1977, in order to obtain the release of a prisoner from East German jails, Bonn was paying close to DM 96,000 per head. Among the diplomatic achievements of the new policy was the institutionalizing of cross-border family reunification: for this the authorities in Pankow charged an additional DM 4,500 per head (a bargain—in 1983 the Romanian dictator Ceauşescu was charging Bonn DM 8,000 a person to allow ethnic Germans to leave Romania). By one estimate, the total amount extracted from Bonn by the GDR, in return for releasing 34,000 prisoners, reuniting 2,000 children with their parents, and 'regulating' 250,000 cases of family reunification, was by 1989 close to DM 3 billion.[9]

One of the unintended consequences of these developments was the virtual disappearance of 'unification' from the German political agenda. To be sure, re-unification of the divided country remained the *Lebenslüge* ('life-lie') of the Federal Republic, as Brandt put it. But by the mid-Eighties, a few years before it unexpectedly took place, re-unification no longer mobilized mass opinion. Polls taken in the Fifties and Sixties suggested that up to 45 percent of the West German population felt unification was the 'most important' question of the day; from the mid-Seventies the figure never exceeded 1 percent.

The third constituency for Bonn's new approach, of course, was the Soviet Union. From Willy Brandt's first negotiations with Brezhnev in 1970, through Gorbachev's visit to Bonn nearly two decades later, all West German plans for 'normalization' to the east passed through Moscow and everyone knew it. In Helmut Schmidt's words, 'naturally, German-Soviet relations stood at the centre of *Ostpolitik*.' Indeed, once the West Germans and Russians had agreed on the permanence of Poland's new frontiers (respecting long-established European practice, no one asked the Poles for their views) and Bonn had consented to recognize the People's Democracies, West Germans and Russians found much common ground.

When Leonid Brezhnev went to Bonn in May 1973, the first such visit by a Soviet Communist Party leader, he and Helmut Schmidt even managed to share warm memories of their common wartime experiences—Schmidt conveniently recalling that he 'fought for Germany by day and at night privately wished for Hitler's defeat'. In his memoirs Willy Brandt, who really had opposed the Third Reich from beginning to end, coolly observes that 'when war reminiscences are exchanged, the fake and the genuine lie very close together'. But if the reminiscences were perhaps illusory, the shared interests were real enough.

---

[9]From the very start of *Ostpolitik*, special attention and privileges were accorded to *Volksdeutsche*, Germans still living beyond the frontiers of Germany, to the east or south. Defined by family or ethnic origin, such people were accorded full citizenship if they could reach the Federal Republic. Hundreds of thousands of residents of Ukraine, Russia, Romania, Hungary and elsewhere suddenly rediscovered German backgrounds they had taken great pains to deny for the previous half century.

The USSR had for many years been pressing for official recognition of its post-war gains and the new frontiers of Europe, preferably at a formal Peace Conference. The Western Allies, the US especially, had long been unwilling to go beyond *de facto* acknowledgement of the *status quo,* pending resolution of the 'German Question' in particular. But now that the Germans themselves were making overtures to their eastern neighbors, the Western position was bound to change; the Soviet leaders were about to realize their hopes. As part of their ambitious strategy of détente with the USSR and China, President Richard Nixon and Henry Kissinger, his National Security Adviser, were more open than their predecessors to negotiations with Moscow—and perhaps less troubled by the nature of the Soviet regime: as Kissinger explained to the US Senate Foreign Relations Committee on Sep 19th 1974, international détente should not be made to wait upon Soviet domestic reforms.

Thus, in December 1971, NATO ministers met in Brussels and agreed in principle to take part in a European Security Conference. Within a year a preparatory session was under way in Helsinki, Finland; and in July 1973, still in Helsinki, the official Conference on Security and Cooperation in Europe opened. Thirty-five countries (including the US and Canada) participated—only Albania declined to attend. Over the ensuing two years the Helsinki conferees drew up conventions, drafted agreements, proposed 'confidence-building' measures to improve East-West relations and much else besides. In August 1975 the Helsinki Accords were unanimously approved and signed.

On the face of things, the Soviet Union was the major beneficiary of the Accords. In the Final Act, under 'Principle I', it was agreed that the 'participating States will respect each other's sovereign equality and individuality as well as all the rights inherent in and encompassed by its sovereignty, including in particular the right of every State to juridical equality, to territorial integrity.' Moreover, in Principle VI, the participating States undertook to 'refrain from any intervention, direct or indirect, individual or collective, in the internal or external affairs falling within the domestic jurisdiction of another participating State, regardless of their mutual relations'.

Brezhnev and his colleagues could not have wished for more. Not only were the political divisions of post-war Europe now officially and publicly accepted, and the sovereignty and territorial integrity of the GDR and other satellite regimes officially conceded; the Western powers had for the first time foresworn all 'armed intervention or threat of such intervention against another participating State'. To be sure, the chances that NATO or the US would ever actually invade the Soviet Bloc had long since been negligible: indeed, the *only* country that had actually engaged in such armed intervention since 1948 was the Soviet Union itself . . . twice.

But it was an illustration of Moscow's endemic insecurity that these clauses in the Helsinki agreements, together with Principle IV affirming that 'the participating States will respect the territorial integrity of each of the participating States', were accorded such significance. Between the agreements with West Germany, and the Helsinki Accords' retrospective confirmation and acceptance of Potsdam, the

Soviet Union had finally achieved its objectives and could rest easy. In return, as it seemed, the Western participants in the Conference had sought and obtained little more than unobjectionable *pro forma* clauses: social, cultural and economic co-operation and exchanges, good faith collaboration to address outstanding and future disagreements, etc, etc.

But also included in the so-called 'third basket' of Helsinki principles was a list of the rights not just of states, but of persons and peoples, grouped under Principles VII ('Respect for human rights and fundamental freedoms, including the freedom of thought, conscience, religion or belief') and VIII ('Equal rights and self-determination of peoples'). Most of the political leaders who signed off on these clauses paid them little attention—on both sides of the Iron Curtain it was generally assumed that they were diplomatic window dressing, a sop to domestic opinion, and in any case unenforceable: under Principles IV and VI, outsiders could not interfere in the internal affairs of signatory states. As one embittered Czech intellectual remarked at the time, Helsinki was in practice a re-run of *Cuius Regio, Eius Religio*: within their borders, rulers were once again licensed to treat their citizens as they wished.

It did not work out that way. Most of the 1975 Helsinki principles and protocols merely gift-wrapped existing international arrangements. But Principle VII not only committed the signatory states to 'respect human rights and fundamental freedoms, including the freedom of thought, conscience, religion or belief, for all without distinction as to race, sex, language or religion.' It also enjoined all thirty-five states to 'promote and encourage the effective exercise of civil, political, economic, social, cultural and other rights and freedoms', and to 'recognize and respect the freedom of the individual to profess and practice, alone or in community with others, religion or belief acting in accordance with the dictates of his own conscience'.

From this wordy and, as it seemed, toothless checklist of rights and obligations was born the Helsinki Rights movement. Within a year of getting their long-awaited international conference agreement, Soviet leaders were faced with a growing and ultimately uncontrollable flowering of circles, clubs, networks, charters and individuals, all demanding 'merely' that their governments stick to the letter of that same agreement, that—as enjoined by the Final Act—they 'fulfill their obligations as set forth in the international declarations and agreements in this field'. Brezhnev had been right to count upon Henry Kissinger and his hard-headed successors to take seriously the non-intervention clauses at Helsinki; but it had never occurred to him (nor indeed to Kissinger) that others might take no less seriously the more utopian paragraphs that followed.[10]

---

[10]The first 'Helsinki Group' was founded on May 12th 1976, in Moscow. Its eleven initial members included Yuri Orlov, Yelena Bonner and Anatoly Sharansky. Helsinki Watch, the international umbrella organization set up specifically to publicize rights abuses in the Helsinki signatory states, was born two years later.

In the short run the Soviet authorities and their colleagues in eastern Europe could certainly suppress easily enough any voices raised on behalf of individual or collective rights: in 1977 the leaders of a Ukrainian 'Helsinki Rights' group were arrested and sentenced to terms ranging from three to fifteen years. But the very emphasis that Communist leaders had placed upon 'Helsinki' as the source of their regimes' international legitimacy would now come to haunt them: by invoking Moscow's own recent commitments, critics (at home and abroad) could now bring public pressure to bear on the Soviet regimes. Against this sort of opposition, violent repression was not just ineffective but, to the extent that it was public knowledge, self-defeating. Hoist by the petard of their own cynicism, Leonid Brezhnev and his colleagues had inadvertently opened a breach in their own defenses. Against all expectation, it was to prove mortal.

XVI

A Time of Transition

'In retrospect our biggest single mistake was to have allowed the elections to go ahead. Our downfall can be traced from there'.
Brigadier Otelo Saraiva de Carvalho

'Spain is the problem, Europe is the solution'.
Ortega y Gasset

'Europe is not just about material results, it is about spirit. Europe is a state of mind'.
Jacques Delors

In Northern Europe, domestic and international change was played out against the ever-present backdrop of these Great Power dealings and the East-West division of the continent. But in Mediterranean Europe local concerns dominated. Until the early Seventies, Spain, Portugal and Greece were peripheral to Europe in more than just a geographical sense. Despite being 'Western' in their Cold War allegiance (Portugal and Greece were members of NATO), all three countries stood otherwise quite apart. Their economies—heavily dependent upon the remittances of a surplus rural workforce employed abroad, and a growing tourist trade—resembled those of other countries on Europe's southern perimeter: Yugoslavia, or Turkey. The standard of living in southern Spain and most of Portugal and Greece was comparable to that of Eastern Europe and parts of the developing world.

All three countries were governed in the early 1970s by authoritarian rulers of a species more familiar in Latin America than Western Europe; the political transformations of the post-war decades seemed largely to have passed them by. In Portugal—ruled by António Salazar from 1932 to 1970—and Spain, where General Franco had staged his military coup in 1936 and ruled unchallenged from 1939 to his death in 1975, hierarchies of authority from another era were frozen into place. In Greece, a military cabal had overthrown king and parliament in 1967; thenceforward, the country was governed by a junta of colonels. The spectre of their unstable past hovered oppressively across the unpromising future prospects of all three countries.

The recent history of Greece, like that of Spain, was heavily back-shadowed by civil war. In the post-World War Two years, the Communist KKE terrorized villages under its control, leaving a legacy of fear and associating the radical Left in many

Greek memories with repression and atrocity. After the Communists abandoned the struggle, in October 1949, it was the Left's turn to suffer sustained repression. Wartime partisans (including many who had fought against the Germans in earlier years) were forced into foreign exile for decades to come. Those who remained, together with their children and even their grandchildren, were forbidden public sector employment until well into the seventies. At the notorious prison on the island of Makronisos, Communists were detained at length and treated with notorious brutality.[1]

But the political divisions of Greece, however tidily they appeared to fold into Cold War categories, were always dominated by distinctive local concerns. In March 1949, at the height of the Tito-Stalin struggle, the slavishly pro-Moscow KKE issued a radio announcement (from Bucharest) endorsing demands for an independent Macedonia. By encouraging the territorial fragmentation of Yugoslavia this was intended to weaken Tito, but it had no such effect. Instead it undercut for a generation the *domestic* credibility of Greek Communism, by suggesting that a Communist victory would result in autonomy for the Macedonian north, with its Slav and Albanian minorities, and thence to the break up of the Greek state.

If this mattered so much, it was because Greek nationalism was peculiarly insecure, even by regional standards. Permanently on the *qui vive* for conflict with their former imperial masters in Turkey, in a state of war with Albania since 1940 (a circumstance left un-remedied until 1985), and unwilling to concede even the fact of a large Slav community abutting their frontiers with Yugoslavia and Bulgaria, Greece's conservative post-war politicians emphatically opted for order and stability over democracy or post-war reconciliation. Conflating old Greek concerns with new international divisions the Greek king, his army and his ministers presented themselves to the West as the most reliable allies in an unstable region.

They were well compensated for their loyalty.[2] In February 1947, the Treaty of Paris obliged Italy to cede the Dodecanese islands to Athens. Greece was a major beneficiary of American aid, both following the pronouncement of the 'Truman Doctrine' and under the Marshall Plan. The country was admitted to NATO in 1952 and the Greek armed forces were the happy recipients of copious practical assistance with planning and matériel. Indeed, the role of the army was to prove crucial. The British had originally hoped to bequeath to liberated Greece a properly non-political army and modern police force; but in the circumstances of time and place, this proved impossible. Instead, the Greek army emerged from eight years of war as uncompromisingly anti-Communist, royalist and undemocratic, its al-

---

[1] The Makronisos' warders' practice of forcing Communists to repent and then turn on those who refused was remarkably similar to Romanian Communist techniques in the prison at Pitesti in the same years, albeit marginally less vicious. See Chapter 6.

[2] At first, as elsewhere in Europe, the US expected to find friends and allies on the centre-left of the Greek political spectrum. It was soon disabused of this, however, and switched to a close and enduring friendship with the nationalist and military Right.

legiance to NATO and to its American colleagues considerably firmer than any commitment to the political institutions or laws of its own state.

Indeed—and much like the traditional Spanish officer corps in this respect—Greek officers saw *themselves*, rather than the ephemeral constitutional documents they were sworn to defend, as the guardians of the nation and its integrity. The army was active from the outset in post-war Greek political life: in the national elections of the early Fifties, the victorious 'Greek Rally' Party was led by Marshal Alexandros Papagos, commander of the government forces in the Civil War. Until 1963 the military were happy enough to give their support to Constantine Karamanlis, who led the re-named Greek Rally party (now the National Radical Union) to election victories in 1956, 1958 and again in 1961—though he was suspected after the last and greatest of these successes of widespread electoral fraud.

Karamanlis was not himself ideologically anti-Communist nor even especially close to the armed forces. But it is not irrelevant that he was born in Greek Macedonia and was profoundly anti-Slav. Of peasant background and Orthodox faith, he was instinctively provincial, nationalist and conservative—a fitting representative of his country and a safe pair of hands in the eyes of American diplomats and Greek officers alike, evincing no desire to enforce civilian oversight of the military or investigate too closely the growing rumors of anti-parliamentary political networks and conspiracies in high places. Under Karamanlis, Greece remained stable, if economically stagnant and more than a little corrupt.

But in May 1963 a left-wing parliamentarian, Dr. Grigoris Lambrakis, was assaulted in Thessaloniki while speaking at a peace rally. His death five days later created a political martyr for the Left and the nascent peace movement in Greece, while the authorities' studied failure to investigate the murky background to Lambrakis' assassination gave rise to widespread suspicion.[3] Six months later Karamanlis narrowly lost the elections to George Papandreou's Center Union, a centrist party backed by the country's growing urban middle class. The following year, at a fresh round of elections, Papandreou's party and its allies did better still, winning an absolute majority of the votes cast and increasing their share from 42 percent to 52.7 percent.

The new parliamentary majority demanded an investigation into the rigging of the 1961 elections, and tensions began to mount between parliament and the young King Constantine. The king's conservative political sympathies were public knowledge, and he was under increasing pressure from the Right to dismiss Papandreou, who was eventually maneuvered into resigning. He was succeeded by a series of interim prime ministers, none of whom could form a stable parliamentary majority. Relations between parliament and court were strained still further when a group

---

[3]And to Costas Gavras' influential 1969 film *Z*, based on the Lambrakis affair.

of liberal-leaning army officers was accused of plotting with George Papandreou's son Andreas. In March 1967, twenty one of them were court-martialed.

Parliamentary government in Greece had by now ceased to function in all but name. Conservatives and army officers warned darkly of growing 'Communist' influence in the country at large. The king would not work with the majority Center Union, which he accused of depending on the votes of the far Left, while the opposition National Radical Union refused to back successive efforts to install 'caretaker' governments. Finally, in April 1967, the National Radical Union itself formed a minority government just long enough for the King to dissolve the parliament and call for new elections.

Popular frustration at the parliamentary stalemate, and a widespread feeling that the king had played an unacceptably partisan role, suggested that the forthcoming elections would produce a further swing to the Left. Proferring just this excuse—the 'Communist threat' insistently invoked in Greece since 1949—and pointing to the undoubted inadequacies of Greece's democratic institutions and the incompetence of its political class, a group of officers working inside the army's long-established right-wing networks seized power on April 21st.

Led by Colonel George Papadopoulos, they poured tanks and paratroopers into the streets of Athens and other Greek cities, arrested politicians, journalists, trade unionists and other public figures, seized control of all the usual strong points and declared themselves the saviors of the nation: 'democracy', as they explained, would be 'placed in a sling'. King Constantine passively, if unenthusiastically, assented and swore the conspirators into office. Eight months later, after a half-hearted attempt at a 'counter-coup', Constantine and his family fled to Rome, un-mourned. The junta appointed a regent and Papadopoulos was named prime minister.

The colonels' coup d'état was a classic *pronunciamento*. Initially violent and always repressive, Papadopoulos and his colleagues dismissed nearly a thousand civil servants, imprisoned or expelled politicians of the left and center, and turned Greece in upon itself for seven stifling years. Anti-modern to the point of parody, the colonels censored the press, outlawed strikes and banned modern music along with mini-skirts. They also banned the study of sociology, Russian and Bulgarian in addition to Sophocles, Euripides and Aristophanes. 'Populist' in style but paternalist in practice, they were obsessed with appearance. Under the colonels' regime long hair was forbidden. The uniforms of palace guards and other ceremonial officials were replaced with gaudily 'traditional' Greek costume. Athens in particular took on a tidy, martial air.

The economic consequences of the Greek coup were mixed. Tourism did not suffer—politically-conscious travelers who boycotted the colonels' Greece were readily replaced by tourists attracted to cheap, if suffocatingly over-regulated resorts. Foreign investment, which in Greece's case had only begun a decade or so before the coup, and a steady increase in GNP—rising at an annual average of 6 percent since 1964—were unaffected by political developments: as in Spain, low wages (abetted by the repression of all labour protest) and a regime predicated on 'law and order' offered a benevolent environment for foreign capital. The junta even had widespread initial support in the rural districts from which the colonels mostly came, especially after they cancelled all peasant debt in 1968.[4]

But the autarkic instincts of the colonels favored a return to old-established national habits of import-substitution—inefficient local manufacturers producing low-quality products and protected against foreign competition. This was bound eventually to bring the military regime into conflict with the country's urban middle class, whose interests as consumers and producers alike would within a few years triumph over their relief at the dismissal of the bickering politicians. And the colonels, mediocre even by the undemanding standards of their kind, had nothing to offer for the future: no project for Greek integration into the emerging and expanding European Community, no strategy for a return to civilian rule.[5]

Moreover the regime, secure enough at home, was increasingly isolated abroad—in December 1969 the Council of Europe unanimously voted to expel Greece; two months later the EEC broke off all negotiations with the junta. More brazenly than most, the colonels' regime rested on force alone. It was thus altogether appropriate that the dictatorship should fall in the course of an incompetent attempt to apply force beyond its frontiers, to resolve the long-running problem of Cyprus.

The island of Cyprus, part of the Ottoman Empire since 1571, had been administered by Britain since 1878 and unilaterally annexed at the outbreak of World War One. In the far-eastern Mediterranean, close to Turkish Anatolia and far removed from the Greek mainland or any other outlying Greek islands, Cyprus nonetheless had a Greek-speaking, Eastern Orthodox majority increasingly disposed to seek union with the Greek state. The Turkish minority, some 18 percent of the island's population, was understandably opposed to any such arrangement and was vociferously supported by the authorities in Ankara. The fate of Cyprus—caught between British efforts to dispose of a troublesome imperial inheritance and longstanding Greek-Turkish hostility—remained troublingly unresolved throughout the Fifties.

Denied their project of '*Enosis*'—union with Greece—the majority of the island's Greek-Cypriot leadership settled somewhat reluctantly for independence, which the UK granted in 1960, retaining only certain transit rights and a strategi-

---

[4]The officers, most of them formed in military cadet schools under the pre-war dictatorship of Ioannis Metaxas, were perhaps not as unpopular as their foreign critics asserted. But they were—rightly—presumed to have the sympathy (and perhaps more) of the United States. What was in essence a belated extension of the Greek civil war of the 1940s rapidly came instead to be seen as the latest *cause célèbre* in Europe's century-old civil war. 'Greece' now replaced 'Spain' as the divining rod for polarized political sentiment.

[5]Since 1962, Greece had 'Associate' status with the European Economic Community.

cally important airbase. The new Republic of Cyprus, its sovereignty and constitution guaranteed by Britain, Turkey and Greece, was ruled by a Greek-Turkish
'partnership' arrangement dominated by the presidency of Archbishop Makarios,
once exiled by London as an armed and violent terrorist, now the respected
spokesman of 'reasonable' Greek Cypriot ambitions.

Meanwhile the island's Greek and Turkish communities lived alongside each
other in suspicious unease, interrupted by sporadic outbursts of inter-communal
violence. The governments in Athens and Ankara both advertised themselves as the
protectors of their respective compatriots and occasionally threatened to intervene. But prudence, and international pressure, kept them from doing so, even
when attacks on Turkish Cypriots in 1963 led to the arrival of a UN Peacekeeping
Force the following year. Despite the Greek Cypriots' near-monopoly of public
employment and positions of authority (loosely comparable to the Protestant majority's exclusion of Catholics from privileges and power in Ulster)—or perhaps because of it—the situation in Cyprus appeared stable. But if Cyprus was no longer
a crisis it remained very much an 'issue'.

Thus in 1973, when students in Athens (first at the Law School, later at the Polytechnic) embarrassed the colonels by publicly opposing their rule for the first time,
the military's response was to divert attention and seek to shore up public support
by re-asserting the Greek claim to Cyprus. General Ioannides, a 'hard-liner' who
displaced Papadopoulos as junta leader following the Polytechnic demonstrations,
plotted with George Grivas and other Greek-Cypriot nationalists to overthrow
Makarios and 're-unite' the island with Greece. On July 15th 1974, units of the
Cypriot National Guard along with hand-picked Greek officers attacked the Presidential Palace, expelled Makarios (who fled abroad) and installed a puppet government in anticipation of direct rule from Athens.

At this juncture, however, the Turkish government announced its own intention
to invade Cyprus in order to protect the interests of the Turkish-Cypriot community, and promptly did so, on July 20th. Within a week, two-fifths of the island was
in Turkish hands. Unable either to prevent or respond to this move by vastly superior Turkish forces, the junta appeared helpless: ordering full mobilization one
day, canceling it the next. Faced with widespread public anger at this national humiliation, the Greek dictators themselves turned to the ageing Karamanlis and invited him to return home from his exile in Paris. By July 24th the former Prime
Minister was back in Athens and had initiated the country's return to civilian rule.

The transition was accomplished with remarkable ease. Karamanlis's New
Democracy party swept home in the November 1974 elections and repeated its
success three years later. A new constitution was approved in June 1975, although
the opposition parties initially protested over the heightened powers granted to the
president of the republic (a post occupied by Karamanlis himself from 1980). With
unexpected alacrity, Greek domestic politics took on a familiar European profile,
divided roughly equally into a center-right (New Democracy) and a center-left (the

Panhellenic Socialist Movement led by the late George Papandreou's American-educated son Andreas).

The smoothness of Greece's return to democracy was due in part to Karamanlis's skill in breaking with his own past, while at the same time conveying an image of seasoned competence and continuity. Rather than re-establish his discredited Center Union he had formed a new party. He called a referendum on the discredited monarchy in December 1974, and when 69.2 percent of the voters demanded its abolition he oversaw the establishment of a republic. In order to avoid alienating the military he resisted calls to purge the army, preferring instead to impose early retirement on the more compromised senior officers while rewarding and promoting loyalists.[6]

With the monarchy out of the way, and the army neutralized, Karamanlis had to address the unfinished business of Cyprus. Neither he nor his successors had any intention of re-opening the *Enosis* question, but nor could they publicly ignore Turkey's presence on the island, even after Makarios's return there in December 1974. In a largely symbolic move that attracted widespread domestic approval on Left and Right alike, Karamanlis pulled Greece out of the military organization of NATO for the next six years in protest at the behavior of a fellow NATO member. Greek-Turkish relations entered an ice age, marked by the Turkish minority's unilateral declaration in February 1975 of a 'Turkish Federated State of Cyprus'—only ever recognized by Turkey itself—and by sporadic diplomatic tiffs over territorial claims in the eastern Aegean.

Cyprus itself thus became an object of international concern, as UN diplomats and lawyers were to spend fruitless decades trying unsuccessfully to resolve the island's divisions. Meanwhile Greek politicians were thereby relieved of responsibility for the island's affairs (though they remained constrained by domestic politics to express a continued interest in its fate) and could turn to more promising horizons. Less than a year after the fall of the colonels, in June 1975, the government in Athens formally applied to join the EEC. On January 1st 1981, in what many in Brussels would come to regard as a regrettable triumph of hope over wisdom, Greece became a full member of the Community.

Unlike Greece, Portugal had no recent experience of even the most vestigial of democracies. Salazar's authoritarian reign had been peculiarly and self-consciously retrograde even by the standards prevailing when he first took over power in 1932—indeed, in its mix of censorious clericalism, corporate institutions and rural under-

---

[6]The junta itself, however, did not escape retribution. Eleven of its leaders were tried and convicted in August 1975. Three were given death sentences, later commuted to life in prison. Papadopoulos died in custody in 1999, unrepentant to the end. Brigadier-General Ioannidis was convicted at a later trial for his role in the suppression of the Polytechnic revolt. He remains in prison at the time of writing.

development, Portugal quite closely resembled post-1934 Austria. Appropriately enough, post-war Portugal was favored by retired Frenchmen nostalgic for Vichy France—Charles Maurras, disgraced leader of the Action Française, was much admired by Salazar and corresponded with him until his death in 1952.[7]

The general standard of living in Salazar's Portugal was more characteristic of contemporary Africa than continental Europe: per capita annual income in 1960 was just $160 (compared with e.g. $219 in Turkey, or $1,453 in the US). The rich were very rich indeed, infant mortality was the highest in Europe, and 32 percent of the population was illiterate. Salazar, an economist who had for some years lectured at the University of Coimbra, was not only unperturbed at Portugal's backwardness, but saw it instead as the key to stability—upon being informed that oil had been discovered in Portugal's Angolan territories he commented merely that this was 'a pity'.

Like the Romanian dictator Ceauşescu, Salazar was obsessed with the avoidance of debt, and conscientiously balanced every annual budget. Fanatically mercantilist, he built up unusually high gold reserves which he took care not to spend on either investment or imports. As a result, his country was locked into poverty, most of the population working on small family farms in the north of the country and *latifundia* further south. With no local capital available to finance domestic industry and foreign investors distinctly unwelcome, Portugal was largely dependent upon the export or re-export of primary commodities, including its own people.

Right up to his death in 1970, it was Salazar's proud boast that not only had he kept Portugal out of the devastating foreign wars of the century, but he had navigated his country between the Scylla of rapacious market capitalism and the Charybdis of state socialism. In fact, he had all too successfully exposed his subjects to the worst of both: material inequality and exploitation for profit were more marked in Portugal than anywhere else in Europe, while the authoritarian state in Lisbon smothered all independent opinion and initiative. In 1969 just 18 percent of the adult population was eligible to vote.

In the absence of domestic opposition, the only resistance to Salazar came from the military, the country's sole independent institution. The Portuguese armed forces were ill paid—rather than expend scarce resources on wages, Salazar actively encouraged impecunious army officers to marry into the better-heeled bourgeoisie. But until 1961 the regime could count on at least their passive loyalty, in spite of two abortive and easily crushed military coup attempts in 1947 and again in 1958. Reform-minded junior officers in the army or navy might chafe at the stagnation around them, but they lacked allies or any popular base.

All that changed in 1961, when Delhi forcibly annexed Portugal's mainland In-

---

[7]Maurras died in 1952, aged 84. Salazar himself, the son of an estate manager, was born in Vimeiro, Portugal, on April 28th 1889, just a week after Hitler. For a man still ruling a European state in the late 1960s he was unusually deeply rooted in the *mores* of the previous century—his mother was born in 1846.

dian territory of Goa and armed revolt broke out in the African colony of Angola. The loss of Goa was a national humiliation, but rebellion in Africa was more serious still. Portugal's considerable African 'provinces', as they were known, comprised Angola, Guinée-Bissau and the Cape Verde Islands in West Africa, and Mozambique in the south-east. Of these Angola, with nearly half a million European residents in a total population of under six million, was by far the most important. Its untapped material wealth—in iron, diamonds and recently-discovered offshore oil—had led Salazar reluctantly to permit foreign investment (notably by the US company Gulf Oil), and in the course of the Sixties the territory was taking on growing economic significance for Portugal itself.

It was also in open revolt. In order to crush the growing Angolan nationalist movement, Lisbon inaugurated in 1967 a 'counter-insurgency' strategy based upon resettlement of the population into large, controllable villages: by 1974 more than one million peasants had been moved. The plan failed to break the insurgency, although it had baneful and enduring effects on Angola's society and rural economy. It did, however, increasingly alienate the soldiers who were called upon to enforce it: both the impecunious officers who had joined the colonial army as a route to upward social mobility and the reluctant conscripts sent abroad to suppress the rebels.

In Angola the rebels were divided between different factions and the Portuguese army was able to contain them, at least for a while. In Mozambique, where 60,000 Portuguese soldiers were kept busy protecting a European settler population numbering just 100,000, or in Guinée and Cape Verde, where the charismatic Amilcar Cabral tied down over 30,000 Portuguese troops in thankless guerilla warfare against ten thousand insurgents, the situation was becoming untenable. By the beginning of the 1970s its African wars were consuming half the annual defense budget of Europe's poorest country. One in every four Portuguese men of military age was being conscripted to serve in Africa—and, after 1967, for a compulsory minimum term of four years. By 1973, 11,000 of them had died there: a mortality rate considerably higher, as a share of the national population, than that suffered by the US Army at the height of the Vietnam War.

Portugal's defense of its colonial holdings was expensive, bloody and increasingly hopeless; the armed forces knew this better than anyone. And they had other reasons to feel frustrated. To secure his own power and distract attention from the country's overseas woes, Marcello Caetano—Salazar's anointed successor—had eased credit restrictions, borrowed heavily from abroad and encouraged the flow of imports. In the years 1970–73, further fuelled by remittances from Portuguese working abroad, the country underwent a brief consumer boom. But it was followed in short order by spiraling inflation brought on by the oil crisis. Wages in the public sector began to fall far behind prices.

For the first time in many years Portugal was hit by strikes. The residents of the shanty towns around the capital, many of them recent arrivals from the impoverished Alentejo region, suffered not just their own endemic indigence but the sight of a new and showy wealth in nearby Lisbon. The army increasingly resented fighting the country's 'dirty wars' in far-away lands on behalf of an unpopular government run by unelected technocrats, and its discontent was now finding a widespread echo at home. The grievances of junior officers and their families, unable to subsist on already low wages further reduced by inflation, were now shared by a rising generation of businessmen frustrated at their rulers' incompetence and who understood that their country's future lay in Europe, not Africa.[8]

On April 25th 1974, officers and men of the Armed Forces Movement (Movimento das Forças Armadas—MFA) ousted Caetano and his colleagues from office and declared a provisional government whose goals were to be democratization, decolonization and economic reform. The coup (like the young officers' *pronunciamento* that first brought Salazar to power in 1926) aroused little resistance, and the leaders of the old regime were allowed to fly into exile—first to Madeira, thence to Brazil. General António de Spínola, former deputy chief of staff of the Portuguese army and governor of Guinée from 1968 to 1972, was appointed by his fellow officers to head the junta. The secret police was abolished, all political prisoners were released, freedom of the press was restored and the leaders of Portugal's Socialist and Communist parties returned from exile, their organizations legally permitted for the first time in nearly half a century.

The revolution was immensely popular everywhere.[9] Spinola brought centrists and socialists into his provisional cabinet and in July he publicly announced plans to offer the African colonies full self-determination. Within a year the colonies were all independent—and Indonesia had seized control of Portuguese East Timor. The decolonization was more than a little chaotic—guerillas in Guinée and Mozambique ignored Spinola's insistence that they first lay down arms and Angola deteriorated into civil war—but seen from Portugal it had the virtue of being quick. It also precipitated, in the wake of the army's retreat and violent clashes in the Angolan capital, Luanda, the return to Portugal of some 750,000 Europeans. Many of them settled in Portugal's more conservative north and would play a significant political role in coming years.

These rapid changes disturbed Spinola, whose conservative instincts were at odds with the increasingly radical projects of his younger colleagues, and in September 1974 he resigned. For the next fourteen months Portugal appeared to be moving towards a full-scale social revolution. With the enthusiastic support of the MFA and Álvaro Cunhal's uncompromisingly Leninist Communist Party (PCP),

---

[8] By 1973, Western Europe accounted for two-thirds of Portugal's imports and exports alike.
[9] The puritanical young officers and their left-wing allies were not, however, well-pleased with the subsequent outpouring of what they regarded as pornographic literature and films, as Portugal compensated for fifty years of cultural constriction. They even attempted at one point to ban the playing of *fados*, the traditional Portuguese folk songs: these, they felt, encouraged 'bitterness and fatalism' and were thus inimical to their goals of enlightenment and social progress.

banks and major industries were nationalized and a massive agrarian reform was undertaken: notably in the Alentejo, the grain-producing region of southern Portugal where most holdings were still in the hands of large, often absentee landlords.

Nationalization was popular in the towns, and agrarian reform in the South—essentially collectivization of the land—was driven initially by 'spontaneous' occupations and land seizures by local tenants and labourers mobilized by the Communists and their allies, the Communists in particular benefiting from their well-deserved reputation as the best-organized and most effective clandestine opponents of the old regime. But the same practices in the center and north of the country, where the land was already sub-divided into thousands of small, family-run property holdings, were decidedly unwelcome. Rural and small-town northern Portugal was also (and still is) actively Catholic, with an average of one priest for every five hundred souls in 1972; the figure for south-central Portugal was 1:4500, and lower still in the far south. The anti-clerical, collectivizing projects of Communist unionists and peasant leaders thus encountered strong and vociferous opposition in the populous northern regions.

In essence, the Portuguese revolutionaries of 1974 were repeating the mistake of the agrarian radicals of the Spanish republic in the Thirties: in seeking to impose a collectivist land reform based on southern social conditions upon the privately-owned and more efficient smallholders of the north, they turned the latter against them. In the Constituent Assembly elections of April 1975 the Communists were held to just 12.5 percent of the vote. Right-of-center parties did better, but the big winner was the Portuguese Socialist Party, founded in exile two years before by Mário Soares, who campaigned very effectively on the slogan 'Socialism, Yes! Dictatorship, No!' and won 38 percent of the vote.

The MFA and the Communists were unhappy with the outcome of the vote, and Cunhal openly acknowledged that if the parliamentary route to power was blocked, an alternative path might have to be taken—as he put it to an Italian journalist in June 1975, 'There is no possibility of a democracy like the one you have in Western Europe . . . Portugal will not be a country with democratic freedoms and monopolies. It will not allow it.' From April to November tensions rose. Foreign commentators warned of an impending Communist coup, and Portugal's NATO allies and western European trade partners held out promises of aid and affiliation if the country abjured Marxist revolution.

Matters came to a head at the end of the year. On November 8th the Constituent Assembly in Lisbon was besieged by building workers and for two weeks there were rumors of an imminent 'Lisbon Commune' and even a civil war between north and south. On November 25th groups of radical soldiers attempted a putsch. Initially they had the tacit support of the PCP, but when it became clear that the bulk of the armed forces and even some of the left-wing officers themselves were opposed to the uprising, even Cunhal backed off. As some of the MFA leaders were later to acknowledge, the outcome of the April 1975 elections had discredited in advance the goals of the revolutionary officers: the Left could have parliamentary democracy or a revolutionary 'transition', but not both.

In February 1976 the Portuguese military, still in effective control of the country nearly two years after their coup, officially handed over power to the civilian authorities. The country was to be governed under a Constitution approved in April 1976 and which continued to echo the rhetoric and ambitions of the post-'74 political mood, committing Portugal to a 'transition to socialism through the creation of conditions for the democratic exercise of power by the working classes.' In the legislative elections of that same month, the Socialists once again came first, though with a slightly reduced vote, and Mário Soares formed Portugal's first democratically-elected government in nearly half a century.

The prospects for Portuguese democracy remained cloudy—Willy Brandt was just one of many sympathetic contemporary observers who saw in Soares another Kerensky, an unwitting stalking horse for undemocratic forces that would replace him at the earliest opportunity. But Soares survived—and more. The armed forces remained confined to barracks, the role of their politicized fringes increasingly marginal. The Communists' vote actually rose—improving to 14.6 percent in 1976 and thence to 19 percent three years later, as the economy deteriorated and Soares' moderate policies frustrated his party's left-wing, to whom he had promised the coming destruction of capitalism in a Socialist Portugal—but at the price of abandoning their insurrectionist ambitions.

In 1977 the Parliament passed an Agrarian Reform Law that confirmed the land collectivization of the immediate past but confined it to the South, with restrictions on the amount of land that could be expropriated from existing owners. This move ended the risk of rural conflict and a conservative backlash, but it could do little in the short run to alleviate the economic mess that democratic Portugal had inherited. Deprived of cheap raw materials from its former colonies (and the captive market they had provided for its otherwise uncompetitive exports), unable to export unskilled labour to Western Europe as in the past, and constrained under the terms of vital IMF loans to balance its budgets and practice fiscal rigor, Portugal suffered years of unemployment and under-consumption.

The military had not completely left the scene: under the 1976 Constitution a 'Council of the Revolution' composed of non-elected representatives of the armed forces retained a right of veto, and in the course of 1980 it rejected twenty three pieces of legislation, including a plan by the right-of-center government elected that year to denationalize domestic banks. But they offered no objection when parliament revised the constitution in the course of the next two years, reducing the power of the executive (abolishing the Council of the Revolution itself in 1982), and quietly removing the anti-capitalist emphasis in the original document.

For the next twenty years the Socialists and their opponents, centrist Social Democrats led by Aníbal Cavaço Silva, were to alternate in office. Mário Soares himself, his anti-capitalist rhetoric long-since abandoned, ascended to the country's

Presidency in 1986, the year Portugal was admitted to the European Community. The country remained strikingly poor by West European standards, a tribute to Salazar's enduring legacy. But against all expectations Portugal had avoided both a 'White Terror' and a 'Red Terror'. The Communists, while still popular in the rural south and the industrial suburbs of Lisbon, remained unrepentantly hard-line under the ageing Cunhal, who stayed in charge until 1992. But their influence was permanently diminished. The repatriated colonials never succeeded in forming a far-right party of embittered nationalists. In the circumstances, the emergence of a democratic Portugal was a very considerable achievement.

To a visitor crossing from France into Spain in, say, 1970, the chasm separating the two sides of the Pyrenees seemed immense. Franco's thirty-year long reign had accentuated the social backwardness and cultural isolation in which Spain had languished for much of the past two centuries, and his authoritarian regime appeared even more at odds with modern European political culture than it had at the outset. At first sight the Sixties appeared to have passed Spain by altogether: rigid censorship, strict enforcement of laws regulating public dress and behavior, an omnipresent police and draconian penal laws for political critics all suggested a land frozen in time, its historical clock set permanently at 1939.[10]

On closer inspection, however, Spain—or at least northern Spain and the cities—was changing quite rapidly. Franco was a rigid and truly reactionary dictator, but unlike his neighbor Salazar he was also an economic realist. In 1959 Spain abandoned the autarkic practices of the past two decades and, at the instigation of a group of Opus Dei ministers, adopted a National Stabilization Plan intended to stifle the country's endemic inflation and open it up to trade and investment. The initial economic impact of the Plan was harsh: devaluation, budget cuts, a credit freeze and wage restrictions—all firmly and uncompromisingly enforced—brought inflation down but forced tens of thousands of Spaniards to seek work abroad.

But the private sector, hitherto constrained by corporatist regulations and a longstanding policy of import substitution, was freer to expand. Tariffs were reduced; Spain joined the World Bank, the IMF and the GATT, and was admitted to the OECD as an Associate Member (in 1962 Franco even applied—unsuccessfully— to join the EEC). The timing of Franco's new economic policy was propitious. The Spanish domestic economy had been protected against competition in the early years of Europe's post-war boom, but was opening itself to foreign commerce at just the right moment. Starting in 1961, GNP began to rise steadily. The percentage of the labor force employed on the land—one worker in two in 1950—fell pre-

---

[10]As recently as 1963 the Spanish leader had not hesitated to execute a captured Communist, Juan Grimau, in defiance of widespread international criticism.

cipitately as rural laborers from the South and West moved north to work in factories and the burgeoning tourist trade: by 1971 only one Spaniard in five was left in agriculture. Already, by the mid-Sixties, Spain had ceased to qualify as a 'developing nation' under UN criteria.

Franco's 'economic miracle' should not be overstated. Spain was not burdened by the residue of empire and thus faced none of the economic or social costs of decolonization. Most of the foreign cash flowing into the country in the Sixties came not from the export of Spanish-produced goods, but rather from overseas remittances by emigrant Spanish workers or else holiday-makers from northern Europe: in short, Spain's economic modernization was largely a by-product of other nations' prosperity. Outside of Barcelona, the Costa Brava, parts of the Basque country and (to a lesser extent) Madrid, the transport, education, medical and service infrastructure of the country still lagged far behind. Even in 1973, per capita income in the country as a whole was still lower than that of Ireland and less than half the EEC average.

Nevertheless, the social consequences of even limited economic modernization were significant. In a time before television Spain may have been largely shielded from the *cultural* impact of the Sixties elsewhere, but the economic disparities and disruption engendered by the Stabilization Plan produced widespread labour discontent. From the later Sixties through Franco's death, strikes, lockouts, demonstrations and widespread demands for collective bargaining and union representation became a fixture of Spanish life. The regime was adamantly opposed to any political concessions; but it could not afford to present too repressive a public face, at a time when so many foreigners were visiting the country—17.3 million in 1966, rising to 34 million the year before Franco's death.

Nor could the Spanish authorities forgo the cooperation and skills of a growing urban work force. They were thus constrained to concede the *de facto* emergence of a labor movement, overwhelmingly based in Catalonia and the heavy industries of the Basque region. Together with the unofficial unions formed by public employees, banking staff and other expanding white-collar occupations, this semi-clandestine network of workers' and employees' representatives could call upon nearly a decade of organization and experience by the time Franco died.

Labor protest in Spain, however, was kept firmly confined to bread and butter issues. By its last years, Franco's regime—rather like that of János Kádár in Hungary—depended not on open and violent repression but rather upon a sort of enforced passive acceptance, a decades-long de-politicization of the culture. Student protesters, who since 1956 had been seeking greater campus autonomy and a relaxing of moral codes and other restrictions, were accorded a certain liberty to organize and protest within strictly circumscribed boundaries; they could even count upon some sympathy from the regime's internal critics—reform-minded Catholics and disappointed 'social-Falangists' among others. But all active expressions of sympathy or collaboration across sectors—with striking miners, for example—were strictly off limits.[11] The same applied to the regime's adult critics.

Indeed, *all* properly political opinions were kept firmly under wraps, and independent political parties were banned. Until 1967 the country lacked even a constitution, and such rights and procedures as existed were largely window dressing for the benefit of Spain's Western partners. Officially a 'regent' for the suspended monarchy, Franco had anointed the young Juan Carlos—grandson of Spain's last king—to succeed him in due course, but for most observers the question of the monarchy played little part in Spanish affairs. Even the Church, still a major presence in the daily life of many Spaniards, played only a limited role in public policy.

Spain's traditional role as a bulwark of Christian civilization against materialism and atheism was a staple of the primary-school curriculum; but the Catholic hierarchy itself (unlike the modernizing 'crypto monks' of Opus Dei) was kept well away from the reins of power, in marked contrast to the neo-Crusading 'National Catholicism' spirit of the regime's first decade.[12] In June 1968, bowing to modern reality, Franco conceded for the first time the principle of religious freedom, allowing Spaniards openly to worship at a church of their choosing. But by then religion itself was entering upon a long decline: in a country that could boast over 8,000 seminarists at the start of the Sixties, there were less than 2,000 twelve years later. Between 1966 and 1975 one third of all Spain's Jesuits left the Order.

The military, too, was kept at a careful distance. Having himself come to power by a military coup, Franco understood very well the risks of alienating a military caste that had inherited an over-developed sense of its responsibility for the preservation of the Spanish state and its traditional values. Throughout the post-war years the Spanish Army was cosseted and flattered. Its victory in the Civil War was celebrated annually in the streets of major cities, its losses ostentatiously memorialized in the monumental Valley of The Fallen, completed in September 1959. Ranks and decorations multiplied: by the time the regime fell there were 300 generals, and the ratio of officers to other ranks was 1:11, the highest in Europe. In 1967, an Institutional Law of the State made the armed forces formally responsible for guaranteeing the nation's unity and territorial integrity and defending 'the institutional system'.

In practice, though, the armed forces had become superfluous. Franco had for decades preserved his military from any foreign or colonial wars. Unlike the French or Portuguese armies, they suffered no humiliating defeats or forced retreats. Spain faced no military threats, and its domestic security was handled by police, gen-

---

[11]One ironic consequence of the carefully calibrated freedoms that Franco allowed to university activists in his last decade is that Spanish students of the Sixties generation typically exaggerate in retrospect the role they were to play in their country's subsequent struggle for democracy.
[12]See Chapter 7. As a result, Catholic leaders, unsullied by any Francoist past, were able to play an active role in the transition to democracy, serving as a 'bridge' between radicals and conservatives.

darmes and special units formed to fight terrorists—real and imaginary. The army, largely confined to a ceremonial role, had become risk averse; its traditional conservatism was expressed increasingly in enthusiasm for the return of the monarchy, an identification that was to prove ironically beneficial in the nation's transition to democracy.

The affairs of the country were run by a restricted network of lawyers, Catholic professors and civil servants, many of them with active interests in the private companies favoured by their policies. But because formal political opposition was banned, it was from inside these same ruling circles—rather than amongst an intelligentsia whose leading lights remained in exile—that reforming ideas and pressure for change would come, prompted by frustration at local inefficiency, foreign criticism or the example of Vatican II.

Franco finally died on November 20th 1975, aged 82. Refusing to the end to consider any serious liberalizations or transfer of authority, he had already outlived his usefulness even to his own supporters, many of whom sympathized with demonstrators who earlier in the year had demanded a lifting of restrictions on the press and political associations. The transition to democracy was thus managed from within the ranks of Franco's own ministers and appointees, which helps account for its speed and success. In the initial stages of Spain's exit from Francoism the traditional forces of democratic change in Spain—liberals, Socialists, Communists, trade unions—played a subordinate role.

Two days after Franco died, Juan Carlos was crowned king. Initially he kept on Carlos Arias Navarro, Franco's last Prime Minister, together with his cabinet colleagues, the better to reassure the army and others that there would be no sudden breach with the past. But in April 1976 Arias incurred royal disfavor when he clamped down on the newly-formed Democratic Coordination, a coalition of still-unauthorized parties of the Left, and arrested its leaders. Within two months the king had replaced Arias with one of his own ministers, Adolfo Suárez González.

At forty four, Suárez was a typical late-Franco era technocrat; indeed, he had served for one year as the head of the Caudillo's own Falangist National Movement. Suárez proved a remarkably astute choice. He formed a new political party, the Center Democratic Union (UCD) and set about persuading the sitting Francoist assembly to accept a national referendum on political reform—essentially, to approve the introduction of universal suffrage and a bi-cameral parliament. Wrong-footed by someone they had supposed to be one of their own, the Francoist old guard agreed—and the referendum passed, on December 15th 1976, with over 94 percent in favor.

In February 1977 Suárez authorized the return of the Spanish Socialist Party (PSOE), the country's oldest political organization, now led by the young Felipe González Márquez from Seville, active in the clandestine movement since his early twenties. At the same time trade unions were legalized and accorded the right to strike. On April 1st Suárez banned and dismantled the National Movement he had once led; a week later he legalized the Spanish Communist Party (PCE), led by Santiago Carrillo and already committed (in striking contrast to its Portuguese comrades) to operating within the confines of a transition to parliamentary democracy.[13]

In June 1977 elections were held to form a Constituent Assembly with the task of writing a new Constitution. The election—the first in Spain since 1936—produced a plurality for Suárez's UCD, which won 165 seats in the Cortes; the second-placed party, González's Socialists, managed just 121, all the other contenders between them taking just 67.[14] In many ways this was the best possible outcome: Suárez's victory reassured conservatives (most of whom had voted for him) that there would be no sharp lurch to the Left, while the absence of a clear majority obliged him to work with Left-wing deputies who thus shared responsibility for the new Constitution that the new Assembly was to draft.

This Constitution (duly confirmed in a second referendum in December 1978) was in most respects quite conventional. Spain was to be a parliamentary monarchy; there was to be no official religion (though in a calculated concession to the Church, Catholicism was recognized as a 'social fact'); the voting age was reduced to eighteen; and the death penalty was abolished. But in a major break with the recent past, the Assembly wrote into Spain's new laws a right of autonomy for the country's historic regions, notably Catalonia and the Basque country.

Article Two of the Constitution affirmed 'the indissoluble unity of the Spanish Nation, common and indivisible *patria* of all Spaniards', but went on to 'recognize and guarantee the right to autonomy of the nationalities and regions that compose it and the solidarity among them all.' The subsequent Statutes of Autonomy acknowledged the ancient fact of linguistic variety and regional sentiment within Spain's hitherto ultra-centralized state; they also recognized the disproportionate demographic significance of Catalonia in particular, and the depth of autonomist sentiment in the Basque country and Catalonia alike. But what was granted some Spaniards could hardly be withheld from others. Within four years Spain was to be divided into seventeen self-administering regions, each with its own flag and capital city. Not just Catalans and Basques, but Galicians, Andalusians, Canaries, Valencians, Navarrese and many others were to be recognized as distinct and separate.[15]

Under the new constitution, however, Madrid retained responsibility for defense, justice and foreign affairs, an unacceptable compromise for Basque nationalists especially. As we have seen, ETA had deliberately stepped up its campaign of violence and assassinations in the months when the new constitution was under dis-

---

[13]One month *before* it was declared legal, the PCE hosted in Madrid a public meeting of the Eurocommunist parties of Western Europe.
[14]The socio-geographical breakdown of the 1977 vote was uncannily close to that of the elections of 1936—the country's political culture had in effect been placed in cold storage for four decades.
[15]Article 151 of the Constitution offered 'home rule' to any region requesting it.

cussion, targeting policemen and soldiers in the hope of provoking a backlash and bringing down a democratic process that seemed increasingly likely to weaken the extremists' case.

In 1981 they might have succeeded. On January 29th, with economic discontent at its peak (see below) and Catalonia, the Basque region, Galicia and Andalucia all embarking upon separatist experiments in home rule, Suárez was forced to resign by his own party—resentful not at his failures (the 1979 general elections under the new constitution had produced another victory for the UCD) but at his achievements—and his autocratic management style. Before another UCD politician, Calvo Sotelo, could succeed him in office, a general strike broke out in the Basque Provinces. To its critics on the Right, democratic Spain appeared leaderless and on the verge of breaking up.

On February 23rd Lt. Colonel Antonio Tejero Molín Molina of the Civil Guard seized the Cortes at gunpoint. In a coordinated move, General Jaime Milans del Bosch, commander of the Valencia military region, declared a state of emergency and called upon the King to dissolve the Cortes and install a military government. Though in retrospect their actions appear theatrical and bumbling, Tejero and Milans del Bosch surely had tradition and precedent on their side. Moreover there was little the Cortes itself, or the various political parties and their supporters, could have done to block a military coup d'état, and the sympathies of the army itself were far from certain.[16]

What determined the outcome, and the shape of subsequent Spanish history, were King Juan Carlos I's outright rejection of the conspirators' demands and his televised speech uncompromisingly defending the Constitution and unambiguously identifying himself and the monarchy with the country's emerging democratic majority. Both sides were probably equally surprised by the courage of a young king who until then had lived in the shadow of his own appointment by the late dictator; but now his fate was irrevocably linked with parliamentary rule. Lacking an institution or a symbol around which to rally their forces, most of those policemen, soldiers and others nostalgic for the old regime turned away from dreams of revolt or restitution and confined themselves instead to supporting Manuel Fraga's Popular Alliance, a newly-formed party committed to fighting 'the most dangerous enemies of Spain: Communism and separatism', but within the law.

The discredit that Tejero had brought on his 'cause' initially afforded an opportunity for the Cortes to cut the military budget and pass a long-overdue bill legalizing divorce. But the UDC majority was increasingly caught between a clericalist and nationalist Right that was unhappy at the speed of change, disturbed by regional autonomy and offended by the relaxed public morals of the new Spain, and a newly assertive Socialist Left, open to compromise on constitutional affairs but

---

[16]There were to be two further plots against king and parliament, in 1982 and 1985, both easily foiled.

presenting a radical face to the country's fractious labor movement and the growing number of unemployed.

As in Portugal, the political transition had come at a difficult economic moment. In large measure this was the responsibility of the last governments of the Franco era, who between 1970 and 1976 had sought to buy popularity by increasing public spending and public sector employment, subsidizing energy costs, holding back prices while letting wages rise, and paying little attention to the long term. By 1977 the consequences of this insouciance were beginning to be felt: in June of that year, at the time of the general election, inflation was running at 26 percent per annum, the state coffers (long starved by Franco's regressive tax regime) were drying up and unemployment was entering a long upward curve. Between 1973 and 1982 the country lost an estimated 1.8 million jobs.[17]

As in the short-lived Republic of the 1930s, Spain was building a democracy in the teeth of an economic recession, and there was much talk of the country going the way of Argentina, with indexed wages and government-subsidized prices degenerating into hyper-inflation. If this was averted, much of the credit must go to the signatories of the so-called Moncloa Pacts of October 1977, the first in a series of negotiated settlements in which politicians, labour leaders and employers agreed to embark upon a broad range of reforms: devaluation of the currency, an incomes policy, controls on government expenditure and structural reforms of the country's huge and wasteful public sector.

The Moncloa Pacts and their successors (the last accord was signed in 1984) worked no miracles. Thanks in part to the second oil shock, the country's balance of payments crisis steadily worsened; many smaller firms folded, and unemployment and inflation rose in tandem, provoking a wave of strikes as well as bitter schisms within the left-wing unions and the Communist Party, reluctant to continue sharing responsibility for the social costs of democratic transition. But without the Pacts these divisions, and their social consequences, would almost certainly have been more severe still.

In the elections of October 1982, at the height of the economic difficulties, the Socialist Party won an absolute majority in the parliament and Felipe González took over as Prime Minister, a post he would hold for the next fourteen years. Suárez's Center Democrats—who had led the transition out of Francoism—were all but eliminated from parliament, winning just two seats. The Communist Party won four, a humiliating defeat that provoked the resignation of Santiago Carrillo. Henceforth Spanish politics were to follow the pattern of the rest of western Europe, regrouping around a center-Left and a center-Right, in this case Fraga's Pop-

---

[17]By the mid-Eighties official unemployment data suggest that more than one in five of the working-age population was out of work. The real figure was probably closer to one in four. In a country still lacking a fully functioning social safety net and where few people had private savings, these figures indicate widespread hardship.

ular Alliance (renamed the People's Party in 1989) which won a surprising 26.5 percent of the vote.

The Socialist Party had campaigned on a populist and anti-capitalist program, promising among other things to preserve workers' jobs and spending power and get Spain out of NATO. Once in power, however, González maintained policies of economic austerity, began the modernization (and later the progressive privatization) of Spanish industry and services, and in 1986 defeated many of his own supporters in a referendum on the question of NATO membership, which he now favored.[18]

These reversals of direction did not endear González to old-line Socialists, whose Party he was now leading away from its longstanding Marxist commitment.[19] But for a politician whose core support came increasingly from men and women too young to remember the Civil War, and whose openly-avowed goal was to overcome Spain's backwardness—the much-debated *atraso* or 'lag' that had afflicted the Peninsula since the end of the Golden Age—the old ideological Left was part of the problem, not the solution. In González's estimation, Spain's future lay not in socialism but in Europe. On January 1st 1986 Spain, accompanied by Portugal, took up full membership of the European Community.

The democratic transition of Mediterranean Europe was quite the most remarkable and unexpected development of the age. By the early eighties, Spain, Portugal and Greece had not merely undergone peaceful conversion to parliamentary democracy: in all three countries the local Socialist Party—clandestine and ostentatiously anti-capitalist just a few years earlier—was now the dominant political force, governing in effect from the center. The regimes of Salazar and Franco disappeared not just from office but from memory, as a new generation of politicians competed for the allegiance of a youthful, 'modern' electorate.

There were several reasons for this. One, already noted, was that in Spain in particular it was the political state, not society at large, which had fallen so very far behind. The economic development of Franco's last decade, and the large-scale social and geographical mobility that it brought about, meant that daily life and expectations in Spain had changed far more than outside observers supposed, who still looked at the country through the prism of the years 1936–56. Young people in Mediterranean Europe did not find it difficult to adapt to social routines long familiar further north; indeed, they were already doing so before the political revolutions. Impatient to be released from the constrictions of another age, they were

---

[18]In 1982, the PSOE campaigned on the slogan 'OTAN, de entrada no!' Four years later, their posters read 'OTAN, de entrada si!'

[19]The traditional Socialist platform of nationalization hardly applied in Spain, where the authoritarian state already owned much of the official economy.

distinctly skeptical of the political rhetoric of Right or Left and unmoved by old loyalties. Visitors to Lisbon or Madrid in the post-transition years were consistently taken aback at the absence of any reference to the recent past, whether in politics or culture.[20]

The coming irrelevance of the 1930s was presciently captured in *La Guerre Est Finie* (The War Is Over), Alain Resnais's sad, elegiac film of 1966 in which the émigré Spanish Communist Diego—portrayed by the incomparable Yves Montand—travels clandestinely from Paris to Madrid, courageously conveying subversive literature and plans for a 'workers' uprising' that he knows will never happen. 'Don't you understand?' he tries to tell his Paris-based Party controllers, who dream of a revival of the hopes of 1936. 'Spain has become the lyrical rallying point of the Left, a myth for veterans of past wars. Meanwhile 14 million tourists vacation in Spain every year. The reality of the world resists us.' It is not by chance that the screenplay for the film was the work of Jorge Semprun, for many decades a clandestine Spanish Communist operative himself before quitting the Party in dismay at its blinkered nostalgia.

By the early Eighties the reluctance of young Spaniards in particular to dwell on the recent past was unmistakable, notably in the ostentatious rejection of old codes of public behavior: in language, in clothing, and above all in sexual *mores*. The popular films of Pedro Almodóvar offer a sort of self-conscious inversion of fifty years of fusty authoritarian rule, a potted exercise in the new counter-cultural conventions. Directed with a cunning, existentialist wink at their subject matter, they typically depict bewildered young women in sexually charged circumstances. In *Pepi, Luci, Bom y otras chicas del montón* (*Pepi, Luci, Bom and Other Girls on the Heap*, 1980), produced just three years after the country's first free elections, the characters laugh knowingly about 'general erections' and the 'war of eroticism that is engulfing us'.

Two years later, in *Laberinto de pasiones* ('Labyrinth of Passion'), camp terrorists and nymphomaniacs exchange scatological banter, debating at one point whether their 'gay little affairs' should come before or after 'a nation's future.' With each film the settings become glossier, the urban locations ever more chic. By 1988, with *Mujeres al borde de un ataque de nervios* (*Women on the Verge of a Nervous Breakdown*), Almodóvar had achieved a convincing cinematic encapsulation of a hectic and self-consciously *modern* society desperately making up for lost time.[21]

It is all the more ironic that these changes were made possible not by cultural or political radicals and innovators but by conservative statesmen from the old regime itself. Constantine Karamanlis, António de Spínola and Adolfo Suárez—like

---

[20]Spain's new constitution of 1978, whose design was aimed above all at reconciling the antagonistic poles of Spanish history—Left/Right; Church/anti-clericals; center/periphery—was conspicuously silent about the regime it replaced.

[21]His films—most recently *La Mala educación* (*Bad Education*, 2004)—were also quite pointedly anti-clerical; perhaps the one respect in which Almodóvar remains consistently faithful to an older tradition of Spanish cultural dissidence.

Mikhail Gorbachev a few years later—were all characteristic products of the system they helped dismantle. Karamanlis, it is true, had been in exile during the colonels' rule; but he was as irreproachably nationalist and narrow-minded as anyone and, furthermore, he bore direct responsibility for the tainted Greek elections of 1961 that played so central a role in discrediting the post-war system and bringing the army to power.

But it was the very reassurance that such men held out to their own constituency that allowed them to dismantle the authoritarian institutions they had once loyally served. And they, in turn, were succeeded by Socialists—Soáres, González, Papandreou—who convincingly reassured their own supporters of their unbroken radical credentials while implementing moderate and often unpopular economic policies forced upon them by circumstances. The transition, in the words of one eminent Spanish commentator, 'required Francoists to pretend they had never been Francoists, and left-wing compromisers to pretend they were still committed to leftist principles'.[22]

The circumstances of the time thus obliged many to abjure virtually overnight long-held positions of principle. The familiar odour of judiciously broken promises and conveniently misplaced memories hung heavy over Mediterranean public life in these years and must go some way to explain the skeptical, apolitical mood of a new generation in all three countries. But those who clung faithfully and unrepentantly to past commitments, from Communists to Falangists, were rapidly overtaken by events. Constancy was no substitute for relevance.

Finally, Spain, Portugal and Greece were able to enter or re-enter the 'West' with such little difficulty, despite their self-imposed political isolation, because their foreign policies had always been compatible—indeed, aligned—with those of NATO or the EEC states. The institutions of the Cold War, not to speak of a common anti-Communism, had facilitated growing communication and collaboration between pluralist democracies and military or clericalist dictatorships. After many years spent meeting, negotiating, planning or just doing business with their unelected counterparts, North Americans and West Europeans had long ceased to take active offence at domestic arrangements in Madrid or Athens or Lisbon.

To most onlookers—including many of their local critics—the unpleasant regimes of southern Europe were thus not so much morally bankrupt as institutionally anachronistic. And, of course, their economies were in essential respects similar to those of other Western nations and already well integrated into international markets for money, goods and labour. Even Salazar's Portugal was recognizably a part of the international system of capitalism—albeit on the wrong end of it. The emerging middle class, in Spain especially, modeled its ambitions no less than its dress upon managers, businessmen, engineers, politicians and civil servants

---

[22]Victor Perez-Diaz, *Spain at the Crossroads. Civil Society, Politics and the Rule of Law* (Cambridge, MA, 1999), p.65

from France or Italy or Britain. For all their backwardness, the societies of Mediterranean Europe already belonged in a world they now aspired to join on equal terms, and the transition out of authoritarian rule was above all facilitated by the opportunity afforded them to do so. Their élites, who had once faced resolutely backward, now looked north. Geography, it appeared, had triumphed over history.

Between 1973 and 1986 the European Community passed through one of its periodic bursts of activism and expansion, what one historian has called its 'sequence of irregular big bangs.' French President Georges Pompidou, released by De Gaulle's death from the mortgage of his patron's disapproval—and more than a little perturbed, as we have seen, by the strategic implications of Willy Brandt's new *Ostpolitik*—made it clear that he would welcome Great Britain's membership of the EC. In January 1972, in Brussels, the EC formally approved the accession of Britain, Ireland, Denmark and Norway, to take effect a year later.

The successful British application was the work of the Conservative Prime Minister Edward Heath, the only British political leader since World War Two unambiguously and enthusiastically in favor of joining his nation's fate to that of its continental neighbors. When the Labour Party returned to office in 1974 and called a referendum on UK membership of the Community, the country approved by 17,300,000 to 8,400,000. But even Heath could not make the British—the English especially—'feel' European, and a significant share of voters on Right and Left alike continued to doubt the benefits of being 'in Europe'. The Norwegians, meanwhile, were quite distinctly of the view that they were better off outside: in a referendum in September 1972, 54 percent of the country rejected EC membership and opted instead for a limited free-trade agreement with the Community, a decision reconfirmed in an almost identical vote twenty two years later.[23]

British membership of the Community would prove controversial in later years, when Prime Minister Margaret Thatcher opposed the emerging projects for ever-closer union and demanded that Britain be refunded her 'overpayments' to the common budget. But in the Seventies London had problems of its own and, despite the price-inflationary impact of membership, was relieved to be part of a trading area that now supplied one third of Britain's inward investment. The first direct elections to a new European Parliament were held in 1979—until then, members of the European Assembly sitting in Strasbourg had been selected by the respective national legislatures—but aroused little popular interest. In the UK the

---

[23]On both occasions the capital, Oslo, voted heavily in favor. But the decision was carried by an anti-European coalition of radicals, environmentalists, 'linguistic nationalists' and farmers from the country's coastal and northern provinces, along with fishermen vehemently opposed to the EEC's restriction of the exclusive coastal fishing zone to just twelve miles. Denmark's entry also brought in Greenland, at the time still governed from Copenhagen. But after Greenland achieved self-rule in 1979, a referendum was called in which the country voted to leave the EEC, the only member-state ever to do so.

turnout was predictably low, just 31.6 percent; but then it was not especially high elsewhere—in France only three out of five electors bothered to vote, in the Netherlands even fewer.

The adhesion of three 'northern tier' countries to the EC was relatively unproblematic for newcomers and old members alike. Ireland was poor but tiny, while Denmark and the UK were wealthy and thus net contributors to the common budget. Like the next round of prosperous additions, in 1995, when Austria, Sweden and Finland joined what was by then the European Union, the new participants added to the coffers and clout of the expanding community without significantly increasing its costs, or competing in sensitive areas with existing members. The newcomers from the South were a different matter.

Greece, like Ireland, was small and poor and its agriculture posed no threat to French farmers. Thus despite certain institutional impediments—the Orthodox Church had official and influential standing and civil marriage, to take one example, was not permitted until 1992—there were no powerful arguments against its admission, which was championed by French President Giscard d'Estaing among others. But when it came to Portugal and (above all) Spain, the French put up strong opposition. Wine, olive oil, fruit and other farm products cost far less to grow and market south of the Pyrenees; were Spain and Portugal to be admitted to the common European market on equal terms, the Iberian farmers would offer French producers stiff competition.

Thus it took nine years for Portugal and Spain to gain entry to the EC (whereas Greece's application went through in less than six), during which time the public image of France, traditionally positive in the Iberian peninsula, fell steeply: by 1983, two-thirds of the way through an acrimonious series of negotiations, only 39 percent of Spaniards had a 'favorable' view of France—an inauspicious beginning to their common future. Part of the problem was that the arrival of the Mediterranean nations entailed more than simply compensating Paris with a further increase in the Community's support payments to French farmers; between them Spain, Portugal and Greece brought an additional 58 million people into the Community, most of them poor and thus eligible for a variety of Brussels-funded programs and subsidies.[24]

Indeed, with the accession of three poor, agrarian countries, the Common Agricultural Fund took on heavy new burdens—and France ceased to be its main beneficiary. Various carefully negotiated deals had thus to be reached to compensate the French for their 'losses'. The newcomers in turn were duly compensated for their own disadvantages and for the long 'transition period' which France succeeded in imposing before allowing their exports into Europe on equal terms. The 'Integrated Mediterranean Programs'—regional subsidies in fact if not yet in name—that were provided to Spain and Portugal upon entry in 1986 had not been

---

[24]This was offset, however, by new investment opportunities for the private sector: the proportion of foreign-owned shares in Spanish companies rose 374 percent in the years 1983–1992.

offered to the Greeks in 1981, and Andreas Papandreou successfully demanded their extension to his country, even threatening to take Greece out of the EC if this was denied![25]

It was in these years, then, that the European Community acquired its unflattering image as a sort of institutionalized cattle market, in which countries trade political alliances for material reward. And the rewards were real. The Spanish and Portuguese did well enough out of 'Europe' (though not as well as France), Spanish negotiators becoming notably adept at advancing and securing their country's financial advantage. But it was Athens that really cleaned up: despite initially falling behind the rest of the Community in the course of the Eighties (and replacing Portugal as the Community's poorest member by 1990), Greece profited greatly from its membership.

Indeed, it was *because* Greece was so poor—by 1990 half of the European Community's poorest regions were Greek—that it did so well. For Athens, EC membership amounted to a second Marshall Plan: in the years 1985–1989 alone, Greece received $7.9 billion from EC funds, proportionately more than any other country. So long as there were no other poor countries waiting in line, this level of redistributive generosity—the price of Greek acquiescence in Community decisions—could be absorbed by the Community's national paymasters, chiefly West Germany. But with the costly unification of Germany and the prospect of a new pool of indigent applicant-states from Eastern Europe, the generous precedents of the Mediterranean accession years would prove burdensome and controversial, as we shall see.

The bigger it grew, the harder the European Community was to manage. The unanimity required in the inter-governmental Council of Ministers ushered in interminable debates. Decisions could take years to be agreed—one directive on the definition and regulation of mineral water took eleven years to emerge from the Council chambers. Something had to be done. There was a longstanding consensus that the European 'project' needed an infusion of purpose and energy—a conference at The Hague back in 1969 was the first of an irregular series of meetings intended to 're-launch Europe'—and the personal friendship of France's President Valéry Giscard d'Estaing and German Chancellor Schmidt in the years 1975–1981 favored such an agenda.

But it was easier to advance by negative economic integration—removing tariffs and trade restrictions, subsidizing disadvantaged regions and sectors—than to agree on purposeful criteria requiring positive *political* action. The reason was simple enough. So long as there was sufficient cash to go around, economic cooperation could be presented as a net benefit to all parties; whereas any political move in the direction of European integration or coordination implicitly threatened na-

---

[25]More than one influential voice was raised in Brussels entreating the European Commission to call his bluff . . .

tional autonomy and restricted domestic political initiative. Only when powerful leaders of dominant states agreed for reasons of their own to work together toward some common purpose could change be brought about.

Thus it was Willy Brandt and Georges Pompidou who had launched the first system of monetary coordination, the 'Snake'; Helmut Schmidt and Giscard d'Estaing who developed it into the European Monetary System (EMS); and Helmut Kohl and François Mitterrand, their respective successors, who would mastermind the Maastricht Treaty of 1992 that gave birth to the European Union. It was Giscard and Schmidt, too, who invented 'summit diplomacy' as a way to circumvent the impediments of a cumbersome supranational bureaucracy in Brussels—a further reminder that, as in the past, Franco-German cooperation was the necessary condition for the unification of Western Europe.

The impulse behind Franco-German moves in the Seventies was economic anxiety. The European economy was growing slowly if at all, inflation was endemic and the uncertainty resulting from the collapse of the Bretton Woods system meant that exchange rates were volatile and unpredictable. The Snake, the EMS and the *écu* were a sort of second-best—because regional rather than international—response to the problem, serially substituting the *Deutschmark* for the dollar as the stable currency of reference for European bankers and markets. A few years later the replacement of national currencies by the *euro*, for all its disruptive symbolic implications, was the logical next step. The ultimate emergence of a single European currency was thus the outcome of pragmatic responses to economic problems, not a calculated strategic move on the road to a pre-determined European goal.

Nevertheless, by convincing many observers—notably hitherto skeptical Social Democrats—that economic recovery and prosperity could no longer be achieved at a national level alone, the successful monetary collaboration of Western European states served as an unexpected stepping stone to other forms of collective action. With no powerful constituency opposed in principle, the Community's heads of state and government signed a Solemn Declaration in 1983 committing them to a future European *Union*. The precise shape of such a Union was then hammered out in the course of negotiations leading to a Single European Act (SEA) which was approved by the European Council in December 1985 and entered into force in July 1987.

The SEA was the first significant revision of the original Rome Treaty. Article One stated clearly enough that 'The European Communities and European political cooperation shall have as their objective to contribute together to making concrete progress towards European unity'. And merely by replacing 'Community' with 'Union' the leaders of the twelve member nations took a decisive step forward in principle. But the signatories avoided or postponed all truly controversial business, notably the growing burden of the Union's agricultural budget. They also stepped cautiously around the embarrassing absence of any common European policy on defense and foreign affairs. At the height of the 'new Cold War' of the

1980s, and on the verge of momentous developments unfolding a few dozen miles to their East, the member states of the European Union kept their eyes resolutely fixed upon the internal business of what was still primarily a common market, albeit one encompassing well over 300 million people.

What they did agree on, however, was to move purposefully towards a genuine single internal market in goods and labour (to be implemented by 1992), and to adopt a system of 'qualified majority voting' in the Union's decision-making process—'qualified', that is, by the insistence of the bigger members (notably Britain and France) that they retain the power to block proposals deemed harmful to their national interest. These were real changes, and they could be agreed to because a single market was favored in principle by everyone from Margaret Thatcher to the Greens, albeit for rather different reasons. They facilitated and anticipated the genuine economic integration of the next decade.

A retreat from the system of national vetoes in the European Council was unavoidable if any decisions were to be taken by an increasingly cumbersome community of states that had doubled its size in just thirteen years and was already anticipating applications for membership from Sweden, Austria and elsewhere. The larger it grew, the more attractive—and somehow 'inevitable'—the future European Union would become to those not yet inside it. To citizens of its member-states, however, the most significant feature of the European Union in these years was not the way in which it was governed (about which most of its people remained entirely ignorant), nor its leaders' projects for closer integration, but the amount of money flowing through its coffers and the way that money was disbursed.

The original Treaty of Rome contained only one agency with a specific remit to identify regions within its member states that needed assistance and then dispense Community cash to them: the European Investment Bank, initiated at Italy's insistence. But a generation later regional expenditures, in the form of cash subsidies, direct aid, start-up funds and other investment incentives were the leading source of budgetary expansion in Brussels and by far the most influential lever at the Community's disposal.

The reason for this was the confluence of regionalist politics *within* the separate member states and growing economic disparities *between* the states themselves. In the initial post-WWII years, European states were still unitary, governed from the center with little regard for local variety or tradition. Only the new Italian constitution of 1948 even acknowledged the case for regional authorities; and even so, the limited local governments that it stipulated remained a dead letter for a quarter of a century. But just when local demands for autonomy became a serious factor in domestic political calculations all over Europe, the EC for its own reasons inaugurated a system of regional funds, beginning in 1975 with the European Regional Development Fund (ERDF).

From the point of view of Brussels-based officials, the ERDF and other so-called 'structural funds' had two purposes. The first was to address the problem of economic backwardness and unevenness within a Community that was still very much guided by a post-war culture of 'growth', as the Single European Act made quite explicit. With each new group of members came new inequalities that required attention and compensation if economic integration was to succeed. Italy's *Mezzogiorno* was no longer the only impoverished zone, as it had once been: most of Ireland; parts of Great Britain (Ulster, Wales, Scotland and the north and west of England); most of Greece and Portugal; southern, central and north-western Spain: all were poor and would need significant subsidies and reallocations of central aid if they were ever to catch up.

In 1982, taking the European Community's average income as 100, Denmark— the wealthiest member—stood at 126, Greece at just 44. By 1989 per capita GDP in Denmark was still more than twice that of Portugal (in the US, the gap between wealthy and poor states was only two-thirds as wide). And these were national averages—regional disparities were greater still. Even wealthy countries had deserving zones: when Sweden and Finland joined the Union in the mid 1990s, their Arctic regions, under-populated and totally dependent on maintenance grants and other subsidies from Stockholm and Helsinki, now qualified for assistance from Brussels too. To correct geographical and market deformations that locked Spain's Galicia or Sweden's Vasterbotten into dependency, agencies in Brussels would devote large amounts of cash—bringing undoubted local benefits but also setting up expensive, cumbersome and occasionally corrupt local bureaucracies in the process.[26]

The second motive behind Europe's enormously costly regional funding projects—between them the various 'Structural' and 'Cohesion' Funds would consume 35 percent of all EU expenditure by the end of the century—was to enable the European Commission in Brussels to bypass uncooperative central governments and collaborate directly with regional interests within the member-states. This strategy proved very successful. Ever since the late 1960s, regionalist sentiment had been growing (in some cases reviving) everywhere. *Quondam* 1968 activists, substituting regional affinity for political dogma, now sought to revive and use the old Occitan language in south-western France. Like their fellow activists in Brittany they found common cause with Catalan and Basque separatists, Scottish and Flemish nationalists, northern Italian separatists and many others, all expressing a common resentment at 'misrule' from Madrid, or Paris, or London or Rome.

The new regionalist politics fell into many over-lapping sub-categories— historical, linguistic, religious; seeking autonomy, self-government or even full national independence—but generally divided into wealthy provinces, resentful at being obliged to subsidize penurious regions of their own country; and historically

---

[26]Of course the Common Agricultural Policy, the other major charge on the EU budget, had long had the effect of exacerbating the very regional distortions that the Cohesion Funds and others were now supposed to help eliminate . . .

disadvantaged or newly de-industrialized zones, angry at being neglected by unresponsive national politicians. In the first category were to be found Catalonia, Lombardy, Belgian Flanders, West Germany's Baden-Württemburg or Bavaria, and the Rhône-Alpes region of south-east France (which together with the Île-de-France comprised nearly 40 percent of French GDP by 1990). In the second category were Andalusia, much of Scotland, French-speaking Wallonia and many others.

Both categories stood to gain from European regional policies. Wealthy regions like Catalonia or Baden-Württemburg set up offices in Brussels and learned how to lobby on their own behalf, for investment or for Community policies favoring local over national institutions. Political representatives from disadvantaged regions were just as quick to manipulate grants and aid from Brussels to increase their local popularity—and thereby pressure compliant authorities in Dublin or London into encouraging and even supplementing Brussels' largesse. These arrangements suited everyone: European coffers might hemorrhage millions to subsidize tourism in the depopulated West of Ireland or to underwrite tax-incentives to attract investors to areas of chronic unemployment in Lorraine or Glasgow; but even if only from enlightened self-interest, the beneficiaries were becoming loyal 'Europeans'. Ireland successfully replaced or updated much of its dilapidated transport and sewerage infrastructure in this way, and among poorer, peripheral member states it was not alone.[27]

The SEA expanded Community powers into many policy areas—the environment, employment practices, local research-and-development initiatives—in which the EC had not previously been involved, all of which entailed the dispensing of Brussels funds directly to local agencies. This cumulative 'regionalization' of Europe was bureaucratic and costly. To take one tiny example that can stand for hundreds: Italy's Alto Adige/South Tyrol region, on the country's northern frontier with Austria, was officially classified by Brussels in 1975 as 'mountainous' (an uncontentious claim); thirteen years later it was officially declared to be over 90 percent 'rural' (no less self-evident to any casual traveler), or—in Brussels jargon—an 'Objective 5–b Area'. In this dual capacity the Alto Adige was now eligible for environmental protection funds; grants to support agriculture; grants to improve vocational training; grants to encourage traditional handicrafts; and grants to ameliorate living conditions in order to retain population.

Accordingly, between 1993 and 1999 the tiny Alto Adige received a total of 96 million *écus* (worth roughly the same amount in 2005 euros). In the so-called 'Third Period' of European structural funding, scheduled to run from 2000–2006, a further 57 million euros were to be put at the province's disposal. Under 'Objective

---

[27]Richer countries were typically less beholden to Brussels and maintained closer control of their affairs. In France, despite the 'decentralization' enshrined in laws passed during the 1980s, the reins of budgetary power stayed firmly in Parisian hands. As a result, prosperous regions of France followed the international trend and benefited from their EU links, but poor districts remained dependent on state aid above all.

Two' these monies were to be disbursed for the sole benefit of the 83,000 residents who lived in 'exclusively' mountainous or 'rural' zones. Since 1990, a government department in Bolzano, the provincial capital, has been devoted exclusively to instructing local residents how to benefit from 'Europe' and European resources. Since 1995 the Province has also maintained an office in Brussels (shared with the neighboring Italian Trentino province and the Austrian region of Tyrol). The official website of the Province of Bolzano (available in Italian, German, English, French and Ladino, a variety of the Swiss *Romansch* dialect) is enthusiastically Europhile, as well it might be.

The result, in the South Tyrol as elsewhere, was that—costly or not—integrating the continent 'from the bottom up', as its advocates insisted, did seem to work. When the 'Council [later the Assembly] of European regions' was launched in 1985 it already comprised 107 member regions, with many more to come. A certain sort of united Europe was indeed beginning to come into focus. Regionalism, once the affair of a handful of linguistic recidivists or nostalgic folklorists, was now offered as an alternate, 'sub-national' identity: displacing the nation itself and all the more legitimate in that it came with the *imprimatur* of official approval from Brussels and even—albeit with distinctly less enthusiasm—from national capitals as well.

The residents of this increasingly parceled Community, whose citizens now professed multiple elective allegiances of variable cultural resonance and daily significance, were perhaps less unambiguously 'Italian' or 'British' or 'Spanish' than in decades past; but they did not necessarily therefore feel more 'European', despite the steady proliferation of 'European' labels and elections and institutions. The lush undergrowth of agencies, media, institutions, representatives and funds brought many benefits but won scant affection. One reason was perhaps the very abundance of official outlets for disbursing and overseeing the administration of European largesse: the already complex machinery of modern state government, its ministries and commissions and directorates, was now doubled and even tripled from above (Brussels) and below (the province or region).

The outcome was not just bureaucracy on an unprecedented scale but also corruption, induced and encouraged by the sheer volume of funding available, much of it requiring the exaggeration and even invention of local needs and thus all but inviting the sorts of venal, local abuses that passed unnoticed by the Community's managers in Brussels but risked discrediting their enterprise even in the eyes of its beneficiaries. Between a reputation for policy-making by distant unelected civil servants, and well-stocked rumors of political back-scratching and profiteering, 'Europe' in these years was not well served by its own achievements.

The familiar shortcomings of local politics—clientelism, corruption, manipulation—that the better-run nation states were thought to have overcome now resurfaced on a continental scale. Public responsibility for occasional 'Euroscandals' was prudently shifted by national politicians onto the shoulders of an invisible class of unelected 'Eurocrats', whose bad name carried no political cost.

Meanwhile the ballooning Community budget was defended by its recipients and promoters in the name of cross-national 'harmonization' or rightful compensation (and fuelled from the Community's seemingly bottomless funds).

'Europe', in short, was coming to represent a significant 'moral hazard', as its carping critics, in Britain in particular, gleefully insisted. The decades-long drive to overcome continental disunity by purely technical measures was looking decidedly political, while lacking the redeeming legitimacy of a traditional political project pursued by an elected class of familiar politicians. Insofar as 'Europe' had a distinctive goal, its economic strategy was still grounded in the calculations and ambitions of the Fifties. As for its politics: the confident, interventionist tone of pronouncements from the European Commission—and the authority and open chequebooks with which European experts descended on distant regions—bespoke a style of government rooted firmly in the social-democratic heyday of the early Sixties.

For all their laudable efforts to transcend the shortcomings of national political calculation, the men and women who were constructing 'Europe' in the Seventies and Eighties were still curiously provincial. Their greatest trans-national achievement of the time, the Schengen Agreement signed in June 1985, is revealingly symptomatic in this respect. Under the terms of this arrangement France, West Germany and the Benelux countries agreed to dismantle their common frontiers and inaugurate a shared regime of passport control. Henceforward it would be easy to cross from Germany to France, just as it had long been unproblematic to move between, say, Belgium and Holland.

But Schengen signatories had to commit themselves in return to ensuring the most stringent visa and customs regimes between themselves and non-participating countries: if the French, for example, were to open their frontiers to anyone crossing from Germany, they had to be sure that the Germans themselves had applied the most stringent criteria at *their* points of entry. In opening the internal frontiers between some EC member states, therefore, the Agreement resolutely reinforced the external borders separating them from outsiders. Civilized Europeans could indeed transcend boundaries—but the 'barbarians' would be kept resolutely beyond them. [28]

---

[28]The 'Schengen zone' has since been expanded to encompass other EU member states, but the UK has remained outside and France, among other participants, has reserved the right to re-impose border controls on security grounds.

XVII

The New Realism

'There is no such thing as Society. There are individual men and women, and there are families'.
Margaret Thatcher

'The French are starting to understand that it is business that creates wealth, determines our standard of living and establishes our place in the global rankings'.
François Mitterrand

'At the end of the Mitterrand experiment, the French Left appeared more devoid of ideas, hopes and support than it has been in its entire history'.
Donald Sassoon

Every politically significant revolution is anticipated by a transformation of the intellectual landscape. The European upheavals of the 1980s were no exception. The economic crisis of the early Seventies undermined the optimism of Western Europe's post-war decades, fracturing conventional political parties and propelling unfamiliar issues to the center of public debate. Political argument on both sides of the Cold War divide was breaking decisively with decades of encrusted mental habits—and, with unexpected speed, forming new ones. For better and for worse, a new realism was being born.

The first victim of the change in mood was the consensus that had hitherto embraced the post-war state, together with the neo-Keynesian economics that furnished its intellectual battlements. By the late 1970s the European welfare state was starting to count the cost of its own success. The post-war baby-boom generation was entering middle age, and government statisticians were already warning of the cost of supporting it in retirement—a problem that loomed closer on the budgetary horizon thanks to widespread reductions in the retirement age. Of West German males aged 60–64, for example, 72 percent were working full time in 1960; twenty years later, only 44 percent of men in this age group were still employed. In the Netherlands the fall was from 81 percent to 58 percent.

Within a few years the largest generational cohort in Europe's recorded history would cease to contribute taxes to the national exchequer and would begin to extract huge sums—whether in the form of guaranteed state pensions or, indirectly but with comparable impact, by making increased demands upon state-maintained medical and social services. Moreover, being also the best-nurtured generation ever, they would almost certainly live longer. And to this concern was now added the growing cost of paying unemployment benefits, by 1980 a major budgetary consideration in every Western European state.

These widespread anxieties were not unfounded. The post-war welfare states rested upon two implicit assumptions: that economic growth and job creation (and thus government income) would continue at the high levels of the fifties and sixties; and that birth-rates would remain well above replacement level, ensuring a ready supply of new tax-payers to pay for their parents'—and grandparents'—retirement. Both assumptions were now open to question, but the demographic miscalculation was the more dramatic of the two. By the beginning of the 1980s, in Western Europe, the population replacement ratio of 2.1 children per woman was being met or exceeded only in Greece and Ireland. In West Germany it stood at 1.4 percent. In Italy it would soon fall lower still: whereas in 1950, 26.1 percent of Italians—more than one in four—was under 14 years old, by 1980 that figure stood at 20 percent, or one in five. By 1990 it would fall to 15 percent, approaching one in seven.[1]

In prosperous Western Europe, then, it appeared that within two decades there would not be enough people around to pay the bills—and prosperity itself seemed to be the culprit, together with reliable contraception and a growing number of women working outside the home.[2] The result was ever higher charges on those in a position to pay. Already the cost of pension and national insurance provision in some places (France, notably) weighed heavily on employers—a serious consideration in a time of endemic high unemployment. But direct charges on the national exchequer were a more immediate concern: as a percentage of GDP, government debt by the mid-1980s was reaching historically high levels—85 percent, in the Italian case. In Sweden, by 1977, one-third of the national product was taken up by social expenditures, a budgetary charge that could only be met either by deficits or else by raising taxes on the very constituencies—employed workers, civil servants and professionals—on whom the Social Democratic consensus had hitherto depended.

Public policy since the 1930s rested on a broadly unquestioned 'Keynesian' consensus. This took for granted that economic planning, deficit financing and full employment were inherently desirable and mutually sustaining. Its critics offered two lines of argument. The first, quite simply, was that the array of social services and provisions to which Western Europeans had become accustomed were not sustainable. The second argument, offered with particular urgency in Britain—where

---

[1] Were it not for the distinctly *upward* curve of the birth rate in immigrant communities from Asia, Africa and the Caribbean, the figures would have been even lower.

[2] In Eastern Europe it was Hungary, where the 'underground' economy (see Chapter 18) furnished many people with a higher standard of living than elsewhere in the Bloc, which first reached comparably low birth-rates in these same years.

the national economy had staggered from crisis to crisis for most of the post-war decades—was that, sustainable or not, the interventionist state was an impediment to economic growth.

The state, these critics insisted, should be removed as far as possible from the market for goods and services. It should not own the means of production, it should not allocate resources, it should not exercise or encourage monopolies, and it should not set prices or incomes. In the view of these 'neo-liberals', most of the services currently furnished by the state—insurance, housing, pensions, health and education—could be provided more efficiently in the private sector, with citizens paying for them out of income no longer (mis-)directed to public resources. In the view of one leading exponent of free-market liberalism, the Austrian economist Friedrich Hayek, even the best-run states are unable to process data effectively and translate it into good policy: in the very act of eliciting economic information they distort it.

These were not new ideas. They were the staple nostrums of an earlier generation of pre-Keynesian liberals, brought up on the free-market doctrines of neo-classical economics. In more recent times they were familiar to specialists from the work of Hayek and his American disciple Milton Friedman. But with the Depression of the 1930s and the demand-led boom of the Fifties and Sixties, such views had been typically dismissed (in Europe at least) as politically myopic and economically anachronistic. Since 1973, however, free-market theorists had re-emerged, vociferous and confident, to blame endemic economic recession and attendant woes upon 'big government' and the dead hand of taxation and planning that it placed upon national energies and initiative. In many places this rhetorical strategy was quite seductive to younger voters with no first-hand experience of the baneful consequences of such views the last time they had gained intellectual ascendancy, half a century before. But only in Britain were the political disciples of Hayek and Friedman able to seize control of public policy and wreak a radical transformation in the country's political culture.

It is more than a little ironic that this should have happened in Britain of all places, for the economy of the UK, though intensively regulated, was perhaps the least 'planned' of any in Europe. There was constant government manipulation of price mechanisms and fiscal 'signals'; but the only ideologically-driven aspect of British economic life were the nationalizations first introduced by the Labour government after 1945. And even though the case for 'state ownership of the means of production, distribution and exchange' (Clause IV of the Labour Party's 1918 constitution) had been retained as Party policy, few of Labour's leaders paid it more than lip service, if that.

The core of Britain's welfare state lay not in economic 'collectivism' but in the country's universalized social institutions, anchored firmly in the early twentieth-century reformism of Keynes's liberal contemporaries. What mattered to most British voters of Left and Right alike was not economic planning or state ownership but free medicine, free public education and subsidized public transport. These facilities were not very good—the cost of running a welfare state in Britain was actually lower than elsewhere, thanks to under-funded services, inadequate public pensions and poor housing provision—but they were widely perceived as an entitlement. However intensely such social goods were condemned by neo-liberal critics as inefficient and under-performing, they remained politically untouchable.

The modern Conservative Party, from Winston Churchill to Edward Heath, had embraced Britain's 'social contract' almost as enthusiastically as the Keynesian 'socialists' of Labour and for many years had kept its feet firmly planted in the middle ground (it was Churchill, after all, who remarked back in March 1943 that 'there is no finer investment for any community than putting milk into babies'). When, in 1970, Edward Heath brought a group of free-marketers together at Selsdon Park near London, to discuss economic strategies for a future Conservative government, his brief and decidedly ambivalent flirtation with their rather moderate proposals brought down upon him a thunderstorm of derisory condemnation. Accused of seeking to return to the Neanderthal primitivism of the economic jungle, 'Selsdon Man' beat a hasty retreat.

If the British political consensus collapsed in the ensuing decade it was not because of ideological confrontation but as a consequence of the continuing failure of governments of *all* colours to identify and impose a successful economic strategy. Starting with the view that Britain's economic woes were the result of chronic under-investment, managerial inefficiency and endemic labour disputes over wages and job demarcation, both Labour and Conservative governments tried to replace the anarchy of British industrial relations with planned consensus along Austro-Scandinavian or German lines—a 'Prices and Incomes Policy' as it was known in Britain, with characteristic empirical minimalism.

They failed. The Labour Party was unable to impose industrial order because its paymasters in the industrial unions preferred nineteenth-century style confrontations on the shop floor—which they stood a good chance of winning—to negotiated contracts signed in Downing Street that would bind their hands for years ahead. The Conservatives, notably Edward Heath's government of 1970–1974, had even less success, largely thanks to the well-founded, historically-engrained suspicion in certain sectors of the British working class—the coalminers above all—of any compromise with Tory ministries. Thus when Heath suggested closing a number of uneconomic coal mines in 1973, and tried to impose legal constraints on the power of trade unions to initiate labour disputes (something the Labour Party had first proposed, then abandoned, a few years before) his government was stymied by a wave of strikes. When he called an election to decide, as he put it, 'who runs the country', he narrowly lost to Harold Wilson, who prudently declined to take up the cudgels himself.

Only under the Labour government of Wilson's successor, James Callaghan, from 1976 to 1979, did a new policy begin to emerge. Driven by desperation and the conditions of an IMF loan, Callaghan and his Chancellor of the Exchequer (the redoubtable Denis Healey) initiated a retreat from the central nostrums of post-war government practice. They embarked on a restructuring program that acknowledged the inevitability of a certain level of unemployment; reduced social transfer payments and labour costs by protecting skilled workers while permitting the emergence of a disfavored periphery of unprotected, non-unionized part-time employees; and set out to control and reduce inflation and government spending even at the price of economic hardship and slower growth.

None of these objectives was openly avowed. The Labour government maintained to the end that it was adhering to its core values and defending the institutions of the welfare state even as it inaugurated a cautiously planned breakout, seeking to achieve by stealth the sorts of reforms that its predecessors had been unable to legislate in the open. The strategy did not work: Labour succeeded only in alienating its own supporters without being able to take any credit for its achievements. By August 1977, thanks in part to the Labour government's deep cuts in public spending, UK unemployment levels had passed 1.6 million and kept on rising. The following year, in Britain's 'Winter of Discontent' of 1978/79, major trade unions undertook a series of angry, concerted strikes against their 'own' government: rubbish went uncollected, the dead were left unburied.[3]

The Prime Minister, James Callaghan, seemed out of touch: in reply to a journalist's question about the growing industrial unrest, he airily announced that there was no need for concern, thereby giving rise to a famous newspaper headline—'Crisis? What Crisis?'—that helped lose him the general election he was forced to hold the following spring. It is more than a little ironic that Labour was constrained to fight the historic election of 1979 on the claim that it had *not* engineered a social crisis by its radical departure from economic convention—when this was exactly what it had done—while the Conservative Party was swept back to power under the energetic leadership of a woman who insisted that it was just such radical treatment that the British malaise required.

Margaret Thatcher was not, on the face of it, a likely candidate for the revolutionary role she was to perform. Born in Grantham, a sleepy, provincial town in Lincolnshire, she was the daughter of an earnest Methodist couple who ran a grocer's shop. She was always a Conservative: her father sat on the local town council as a Conservative; the young Margaret Roberts (as she then was) won a scholarship to Oxford—where she studied chemistry—and rose to be President of the University's Conservative Society. In 1950, at the age of 25, she was an (unsuccessful)

---

[3] The highest level of resentful anger was to be found in the public service unions, covering underpaid government employees from dustmen to nurses. The major *industrial* unions were far more sanguine about Callaghan's cuts: so long as Labour kept its promise to protect the traditional skilled industrial workers and leave their privileges intact, their leaders were pleased to tolerate the government's apostasy. They were rather taken aback to discover that no such deals could be cut with Mrs. Thatcher.

Conservative candidate in the General Elections, the youngest woman candidate in the country. A chemist and subsequently a tax lawyer by profession, she first entered Parliament in 1959, winning a seat in the solidly conservative borough of Finchley which she would continue to represent until she entered the House of Lords in 1992.

Until she successfully beat off much more senior Conservative figures to win her party's leadership in 1975, Margaret Thatcher was best known in Britain as the Education Minister in Heath's Conservative government who, in order to meet budget-cutting targets, abolished the provision of free milk in British schools: a decision (taken reluctantly) that led to the sobriquet 'Maggie Thatcher Milk Snatcher' and gave the first hint of her future trajectory. Yet this decidedly unfavorable public image proved no impediment to Mrs. Thatcher's advance—her willingness to court and confront unpopularity not only did her no harm among colleagues, but may even have been part of her appeal.

And she unquestionably had appeal. Indeed, a surprisingly broad range of hardbitten statesmen in Europe and the United States confessed, albeit off the record, to finding Mrs. Thatcher rather sexy. François Mitterrand, who knew something about such things, once described her as having 'the eyes of Caligula but the mouth of Marilyn Monroe.' She could bully and browbeat with less mercy than any British politician since Churchill, but she also seduced. From 1979 to 1990 Margaret Thatcher bullied, browbeat—and seduced—the British electorate into a political revolution.

'Thatcherism' stood for various things: reduced taxes, the free market, free enterprise, privatization of industries and services, 'Victorian values', patriotism, 'the individual'. Some of these—the economic policies—were an extension of proposals already circulating in Conservative and Labour circles alike. Others, notably the 'moral' themes, were more popular among Conservative Party stalwarts in rural constituencies than with the electorate at large. But they came in the wake of a backlash against the libertarianism of the Sixties and appealed to many of Mrs. Thatcher's admirers in the working- and lower-middle classes: men and women who had never really been comfortable in the company of the progressive intelligentsia that dominated public affairs in these years.

But what Thatcherism stood for more than anything else was the 'smack of firm government'. By the end of the Seventies there was much anxious debate about Britain's purported 'ungovernability', the widely-shared perception that the political class had lost control, not just of economic policy but of the workplace and even the streets. The Labour Party, traditionally vulnerable to the charge that it could not be counted upon to steer the economy, was now open to the accusation, following the 'Winter of Discontent', that it could not even run the state. In their 1979 election campaign, the Tories made great play not just with the need for economic rigour and proper money management, but with the nation's ostensible longing for strong, confident rulers.

Margaret Thatcher's first election victory was not particularly remarkable by historical standards. Indeed, under Mrs. Thatcher's leadership the Conservative Party never actually gained many votes. It did not so much win elections as watch Labour lose them, many Labour voters switching to Liberal candidates or else abstaining altogether. In this light, Margaret Thatcher's radical agenda and determination to see it through can seem out of all proportion to her national mandate, an unexpected and even risky break with the longstanding British tradition of governing from as close to the political centre as possible.

But it seems clear in retrospect that this was just what accounted for Margaret Thatcher's success. Her refusal to be moved even when her monetarist policies were apparently failing (to those Conservatives in October 1980 who begged her to reverse tack and make a U-turn in policy she responded: 'You turn if you want. The lady's not for turning'); her happy adoption of the Soviet description of her as the 'Iron Lady'; her palpable pleasure at engaging and defeating a string of opponents, from the Argentine military junta in the Falklands' War to the miners' union leader Arthur Scargill; the handbag waved aggressively at assembled European Community leaders as she demanded 'our money back': all these suggest a clear appreciation that her primary political asset was the very obstinacy, the obdurate refusal to compromise, that so outraged her critics. As every opinion poll suggested, even those who didn't care for Thatcherite policies often conceded a certain reluctant admiration for the woman herself. The British were once again being *ruled*.

Indeed, and for all her talk of the individual and the market, Margaret Thatcher presided over a remarkable and somewhat disconcerting revival of the British state. In administration she was an instinctive centralizer. To ensure that her writ carried throughout the land, she reduced the powers and budgets of local government (the 1986 Local Government Act dismantled Britain's metropolitan authorities, taking their powers back to London, just as the rest of Europe was engaged in a large-scale *de*centralization of power). The direction of educational policy and regional economic planning reverted to central government departments under direct political control, while government ministries themselves found their traditional freedom of maneuver increasingly constrained by a Prime Minister who depended far more on a small coterie of friends and advisers than on the traditional élite corps of senior civil servants.

Margaret Thatcher instinctively (and correctly) suspected the latter, like their peers in the educational and judicial establishment, of preferring the old state-subsidized paternalism. In the complex conventions of Britain's class-conscious politics, Margaret Thatcher—a lower-middle class upstart with a soft spot for *nouveau riche* businessmen—was not much liked by the country's venerable governing élite and she returned the sentiment with interest. Older Tories were shocked at her unsentimental scorn for tradition or past practice: at the height of the privatization craze, former Prime Minister Harold Macmillan accused her of selling the 'family silver'. Her predecessor, Edward Heath, who had once angrily described the well-publicized undertakings of a corrupt British businessman as 'the unacceptable face of capitalism', abhorred both Thatcher and her policies. She could not have cared less.

The Thatcherite revolution strengthened the state, cultivated the market—and set about dismantling the bonds that had once bound them together. She destroyed forever the public influence exercised by Britain's trade unions, passing laws that limited union leaders' ability to organize strikes, and then getting them enforced in the courts. In a highly symbolic confrontation in 1984–85, pitting the armed state against a doomed community of industrial proletarians, she crushed a violent and emotional effort by the National Union of Miners to break her government's policy of closing inefficient mines and ending subsidies to the coal industry.

The miners were badly led, their cause hopeless, their strike prolonged more from desperation than calculation. But the fact that Margaret Thatcher won a battle that Edward Heath had lost (and that successive Labour leaders had ducked) immensely strengthened her hand—as did an unsuccessful attempt by the Provisional IRA to assassinate her in the midst of the strike. Thatcher, like all the best revolutionaries, was fortunate in her enemies. They allowed her to claim that she alone spoke for the frustrated, over-regulated, little people whom she was freeing from decades of domination by vested interests and by the subsidized, parasitical beneficiaries of taxpayer largesse.

There is no doubt that Britain's economic performance *did* improve in the Thatcher years, after an initial decline from 1979–81. Thanks to a shakeout of inefficient firms, increased competition and the muffling of the unions, business productivity and profits rose sharply. The Treasury was replenished (on a one-time basis) with the proceeds from the sale of nationally-owned assets. This had not been part of the original Thatcher agenda in 1979, nor was privatization as such an ideologically-charged idea—it was the Labour Party, after all, that sold off the nation's share in British Petroleum in 1976 (at the IMF's bidding). But by 1983 the political as well as the financial benefit of liquidating the country's state-owned or state-run assets led the Prime Minister to inaugurate a decade-long national auction, 'liberating' producers and consumers alike.

Everything, or almost everything, was put on the privatization block. In the first round were smaller firms and units, mostly in manufacturing, in which the state held a partial or controlling interest. These were followed by hitherto 'natural' monopolies like the telecommunications network, energy utilities, and air transportation, beginning with the sale of British Telecom in 1984. The government also sold off much of the country's post-war public housing stock: at first to its current occupants but eventually to allcomers. Between 1984 and 1991, one-third of all the world's privatized assets (by value) were accounted for by UK sales alone.

Despite this apparent dismantling of the public sector, the share of Britain's GDP absorbed by public expenditure remained virtually the same in 1988 (41.7 percent) as it had ten years earlier (42.5 percent), notwithstanding Thatcher's promises to 'get the state off people's backs'. This was because the Conservative government had to pay unprecedented sums in unemployment benefit. The 'scandalously' high figure of 1.6 million jobless that had so damaged Callaghan's government in 1977 had reached 3.25 million by 1985 and remained one of the highest in Europe for the rest of Mrs. Thatcher's time in office.

Many of those who lost jobs in inefficient (and previously state-subsidized) industries like steel, coal-mining, textiles and shipbuilding would never find work again, becoming lifelong dependents of the state in all but name. If their former employers went on in some cases (steel, notably) to become profitable private companies it was less through the miracle of private ownership than because Margaret Thatcher's governments had relieved them of high fixed labour costs, 'socializing' the expense of superfluous workers in the form of state-subsidized unemployment.

There was something to be said for the privatization of certain public industries and services. For many years vital economic assets had been held in the public sector with little thought given to investment or modernization. They had been starved of cash, their performance cushioned against pressure from competition and consumer alike, their managers hamstrung by bureaucratic inertia and political meddling.[4] Thanks to Mrs. Thatcher there emerged in Britain a much-expanded market for goods, services and, eventually, labour. There was more choice and (though this took longer and remained imperfect) more price competition. When her successor, John Major, kept Britain out of the 'social chapter' of the European Union treaty, Jacques Delors accused him of having made the UK a 'paradise for foreign investment': a charge to which Thatcherites could justifiably and happily plead guilty.

As an *economy*, then, Thatcherized Britain was a more efficient place. But as a *society* it suffered meltdown, with catastrophic long-term consequences. By disdaining and dismantling all collectively-held resources, by vociferously insisting upon an individualist ethic that discounted any unquantifiable assets, Margaret Thatcher did serious harm to the fabric of British public life. Citizens were transmuted into shareholders, or 'stakeholders', their relationship to one another and to the collectivity measured in assets and claims rather than in services or obligations. With everything from bus companies to electric supply in the hands of competing private companies, the public space became a market place.

If—as Mrs. Thatcher asserted—there is 'no such thing as Society', then in due course people must lose respect for socially-defined goods. And so they did, as late-Thatcherite Britain began to take on some of the more unappealing characteristics of the American model that the Iron Lady so admired. Services that re-

---

[4] In 1996 (its last year of existence) Britain's nationalized railway network 'boasted' the lowest public subsidy for a railway in Europe. In that year the French were planning for their railways an investment rate of £21 per head of population; the Italians £33; the British just £9.

POSTWAR: A HISTORY OF EUROPE SINCE 1945

mained in public hands were starved of resources, while significant wealth accumulated in the 'emancipated' sectors of the economy—notably the City of London, where investment bankers and stockbrokers benefited greatly from the 'Big Bang' of 1986, when Britain's financial markets were deregulated and opened to international competition. Public spaces fell into neglect. Petty crime and delinquency rose in line with the growing share of the population caught in permanent poverty. Private affluence was accompanied, as so often, by public squalor.[5]

But there were limits to Margaret Thatcher's reach. The typical 'Thatcherite' voter—caricatured as a thirty-something realtor in the eastern suburbs of London, under-educated but well-remunerated, with material assets (house, car, foreign vacations, a handful of shares in mutual funds and a private pension scheme) of which his parents could only have dreamed—might have entered the world of Thatcherite individualism. But he and his family were still entirely dependent upon the state for the provision of vital services: free education, virtually free medicine, and subsidized transport. Thus when Mrs. Thatcher and her successor John Major so much as hinted that they might begin privatizing the National Health Service or charging fees for state education, public support evaporated—among precisely those newly-prosperous but highly vulnerable sectors of the population that had been attracted to Thatcherism in the first place.

Five years after Mrs. Thatcher's departure, John Major did indeed succeed in pushing through the privatization of the railway services. The Conservatives were encouraged by the prospect of further profit from the sale of public assets into private ownership; but their chief motive was Major's need to be seen to be privatizing *something*—Mrs. Thatcher had by then sold off just about everything else, and privatization was the Conservative Party's sole and only program. But the incompetence and malfeasance of the procedure, and the disasters that followed—culminating in a series of tragic and palpably avoidable train crashes—helped bring about not just the defeat of the Conservative government two years later, but the end of a cycle of privatizations and the retrospective discrediting of the more extreme incarnations of Thatcherism itself.

Among Margaret Thatcher's chief victims was her very own Conservative Party. By the time the Iron Lady had finished with it, the Tory Party—Britain's 'natural' party of government for nearly a century—had no program, no leaders and, as it appeared to many, no soul. This seems a harsh judgment to make of a woman who led her party to three electoral victories in succession and governed virtually alone for nearly twelve years. But that of course is the point: Margaret Thatcher governed *alone*. In the words of Frederick the Great, 'The people say what they like and then

---

[5] And private poverty, too. By breaking the link between pensions and wages, Thatcher sharply reduced the retirement income of most of her fellow citizens. By 1997 UK public pensions were just 15 percent of average earnings: the lowest ratio in the EU.

I do what I like.' Any colleague who differed from her on any significant issue and who was thus not 'one of us', was cast into the outer darkness.

Most of Mrs Thatcher's Tory contemporaries, not to mention the party's cohort of elder statesmen whom she thrust aside as soon as she dared, were genuine *conservatives*, old enough in many cases to remember the bitter political divisions of the inter-war years and wary of arousing the demon of class warfare. Thatcher was a *radical*, bent upon destruction and innovation; she scorned compromise. For her, class warfare, suitably updated, was the very stuff of politics. Her policies, often dreamed up at very short notice, were secondary to her goals; and these in turn were in large measure a function of her style. Thatcherism was about *how* you govern, rather than what you do. Her unfortunate Conservative successors, cast out upon the blasted landscape of post-Thatcherism, had no policies, no goals—and no style.[6]

Margaret Thatcher may have destroyed the Conservative Party but she must be credited with the salvation and re-birth of Labour. In the short-run, of course, she crushed her Labour opponents—indeed, she could not have wrought the changes she did but for their stunning incompetence. While some Labour Party leaders in 1979 understood the problems they faced, they could carry neither conviction nor their supporters. With Thatcher in power, the British Labour movement entered a decade of turmoil. The party's militant and unionist core saw the world much as Mrs. Thatcher did, but from the other side of the mirror: Britain must choose between a protectionist, collectivist, egalitarian, regulatory state and open markets, untrammeled competition, privatized resources and a minimum of shared goods and services. The choice, thanks to the Iron Lady, was once again clear: socialism or capitalism.

Labour's traditional moderates, like their Conservative counterparts, were in despair. Some of them—notably Roy Jenkins, a former President of the European Commission—abandoned Labour and formed a short-lived Social Democratic Party that would in due course merge with the Liberals, Britain's perennial third party. But most stayed, albeit with trepidation. Their pessimism was well-founded. Led by the intellectually appealing but politically ineffectual Michael Foot, the party fought the 1983 general election on a shamelessly anachronistic program committed to undoing not just Thatcherism but many of the compromises of Labour's own past governments. The UK would retreat from the international economic arena (and from its unswerving fealty to the American alliance). There was to be no truck with privatization, open markets, 'Europe' or any other alien proj-

---

[6] In the decade following her retirement, Margaret Thatcher's heirs at the Conservative helm declined from the tiresomely humdrum (John Major), through the bumptiously inadequate (William Hague), to the terminally inept (Iain Duncan Smith). After the long reign of the Sun Queen there ensued a deluge of mediocrity.

ect. Safe behind the protective walls of a closed economy, the Little Englanders of Britain's Left would defiantly build, at last, the New Jerusalem so often traduced by their colleagues.

Labour's election manifesto of 1983 was succinctly and presciently described by one of the Party's own dispirited parliamentarians as 'the longest suicide note in History'. Buoyed by her recent victory in the Falklands War, in which she had established a party monopoly upon 'patriotism' and displayed once again her unusual taste for confrontation,[7] Mrs. Thatcher won the election of June 1983 by a near-record margin. The Labour Party lost over three million voters, and 160 seats in Parliament. Its share of the vote fell to 27.6 percent, the party's worst performance since the First World War. Whether the British people wanted what Mrs. Thatcher was selling remained uncertain (the Conservative vote did not rise); but they decidedly did *not* want the alternative on offer.

It took the Labour Party fourteen years and three different leaders to recover from the catastrophe of 1983. Politically, the party had to isolate and destroy the influence of Trotskyites and other 'hard' Left activists in some of its regional strongholds (notably Liverpool). Sociologically, it needed to come to terms with its failure to keep abreast with the concerns and aspirations of a new middle class, without whose support it could never again be elected to office, and which outnumbered the evaporating core of industrial proletarians and public sector employees on whom Labour (like all Social Democratic parties) had traditionally relied. Intellectually, Labour's leaders needed to identify a new set of policy objectives—and a new language in which to present them.

By the mid-Nineties these goals had been reached—if only cosmetically. The party changed its name to *New* Labour in 1996, a year after its incoming leader, Tony Blair, persuaded his colleagues finally to abandon the controversial Clause IV committing the party to nationalization. When Labour at last returned to power in 1997, comprehensively defeating an exhausted Conservative party, there was no talk of unraveling the Thatcherite revolution. Instead New Labour's campaign, aimed almost exclusively at marginal, 'soft' Conservative voters, inveighed against high taxes, corruption and inefficiency—the very objects of Mrs. Thatcher's own attacks a generation before.

If Tony Blair and his colleagues drew a discreet veil over the Thatcherite era, this was not by chance. Blair's successes rested squarely upon a threefold inheritance from Mrs. (now Lady) Thatcher. First, she 'normalized' the radical dismantling of the public sector in industry and services and its replacement with the 'privatized', entrepreneurial Britain whose praises Blair sang with such gusto. Second, and in the process, she had destroyed the old Labour Party and facilitated the task of those

---

[7] As she explained to the Scottish Tory Party Conference, on May 14th 1982: 'It is exciting to have a real crisis on your hands, when you have spent half your political life dealing with humdrum issues like the environment.'

who fought to reform it: Blair had merely to reap the rewards of their work. And third, as we have seen, her asperity and her intolerance of dissent and disagreement had fractured her own party and rendered it unelectable.

Riding on Thatcher's coat-tails, Tony Blair shared many of her prejudices, albeit in a less abrasive key. Like her, he intensely disliked the old political vocabulary. In his case this meant avoiding all talk of 'class', an antiquated social category displaced in New Labour's rhetorical boilerplate by 'race' or 'gender'. Like Mrs. Thatcher, Blair showed very little tolerance for decentralized decision-making or internal dissent. Like her, he preferred to surround himself with private-sector business-men.[8] And although New Labour remained vaguely committed to 'society', its Blairite leadership group was as viscerally suspicious of 'the state' as the most doc-trinaire of Thatcherites.

This, then, is the measure of Margaret Thatcher's achievement. Not only did she destroy the post-war consensus but she forged a new one. Before she rose to power the default position in British public policy was that the state is the natural fount of legitimacy and initiative. By the time she departed the scene, this was on the way to becoming a minority view even in Britain's profoundly state-bound Labour Party. For the first time in two generations the role of the state had been put up for discussion and fewer and fewer voices were heard in its defense, at least within the political mainstream. To be sure, there were those who continued to believe that the Thatcherite revolution wrought havoc, and that a return to direct state man-agement of services (if not public ownership of production) was still be desired. But in the wake of Mrs. Thatcher theirs was a case that had to be made—and ex-cept with respect to core social goods like education and medicine, it was no longer guaranteed a sympathetic hearing.

It is sometimes suggested that Thatcher's role in this change has been exagger-ated, that circumstances would have propelled Britain in a 'Thatcherite' direction in any event: that the post-war social pact was already running out of steam. Per-haps. But it is hard even in retrospect to see just who but Mrs. Thatcher could have performed the role of gravedigger. It is the sheer *scale* of the transformation she wrought, for good and ill, that has to be acknowledged. To anyone who had fallen asleep in England in 1978 and awoken twenty years later, their country would have seemed unfamiliar indeed: quite unlike its old self—and markedly different from the rest of Europe.

France, too, changed dramatically in the course of these years, and with some of the same consequences. But whereas in Britain the core assumptions of the post-war consensus were shattered by a revolution from the Right, in France it was the

---

[8] With perhaps this difference: whereas Margaret Thatcher believed in privatization as something akin to a moral good, Tony Blair just likes rich people.

revival and transformation of the non-Communist *Left* that broke the political mould. For many years, French politics had been held in thrall to the parallel and opposed attractions of the Communist Party on the Left and the Gaullists on the Right. Together with their junior partners on Left and Right alike, Communists and Gaullists faithfully incarnated and extended a peculiarly French tradition of political allegiance determined by region, occupation and religion.

These rigidities of French political sociology, unbroken since the mid-nineteenth century, were already under siege, as we have seen, from the social and cultural shifts of the Sixties. The Left could no longer count on a proletarian bloc vote. The Right was no longer bound together by the person and aura of De Gaulle, who had died in 1970; and the fundamental measure of political conservatism in France—the propensity of conservative voters to be practicing Catholics—was being undermined by the decline in public religious observance, as the churches of village and small-town France lost their parishioners, and especially their parishioners' children, to the metropolitan centers.

But a deeper change was also under way. In the course of the 1970s and early 1980s, traditional French society and an older way of life—variously and affectionately described and recalled as *la France profonde, la douce France, la bonne vieille France, la France éternelle*—seemed, to the French, to be disappearing before their eyes. The agricultural modernization of the 1950s and 1960s, the migration of the sons and daughters of peasants to the cities, had been steadily depleting and depopulating the French countryside. The revitalized national economy was effecting a transformation in the jobs, travel patterns, and leisure time of a new class of city-dwellers. Roads and railways that had gathered weeds and grime for decades were rebuilt, re-landscaped, or replaced by a virtually new network of national communications. Towns and cities themselves, long preserved in the dowdy urban aspic of decay and underinvestment, were becoming crowded and energetic.

The French were not always comfortable with the speed of change. Political movements emerged to protest at the acceleration and urbanization of social life, the growth of cities and depopulation of the countryside. One legacy of the Sixties—the renewed interest in local and regional languages and culture—seemed to threaten the very territorial integrity and unity of France itself. To fearful contemporaries their country appeared to be modernizing and splitting apart all at once. But the state remained above the fray. In Britain the relationship between an all-embracing state and an inefficient economy, upon which Margaret Thatcher placed such pejorative emphasis, appeared self-evident to many. But in France it was the state itself that seemed to hold the key to the country's economic resurgence. Its managers were the country's intellectual élite; its planners saw themselves as a class of disinterested civil servants unaffected by the nation's ephemeral ideological passions and social eruptions. Politics in France divided the nation bitterly over the question of *who* would gain power and to what social ends; but concerning the question of *how* they would wield that power there was a remarkable practical consensus.

From 1958 to 1969 the French state had been ruled by Charles De Gaulle. The President's self-consciously traditional style, and his avowed unconcern for the minutiae of economic planning, had proved no impediment to change. Quite the contrary: it was under the camouflage of a semi-authoritarian constitution, tailored to the requirements of a charismatic military autocrat, that France had begun the disruptive modernization that helped spark the protests of 1968—indeed, it was the unsettling mix of old-fashioned paternal authority and destabilizing social changes that brought those protests about.

De Gaulle's opponents and critics made much play with the 'undemocratic' way in which the General had seized and exercised power—'le coup d'état permanent' as François Mitterrand called it in a pamphlet published in 1965—but the resources and trappings of virtually unrestricted presidential power proved no less appealing to his successors of all political stripes. And the distinctive system of direct presidential election cast a shadow across the country's quinquennial parliamentary elections, placing a premium upon the political skills and personality of individual candidates around whom political parties had perforce to regroup. It was in this setting that the redoubtable Mitterrand was himself to excel.

François Mitterrand, like Margaret Thatcher, was an implausible candidate for the role he was to play in his country's affairs. Born to a practicing Catholic family in conservative south-western France, he was a right-wing law student in the 1930s and an activist in some of the most extreme anti-democratic movements of the age. He spent most of World War Two as a junior servant of the collaborationist government in Vichy, switching his allegiance just in time to be able to claim postwar credentials as a resister. His parliamentary and ministerial career in the Fourth Republic was pursued in various minor parties of the center-Left, none of them bearing any allegiance to the Marxist mainstream.

Even when he ran unsuccessfully for president in 1965 with the support of the parties of the official Left, Mitterrand was in no sense their candidate and took care to keep his distance from them. It was only after the implosion of the old Parti Socialiste in 1969, following its electoral humiliation in 1968, that Mitterrand began to plot his role in its renaissance: a take-over bid launched in 1971 with the appearance of a new Socialist Party led by Mitterrand and a new generation of ambitious young men recruited to serve him.

The relationship binding Mitterrand and the remnants of French Socialism's proud heritage was mutually instrumentalist. The Party needed Mitterrand: his good showing in the presidential election of 1965, when he secured the backing of 27 percent of registered voters (including many in conservative bastions of the East and West) and forced De Gaulle into a run-off, revealed him to be a vote-winner— as early as 1967, during a *parliamentary* election, Mitterrand badges and photos were selling well. The country was entering a new age of televised, personalized politics—as Michel Durafour, the mayor of St Etienne, glumly noted in 1971: 'France lives only in anticipation of the next presidential election.' Mitterrand would be a trump card for the Left.

Mitterrand, in turn, needed the Socialists. Lacking an organization of his own, more than a little tainted by the compromises and scandals of the Fourth Republic in whose governments he had served, this consummate opportunist used the Socialist Party to recycle himself as a man of the committed Left while keeping clear of the burdensome doctrinal baggage with which the old Left was freighted. He once described his religious allegiances thus: *'Je suis né chrétien, et je mourrai sans doute en cet état. Dans l'intervalle . . .'* ('I was born Christian and shall doubtless die in that condition. But meanwhile . . .'). In much the same cynical vein he might have added that he was born a conservative and would die one, but managed to become a Socialist in the meantime.

This marriage of convenience worked better than either party could have imagined. In the course of the 1970s, as the British Labour Party was entering its terminal decline, so France's Socialists were on the verge of their greatest success. The twin impediments to the re-emergence of a left majority in France had been De Gaulle's personal appeal, and the fear of many voters that a government of the Left would be dominated by the Communists. By 1970, De Gaulle was dead; within ten years, so were the prospects of the Communists. For the former Mitterrand could take no direct credit, but the latter was unquestionably his achievement.

Acknowledging the logic of necessity, and lacking the ideological delicacy of his genuinely Socialist predecessors, Mitterrand at first aligned his new Socialist Party with the Communists; in 1972 he formed an electoral coalition with them behind a vaguely-worded, anti-capitalist Common Programme. By the elections of 1977 the Communists, the dominant party of the Left since 1945, were ten percentage points behind Mitterrand's Socialists. Only then did Georges Marchais, the PCF's lackluster General Secretary, begin to realize the mistake his Party had made in aligning its fate with that of Mitterrand's young and energetic party—a decision taken partly under the optimistic, ecumenical influence of 'Eurocommunism'—but it was too late.

After improving upon his 1965 showing in the 1974 Presidential election, when he was narrowly beaten by Giscard d'Estaing after standing as the candidate of the united Left, Mitterrand had forged a superb electoral machine, turning the Socialist Party into a catch-all movement appealing across the whole spectrum of French society, including Catholics, women, farmers and small shopkeepers, all hitherto hostile to the Socialists.[9] His own image had mellowed with age: huge campaign billboards across France in the spring of 1981 showed Mitterrand's portrait in soft

---

[9] A 1979 poll revealed that the electoral profile of Mitterrand's *Parti Socialiste* uncannily reflected that of the country at large, something no other party could claim.

focus, set against the same timeless bucolic rural landscape once favored in Pétainist propaganda on those same billboards, under the promise 'La Force Tranquille'—Quiet Strength.

The Communists, meanwhile, were weak—the Soviet invasion of Afghanistan in 1979 was an acute embarrassment, as were their own declining polls. During the course of the 1970s the Communist Party had ceased to be a fixed star in the ideological firmament: its prestige had collapsed along with its vote, even in the industrial 'Red Belt' of Paris that it had dominated since the mid-twenties. Nevertheless, Marchais was determined to stand as a candidate in the forthcoming presidential elections: partly out of habit, partly from hubris, but mostly from a growing awareness of the need to cut the PCF loose from the poisoned embrace of its Socialist comrades.

At the first round of the 1981 Presidential election the two conservative candidates, Giscard d'Estaing and the young Jacques Chirac, together outpolled Mitterrand and Marchais (the latter winning just 12.2 percent of the vote). But in the run-off two weeks later between the two best-placed candidates, Mitterrand secured the backing of Socialists, Communists, environmentalists and even the normally uncooperative Trotskyists, more than doubled his first-round share and defeated Giscard to become the first directly-elected Socialist head of state in Europe. He promptly dissolved parliament and called legislative elections at which his own party trounced Communists and Right alike, winning for itself an absolute majority in the Assemblée Nationale. The Socialists were in complete control of France.

The spontaneous celebrations that greeted the Socialists' victories were unprecedented. For the tens of thousands of (mostly young) Mitterrand supporters who danced in the streets this was the '*grand soir*', the revolutionary eve, the threshold of a radical break with the past. On the basis of electoral data alone that would have been a curious claim. As in past electoral upheavals—the French Popular Front victory in April 1936 to which Mitterrand's achievement was immediately compared, or Margaret Thatcher's election in 1979—the French vote in 1981 was not radically re-distributed. Indeed, Mitterrand actually fared *worse*, in the initial voting, than in his earlier bids for the presidency in 1965 and 1974.

What made the difference was the discipline showed by Left voters this time around in coalescing behind Mitterrand at the second round rather than abstaining in sectarian obstinacy, and the division of opinion on the *Right*. Of those who voted for Chirac in the initial round of the 1981 presidential election, 16 percent gave their votes to Mitterrand two weeks later—rather than re-elect the outgoing president Giscard d'Estaing: a man heartily disliked by Chirac's Gaullist supporters. Had the Right not divided thus there would have been no President Mitterrand, no Socialist sweep in the ensuing legislative elections—and no *grand soir* of radical expectations.

It is worth emphasizing this because so much seemed to hang on the outcome of the 1981 election. In retrospect it is clear, as Mitterrand himself understood, that his achievement in 1981 was to 'normalize' the process of alternation in the French Republic, to make it possible for the Socialists to be treated as a normal party of government. But to Mitterrand's supporters in 1981 the picture looked very different. Their goal was not to normalize the alternation of power in the future but to seize it and use it, here and now. They took for good coin their leader's promises of radical transformation, his undertaking to sweep away not just the corruption and *ennui* of the Giscard years but also the very capitalist system itself. Excluded from office for so long, France's Socialist militants had remained free to dream a dream of revolution.

For the Left had not exercised power in France for many decades; indeed, it had *never* exercised power untrammeled by coalition partners, uncooperative bankers, foreign exchange crises, international emergencies and a litany of other excuses for its failure to implement socialism. In 1981, as it seemed, none of these applied and there would be no excuse for backsliding. Moreover, the association of control of the state with implementation of revolutionary change was so deeply embedded in radical political culture in France that the mere fact of winning the election was itself taken as signifying a coming social confrontation.

Like Marx himself, the French Left identified all *real* change with political revolution in general and the great French Revolution in particular. Enthusiastic comparisons were thus made with 1871 and even 1791. Nothing Mitterrand had said in the campaign had led the more committed of his followers to think otherwise. In order to 'dish' the Communists and the left wing of his own party, Mitterrand had stolen their revolutionary clothes. His election campaign aroused expectations that he was now expected to fulfill.

Thus the Mitterrand years began with an ambitious and radical agenda: a blend of morally uplifting and overdue social reforms (of which the abolition of capital punishment was the most significant) with a phantasmagoric programme of 'anti-capitalist' legislation. Wages were raised, the retirement age lowered, working hours reduced. But the core element of the programme was an unprecedented schedule of nationalizations. In its first year of office the new Socialist government of Prime Minister Pierre Mauroy took into state control, *inter alia*: 36 banks; two major finance houses; five of France's largest industrial corporations (including Thomson-Brandt, the country's major electrical and electronic products manufacturer); and Usinor and Sacilor, France's giant iron and steel groups.

There was no pre-determined economic strategy behind these moves. There *was* talk of invigorating the slowing French economy by the injection of government capital; but this was not a new idea, nor a particularly Socialist one: Prime Minister Chirac, back in the mid-Seventies, had briefly entertained similarly demand-led projects for growth. The prime function of the nationalizations of 1981–82, like the exchange controls that accompanied them, was to symbolize the anti-capitalist *intent* of the new regime; to confirm that the elections of 1981 had really changed something more than just the personnel of government.

In reality, it was clear from the outset to those concerned that state-owned banks, for example, could only function if permitted 'total autonomy of decision and action', thus eliminating the regulatory and socially redistributive goals that had been adduced to justify their take-over in the first place. This pragmatic concession illustrates the broader impediment facing the Mitterrand 'revolution'. For a year the new regime strove boldly to present a radical face to France and the world. At first this was convincing—Jacques Attali, Mitterrand's close adviser, recorded that US officials (always on the lookout for such backsliding) claimed to see little difference between French economic policy and that of the Soviet Union.

But for France to take a 'Socialist' path in 1982 would have meant imposing not just exchange controls but a whole gamut of regulations cutting the country off from its commercial partners and putting the economy on a virtually autarkic footing. To take France out of international financial markets would not perhaps have been so unimaginable an undertaking as it would later become: in 1977 the market capitalization of IBM alone was twice that of the entire Paris Bourse. Of greater significance was the fact that such a move would have triggered France's separation and perhaps even departure from the European Community, whose agreements on tariffs, markets and currency alignments—not to mention impending plans for a single market—already severely restricted the options open to member states.

These considerations appear to have concentrated Mitterrand's thinking—aided, no doubt, by evidence of mounting panic in business circles and signs that currency, valuables and people were moving abroad with increasing urgency, precipitating an economic crisis. On June 12th 1982, the President decided upon a 'U' turn. Rejecting the advice of his more radical counselors, Mitterrand authorized his government to freeze prices and wages for a four-month period; cut public spending (which had been generously increased the previous year); raise taxes; give priority to the struggle with inflation (rather than print money, as he had been urged to do)—in effect adopting the economic strategy of the conservative economist Raymond Barre whose 1977 'Plan', never implemented, would have introduced into France a dose of Thatcherism *avant l'heure*; and abandoned forthwith all reference to a 'French path to Socialism'.

The President's Communist allies and some of his Socialist colleagues were deeply shocked. But they should not have been surprised. The supreme pragmatist, Mitterrand grasped readily enough that it was unthinkable for France even to contemplate choosing between remaining in the Western economic (and political) orbit and casting itself out into a doubtfully sustainable middle route between capitalism and Communism. Making a lasting virtue out of passing necessity, he duly re-fashioned himself as a leading 'Europeanist'. France would build a better society *through* European unification rather than against it. Rather than struggle against capitalism France would invent a superior version.

By 1984 Mitterrand had removed the four Communist ministers in his government; publicly proclaimed the virtues of a 'mixed' economy; appointed a young and technocratic prime minister, Laurent Fabius; handed the management of economic affairs, finance, and the budget to Jacques Delors, with instructions to stabilize the French economy[10]; and even, in a prominent speech in April of that year, called for a French modernization 'à l'américaine'.

Mitterrand had France on his side—in 1983 only 23 percent of his own Socialist voters regretted his failure to 'put Socialism into practice'. Whether they wanted him to 'modernize' with quite so much enthusiasm is less certain, but modernize he did. Without explicitly abandoning the less controversial of his early reforms—administrative decentralization, the overhaul of social security, the securing of workplace rights for women and a long-awaited reform of the judiciary—Mitterrand devoted the rest of his long reign (he retired in 1995 after two seven-year presidential terms, dying at the age of eighty the following year) to expensive public works of questionable aesthetics and utility; the re-establishment of French international initiative[11]; ... and to overseeing the restoration into private hands of the many services and industries he had only recently taken into public control.

The initial drive to privatize France's huge public sector was undertaken by the conservative parliamentary majority that emerged victorious from the 1986 elections. But successive governments of all stripes pursued the same goal—indeed, the Socialist governments of Mitterrand's final years were by far the most energetic privatizers of all. The first assets to be sold into private hands, following the British model of public offerings, were the major banks and TF1, one of three national television channels. There followed public holding companies, insurance concerns, chemical and pharmaceutical corporations and the giant oil conglomerates Total and Elf.

In contrast to Mrs. Thatcher and her heirs, however, the French were cautious about selling off public utilities, or 'strategic' firms like the Renault car company (only recently saved from bankruptcy by a huge capital grant from the state in 1985). In markets as in gardens, the French were suspicious of unplanned growth. They preferred to retain a certain capacity to intervene, typically by keeping a portion of even privatized firms in state hands. Privatization itself, in France, was thus a distinctly regulated affair—controlling shares were carefully directed towards enterprises and businesses on whom the state could rely, and international investors remained for many years understandably suspicious. Nevertheless, by French standards the changes were momentous, bringing the country sharply back into line with European and international developments.

This is perhaps an appropriate moment to say something about the privatiza-

---

[10] A former banker and one-time adviser to Gaullist Prime Minister Jacques Chaban-Delmas, Delors would go on to preside over the European Commission from 1985–1995.
[11] Even at the height of popular discontent with government policy, in the economic slump of the mid-1980s, 57 percent of electors declared themselves pleased with Mitterrand's *foreign* policy.

tion wave that broke upon the shores of Western Europe in the 1980s and was to roll across the continent in the course of the following decade. It did not come altogether out of the blue. British Petroleum had been progressively sold off, beginning in 1977, as we have seen; the West German government had dispensed with the chemical combine Preussag by a public share issue as early as 1959 and sold its shares in Volkswagen a few years later; even the Austrian state had sold 40 percent of its shares in two nationalized banks in the course of the 1950s and relinquished its sizeable holding in Siemens in 1972.

But these were sporadic, and—as it were—*pragmatic* privatizations. What happened in the nineteen-eighties was something quite different, pressed upon governments from two quite distinct directions. In the first place, accelerating developments in technology—notably in telecommunications and the financial markets—were undermining the old 'natural' monopolies. If governments could no longer harness the airwaves, or the movement of money, for their own exclusive use, it made little sense for them to 'own' them. There remained a powerful political or social case for the state retaining part of a given sector—a public television channel, say, or the post office; but competition was now unavoidable.

In the second place, governments were being driven to sell public assets out of short-term economic necessity. Pressed by inflation, the oil crisis of 1979–80, large annual deficits and growing government indebtedness, finance ministers looked upon the sale of publicly-owned assets as doubly beneficial. The state would off-load loss-making industries or services; and the monies thus raised would help balance the budget, albeit on a one-time basis. Even if an industry or service remained in partial public-ownership (the state typically keeping the unprofitable parts that private buyers didn't want), the injection of cash from share sales could be applied to future investment. For this reason even many public sector managers were enthusiastic partisans of such partial sales, having long resented the diversion of their profits to help make good national budgetary shortfalls.

There was considerable variation in the form and extent of European public ownership and control. The public industrial sector was smallest in Holland, Denmark and Sweden, most extensive in Italy, France, Spain and Austria. Excluding health and social services, the share of the workforce in the early eighties directly employed by the state varied from 15 percent in West Germany to 28 percent in Italy and nearly one in three in Austria. In some countries—Austria, Spain and Italy—the public sector was organized into huge industrial holding companies, of which Italy's IRI was the largest.[12]

Elsewhere the state's interest was filtered through a National Investment Bank and Industrial Guarantee Fund—as in the Netherlands—or its Belgian equivalent,

---

[12] In 1982 IRI (*Instituto per la Ricostruzione Industriale*) controlled, among much else, all of Italy's cast-iron manufacturing, two-thirds of its special steel output, one quarter of its ice-cream production and 18 percent of its peeled tomatoes.

the Société Nationale d'Investissement. The steel industry alone was supported in a wide variety of ways: in Britain the Treasury habitually wrote off the debts of state-owned companies; in France the government provided loans at low rates of interest and intervened politically to favor local producers over foreign competition; in West Germany private sector steel manufacturers received direct cash subsidies.

Given such national disparities, the forms of privatization in Europe naturally diverged significantly. In every case, however, they entailed some element of deregulation; the liberalization of markets; and the introduction of new financial instruments to facilitate the sale and re-sale of shares in partly- or wholly-privatized companies. In West Germany, where the main export sectors (cars, mechanical engineering, chemical and electronics companies) were already in private hands, the impediment to efficiency and competition came not from state control but rather from high fixed costs and labour-market regulations. *Privatization* in Germany, when it came, was primarily the responsibility of the *Treuhandgesellschaft*, the public corporation established in 1990 to dispose of former East German state-owned enterprises.[13]

In Italy, the chief stumbling block on the road to privatization was the vested interest not of the state but of political parties. The Christian Democrats and Socialists in particular used the state sector and public holding companies to reward colleagues and bribe supporters, often favoring them with public contracts and absorbing them into the *sottogoverno* or submerged power structure that underpinned their dominion. But in spite of this powerful disincentive the Italian private sector grew steadily in this period, especially among manufacturing firms employing fewer than one hundred persons—far more numerous in Italy than in Britain, France or Germany.

Already in 1976 the Constitutional Court had ended the monopoly of RAI, the state-run radio and television networks. A few years later Alfa Romeo, at that point still operated under the aegis of a public holding company, was 'made over' to FIAT. Within six years the major holding companies themselves—IRI, INA, ENI, and ENEL[14]—had all been converted to public joint-stock companies. They had no value in themselves—quite the reverse: in 1984 IRI was losing 4.5 million lire per annum for every one of its 500,000 employees. But they were able to issue bonds that were convertible to shares in the companies under their control now scheduled for privatization.

The situation in countries newly-emerged from authoritarian rule was rather different. The public sector in post-Franco Spain, for example, actually *expanded*.

---

[13] The original goal of the *Treuhand* was to convert as many as possible of the nine thousand East German companies (employing seven million men and women) into real businesses and liquidate the rest. But under political pressure it preferred to rehabilitate or consolidate many of the unprofitable concerns, ironically thereby creating a new, semi-public sector subsidized from public funds. See Chapter 21.
[14] Instituto per la Ricostruzione Industriale, Instituto Nazionale delle Assicurazioni, Ente Nazionale Idrocarburi, Ente Nazionale per l'Energia Elettrica.

Public expenditure as a share of GNP rose steadily, as the centrists in government from 1976 to 1982 pursued the old regime's strategy of avoiding social confrontation by simply transferring failed private companies to the state. They could hardly do otherwise—for varying reasons, nationalization in this form was the preference of workers, owners, national politicians and regional authorities alike. In any case, one of the chief general arguments for cutting the public sector—that the welfare state it incarnated was too costly to maintain—did not apply in Spain, or Portugal or Greece. There was no welfare state to dismantle.

Nevertheless, even in the absence of European-level social services and protections, the public sector—saddled with the abandoned and unprofitable refuse from Spanish capitalism's accelerated and cosseted adolescence—was hopelessly overburdened. Already in 1976 *INI* (Instituto Nacional de Industria) alone had a stake in 747 (mostly unprofitable) industrial companies and a controlling interest in 379 others. Some measure of privatization and de-regulation was inevitable if Spain were ever to be solvent. As in France, it was a Socialist government that initiated this process, introducing private pension funds in 1987 and abolishing the state television monopoly two years later.

In post-revolutionary Portugal, Article 85 of the Constitution and a subsequent 1977 law explicitly forbade private enterprise in banking, insurance, transport, posts and telecommunications, electricity production and distribution, petroleum refining and the arms industry. The Socialist administration of Mário Soares sought in 1983 to introduce some flexibility by allowing the private sector to compete with the state in banking and insurance, and authorizing joint-stock companies to form in the steel, petroleum, chemical and arms industries. But it would be some time before the remaining protected sectors were opened even to limited competition.

Mediterranean Europe—like post-Communist Central Europe a few years later—would probably have been even slower to relinquish state controls but for the impact of the European Community/Union. The fixed currency parities of the European Monetary System (EMS) after 1979 were an early constraint—one reason why the Mitterrand governments started selling public assets was to reassure currency markets and thus maintain the franc at its agreed level in EMS. But Brussels' chief means of leverage were the rules being drawn up for the operation of a single European market. The latter obliged all businesses—public and private alike—to conform to norms of open competition within and eventually between countries. There was to be no favoring of national 'champions', or hidden subsidies or other advantage for publicly-owned or controlled enterprises competing for contracts or custom.

However much these regulations were circumvented in practice, their mere existence obliged state-owned firms to comport themselves in the marketplace no differently from private ones—at which point there was little reason to maintain the state's involvement in their affairs. The Italian response was typical of that of many other member states of the Community: in 1990 Italy adopted new regulations that echoed the relevant clauses of the Single European Act, requiring all state-owned firms to apply the principle of open and equal competition in all their dealings—except in the case of firms and undertakings where a state monopoly was 'vital to its tasks', a clause whose flexibility and vagueness allowed governments to adapt to European norms while staying sensitive to local pressures.

Despite the excited talk in Brussels (and London) of increased openness and 'competitiveness' the European privatization fever of these years probably wrought less change than its supporters promised or expected. Critics had warned that the result would not be more competition but simply a transfer of concentrated economic power from the public to the private sphere and this is what happened. Thanks to complicated cross-shareholding arrangements, many large private firms in France, for example, mimicked the behaviour of the old public companies. They monopolized whole sectors and were no more responsive to their small 'stakeholders' than they had been to taxpayers or consumers when administered under public management.

Ironically, privatization and increased competition also had little immediate impact upon the size of the state sector itself. We have already seen that in Thatcher's Britain the scope of the state actually *expanded*. So it was elsewhere. Between 1974 and 1990 (thanks in some measure to endemic private-sector unemployment) the share of the employed workforce in public service actually grew: from 13 percent to 15.1 percent in Germany; from 13.4 percent to 15.5 percent in Italy; from 22.2 percent to 30.5 percent in Denmark. Most of these government employees, however, were now in the tertiary sector rather than in manufacturing: providing and administering services (financial, educational, medical and transportation) rather than making things.

Economic liberalization did not signal the fall of the welfare state, nor even its terminal decline, notwithstanding the hopes of its theorists. It did, though, illustrate a seismic shift in the allocation of resources and initiative from public to private sectors. This change went far beyond the technical question of who owned which factories, or how much regulation there was to be in any given industry. For nearly half a century Europeans had watched the state, and public authorities, play a steadily more prominent part in their affairs. This process had become so commonplace that the premise behind it—that the activist state was a necessary condition of economic growth and social amelioration—was largely taken for granted. Without the cumulative unraveling of this assumption in the course of the waning decades of the century, neither Thatcherism nor the Mitterrand *volte-face* would have been possible.

XVIII

The Power of the Powerless

'Marxism is not a philosophy of history, it is *the* philosophy of history, and
to renounce it is to dig the grave of Reason in history'.
Maurice Merleau-Ponty

'I talk about rights because they alone will enable us to leave this magic
lantern show'.
Kazimierz Brandys

'Totalitarian society is the distorted mirror of the whole of modern
civilization'.
Václav Havel

'The pressure of the state machine is nothing compared with the pressure
of a convincing argument'.
Czeslaw Milosz

Behind the long 'Social-Democratic moment' in Western Europe there had lain not
just pragmatic faith in the public sector, or allegiance to Keynesian economic principles, but a sense of the shape of the age that influenced and for many decades stifled even its would-be critics. This widely-shared understanding of Europe's recent
past blended the memory of Depression, the struggle between Democracy and
Fascism, the moral legitimacy of the welfare state, and—for many on both sides of
the Iron Curtain—the expectation of social progress. It was the Master Narrative
of the twentieth century; and when its core assumptions began to erode and crumble, they took with them not just a handful of public-sector companies but a whole
political culture and much else besides.

If one were seeking a symbolic moment when this transformation was accomplished, a hinge on which post-war Europe's self-understanding turned, it came in
Paris on December 28th 1973 with the first Western publication of Aleksandr
Solzhenitsyn's *The Gulag Archipelago*. Reviewing the English translation in the
Guardian, W. L. Webb wrote 'To live now and not to know this work is to be a kind
of historical fool, missing a crucial part of the consciousness of the age.' The irony,
as Solzhenitsyn himself acknowledged, was that the message of the book—that
'real existing Socialism' was a barbaric fraud, a totalitarian dictatorship resting
upon a foundation of slave labour and mass murder—was hardly new.

Solzhenitsyn himself had written about the subject before, and so had numberless victims, survivors, observers and scholars. *The Gulag Archipelago* added hundreds of pages of detail and data to earlier testimonies, but in its moral fervor and emotional impact it was not obviously a greater work of witness than Evgenia Ginzburg's *Journey into the Whirlwind*, published in 1967; Margarete Buber-Neumann's memoir of her experiences in both Soviet and Nazi camps, first published in German in 1957; Wolfgang Leonhard's disabused account of his own misplaced faith, which appeared in 1955; or even earlier demolitions of the Soviet myth by Victor Serge and Boris Souvarine.[1]

But timing was all. Intellectual critics of Communism had never been lacking; however their impact had for many decades been blunted by a widespread desire in Western Europe (and, as we have seen, in Eastern Europe through the 1960s) to find some silver lining, however dim, in the storm cloud of state socialism that had rolled across much of the continent since it first broke upon Russia in 1917. 'Anti-Communism', whatever its real or imputed motives, suffered the grievous handicap of appearing to challenge the shape of History and Progress, to miss the 'bigger picture', to deny the essential contiguity binding the democratic welfare state (however inadequate) to Communism's collectivist project (however tainted).

That is why opponents of the post-war consensus were so marginalized. To suggest, as Hayek and others had done, that market-restraining plans for the common good, albeit well-intentioned, were not just economically inefficient but also and above all the first step on the road to serfdom, was to tear up the road map of the twentieth century. Even opponents of Communist dictatorship like Arthur Koestler, Raymond Aron, Albert Camus or Isaiah Berlin, who tried to insist upon the distinction between social-democratic reforms for the common benefit and party dictatorships established in the name of a collectivist myth, appeared to many of their 'progressive' critics to echo and thus serve partisan political allegiances taken up in the Cold War.

Accordingly, they fell foul of a widespread reluctance, especially on the part of the Sixties generation, to abandon the radical catechism. It was one thing to sneer knowingly at Stalin, now long dead and anyway condemned by his own heirs. It was quite another to acknowledge that the fault lay not in the man but the system. And to go further, to impute responsibility for the crimes and misdemeanors of Leninism to the project of radical utopianism itself was to mine the very buttresses of modern politics. As the British historian E. P. Thompson, something of a cult figure to a younger generation of 'post-Communist Marxists', wrote accusingly to

---

[1] Evgenia Ginzburg, *Journey into the Whirlwind* (Harcourt, 1967); Margarete Buber-Neumann, *Von Potsdam nach Moskau: Stationen eines Irrweges* (Stuttgart: Deutsche Verlags-Anstalt, 1957); Wolfgang Leonhard, *Child of the Revolution* (Pathfinder Press, 1979), first published in Cologne in 1955 as *Die Revolution entlässt ihre Kinder*; Victor Serge, *Mémoires d'un révolutionnaire* (Paris, 1951); Boris Souvarine, *Stalin. A Critical Survey of Bolshevism* (first published in English in 1939).

THE POWER OF THE POWERLESS

Leszek Kolakowski (after Kolakowski published a damning indictment of Soviet Communism in the wake of 1968): *your* disenchantment is a threat to *our* Socialist faith.

By 1973, however, that faith was under serious assault not just from critics but from events themselves. When *The Gulag Archipelago* was published in French, the Communist daily newspaper *l'Humanité* dismissed it, reminding readers that since 'everyone' already knows all about Stalin, anyone rehashing all *that* could only be motivated by 'anti-Sovietism'. But the accusation of 'anti-Sovietism' was losing its force. In the wake of the Soviet invasion of Prague and its repressive aftermath, and of reports filtering out of China about the Cultural Revolution, Solzhenitsyn's root and branch condemnation of the whole Communist project rang true—even and perhaps especially to erstwhile sympathizers.

Communism, it was becoming clear, had defiled and despoiled its radical heritage. And it was continuing to do so, as the genocide in Cambodia and the widely-publicized trauma of the Vietnamese 'boat people' would soon reveal.[2] Even those in Western Europe—and they were many—who held the United States largely responsible for the disasters in Vietnam and Cambodia, and whose anti-Americanism was further fuelled by the American-engineered killing of Chile's Salvador Allende just three months before the publication of *The Gulag Archipelago*, were increasingly reluctant to conclude as they had once done that the Socialist camp had the moral upper hand. American imperialism was indeed bad—but the other side was worse, perhaps far worse.

At this point the traditional 'progressive' insistence on treating attacks on Communism as implicit threats to *all* socially-ameliorative goals—i.e. the claim that Communism, Socialism, Social Democracy, nationalization, central planning and progressive social engineering were part of a common political project—began to work against itself. If Lenin and his heirs had poisoned the well of social justice, the argument ran, we are *all* damaged. In the light of twentieth-century history the state was beginning to look less like the solution than the problem, and not only or even primarily for economic reasons. What begins with centralized planning ends with centralized killing.

That, of course, is a very 'intellectual' sort of conclusion, but then the impact of the retreat from the state was felt most immediately by intellectuals—appropriately enough, since it was intellectuals who had been most zealous in promoting social improvement from above in the first place. As Jiří Gruša, the Czech writer, was to observe in 1984: It was we [writers] who glorified the modern state.' By it very nature, modern tyranny—as Ignazio Silone noted—requires the collaboration of intellectuals. It was thus altogether appropriate that it was the disaffec-

---

[2] Between 1975 and 1981 France alone took in 80,000 refugees from Indo-China.

tion of Europe's intellectuals from the grand narrative of progress that triggered the ensuing avalanche; and somehow fitting that this disaffection was most marked in Paris, where the narrative itself had first taken intellectual and political shape two centuries earlier.

France in the Seventies and Eighties was no longer Arthur Koestler's 'burning lens of Western Civilization', but French thinkers were still unusually predisposed to engage universal questions. Writers and commentators in Spain or West Germany or Italy in these years were much taken up with local challenges—though the terrorist threat that preoccupied them carried implications of its own for the discrediting of radical utopianism. Intellectuals in the UK, never deeply touched by the appeal of Communism, were largely indifferent to its decline and thus kept their distance from the new Continental mood. In France, by contrast, there had been widespread and longstanding local sympathy for the Communist project. As anti-Communism gathered pace in French public discussion, abetted by the steady decline in the Communist Party's vote and influence, it was thus fuelled by local recollection and example. A new generation of French intellectuals transited with striking alacrity out of Marxism, driven by a sometimes unseemly haste to abjure their own previous engagement.

In condemning the distortions of radical utopianism, the young Parisian 'new philosophers' of the mid-Seventies like André Glucksmann or Bernard-Henri Lévy were in most respects unoriginal. There was little in Glucksmann's *Les Maîtres Penseurs*—published to universal acclaim in March 1977—that Raymond Aron had not said better in his *Opium des Intellectuels* twenty two years earlier. And there was nothing in Lévy's *Barbarie à Visage Humain*, which appeared two months after Glucksmann's essay, which French readers could not have found in Albert Camus's *L'Homme révolté*. But whereas Camus's essay was cuttingly dismissed by Jean-Paul Sartre when it came out in 1951, Lévy and Glucksmann were influential bestsellers. Times had changed.

The parricidal quality of this local intellectual earthquake is obvious. Its ostensible target was the calamitous Marxist detour in Western thought; but much of its fire was directed above all at those dominant figures of post-war intellectual life, in France and elsewhere, who had peered across the touchlines of History, cheering on the winners and politely averting their eyes from their victims. Sartre, by far the best known of these fellow-travelers, himself fell from favour in these years, even before his death in 1980, his creative legacy sullied by his apologetics first for Soviet Communism, later for Maoism.[3]

The climate change in Paris extended beyond a settling of scores across a gen-

---

[3] In 1963, long after he had lost interest in France's own Communists, the author of *Les Mains Sales* could still be heard in Prague enthusing about Socialist Realism to a bemused audience of Czech writers and intellectuals.

eration of engaged intellectuals. In 1978 Karl Popper's *The Logic of Scientific Discovery* appeared in French for the first time, the harbinger of a steady absorption into the French mainstream of a whole corpus of 'Anglo-American' scholarship in philosophy and the social sciences of which the local intellectual culture had for decades remained in near ignorance. In the same year the historian François Furet published his path-breaking *Penser la Révolution Française*, in which he systematically dismantled the 'revolutionary catechism' through which the French had for many decades been taught to understand their country and its past.

In this 'catechism' as Furet dissected it, the French Revolution had been the ur-moment of modernity: the confrontation that triggered France's division into opposing political cultures of Left and Right, ostensibly determined by the class identities of the antagonists. That story, which rested upon the twin pillars of early-nineteenth century liberal optimism and a Marxist vision of radical social transformation, had now, in Furet's account, run into the ground—not least because Soviet Communism, the revolutionary heir-presumptive in this morality tale of purposeful radical transformation, had retroactively polluted the whole inheritance. The French Revolution, in Furet's words, was 'dead'.

The political implications of Furet's thesis were momentous, as its author well understood. The failings of Marxism as a politics were one thing, which could always be excused under the category of misfortune or circumstance. But if Marxism were discredited as a Grand Narrative—if neither reason nor necessity were at work in History—then all Stalin's crimes, all the lives lost and resources wasted in transforming societies under state direction, all the mistakes and failures of the twentieth century's radical experiments in introducing Utopia by *diktat*, ceased to be 'dialectically' explicable as false moves along a true path. They became instead just what their critics had always said they were: loss, waste, failure and crime.

Furet and his younger contemporaries rejected the resort to History that had so coloured intellectual engagement in Europe since the beginning of the 1930s. There is, they insisted, no 'Master Narrative' governing the course of human actions, and thus no way to justify public policies or actions that cause real suffering today in the name of speculative benefits tomorrow. Broken eggs make good omelettes. But you cannot build a better society on broken men. In retrospect this may appear a rather lame conclusion to decades of intense theoretical and political debate; but for just that reason it illustrates rather well the extent of the change.

In *Ma Nuit Chez Maud*, Eric Rohmer's 1969 *conte moral*, a Communist philosopher and his Catholic colleague argue at considerable length over the competing claims of Pascal's wager on God and the Marxist bet on History. What is striking in retrospect is not the conversation itself, which will be familiar to anyone old enough to remember the Sixties in continental Europe, but the seriousness with which it was taken not just by the on-screen protagonists but by millions of contemporary viewers. Ten years later the topic, if not the film, was already a period piece. The resort to History in defense of unpalatable political choices had begun to seem morally naïve and even callous. As Camus had noted many years before, 'Responsibility towards History releases one from responsibility towards human beings'.[4]

The new uncertainty about 'History' (and history) inaugurated a disagreeable decade for West European intellectuals, uneasily aware that the disintegration of great historical schemes and master narratives boded ill for the chattering classes who had been most responsible for purveying them, and who were now themselves—as it seemed to many of them—the object of humiliating indifference. In September 1986, in a revealing solipsistic aside to a French journalist, French sociologist Pierre Bourdieu bemoaned the fallen condition of the engaged public thinker: 'As for me, I think that if there is a great cause left today it's the defense of the intellectuals'.[5]

Intellectual self-abnegation before History was once described by Isaiah Berlin as 'the horrible German way out of the burden of moral choice'. This is a little hard on Germans, who were hardly the only Europeans to abase themselves on the altar of historical necessity, though it is true that the idea had its roots in German romantic philosophy. But it points to an emerging vacuum in European political ideas: if there was no 'great cause' left; if the progressive legacy had run into the ground; if History, or necessity, could no longer be credibly invoked in defense of an act, a policy or a programme; then how should men decide the great dilemmas of the age?

This was not a problem for Thatcherite radicals, who treated public policy as an extension of private interests and for whom the marketplace was a necessary and sufficient adjudicator of values and outcomes. Nor were the times unusually troubling for Europe's traditional conservatives, for whom the measure of good and evil in human affairs remained anchored in religious norms and social conventions, bruised but not yet altogether displaced by the cultural *tsunami* of the Sixties. It was the progressive *Left*, still the dominant presence in European political and cultural exchanges, which was urgently in need of a different script.

What it found, to its collective surprise, was a new political vernacular—or, rather, a very old one, freshly rediscovered. The language of rights, or liberties, was firmly inscribed in every European constitution, not least those of the Peoples' Democracies. But as a way of thinking about politics, 'rights talk' had been altogether unfashionable in Europe for many years. After the First World War rights—notably the right to self-determination—had played a pivotal role in international debate over a post-war settlement, and most of the interested parties at the Versailles

---

[4] 'La responsabilité envers l'Histoire dispense de la responsabilité envers les êtres humains'.
[5] 'Pour ma part, je pense que s'il y a une grande cause aujourd'hui, c'est la défense des intellectuals.' See *Le Nouvel Observateur*, #1140, septembre 1986, 'Les Grandes Causes, ça existe encore?'

Peace Conference had invoked their rights quite vociferously when pressing their case upon the Great Powers. But these were *collective* rights—the rights of nations, peoples, minorities.

Moreover, the record of collectively-asserted rights was an unhappy one. Where the rights of more than one ethnic or religious community had clashed, usually over a conflicting territorial claim, it had been depressingly obvious that force, not law, was the only effective way to establish precedence. Minority rights could not be protected within states, nor the rights of weak states secured against the claims of their more powerful neighbors. The victors of 1945, looking back on the dashed hopes of Versailles, concluded as we have seen that *collective* interests were better served by the painful but effective solution of territorial regrouping (ethnic cleansing as it would later be known). As for stateless persons, they would no longer be treated as a judicial anomaly in a world of states and nations, but as individual victims of persecution or injustice.

Post-1945 rights talk thus concentrated on individuals. This too was a lesson of war. Even though men and women were persecuted in the name of their common identity (Jews, gypsies, Poles, etc) they suffered as individuals; and it was as individuals with individual rights that the new United Nations sought to protect them. The various Conventions on Human Rights, Genocide or Social and Economic Rights that were incorporated into international law and treaties had a cumulative impact upon public sensibilities: they combined an eighteenth-century, Anglo-American concern for individual liberties with a very mid-twentieth-century emphasis upon the obligations of the state to ensure that a growing spectrum of greater and lesser claims were met—from the right to life to the 'right' to 'truth in advertising' and beyond.

What propelled this legal rhetoric of individual rights into the realm of real politics was the coincidence of the retreat of Marxism with the international Conference on Security and Cooperation in Europe, which had opened in Helsinki the same year that *The Gulag Archipelago* was published in Paris. Until then, talk of 'rights' had long been disfavored among left-leaning European intellectuals, echoing Marx's famous dismissal of 'the so-called rights of man' as egoistic and 'bourgeois'. In progressive circles, terms such as 'Freedoms' or 'Liberty or 'Rights', and other abstractions associated with 'man in general', were taken seriously only when preceded by an adjectival modifier: 'bourgeois', or 'proletarian' or 'Socialist'.

Thus in 1969 a group of intellectuals on the left of the French Parti Socialiste Unifié criticized their own party (led at the time by Michel Rocard and Pierre Mendès-France) for supporting the reformers in Prague. The latter, they declared, had been 'the willing victims of petty-bourgeois ideologies (humanism, freedom, justice, progress, universal secret suffrage, etc).' This was no isolated instance. In the course of the 1960s many left-leaning Western commentators whose politics were otherwise quite moderate avoided mention of 'rights' or 'liberties' for fear of appearing naïve. In Eastern Europe reform Communists and their supporters had also avoided such language: in their case because of its defilement and devaluation in official rhetoric.

But from the mid-seventies it became increasingly common to find speeches and writings from all across the political spectrum in Western Europe unrestrainedly invoking 'human rights' and 'personal liberties'. As one Italian observer remarked in 1977, the idea and ideal of 'undivided' freedom was being openly discussed on the Left 'without mystification or demagogy' for the first time since the war.[6] This did not necessarily translate immediately into politics—for much of the Eighties West European Labour and Socialist parties floundered quite helplessly, resorting in many cases to the illicit appropriation of their opponents' programmes to cover their own nakedness. But their new openness to the vocabulary of rights and liberties did give Western European scholars and intellectuals access to the changing language of political opposition in *Eastern* Europe and a way of communicating across the divide—just in time, for it was *east* of the Iron Curtain that truly original and significant change was now under way.

In 1975 the Czech reform communist Zdeněk Mlynář wrote an 'Open Letter to the Communists and Socialists of Europe', addressed above all to Eurocommunists and appealing for support against the repression of dissent in Czechoslovakia. The illusions of reform Communism died hard. But Mlynář was already in a minority, his faith in both Socialism and its Western sympathizers already regarded with bemusement by most of Communism's domestic critics in the Soviet bloc.

These critics, not yet called 'dissidents' (a term generally disfavoured by those it described), had for the most part turned away from the regime and the 'Socialist' language it espoused. In the aftermath of 1968 that language, with its wooden embrace of 'peace' and 'equality' and 'fraternal goodwill', rang peculiarly false—especially to the Sixties activists who had taken it seriously. The latter—overwhelmingly students, scholars, journalists, playwrights and writers—had been the chief victims of the repression in Czechoslovakia especially, where the Party leadership under Gustav Husák (the 'President of Forgetting') correctly calculated that its best hope of re-establishing 'order' lay in mollifying popular discontent with material improvements while energetically silencing all dissenting voices and references to the recent past.

Forced underground—quite literally in the Czech case, where many unemployed professors and writers found work as stokers and boilermen—the regime's opponents could hardly engage in a *political* debate with their oppressors. Instead,

---

[6] Antonino Bruno, *Marxismo e Idealismo Italiano* (1977), pp.99–100.

abandoning Marxist vocabulary and the revisionist debates of earlier decades, they made a virtue of their circumstances and espoused deliberately 'un-political' themes. Of these, thanks to the Helsinki Accords, 'rights' were by far the most accessible.

All Soviet bloc constitutions paid formal attention to the rights and duties of the citizen; the package of additional and quite specific rights agreed to at Helsinki thus furnished Communism's domestic critics with a strategic opening. As the Czech historian Petr Pithart noted, the point was not to demand some rights as yet un-possessed—a sure invitation to further repression—but to claim those that the regime already acknowledged and that were enshrined in law, thus conferring upon the 'opposition' a moderate, almost conservative air, while forcing the Party onto the defensive.

Taking seriously the letter of 'Socialist' law was more than just a tactic, a device for embarrassing Communism's rulers. In closed societies where everything was political—and politics as such were thus precluded—'rights' offered a way forward, a first breach in the curtain of pessimism shrouding Eastern Europe in the 'silent Seventies', an end to the regime's monopoly on language-as-power. Moreover the constitutional rights of persons, by their very nature, bear formal witness to the existence of persons as such, with claims upon one another and upon the community. They describe a space between helpless individuals and the all-powerful state.

The movement for rights ('human rights'), as the young Hungarian theorist Miklós Haraszti conceded, was an acknowledgement that the necessary corrective to Communism's defects was not a better Communism but the constitution—or reconstitution—of civil (i.e. 'bourgeois') society. The irony of inverting Marxism's agenda and seeking to replace the Socialist state with bourgeois society was not lost on intellectuals in Prague or Budapest. But as Haraszti's Hungarian colleague Mihaly Vajda explained, the supremacy of the bourgeois looked decidedly preferable to their country's 'unbearable historical experience of the tyranny of the citizen'.

The significance of efforts to reconstitute civil society—a nebulous phrase describing an uncertain objective but one widely espoused by the intellectual opposition in Eastern Europe from the mid-Seventies onward—was that they recognized the impossibility after 1968 of trying to reform the Party-state. Few seriously expected Husák in Prague, or Honecker in Berlin (much less the Soviets themselves), to concede the logic of 'rights-talk' and take their own constitutions seriously. To speak of rights in theory was precisely to illustrate their absence in practice, to remind observers at home and abroad of just how un-free these societies actually were. Instead of engaging the Communist authorities, the new opposition was deliberately talking past them.

For dissidents like Haraszti, or Adam Michnik in Poland, whose 1976 essay 'A New Evolutionism' laid out much of the strategy of the Polish opposition in coming years, this was a radical departure from their youthful engagement with Marxism and its socio-economic priorities. For those who had never been remotely drawn to Marxist debates, like Václav Havel, the transition was much easier. The son of a wealthy Prague businessman whose family was dispossessed by the Communist government after 1948, Havel evinced none of the youthful revolutionary enthusiasm of his engaged contemporaries, nor did he play a very active part in their reformist efforts before 1968. Havel's relationship with the Communist authorities was always antagonistic, thanks in large part to his bourgeois origins, but it had never been political.

In the course of the Seventies and Eighties, as he was harassed, arrested and ultimately imprisoned for his activities, Havel was to become a supremely political figure. But his 'message' remained resolutely un-political. The point, he insisted, was not to argue with those in power. It was not even primarily to *tell* the truth, though in a regime based on lies this was important. The only thing that made sense in the circumstances of the time, he wrote, was to 'live in truth'. All else was compromise—'The very act of forming a political grouping forces one to start playing a power game, instead of giving truth priority.'

The objective, as Havel explained in a 1984 essay reflecting on the goals and tactics of Czechoslovakia's fragile intellectual opposition, should be to act with autonomy, whatever the regime tries to impose on you; to live *as if* one were truly free. This was hardly a prescription for most people, as Havel well understood: 'These are perhaps impractical methods in today's world and very difficult to apply in daily life. Nevertheless, I know no better alternative.'

Havel's position was not without precedents, even in recent times. Ludvík Vaculík, addressing the Fourth Congress of the Czechoslovak Writers' Union in June 1967, had recommended a similar 'as if' strategy to his colleagues even then. We should, he told them, 'play at being citizens . . . make speeches as if we were grown-up and legally independent.' But in the more optimistic atmosphere of the Sixties Vaculík and others could still hope for some accommodation and adaptation from those in power. By the time Michnik or Havel were espousing similar arguments, circumstances had changed. The point was no longer to advise the government how to govern, but to suggest to the nation—by example—how it might live.

In the circumstances of the Seventies, the idea that Eastern European intellectuals could 'suggest to the nation' how it should comport itself might appear more than a little ambitious—most intellectuals were in no position to suggest much of anything even to one another, far less to their fellow citizens at large. The intelligentsia in Hungary and Poland especially was largely ignorant of conditions and opinion in the industrial centers, and even more cut off from the world of the peasantry. Indeed it might be said that thanks to Communism—a political system which, in the words of the Hungarian dissidents Ivan Szelenyi and George Konrád, put 'intellectuals on the road to class power'—the old Central-European distinction between 'intelligentsia' and 'people' (more applicable in aristocratic societies like Hungary and Poland than in plebeian ones like Czechoslovakia, but artificially instituted even there after 1948) had resurfaced in an acute form.

The first to bridge this gap were the Poles. In 1976, following a series of strikes protesting at sharp increases in the price of food, the regime struck back hard, beating and arresting workers in the industrial towns of Ursus and Radom. In a response that broke quite deliberately with the mutual indifference of worker and intellectual protests a few years before, Jacek Kuroń and a few colleagues announced the formation in September 1976 of KOR, an acronym for the Committee for the Defense of Workers. The object of KOR, and a Committee for the Defense of Human and Civil Rights (ROPCiO) founded a few months later, was to publicize the assault on workers' civil liberties, assist in their legal defense, and form a common front. Three years later, in December 1979, the intellectual leaders of KOR—some Jewish, some Catholic, some former Communists, others not—would be responsible for the framing and publication of a 'Charter of Workers' Rights'.

The creation—or, rather, the assertion—of an autonomous civil sphere in Poland thus grew out of a social confrontation. Across the border in Czechoslovakia, in even less promising political circumstances, it was born of a legal opportunity. In January 1977 a group of Czechoslovak citizens signed a document (initially published as a manifesto in a West German newspaper) criticizing their government for its failure to implement the human rights provisions of the Czechoslovak Constitution, the Final Act of the 1975 Helsinki Accords, and United Nations covenants on political, civil, economic, and cultural rights, all of which Prague had signed—and, in the case of Helsinki Decree 120, formally incorporated into the Czech Legal Code.[7]

The signatories of this document ('Charter 77' as it became known) described themselves as a 'loose, informal, and open association of people . . . united by the will to strive individually and collectively for respect for human and civil rights in our country and throughout the world.' They took care to emphasize that Charter 77 was not an organization, had no statutes or permanent organs, and 'does not form the basis for any oppositional political activity,' a stipulation intended to keep their act within the bounds of Czechoslovak law.

Charter 77 was always the work of a tiny network of courageous indivuduals who represented no-one but themselves: 243 people signed the original document, and they were joined by just 1,621 others (in a population of 15 million) in the course of the next decade. The Charter's first spokesmen were Havel, Jiří Hájek (the country's foreign minister under Dubček) and the elderly Jan Patočka, Czechoslovakia's leading philosopher, all of them isolated intellectuals without public standing or

---

[7] Curiously, it was the Czechoslovak government's decision to ratify the UN human rights Covenants in 1976—the 35th state to do so—that made those Covenants binding under international law.

influence; but this did not stop the authorities reacting furiously to their manifesto, 'an antistate, antisocialist, demagogic, abusive piece of writing'. Individual signatories were variously described—in language drawn verbatim from the show trials of the Fifties—as 'traitors and renegades,' 'a loyal servant and agent of imperialism', 'a bankrupt politician' and 'an international adventurer'. Retaliation and intimidation were deployed against the signatories, including dismissal from work, denial of schooling for their children, suspension of drivers' licenses, forced exile and loss of citizenship, detention, trial, and imprisonment.

The harsh treatment of the signatories of Charter 77 and the Czechoslovak government's vindictive persecution of a new generation of young musicians (notably the rock group The Plastic People of the Universe) prompted the formation in April 1978 of a support group, the 'Committee for the Defense of the Unjustly Persecuted' (VONS), with goals similar to those of KOR. The response of the Prague regime to this latest development was to arrest six of the leading figures in VONS, including Havel, and try them for subversion the following year. In October 1979 they were sentenced to prison terms of up to five years.

In the wake of 1968 the Communist regimes had all (with the exception of Ceauşescu's Romania) adopted in practice the approach of Kádár's Hungary. They no longer even pretended to seek the genuine allegiance of their subjects, asking only that people proffer the outward symbols of public conformity. One goal of the Charter, like VONS—or KOR—was to overcome the resulting cynical indifference to public affairs among their fellow citizens. Havel in particular laid stress on the need to deprive governments of the satisfaction of seeing people heedlessly abase themselves in order to pass unnoticed. Otherwise, he wrote, the regime can count upon an 'outpost in every citizen'—a theme illustrated in his classic essay 'The Power of the Powerless' by the example of the greengrocer who ritually hangs in his shop-window the sign 'Workers of the World, Unite!'.

Some of the concerns of the dissenting intelligentsia were better adapted than others to this effort to overcome public apathy and fear. The emerging environmental catastrophe, already mentioned in Chapter 15, was one. In Slovakia, according to the regime's own figures, 45 percent of the 3,500 miles of rivers in Slovakia were 'dangerously' polluted in 1982. Four-fifths of the well water in the eastern part of the republic was unusable for human consumption. This was largely due to the over-use of fertilizer on the collective farms of the area, leading to soil-poisoning and crop failures like those experienced in the black soil areas of the Soviet Union.

By the early Eighties northern Bohemia had the worst air pollution in Europe, thanks to the use of (cheap) brown coal in industrial and energy production there. Of 73.5 billion kwh of power generated in the region, 64 billion came from plants burning this high-sulphur fuel. As a result, by 1983 some 35 percent of all Czech forests were dead or dying, and one-third of all Czech watercourses were too polluted even for industrial use. In Prague itself the government was forced to set up a special hospital service dealing with the respiratory ailments of children. Ivan Klíma, in a short story called '*A Christmas Conspiracy*', described stepping out into the streets of the Czech capital: 'The dark, cold mist smelled of smoke, sulphur and irritability.'

Under Socialism it was the state that polluted. But it was society that suffered, and pollution was thus a subject about which everyone cared. It was also implicitly political: the reason that it was so hard to protect the environment was that no-one had an interest in taking preventive measures. Only effective and consistently applied official sanctions could have enforced improvements, and these would have had to come from the same authority which was encouraging the wastage in the first place. Any factory or farm manager imprudent enough to risk his 'quotas' by applying pollution-control measures on his own initiative would have been in serious trouble. The Communist economic system was inherently prejudicial to its environment, as more and more people came to appreciate.[8]

Writers and scholars, reasonably enough, were preoccupied with censorship. The impediments to publication, or performance, varied considerably from one Communist country to another. In Czechoslovakia, since 1969, the authorities were unabashedly repressive: not only were thousands of men and women excluded from print or public appearance, but a very broad swathe of themes, persons and events could not even be mentioned. In Poland, by contrast, the Catholic Church and its institutions and newspapers provided a sort of semi-protected space in which a degree of literary and intellectual freedom could be practiced, albeit cautiously.

Here, as in Hungary, the problem was often one of *self*-censorship. In order to secure access to an audience, intellectuals, artists or scholars were always tempted to adapt their work, to trim or hedge an argument in anticipation of likely official objections. The professional and even material benefits of such adjustment were not to be neglected, in societies where culture and the arts were taken very seriously; but the moral cost in self-respect could be considerable. As Heine had written a hundred and fifty years before, in terms many Eastern European intellectuals would immediately have recognized, 'these executioners of thought make criminals of us. For the author . . . frequently commits infanticide: he kills his own thought-child in insane terror of the censor's mind.'

This was one kind of partial complicity. Silence—the internal emigration of the 'Ketman' in Czesław Miłosz's *Captive Mind*—was another. But those who did speak

---

[8] But even environmentalism had its internal dissidents. Milan Šimečka, the Slovak writer, warned his colleagues (Havel among them) against underestimating the benefits of modernity: 'I am of the opinion that even the pollution that accompanies industrial prosperity is better than the chaos and brutality which plagues those societies in which people are unable to satisfy their basic needs.' Milan Šimečka, 'A World With Utopias or Without Them', *Cross-Currents*, 3 (1984), p. 26.

out, circulating their work in illicit carbon copies, faced the gloomy prospect of near-invisibility, of having their ideas and their art confined to a tiny, closed audience—experiencing at best what one Czech intellectual morosely called the onanistic satisfaction of publishing *samizdat* for the same two thousand intellectuals, all of whom also write it.

Moreover, courage did not in itself ensure quality. The non-conformist, oppositional and frequently dangerous aspect of underground writing conferred on it (especially among its admirers in the West) an aura of romance and a sometimes overstated significance. Original and radical ideas could indeed blossom and thrive in the decaying compost-heap of the Soviet bloc—the writings of Havel and Michnik are the best but by no means the only instances of this, the *Fleurs du Mal* of Communism.[9] But for many others, being unpublished was no guarantee of quality. There is no 'muse of censorship' (George Steiner). Just because the regime didn't like you doesn't mean you were talented.

Thus the reputation of even some of the best known opposition intellectuals was to shrivel and shrink when exposed to a free market in ideas. Hungary's George Konrád—whose rather self-indulgent essays on 'Antipolitics' were widely admired in the Eighties—was one of many who would drop from sight after 1989. Others, like the East German novelist Christa Wolf, understood well that it was the very difficulties of being a writer under Communism that furnished her with both subject matter and a certain energy (and public standing). That is one reason why many intellectuals in Communist societies preferred to forego the opportunity of emigration and exile—better to be persecuted and significant than to be free but irrelevant.

The fear of irrelevance lay behind another consideration in these years, the widespread insistence upon the urgency of 'getting back' to Europe. Like censorship, this was a concern limited to intellectuals—indeed mostly to writers from the western provinces of the former Habsburg Empire, where the backwardness and under-development imposed by Soviet writ had been especially painful. The best-known spokesman for this sentiment was the Czech novelist and screenwriter Milan Kundera, writing from exile in Paris, for whom the tragedy of *Central* Europe (a geographical term revived explicitly to make Kundera's point) was its takeover by an alien, Asian dictatorship.

Kundera himself was not much appreciated in his homeland, where both his exile and his success were resented by those of his peers who had chosen (in their own account) to forego both. But his general thesis was widely shared, particularly in so far as it was addressed to Western readers, accused of neglecting and ignor-

---

[9] Yugoslavia is the exception that illustrates the rule: 'As there had never been an official culture established in Yugoslavia (which did not prevent the existence of official figures in cultural life), there could never be its natural opposite, an underground, alternative or parallel culture, such as was richly cherished by other socialist countries.' Dubravka Ugresic, *The Culture of Lies* (1998), page 37.

ing the 'other' West to their East—a theme already adumbrated by Miłosz back in the 1950s when he remarked that a 'chapter in a hypothetical book on postwar Polish poetry should be dedicated to irony and even derision in the treatment of the Western European and particularly French intellectuals.'

For Kundera, who was skeptical of citizens' initiatives like Charter 77, the Czech condition under Communism was an extension of the older problem of national identity and destiny in Europe's heartland, where small nations and peoples were always at risk of disappearing. The point of intellectual opposition there and abroad, he felt, was to bring *this* concern to international attention, not waste time trying to change Moscow's 'Byzantine' empire. Central Europe, moreover, was the 'destiny of the West, in concentrated form'. Havel concurred: Communism was the dark mirror that history was holding up to the West.

Poles like Michnik did not use the term 'Central Europe', or speak so much of 'returning to Europe': partly because, unlike the Czechs, they were in a position to pursue closer, attainable objectives. This is not to suggest that Poles and others did not dream of one day sharing in the benefits of the new European Community— of exchanging the failed myth of Socialism for the successful fable of 'Europe'. But they had more immediate priorities, as we shall see.

East Germans, too, had concerns of their own. One of the paradoxes of *Ostpolitik*, as practiced by Brandt and his successors, was that by transferring large sums of hard currency into East Germany and showering the GDR with recognition, attention, and support, West German officials unintentionally foreclosed any chance of internal change, including reform of Eastern Germany's polluted, antiquated industrial economy. By 'building bridges', twinning towns, paying their respects, and distancing themselves from Western criticism of East bloc regimes, Bonn's statesmen afforded the leadership of the GDR a false sense of stability and security.

Moreover, by 'buying out' political opponents and prisoners, West Germany deprived the East German opposition of some of its best known dissenters. No other Communist society had a Western *doppelganger*, speaking the same language. The temptation to leave was thus always there and the 'right to movement' typically headed the list of rights that preoccupied writers and artists in the GDR. But many 'internal' critics of the East German regime chose to abandon neither their country nor their old ideas. Indeed, by the end of the Seventies the GDR was the *only* European Communist state that could still boast an informal and even intra-Party Marxist opposition. Its best known dissidents all attacked Communist authority from the *Left*—a stance that rendered them both inaudible and irrelevant elsewhere in Eastern Europe, as the Czech writer Jiří Pelikán tartly observed.

Thus Rudolf Bahro, who after years of persecution was deported west in 1979, was best-known for his essay *The Alternative*, an explicitly Marxist critique of 'real existing Socialism'. Robert Havemann, an older Communist who was prosecuted and fined in these years for his engagement on behalf of the folk singer Wolf Biermann (expelled West in 1976) castigated the ruling party not for abusing rights but for betraying its ideals and encouraging mass consumption and the private ownership of consumer goods. Wolfgang Harich, a leading figure in GDR philosophy circles and a longtime critic of the regime's 'bureaucratic' deviation, was equally vociferous in his opposition to the 'illusions of consumerism', against which he saw it as the task of the ruling party to re-educate the populace.

What opposition there was in the GDR to Communism as such tended to coalesce, as in Poland, around the churches: in Germany the Protestant *Bund der Evangelischen Kirchen*. Here the new language of rights and liberties abutted that of the Christian faith, and (again, as in Poland) was reinforced by association with the only surviving pre-Socialist institution. The influence of the churches also accounts for the prominence of the 'peace' question in East German dissident circles.

Elsewhere in eastern Europe the Western 'peaceniks' and activists for nuclear disarmament were regarded with considerable suspicion. They were seen at best as naïve innocents, more likely the mindless instruments of Soviet manipulation.[10] Václav Havel, for one, regarded the growing west European anti-war movement of the early 1980s as the perfect vehicle for engaging, diverting and *neutralizing* the western intelligentsia. : 'peace', he insisted, is not an option in countries where the state is permanently at war with society. Peace and disarmament under prevailing conditions would leave western Europe free and independent, while maintaining eastern Europe under Soviet control. It was a mistake to separate the 'peace' question from the demand for rights and liberties. Or, as Adam Michnik put it, 'the condition for reducing the danger of war is full respect of human rights'.

But in East Germany the peace movement found a deep local resonance. No doubt this was in part thanks to links with West Germany. But there was something else. The GDR—an accidental state with neither history nor identity—could with some shard of plausibility describe peace, or at least 'peaceful coexistence', as its true *raison d'être*. Yet at the same time it was by far the most militarized and militaristic of the socialist states: from 1977 'Defense Studies' were introduced into East German schools, and the state Youth Movement was unusually para-military even by Soviet standards. The tension generated by this glaring paradox found its outlet in an opposition movement which derived a large part of its support from its concentration on the issue of peace and disarmament.

In 1962 the East German regime had introduced a compulsory military service of eighteen months for all men aged 18–50. But two years later it added an escape clause: those who wished to be excused military service on moral grounds could join the *Bausoldaten*, an alternative labor unit. Although membership of the latter could prove a handicap in later life, its mere existence meant the GDR acknowledged the fact and the legitimacy of conscientious objection. By 1980

---

[10] With good reason. As we have since learned, the British and West German peace movements of the time were thoroughly penetrated by Soviet and East German intelligence.

thousands of East German men had passed through the *Bausoldaten* and represented a substantial potential network for peace activists.

Thus when Lutheran pastors began in 1980 to offer support and protection to the early peace activists, they were able to do so to a considerable extent without incurring state disapproval. The nascent peace movement then spread from the churches to the universities, inevitably raising not only calls for disarmament, but also the demand for the right to articulate these calls without hindrance. In this indirect way dissenting East Germans belatedly found a way to communicate (and catch up) with the opposition elsewhere in the bloc.

Romanians had no such luck. The appearance of Charter 77 prompted a courageous letter of support from the writer Paul Goma and seven other Romanian intellectuals, all of whom were promptly suppressed. But otherwise Romania remained as silent as it had been for three decades. Goma was forced into exile: no-one took his place. For this the West bore a measure of responsibility—even if a Romanian Charter 77 or a local version of Poland's *Solidarity* (see Chapter 19) had arisen, it is unlikely that it would have received much Western support. No US President ever demanded that the dictator Nicolai Ceauşescu 'let Romania be Romania'.

Even the Soviet Union allowed a tightly restricted liberty of action to certain intellectuals—mostly prominent scientists, always a privileged category. The biologist Zhores Medvedev, whose 1960s exposure of Lysenko had long circulated in *samizdat*, was first harrassed and then deprived of his citizenship. He settled in the UK in 1973. But Andrei Sakharov, the country's best-known nuclear physicist and a longstanding critic of the regime, remained at liberty—until his public opposition to the 1979 invasion of Afghanistan rendered his presence intolerable. Sakharov was too embarrassing to ignore (he had been awarded the Nobel Peace Prize in 1975) but too important to send abroad. He and his wife Yelena Bonner were forced instead into (internal) exile in the closed city of Gorky.

But Sakharov always insisted he was calling the Soviet Union to account for its shortcomings and its persecution of critics, rather than seeking its overthrow—a stance that put him somewhere between an older generation of reform Communists and the new Central European dissidents. Others, less prominent and avowedly anti-Soviet, were treated much more harshly. The poet Natalya Gorbanevskaya spent three years in a prison psychiatric hospital, diagnosed along with hundreds of others with 'sluggish schizophrenia'. Vladimir Bukovsky, the best known of the younger radicals, spent twelve years in Soviet prisons, labour camps and psychiatric wards before international outcry at his treatment led to his exchange for Luis Corvalán, a Chilean Communist, in 1976.

Except for such occasional protests on behalf of individuals, and a concerted campaign on behalf of the right of Soviet Jews to emigrate, the West paid remarkably little attention to the *domestic* affairs of the USSR—much less than was, by the early 1980s, being directed towards internal opposition in Poland or even Czechoslovakia, for example. It was not until 1983 that the Soviet Union withdrew from the World Psychiatric Association, when the latter—with shameful tardiness—finally began to criticize its abuses.

But with or without external prompting, the overwhelming majority of the Soviet intelligentsia was never going to follow the example being set, however tentatively, elsewhere in Eastern Europe. The fear inspired by Stalin's repression hung like a pall across the moral landscape three decades after his death, even if no-one actually spoke of it, and all but the most outspoken and courageous critics took care to stay within the bounds of legitimate Soviet themes and language. They assumed, reasonably enough, that the Soviet Union was here to stay. Writers like Andrei Amalrik, whose essay 'Will the Soviet Union Survive until 1984?' first appeared in the West in 1970, and was re-published in expanded form ten years later, were prophetic but atypical. In contrast to the puppet regimes it had installed at its boundaries, the Soviet Union by 1983 had been in place for longer than most of its citizens could remember and appeared fundamentally stable.

The intellectual opposition in Central Europe had little immediate impact. This surprised no-one: the new realism of the Seventies-era dissidents encompassed not just a disabused grasp of Socialism's failure but also a clear-sighted appreciation of the facts of power. There were limits, moreover, on what could be asked of people: in his 'Essay on Bravery' the Czechoslovak writer Ludvík Vaculík argued persuasively that one can ask only so much of ordinary people struggling to get through their daily lives. Most people lived in a sort of moral 'grey zone', a safe if stifling space in which enthusiasm was replaced by acceptance. Active, risk-laden resistance to authority was hard to justify because—again, for most ordinary people—it appeared unnecessary. 'Un-heroic, realistic deeds' were the most one could expect.

The intellectuals were talking for the most part to one another rather than addressing the community at large: in some cases they were offering implicit amends for their earlier enthusiasms. Moreover, they were the heirs (in certain instances quite literally the children) of the ruling class of the first generation of Socialist power—education and privilege having passed reasonably efficiently down the generations, especially in Poland and Hungary. That did not always endear them to the mass of the population. As in the past, when they had spoken *for* the regimes they now opposed, they were a tiny minority of the population and represented only themselves.

Thus when George Konrád wrote somewhat sententiously that 'no thinking person should want to drive others from positions of political power in order to occupy them for himself', he was acknowledging a simple truth—no 'thinking person' was in a position there and then to do any such thing. This same appreciation of the grim facts of life also forms a backdrop to the opposition's insistence on non-violence: not only in Czechoslovakia, where passivity in the face of authority had a long history; or in the GDR, where the Lutheran Church was increasingly influential in opposition circles; but even in Poland, where it represented for Michnik and others both a pragmatic and an ethical bar to dangerous and pointless 'adventures'.

The achievement of the new opposition lay elsewhere. In the East as in the West, the Seventies and Eighties were a time of cynicism. The energies of the Sixties had dissipated, their political ideals had lost moral credibility, and engagement in the public interest had given way to calculations of private advantage. By forging a conversation about rights, by focusing attention on the rather woolly concept of 'civil society', by insistently talking about the silences of Central Europe's present and its past—by moralizing shamelessly in public, as it were—Havel and others were building a sort of 'virtual' public space to replace the one destroyed by Communism.

One thing the dissident intellectuals did *not* talk about very much was economics. This, too, was a kind of realism. Ever since Stalin, economic—or, more precisely, industrial—growth had been both the goal of Socialism and the main measure of its success. Economics, as we saw in Chapter 13, had been the overriding concern of an earlier generation of reformist intellectuals: reflecting back at the Communist regime its own obsessions and echoing an assumption—shared by Marxists and many non-Marxists alike—that all politics are ultimately *about* economics. Critical discussion couched in the form of recommendations for economic reform had been the nearest thing to a licensed opposition in the revisionist decade between 1956 and 1968.

But by the middle of the 1970s it was hard for any well-informed observer of the Soviet bloc to take seriously the prospect of economic reform from within, and not only because the language of Marxist economics had collapsed after decades of unseemly abuse. From 1973 the economies of Eastern Europe were falling sharply behind even Western Europe's reduced growth rates. Except for a brief blip in the finances of the oil-rich Soviet Union, brought on by the rise in energy prices, the inflation of the Seventies and the 'globalizing' of trade and services in the Eighties put the economies of the Soviet bloc at an insuperable disadvantage. In 1963 the international trade of Comecon countries had been 12 percent of the world total. By 1979 it was down to 9 percent and falling fast.[11]

The countries of the Soviet bloc could not compete on quality with the industrial economies of the West; nor did any of them except the USSR itself have a sustainable supply of raw materials to sell to the West, so they could not even compete with undeveloped countries. The closed Comecon system precluded participation in the new trading networks of Western Europe and GATT, and Com-

---

[11] During the 1980s Poland and Czechoslovakia both slipped into negative economic growth—their economies actually shrinking. The economy of the USSR itself had probably been shrinking since 1979.

munist states could in any case not adapt their economies to world price levels without risking the fury of domestic consumers (which is what happened in Poland in 1976).

The crippling defect of Communist economies by this time was endemic, ideologically-induced inefficiency. Because of an unbending insistence upon the importance of primary industrial output for the 'construction of socialism', the Soviet bloc missed the switch from extensive to intensive, high-value production that transformed Western economies in the course of the Sixties and Seventies. Instead it remained reliant upon a much earlier model of economic activity, redolent of Detroit or the Ruhr in the 1920s, or late nineteenth-century Manchester.

Thus Czechoslovakia—a country with very limited resources in iron—was by 1981 the world's third largest (per capita) exporter of steel. To the bitter end, the GDR was planning ever-expanded production of obsolete heavy industrial goods. No-one who had any choice actually wanted to buy Czech steel or East German machines, except at heavily subsidized prices: these goods were thus produced and sold at a loss. In effect, Soviet-style economies were now *subtracting* value—the raw materials they imported or dug out of the ground were worth more than the finished goods into which they were transformed.

Even in areas of comparative advantage the Soviet economy took its toll. Just as Hungary was Comecon's chosen manufacturer of trucks and buses, so the GDR in the 1980s was assigned the task of manufacturing computers. But not only were the machines produced in East Germany unreliable and outdated; the centralized system was simply unable to make enough of them. By 1989, East Germany (with a population of 16 million) was turning out just one-fiftieth the number of computers manufactured in Austria (population: 7.5 million)—and as a producer of computers Austria was a negligible competitor in the international market. 'Comparative advantage' in this case was thus strictly relative—the GDR was spending millions of marks producing unwanted goods that were available at lower cost and in better quality on the world market.

Much of the responsibility for all this lay with the inherent defects of centralized planning. By the late 1970s Gosplan, the Soviet central economic planning agency, had forty departments for different branches of the economy and twenty seven separate economic ministries. The obsession with numerical targets was notorious to the point of self-parody: Timothy Garton Ash cites the example of 'The People's Economy Plan for the Borough of Prenzlauer Berg' (in East Berlin), where it was announced that 'Book-holdings in the libraries are to be increased from 350,000 to 450,000 volumes. The number of borrowings is to be increased by 108.2 percent'.[12]

---

[12] Timothy Garton Ash, *The Uses of Adversity* (NY, 1989), page 9.

Fixed price systems made it impossible to ascertain real costs, to respond to needs or to adapt to resource constraints. Administrators at every level were frightened of taking risks and innovating, lest they reduce aggregate output in the short term. In any case, they had no incentive: they were secure in their posts no matter how incompetent, thanks to Brezhnev's well-known preference for the 'stability of cadres' (the watchword from 1971 onwards). Meanwhile, in order to make sure that they would meet targets set from above, factory foremen and managers took great pains to *hide* reserves of material and labour from the authorities. Waste and shortage were thus mutually self-sustaining.

The predictable effect of such a system was to encourage not just stagnation and inefficiency but a permanent cycle of corruption. It is one of the paradoxes of the Socialist project that the absence of property tends to generate more corruption, not less. Power, position and privilege cannot be directly bought, but depend instead upon mutually-reinforcing relationships of patronage and clientelism. Legal rights are replaced by sycophancy, which is duly rewarded with job security or advancement. To achieve even modest and legitimate objectives—medical treatments, material necessities, educational opportunities—people are required to bend the law in a variety of minor but corrupting ways.

This accounts in large measure for the marked increase in cynicism in these years. One example can stand for many: Tractor plants, or truck manufacturers, did not bother to make sufficient spare parts because they could more easily meet their 'norms' by building large machines—with the result that when these large machines broke down, there were no replacement parts available. Official data published only the total number of machines of all sorts produced in a given sector; they did not say how many were still in working order. The workers, of course, knew better.

The Socialist social contract was tartly summed up in the popular joke: 'you pretend to work, we pretend to pay you'. Many workers, especially the less-skilled, had a stake in these arrangements, which—in return for political quiescence—offered social security and a low level of pressure at the workplace. As East Germany's official *Small Political Dictionary* put it, with unintended irony, 'in socialism, the contradiction between work and free time, typical of capitalism, is removed.'

The only parts of a typical Communist economy that worked relatively efficiently by 1980 were the high-technology defense industries and the so-called 'second economy'—the black market in goods and services. The importance of this second economy—whose very existence could not be officially acknowledged—was testimony to the sad state of the official one. In Hungary, by the early eighties, it is estimated that a mere 84,000 artisans—operating exclusively in the private sector— were meeting nearly 60 percent of local demand for services, from plumbing to prostitution.

Add to this private peasant production, along with public resources (bricks, copper wire, typefaces) 'diverted' for use by workers in private enterprise, and it can be seen that Soviet-style Communism—much like Italian capitalism—relied for its survival on a parallel economy.[13] The relationship was symbiotic: the Communist state could sustain its public monopoly only by channeling into the private sphere all activities and needs that it could neither deny nor meet; while the second economy depended upon the official one for resources, but above all for the very inefficiency of the public sector which guaranteed it a market and artificially elevated its value and thereby its profits.

Economic stagnation was in itself a standing rebuke to Communism's claims to superiority over capitalism. And if not a stimulus to opposition, it was certainly a source of disaffection. For most people living under Communism in the Brezhnev era, from the late Sixties through the early Eighties, life was no longer shaped by terror or repression. But it was grey and drab. Adults had fewer and fewer children; they drank more—the per capita annual consumption of alcoholic spirits in the Soviet Union quadrupled in these years—and they died young. Public architecture in Communist societies was not only aesthetically unappealing, it was shoddy and uncomfortable, a faithful mirror of the shabby authoritarianism of the system itself. As a Budapest taxi-driver once remarked to the present author, pointing to the serried ranks of dank, grimy apartment blocks that disfigure the city's outer suburbs: 'We live in those. Typical Communist building—summer is hot, winter very cold.'

Apartments, like much else in the Soviet bloc, were cheap (rent averaged 4 percent of a typical household budget in the USSR), because the economy was regulated not by price but by scarcity. This had its advantages for the authorities—the arbitrary allocation of scarce commodities helped maintain loyalty—but it carried with it a serious risk, which most Communist leaders understood very well. Ever since it had become clear by the end of the Sixties that the future promise of 'Socialism' could no longer be counted upon to bind citizens to the regime, Communist rulers had opted instead to treat their subjects as consumers and replace (socialist) utopia tomorrow with material abundance today.

This choice was made quite consciously. As Vasil Bil'ák, the Czech hardliner who was instrumental in inviting the Soviets to invade his country in 1968, put it to his party's Ideological Commission in October 1970: '[In 1948] we had posters in the shop windows about how socialism is going to look, and people were receptive to it. That was a different kind of excitement and a different historical time, and today we can't put up posters about how socialism is going to look, but today

---

[13] In agriculture, much of the Soviet Union, Hungary and Romania once again resembled the great nineteenth-century landed estates: poorly-paid, under-performing, inadequately-equipped agricultural labourers did the minimum for their absent employers while saving their energy for the real labour they put into family plots.

shop windows have to be full of goods so that we can document that we are moving to socialism and that we have socialism here'.[14]

Consumerism, then, was to be encouraged as the measure of Socialism's success. This was not the same as Khrushchev's famous 1959 'kitchen debate' with Nixon, when he assured the American Vice-President that Communism would outperform capitalism in the foreseeable future. Bil'ák—like Kádár in Hungary—had no such illusions. He was content for Communism to be a pale imitation of capitalism, so long as the goods on offer kept consumers happy. East Germany's Erich Honecker, who replaced the unmourned Walter Ulbricht as party leader in 1971, likewise set out to offer the citizens of the GDR a modest adaptation of West Germany's 1950's 'miracle'.

This strategy was moderately successful for a while. The standard of living in Czechoslovakia, Hungary and Poland improved through the 1970s, at least when measured by retail consumption. The number of cars and televisions—the iconic consumer durables of the age—rose steadily: in Poland the number of privately-owned cars per head of the population increased fourfold between 1975 and 1989. By the end of the eighties there were four televisions for every ten people in Hungary; the figures for Czechoslovakia were similar. If buyers were willing to accept poor quality, indifferent styling and little choice, they could usually find what they wanted, in official shops or through the 'private' sector. In the Soviet Union, however, such 'optional' goods were harder to find—and relatively more expensive.

The same was true of basic necessities. In March 1979 a shopper in Washington DC would have had to work 12.5 hours to afford a generic 'basket' of basic foods (sausages, milk, eggs, potatoes, vegetables, tea, beer, etc). A similar basket would 'cost' 21.4 work-hours in London, but 42.3 work-hours in Moscow, despite high levels of subsidy.[15] Moreover the Soviet or East European consumer had to spend many more hours finding and purchasing foods and other goods. Measured in time and effort, if not in rubles or crowns or forints, life under Communism was expensive as well as exhausting.

The problem with defining Communism by its success in satisfying private consumers was that the whole economy was geared, as noted above, to the high-volume manufacture of industrial machinery and raw materials. Except for food, Communist economies did not produce the things that consumers wanted (and they were not very efficient at producing food, either—the Soviet Union had long since become a net *importer* of grain, tripling its food imports between 1970 and 1982 alone). The only way around this impediment was to import consumer goods from

---

[14] I am grateful to Dr Paulina Bren for this reference.

[15] In the Brezhnev years a pound of beef cost three and a half rubles to produce but was sold in shops for two rubles. The European Community subsidized its farmers too, and in approximately the same proportions. The difference, of course, was that Western Europe could afford a Common Agricultural Policy and the Soviet Union could not.

abroad, but these had to be paid for with hard currency. The latter could only be acquired by exports: but except for Soviet oil the world market had little use for Socialist output unless sold at a sharp discount and in many cases not even then. In practice, the only way to stock the shelves in the East was to borrow money from the West.

The West was certainly keen to oblige. The IMF, the World Bank and private bankers were all happy to lend to Soviet bloc countries: the Red Army was a reassuring guarantee of stability, and Communist officials misrepresented their countries' output and resources to convincing effect.[16] In the course of the 1970s alone Czechoslovakia's hard currency debt rose twelve-fold. Poland's hard currency debt increased some 3,000 percent, as First Secretary Gierek and his colleagues sucked in subsidized Western goods, introduced expensive new social insurance programs for peasants and froze food prices at 1965 levels.

Once borrowing at these levels took off it was hard to contain. Gierek's food price increases of 1976 triggered angry riots and were quickly repealed, the regime choosing instead to keep borrowing: between 1977 and 1980 one-third of Poland's external line of credit was used to subsidize domestic consumption. Communist economists in Prague recommended phasing out subsidies and introducing 'real' prices, but their political masters feared the social consequences of such a retreat and preferred to increase their debts instead. As in the inter-war years, the fragile little states of eastern Europe were once again borrowing capital from the West to finance their autarkic economies and avoid hard choices.

Miklós Németh, the last Communist prime minister of Hungary, was to acknowledge as much a few years later. A loan of one billion Deutschmarks from Bonn, granted in October 1987 and portrayed by West German politicians as a contribution to Hungarian economic 'reform', was in reality disbursed thus: 'we spent two thirds of it on interest and the remainder importing consumer goods to ease the impression of economic crisis.' By 1986 Hungary's *official* deficit on current account was $ 1.4 billion per annum. Between 1971 and 1980 Poland's hard currency debt had risen from $1 billion to $20.5 billion, with worse to come. By its own reckoning the GDR in its last years was spending over 60 percent of its yearly export earnings just to cover the (very generously discounted) interest on its Western debts. Yugoslavia, always a favored client (from 1950 through 1964 the US had covered three-fifths of Belgrade's annual deficits) received generous loans and stand-by arrangements on the basis of official data that bore not even a passing relationship to reality.

Taken as a whole, eastern Europe's hard currency debt, which stood at $6.1 billion in 1971, grew to $66.1 billion in 1980. By 1988 it would reach $95.6 billion. These figures did not include Romania, where Ceaușescu had paid off his country's for-

---

[16] Hungary joined the IMF in May 1982, to mutual self-congratulation. Only in 1989 did it emerge that its government had seriously understated its internal and external debt for the previous decade.

eign loans on the backs of his long-suffering subjects; and they might well have been even higher but for some latitude on price-setting introduced in Hungary over the course of the Seventies. But their message was clear: the Communist system was living not just on loans but on borrowed time. Sooner or later it would be necessary to make painful and socially disruptive economic adjustments.

In years to come Markus Wolf, the East German spymaster, would claim that by the late 1970s he had already concluded that the GDR 'wouldn't work' and he was certainly not alone. Economists like Hungary's Támás Bauer and his Polish contemporary Leszek Balcerowicz knew perfectly well how fragile the Communist house of cards had become. But so long as the capitalists would underwrite it, Communism could survive. Leonid Brezhnev's 'era of stagnation' (Mikhail Gorbachev) fostered many illusions, and not only at home. In 1978, when a World Bank Report actually determined that the GDR had a higher standard of living than Great Britain, Prince Potemkin must surely have smiled in his far-off grave.

But Communists understood something that the bankers of the West had missed. Economic reform in the Soviet bloc had not merely been postponed. It was out of the question. As Amalrik had predicted in *Will the USSR Survive Until 1984?*, the Communist élite 'look upon the regime as a lesser evil compared with the painful process of changing it.' Economic reforms of even the most localized and micro-efficient kind would have immediate political ramifications. The economic arrangements of socialism were not an autonomous zone; they were thoroughly integrated into the political regime itself.

It was not by chance that the East European satellite states were all run by ageing, conservative time-servers. In a new age of realism Edward Gierek in Warsaw (born 1913), Gustav Husák in Prague (born 1913), Erich Honecker in Berlin (born 1912), János Kádár in Budapest (born 1912) and Todor Zhivkov in Sofia (born 1911)—not to speak of Enver Hoxha in Tirana (born 1908) and Josip Broz Tito in Belgrade (born 1892)—were the most realistic of all. Like Leonid Brezhnev—born 1906, Seven Orders of Lenin, four-time Hero Of The Soviet Union, winner of the Lenin Peace Prize, General Secretary and, since 1977, Head of State—these men had grown old in the old ways. They had little incentive to pull the rug out from under themselves. They had every intention of dying in their beds.[17]

The fact that 'real existing Socialism' was dysfunctional and discredited did not in itself seal its fate. In his 1971 Nobel Prize acceptance speech (delivered in his absence), Aleksandr Solzhenitsyn had rousingly asserted that 'once the lie has been dispersed, the nakedness of violence will be revealed in all its repulsiveness, and then violence, become decrepit, will come crashing down.' But this was not quite true. The nakedness of Soviet violence had long since been revealed—and would be ex-

---

[17] Moreover, like Brezhnev himself, they were among the leading consumers of the age. In a Soviet joke from the time, the Soviet leader is showing his mother his *dacha*, his cars and his hunting lodges. 'It's wonderful, Leonid,' she says. 'But what if the Communists come back to power?'

posed again in the disastrous 1979 invasion of Afghanistan—and the lie of Communism was progressively dispersed and dispelled in the course of the years after 1968.

But the system had not yet come crashing down. Lenin's distinctive contribution to European history had been to kidnap the centrifugal political heritage of European radicalism and channel it into power through an innovative system of monopolized control: unhesitatingly gathered and forcefully retained in one place. The Communist system might corrode indefinitely at the periphery; but the initiative for its final collapse could only come from the centre. In the story of Communism's demise, the remarkable flowering in Prague or Warsaw of a new kind of opposition was only the end of the beginning. The emergence of a new kind of leadership in Moscow itself, however, was to be the beginning of the end.

XIX

The End of the Old Order

'We cannot go on living like this'.
Mikhail Gorbachev (to his wife, March 1985)

'The most dangerous time for a bad government is when it starts to
reform itself'.
Alexis De Tocqueville

'We have no intention of harming or destabilizing the GDR'.
Heinrich Windelen, West-German Minister for inter-German relations

'Historical experience shows that Communists were sometimes forced by
circumstances to behave rationally and agree to compromises'.
Adam Michnik

'People, your government has returned to you'.
Václav Havel, Presidential Address, January 1st 1990

The conventional narrative of Communism's final collapse begins with Poland. On October 16th 1978, Karol Wojtyła, Cardinal of Craków, was elected to the Papacy as John Paul II, the first Pole to hold the office. The expectations aroused by his election were unprecedented in modern times. Some in the Catholic Church regarded him as a likely radical—he was young (just fifty-eight when elected pope in 1978, having been appointed Archbishop of Craków while still in his thirties) but already a veteran of the Second Vatican Council. Energetic and charismatic, this was the man who would complete the work of Popes John XXIII and Paul VI and who would lead the Church into a new era, a pastor rather than a Curial bureaucrat.

Conservative Catholics, meanwhile, took comfort in Wojtyła's reputation for unbending theological firmness and the moral and political absolutism born of his experience as a priest and prelate under communism. This was a man who, for all his reputation as a 'pope of ideas', open to intellectual exchange and scholarly debate, would not compromise with the Church's enemies. Like Cardinal Joseph Ratzinger, the powerful head of the Congregation for the Doctrine of the Faith (and his successor as Pope), Wojtyła had been startled out of his early reforming enthusiasm by the radical aftershock of John XXIII's reforms. By the time of his election he was already an administrative as well as a doctrinal conservative.

Karol Wojtyła's Polish origins and his tragic early life help to explain the unusual strength of his convictions and the distinctive quality of his papacy. He lost his mother when he was eight (he would lose his only sibling, his older brother Edmund, three years later; his last surviving close relative, his father, died during the war when Wojtyła was nineteen). Following his mother's death he was taken by his father to the Marian sanctuary at Kalwaria Zebrzydowska and made frequent pilgrimages there in following years—Zebrzydowska, like Częstochowa, is an important center of the cult of the Virgin Mary in modern Poland. By the age of fifteen Wojtyła was already the president of the Marian sodality in Wadowice, his home town, an early hint of his inclination to Mariolatry (which in turn contributed to his obsession with marriage and abortion).

The new Pope's Christian vision was rooted in the peculiarly messianic style of Polish Catholicism. In modern Poland he saw not only the embattled eastern frontier of the True Faith, but also a land and a people chosen to serve as the example and sword of the Church in the struggle against Eastern atheism and Western materialism alike.[1] Together with his long service in Craków, isolated from Western theological and political currents, this probably explained his tendency to embrace a parochial and sometimes troubling Polish-Christian vision.[2]

But it also explains the unprecedented enthusiasm for him in the country of his birth. From the outset, the pope broke with his predecessors' cosmopolitan Roman acquiescence in modernity, secularism, and compromise. His campaign of international appearances—complete with carefully staged performances in huge open arenas, accompanied by oversized crucifixes and a paraphernalia of light, sound, and theatrical timing—was not undertaken without design. This was a Big Pope, taking himself and his Faith to the world: to Brazil, Mexico, the US, and the Philippines; to Italy, France, and Spain; but above all to Poland itself.

Abandoning the cautious 'Ostpolitik' of his predecessors, John Paul II arrived in Warsaw on June 2nd 1979 for the first of three dramatic 'pilgrimages' to Communist Poland. He was met with huge, adoring crowds. His presence affirmed and reinforced the influence of the Catholic Church in Poland; but the Pope was not interested in merely endorsing Christianity's passive survival under Communism. To the occasional discomfort of his own bishops he began explicitly discouraging

---

[1] It is of course the business of the Catholic Church to inveigh against material idols and the sin of pride. But Karol Wojtyła went much further. In his 1975 Lenten Exercises at the Vatican, three years before becoming Pope, he explicitly announced that of the two threats to the Church, consumerism and persecution, the former was by far the graver danger and thus the greater enemy.

[2] Witness his initial support for a projected Carmelite convent at Auschwitz, later withdrawn in the face of international protest. His thoughtless description of Poland under martial law as a 'vast concentration camp' reflects a similar limitation.

Catholics in Poland and everywhere else in Eastern Europe from any compromise with Marxism, and offered his Church not merely as a silent sanctuary but as an alternative pole of moral and social authority.

As Poland's Communists well understood, such a change in the position of the Catholic Church—from compromise to resistance—could have a destabilizing local impact, posing an open challenge to the Party's monopoly of authority. In part this was because Poles remained overwhelmingly and enthusiastically Catholic; in large measure it was because of the man himself. But there was very little they could do—to forbid the Pope to visit Poland or to speak there would only have strengthened his appeal and further alienated millions of his admirers. Even after the imposition of martial law, when the Pope returned to Poland in June 1983 and spoke to his 'compatriots' in St John's Cathedral in Warsaw of their 'disappointment and humiliation, their suffering and loss of freedom', the Communist leaders could only stand and listen. 'Poland', he told an uncomfortable General Jaruzelski in a televised speech, 'must take her proper place among the nations of Europe, between East and West.'

The Pope, as Stalin once observed, has no divisions. But God is not always on the side of the big battalions: what John Paul II lacked in soldiers he made up in visibility—and timing. Poland in 1978 was already on the edge of social upheaval. Ever since the workers' revolts of 1970, and again in 1976, both prompted by sharp increases in the price of food, First Secretary Edvard Gierek had tried hard to avert domestic discontent—mostly, as we have seen, by borrowing heavily abroad and using the loans to supply Poles with subsidized food and other consumer goods. But the strategy was failing.

Thanks to the emergence of Jacek Kuroń's KOR, the intellectual opposition and workers' leaders now cooperated far more than in the past. In response to the cautious appearance of 'free' (i.e. illegal) trade unions in a number of industrial and coastal towns, beginning in Katowice and Gdansk, the leaders of KOR drew up a 'Charter of Workers' Rights' in December 1979: its demands included the right to autonomous, non-Party unions and the right to strike. The predictable response of the authorities was to arrest intellectual activists and sack the offending workers—among them the then-unknown electrician Lech Walesa and fourteen other employees at Elektromontaz in Gdansk.

Whether the semi-clandestine movement for workers' rights would have continued to grow is not clear. Its spokesmen were certainly emboldened by the Pope's recent visit and their sense that the regime would be reluctant to strike back violently for fear of international disapproval. But theirs was still a tiny and haphazard network of activists. What triggered mass backing was the Communist Party's attempt—for the third time in a decade—to resolve its economic difficulties by announcing, on July 1st 1980, an immediate increase in the price of meat.

The day after the announcement, KOR declared itself a 'strike information agency'. In the next three weeks protest strikes spread from the Ursus tractor plant (scene of the 1976 protests) to every major industrial city in the country, reaching Gdansk and its Lenin Shipyard on August 2nd. There the shipbuilders occupied the yard and formed themselves into an unofficial trade union, *Solidarność* ('Solidarity')—led by Walesa, who on August 14th 1980 climbed over the shipyard wall and into the leadership of a national strike movement.

The authorities' instinctive response—to arrest 'ringleaders' and isolate the strikers—having failed, they opted instead to buy time and divide their opponents. In an unprecedented move, representatives of the Politburo were sent to Gdansk to negotiate with 'reasonable' workers' leaders, even as Kuroń, Adam Michnik and other KOR leaders were temporarily detained for questioning. But other intellectuals—the historian Bronisław Geremek, the Catholic lawyer Tadeusz Mazowiecki—arrived in Gdansk to help the strikers negotiate, and the strikers themselves insisted that they be represented by their own choice of spokesmen: notably the increasingly prominent Walesa.

The regime was forced to relent. On September 1st the police released all remaining detainees, and two weeks later the Polish Council of State officially conceded the strikers' chief demand, the right to form and register free labor unions. Within eight weeks the informal network of strikes and *ad hoc* unions that now criss-crossed Poland had coalesced into a single organization whose existence the authorities could no longer pretend to deny: on November 10th 1980, Solidarity became the first officially registered independent trade union in a Communist country, with an estimated ten million members. At its founding national Congress the following September Walesa was elected president.

From November 1980 until December 1981 Poland lived in an excited, uneasy limbo. Walesa's advisers—mindful of past mistakes and wary of provoking a backlash from the humiliated Communist leadership—urged caution. This was to be a 'self-limiting revolution'. Jacek Kuroń, with the memory of 1956 and 1968 firmly in mind, insisted upon his continuing commitment to a 'socialist system' and reiterated Solidarity's acceptance of the 'Party's leading role'—no-one wanted to give the authorities in Warsaw or Moscow an excuse to send in the tanks.

The self-imposed restraints paid off, up to a point. Overtly political issues—disarmament, or foreign policy—were kept off Solidarity's public agenda, which focused instead upon KOR's established strategy of 'practicing society': building links with the Catholic Church (of particular interest to Adam Michnik, who was determined to overcome the traditional anti-clericalism of the Polish Left and forge an alliance with the newly-energized Catholic leadership); forming local unions and factory councils; pressing for workplace self-management and social rights (the latter borrowed verbatim from the Conventions of the Geneva-based International Labour Organization).

But under Communism, even such cautiously 'non-political' tactics were bound

THE END OF THE OLD ORDER

to run up against the Party's reluctance to concede *any* real authority or autonomy. Moreover, the economy continued to implode: industrial productivity collapsed in the course of 1981, as Poland's newly unionized workers held meetings, protests and strikes to press their demands. Seen from Warsaw, and especially from Moscow, the country was adrift and the regime was losing control. It was also setting a bad example to its neighbors. Despite the best efforts of its cautious leaders, Solidarity was doomed to arouse the ghosts of Budapest and Prague.

General Wojciech Jaruzelski had risen from defense minister to prime minister in February 1981, replacing the now-disgraced Gierek. In October he succeeded Stanisław Kania as Party Secretary. Ensured of the support of the army, and with the Soviet leadership encouraging firm action to halt Poland's drift out of control, he moved swiftly to put an end to a situation that both sides knew could not last indefinitely. On December 13th 1981—just as US-Soviet nuclear disarmament talks were getting under way in Geneva—Jaruzelski declared martial law in Poland, ostensibly to forestall a Soviet intervention. Solidarity's leaders and advisers were swept up into prison (though the union itself was not formally banned until the following year, at which point it went 'underground'[3]).

In post-'89 retrospect the rise of Solidarity appears as the opening fusillade in the final struggle against Communism. But the Polish 'revolution' of 1980–81 is better understood as the last in a rising crescendo of workers' protests that began in 1970 and were directed against the Party's repressive and incompetent management of the economy. Cynical incompetence, careerism and wasted lives; price increases, protest strikes and repression; the spontaneous emergence of local unions and the active engagement of dissident intellectuals; the sympathy and support of the Catholic Church: these were familiar staging posts in the re-birth of a civil society, movingly portrayed by Andrzej Wajda in *Man of Marble* (1977) and *Man of Iron* (1981), his didactic cinematic account of the betrayed illusions and reborn hopes of Communist Poland.

But that is all they were. They were not in themselves a harbinger of the downfall of Communist power. As Michnik, Kuroń and others continued to insist, before the imposition of martial law and after, Communism might be progressively eroded from within and from below, but it could not be overthrown. Open confrontation would be catastrophic, as history had convincingly demonstrated. Yes, martial law (which remained in force until July 1983) and the ensuing 'state of war' were an admission of a certain kind of failure on the part of the authorities—no other Communist state had ever been driven to such measures and Michnik himself called it 'a disaster for the totalitarian state' (while at the same time conceding that it was a serious 'setback for the independent society'). But Communism was

---

[3]With the encouragement of the Vatican, the US would provide significant financial support for Solidarity in its clandestine years—by some estimates as much as $50 million.

about power, and power lay not in Warsaw but in Moscow. The developments in Poland were a stirring prologue to the narrative of Communism's collapse, but they remained a sideshow. The real story was elsewhere.

The clamp-down in Poland further contributed to the steady cooling of East-West relations that began in the late 1970s. The 'second Cold War', as it became known, should not be exaggerated: although at one point both Leonid Brezhnev and Ronald Reagan accused the other of contemplating and even planning for a nuclear war, neither the Soviet Union nor the US had any such intentions.[4] With the conclusion of the Helsinki Accords it seemed to Washington *and* Moscow that the Cold War was ending to their own advantage. Indeed, the situation in Europe suited both great powers, with the US now comporting itself rather like czarist Russia in the decades following Napoleon's defeat in 1815: i.e. as a sort of continental policeman whose presence guaranteed that there would be no further disruption of the status quo by an unruly revolutionary power.

Nevertheless, East-West relations *were* deteriorating. The Soviet invasion of Afghanistan in December 1979, undertaken largely at the instigation of Foreign Minister Andrei Gromyko in order to restore a stable and compliant regime on the Soviet Union's sensitive southern borders, prompted a US boycott of the upcoming 1980 Olympic Games in Moscow (a compliment duly repaid when the Soviet bloc spurned the Los Angeles Olympics in 1984) and caused President Jimmy Carter publicly to revise 'my own opinion of what the Soviets' ultimate goals are' (*The New York Times*, January 1st 1980). The invasion also confirmed Western leaders in the wisdom of their decision, taken at a NATO summit just two weeks earlier, to install 108 new Pershing II and 464 Cruise missiles in Western Europe—itself a response to Moscow's deployment in Ukraine of a new generation of SS20 medium-range missiles. A new arms race appeared to be gathering speed.

No-one, least of all the leaders of Western Europe whose countries would have been the first to suffer in a nuclear exchange, had any illusions about the value of nuclear missiles. As instruments of war such weapons were uniquely unhelpful—in contrast to spears, they really were only good for sitting on. Nonetheless, as a deterrent device a nuclear arsenal had its uses—if your opponent could be convinced that it might, ultimately, be used. There was, in any case, no other way to defend Western Europe against a Warsaw Pact that by the early 1980s boasted more than fifty infantry and armored divisions, 16,000 tanks, 26,000 fighting vehicles and 4,000 combat aircraft.

That is why British Prime Ministers (both Margaret Thatcher and before her

---

[4]Though early in his presidency, in November 1981, Reagan did let slip the thought that a nuclear war in Europe need not lead to a strategic exchange. Washington's West European allies were at least as alarmed as Moscow and both protested vociferously.

James Callaghan), West German Chancellors and the leaders of Belgium, Italy and the Netherlands all welcomed the new battlefield missiles and authorized them to be stationed on their soil. In his new-found enthusiasm for the Western alliance, French President François Mitterrand was especially keen: in a dramatic speech to a somewhat bemused Bundestag in January 1983 he impressed upon West Germans the urgent need to hold firm and adopt the latest American missiles.[5]

The 'new' Cold War re-opened a prospect of terror out of all apparent proportion to the issues at stake—or the intentions of most of the participants. In Western Europe the anti-nuclear peace movement underwent a revival, strengthened by a new generation of 'green' activists. In Britain an enthusiastic and decidedly English assortment of feminists, environmentalists and anarchists, together with their assembled friends and relations, mounted a prolonged siege of the cruise missile site at Greenham Common—to the bewilderment of its long-suffering American garrison.

The opposition was greatest in West Germany, where the Social Democratic Chancellor Helmut Schmidt was forced to step down after the left wing of his own party voted against the new missiles—which were then approved and installed by his Christian Democratic successor Helmut Kohl.[6] The mirage of a de-nuclearized, neutral zone in central Europe was still dear to many Germans, and prominent West German Greens and Social Democrats added their voices to official East German appeals against nuclear weapons—at a demonstration in Bonn in October 1983 former Chancellor Willy Brandt urged a sympathetic crowd of 300,000 people to demand that their government unilaterally renounce any new missiles. The so-called 'Krefeld Appeal' against the deployment of Cruise and Pershing missiles in the Federal Republic gathered 2.7 million signatures.

Neither the invasion of Afghanistan nor the 'state of war' in Poland aroused comparable concern in Western Europe even in official circles (indeed, Chancellor Helmut Schmidt's first response to Jaruzelski's declaration of martial law was to send a high-level personal representative to Warsaw in February 1982 to help overcome Polish 'isolation'[7]). As for the 'peaceniks', they were far less troubled by repression in Warsaw than by the bellicose rhetoric emanating from Washington. Although NATO's decision to deploy new missiles had been accompanied by the offer of negotiations to reduce such weapons (the so-called 'twin track' approach), it seemed increasingly obvious that the US under its new president had adopted a new and aggressive strategy.

Much of the belligerence in Washington was just rhetoric—when Ronald Rea-

---

[5]There was, of course, never any question of Pershings or Cruises being deployed in France itself . . .
[6]It emerged after 1990 that at least 25 Bundestag members in these years were paid agents of the GDR.
[7]On December 13th 1981, the day martial law was declared in Poland, Schmidt was in the GDR holding 'summit talks' with his counterpart Erich Honecker and was somewhat put out, less by the imprisonment of hundreds of Polish dissidents than by the potentially 'destabilizing' impact of Polish developments on improving inter-German relations.

gan demanded that 'Poland be Poland', or dubbed Moscow an 'evil empire' (in March 1983) he was playing to a domestic audience. The same president, after all, was initiating talks on nuclear arms reduction and offering to withdraw his own intermediate-range missiles if the Soviets dismantled theirs. But the United States was indeed embarking upon a major program of rearmament. In August 1981 Reagan announced that the US would stockpile neutron bombs. The MX missile system, in breach of the Strategic Arms Limitation Treaties, was announced in November 1982, followed five months later by the Strategic Defense Initiative ('Star Wars'), prompting a Soviet protest on the credible grounds that it breached the 1972 Anti-Ballistic Missile Treaty. Official military aid and clandestine support to Afghanistan and Central America was steadily augmented. In 1985 US defense spending rose by 6 percent, an unprecedented peacetime increase.[8]

Back in September 1981 Reagan had warned that without a verifiable nuclear arms agreement there would be an arms race and that if there were an arms race the US would win it. And so it proved. In retrospect, the American defense build-up would come to be seen as the cunningly crafted lever that bankrupted and ultimately broke the Soviet system. This, however, is not quite accurate. The Soviet Union could ill afford the armaments race upon which it had begun to embark as early as 1974. But bankruptcy alone would not have brought Communism to its knees.

The Second Cold War, and America's public belligerence, undoubtedly increased the strains on a creaking and dysfunctional system. The Soviet Union had built a military machine that defeated Hitler, occupied half of Europe and matched the West weapon for weapon for forty years—but at a terrible price. At their peak, somewhere between 30–40 percent of Soviet resources were diverted to military spending, four to five times the American share. It was already obvious to many Soviet experts that their country could not indefinitely maintain such a burden. In the long run the economic bill for this generations-long military build-up must come due.

But in the short run at least, foreign tensions probably helped shore up the regime. The Soviet Union might be a continent-size Potemkin village—'Upper Volta with missiles' in Helmut Schmidt's pithy description—but it did, after all, have those missiles and they conferred a certain status and respect upon their owners. Moreover the ageing Soviet leaders, KGB director Yuri Andropov in particular, took the American threat very seriously. Like their counterparts in Washington they really believed the other side was contemplating pre-emptive nuclear war.

---

[8]Thanks to an ever-larger GDP, the defense element in American public expenditure had fallen steadily in relative terms from the mid-Fifties through 1979, even during the Vietnam years. It then increased dramatically: as a percentage of Federal outlay, defense spending in 1987 was up by 24 percent on 1980 levels.

Reagan's hard line, and in particular his Strategic Defense Initiative, made the old Soviet leadership even less disposed to compromise.

The real military dilemma facing the Soviet leaders was neither in Europe nor in Washington, but rather in Kabul. *Pace* Jimmy Carter's late-found sensitivity to Soviet strategic ambitions, the 1979 invasion of Afghanistan did not open a new front in Communism's strategic struggle with the free world. It was born, rather, of domestic anxiety. The 1979 Soviet census revealed an unprecedented increase in the (largely Muslim) population of Soviet Central Asia. In Soviet Kazakhstan and the republics abutting the Afghan frontier—Turkmenistan, Uzbekistan and Tajikistan—the numbers were up by over 25 percent since 1970. Over the course of the following decade, whereas the Ukrainian population would grow by just 4 percent, that of Tajikistan increased by nearly half. European Russia, as it seemed to its leaders, was under demographic threat from its internal minorities: as the ailing Leonid Brezhnev acknowledged to his Party's 26th Congress in February 1981, there were still 'nationality questions' that needed addressing.

Had the occupation of Afghanistan succeeded in installing a secure, friendly regime in Kabul, the Soviet leaders could have chalked up a double success. They would have re-affirmed Moscow's faltering presence in the Middle East while sending a 'clear message' to a new generation of Soviet Muslims tempted by dreams of independence. But the Soviets, of course, failed in Afghanistan. Brezhnev, Gromyko and their generals ignored not just the lessons of Vietnam, repeating many of the Americans' errors; they also forgot czarist Russia's own failures in the same region eighty years earlier. Instead, the USSR's disastrous attempt to sustain a puppet regime in unfamiliar, hostile territory aroused an intransigent opposition of guerrillas and zealots (*mujahidin*), armed and financed from abroad. And rather than 'addressing' the empire's own nationality questions, it served only to inflame them: the Soviet-backed 'Marxist' authorities in Kabul did little for Moscow's standing in the Islamic world, at home or abroad.

Afghanistan, in short, was a catastrophe for the Soviet Union. Its traumatic impact upon a generation of conscripted soldiers would emerge only later. By the early-1990s it was estimated that one in five veterans of the Afghan wars were confirmed alcoholics; in post-Soviet Russia many of the others, unable to find regular work, drifted into far-right nationalist organizations. But long before then even the Soviet leaders themselves could see the scale of their mis-step. In addition to the cost in men and matériel, the decade-long war of attrition in the Afghan mountains constituted an extended international humiliation. It excluded for the foreseeable future any further deployment of the Red Army beyond its frontiers: as Politburo member Yegor Ligachev would later acknowledge to the American journalist David Remnick, after Afghanistan there could no longer be any question of applying force in Eastern Europe.

It says something about the underlying fragility of the Soviet Union that it was so vulnerable to the impact of one—albeit spectacularly unsuccessful—neo-colonial adventure. But the disaster in Afghanistan, like the cost of the accelerating arms race of the early '80s, would not in itself have induced the collapse of the system. Sustained by, fear, inertia and the self-interest of the old men who ran it, Brezhnev's 'era of stagnation' might have lasted indefinitely. Certainly there was no countervailing authority, no dissident movement—whether in the Soviet Union or its client states—that could have brought it low. Only a Communist could do that. And it was a Communist who did.

The guiding premise of the Communist project was its faith in the laws of history and the interests of the collectivity, which would always trump the motives and actions of individuals. It was thus ironically appropriate that its destiny should in the end have been determined by the fate of men. On November 10th 1982, at the age of 76, Leonid Brezhnev finally gave up the ghost, having long since come to resemble it. His successor, Andropov, was already 68 and not in good health. In just over a year, before he could implement any of the reforms that he planned, Andropov died and was replaced as General Secretary by Konstantin Chernenko, himself aged 72 and in such poor health that he could hardly complete his speech at Andropov's funeral in February 1984. Thirteen months later he, too, was dead.

The death in quick succession of three old Communists, all of them born before World War One, was somehow symptomatic: the generation of Party leaders with first-hand memories of the Soviet Union's Bolshevik origins, and whose lives and careers had been blighted by Stalin, was now disappearing. They had inherited and overseen an authoritarian, gerontocratic bureaucracy, whose overwhelming priority was its own survival: in the world that Brezhnev, Andropov and Chernenko had grown up in, merely dying in your bed was no insignificant accomplishment. Henceforth, however, that world would be run by younger men: no less instinctively authoritarian, but who would have little option but to address the problems of corruption, stagnation and inefficiency that plagued the Soviet system from top to bottom.

Chernenko's successor, duly promoted to Secretary General of the Communist Party of the Soviet Union on March 11th 1985, was Mikhail Sergeyevich Gorbachev. Born in a village of the southern Stavropol region in 1931, he had been elected to the Central Committee at the age of 41. Now, just thirteen years later, he was at the head of the Party. Gorbachev was not only twenty years younger than his Soviet precursors: he was also younger than every American president until Bill Clinton. His rapid rise had been encouraged and facilitated by Andropov and he was widely seen as a likely reformer.

A reformer: but hardly a radical. Mikhail Gorbachev was very much an *apparatchik*. He had risen through the Party, from First Secretary of the Stavropol district Young Communists in 1956 through secretary of the regional state farms committee to member of the Supreme Soviet (elected in 1970). The new leader incarnated many of the sentiments of his Communist generation: never openly critical of the Party or its policies, he was nonetheless deeply affected and excited by the revelations of 1956, only to be let down by the mistakes of the Khrushchev era and disappointed at the repression and inertia of the Brezhnev decades that followed.

Mikhail Gorbachev was in this sense a classic reform Communist—it is no coincidence that he was close friends at the Moscow University Law Faculty in the early Fifties with Zdeněk Mlynář, who would go on to play a central role in the Prague Spring of 1968. But like all the reform Communists of his generation, Gorbachev was first a Communist and only then a reformer. As he explained to the French Communist newspaper *L'Humanité* in a February 1986 interview, the Communism of Lenin remained for him a fine and unsullied ideal. Stalinism? 'A concept made up by opponents of Communism and used on a large scale to smear the Soviet Union and socialism as a whole'.[9]

No doubt that is what a Secretary General of the Soviet Party *would* say, even in 1986. But Gorbachev certainly believed it, and the reforms he initiated were quite consciously Leninist—or 'Socialist'—in intent. Indeed Gorbachev may well have been more ideologically serious than some of his Soviet predecessors: it is not by chance that whereas Nikita Khrushchev had once famously declared that, were he British, he would vote Tory, Mikhail Gorbachev's favorite foreign statesman was Felipe González of Spain, whose brand of social democracy the Soviet leader came in time to think of as closest to his own.

To the extent that hopes were vested in Gorbachev, this reflected more than anything the absence of any domestic opposition in the Soviet Union. Only the Party could clean up the mess it had made, and by good fortune the Party had elected as its leader a man with both the energy and the administrative experience to make the effort. For in addition to being unusually well educated and widely read for a senior Soviet bureaucrat, Gorbachev displayed a distinctively Leninist quality: he was willing to compromise his ideals in order to secure his goals.

There was nothing mysterious about the difficulties that Gorbachev had inherited as General Secretary of the CPSU. Impressed by what he saw during travels in Western Europe during the seventies, the new leader intended from the outset to devote his main efforts to an overhaul of the Soviet Union's moribund economy and the intertwined inefficiencies and corruption of its top-heavy institutional apparatus. Foreign debt was rising steadily, as the international price of oil, the Soviet Union's major export, fell from its late '70s peak: $30.7 billion by 1986, the debt would reach $54 billion by 1989. The economy, which had hardly grown through the course of the 1970s, was now actually shrinking: always qualitatively lagging, Soviet output was now quantatively inadequate as well. Arbitrarily-set central plan-

---

[9]In fact Gorbachev's own family had suffered greatly under Stalin: both of his grandfathers were imprisoned or exiled in the course of the dictator's purges. But the new Soviet leader did not even acknowledge the fact until November 1990.

ning targets, endemic shortages, supply bottlenecks and the absence of price or market indicators effectively paralyzed all initiative.

The starting point for 'reform' in such a system, as Hungarian and other Communist economists had long appreciated, was decentralization of pricing and decision-making. But this encountered near-insuperable obstacles. Outside of the Baltics almost no-one in the Soviet Union had any first-hand experience of independent farming or a market economy: of how to make something, to price it or find a buyer. Even after a 1986 Law on Individual Labour Activity authorized limited (small-scale) private enterprise, there were surprisingly few takers. Three years later there were still just 300,000 businesspeople in the whole Soviet Union, in a population of 290 million.

Moreover, any would-be economic reformer faced a chicken-egg dilemma. If economic reform began with decentralization of decision-making, or the granting of autonomy to local businesses and the abandoning of directives from afar, how were producers, managers or businessmen to function without a market? In the short-run there would be *more* shortages and bottlenecks, not fewer, as everyone retreated to regional self-sufficiency and even to a local barter economy. On the other hand a 'market' could not just be announced. The very word posed serious political risks in a society where 'capitalism' had been officially excoriated and abhorred for decades (Gorbachev himself avoided all mention of a market economy until late in 1987, and even then only ever spoke of a 'socialist market').

The reforming instinct was to compromise: to experiment with the creation—from above—of a few favored enterprises freed from bureaucratic encumbrances and assured a reliable supply of raw materials and skilled labor. These, it was reasoned, would serve as successful and even profitable models for other, similar, enterprises: the goal was controlled modernization and progressive adaptation to pricing and production in response to demand. But such an approach was foredoomed by its operating premise—that the authorities could create efficient businesses by administrative fiat.

By pumping scarce resources into a few model farms, mills, factories or services the Party was indeed able to forge temporarily viable and even notionally profitable units—but only with heavy subsidies and by starving less-favored operations elsewhere. The result was even more distortion and frustration. Meanwhile farm managers and local directors, uncertain of the way the wind was blowing, hedged their bets against the return of planned norms and stockpiled anything they could lay their hands on lest centralized controls tighten up again.

To Gorbachev's conservative critics this was an old story. Every Soviet reform program since 1921 began the same way and ran out of steam for the same reasons, starting with Lenin's New Economic Policy. Serious economic reforms implied the relaxation or abandonment of controls. Not only did this initially exacerbate the problems it was designed to solve, it meant just what it said: a loss of control. But

Communism depended upon control—indeed Communism *was* control: control of the economy, control of knowledge, control of movement and opinion and people. Everything else was dialectics, and dialectics—as a veteran Communist explained to the young Jorge Semprún in Buchenwald—'is the art and technique of always landing on your feet'.[10]

It soon became obvious to Gorbachev that to land on his feet as he wrestled with the Soviet economy he must accept that the Soviet economic conundrum could not be addressed in isolation. It was but a symptom of a larger problem. The Soviet Union was run by men who had a vested interest in the political and institutional levers of a command economy; its endemic minor absurdities and quotidian corruption were the very source of their authority and power. In order for the Party to reform the economy it would first have to reform itself.

This, too, was hardly a new idea—the periodic purges under Lenin and his successors had typically proclaimed similar objectives. But times had changed. The Soviet Union, however repressive and backward, was no longer a murderous totalitarian tyranny. Thanks to Khrushchev's monumental housing projects most Soviet families now lived in their own apartments. Ugly and inefficient, these low-rent flats nonetheless afforded ordinary people a degree of privacy and security unknown to earlier generations: they were no longer so exposed to informers or likely to be betrayed to the authorities by their neighbors or their in-laws. The age of terror was over for most people and, for Gorbachev's generation at least, a return to the time of mass arrests and party purges was unthinkable.

In order to break the stranglehold of the Party *apparat* and drive forward his plans for economic restructuring, then, the General Secretary resorted instead to '*glasnost*'—'openness': official encouragement for public discussion of a carefully restricted range of topics. By making people more aware of impending changes and heightening public expectation, Gorbachev would forge a lever with which he and his supporters might pry loose official opposition to his plans. This too was a vintage ploy, familiar to reforming czars among others. But for Gorbachev the urgency of the need for official openness was brought home to him by the catastrophic events of April 26th 1986.

On that day, at 1.23 am, one of the four huge graphite reactors at the nuclear power plant in Chernobyl (Ukraine) exploded, releasing into the atmosphere 120 million curies of radioactive matériel—more than one hundred times the radiation of Hiroshima and Nagasaki *combined*. The plume of atomic fallout was carried north-west into Western Europe and Scandinavia, reaching as far as Wales and Sweden and exposing an estimated five million people to its effects. In addition to the 30 emergency workers killed on the spot, some 30,000 people have since

---

[10] '*Mais c'est quoi, la dialectique?*' '*C'est l'art et la manière de toujours retomber sur ses pattes, mon vieux!*' Jorge Semprún, *Quel Beau Dimanche* (Paris: Grasset, 1980), p. 100

died from complications caused by exposure to radiation from Chernobyl, including more than 2,000 cases of thyroid cancer among residents in the immediate vicinity.

Chernobyl was not the Soviet Union's first environmental disaster. At Cheliabinsk-40, a secret research site near Ekaterinburg in the Ural Mountains, a nuclear waste tank exploded in 1957, severely polluting an area 8 km wide and 100 km long. 76 million cubic metres of radioactive waste poured into the Urals river system, contaminating it for decades. 10,000 people were eventually evacuated and 23 villages bulldozed. The reactor at Cheliabinsk was from the first generation of Soviet atomic constructions and had been built by slave labour in 1948–51.[11]

Other man-made environmental calamities on a comparable scale included the pollution of Lake Baikal; the destruction of the Aral Sea; the dumping in the Arctic Ocean and the Barents Sea of hundreds of thousands of tons of defunct atomic naval vessels and their radioactive contents; and the contamination by sulphur dioxide from nickel production of an area the size of Italy around Norilsk in Siberia. These and other ecological disasters were all the direct result of indifference, bad management and the Soviet 'slash and burn' approach to natural resources. They were born of a culture of secrecy. The Cheliabinsk-40 explosion was not officially acknowledged for many decades, even though it occurred within a few kilometers of a large city—the same city where, in 1979, several hundred people died of anthrax leaked from a biological weapons plant in the town centre.

The problems with the USSR's nuclear reactors were well known to insiders: two separate KGB reports dated 1982 and 1984 warned of 'shoddy' equipment (supplied from Yugoslavia) and serious deficiencies in Chernobyl's reactors 3 and 4 (it was the latter that exploded in 1986). But just as this information had been kept secret (and no action taken) so the Party leadership's first, instinctive response to the explosion on April 26th was to keep quiet about it—there were, after all, fourteen Chernobyl-type plants in operation by then all across the country. Moscow's first acknowledgement that anything untoward had happened came fully four days after the event, and then in a two-sentence official communiqué.

But Chernobyl could not be kept secret: international anxiety and the Soviets' own inability to contain the damage forced Gorbachev first to make a public statement two weeks later, acknowledging some but not all of what had taken place, and then to call upon foreign aid and expertise. And just as his fellow citizens were thus made publicly aware for the first time of the scale of official incompetence and indifference to life and health, so Gorbachev was forced to acknowledge the extent of his country's problems. The bungling, the mendacity and the cynicism of the men responsible both for the disaster and the attempt to cover it up could not be

---

[11]This was the subject of a book by Zhores Medvedev, *Nuclear Disaster in the Urals*, published in exile in 1979.

dismissed as a regrettable perversion of Soviet values: they *were* Soviet values, as the Soviet leader began to appreciate.

Beginning in the autumn of 1986 Gorbachev shifted gears. In December of that year Andrei Sakharov, the world's best-known dissident, was liberated from house arrest in Gorky (Nizhniy Novgorod), a harbinger of the large-scale release of Soviet political prisoners that began the following year. Censorship was relaxed—1987 saw the long-delayed publication of Vassily Grossman's *Life and Fate* (twenty six years after M.A. Suslov, the Party's ideological commissar, had predicted that it could not be released for 'two or three centuries'). The police were instructed to cease jamming foreign radio broadcasts. And the Secretary General of the CPSU chose the occasion of his televised speech to the Party Central Committee in January 1987 to make the case for a more inclusive democracy, over the heads of the Party conservatives and directly to the nation at large.

By 1987 more than nine out of ten Soviet households possessed a television, and Gorbachev's tactic was initially a striking success: by creating a *de facto* public sphere for semi-open debate about the country's woes, and breaking the governing caste's monopoly of information, he was forcing the Party to follow suit—and making it safe for hitherto silent reformers within the system to speak out and give him their backing. In the course of 1987–88 the General Secretary was, almost despite himself, forging a national constituency for change.

Informal organizations sprang up: notably 'Club Perestroika', formed in Moscow's Mathematical Institute in 1987, which in turn gave birth to 'Memorial', whose members devoted themselves to 'keeping alive the memory of the victims' of the Stalinist past. Initially taken aback at their own very existence—the Soviet Union, after all, was still a one-party dictatorship—they soon flourished and multiplied. By 1988 Gorbachev's support came increasingly from outside the Party, from the country's newly emerging public opinion.

What had happened was that the logic of Gorbachev's reformist goals, and his decision, in practice, to appeal to the nation against his conservative critics within the apparatus, had transformed the dynamic of *perestroika*. Having begun as a reformer within the ruling Party, its General Secretary was now increasingly working against it, or at least trying to circumvent the Party's opposition to change. In October 1987 Gorbachev spoke publicly of Stalinist crimes for the first time and warned that if the Party did not champion reform it would lose its leading role in society.

In the Party conference of June 1988 he reiterated his commitment to reform and to the relaxation of censorship, and called for the preparation of open (i.e. contested) elections to a Congress of People's Deputies for the following year. In October 1988 he demoted some of his leading opponents—notably Yegor Ligachev, a longstanding critic—and had himself elected President of the Supreme Soviet (i.e. head of state), displacing Andrei Gromyko, last of the dinosaurs. Within the Party he still faced strong rearguard opposition; but in the country at large his popularity was at its peak, which was why he was able to press forward—and indeed had little option but to do so.[12]

The elections of May/June 1989 were the first more or less free vote in the Soviet Union since 1918. They were not multi-party elections—that would not happen until 1993, by which time the Soviet Union itself was long gone—and the outcome was largely pre-determined by restricting many seats to Party candidates and forbidding internal Party competition for them; but the Congress they elected included many independent and critical voices. Its proceedings were broadcast to an audience of some 100 million spectators, and demands by Sakharov and others for further change—notably the dethroning of the increasingly discredited Party from its privileged position—could not be swept aside, even by an initially reluctant Gorbachev. The Communists' monopoly of power was slipping away, and with Gorbachev's encouragement the Congress would duly vote the following February to remove from the Soviet constitution the key clause—Article Six—assigning the Communist Party a 'leading role'.[13]

The course of Soviet domestic upheaval from 1985 to 1989 was facilitated by a major shift in Soviet foreign policy under Gorbachev and his new Foreign Minister Edvard Shevardnadze. From the outset Gorbachev made clear his determination to unburden the USSR at the very least of its more onerous military encumbrances. Within a month of coming to power he had halted Soviet missile deployments and gone on to offer unconditional negotiations on nuclear forces, starting with a proposal that both superpowers halve their strategic arsenals. By May 1986, after a surprisingly successful 'summit' meeting with Reagan in Geneva (the first of an unprecedented five such encounters), Gorbachev agreed to allow US 'forward-based systems' to be excluded from strategic arms talks, if that would help get these under way.

There followed a second, Reykjavik, summit in October 1986 where Reagan and Gorbachev, while failing to reach agreement on nuclear disarmament, nonetheless laid the basis for future success. By late 1987 Shevardnadze and US Secretary of State George Schultz had drafted an Intermediate Range Nuclear Forces Treaty, signed and ratified the following year. This Treaty, by endorsing Ronald Reagan's earlier 'zero option' proposal, constituted Soviet acceptance that a nuclear war in Europe was un-winnable—and served as the prologue to an even more important treaty, signed in 1990, strictly limiting the presence and operation of *conventional* forces on the European continent.

Seen from Washington, Gorbachev's concessions on arms naturally appeared as

---

[12]In an opinion poll taken some months later, in January 1990, Gorbachev ranked just after Peter The Great in public favour—but far behind both Karl Marx and V.I.Lenin . . .
[13]It was Sakharov who forced the issue into the open by demanding—on live television—the abrogation of Article Six and the return to the peoples' representatives of the power 'stolen' by the Party in 1918. Gorbachev himself finally switched off Sakharov's microphone, but too late.

a victory for Reagan—and thus, in the zero-sum calculus of Cold War strategists, a defeat for Moscow. But for Gorbachev, whose priorities were domestic, securing a more stable international environment was a victory in itself. It bought him time and support for his reforms at home. The true significance of this sequence of meetings and accords lay in the Soviet recognition that military confrontation abroad was not only expensive but also dysfunctional: as Gorbachev expressed it in October 1986 in the course of a visit to France, 'ideology' was not an appropriate basis for foreign policy.

These views reflected the advice he was beginning to get from a new generation of Soviet foreign affairs experts, notably his colleague Aleksandr Yakovlev, to whom it had become clear that the USSR could exercise more control over its foreign relations by well-calculated concessions than by fruitless confrontation. In contrast to the intractable problems he faced at home, foreign policy was an arena in which Gorbachev exercised direct control and could thus hope to effect immediate improvements. Moreover the strictly Great-Power dimension of Soviet foreign relations should not be exaggerated: Gorbachev placed at least as much importance on his relations with western Europe as on his dealings with the US—he made frequent visits there and established good relations with González, Kohl and Thatcher (who famously regarded him as a man with whom she 'could do business').[14]

Indeed, in important respects Gorbachev thought of himself above all as a *European* statesman, with European priorities. His focus upon ending the arms race and the stockpiling of nuclear weapons was closely tied to a new approach to the Soviet Union's role as a distinctively *European* power. 'Armaments', he declared in 1987, 'should be reduced to a level necessary for strictly defensive purposes. It is time for the two military alliances to amend their strategic concepts to gear them more to the aims of defense. Every apartment in the 'European home' has the right to protect itself against burglars, but it must do so without destroying its neighbors' property.'

In a similar spirit and for the same reasons, the Soviet leader understood from the outset the urgent need to extract the Soviet Union from Afghanistan, the 'bleeding wound' as he described it to a Party Congress in February 1986. Five months later he announced the withdrawal of some 6,000 Soviet troops, a redeployment completed in November of the same year. In May 1988, following an accord reached at Geneva with Afghanistan and Pakistan and guaranteed by both great powers, Soviet troops began to leave Afghanistan: the last remaining soldiers of the Red Army departed on February 15th 1989.[15]

Far from addressing the Soviet nationalities question, the Afghan adventure

---

[14]He also made a point, at Chernenko's funeral in March 1985, of meeting and greeting Alessandro Natta, the head of the Italian Communist Party, until then perennially in Moscow's bad graces.
[15]In an ironically apposite echo of the American fiasco in Vietnam, the puppet regime in Kabul—now bereft of armed support from abroad—limped on until 1992 before succumbing (its international guarantors notwithstanding) to the forces of the Taliban.

had, as was by now all too clear, exacerbated it. If the USSR faced an intractable set of national minorities, this was in part a problem of its own making: it was Lenin and his successors, after all, who invented the various subject 'nations' to whom they duly assigned regions and republics. In an echo of imperial practices elsewhere, Moscow had encouraged the emergence—in places where nationality and nation-hood were unheard of fifty years earlier—of institutions and intelligentsias grouped around a national urban center or 'capital'. Communist Party First Secretaries in the Caucasus, or the central Asian republics, were typically chosen from the dom-inant local ethnic group. To secure their fiefdom these men were understandably drawn to identify with their 'own' people, particularly once fissures began to ap-pear in the central apparatus. The Party was starting to fracture under the cen-trifugal pull of anxious local administrators protecting their own interests.

Gorbachev seems not fully to have understood this process. 'Comrades', he in-formed the Party in 1987, 'we can truly say that for our country the nationalities issue has been resolved'. Perhaps he did not altogether believe his own claims; but he certainly thought that some loosening of central control and addressing of long-standing grievances would suffice (in 1989 the Crimean Tartars, for example, were finally allowed to return home after many decades of Asian exile). In a continen-tal empire of over one hundred ethnic groups from the Baltic to the Sea of Okhotsk, most of whom had longstanding grievances that *glasnost* now encouraged them to air, this was to prove a serious miscalculation.

The inadequacy of Gorbachev's response to demands for autonomy at the So-viet empire's far-flung margins should not come as a surprise. Gorbachev was from the outset, as we have seen, a 'reform Communist', albeit a very unusual one: sym-pathetic to the need for change and renewal but reluctant to assault the core tenets of the system under which he had grown up. Like many in his generation in the Soviet Union and elsewhere he genuinely believed that the only path to improve-ment lay through a return to Leninist 'principles'. The idea that it was the Leninist project itself that might be at fault remained alien to the Soviet leader until very late—only in 1990 did he finally permit the domestic publication of overtly anti-Leninist writers such as Aleksandr Solzhenitsyn.

The spirit of Gorbachev's early goals is exemplified in the inimitable tone of the new-found official tolerance for pop music, as expressed by *Pravda* in October 1986: 'Rock and roll has a right to exist but only if it is melodious, meaningful and well-performed.' That is precisely what Mikhail Gorbachev wanted: a melodious, meaningful and well-performed Communism. Necessary reforms would be un-dertaken and appropriate freedoms granted, but there was to be no unregulated licence—as late as February 1988 the government was still clamping down firmly on independent publishing houses and printers.

It is one of the curiosities of Communist reformers that they always set out with the quixotic goal of reforming some aspects of their system while keeping oth-ers unaffected—introducing market-oriented incentives while maintaining central planning controls, or allowing greater freedom of expression while retaining the Party's monopoly of truth. But partial reform or reform of one sector in isolation from others was inherently contradictory. 'Managed pluralism' or a 'socialist market' was doomed from the start. As for the idea that the 'leading role' of the Communist Party could be sustained while the Party itself shed merely the pathological excrescences of seven decades of absolute power, this suggests a certain political naiveté on Gorbachev's part. In an authoritarian system power is indivisible—relinquish it in part and you must eventually lose it all. Nearly four centuries earlier, the Stuart monarch James I understood these things much better—as he put it in a succinct rebuff to Scottish Presbyterians protesting at the power vested in his bishops: 'No Bishop, no King'.

Gorbachev and his controlled revolution were in the end swept aside by the scale of the contradictions they aroused. Looking back, he observed with some regret that 'naturally, I feel troubled by the fact that I did not succeed in keeping the entire process of *perestroika* within the framework of my intentions'. But the intentions and the framework were incompatible. Once the sustaining supports of censorship, control and repression were removed, everything of consequence in the Soviet system—the planned economy, the public rhetoric, the monopoly of the Party—just collapsed.

Gorbachev did not achieve his objective, a reformed and efficient Communism, shorn of its dysfunctions. Indeed, he failed utterly. But his achievement was impressive none the less. In the USSR there were no independent or even semi-autonomous institutions for critics and reformers to mobilize on their behalf: the Soviet system could only ever have been dismantled from inside and by initiative coming from above. By introducing first one element of change and then another and then another, Gorbachev progressively eroded the very system through which he had risen. Employing the vast powers of a Party General Secretary, he eviscerated the Party dictatorship from within.

This was a remarkable and unprecedented feat. No-one could have predicted it in 1984, when Chernenko died, and no-one did. Gorbachev, in the view of one of his close advisers, was 'a genetic error of the system'.[16] In retrospect it has become tempting to conclude that his ascent was uncannily timely—as the Soviet system was tottering, so there emerged a leader who understood what was happening and successfully sought an exit strategy from empire. Cometh the hour, cometh the man? Perhaps. And Mikhail Gorbachev certainly was not just another apparatchik.

But he surely had no idea what he was doing and would have been horrified had he known. His critics were more perspicacious. On the one hand, Party hardliners understandably hated Gorbachev—many of them warmly endorsed the notorious letter published in the newspaper *Sovetskaya Rossiya* on March 13th 1988 in which

---

[16]Andrei Grachev, quoted in Archie Brown, *The Gorbachev Factor* (Oxford, 1997), p.88.

Nina Andreyeva, a Leningrad schoolteacher, angrily warned (reasonably enough, as it transpired) that the new reforms would inevitably lead the country back to capitalism. On the other hand, Gorbachev never had the unconditional support of radical reformers, who grew increasingly frustrated with his apparent indecisiveness. It was one of Gorbachev's weaknesses that in order to keep control of events he felt constrained to occupy the center ground whenever possible, encouraging new ideas but then slipping back into the arms of Party conservatives just as radical reformers like Yakovlev or Boris Yeltsin were pressing him to go much further. These vacillations, Gorbachev's seeming reluctance to press the logic of his initiatives, and his insistence on not going too far or too fast left many of his early admirers feeling let down.

The trouble was that by relinquishing the Party's monopoly of power and initiative, Gorbachev commensurately reduced his own influence as well. He was thus obliged to forge tactical alliances and trim between the extreme positions of others. This is a familiar if uncomfortable necessity for democratic politicians; but in the eyes of a nation accustomed to seventy years of dictatorship such maneuverings simply made Gorbachev appear weak. From the early months of 1989 onwards the Soviet President fell steadily in opinion polls. By the autumn of 1990 Gorbachev would have the support of just 21 percent of the public.

Long before his fall from power, then, Gorbachev had decidedly fallen from grace. But only at home: elsewhere, 'Gorbymania' flourished. On his increasingly frequent visits abroad Gorbachev was fêted by west European politicians and cheered by enthusiastic crowds. Late in 1988, Margaret Thatcher—one of Gorbachev's most ardent fans—pronounced the Cold War 'over'. Seen from Eastern Europe this might have been thought a little premature; but there too Mikhail Gorbachev was wildly popular.

In the 'peoples' democracies' the Soviet leader's domestic travails, though duly noted, counted for less than his foreign pronouncements, notably a widely reported speech to the United Nations on December 7th 1988. After announcing unilateral cuts in Soviet conventional forces in Europe, Gorbachev went on to advise his audience that 'Freedom of choice is a universal principle. There should be no exceptions.' This was more than just a renunciation of the 'Brezhnev Doctrine', an acknowledgement that Moscow would not use force to impose its version of 'Socialism' upon fraternal states. What Gorbachev was conceding—and was immediately understood to have conceded—was that the citizens of the satellite states were now at liberty to go their own way, Socialist or not. Eastern Europe was about to re-enter history.

Under Mikhail Gorbachev's leadership, the Soviet Union since 1985 had progressively removed itself from direct oversight of its client states. But the implications of this growing detachment remained unclear. The peoples' democracies were still run by authoritarian party cliques whose power rested upon a massive repressive apparatus. Their police and intelligence services remained closely bound and beholden to the Soviet Union's own security apparatus and continued to operate semi-independently of local authorities. And while the rulers in Prague or Warsaw or East Berlin were starting to appreciate that they could no longer count on Moscow's unconditional support, neither they nor their subjects had a clear sense of what this meant.

The situation in Poland encapsulated these uncertainties. On the one hand, the declaration of martial law had re-asserted the authoritarian rule of the Communist Party. On the other hand, the suppression of Solidarity and the silencing of its leaders did nothing to ease the country's underlying problems. Quite the contrary: Poland was still in debt, but now—thanks to international condemnation of the repression—its rulers could no longer extricate themselves from difficulty by further borrowing abroad. In effect, Poland's rulers were facing the same dilemma they had tried to address in the 1970s, but with even fewer options.

Meanwhile, the opposition might have been criminalized but it had not evaporated. Clandestine publishing continued, as did lectures, discussions, theatrical performances and much else. Solidarity itself, though banned, maintained a virtual existence, especially after its best-known spokesman, Lech Wałesa, was released from internment in November 1982 (and was awarded the Nobel Peace Prize, in absentia, the following year). The regime could not take the risk of forbidding a return visit from the Pope, in June 1983, after which the Church became ever more engaged in underground and semi-official activities

The political police favored repression: in one notorious instance in 1984 they orchestrated the kidnap and murder of a popular radical priest, Father Jerzy Popiełuszko—*pour décourager les autres*. But Jaruzelski and most of his colleagues already understood that such provocations and confrontations would no longer work. Popiełuszko's funeral drew a crowd of 350,000; and far from frightening off opposition the incident merely publicized the scale of popular support for the Church and for Solidarity, legal or no. By the mid-'80s Poland was fast approaching a stand-off between a recalcitrant society and an increasingly desperate state.

The natural instinct of the Party leadership (in Warsaw as in Moscow) was to propose 'reforms'. In 1986 Jaruzelski, now state President, released Adam Michnik and other Solidarity leaders from prison and through a newly installed 'Ministry of Economic Reform' offered a modest raft of economic changes designed, among other objectives, to attract renewed foreign funding of Poland's national debt, now fast approaching $40 billion.[17] In a bizarre nod to democracy, the government actually began asking Poles in 1987 what sort of economic 'reform' they would like: 'Would you prefer', they were asked, 'a fifty percent rise in the price of bread and

---

[17]In 1986 the US lifted its veto on Polish membership of the IMF, in return for the release of all remaining political prisoners and a general amnesty.

one hundred percent on petrol, or sixty percent for petrol and a hundred percent for bread?' Unsurprisingly, the public's response was, in essence, 'none of the above'.

The question—and the decision to pose it—nicely illustrated the political as well as the economic bankruptcy of Poland's Communist rulers. Indeed, it says something about the authorities' crumbling credibility that Poland's membership of the IMF was made possible in part by the *consent* of Solidarity itself. Despite being banned, the union had managed to maintain its organization abroad and it was Solidarity's Brussels office that advised the IMF Managing Director in September 1985 to admit Poland—while insisting that Jaruzelski's partial improvements were foredoomed and that only a package of thoroughgoing reforms could address the country's troubles.[18]

By 1987 the most arresting aspect of the Polish situation was the sheer helplessness of the Party and its organs. Without actually facing any visible threat to its monopoly of power, the Polish United Workers Party was slipping into irrelevance. The 'counter-society' theorized by Michnik and others a decade earlier was emerging as a *de facto* source of authority and initiative. After 1986, debate within the Polish opposition turned not so much on teaching society to be free as on how much the opposition should agree to engage with the regime, and to what end.

A group of young economists at Warsaw's School of Planning and Statistics, led by Leszek Balcerowicz, was already drawing up plans for an autonomous private business sector freed from central planning—i.e. a market; these and other proposals were intensely debated among 'unofficial' Poles and widely discussed abroad. But the guiding tenets of political 'realism' and the 'self-limiting' objectives of 1980–81 remained in force—confrontation and violence, which could only play into the hands of Party hardliners, were studiously and successfully avoided. Conversations were one thing, 'adventures' something else.

The trigger for the Party's final eclipse, predictably enough, was yet another attempt to 'reform' the economy—or, more modestly, to reduce the country's unsustainable debt. In 1987 consumer prices were raised by some 25 percent; in 1988 by a further 60 percent. As in 1970, 1976 and again in 1980, so now: the sharp price rises sparked a round of strikes, culminating in a massive movement of stoppages and occupations in the spring and summer of 1988. In the past, lacking any leverage over the workforce, the Communist authorities had either abandoned efforts to raise prices or else resorted to force—or both. On this occasion they had a third option—appealing to the workers' own leaders for help. In August 1988 General Czesław Kiszczak, the Interior Minister, urged Lech Wałesa—nominally a private citizen, the unacknowledged leader of an unrecognized organization—to meet him and negotiate an end to the country's labor protests. Initially reluctant, Wałesa at last agreed.

---

[18]See Harold James, *International Monetary Cooperation since Bretton Woods* (IMF + Oxford University Press, 1996), p. 567.

Wałesa had little difficulty appealing to the strikers—the moral authority of Solidarity had only grown in the years since 1981—but the underlying issues remained: the country's inflation rate was now approaching 1000 percent p.a. There ensued four months of sporadic unofficial contacts between Solidarity and the government, stimulating more public calls for 'reform'. Drifting helplessly, the authorities oscillated between gestures and threats: replacing ministers, denying any plans for negotiations, promising economic change, threatening to close the Gdansk shipyard. The public's confidence in the state, such as it was, collapsed.

On December 18th 1988—symptomatically if coincidentally just one week after Gorbachev's seminal UN speech—a Solidarity 'Citizens Committee' was formed in Warsaw to plan for full-scale negotiations with the government. Jaruzelski, his options seemingly exhausted, at last conceded the obvious and forced a somewhat reluctant Central Committee to agree to talks. On February 6th 1989 the Communists officially recognized Solidarity as a negotiating partner and opened 'round table' negotiations with its representatives. The talks lasted until April 5th. On that day (once again a week after major Soviet developments, this time the open elections to the Congress of Peoples' Deputies), all sides agreed to the legalization of independent trade unions, far-reaching economic legislation and, above all, a new elected Assembly.

In hindsight the outcome of the round-table talks was a negotiated termination of Communism in Poland, and at least to some of the participants this much was already clear. But no-one anticipated the *speed* of the dénouement. The elections to be held on June 4th, while allowing an unprecedented element of real choice, were rigged to ensure a Communist majority: voting for the national Senate was to be genuinely open, but in the elections to the Sejm (Parliamentary Assembly) half the seats were reserved for official (i.e. Communist) candidates. And by scheduling the elections so soon, the government hoped to capitalize on the disorganization and inexperience of its opponents.

The results came as a shock to everyone. Backed by Adam Michnik's impromptu new daily 'Election Gazette' (*Gazeta Wyborcza*), Solidarity won 99/100 seats for the Senate and all the seats it was allowed to contest for the Sejm. Meanwhile only two of the Communist candidates standing for 'reserved' seats secured the 50 percent of the vote required to take up their places. Faced with a complete rout and unprecedented public humiliation, the Communist rulers of Poland had the option of ignoring the vote; declaring martial law once again; or else accepting defeat and relinquishing power.

Put thus, the choice was clear—as Gorbachev made quite explicit to Jaruzelski in a private phone conversation, the election must stand. Jaruzelski's first thought was to secure a face-saving compromise by inviting Solidarity to join him in a coalition government, but this was rebuffed. Instead, after some weeks of further negotiation and unsuccessful Communist efforts to nominate their own prime minister, the Party leadership bowed to the inevitable and on September 12th 1989 Tadeusz Mazowiecki was approved as post-war Poland's first non-Communist Prime Minister (although the Communists retained control of certain key ministries).

Meanwhile, in a shrewd political move, the Solidarity parliamentary group simultaneously voted to make Jaruzelski Head of State, effectively co-opting the Communist 'moderates' into the ensuing transition and easing their embarrassment. The following month Mazowiecki's government announced plans to institute a 'market economy', presented in a stabilization program—the so-called 'Balcerowicz Plan'—that was approved by the Sejm on December 28th. One day later, the 'leading role' of Poland's Communist Party was formally excised from the country's constitution. Within four weeks, on January 27th 1990, the Party itself had been dissolved.

The helter-skelter quality of the last months of Communist Poland should not blind us to the long and quite slow build up that went before. Most of the actors in the drama of 1989—Jaruzelski, Kiszczak, Wałesa, Michnik, Mazowiecki—had already been on the stage for many years. The country had passed from a brief flourish of relative liberty in 1981 into martial law, followed by a lengthy, uncertain purgatory of repressive semi-tolerance that finally unraveled in a re-run of the previous decade's economic crises. For all the strength of the Catholic Church, the countrywide popularity of Solidarity, and the Polish nation's abiding loathing of its Communist rulers, the latter clung to power for so long that their final fall came as something of a surprise. It had been a long goodbye.

In Poland, martial law and its aftermath revealed the limits and inadequacies of the Party; but while repression solidified the opposition it also made it cautious. In Hungary, a comparable caution was born of very different experience. Two decades of ambiguous tolerance had obscured the precise limits of officially condoned dissent. Hungary, after all, was the Communist state where Hilton opened its first hotel behind the Iron Curtain, in December 1976; where Billy Graham undertook not one but *three* public tours in the course of the Eighties; and which was visited (and implicitly favored) by two US secretaries of State and Vice-President George Bush in that same decade. By 1988 Communist Hungary had a decidedly 'good' image.

Partly for this reason, opposition to Party rule took a long time to emerge into the open. Dissimulation and maneuver seemed the better part of valor, especially to anyone who remembered 1956; and life in János Kádár's Hungary was tolerable, if drab. In reality, the official economy, as we saw in the previous chapter, was in no better condition than that of Poland, despite various reforms and 'New Economic Mechanisms.' To be sure, the 'black' or parallel economy enabled many people to get by on a standard of living somewhat higher than that of Hungary's neighbors. But as research by Hungarian social statisticians was already revealing, the country was suffering significant inequalities of income, health and housing;

social mobility and welfare were actually behind the West; and the long work hours (many people worked two or even three jobs), high levels of alcoholism and mental disorder, together with the highest suicide rate in eastern Europe, were taking their toll on the population.

There was, then, ample ground for discontent. But there was no organized *political* opposition. Although some independent organizations surfaced in the course of the 1980s, they were mostly confined to environmental issues or to protests against Romania's mistreatment of its Hungarian minority—an issue on which they could count on the Communists' tacit sympathy (which explains official tolerance of the decidedly nationalist Hungarian Democratic Forum, formed in September 1987). Hungary remained a 'socialist republic' (as it was officially described in the Constitutional revision of 1972). Dissent and criticism were largely confined within the ruling Party, although in the elections of June 1985 multiple candidacies were permitted for the first time and a handful of officially-approved independents got elected. But it was not until 1988 that serious changes began.

The catalyst for change in Hungary was the frustration of younger, 'reform' Communists—openly enthusiastic about the transformations Gorbachev was working in the CPSU—at the inflexibility of their own ageing Party leadership. In May 1988, at a special Communist Conference called for the purpose, they at last succeeded in removing the 76-year-old Kádár from the leadership and replacing him with Károly Grósz, the Prime Minister. The strictly practical consequences of this internal Party coup were limited to an economic austerity program aimed at strengthening 'market forces'; but it had great symbolic force.

János Kádár had ruled Hungary ever since the revolution of 1956, in whose suppression he played the major part. Despite his rather favorable image abroad, he incarnated for Hungarians the official lie at the heart of 'goulash Communism': that the Hungarian reform movement had been nothing but a 'counter-revolution'. Kádár was also the living embodiment of the conspiracy of silence surrounding Imre Nagy ever since his kidnapping, secret trial and even more secret execution and burial three decades before.[19] The removal of Kádár thus seemed to suggest that something fundamental had shifted in Hungarian public life—an impression confirmed when his successors not only allowed a group of dissident young Communists and others to form Fidesz (Young Democrats), but in November 1988 officially condoned the appearance of independent political parties.

In the early months of 1989 the Communist legislature passed a series of measures recognizing the right of free assembly; officially sanctioning 'transition' to a multi-party system; and, in April, formally jettisoning 'democratic centralism' in the Party itself. Of even greater moment, Hungary's Communist rulers—tacitly acknowledging that their Party could not hope to maintain its control of the coun-

---

[19]Officially the site of Nagy's grave had remained unknown for thirty years; in fact its location, in an obscure and unmarked corner of the Budapest Municipal Cemetery, was public knowledge.

try unless it came clean about its past—announced their intention to exhume and rebury the troublesome remains of Imre Nagy. At the same time Imre Pozsgay and other reformers in the Hungarian Politburo convinced their colleagues to open a commission of inquiry into the events of 1956 and officially redefine them: no longer a 'counter-revolution', they were now officially a 'popular uprising against an oligarchic rule that had debased the nation.'

On June 16th 1989—the thirty-first anniversary of his death—the remains of Imre Nagy and four of his colleagues were ceremoniously reburied as national heroes. An estimated 300,000 Hungarians lined the streets, with millions more watching the proceedings live on television. Among the speakers at the graveside was Viktor Orbán, the young leader of the Young Democrats, who could not help noting that some of the Communists present at Nagy's reburial were the same who, just a few years before, had so strenuously falsified the very revolution whose praises they were now singing.

This was true. It was a curiosity of the Hungarian exit from Communism that it was conducted by Communists themselves—only in June were round-table talks convened with opposition parties, in conscious imitation of the Polish precedent. This induced a certain skepticism among anti-Communist Hungarians, for whom Nagy's resurrection, like his earlier execution, was an intra-Party affair of little concern to Communism's many victims. But it would be wrong to underestimate the symbolic force of the reburial of Nagy. It was an admission of defeat, an acknowledgement that the Party and its leadership had lived and taught and imposed a lie.

When János Kádár died just three weeks later—on the very day that the Hungarian Supreme Court pronounced Nagy's full rehabilitation—Hungarian Communism died with him. All that remained was to agree on the formalities of its passing. The 'leading role' of the Party was abolished; multi-party elections were scheduled for the following March; and on October 7th the Communists—the Hungarian Socialist Workers Party—re-baptized themselves the Hungarian Socialist Party. On October 23rd Parliament, still overwhelmingly composed of Communist deputies elected under the old Party regime, in turn voted to rename the country itself as, simply, the Hungarian Republic.

The Hungarian 'revolution' of 1989 had two distinguishing features. The first, as we have seen, is that it was the only passage from a Communist regime to a genuine multi-party system effected entirely from within. The second point of note is that whereas in Poland, as later in Czechoslovakia and elsewhere, the events of 1989 were largely self-referential, the Hungarian transition played a vital role in the unraveling of another Communist regime, that of East Germany.

To outside observers, the German Democratic Republic appeared among the least vulnerable of Communist regimes, and not only because it was universally assumed that no Soviet leader would ever allow it to fall. The physical environment

of the GDR, notably its cities, might appear tawdry and dilapidated; its security police, the Stasi, were notoriously omnipresent; and the Wall in Berlin remained a
moral and aesthetic outrage. But the East German economy was widely believed
to be in better shape than that of its socialist neighbors. When First Secretary Erich
Honecker boasted at the country's fortieth anniversary celebrations in October
1989 that the GDR was one of the world's top ten economic performers, his guest
Mikhail Gorbachev was heard to emit an audible snort; but if nothing else, the
regime was efficient in the manufacture and export of bogus data: many Western
observers took Honecker at his word.

The GDR's most enthusiastic admirers were to be found in the Federal Republic. The apparent success of *Ostpolitik* in defusing tensions and facilitating human
and economic communications between the two halves of Germany had led virtually the entire political class to invest their hopes in its indefinite prolongation.
West German public figures not only encouraged illusions among the *nomenklatura* of the GDR, they deluded themselves. Simply by repeating that *Ostpolitik*
was having the effect of easing tensions to the east, they came to believe it.

Preoccupied with 'peace,' 'stability,' and 'order,' many West Germans thus ended
up sharing the point of view of the Eastern politicians with whom they were doing
business. Egon Bahr, a prominent Social Democrat, explained in January 1982 (immediately following the declaration of martial law in Poland) that Germans had re-
nounced their claim to national unity for the sake of peace and the Poles would just
have to renounce *their* claim to freedom in the name of the same 'highest priority.'
Five years later the influential writer Peter Bender, speaking at a Social Democratic Party symposium on 'Mitteleuropa', proudly insisted that 'in the desire for détente we have more in common with Belgrade and Stockholm, *also with Warsaw
and East Berlin* [emphasis added], than we do with Paris and London.'

In later years it would emerge that on more than one occasion national leaders
of the SPD made confidential and decidedly compromising statements to high-
ranking East Germans visiting the West. In 1987 Björn Engholm praised the domestic policies of the GDR as 'historic', while the following year his colleague Oskar
Lafontaine promised to do everything in his power to make sure that West German
support for East German dissidents remained muted. 'The Social Democrats,' he
assured his interlocutors, 'must avoid everything that would mean a strengthening
of those forces.' As a Soviet report to the GDR Politburo noted in October 1984,
'Many arguments that had previously been presented by us to the representatives
of the SPD have now been taken over by them'.[20]

The illusions of West German Social Democrats are perhaps understandable.
But they were shared with almost equal fervour by many Christian Democrats too.
Helmut Kohl, the West German Chancellor since 1982, was just as keen as his op-

---

[20]I am grateful to Professor Timothy Garton Ash for this reference.

ponents to cultivate good relations with the GDR. At the Moscow funeral of Yuri Andropov in February 1984 he met and spoke with Erich Honecker—and did so again at the burial of Chernenko the following year. Agreements were reached between the two sides over cultural exchange and the removal of mines on the inter-German border. In September 1987 Honecker became the first East German leader to visit the Federal Republic. Meanwhile West German subsidies for the GDR continued apace (but no support was ever forthcoming for East Germany's internal opposition).

Flush with West German sponsorship, confident of Moscow's backing and at liberty to export to the West its more troublesome dissidents, the East German regime might have survived indefinitely. It certainly appeared immune to change: in June 1987 demonstrators in East Berlin opposed to the Wall and chanting praise for the distant Gorbachev were summarily dispersed. In January 1988 the government did not hesitate to imprison and expel well over a hundred demonstrators who were commemorating the 1919 murder of Rosa Luxemburg and Karl Liebknecht with signs quoting Luxemburg herself: 'Freedom is also the freedom of those who think differently'. In September 1988 Honecker, on a visit to Moscow, publicly praised Gorbachev's *perestroika*—only to make a point of studiously avoiding its implementation upon his return home.[21]

Notwithstanding the unprecedented developments then unfolding in Moscow, Warsaw and Budapest, the East German Communists were still rigging votes in a manner familiar from the 1950s. In May 1989 the official outcome of the GDR municipal elections—98.85 percent for government candidates—was so egregiously fabricated that it aroused nationwide protests from priests, environmental groups and even critics within the ruling party. The Politburo studiously ignored them. But now, for the first time, East Germans had a choice. They no longer had to accept the status quo, risk arrest or else essay a hazardous escape to the West. On May 2nd 1989, in the course of relaxing the control of movement and expression within Hungary itself, the authorities in Budapest had removed the electrified fence along the country's western frontier, although the border itself remained formally closed.

East Germans began to swarm into Hungary. By July 1st 1989 some 25,000 of them had made their way to 'vacation' there. Thousands more followed, many of them seeking temporary refuge in West German embassies in Prague and Budapest. A few made their way across the still-closed Austro-Hungarian frontier without being stopped by border guards, but most just stayed in Hungary. By early September there were 60,000 GDR citizens in Hungary, waiting. Asked on a Hungarian television news program on September 10th what his government's response would be if some of these people started walking west, the Hungarian Foreign

---

[21]It appears that Honecker had calculated, reasonably enough, that Gorbachev would not last and could safely be ignored.

Minister Gyula Horn replied: 'We will allow them through without any further ado and I assume that the Austrians will let them in.' The door to the West was officially open: within seventy-two hours some 22,000 East Germans had rushed through it.

The East German authorities protested furiously—the Hungarian move implied a breach of the longstanding agreement between Communist governments not to allow their countries to be used as escape routes from fraternal neighbors. But the authorities in Budapest merely insisted that they were bound by their signature to the Helsinki Final Act. The people took them at their word. In the course of the next three weeks the GDR authorities confronted a public-relations disaster as tens of thousands of their fellow citizens tried to get out through the new exit route.

In an attempt to take control of events the GDR rulers offered East German refugees in the embassies in Prague and Warsaw safe passage back through their own country and on to West Germany in a sealed train. This, however, merely exacerbated the regime's mounting humiliation: as the train passed through the GDR it was greeted by tens of thousands of cheering, envious locals. An estimated five thousand people tried to clamber aboard when the refugee train stopped briefly in Dresden; when the police beat them back a riot ensued—all under the eyes of the world's media.

The regime's travails emboldened its critics. The day after Hungary opened its borders a group of East German dissenters in East Berlin founded Neues Forum ('New Forum'), followed a few days later by another citizens' movement, 'Democracy Now', both groups pressing for a democratic 'restructuring' of the GDR. On Monday October 2nd, in Leipzig, a crowd of 10,000 demonstrated in frustration at the Honecker regime's refusal to reform itself—the largest public gathering in East Germany since the ill-fated Berlin uprising of 1953. The 77–year old Honecker remained impervious. East Germans seeking to emigrate, he declared in September, had been 'blackmailed through enticements, promises and threats to renounce the basic principles and fundamental values of socialism.' To the increasing anxiety of younger colleagues—who could no longer ignore the scale of the challenge facing them—the leadership appeared helpless: frozen in place. On October 7th, to honor the fortieth anniversary of the founding of the GDR, Mikhail Gorbachev came and spoke, memorably advising his stone-faced host that 'life punishes those who delay.' To no avail: Honecker pronounced himself satisfied with things the way they were.

Encouraged by the Soviet leader's visit—not to speak of developments abroad—demonstrators in Leipzig and other cities began holding regular demonstrations and 'vigils' for change. The Monday gatherings in Leipzig, now a regular fixture, had grown to 90,000 by the week following Gorbachev's speech, the assembled crowds all proclaiming 'We are the people!' and calling upon 'Gorby' to help them. The following week the numbers had grown again; an increasingly agitated Honecker was now proposing to use force to put down any further show of opposition.

The prospect of outright confrontation appears finally to have concentrated the mind of Honecker's Party critics. On October 18th some of his colleagues, led by Egon Krenze, staged a coup and removed the old man from power, after 18 years.[22] Krenze's first act was to fly to Moscow, endorse (and seek the endorsement of) Mikhail Gorbachev and return to Berlin to prepare a cautious East German *perestroika*. But it was too late. At the most recent Leipzig demonstration, an estimated 300,000 people had come together to press for change; on November 4th half a million East Germans gathered in Berlin to demand immediate reforms. Meanwhile, on that same day, Czechoslovakia opened its border; in the next forty-eight hours 30,000 people left through it.

By now the authorities were truly panicked. On November 5th, the GDR government hesitantly proposed a mildly liberalized travel law, only to have it dismissed by critics as pitifully inadequate. The East German cabinet then dramatically resigned, followed by the Politburo. The following evening—November 9th, anniversary of both the Kaiser's abdication and *Kristallnacht*—Krenze and his colleagues proposed yet another travel law to head off the stampede. At a news conference carried live on German television and radio, Günter Schabowski explained that the new provisions, in immediate effect, authorized foreign travel without advance notice and permitted transit through the border crossings into West Germany. The Wall, in other words, was now open.

Before the broadcast was even finished people were in the streets of East Berlin and heading for the border. Within hours, fifty thousand people had poured into West Berlin: some forever, others just going to look. By the following morning the world had changed. As anyone could see, the Wall had been breached for good and there could be no return. Four weeks later the Brandenburg Gate, straddling the East-West border, was reopened; over the Christmas holidays of 1989, 2.4 million East Germans (1 in 6 of the total population) visited the West. This had most decidedly *not* been the intention of the GDR rulers. As Schabowski himself later explained, the authorities had 'no clue' that opening the Wall might bring about the downfall of the GDR—quite the contrary: they saw it as the beginning of 'stabilization'.

In taking the hesitant decision to open the border the GDR leaders had hoped merely to release a safety valve, perhaps secure a little popularity, and above all buy

---

[22]Three days after Gorbachev's visit Honecker received a visiting Chinese dignitary and compared the unrest in the GDR with China's recent 'counter-revolution'. It seems likely that he was at least contemplating a German re-play of the Tiananmen Square massacre—one reason why his colleagues took the decision to oust him.

enough time to propose a program of 'reforms'. The Wall, after all, was opened for much the same reason that it had been erected and closed a generation earlier: to staunch a demographic hemorrhage. In 1961 this desperate ploy had succeeded; in 1989, too, it worked after a fashion—surprisingly few East Germans remained permanently in West Berlin or emigrated to West Germany once they were reassured that if they returned they would not find themselves imprisoned again. But the price of that reassurance was the fall of more than just the regime.

In the aftermath of the fall of the Wall, the SED went through the—by now familiar—last rites of a dying Communist Party. On December 1st the Volkskammer (GDR Parliament) voted 420–0 (with five abstentions) to delete from the GDR constitution the clause declaring that the state is 'led by the working class and its Marxist-Leninist party'. Four days later the Politburo resigned once again; a new leader—Gregor Gysi—was chosen; and the party's name duly changed, to the Party of Democratic Socialism. The old Communist leadership (including both Honecker and Krenze) was expelled from the party; round table (again) discussions were begun with representatives of Neues Forum (by general consent the most visible of the opposition groups), and free elections were scheduled.

But even before the latest (and last) GDR government under Dresden Party boss Hans Modrow had started drafting a 'Party action program', its actions and intentions were all but irrelevant. East Germans, after all, had an option that was not available to other subject-peoples—there was no 'West Czechoslovakia', or 'West Poland'—and they were not about to forego it. The goalposts were shifting: in October 1989 the Leipzig demonstrators had chanted 'Wir sind das Volk'—'We are the people'. By January 1990 the same crowds were proclaiming a subtly different demand: 'Wir sind *ein* Volk'—'We are one people'.

Because the death of German Communism would thus entail, as we shall see in the next chapter, the death of a German state—by January 1990 the point had become not just to get *out* of Socialism (much less 'reform' it) but to get *into* West Germany—it is not clear in retrospect how to interpret the hopes of the crowds who brought down the GDR in the autumn of 1989. What *is* clear, however, is that neither the Party (as in Hungary), nor the opposition (as in Poland) can claim much credit for the course of events. We have seen how slow the Party was to grasp its predicament; but its intellectual critics were not much quicker.

On November 28th Stefan Heym, Christa Wolf and other East German intellectuals issued an appeal 'For Our Land', to save socialism and the GDR and stand firm against what Heym described as the 'glittering rubbish' of the West. Bärbel Bohley, the leading figure in Neues Forum, even described the opening of the Berlin Wall as 'unfortunate', because it forestalled 'reform' and precipitated elections before the parties or the voters were 'ready'. Like many of East Germany's 'dissenting' intellectuals (not to speak of their West German admirers) Bohley and her colleagues still envisaged a reformed Socialism, shorn of secret policemen and a ruling party but keeping a safe distance from its predatory capitalist *doppelganger* to the west. As events were to show, this was at least as unrealistic as Erich Honecker's fantasy of a return to neo-Stalinist obedience. Neues Forum thus condemned itself to political irrelevance, its leaders reduced to carping resentfully at the improvidence of the masses.[23]

The German uprising of 1989, then, was perhaps the only truly popular—i.e. mass—revolution of that year (and indeed the only successful popular revolt in German history).[24] The fall of Communism in neighboring Czechoslovakia, although coming at the same time as the transformation in East Germany, followed a significantly different path. In both countries the Party leadership was rigid and repressive, and the rise of Gorbachev was at least as unwelcome to the regime in Prague as it was in Pankow. But there the similarities end.

As in Hungary, so in Czechoslovakia, Communist rule rested uneasily upon the silent memory of a stolen past. But whereas in the Hungarian case Kádár had semi-successfully distanced himself and his party from their Stalinist inheritance, the leaders of Czechoslovakia had managed no such transition. Nor had they sought it. The Warsaw Pact invasion of 1968 and the subsequent 'normalization' lived on in Gustav Husák, in power since 1969. Even when Husák, now 75, resigned as General Secretary of the Party in 1987 (while remaining state President), he was replaced by Miloš Jakeš—younger, to be sure, but best known for his prominent role in the mass purges of the early Seventies.

The Czechoslovak Communists were actually rather successful at maintaining total control to the very end. Neither the Catholic Church (always a minor player in Czech, if not Slovak affairs) nor the intellectual opposition gained significant support in society at large. Thanks to the brutally efficient management of the purges, most of the country's intelligentsia, from playwrights to historians to Sixties-era reform Communists, had been expunged not just from their jobs put from public visibility. Until 1989 some of Czechoslovakia's most outspoken domestic critics of Communism, beginning with Václav Havel himself, were better-known abroad than in their own country. As we saw in the last chapter, Havel's own civic organization, Charter 77, managed fewer than two thousand signatories in a population of 15 million.

Of course, people were afraid to take the risk of openly criticizing the regime;

---

[23]To be fair, the East German dissidents genuinely misread the courage of the crowds in November 1989 as the basis for a renewed socialist republic. On the other hand, the source of that misreading was their blind failure to understand what 'socialism' had come to mean—and their own investment in its survival.

[24]In certain respects its Polish equivalent came in 1980–81—the political transition in Poland a decade later was an altogether more calculated and negotiated affair.

but it has to be said that most Czechs and Slovaks were not actively unhappy with their lot. The Czechoslovak economy, like most other Eastern European economies since the early Seventies, had been deliberately geared to supplying basic consumer goods, and in the Czech case something more. Indeed, Communist Czechoslovakia consciously mimicked aspects of Western consumer society—notably television programming and popular leisure pursuits—albeit in a mediocre key. Life in Czechoslovakia was dull, the environment was deteriorating and younger people especially chafed at the omnipresent and censorious authorities. But in return for avoiding confrontation with the regime and paying lip service to its turgid rhetoric, people were left to their own devices.

The regime kept a tight and even brutal lid on any signs of dissent. Demonstrators in Prague and elsewhere who came out to mark the twentieth anniversary of the invasion in August 1988 were arrested; unofficial efforts to hold an 'East-West' seminar in Prague were quashed. In January 1989, on the twentieth anniversary of Jan Palach's suicide in Wenceslas Square, Havel and thirteen other Charter 77 activists were arrested and once again imprisoned (though in contrast with the harsh treatment meted out to him in earlier years, Havel—now an international figure whose mistreatment might embarrass his jailers—was released in May).

In the course of the spring and summer of 1989 informal networks and groups sprang up around the country, in hopeful imitation of developments in neighboring lands: following the 'John Lennon Peace Club' formed in December 1988 there came the 'Prague Mothers' protest of May 1989, followed by environmentalist demonstrations in Bratislava the following month. None of these tiny and easily-contained bubbles of civic initiative posed any threat to the police or the regime. But in August, just as Mazowiecki was finalizing plans for his government in Warsaw and shortly before the Hungarian borders were flung open, demonstrators filled the streets of the Czech capital to commemorate, once again, the overthrow of the Prague Spring.

On this occasion, however, the Czech police were decidedly more restrained. The Jakeš regime had decided to trim a little, offering at least the appearance of acknowledging the change of mood in Moscow, while altering nothing of substance in its rule. The same calculation doubtless explains the authorities' hands-off approach to the next major public demonstration on October 28th, the anniversary of the foundation of the Czechoslovak state in 1918 (officially ignored since 1948). But there was still no great public pressure upon the Communist leadership—even the announcement on November 15th that exit visas would no longer be required for travel to the West was less a concession to demand than a strategic imitation of changes elsewhere.

It was this apparent lack of real reforming intent on the part of the party chiefs, and the absence of any effective external opposition—the summer demonstrations lacked common objectives and no leaders had yet emerged to channel discontent into a programme—that lent credence to a widespread suspicion that what followed was in some measure a staged 'plot': an attempt by would-be reformers in the administration and police to jump-start the moribund Party in the direction of a Czech *perestroika*.

This is not as bizarre as it may sound in retrospect. On November 17th the Prague police officially approved a student march through the inner-city to commemorate yet another gloomy date, the 50th anniversary of the Nazi murder of a Czech student, Jan Opletal. But when the marching students began to chant anti-Communist slogans the police attacked, scattering the crowd and beating up isolated victims. The police themselves then encouraged the rumour that—in a replay of Opletal's own murder—one of the students had been killed. This was later acknowledged to be a false report; but meanwhile it had the predictable effect of provoking anger among the students themselves. In the course of the next forty eight hours tens of thousands of students were mobilized, the universities were occupied and huge crowds began to gather in the streets to protest. Now, however, the police merely stood by.

If there ever had been a plot it decidedly backfired. To be sure, the events of November 17th and their aftermath dislodged the neo-Stalinist leadership of the Communist Party: within a week the entire Praesidium, led by Jakeš, had resigned. But their successors had absolutely no popular credibility and were in any case immediately submerged by the speed of events. On November 19th Václav Havel, who had been consigned to virtual house arrest in rural northern Bohemia, returned to a capital city in turmoil, where the Communists were rapidly losing power but there was as yet no-one around to take it out of their hands.

Installing himself—appropriately enough—in a Prague theater, Havel and his friends from Charter 77 formed Občanské Fórum (Civic Forum), an informal and fluid network that metamorphosed within days from a debating society to a civic initiative and thence into a shadow government. The discussion in Civic Forum was driven partly by the longstanding goals of its best-known participants, but mostly by the spectacularly accelerating course of events in the streets outside. The first thing the Forum did was to demand the resignation of the men responsible for the invasion of '68 and its aftermath.

On November 25th, the day after the Party leaders duly resigned en masse, a crowd of half a million people gathered at the Letná stadium in Prague, not so much to demand particular reforms as to make their presence known, after two decades of cowed public silence: to themselves and to one another. That same night Havel was granted an unprecedented interview on Czech television. The following day he addressed a crowd of 250,000 in Wenceslas Square, sharing a platform with the Communist Prime Minister Ladislav Adamec—and Alexander Dubček.

By now it had become clear to the emerging leadership of Civic Forum that they were, despite themselves, running a revolution. In order to provide some direction—and to have something to say to the massed crowds outside—a group led by the historian Petr Pithart drew up the 'Programmatic Principles of Civic Forum'. These contained a brief summary of the general objectives of the Forum and are an instructive guide to the mood and priorities of the men and women of 1989. 'What do we want?' the program asks. 1: A state of law. 2: Free elections. 3: Social justice. 4: A clean environment. 5: An educated people. 6: Prosperity. 7: Return to Europe.

The mixture of boilerplate political demands, cultural and environmental ideals, and the invocation of 'Europe' is characteristically Czech and owed much to various Charter 77 pronouncements over the previous decade. But the tone of the Programme nicely captured the mood of the crowds in the heady days of November: pragmatic, idealistic and wildly ambitious all at once. The mood in Prague and the rest of the country was also more avowedly optimistic than in any of the other Communist 'transitions'. This was an effect of acceleration.[25]

Within a week of the bloody repression of the student demonstrators the Party leadership had resigned. One week later Civic Forum and Public Against Violence (PAV—its Slovak *alter ego*) had been legalized and were negotiating with the government. On November 29th the Federal Assembly, responding meekly to a Civic Forum demand, removed from the Czechoslovak constitution the seminal clause guaranteeing the Communist Party its 'leading role'. At this point the Adamec government proposed a new governing coalition as a compromise but the representatives of Civic Forum—boosted by large and determined crowds now in permanent occupation of the streets—rejected it out of hand.

By now the Communists could hardly fail to note events abroad: not only had their colleagues in the former East German leadership been expelled on December 3rd; but Mikhail Gorbachev was sitting down to dinner with President Bush in Malta and the Warsaw Pact states were preparing publicly to renounce their 1968 invasion of Czechoslovakia. Discredited and disqualified by their own paymasters, the remaining members of the Husák group of Czech and Slovak Communists, including Prime Minister Adamec, resigned.

After a two-day 'Round Table' meeting (the briefest of all the round tables of the year) the Civic Forum leaders now agreed to join a cabinet. The Prime Minister—the Slovak Marián Čalfa—was still a Party member, but a majority of the ministers—for the first time since 1948—were non-Communists: Jiří Dienstbier of Charter 77 (a stoker until just five weeks earlier) was to be foreign minister; the Catholic lawyer Jan Čarnogurský of PAV was to be Deputy Prime Minister; Vladimír Kusý of Civic Forum was information minister; and the hitherto obscure free-market economist Václav Klaus was to direct the Ministry of Finance. The new government was sworn in on December 10th by President Husák, who then promptly resigned

---

[25]The author, who was in Prague at this time, can vouch for the intoxicating feeling that history was being made by the hour.

The re-emergence of Alexander Dubček from two decades of obscurity had opened the possibility that he might be chosen to replace Husák as President—in part as a symbol of continuity with the thwarted hopes of 1968, in part to assuage the wounded feelings of the Communists and maybe even mollify hard-liners in the police and other services. But as soon as he began to make public speeches it became embarrassingly clear that poor Dubček was an anachronism. His vocabulary, his style, even his gestures were those of the reform Communists of the Sixties. He had learned nothing, it seemed, from his bitter experiences, but spoke still of resurrecting a kinder, gentler, Czechoslovak path to Socialism. To the tens of thousands of young people in the streets of Prague, or Brno, or Bratislava he was at first a historical curiosity; soon he became an irritating irrelevance.[26]

By way of compromise Dubček was elected chairman (i.e. Speaker) of the Federal Assembly. It fell to Václav Havel himself to become President—a notion so bizarrely implausible just five weeks before that he had gently dismissed the suggestion when it was first mooted by cheering crowds in the streets of Prague: 'Havel na Hrad!' ('Havel to the Castle'). By December 7th, however, the playwright had come around to the view that his acceptance of the post might be the best way to facilitate the country's exit from Communism; on December 28th 1989 the same Communist Assembly which had dutifully rubber-stamped the legislation that had hitherto consigned Havel and others to years of imprisonment now elected him President of the Czechoslovak Socialist Republic. On New Year's Day 1990 the new President amnestied 16,000 political prisoners; the following day the political police itself was disbanded.

Czechoslovakia's remarkably expeditious and peaceful exit from Communism— the so-called 'velvet revolution'—was made possible by a confluence of circumstances. As in Poland, the intellectual opposition was united above all by the memory of past defeats and a determination to avoid outright confrontation—it was not for nothing that the leading civic organization in Slovakia called itself 'Public Against Violence'. As in the GDR, the utter bankruptcy of the ruling Party became clear so fast that the option of an organized rearguard action was excluded almost from the start.

But the role of Havel was equally crucial—no one individual of comparable public standing emerged in any other Communist country, and while most of the practical ideas and even the political tactics of Civic Forum might have been forthcoming in his absence, it was Havel who caught and channeled the public mood, moving his colleagues forward while keeping the expectations of the crowds

---

[26]A cartoon in one of the ephemeral Prague student newspapers of December 1989 perfectly captures the generation gap. A paunchy middle-aged man in an undershirt stares with distaste into his shaving mirror at a blowsy woman in the doorway, a dirty nightgown draped over her shoulders, her hair in rollers, a cigarette dangling from her lips. 'Don't you recognize me?' she taunts him. 'I'm your dream of 1968.'

within manageable bounds. The impact of Havel and his public appeal cannot be overstated. Like Tomáš Masaryk, with whom he came increasingly to be compared, the improbably charismatic Havel was now widely regarded by many as something akin to a national saviour. One Prague student poster from December 1989, in a possibly unintended but highly apposite religious allusion, depicted the incoming President with the words 'He gave Himself to us.'

It was not just Havel's multiple incarcerations and his unflinching record of moral opposition to Communism that placed him upon this pedestal: it was also his distinctively apolitical disposition. It was not in spite of his theatrical preoccupations that his fellow-citizens turned to Havel, it was because of them. As one Italian commentator observed of Havel's emerging role on the Czechoslovak political stage, his distinctive voice allowed him to articulate the feelings of a silenced nation: '*Se un popolo non ha mai parlato, la prima parole che dice è poesia*'.[27] For just these reasons it was Havel—notably skeptical of the seductions of capitalism (in contrast to his Finance Minister Klaus)—who alone could bridge the uncomfortable gap separating the mendacious but seductive egalitarianism of a defunct Communism from the uncomfortable realities of the free market.

In Czechoslovakia such a bridge was important. For all that it was in many respects the most western of the European Communist lands, Czechoslovakia was also the only one with a markedly egalitarian and left-leaning political culture: this, after all, was the only country in the world where almost two voters in five had ever chosen a Communist Party in free elections, back in 1946. In spite of forty years of 'real existing Socialism'—and twenty years of deadening 'normalization'—something of this political culture still endured: in the first post-Communist elections, held in June 1990, 14 percent of the electorate opted for the Communist Party. It was the enduring presence of this sizeable core of Communist supporters—together with the much larger penumbra of apolitical citizens not sufficiently dissatisfied to protest their condition—that had led dissident writers like Ludvík Vaculík to question the likelihood of great changes in the immediate future. History seemed to be against the Czechs and Slovaks: ever since 1938, Czechoslovakia had never quite managed to recover control of its own destiny.

Thus, when the people themselves finally seized the initiative in November 1989, the ensuing velvet revolution appeared almost too good to be true. Hence the talk of police plots and manufactured crises, as though Czechoslovak society had so little self confidence that even the initiative to destroy Communism must have come from the Communists themselves. Such skepticism was almost certainly misplaced—all the evidence that has since emerged suggests that on November 17th the Czech security police simply went too far. There was no 'plot' to force the hand

---

[27]'If a people have never spoken, the first words they utter are poetry.' Ferdinando Camon in *La Stampa*, 'Tutto Libri', December 16th 1989.

of the ruling clique. In 1989 the people of Czechoslovakia really did take charge of their destiny.

The Romanian case was another matter. There it seems clear that in December 1989 one faction within the ruling Romanian Workers' Party did indeed decide that its best chance of survival lay in forcibly removing the ruling coterie around Nicolae Ceauşescu. Romania, of course, was not a typical Communist state. If Czechoslovakia was the most western of the Communist satellite countries, Romania was the most 'oriental'. Under Ceauşescu, Communism had degenerated from national Leninism to a sort of neo-Stalinist satrapy, where Byzantine levels of nepotism and inefficiency were propped in place by a tentacular secret police.

Compared with Dej's vicious dictatorship of the Fifties, Ceauşescu's regime got by with relatively little overt brutality; but the rare hints of public protest—strikes in the Jiu mining valley in August 1977, for example, or a decade later at the Red Star tractor works in Braşov—were violently and effectively suppressed. Moreover, Ceauşescu could count not only on a cowed population but also upon a remarkable lack of foreign criticism for his actions at home: eight months after imprisoning the strike leaders in the Jiu Valley (and murdering their leaders) the Romanian dictator was visiting the United States as the guest of President Jimmy Carter. By taking his distance from Moscow—we have seen how Romania abstained from the 1968 invasion of Czechoslovakia—Ceauşescu bought himself freedom of maneuver and even foreign acclaim, particularly in the early stages of the 'new' Cold War of the 1980s. Because the Romanian leader was happy to criticize the Russians (and send his gymnasts to the Los Angeles Olympics), Americans and others kept quiet about his domestic crimes.[28]

Romanians, however, paid a terrible price for Ceauşescu's privileged status. In 1966, to increase the population—a traditional 'Romanianist' obsession—he prohibited abortion for women under forty with fewer than four children (in 1986 the age barrier was raised to forty-five). In 1984 the minimum marriage age for women was reduced to fifteen. Compulsory monthly medical examinations for all women of childbearing age were introduced to prevent abortions, which were permitted, if at all, only in the presence of a Party representative. Doctors in districts with a declining birth rate had their salaries cut.

The population did not increase, but the death rate from abortions far exceeded that of any other European country: as the only available form of birth control, illegal abortions were widely performed, often under the most appalling and dangerous conditions. Over the ensuing twenty-three years the 1966 law resulted in the death of at least ten thousand women. The real infant mortality rate was so high

---

[28]At least until the rise of Mikhail Gorbachev, after which the West had no further use for an anti-Soviet maverick.

A 'Wanted' poster for the Baader-Meinhof Group, 1972 (Ulrike Meinhof and Andreas Baader, top left). 'Extra-parliamentary' radicals in Germany turned to terrorism to 'strip the veil' from the Federal Republic and reveal 'the civilized extermination technology of the New Order of Bretton Woods'.

The opening day of the April 1982 trial of 63 Red Brigade members accused of killing former Italian premier Aldo Moro. In Italy left terrorists emphasized their (illusory) links to the proletariat, but it was right terrorists who posed the greater danger (and killed more people).

Members of ETA ('Basque Homeland and Liberty'), 1982. Frustrated by their growing isolation from a prosperous local population (many from elsewhere in Spain) unmoved by the mirage of an 'independent Basquia', ETA gunmen killed an annual average of 34 people through the Eighties.

'. . . I found a big stone to throw at a soldier. . . . I'm going to get a gun when I'm a little older . . .' (Belfast children's chant, circa 1976). The thirty-year-long, three-way confrontation between IRA gunmen, Protestant gunmen and the British Army resulted in nearly two thousand deaths.

Portuguese workers arriving in France, 1970. By 1973 foreigners comprised 11 percent of France's workforce. In West Germany there were nearly three million 'guest workers', mostly from Mediterranean countries. Europe's 'economic miracle' depended heavily on the contribution of these migrants—and the remittances they sent home.

Italian women demonstrating for divorce law reform, 1974. Post-war west European welfare legislation chiefly benefitted employed workers and families. Issues of particular concern to women—abortion, contraception, divorce—had to await the Sixties in northern Europe, the Seventies elsewhere.

Francisco Franco and his anointed successor, Prince Juan Carlos, October 1971. The Generalissimo (who died in 1975) would have been very disappointed in his protégé: as King, Juan Carlos thwarted a military coup in 1981 and proved a staunch and popular defender of democratic Spain.

Portugal's first parliamentary elections, April 1975. In retrospect the transition to parliamentary democracy in Mediterranean Europe appears smooth and even inevitable. At the time, however, many on Left and Right alike expected something else and were surprised (and disappointed) at the outcome.

Chancellor Willy Brandt—and GDR premier Willi Stoph—in Erfurt, March 1970, during the first inter-German talks. Brandt's Ostpolitik *opened contacts and eased tensions in central Europe—but to some West Germany seemed to be legitimizing and even propping up its Communist neighbours.*

'The eyes of Caligula and the mouth of Marilyn Monroe'. Margaret Thatcher's success in extracting a huge EEC budget rebate for Britain owed much to her skill at seducing and browbeating not just the British electorate but even seasoned cynics like François Mitterrand.

John Paul II on his first papal visit to Poland in June 1979. Though Karol Wojtyła did not single-handedly bring down Communism—as many fondly believed— his contribution to the discrediting of the regime in Poland was immense.

Adam Michnik in Gdansk, 1984. Michnik was one of the most courageous and original critics of Communism in eastern Europe. Notably influential was his emphasis upon non-violence and upon eroding Communist power from within, rather than seeking to confront or overthrow it.

Mikhail Gorbachev basking in popular adulation: Prague, April 1987. The last Soviet leader was never as popular at home as he was farther west; but success abroad encouraged him to pursue reform at home, perhaps beyond his initial intentions.

East German refugees in a sealed train, heading through Prague to the West, November 1989. The Bolshevik Revolution began with Lenin crossing Germany in a sealed train, so sending Communist citizens to freedom this way was altogether fitting.

Prague, November 1989. Even the 'Velvet Revolution' had its brutal prologue. But outside Romania the transitions of 1989 saw little serious violence—perhaps because many Communist cadres understood better than their critics that these regimes were doomed.

Alexander Dubček and Václav Havel, Prague, November 24th 1989. A plan to name Dubček President of post-Communist Czechoslovakia quickly aborted: to the revolutionaries of 1989—who chose Havel instead—the hero of 'reform Communism' was as irrelevant and dated as Stalinism itself.

that after 1985 births were not officially recorded until a child had survived to its fourth week—the apotheosis of Communist control of knowledge. By the time Ceauşescu was overthrown the death rate of new-born babies was twenty-five per thousand and there were upward of 100,000 institutionalized children.

The setting for this national tragedy was an economy that was deliberately turned backward, from subsistence into destitution. In the early Eighties, Ceauşescu decided to enhance his country's international standing still further by paying down Romania's huge foreign debts. The agencies of international capitalism— starting with the International Monetary Fund—were delighted and could not praise the Romanian dictator enough. Bucharest was granted a complete rescheduling of its external debt. To pay off his Western creditors, Ceauşescu applied unrelenting and unprecedented pressure upon domestic consumption.

In contrast to Communist rulers elsewhere, unrestrainedly borrowing abroad to bribe their subjects with well-stocked shelves, the Romanian *Conducator* set about exporting every available domestically-produced commodity. Romanians were forced to use 40–watt bulbs at home (when electricity was available) so that energy could be exported to Italy and Germany. Meat, sugar, flour, butter, eggs, and much more were strictly rationed. To ratchet up productivity, fixed quotas were introduced for obligatory public labour on Sundays and holidays (the *corvée*, as it was known in *ancien régime* France).

Petrol usage was cut to the minimum: in 1986 a program of horse-breeding to substitute for motorized vehicles was introduced. Horse-drawn carts became the main means of transport and the harvest was brought in by scythe and sickle. This was something truly new: all socialist systems depended upon the centralized control of systemically induced shortages, but in Romania an economy based on over-investment in unwanted industrial hardware was successfully switched into one based on pre-industrial agrarian subsistence.

Ceauşescu's policies had a certain ghoulish logic. Romania did indeed pay off its international creditors, albeit at the cost of reducing its population to penury. But there was more to Ceauşescu's rule, in his last years, than just crazy economics. The better to control the country's rural population—and increase still further the pressure on peasant farmers to produce food for export—the regime inaugurated a proposed 'systematization' of the Romanian countryside. Half of the country's 13,000 villages (disproportionately selected from minority communities) were to be forcibly razed, their residents transferred into 558 'agro-towns'. Had Ceauşescu been granted the time to carry through this project it would utterly have destroyed what little remained of the country's social fabric.

The rural 'systemization' project was driven forward by the Romanian dictator's mounting megalomania. Under Ceauşescu the Leninist impulse to control, centralize and plan every detail of daily life graduated into an obsession with homogeneity and grandeur surpassing even the ambitions of Stalin himself. The enduring physical incarnation of this monomaniacal urge was to be the country's capital, scheduled for an imperial make-over on a scale unprecedented since Nero. This project for the 'renovation' of Bucharest was to be aborted by the coup of December 1989; but enough was done for Ceauşescu's ambition to be indelibly etched into the fabric of the contemporary city. A historic district of central Bucharest the size of Venice was completely flattened. Forty thousand buildings and dozens of churches and other monuments were razed to make space for a new 'House of the People' and the five-kilometer-long, 150–meter-wide Victory of Socialism Boulevard.

The whole undertaking was mere façade. Behind the gleaming white frontages of the boulevard were run up the familiar dirty, grim, pre-cast concrete blocks. But the façade itself was aggressively, humiliatingly, unrelentingly uniform, a visual encapsulation of totalitarian rule. The House of the People, designed by a twenty-five-year-old architect (Anca Petrescu) as Ceauşescu's personal palace, was indescribably and uniquely ugly even by the standards of its genre. Grotesque, cruel and tasteless it was above all *big* (three times the size of the Palace of Versailles . . .). Fronted by a vast hemicycle space that can hold half a million people, its reception area the size of a football pitch, Ceauşescu's palace was (and remains) a monstrous lapidary metaphor for unconstrained tyranny, Romania's very own contribution to totalitarian urbanism.

Romanian Communism in its last years sat uneasily athwart the intersection of brutality and parody. Portraits of the Party leader and his wife were everywhere; his praise was sung in dithyrambic terms that might have embarrassed even Stalin himself (though not perhaps North Korea's Kim Il Sung, with whom the Romanian leader was sometimes compared). A short list of the epithets officially-approved by Ceauşescu for use in accounts of his achievements would include: The Architect; The Creed-shaper; The Wise Helmsman; The Tallest Mast; The Nimbus of Victory; The Visionary; The Titan; The Son of the Sun; A Danube of Thought; and The Genius of the Carpathians.

What Ceauşescu's sycophantic colleagues really thought of all this they were not saying. But it is clear that by November 1989—when, after sixty-seven standing ovations, he was re-elected Secretary General of the Party and proudly declared that there were to be no reforms—a number of them had begun to regard him as a liability: remote and out of touch not just with the mood of the times but with the rising level of desperation among his own subjects. But so long as he had the backing of the secret police, the Securitate, Ceauşescu appeared untouchable.

Appropriately enough, then, it was the Securitate who precipitated the regime's fall when, in December 1989, they tried to remove a popular Hungarian Protestant pastor, Lázslo Tökés, in the western city of Timisoara. The Hungarian minority, a special object of prejudice and repression under Ceauşescu's rule, had been encouraged by developments just across the border in Hungary and were all the more resentful at the continuing abuses to which they were subject at home. Tökés became a symbol and focus for their frustrations and, when the regime targeted him on December 15th, the church in which he had taken refuge was surrounded by parishioners holding an all-night vigil in his support.

The following day, as the vigil turned unexpectedly into a demonstration against the regime, the police and the army were brought out to shoot into the crowd. Exaggerated reports of the 'massacre' were carried on Voice of America and Radio Free Europe and spread around the country. To quell the unprecedented protests, which had now spread from Timisoara to Bucharest itself, Ceaușescu returned from an official visit to Iran. On December 21st he appeared on a balcony at Party headquarters with the intention of making a speech denouncing the 'minority' of 'troublemakers'—and was heckled into shocked and stunned silence. The following day, after making a second unsuccessful attempt to address the gathering crowds, Ceaușescu and his wife fled from the roof of the Party building in a helicopter.

At this point the balance of power swung sharply away from the regime. At first the army had appeared to back the dictator, occupying the streets of the capital and firing on demonstrators who tried to seize the national television studios. But from December 22nd the soldiers, now directed by a 'National Salvation Front' (NSF) that took over the television building, switched sides and found themselves pitted against heavily armed *Securitate* troops. Meanwhile the Ceaușescus were caught, arrested and summarily tried. Found guilty of 'crimes against the state' they were hastily executed on Christmas Day, 1989.[29]

The NSF converted itself into a provisional ruling council and—after renaming the country simply 'Romania'—appointed its own leader Ion Iliescu as President. Iliescu, like his colleagues in the Front, was a former Communist who had broken with Ceaușescu some years before and who could claim some slight credibility as a 'reformer' if only by virtue of his student acquaintance with the young Mikhail Gorbachev. But Iliescu's real qualification to lead a post-Ceaușescu Romania was his ability to control the armed forces, especially the Securitate, whose last hold-outs abandoned their struggle on December 27th. Indeed, beyond authorizing on January 3rd 1990 the re-establishment of political parties, the new President did very little to dismantle the institutions of the old regime.

As later events would show, the apparatus that had ruled under Ceaușescu remained remarkably intact, shedding only the Ceaușescu family itself and their more egregiously incriminated associates. Rumours of thousands killed during the protests and battles of December proved exaggerated—the figure was closer to one hundred—and it became clear that for all the courage and enthusiasm of the huge crowds in Timisoara, Bucharest and other cities the real struggle had been between the 'realists' around Iliescu and the old guard in Ceaușescu's entourage. The victory of the former ensured for Romania a smooth—indeed suspiciously smooth—exit out of Communism.

---

[29]The trial and execution by firing squad were filmed for television, but not shown until two days later.

The absurdities of late-era Ceauşescu were swept away, but the police, the bureaucracy and much of the Party remained intact and in place. The names were changed—the Securitate was officially abolished—but not their ingrained assumptions and practices: Iliescu did nothing to prevent riots in Tirgu Mures on March 19th, where eight people were killed and some three hundred wounded in orchestrated attacks on the local Hungarian minority. Moreover, after his National Salvation Front won an overwhelming majority in the elections of May 1990 (having earlier promised not to contest them), and he himself was formally re-elected President, Iliescu did not hesitate in June to bus miners in to Bucharest to beat up student protesters: twenty-one demonstrators were killed and some 650 injured. Romania still had a very long road to travel.

The 'palace coup' quality of Romania's revolution was even more in evidence to the south, where the Central Committee of the Bulgarian Communist Party unceremoniously ejected Todor Zhivkov from power at the advanced age of 78. The longest-serving leader in the Communist bloc—he had risen to the head of the Party in 1954—Zhivkov had done his best, in characteristic Bulgarian style, to hew closely to the Russian model: in the early Eighties he instituted a 'New Economic Mechanism' to improve production, and in March 1987, following Moscow's lead, he promised an end to 'bureaucratic' control of the economy, assuring the world that Bulgaria could now point to a *perestroika* of its own.

But the continuing failures of the Bulgarian economy, and the Communist leadership's growing insecurity as the new shape of affairs in Moscow became clear, led Zhivkov to seek out an alternative source of domestic legitimacy: ethnic nationalism. The significant Turkish minority in Bulgaria (some 900,000 in a population of fewer than nine million) was a tempting target: not only was it ethnically distinct and of a different religion but it was also the unfortunate heir and symbol of an era of hated Ottoman rule only now passing from direct memory. As in neighboring Yugoslavia, so in Bulgaria: a tottering Party autocracy turned the full fury of ethnic prejudice upon a helpless domestic victim.

In 1984 it was officially announced that the Turks of Bulgaria were not 'Turks' at all but forcibly-converted Bulgarians who would now be restored to their true identity. Muslim rites (such as circumcision) were restricted and criminalized; the use of the Turkish language in broadcasting, publications and education was proscribed; and in a particularly offensive (and angrily resented) move, all Bulgarian citizens with Turkish names were instructed henceforth to assume properly 'Bulgarian' ones instead. The outcome was a disaster. There was considerable Turkish resistance—which in turn aroused some opposition among Bulgarian intellectuals. The international community protested loudly; Bulgaria was condemned at the UN and in the European Court of Justice.

Meanwhile Zhivkov's fellow Communist oligarchs abroad took their distance from him. By 1989 the Bulgarian Communists were more isolated than ever and not a little perturbed at the course of events next door in Yugoslavia, where the Party seemed to be losing control. Things were brought to a head by the exodus to Turkey, during the summer of 1989, of an estimated 300,000 ethnic Turks—another public relations calamity for the regime, and an economic one too, as the country began to run short of manual laborers.[30] When the police over-reacted on October 26th to a small gathering of environmentalists in a Sofia park—arresting and beating activists from the *Ecoglasnost* group for circulating a petition—party reformers led by foreign minister Petar Mladenov decided to act. On November 10th (not coincidentally the day after the fall of the Berlin Wall) they ousted the hapless Zhivkov.

There followed the by-now familiar sequence of events: the release of political prisoners; sanctioning of political parties; removal from the constitution of the Communists' 'leading role'; a 'round table' to plan for free elections; a change in the name of the old party, now dubbed the 'Bulgarian Socialist Party'; and in due course the elections themselves, which—as in Romania—the former Communists easily won (there were widespread allegations of electoral fraud).

In Bulgaria the political 'opposition' had emerged largely after the fact and as in Romania there were suggestions that it was in some measure fabricated for their own purposes by dissident Communist factions. But the changes were nonetheless real. At the very least, Bulgaria successfully avoided the catastrophe awaiting Yugoslavia: on December 29th, in the face of angry nationalist protests, Muslims and Turks were granted full and equal rights. By 1991, a mainly Turkish party, the Movement for Rights and Freedom, had secured enough electoral backing to hold the balance of seats in the country's national Assembly.

Why did Communism collapse so precipitously in 1989? We should not indulge the sirens of retrospective determinism, however seductive. Even if Communism was doomed by its inherent absurdities, few predicted the timing and the manner of its going. To be sure, the ease with which the illusion of Communist power was punctured revealed that these regimes were even weaker than anyone supposed, and this casts their earlier history in a new light. But illusory or no, Communism lasted a long time. Why did it not last longer?

One answer is a version of the 'domino theory'. Once Communist leaders started falling in one place their legitimacy elsewhere was fatally impaired. The credibility of Communism rested in part upon its claim to embody necessity, to be the logical product of historical progress, a fact of political life, an inevitable presence on the modern landscape. Once this was shown to be palpably untrue—in Poland, for

---

[30]Officially, of course, the Turks didn't exist: 'There are no Turks in Bulgaria' (Dimitur Stoyanov, Interior Minister).

example, where Solidarity had apparently put History into reverse—then why continue to believe it in Hungary, or Czechoslovakia? We have already seen that the example of others clearly weighed in the balance.

Nevertheless, the striking aspect of Communism's collapse in Europe was not contagion *per se*: all revolutions spread in this way, corroding the legitimacy of established authorities by cumulative example. That is what happened in 1848, 1919 and, in a minor key, in 1968. The novelty of 1989 was the sheer *speed* of the process. As late as October 1989 Imre Pozsgay in Hungary, or Egon Krenze in East Germany, fondly supposed that they could control and manage their version of *perestroika*. Most of their opponents tended to agree and continued to look for some interim compromise. Back in 1980 Adam Michnik had written that 'a hybrid society is conceivable, one where totalitarian organization of the state will co-exist with democratic institutions of society'; well into the summer of 1989 he had little reason to expect anything else.

One novel factor was the role of the communications media. Hungarians, Czechs and Germans in particular were able to see their own revolution on the television news each evening. For the population of Prague, repeated television re-runs of the events of November 17th constituted a sort of instant political education, drumming home a double message: 'they are powerless' and 'we did it.' As a consequence, Communism's crucial asset, its control and monopoly of information, was lost. The fear of being alone—the impossibility of knowing whether your own feelings were shared by others—was dissipated for ever. Even in Romania the take-over of the national television studios was the determining moment in the uprising. Not for nothing was the gruesome fate of the Ceauşescus filmed for broadcast to a national audience. This was not a new pattern, of course—throughout the twentieth century radio stations and post offices were the first objectives of revolutionary crowds, from Dublin to Barcelona. But television is *fast*.

The second marked characteristic of the revolutions of 1989 was their pacific quality. Romania was the exception, of course; but given the nature of Ceauşescu's regime this was to be expected. The real surprise was that even in Timisoara and Bucharest the scale of bloodshed was far less than everyone feared. In part this, too, was a function of television. With the whole population—not to speak of much of the rest of the world—observing their every move, the Communist regimes were stymied. To be observed in this way was itself a loss of authority and severely restricted their range of options.[31]

To be sure, such considerations did not inhibit the Communist authorities in China, who shot down hundreds of peaceful demonstrators in Tiananmen Square on June 4th of that same year. Nicolae Ceauşescu would not have hesitated to em-

---

[31]Such considerations did not always apply in remote rural communities and small provincial towns, where the police continued to the very end to operate unhindered by television cameras or public disapproval.

ulate Beijing had he been able to do so. And we have seen that Erich Honecker at least contemplated something similar. But for most of their colleagues that was no longer an option. At some crucial moment all dying authoritarian regimes vacillate between repression and compromise. In the case of the Communists, confidence in their own capacity to rule was evaporating so rapidly that the chances of clinging to power by force alone began to seem slim—and the benefits of doing so by no means clear. In the calculus of self-interest the balance of advantage to most Communist bureaucrats and party *apparatchiks* was rapidly swinging the other way—better to swim with the current than be washed away in a tidal wave of change.

That calculation might have looked different had the crowds been angry or their leaders belligerently determined to wreak revenge upon the old order. But for many reasons—including the example of Tiananmen itself, unfolding on television the very day of the Polish elections—the men and women of 1989 consciously eschewed violence. It was not just the Polish revolution that was 'self-limiting'. With decades of violence to their discredit, and all the guns and bullets on their side, the Communist regimes had very effectively taught their own subjects the impropriety and imprudence of resorting to force. With the police still breaking heads in Berlin and Prague until the dying hours of the old regime, Slovaks were not the only 'Public Against Violence'.

Distaste for violence was all that many of the revolutionaries of 1989 had in common. They were an unusually motley group, even by the standards of most previous insurrections. The balance varied from place to place but typically 'the people' included a mix of reform Communists, social democrats, liberal intellectuals, free-market economists, Catholic activists, trade unionists, pacifists, some unreconstructed Trotskyists and others besides. This very variety was itself part of their strength: it constituted *de facto* precisely the informal complex of civil and political organizations which is so inimical to a one-party state.

At least one significant fault line—that separating liberal democrats from populist nationalists—could already be detected, distinguishing Mazowiecki from Walesa, for example, or Hungary's left-leaning Free Democrats (led by János Kis and other dissident intellectuals) from old-line nationalists in the Democratic Forum. There was also (as we have seen) a distinct generational aspect to the crowds of 1989. Many of the seasoned leaders of the intellectual opposition shared a common history with the regime's own critics within the Party. To students and other young people, however, they thus appeared cast in the same mould: part of a past that could not and should not be revived. In the image of its 26-year-old leader Viktor Orbán, Fidesz in Hungary was originally designated as a political party exclusively for people under thirty.[32]

---

[32]A backhanded nod to the Sixties' only lasting monument, the idea that youth is an inherently superior condition—in the words of Jerry Rubin: 'Never trust anyone over 30.'

The memories and illusions of the 'Dubček generation' were not shared by their children, who evinced little interest in remembering 1968 or saving the 'good' aspects of the GDR. The new generation was less concerned with engaging its rulers in debate, or offering radical alternatives to their rule, than in simply getting out from under it. This contributed to the carnival-like aspect of 1989 remarked upon by some observers in Poland and Czechoslovakia; it also contributed to the unconcern with violent retribution. Communism was no longer an obstacle so much as an irrelevance.

This can be seen best in the language in which the objectives of 1989 were commonly expressed. The theme of 'returning to Europe' was not new. Long before Communism, the continent's eastern half had been the Europe that sought recognition and acknowledgement; *Western* Europe was the Europe that 'knew' itself and from whom the acknowledgement was so longingly sought.[33] With the coming of the Soviet bloc, the sense that their part of Europe was severed from its roots had become a leitmotif of intellectual dissent and opposition across the region.

But the lament for their lost European identity had acquired special significance for Eastern Europeans in recent years with the emergence in the West of something new: an institutional entity—a 'European Community', a 'European Union'—built around self-consciously 'European' values with which East Europeans could all too readily identify: individual rights, civic obligations, the freedom of expression and movement. Talk of 'Europe' became less abstract and therefore, among other things, more interesting to young people. No longer just a lament for the lost culture of old Prague or Budapest, it now represented a concrete and attainable set of political goals. The opposite of Communism was not 'capitalism' but 'Europe'.

This was more than just a matter of rhetoric. Whereas the old Communist cadres could convincingly (and even with conviction) point to the depredations of an abstraction called 'capitalism', they had nothing to offer in place of 'Europe'— because it represented not an ideological alternative but simply the political norm. Sometimes the thought was inflected as 'the market economy', sometimes as 'civil society'; but in either case 'Europe' stood—squarely and simply—for normalcy and the modern way of life. Communism was now no longer the future—its insistent trump card for six decades—but the past.

Naturally, there were variations. Nationalists and even some political and religious conservatives—many of them active and influential in 1989—were not disposed to think so much of Europe as of 'Poland' or 'Hungary'. And some of them were perhaps less interested in freedom and individual rights than others. The immediate priorities of the crowd also varied—the idea of somehow returning to Europe was more important in mobilizing popular sentiment in Czechoslovakia

---

[33]This line of reasoning was developed by Voltaire, among others, and is elegantly explicated by Larry Wolff in *Inventing Eastern Europe* (Stanford, 1994).

than in Romania, to take an obvious example, where removing a dictator and putting food on the table took precedence. And whereas some of the leaders of 1989 set out from the start to build a market economy (when forming his first government in September 1989 Tadeusz Mazowiecki memorably declared that he was 'looking for my Ludwig Erhard!') others—notably Havel—preferred to focus upon the civic foundations of democracy.

The significance of these nuances would only emerge later. It may be appropriate here, however, to offer an observation concerning the place of the *United States* in this story. Eastern Europeans, especially East Berliners, were perfectly well aware of the US's role in containing the Soviet Union. They also understood the nuances distinguishing West European politicians—who, for the most part, were content to live with Communism so long as it left them alone—from American politicians like Ronald Reagan who openly described it as an 'evil empire'. Solidarity was financed largely from the US and it was the US that gave the most insistent official encouragement to protesters in Berlin and elsewhere—once it was clear that they would probably win.

But it should not be concluded from this, as it sometimes is, that Eastern Europe's captive peoples were yearning to become . . . American; much less that it was American encouragement or support that precipitated or facilitated their liberation.[34] The US played a remarkably small part in the dramas of 1989, at least until after the fact. And the American social model itself—the 'free market'—was only occasionally posited as an object of admiration or emulation by the crowds or their spokesmen. For most people who had lived under Communism, liberation by no means implied a yearning for untrammeled economic competition, much less the loss of free social services, guaranteed employment, cheap rents or any of Communism's other attendant benefits. It was, after all, one of the attractions of 'Europe', as imagined from the East, that it held out the prospect of affluence *and* security, liberty *and* protection. You could have your socialist cake and eat it in freedom.

Such euro-dreams were harbingers of disappointments to come. But few saw this at the time. In the marketplace of alternative models, the American way of life was still a minority taste and America, for all its global clout, was a long way away. The other superpower, however, was right on the doorstep. The satellite states of eastern Europe were all colonies of the Communist empire based in Moscow. Accordingly, there is only so much about the changes of 1989 that can be attributed to indigenous social or political forces—whether they were underground Catholic organizations in Slovakia, rock-music groups in Poland or free-thinking intellectuals everywhere. In the last analysis, it was always Moscow that counted.

---

[34]Even Reagan's initial response to the declaration of martial law in Poland was distinctly lukewarm. Only after loud public criticism (from Henry Kissinger, among others) did official Washington adopt the hard-line stance for which it became better known.

In the heady afterglow of liberation, many East Europeans belittled the significance of Moscow, the better to highlight their own achievement. In January 1992,
Democratic Forum's József Antall, now prime minister of Hungary, bemoaned to
a Hungarian audience the West's lack of appreciation for Central Europeans' heroic
role in the downfall of communism: 'This unrequited love must end because we
stuck to our posts, we fought our own fights without firing one shot and we won
the third world war for them.' Antall's embittered account, however flattering to his
audience, misses the seminal truth about 1989: if Eastern Europe's crowds and intellectuals and trade union leaders 'won the third world war' it is, quite simply, because Mikhail Gorbachev let them.

On July 6th 1989, Gorbachev addressed the Council of Europe in Strasbourg and
informed his audience that the Soviet Union would not stand in the way of reform
in Eastern Europe: that was 'entirely a matter for the people themselves.' At a conference of eastern bloc leaders in Bucharest on July 7th 1989, the Soviet leader affirmed each socialist state's right to follow its own trajectory without external
interference. Five months later, in a stateroom on the SS Maxim Gorky off Malta,
he assured President Bush that force would not be used to keep Eastern Europe's
Communist regimes in power. There was no ambiguity about his position. Gorbachev, as Michnik had remarked in 1988, was 'the prisoner of his foreign policy
successes.' Once an imperial metropole had so publicly acknowledged that it would
not, could not hang on to its colonial periphery—and had been universally acclaimed for saying so—its colonies were lost and with them the empire's indigenous collaborators. All that remained to be determined was the manner and
direction in which they fell.

The collaborators themselves certainly understood what was happening: between July 1988 and July 1989 Károly Grósz and Miklós Németh, the leading reformers in the Hungarian Party, made four separate visits to Moscow to meet
Mikhail Gorbachev. Their colleague Rezsö Nyers also spoke with him in Bucharest
on July 7th 1989, the day after Kádár's death, by which date it was already clear that
their cause was lost. Gorbachev did nothing actively to precipitate or encourage the
revolutions of 1989: he merely stood aside. In 1849 Russian intervention had sealed
the fate of the Hungarian and other revolutions of that year; in 1989 Russian abstention helped assure their success.

Gorbachev did more than just let the colonies go. By indicating that he would
not intervene he decisively undermined the only real source of political legitimacy
available to the rulers of the satellite states: the promise (or threat) of military intervention from Moscow. Without that threat the local regimes were politically
naked. Economically they might have struggled for a few more years, but there, too,
the logic of Soviet retreat was implacable: once Moscow started charging world
market prices for its exports to Comecon countries (as it did in 1990) the latter,
heavily dependent on imperial subsidies, would have collapsed in any event.

As this last example suggests, Gorbachev was letting Communism fall in eastern Europe in order to save it in Russia itself—just as Stalin had built the satellite regimes not for their own sake but as a security for his western frontier. Tactically Gorbachev miscalculated badly—within two years the lessons of Eastern Europe would be used against the region's liberator on his home territory. But strategically his achievement was immense and unprecedented. No other territorial empire in recorded history ever abandoned its dominions so rapidly, with such good grace and so little bloodshed. Gorbachev cannot take direct credit for what happened in 1989—he did not plan it and only hazily grasped its long-term import. But he was the permissive and precipitating cause. It was Mr Gorbachev's revolution.

PART FOUR

After the Fall: 1989–2005

XX

A Fissile Continent

'I don't have to do anything to stop it; the Soviets will do it for me. They will never allow this greater Germany just opposite them'.
François Mitterrand, November 28th 1989

'When we started, we did not understand the depth of the problems we faced'.
Mikhail Gorbachev, 1990

'Our country has not been lucky. It was decided to carry out this Marxist experiment on us. In the end we proved that there is no place for this idea—it has simply pushed us off the path taken by the world's civilized countries'.
Boris Yeltsin, 1991

'The existence of the Czech nation was never a certainty, and precisely this uncertainty constitutes its most striking aspect'.
Milan Kundera

Liberated from Communism, eastern Europe underwent a second and even more striking transformation. In the course of the 1990s four established states disappeared from the map of the continent and fourteen countries were born—or resuscitated. The six westernmost republics of the Soviet Union—Estonia, Latvia, Lithuania, Belarus, Ukraine and Moldova—became independent states, together with Russia itself. Czechoslovakia became two separate countries—Slovakia and the Czech Republic. And Yugoslavia broke apart into its constituent units: Slovenia, Croatia, Bosnia-Herzegovina, Serbia-Montenegro and Macedonia.

This making and breaking of nations was comparable in scale to the impact of the Versailles treaties that followed World War One—and in certain respects more dramatic. The emergence of nation-states at Versailles was the culmination of a long drawn-out process with its roots in the mid-nineteenth century or before; it came as no surprise. But the prospect of something similar occurring in the late twentieth century was anticipated by almost no-one. Indeed, three states that were to disappear in the course of the 1990s—Czechoslovakia, Yugoslavia and the USSR—were themselves of post-1918 vintage.

It is not, however, a coincidence that these were the last remaining multi-ethnic, federal states in the region. The territorial fission of the Nineties accompanied the extinction of the last of Europe's four continental empires—that of Russia. It was, in effect, a delayed epilogue to the post-imperial state-making that had followed the fall of the other three: Ottoman Turkey, Habsburg Austria and Wilhelmine Germany. But the logic of imperial break-up would not in itself have triggered the institutional re-arrangement of Eastern Europe. As so often in the past, the fate of the region was determined by events in Germany.

Credit for German re-unification—a unique case of fusion in a decade of fission—must go in the first instance to Helmut Kohl. The West German Chancellor was initially as hesitant as everyone else—on November 28th 1989 he presented to the Bundestag a *five-year* program of cautious steps toward German unity. But after listening to East German crowds (and assuring himself of the support of Washington) Kohl calculated that a unified Germany was now not merely possible but perhaps urgent. It was clear that the only way to staunch the flow west (2,000 people a day at one point) was to bring West Germany east. In order to keep East Germans from leaving their country, the West German leader set about abolishing it.

As in the 19th century, German unification was in the first instance to be achieved by a currency union; but political union inevitably followed. Talk of a 'confederation', which the West Germans had initially encouraged and Hans Modrow's GDR cabinet had eagerly pursued, was precipitately dropped and in the hastily called East German elections of March 1990 Christian Democrat candidates ran on a unification ticket. Their 'Alliance for Germany' won 48 percent of the vote: the Social Democrats, handicapped by their well-advertised ambivalence on the subject, won just 22 percent.[1] The former Communists—now the Party of Democratic Socialism—secured a respectable 16 percent showing; but Alliance '90, a coalition of former dissidents including Bärbel Bohley's *Neues Forum*, won just 2.8 percent.[2]

The first act of the new majority in the GDR Volkskammer, represented by a CDU-SPD-Liberal coalition led by Lothar de Maizière, was to commit their country to German unity.[3] On May 18th 1990 a 'monetary, economic and social union' was signed between the two Germanies, and on July 1st its crucial clause—the extension of the Deutschmark to East Germany—came into force. East Germans could now exchange their virtually useless East German marks—up to the equivalent of DM 40,000—at a hugely advantageous rate of 1:1. Wages and salaries in the

---

[1] In August 1989 the deputy chairman of the Social Democratic Party had criticized the Kohl government for 'aggravating' the crisis by welcoming East German refugees who were seeking to come west via the newly opened Hungarian border. However in Berlin (a traditional SPD stronghold) the SPD did much better in the elections of 1990, winning 35 percent of the vote.

[2] Bohley's own response was to observe somewhat sourly: 'We wanted justice and we got the *Rechtstaat* [constitutional state].'

[3] De Maizière's second act was at last to acknowledge East Germany's shared responsibility for the Holocaust and allocate DM6.2 million for reparations.

GDR would henceforth be paid in Deutschmarks at parity—a dramatically effective device for keeping East Germans where they were, but with grim long-term consequences for East German jobs and the West German budget.

On August 23rd, by pre-agreement with Bonn, the Volkskammer voted to accede to the Federal Republic. A week later a Treaty of Unification was signed, by which the GDR was absorbed into the FRG—as approved by its voters in the March elections and permitted under Article 23 of the 1949 Basic Law. On October 3rd the Treaty entered into force: the GDR 'acceded' to the Federal Republic and ceased to exist.

The division of Germany had been the work of the victors of World War Two and its reunification in 1990 would never have come about without their encouragement or consent. East Germany was a Soviet satellite state, with 360,000 Soviet troops still stationed there in 1989. West Germany, for all its independence, was not free to act autonomously on *this* matter. As for Berlin, until a final peace settlement was reached it remained a city whose fate formally depended upon the original occupying powers—France, Britain, the US and the Soviet Union.

Neither the British nor the French were in any particular hurry to see Germany reunited. To the extent that West Europeans even thought about a unified Germany they assumed—reasonably enough—that it would come at the *end* of a long process of change in Eastern Europe, not right at the outset. As Douglas Hurd (the British foreign secretary) observed in December 1989, reflecting on the imminent conclusion of the Cold War: This was 'a system . . . under which we've lived quite happily for forty years.'

His Prime Minister, Margaret Thatcher, made no secret of her fears. In her memoirs she recalls a hastily convoked meeting with French President Mitterrand: 'I produced from my handbag a map showing the various configurations of Germany in the past, which were not altogether reassuring about the future . . . [Mitterrand] said that at moments of great danger in the past France had always established special relations with Britain and he felt such a time had come again . . . It seemed to me that although we had not discovered the means, at least we both had the will to check the German juggernaut. That was a start.'

Mrs Thatcher—and she was not alone—was also worried that German unification might de-stabilize Mikhail Gorbachev, possibly even leading to his fall (by analogy with Nikita Khrushchev's disgrace following his Cuban humiliation). But the British, for all their anxieties, had nothing to offer by way of an alternative to the course of events then unfolding in Germany and they duly acquiesced. Mitterrand was not so easily appeased. More than anyone else, the French were truly disturbed by the collapse of the stable and familiar arrangements in Germany and in the Communist bloc as a whole.[4]

---

[4]It is no coincidence that Mitterrand was the only major Western political figure to accommodate himself without hesitation to the apparent overthrow of Gorbachev in the abortive Moscow coup of the following year.

The first reaction from Paris was to try and block any move to German unification—Mitterrand even going so far as to visit the GDR in December 1989 in a show of support for its sovereignty. He declined Helmut Kohl's invitation to attend a ceremony to mark the re-opening of the Brandenburg Gate, and tried to convince Soviet leaders that, as traditional allies, France and Russia had a common interest in blocking German ambitions. Indeed, the French were banking on Gorbachev to veto German unity—as Mitterrand explained to his advisers on November 28th 1989, 'I don't have to do anything to stop it, the Soviets will do it for me. They will never allow this greater Germany just opposite them.'

But once it became clear that this was not so—and following Kohl's decisive victory in the East German elections—the French President adopted a different tack. The Germans could have their unity, but at a price. There must be no question of an enhanced Germany taking an independent path, much less reverting to its old middle-European priorities. Kohl must commit himself to pursuing the European project under a Franco-German condominium, and Germany was to be bound into an 'ever-closer' union—whose terms, notably a common European currency, would be enshrined in a new treaty (to be negotiated the following year in the Dutch city of Maastricht)[5].

The Germans agreed readily enough to all the French conditions (though the maladroit character of France's diplomatic maneuvers chilled relations for a while)—an echo of earlier days, when Bonn agreed after 1955 to confine 'Europe' to the original six countries in order to assuage French anxiety over the restoration of full sovereignty to Germany. Kohl even concurred in the coming months over a range of minor concessions designed to reward Paris for its forbearance.[6] Unification was well worth some appeasement of Germany's nervous European neighbours. In any case Kohl—born in Ludwigshafen and like his fellow Rhinelander Adenauer instinctively disposed to look west—was not unduly troubled at the idea of tying Germany ever more closely to the European Community.

But most important of all, the German Chancellor had the wind in his sails, as any contemporary photograph of him will confirm: German unification had the full backing of the United States. Like everyone else, the administration of President George Bush initially supposed along with its allies that German unification could only come at the end of the series of unpredictable changes unfolding in the USSR and Eastern Europe, and then only with Soviet consent. But Washington was quicker to catch the prevailing mood, especially after a February 1990 poll

---

[5]It is not a little ironic that Mitterrand's successors are now having to grapple with the budgetary constraints and social consequences of that same treaty.

[6]Not the least of which was the appointment of Mitterrand's crony Jacques Attali as head of a new institution—the European Bank for Reconstruction and Development (EBRD)—with a remit to invest in the rebuilding of Eastern Europe. After spending millions refurbishing a prestigious building for himself—but very little on the bank's putative beneficiaries—Attali was ignominiously removed. The experience did no discernible damage to his considerable self-esteem.

showed that 58 percent of West Germans favored a united and *neutral* Germany. This was the very outcome the US (and many West German politicians) feared most: an enlarged Germany, neutral and unattached in the middle of Europe, destabilizing and unsettling its neighbours on both sides.

The US thus committed itself wholeheartedly to support for Kohl's objectives, to ensure that Germans were never required to choose between unity and the Western alliance. Under pressure from Washington, the French and British accordingly agreed to sit down with the Soviet Union and representatives of the two Germanies and thrash out the terms of the emergence of a new Germany. These so-called '4+2' talks, conducted by foreign ministers from February to September 1990, culminated in a Treaty on the Final Settlement with Respect to Germany, signed in Moscow on September 12th.

With this treaty, which formally recognized the borders of a future Germany as those of the two present German states, the four-power status of Berlin was brought to an end, expiring at midnight on October 2nd 1990. The Soviet Union agreed to allow a united Germany to remain in NATO, and terms were reached for the withdrawal of the Red Army and the departure of all foreign troops from Berlin (to be completed four years hence, after which only a small complement of NATO troops would remain on German soil).

Why did Mikhail Gorbachev so readily allow German unification to go forward? For decades the Soviet Union's primary strategic objective had been to maintain the territorial *status quo* in central Europe: Moscow—like London, Paris and Washington—had become comfortable with a divided Germany and had long since abandoned Stalin's post-war goal of extricating Bonn from the Western alliance. And unlike the French and the British, the Soviet leadership was still in a position to block the process of unification, at least in principle.

Gorbachev, like everyone else in 1990, was flying blind. No-one, in East or West, had a plan telling them what to do if the GDR disintegrated; and there were no blueprints for German unification. But the Soviet leader, unlike his western counterparts, had no good options. He could not realistically hope to prevent German unity except by reversing his benign public announcements of recent years and seriously damaging his own credibility. He did initially oppose the absorption of a united Germany into NATO; and even after conceding the point in principle[7] continued to insist that NATO troops not be allowed to move 300 kilometers east to the Polish border—something US Secretary of State James Baker actually promised to his Soviet counterpart in February 1990. But when that promise was later broken Gorbachev was helpless to intervene.

What he *was* able to do was extract, quite literally, a price for his concessions.

---

[7]There is some evidence that Gorbachev conceded this crucial point inadvertently, when he acceded in May 1990 to President Bush's suggestion that Germany's right of self-determination should include the freedom to 'choose its alliances'.

As the West German Chancellor had foreseen, the USSR was open to financial persuasion. Gorbachev tried at first to hold the unification negotiations hostage for a ransom of $20 billion, before finally settling for approximately $8 billion, together with some $2 billion more in interest-free credits. Overall, from 1990 through 1994, Bonn transferred to the Soviet Union (and latterly Russia) the equivalent of $71 billion (with a further $36 billion going to the former Communist states of Eastern Europe). Helmut Kohl also agreed to alleviate Soviet (and Polish) fears of German irredentism by pledging, as we have seen, to accept as permanent his country's eastern boundaries, a commitment enshrined the following year in a Treaty with Poland.

Having secured the best terms it could, Moscow agreed to abandon the GDR. Playing Sidney Greenstreet to Washington's Bogart, the Soviet Union made the best of a bad hand and relinquished its diminutive, resentful East German sidekick with the requisite protestation but few real regrets. It made more sense to build a strategic relationship with a friendly and appreciative new Germany than to make an enemy of it, and from the Soviet perspective a united Germany, firmly grasped—and contained—in the Western embrace, was not such a bad outcome.

The GDR was not much loved. But it did not pass entirely unlamented. In addition to West German intellectuals like Günter Grass and Jürgen Habermas who feared for the soul of a reunited 'greater' Germany[8], many East Germans who had known no other homeland had mixed feelings when 'their' Germany was swept away from under them. Two generations had grown up in the GDR. They might not have believed its more egregiously absurd self-descriptions, but they could not be entirely deaf to official propaganda. We should not be surprised to learn that long after 1989 children in eastern German secondary schools continued to believe that East German troops had fought alongside the Red Army to liberate their country from Hitler.

This inculcated misperception was part of the GDR's core identity and did nothing to ease its disoriented former citizens' transition 'back' into Germany, particularly as 'their' Germany was systematically excised from the official record. The names of towns, streets, buildings and counties were changed, often reverting to pre-1933 usage. Rituals and memorials were restored. This was not the recovery of history, however, but rather its erasure—it was as though the GDR had never been. When Erich Mielke was prosecuted and sentenced for murder it was not for crimes he authorized as head of the Stasi but rather for a political assassination committed in the 1930s, the evidence provided by Nazi interrogation records.

Rather than engage the GDR's troubled history, in other words, its former subjects were encouraged to forget it—an ironic replay of West Germany's own age of

---

[8]In Grass's view, modern German history consists of a perennial disposition to bloat and expand, followed by desperate attempts at constraint by the rest of the continent—or in his words: 'Every few years, for our all-German constipation, we are given a Europe-enema.'

forgetting in the Fifties. And as in the early years of the Federal Republic, so after 1989: prosperity was to be the answer. Germany would buy its way out of history. To be sure, the GDR was a decidedly suitable case for treatment. It was not just its institutions that were falling apart—much of its material infrastructure was decrepit. Two dwellings in five were built before 1914 (in West Germany in 1989 the figure was less than one in five); a quarter of all houses lacked a bath, one third had only an outdoor toilet, and more than 60 percent lacked any form of central heating.

As in its dealings with Moscow, Bonn's response was to throw very large sums of money at the problem. In the three years following unification total transfers from Western into Eastern Germany amounted to the equivalent of 1,200 billion euros; by the end of 2003 the cost of absorbing the former GDR had reached 1.2 *trillion* euros. East Germans were subsidized into the Federal Republic: their jobs, pensions, transport, education and housing underwritten by huge increases in government expenditure. In the short run this worked—confirming East Germans' faith not so much in the free market as in the unplumbed resources of the West German exchequer. But after the first flush of reunion, many 'Ossies' were actually put off by the patronizing triumphalism of their Western cousins—a sentiment on which the former Communists would trade with some success in future elections.

Meanwhile, to avoid upsetting West German voters—by no means all of whom had greeted unification with unalloyed enthusiasm—Kohl chose not to raise taxes. Instead, in order to meet its vast new commitments the Federal Republic—which had hitherto run substantial current account surpluses—had no choice but to go into deficit. The Bundesbank, aghast at the inflationary impact of such a policy, accordingly began steadily to raise interest rates, starting in 1991—at precisely the moment when the Deutschmark was being locked for ever into a planned European currency. The knock-on effect of these interest rates—increased unemployment and slower economic growth—would be felt not just in Germany but throughout the European Monetary System. In effect, Helmut Kohl exported the cost of his country's unification and Germany's European partners were made to share the burden.

Mikhail Gorbachev's concessions on Germany surely contributed to the decline in his domestic standing—indeed he had warned James Baker that a united Germany inside NATO might 'be the end of *perestroika*'. To lose the other east European satellite states could be attributed to misfortune; but to relinquish Germany as well looked like carelessness. The Soviet Defense Minister, Marshall Sergei Akhromeyev, was convinced that Gorbachev could have got better terms from the West had he paid attention to the problem in time; and he was not alone. But that, of course, was Gorbachev's problem: by the end of the 1980s he was so absorbed in domestic challenges that his response to the rapid onset of problems in the USSR's 'near-West' was, as we have seen, to leave the latter increasingly to its own devices.

But benign neglect was not an option when it came to addressing comparable challenges within the Soviet Union's own frontiers. The Russian empire had grown by conquest and accretion over the centuries and much of what had once been foreign territory was now intimately associated with the homeland. There appeared to be no question of 'releasing' it in the sense that Poland or Hungary had now been 'released'. But the more recent Soviet conquests remained only half-digested and vulnerable, as we have seen, to foreign influence and example: in central Asia, in the Caucasus, but above all on the far western edge of the empire along the Baltic Sea.

The Baltic republics of the Union—Estonia, Latvia and Lithuania—were distinctive in three significant respects. In the first place they were more exposed to the West than any other region of the Soviet Union proper. Estonians especially were in touch with the Scandinavian countries, watching Finnish television since the 1970s and ever-conscious of the contrast between their own condition and that of their prosperous neighbours. Lithuanians, whose primary historical and geographical affinity was with neighbouring Poland, could hardly fail to notice that even under Communism Poles were decidedly freer and better off than them.

Secondly, and despite the unflattering comparison with foreign neighbours, the Baltic states were nonetheless prosperous by Soviet standards. They were the major Soviet producers of a large number of industrial products—railroad cars, radio sets, paper goods—as well as a leading source of fish, dairy produce and cotton. Between the commodities that they produced and those that passed through their docks Estonians, Latvians and Lithuanians had at least a passing acquaintance with a way of life and a standard of living of which most of the rest of the Soviet Union could but dream.

But the third distinguishing feature of the Baltic republics, and by far the most significant, was that they alone had a recent history of genuine independence. After initially winning their freedom in 1919 following the collapse of the Czarist Empire they had been forcibly re-absorbed twenty years later by the Romanovs' Soviet heirs, in the secret clauses of the August 1939 Molotov-Ribbentrop Pact. But the invasion of 1940 was still very much part of living memory. In the Baltics, Gorbachev's *glasnost*—which elsewhere in the Soviet Union prompted demands for greater civil or economic rights—inevitably re-opened the question of independence. *Samizdat* in this region was always and necessarily nationalist in tone.

An additional reason for this was the 'Russian' question. In 1945 the population of all three Baltic republics was quite homogenous, with most residents belonging to the dominant national group and speaking the local language. But by the early 1980s, thanks to forced expulsions during and after the war and a steady inflow of Russian soldiers, administrators and workers, the population was far more mixed, especially in the northern republics. In Lithuania some 80 percent of the residents of the republic were still Lithuanian; but in Estonia only an estimated 64 percent of the population was ethnically Estonian and Estonian-speaking; while in Latvia the share of native Latvians in the population, at the 1980 census, was 1.35 million out of a total of some 2.5 million: just 54 percent. The countryside was still peopled by Balts, but the cities were increasingly Russian, and Russian-speaking: a much resented transformation.

The first stirrings of protest in the region were thus directed at questions of language and nationality, and the associated memory of Soviet deportations to Siberia of thousands of local 'subversives'. On August 23rd 1987, there were simultaneous demonstrations in Vilnius, Riga and Tallinn to mark the anniversary of the Molotov-Ribbentrop Pact, followed three months later in Riga alone by a public meeting to commemorate the anniversary of the 1918 declaration of Latvian independence. Emboldened by their success—or, more precisely, by the authorities' unprecedented tolerance of such public expressions of implied dissent—independent groups and gatherings started to emerge across the region.

Thus on March 25th 1988 in Riga hundreds gathered to commemorate the Latvian deportations of 1949, followed by a demonstration in June to mark the expulsions of 1940. There followed an uncharacteristically lively meeting of the hitherto quiescent Latvian Writers' Union, with talk of a 'Latvian Popular Front'. A few weeks later, under the auspices of the ostensibly a-political 'Environmental Protection Club' (EPC), the Latvian National Independence Movement was born. The course of events in Estonia was virtually identical: following the commemorations of 1987 and a series of environmentalist protests there was born first the 'Estonian Heritage Society', dedicated to the preservation and restoration of local cultural monuments; then, in April 1988, a 'Popular Front of Estonia'; and finally, in August—one month after its Latvian confrère—the Estonian National Independence Movement.

The most dramatic aspect of these nascent political movements in Estonia and Latvia was their mere existence—and their unusually subversive nomenclature. But it was in Lithuania, where the Russian presence was far less obtrusive, that the challenge to Soviet power was made explicit. On July 9th 1988 a demonstration in Vilnius to demand environmental protections, democracy and greater autonomy for Lithuania attracted 100,000 people in support of Sajudis, the newly-formed 'Lithuanian Reorganization Movement', openly critical of the Lithuanian Communist Party for its 'subservience' to Moscow and with 'Red Army Go Home' emblazoned on their banners . By February 1989 Sajudis had been transformed into a nationwide political party. The following month, in the elections to the Soviet Congress of People's Deputies, it won 36 of Lithuania's 42 seats.

The elections in all three republics were a marked victory for independent candidates and triggered a growing awareness of a common Baltic trajectory. This was symbolically re-confirmed on August 23rd 1989 by the forging of a human chain ('Hands across the Baltic') 650 kilometers in length, reaching from Vilnius through Riga to Tallinn, to mark the 50th anniversary of the Molotov-Ribbentrop Pact. An estimated 1.8 million people—one quarter of the entire population of the region—

took part. With the Estonian and Latvian independence movements now echoing their Lithuanian counterpart and openly proclaiming national independence as their goal, confrontation with Moscow seemed inevitable.

And yet it came very slowly. The Baltic independence movements spent 1989 pressing against the frontiers of the permissible. When the newly independence-minded Supreme Soviets of first Lithuania and then Latvia tried to imitate an Estonian law of November 1988 authorizing the privatization of local state enterprises, Moscow voided the decrees, as it had earlier voided the Estonian initiative; but otherwise the government refrained from any involvement. When, on October 8th 1989 (the day after Gorbachev's public warning in East Berlin that 'life punishes those who delay'), the Latvian Popular Front proclaimed its intention to move towards full independence, the Soviet authorities were too preoccupied with the escalating crisis in Germany to take any action.

But on December 18th the Lithuanian Communist Party split; an overwhelming majority declaring itself for immediate independence. Now Gorbachev could no longer remain silent. He traveled to Vilnius on January 11th 1990 to advise against the proposed secession, urging 'moderation'. However—and not for the first time—his own example was working against him. Emboldened by the electoral victory of Sajudis, by the Soviet President's own success in getting the Soviet Central Committee to abandon the constitutional guarantee of the Party's 'leading role'[9], and by the '4+2' negotiations then under way, the Lithuanian Supreme Soviet on March 11th voted 124–0 to restore Lithuanian independence, symbolically reinstating the 1938 'Constitution of the State of Lithuania' and nullifying the authority in the Republic of Lithuania of the Constitution of the USSR.

It says a lot about the uncertain state of affairs in 1990—when even the government of the Russian Republic itself was now asserting its 'sovereignty' and the precedence of Russian laws over 'all-Union' decrees—that the Soviet rulers' response to the Vilnius declaration was to initiate nothing more threatening than an economic boycott: unable to prevent a Lithuanian breakaway, Gorbachev was nonetheless still capable of forestalling the military intervention that many of his hard-line colleagues were now demanding. Even the boycott itself was abandoned in June, in return for a Lithuanian agreement to 'suspend' the full implementation of its declaration of independence.

After a hectic six months during which virtually every other major Soviet republic asserted its 'sovereignty' if not yet its full independence, Gorbachev's position was becoming untenable. His efforts to rein in the Baltic initiatives had substantially weakened his image as a 'reformer', while his failure to suppress talk of autonomy, sovereignty and independence was stirring up resentment among his colleagues and—more ominously—in the army and security forces. On December

---

[9]Note that just eight weeks earlier Gorbachev had adamantly refused to consider any such change.

20th 1990 his Foreign Minister, Edvard Shevardnadze, resigned and warned publicly of the growing risk of a coup.

On January 10th 1991, with the US and its allies thoroughly distracted by the Gulf War then getting under way in Iraq, Gorbachev issued an ultimatum to the Lithuanians, demanding in his capacity as President of the Union that they adhere forthwith to the Constitution of the USSR. The following day soldiers from the élite forces of the KGB and the Soviet Ministry of the Interior seized public buildings in Vilnius and installed a 'National Salvation Committee'. Twenty four hours later they attacked the radio and television studios in the city, turning their guns on a large crowd of demonstrators who had gathered there: fourteen civilians were killed, 700 wounded. A week later troops from the same units stormed the Latvian Ministry of the Interior in Riga, killing four people.

The bloodshed in the Baltics signaled the opening of the endgame in the Soviet Union. Within a week over 150,000 people had gathered in Moscow to demonstrate against the shootings. Boris Yeltsin, erstwhile First Secretary of the Moscow City Committee and—since May 1990—Chairman of the Russian Supreme Soviet, traveled to Tallinn to sign a mutual recognition of 'sovereignty' between Russia and the Baltic Republics, bypassing altogether the Soviet authorities. In March 1991 referenda in Latvia and Estonia confirmed that electors there too overwhelmingly favored full independence. Gorbachev, who had half-heartedly started to repress the recalcitrant republics, now reverted to his earlier stance and vainly sought a *modus vivendi* with them instead.

But the Soviet President was now under attack from both sides. His reluctance to crush the Balts definitively alienated his military allies (two of the generals who staged the attacks in Vilnius and Riga would figure prominently in the subsequent coup in Moscow). But his former friends and admirers no longer trusted him. Yeltsin in March 1991 publicly denounced Gorbachev's 'lies and deceptions' and called for his resignation, defying official pressure to remain silent or face impeachment. Meanwhile the Baltic example was being taken up in other republics.

So long as the overarching structures of Soviet power remained secure, Communist rulers from Ukraine to Kazakhstan had confined their 'reforms' to cautious mimicry of Gorbachev himself. But following the débâcle in the Baltics the same well-honed antennae that attuned them to *perestroika* now signaled that the Union itself might well be doomed; in any case they could see for themselves that in certain ruling circles the Soviet President was a marked man. Thus whereas the new politics of the Baltic republics reflected a genuine and widespread national renaissance, moves towards 'sovereignty' in many of the other republics were typically a more variable mixture of national feeling and *nomenklatura* self-preservation. There was also a growing element of fear: a sense that if security and authority were crumbling at the apex—or, worse, might soon be forcibly and unilaterally reasserted by Gorbachev's foes—then it would be prudent to gather the essential reins of power into local hands. Finally, there was a dawning awareness among Soviet managers that should the center fall apart an awful lot of valuable public assets would be up for grabs: party property, mineral rights, farms, factories, tax revenues and so forth.

By far the most important of the would-be 'sovereign' republics now asserting their distinctive claims was Ukraine.[10] Like the Baltic republics, Ukraine had a history of independence (albeit chequered), last asserted and promptly lost in the aftermath of World War One. It was also intimately associated with Russia's own history: in the eyes of many Russian nationalists, Kievan 'Rus'—the thirteenth-century kingdom based on the Ukrainian capital and reaching from the Carpathians to the Volga—was as integral to the core identity of the empire as Russia itself. But of more immediate and practical consideration were the material resources of the region.

Sitting squarely athwart Russia's access routes to the Black Sea (and the Mediterranean) as well as to central Europe, Ukraine was a mainstay of the Soviet economy. With just 2.7 percent of the land area of the USSR it was home to 18 percent of its population and generated nearly 17 percent of the country's Gross National Product, second only to Russia itself. In the last years of the Soviet Union Ukraine contained 60 percent of the country's coal reserves and a majority share of the country's titanium (vital for modern steel production); its unusually rich soil was responsible for over 40 percent of Soviet agricultural output by value.

The disproportionate importance of Ukraine in Russian and Soviet history was reflected in the Soviet leadership itself. Both Nikita Khrushchev and Leonid Brezhnev were Russians who hailed from eastern Ukraine—Khrushchev returning there in the 1930s as First Secretary of the Ukrainian Party. Konstantin Chernenko was the son of Ukrainian 'kulaks' deported to Siberia, while Yuri Andropov had risen to the top as a consequence of occupying the strategically central post of KGB head in Ukraine. But this close association between the Ukrainian republic and the Soviet leadership did not imply any special regard for its inhabitants.

Quite the contrary. For much of its history as a Soviet republic, Ukraine was treated as an internal colony: its natural resources exploited, its people kept under close surveillance (and, in the 1930s, exposed to a program of punitive repression that amounted to near-genocide). Ukrainian products—notably food and ferrous metals—were shipped to the rest of the Union at heavily subsidized prices, a practice that continued almost to the end. Following World War Two, the Ukrainian Socialist Republic was considerably enlarged by the annexation from Poland of eastern Galicia and western Volhynia: the local Polish population, as we have seen, was expelled westwards in exchange for ethnic Ukrainians forced out of Poland itself.

---

[10]The five central Asian republics—Kazakhstan, Kirghizia, Tadjikistan, Turkmenia and Uzbekistan—between them covered more land (18 percent of Soviet territory) than any republic other than Russia itself, although their combined share of Soviet GNP in September 1991 was just 9.9 percent. But their story falls outside the bounds of the present book.

These population exchanges—and the wartime extermination of much of the local Jewish community—resulted in a region that was by Soviet standards quite homogenous: thus whereas the Russian Republic in 1990 contained over one hundred minorities, thirty one of them living in autonomous regions, Ukraine was 84 percent Ukrainian. Most of the rest of the population were Russians (11 percent), with the remainder comprising small numbers of Moldovans, Poles, Magyars, Bulgarians and the country's surviving Jews. Perhaps more to the point the only significant minority—the Russians—was concentrated in the industrial east of the country and in the capital Kiev.

Central and Western Ukraine, notably around Lviv, the second city, was predominantly Ukrainian in language and Eastern Orthodox or else Uniate (Greek-rite Catholic) in religion. Thanks to the relative tolerance of the Habsburgs, Ukrainians in Galicia had been allowed to preserve their native tongue. Depending upon district, anything from 78 percent to 91 percent of the local inhabitants used it as their first language in 1994, whereas in the territories once ruled by the Czar even those who identified themselves as Ukrainians often spoke Russian more readily.

The Soviet constitution, as we have seen, ascribed national identities to the residents of its separate republics and indeed defined all its citizens by ethnic-national categories. As elsewhere, so in Ukraine—particularly the recently-annexed Western Ukraine—this had self-fulfilling consequences. In earlier times, when the local language was mostly confined to the remote countryside, and the cities were Russian-speaking and Soviet-dominated, the theoretically decentralized and federal character of this union of national republics was of interest only to scholars and Soviet apologists. But with the growing number of urban-dwelling Ukrainian-speakers, Ukrainian-language media, and a political élite now identifying itself with self-consciously 'Ukrainian' interests, Ukrainian nationalism was the predictable accompaniment to Soviet fragmentation.[11]

A non-Party movement—RUKH (the 'People's Movement for *Perestroika*')—was founded in Kiev in November 1988, the first autonomous Ukrainian political organization for many decades. It gathered considerable support, notably in the major cities and from '60s-era reform Communists; but in marked contrast to independence movements in the Baltic it could not automatically count on mass backing and did not reflect any groundswell of national sentiment. In elections to the Ukrainian Supreme Soviet in March 1990 the Communists secured a clear majority; RUKH won less than a quarter of the seats.

Thus it was not Ukrainian nationalists who were to seize the initiative but rather the Communists themselves. The Communists in the Ukrainian Soviet voted, on

[11]But mostly unpredicted. For an impressive exception, see the essays by Roman Szporluk: written over the course of the Seventies and Eighties and gathered in *Russia, Ukraine and the Break-Up of the Soviet Union* (Hoover Institution, Stanford, 2000).

July 16th 1990, to declare Ukrainian 'sovereignty' and asserted the republic's right to possess its own military and the primacy of its own laws. And it was under the direction of Leonid Kravchuk—a Communist *apparatchik* and former 'Secretary for ideological questions' of the Ukrainian Party—that Ukrainians took part in a March 1991 all-Union referendum and indicated their continuing support for a federal system, albeit 'renewed' (in Gorbachev's term). Only in Western Ukraine, where voters were asked whether they favored outright independence over intra-federal sovereignty, were the Ukrainian Communists outflanked by those seeking a complete break with Moscow: 88 percent voted yes. Kravchuk and his fellow Party leaders duly took note, while cautiously awaiting the outcome of developments elsewhere.

This pattern was repeated in the smaller western Soviet republics as well, varying according to local circumstances. Byelorussia (or 'Belarus'), to the north of Ukraine, had no comparable national identity or traditions. The ephemeral independent 'Belarusan (*sic*) National Republic' of 1918 never secured external recognition and many of its own citizens felt closer allegiance to Russia, or else Poland or Lithuania. After World War Two, with the annexation of parts of eastern Poland, the Belorussian Soviet Socialist Republic contained a significant minority of Russians, Poles and Ukrainians. Belarussians themselves—though by far the largest linguistic community in the republic—showed no sign of wanting or expecting sovereignty of any kind; nor could their country, heavily dependent on Russia, hope to sustain genuine independence.

A poor, marshy region better suited to livestock-rearing than large scale agriculture, Belarus had been devastated by the war. Its most significant contribution to the post-war Soviet economy was in chemicals and flax—and in its strategic position athwart major gas lines and communication links from Moscow to the Baltic Sea. The nearest thing to an independence movement was Adradzhenne ('Rebirth'), an organization based in the capital Minsk that emerged in 1989 and closely echoed the Ukrainian RUKH. In Belarus as in Ukraine, the Soviet elections of 1990 saw the Communists returned in a clear majority; and when the Ukrainian Soviet declared itself 'sovereign' in July 1990 its northern neighbour duly followed suit two weeks later. In Minsk as in Kiev, the local *nomenklatura* was moving prudently, waiting upon events in Moscow.

Soviet Moldavia, squeezed between Ukraine and Romania, was a different and rather more interesting case.[12] The territory in question—'Bessarabia' as it was better-known under the Czars—had see-sawed back and forth between Russia and Romania over the course of the century and the fortunes of war. Its four and a half million residents were predominantly Moldavian, but with large Russian and

---

[12]And should not be confused with historical Moldavia just across the Prut river in Romania.

Ukrainian minorities and quite a significant number of Bulgarians, Jews, gypsies and Gagauz (a Turkic-speaking Orthodox people living near the Black Sea). In this characteristically imperial mix of peoples the majority were Romanian-speakers; but under Soviet rule—the better to separate them from neighbouring Romanians—the citizens of Moldavia had been constrained to write their language in Cyrillic and describe themselves not as Romanians but as 'Moldovans'.

National identity here was thus more than a little uncertain. On the one hand many of its people, especially in the capital Chisinau (Kishinev), spoke Russian well and thought of themselves as Soviet citizens; on the other hand the Romanian connection (in history and in language) provided a bridge to Europe and a basis for burgeoning demands for increased autonomy. When a 'Popular Front' movement emerged in 1989 its primary objective was the demand that Romanian become the official language of the republic, a concession that the local Communist authorities granted that same year. There was also some incendiary talk, mostly speculative and actively discouraged from Bucharest, of Moldova 'rejoining' Romania itself.

Following the 1990 elections, in which the Popular Front won a majority, the new government proceeded first to change the name of the republic from the Moldavian Soviet Socialist Republic to the 'Soviet Socialist Republic of Moldova' (later plain 'Republic of Moldova') and then, in June, to declare itself sovereign. These largely symbolic moves caused rising anxiety and talk of pre-emptive separatism among Russian-speakers as well as the tiny Gagauz community. Following a referendum on autonomy in the autumn of 1990 the Communist leadership in Tiraspol—the main town in eastern Moldova, across the Dniester river, where Russians and Ukrainians formed a local majority—declared a Transnistrian Autonomous Soviet Socialist Republic, echoing a similarly 'autonomous' Gagauz Soviet Socialist Republic in the southeast.

Given that there are at most 160,000 Gagauz, and that 'Transnistria' is a banana-shaped sliver of land, just 4,000 square kilometers in area with a population of fewer than 500,000, the emergence of such 'autonomous republics' might seem absurd, the *reductio ad absurdum* of 'invented traditions' and 'imagined nations'. But whereas the Gagauz republic never got beyond proclaiming its existence (the future Moldovan state would re-incorporate it peacefully, against a right to secede should Moldova ever 'rejoin' Romania), Transnistrian 'independence' was underwritten by the presence of the Soviet (later Russian) XIVth Army, which helped its clients fight off initial Moldovan attempts to recover the territory.

In the increasingly uncertain mood of the times, Soviet (and later Russian) authorities were not at all reluctant to offer patronage to a micro-state that was of necessity loyal to Moscow, wholly dependent on Russian goodwill and whose rulers were local Communist satraps who had seized control of the territory and would convert it in short order into a haven for smugglers and money-launderers.

Transnistria being the source of 90 percent of Moldova's electricity, the new rulers even had a legitimate economic resource of sorts, one that they could threaten to withhold should Chisinau refuse to cooperate.

Transnistrian independence was not recognized by Moldova or anyone else: even Moscow never went so far as to accord the breakaway region official legitimacy. But the scission in tiny Moldova offered a foretaste of more serious troubles to come a few hundred kilometers further east, in the Caucasus. There the longstanding antagonisms between Armenians and Azeris, complicated in particular by the presence in Azerbaijan of a substantial Armenian minority in the region of Nagorno-Karabakh, had already resulted in violent clashes both with each other and with Soviet troops in 1988, with hundreds of casualties.[13] In the Azerbaijan capital of Baku there were further clashes in January of the following year.

In neighbouring Georgia, twenty demonstrators were shot during clashes in the capital Tbilisi between nationalists and soldiers in April 1989, as tensions rose between crowds demanding secession from the Union and authorities still committed to preserving it. But Soviet Georgia, like the neighbouring Soviet republics of Armenia and Azerbaijan, was too geographically vulnerable and ethnically complex to be able to contemplate with equanimity the insecurity that must accompany Soviet collapse. Accordingly the local authorities decided to anticipate that eventuality by precipitating it, the ruling Communist parties re-defining themselves as national independence movements and regional Party leaders—of whom by far the best known was Edvard Shevardnadze in Georgia—positioning themselves to seize power as soon as it fell into the street.

By the spring of 1991, then, everyone at the peripheries was waiting to see what would happen at the centre. The key, of course, was Russia itself—by far the dominant republic of the Union, with half the country's population, three-fifths of its Gross National Product and three-quarters of its land mass. In a certain sense the country of 'Russia' as such did not exist: it had for centuries been an empire, whether in fact or in aspiration. Spread across eleven time zones and encompassing dozens of different peoples, 'Russia' had always been too big to be reduced to a single identity or common sense of purpose.[14]

During and after the Great Patriotic War the Soviet authorities had indeed played the Russian card, appealing to national pride and exalting the 'victory of the Russian people'. But the Russian people had never been assigned 'nationhood' in the way that Kazakhs or Ukrainians or Armenians were officially 'nations' in So-

---

[13]The Azeris being of Turkic origin, part of the background to these tensions can be traced to the Armenian massacres of World War One in Ottoman Turkey.
[14]The characteristic Russian self-image, an unstable alloy of insecurity and hubris, is nicely captured in remarks by the liberal philosopher Peter Chaadayev, from his 'Philosophical Letters' of 1836: 'We are one of those nations which do not seem to be an integral part of the human race, but which exist only to give some great lesson to the world. The instruction which we are destined to give will certainly not be lost: but who knows the day when we shall find ourselves a part of humanity, and how much misery we shall experience before the fulfillment of our destiny.'

viet parlance. There was not even a separate 'Russian' Communist Party. To be Russian was to be Soviet. There was a natural complementarity between the two: in a post-imperial age the Soviet Union provided cover for the Russian imperial state, while 'Russia' furnished the Soviet Union with historical and territorial legitimacy. The boundaries between 'Russia' and 'the Soviet Union' were thus kept (deliberately) blurred.[15]

By the time of Gorbachev there was a marked increase in the emphasis on 'Russianness', for some of the same reasons that the East German state had begun to take a very public pride in Frederick the Great and to exalt the properly *German* qualities of the German Democratic Republic. In the declining years of the peoples' republics, patriotism re-emerged as a serviceable substitute for socialism. For just this reason it was also the easiest and least threatening form of political opposition. In Russia or the GDR, as in Hungary, intellectual critics might suffer persecution but muted expressions of nationalism were not necessarily repressed or even discouraged—they could be channeled to the authorities' advantage. The revival of 'Great Russian chauvinism' in Soviet publications and the media should be understood in this light. It was also, of course, an additional source of anxiety for vulnerable national minorities.

This was the setting for the unexpected emergence of Boris Yeltsin. A conventional Brezhnev-era *apparatchik*, specializing in industrial construction before becoming a Central Committee Secretary, Yeltsin rose steadily through the ranks of the Party—until he was summarily demoted in 1987 for over-reaching himself in his criticisms of senior colleagues. At this crucial juncture Yeltsin, who had had ample opportunity to observe just how effectively the Party and state bureaucracy could prevent any real change, had the political instinct to re-programme himself as a distinctively *Russian* politician: emerging first as a deputy for the Russian Federation after the March 1990 elections and then as Chairman of the Russian Supreme Soviet—i.e. the Russian Parliament.

It was from this influential and visible perch that Boris Yeltsin became the country's leading reformist, ostentatiously quitting the Communist Party in July 1990 and using his power-base in *Russian* Moscow, as it were, to take aim at erstwhile comrades across the way in *Soviet* Moscow. His primary target was now Gorbachev himself (despite the fact that Yeltsin had initially been a firm backer of the Soviet President, in whose native Sverdlovsk region he had worked for over a decade). The Soviet leader's failings were becoming ever more painfully evident—and his popularity was sinking fast, as Yeltsin could not fail to observe.

Gorbachev's major tactical mistake in domestic affairs had been to encourage the emergence of a national legislature with national visibility, real powers and

---

[15]That is one reason why the end of the Soviet Union was and is a source of genuine regret among many Russians. 'Independence' for everyone else meant something gained; independence for Russia itself constituted an unmistakable loss.

considerable independence. Yeltsin and his Russian supporters were much quicker than Gorbachev himself to appreciate that this new, openly-elected Soviet would be a natural forum for the expression of discontents of all sorts; and Yeltsin became particularly adept at aligning Russia's own interests with those of the various nations and republics. Gorbachev was alert to the threat that such alliances posed to the very Union itself: but by now it was too late for him to do anything except align himself uneasily and unconvincingly with Soviet functionaries nostalgic for the old Party monopoly—the same monopoly that he had done so much to break.

Thus while Gorbachev was still 'triangulating' between the desirable and the possible, arguing for a 'controlled federalism' (a characteristically Gorbachevian compromise), Yeltsin was passionately and very publicly defending the struggles for Baltic independence. In April 1991 Gorbachev reluctantly conceded to republics the right of secession in a new Union constitution; but this bow to reality merely weakened him further, convincing his conservative foes that Gorbachev would have to be removed if order was to be restored. Meanwhile, on June 12th 1991, Yeltsin, who had long since overtaken Gorbachev in national popularity polls, was elected President of the Russian Soviet Republic—the first ever democratically chosen leader of Russia.[16]

The following month, on July 12th, the Supreme Soviet of the USSR voted in favor of a new Union: de-centralized and allowing considerable latitude for dissenting member-states. Together with the popular election of the now openly anti-Communist Yeltsin, this finally tipped the scales. Party conservatives were becoming desperate and a group of highly-placed officials—including the Prime Minister, the Defense Minister, the Interior Minister and Vladimir Kryuchkov, the head of the KGB—began to prepare for a coup. That something of the sort was brewing was by now an open secret in Moscow—as early as June 20th the American ambassador had actually warned Gorbachev of a conspiracy, to no avail.

The putsch itself was timed to coincide with Gorbachev's annual vacation in the Crimea; the last Party leader to be forcibly deposed, Nikita Khrushchev, had also been relaxing in the Soviet south when his colleagues in Moscow staged his surprise removal. The 1991 plotters were thus unabashedly reverting to earlier Soviet practices. Accordingly, on August 17th Gorbachev was asked to agree to hand his Presidential powers to an 'Emergency Committee'. When he refused, the Emergency Committee announced on August 19th that the President was unable to exercise his authority 'for health reasons' and that the Committee would thus assume full powers. The Soviet Vice-President Gennady Yanaev signed a decree stripping Gorbachev of his authority and a six-month 'state of emergency' was declared.

But although Gorbachev was helpless, for all practical purposes a prisoner in his Black Sea villa at the southern promontory of the Crimea, the plotters were not

---

[16]Yeltsin received 57 percent of the vote in a turnout of 74 percent.

much better off. In the first place, the mere fact that they had had to declare an emergency and announce virtual martial law merely in order to replace one Communist leader with another demonstrated how far the traditional structures of the Soviet Union had unraveled. The plotters did not have the unanimous support of their own agencies—crucially a majority of senior KGB officers refused to back Kryuchkov. And while there was no doubt about what the plotters were *against*, they were never able to offer any clear indication of what it was they were *for*.

In addition, the plotters were an unintentional caricature of everything that was wrong with the Soviet past: old, grey men from the Brezhnev era, slow and wooden in speech, out of touch with changes in a country whose clock they were clumsily trying to turn back thirty years. In times past when such men as these schemed in the Kremlin they were hidden from public view, their only appearances confined to distant viewing stands at public ceremonies. Now, however, they were constrained to appear on television and to the press to explain and defend their actions—and the public was given ample opportunity to observe close-up the physiognomy of official Socialism in its dotage.

Meanwhile Boris Yeltsin seized the moment. His standing had been further elevated by a personal meeting with George Bush, during the American President's visit to the USSR just three weeks before. Now, on August 19th, he publicly denounced the Kremlin takeover as an illegal coup d'état and placed himself at the head of the resistance to it, directing operations from his headquarters in the Russian Parliament and mobilizing the crowds surrounding it to defend democracy against the tanks. At the same time, in the full glare of the assembled international media, Yeltsin engaged in lengthy conversations and negotiations with world leaders—all but one of whom offered him their full public support and studiously withheld any recognition from the increasingly isolated conspirators.[17]

The resistance was no mere formality: on the night of August 20th–21st three demonstrators died in clashes with the army. But the leaders of the coup—having lost the public initiative—now began to lose their nerve. They did not have the broad support of the armed forces that they would have needed to secure the country, and with every hour of the stand-off in the streets of Moscow (and Leningrad) they were losing their crucial asset: fear. Instead of being intimidated by developments in the Kremlin, democrats and nationalists were emboldened by them: in the midst of the uncertainty, on August 20th, Estonia declared itself independent, with Latvia following suit the next day. On August 21st one of the coup leaders, Boris Pugo (the Interior Minister and former head of the KGB in Latvia), committed suicide; at Yeltsin's behest his colleagues were arrested. That same day an exhausted and anxious Gorbachev was flown back to Moscow.

---

[17] The exception was French President François Mitterrand, still uncomfortable with the destabilization of eastern Europe and a little too quick to acknowledge the plotters' success in restoring the *status quo ante*.

Formally speaking, Gorbachev resumed his powers; but in reality everything had changed for ever. The Communist Party of the Soviet Union (CPSU) was terminally discredited—it was not until August 21st that Party spokesmen publicly condemned their colleagues' coup, by which time the plotters were already in prison and Yeltsin had taken advantage of the Party's fatal hesitations to ban it from operating within the Russian federation. Gorbachev, who seemed dazed and uncertain when seen in public, was understandably slow to grasp the import of these developments. Rather than praise Yeltsin, the Russian Parliament or the Russian people for their success, he spoke to the cameras about *perestroika* and the indispensable role the Party would continue to have in renewing itself, promoting reforms, etc.

This approach still played well in the West, where it was widely assumed (and hoped) that after the abortive coup things would carry on much as before. But in the Soviet Union itself Gorbachev's anachronistic reiterations of failed goals, and his apparent ingratitude to his rescuers, were a revelation. Here was a man who had been overtaken by History and didn't know it. For many Russians the events of August had been a true revolution, a genuinely popular uprising not *for* the reformers and their Party but *against* them: the CPSU, as the demonstrators shouted at Gorbachev on his belated arrival at the Russian Parliament, was 'a criminal enterprise' whose own government ministers had tried to overthrow the constitution. By the time a chastened Gorbachev got the point, suspended the CPSU and (on August 24th) resigned as its General Secretary, it was too late. Communism was now irrelevant, and so too was Mikhail Gorbachev.

Of course, the former General Secretary was still President of the Soviet Union. But the relevance of the Union itself was now directly in question. The failed putsch had been the last and greatest impulse to secession. Between August 24th and September 21st Ukraine, Belarus, Moldova, Azerbaijan, Kyrgyzstan, Uzbekistan, Georgia, Tajikistan and Armenia followed the Baltic republics and declared themselves independent of the Soviet Union—most of them making the announcement in the confused and uncertain days that followed Gorbachev's return.[18] Following Kravchuk's lead in Ukraine, regional First Secretaries like Nursultan Nazarbaev of Kazakhstan, Askar Akaev in Kyrgyzstan, Gaidar Aliev in Azerbaijan, Stanislav Shushkevich in Belarus and others cannily distanced themselves from their long-standing Party affiliation and re-situated themselves at the head of their new states, taking care to nationalize as quickly as possible all the local Party's assets.

Gorbachev and the Supreme Soviet in Moscow could do little more than acknowledge reality, recognize the new states and lamely propose yet another 'new'

---

[18]Even in Ukraine, where many Russian-speakers had been wary of talk about national independence, the coup of August had a dramatic impact on the public mood: on August 24th the Ukrainian Supreme Soviet voted for independence, subject to a referendum, by 346 votes to 1. When the national referendum was held on December 1st, 90.3 percent (in a turnout of 84 percent of the electorate) voted to leave the Soviet Union.

constitution that would embrace the independent republics in some sort of confederal arrangement. Meanwhile, a few hundred yards away, Boris Yeltsin and the Russian parliament were establishing an independent Russia. By November Yeltsin had taken under Russian control virtually all financial and economic activity on Russian territory. The Soviet Union was now a shell state, emptied of power and resources.

By this time the core institutions of the USSR were either in the hands of independent states or else had ceased to exist: on October 24th the KGB itself was formally abolished. When Gorbachev proposed a new 'Treaty on the Economic Community of Sovereign States' most of the independent republics simply refused to sign. At the October sessions of the Supreme Soviet of the USSR the western republics were absent. Finally, on December 8th, the presidents and prime ministers of Russia, Ukraine and Belarus—the core Slav states of the Soviet empire—took it upon themselves to meet near Minsk and denounce the Union Treaty of 1922, in effect abolishing the Soviet Union. In its place they proposed establishing a Commonwealth of Independent States (CIS).

Upon hearing of this, Gorbachev in Moscow angrily denounced the move as 'illegal and dangerous'. But the opinions of the President of the Soviet Union were no longer a matter of concern to anyone: as Gorbachev at last was coming to appreciate, he was effectively in charge of nothing. Nine days later, on December 17th, Gorbachev met with Yeltsin and they agreed (or, rather, Gorbachev conceded) that the Soviet Union must be formally abolished: its ministries, embassies and armies were to pass under Russian control, its place under international law to be inherited by the Russian Republic.

Twenty-four hours later Gorbachev announced his intention to resign as Soviet President. On Christmas Day 1991 the Russian flag replaced the Soviet insignia atop the Kremlin: Mikhail Gorbachev ceded his prerogatives as Commander-in-Chief to President Yeltsin of Russia and stepped down from his post. Within forty-eight hours Gorbachev had vacated his office and Yeltsin moved in. At midnight on December 31st 1991 the Union of Soviet Socialist Republics ceased to exist.

The disappearance of the Soviet Union was a remarkable affair, unparalleled in modern history. There was no foreign war, no bloody revolution, no natural catastrophe. A large industrial state—a military superpower—simply collapsed: its authority drained away, its institutions evaporated. The unraveling of the USSR was not altogether free of violence, as we have seen in Lithuania and the Caucasus; and there would be more fighting in some of the independent republics in the coming years. But for the most part the world's largest country departed the stage almost without protest. To describe this as a bloodless retreat from Empire is surely accurate; but it hardly begins to capture the unanticipated *ease* of the whole process.

Why, then, was it all so apparently painless? Why, after decades of internal violence and foreign aggression, did the world's first Socialist society implode without even trying to defend itself? One answer, of course, is that it never really existed in the first place: that, in the words of the historian Martin Malia, 'there is no such thing as socialism, and the Soviet Union built it.' But if this accounts for the futility of Communist authority in the satellite states, held in place by nothing more than the shadow of the Red Army, it does not quite suffice to explain what happened in the imperial homeland itself. Even if the *society* that Communism claimed to have built was essentially fraudulent, the Leninist *state*, after all, was decidedly real. And it was a home-grown product.

Part of the answer is Mikhail Gorbachev's unintended success in eviscerating the administrative and repressive apparatus on which the Soviet state depended. Once the Party lost its grip, once it was clear that the army or the KGB would not be deployed without mercy to break the regime's critics and punish dissent—and this did not become clear until 1991—then the naturally centrifugal tendencies of a huge land empire came to the fore. Only then did it become evident—seventy years of energetic claims to the contrary notwithstanding—that there was indeed no Communist society as such: only a wilting state and its anxious citizens.

But—and this is the second aspect of the explanation—the Soviet state did *not* in fact disappear. The USSR shattered, rather, into a multiplicity of little successor states, most of them ruled by experienced Communist autocrats whose first instinct was to reproduce and impose the systems and the authority they had hitherto wielded as Soviet managers. There was no 'transition to democracy' in most of the successor republics; that transition came—if it came at all—somewhat later. Autocratic state power, the only kind that most denizens of the domestic Soviet empire had ever known, was not so much dethroned as downsized. From the outside this was a dramatic change; but experienced from within its implications were decidedly less radical.

Moreover, whereas the local Communist secretaries who metamorphosed so smoothly into national state presidents had every reason to act decisively to secure their fiefdom, the Soviet authorities at the center had no territorial fiefdom of their own to protect. All they could offer was a return to the decrepit structures that Gorbachev had so enthusiastically cut down; unsurprisingly, they lacked the will to battle on.[19] The only former Communist leader with a power base in Moscow itself was Boris Yeltsin; he, as we have seen, did indeed act decisively—but on behalf of a renascent 'Russia'.

Thus the efflorescence of successor states should not be interpreted as evidence that the Soviet Union collapsed under the weight of a hitherto quiescent, newly reawakened nationalism in its constituent republics. With the exception of the Baltic countries, whose trajectory more closely resembled that of their western neigh-

---

[19]The will, but not the means. Had Gorbachev—or the August plotters—chosen to use the army to crush all opposition, it is by no means sure that they would have failed.

bours, the Soviet republics were themselves a product of Soviet planning and—as we have seen—were typically quite ethnically complex. Even in the newly-independent states there were many vulnerable minorities (especially the omnipresent Russians)—erstwhile Soviet citizens with good reason to regret the loss of 'imperial' protection and who would prove distinctly ambivalent about their new circumstances.

They were not alone. When President George Bush visited Kiev on August 1st 1991 he made a point of publicly recommending to Ukrainians that they remain in the Soviet Union. 'Some people' he declared, 'have urged the United States to choose between supporting President Gorbachev and supporting independence-minded leaders throughout the USSR. I consider this a false choice. President Gorbachev has achieved astonishing things . . . We will maintain the strongest possible relationship with the Soviet Government of President Gorbachev.' This rather ham-fisted attempt to shore up the increasingly vulnerable Soviet President was not quite tantamount to an endorsement of the Soviet Union . . . but it came perilously close.

The American President's publicly-aired caution is a further salutary reminder of the limited part played by the USA in these developments. *Pace* the self-congratulatory narrative that has entered the American public record, Washington did not 'bring down' Communism—Communism imploded of its own accord. Meanwhile, if his Ukrainian audience ignored Bush's advice and voted overwhelmingly a few months later to quit the Union for good, it was not out of a sudden access of patriotic enthusiasm. Independence in Ukraine, or Moldova, or even Georgia, was not so much about self-determination as self-preservation—a sound basis for state-making, as it turned out, but a poor foundation for democracy.

Nothing in its life so became the Soviet Union as the leaving of it. Much the same was true of the break-up of Czechoslovakia, the 'velvet divorce' between Slovaks and Czechs that was peaceably and amicably consummated on January 1st 1993. At first glance this would appear a textbook instance of the natural onrush of ethnic sentiments into the vacuum left by Communism: the 'return of history' in the form of national revival. And that, of course, is how it was advertised by many of the local protagonists. But on closer inspection the division of Czechoslovakia into two separate states—Slovakia and the Czech Republic—illustrates once again, on a provincial scale and at the heart of Europe, the limitations of such an interpretation.

There was certainly no shortage of 'history' on which to call. Czechs and Slovaks, however indistinguishable they might appear to perplexed outsiders, had markedly different pasts. Bohemia and Moravia—the historical territories comprising the Czech lands—could boast not merely a remarkable medieval and Renaissance past at the heart of the Holy Roman Empire but also a pre-eminent share in the industrialization of central Europe. Within the Austrian half of the Habsburg

Empire Czechs enjoyed growing autonomy and a marked prosperity. Their major city, Prague—one of the aesthetic glories of the continent—was by 1914 a significant center of modernism in the visual arts and literature.

Slovaks, by contrast, had little to boast about. Ruled for centuries from Budapest they lacked any distinctive national story—within the Hungarian half of the Empire they were regarded not as 'Slovaks' but as slav-language-speaking peasants of rural northern Hungary. The urban inhabitants of the Slovak region were predominantly Germans, Hungarians or Jews: it was not by chance that the largest town in the area, an unprepossessing conurbation on the Danube a few kilometres east of Vienna, was variously known as Pressburg (to German-speaking Austrians) or Pozsony (to Hungarians). Only with the independence of Czechoslovakia in 1918, and the Slovaks' somewhat reluctant incorporation therein, did it become the second city of the new state under the name Bratislava.

The inter-war Republic of Czechoslovakia was democratic and liberal by prevailing regional standards, but its centralized institutions strongly favored the Czechs, who occupied almost all positions of power and influence. Slovakia was a mere province and a poor and rather disfavored one at that. The same impulse that led many of the country's three million German-speaking citizens to listen to pro-Nazi separatists thus also drove a certain number of Czechoslovakia's two and a half million Slovaks to look with sympathy upon Slovak populists demanding autonomy and even independence. In March 1939, when Hitler absorbed the Czech regions into the 'Protectorate of Bohemia and Moravia', an authoritarian, clericalist Slovak puppet state was established under Father Józef Tiso. The first ever independent state of Slovakia thus emerged at Hitler's behest and over the corpse of the Czechoslovak Republic.

Just how popular Slovakia's wartime 'independence' ever was is hard to know after the fact. In the post-war years it was discredited both by its own record (Slovakia deported to death camps virtually all of its 140,000 pre-war Jewish population) and by its intimate dependence upon its Nazi patron. After its liberation, Czechoslovakia was re-established as a single state and expressions of Slovak nationalism were frowned upon. Indeed in the early Stalinist years, 'Slovak bourgeois nationalism' was one of the accusations levied at putative defendants in the show trials then being prepared—Gustav Husák spent six years in prison on the charge.

But in time the Communists in Czechoslovakia, as elsewhere, came to see the advantage of encouraging a moderate degree of national feeling. Reflecting a growing sentiment in Bratislava the reformers of 1968 (many of them of Slovak origin) proposed, as we have seen, a new federal constitution to comprise two distinct Czech and Slovak Republics; of all the significant innovations discussed or implemented in the Prague Spring this was the only one to survive the subsequent 'normalization'. Having initially treated Catholic, rural Slovakia as hostile territory the Party authorities now came if anything to favor it (see Chapter 13).

Slovakia's backwardness—or rather, the absence there of large concentrations of educated middle-class urbanites—now worked to its advantage. With fewer cars or televisions and worse communications than the more advanced western provinces, Slovaks appeared less vulnerable to foreign influence than Prague-based radicals and dissidents with their access to foreign media. Accordingly they suffered far less in the repression and purges of the seventies. Now it was *Czechs* who were on the receiving end of official disfavour. [20]

With this history in mind, the break up of Czechoslovakia after 1989 would appear, if not a foregone conclusion, then at the very least a logical outcome of decades of mutual ill-feeling: suppressed and exploited under Communism but not forgotten. But it was not thus. In the three years separating the end of Communism from the final split, every public opinion poll showed that some form of common Czecho-Slovak state was favored by a majority of Czechs *and* Slovaks. Nor was the political class deeply divided over the issue: in both Prague and Bratislava it was broadly agreed from the outset that the new Czechoslovakia would be a federation, with considerable autonomy for its separate parts. And the new President, Václav Havel, was a firm and very public believer in maintaining Czechs and Slovaks in the same country.

The initial unimportance of the 'national' question can be seen from the results of the first free elections, in June 1990. In Bohemia and Moravia Havel's Civic Forum secured half of the vote, with most of the remainder divided between Communists and Christian Democrats. In Slovakia the picture was more complex: Civic Forum's sister party Public Against Violence (PAV) emerged as the largest group, but a sizeable share of the vote was split between Christian Democrats, Communists, Hungarian Christian Democrats and Greens.[21] But the newly re-emergent Slovak National Party scored just 13.9 percent in the elections to a Slovak National Council, 11 percent in the vote for delegates to the Federal Assembly (parliament). Less than one Slovak voter in seven opted for the only party which favored dividing the country into its separate ethnic constituencies.

But in the course of 1991 Civic Forum began to disintegrate. An alliance based upon a common foe (Communism) and a popular leader (Havel), it now had neither: Communism was gone and Havel was the President of the Republic, ostensibly above the political fray. Political differences between erstwhile colleagues now came to the fore, with doctrinal free-marketeers led by Finance Minister Václav Klaus (a self-described Thatcherite) increasingly influential. In April 1991, follow-

---

[20]This occasioned some ill-feeling among Czechs. On a visit to Prague in 1985 the present author was regaled by liberal Czechs with accounts of the privileges accorded by the regime to the Slovak minority. Schoolteachers from Slovakia—recruited to teach in Prague's elementary schools and deemed by parents to be hopelessly provincial and inadequate to the task—were a particular target of resentment.
[21]The appearance of a separate Hungarian party reflects the presence on Slovak territory of some 500,000 Hungarians, 10 percent of the population of Slovakia.

ing parliamentary approval of a broad law on the privatization of state-owned enterprises, Civic Forum split and Klaus's (dominant) faction became the Civic Democratic Party.

Klaus was determined to drive the country rapidly forward towards 'capitalism'. But whereas there was a real constituency in the Czech lands for such an objective this was not the case in Slovakia. Privatization, the free market and a reduced state sector held little appeal for most Slovaks, who depended far more than Czechs upon jobs in unprofitable, outdated state-owned factories, mines and mills—'enterprises' for whose products there was no longer a protected market and that were unlikely to attract foreign capital or private investors. In the eyes of certain business and political circles in Prague, Slovakia was a burdensome inheritance.

Meanwhile Public Against Violence also broke apart, for analogous reasons. Its most effective public figure was now Vladimír Mečiar, an ex-boxer who played a relatively minor role in the events of 1989 but had since proved far more adept than his colleagues at maneuvering through the shoals of democratic politics. Following the June election he had formed a government in the Slovak National Council, but his rebarbative personal style produced a split in his coalition and Mečiar was replaced by the Catholic politician Ján Čarnogurský. Mečiar duly departed PAV, forming instead his own Movement for a Democratic Slovakia.

From the Fall of 1991 into the summer of 1992 representatives from the Czech and Slovak administrations conducted lengthy negotiations, seeking an agreed basis for a decentralized, federal constitution—the preference of the clear majority of politicians and voters on both sides. But Mečiar, in order to establish a constituency for himself and his party, now took up the cause of Slovak nationalism—a subject in which he had not previously evinced great interest. Slovaks, he informed his audiences, were threatened by everything from Czech privatization plans to Hungarian separatism to the prospect of absorption into 'Europe'. Their national existence (not to mention their livelihoods) was now at stake.

Buoyed by such rhetoric and his kitschy but charismatic public style, Mečiar led his new party to a clear victory at the Federal elections of June 1992 with nearly 40 percent of the vote in Slovakia. Meanwhile, in the Czech regions, Václav Klaus's new Civic Democratic Party, in alliance with Christian Democrats, also emerged victorious. With Klaus now prime minister of the Czech region, both autonomous halves of the federal republic were in the hands of men who—for different but complementary reasons—would not be sorry to see the country fall apart. Only the Federal President himself now stood, in constitutional form and in his own person, for the ideal of a united, federal Czechoslovakia.

But Václav Havel was no longer as popular—and therefore as influential—as he had been less than two years before. In his very first official journey as President he had traveled not to Bratislava but to Germany—an understandable move in the light of longstanding Czech-German animosity and his country's need to make friends in Western Europe, but a tactical misstep nonetheless from the point of view of Slovak sensibilities. And Havel was not always well served by his staff: in March 1991 his spokesman Michael Žantovský declared that Slovak politics were increasingly in the hands of ex-Communists and 'people who recall the Slovak state as the golden period of the Slovak nation'. [22]

Žantovský's assertion was not altogether mistaken, but in context it would prove more than a little self-fulfilling. Like other former Czech dissidents, Havel and his colleagues were not always inclined to think well of Slovaks. They rather looked upon them as parochial chauvinists: at best naively chasing the mirage of sovereignty, at worst nostalgic for the wartime puppet state. Ironically, Klaus did not share such liberal prejudices, nor did he care one way or the other about Slovakia's past. Like Mečiar, he was a realist. The two men, now the most powerful politicians in their respective regions, spent the next few weeks ostensibly negotiating the terms of a state treaty for a federal Czechoslovakia.

Whether they ever could have achieved agreement is unlikely: Mečiar demanded currency-issuing and borrowing rights for a virtually sovereign Slovak republic; a moratorium on privatization; the restoration of Communist-era subsidies; and a raft of other measures - all of which were anathema to Klaus, doggedly pursuing his plan for a forced march to the unrestricted market. Indeed, their meetings in the course of June and July 1992 were not really negotiations at all: Klaus purported to be surprised and upset by Mečiar's demands, but these were hardly a secret in view of Mečiar's many speeches on the subject. In practice it was Klaus who was maneuvering the Slovak leader towards a break, rather than the other way around.

In consequence, even though the majority of Slovak deputies in the Slovak National Council and in the Federal Assembly would have been quite content to approve a state treaty affording each half of the country full autonomy and equal status in a federal state, they found themselves instead facing a *fait accompli*. With negotiations stalled, Klaus in effect told his Slovak interlocutors: Since we appear to be unable to reach an agreement, we might as well abandon these fruitless efforts and go our separate ways. The Slovaks, faced with the apparent fulfillment of their own wishes, were trapped into assent—in many cases against their own better judgment.

On July 17th 1992 the Slovak National Council accordingly voted to adopt a new flag, a new constitution and a new name: the Slovak Republic. A week later Klaus and Mečiar, the latter still a trifle dazed by his own 'success', agreed to divide their country with effect from January 1st 1993. On that day Czechoslovakia disappeared and its two republics re-emerged as separate states, with Klaus and Mečiar as their respective Prime Ministers. Václav Havel, whose efforts to bind the country together had been increasingly forlorn—and altogether ignored in the final months—ceased

---

[22]Quoted in *Mladá Fronta dnes* 12th March 1991. See Abby Innes, *Czechoslovakia: The Short Goodbye* (Yale U.P., Newhaven, 2001), page 97.

to be President of Czechoslovakia and was reincarnated as President of the fore-shortened Czech Republic.[23]

Whether divorce was good for the two partners remained unclear for some time—neither the Czech Republic nor Slovakia flourished in the initial post-Communist decade. Klaus's 'shock therapy' and Mečiar's national-Communism both failed, albeit in different ways. But although Slovaks came to regret their dalliance with Vladimír Mečiar, and Klaus's star waned in Prague, nostalgia for Czechoslovakia was never much in evidence. The Czechoslovak divorce was a manipulated process in which the Czech Right brought about what it claimed not to seek while Slovak Populists achieved rather more than they had intended; not many people were overjoyed at the result, but nor was there lasting regret. As in the break up of the Soviet Union, the power of the state and the political machinery it had spawned were not threatened: merely duplicated.

The division of Czechoslovakia was a product of chance and circumstances. It was also the work of men. With other people in control—with different outcomes at the elections of 1990 and 1992—the story would not have been the same. Contagion played a small part as well: the example of the Soviet Union—and events unfolding in the Balkans—made a schism between the two 'national republics' of one small central European state seem less absurd or impermissible than it might otherwise have appeared. Had a federal state treaty been agreed upon by 1992—had Czechoslovakia endured for a few years longer—it is highly unlikely that anyone in Prague or Bratislava would have seen much point in pursuing their quarrels, with the prospect of admission to the European Union absorbing their attention and the bloody massacres in nearby Bosnia concentrating their minds.

---

[23]The political split proved easier to manage than the economic one—it was not until 1999 that agreement over the division of Czechoslovakia's federal assets was finally reached.

XXI

The Reckoning

'If there is ever another war in Europe, it will come out of some damned
silly thing in the Balkans'.
Otto von Bismarck

'It seems as if these feuding peasants could hardly wait for the invasion of
their country so they could hunt down and kill one another'.
Milovan Djilas, **Wartime** *(1977)*

'We've got no dog in this fight'.
James Baker, US Secretary of State (June 1991)

'The worst thing about Communism is what comes after'.
Adam Michnik

'Truth is always concrete.'
G. W. Hegel

The peaceful fragmentation of Czechoslovakia contrasts dramatically with the catastrophe that befell Yugoslavia in the same years. Between 1991 and 1999 hundreds
of thousands of Bosnians, Croats, Serbs and Albanians were killed, raped or tortured by their fellow citizens; millions more were forced out of their homes and into
exile. Struggling to account for massacres and civil war on a scale not seen since
1945—in a country long regarded by Western radicals as something of a model socialist society—foreign commentators have typically proposed two contrasting explanations.

One view, widely circulated in Western media and taken up in the public statements of European and American statesmen, presents the Balkans as a hopeless
case, a cauldron of mysterious squabbles and ancient hatreds. Yugoslavia was
'doomed'. It consisted, in the words of a much-cited *bon mot*, of six republics, five
nations, four languages, three religions and two alphabets, all held together by a single party. What happened after 1989 was simple: the lid having been removed, the
cauldron exploded.

According to this account, 'age-old' conflicts—in what the Marquis de Salaberry
had described in 1791 as 'the unpolished extremities' of Europe—bubbled over
much as they had done in centuries past. Murderous animosities, fuelled by mem-

ories of injustice and vengeance, took over a whole nation. In the words of the US Secretary of State Lawrence Eagleburger, speaking in September 1992: 'Until the Bosnians, Serbs and Croats decide to stop killing each other, there is nothing the outside world can do about it'.

In a contrasting interpretation, some historians and foreign observers asserted that—on the contrary—the Balkan tragedy was largely the fault of outsiders. Thanks to outside intervention and imperial ambition, the territory of former Yugoslavia had over the course of the past two centuries been occupied, divided and exploited to the advantage of others—Turkey, Britain, France, Russia, Austria, Italy and Germany. If there was bad blood between the peoples of the region it should be traced to imperial manipulation rather than to ethnic hostility. It was the irresponsible interference of foreign powers, so the argument runs, that exacerbated local difficulties: had the German Foreign Minister Hans-Dietrich Genscher, for example, not insisted in 1991 on 'prematurely' recognizing the independence of Slovenia and Croatia, the Bosnians might never have followed suit, Belgrade would not have invaded, and a decade of disaster could have been averted.

Whatever one thinks of these two readings of Balkan history, it is striking to note that despite their apparent incompatibility they have one important feature in common. Both diminish or ignore the role of the Yugoslavs themselves, dismissed as victims either of fate or the manipulations and mistakes of others. To be sure, there was a lot of history buried in the mountains of the former Yugoslavia, and many bad memories too. And outsiders did indeed contribute crucially to the country's tragedy, though mostly through irresponsible acquiescence in local crimes. But the break up of Yugoslavia—resembling in this respect the dismantling of other former Communist states—was the work of men, not fate. And the overwhelming responsibility for Yugoslavia's tragedy lay not in Bonn or any other foreign capital, but with the politicians in Belgrade.

When Josip Broz Tito died in 1980, at the age of 87, the Yugoslavia he had reassembled in 1945 had a real existence. Its constituent republics were separate units within a federal state whose presidency comprised representatives from all six republics, as well as two autonomous regions (the Vojvodina and Kosovo) within Serbia. The different regions had very different pasts. Slovenia and Croatia in the north were primarily Catholic and had once been part of the Austro-Hungarian Empire as too, albeit for a shorter time, had Bosnia. The southern part of the country (Serbia, Macedonia, Montenegro and Bosnia) was for centuries under Ottoman Turkish rule, which accounts for the large number of Muslims in addition to the predominantly Orthodox Serbs.

But these historical differences—though genuine enough and exacerbated by the experience of World War Two—had been attenuated in subsequent decades. Economic change brought hitherto isolated rural populations into sometimes uneasy contact in towns like Vukovar or Mostar; but the same changes also accelerated integration across old social and ethnic boundaries.

Yugoslavia 1945–91

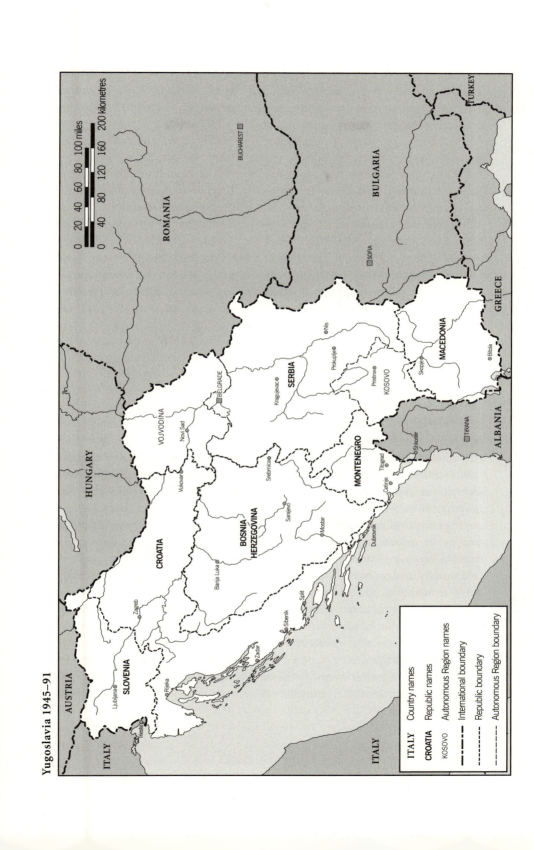

Thus although the Communist myth of fraternal unity required turning a blind eye and a deaf ear to wartime memories and divisions—the history textbooks of Tito's Yugoslavia were prudently unforthcoming about the bloody civil wars that had marked the country's common past—the benefits of such official silences were real. The rising post-war generation was encouraged to think of itself as 'Yugoslav', rather than 'Croat' or 'Macedonian'; and many—especially the young, the better educated and the burgeoning number of city-dwellers—had adopted the habit.[1] Younger intellectuals in Ljubljana or Zagreb were no longer much interested in the heroic or troubled past of their ethnic forebears. By 1981 in cosmopolitan Sarajevo, the capital of Bosnia, 20 percent of the population described themselves as 'Yugoslavs'.

Bosnia had always been the most ethnically variegated region of Yugoslavia and was thus perhaps not typical. But the whole country was an interwoven tapestry of overlapping minorities. The 580,000 Serbs living in Croatia in 1991 were some 12 percent of the population of that republic. Bosnia in the same year was 44 percent Muslim, 31 percent Serb and 17 percent Croat. Even tiny Montenegro was a mix of Montenegrins, Serbs, Muslims, Albanians and Croats—not to speak of those who opted to describe themselves to census-takers as 'Yugoslavs'. Residents of ethnically mixed regions often had little sense of their friends' or neighbors' nationality or religion. 'Inter-marriage' was increasingly common.

Indeed the 'ethnic' fault-lines within Yugoslavia were never very well defined. The linguistic distinctions can serve as a representative illustration. Albanians and Slovenes speak distinct languages. Macedonians speak Macedonian (i.e. Bulgarian, with minor variations). But the differences between the 'Serb' and 'Croat' forms of 'Serbo-Croatian' as spoken by the overwhelming majority of the population were, and are, small indeed. Serbs use the Cyrillic alphabet and Croats (and Bosnians) the Latin alphabet; but beyond some literary and scholarly terms, occasional spelling variations and a different pronunciation of the letter 'e' ('ye' in the 'Iékavian' or Croat form, 'e' in the 'Ekavian' or Serb variant) the two 'languages' are identical. Moreover, Montenegrins write in Cyrillic (like Serbs) but pronounce in the 'Iékavian' manner, like Croats and Bosnians—as do the Serb residents of Bosnia. Only the historical inhabitants of Serbia proper use the 'Ekavian' variant—and when Bosnian Serb nationalist leaders sought after 1992 to impose official 'Serbian' (i.e. 'Ekavian') pronunciation on their fellow Bosnian Serbs in the zone they had carved out of Bosnia, they encountered overwhelming resistance.

Thus the 'Croat' language recognized in 1974 as the official language of the republic of Croatia—meeting the demands of a 1967 'Declaration on Language' drawn up by a group of Zagreb intellectuals—was above all an identity tag: a way

---

[1]Zagreb, Belgrade and Skopje (the capital of Macedonia) were all among the fastest growing cities of Central Europe between 1910 and 1990.

for Croats to protest against Tito's suppression of all expressions of national identity in his federation. The same was true of certain Serb writers' obsession with preserving or re-affirming 'pure' Serbian. It seems fair to conclude that—in contrast to conventional differences between dialects of a single national language, where indigenous usage varies widely but educated élites tend to share a common 'correct' form—in former Yugoslavia it was the mass of the population who actually spoke an interchangeable single language, while a minority of nationalists sought to differentiate themselves by accentuating the narcissism of small differences.

The much invoked religious differences are no less misleading. The distinction between Catholic Croats and Orthodox Serbs, for example, mattered far more in earlier centuries—or in World War Two, when the Ustashe in Zagreb wielded Catholicism as a weapon against Serbs and Jews alike.[2] By the 1990s religious practice in the fast growing cities of Yugoslavia was on the wane and only in the countryside did the correspondence between religion and national sentiment still count for something. Many ostensibly Muslim Bosnians were thoroughly secularized—and in any case had little in common with Muslim Albanians (by no means all Albanians were Muslim, though this fact passed largely unnoticed by their enemies). Thus while there is no doubt that the old Ottoman practice of defining nationality by religion had left its mark, mostly by exaggerating the place of Orthodox Christianity among the southern Slavs, the evidence of this was increasingly attenuated.

Although an older generation of Yugoslavs continued to hold many of the prejudices of an earlier time—the future Croatian President Franjo Tudjman was notoriously ecumenical in his prejudices, despising Muslims, Serbs and Jews alike—probably the only generalized discrimination in recent years was the one directed at the Albanian minority in the south, castigated by many Slovenes, Croats, Serbs, Macedonians and Montenegrins as criminal and shiftless. These sentiments were strongest in Serbia.[3]

There were various reasons. Albanians were the fastest growing group in the country. Whereas in 1931 Albanians had been just 3.6 percent of the population of Yugoslavia, they were already 7.9 percent by 1948 (thanks to post-war immigration from neighbouring Albania proper). By 1991, thanks to their far higher birthrate (eleven times that of the Serb or Croat communities), the estimated 1,728,000 Albanians in Yugoslavia constituted 16.6 percent of the federal total. Most of the Albanian citizens of Yugoslavia lived in Serbia, in the autonomous region of Kosovo,

---

[2] 'We shall kill some Serbs, deport others, and oblige the rest to embrace Catholicism'—thus the Ustashe Minister of Religion in Zagreb, July 22nd 1941.

[3] On a 'fact-finding' visit to Skopje just after the 1999 Kosovo war the present author was 'confidentially' informed by the Macedonian Prime Minister that Albanians (including his own ministerial colleague who had just left the room) were not to be trusted: 'You can't believe anything they say—they just are not like us. They are not *Christian*.'

where they made up 82 percent of the local population and vastly outnumbered the 194,000 Serbs—although it was the latter who enjoyed the better jobs, housing and other social privileges.

Kosovo had historic significance for Serb nationalists as the last holdout of medieval Serbia against the advance of the Turks and the site of a historic battlefield defeat in 1389. The local Albanian predominance was thus regarded by some Serb intellectuals and politicians as both demographically troubling and historically provocative—especially since it echoed the Serbs' displacement by Muslims as the largest minority in the adjacent Bosnian republic. Serbs, it appeared, were losing out—to hitherto subservient minorities who had benefitted from Tito's rigorous enforcement of federal equality.[4] Kosovo was thus a potentially explosive issue, for reasons linked only tenuously to 'age-old' Balkan feuds: as André Malraux shrewdly advised a Yugoslav visitor to France back in the Sixties, *'Le Kosovo c'est votre Algérie dans l'Orléanais'*.

Whereas Serb dislike of Albanians fed on proximity and insecurity, in the far north of Yugoslavia the growing distaste for feckless southerners was ethnically indiscriminate and based not on nationality but economics. As in Italy, so in Yugoslavia, the more prosperous north was increasingly resentful of impoverished southerners, sustained—as it seemed—by transfers and subsidies from their more productive fellow citizens. The contrast between wealth and poverty in Yugoslavia was becoming quite dramatic: and it correlated provocatively with geography.

Thus while Slovenia, Macedonia and Kosovo all had approximately the same share (8 percent) of the national population, in 1990 tiny Slovenia was responsible for 29 percent of Yugoslavia's total exports while Macedonia generated just 4 percent and Kosovo 1 percent. As best one can glean from official Yugoslav data, per capita GDP in Slovenia was double that of Serbia proper, three times the size of per capita GDP in Bosnia and eight times that of Kosovo. In Alpine Slovenia the illiteracy rate in 1988 was less than 1 percent; in Macedonia and Serbia it was 11 percent. In Kosovo it stood at 18 percent. In Slovenia by the end of the 1980s the infant mortality rate was 11 deaths per 1,000 live births. In neighbouring Croatia the figure was 12 per 1,000; in Bosnia, 16 per 1,000. But in Serbia the figure was 22 per 1,000, in Macedonia, 45 per 1,000 and in Kosovo, 52 per 1,000.

What these figures suggest is that Slovenia and (to a lesser extent) Croatia already ranked alongside the less prosperous countries of the European Community, while Kosovo, Macedonia and rural Serbia more closely resembled parts of Asia or Latin America. If Slovenes and Croats were increasingly restive in their common Yugoslav home, then, this was not because of a resurfacing of deep-rooted religious

---

[4]This was not, of course, the way things appeared to Croats and others, who could point to Serb domination of the national army (60 percent of the officer corps was Serb by 1984, a fair reflection of Serb presence in the population at large but no more reassuring for that) and Belgrade's disproportionate share of investment and federal expenditure.

or linguistic sentiments or from a resurgence of ethnic particularism. It was because they were coming to believe that they would be a lot better off if they could manage their own affairs without having to take into account the needs and interests of underachieving Yugoslavs to their south.

Tito's personal authority and his vigorous repression of serious criticism kept such dissenting opinion well out of public view. But after his death the situation deteriorated fast. During the Sixties and early Seventies, when the West European boom was sucking in Yugoslav labor and sending back substantial hard currency remittances, over-population and under-employment in the south posed less of a problem. From the end of the Seventies, however, the Yugoslav economy started to unravel. Like other Communist states Yugoslavia was heavily indebted to the West: but whereas the response in Warsaw or Budapest was to keep borrowing foreign cash, in Belgrade they resorted instead to printing more and more of their own. Through the course of the 1980s the country moved steadily into hyper-inflation. By 1989 the annual inflation rate was 1,240 percent and rising.

The economic mistakes were being made in the capital, Belgrade, but their consequences were felt and resented above all in Zagreb and Ljubljana. Many Croats and Slovenes, Communists and non-Communists alike, believed that they would be better off making their own economic decisions free of the corruption and nepotism of the ruling circles in the Federal capital. These sentiments were exacerbated by a growing fear that a small group of *apparatchiks* around Slobodan Milošević, the hitherto obscure President of the League of Communists in his native Serbia, was making a bid for power in the political vacuum that followed Tito's death—by arousing and manipulating Serb national emotions.

Milošević's behavior was not inherently unusual for Communist leaders in these years. In the GDR the Communists, as we have seen, sought to curry favor by invoking the glories of eighteenth-century Prussia; and 'national Communism' had been on display for some years in neighboring Bulgaria and Romania. When Milošević ostentatiously welcomed a patriotic Memorandum from the Serbian Academy of Arts and Sciences in 1986, or visited Kosovo the following year to show his sympathy for Serb complaints about Albanian 'nationalism', his calculations were not very different from those of other East European Communist leaders of the time. In the era of Gorbachev, with the ideological legitimacy of Communism and its ruling party waning fast, patriotism offered an alternative way of securing a hold on power.

But whereas in the rest of eastern Europe this resort to nationalism and the attendant invocation of national memories only risked arousing anxiety among *foreigners*, in Yugoslavia the price would be paid at home. In 1988 Milošević, the better to strengthen his position within the Serbian republic, began openly encouraging nationalist meetings at which the insignia of the wartime Chetniks were on public display for the first time in four decades—a reminder of a past that Tito had suppressed and a move calculated to arouse real disquiet among Croats in particular.

Nationalism was Milošević's way of securing a hold over Serbia—confirmed in May 1989 with his election to the Presidency of the Serbian republic. But to preserve and strengthen Serbia's influence over Yugoslavia as a whole he needed to transform the federal system itself. The carefully calculated balance of influence between the various constituent republics had been fostered first by Tito's charismatic leadership and then by a revolving presidency. In March 1989 Milošević set out to topple this arrangement.

By forcing through an amendment to Serbia's own constitution he 'absorbed' the hitherto autonomous provinces of Kosovo and Vojvodina into Serbia proper—while allowing them to retain their two seats in the federal presidency. Henceforth Serbia could count on four of the eight federal votes in any dispute (Serbia, Kosovo, Vojvodina and the compliant pro-Serbian republic of Montenegro). Since Milošević's goal was to forge a more unitary (Serb-led) state, something that the other four republics would naturally resist, the federal system of government was effectively stalemated. From the perspective of Slovenia and Croatia especially, the course of events pointed to only one possible solution: since they could no longer expect to advance or preserve their interests through a dysfunctional federal system, their only hope was to take their distance from Belgrade, if necessary by declaring complete independence.

Why, by the end of 1989, had matters already reached this pass? Elsewhere the route out of Communism was 'democracy': party functionaries and bureaucrats from Russia to the Czech Republic transformed themselves in a matter of months from *nomenklatura* yes-men into glib practitioners of pluralist party politics. Survival depended upon re-calibrating one's public allegiances with the conventional party alignments of a liberal political culture. However implausible the transition in many individual cases, it worked. And it did so because there was no alternative. In most post-Communist countries the 'class' card was discredited and there were few internal ethnic divisions on which to prey: accordingly a new set of public categories—'privatization' or 'civil society' or 'democratization' (or 'Europe', which encompassed all three) occupied most of the new political terrain.

But Yugoslavia was different. Just because its various populations were so very intermingled (and had not undergone the genocides and population transfers that had re-arranged places like Poland or Hungary in earlier decades), the country offered fertile opportunities for demagogues like Milošević, or Franjo Tudjman, his Croat counterpart. In fashioning *their* exit from Communism around a new political constituency they could play an ethnic card no longer available elsewhere in Europe—and substitute it for a concern with democracy.

In the Baltic states, or Ukraine, or Slovakia, post-Communist politicians could resort to national independence as a route out of the Communist past—building a new state and a new democracy all at once—without having to worry unduly about the presence of national minorities. But in Yugoslavia, the break-up of the federation into its constituent republics would in every case except Slovenia leave a significant minority or group of minorities stranded in someone else's country. Under these circumstances, once one republic declared itself independent, others would feel bound to follow suit. In short, Yugoslavia now faced the same intractable issues that Woodrow Wilson and his colleagues had failed to resolve at Versailles seventy years earlier.

The catalyst, as many had foreseen, was Kosovo. Throughout the 1980s there had been sporadic Albanian demonstrations and protests at Belgrade's mistreatment of them, notably in the local capital Pristina. Their institutions had been closed down, their leaders dismissed, their daily routines constrained by harsh policing and, from March 1989, by a curfew. The Serbian constitutional amendments effectively stripped the Albanians, already a depressed and deprived underclass, of any autonomy or political representation—a course of events celebrated and underscored by Milošević's visit to the province in June 1989 to celebrate the 600th anniversary of the 'Battle of Kosovo'.

In a speech to a crowd estimated at nearly one million people, Milošević reassured the local Serbs that they had once again 'regained their state, national, and spiritual integrity.... Hitherto, thanks to their leaders and politicians and their vassal mentality [Serbs] felt guilty before themselves and others. This situation lasted for decades, it lasted for years and here we are now at the field of Kosovo to say that this is no longer the case'. A few months later, following bloody clashes between police and demonstrators with many dead and injured, Belgrade shut down the provincial Kosovo Assembly, placing the region under direct rule from Belgrade.

The course of events in the far south of the country directly affected decisions made in the northern republics. At best mildly sympathetic to the Albanians' plight, Ljubljana and Zagreb were far more directly concerned at the rise of Serbian authoritarianism. At the Slovene elections of April 1990, although a majority of the voters still favoured remaining in Yugoslavia they gave their backing to non-Communist opposition candidates openly critical of existing federal arrangements. The following month, in neighboring Croatia, a new nationalist party won an overwhelming majority and its leader, Franjo Tudjman, took over as President of the republic.

The last straw, revealingly, came in December 1990 when—under Milošević's direction—the Serbian leadership in Belgrade seized without authorization 50 percent of the entire drawing rights of the Yugoslav federation to cover back pay and bonuses for federal employees and state enterprise workers. The Slovenes—whose 8 percent of the population contributed one-quarter of the federal budget—were especially incensed. The following month the Slovene Parliament announced that it was withdrawing from the federal fiscal system and proclaimed the republic's independence, though without initiating any moves to secede. Within a month the Croat Parliament had done likewise (the Macedonian Parliament in Skopje duly followed suit).

The consequences of these developments were initially unclear. The substantial

Serb minority in south-eastern Croatia—notably in a long-established frontier region of Serb settlement, the Krajina—was already clashing with Croat police and calling upon Belgrade for help against its 'Ustashe' repressors. But Slovenia's distance from Belgrade, and the presence of less than 50,000 Serbs in the republic, gave grounds for hope that a peaceful exit might be engineered. Foreign opinion was divided: Washington, which had suspended all economic aid to Yugoslavia because of the Serbian measures in Kosovo, nevertheless publicly opposed any moves to secede.

Anticipating President Bush in Kiev a few weeks later, Secretary of State James Baker visited Belgrade in June 1991 and assured its rulers that the US supported 'a democratic and unified Yugoslavia'. But by then a 'democratic and unified' Yugoslavia was an oxymoron. Five days after Baker spoke both Slovenia and Croatia took control over their frontiers and initiated unilateral secession from the federation, with the overwhelming support of their citizens and the tacit backing of a number of prominent European statesmen. In response the federal army moved up to the new Slovene border. The Yugoslav war was about to begin.

Or, rather, the Yugoslav *wars*, for there were five. The Yugoslav attack on Slovenia in 1991 lasted just a few weeks, after which the army withdrew and allowed the secessionist state to depart in peace. There then followed a far bloodier war between Croatia and its rebellious Serb minority (backed by the army of 'Yugoslavia'—in practise Serbia and Montenegro) that lasted until an unsteady cease-fire brokered by the UN early the following year. After the Croats and Muslims of Bosnia voted for independence in March 1992, the Serbs of Bosnia declared war on the new state and set about carving out a 'Republika Srpska', again with the backing of the Yugoslav army, laying siege to a number of Bosnian towns—notably the capital, Sarajevo.

Meanwhile, in January 1993, a separate civil war broke out between the Croats and Muslims of Bosnia, with some Croats attempting to carve out an ephemeral statelet in the Croat-dominated region of Herzegovina. And finally, after these other conflicts had been brought to an end (though not before the Croat-Serb war broke out afresh in 1995 with a successful move by Zagreb to recapture the Krajina, lost to Serb forces three years before), came the war in and over Kosovo: having effectively lost everywhere else, Milošević turned back to Kosovo and was only prevented from destroying or expelling its Albanian population by an unprecedented attack on Serbia itself by NATO forces in the spring of 1999.

In each of these conflicts there was both an internal dynamic and external engagement. Slovenian and Croatian independence was driven forward by well-founded domestic considerations, as we have seen. But it was the hasty German—and subsequently European Community—recognition of the two new states that confirmed their official existence for friend and foe alike. Because an independent Croatia now existed, hysterical propaganda on radio and television stations in Belgrade could start to play on the fears of Serbs resident in the new state, invoking memories of wartime massacres and urging Serbs to take up arms against their 'Ustashe' neighbors.

In Bosnia, where Serbs were present in far larger numbers, the prospect of an independent Bosnia with a Croat-Muslim majority aroused similar anxieties. Whether Bosnian independence was unavoidable remains unclear: this was the most integrated of the pre-war republics, with the most to lose from any move to separate by force its constituent communities who were spread like a patchwork all across its territory, and before the rise of Milošević none of its ethnic or religious minorities had shown any sustained desire for institutional separation. But once its northern neighbors had seceded, the issue was moot.

After 1991 the Croats and Muslims of Bosnia were bound to prefer sovereign independence to minority status in what remained of Milošević's Yugoslavia, and they voted accordingly in a referendum at the end of February 1992. However the Serbs of Bosnia, now exposed for some months to talk from Belgrade not merely of *Ustashe* massacres but of a coming Muslim *jihad*, were no less understandably disposed to prefer union with Serbia, or at least their own autonomous region, to minority status in a Muslim-Croat state ruled from Sarajevo. Once Bosnia (or rather its Muslim and Croat leaders—the Serbs boycotted both the referendum and the parliamentary vote) declared itself independent in March 1992 its fate was sealed. The following month Bosnian Serb leaders declared the Republika Srpska and the Yugoslav army marched in to help them secure territory and 'cleanse' it.

The Serb-Croat and Serb-Bosnian wars wrought a terrible toll on their peoples. Although there was initially some open warfare between more or less regular armies, particularly in and around strategic cities like Sarajevo or Vukovar, much of the fighting was conducted by irregulars, notably Serb irregulars. These were little more than organized bands of thugs and criminals, armed by Belgrade and led either by professional felons like 'Arkan' (Zeljko Raznatovic), whose 'Serb Volunteer Guard' (the 'Tigers') massacred hundreds in eastern districts of Croatia and Bosnia; or else by former Yugoslav Army officers like Lt. Colonel Ratko Mladić (described by American diplomat Richard Holbrooke as 'a charismatic murderer'), who placed himself in charge of the Bosnian Serb forces from 1992 and helped organize the first attacks on Croat villagers living in majority-Serb communities in the Krajina.

The primary strategic objective was not so much the defeat of opposing forces as the expulsion of non-Serb citizens from their homes, land and businesses in the territories claimed for Serbs.[5] This 'ethnic cleansing'—a new term for a very old practice—was engaged in by all sides, but Serb forces were far and away the worst offenders. In addition to those who were killed (an estimated 300,000 by the end

---

[5]Since ethnic identity in Yugoslavia could not be ascertained from appearance or speech, roaming militias relied on villagers 'fingering' their neighbours—families with whom they had often lived at peace, sometimes as friends, for years and even decades.

of the Bosnian war), millions were forced into exile. Applications to the European Community for asylum more than tripled between 1988 and 1992: in 1991 Germany alone faced requests for asylum from 256,000 refugees. In the first year of the wars in Croatia and Bosnia there were 3 million people from Yugoslavia (one in eight of the pre-war population) seeking refuge abroad.

The international community was thus hardly unaware of the Yugoslav tragedy—which in any case was unfolding in real time on the television screens of the world, with harrowing pictures of starving Muslims in Serb prison camps and worse. The Europeans were the first to try and intervene, sending an EC ministerial team to Yugoslavia in June 1991—it was on this occasion that the unfortunate Jacques Poos, foreign minister of Luxembourg, unburdened himself of the deathless claim that 'the hour of Europe' had dawned. But despite establishing high-level commissions to enquire and arbitrate and propose, the European Community and its various agencies proved quite helpless—not least because its members were divided between those, like Germany and Austria, who favored the seceding republics and others, led by France, who wanted to retain existing borders and states and who for this reason among others were not altogether unsympathetic to Serbia.

Since the US (and therefore NATO) remained resolutely above the fray, that left only the United Nations. But beyond imposing sanctions on Belgrade, there appeared little the UN could do. Historically, soldiers under UN command were introduced into war-torn regions and countries to secure and keep a peace: but in Yugoslavia there was as yet no peace to keep, and there existed neither the will nor the means to bring it about on the ground. As in the comparable case of the Spanish Civil War, an ostensibly neutral international stance in practice favoured the aggressor in a civil conflict: the international arms embargo imposed on former Yugoslavia did nothing to restrain the Serbs, who could call on the substantial arms industry of the old Yugoslav federation, but it severely hampered the Bosnian Muslims in their struggles and goes a long way to account for their substantial military losses between 1992 and 1995.

The only practical achievement of the international community before 1995 was to install a 14,000-strong UN Protection Force in Croatia to separate Croats and Serbs after the fighting there had subsided, followed by the insertion into selected towns in Bosnia—designated as 'Safe Areas'—of a few hundred uniformed UN peacekeepers to protect the growing numbers of (mostly Muslim) refugees herded into these areas. Later came the establishment of UN-authorized 'no-fly zones' in parts of Bosnia, intended to restrict Yugoslavia's freedom to threaten civilians (or break UN-imposed sanctions).

Of greater long-term significance, perhaps, was the setting up in The Hague, in May 1993, of an International Tribunal for War Crimes. The mere existence of such a court confirmed what was by now obvious—that war crimes, and worse, were being perpetrated just a few score miles south of Vienna. But since most of the presumptive criminals, including Mladić and his fellow Bosnian Serb Radovan

Karadžić (President of Republika Srpska), were actively pursuing their crimes with impunity, the Court remained as yet a ghostly and irrelevant side-show.

The situation began to change only in 1995. Until then all talk of foreign intervention had been stymied by the claim—energetically propounded by French and British officers in and out of the UN forces—that the Bosnian Serbs were strong, determined and well armed. They should not be provoked: any serious attempt to enforce a peace settlement in Bosnia against their will or their interests, it was suggested, would not only be unfair but could make matters worse . . . a line of reasoning slyly encouraged from Belgrade by Milošević, who nevertheless claimed somewhat implausibly to play little part in the decisions of his fellow Serbs in Bosnia.

Thus accorded a virtual free hand[6], the Bosnian Serbs proceeded nevertheless to overplay it. Even though it was broadly agreed by the international community (including a 'Contact Group' of foreign diplomats tirelessly seeking an agreement) that a 'Muslim-Croat' Federation (formed in March 1994 in a ceremony in Washington that put an end to Croat-Muslim fighting) should receive 51 percent of a newly federal Bosnia, with the Serbs getting 49 percent, the Serb leaders based in the town of Pale took no notice and continued their attacks. In February 1994 their forces had lobbed a mortar shell from the surrounding mountains into the marketplace of Sarajevo, killing sixty-eight people and wounding hundreds more. Following this NATO—with UN backing—threatened air strikes in the event of further attacks and there was a temporary lull.

But in May of 1995, in retaliation for some Bosnian military advances and Croatia's successful recapturing of the Krajina (putting the lie to the myth of Serbian military prowess), Serbian shelling of Sarajevo resumed. When NATO planes bombed Bosnian Serb installations in response, the Serbs seized 350 UN peacekeepers as hostages. Terrified for the fate of their soldiers, Western governments importuned the UN and NATO to desist. The international presence, far from constraining the Serbs, now offered them additional cover.

Bolstered by this evidence of Western pusillanimity, on July 11th Bosnian Serb forces under Mladić brazenly marched into one of the so-called UN 'Safe Areas', the eastern Bosnian town of Srebrenica, by then overflowing with terrified Muslim refugees. Srebrenica was officially 'protected' not just by UN mandate but by a 400–strong peacekeeping contingent of armed Dutch soldiers. But when Mladić's men arrived the Dutch battalion laid down its arms and offered no resistance whatsoever as Serbian troops combed the Muslim community, systematically separating men and boys from the rest. The next day, after Mladić had given his 'word of honor as an officer' that the men would not be harmed, his soldiers marched the

---

[6]Between 1992 and 1994 the UN agencies in the Balkans were all but complicit with the Bosnian Serbs—allowing them, for example, an effective veto over what and who could enter and leave the besieged city of Sarajevo.

Muslim males, including boys as young as thirteen, out into the fields around Srebrenica. In the course of the next four days nearly all of them—7,400—were killed. The Dutch soldiers returned safely home to Holland.

Srebrenica was the worst mass murder in Europe since World War Two: a war crime on the scale of Oradour, Lidice or Katyn, carried out in full view of international observers. Within days the news of what appeared to have taken place at Srebrenica was broadcast worldwide. Yet the only immediate response was an official warning from NATO to the Serbs that there would be a resumption of air strikes if other 'safe areas' were attacked. It was not until August 28th, a full seven weeks later, that the international community finally responded—and only because the Bosnian Serbs, assuming reasonably enough that they had *carte blanche* to commit massacres at will, made the mistake of shelling the Sarajevo marketplace for a second time: killing another thirty-eight civilians, many of them children.

Now, at last, NATO acted. Overcoming a lingering reluctance on the part of the UN leadership, certain European leaders and even some of his own military, President Clinton authorized a serious and sustained bombing campaign designed to reduce and ultimately eliminate the Serbian capacity to cause further harm. It was late in coming, but it worked. The much-vaunted Serb fighting machine evaporated. Faced with a prolonged, open-ended assault on their positions and with no backing from Milošević (who now took great care to emphasize his distance from the men of Pale) the Bosnian Serbs folded.

With the Serbs out of the picture and the US now very much in, it proved surprisingly easy to introduce peace—or at least the absence of war—into the Balkans. On October 5th President Clinton announced a cease-fire, declaring that the parties had agreed to attend peace talks in the US. On November 1st the talks began, at a US Air Force base in Dayton, Ohio. Three weeks later they concluded with an agreement signed in Paris on December 14th 1995.[7] Tudjman represented Croatia, Alija Izetbegović spoke for the Bosnian Muslims and Slobodan Milošević signed on behalf of both Yugoslavia and the Bosnian Serbs.

The objective of Dayton, from the American perspective, was to find a solution to the Yugoslav wars that did not entail a partition of Bosnia. Partition would have represented a victory for the Serbs (who would then have sought to join their share to Serbia proper and forge the Greater Serbia of nationalist dreams); and it would have put an international *imprimatur* on ethnic cleansing as state-making. Instead, a complicated tripartite system of governance was established, in which the Serbs, Muslims and Croats of Bosnia all had a degree of administrative and territorial autonomy but within a single Bosnian state whose external boundaries would remain unaltered.

Formally, then, Bosnia survived its civil war. But the effects of terror and ex-

---

[7]It was at French insistence that the signing ceremony was held in Paris—an exercise in ceremonial overcompensation that only drew attention to France's previous reluctance to act against the Serbs.

pulsion could not be undone. Most of those expelled from their homes (Muslims, above all) never returned, despite assurance and encouragement from local and international authorities. Indeed there were to be further 'cleansings'—this time of Serbs, systematically expelled by Zagreb from the newly retaken Krajina or else pressured by their own armed militias to leave their homes in Sarajevo and elsewhere and 'resettle' in predominantly Serb areas. But on the whole the peace was kept and Bosnia held together—by a 60,000-strong NATO army acting as an Implementation Force (later Stabilization Force) and a civilian High Representative empowered to administer the country until it could assume responsibility for its own affairs.

Both the High Representative and the international troops are still in Bosnia and continue to oversee its affairs at the time of writing (ten years after Dayton)—an indication of the calamitous condition of the country following the war and of the continuing ill-feeling and lack of cooperation among the three communities.[8] Bosnia became host to a raft of international agencies: governmental, intergovernmental and non-governmental. Indeed the Bosnian economy after 1995 depended almost entirely upon the presence and expenditures of these agencies. A World Bank estimate of January 1996 suggested that in order to recover Bosnia would need $5.1 billion over three years. This has proven wildly optimistic.

Once the Bosnian war ended, and with the various international agencies in place to help secure the peace, international interest subsided. The European Union, as usual, was transfixed by its own institutional concerns; while Clinton, taken up first with domestic election issues and then with NATO expansion and the instability of Yeltsin's Russia, ceased to focus on the Balkan crisis. But even though Slovenia, Croatia and Bosnia were now ostensibly independent states, the Yugoslav problem had not been resolved. Slobodan Milošević was still in control of what remained of his country and the issue on which he had ridden to power in the first place was about to explode.

The Albanians of Serbia had continued to suffer discrimination and repression—indeed, with international attention deflected to the crisis farther north they were more vulnerable than ever. Following Dayton, Milošević's international fortunes had decidedly improved: although he had not succeeded in getting all sanctions removed (his chief purpose in cooperating so readily with the American peace moves in Bosnia), Yugoslavia ceased to be quite the pariah it had been. And so, with a series of defeats to his name and Serb nationalist politicians in Belgrade criticizing him for compromising with Serbia's 'enemies', Milošević turned back to Kosovo.

By the spring of 1997 Elisabeth Rehn, the UN special rapporteur for human rights, was already warning of impending disaster in the Kosovo province, as Bel-

---

[8]The NATO-led Stabilization Force was replaced by the European Union's EUFOR on December 2nd 2004.

grade pressed down upon the Albanian majority there, rejecting all demands for local autonomy and depriving the local population of even the minimum of institutional representation. Bypassing the helpless and humiliated moderate leadership of Ibrahim Rugova, a younger generation of Albanians—armed and encouraged from Albania itself—abandoned non-violent resistance and turned increasingly to the KLA (Kosovo Liberation Army).

Originating in Macedonia in 1992, the KLA was committed to armed struggle for Kosovo's independence (and perhaps union with Albania). Its tactics—consisting mostly of guerilla attacks on isolated police stations—offered Milošević an opportunity to condemn *all* Albanian resistance as 'terrorist' and authorize a campaign of increasing violence. In March 1998, after Serb forces—armed with mortars and backed with combat helicopters—killed and wounded dozens of people in massacres at Drenica and other Albanian villages, the international community at last responded to pleas from Rugova and began to pay closer attention. But when both the US and the EU expressed themselves 'appalled by the police violence in Kosovo', Milošević's belligerent response was to warn that 'terrorism aimed at the internationalization of the issue will be most harmful to those who resorted to these means.'

By now all the Kosovo Albanian leadership—most of it in exile or in hiding—had decided that only complete separation from Serbia could save their community. Meanwhile the US and the ongoing 'Contact Group' countries continued to try to mediate between Milošević and the Albanians—partly to broker a 'just' solution, partly to head off a broader war in the south Balkans. This was not an unreasonable fear: if Yugoslavia could not be brought to treat its Albanian citizens decently—and they opted to secede—this could have serious consequences for neighboring Macedonia, with a large and unhappy Albanian minority of its own.

Newly independent Macedonia, known at Greek insistence as the Former Yugoslav Republic of Macedonia (FYROM)[9], was a historically sensitive zone. Its frontiers with Bulgaria, Greece and Albania had all been disputed before and after both World Wars. It was looked upon with suspicion by all its neighbors—on whom the landlocked little state is utterly dependent for trade and access to the outside world. And its survival following the break-up of Yugoslavia was by no means a sure thing. But if Macedonia were to collapse, then Albania, Bulgaria, Greece and even Turkey might be drawn into the conflict.

Thus Milošević's continued mistreatment—massacres—of the Albanians in Kosovo was bound to bring down upon him the disapproval and ultimate inter-

---

[9]The ageing Greek Prime Minister Andreas Papandreou, manipulating nationalist sentiment for electoral advantage, claimed that the term 'Macedonia' was part of his country's ancient heritage and could apply to only the northernmost region of Greece itself. If the Slav state carved out of southern Yugoslavia called itself by that name it must harbour irredentist ambitions. What Papandreou could not acknowldge was that many of the 'Greeks' of Greek Macedonia were themselves of Slav descent—albeit officially Hellenized for patriotic ends.

vention of the Western powers. Curiously, he seems never fully to have grasped this, despite serial warnings through the summer of 1998 from the US Secretary of State Madeleine Albright (who said she would hold Milošević 'personally responsible'), President Jacques Chirac of France, and NATO Secretary-General Javier Solana. Like Saddam Hussein a few years later, Milošević was isolated and insulated from Western opinion and over-confident of his own ability to manipulate foreign statesmen and maneuver between them.

This was not entirely Milošević's fault. Flattered by frequent visits from certain American diplomats—vaingloriously over-confident of their negotiating prowess—Milošević had good reason to think that he was seen in the West not as an intransigent foe but as a privileged interlocutor.[10] And the Yugoslav dictator was well aware of the international community's overarching concern to avoid any further redrawing of international boundaries. As late as July 1998, despite clear evidence that the situation in Kosovo was now desperate, the Contact Group of foreign ministers publicly ruled out independence as a solution.

What Milošević quite failed to grasp was the transformative impact of the Bosnian catastrophe upon international opinion. Human rights—ethnic cleansing in particular—were now high on everyone's agenda, if only out of a gnawing collective guilt at the world's previous failure to act in time. In June 1998 the War Crimes Tribunal in The Hague declared itself competent to exercise jurisdiction over crimes committed in Kosovo—Louise Arbour, the chief prosecutor, claiming that the scale and nature of the fighting in the province qualified it as an armed conflict under international law—and on July 19th the US Senate urged the Hague officials to indict Milošević with 'war crimes, crimes against humanity and genocide'.

The plausibility of such charges was mounting fast. Not only were hundreds of Albanian 'terrorists' now being killed by special police units drafted in from Serbia, but there was growing evidence that under the cover of this conflict Belgrade was planning to 'encourage' the departure of the Albanian population, forcing them to flee their land and livelihoods in order to save their lives. Throughout the winter of 1998–99 there were reports of Serb police actions—sometimes in response to KLA attacks, more typically involving mass executions of one or more extended families—intended to terrorize whole communities into abandoning their villages and fleeing across the borders into Albania or Macedonia.

The international response was now increasingly divided. The US and most of its NATO partners openly favored some form of military intervention on behalf of the besieged Albanians as early as October 1998. But at the UN (which would have had to authorize such intervention in the ostensibly 'domestic' affairs of a sover-

---

[10]In the winter of 1996, following palpably fraudulent results in local elections, Serb students demonstrated for three months in the streets of Belgrade, protesting Milošević's dictatorship and demanding change. They received no support or encouragement from the Western powers, however, who looked upon Milošević as a stabilizing factor in the post-Dayton years and did nothing to weaken his position.

eign state) there was strong opposition from China and Russia—whose parliament passed a resolution labeling any future NATO action as 'illegal aggression'. Within the EU and NATO itself Greece, for its own reasons, opposed any intervention in Yugoslav affairs. Meanwhile Ukraine and Belarus offered 'unconditional solidarity' and 'moral support' to their fellow Slavs in Serbia.

The apparent stalemate might have continued indefinitely had Belgrade not upped the ante with a series of brutal mass murders in early 1999, first on January 15th at the village of Racak in southern Kosovo and then in March all across the province. The Racak attack, in which 45 Albanians were killed (23 of them apparently executed), served finally—like the marketplace massacre in Sarajevo—to stimulate the international community to action.[11] After fruitless negotiations at Rambouillet between Madeleine Albright and a Yugoslav delegation, which ended with a predictable refusal by Belgrade to withdraw its forces from Kosovo and accept a foreign military presence there, intervention became inevitable. On March 24th, and despite the absence of formal UN approval, NATO ships, planes and missiles went into action over Yugoslavia, in effect declaring war on the Belgrade regime.

The final Yugoslav war lasted just under three months, in the course of which NATO forces wrought serious damage in Serbia proper but had only limited success in preventing the ongoing expulsion of the Albanian population from Kosovo: in the course of the war 865,000 refugees (half the Albanian population of Kosovo) fled into makeshift camps across the border in Montenegro, Bosnia, Albania and the ethnically Albanian regions of western Macedonia. But in spite of President Clinton's imprudently public insistence that there should be no NATO ground troops engaged—obliging the alliance to conduct a war from the air with inevitable mishaps that played into Yugoslav propaganda and the Serb cult of victimhood—the outcome was a foregone conclusion. On June 9th Belgrade agreed to remove all its troops and police from Kosovo, NATO attacks were suspended, and the UN duly mandated a 'temporary' occupation of the province by a NATO-led Kosovo Force (KFOR).

The occupation of Kosovo marked the end of the decade-long cycle of Yugoslav wars—and also the beginning of the end for Milošević himself. His credibility undermined by this latest and worst setback for the Serb nationalist project, Milošević was overwhelmingly defeated in the Yugoslav presidential election of September 2000 by an opposition candidate, Vojislav Koštunica. When Milošević cynically conceded that Koštunica had more votes, but declared that the margin was so close that a runoff was needed, he at last aroused a storm of popular protest among the longsuffering Serbs themselves. Tens of thousands of protesters took to the streets of Belgrade and on October 5th Milošević finally conceded defeat and stepped down. Six months later the government of Serbia, increasingly desperate for West-

---

[11]And as with the Sarajevo atrocity, Belgrade and its apologists insisted either that it never happened or, when that became untenable, that it was a staged 'provocation' by the victims themselves.

ern economic assistance, agreed to arrest Milošević and hand him over to the Hague Tribunal where he was charged with genocide and war crimes.

Who was to blame for the tragedy of Yugoslavia? There was certainly enough responsibility to go around. The United Nations showed little initial concern—its inadequate and unconcerned Secretary-General, Boutros Boutros-Ghali, described Bosnia as 'a rich man's war'—and when its representatives did arrive in the Balkans they spent most of their time blocking any decisive military action against the worst offenders. The Europeans were little better. France in particular displayed a distinct reluctance to place any blame for the course of events upon Serbia—and indeed a marked disinclination to get involved at all.

Thus when, in September 1990, Washington sought to place Yugoslavia on the agenda of an upcoming OSCE summit in Paris, François Mitterrand accused the Americans of 'over-dramatizing' and refused. Four months later, when the issue arose again, the French foreign office now claimed that it was 'too late' for foreign intervention . . . Paris remained similarly uncooperative even after international forces had been obliged to engage in the region: the French General Bernard Janvier, commander of the UN Protection Force in Bosnia, personally forbade air strikes against the Bosnian Serb forces at Srebrenica.[12] As for the Dutch government, it went so far as to veto *any* NATO strikes on Bosnian Serb strongholds until all Dutch soldiers were safely out of the country.

Other countries performed a little better, but not much. Although London eventually backed American pressure to intervene, the British authorities spent the first crucial years of the Yugoslav conflict quietly impeding any direct engagement on the part of the EC or NATO. And the British treatment of Yugoslav refugees was shameful: in November 1992, as the flow of desperate, homeless Bosnians built to its peak, London announced that no Bosnian could travel to the UK without a visa. This was perfidious Albion at its most cynical. Since there was no British embassy in Sarajevo to issue such visas, the only way a Bosnian family could secure them was by making its way to a British embassy in a third country . . . at which point the UK government would and did claim that since they had found asylum somewhere else, Britain need not admit them. Thus whereas Germany, Austria and the Scandinavian countries played generous host to hundreds of thousands of Yugoslav refugees between 1992 and 1995, the UK actually saw a *decline* in the number of asylum seekers in these same years.

Although it took Washington an extraordinarily long time to focus upon events in the Balkans, once the US did engage there its record is distinctly better. Indeed the fact that it was American initiative that drove forward each stage of interna-

---

[12]Janvier's performance aroused demands in France and elsewhere that he be co-indicted for responsibility in the subsequent massacre.

tional intervention was a source of serial humiliation for the Western European allies. But the US, too, dragged its feet—for the most part because the American defense establishment was reluctant to take any risks and because many US politicians continued to believe that their country had 'no dog' in this war. The idea of deploying NATO in these novel circumstances—or that the US might unilaterally intervene in the domestic affairs of a sovereign state with which it had no quarrel—was not an easy sell. It was, as Secretary of State Warren Christopher observed at the height of the Bosnian war, 'a problem from hell'.

As for the Yugoslavs themselves, no-one emerges with honour. The failure of the Yugoslav federal system was precipitated by Belgrade, but Ljubljana and Zagreb were not sorry to see it go. Bosnian Muslims, it is true, had only restricted opportunities to commit war crimes of their own—for the most part they were on the receiving end of other people's aggression. Theirs is the saddest loss of all—and the destruction of Sarajevo a particular source of grief. On its restricted scale the Bosnian capital was a genuinely cosmopolitan city: perhaps the last of the multi-ethnic, multi-lingual, ecumenical urban centers that were once the glory of central Europe and the eastern Mediterranean. It will be rebuilt but it can never recover.

Armed Croats, on the other hand, were responsible for innumerable acts of violence against civilians—under direction from Zagreb and on their own initiative. In Mostar, a town in western Bosnia with an unusually high percentage of interfaith marriages, Croat extremists deliberately set about expelling Muslims and mixed families from the western half of the city. They then replaced them with Croat peasants driven into the town and radicalized by their own experience of ethnic cleansing in the villages, and set siege to the Muslim eastern districts. In the meantime, in November 1993, they systematically destroyed the sixteenth-century Ottoman bridge across the Neretva river, a symbol of the town's integrated and ecumenical past.

The Croats, then, had little to boast of—and of all the post-Communist leaders who emerged from the rubble, Franjo Tudjman was one of the more egregiously unattractive. More than anyone else he made it a personal project to erase the Yugoslav past from his fellow citizens' memory: by March 1993 the very word 'Yugoslavia' had been removed from textbooks, readers, encyclopedias, book titles and maps published in the new Croatia. Only after Tudjman's death could the Croat state he had founded begin credibly to re-position itself as a candidate for membership of the international community.

But in the end the primary responsibility for the Yugoslav catastrophe must rest with the Serbs and their elected leader Slobodan Milošević. It was Milošević whose bid for power drove the other republics to leave. It was Milošević who then encouraged his fellow Serbs in Croatia and Bosnia to carve out territorial enclaves and who backed them with his army. And it was Milošević who authorized and directed the sustained assault on Yugoslavia's Albanian population that led to the war in Kosovo.

Belgrade's actions were a disaster for Serbs everywhere. They lost their land in the Krajina region of Croatia; they were forced to accept an independent Bosnia and abandon plans to carve from it a sovereign Serb state; they were defeated in Kosovo, from which most of the Serb population has since fled in justified fear of Albanian retribution; and in the rump state of Yugoslavia (from which even Montenegro has sought to secede) their standard of living has fallen to historic lows. This course of events has further exacerbated a longstanding Serb propensity for collective self-pity at the injustice of history and it is true that in the longer run the Serbs may well be the greatest losers in the Yugoslav wars. It says something about the condition of their country that today even Bulgaria and Romania rank above Serbia in present living standards and future prospects.

But this irony should not blind us to Serb responsibility. The appalling ferocity and sadism of the Croat and Bosnian wars—the serial abuse, degradation, torture, rape and murder of hundreds of thousands of their fellow citizens—was the work of Serb men, mostly young, aroused to paroxysms of casual hatred and indifference to suffering by propaganda and leadership from local chieftains whose ultimate direction and power came from Belgrade. What followed was not so unusual: it had happened in Europe just a few decades before, when—all across the continent and under the warrant of war—ordinary people committed quite extraordinary crimes.

There is no doubt that in Bosnia especially there was a history upon which Serb propaganda could call—a history of past sufferings that lay buried just beneath the misleadingly placid surface of post-war Yugoslav life. But the decision to arouse that memory, to manipulate and to exploit it for political ends, was made by men: one man in particular. As Slobodan Milošević disingenuously conceded to a journalist during the Dayton talks, he had never expected the wars in his country to last so long. That is doubtless true. But those wars did not just break out from spontaneous ethnic combustion. Yugoslavia did not fall: it was pushed. It did not die: it was killed.

Yugoslavia was the worst case, but post-Communism was difficult everywhere. The path from authoritarianism to democracy in Portugal or Spain accompanied the accelerated modernization of a backward agrarian economy—a combination with which the rest of Western Europe was familiar from its own past. But the exit from Communism had no precedent. The much-anticipated passage from capitalism to socialism had been theorized *ad nauseam* in academies, universities and coffee bars from Belgrade to Berkeley; but no-one had thought to offer a blueprint for the transition from socialism to capitalism.

Of Communism's many encumbering legacies, the economic inheritance was the most tangible. The obsolescent industrial plant of Slovakia, or Transylvania, or Silesia, coupled economic dysfunction with environmental irresponsibility. The two were closely related: the poisoning of Lake Baikal, the death of the Aral Sea, the acid rain falling across the forests of Northern Bohemia represented not just ecological catastrophe but a huge mortgage on the future. Before there could be investment in new industries the old ones would need to be dismantled and someone would have to make good the damage they had wrought.

In the eastern *Länder* of Germany the bill for undoing the damage of Communism was assumed by the Federal government. The *Treuhand* (see Chapter 17) spent billions of Deutschmarks over the next four years buying up and selling off obsolete industrial plants and factories, paying off their redundant employees and making good—so far as possible—the consequences of their activities. But even though the results were patchy and nearly bankrupted the Federal treasury, the former East Germans were fortunate nonetheless: *their* transition out of Communism was paid for by Western Europe's strongest economy. Elsewhere the cost of reinventing economic life had to be borne by the victims themselves.

The basic choice facing post-Communist governments was either to attempt a one-time, overnight transformation from subsidized socialist economies into market-driven capitalism—the 'big bang' approach—or else proceed cautiously to dismantle or sell off the more egregiously malfunctioning sectors of the 'planned economy' while preserving as long as possible those features which mattered most to the local population: cheap rents, guaranteed jobs, free social services. The first strategy conformed best to the free-market theorems beloved of an emerging generation of post-Communist economists and businessmen; the second was more politically prudent. The problem was that either approach must in the short term (and perhaps the not-so-short term) cause significant pain and loss: in Boris Yeltsin's Russia, where *both* were applied, the economy shrank dramatically for eight years—the biggest peacetime setback for a major economy in modern history.

It was in Poland, under the determined supervision of Leszek Balcerowicz (first as finance minister, later as head of the country's central bank), that the 'big bang' approach was applied earliest and with the greatest consistency. Obviously, Balcerowicz argued, his country—insolvent in all but name—could not recover without international aid. But that aid would not be forthcoming unless Poland put in place credible structures of the kind that would reassure Western bankers and lending agencies. It was not the International Monetary Fund that was forcing harsh measures on Poland; rather, by anticipating IMF strictures, Poland would merit and receive the help it needed. And the only way to do this was *fast*, during the post-Communist honeymoon and before people realized how painful the process would be.

Thus on January 1st 1990 the first post-Communist government of Poland embarked on an ambitious program of reforms: building up foreign reserves, removing price controls, tightening credit and cutting subsidies (i.e. allowing enterprises to fail)—all at the expense of domestic real wages, which immediately fell some 40 percent. Except for the explicit recognition of the inevitability of unemployment (softened by the establishment of a fund to support and help retrain those forced out of work) this was not very different from what had twice been unsuccessfully attempted during the 1970s. What had changed was the political climate.

In neighboring Czechoslovakia, under the guidance of finance minister (later Prime Minister) Václav Klaus, a similarly ambitious program was pursued—with an additional emphasis upon currency convertibility, the liberalization of foreign trade, and privatization, all in keeping with Klaus's openly avowed 'Thatcherism'. Like Balcerowicz and some of the young economists in the Kremlin, Klaus favoured 'shock therapy': finding nothing worth preserving in socialist economics he saw no benefit in delaying the switch to capitalism.

At the other extreme stood men like Slovakia's Mečiar, Romania's Iliescu or Ukraine's Prime Minister (and subsequently President) Leonid Kuchma. Wary of upsetting their constituents they delayed the introduction of change as long as possible—Ukraine's first 'economic reform program' was announced in October 1994—and proved singularly reluctant to liberalize domestic markets or reduce the state's share in the economy. In September 1995 Kuchma would defend his position—in terms familiar to historians of the region—by warning against 'blindly copying foreign experience'.

After passing through a slough of economic despond in the early 1990s the first tier of former Communist states re-emerged on a more secure foundation, able to attract Western investors and envisage an eventual ascent into the European Union. The relative success of the Polish or Estonian economic strategies when compared to the fortunes of Romania or Ukraine is obvious to any visitor—indeed, at the level of small business activity or even public optimism, the more successful eastern European countries have fared better than former East Germany, for all the latter's apparent advantages.

It is tempting to conclude that the more 'advanced' post-Communist states like Poland—or the Czech Republic, Estonia, Slovenia and perhaps Hungary—were thus able in the course of a few uncomfortable years to bridge the gap from state socialism to market capitalism, albeit at some cost to their older and poorer citizens; meanwhile a second tier of countries in the Balkans and the former Soviet Union was left to struggle in their wake, held back by an incompetent and corrupt ruling elite unable and unwilling to contemplate the necessary changes.

This is very broadly true. But even without Klaus or Balcerowicz or their Hungarian and Estonian counterparts, some former-Communist states were always going to do better than others in the passage to a market economy: either because they were already embarked upon it before 1989—as we have seen—or else because their Soviet-era distortions were not as pathological as those of their less fortunate neighbours (the comparison between Hungary and Romania is telling in this respect). And of course the miracles of economic transformation on offer in the capital cities of certain countries—in Prague or Warsaw or Budapest, for example—are not always replicated in their distant provinces. As in the past, so today: the real boundaries in central and eastern Europe are not between countries but between prosperous urban centers and a neglected and impoverished rural hinterland.

Rather more revealing than the differences between the post-Communist experiences of these lands are their similarities. In every country, after all, the new ruling elites faced the same strategic choices. The 'market-economic romance', as Russian Premier Viktor Chernomyrdin termed it dismissively in January 1994, was universal.[13] So, too, were the general economic objectives: liberalization of the economy, transition to some form of free market and access to the European Union—with its seductive promise of foreign consumers, investment and regional support funds to ease the pain of dismantling the command economy. These were outcomes that almost everyone sought—and in any case there was, as it seemed to most informed opinion, no alternative.

If there were deep differences in public policy in post-Communist societies, then, it was not because of any widespread division of opinion over where these countries had to go or how to get there. The real issue was how to dispose of resources. The economies of the Communist states may have been distorted and inefficient, but they included vast and potentially lucrative assets: energy, minerals, arms, real property, communications media, transportation networks and much else. Moreover, in post-Soviet societies the only people who knew how to manage a laboratory, a farm or a factory—who had experience of international trade or of running a large institution—and who knew how to get things done were the Party's own people: the intelligentsia, the bureaucracy and the *nomenklatura*.

These were the people who would be in charge of their countries after 1989 no less than before—at least until a new, post-Communist generation could emerge. But they would now be operating under a new guise: instead of working for the Party they would be in various political parties competing for power; and instead of being employed by the state they would be independent operators in a competitive market for skills, goods and capital. When the state sold its interest in everything from drilling rights to apartment blocks, these were the men (and they were mostly men, Ukraine's future prime minister Yulia Timoshenko being a notable exception) who would do the selling—and the buying.

Capitalism, in the gospel that spread across post-Communist Europe, is about markets. And markets mean privatization. The fire-sale of publicly owned commodities in post-1989 eastern Europe had no historical precedent. The cult of privatization in western Europe that had gathered pace from the late Seventies (see Chapter 16) offered a template for the helter-skelter retreat from state ownership in the East; but otherwise they had very little in common. Capitalism, as it had

---

[13]Among a younger generation, business-oriented and impatient to escape their country's encumbering past, it even brought forth a new conformism to substitute for the wooden public language of Communism: uncritical adulation for the mantras of neo-classical economics blissfully unclouded by any familiarity with their social cost.

emerged in the Atlantic world and Western Europe over the course of four centuries, was accompanied by laws, institutions, regulations and practices upon which it was critically dependent for its operation and its legitimacy. In many post-Communist countries such laws and institutions were quite unknown—and dangerously underestimated by neophyte free-marketers there.

The result was privatization as kleptocracy. At its most shameless, in Russia under the rule of Boris Yeltsin and his friends, the post-transition economy passed into the hands of a small number of men who became quite extraordinarily rich—by the year 2004 thirty-six Russian billionaires ('oligarchs') had corralled an estimated $110 billion, one quarter of the country's entire domestic product. The distinction between privatization, graft and simple theft all but disappeared: there was so much—oil, gas, minerals, precious metals, pipelines—to steal and no-one and nothing to prevent its theft. Public assets and institutions were pulled apart and re-allocated to one another by officials extracting and securing quite literally anything that moved or could be legally re-assigned to private parties.

Russia was the worst case, but Ukraine came a close second. Kuchma and other politicians were elected with huge cash backing from 'businessmen' in the form of down payments on future income: in post-Soviet Ukraine, as these people well understood, power led to money, not the other way around. Public goods, state loans or subsidies passed directly from the hands of government to the pockets of a few clans, much of it then transiting on to private accounts overseas. The new 'capitalists' in these countries did not actually make anything; they merely laundered public assets for private benefit.

Nepotism flourished, much as it had under Communism but for far greater private gain: when Ukraine's Kryvorizhstal, one of the largest steel plants in the world—with 42,000 employees and an annual pre-tax profit of $300 million (in a country whose average income was $95 a month)—was belatedly put up for sale in June 2004, no-one in Kiev was surprised to learn that the successful 'bidder' was Viktor Pinchuk, one of the country's wealthiest businessmen and the son-in-law of the Ukrainian President.

In Romania and Serbia, state assets suffered a similar fate or else were not sold off at all, local political chieftains riding out the initial talk of privatization and preferring to maintain their power and influence the old way. Like Albanians at about the same time, Romanians seeking instant market gratification were offered pyramid schemes instead, promising huge short-term gains without risk. At its peak one such operation, the 'Caritas' scam, which ran from April 1992 to August 1994, had perhaps four million participants—nearly one in five of the Romanian population.

Like 'legitimate' privatization, these pyramid schemes (they were common in Russia, too) mostly functioned to channel private cash into mafias based in old Party networks and the former security services. Meanwhile, fourteen years after the fall of Ceaușescu, 66 percent of Romanian industry was still in state ownership, although some of the more profitable and attractive enterprises had changed hands.

Foreign investors remained for many years understandably wary of risking their capital in such countries: the prospect of substantial returns had to be offset against the chronic absence of legal protections.

Elsewhere in Central Europe the balance of risk favoured foreign investors, if only because the prospect of EU membership was accelerating the necessary institutional reform and legislation. Even so, much of the initial privatization in Hungary or Poland consisted either of the transformation of Communist-era black market activities into legitimate business; or else a quick sale of the more obviously viable bits of state enterprises to local entrepreneurs backed by foreign cash. Three years after the revolution only 16 percent of Poland's state-owned businesses had been sold into private hands. In the Czech Republic an ingenious voucher scheme, offering people the chance to purchase stock in state enterprises, was supposed to transform the citizenry into a nation of capitalists: but its main effect over the next few years was to lay the groundwork for future scandals and a political backlash against rampant 'profiteering'.

One reason for the distortions attendant upon privatization in post-Communist Europe was the virtual absence of Western engagement. To be sure, Moscow or Warsaw was initially awash in young American economists offering to teach their hosts how to build capitalism, and German firms in particular showed an early interest in relatively upscale Communist companies like the Czech car manufacturer Škoda.[14] But there was virtually no engagement by foreign governments, no Marshall Plan or anything remotely resembling it: except in Russia, where considerable sums in grants and loans flowed in from Washington to help shore up the Yeltsin regime—and flowed out again into the pockets of Yeltsin's friends and backers.

Instead, foreign investment resembled not the sustained post-World War Two effort that helped reconstruct Western Europe but rather the piecemeal private-sector involvement that had followed the Versailles settlement: invested in good times and withdrawn when the going got tough.[15] As in the past, therefore, eastern Europeans have had to compete with the West on a markedly uneven playing field, lacking local capital and foreign markets and able to export only low-margin foods and raw materials or else industrial and consumer goods kept cheap thanks to low wages and public subsidy.

Unsurprisingly, many new post-Communist governments were tempted, like their inter-war predecessors, to shield themselves against the political costs of this

---

[14]Giving rise to nationalist jitters at the prospect of Prague's re-absorption into a Greater German Co-Prosperity Sphere—and a popular joke: "I have some good news and some bad news about Czechoslovakia's post-Communist prospects." "What's the good news?" "The Germans are coming!" "And the bad news?" "The Germans are coming."

[15]A notable exception to this story is Estonia, which has benefitted hugely from its virtual adoption by its Scandinavian neighbours. In 1992, when it left the ruble zone, 92 percent of Estonia's trade was with the former Soviet Union. Five years later over three quarters of that trade was with the West, much of it across the Baltic.

situation by instituting protections—in this case, laws restricting foreign owner-ship of land and companies. Somewhat unreasonably castigated by foreign critics as 'nationalist', these echoes of earlier efforts at autarky predictably achieved little: by inhibiting outside investment and distorting the local market they merely tweaked the privatization process still further towards corruption.[16]

Thus for every crooked Russian oligarch with a second home in London or Cannes, or enthusiastic young Polish businessman with a BMW and a cell phone, there were millions of disgruntled pensioners and laid-off workers for whom the transition to capitalism was at best an ambiguous benefit—not to speak of the millions of peasants who could neither be redeployed nor rendered economically self-sustaining: in Poland by the end of the twentieth century agriculture generated only 3 percent of GDP—but still occupied one-fifth of the working population. Un-employment remained endemic in many places—and with the loss of a job went the cheap facilities and other benefits that had traditionally accompanied work in these countries. With prices rising steadily, whether from inflation[17] or in antici-pation of European entry, anyone on a fixed income or a state pension (which meant most of the teachers, doctors and engineers who had once been the pride of Socialism) had good cause to wax nostalgic for the past.

Many people in Eastern Europe—above all those over forty—complained bit-terly of what they had lost in material security and cheap board, lodging and serv-ices; but this did not mean that they were necessarily longing to return to Communism. As one fifty-year-old retired Russian military engineer living with her pensioner husband on $448 a month explained to foreign journalists in 2003: 'What we want is for our life to be as easy as it was in the Soviet Union, with the guaran-tee of a good, stable future and low prices—and at the same time this freedom that did not exist before'.

Opinion polls of Latvians, who would be horrified to imagine a return to Rus-sian rule, nevertheless suggest that peasants especially are convinced they were bet-ter off in Soviet times. And they may be right, and not only if they are peasants. In the late Eighties, before the revolutions, East Europeans were avid cinemagoers. By 1997 cinema attendance in Latvia had fallen by 90 percent. The same was true everywhere—in Bulgaria it was down 93 percent, in Romania it was down by 94 percent, in Russia it had fallen 96 percent. Interestingly, cinema attendance in Poland in the same years was only down by 77 percent, in the Czech Republic by 71 percent, in Hungary by 51 percent. In Slovenia it had hardly fallen at all. These data suggest a direct relationship between prosperity and film-going and confirm the explanation offered in one Bulgarian poll for the decline in local cinema at-

---

[16]And inefficiency—one irony of ritualized privatization in eastern Europe was that once collective farms were broken up into tiny plots they could no longer be worked by tractor but only by hand.
[17]It is estimated that inflation in post-Communist Ukraine reached an annual rate of 5,371 percent in 1993.

tendance: since the fall of Communism there was a better choice of films . . . but people could no longer afford the tickets.

In the circumstances, the difficult and incomplete economic transformation of Eastern Europe prompts the Johnsonian observation that though it was not done well, one is surprised to find it done at all. Much the same might be said of the transition to democracy. With the exception of Czechoslovakia, none of the formerly Communist societies between Vienna and Vladivostok had any living memory of genuine political freedom and many local commentators were pessimistic about the chances for pluralist politics. If capitalism without legal restraints descends readily into theft, then—in the absence of agreed and understood boundaries to public rhetoric and political competition—democracy, it was feared, risks slipping into competitive demagogy.

This was not an unreasonable fear. By concentrating power, information, initiative and responsibility into the hands of the party-state, Communism had given rise to a society of individuals not merely suspicious of one another and skeptical of any official claims or promises, but with no experience of individual or collective initiative and lacking any basis on which to make informed public choices. It was not by chance that the most important journalistic initiative in post-Soviet states was the appearance of newspapers devoted to providing hard information: *Facts and Arguments* in Moscow, *Facts* in Kiev.

It was older people who were least equipped to negotiate the transition to an open society. The younger generation had better access to information—from foreign television and radio and, increasingly, from the internet. But while this made many young voters in these countries more cosmopolitan and even sophisticated, it also opened a breach with their parents and grandparents. A survey of young Slovaks taken a decade after their country's independence revealed a clear generation gap. Young people were utterly disconnected from the pre-1989 past, of which they had little knowledge; conversely they complained that in the brave new world of post-Communist Slovakia their parents were adrift and helpless: they could offer neither help nor advice to their children.

This generation gap would have political consequences everywhere, with older and poorer voters proving periodically susceptible to the appeal of parties offering nostalgic or ultra-nationalist alternatives to the new liberal consensus. Predictably, this problem was worst in parts of the former Soviet Union, where the disruption and dislocation was worst and democracy hitherto unknown. Grindingly poor, insecure, and resentful at the conspicuous new wealth of a tiny minority, elderly—and not-so-elderly—voters in Russia and Ukraine especially were easily attracted to authoritarian politicians. Thus while it proved easy enough in post-Communist lands to invent model constitutions and democratic parties it was another matter altogether to forge a discriminating electorate. Initial elections everywhere tended to favour the liberal or right-of-center alliances that had brokered the overthrow of the old regime; but the backlash brought on by economic hardships and inevitable disappointments frequently worked to the advantage of the former Communists, now recycled in nationalist guise.

This transformation of the old *nomenklatura* was less bizarre than it might have appeared to outside observers. Nationalism and Communism had more in common with one another than either had with democracy: they shared, as it were, a political 'syntax'—while liberalism was another language altogether. If nothing else, Soviet Communism and traditional nationalists had a common foe—capitalism, or 'the West'—and their heirs would prove adept at manipulating a widespread envious egalitarianism ('at least back then we were *all* poor') into blaming post-Communist woes on foreign interference.

There was thus nothing especially incongruous about the rise of Corneliu Vadim Tudor, for example: a well-known literary sycophant at the court of Nicolae Ceauşescu who devoted himself to writing odes to the glory of the *Conducator* before switching from national communism to ultra-nationalism. In 1991, backed by émigré cash, he founded the Greater Romania Party, whose platform combined irredentist nostalgia with attacks on the Hungarian minority and openly espoused anti-Semitism. In the presidential elections of December 2000, one Romanian voter in three opted for Tudor over the only available alternative, the former Communist *apparatchik* Ion Iliescu.[18]

Even when nationalist politicians began as critics of Communism—as in the case of the Russian 'national-patriotic' movement *Pamyat* ('Memory')—they slipped comfortably enough into a symbiotic sympathy for the Soviet past, blending a sort of nationalist *ressentiment* with nostalgia for the Soviet heritage and its monuments. The same conflation of patriotic rhetoric with regret for the lost world of Soviet-style authoritarianism accounted for the popularity of the new nationalists in Ukraine, Belarus, Serbia and Slovakia—and has its counterparts in the various farmers' and 'popular' parties that sprang up in Poland at the end of the Nineties, notably Andrzej Lepper's widely supported Self-Defence Party.

Although recycled Communists made alliances everywhere with genuine nationalists[19], the appeal of outright nationalism proved strongest and most enduring in Russia. This was not surprising: in the words of Vladimir Zhirinovsky, a fiery new public figure who built his electoral appeal on unapologetic old-Russian xenophobia, 'The Russian people have become the most humiliated nation on the planet'. Whatever its limitations, the Soviet Union had been a world power: a territorial and cultural giant, the legitimate heir and extension of Imperial Russia. Its disintegration was a source of deep humiliation to older Russians, many of whom shared the resentment of the Soviet military at NATO's absorption of the Russian

---

[18]But Romania is perhaps unique. In the Bucharest mayoral elections of 1998 the Romanian Workers' Party blanketed the city with posters of Nicolae Ceauşescu. 'They shot me', the posters read. 'Do you live any better? Remember all I did for the Romanian people'.

[19]And even on occasion with unreconstructed Fascists, nostalgic for the better days of World War Two—notably in Croatia.

'near West' and their country's inability to prevent it. The wish to recover some international 'respect' drove much of Moscow's post-Soviet foreign policy and accounts both for the nature of the presidency of Vladimir Putin and the broad support on which Putin could draw, despite (and because of) his increasingly illiberal domestic policies.

For obvious reasons the citizens of Russia's former empire in central Europe were not disposed to nostalgia in this form. But the lost world of Communism held some appeal even in East Germany, where polls in the mid-'90s showed a widespread belief that, except for travel, the electronic media and freedom of expression, life had been better before 1989. In other countries even the old Communist-era media aroused a certain affection—in 2004 the most popular program on Czech television was re-runs of '*Major Zeman*', an early Seventies detective series whose scripts were little more than propaganda exercises for post-'68 'normalization'.

Only in the Czech Republic (together with France and the states of the former USSR) did the Communist Party brazenly retain its name. But in every post-Communist country of central Europe roughly one voter in five could be found supporting comparable 'anti-' parties: anti-American, anti-EU, anti-Western, anti-privatization . . . or more commonly all the above. In the Balkans especially, 'anti-Americanism' or 'anti-Europeanism' was typically a code for anti-capitalism, a cover for ex-Communists who could not openly express nostalgia for the old days but traded on it just the same in their disguised public pronouncements.

This protest vote indirectly illustrated the unavoidable consensus which bound the political mainstream: there was only one possible future for the region, and that was in the West, in the European Union, and in the global market, whatever it took. On these goals there was little to distinguish the major competing parties, all of which would win elections by criticizing the 'failed' policies of their opponents and then proceed to implement a strikingly similar program. The result in Central and Eastern Europe was a new 'wooden' language of public policy—'democracy', 'market', 'budget deficit', 'growth', 'competition'—of very little meaning or concern to many citizens.

Voters who wished to register their protest or express their pain were thus drawn to the margins. In the early Nineties observers saw in the rise in post-Communist Europe of national-populist fringe parties and their demagogic leaders a dangerously anti-democratic reaction, the atavistic retreat of a backward region imprisoned for half a century in a time-warp. In more recent years, however, the success of Jörg Haider in Austria, Jean-Marie Le Pen in France and their close counterparts everywhere from Norway to Switzerland has tended to dilute the patronizing tone of Western European commentary. Atavism is no respecter of frontiers.

The success of political democracy in many former Communist countries had ambiguous consequences for the intellectuals who had done so much to bring it about. Some, like Adam Michnik in Poland, maintained an influential voice through journalism. Others, like János Kis in Hungary, passed from intellectual dissent into parliamentary politics (in Kis's case as leader of the Free Democrats) only to move back into academic life after a few turbulent years in the public eye. But most of the opposition intellectuals of earlier years did not make a successful conversion into post-Communist politicians or public figures, except as transitional figureheads, and many who tried proved sadly inept. Václav Havel was unique—and even he was not particularly successful.

As Edmund Burke had dismissively observed of an earlier generation of revolutionary activists: 'The best were only men of theory'. Most of them were quite unprepared for the messy political and technical issues of the coming decade. They were also quite unprepared for the dramatic fall in the public status of intellectuals in general, as reading habits changed and a younger generation turned away from traditional sources of guidance and opinion. By the mid-Nineties some of the once-influential periodicals of an older intellectual generation had become sadly marginal.

Barbara Toruńczyck's *Zeszyty Literackie*, a widely admired literary journal published from Paris by a '68 generation Polish exile, had played a major role in sustaining Polish cultural debate before 1989. Now, after its triumphant establishment in the capital of its liberated homeland, it struggled to maintain a readership of 10,000. *Literární Noviný*, the oldest and most influential Czech cultural weekly, did barely better, with a circulation of less than 15,000 by 1994. These figures, pro-rated to population, would not have seemed so unworthy to the publishers of literary magazines and periodicals in most Western countries; but in Central Europe their increasingly marginal place represented a traumatic shift in cultural priorities.

One of the reasons for the decline of the intellectuals was that their much remarked-upon emphasis on the *ethics* of anti-Communism, the need to construct a morally aware civil society to fill the anomic space between the individual and the state, had been overtaken by the practical business of constructing a market economy. Within a few short years 'civil society' in Central Europe had become an archaic notion, of interest only to a handful of foreign sociologists. Something rather similar had happened after World War Two in western Europe (see Chapter 3), when the high moral tone of the wartime Resistance had been dispelled and displaced first by the practical business of reconstruction and then by the Cold War. But whereas French or Italian writers in those years still had a sizeable audience—thanks in part to their loudly advertised political engagement—their Hungarian or Polish counterparts were not so fortunate.

The intellectuals who *did* make a successful leap into democratic public life were usually 'technocrats'—lawyers or economists—who had played no conspicuous part in the dissenting community before 1989. Not having performed a hitherto heroic role they offered more reassuring models for their similarly un-heroic fellow citizens. Shortly after he succeeded Havel as Czech President in 2003, Václav Klaus put the point very bluntly in a presidential address: 'I am a bit like all of you. Neither a former communist nor a former dissident; neither a henchman nor a moralist, whose very presence on the scene is a reminder of the courage you did not have: your bad conscience.'

Allusions to bad conscience raised the troubling question of retribution—of what people had done in the Communist past and what (if anything) should happen to them now. This was to prove a traumatic dilemma for almost every post-Communist regime. On the one hand there was broad agreement, and not just among moralizing intellectuals, that political crimes committed in the Soviet-era should be brought to light and their perpetrators punished. Unless the truth about the Communist past was publicly acknowledged the already difficult transition to freedom would be made harder still: apologists for the old regime would whitewash its sins and people would forget what 1989 had been about.

On the other hand, Communists had been in government for over forty years in all these countries—fifty years in the Baltic states, seventy in the Soviet Union itself. The party-state had exercised a monopoly of power. Its laws, its institutions and its police had been the only force in the land. Who was to say, in retrospect, that Communists had not been the legitimate rulers? They had certainly been recognized as such by foreign governments, and no international court or tribunal had ever declared Communism to be a criminal regime. How, then, could someone be punished retroactively for obeying Communist laws or working for the Communist state?

Moreover, some of those who were most prominent in early calls for vengeance against Communist tyranny were of doubtful provenance themselves—anti-Communism in the confused mood of the early '90s often overlapped with a certain nostalgia for the regimes the Communists had replaced. Separating condemnation of Communism from rehabilitation of its Fascist predecessors was not always going to be easy. Many reasonable people conceded that it would be necessary to draw a line under the Stalinist era: it was too late to punish those who had collaborated in the coups and show trials and persecutions of the 1950s, and most of their victims were dead.

Such matters, it was felt, were best left for historians, who would now have access to archives and could get the story right for the benefit of future generations. Concerning the *post*-Stalinist decades, however, there was wide agreement that there ought to be some public reckoning with the most egregious crimes and criminals: Czech Communist leaders who had collaborated in the overthrow of the Prague Spring; Polish policemen responsible for the assassination of Father Popiełuszko (see Chapter 19); East German authorities who ordered the shooting of anyone trying to scale the Berlin Wall, and so on.

But this still left unresolved two much harder dilemmas. What should be done with former Communist Party members and police officials? If they were not accused of specific crimes, then should they suffer any punishment at all for their past acts? Should they be allowed to participate in public life—as policemen, politicians, even prime ministers? Why not? After all, many of them had cooperated actively in the dismantling of their own regime. But if not, if there were to be restrictions placed on the civic or political rights of such people, then how long should such restrictions apply and how far down the old *nomenklatura* should they reach? These questions were broadly comparable to those faced by Allied occupiers of post-war Germany trying to apply their program of de-Nazification—except that after 1989 the decisions were being taken not by an army of occupation but by the parties directly concerned.

This was one thorny problem. The second was in some ways more complicated still, and only emerged over the course of time. The Communist regimes did not merely force their rule upon a reluctant citizenry; they encouraged people to collude in their own repression, by collaborating with the security agencies and reporting the activities and opinions of their colleagues, neighbours, acquaintances, friends and relations. The scale of this subterranean network of spies and informers varied from country to country but it was present everywhere.

The consequence was that while the whole society thus fell under suspicion—who might not have worked for the police or the regime at some moment, even if only inadvertently?—by the same token it became hard to distinguish venal and even mercenary collaboration from simple cowardice or even the desire to protect one's family. The price of a refusal to report to the Stasi might be your children's future. The grey veil of moral ambiguity thus fell across many of the private choices of helpless individuals.[20] Looking back, who—save a handful of heroic and unwavering dissidents—could pass judgment? And it is striking that many of those same former dissidents—Adam Michnik prominent among them—were the most vigorously opposed to any retribution for their fellow citizens.

For all that these difficulties were common to every post-Communist state, each country dealt with them in its own way. In places where there never really was a transition—where Communists or their friends remained in power under a new nomenclature and with freshly laundered 'Western' agendas—the past remained untouched. In Russia, as in Ukraine or Moldova or what remained of Yugoslavia, the issue of retribution never really arose and high-ranking officials from the old regime were quietly recycled back into power: under Vladimir Putin, Communist-era *siloviki* (prosecutors, police, and military or security personnel) constituted over half the President's informal cabinet.

In Germany, on the other hand, revelations concerning the size and reach of the state security bureaucracy had astonished the nation. It turned out that in addition to its 85,000 full-time employees the Stasi had approximately 60,000 'unofficial collaborators', 110,000 regular informers and upwards of half a million 'part-time' informers, many of whom had no means of knowing that they even fell into such

---

[20]Though not, perhaps, across the self-serving moves of certain prominent writers—who would have risked little by declining their services: e.g. Christa Wolf, whose much-vaunted literary ambivalence appears somehow less admirable in the light of later revelations of her cooperation with the Stasi.

a category.[21] Husbands spied on wives, professors reported on students, priests informed on their parishioners. There were files on 6 million residents of former East Germany, one in three of the population. The whole society had in effect been infiltrated, atomized and polluted by its self-appointed guardians.

To lance the boil of mutual fear and suspicion, the Federal Government in December 1991 appointed a Commission under the former Lutheran minister Joachim Gauck to oversee the Stasi files and prevent their abuse. Individuals would be able to ascertain whether they had a 'file' and then, if they wished, come and read it. People would thus learn—sometimes with devastating domestic consequences—who had been informing on them; but the material would not be open to the public at large. This was an awkward compromise but, as it turned out, quite successful: by 1996, 1,145,000 people had applied to see their files. There was no way to undo the human damage, but because the Gauck Commission was trusted not to abuse its powers the information it controlled was hardly ever exploited for political advantage.

It was fear of just such exploitation that inhibited similar procedures elsewhere in Eastern Europe. In Poland, accusations of past collaboration became a familiar way of discrediting political opponents—in 2000, even Lech Wałesa was accused of collaborating with the former special services, though the charge never stuck. One post-Communist Interior Minister even threatened to publish the names of all his political opponents who were tarnished by the brush of collaboration; it was in anxious anticipation of just such behaviour that Michnik and others had favoured simply drawing a final line under the Communist past and moving on. Consistent with this view, Michnik even opposed efforts in 2001 to try the former Communist President Jaruselski (then aged 78) for giving orders back in 1970 to shoot striking workers. In 1989 the recent memory of martial law and its aftermath had made it seem unwise to open up the past and assess guilt; by the time it was safe to do so the opportunity had passed, popular attention was elsewhere and the quest for belated retroactive justice looked more like political opportunism.

In Latvia it was decreed that anyone with a record of KGB involvement would be barred from public office for ten years. From 1994 Latvian citizens were at liberty, following the German model, to see their own Communist-era police files; but the contents were made public only if a person ran for office or sought employment in law enforcement. In Bulgaria the new government, drawing on the practice of post-Vichy France, established tribunals with the authority to impose 'civic degradation' upon those guilty of certain offenses associated with the previous regime.

In Hungary, the benign role of the Communist Party in its transition out of

---

[21]By way of comparison, the Gestapo in 1941 had a staff of fewer than 15,000 to police the whole of greater Germany.

power made it hard to justify purging or punishing it for earlier sins—particularly since in post-Kádár Hungary the main point of contention was of course 1956, a date which would soon be ancient history for a majority of the population. In neighbouring Romania, where there were indeed ample recent grounds for retribution, efforts to mount a local version of the Gauck Commission foundered for some years on the firm opposition of the post-Communist political elite, many of whose luminaries (beginning with President Iliescu himself) would certainly be implicated in any serious interrogation of the Ceaușescu regime's activities. Eventually a 'National College for the Study of the "Securitate" Archives' was inaugurated, but it could never aspire to the authority of the German original.

In none of these countries was the problem of coming to terms with the Communist past resolved to everyone's satisfaction or with complete fairness. But in Czechoslovakia the solution that was adopted aroused controversy reaching well beyond the country's borders. Stalinism here had come later and lasted longer than elsewhere, and the ugly memory of 'normalization' was still very much alive. At the same time Communism had a firmer political basis in the Czech region than anywhere else in Eastern Europe. Finally, there was a certain national discomfort at the memory of Czechoslovakia's apparent serial failure to resist tyranny—in 1938, in 1948 and after 1968. For one reason or another, the whole country—as it seemed to its more uncompromising domestic critics—suffered from a bad conscience. Václav Klaus knew whereof he spoke.

The first post-Communist Czechoslovak legislation—a 1990 law rehabilitating everyone illegally sentenced between 1948 and 1989 and eventually paying out 100 million euros in compensation—provoked little debate. But it was followed by a 'lustration'[22] law (renewed for five years in 1996 and renewed again when it expired early in the twenty-first century) whose purpose was to vet all public officials or would-be public officials for links to the old security services. This legitimate-sounding objective led, however, to widespread opportunities for abuse. Many of the names found on the old secret police informer lists were, it transpired, merely 'candidates': men and women whom the regime was hoping to force into compliance. They included a number of the best-known Czech writers, some of them not even resident in the country.

The secret police lists soon found their way into the press, published and publicized by politicians and parliamentary candidates hoping to discredit their opponents. In the course of the mud-slinging even Havel was mentioned as a one-time candidate for recruitment into the police network of spies. And, as some critics had warned, while the secret police files furnished copious data about those they sought to recruit they were all but silent on the identities of the policemen doing the recruiting. A cartoon in the daily *Lidové Noviný* showed two men talking in front of

---

[22]From the Czech *lustrace*, meaning 'bringing to light', though the translation carries purgative connotations as well.

the parliament in Prague: I am not worried about lustrations', says one of them.' I was not an informer. 'I was just giving orders'.[23]

Lustration was not a penal procedure, but it did cause acute embarrassment to many of its victims, unjustly 'named and shamed'. More seriously, perhaps, it was from the outset an overtly political device. It was one of the issues on which the old Civic Forum alliance broke up—longstanding dissidents (Havel included) opposed the new law while Klaus enthusiastically supported it as a way 'to clarify who stands where' (and embarrass his ex-dissident critics, some of them erstwhile reform Communists). It is noteworthy that Vladimír Mečiar in Slovakia also opposed the lustration law, not least because of his own widely rumored links to the former secret police—though once he had taken his country into independence he made copious use of the information in police files for his own political ends.

In the first twelve years of its application, the lustration law did relatively little direct damage. It was applied to some 300,000 people who applied for clearance: an estimated 9,000 of them did not pass, a strikingly small number compared to the half a million Czechs and Slovaks who lost their jobs or were purged from the Party after 1968. But the more lasting impact of the legislation was the bad taste it left behind, contributing to a widespread cynicism in Czech society about the way in which the 'velvet revolution' had played itself out. 'Lustration' in the Czech Republic seemed to be more about legitimizing an incoming elite than dealing honestly with the outgoing past.

In July 1993 the Czech parliament adopted a 'Law on the Illegality of and Resistance to the Communist Regime', in effect declaring the Communist Party a criminal organization. In theory this should have criminalized millions of former Party members, but its impact was purely rhetorical and no action followed. Far from discrediting Communism and legitimizing its overthrow, the law merely reinforced the skeptical detachment of the public at whom it was directed. Ten years after the law was passed, opinion polls revealed that one Czech voter in five favored the unreconstructed (and perfectly legal) Communist Party, which remained the largest political organization in the country, with 160,000 members.

---

[23]I am indebted to Dr Jacques Rupnik for the reference.

XXII

The Old Europe—and the New

'You have to wonder why Europe does not seem capable of taking decisive
action in its own theatre'.
Richard Holbrooke

'*Si c'était à refaire, je commençerais par la culture*' ('If I were starting over, I
would begin with culture'.)
Jean Monnet

'It is always possible to bind together a considerable number of people in
love, so long as there are other people left over to receive the
manifestations of their aggressiveness'.
Sigmund Freud

'What is the explanation of this curious combination of the permanent
unemployment of eleven percent of the population with a general sense of
comparative prosperity on the part of the bulk of the population?'
Beatrice Webb (1925)

The fissile political temper of the Nineties was not confined to the countries of the
former Communist East. The same urge to escape the bonds of centralized rule—
or else to relinquish responsibility for impoverished fellow citizens in distant
provinces—was felt in the West. From Spain to the United Kingdom the established
territorial units of Western Europe were subjected to extensive administrative decentralization, though they all managed more or less to retain at least the form of
the conventional national state.

In some places this centrifugal propensity had already surfaced decades earlier,
as we saw in Chapter 16. In Spain, where the longstanding demand for autonomy
in Catalonia or the Basque region had been recognized by the new constitution,
Catalonia especially had emerged within a generation as virtually a state-within-
a-state, with its own language, institutions and governing councils. Thanks to a 1983
Law of Linguistic Normalization (*sic*), Catalan was to become the 'dominant language of instruction'; ten years later the Generalitat (Catalan parliament) decreed
the exclusive use of Catalan in kindergarten and infant schools. Not surprisingly,
even though Castilian Spanish remained in use everywhere, many younger people
were more comfortable speaking Catalan.

None of the other Spanish regions was to acquire quite this level of national distinctiveness; but then none of them carried the same weight within the country as a whole. In 1993 Catalonia, one of seventeen Spanish regions, accounted for a fifth of the country's GNP. Over a quarter of all foreign investment in Spain came to Catalonia, much of it to the flourishing provincial capital, Barcelona; per capita income in the province as a whole was more than 20 percent above the national average. If Catalonia were an independent country it would count among the more prosperous states on the European continent.

One reason for the rise of a distinctive Catalan identity was an easily stoked resentment at the substantial contribution Catalans were expected to make to the national exchequer, thanks in part to the setting up in 1985 of an Inter-Territorial Compensation Fund to assist Spain's poorest regions. But Catalonia—like the Basque country, Galicia, Navarre and other newly assertive autonomous provinces—also benefited from the hollowing out of 'Spanishness'. Franco had exploited to exhaustion the traditional gamut of national claims—the glory of Empire, the honour of the military, the authority of the Spanish Church—and after his fall many Spaniards had scant interest in the rhetoric of heritage or tradition.

Indeed, rather like an earlier generation of post-authoritarian Germans, the Spanish were decidedly inhibited about 'talking national'. Regional or provincial identification, on the other hand, was unpolluted by authoritarian association: on the contrary, it had been a favorite target of the old regime and could thus credibly be presented as an integral aspect of the transition to democracy itself. This association between autonomy, separatism and democracy was less clear in the Basque case, where ETA pursued its murderous path (even mounting assassination attempts in 1995 on both the king and the prime minister). Moreover, whereas the six million Catalans were prospering, the old industrial districts of the Basque country were in decline. Unemployment was endemic and income levels in the region were lower than in Catalonia, hovering close to the national average.

If Basque nationalists failed to capitalize on these problems it was in large measure because many of the region's two million inhabitants were new to the area—by 1998 only one person in four could even speak *Euskera*, the Basque language. Not surprisingly, they showed little interest in separatist movements: just 18 percent of Basques expressed support for independence, preferring the regional autonomy they had already secured. Even a majority of the Basque National Party's voters felt the same way. As for Herri Batasuna, the political wing of ETA, it was losing votes to moderate autonomists and even mainstream Spanish parties. By the end of the decade it had declined into an all-purpose outsiders' party for disaffected Greens, feminists, Marxists and anti-globalizers.

In Spain, the splintering of the nation-state was driven by past memories. In Italy it was more often the product of present discontents. The traditionally dissident regions of Italy were in the far north: frontier zones where the local population had been assigned Italian identity within living memory—often as a result of war and

London, Dublin and even Washington to intervene with more energy than they had mustered hitherto and press at least an interim agreement on the warring parties. Whether the Good Friday Agreement, signed in April 1998, could resolve the national question in Ireland remained unclear. The interim solution on which both sides reluctantly concurred left much unresolved. Indeed, the terms of the accord brokered by the Prime Ministers of Ireland and the UK, with assistance from President Clinton—local self-government by an Assembly based in Ulster, with guarantees of representation for the Catholic minority, an end to the Protestant monopoly of police and other powers, confidence-building measures across the two communities and a standing Inter-Governmental Conference to oversee implementation—contained much that could have been imagined, with good will on all sides, twenty years earlier. But as an armistice in Ireland's Hundred Years War the agreement seemed likely to hold for a while. Not for the first time in such matters, the ageing radicals at the head of the insurgency appeared to have been won over by the prospect of office.

Moreover the Republic of Ireland itself underwent an unprecedented socioeconomic transformation in the course of the 1990s and now bore little discernable resemblance to the 'Eire' of nationalist imaginings. From the perspective of youthful Dublin, absorbed in its newfound role as a multi-cultural, low-tax outrider for post-national Euro-prosperity, the sectarian preoccupations of the Provisional IRA had come to be regarded in much the same way as the imperial, unionist obsessions of the Orange Order were seen in London: bizarre antiquarian relics of another age.

To anyone familiar with their earlier history, the new politics of sub-national particularism in the larger states of western Europe might appear simply as the reversion to type following the centralizing detour of the previous century. Even the outstanding contemporary European exception to this pattern actually illustrates the rule: Germany, the largest European state west of the former Soviet Union, did *not* experience a comparable separatist resurgence. This was not because of any peculiarities of its history but because post-Nazi Germany was *already* a truly federal republic.

Whether they were mapped directly on to ancient states (as in the case of Bavaria) or were newly conceived territorial combinations of once-independent principalities and republics (like Baden-Württemburg or NordRhein-Westfalen), the *Länder* of modern Germany exercised a considerable degree of financial and administrative autonomy in many of those aspects of government that impinge most directly upon people's daily lives: education, culture, the environment, tourism and local public radio and television. To the limited extent that *territorially*-defined identity politics might have appealed to Germans—and here Germany's distinctive past probably *did* play an inhibiting role—the *Länder* thus offered a serviceable surrogate.

Indeed it was not in western Europe's largest country but instead in one of its smallest that the politics of national separatism took their most concentrated form. Belgium, a country the size of Wales with a population density exceeded only by the adjacent Netherlands, was the one West European state whose internal schisms bore some resemblance to contemporary developments in the post-Communist east. Its story may thus cast light on why, after the separatist wave of the late twentieth century had receded, the national states of *Western* Europe remained intact.

By the 1990s the towns and valleys of Wallonia were sunk into post-industrial decline. Coal mining, steel making, slate and metallurgical industries, textile production—the traditional cradle of Belgium's industrial wealth—had virtually disappeared: Belgian coal production in 1998 was less than two million tons per year, down from twenty-one million tons in 1961. In what was once Europe's most profitable industrial region there remained only the decrepit mills of the Meuse valleys above Liège and the gaunt, silent mining installations around Mons and Charleroi. Most of the former miners, steel-workers and their families in these communities now depended upon a welfare system administered from the country's bi-lingual capital and paid for—as it seemed to Flemish nationalists—out of the taxes of gainfully employed northerners.

For Flanders had boomed. In 1947 over 20 percent of the Flemish workforce was still in agriculture; fifty years later fewer than 3 percent of Dutch-speaking Belgians derived their income from the land. In the decade from 1966 to 1975 the Flemish economy grew at the unprecedented rate of 5.3 percent per annum; even during the economic trough of the late Seventies and early Eighties it continued to grow, at a rate nearly twice that of Wallonia. Unencumbered by old industry or an unemployable workforce, towns like Antwerp and Ghent flourished with the growth of services, technology and commerce, aided by their location athwart Europe's 'golden banana', running from Milan to the North Sea. There were now more Dutch speakers than French speakers in the country (by a proportion of three to two), and they produced and earned more per capita. The Belgian north had overtaken the south as the privileged, dominant region—a transformation accompanied by a crescendo of demands from the Flemish for political gains to match their newfound economic dominance.

Belgium, in short, combined all the ingredients of nationalist and separatist movements across Europe: an ancient territorial division[1] reinforced by an equally venerable and seemingly insuperable linguistic gulf (whereas many residents of the Dutch-speaking regions have at least a passive acquaintance with French, most Walloons speak no Dutch) and underpinned by stark economic contrasts. And there was a further complication: for most of Belgium's short history the impoverished communities of rural Flanders had been dominated by their urban, in-

---

[1] Julius Caesar's *Gallia Belgica* lay athwart the line that was to separate Gallo-Roman territories from the Franks and mark the boundary thenceforth demarcating Latinate, French-dominated Europe from the Germanic north.

Belgium in 2005

Map legend:

- Dutch-speaking areas
- French-speaking areas
- German-speaking areas
- Language-area boundary
- Regional boundary
- International boundary
- City
- Brussels

Scale:
0 10 20 30 miles
0 10 20 30 40 50 kilometres

Map labels:

NETHERLANDS
GERMANY
LUXEMBOURG
FRANCE

FLANDERS
WEST-VLAANDEREN
OOST-VLAANDEREN
ANTWERPEN
LIMBURG
VLAAMS-BRABANT
BRABANT-WALLON
WALLONIA
HAINAULT
NAMUR
LIÈGE
LUXEMBOURG
BRUSSELS

Cities: Oostende, Zeebrugge, Brugge, Ypres, Kortrijk, Gent, St-Niklaas, Antwerpen, Turnhout, Mechelen, Hasselt, Maastricht, Leuven, Liège, Namur, Charleroi, Mons, Arlon

Surrounding cities: Dunkerque, Lille, Charleville-Mézières, St-Quentin, Laon, Aachen, Trier, Luxembourg, Essen, Duisburg, Düsseldorf, Solingen, Leverkusen, Cologne, Bonn, Krefeld, Neuss, Mönchengladbach, Eindhoven dustrialized, French-speaking Walloon compatriots. Flemish nationalism had been shaped by resentment at the obligation to use French, at the French-speakers' apparent monopoly of power and influence, at the francophone élite's arrogation to itself of all the levers of cultural and political authority.

Flemish nationalists, then, had traditionally taken for themselves a role comparable to that of Slovaks in pre-divorce Czechoslovakia—even to the extent of actively collaborating with the occupiers during World War Two in the forlorn hope of some crumbs of separatist autonomy from the Nazi table. But by the 1960s the economic roles had been reversed: Flanders was now presented by its nationalist politicians not in the image of backward, under-privileged Slovakia but rather as Slovenia (or—as they might prefer—Lombardy): a dynamic modern nation trapped in an anachronistic and dysfunctional state.

These two self-ascribed identities—repressed linguistic minority and frustrated economic dynamo—were now *both* woven into the fabric of Flemish separatist politics, such that even after the old injustices had been swept away and the Dutch-speaking provinces of the north had long since won the right to the use of their own language in public affairs, the remembered resentments and slights simply attached themselves to new concerns instead, bequeathing to Belgian public policy debates an intensity—and a venom—which the issues alone could never explain.

One of the crucial symbolic moments in the 'language war' came in the Sixties— fully half a century after Dutch had been officially approved for use in Flemish schools, courts and local government, and four decades after its use there was made mandatory—when Dutch-speaking students at the University of Leuven (Louvain) objected to the presence of French-speaking professors at a university situated within the Dutch-speaking province of Flanders-Brabant. Marching to the slogan of '*Walen buiten!*' ('Walloons Out!') they succeeded in breaking apart the university, whose francophone members headed south into French-speaking Brabant-Wallon and established there the University of Louvain-la-Neuve (in due course the university library, too, was divided and its holdings redistributed, to mutual disadvantage).

The dramatic events at Leuven—a curiously parochial and chauvinist echo of contemporary student protests elsewhere—brought down a government and led directly to a series of constitutional revisions (seven in all) over the course of the ensuing thirty years. Although devised by moderate politicians as concessions to satisfy the demands of the separatists, the institutional re-arrangements of Belgium were always understood by the latter as mere stepping stones on the road to ultimate divorce. In the end neither side quite achieved its aims, but they did come close to dismantling the Belgian unitary state.

The outcome was byzantine in its complexity. Belgium was sub-divided into three 'Regions': Flanders, Wallonia, and 'Brussels-Capital', each with its own elected parliament (in addition to the national parliament). Then there were the three formally instituted 'Communities': the Dutch-speaking, the French-speaking, and the German-speaking (the latter representing the approximately 65,000 German speakers who live in eastern Wallonia near the German border). The communities, too, were assigned their own parliaments.

The regions and the linguistic communities don't exactly correspond—there are German speakers in Wallonia and a number of French-speaking towns (or parts of towns) within Flanders. Special privileges, concessions, and protections were established for all of these, a continuing source of resentment on all sides. Two of the regions, Flanders and Wallonia, are effectively unilingual, with the exceptions noted. Brussels was pronounced officially bilingual, even though at least 85 percent of the population speaks French.

In addition to the regional and linguistic Communities, Belgium was also divided into ten provinces (five each in Flanders and Wallonia). These, too, were assigned administrative and governing functions. But in the course of the various constitutional revisions real authority came increasingly to lie either with the region (in matters of urbanism, environment, the economy, public works, transport and external commerce) or the linguistic community (education, language, culture and some social services).

The outcome of all these changes was comically cumbersome. Linguistic correctness (and the constitution) now required, for example, that all national governments, whatever their political color, be 'balanced' between Dutch- and French-speaking ministers, with the prime minister the only one who has to be bilingual (and who is therefore typically from Flanders). Linguistic equality on the Cour d'Arbitrage (Constitutional Court) was similarly mandated, with the presidency alternating annually across the language barrier. In Brussels, the four members of the executive of the capital region would henceforth sit together (and speak in the language of their choice) to decide matters of common concern; but for Flemish or Francophone 'community' affairs they would sit separately, two by two.

As a consequence Belgium was no longer one, or even two, states but an uneven quilt of overlapping and duplicating authorities. To form a government was difficult: it required multi-party deals within and across regions, 'symmetry' between national, regional, community, provincial, and local party coalitions, a working majority in both major language groups, and linguistic parity at every political and administrative level. And when a government *was* formed it had little initiative: even foreign policy—in theory one of the last remaining responsibilities of the national government—was effectively in the hands of the regions, since for contemporary Belgium it mostly means foreign trade agreements and these are a regional prerogative.

The politics of this constitutional upheaval were just as convoluted as the institutional reforms themselves. On the Flemish side, extreme nationalist and separatist parties emerged to press for the changes and benefit from the new opportunities to which they gave rise. When the Vlaams Blok, spiritual heir to the wartime ultranationalists, rose to become the leading party in Antwerp and some Dutch-speaking suburbs north of Brussels, the more traditional Dutch-speaking parties felt obliged to adopt more sectarian positions in order to compete.

Similarly, in Wallonia and Brussels, politicians from the French-speaking mainstream parties adopted a harder 'communitarian' line, the better to accommodate Walloon voters who resented Flemish domination of the political agenda. As a result, all the mainstream parties were eventually forced to split along linguistic and community lines: in Belgium the Christian Democrats (since 1968), the Liberals (since 1972), and the Socialists (since 1978) all exist in duplicate, with one party of each type for each linguistic community. The inevitable result was a further deepening of the rift between the communities, as politicians now addressed only their own 'kind'.[2]

A high price was thus paid to mollify the linguistic and regional separatists. In the first place, there was an economic cost. It was not by chance that by the end of the twentieth century Belgium had the highest ratio of public debt to gross domestic product in Western Europe—it is expensive to duplicate every service, every loan, every grant, every sign. The established practice of using public money (including EU regional grants) on a proportional basis to reward clients of the various community 'pillars' was now applied to the politics of the language community: ministers, state secretaries, their staffs, their budgets and their friends are universal, but only in Belgium does each come attached to a linguistic *doppelganger*.

By the end of the century 'Belgium' had taken on a decidedly *pro forma* quality. Entering the country by road, a traveler could be forgiven for overlooking the rather apologetic signpost inscribed with a diminutive 'België' or 'Belgique'. But visitors could hardly miss the colorful placard informing them of the province (Liège, say, or West-Vlaanderen) that they had just entered, much less the information board (in Dutch or French but not both) indicating that they were in Flanders or Wallonia. It is as though the conventional arrangements had been handily inverted: the country's international borders were a mere formality, but its internal frontiers were imposing and very real. Why, then, did Belgium not simply come apart?

There are three factors that help account for Belgium's improbable survival, and more broadly for the persistence of all the states of Western Europe. In the first place, with the passing of generations and the implementation of constitutional reforms, the separatist case lost its urgency. The old communitarian 'pillars'— hierarchically organized social and political networks that substituted for the nation-state—were already in decline. A younger generation of Belgians was prov-

---

[2]The main newspapers, *Le Soir* and *De Standaard*, have almost no readers outside the French- and Dutch-speaking communities respectively. As a result, neither takes much trouble to report news from the other half of the country. When someone speaks Dutch on Walloon television (and vice-versa) subtitles are provided. Even the automatic information boards on interregional trains switch back and forth between Dutch and French (or to both, in the case of Brussels) as they cross the regional frontiers. It is only partly a jest to say that English is now the common language of Belgium.

ing far less susceptible to appeals based on sectarian affinity even if older politicians were slow to appreciate the fact.

The decline in religious practice, the accessibility of higher education, and the move from countryside to town loosened the grip of the traditional parties. For obvious reasons this was especially true of the 'new' Belgians: the hundreds of thousands of second- and third-generation immigrants from Italy, Yugoslavia, Turkey, Morocco or Algeria. Like the new Basques, these people have pressing concerns of their own and little interest in the dusty agendas of ageing separatists. Opinion polls through the Nineties indicated that most people, even in Flanders, no longer put regional or language issues at the head of their concerns.

Secondly, Belgium was *rich*. The obvious difference between Belgium and other, less fortunate parts of Europe where nationalists were able successfully to exploit communal sensibilities is that for the vast majority of residents of modern Belgium life was both tranquil and materially sufficient. The country is at peace—if not with itself then at least with everyone else—and the same prosperity that underwrote the 'Flemish miracle' also attenuated the politics of linguistic resentment. This observation applies with equal force to Catalonia or even to parts of Scotland, where the more extreme exponents of the case for national independence saw their arguments steadily defanged by the demobilizing effects of unaccustomed affluence.

The third reason for the survival of Belgium—and of Western Europe's other internally fragmented nation-states—has less to do with economics than with geography, though the two are closely related. If Flanders—or Scotland—could in the end remain comfortably part of Belgium or the UK it was not because they lacked the intensity of national sentiment that appeared to have re-surfaced in former Communist lands. Quite the contrary: the desire for self-rule was palpably stronger in Catalonia, say, than in Bohemia; and the gulf separating Flamands from Walloons was far wider than that between Czechs and Slovaks or even Serbs and Croats. What made the difference was the fact that the states of Western Europe were no longer free-standing national units with a monopoly of authority over their subjects. They were also and increasingly part of something else as well.

The formal mechanism for a move towards full European *Union* was set out in the Single European Act (SEA) of 1987; but what really drove the process forward was the end of the Cold War. The SEA had committed the twelve members of the Community to achieving by 1992 the full and free circulation of goods, services, capital and people—hardly a breakthrough, since these same objectives were already envisaged in principle decades before. It was the Maastricht Treaty of that year, and its successor Treaty of Amsterdam five years later, that propelled the Union's members into a truly novel set of institutional and financial arrangements, and these were the direct outcome of radically changed external circumstances.

From Community to Union: The EU 1957–2003

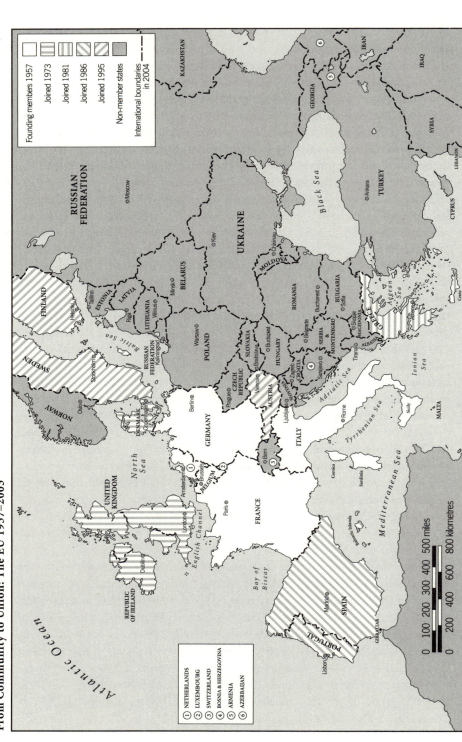

Legend:
- Founding members 1957
- Joined 1973
- Joined 1981
- Joined 1986
- Joined 1995
- Non-member states
- International boundaries in 2004

1. NETHERLANDS
2. LUXEMBOURG
3. SWITZERLAND
4. BOSNIA & HERZEGOVINA
5. ARMENIA
6. AZERBAIJAN

Scale: 0 100 200 300 400 500 miles
0 200 400 600 800 kilometres

At Maastricht, it was the much-publicized agreement to establish a common European currency that caught public attention. The French, to overcome their anxiety at German unification, bound the Federal Republic firmly into the 'West' by getting Bonn to agree to abandon the *Deutschmark* for a single European currency unit—the *euro*—and by committing the enlarged German state to operating within the constraints of a European Union bound by an ever-denser mesh of laws, rules and agreements Bonn, in return, insisted that the new currency be a carbon copy of the old *Deutschmark*, regulated—like the German currency—by an autonomous board of central bankers and committed to the fiscal principles of the German central bank: low inflation, tight money, and minimal deficits. The German negotiators—wary of the profligate tendencies of 'Club Med' countries like Italy or Spain—imposed draconian conditions for membership of the new currency, with the European Commission authorized to impose fines upon reprobate governments.

At Bonn's behest, Europe's finance ministers would thus be bound, Ulysses-like, to the euro-mast: unable to respond to the Siren-calls of voters and politicians for easier money and increased public spending. These terms, designed to insure that the new euro would be as inflation-proof as the *Deutschmark* itself, were not universally popular—in the poorer member states it was widely and rightly feared that they would constrain public policy and perhaps even prevent growth. And so, in order to make the Maastricht conditions more palatable, cash bonuses were made available to recalcitrant governments: Jacques Delors, the Commission President, all but bribed the finance ministers of Greece, Spain, Portugal and Ireland, promising large increases in EU structural funds in return for their signatures on the Treaty.

The UK and Denmark, meanwhile, signed the main body of the Treaty but opted out of the proposed common currency—partly in anticipation of its economically restrictive impact; partly because of its symbolic resonance in nations already more reluctant than most to abandon the trappings of sovereignty to transnational agencies; and in the case of the UK because—as so often in the past—the march to Union was regarded with acute misgivings as a further step towards a European super state.[3]

To be sure, the Maastricht Treaty made much play with 'subsidiarity'—a sort of Occam's Razor for eurocrats, stating that 'the Union does not take action (except in the areas which fall within its exclusive competence) unless it is more effective than action taken at national, regional or local level'. But even this had different meanings for different ears: in France it meant limiting the power of supernational bodies beyond Paris's control; for the Germans, it implied special privileges and

---

[3]The more historically disposed perhaps called to mind the passage in the *Mémorial de Sainte-Hélène* by the Comte de Las Cases, where the exiled Napoléon Bonaparte envisages a future 'association européenne' with 'one code, one court, one currency'.

powers for regional governments; for the British it represented a device for block-ing institutional integration.

Maastricht had three significant side-effects. One of them was the unforeseen boost it gave to NATO. Under the restrictive terms of the Treaty it was clear (as the French at least had intended) that the newly liberated countries of eastern Europe could not possibly join the European Union in the immediate future—neither their fragile legal and financial institutions nor their convalescent economies were remotely capable of operating under the strict fiscal and other regulations the Union's members had now imposed upon all present and future signatories.

Instead, it was suggested in the corridors of Brussels that Poland, Hungary and their neighbours might be offered early membership of NATO as a sort of com-pensation: an interim prize. The symbolic value of extending NATO in this way was obviously considerable, which is why it was immediately welcomed in the new candidate member-states. The practical benefits were less obvious (unlike the dam-age to relations with Moscow which was real and immediate). But because Wash-ington had reasons of its own for favouring the expansion of the North Atlantic Defense community, a first group of central European nations was duly admitted to NATO a few years later.[4]

The second impact was on European public awareness. The Maastricht Treaty provoked an unprecedented level of interest in what had hitherto been the ob-scure workings of the European Union and its anonymous bureaucracy. Even though the Treaty was approved in every country where it was put to a national vote (albeit by just 50.1 percent in the French case) it aroused sufficient opposition to place the question of 'Europe' on domestic political agendas, often for the first time. For four decades, the institutions and rules of a new continental system had been quietly designed and decided in obscure Benelux towns with no reference to public wishes or democratic procedure. Those days, it appeared, were over.

The third consequence of Maastricht was that it cleared the way for the coming together not, indeed, of Europe, but at least of its western half. The end of the Cold War, and the EU's commitment to a single market, removed the impediments to membership for the remaining members of the old European Free Trade Area.[5] Sweden, Finland and Austria all duly applied, no longer constrained by their com-mitment to neutrality (or, in the Finnish case, by the need to maintain good rela-tions with Moscow) and increasingly nervous at being left out of the common European space.

The accession negotiations with the new applicants were completed in just three

---

[4]Poland, Hungary and the Czech Republic joined in 1999, just in time to be (somewhat reluctantly) com-mitted to NATO's engagement in Kosovo. Bulgaria, Romania, Estonia, Latvia, Lithuania, Slovakia and Slovenia were admitted in 2004.
[5]The economic recession of the early Nineties also helped, contributing to a widespread view in Swe-den especially that the country's exporters could not survive without unrestricted access to the Euro-pean market.

'easy' cases: small countries like Slovenia or Hungary, contiguous to the Union's existing borders and with relatively modernized economies, which posed only a limited challenge to the EU's institutional framework and its budget. But it soon became clear that this might be politically imprudent—left out in the cold Romania, or Poland, could drift into dangerously undemocratic waters—and so, beginning in 1998, the European Union officially initiated the accession process of all ten eastern European applicants together with Cyprus. Malta was added to the list shortly afterwards. Turkey, however, was held back.

From this point the enlargement took on a dynamic of its own, notwithstanding continuing misgivings on the part of a number of existing EU members and, to judge from opinion polls, widespread lack of enthusiasm among their populations. Bilateral accession negotiations were set in motion, first with a presumptive inner core of candidates: Cyprus, the Czech Republic, Estonia, Hungary, Poland and Slovenia; and then, a year later, with the rest: Bulgaria, Romania, Slovakia, Latvia, Lithuania and Malta. Poland's presence in the first group, in spite of the economic difficulties it posed, was explained by its size and prominence. Slovakia, conversely, was 'relegated' to the second tier in response to the stagnation and corruption wrought there by Mečiar's authoritarian rule—and as a warning and example to others.

There followed five years of intense and sometimes acrimonious negotiations. 'Brussels' descended upon the capitals of all the candidate countries, showering them with advisors, recommendations, examples, programmes and instructions in an effort to bring their institutions, laws, regulations, practices and civil services up to a minimum standard compatible with those of the Union. The applicants, in turn, pressed as hard as they dared for assurances that they would have free access to EU consumers, while defending their domestic market from being overwhelmed by more attractive and efficient goods and services from the West.

The struggle was decidedly unequal. Whereas the EU was the longstanding and openly avowed object of Eastern desires, the putative new members could offer little in return except the promise of good behaviour. And thus it was agreed that while the new members would be accorded a few limited concessions—among them temporary restraints upon foreign purchases of land, a sensitive political issue—they would have to accept that the EU, despite its commitment to a single market, was going to impose considerable restrictions upon their own export of goods and, especially, people.

In response to wildly exaggerated estimates of likely population flows (one European Commission report published in 2000 prophesied an annual exodus of 335,000 from the ten eastern accession states if the frontiers were opened without restriction), most of the Western member-states insisted on quotas being placed on the number of eastern Europeans who could move to the West—in blatant disregard of the spirit and indeed the letter of a decade of proclamations and treaties. Germany, Austria and Finland imposed strict limits for two years with an option to extend these for a further five. Belgium, Italy and Greece followed suit. Only the UK and Ireland declared their willingness to conform to the 'open door' principles of the Union—while announcing that welfare benefits for work-seekers from Eastern Europe would be kept to a minimum.

The eastward extension of agricultural subsidies and other benefits was also placed within strict limits. In part, as the Commission's *Transition Report 2003* put it, this was because of 'questions about the accession countries' capacities to absorb and use efficiently the post-accession grants from the EU's cohesion and structural funds'. But the main reason was simply to hold down the cost of enlargement and minimize competition for Western producers. Not until 2013 would East European farmers get the same subsidies as those already being paid out in the West— by which time, it was hoped, most of them would have retired or gone out of business.

By the time the negotiations were complete, the terms agreed and the 97,000 pages of the Union's *acquis communautaire* duly incorporated into the governing codes of the applicant states, the actual enlargement itself came as something of an anti-climax. Having waited fifteen years to join, most of the new states could be forgiven for lacking the enthusiasm they might have exhibited a decade earlier. In any case, many of the practical benefits of Western engagement had already been discounted—notably in car manufacturing, where former Communist states had a ready supply of cheap, skilled labour and in which companies like Volkswagen, Renault and Peugeot-Citroën invested heavily during the Nineties. Between 1989 and 2003 the cumulative total of foreign direct investment for Eastern Europe as a whole had reached $117 billion.

By the early twenty-first century, foreign investment in former Communist Europe was actually tailing off. Ironically, this was largely a result of the coming EU enlargement. Once they were inside the Union it would certainly be easier to do business in and with countries like Poland or Estonia. And they in turn would be able to sell more to the West: Poland expected to double its food exports to the EU within three years of joining. But these were the fruits of relative backwardness. Once they were inside the EU, wages and other costs in the countries of Eastern Europe would begin to rise to Western levels. The region's cost advantage over factories in India, or Mexico, would be lost. Profit margins—at least in the manufacturing sector—would start to fall.

Meanwhile, thanks to the heavy cost of unraveling the Communist economies, East Europe on the eve of accession remained far behind the countries of the EU. Per capita GDP even in the most prosperous new member states was far below their Western neighbours: in Slovenia it stood at 69 percent of the EU average, in the Czech Republic at 59 percent, in Hungary 54 percent. In Poland it was just 41 percent, in Latvia, the poorest new member, 33 percent. Even if the economies of the new EU states kept growing on average 2 percent faster than those of the existing members[7], it would take Slovenia twenty-one years to catch up with France. For Lithuania the time lag would be fifty-seven years. The citizens of former-Communist states had no access to such data, of course. But most had few illusions about the difficulties ahead. When Czechs were asked, in a series of opinion polls in 2000, how long they thought it would be before their situation 'improved', 30 percent of respondents answered 'within five years'; 30 percent answered 'in ten years'; 30 percent answered 'fifteen years or more'; and 10 percent said 'never'.

Nonetheless, for all the justified skepticism of the beneficiaries, the formal implications of the EU's 'big-bang' enlargement were real enough. When the accession treaty, signed in Athens in April 2003, came into force on May 1st 2004, the European Union grew at a single stroke from fifteen to twenty-five members (Bulgaria and Romania were held back, their accession anticipated for 2007). Its population increased by one-fifth (though its economy was expanded by less than 5 percent); its land mass by almost as much. And the frontiers of 'Europe', which as recently as 1989 had reached no further east than Trieste, now extended into what had once been the USSR.

At the dawn of the twenty-first century the European Union faced a daunting range of problems: some old, some new and some of its own making. Its economic troubles were perhaps the most familiar and in the end the least serious of its concerns. With or without the new member states the EU continued to spend—as it had done from the outset—hugely disproportionate sums of money on its farmers. Forty percent of the Union's budget—or $52 billion in 2004—went on politically motivated 'farm support payments', many of them to large mechanized agri-businesses in France or Spain that hardly needed the help.

Even after agreement had been reached to reduce these subsidies and cut the Common Agricultural Program it was anticipated that farm price supports would still constitute over a third of the EU's total expenditure well into the second decade of the new century, placing an intolerable burden upon the budget. The problem was not that the Union was poor. Quite the contrary: the collective wealth and resources of its members were comparable to those of the US. But its budget, in the words of an independent report commissioned by Brussels in 2003, was a 'historical relic'.

The European Union had started out, half a century before, as a customs union—a 'common market'—bound together by not much more than a common external tariff. Its pattern of expenditure was driven and then constrained by ne-

---

[7]A highly optimistic assumption. In the years following their accession to the EC in 1986, the economies of Spain and Portugal grew on average between 1 percent and 1.5 percent faster than the rest of the Community.

An Ever-Expanding Union? The EU in 2004

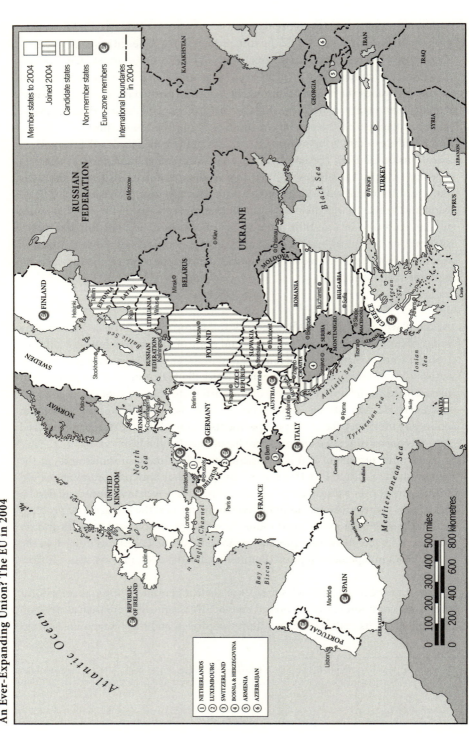

Legend:
- Member states to 2004
- Joined 2004
- Candidate states
- Non-member states
- Euro-zone members €
- International boundaries in 2004

1 NETHERLANDS
2 LUXEMBOURG
3 SWITZERLAND
4 BOSNIA & HERZEGOVINA
5 ARMENIA
6 AZERBAIJAN

Scale:
0 100 200 300 400 500 miles
0 200 400 600 800 kilometres

gotiated agreements on tariffs, prices, subsidies and supports. Over the years its ambitions had expanded into the realms of culture, law, government and politics and it had taken on—in Brussels and elsewhere—many of the external trappings of a conventional government.

But whereas conventional governments are free to raise money to meet their anticipated costs, the European Union had and has very few revenue-raising capacities of its own. Its income derives from fixed rates of customs duty, agricultural levies, a Union-wide indirect sales tax (VAT) and, above all, contributions from member-states capped at just 1.24 percent of Gross National Income (GNI). Thus very little of the EU's income is under the direct control of the Union's own administration—and all of it is vulnerable to political pressures within the separate member-states.

Most of the latter are recipients of EU largesse rather than contributors to its budget. In 2004, following its enlargement to the East, nineteen of the Union's member countries received from Brussels more than they paid in. The cost of running the Union was in practice met by net contributions from just six member states: the UK, France, Sweden, Austria, the Netherlands and Germany. Ominously for the Union's future prospects, all six countries petitioned the Commission in December 2003 to have national contributions to the EU budget reduced in future from 1.24 percent of GNI to just 1 percent.

The Union's budget, tiny in comparison to that of even the smallest member-state and mostly spent on structural funds, price supports and the EU's own costly administration, is thus a permanent hostage to the interests of its contributors and recipients alike. The levers of the Union's economic machinery depend for their efficiency upon the consent of all its constituent parts. Where everyone more or less concurs on the principle and benefits of a given policy—on open internal borders, or unrestricted markets for goods and services—the EU has made remarkable progress. Where there is real dissent from a handful of members (or even just one, particularly if it is a major contributor), policy stalls: tax harmonization, like the reduction of agricultural supports, has been on the agenda for decades.

And sometimes the clock runs backwards. After two decades of Brussels-driven efforts to eliminate state subsidies for favoured national 'champions' and thereby secure a level playing field in intra-European economic competition, the EU's single market commissioner (the Dutchman Frits Bolkestein) expressed his surprise in July 2004 at watching France and Germany revert to the 'protectionist' policies of the Seventies in defense of threatened local firms. But then both Berlin and Paris, unlike the unelected commissioners in Brussels, have tax-paying voters whom they simply cannot ignore.

These paradoxes of union are nicely captured in the tribulations of the euro. The problem with a common currency lay not in the technical substitution of a single unit of reference for a multitude of national currencies—this process was already under way long before the abolition of the franc or the lira or the drachma and turned out to be surprisingly smooth and painless[8]—but in the prerequisite harmonization of national economic policies. To avoid the moral hazard and practical risks of free riders, Bonn, as we have seen, had insisted upon what became known as the 'growth and stability pact'.

Countries wishing to join the euro were obliged to hold their public debt down to no more than 60 percent of Gross Domestic Product, and were expected to run budget deficits of no more than 3 percent of same. Any country that failed these tests would be subject to sanctions, including substantial fines, imposed by the Union. The point of these measures was to ensure that no euro-zone government would let down its fiscal guard, overrun its budget at will and thus place unfair strains on the economies of other euro-zone members who would have to bear the burden of ensuring the stability of the common currency.

To everyone's surprise the traditionally spendthrift southern tier proved surprisingly disciplined. Spain 'qualified' for euro membership by what one Spanish observer tartly described as a combination of *fortuna* and *virtu*: an upswing in the economy allowed the government to pay down the country's public debt just in time for the 1999 introduction of the currency. Even Italy managed to pass the Teutonic tests (which many Italians rightly suspected had been set up to keep them out), albeit with more than a little juggling of figures and the one-time sale of public assets. By 2003 the euro-zone encompassed twelve countries, ranging from Ireland to Greece.

But—as many skeptics had predicted—the strains of a 'one size fits all' currency soon began to tell. The newly established European Central Bank (ECB) in Frankfurt maintained from the outset a relatively high interest rate, to support the new currency and secure it against inflation. But the economies of the euro-zone states differed with respect both to their level of development and their point in the economic cycle. Some, like Ireland, were booming; others—notably Portugal—lagged far behind and could have used the boost to domestic activity as well as exports that would traditionally have been achieved by lowering interest rates and 'softening' the currency.

Shorn of the power to implement such measures, the government of Portugal was obliged by the terms of the 'pact' to reduce government expenditure—or else face substantial fines—just when it ought, in conventional economic theory, to have been spending its way out of recession. This did not make for domestic popularity; but at least the country could boast that it had not reneged on the terms of its participation in the new currency: by 2003 Lisbon had successfully reduced government debt to 59.4 percent of GDP and the annual deficit to 2.8 percent, squeezing under the official limits.

---

[8]On January 1st 2002 a total of 600,000,000,000 euros in cash was seamlessly distributed and introduced across the euro-zone countries, a remarkable technical achievement.

The next year, however, France ran a deficit of nearly 4.1 percent—and *Germany*, its ageing economy finally paying the price for unification, followed suit with a deficit of 3.9 percent and a debt ratio of nearly 65 percent. Given the size of their respective economies, the fact that neither France nor Germany was adhering to its own rules represented a significant challenge to the whole agreement. But this time, when the Commission set in motion the penalty proceedings, Paris and Berlin made it clear that they regarded the 'temporary' deficits as economically unavoidable and had no intention of paying fines or even committing themselves to doing significantly better the following year.

The Union's smaller states—both those like Greece or Portugal which had striven mightily and at some cost to meet the pact's terms and those such as the Netherlands and Luxembourg which feared for the stability of what was now *their* currency too—duly cried foul, but the lesson was clear. Within less than a decade of its appearance, the growth and stability pact was dead. Just how much the euro would actually suffer if the participating countries were allowed more flexibility in their domestic budgets was by no means clear. There were many who felt that the real problem lay not with national governments but rather with the rigid and seemingly unresponsive Central Bank, immovably insistent upon its complete independence and still fighting the anti-inflationary battles of the 1970s.

The difficulties of the euro pointed to a broader shortcoming in the European project: its extraordinarily unwieldy system of government. The problem lay in the original conception. Jean Monnet and his heirs had deliberately eschewed any effort to imagine, much less implement, a democratic or federal system. Instead they had driven forward a project for the modernization of Europe from above: a strategy for productivity, efficiency and economic growth conceived on Saint-Simonian lines, managed by experts and officials and with scant attention paid to the wishes of its beneficiaries. The energies of its proponents and exponents were largely devoted to the complex *technical* dimensions of 'building Europe'. To the extent that other concerns ever arose, they were serially postponed.

By the 1990s, then, the European Union was still run along lines that had been laid down decades before and mostly for managerial convenience. The unelected Commission in Brussels administered a substantial bureaucracy, initiating policies and implementing agendas and decisions subject to the approval of a Council of Ministers from the member-states. An unwieldy European Parliament, sitting variously in Strasbourg and Brussels and directly elected since 1979, exercised a slowly expanding oversight role (in the original Rome Treaty its function had been strictly consultative) but no power of initiative.

Uncontentious decisions were typically made in Brussels by experts and civil servants. Policies likely to affect significant electoral constituencies or national interests were hammered out in the Council of Ministers and produced complicated compromises or else expensive deals. Whatever could not be resolved or agreed was simply left in abeyance. The dominant member states—Britain, Germany and above all France—could not always count on getting what they wanted; but whatever they truly did *not* want did not come to pass.

This was a unique set of arrangements. It bore no relation to the condition of the separate states of North America in 1776, all of which had emerged as satellites of a single country—Britain—whose language, culture and legal system they shared. Nor was it really comparable to the Swiss Confederation, although that analogy was occasionally suggested: in their centuries-old web of overlapping sovereignties, administrative enclaves and local rights and privileges the cantons of Switzerland more closely resemble old-regime France without the king.[9]

The member-states of the European Union, by contrast, remained completely independent and separate units in a voluntary association to which they had, over time, conceded a randomly accumulated set of powers and initiatives without ever saying what principle lay behind the arrangement and how far this common undertaking was to go. 'Brussels'—an appropriately anonymous headquarters for an undefined administrative entity, neither democratic nor authoritarian—governed only through the consent of its member governments. From the outset it had presented itself to all of these as a straightforwardly positive-sum undertaking: the Community/Union would contribute to its members' well-being without subtracting anything of significance from their independence. But this could not continue indefinitely.

What brought matters to a head was not the inherently complicated and incremental nature of the Union's system of rule, but the impossibility of maintaining it with twenty-five members. Hitherto the chairmanship of the Council of Ministers rotated every six months, with each country getting to host a self-promoting bi-annual European conference—a system already much disliked by the Union's full-time administrators. The prospect of such a circus shambling around through twenty-five different capitals, from Lisbon to Ljubljana, was plainly absurd. Moreover, a decision-taking system designed for six member-states and already cumbersome for twelve, much less fifteen, would simply grind to a halt with fifty European Commissioners (two from each country), or a European Council representing twenty-five member-states—each with a power of veto.

The likely difficulties were all too well foreshadowed at a meeting in Nice in December 2000. Ostensibly called to lay the groundwork for enlargement and to devise a new voting system in the EU Council of Ministers—one that would weight member-states' votes by population while still ensuring that majority decisions could be reached—the conference ended in acrimonious and deeply embarrassing horse trading. The French insisted on maintaining parity with Germany (despite

---

[9] If they still worked as smoothly as they did it was at least in part because the federal machinery was so very well oiled, not least by money: in the 1990s Switzerland was still by most measures the world's wealthiest country.

a population disparity of twenty million people) while countries like Spain and Poland, the latter accorded observer status at the meeting, sought to maximize their own future voting strength in the Council by selling their backing to the highest bidder.

The unseemly scramble for influence at Nice, as leading European statesmen like Tony Blair, Jacques Chirac and Gerhard Schroeder spent sleepless nights bargaining and bickering for status and influence in their common European home, illustrated the price that was now being paid for previous neglect of constitutional niceties. By bringing the Union to a new low, Nice led directly to the establishment of a 'European Convention': a sort of unelected constituent assembly authorized to produce a practical system of governance for an enlarged 'Europe' and, it was hoped, some credible account of the purposes of the whole thing. Following a certain amount of (by now familiar) lobbying from Paris, the presidency of the Convention was assigned to the ageing but ever-vainglorious Valéry Giscard d'Estaing.

After two years of deliberations, the Convention emitted something more than a draft but decidedly less than a constitution. Shorn of its portentous Giscardian preamble (immediately and unfavourably contrasted with the elegant brevity of its Jeffersonian predecessor) the Convention's document offered little by way of classic constitutional proposals—no sweeping definitions of individual liberty, no clear statement concerning the division of powers, etc. In this respect, as many had predicted, it was a disappointment.

But Giscard's text—which after some discussion was adopted as a Constitutional Treaty in Rome in 2004—*did* provide a working blueprint for the practical management of the Union's affairs: improved systems of coordination on defense and immigration; a simplified and unified summary of EU law; a Charter of Fundamental Rights for EU citizens aimed at further strengthening the authority of the European courts; a clear and even ambitious account of the Union's formal competence and authority.

Above all, the proposed constitution would have served to reduce—over time— the top-heavy system of national representation in the Commission; and it devised a system for voting in the European Council that proved, after a certain amount of haggling, to be acceptable to all parties as well as demographically equitable. Whether the new dispositions would produce clear-cut majorities on difficult issues remained uncertain: all the more so since for truly contentious topics like taxation and defense it was nonetheless agreed—at British insistence but to the unspoken relief of many other countries—to retain the old Gaullist device of national vetoes. And no-one was in any doubt that for all the careful distribution of weighted votes, real power still lay with the biggest countries—as Ortega y Gasset had already concluded in 1930, 'Europe' was for practical purposes 'the trinity of France, England, Germany'. But at least—and always assuming that the constitution was to be ratified in every member-state, which proved to be an unforeseen impediment—it would now be possible to reach decisions.

By 2004, then, the European Union had—to the surprise of many observers—seemingly overcome, or at least alleviated, the practical difficulties of governing an unwieldy and inchoate community of twenty-five separate states. But what it had not done—what neither Giscard's Convention, nor the various Treaties, nor the European Commission and its multifarious reports and programmes, nor the expensive publications and websites designed to educate the European public about the Union and its workings had even begun to do—was to address the chronic absence of interest on the part of the European public.

If the technocrats who built the institutions of the new 'Europe' had shown a haughty unconcern for the opinions of the public at large, this sentiment was now being repaid in kind and in earnest. Reflecting bleakly upon his Labour Party colleagues' obsession with the techniques and rules of party-political management, the British Prime Minister Clement Attlee used to advise against the 'fundamental fallacy' of believing that 'it is possible by the elaboration of machinery to escape the necessity of trusting one's fellow human beings'.[10] But this was just the premise on which the institutions of post-war European unity had been built, with consequences that were at last becoming apparent. The EU was suffering from a serious 'democratic deficit'.

With each direct election to the European parliament the turnout fell; the only exceptions to this rule were those occasions where national and European elections coincided and voters who had been mobilized around local or national issues took the occasion to vote in the European polls as well. Otherwise the decline was unbroken—in France it fell from 60 percent in 1979 to 43 percent in 2004; in Germany from 66 percent to 43 percent; in the Netherlands from 58 percent to 39 percent.[11]

The contrast between the level of interest that electors exhibited for national politics and their growing unconcern for the parliament in Strasbourg is especially revealing. At the European elections of June 2004, the first since the Union's enlargement, the vote in the UK was down by 20 percentage points from the most recent national elections, in Spain by 23 percentage points; Portugal saw a drop of 24 percentage points, Finland 39 percentage points, Austria 42 percentage points and Sweden 43 percentage points (from an 80 percent turnout in Sweden's own elections to just 37 percent for the European vote).

The pattern is far too consistent to attribute to local circumstances. Moreover—and with more serious implications for the Union's future—it was closely replicated in the new member-states of the East, even though this was their first opportunity to vote in an election to the parliament of Europe that they had waited so long to

---

[10]Quoted in Kenneth Harris, *Attlee* (London, 1984), p. 63.
[11]The decline in the Dutch vote may be especially ominous. Once the kernel of European enthusiasm and a generous contributor to EC and EU funds, the Netherlands in recent years has been retreating into itself—a development both illuminated and accelerated by the rise of Pim Fortuyn and his subsequent assassination.

join. In Hungary the turnout in the June 2004 European elections fell short of the last national elections by 32 percentage points; in Estonia by 31 points; in Slovakia, where the latest national elections had seen a 70 percent turnout, the share of the electorate that bothered to come and vote in the European elections was 17 percent. In Poland the turnout of just 20 percent represented a 26-point decline from the national elections of 2001 and was the lowest since the fall of Communism.

Why were Europeans, 'old' and 'new' alike, so profoundly indifferent to the affairs of the European Union? In large part because of a widespread belief that they had no influence over them. Most European governments had never held a vote to determine whether or not they should join the EU or the euro-zone—not least because in those countries where the issue *had* been put to a national referendum it was rejected, or else passed by the narrowest of margins. So the Union was not 'owned' by its citizens—it seemed somehow to stand apart from the usual instruments of democracy.

Moreover there was a widespread (and accurate) sentiment among European publics that of all the institutions of the EU, the 732 elected Members of the European Parliament were the least significant. Real power lay with a Commission appointed by national governments and a Council of Ministers comprising their representatives. *National* elections, in short, were where the crucial choices were to be made. Why waste time selecting the monkey when you should be paying attention to the choice of organ grinder instead?

On the other hand, as was becoming increasingly clear to even the most casual citizen, the 'faceless' men and women in Brussels now wielded real power. Everything from the shape of cucumbers to the color and wording of a person's passport was now decided in Brussels. 'Brussels' could give (from milk subsidies to student scholarships) and 'Brussels' could take away (your currency, your right to dismiss employees, even the label on your cheese). And every national government had at one time or another over the past two decades found it convenient to blame 'Brussels' for unpopular laws or taxes, or economic policies which it tacitly favoured but for which it was reluctant to take responsibility.

In these circumstances, the Union's democratic deficit could easily turn from unconcern into hostility, into a sense that decisions were being taken 'there' with unfavourable consequences for us 'here' and over which 'we' had no say: a prejudice fuelled by irresponsible mainstream politicians but fanned by nationalist demagogues. It was not by chance that in the same European elections of 2004 that saw such a sharp falling off in voter interest, many of those who *did* bother to turn up at the polls gave their support to overtly—sometimes rabidly—anti-EU candidates.

In western Europe the enlargement itself helped trigger this backlash. In Britain the Europhobic UK Independence Party and the white-supremacist British National Party between them took 21 percent of the vote, promising to keep the UK clear of 'Europe' and protect it from the anticipated onrush of immigrants and asylum-seekers. In Belgium the Vlaams Blok, in Denmark the Dansk Folkeparti (People's Party), and in Italy the Northern League all played on a similar register—as they had done in the past, but with rather more success on this occasion.

In France, Jean-Marie Le Pen's Front National took a similar position; but French doubts over European enlargement were not confined to the political extremes. It was an open secret that the French political establishment had long been opposed to expanding the EU and thereby diluting French influence: Mitterrand, Chirac and their diplomatic representatives had all worked hard to postpone the inevitable for as long as possible. Public opinion echoed these sentiments: in a poll taken four months before the new members were due to join the Union 70 percent of French voters declared the EU 'unprepared' for their arrival, while 55 percent opposed their inclusion altogether (compared to 35 percent of EU voters as a whole).[12]

But antipathy towards the EU also played a part in Eastern Europe. In the Czech Republic, the Civic Democratic Party—aligned with Václav Klaus and loudly skeptical of the EU and its 'over-mighty' powers—was the clear victor in 2004, winning 38 percent of the country's European Parliamentary seats. In neighbouring Poland Euroskeptic parties of the far Right actually did better than the ruling center-left coalition—not surprisingly, perhaps, considering that in a Eurobarometer poll taken a few months previously only just over half the Polish electorate thought that the European Union was a 'good thing'.

And yet, taken all in all, the EU *is* a good thing. The economic benefits of the single market have been real, as even the most ardent British Euroskeptics had come to concede, particularly with the passing of the passion for 'harmonizing' that marked the Commission Presidency of Jacques Delors. The newfound freedom to travel, work and study anywhere in the Union was a boon to young people especially. And there was something else. In relative terms, the so-called 'social' element in the EU budget was tiny—less than 1 percent of the European-area GNP. But from the late Eighties, the budgets of the European Community and the Union nevertheless had a distinctly redistributive quality, transferring resources from wealthy regions to poorer ones and contributing to a steady reduction in the aggregate gap between rich and poor: substituting, in effect, for the nationally based Social-Democratic programmes of an earlier generation.[13]

In recent years the citizens of Europe had even acquired their own court. The European Court of Justice (ECJ), set up in 1952 under the same Treaty of Paris that established the European Coal and Steel Community, had started out with the lim-

---

[12]It is perhaps worth adding that in January 2004 only one French adult in fifty could name the ten new EU member states.
[13]Not everywhere, however: in the UK—as in the US—the income spread between the wealthy and the rest grew steadily wider from the late 1970s.

ited task of ensuring that EC legislation ('Community law') was interpreted and applied in the same way in each member-state. But by the end of the century its judges—originally one from each member-state—were authorized to settle legal disputes between member-states and EU institutions, as well as to hear cases brought against lower court decisions or even against national governments. The ECJ had, in effect, assumed many of the powers and attributes of a pan-European Court of Appeals.[14]

As the example of the Court suggests, the rather indirect and often unintentional manner in which the Union's institutions emerged had its advantages. Very few lawyers or legislators in even the most pro-European states of the European 'core' would have been willing to relinquish local legal supremacy had they been asked to do so at the outset. Similarly, if a clearly articulated 'European project', describing the goals and institutions of the Union as they later evolved, had ever been put to the separate voters of the states of western Europe it would surely have been rejected.

The advantage of the European idea in the decades following World War Two had thus lain precisely in its imprecision. Like 'growth' or 'peace'—with both of which it was closely associated in the minds of its proponents—'Europe' was too benign to attract effective opposition.[15] Back in the early Seventies, when the French President Georges Pompidou first took to speaking airily of a 'European Union', Foreign Minister Michel Jobert once asked his colleague Edouard Balladur (the future French Premier) what exactly it meant: 'Nothing' replied Balladur. 'But then that is the beauty of it.' Pompidou himself dismissed it as 'a vague formula . . . in order to avoid paralyzing doctrinal disputes'.[16]

Of course it is this formulaic vagueness, combined with the all-too-precise detail of EU legislative directives, which has given rise to the democratic deficit: it is hard for Europeans to care about a Union whose identity was for so long unclear, but which at the same time appears to impinge upon every aspect of their existence. And yet, for all its faults as a system of indirect government, the Union has certain interesting and original attributes. Decisions and laws may be passed at a transgovernmental level, but they are implemented by and through national authorities. Everything has to be undertaken by agreement, since there are no instruments of coercion: no EU tax collectors, no EU policemen. The European Union thus represents an unusual compromise: international governance undertaken by national governments.

Finally, while the European Union has neither means nor mechanisms to pre-

---

[14]The ECJ should not be confused with the European Court of Human Rights, set up under the auspices of the Council of Europe to enforce the 1953 Convention for the Protection of Human Rights and Fundamental Freedoms.

[15]In Giscard's 'Constitution for Europe', Article 3(I) defines the Union's aims as being 'to promote peace, its values, and the well-being of its peoples'.

[16]Quoted by Andrew Moravscik in *The Choice for Europe* (New York, 1998),. p. 265.

vent its member-states coming to blows, its very existence renders the idea some-how absurd. The lesson that war was too high a price to pay for political or terri-torial advantage had already been brought home to the victors after World War One, though it took a second war to convey the same lesson to the *losing* side. But just because a third intra-European war would have been catastrophic and perhaps terminal does not mean it could not have happened, at least in the early post-war years.

By the end of the century, however, the elites and institutions of the European Union were so intertwined and interdependent that armed conflict, while never im-possible, had become somehow inconceivable. That is why 'Europe' was such an ob-ject of desire to aspirant members like Latvia or Poland, an escape route out of their past and an insurance policy for the future. But it is also, ironically, why the EU's own leaders proved so fatuously helpless when confronted with the reality of war in the Balkans.

Its humiliation over Yugoslavia[17] is a reminder that the European Union cannot escape the defects of its virtues. By *not* being a state the Union has been able to bind some 450 million people into a single, loosely articulated community with re-markably little dissent. But because it is not a state—because its citizens' primary loyalties remain to the country in which they find themselves, whose laws they obey, whose language they speak and whose taxes they pay—the EU has no mech-anism for determining or enforcing its own security interests.

This does not mean that 'Europe' has no common foreign policy. On the con-trary, the European Community and its successor the EU have for many decades been extremely effective in advancing and defending their interests in international forums and against foreign competitors. But those interests have from the outset been defined in overwhelmingly economic—or more precisely, protectionist—terms. European economics ministers and trade commissioners have engaged in open combat with Washington over tax breaks for American exporters or import restrictions on European products.

More controversially, the EU has also fought very effectively to maintain high external tariffs in defense of Europe's subsidized farmers—restraining open trade in commodities like sugar, for example, to the detriment of farmers in Africa or Central America.[18] But whereas the separate member states of the EU—even the most powerful ones—have been pleased to pass on to Brussels responsibility for

---

[17]Mordantly predicted at the time by the US Secretary of State Lawrence Eagleburger, who foresaw that the Europeans 'will screw up and this will teach them a lesson'.

[18]The EU was not alone in subsidizing its own farmers to the detriment of others. It was not even the worst offender: Norway, Switzerland, Japan and the US all pay out more in per capita terms. But the EU appeared somehow more hypocritical. While Brussels preaches virtue to the world at large, its own practice is often quite selective. East Europeans, instructed to incorporate and adopt a veritable library of European Union regulations, could hardly fail to notice the frequency with which West European gov-ernments exempted themselves from those same rules.

presenting their economic case in the World Trade Organization and elsewhere, they have reserved for themselves *the* vital attribute of any modern state. The European Union has no army.

In part this is an accident of history. In the early 1950s there were many who thought that in future the Western Europeans could and should organize their military affairs collectively—at an August 1950 meeting of the Council of Europe's Consultative Assembly, Paul Reynaud of France even argued the case for a European Minister of War. But the defeat of the proposal for a European Defense Force (see Chapter 8), and the incorporation of West Germany into NATO, put an end to such ideas for a generation; instead Western Europe snuggled comfortably under the American nuclear umbrella.

Following the end of the Korean War and the retreat from empire, every Western European country cut its defense budget. With the fall of Communism, spending on the military reached new lows. In the late Eighties the average share of defense spending in NATO members' budgets had already declined to 3.4 percent of GNP; by 2003 Denmark was spending just 1.6 percent of GNP on defense; Italy 1.5 percent; Spain a mere 1.4 percent. Only the French and British spent substantially more, though in neither case did spending now exceed 5 percent—negligible by historical standards.

Moreover, none of the armed forces of Europe was under 'European' control or likely to be in the foreseeable future, despite plans announced in 2000 for a European 'Rapid Reaction Force'. Although there had for some years been a European Commissioner for External Relations, since the Treaty of Amsterdam his functions were duplicated (and his authority thereby diminished) by a High Representative for the Common Foreign and Security Policy, answerable only to the EU Council of Ministers. And neither the Commissioner nor the High Representative had any authority to initiate his own policy, despatch armed forces or speak for the foreign policies or ministers of the member-states unless previously instructed. Henry Kissinger's sardonic question of an earlier decade—'If I want to phone Europe, what number do I call?'—had lost none of its force.

But these limitations—the fact that in spite of its size and wealth the EU was not a state, much less a great power—paradoxically served to enhance its image, at home and abroad. In this respect at least the EU was indeed coming to resemble Switzerland, a repository of international agencies and cooperation, an exemplar of 'post-national' strategies for problem solving and social cohesion: not so much a network of institutions or a corpus of laws but rather a set of values—'European values'—embodied in the new Charter of Fundamental Rights.

If the values and norms of this new Europe were under pressure at the end of the twentieth century it was not from the established nation-states against which the European idea had been traditionally but misleadingly juxtaposed. Instead, both the EU *and* its various member-states were now facing an unprecedented wave of economic and social challenges brought upon them by forces largely beyond their control, most of them associated in one way or another with what it was becoming customary to designate as globalization.

There was nothing especially mysterious about globalization. It wasn't even unprecedented—the impact on the world economy of new and rapid networks of transport and communications at the end of the *nineteenth* century was at least as dramatic as the transformation wrought by the Internet and the deregulation and liberalization of financial markets a century later. Nor was there anything new about the unequal global distribution of the benefits of liberalized trade—particularly when, at the end of the twentieth century no less than in the years before 1914, international trade regimes were so consistently accommodating to the interests of the powerful and wealthy.

But from the European perspective the latest transformations in the world economy were distinctive in one important respect. At the end of the nineteenth century the European states were just beginning to expand their domestic reach: in time many of them would own, operate or regulate large sectors of the economy. Government expenditure—financed out of new, progressive taxes—would increase dramatically, partly to pay for wars but increasingly for the purpose of servicing social and welfare needs for which the state was now assuming responsibility.

The economic internationalization of the nineteen-nineties, however, followed closely in the wake of the first great wave of European privatizations and provided the impetus for more to come (see Chapter 17). The European state was now in retreat—first in Britain, then much of Western Europe and finally in the former-Communist East—a process further abetted by the implementation after 1987 of the Single European Act, with its provisions for open competition within and across borders. Through mergers, acquisitions and the internationalization of their operations, companies and corporations now operated on a global scale. The production and distribution of goods was often beyond the control of individual countries.

As for money, it was beginning to multiply and migrate in ways that would have been unthinkable a few years before. In 1980 the sum of all international bank lending was $324 billion a year; by 1991 that figure had grown to $7.5 trillion—a 2,000 percent increase in just over a decade. And this was just the beginning. Controls on the movement of capital—eliminated by most European states in the course of the early Eighties—now appeared as antiquated as food rationing. The 'crash' of September 1992—when first the UK and then Italy were forced out of the European Monetary System and obliged to devalue by private speculators and institutional investors whose activities they were powerless to prevent—was a highly symbolic moment.

The advantages of this revolution in the international economy were self-evident. Investment capital, no longer restrained by national frontiers, exchange-rate regimes or local currency regulation, flowed unchecked wherever it was needed (and could anticipate a profit)—by 1990 foreigners already held 34 percent of German debt. But there were disadvantages too: European manufacturers, their profit margins constrained by the high wages and overhead costs of employing skilled labor in Germany or France or Sweden, were now at liberty to seek out not only international investors but also a more malleable and inexpensive foreign workforce.

Instead of importing into Europe cheap workers from poor countries—as in the past—German or British or French firms now found it more efficient to export their factories instead, installing them in Brazil or Nigeria, Portugal or Romania and then directly selling the finished product to markets all over the world. This further accelerated the de-industrialization of Western Europe, adding to the already chronic unemployment in many regions—and increasing the burden on state-provided unemployment compensation and other social services.

When the last coalmine in France—at Creutzwald in the Moselle—closed in April 2004, no-one even pretended that the former miners would ever find regular work again. Unemployment in the Moselle district hovered around 10 percent of the active population; further north, in the former mining towns along the Belgian border, it was 15 percent. France as a whole had lost 1.5 million industrial jobs in the last three decades of the century, most of them since 1980. Spain, which very quickly lost any comparative advantage that accrued to it from being one of Western Europe's more backward economies, shed 600,000 jobs in the twenty years following the transition to democracy. At the height of the recession of the mid-1990s, 44 percent of the country's under-25 workforce was unemployed.

Unemployment was not new. And given the generous welfare net available in most EU countries, the economic impact of joblessness on individuals and communities was in no way comparable to the devastation of the inter-war years (its psychological consequences are another matter). But what *was* distinctive about the social costs of economic disruption in the last years of the twentieth century was that they were taking place in a time of plenty. Privatization and the opening of the financial markets had created great wealth, albeit for a relative few; in certain places—London, say, or Barcelona—its consequences were strikingly visible. And thanks to the shrinking of distances and the increased speed of communications—via computers and the electronic media—information about the way other people lived was immediately and copiously available to all.

It was this sense of glaring contrasts between wealth and poverty, prosperity and insecurity, private affluence and public squalor, that drove a growing skepticism in Europe about the loudly touted virtues of unregulated markets and untrammeled globalization—even as many Europeans were themselves the indirect beneficiaries of the changes they deplored. In the past, such sentiments—added to pressure from organized labour and the self-interest of politicians—might have favoured a retreat to some form of limited protectionism.

But governments' hands were now tied and organized labour, in the traditional sense, hardly existed anymore. Only in France did a unionized workforce succeed with the help of public opinion in temporarily blocking the sell-off of public companies: and even then only in special instances like Electricité de France, an icon of the post-war nationalized sector whose employees were among the few remaining members of the once-giant (Communist-led) Confédération Générale du Travail (CGT). In the last years of the century, even as the rest of the European energy market was deregulated, EdF remained in state ownership.

But the CGT, once the dominant blue-collar union in France, was a shadow of its former self—the French union movement as a whole had lost two-thirds of its members since 1980—and the workers it represented were no longer typical of the laboring population in France or elsewhere. Work itself had changed. What was emerging in many places was a novel, four-class system. At the top was the new professional stratum: metropolitan, cosmopolitan, affluent and educated—often attached to banks and other financial agencies, the primary beneficiaries of the new global economy. Then came a second tier, a protected core of traditional employees—in factories, service industries or the public sector—their jobs reasonably secure and many of their traditional benefits and guarantees still intact.

A third tier consisted of small businesses and services—corner-storekeepers, travel agents, tailors, electronic repairmen and the like—more often than not owned and staffed by immigrant communities or their descendants (Arabs in France, Turks or Kurds in Germany, South Asians in Britain). To these should be added the very sizeable and typically family-based 'grey' economy in Southern Europe. In Italy, where everything from shoes to textiles to machine parts was often produced and distributed below the radar of officialdom, it was estimated in 1997 that the 'informal' sector contributed at least one quarter of the country's Gross Domestic Product. In Portugal the national figure—inevitably an estimate—was 22 percent; but in some regions—like the town of Braga in the far north of the country—'unofficial' workers constituted as much as 45 percent of the local labour force.

And then came the fourth tier—the fastest growing: people employed (if at all) in jobs that lacked both the long-term security of traditional skilled work and the benefits that had become standard in the boom years of the Fifties and Sixties. To be sure, unemployment figures in some countries—Britain, or the Netherlands—did eventually fall to gratifyingly low levels: proof, it was widely bruited, of the virtuous workings of the unhindered and globalized market. But many of those who no longer figured on unemployment rolls—women and young people especially—were now doing low-paid, part-time work without benefits; or else were employed on fixed-term contracts in job programmes subsidized or under-written by the state.

Those whose wages were too low to support them and their families could still turn to the welfare state, and many did. In the UK, where the Thatcherite assault on state and society alike had been felt most acutely, 14 million people now lived in poverty, including 4 million children.[19] One person in six depended upon Income Support or Family Credit programmes to keep them above the poverty line. Homelessness, which in northern Europe at least had been effectively eradicated by the end of the 1950s, was once again on the increase: in the course of the Thatcher years the number of homeless in London alone rose ten-fold. By the mid-'90s it had reached 80,000. Within a few miles of some of the most expensive real estate in the world parts of the British capital were beginning to resemble the 'Outcast London' of late-Victorian notoriety.[20]

Whereas, in the past, economic upswings had tended to lift many of the poor into better paid and more secure employment, this was no longer happening. Europe, in other words, was developing an under-class in the midst of plenty. As the French sociologist André Gorz had predicted back in the 1960s, the end of the industrial era would see the birth of a new caste of casual, temporary workers—a 'non-class of non-workers'—at once marginal to modern life and yet somehow right at its heart.[21]

Like its American equivalent, the European under-class was determined not only by poverty and unemployment (or under-employment) but also and increasingly by race: in the mid-'90s the unemployment rate in London for young *black* men was 51 percent. The poor, like Europe as a whole by the end of the century, were strikingly multinational—or 'multicultural' as it had become custom to describe it, in acknowledgement of the fact that many dark-skinned Dutchmen or Germans or Brits were the native-born children or even grandchildren of the original Moroccan or Turkish or Pakistani immigrants. Towns like Rotterdam or Leicester were now multi-lingual and multi-colored in a way that would have amazed anyone returning after an absence of even just two decades. In 1998, white children were a minority in the local authority (i.e. public) secondary schools of inner London.

Europe's major cities, London above all, were now truly cosmopolitan. If the high-paying city jobs were still going to white Europeans (and North Americans) nearly all the low-paying work, from street-cleaning to child-care, was now done not by traditional 'second-class' Europeans from the *Alentejo* or the *Mezzogiorno* but by 'minorities', often black or brown, many of them without working papers.

---

[19]In 1995, according to a UNICEF study, one British child in five lived in poverty, compared with one in ten in Germany and one in twenty in Denmark.

[20]Invoking slightly different criteria to make a similar point, the Cambridge political theorist John Dunn divides the workforces of wealthy countries into 'those who can individually take very good care of themselves on the market . . . , those who can hold their own only because they belong to surviving units of collective action with a threat advantage out of all proportion to the value of individual members' labour, and those who are already going under, because no one would chose to pay much for their labour'. Dunn, *The Cunning of Unreason. Making Sense of Politics* (London, 2000), p. 333.

[21]Gorz, as befitted a man of his time and politics, assumed that this new class would in turn fuel a new generation of radical social movements. To date there is little evidence of this.

According to official figures the net increase in foreigners living in London and the south-east of England in the years 1992–2002 was 700,000; but the actual number was distinctly higher.

Immigration, though perennially discouraged and rigorously controlled throughout Western Europe, was thus still a major demographic factor: of those same inner-London children of 1998, one third did not use English as their first language. These were frequently the offspring of refugees, 'asylum-seekers' in the jargon of the day, whose numbers had ballooned in the wake of the Yugoslav wars; but also of migrant workers from Central and South-East Asia, the Middle East and much of Africa—many of them illegal and thus undocumented.

In Germany, whose asylum facilities were (and remain) by far the most generous in Europe[22] but where it was traditionally very difficult for immigrants to obtain full citizenship, it was estimated that there were five million such people—counting families and dependants—by the end of the century. The majority of asylum applications to Germany by the beginning of the new century came from Iraq, Turkey and the countries of former Yugoslavia, but there were also growing numbers from Iran, Afghanistan, Russia and Vietnam.

The fear that Western Europe might be 'overrun' by 'economic refugees', illegal immigrants, asylum-seekers and the like contributed to a widespread lack of enthusiasm for EU enlargement. Already by the 1980s undocumented workers from Poland were present in large numbers in the British and German building trades. But the problem was not so much Poland, or Hungary, or the other would-be accession states of Central Europe, but rather the lands to their east. In 1992 Poland itself had 290,000 'irregular' immigrants, mostly from Bulgaria, Romania and the former USSR; Hungary, with a population of just 10 million, was home to over 100,000 asylum-seekers. Whereas life there—or in Slovakia or the Czech Republic—was hard, it was not intolerable and the gap separating these countries from their Western neighbours was already being bridged, however slowly. The gulf between Central Europe and the rest of post-Communist Europe, however, yawned far greater.

Thus whereas by the late-Nineties the average monthly wage in Poland and the Czech Republic was already approaching $400, in Belarus, Ukraine and Romania it hovered around $80; in Bulgaria at under $70; and in Moldova at just $30—itself a misleading average, since outside of the capital, Chisinau, incomes were lower still, in a population of whom 48 percent still worked on the land. And unlike Poland, or even Bulgaria, the condition of the former Soviet republics was not improving: by the year 2000, one Moldovan in two was earning less than $220 a year—just $19 a month.

In such circumstances the only hope for Moldovans—or Ukrainians, or indeed

---

[22]In 1992 alone, the Federal Republic opened its doors to nearly a quarter of a million Yugoslav refugees. Britain admitted 4,000; France just 1,000.

many Russians outside of the major conurbations—was to find work in the West. And so an alarming number of them—young women above all—ended up in the hands of criminal syndicates, shipped into the EU through Romania and the Balkans to be employed at best as indentured servants in workshops and restaurants, at worst and more often as prostitutes: in Germany or Italy—or even Bosnia, servicing a well-paid clientele of Western soldiers, administrators and 'aid-workers'. Involuntary Moldovan and Ukrainian 'guest-workers' thus joined the Roma (Gypsies) at the bottom of the continent's multi-cultural heap.[23]

The victims of the sex trade were largely invisible—like earlier generations of white migrants from Europe's fringes they blended easily enough into the local majority, which is why they proved so hard for police and social services to trace. But most of the people whom French sociologists and critics had taken to describing as *les exclus* ('the excluded') were perfectly visible. The new under-class consisted of people excluded not so much from work as from 'life chances': individuals stranded outside the economic mainstream, their children poorly educated, their families marooned in barrack-like apartment blocks at the edge of cities, bereft of shops, services and transport. In 2004, a study by the French interior ministry concluded that some two million such people lived in urban ghettos blighted by social exclusion, racial discrimination and high levels of domestic violence. In some of these *quartiers chauds* youth unemployment had reached 50 percent; the worst affected were young people of Algerian or Moroccan descent.

All too often this under-class was distinguished not just by colour but by creed. For in addition to being multi-cultural the European Union was now increasingly multi-religious. Christians remained in the overwhelming majority, albeit non-practicing in most cases. Jews were now a small minority, their numbers significant only in Russia, France and to a much lesser extent the UK and Hungary. But Hindus and above all Muslims were now a substantial and visible presence in the UK, Belgium, the Netherlands and Germany, as well as in the main cities of Scandinavia, Italy and Central Europe. And—uniquely among the major world religions in Europe—the number of adherents to Islam was rising rapidly.

By the first years of the twenty-first century there were perhaps six million Muslims in France (the majority of North African extraction) and almost as many in Germany (chiefly of Turkish or Kurdish background). Together with the nearly two million Muslims in the UK (mostly from Pakistan and Bangladesh) and a significant presence in the Benelux countries and Italy, these figures suggested a total of perhaps fifteen million Muslims in the Union as a whole.

The Muslim presence in communities that were hitherto overwhelming secu-

---

[23]At the end of the twentieth century there were an estimated 5 million Gypsies in Europe: some 50,000 in Poland, 60,000 in Albania, half a million in Hungary, perhaps 600,000 each in Bulgaria, the former Yugoslavia and the Czech Republic and at least 2 million in Romania. The prejudice and abuse to which they were exposed was common to every country in which the Gypsies lived (not to mention places like Britain to which they were forbidden entry).

lar posed difficult questions of social policy: what provision should be made for the wearing of religious clothing or symbols in public schools? How far should the state encourage (or discourage) separate cultural institutions and facilities? Was it good policy to support multi-cultural (and thus effectively separate) communities or should the authorities seek rather to facilitate and even enforce integration? Official policy in France advocated cultural integration and forbade the display of signs of faith in school; elsewhere, notably in Britain and the Netherlands, there was a broader tolerance for cultural distinction and assertive religious self-identification. But opinion everywhere was divided (see Chapter 23).

If such questions had risen rapidly to the top of national political agendas, and were increasingly entangled in debates over immigration and asylum, it was because of growing anxiety all across the continent at the rise of a new generation of xenophobic parties. Some of these parties had roots in an earlier age of sectarian or nationalist politics; others—like the surprisingly successful Dansk Folkeparti or the List Pim Fortuyn in the Netherlands—were of very recent provenance. But all of them had proven unexpectedly adept at exploiting 'anti-immigrant' sentiment.

Whether, like the British National Party, they railed against 'ethnic minorities' or, like the Front National's Jean-Marie Le Pen, they targeted 'immigrants'—in German the preferred term was 'foreigners' or 'aliens'—the parties of the far Right found rich pickings in these years. On the one hand slower growth combined with vulnerability to global economic forces was exposing many working people to a level of economic insecurity unprecedented in living memory. On the other hand the old organs of the political *Left* were no longer in place to corral and mobilize that insecurity under the banner of class: it was not by chance that the Front National often got its best results in districts that had once been bastions of the French Communist Party.

The presence in increasing numbers of a visible and culturally alien minority in their midst—and the prospect of even more foreigners feeding at the welfare trough or taking 'our' jobs once the floodgates from the East were opened—was icing on the cake for the new Right. Charging that the 'boat is full'—or that their governments had abandoned control of its frontiers to 'cosmopolitan interests' or the 'bureaucrats of Brussels'—populist demagogues promised to stop immigration, repatriate 'foreigners' and return the state to its embattled white citizenry, outsiders in their own country.

Compared with the Fascism of an earlier age this latest manifestation of xenophobia might appear mild—though Germany saw a wave of hate crimes against foreigners and minorities in the early Nineties that prompted some commentators to raise broader concerns: Günter Grass pointed accusingly to the self-centered indifference of West German political culture and the country's myopic enthusiasm for an 'unmerited' unity, arguing that responsibility for the racist violence (especially in the festering, defunct industrial towns of the former GDR where anti-foreigner feeling was most intense) should be placed squarely at the feet of the country's complacent and amnesiac political elite.

But even if the level of violence was contained, the scale of public support for the new Right was cause for serious concern. Under Jörg Haider, its youthful and telegenic leader, the Freedom Party (FP) in neighbouring Austria—heir to the post-war League of Independents but ostensibly purged of the latter's Nazi associations—rose steadily in the polls, presenting itself as the defender of the 'little people' left behind by the mutually beneficial collaboration of the two big parties and threatened by the hordes of 'criminals', 'drug-users' and other 'foreign rabble' now invading their homeland.

To avoid falling foul of the law, Haider was generally careful to avoid behaviour that would tar him too obviously with the brush of Nazi nostalgia. For the most part the Austrian (like Jean-Marie Le Pen) revealed his prejudices only indirectly—for example, by naming, as instances of whatever it was in public life that offended him, people who just happened to be Jewish. Both he and his audiences were more comfortable with newer targets like the European Union: 'We Austrians should answer not to the EU, not to Maastricht, not to some international idea or other, but to this our Homeland'.

In the Austrian parliamentary elections of 1986, Haider's Freedom Party won 9.7 percent of the vote. Four years later it had risen to 17 percent. In the elections of October 1994 it rocked the Viennese establishment by reaching 23 percent, just four points short of the People's Party which had governed the country for the first twenty-five years after the war and which still dominated Austria's rural provinces. Even more ominously, Haider had bitten deep into the traditionally Socialist electorate of working-class Vienna. Considering that (according to 1995 opinion polls) one Austrian in three believed with Haider that 'guest-workers' and other foreigners in Austria had too many benefits and privileges, this was hardly surprising.

Haider's influence peaked at the very end of the century, in the wake of the elections of October 1999 when his party received the backing of 27 percent of Austria's voters: pushing the People's Party into third place and coming within 290,000 votes of the first-place Socialists. In February 2000, to somewhat exaggerated gasps of horror from Austria's European partners, the People's Party formed a coalition government with the Freedom Party (though not including Haider himself). But the new Austrian Chancellor, Wolfgang Schüssel, had made a shrewd calculation: the Freedom Party was a movement of protest, an anti-'them' party that appealed to 'the ripped-off, lied-to little people' (to quote Pierre Poujade, the eponymous populist prototype). Once in government, exposed to the wear and tear of office and constrained to share responsibility for unpopular policies, it would soon lose its appeal. In the elections of 2002 the FP scored just 10.1 percent (while the People's Party had risen to nearly 43 percent). In the European elections of 2004 Haider's party was reduced to 6.4 percent of the vote.

The rise and decline of Haider (who remained nevertheless a popular governor of his native Carinthia) was emblematic of the trajectory of anti-foreigner parties elsewhere. After winning 17 percent of the vote in 2002, in the wake of its leader's assassination, the List Pim Fortuyn rose briefly into the ranks of Dutch government only to see its support collapse to just 5 percent at the subsequent election and its parliamentary representation fall from 42 to 8. In Italy the Lega Nord's ascent into government under the wing of Berlusconi precipitated a steady fall in its support.

In Denmark, the Dansk Folkeparti had risen from obscure beginnings in 1995 to become by 2001 the country's third-largest parliamentary group. By staying out of office and focusing almost exclusively on the immigration issue, the party and its leader Pia Kjærsgaard were able to leverage their influence out of all proportion to size. Both the leading Danish parties—Liberals and Social Democrats—now competed to outbid the other in their newfound 'firmness' on laws governing asylum and foreign residents. 'We'—as Kjærsgaard put it after her party won 12 percent of the vote in the elections of 2001—'are in charge'.[24]

In the sense that there was now almost no mainstream politician of Left or Right who dared appear 'soft' on such issues, she was right. Even the tiny, thuggish British National Party (BNP) was able to cast a shadow on the policies of New Labour governments in the UK. Traditionally marginal—its best recent performance had been 7 percent of the vote in 1997 in an East London district where Bengalis had replaced Jews as the local ethnic minority—the BNP won 11,643 votes (14 percent) four years later in two districts of Oldham, a former mill town in Lancashire where race riots had broken out shortly before the elections.

These were negligible figures compared with developments on the Continent and the BNP came nowhere near winning a parliamentary seat. But because (according to opinion polls) its concerns appeared to reflect a widespread national unease, the hard Right was able to frighten Prime Minister Tony Blair into tightening still further the UK's already ungenerous provisions for would-be immigrants and refugees. It says something about the mood of the time that a New Labour government with an overwhelming parliamentary majority and nearly 11 million voters at the 2001 elections should nonetheless have been moved to respond in this way to the propaganda of a neo-Fascist clique which attracted the support of just 48,000 electors in the country at large: one-fifth of 1 percent of the vote and only 40,000 more votes than the Monster Raving Loony Party.

France was another matter. There the Front National had an issue—immigrants; mass backing—2.7 million voters at the general elections of 1986; and a charismatic leader brilliantly adept at converting generalized public dissatisfaction into focused anger and political prejudice. To be sure, the far Right would never have done so

---

[24]The Dansk Folkeparti originated in a breakaway from the Danish Progress Party, itself a product of the anti-tax movements of the early 1970s (see Chapter 14) but considered by a new generation of radicals to be too 'soft' on the EU and insufficiently anti-immigrant.

well had Mitterrand not cynically introduced into France in 1986 a system of proportional representation designed to engineer the parliamentary success (and thus national visibility) of the *Front National*—and thereby divide and weaken France's mainstream conservative parties.

But the fact remains that 4.5 million French voters backed Le Pen in the presidential elections of 1995: a number that rose to 4.8 million in April 2002 when the FN leader achieved an unprecedented success, taking second place in a presidential election with 17 percent of the vote and forcing the Left's candidate, the hapless Socialist Prime Minister Lionel Jospin, out of the race. In France, too, the conclusion reached by mainstream politicians was that they must somehow draw the sting of Le Pen's appeal by appropriating his concerns and promising tough measures to address 'security' and immigration, without explicitly condoning either Le Pen's language—or his program ('France for the French' and repatriation for everyone else).

Despite Le Pen's own links to an older tradition of far-Right politics—through his youthful support for the Poujadists, his passage through the shadowy organizations of the far-Right during the Algerian war, and his carefully phrased defense of Vichy and the Pétainist cause—his movement, like its counterparts all across the continent, could not be dismissed as simply an atavistic, nostalgic regurgitation of Europe's Fascist past. Certainly Fortuyn or Kjærsgaard could not be categorized thus. Indeed both took care to emphasize their desire to preserve their countries' traditional tolerance—under threat, they asserted, from the religious fanaticism and retrograde cultural practices of the new Muslim minorities.

Nor was Austria's Freedom Party a Nazi movement; and Haider was not Hitler. On the contrary, he took ostentatious care to emphasize his post-war credentials. Born in 1950 he had, as he repeatedly reminded audiences, '*die Gnade der späten Geburt*': the good fortune of a late birth. Part of Haider's success—like that of Christoph Blocher, whose Swiss People's Party won 28 percent of the popular vote in 2003 on an anti-immigrant, anti-EU ticket—came from his skill at burying a racist sub-text under the image of a modernizer, a national-populist of the liberal persuasion. This played surprisingly well to youthful voters: at one point the Freedom Party was the leading party in Austria among the under-thirties.[25]

In Austria as in France it was the fear and hatred of immigrants (in France from the south, in Austria from the east, in both cases from lands over which they once ruled) that has replaced the old obsessions—anti-semitism especially—as the tie that binds the far Right. But the new anti-system parties also benefited from something else: clean hands. Excluded from office, they were untainted by the corruption which seemed, by the early Nineties, to be gnawing at the roots of the European

---

[25]In Switzerland, where anti-immigrant prejudice was especially widespread in the German-speaking cantons, the racism was not always buried: one election poster showed an array of dark-skinned faces over the caption 'The Swiss are becoming Negroes'.

system. Not just in Romania or Poland or (above all) Russia, where it could be explained away as the collateral cost of a transition to capitalism: but in the democratic heartlands of the continent.

In Italy, where ever since the war the Christian Democrats had enjoyed a cozy and profitable relationship with bankers, businessmen, contractors, city bosses, state employees and—it was widely rumored—the Mafia, a new generation of young magistrates began courageously to chip away at decades of barnacled public silence. Ironically it was the Socialist Party that fell first, brought down by the *tangentopoli* ('bribe city') scandal in 1992 that followed investigations into its management of the city of Milan. The party was disgraced and its leader, the former Prime Minister Bettino Craxi, was forced to flee across the Mediterranean into exile in Tunisia.

But the Socialists' affairs were inextricably intertwined with those of the Christian Democrats, their long-time coalition partner. Both parties were further discredited by the wave of arrests and charges that followed, and they took down with them the whole web of political arrangements and accommodations that had shaped Italian politics for two generations. In the elections of 1994, *all* the country's leading political parties except the former-Communists and the ex-Fascists were virtually wiped out—though the only lasting beneficiary of this political earthquake was a former lounge singer, the louche media magnate Silvio Berlusconi, who entered politics not so much to further the national house-cleaning as to ensure that his *own* business dealings remained safely unaffected.

In Spain it was a scandal of a rather different sort that ended the political career of Felipe González, when it was revealed in the mid-'90s (by an enthusiastic younger generation of investigative reporters in the dailies *El Mundo* and *Diario 16*) that his government had conducted a 'dirty war' against Basque terrorism during the years 1983–87, allowing and encouraging death squadrons to practice kidnapping, torture and assassination, both in Spain and even across the frontier in the Basque regions of France whence ETA frequently operated (see Chapter 14).

In view of ETA's reputation, this might not have sufficed to discredit the charismatic González—thanks to the cynical public mood of the late Franco years many of his contemporaries had grown up with a distinctly instrumental view of the state and its laws—were it not for parallel revelations of graft and influence-peddling by González's Socialist colleagues that echoed the Italian example and aroused widespread anxiety over the moral condition of a Spanish democracy still in its infancy.

In France—or Germany, or Belgium—the spate of scandals that disfigured public life in the Nineties suggested not so much the fragility of institutions and *mores* as the rising cost of practicing democracy under modern conditions. Politics—staff, advertising, consultancies—are expensive. Public cash for political parties was strictly limited in Europe by law and tradition and usually made available only for the purpose of standing at elections. If they needed more, politicians had in the past turned to their traditional backers: party members, mass unions (on the Left) and private businessmen and corporations. But these resources were drying up: party membership figures were falling, mass unions were on the decline and with a growing cross-party policy consensus on economic affairs, companies and private individuals saw little reason to contribute generously to any one party.

Perhaps understandably, in any case more or less universally, the major political parties of Western Europe began to seek out alternative ways to attract funding—just at the time when, thanks to the abolition of controls and the globalization of business, there was a whole lot more money around. Gaullists *and* Socialists in France—like the Christian Democrats in Germany and New Labour in Britain—were revealed to have raised cash over the past two decades in a variety of shady ways: whether by selling favours, peddling influence or simply leaning rather more insistently than in the past upon conventional contributors.

Things went a little further in Belgium: one scandal among many—the so-called Dassault/Agusta affair—can serve as an illustration. At the end of the 1980s, the Belgian government contracted to purchase forty-six military helicopters from the Italian firm Agusta and to give the French company Dassault the job of refitting its F-16 aircraft. Competing bidders for the contracts were frozen out. In itself this was not unusual, and the fact that three countries were involved even lends an ecumenically pan-European quality to the affair.

But it later emerged that Belgium's Socialist Party (in government at the time) had done rather nicely from kickbacks on both deals. Shortly thereafter, one leading Socialist politician who knew too much, André Cools, was killed in a parking lot in Liège in 1991; another, Etienne Mange, was arrested in 1995; and a third, Willy Claes, a former prime minister of Belgium, sometime (1994–1995) secretary-general of NATO and foreign minister when the deals were made, was found guilty in September 1998 of taking bribes for his party. A fourth suspect, the former army general Jacques Lefebvre who was closely involved in the affair, died in mysterious circumstances in March 1995.

If this is a peculiarly Belgian story ('*La Belgique*' according to Baudelaire, '*est sans vie, mais non sans corruption*') it is perhaps because the duplication and dilution of constitutional authority there had led not just to the absence of government oversight but to the near-collapse of much of the apparatus of the state, including the criminal justice system. Elsewhere, with the exception of Italy as noted above, there was strikingly little evidence of *personal* corruption—most of the crimes and misdemeanors were undertaken quite literally for the good of the party[26]—but a number of very prominent men were nevertheless forced abruptly out of public life.

These included not just González, the French ex-Prime Minister Alain Juppé and the historic leaders of Italy's Christian Democrats; but even former German Chan-

---

[26]With one exception: Edith Cresson—a former French Socialist Prime Minister turned EU Commissioner—contributed to the discrediting of the whole Commission when it was revealed in 1999 that she had used her power in Brussels to invent a well-paid consultancy for her former dentist.

cellor Helmut Kohl, the hero of unification, whose reputation was cast under a cloud when he refused to divulge the names of secret donors to his party's funds. Had he not been protected by his office, French President Jacques Chirac—mayor of Paris during a time when the city was awash in party-political graft and favour-peddling—would surely have joined their ranks.

What is perhaps most striking about these developments is how relatively *little* discredit they seem to have brought upon the political system as a whole. The decline in turnout at elections certainly bespeaks a general loss of interest in public affairs; but this could already be detected decades earlier in rising abstention rates and the diminished intensity of political argument. The real surprise is not the rise of a new cohort of right-wing populist parties but their consistent failure to do even better than they have, to capitalize on the disruption and discontent since 1989.

There was a reason for this. Europeans may have lost faith in their politicians, but at the core of the European system of government there is something that even the most radical anti-system parties have not dared to attack head on and which continues to attract near-universal allegiance. That something is certainly not the European Union, for all its manifold merits. It is not democracy: too abstract, too nebulous and perhaps too often invoked to stand in isolation as an object for admiration. Nor is it freedom or the rule of law—not seriously threatened in the West for many decades and already taken for granted by a younger generation of Europeans in all the member states of the EU. What binds Europeans together, even when they are deeply critical of some aspect or other of its practical workings, is what it has become conventional to call—in disjunctive but revealing contrast with 'the American way of life'—the 'European model of society'.

XXIII

The Varieties of Europe

'We were wise indeed, could we discern truly the signs of our own time; and by knowledge of its wants and advantages, wisely adjust our own position in it. Let us, instead of gazing wildly into the obscure distance, look calmly around us, for a little, on the perplexed scene where we stand'.
Thomas Carlyle

'The Creator of Europe made her small and even split her up into little parts, so that our hearts could find joy not in size but in plurality'.
Karel Čapek

'In Europe we were Asiatics, whereas in Asia we, too, are Europeans'.
Fyodor Dostoevsky

When Communism fell and the Soviet Union imploded, they took with them not just an ideological system but the political and geographical coordinates of an entire continent. For forty-five years—beyond the living memory of most Europeans—the uneasy outcome of World War Two had been frozen in place. The accidental division of Europe, with all that it entailed, had come to seem inevitable. And now it had been utterly swept away. In retrospect the post-war decades took on a radically altered significance. Once understood as the onset of a new era of permanent ideological polarization they now appeared for what they were: an extended epilogue to the European civil war that had begun in 1914, a forty-year interregnum between the defeat of Adolf Hitler and the final resolution of the unfinished business left behind by his war.

With the disappearance of the world of 1945–1989, its illusions came into better focus. The much-heralded 'economic miracle' of post-war Western Europe had returned the region to the standing in world trade and output that it had lost in the course of the years 1914–45, with rates of economic growth subsequently settling back into levels broadly comparable to those of the late nineteenth century. This was no small achievement, but it was not quite the breakthrough into infinitely incremental prosperity that contemporaries had once fondly supposed.

Moreover, the recovery had been achieved not in spite of the Cold War but because of it. Like the Ottoman threat in an earlier time, the shadow of the Soviet empire shrank Europe but imposed upon the surviving rump the benefits of unity. In the absence of the imprisoned Europeans to their east the citizens of western Europe had flourished: free of any obligation to address the poverty and backwardness of the successor states to the old continental empires and secured by the American military umbrella against the political backwash of the recent past. Viewed from the East this was always tunnel vision. After the collapse of Communism and the break-up of the Soviet empire, it could no longer be sustained.

On the contrary. The happy cocoon of post-war Western Europe—with its economic communities and free-trade zones, its reassuring external alliances and redundant internal frontiers—seemed suddenly vulnerable, called upon to respond to the frustrated expectations of would-be 'Euro-citizens' to its East and no longer anchored to a self-evident relationship with the great power across its western ocean. Constrained once again to acknowledge their continent's broad eastern marches when sketching a common European future, Western Europeans were perforce drawn back into the common European past.

As a consequence, the years 1945–1989 took on a parenthetical quality. Open warfare between states, a constituent feature of the European way of life for three hundred years, had reached apocalyptic levels between 1913 and 1945: some sixty million Europeans died in wars or state-sponsored killing in the first half of the twentieth century. But from 1945 to 1989 inter-state war disappeared from the continent of Europe.[1] Two generations of Europeans grew up under the hitherto inconceivable impression that peace was the natural order of things. As an extension of politics, war (and ideological confrontation) was outsourced to the so-called Third World.

That said, it is worth recalling that while remaining at peace with their neighbors the Communist states practiced a distinctive form of permanent warfare upon their own societies: mostly in the form of rigorous censorship, enforced shortages and repressive policing but occasionally breaking into open conflict—notably in Berlin in 1953, in Budapest in 1956, in Prague in 1968 and in Poland sporadically from 1968 to 1981 and under martial law thereafter. In Eastern Europe the post-war decades thus appear rather different in collective memory (though no less parenthetical). But compared with what had gone before, Eastern Europe too had lived through an age of unusual, albeit involuntary, calm.

Whether the post-World War Two era, now fast retreating into memory with the onset of new world (dis-)orders, would become an object of nostalgic longing and regret depended very much on where and when you were born. From both sides of the Iron Curtain the children of the Sixties—i.e. the core cohort of the baby-boomer generation, born between 1946 and 1951—certainly looked back with affection upon 'their' decade and continued to harbour fond memories and an

---

[1] Even taking into account the Yugoslav wars of the Nineties, the number of war-related deaths in Europe in the second half of the century was less than one million.

exaggerated sense of its significance. And in the West, at least, their parents remained grateful for the political stability and material security of the era, contrasted with the horrors that had gone before.

But those too young to recall the Sixties were often resentful of the solipsistic self-aggrandizement of its ageing memorialists; while many older people who had lived out their lives under Communism recalled not just secure jobs, cheap rents and safe streets but also and above all a grey landscape of wasted talents and blighted hopes. And on both sides of the divide there were limits to what could be recovered from the rubble of twentieth-century history. Peace, prosperity and security, to be sure; but the optimistic convictions of an earlier age were gone for good.

Before he committed suicide in 1942 the Viennese novelist and critic Stefan Zweig wrote longingly of the lost world of pre-1914 Europe, expressing 'pity for those who were not young during those last years of confidence'. Sixty years later, at the end of the twentieth century, almost everything else had been recovered or rebuilt. But the confidence with which Zweig's generation of Europeans entered the century could never be entirely recaptured: too much had happened. Inter-war Europeans recalling the *Belle Epoque* might murmur 'if only'; but in the aftermath of World War Two the overwhelming sentiment among anyone reflecting on the continent's thirty-year catastrophe had been 'never again'.[2]

In short, there was no way back. Communism in Eastern Europe had been the wrong answer to a real question. That same question in Western Europe—how to overcome the catastrophe of the first half of the twentieth century—had been addressed by setting recent history aside altogether, recapitulating some of the successes of the second half of the *nineteenth* century—domestic political stability, increased economic productivity and a steady expansion in foreign trade—and labeling them 'Europe'. After 1989, however, prosperous, post-political Western Europe was faced once again with its eastern twin and 'Europe' had to be rethought.

The prospect of abandoning the cocoon was not universally welcomed, as we have seen, and writing in March 1993 for the Polish journal *Polityka* Jacek Kuroń did not exaggerate when he surmised that 'certain Western political figures are nostalgic for the old world order and the USSR'. But that 'old world order'—the familiar *stasis* of the past four decades—was gone forever. Europeans were now confronted not just with an uncertain future but also with a rapidly changing past. What had recently been very straightforward was now, once again, becoming rather complicated. The end of the twentieth century saw half a billion people on the western promontory of the Eurasian land mass increasingly taken up with the interro-

---

[2]Raymond Aron (born in 1905) shared some of Zweig's wistful memories, if not his despair: 'Ever since, under a July sun, bourgeois Europe entered the century of wars, men have lost control of their history'.

gation of their own identity. Who are Europeans? What does it mean to be European? What *is* Europe—and what kind of a place do Europeans want it to be?

There is little to be gained by seeking to distill the essence of 'Europe'. The 'Idea of Europe'—itself a much debated topic—has a long history, some of it quite reputable. But although a certain 'idea' of Europe—reiterated in assorted conventions and treaties—informs the Union to which most Europeans now belong, it offers only a very partial insight into the life they lead there. In an age of demographic transition and resettlement, today's Europeans are more numerous and heterogeneous than ever before. Any account of their common condition at the dawn of the twenty-first century must begin by acknowledging that variety, by mapping the overlapping contours and fault-lines of European identity and experience.

The term 'mapping' is used advisedly. Europe, after all, is a place. But its frontiers have always been more than a little fluid. The ancient boundaries—of Rome and Byzantium, of the Holy Roman Empire and Christian Europe—correspond closely enough with later political divisions to suggest some genuine continuity: the uneasy encounter-points of Germanic and Slav Europe were as clear to an eleventh-century writer like Adam of Bremen as they are to us; the medieval frontiers of Catholic and Orthodox Christianity, from Poland to Serbia, were much as we find them today; and the concept of a Europe divided between east and west at the Elbe would have been familiar to the ninth-century administrators of the Carolingian Empire, had they thought in such terms.

But whether those long-established boundary lines are any guide to the whereabouts of *Europe* always depended upon where you happen to stand. To take one well-known case: by the eighteenth century most Hungarians and Bohemians had been Catholic for centuries and many of them were German speakers. But for enlightened Austrians, 'Asia' nevertheless began at the Landstrasse, the high road leading east out of Vienna. When Mozart headed *west* from Vienna en route for Prague in 1787, he described himself as crossing an *oriental* border. East and West, Asia and Europe, were always walls in the mind at least as much as lines on the earth.

Because much of Europe until recent times was not divided into states but instead accommodated within empires, it helps to think of the external markers of the continent not as frontiers but as indeterminate boundary-regions—marches, *limes, militärgrenze, krajina*: zones of imperial conquest and settlement, not always topographically precise but delimiting an important political and cultural edge. From the Baltic to the Balkans, such regions and their inhabitants have for centuries understood themselves as the outer guard of civilization, the vulnerable and sensitive point where the familiar world ends and barbarians are kept at bay.

But these borderlands are fluid and have often shifted with time and circumstance: their geographical implications can be confusing. Poles, Lithuanians and Ukrainians have all presented themselves in their literature and political myths as guarding the edges of 'Europe' (or Christianity).[3] But as a brief glance at a map suggests, their claims are mutually exclusive: they can't all be right. The same is true of competing Hungarian and Romanian narratives, or the insistence of both Croats and Serbs that it is *their* southern border (with Serbs and Turks respectively) that constitutes the vital outer defensive line of civilized Europe.

What this confusion shows is that the outer boundaries of Europe have for centuries been sufficiently significant for interested parties to press with great urgency their competing claims to membership. Being 'in' Europe offered a degree of security: an assurance—or at least a promise—of refuge and inclusion. Over the centuries it came increasingly to serve as a source of collective identity. Being a 'border-state', an exemplar and guardian of the core values of European civilization, was a source of vulnerability but also pride: which is why the sense of having been excluded and forgotten by 'Europe' made Soviet domination so particularly humiliating for many central and eastern European intellectuals.

Europe, then, is not so much about *absolute* geography—where a country or a people actually are—as *relative* geography: where they sit in relation to others. At the end of the twentieth century, writers and politicians in places like Moldova, Ukraine or Armenia asserted their 'Europeanness' not on historical or geographical grounds (which might or might not be plausible) but precisely as a defense *against* history and geography alike. Summarily released from Muscovite empire, these post-imperial orphan states looked now to another 'imperial' capital: Brussels.[4]

What these peripheral nations hoped to gain from the distant prospect of inclusion in the new Europe was less important than what they stood to lose by being left out of it. The implications of exclusion were already clear to even the most casual visitor by the early years of the new century. Whatever was once cosmopolitan and 'European' in cities like Cernovitz in Ukraine or Chisinau in Moldova had long since been beaten out of them by Nazi and Soviet rule; and the surrounding countryside was even now 'a pre-modern world of dirt roads and horse-drawn carts, of outdoor wells and felt boots, of vast silences and velvet-black nights'.[5] Identification with 'Europe' was not about a common past, now well and truly destroyed. It was about asserting a claim, however flimsy and forlorn, upon a common future.

The fear of being left out of Europe was not confined to the continent's outer perimeter. From the perspective of Romanian-speaking Moldovans, their neighbors

---

[3]Many Poles, it should be noted, also insist upon their country's place at the *centre* of Europe—a revealing confusion.
[4]Much the same is true of Albanian Kosovars. Liberated by NATO from Serbian oppression, they aspire to independent statehood less from nationalistic ambition than as a surety against the risk of being left *in* Serbia—and *out* of Europe.
[5]Anna Reid, *Borderland. A Journey through the history of Ukraine* (2000), p. 20. Hence the place of 'Europe' in the language and hopes of the Ukrainian revolution of December 2004.

to the West in Romania proper were blessed by history. Unlike Moldova they were seen by the West as legitimate if under-performing contenders for EU membership and were thus assured of a properly *European* future. But seen from Bucharest the picture changes: it is Romania itself that is at risk of being left out. In 1989, when Nicolae Ceaușescu's colleagues finally began to turn on him, they wrote a letter accusing the *Conducator* of trying to tear their nation away from its European roots: 'Romania is and remains a European country. . . . You have begun to change the geography of the rural areas, but you cannot move Romania into Africa.' In the same year the elderly Romanian playwright Eugène Ionesco described the country of his birth as 'about to leave Europe for good, which means leaving history.' Nor was this a new concern: in 1972 E. M. Cioran, looking back at his country's grim history, echoed a widespread Romanian insecurity: 'What depressed me most was a map of the Ottoman Empire. Looking at it, I understood our past and everything else'.[6]

Romanians—like Bulgarians, Serbs and others with good reason to believe that 'core' Europe sees them as outsiders (when it sees them at all)—alternate between defensively asserting their ur-European characteristics (in literature, architecture, topography, etc) or else acknowledging the hopelessness of their cause and fleeing West. In the aftermath of Communism, both responses were in evidence. While the former Romanian Prime Minister, Adrien Nastase, was describing for readers of *Le Monde* in July 2001 the 'added value' that Romania brings to Europe, his fellow Romanians constituted over half the total number of aliens apprehended while illegally crossing the Polish-German border. In a poll taken early in the new century, 52 percent of Bulgarians (and an overwhelming majority of those under 30) said that, given the chance, they would emigrate from Bulgaria—preferably to 'Europe'.

This sense of being on the periphery of someone else's centre, of being a sort of second-class European, is today largely confined to former Communist countries, nearly all of them in the zone of small nations that Tomáš Masaryk foresaw coming into being, from North Cape to Cape Matapan in the Peloponnese. But it was not always so. Within recent memory the continent's other margins were at least as peripheral—economically, linguistically, culturally. The poet Edwin Muir described his childhood move from the Orkneys to Glasgow in 1901 as 'one hundred and fifty years covered in a two days' journey'; it is a sentiment that would not have been out of place half a century later. Well into the 1980s the highlands and islands at Europe's edges—Sicily, Ireland, northern Scotland, Lapland—had more in common with one another, and their own past, than with the prosperous metropolitan regions of the centre.

Even now—indeed above all now—fault lines and boundaries cannot be counted upon to follow national frontiers. The Council of Baltic Sea States is a case in point. Established in 1992, it comprises Scandinavian participants: Denmark, Fin-

---

[6]See Tony Judt, 'Romania: Bottom of the Heap', *New York Review*, November 1st 2001.

mained decidedly more equal than others. Two and a half centuries after Voltaire drew the contrast between a Europe that 'knows' and a Europe that 'waits to be known', that distinction retained much of its force. Power, prosperity and institutions were all clustered into the continent's far western corner. The moral geography of Europe—the Europe in Europeans' heads—consisted of a core of 'truly' European states (some of them, like Sweden, geographically quite peripheral) whose constitutional, legal and cultural values were held up as the model for lesser, aspirant Europeans: seeking, as it were, to become truly themselves.[11]

Eastern Europeans, then, were expected to know about the West. When knowledge flowed in the opposite direction, however, it was not always in very flattering ways. It is not just that impoverished eastern and southern Europeans travelled north and west to sell their labour or their bodies. By the end of the century certain eastern European cities, having exhausted their appeal as rediscovered outposts of a lost central Europe, had begun to reposition themselves in a profitable niche market as cheap and tawdry vacation spots for down-market mass tourism from the West. Tallinn and Prague in particular established an unenviable reputation as the venue for British 'stag flights'—low-cost package weekends for Englishmen seeking abundant alcohol and cheap sex.

Travel agents and tour organizers whose clientele would once have settled for Blackpool or (more recently) Benidorm now reported rapturous enthusiasm for the exotic treats on offer in the European east. But then the English, too, were peripheral in their way—which is why Europe remained for so many of them an exotic object. In 1991 the Sofia weekly *Kultura* asked Bulgarians to which foreign culture they felt closest: 18 percent answered 'French', 11 percent 'German' (and 15 percent 'American'). But only 1.3 percent acknowledged feeling any closeness to 'English culture'.

The undisputed *centre* of Europe, for all its post-unification woes, was still Germany: in population and output by far the largest state in the EU, it was the very kernel of 'core Europe', as every Chancellor from Adenauer to Schröder had always insisted it must be. Germany was also the only country that straddled the former divide. Thanks to unification, immigration and the arrival of the Federal government, Greater Berlin was now six times the area of Paris—a symbol of the relative standing of the Union's two leading members. Germany dominated the European economy. It was the largest trading partner of most member-states of the EU. Two-thirds of the Union's net income came from the Federal Republic alone. And despite being its primary paymasters—or maybe for that reason—Germans remained among the EU's most committed citizens. German statesmen would pe-

---

[11]In June 2004 the present author received the following greeting from a correspondent in the foreign ministry in Zagreb: 'Things here good. Croatia got EU membership invitation. This will change many mental maps'.

riodically propose the creation of a 'fast-track' of states committed to a fully integrated federal Europe, only to retreat in undisguised frustration at their partners' procrastination.

If Germany—to pursue the Voltairian image a little further—was the country that 'knew' Europe best, it was appropriate that at the beginning of the twenty-first century two other former imperial states should have been most insistently seeking to be 'known' by it. Like Germany, Russia and Turkey had once played an imperial role in European affairs. And many Russians and Turks had shared the uncomfortable fate of Europe's ethnic German communities: displaced heirs of an autocratic power now reduced to resented and vulnerable minorities in someone else's nation state, the tidal refuse of imperial retreat. In the late 1990s it was estimated that more than one hundred million Russians lived outside of Russia in the independent countries of eastern Europe.[12]

But there the resemblance ended. Post-Soviet Russia was a Eurasian empire rather than a European state. Preoccupied with violent rebellions in the Caucasus, it was maintained at a distance from the rest of Europe by the new buffer states of Belarus, Ukraine and Moldova as well as by its own increasingly illiberal domestic politics. There was no question of Russia joining the EU: new entrants, as we have seen, were required to conform to 'European values'—with respect to the rule of law, civic rights and freedoms and institutional transparency—that Vladimir Putin's Moscow was very far from acknowledging, much less implementing.[13] In any event, Russian authorities were more interested in building pipelines and selling gas to the EU than in joining it. Many Russians, including residents of the western cities, did not instinctively think of themselves as Europeans: when they traveled west they spoke (like the English) of 'going to Europe'.

Nevertheless, Russia had been a 'hands-on' European power for three hundred years and the legacy remained. Latvian banks were the target of takeovers by Russian businessmen. A Lithuanian president, Rolandas Paksas, was forced out of office in 2003 under suspicion of close links with the Russian mafia. Moscow retained its Baltic enclave around Kaliningrad and continued to demand unrestricted transit (through Lithuania) for Russian freight and military traffic, as well as visa-free travel for Russian citizens visiting the EU. Laundered cash from the business un-

---

[12]Hungarians in twenty-first-century Romania, Slovakia and Serbia were another, smaller post-imperial minority: once dominant, now vulnerable. In the Vojvodina region of northern Serbia, Hungarians who had lived there for centuries were periodically assaulted and their properties vandalized by Serb youths. The response of the authorities in Belgrade, who appeared to have learned nothing and forgotten nothing from the catastrophe of the Nineties, was depressingly predictable: the attacks were not 'serious' and in any case, 'they' started it.

[13]Quite the opposite. In a series of measures in the spring and summer of 2004 the authorities significantly curtailed both the rights of the press and the already restricted opportunities for public protest. Russia's brief window of freedom—actually disarray and the absence of constraint rather than genuine constitutionally protected liberty—was fast closing. In 2004, Russian observers estimated that KGB-trained officials occupied one in four of civilian administrative posts in the country.

dertakings of Russian oligarchs was funnelled through the property market in London and the French Riviera.

In the short run, Russia was thus a decidedly uncomfortable presence on Europe's outer edge. But it was not a threat. The Russian military was otherwise engaged and anyway in dilapidated condition. The health of the Russian population was a matter of serious concern—life expectancy for men especially was falling precipitately and international agencies had for some time been warning that the country had seen a revival of tuberculosis and was on the verge of an AIDS epidemic—but this was primarily a source of concern for Russians themselves. For the immediate future Russia was decidedly preoccupied with its own affairs.

In the longer run, the simple fact of Russia's proximity, its sheer size and unmatched fossil-fuel reserves, must inevitably cast a shadow on the future of an energy-poor European continent. Already in 2004, half of Poland's natural gas and 95 percent of its oil came from Russia. But in the meantime what the Russian authorities and individual Russians were seeking from Europe was 'respect'. Moscow wished to be more intimately involved in intra-European decision making, whether in NATO, in the administration of Balkan settlements, or in trade agreements (both bilateral and through the World Trade Organization): not because decisions taken in Russia's absence would necessarily be prejudicial to its interests but as a point of principle.

European history, it seemed to many observers, had come full circle. As in the 18th century so in the 21st: Russia was both in Europe and outside it, Montesquieu's 'nation d'Europe' and Gibbon's 'Scythian wilderness'. For Russians, the European West remained what it had been for centuries, a contradictory object of attraction and repulsion, of admiration and *ressentiment*. Russia's rulers and people alike remained markedly sensitive to outside opinion while evincing deep suspicion of all foreign criticism or interference. History and geography had bequeathed to Europeans a neighbour they could neither ignore nor accommodate.

The same might once have been said of Turkey. For nearly seven hundred years the Ottoman Turks had been Europe's 'other', supplanting the Arabs who had occupied the role for the previous half millennium. For many centuries 'Europe' began where the Turks ended (which was why Cioran was so depressed to be reminded of Romania's long years under Ottoman rule); and it was commonplace to speak of Christian Europe being periodically 'saved'—whether at the gates of Vienna, or Budapest, or at the 1571 Battle of Lepanto—from the jaws of Turkish Islam. From the mid-eighteenth century, as Ottoman Turkey slipped into decline, the 'Eastern Question'—how to manage the Ottoman Empire's decline and what to do with the territories now emerging from centuries of Turkish rule—was the most pressing challenge facing European diplomats.

Turkey's defeat in World War I, the overthrow of the Ottomans, and their replacement by Kemal Ataturk's ostentatiously secular, modernizing state, had taken the Eastern Question off the European agenda. Now governed from Ankara, the

Turks had troubles enough of their own; and although their removal from the Balkans and the Arab Middle East had bequeathed a tangled web of conflicts and choices with momentous long-term consequences for Europe and the world, the Turks themselves were no longer part of the problem. Had it not been for Turkey's strategic location athwart the Soviet Union's sea route to the Mediterranean, the country might well have disappeared altogether from Western consciousness.

Instead, Ankara became for the duration of the Cold War an accommodating participant in the Western alliance, contributing to NATO a rather significant contingent of soldiers. American missiles and bases were established in Turkey as part of the *cordon sanitaire* ringing the Soviet frontiers from Baltic to Pacific, and Western governments not only furnished Turkey with copious sums in aid but looked benevolently and uncritically upon its unstable dictatorial regimes—often the outcome of military coups—and their unrestrained abuse of minority rights (notably those of the Kurds in the country's far east, one fifth of the total population). Meanwhile, Turkish 'guest workers', like the rest of the Mediterranean basin's surplus rural population, migrated in large numbers to Germany and other Western European lands in search of jobs.

But the Ottoman legacy would return to haunt the new Europe. With the end of the Cold War, Turkey's distinctive location took on a different significance. The country was no longer a frontier outpost and barrier state in an international geopolitical confrontation. Instead it was now a conduit, caught between Europe and Asia, with ties and affinities in both directions. Although Turkey was formally a secular republic, most of its seventy million citizens were Muslims. Many older Turks were not especially orthodox, but with the rise of radical Islam there were growing fears that even Ataturk's ruthlessly imposed secular state might prove vulnerable to a new generation rebelling against their secularized parents and looking for roots in an older heritage of Ottoman Islam.

But Turkey's educated professional and business elites were disproportionately located in the European city of Istanbul and identified enthusiastically with Western dress, culture and practices. Like other ambitious eastern Europeans they saw Europe—European values, European institutions, European markets and careers— as the only possible future for them and their ambivalently situated country. Their goal was clear: to escape out of history and into 'Europe'. Moreover, this was one objective they shared with the traditionally influential officer corps, who identified wholeheartedly with Ataturk's dream of a secular state and expressed open irritation at creeping Islamisation in Turkish public life.

However, Europe—or at least Brussels—was more than a little hesitant: Turkey's application to join the European Union lay unaddressed for many years. There were good reasons for caution: Turkey's prisons, its treatment of domestic critics and its inadequate civil and economic codes were just some of many issues that would need to be addressed before it could hope to get beyond a strictly trading relationship with its European partners. Senior European commissioners like the

Austrian Franz Fischler openly voiced doubts about the country's long-term democratic credentials. And then there were practical difficulties: as a member-state Turkey would be the second largest in the Union after Germany, as well as one of the poorest—the gulf between its prosperous western edge and the vast, impoverished east was huge and, given the opportunity, millions of Turks might well head west into Europe in search of a living wage. The implications for national immigration policies, as well as for the EU's budget, could hardly be ignored.

But the real impediments lay elsewhere.[14] If Turkey entered the EU, the Union would have an external frontier abutting Georgia, Armenia, Iran, Iraq and Syria. Whether or not it made geographical sense to take 'Europe' to within one hundred miles of Mosul was a legitimate question; in the circumstances of the time it was unquestionably a security risk. And the further Europe stretched its frontiers, the more it was felt by many—including the drafters of the constitutional document of 2004—that the Union should explicitly state what it was that defined their common home. This, in turn, induced a number of politicians in Poland, Lithuania, Slovakia and elsewhere—not to mention the Polish Pope in Rome—to try unsuccessfully to insert into the preamble to a new European constitutional text a reminder that Europe was once *Christian* Europe. Had not Václav Havel, speaking at Strasbourg in 1994, reminded his audience that the 'European Union is based on a large set of values, with roots in antiquity and Christianity'?

Whatever else they were, Turks were assuredly not Christian. The irony was that precisely for this reason—because they could not define themselves as Christian (or 'Judeo-Christian')—would-be European Turks were even more likely than other Europeans to emphasize the secular, tolerant and liberal dimensions of European identity.[15] They were also, and with increasing urgency, trying to invoke European values and norms as a lever against reactionary influences in Turkish public life—a goal that the member-states of Europe itself had long encouraged.

But although in 2003 the Turkish parliament finally removed, at European bidding, many longstanding restrictions on Kurdish cultural life and political expression, the lengthy hesitation-waltz performed by governments and officials at Brussels had begun to exact a price. Turkish critics of EU membership pointed insistently to the humiliation of a once-imperial nation, now reduced to the status of a supplicant at the European door, importuning support for its application from its former subject nations. Moreover, the steady growth of religious sentiment in Turkey not only produced an electoral victory for the country's moderate Islamist party but encouraged the national parliament to debate a motion to make adultery, once again, a criminal offence.

---

[14]Including the domestic political calculations of Greek politicians, who for many years used their vote in Brussels to hinder and block any movement on Turkey's candidacy.
[15]In addition they were wont to see as 'European' an idealized free-market, contrasting it with the graft and cronyism of Turkey's own economy.

In response to explicit warnings from Brussels that this could definitively jeopardize Ankara's application to join the EU, the motion was abandoned and in December 2004 the European Union at last agreed to open accession talks with Ankara. But the damage was done. Opponents of Turkish membership—and there were many, in Germany[16] and France as well as closer to home in Greece or Bulgaria—could point once again to its unsuitability. In 2004 the retiring Dutch EU Commissioner Frits Bolkestein warned of the coming 'Islamisation' of Europe. The likelihood of negotiations proceeding smoothly diminished still further—Günter Verheugen, the EU Commissioner for enlargement, acknowledged that he did not expect Turkey to become a member of the Union 'before 2015'. Meanwhile, the cost of future rejection or further delays—to Turkish pride and the political stability of Europe's vulnerable edge—ratcheted up another notch. The Eastern Question was back.

That history should have weighed so heavily upon European affairs at the start of the twenty-first century was ironic, considering how lightly it lay upon the shoulders of contemporary Europeans. The problem was not so much education—the teaching or mis-teaching of history in schools, though in some parts of southeastern Europe this too was a source of concern—as the public uses to which the past was now put. In authoritarian societies, of course, this was an old story; but Europe, by its self-definition, was post-authoritarian. Governments no longer exercised a monopoly over knowledge and history could not readily be altered for political convenience.

Nor was it, for the most part. The threat to history in Europe came not from the deliberate distortion of the past for mendacious ends, but from what might at first have seemed a natural adjunct to historical knowledge: nostalgia. The final decades of the century had seen an escalating public fascination with the past as a detached artifact, encapsulating not recent memories but *lost* memories: history not so much as a source of enlightenment about the present but rather as an illustration of how very different things had once been. History on television—whether narrated or performed; history in theme parks; history in museums: all emphasized not what bound people to the past but everything that separated them from it. The present was depicted not as heir to history but as its orphan: cut off from the way things were and the world we have lost.

In eastern Europe, nostalgia drew directly upon regret for the lost certainties of Communism, now purged of its darker side. In 2003 the Museum of Decorative Arts in Prague mounted an exhibition of 'pre-revolutionary clothing': boots, underwear, dresses and the like from a world that had only ended fourteen years be-

---

[16]The Christian Democratic Union in Germany was officially opposed to Turkey joining the EU.

fore but was already an object of detached fascination. The exhibition attracted many older people for whom the grey sameness of the shoddily-made items on display must have been a recent memory. And yet the response of visitors suggested a degree of affection and even regret that caught the curators quite by surprise.

Ostalgie, as it was known in Germany, drew on a similar vein of forgetful remembering. Considering that the GDR—to adapt Mirabeau's description of Hohenzollern Prussia—was little more than a security service with a state, it demonstrated in the glow of retrospect a remarkable capacity to evoke affection and even longing. While Czechs were admiring their old clothes, Germans were flocking to *Goodbye Lenin*: a film whose ostensible mocking of the shortages, dogmas and general absurdity of life under Erich Honecker was knowingly offset by a certain sympathy for its subject and more than a little ambivalence at its sudden loss.

But Germans and Czechs, like other central Europeans, have had all too much experience of sudden, traumatic national re-starts. Their selective nostalgia for whatever might be retrieved from the detritus of lost pasts made a lot of sense—it was not by chance that Edgar Reitz's *Heimat: Eine Deutsche Chronik* attracted an average of nine million West German viewers per episode when it was televised in 1984. The obsession with nostalgia that swept across the rest of *Western* Europe in the last years of the old century, giving rise to heritage industries, memorials, reconstructions, reenactments and renovations, is not so readily accounted for.

What the historian Eric Hobsbawm described in 1995 as 'the great age of historical mythology' was not of course unprecedented—Hobsbawm himself had written brilliantly about the 'invention of tradition' in nineteenth-century Europe, at the dawning of the national age: the sort of *ersatz* culture dismissed by Edwin Muir (writing of Burns and Scott in *Scotland 1941*) as 'sham bards for a sham nation'. But the creative re-imagining of the national past in France and the UK at the end of the twentieth century was of another order altogether.

It was not by chance that history-as-nostalgia was so very pronounced in these two national settings in particular. Having entered the twentieth century as proud imperial powers, both countries had been stripped of territory and resources by war and decolonization. The confidence and security of global empire had been replaced by uneasy memories and uncertain future prospects. What it meant to be French, or British, had once been very clear, but no longer. The alternative, to become enthusiastically 'European', was far easier in small countries like Belgium or Portugal, or in places—like Italy or Spain—where the recent national past was best left in shadow.[17] But for nations reared within living memory on grandeur and glory, 'Europe' would always be an uncomfortable transition: a compromise, not a choice.

---

[17]Democratic Spain did indeed develop an official 'heritage' industry, fostered by its *Patrimonio Nacional*, but the latter took care to emphasize the country's distant Golden Age rather than its recent history.

Institutionally speaking, the British turn to nostalgia began almost immediately after World War Two, when the Labour Minister Hugh Dalton established a 'National Land Fund' to acquire sites and buildings of 'beauty and history' for the nation, to be administered by a National Trust. Within a generation 'NT' properties—parks, castles, palaces and 'areas of outstanding natural beauty' had become prominent tourist attractions: some of them still occupied by their original owners, who had bequeathed their heirlooms to the nation in return for significant fiscal relief.

From the Fifties through the Seventies a reassuring version of the recent past surfaced and resurfaced in the form of war films, costume dramas and clothing: the recycling of Edwardian fashion, from teddy boys to hirsute facial ornaments, was a particular feature of this trend—culminating, in 1977, in a self-consciously 'retro' and nostalgic celebration of the Queen's Silver Jubilee amid street parties, photographic exhibits and nationwide invocation of older and better times. But after the Thatcherite revolution of the Eighties even this element of continuity was lost. In the course of that decade the Britain—more precisely the England—that could feel a certain warm glow of recognition when looking back to the '40s, or even to 1913, was quite swept away.

In its place there emerged a country incapable of relating to its immediate past except through the unintentional irony of denial, or else as a sort of disinfected, disembodied 'heritage'. The denial was well captured by the insecurities of the old educational establishment of Oxford and Cambridge, humiliatingly constrained in the new Blairite atmosphere of egalitarian opportunism to insist on their 'anti-élitism'; or in the grotesque self-deprecation of cultural institutions like London's Victoria and Albert Museum, reduced in the 1990s to marketing itself with wink and nod as 'an ace caff' with quite a nice museum attached'.

As for the nation's heritage, it was quite avowedly transformed into a business proposition, the 'heritage industry': promoted and underwritten by a new government 'Department of National Heritage'. Established in 1992 by a Conservative government but in conformity with plans originally drafted under Labour, the new ministry would later be absorbed under Tony Blair's New Labour governments into a revealingly labeled 'Department for Culture, Media and Sport'. The ecumenical background is significant: heritage was not a political-party project. The past was not abused or exploited; it was sanitized and given a happy face.

Barnsley, at the heart of the defunct South Yorkshire coalfield, was a case in point. Once an important mining hub, Barnsley in the post-Thatcher era had been transformed beyond recognition. Its town center was eviscerated, its civic core ripped up and replaced by tawdry pedestrian malls encased in concrete parking garages. All that remained were the town hall and a handful of neighbouring buildings, architectural relics of Barnsley's nineteenth-century municipal glory, to which visitors were directed by fake-ancient, 'olde-worlde' signposts. Meanwhile, bookstalls in the local market now specialized in selling local nostalgia to the area's

viewer: 'America is the place to come when you are young and single. But if it is time to grow up, you should return to Europe'.

The image of America as the perennial land of youth and adventure—with twenty-first-century Europe cast as an indulgent paradise for the middle-aged and risk-averse—had wide currency, especially in America itself. And indeed Europe *was* growing older. Of the twenty countries in the world in 2004 with the highest share of people over sixty, all but one were in Europe (the exception was Japan). The birth rate in many European countries was well below replacement levels. In Spain, Greece, Poland, Germany and Sweden, fertility rates were below 1.4 children per woman. In parts of Eastern Europe (Bulgaria and Latvia, for example, or Slovenia) they were closer to 1.1, the lowest in the world. Projected forward through 2040 these data suggested that many European countries could expect population to fall by one fifth or more.

None of the traditional explanations for fertility decline seemed to account for Europe's incipient demographic crisis. Poor countries like Moldova and rich ones like Denmark faced the same challenge. In Catholic countries like Italy or Spain, young people (married and unmarried alike) often lived in their parents' homes well into their thirties, whereas in Lutheran Sweden they had their own homes and access to generous levels of state-funded child-support and maternity leave. But although Scandinavians were having slightly more children than Mediterranean Europeans, the differences in fertility were less striking than the similarities. And the figures everywhere would have been lower still but for immigrants from outside Europe, who boosted the overall population numbers and had a much greater propensity to procreate. In Germany in 1960 the number of children born with one foreign parent was just 1.3 percent of the total for the year. Forty years later that figure had risen to one child in five.

The demographic scene in Europe was not actually so very different from that across the Atlantic—by the start of the new millennium the indigenous American birth-rate had also fallen below replacement levels. The difference was that the number of immigrants entering the US was so much larger—and they were disproportionately young adults—that overall fertility in the US looked set comfortably to outdistance that of Europe for the foreseeable future. And although the demographic troughs meant that both America and Europe might have trouble meeting public pension and other commitments in the decades ahead, the welfare systems of Europe were incomparably more generous and thus faced the greater threat.

Europeans were confronted with an apparently straightforward dilemma: what would happen if (when?) there weren't enough young people working to cover the costs of a burgeoning community of retired citizens, now living much longer than in the past, paying no taxes and placing growing strain on medical services into the bargain?[9] One answer was to reduce retirement benefits. Another was to raise the threshold at which those benefits were paid—i.e. make people work longer before retirement. A third alternative was to extract more taxes from the pay packets of those still in work. A fourth option, only really considered in Britain (and then half-heartedly), was to imitate the US and encourage or even oblige people to turn to the private sector for social insurance. All of these choices were potentially politically explosive.

For many free-market critics of Europe's welfare states, the core problem facing Europe was not demographic shortfall but economic rigidity. It wasn't that there weren't, or wouldn't be, enough workers—it was that there were too many laws protecting their salaries and their jobs, or else guaranteeing such elevated unemployment and pension payments that they lacked all incentive to work in the first place. If this 'labour-market inflexibility' were addressed and costly social provisions reduced or privatized, then more people could enter the workforce, the burden on employers and taxpayers would be alleviated, and 'Eurosclerosis' could be overcome.

As a diagnosis this was both true and false. There was no question that some of the rewards of the welfare state, negotiated and locked into place at the peak of the post-war boom, were now a serious burden. Any German worker who lost his or her job was entitled to 60 percent of their last wage packet for the next thirty-two months (67 percent if they had a child). After that the monthly payments fell to 53 percent (or 57 percent) of their last wage packet—indefinitely. Whether this safety net discouraged people from seeking paid work was unclear. But it came at a price. A penumbra of regulations designed to protect the interests of employed workers made it hard for employers in most EU countries (notoriously France) to sack full-time workers: their consequent reluctance to hire contributed to stubbornly high rates of youth unemployment.

On the other hand, the fact that they were highly regulated and inflexible by American standards did not mean that Europe's economies were necessarily inefficient or unproductive. In 2003, when measured in terms of productivity per hour worked, the economies of Switzerland, Denmark, Austria and Italy were all comparable to the US. By the same criterion Ireland, Belgium, Norway, the Netherlands and France (sic) all out-produced the US. If America was nevertheless more productive overall—if Americans made more goods, services and money—it was because a higher percentage of them were in paid jobs; they worked longer hours than Europeans (three hundred more hours per year on average in 2000); and they had far fewer and shorter holidays.

Whereas the British were legally entitled to 23 paid vacation days annually, the

[9]In France in 1960 there were four workers for every pensioner. In 2000 there were two. By 2020, on present trends, there would be just one.

French to 25 and the Swedes to 30 or more, many Americans had to settle for less than half as much paid vacation, depending where they lived. Europeans had made a deliberate choice to work less, earn less—and live better lives. In return for their uniquely high taxes (another impediment to growth and innovation, in the eyes of Anglo-American critics) Europeans received free or nearly free medical services, early retirement and a prodigious range of social and public services. Through secondary school they were better educated than Americans. They lived safer and—partly for that reason—longer lives, enjoyed better health (despite spending far less[10]) and had many fewer people in poverty.

This, then, was the 'European Social Model'. It was without question very expensive. But for most Europeans its promise of job security, progressive tax rates and large social transfer payments represented an implicit contract between government and citizens, as well as between one citizen and another. According to the annual 'Eurobarometer' polls, an overwhelming majority of Europeans took the view that poverty was caused by social circumstances and not individual inadequacy. They also showed a willingness to pay higher taxes if these were directed to alleviating poverty.

Such sentiments were predictably widespread in Scandinavia. But they were almost as prevalent in Britain, or in Italy and Spain. There was a broad international, cross-class consensus about the duty of the state to shield citizens from the hazards of misfortune or the market: neither the firm nor the state should treat employees as dispensable units of production. Social responsibility and economic advantage should not be mutually exclusive—'growth' was laudable, but not at all costs.

This European model came in more than one style: the 'Nordic', the 'Rhineland', the 'Catholic', and variations within each. What they had in common was not a discrete set of services or economic practices, or a particular level of state involvement. It was, rather, a sense—sometimes spelled out in documents and laws, sometimes not—of the balance of social rights, civic solidarity and collective responsibility that was appropriate and possible for the modern state. The aggregate outcomes might look very different in, say, Italy and Sweden. But the social consensus they incorporated was regarded by many citizens as formally binding—when, in 2004, the Social Democratic Chancellor of Germany introduced changes in the country's welfare payments, he ran into a firestorm of social protest, just as a Gaullist government had done ten years earlier when proposing similar reforms in France.

---

[10]In 2004, health costs absorbed 8 percent of GDP in Sweden but 14 percent in the USA. Four-fifths of the cost was born by the government in Sweden, less than 45 percent by the Federal government in the US. The rest was a direct burden on American businesses and their employees. Forty-five million Americans had no health insurance.

Ever since the 1980s there had been various attempts to resolve the choice between European social solidarity and American-style economic flexibility. A younger generation of economists and entrepreneurs, some of whom had spent time in US business schools or firms and were frustrated at what they saw as the inflexibility of the European business environment, had impressed upon politicians the need to 'streamline' procedures and encourage competition. The aptly named 'Gauche Américaine' in France set out to release the Left from its anti-capitalist complex while retaining its social conscience; in Scandinavia, the inhibiting effect of high taxation was discussed (if not always conceded) even in Social Democratic circles. The Right had been brought to acknowledge the case for welfare; the Left would now recognize the virtues of profit.

The effort to combine the best of both sides overlapped, not coincidentally, with the search for a project to replace the defunct debate between capitalism and socialism that had formed the core of Western politics for over a century. The result, for a brief moment at the end of the 1990s, was the so-called 'Third Way': ostensibly blending enthusiasm for unconstrained capitalist production with due consideration for social outcomes and the collective interest. This was hardly new: it added little of substance to Ludwig Erhard's 'Social Market economy' of the 1950s. But politics, especially post-ideological politics, is about *form*; and it was the form of the Third Way, modeled on Bill Clinton's successful 'triangulation' of Left and Right and articulated above all by New Labour's Tony Blair, which seduced observers.

Blair, of course, had certain advantages unique to his time and place. In the UK, Margaret Thatcher had moved the political goalposts far to the Right, while Blair's predecessors in the Labour leadership had done the hard work of destroying the Party's old Left. In a post-Thatcher environment, Blair could thus sound plausibly progressive and 'European' merely by saying positive things about the desirability of well-distributed public services; meanwhile his much-advertised admiration for the private sector, and the business-friendly economic environment his policies sought to favour, placed him firmly in the 'American' camp. He spoke warmly of bringing Britain into the European fold; but insisted nonetheless on keeping his country exempt from the social protections of European legislation and the fiscal harmonization implicit in the Union's 'single market'.

The Third Way was marketed as *both* a pragmatic solution to economic and social dilemmas *and* a significant conceptual breakthrough after decades of theoretical stagnation. Its continental admirers, heedless of the aborted 'third ways' in their own national pasts—notably the popular Fascist 'third way' of the 1930s— were keen to sign on. Under Jacques Delors (1985–1995) the European Commission had appeared a trifle preoccupied with devising and imposing norms and rules—substituting 'Europe' for the lost inheritance of Fabian-style bureaucratic socialism. Brussels, too, seemed in need of a Third Way: an uplifting story of its own that could situate the Union between institutional invisibility and regulatory excess.[11]

Blair's new-look politics would not long survive the disastrous decision to embroil his country and his reputation in the 2003 invasion of Iraq—a move which merely reminded foreign observers that New Labour's Third Way was inseparably intertwined with the UK's reluctance to choose between Europe and the United States. And the evidence that Britain, like the US, was seeing a dramatic rise in the numbers of the poor—in contrast to the rest of the EU where poverty was increasing modestly, if at all—severely diminished the appeal of the British model. But the Third Way was always going to have a short shelf life. Its very name implied the presence of two extremes—ultra free-market capitalism and state socialism—both of which no longer existed (and in the case of the former had always been a figment of doctrinal imaginations). The need for a dramatic theoretical (or rhetorical) breakthrough had passed.

Thus privatization in the early 1980s had been controversial, provoking widespread discussion of the reach and legitimacy of the public sector and calling into question the attainability of social-democratic objectives and the moral legitimacy of the profit motive in the delivery of public goods. By 2004, however, privatization was a strictly pragmatic business. In eastern Europe, it was a necessary condition for membership of the EU, in conformity with Brussels' strictures against market-distorting public subsidies. In France or Italy, the sale of publicly owned assets was now undertaken as a short-term book-keeping device to reduce the annual deficit and stay within euro-zone rules.

Even Tony Blair's own Third Way projects—for the semi-privatization of London's Underground, for example, or the introduction of 'competition' into hospital services—were embarked upon as cost-efficiency calculations with side-benefits to the national budget. To the extent that they were tied to an argument of social principle, this was tacked on as an unconvincing afterthought. And Blair's appeal was diminishing with time (as the sharply reduced scale of his third electoral victory, in May 2005, was to show). Despite cutting government expenditure, opting out of the European social charter, reducing company taxation and welcoming inward investment with all manner of sweeteners, the UK remained stubbornly unproductive. When measured by output-per-hour it consistently underperformed its 'sclerotic', regulation-bound EU partners.

Moreover, a New Labour plan to avoid the coming crisis of Europe's underfunded public pension schemes—by passing the liability on to the private sector— was already doomed to failure within less than a decade of its proud inauguration. In the UK, like the US, companies that invested their pension funds in a skittish

---

[11]Under Delors' successors the pendulum has shifted: the Commission is still as active as ever, but its efforts are directed to *de*-regulating markets.

stock market had little hope of meeting long-term commitments to their employ-ees, especially as those employees—no less than pensioners dependent upon pub-lic funding—would now be living much longer than before. Most of them, it was becoming clear, would never see a full company pension . . . unless the state was forced back into the pensions business to make up the shortfall. The Third Way was beginning to look an awful lot like a game of Three-Card Monte.

At the beginning of the twenty-first century, the dilemma facing Europeans was not Socialism or Capitalism, Left versus Right, or the Third Way. It was not even 'Europe' versus 'America', since that choice had now been effectively resolved in most people's minds in favour of Europe. It was, rather, a question—*the* question—which history had placed upon the agenda in 1945 and which had qui-etly but insistently dislodged or outlived all other claims upon Europeans' atten-tion. What future was there for the separate European nation-states? Did they *have* a future?

There could be no going back to the world of the autonomous, free-standing nation-state, sharing nothing with its neighbour but a common border. Poles, Ital-ians, Slovenes, Danes—even the British—were now Europeans. So, too, were mil-lions of Sikhs, Bengalis, Turks, Arabs, Indians, Senegalese and others besides. In their economic lives, everyone whose country was in the European Union—or wanted to be—was now irrevocably European. The EU was the world's largest in-ternal single market, the world's biggest trader in services, and its member-states' unique source of authority in all matters of economic regulation and legal codes.

In a world where comparative advantage in fixed-factor endowments—energy, minerals, farmland, even location—counted for less than policies facilitating edu-cation, research and investment, it mattered hugely that the Union exercised in-creasing initiative in these areas. Just as states had always been vital in the constituting of markets—making rules governing exchange, employment and movement—so it was now the EU that made those rules; thanks to its own cur-rency it also exercised a near monopoly on the markets in money itself. The only vital economic activity left to national rather than European initiative was taxation rates—and only because the UK insisted upon it.

But men live not in markets but in communities. For the past few hundred years those communities have been grouped, voluntarily or (more often) coer-cively, in states. After the experiences of 1914–45, Europeans everywhere felt an urgent need for the state: the politics and social agendas of the 1940s reflect this anxiety above anything else. With economic prosperity, social peace and inter-national stability, however, that need slowly evaporated. In its place came suspi-cion of intrusive public authority and a desire for individual autonomy and the removal of constraints on private initiative. Moreover, in the era of the super-powers, the fate of Europe seemed largely to have been taken out of its hands.

The European nation-states thus appeared increasingly supererogatory. However: since 1990—and *e fortiori* since 2001—those states appear, once again, to matter quite a lot.

The early modern state had two, intimately related functions: raising taxes and making war. Europe—the European Union—is not a state. It does not raise taxes and it has no capacity for making war. As we have seen, it took a very long time indeed for it to acquire even the rudiments of a military capacity, much less a foreign policy. For most of the first half century following the end of World War Two this was not a handicap: the prospect of undertaking another European war was abhorrent to almost all Europeans, and their defense against the only likely enemy had been sub-contracted across the Atlantic.

But in the aftermath of September 11th 2001 the limitations of a post-national prescription for a better European future became clear. The traditional European state, after all, not only made war abroad but enforced the peace at home. This, as Hobbes long ago realized, is what gives the state its distinctive and irreplaceable legitimacy. In countries where violent political warfare against unarmed civilians had been endemic in recent years (Spain, the UK, Italy and Germany) the importance of the state—its policemen, its army, its intelligence services and its judicial apparatus—was never forgotten. In an age of 'terrorism', the state's monopoly of armed power is an attractive reassurance to most of its citizens.

Keeping citizens safe is what states do. And there was no sign that Brussels (the European Union) would or could take on this responsibility in the foreseeable future. In this vital respect the state remained the core legitimate representative of its citizens, in a way that the transnational union of Europeans, for all its passports and parliaments, could not hope to match. Europeans might enjoy the freedom to appeal over the heads of their own governments to European judges, and it remained a source of wonder to many that national courts in Germany or Britain complied so readily with judgments emanating from Strasbourg or Luxembourg. But when it came to keeping the gunman and the bomber away, responsibility and thus power remained firmly in Berlin or London. What, after all, should a citizen of Europe do if her house were fire-bombed? Call a bureaucrat?

Legitimacy is a function of capacity: it is in part because the disarticulated, ultra-federal state of Belgium, e.g. has sometimes appeared unable to keep its citizens safe that its legitimacy has been called into question. And although the capacity of the state begins with arms it does not end there, even today. So long as it is the state—rather than a trans-state entity—which pays pensions, insures the unemployed and educates children, then that state's monopoly of a certain sort of political legitimacy will continue unchallenged. Over the course of the twentieth century the European nation-state took on considerable responsibilities for its citizens' welfare, security and well-being. In recent years it has shed its intrusive oversight of private morality and some—but not all—of its economic initiative. The rest remains intact.

Legitimacy is also a function of territory. The European Union, as many observers have noted, is an utterly original animal: it is territorially defined without being a consistent territorial entity. Its laws and its regulations are territory-wide, but its citizens cannot vote in each other's national elections (while being free to cast their vote in local and European ballots). The geographical reach of the Union is quite belied by its relative unimportance in Europeans' daily affairs when compared to the country of their birth or residence. To be sure, the Union is a major provider of economic and other services. But this defines its citizens as consumers rather than participants—'a community of passive citizens . . . governed by strangers'—and thus risks provoking unflattering comparisons with pre-democratic Spain or Poland, or the quiescent political culture of Adenauer's West Germany: unpromising precedents for such an ambitious undertaking.

Citizenship, democracy, rights and duty are intimately bound up with the state—particularly in countries with a living tradition of active citizen participation in public affairs. Physical proximity matters: to participate in the state you need to feel part of it. Even in an age of super-fast trains and real-time electronic communication it is not clear how someone in Poimbra, say, or Rzeszow, can be an active citizen of *Europe*. For the concept to retain any meaning—and for Europeans to remain political in any useful sense—their reference for the foreseeable future will remain Lisbon, or Warsaw: not Brussels. It is not by chance that in the modern age giant states—China, Russia, the US—have either been governed by authoritarian rule or else have remained resolutely centrifugal, their citizens more than a little suspicious of the federal capital and all its works.

Appearances, then, were misleading. The European Union in 2005 had not superceded conventional territorial units and would not be doing so for the foreseeable future. Six decades after Hitler's defeat, the multiple identities, sovereignties and territories that together defined Europe and its history certainly overlapped and inter-communicated more than at any time in the past. What was new, and thus rather harder for outside observers to catch, was the possibility of being French *and* European, or Catalan *and* European—or Arab *and* European.

Distinctive nations and states had not vanished. Just as the world was not converging on a single 'American' norm—the developed capitalist societies exhibited a wide range of social forms and very different attitudes toward both the market and the state—so Europe too contained a distinctive palate of peoples and traditions. The illusion that we live in a post-national or post-state world comes from paying altogether too much attention to 'globalized' economic processes . . . and assuming that similarly transnational developments must be at work in every other sphere of human life. Seen uniquely through the lens of production and exchange, Europe had indeed become a seamless flow chart of transnational waves. But viewed as a site of power or political legitimacy or cultural affinities Europe remained what it had long been: a familiar accumulation of discrete

Boris Yeltsin and Mikhail Gorbachev, Moscow 1991. The scandals of Yeltsin's presidency should not obscure his achievements. He was much quicker than Gorbachev to understand what was happening and to adapt—notably to the re-emergence of national states in the wake of empire.

The first Moscow consignment of Big Macs, January 1st 1990. Western commodities and cash poured into the post-Communist vacuum. But the unregulated economy quickly fell prey to a small number of 'oligarchs' who became quite extraordinarily rich: capitalism as kleptocracy.

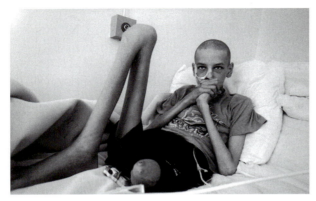

Minsk, Belarus, 1999: The Children's Cancer Hospital. Thirty thousand people died as a result of the Chernobyl explosion in 1986. One Belarusian in four was poisoned. Nor was Chernobyl the first nuclear disaster in Soviet history— merely the worst.

The Aral Sea, Uzbekhistan, October 1997. Communist industrial policy coupled economic dysfunction with environmental irresponsibility. The death of the Aral Sea—like the poisoning of Lake Baikal—was an ecological catastrophe and a huge mortgage on the future.

Demonstrators in Kiev in September 1991 (one week after Ukrainian independence) holding photos of NKVD victims. The memory of Soviet repression was especially strong in Ukraine, subjected by Stalin to an induced, punitive famine that amounted to near-genocide.

Gypsies (Roma) in Bucharest, 1996. An estimated five million Gypsies live in Europe, at least two million in Romania alone. They are everywhere exposed to prejudice and abuse (or else—as in the UK—forbidden to enter).

This Romanian woman was on sale for $800, Bucharest, December 2002. The east European sex trade was reaching epidemic proportions. Criminal syndicates tricked or abducted girls from Romania and the former USSR into prostitution in western Europe and the Balkans.

While awaiting entry to the EU, Hungary joined NATO as a second best (in 1999)—and was promptly committed (somewhat reluctantly) to the war in Kosovo. The banner over the NATO stand at Budapest's 1997 International Fair reads 'At NATO's gate'.

Serbs in June 1989 commemorating the 600th anniversary of the 'Battle of Kosovo': the last stand of medieval Serbia against the advancing Turks. Slobodan Milošević wilfully fanned historical grievances, promising to defend Serb 'national and spiritual integrity'.

Victims of the July 1995 Srebrenica massacre. As a UN peacekeeping contingent of armed Dutch soldiers stood by, Serb irregulars under Ratko Mladić marched 7,400 Bosnian men and boys out of the town and shot them.

Kosovar Albanians, March 21st 1999. In the final act of the Yugoslav wars, Milošević sought to terrorize the Albanian community into departing. This blatant exercise in ethnic cleansing belatedly triggered armed intervention by NATO, its first ever.

*Turkey—an overwhelmingly Muslim country in Asia Minor—has a decidedly European 'vocation'.
Here his supporters, waving the flags of Turkey and the EU, greet Prime Minister Erdogan as he
returns to Ankara in December 2004, after securing a starting date for EU membership talks.*

*France—an EU founding member—rejected the proposed 'European Constitution' in a national
referendum, May 2005. Some French voters feared too little European regulation; some feared too
much European regulation. Many just feared too much Europe—Turkey above all.*

Jörg Haider, leader of Austria's far-Right Freedom Party. Despite occasional lapses, Haider successfully distanced himself from Austria's Nazi past while attacking other parties and 'foreign rabble'. The caption reads 'He didn't lie to you!'

'Vote Danish!' Pia Kjaersgaard, whose Danish People's Party won 12 percent of the vote in 2001. Even in Scandinavia the new populism prompted mainstream parties to show their own 'firmness' by restricting asylum and foreigners' rights.

Tony Blair's 'Third Way' between the European 'model' and the unrestricted market—like his efforts to triangulate between the EU and London's 'special relationship' with Washington—had limited success. When offered the chance, many Brits sought medical care on the Continent.

Moroccans in the Andalucian city of Almería protesting against Spanish racism, February 2000. While much of western Europe had become increasingly multicultural, the incidence of prejudice and tension remained high—notably along the EU's porous Mediterranean frontier.

Somalis in front of Santa Maria Novella, Florence, 1997. By the year 2000 there were some fifteen million Muslims in the EU. Islam was Europe's fastest growing religion—an ironic legacy of Christian Europe's imperial past.

Jacques Chirac at a ceremony commemorating the round-up of 13,000 Parisian Jews in July 1942. To his great credit, Chirac was the first French president to acknowledge France's role in the Final Solution: he declared the anniversary a day of 'mourning and shame for the French'.

German Chancellor Gerhard Schroeder, speaking on the sixtieth anniversary of the liberation of Auschwitz. The wartime destruction of Europe's Jews, conspicuously absent from public consciousness in the initial post-war decades, had become the centerpiece of European official memory: in Germany and everywhere else.

state-particles. Nationalism had largely come and gone[12]; but nations and states remained.

Considering what Europeans had done to one another in the first half of the twentieth century, this was rather remarkable. It certainly could not have been predicted from the rubble of 1945. Indeed, the re-emergence of Europe's battered peoples and their distinctive national cultures and institutions from the wreckage of the continent's thirty years' war might well be thought an even greater achievement than their collective success in forging a transnational Union. The latter, after all, had been on various European agendas well before the Second World War and was if anything facilitated by the devastation wrought by that conflict. But the resurrection of Germany, or Poland, or France, not to speak of Hungary or Lithuania, had seemed altogether less likely.

Even less predictable—indeed quite unthinkable just a few short decades before—was Europe's emergence in the dawn of the twenty-first century as a paragon of the international virtues: a community of values and a system of inter-state relations held up by Europeans and non-Europeans alike as an exemplar for all to emulate. In part this was the backwash of growing disillusion with the American alternative; but the reputation was well earned. And it presented an unprecedented opportunity. Whether Europe's burnished new image, scrubbed clean of past sins and vicissitudes, would survive the challenges of the coming century, however, would depend a lot on how Europeans responded to the non-Europeans in their midst and at their borders. In the troubled early years of the twenty-first century that remained an open question.

One hundred and seventy years earlier, at the dawn of the nationalist era, the German poet Heinrich Heine drew a revealing distinction between two sorts of collective sentiment: 'We [Germans]', he wrote,

> were ordered to be patriots and we became patriots, for we do everything our rulers order us to do. One must not think of this patriotism, however, as the same emotion which bears this name here in France. A Frenchman's patriotism means that his heart is warmed, and with this warmth it stretches and expands so that his love no longer embraces merely his closest relative, but all of France, the whole of the civilized world. A German's patriotism means that his heart contracts and shrinks like leather in the cold, and a German then hates everything foreign, no longer wants to become a citizen of the world, a European, but only a provincial German.

---

[12] In Europe, but not in America. In international surveys at the end of the twentieth century, the number of Americans claiming to be 'very proud' of their country exceeded 75 percent. In Europe only the Irish and the Poles exhibited similar patriotic verve; elsewhere the number of 'very proud' people ranged from 49 percent (Latvians) to 17 percent (former West Germans).

France and Germany, of course, were no longer the critical references. But the choice posed by Heine's two kinds of patriotism speaks quite directly to the contemporary European condition. If the emerging Europe were to take a 'Germanic' turn, contracting 'like leather in the cold' to a defensive provincialism—an eventuality suggested by the referendums in France and the Netherlands in the spring of 2005, when clear majorities rejected the proposed European 'Constitution'—then the opportunity would be missed and the European Union would never transcend its functional origins. It would remain no more than the sum and highest common factor of its members' separate self-interests.

But if patriotism for Europe could find a way to reach beyond itself, to capture the spirit of Heine's idealized France, 'stretching and expanding to embrace the whole of the civilized world', then something more was now possible. The twentieth century—America's Century—had seen Europe plunge into the abyss. The old continent's recovery had been a slow and uncertain process. In some ways it would never be complete: America would have the biggest army and China would make more, and cheaper, goods. But neither America nor China had a serviceable model to propose for universal emulation. In spite of the horrors of their recent past—and in large measure because of them—it was *Europeans* who were now uniquely placed to offer the world some modest advice on how to avoid repeating their own mistakes. Few would have predicted it sixty years before, but the twenty-first century might yet belong to Europe.

Epilogue

Epilogue

From the House of the Dead

AN ESSAY ON MODERN EUROPEAN MEMORY

'The problem of evil will be the fundamental problem of postwar intellectual life in Europe—as death became the fundamental problem after the last war'.
Hannah Arendt (1945)

'Forgetting, I would even go so far as to say historical error, is a crucial factor in the creation of a nation; thus the progress of historical studies is often a danger for national identity ... The essence of a nation is that all individuals have many things in common, and also that they have forgotten many things'.
Ernest Renan

'All historical work on the events of this period will have to be pursued or considered in relation to the events of Auschwitz ... Here, all historicization reaches its limits'.
Saul Friedlander

For Jews, concluded Heinrich Heine, baptism is their 'European entry ticket'. But that was in 1825, when the price for admission to the modern world was the relinquishing of an oppressive heritage of Jewish difference and isolation. Today, the price of admission to Europe has changed. In an ironic twist that Heine—with his prophetic intimations of 'wild, dark times rumbling towards us'—would have appreciated better than anyone, those who would become full Europeans in the dawn of the twenty-first century must first assume a new and far more oppressive heritage. Today the pertinent European reference is not baptism. It is extermination.

Holocaust recognition is our contemporary European entry ticket. In 2004 President Kwasniewski of Poland—seeking to close a painful chapter in his nation's past and bring Poland into line with its EU partners—officially acknowledged the wartime sufferings of Polish Jews, including their victimization at the hands of Poles themselves. Even Romania's outgoing President Iliescu, in a concession to his country's ambition to join the European Union, was constrained the following year to concede what he and his colleagues had long and strenuously denied: that Romania, too, played its part in the destruction of the Jews of Europe ...

To be sure, there are other criteria for full participation in the family of Europe. Turkey's continuing refusal to acknowledge the 'genocide' of its Armenian population in 1915 will be an impediment to its application for EU membership, just as Serbia will continue to languish on the European doorstep until its political class takes responsibility for the mass murders and other crimes of the Yugoslav wars. But the reason crimes like these now carry such a political charge—and the reason 'Europe' has invested itself with the responsibility to make sure that attention is paid to them and to define 'Europeans' as people who *do* pay attention to them—is because they are partial instances (in this case before and after the fact respectively) of *the* crime: the attempt by one group of Europeans to exterminate *every* member of another group of Europeans, here on European soil, within still living memory.

Hitler's 'final solution to the Jewish problem' in Europe is not only the source of crucial areas of post-war international jurisprudence—'genocide' or 'crimes against humanity'. It also adjudicates the moral (and in certain European countries the legal) standing of those who pronounce upon it. To deny or belittle the *Shoah*—the Holocaust—is to place yourself beyond the pale of civilized public discourse. That is why mainstream politicians shun, so far as they can, the company of demagogues like Jean-Marie Le Pen. The Holocaust today is much more than just another undeniable fact about a past that Europeans can no longer choose to ignore. As Europe prepares to leave World War Two behind—as the last memorials are inaugurated, the last surviving combatants and victims honoured—the recovered memory of Europe's dead Jews has become the very definition and guarantee of the continent's restored humanity. It wasn't always so.

There was never any mystery about what had happened to Europe's Jews. That an estimated 6 million of them were put to death during the Second World War was widely accepted within a few months of the war's end. The handful of survivors, whether in the displaced persons' camps or in their countries of origin, paid implicit witness to the number of dead. Of 126,000 Jews removed from Austria, 4,500 returned after the war. In the Netherlands, where there had been 140,000 Jews before the war, 110,000 were deported—of whom fewer than 5,000 returned. In France, of 76,000 (mostly foreign-born) Jews who were deported during the years 1940–44, less than 3 percent survived. Further east, the figures were even worse: of Poland's pre-war population of over 3 million Jews, fully 97.5 percent were exterminated. In Germany itself, in May 1945, there remained just 21,450 of the country's 600,000 Jews.

The returning remnant was not much welcomed. After years of anti-Semitic propaganda, local populations everywhere were not only disposed to blame 'Jews' in the abstract for their own suffering but were distinctly sorry to see the return of men and women whose jobs, possessions and apartments they had purloined. In the 4th arrondissement of Paris, on April 19th 1945, hundreds of people demonstrated in protest when a returning Jewish deportee tried to reclaim his (occupied) apartment. Before it was dispersed, the demonstration degenerated into a near-riot, the crowd screaming *'La France aux français!'* The venerable French Catholic philosopher Gabriel Marcel would doubtless not have resorted to such language. But he was not embarrassed to write a few months later, in the journal *Témoignage Chrétien*, of the 'overweening presumption' of 'the Jews' and their urge to 'take everything over'.

Little wonder that the future French government minister Simone Weil could write, of her return from Bergen Belsen: 'We had the feeling that our lives did not count; and yet there were so very few of us'. In France (as in Belgium) deported re-sisters who had survived and now returned were treated as heroes: the saviours of their nation's honour. But Jews, deported not for their politics but on account of their race, could serve no such useful purpose. In any case De Gaulle (like Churchill) was curiously blind to the racial specificity of Hitler's victims, under-standing Nazism in the context of Prussian militarism instead. At Nürnberg, the French prosecutor François de Menthon was uncomfortable with the very concept of 'crimes against humanity'—he preferred 'crimes against peace'—and through-out the trial he made no reference to the deportation or murder of Jews.[1]

Nearly three years later an editorial in *Le Monde* on January 11th 1948, headed 'The survivors of the death camps', managed to speak movingly of '280,000 de-portees, 25,000 survivors' without once mentioning the word 'Jew'. Under legisla-tion passed in 1948, the term *'déportés'* could be applied only to French citizens or residents deported for political reasons or for resisting the occupier. No distinction was made regarding the camp to which someone was sent or their fate upon ar-rival. Thus Jewish children who were locked into trains and shipped to Auschwitz for gassing were described in official documents as 'political deportees'. With mor-dant if unintended irony these children, most of whom were the sons and daugh-ters of foreign-born Jews and who had been forcibly separated from their parents by French gendarmes, were then commemorated in documents and upon plaques as having 'died for France'.[2]

In Belgium, Catholic parties in the first post-war parliament protested at the idea of any compensation being paid to 'Jews arrested simply for a racial motive'—most of whom, it was hinted, were probably black-marketeers. Indeed, in Belgium the exclusion of Jews from any post-war benefits was taken a step further. Since 95 percent of the Jews deported from Belgium had been foreign nationals or stateless, it was determined by a post-war law that—unless they had also fought in the or-

---

[1] The American prosecutor Telford Taylor was struck by this in retrospect but acknowledges that he did not even notice it at the time—a revealing admission. See Telford Taylor, *The Anatomy of the Nurem-berg Trials* (NY, 1992), p. 296.

[2] In the town of Pithiviers, near Orléans, where Jewish children rounded up in Paris were kept until their shipment east, a monument was actually erected in 1957 bearing the inscription '*A nos déportés morts pour la France*'. Only in 1992 did the local municipality erect a new plaque, more accurate if less reas-suring. It reads: 'To the memory of the 2300 Jewish children interned at the Pithiviers camp from July 19th to September 6th 1942, before being deported and murdered in Auschwitz'.

POSTWAR: A HISTORY OF EUROPE SINCE 1945

ganized resistance movements—surviving Jews who ended up in Belgium after the war would not be eligible for any public aid. In October 1944, the Belgian authorities automatically ascribed the nationality 'German' to any Jewish survivor in Belgium who could not prove his or her Belgian citizenship. Theoretically this abolished all wartime 'racial' distinctions—but it also turned surviving Jews into *de facto* enemy aliens who could be interned and whose property was seized (and not returned until January 1947). Such rulings had the attendant benefit of marking these Jews for eventual return to Germany, now that they were no longer threatened by Nazi persecution.

In the Netherlands, where, according to the Dutch resistance paper *Vrij Nederland*, the Nazis themselves had been taken aback at the alacrity with which local citizens and civic leaders cooperated in their own humiliation, the handful of returning Jews was decidedly unwelcome. One of them, Rita Koopman, recalled being greeted thus upon her return: 'Quite a lot of you came back. Just be happy you weren't here—how we suffered from hunger!' Indeed, the Dutch did suffer greatly through the 'Hunger Winter' of 1944–45 and the many houses vacated by deported Jews, in Amsterdam especially, were a valuable source of wood and other supplies. But for all the enthusiastic cooperation of Dutch wartime officialdom in identifying and rounding up the country's Jews, the post-war authorities—their own conscience clear—felt no obligation to make any particular amends to Jews. Instead, they made a rather self-congratulatory point of refusing to distinguish among Dutch citizens on racial or any other grounds and thus froze the country's lost Jews into retrospective anonymity and invisibility. In the Fifties, the Catholic prime ministers of the Netherlands even declined to contribute to a proposed international monument at Auschwitz, dismissing it as 'Communist propaganda'.

In eastern Europe there was of course never much question of recognizing Jewish suffering, much less compensating it. In the immediate post-war years Jews in this region were concerned above all with merely staying alive. Witold Kula, a non-Jewish Pole, wrote in August 1946 of a train journey from Łódz to Wrocław where he witnessed the anti-Semitic mocking of a Jewish family: 'The average Polish intellectual doesn't realize that a Jew in Poland today cannot drive a car, doesn't risk a train journey, dare not send his child on a school outing; he cannot go to remote localities, prefers big cities even to medium-sized ones and is ill-advised to take a walk after nightfall. You would have to be a hero to go on living in such an atmosphere after six years of torment'.

After Germany's defeat, many Jews in eastern Europe pursued their wartime survival strategy: hiding their Jewish identity from their colleagues, their neighbours and even their children, blending as best they could into the post-war world and resuming at least the appearance of normal life. And not only in eastern Europe. In France, although new laws forbade the overt anti-Semitic rhetoric of pre-war public life, the legacy of Vichy remained. The taboos of a later generation had not yet taken hold, and behaviour that would in time be frowned upon was still acceptable. As in the Thirties, the Left was not immune. In 1948 the Communist parliamentarian Arthur Ramette drew attention to certain prominent Jewish politicians—Léon Blum, Jules Moch, René Mayer—in order to contrast them with the parliamentarians of his own party: 'We Communists have only French names' (a claim as unseemly as it was untrue).

In these circumstances, the choice for most of Europe's Jews seemed stark: depart (for Israel once it came into existence, or America after its doors were opened in 1950) or else be silent and, so far as possible, invisible. To be sure, many of them felt an overwhelming urge to speak and bear witness. In Primo Levi's words, he was driven by an 'absolute, pathological narrative charge' to write down what he had just experienced. But then Levi's own fate is instructive. When he took *Se questo è un uomo*, the story of his incarceration in Auschwitz, to the leading left-wing Italian publisher Einaudi in 1946, it was rejected out of hand: Levi's narrative of persecution and survival, beginning with his deportation as a Jew rather than as a resister, did not conform to uplifting Italian accounts of nationwide anti-Fascist resistance.

Se questo è un uomo was published instead by a small press in just 2,500 copies—most of which were remaindered in a warehouse in Florence and destroyed in the great flood there twenty years later. Levi's memoir was not published in Britain until 1959, when *If This Is a Man* sold only a few hundred copies (nor did the US edition, under the title *Survival in Auschwitz*, begin to sell well until twenty years later). Gallimard, the most prestigious of the French publishing houses, for a long time resisted buying anything by Levi; only after his death in 1987 did his work, and his significance, begin to gain recognition in France. Like his subject, then, Primo Levi remained largely inaudible for many years: no-one was listening. In 1955 he noted that it had become 'indelicate' to speak of the camps: 'One risks being accused of setting up as a victim, or of indecent exposure'. Giuliana Tedeschi, another Italian survivor of Auschwitz, made the same point: 'I encountered people who didn't want to know anything, because the Italians, too, had suffered, after all, even those who didn't go to the camps. . . . They used to say, "For heaven's sake, it's all over," and so I remained quiet for a long time'.[3]

Even in Great Britain the Holocaust was not discussed in public. Just as the representative concentration camp for the French was Buchenwald, with its well-organised committees of Communist political prisoners, so in post-war Britain the iconic image of a Nazi camp was not Auschwitz but Bergen-Belsen (liberated by British troops); and the skeletal survivors recorded on film and shown in cinema newsreels at the end of the war were not typically identified as Jews.[4] In post-war

[3]Giuliana Tedeschi is quoted by Nicola Caracciolo in *Uncertain Refuge: Italy and the Jews During the Holocaust* (University of Illinois Press, 1995), p. 121.
[4]In post-war Britain, an unusually thin or sickly person might be described as looking 'like something out of Belsen'. In France, fairground chambers of horror were labelled 'Buchenwalds'—as an inducement to voyeuristic trade.

Britain, too, Jews often preferred to maintain a low profile and keep their memories to themselves. Writing in 1996 of his English childhood as the son of camp survivors, Jeremy Adler recalled that whereas there were no taboos at home about discussing the Holocaust, the topic remained off limits everywhere else: 'My friends could boast of how dad had fought with Monty in the desert. My own father's experiences were unmentionable. They had no place until recently. The public cycle from repression to obsession in Britain took about fifty years'.[5]

In retrospect it is the universal character of the neglect that is most striking. The Holocaust of the Jews was put out of mind not only in places where there were indeed good reasons not to think about it—like Austria, say (which had just one-tenth the population of pre-war Germany but supplied one in two of all concentration camp guards), or Poland; but also in Italy—where most of the nation had no cause for shame on this score—or in Britain, where the war years were otherwise looked upon with pride and even some nostalgia. The rapid onset of the Cold War contributed, of course.[6] But there were other reasons too. For most Europeans, World War Two had not been about the Jews (except in so far as they were blamed for it), and any suggestion that Jewish suffering might claim pride of place was deeply resented.

The Holocaust was only one of many things that people wanted to forget: 'In the fat years after the war . . . Europeans took shelter behind a collective amnesia' (Hans-Magnus Enzensberger). Between their compromises with Fascist administrators and occupying forces, their collaboration with wartime agencies and rulers and their private humiliations, material hardships and personal tragedies, millions of Europeans had good reasons of their own to turn away from the recent past, or else mis-remember it to better effect. What the French historian Henry Rousso would later dub the 'Vichy syndrome'—the decades-long difficulty of acknowledging what had really happened during the war and the overwhelming desire to block the memory or else recast it in a usable way that would not corrode the fragile bonds of post-war society—was by no means unique to France.

Every occupied country in Europe developed its own 'Vichy syndrome'. The

---

[5]See *The Times Literary Supplement* for October 4th 1996. Jews were not the first people in Britain to opt for discretion where the Holocaust was concerned. The wartime government under Churchill chose not to deploy information about the death camps in its propaganda against Germany lest this incite an increase in anti-Semitic feelings—already quite high in some parts of London, as wartime intelligence reports had noted.

[6]Especially in America. In 1950 the Displaced Persons' Commission of the US Congress stated that 'The Baltic Waffen SS units are to be considered as separate and distinct in purpose, ideology, activities and qualifications from the German SS. Therefore the Commission holds them not to be a movement hostile to the government of the United States'. The Baltic Waffen SS had been among the most brutal and enthusiastic when it came to torturing and killing Jews on the Eastern Front; but in the novel circumstances of the Cold War they were of course 'our' Nazis. I am grateful to Professor Daniel Cohen of Rice University for this information.

wartime privations of Italians, for example, both at home and in prison camps, diverted public attention from the suffering Italians had caused to others—in the Balkans, for example, or in Italy's African colonies. The stories that the Dutch or the Poles told themselves about the war would sustain the national self-image for decades—the Dutch in particular setting great store by their image as a nation that had resisted, while forgetting as best they could that 23,000 Dutchmen volunteered for the Waffen SS: the largest contingent from Western Europe. Even Norway had somehow to digest the memory that more than one in five of its military officers had voluntarily joined Vidkun Quisling's neo-Nazi *Nasjonal Samling* ('National Rally') before or after April 1940. But whereas liberation, resistance and deportees—even heroic defeats like Dunkirk or the Warsaw Rising of 1944—could all be put to some service in compensatory national myth-making, there was nothing 'usable' about the Holocaust.[7]

In certain respects it was actually easier for *Germans* to engage and acknowledge the scale of their crime. Not, of course, at first: we have seen how 'de-Nazification' failed. History teaching in the early Federal Republic stopped with the Wilhelminian Empire. With the rare exception of a statesman like Kurt Schumacher—who warned his fellow countrymen as early as June 1947 that they had better learn to 'talk for once about the Jews in Germany and the world'—German public figures in the Forties and Fifties managed to avoid any reference to the Final Solution. The American writer Alfred Kazin remarked upon the fact that for his students in Cologne in 1952 'the war was over. The war was not to be mentioned. Not a word was said by my students about the war'. When West Germans looked back it was to memories of their own sufferings: in polls taken at the end of the Fifties an overwhelming majority identified the Allied post-war occupation as 'the worst time of their lives'.

As some observers had already predicted in 1946, the Germans successfully distanced themselves from Hitler: evading both punishment and moral responsibility by offering the Führer to the world as a scapegoat. Indeed there *was* considerable resentment at what Hitler had wrought—but at the harm he had brought down upon the heads of Germans rather than because of what he and Germans had done to others. Targetting the Jews, as it seemed to many Germans in these years, was not so much Hitler's greatest crime as his greatest *error*: in a 1952 survey, nearly two out of five adults in West Germany did not hesitate to inform pollsters that they thought it was 'better' for Germany to have no Jews on its territory.

Attitudes like these were facilitated by the relative absence of nearby reminders of Nazi atrocities; the Nazis had carefully located their main death camps far from the 'Old Reich'. Not that proximity in itself was any guarantee of sensibility. The fact that Dachau was a suburb of Munich, a tram-ride from the city centre, did not in

---

[7] Except of course in Israel.

itself advance local understanding of what had taken place there: in January 1948 the Bavarian parliament unanimously voted to convert the site of the Nazi camp there into an *Arbeitslager*, a forced labour camp for 'work-shy, a-social elements'. As Hannah Arendt observed on visiting Germany in 1950: 'Everywhere one notices that there is no reaction to what has happened, but it is hard to say whether this is due to an intentional refusal to mourn or whether it is the expression of a genuine emotional incapacity'. In 1955 a Frankfurt court acquitted one Dr Peters, the general manager of a company that provided the SS with Zyklon-B gas, on the grounds that there was 'insufficient proof' that it had been used to kill deportees.

At the same time, however, Germans—uniquely in Europe—could not deny what they had done to the Jews. They might avoid mention of it; they might insist upon their own sufferings; they might pass the blame up to a 'handful' of Nazis. But they could not sidestep responsibility for the subject by attributing the crime of genocide to someone else. Even Adenauer, though he confined himself in public to expressions of sympathy for Jewish 'victims' without ever naming those who victimized them, had been constrained to sign the reparations treaty with Israel. And whereas neither the British, nor the French, nor even his fellow Italians showed any interest in the memoirs of Primo Levi, *The Diary of Anna Frank* (admittedly a more accessible document) was to become the best-selling paperback in German history, with over 700,000 copies sold by 1960.

The trigger for German self-interrogation, as we have seen, was a series of trials prompted by belated investigations into German crimes on the eastern front. Beginning in Ulm in 1958 with proceedings against members of wartime 'Intervention Groups', followed by the arrest and prosecution of Adolf Eichmann, and culminating in the Frankfurt trials of Auschwitz guards between December 1963 and August 1965, these proceedings were also the first opportunity since the end of the war for camp survivors to speak publicly about their experiences. At the same time the Federal Republic's twenty-year Statute of Limitations for murder was extended (though not yet abolished).

This change in mood was driven in large measure by a wave of anti-Semitic vandalism at the end of the Fifties and by growing evidence that young Germans were utterly ignorant about the Third Reich: their parents had told them nothing and their teachers avoided the subject. Beginning in 1962, ten West German *Länder* announced that henceforth the history of the years 1933–1945—including the extermination of the Jews—would be a required subject in all schools. Konrad Adenauer's initial post-war assumption was thus reversed: the health of German democracy now required that Nazism be remembered rather than forgotten. And attention was increasingly directed to genocide and 'crimes against humanity', rather than the 'war crimes' with which National Socialism had hitherto been primarily associated. A new generation was to be made aware of the nature—and the scale—of Nazi atrocities. No longer would popular magazines like *Stern* and *Quick* be able to downplay the significance of the camps, as they had done in the Fifties,

or sing the praises of 'good' Nazis. A certain public awareness of the unacceptability, the indecency of the recent German past began to take hold.

The change should not be exaggerated. During the Sixties both a West German
Chancellor (Kiesinger) and the Federal President (Hans Lübke) were former
Nazis—a glaring contradiction in the Bonn Republic's self-image that younger
commentators duly noted, as we saw in Chapter 12. And it was one thing to tell the
truth about the Nazis, quite another to acknowledge the collective responsibility of
the German people, a subject on which most of the political class was still silent.
Moreover, while the number of West Germans who believed that Hitler would
have been one of Germany's greatest statesmen 'but for the war' fell from 48 percent in 1955 to 32 percent in 1967, the latter figure (albeit composed overwhelmingly
of older respondents) was hardly reassuring.

The real transformation came in the following decade. A series of events—the
Six-Day Arab-Israeli War of 1967, Chancellor Brandt dropping to his knees at the
Warsaw Ghetto memorial, the murder of Israeli athletes at the 1972 Munich
Olympics and, finally, the German telecast of the 'Holocaust' mini-series in January 1979—combined to place Jews and their sufferings at the head of the German
public agenda. Of these the television series was by far the most important. The
purest product of American commercial television—its story simple, its characters
mostly two-dimensional, its narrative structured for maximum emotional
impact—'Holocaust' (as noted in Chapter 14) was execrated and abominated by European cinéastes from Edgar Reitz to Claude Lanzmann, who accused it of turning German history into American soap opera and rendering accessible and
comprehensible that which should always remain unspeakable and impenetrable.

But these very limitations account for the show's impact. It ran for four consecutive nights on West German national television and was watched by an estimated twenty million viewers—well over half the adult population. It also
happened to coincide with another trial, of former guards from the Majdanek
death camp: a reminder to viewers that this was unfinished business. The public
impact was enormous. Five months later the Bundestag voted to abolish the Statute
of Limitations for murder (though it should be recorded that among those who
voted against was the future Chancellor Helmut Kohl). Henceforward Germans
would be among the best-informed Europeans on the subject of the *Shoah* and at
the forefront of all efforts to maintain public awareness of their country's singular
crime. Whereas in 1968 there had been just 471 school groups visiting Dachau, by
the end of the Seventies the annual number was well in excess of five thousand.

Knowing—and publicly acknowledging—what Germans had done to Jews four
decades earlier was a considerable advance; but situating it in German and European history remained a difficult and unresolved dilemma, as the 'historians' clash'
of the Eighties was to demonstrate. Some conservative scholars, among them the
hitherto well-respected historian Ernst Nolte, were uncomfortable with the insistence on treating Hitler, his movement and his crimes as unique and *sui generis*. If

we are to understand Nazism, they insisted, we have to situate it in its time and place. According to Nolte, the rise of National Socialism, and some of its more grotesque practices, were above all a response to Bolshevism: they followed and in some measure imitated the example and the threat offered by Lenin and his heirs. That doesn't diminish the crimes of Nazism, Nolte argued in a notorious article in the *Frankfurter Allgemeine Zeitung* in June 1986; but without the Bolshevik precedent they cannot be fully explained. It was time to reconsider the Nazi era, situating the Holocaust in a broader pattern of modern genocides.

The reaction to Nolte came above all from Jürgen Habermas, who—like Enzensberger, Günter Grass and other members of the 'skeptical generation'—was old enough to remember Nazism and thus intensely suspicious of any attempt to 'limit' German responsibilities. Nonsense, Habermas replied to Nolte: the point about Nazism is not to 'situate' or 'historicize' it—that is precisely the temptation which no German would ever again have the right to indulge. The Nazi crime—the German crime—was unique: unique in its scale, unique in its ambition, unique in its un-plumbed evil. Contextualization in Nolte's sense, with the implicit relativisation of German responsibility that must inevitably ensue, was simply proscribed.

But Habermas's uncompromising stance set a standard to which few of his countrymen (including historians, for whom comparison and context are the lifeblood of their discipline) could be expected to adhere for long. The new salience of the Holocaust in German public discussion—culminating in the Nineties in copious displays of official remorse for past shortcomings, with Germans indulging in what the writer Peter Schneider called 'a kind of self-righteous self-hate'—could not last indefinitely. To ask each new generation of Germans to live forever in Hitler's shadow, to require that they take on responsibility for the memory of Germany's unique guilt and make it the very measure of their national identity, was the least that could be demanded—but far too much to expect.

Elsewhere in Western Europe the process of remembering and acknowledging had first to overcome self-serving local illusions—a process that typically took two generations and many decades. In Austria—where the television 'Holocaust' was broadcast just two months after its German showing but with no remotely comparable impact—it was not until the country's President, Kurt Waldheim, was revealed in the mid-Eighties to have played a role in the Wehrmacht's brutal occupation of wartime Yugoslavia that (some) Austrians began a serious, and still incomplete, interrogation of their country's Nazi past. Indeed, the fact that Waldheim had previously served as UN Secretary General without anyone in the international community troubling themselves over his war record fuelled the suspicions of many Austrians that they were being held to uniquely high standards. Austria, after all, had had a post-war Jewish Chancellor (the Socialist Bruno Kreisky), which was more than could be said for the Germans.

But no-one expected very much of the Austrians. Their largely untroubled relationship to recent history—as late as 1990, nearly two Austrians in five still

thought of their country as Hitler's victim rather than his accomplice and 43 percent of Austrians thought Nazism 'had good and bad sides'—merely confirmed
their own and others' prejudices.[8] Austria's Alpine neighbour Switzerland was another matter. For forty years after 1945, Switzerland secured a free pass for its
wartime record. Not only was it forgotten that the Swiss had made strenuous efforts to keep Jews out; on the contrary, in popular fiction and in films everywhere
the country was represented as a safe, welcoming haven for any persecuted person
who could reach its borders. The Swiss basked in their clear conscience and the envious admiration of the world.

In fact, by 1945 the Swiss had taken in just 28,000 Jews—seven thousand of
them before the war began. Wartime refugees were refused work permits—they
were supported from payments levied upon wealthy Jewish residents. Not until June
1994 did the authorities in Bern officially acknowledge that the Swiss request (made
to Berlin in October 1938) for the letter 'J' to be stamped on the passports of all German Jews—the better to keep them out—was an act of 'intolerable racial discrimination'. If this were the extent of Swiss misbehaviour there would hardly have
been much fuss—London and Washington never actually requested an identification tag on Jewish passports, but when it came to saving Jewish refugees the British
and American records are hardly a source of pride. But the Swiss went considerably further.

As became painfully clear in the course of official investigations conducted
through the 1990s, Switzerland not only trafficked in looted gold and made a substantial practical contribution to the German war effort (see Chapter 3), but Swiss
banks and insurance companies had knowingly pocketed indecently large sums of
money belonging to Jewish account holders or to the claimants of insurance policies on murdered relatives. In a secret post-war agreement with Communist
Poland—first made public in 1996—Bern even offered to assign the bank accounts
of dead Polish Jews to the new authorities in Warsaw, in return for indemnity payments to Swiss banks and businesses expropriated after the Communists' take-
over.[9] Once this sort of evidence started to emerge, the country's burnished
reputation came apart, and no amount of (grudgingly conceded) amends and payments and 'victims' funds' are going to put it back together very soon. A September 13th 1996 editorial in Germany's *Die Zeit*—noting that Switzerland had at last
been caught by 'the long shadow of the Holocaust'—smacked more than a little of
Schadenfreude. But it was the simple truth.

The burnished image of wartime Holland—where almost everyone was believed to have 'resisted' and done their best to impede German plans—was en-

---

[8] In October 1991, following the desecration of tombs in Vienna's Jewish cemetery, Gallup polled Austrians on their attitude to Jews: 20 percent thought 'positions of authority' should be closed to Jews; 31
percent declared that they 'would not want a Jew as a neighbour'; fully 50 percent were ready to agree
with the proposition that 'Jews are responsible for their past persecution'.
[9] The Poles happily agreed—for these purposes Warsaw saw no impediment to defining Jews as Poles . . .

gaged and discredited somewhat earlier, and by local initiative. By the mid-Sixties multi-volume official histories of the Second World War provided copious information about the *what* of the Netherlands' wartime experience, including the deportations, but studiously avoided addressing in detail the *who*, the *how* and the *why* of the Jewish catastrophe in particular. In any case, few people read them. But in April 1965 a Dutch historian—Jacob Presser—published *Ondergang*, the first full history of the extermination of Dutch Jewry; it sold 100,000 copies in 1965 alone and precipitated a torrent of public interest in its subject.[10] It was followed in short order by an avalanche of television documentaries and other programmes about the wartime occupation—one of which, *De bezetting* ('The Occupation'), was to run for over two decades—and by a shift in official mood. It was in 1965 that a Dutch government, for the first time, offered to contribute to the memorial at Auschwitz—though it took another seven years before the Netherlands at last agreed to pay to surviving Jewish deportees the pension that had been accorded resisters and other Nazi victims since 1947.

As in Germany, the trigger for Dutch interest in their occluded past was the Israeli and German trials of the early Sixties. And in the Netherlands as elsewhere, the post-war baby-boomers were curious about recent history and more than a little skeptical of the story they had been told—or, rather, not told—by the 'silent generation' of their parents. The social changes of the Sixties helped breach the wall of official silence about the occupation: the breaking of social and sexual taboos—which in parts of the Netherlands, notably Amsterdam, had deeply disruptive implications for a hitherto conservative society—drew in its train a suspicion of other received practices and cultural truisms. For a new cohort of readers the core-text of the Dutch Holocaust—Anne Frank's diary—was now read in a very different light: Anne and her family, after all, were betrayed to the Germans by their Dutch neighbours.

By the end of the century, the years 1940–45 had become the most thoroughly studied period in Dutch history But although the truth about the contribution of the Dutch to the identification, arrest, deportation and death of their Jewish fellow citizens first became public knowledge in the Sixties, it took a long time for the full implications to sink in: not until 1995 did a reigning head of state—Queen Beatrice—publicly acknowledge the tragedy of the Dutch Jews, in the course of a visit to Israel. Perhaps only in the mid-Nineties, with the image of armed Dutch UN peacekeepers standing placidly aside to let Serbian militia round-up and murder seven thousand Muslims at Srebrenica, did the lesson finally strike home. A long-postponed national debate about the price the Dutch have paid for their heritage of order, co-operation and obedience could at last begin.

In their defense, the Dutch—like the Belgians, the Norwegians, the Italians (after

---

[10] *Ondergang* was published in English in 1968 as *The Destruction of the Dutch Jews*.

September 1943) and most of occupied eastern Europe—could claim that however shameful the cooperation of individual bureaucrats, policemen and others with the occupying authorities, the initiative always came from above: from the Germans. This is not as true as was once believed, and in certain places—notably territories like Slovakia or Croatia (or Hungary in the final months of the war) where local puppet governments pursued criminal projects of their own—it was only ever a half-truth. But in occupied western Europe, with one outstanding exception, there were no popularly accredited local regimes, no ostensibly legitimate national governments exercising authority and thus fully responsible for their actions. The Germans could not have done what they did in occupied Norway or Belgium or Holland without the collaboration of the locals (in the one country—Denmark— where that collaboration was not forthcoming, the Jews survived). But in all these cases it was the Germans who issued the orders.

The exception, of course, is France. And it is the tortured, long-denied and serially incomplete memory of France's war—of the Vichy regime and its complicitous, pro-active role in Nazi projects, above all the Final Solution—that has back-shadowed all of Europe's post-war efforts to come to terms with World War Two and the Holocaust. It is not that France behaved the worst. It is that France mattered most. Until 1989, Paris—for reasons discussed in this book—was still the intellectual and cultural capital of Europe: perhaps more so than at any time since the Second Empire. France was also by far the most influential state in continental western Europe, thanks to Charles De Gaulle's remarkable achievement in reestablishing his country in the corridors of international power. And it was France—French statesmen, French institutions and French interests—that drove forward, on French terms, the project for a united continent. Until France could look its past in the face, a shadow would hang over the new Europe—the shadow of a lie.

The Vichy problem can be simply stated. Marshall Pétain's regime had been voted into office in July 1940 by the last parliament of France's Third Republic; it was thus the only wartime regime that could claim some continuity, however spurious, with pre-war democratic institutions. At least until the end of 1942, an overwhelming majority of French men and women regarded Vichy and its institutions as the legitimate authority in France. And for the Germans, Vichy was an immense convenience—it saved them the trouble of installing a costly occupation regime of their own in so large a country as France, while furnishing them with everything they needed from such a regime: acquiescence in defeat, 'war reparations', raw materials, cheap labor . . . and much else besides.

For Vichy did more than accommodate itself and its subjects to France's defeat and run their country for Germany's convenience. Under Pétain and his Prime Minister, Pierre Laval, France initiated collaborative projects of its own: notoriously the introduction in 1940 and 1941 of 'Jewish laws' without any German pressure to do so, and the arrangement whereby French authorities themselves would round up the country's Jewish population (beginning with the many foreign-born Jews resident there) to meet quotas being demanded by the Nazi authorities as the Final Solution got under way. As a consequence of this successful assertion of French administrative autonomy, most of the Jewish deportees from France never even saw a foreign uniform until they were handed over to Germans for final trans-shipment to Auschwitz from the train yards at Drancy (north of Paris). Until then the whole affair was in French hands.

Following the Liberation, for all the obloquy poured upon Pétain and his collaborators, his regime's contribution to the Holocaust was hardly ever invoked, and certainly not by the post-war French authorities themselves. It was not just that the French successfully corralled 'Vichy' into a corner of national memory and then mothballed it. They simply didn't make the link between Vichy and Auschwitz. Vichy had betrayed France. Collaborators had committed treason and war crimes. But 'crimes against humanity' were not part of the French juridical lexicon. They were the affair of Germans.

This situation still obtained twenty years later. When the present author studied French history in the UK in the late Sixties the scholarly literature on Vichy France—such as it was—paid almost no attention to the 'Jewish' dimension. 'Vichy studies' in France and elsewhere focused on the question of whether the Pétainist regime was 'Fascist' or 'reactionary', and how far it represented continuity or a break with the country's republican past. There was still a respected school of French historians who argued that the Pétainist 'shield' had protected France from 'Polonisation'—as though Hitler ever intended to treat his western conquests with the barbarous ferocity visited upon the East. And any questioning of the myth of a heroic, nationwide resistance was still off limits—in historiography as in national life.

The only concession French authorities in those years would make to the changing mood abroad came in December 1964 when the National Assembly belatedly incorporated the category of 'crimes against humanity' (first defined in the London accords of August 8th 1945) into French law and declared them imprescriptable. But this too had nothing to do with Vichy. It was a response to the Auschwitz Trial then under way in Frankfurt, and was intended to facilitate any future prosecution on French soil of individuals (whether German or French) for their direct participation in the Nazis' exterminatory schemes. Just how very far it was from official thinking to re-open the question of France's *collective* responsibility became clear in 1969, when the government forbade French television to show *Le Chagrin et la Pitié* ('The Sorrow and the Anger') by Marcel Ophuls.

Ophuls' film, a documentary about the wartime occupation of Clermont Ferrand in central France, was based on interviews with French, British and German subjects. There was almost nothing in it about the Holocaust and not much about Vichy: its theme was the widespread venality and daily collaboration of the war years: Ophuls was peering behind the self-serving post-war story of resistance.

But even this was too much for the authorities in the last year of De Gaulle's presidency. And not just the authorities: when the film was finally released two years later, not on national television but in a small cinema in Paris's *Quartier Latin*, one middle-aged woman was heard to comment, upon exiting the cinema: 'Shameful—but what do you expect? Ophuls is Jewish, isn't he?'

It is a point of some note that in France, uniquely, the breakthrough into a more honest engagement with wartime history was the work of *foreign* historians, two of whom—Eberhard Jäckel in Germany and Robert Paxton in the US, both of whose major books were published between the end of the Sixties and the mid-Seventies—were the first to use German sources to demonstrate how much of Vichy's crimes were undertaken at French initiative. This was not a subject that any native-born scholar had felt comfortable addressing: thirty years after the Liberation of France, national feelings were still acutely sensitive. As late as 1976, on learning the details of an exhibition planned to memorialize French victims at Auschwitz, the *Ministère des Anciens Combattants* (Ministry of Veterans' Affairs) requested certain changes—the names on the list 'lacked a properly French resonance'."[11]

As so often in France in those years, such sentiments probably had more to do with wounded pride than with unadorned racism. As recently as 1939, France had been a major international power. But in three short decades it suffered a shattering military defeat, a demeaning occupation, two bloody and embarrassing colonial withdrawals, and (in 1958) a regime change in the form of a near-coup. La Grande Nation had accumulated so many losses and humiliations since 1914 that the compensatory propensity to assert national honour on every possible occasion had become deeply ingrained. Inglorious episodes—or worse—were best consigned to a memory-hole. Vichy, after all, was not the only thing that the French were in a hurry to put behind them—no-one wanted to talk about the 'dirty wars' in Indo-China and Algeria, much less the torture practised there by the army.

De Gaulle's departure changed little in this respect, even though a younger generation of Frenchmen and -women showed scant interest in national glory and had no personal investment in the myths surrounding France's recent history. In coming years the French undoubtedly became more aware of the Holocaust and sensitive to Jewish suffering in general—in part thanks to the outrage that followed De Gaulle's notorious press conference of November 27th 1967, in the aftermath of Israel's victory in the Six-Day War, when the French President referred to Jews as 'a people sure of themselves and domineering'. And the 1985 documentary film *Shoah*, by the French director Claude Lanzmann, had a dramatic impact upon French audiences, despite (or perhaps because of) being concerned almost exclusively with the extermination of Jews in the East.

---

[11] See Sonia Combe, *Archives interdites: Les peurs françaises face à l'histoire contemporaine* (Paris: Albin Michel, 1994), p. 14.

But even though French historians—following in the wake of their foreign colleagues—were now establishing beyond question the overwhelming responsibility of France's wartime rulers for the fate of Jews deported from French soil, the official French stance never varied. From Georges Pompidou (president from 1969 to 1974) through Valéry Giscard d'Estaing (1974–1981) and on to François Mitterrand (1981–1995), the line remained the same: whatever was done under or by the Vichy regime was the affair of Vichy. Vichy may have taken place in France and been the work of certain Frenchmen. But Vichy was an authoritarian parenthesis in the history of the French Republic. Vichy, in other words, was not 'France', and thus France's public conscience was clear.

President Mitterrand, the last French head of state to experience World War Two as an adult (he was born in 1916), had special reason to maintain this Jesuitical distinction. A former Vichyite civil servant, Mitterrand built his subsequent political career in large measure by obscuring the compromises and ambiguities of his own biography and by projecting those ambiguities onto the country at large. He studiously avoided any reference to Vichy on public occasions; and while he was never reluctant to speak out about the Holocaust in general—whether in Jerusalem in 1982 or at home on the fiftieth anniversary of the July 1942 round-up of 12,884 Parisian Jews—he never let slip any suggestion that this was an affair in which France had debts to pay.

The taboo that Mitterrand enforced, embodied and would surely have taken to his grave was finally broken (as so often in this matter) by a series of trials. In 1994, after nearly fifty years in hiding, Paul Touvier—an activist in Vichy's wartime Milice—was caught and brought to trial for the murder of seven French Jews in June 1944 near Lyon. In himself Touvier was unimportant: a cog in the Vichy machinery and a collaborator of Klaus Barbie, the Gestapo head in Lyon who had been captured and tried in 1987. But Touvier's trial—and the evidence that came out concerning the Vichy authorities' collaboration with the Gestapo and their role in the deportation and murder of Jews—served as a kind of *ersatz* for other trials that never happened: notably that of René Bousquet, the senior police administrator at Vichy. The prosecution of Bousquet, who in 1942 personally negotiated with the German authorities for the delivery of Jews, might have provided France with an occasion to confront the truth about Vichy. And not just Vichy, for Bousquet had lived unscathed for many decades in post-war France, protected by friends in very high places—including Mitterrand himself. But before he could be brought to trial Bousquet was conveniently assassinated (by a 'lunatic') in June 1993.

In the wake of Touvier's condemnation, and in the absence of Bousquet, the French judiciary at last found the courage (after Mitterrand's death) to inculpate, arrest and prosecute another major figure, Maurice Papon. A sometime government minister and police chief of Paris under De Gaulle, Papon had been employed as secretary-general of the Bordeaux administrative region during the war.

This was a purely bureaucratic post, and his stint in Bordeaux in the service of Pétain had proven no impediment to Papon's successful post-war career as a public servant. While in Bordeaux, however, Papon had been directly responsible for authorising the arrest and despatch of the region's Jews to Paris and thence into deportation. It was for this—now defined under French law as a crime against humanity—that he was placed on trial in 1997.

The Papon trial, which lasted six months, revealed no new evidence—except perhaps about the man himself, who displayed an astonishing absence of pity or remorse. And of course the trial came fifty years too late: too late to punish the octogenarian Papon for his crimes; too late to avenge his victims; and too late to save the honour of his country. A number of French historians, called to testify as expert witnesses, declined to appear. Their task, they insisted, was to recount and explain what had happened in France fifty years before, not deploy that knowledge in a criminal prosecution.[12] But the trial was exemplary nonetheless. It demonstrated conclusively that the fine distinction between 'Vichy' and 'France' so carefully drawn by everyone from De Gaulle to Mitterrand had never existed. Papon was a Frenchman who served the Vichy regime and the subsequent French Republic: both of which were fully aware of his activities in the Bordeaux prefecture and neither of which was troubled by them.

Moreover, Papon was not alone—indeed both the man and his record were decidedly commonplace. Like so many others, all he had done was sign the death warrants of people he never met and to whose fate he was indifferent. The most interesting thing about Papon's case (and that of Bousquet, too) was why it had taken official France nearly fifty years to locate them in its midst—and why, at the very end of the century, the crust of silence finally broke open. There are many explanations, not all of them flattering to the French political class or national media. But the passage of time, together with the psychological significance of the ending of an era, is perhaps the most pertinent.

So long as François Mitterrand remained in office, he incarnated in his very person the national inability to speak openly about the shame of the occupation. With Mitterrand's departure, everything changed. His successor, Jacques Chirac, had been just eleven years old when France was liberated in 1944. Within weeks of taking office, on the fifty-third anniversary of the same round-up of Parisian Jews about which Mitterrand had always been so circumspect, President Chirac broke a fifty-year taboo and pointedly acknowledged for the first time his country's role in the extermination of the Jews of Europe. Ten years later, on March 15th 2005, at the newly inaugurated Holocaust Museum in Jerusalem, Chirac's Prime Minister,

---

[12] Professor Paxton of Columbia University, who had initiated historical investigation into Vichy's crimes nearly a quarter of a century earlier (when most of his French colleagues were otherwise engaged), took a less monastic view of his professional calling and gave important testimony.

Jean-Pierre Raffarin, solemnly declared: '*La France a parfois été le complice de cette infamie. Elle a contracté une dette imprescriptible qui l'oblige*'. 'France was at times an accomplice in this shame. She is bound forever by the debt she has incurred'.

By the end of the twentieth century the centrality of the Holocaust in Western European identity and memory seemed secure. To be sure, there remained those occasional individuals and organisations—'revisionists'—who persisted in trying to show that the mass extermination of the Jews could not have taken place (though they were more active in North America than in Europe itself). But such people were confined to the extreme political margins—and their insistence upon the technical impossibility of the genocide paid unintended homage to the very enormity of the Nazi crime. However, the compensatory ubiquity with which Europeans now acknowledged, taught and memorialized the loss of their Jews did carry other risks.

In the first place, there was always the danger of a backlash. Occasionally even mainstream German politicians had been heard to vent frustration at the burden of national guilt—as early as 1969 the Bavarian Christian Social leader Franz-Josef Strauss relieved himself in public of the thought that 'a people that has achieved such remarkable economic success has the right not to have to hear anymore about "Auschwitz".' Politicians of course have their reasons.[13] What was perhaps more indicative of a coming cultural shift was a widespread urge, at the beginning of the twenty-first century, to re-open the question of *German* suffering after years of public attention to Jewish victims.

Artists and critics—among them Martin Walser, Habermas's contemporary and an influential literary voice in the post-war Federal Republic—were now starting to discuss another 'unmanaged past': not the extermination of the Jews but the under-acknowledged other side of recent German history. Why, they asked, after all these years should we not speak of the burning of Germany's cities, or even of the uncomfortable truth that life in Hitler's Germany (for Germans) was far from unpleasant, at least until the last years of World War II? Because we should speak instead of what Germany did to the Jews? But we've spoken of this for decades; it has become a routine, a habit. The Federal Republic is one of the most avowedly philo-Semitic nations in the world; for how much longer must we (Germans) look over our shoulder? New books about 'the crimes of the Allies'—the bombing of Dresden, the burning of Hamburg and the wartime sinking of German refugee

---

[13]When US President Ronald Reagan, on a visit to West Germany in 1985, was advised to avoid the military cemetery at Bitburg (site of a number of SS graves) and pay his respects at a concentration camp instead, Chancellor Kohl wrote to warn him that this 'would have a serious psychological effect on the friendly sentiments of the German people for the United States of America.' The Americans duly capitulated; Reagan visited Belsen *and* Bitburg . . .

ships (the subject of *Im Krebsgang*, 'Crabwise', a 2002 novel by Günter Grass)—sold in huge numbers.

In the second place, the new-found salience of the Holocaust in official accounts of Europe's past carried the danger of a different sort of distortion. For the really uncomfortable truth about World War Two was that what happened to the Jews between 1939 and 1945 was not nearly as important to most of the protagonists as later sensibilities might wish. If many Europeans had managed to ignore for decades the fate of their Jewish neighbours, this was not because they were consumed with guilt and repressing unbearable memories. It was because—except in the minds of a handful of senior Nazis—World War Two was not about the Jews. Even for Nazis the extermination of Jews was part of a more ambitious project of racial cleansing and resettlement.

The understandable temptation to read back into the 1940s the knowledge and emotions of half a century later thus invites a rewriting of the historical record: putting anti-Semitism at the centre of European history. How else, after all, are we to account for what happened in Europe in those years? But that is too easy—and in a way too comforting. The reason Vichy was acceptable to most French people after the defeat of 1940, for example, was not that it pleased them to live under a regime that persecuted Jews, but because Pétainist rule allowed the French to continue leading their lives in an illusion of security and normality and with minimum disruption. How the regime treated Jews was a matter of indifference: the Jews just hadn't mattered that much. And much the same was true in most other occupied lands.

Today we may find such indifference shocking—a symptom of something gravely amiss in the moral condition of Europe in the first half of the twentieth century. And we are right to recall that there were also those in every European country who *did* see what was happening to Jews and did their best to overcome the indifference of their fellow citizens. But if we ignore that indifference and assume instead that most other Europeans experienced the Second World War the way Jews experienced it—as a *Vernichtungskrieg*, a war of extermination—then we shall furnish ourselves with a new layer of mis-memory. In retrospect, 'Auschwitz' is the most important thing to know about World War Two. But that is not how things seemed at the time.

It is also not how things seemed in eastern Europe. To east Europeans, belatedly released after 1989 from the burden of officially mandated Communist interpretations of World War Two, the *fin-de-siècle* Western preoccupation with the Holocaust of the Jews carries disruptive implications. On the one hand, eastern Europe after 1945 had much more than western Europe to remember—and to forget. There were more Jews in the eastern half of Europe and more of them were killed; most of the killing took place in this region and many more locals took an active part in it. But on the other hand, far greater care was taken by the post-war authorities in eastern Europe to erase all public memory of the Holocaust. It is not that the horrors and crimes of the war in the east were played down—on the contrary, they were repeatedly rehearsed in official rhetoric and enshrined in memorials and textbooks everywhere. It is just that Jews were not part of the story.

In East Germany, where the burden of responsibility for Nazism was imputed uniquely to Hitler's West German heirs, the new regime paid restitution not to Jews but to the Soviet Union. In GDR school texts, Hitler was presented as a tool of monopoly capitalists who seized territory and started wars in pursuit of the interests of big business. The 'Day of Remembrance' inaugurated by Walter Ulbricht in 1950 commemorated not Germany's victims but eleven million dead 'fighters against Hitler fascism'. Former concentration camps on East German soil—notably Buchenwald and Sachsenhausen—were converted for a while into 'special isolation camps' for political prisoners. Many years later, after Buchenwald had been transformed into a memorial site, its guidebook described the stated aims of 'German fascism' as 'Destruction of Marxism, revenge for the lost war and brutal terror against all resisters'. In the same booklet, photos of the selection ramp at Auschwitz were captioned with a quote from the German Communist Ernst Thälmann: 'The bourgeoisie is serious about its aim to annihilate the party and the entire avant-garde of the working class'.[14] This text was not removed until after the fall of Communism.

The same version of events could be found throughout Communist Europe. In Poland it was not possible to deny or minimize what had taken place in extermination camps at Treblinka or Majdanek or Sobibor. But these places no longer existed—the Germans had taken extraordinary pains to obliterate them from the landscape before fleeing the advancing Red Army. And where the evidence did survive—as at Auschwitz, a few kilometres from Crakow, Poland's second city—it was retrospectively assigned a different meaning. Although 93 percent of the estimated 1.5 million people murdered at Auschwitz were Jews, the museum established there under the post-war Communist regime listed the victims only by nationality: Polish, Hungarian, German, etc. Polish schoolchildren were indeed paraded past the shocking photos; they were shown the heaps of shoes, hair and eyeglasses. But they were not told that most of it belonged to Jews.

To be sure, there was the Warsaw Ghetto, whose life and death were indeed memorialized on the site where the ghetto had stood. But the Jewish revolt of 1943 was occluded in Polish memory by the Poles' own Warsaw uprising a year later. In Communist Poland, while no-one denied what Germans had done to Jews, the subject was not much discussed. Poland's 're-imprisonment' under the Soviets, together with the widespread belief that Jews had welcomed and even facilitated the Communist takeover, muddied popular recall of the German occupation. In any case, Poles' own wartime suffering diluted local attention to the Jewish Holocaust

---

[14]Quoted by Ian Buruma in 'Buchenwald', *Granta* 42, 1992.

and was in some measure competitive with it: this issue of 'comparative victimhood' would poison Polish-Jewish relations for many decades. The juxtaposition was always inappropriate. Three million (non-Jewish) Poles died in World War II; proportionately lower than the death rate in parts of Ukraine or among Jews, but a terrible figure notwithstanding. Yet there was a difference. For Poles, it was difficult to survive under German occupation, but in principle you could. For Jews it was possible to survive under German occupation—but in principle you could not.

Where a local puppet regime had collaborated with its Nazi overlords, its victims were duly memorialized. But scant attention was paid to the fact that they were disproportionately Jews. There were national categories ('Hungarians') and above all social categories ('workers'), but ethnic and religious tags were studiously avoided. The Second World War, as we have seen (see Chapter 6), was labelled and taught as an anti-Fascist war; its racist dimension was ignored. In the 1970s, the government of Czechoslovakia even took the trouble to paint over the inscriptions on the walls of Prague's Altneuschul (Old-New Synagogue) that gave the names of Czech Jews killed in the *Shoah*.

When re-casting recent history in this region, the post-war Communist authorities could certainly count on an enduring reservoir of anti-Jewish feeling—one reason they went to some trouble to suppress evidence of it even in retrospect (during the Seventies Polish censors consistently banned allusions to the country's inter-war anti-Semitism). But if east Europeans paid less attention in retrospect to the plight of the Jews, it was not just because they were indifferent at the time or preoccupied with their own survival. It is because the Communists imposed enough suffering and injustice of their own to forge a whole new layer of resentments and memories.

Between 1945 and 1989 the accumulation of deportations, imprisonments, show trials and 'normalizations' made almost everyone in the Soviet bloc either a loser or else complicit in someone else's loss. Apartments, shops and other property that had been appropriated from dead Jews or expelled Germans were all too often re-expropriated a few years later in the name of Socialism—with the result that after 1989 the question of compensation for past losses became hopelessly tangled in dates. Should people be recompensed for what they lost when the Communists seized power? And if such restitution were made, to whom should it go? To those who had come into possession of it after the war, in 1945, only to lose it a few years later? Or should restitution be made to the heirs of those from whom businesses and apartments had been seized or stolen at some point between 1938 and 1945? Which point? 1938? 1939? 1941? On each date there hung politically sensitive definitions of national or ethnic legitimacy as well as moral precedence.[15]

---

[15]When the Czechoslovak parliament voted in 1991 to restitute property seized after the war it explicitly limited the benefits to those expropriated after *1948*—so as to exclude Sudeten Germans expelled in 1945–46, before the Communists seized power.

And then there were dilemmas peculiar to the internal history of Communism itself. Should those responsible for inviting Russian tanks in to crush the 1956 Hungarian revolution or suppress the Prague Spring of 1968 be arraigned for these crimes? In the immediate aftermath of the 1989 revolutions many thought they should. But some of their victims were former Communist leaders. Who deserved the attention of posterity: obscure Slovak or Hungarian peasants thrown off their property, or the Communist apparatchiks who ejected them but who themselves fell victim a few years later? Which victims—which memories—should have priority? Who was to say?

The fall of Communism thus brought in its wake a torrent of bitter memories. Heated debates over what to do with secret police files were only one dimension of the affair (see Chapter 21). The real problem was the temptation to overcome the memory of Communism by inverting it. What had once been official truth was now discredited root and branch—becoming, as it were, officially false. But this sort of taboo-breaking carries its own risks. Before 1989 every anti-Communist had been tarred with the 'Fascist' brush. But if 'anti-Fascism' had been just another Communist lie, it was very tempting now to look with retrospective sympathy and even favour upon *all* hitherto discredited anti-Communists, Fascists included. Nationalist writers of the nineteen-thirties returned to fashion. Post-Communist parliaments in a number of countries passed motions praising Marshal Antonescu of Romania or his counterparts elsewhere in the Balkans and central Europe. Execrated until very recently as nationalists, Fascists and Nazi collaborators, they would now have statues raised in honour of their wartime heroism (the Romanian parliament even accorded Antonescu one minute's silence).

Other taboos fell along with the discredited rhetoric of anti-Fascism. The role of the Red Army and the Soviet Union could now be discussed in a different light. The newly liberated Baltic states demanded that Moscow acknowledge the illegality of the Molotov-Ribbentrop Pact and Stalin's unilateral destruction of their independence. The Poles, having at last (in April 1995) secured Russian acknowledgement that the 23,000 Polish officers murdered in Katyn forest were indeed killed by the NKVD and not the Wehrmacht, demanded full access to the Russian archives for Polish investigators. As of May 2005 neither request seemed likely to meet with Russian acquiescence and the memories continued to rankle.[16]

The Russians, however, had memories of their own. Seen from the satellite countries, the Soviet version of recent history was palpably false; but for many Russians themselves it contained more than a grain of truth. World War Two *was* a 'Great Patriotic War'; Soviet soldiers and civilians *were*, in absolute numbers, its greatest victims; the Red Army *did* liberate vast swathes of eastern Europe from the

---

[16]Under President Putin, Russia continues to insist that the Balts were liberated by the Red Army, after which they voluntarily joined the Union of Soviet Socialist Republics.

horrors of German rule; and the defeat of Hitler *was* a source of unalloyed satisfaction and relief for most Soviet citizens—and others besides. After 1989, many in Russia were genuinely taken aback at the apparent ingratitude of erstwhile fraternal nations, who had been released in 1945 from the German yoke thanks to the sacrifices of Soviet arms.

But for all that, Russian memory was divided. Indeed, that division took institutional form, with two civil organizations coming into existence to promote critical but diametrically opposed accounts of the country's Communist past. *Memorial* was founded in 1987 by liberal dissidents with the goal of obtaining and publishing the truth about Soviet history. Its members' particular concerns were with human-rights abuse and the importance of acknowledging what had been done in the past in order to forestall its recurrence in the future. *Pamiat'*, formed two years earlier, also sought to recover and honour the past (its name means 'memory' in Russian) but there the resemblance ceases. The founders of *Pamiat'*, anti-Communist dissidents but far from liberal, wanted to offer an improved version of the Russian past: sanitized of Soviet 'lies' but also free of other influences foreign to Russia's heritage, above all that of 'Zionists'. Within a few years *Pamiat'* had branched out into nationalist politics, wielding Russia's neglected and 'abused' history as a weapon with which to ward off 'cosmopolitan' challenges and interlopers.

The politics of aggrieved memories—however much these differed in detail and even contradicted one another—constituted the last remaining bond between the former Soviet heartland and its imperial holdings. There was a shared resentment at the international community's under-appreciation for their past sufferings and losses. What of the victims of the Gulag? Why had they not been compensated and memorialized like the victims and survivors of Nazi oppression? What of the millions for whom wartime Nazi oppression became postwar Communist oppression with no discernible caesura? Why did the West pay so little attention?

The desire to flatten out the Communist past and indict it en bloc—to read everything from Lenin to Gorbachev as an uninflected tale of dictatorship and crime, a seamless narrative of regimes and repressions imposed by outsiders or perpetrated in the people's name by unrepresentative authorities—carried other risks. In the first place it was bad history, eliminating from the record the genuine enthusiasms and engagements of earlier decades. Secondly, the new orthodoxy had contemporary political implications. If Czechs—or Croats or Hungarians or anyone else—had played no active part in the dark side of their own recent past; if eastern European history since 1939—or, in the Russian case, from 1917 to 1991—was exclusively the work of others, then the whole era became a sort of parenthesis in the national story: comparable to the place assigned to Vichy in post-war French consciousness, but covering a vastly longer period and an even grimmer archive of bad memories. And the consequences would be similar: in 1992, Czechoslovak au-

POSTWAR: A HISTORY OF EUROPE SINCE 1945

thorities banned a BBC documentary film about the 1942 assassination in Prague of Reinhard Heydrich from the Karlovy Vary film festival, because it showed 'unacceptable' footage of Czechs demonstrating support for the wartime Nazi regime.

With this post-Communist re-ordering of memory in eastern Europe, the taboo on comparing Communism with Nazism began to crumble. Indeed politicians and scholars started to insist upon such comparisons. In the West this juxtaposition remained controversial. Direct comparison between Hitler and Stalin was not the issue: few now disputed the monstrous quality of both dictators. But the suggestion that Communism itself—before and after Stalin—should be placed in the same category as Fascism or Nazism carried uncomfortable implications for the West's own past, and not only in Germany. To many western European intellectuals, Communism was a failed variant of a common progressive heritage. But to their central and east European counterparts it was an all too successful local application of the criminal pathologies of twentieth-century authoritarianism and should be remembered thus. Europe might be united, but European memory remained deeply asymmetrical.

The Western solution to the problem of Europe's troublesome memories has been to fix them, quite literally, in stone. By the opening years of the twenty-first century, plaques, memorials and museums to the victims of Nazism had surfaced all across western Europe, from Stockholm to Brussels. In some cases, as we have seen, they were amended or 'corrected' versions of existing sites; but many were new. Some aspired to an overtly pedagogical function: the Holocaust Memorial which opened in Paris in January 2005 combined two existing sites, the 'Memorial to the Unknown Jewish Martyr' and a 'Centre for Contemporary Jewish Documentation'. Complete with a stone wall engraved with the names of 76,000 Jews deported from France to Nazi death camps, it echoed both the US Vietnam Memorial and—on a much reduced scale—the ambitions of the Holocaust Memorial Museum in Washington, DC, or Yad Vashem in Jerusalem. The overwhelming majority of such installations were indeed devoted—in part or whole—to the memory of the Holocaust: the most impressive of them all was opened in Berlin on May 10th 2005.

The explicit message of the latest round of memorials contrasts sharply with the ambiguity and prevarication of an earlier generation of lapidary commemorations. The Berlin memorial, occupying a conspicuous 19,000-square metre site adjacent to the Brandenburg Gate, is the most explicit of them all: far from commemorating ecumenically the 'victims of Nazism' it is, quite avowedly, a 'Memorial to the Murdered Jews of Europe'.[17] In Austria, young conscientious ob-

---

[17] The memorial was not uncontroversial: in addition to many who disliked its abstract conception there were those, including a Christian Democrat Mayor of the city, Eberhard Diepgen, who criticized it for helping turn Berlin into 'the capital of repentance'.

jectors could now choose to replace military service with a period in the state-financed *Gedenkdienst* ('Commemorative Service', established in 1991), working at major Holocaust institutions as interns and guides. There can be little doubt that Western Europeans—Germans above all—now have ample opportunity to confront the full horror of their recent past. As the German Chancellor Gerhard Schroeder reminded his audience on the sixtieth anniversary of the liberation of Auschwitz, 'the memory of the war and the genocide are part of our life. Nothing will change that: these memories are part of our identity'.

Elsewhere, however, shadows remain. In Poland, where a newly established Institute of National Memory has striven hard to encourage serious scholarly investigation into controversial historical subjects, official contrition for Poland's own treatment of its Jewish minority has aroused vociferous objections. These are depressingly exemplified in the reaction of Nobel Peace Prize winner and Solidarity hero Lech Wałesa to the publication in 2000 of Jan Tomasz Gross's book *Neighbours*, an influential study by an American historian of a wartime massacre of Jews by their Polish neighbours: 'Gross', Wałesa complained in a radio interview, was out to sow discord between Poles and Jews. He was a 'mediocre writer . . . a Jew who tries to make money'.

The difficulty of incorporating the destruction of the Jews into contemporary memory in post-Communist Europe is tellingly illustrated by the experience of Hungary. In 2001 the government of Viktor Orbán inaugurated a Holocaust Memorial Day, to be commemorated annually on April 16th (the anniversary of the establishment in 1944 of a ghetto in wartime Budapest). Three years later Orbán's successor as prime minister, Péter Medgyessy, opened a Holocaust Memorial Centre in a Budapest house once used to intern Jews. But much of the time this Holocaust Centre stands nearly empty, its exhibits and fact sheets seen by a thin trickle of visitors—many of them foreign. Meanwhile, on the other side of town, Hungarians have flocked to the *Terrorhaza*.

The *Terrorhaza* ('House of Terror'), as its name suggests, is a museum of horrors. It tells the story of state violence, torture, repression and dictatorship in Hungary from 1944 to 1989. The dates are significant. As presented to the thousands of schoolchildren and others who pass through its gloomy, Tussaud-like reproduction of the police cells, torture equipment and interrogation chambers that were once housed there (the House of Terror is in the headquarters of the former Security Police), the *Terrorhaza*'s version of Hungarian history draws no distinction between the thugs of Ferenc Szálasi's Arrow Cross party, who held power there from October 1944 to April 1945, and the Communist regime that was installed after the war. However, the Arrow Cross men—and the extermination of 600,000 Hungarian Jews to which they actively contributed—are represented by just three rooms. The rest of the very large building is devoted to a copiously illustrated and decidedly partisan catalogue of the crimes of Communism.

The not particularly subliminal message here is that Communism and Fascism are equivalent. Except that they are not: the presentation and content of the Budapest *Terrorhaza* makes it quite clear that, in the eyes of the museum's curators, Communism not only lasted longer but did far more harm than its neo-Nazi predecessor. For many Hungarians of an older generation, this is all the more plausible for conforming to their own experience. And the message has been confirmed by post-Communist Hungarian legislation banning public display of *all* representations of the country's undemocratic past: not just the swastika or the Arrow Cross symbol but also the hitherto ubiquitous red star and its accompanying hammer and sickle. Rather than evaluate the distinctions between the regimes represented by these symbols, Hungary—in the words of Prime Minister Orbán at the opening of the Budapest House of Terror on February 24th 2002—has simply 'slammed the door on the sick twentieth century'.

But that door is not so easy to close. Hungary, like the rest of central and eastern Europe, is still caught in the backdraft.[18] The same Baltic states which have urged upon Moscow the duty to acknowledge its mistreatment of them have been decidedly slow to interrogate their own responsibilities: since winning their independence neither Estonia nor Latvia nor Lithuania has prosecuted a single case against the surviving war criminals in their midst. In Romania—despite former President Iliescu's acknowledgement of his country's participation in the Holocaust—the 'Memorial of the Victims of Communism and anticommunist Resistance' inaugurated at Sighet in 1997 (financed in part by the Council of Europe) commemorates assorted inter-war and wartime Iron Guard activists and other Romanian Fascists and anti-Semites, now recycled as martyrs to Communist persecution.

In support of their insistence upon 'equivalence', commentators in eastern Europe can point to the cult of the 'victim' in contemporary Western political culture. We are moving from winners' history to victims' history, they observe. Very well, then let us be consistent. Even if Nazism and Communism were utterly different in intent—even if, in Raymond Aron's formulation, 'there is a difference between a philosophy whose logic is monstrous, and one which can be given a monstrous interpretation'—that was scant consolation to their victims. Human suffering should not be calibrated according to the goals of the perpetrators. In this way of reasoning, for those being punished or killed there, a Communist camp is no better or worse than a Nazi camp.

Similarly, the emphasis upon 'rights' (and restitution for their abuse) in modern international jurisprudence and political rhetoric has furnished an argument for those who feel that *their* sufferings and losses have passed unrecognized—and

---

[18]In March 2004 eighty-four Hungarian writers, including Péter Esterházy and György Konrád, left the country's Writers' Union in protest at its tolerance of anti-Semitism. The occasion for the walk out were comments by the poet Kornel Döbrentei following the award of the Nobel Prize for Literature to the Holocaust survivor Imre Kertész. The prize, according to Döbrentei, was 'conscience money' for a writer who was just indulging the 'taste for terror' of 'his minority'.

uncompensated. Some conservatives in Germany, taking their cue from international condemnation of 'ethnic cleansing', have re-opened the claims of German communities expelled from their lands at the end of the Second World War. Why, they ask, was theirs a lesser form of victimhood? Surely what Stalin did to the Poles—or, more recently, what Milošević did to the Albanians—was no different in kind from what Czechoslovakia's President Beneš did to the Sudeten Germans after World War Two? By the early years of the new century there was talk in respectable circles of establishing in Berlin yet another memorial: a 'Center Against Expulsions', a museum devoted to all victims of ethnic cleansing.

This latest twist, with its suggestion that *all* forms of collective victimhood are essentially comparable, even interchangeable, and should thus be accorded equal remembrance, aroused a spirited rebuttal from Marek Edelman, the last surviving commander of the Warsaw Ghetto uprising, when he signed a petition in 2003 opposing the proposed Center. 'What sort of remembrance! Did they suffer that much? Because they lost their houses? Of course it is sad when you are being forced to leave your house and abandon your land. But the Jews lost their houses *and* all of their relatives. Expulsions are about suffering, but there is so much suffering in this world. Sick people suffer, and nobody builds monuments to honour them' (*Tygodnik Powszechny*, August 17th 2003).

Edelman's reaction is a timely reminder of the risks we run by indulging to excess the cult of commemoration—and of displacing perpetrators with victims as the focus of attention. On the one hand there is no limit in principle to the memories and experiences worthy of recall. On the other hand, to memorialize the past in edifices and museums is also a way to contain and even neglect it—leaving the responsibility of memory to others. So long as there were men and women around who really did remember, from personal experience, this did not perhaps matter. But now, as the 81-year-old Jorge Semprún reminded his fellow survivors at the sixtieth anniversary of the liberation of Buchenwald on April 10th 2005, 'the cycle of active memory is closing'.

Even if Europe *could* somehow cling indefinitely to a living memory of past crimes—which is what the memorials and museums are designed, however inadequately, to achieve—there would be little point. Memory is inherently contentious and partisan: one man's acknowledgement is another's omission. And it is a poor guide to the past. The first post-war Europe was built upon deliberate *mis*-memory—upon forgetting as a way of life. Since 1989, Europe has been constructed instead upon a compensatory surplus of memory: institutionalised public remembering as the very foundation of collective identity. The first could not endure—but nor will the second. Some measure of neglect and even forgetting is the necessary condition for civic health.

To say this is not to advocate amnesia. A nation has first to have remembered something before it can begin to forget it. Until the French understood Vichy as it was—and not as they had chosen to misremember it—they could not put it aside and move on. The same is true of Poles in their convoluted recollection of the Jews who once lived in their midst. The same will be true of Spain, too, which for twenty years following its transition to democracy drew a tacit veil across the painful memory of the civil war. Public discussion of that war and its outcome is only now getting under way.[19] Only after Germans had appreciated and digested the enormity of their Nazi past—a sixty-year cycle of denial, education, debate and consensus— could they begin to live with it: i.e. put it behind them.

The instrument of recall in all such cases was not memory itself. It was *history*, in both its meanings: as the passage of time and as the professional study of the past—the latter above all. Evil, above all evil on the scale practiced by Nazi Germany, can never be satisfactorily remembered. The very enormity of the crime renders all memorialisation incomplete.[20] Its inherent implausibility—the sheer difficulty of conceiving of it in calm retrospect—opens the door to diminution and even denial. Impossible to remember as it truly was, it is inherently vulnerable to being remembered as it wasn't. Against *this* challenge memory itself is helpless: 'Only the historian, with the austere passion for fact, proof, evidence, which are central to his vocation, can effectively stand guard'.[21]

Unlike memory, which confirms and reinforces itself, history contributes to the disenchantment of the world. Most of what it has to offer is discomforting, even disruptive—which is why it is not always politically prudent to wield the past as a moral cudgel with which to beat and berate a people for its past sins. But history does need to be learned—and periodically re-learned. In a popular Soviet-era joke, a listener calls up 'Armenian Radio' with a question: 'Is it possible', he asks, 'to foretell the future?' Answer: 'Yes, no problem. We know exactly what the future will be. Our problem is with the past: that keeps changing'.

So it does—and not only in totalitarian societies. All the same, the rigorous investigation and interrogation of Europe's competing pasts—and the place occupied by those pasts in Europeans' collective sense of themselves—has been one of the unsung achievements and sources of European unity in recent decades. It is, however, an achievement that will surely lapse unless ceaselessly renewed. Europe's barbarous recent history, the dark 'other' against which post-war Europe was laboriously constructed, is already beyond recall for young Europeans. Within a generation the memorials and museums will be gathering dust—visited, like the battlefields of the Western Front today, only by aficionados and relatives.

If in years to come we are to remember why it seemed so important to build a

---

[19]The last statue of Franco in Madrid was quietly removed at dawn, in front of an audience of one hundred onlookers, on March 17th 2005.
[20] 'We, the survivors, are not the true witnesses. . . . We are . . . an anomalous minority: we are those who by their prevarications, or their attributes or their good luck did not touch bottom. Those who did so, those who saw the Gorgon, have not returned to tell about it, or they returned mute.' Primo Levi, *The Drowned and the Saved* (NY, 1988), pp. 83–84.
[21]Yosef Hayim Yerushalmi, *Zakhor: Jewish History and Jewish Memory* (Seattle, 1982), p. 116.

certain sort of Europe out of the crematoria of Auschwitz, only history can help us. The new Europe, bound together by the signs and symbols of its terrible past, is a remarkable accomplishment; but it remains forever mortgaged to that past. If Europeans are to maintain this vital link—if Europe's past is to continue to furnish Europe's present with admonitory meaning and moral purpose—then it will have to be *taught* afresh with each passing generation. 'European Union' may be a response to history, but it can never be a substitute.

Photo Credits

Part Three Insert

Page 1, top (Baader-Meinhof poster): AKG Images; bottom (Red Brigades terrorists) Bettmann/Corbis.

Page 2, top (ETA terrorists, 1982): Magnum/Harry Gruyaert; bottom (Belfast children, 1976): Davis Factor/Corbis.

Page 3, top (Portuguese immigrant workers, France, 1970): J. Pavlosky/Rapho; bottom (Italian women divorce protest, 1974): Contrasto/Katz Pictures.

Page 4, top (Juan Carlos and Franco, 1971): Bettmann/Corbis; bottom (Lisbon woman newspaper vendor): Magnum/Jean Gaumy.

Page 5, top (Brandt in Erfurt, 1970): AKG Images; bottom (Mitterrand and Thatcher, 1984): Bryn Colton/Assignments Photographers/Corbis.

Page 6, top (John Paul II in Poland, 1979): Topham Picture Library; middle (Michnik in Gdansk, 1984): Wostok Press; bottom (Gorbachev in Prague, 1987): Peter Turnley/Corbis.

Page 7, top (train with East German refugees): Marc Deville/Gamma/Katz Pictures; middle (Prague student protest, 1989): Lubomir Kotek/AFP/Getty Images; bottom (Havel and Dubček, 1989): Chris Niedenthal/*Time Life*/Getty Images.

Page 8 (Lenin statue, Hungary, 1990): Wostok Press.

Part Four Insert

Page 1, top (Yeltsin and Gorbachev, 1991): Wostok Press; bottom (McDonald's in Moscow, 1990): Sergei Guneyev/*Time Life*/Getty Images.

Page 2, top (Chernobyl effects, Belarus): Magnum/Paul Fusco; middle (Aral Sea disaster, 1997): Magnum/Francesco Zizola; bottom (Ukrainian demonstration, 1991): Alain Nogues/Sygma/Corbis.

Page 3, top (Gypsy poverty, Bucharest, 1996): Wostok Press; middle (eastern European sex trade, 2002): Sasha Bezzubov/Corbis; bottom (NATO at fair in Hungary, 1997): Wostok Press.

Page 4, top (Serb 1389–1989 commemoration, 1989): Wostok Press; middle (Srebrenica massacre graves): Danilo Krstanovic/Reuters; bottom (Albanian refugees, 1999): David Brauchli/Getty Images.

Page 5, top (Turkey and EU, 2004): European Press Photo Agency/Kerim Okten; bottom (French "NON EU" sign): Alternative Libertaire.

Page 6, top (Haider, 1995): Viennareport/Sygma/Corbis; middle (Kjaersgaard, 1998): Dean Francis/Sygma/Corbis; bottom (Blair and NHS reform, 2004): David Bebber/Reuters/Corbis.

Page 7, top (Moroccans in Spain, 2000): J. M. Bendich/Sygma/Corbis; bottom (Somali immigrants in Italy, 1997): Magnum/John Vink.

Page 8, top (Chirac at commemoration): Jacques Langevin/Sygma/Corbis; bottom (Schroeder at commemoration): Arnd Wiegmann/Reuters.

Index